The Genealogical Services Directory

Family
and
Local History
Handbook

Edited & Compiled

by

Robert Blatchford

Contents

7 Feature Articles

4

Editorial

It seems such a short time since the first edition was published and now in 2002 the sixth is here. With each edition the preparatory work has increased. The article commissions and information verification takes place over several months. Once the material is gathered together the work of designing and creating the book begins and the days become exceedingly long. We are often asked about the preparation of the book. My answer is always the same. Everything is prepared in house and the only task not done by us is the actual printing.

For those of you who are technically minded the *Handbook* is produced electronically. It does not see paper until it is printed. Apple Macintosh computers, a G4 and a G3 PowerBook, are used for all the design and layout work. As for the software Quark Xpress 4 and Adobe Photoshop 6 are the principal players.

This our sixth edition has to be our *best* yet. I am constantly surprised by the critical acclaim we receive for each edition. Again we have been able to commission leading family and local historians to provide articles on many interesting subjects.

In the 5th Edition the Local History Section was expanded and for this edition it is the turn of the military history section. There are many topics such as *Records of the British Army*, *The Anglo Boer War*, the *RFC and RAF Register* as well as *Martin Fletcher*'s article *The Nation's Lost Sons* covering the identification of remains found in the World War I battlefields.

I must acknowledge all the many people, too numerous to name individually who have helped in so many ways. I am especially grateful to my wife, Elizabeth, and the family for their patience and forbearance. The technical help and advice from Alan and Sandra Williamson has been invaluable, as is the support from the BALH and Michael Cowan. I cannot fail to mention Nancy Redpath and Daphne Hambrook for their invaluable help in the last frantic days before the files go to the printer

Please support our advertisers as their contribution to the production of the *Handbook* is essential. If you do respond to their advertisement please tell them you saw their advertisement in *The Family and Local History Handbook*

Suggestions from our readers are always welcome and where possible they are implemented in the next edition. We hope that you, our readers, enjoy this 6th edition as much as the previous ones.

Robert Blatchford

tracing the birth parents of adopted persons in England and Wales

federation of FAMILY HISTORY SOCIETIES

research services: a code of practice for family historians

federation of FAMILY HISTORY SOCIETIES

the strays clearing house and the national strays index

federation of FAMILY HISTORY SOCIETIES

in search of your soldier ancestors

federation of FAMILY HISTORY SOCIETIES

you and your record office: a code of practice for family historians using county record offices

federation of FAMILY HISTORY SOCIETIES

new to family history: can we help?

federation of FAMILY HISTORY SOCIETIES

For information on the Federation of Family History Societies
and its member societies in the UK and overseas
visit our website: www.ffhs.org.uk
or
e-mail: info@ffhs.org.uk
or write to
The Administrator, Maggie Loughran
PO Box 2425, Coventry, CV5 6YX UK

Family History and Local History
– You can't have one without the other
Alan Crosby discusses the connection ....

I often give talks in this subject to organisations involved in both areas of research and I find that almost without exception people are excited by the challenge and the opportunities which linking these two themes can offer. It is in some ways obvious that the two subjects do go together, and are inextricably entwined. We cannot understand local communities - their origins, development and character - without giving the fullest possible attention to the people who made up those communities. After all, the farms and the fields, the streets and the houses, the industries and the churches, are all the product of untold human endeavour over the centuries.

If we ignore the people we ignore the reason why, and that is absurd. Yet, at the same time, we cannot really understand the lives of individuals and the stories of families unless we consider their world, the environment they lived in and the lifestyles they enjoyed (or, maybe, didn't enjoy but rather suffered!).

How often, in researching your family history, have you wondered about what it was like for the people whose names, dates and brief historical record you have uncovered? What sort of housing did they live in, what clothes did they wear, what were their working conditions, what was the landscape which they knew from day to day and how did they fit into local society? Have you asked yourself why they moved from one place to another, what they felt about their fellow-citizens, how greater and lesser events impinged upon them, and what rituals and customs they encountered in birth, marriage and death. What sort of education was available to them - if any - and how did they tackle the burdens and oppressions of poverty, early and sudden death, natural disaster, illness and ill-health. What lightened their lives and what did they look forward to?

Local history can answer many such questions. It can set the lives of your forebears firmly in their proper context, helping to explain why they did what they did and what they met along life's path. All over the British Isles local history is a 'growth industry'. There are many hundreds of societies which are devoted to furthering the cause of local history - undertaking research, using original sources; holding lecture meetings and field visits; publishing the fruits of research and writing; campaigning for the extraordinarily rich heritage which is the legacy of the past and seeking to ensure its conservation and enhancement for future generations.

> **Local History can answer many such questions. It can set the lives of your forebears....**

Local history is endlessly diverse, full of rewards and unexpected surprises, and something which is available and accessible to everybody. The British Association for Local History helps to further the cause of this fascinating and valuable subject. BALH promotes the study of, and interest in, our local heritage and history.

All those who are interested in the history of the family will find that the study of local history can provide a much clearer and deeper understanding of where we came from and how it was in the past.

This article previously appeared in the 5th Edition

Starting Out
A Beginners Guide to Family History
Doreen Hopwood *guides you through the early stages*

Every family has its own, unique history, and our ancestors have helped to make us what we are today. For those of you about to embark on the ancestral trail, here are some basic guidelines to help you to proceed effectively and efficiently.

Until recently, it was the families of the rich and famous (or infamous!) whose histories were researched, but the same investigative techniques must be applied whatever the status of the family in order to produce a family tree. Patience and perseverance are two "musts" for the prospective family historian, along with a "sense of the past". As research takes you back in time, be prepared for surprises – and maybe the odd shock! We need to step back into the contemporary world of our forebears to understand their daily lives and you'll soon find yourselves delving into local and social history to find out more. What did a puddler do for a living? Court Heneage in Aston Manor may sound like a very grand address, but was a set of back to back houses in Victorian Birmingham!

Success with research may also depend on the survival of records, whether your family moved frequently, their status and even the popularity of the surname being studied. Perhaps you have an unusual surname and want to find out more - but be aware that in the nineteenth century many of our ancestors were illiterate and you may well encounter changes in spelling as they were written down as they sounded. On the plus side, however, names like Jones aren't prone to this problem!

Whilst this directory contains information about all of the major repositories in the United Kingdom – the Public Record Office, the Family Records Centre, county record offices and libraries – these are NOT the places to start your research. Your first steps should be to talk to members of your family and gather together as much information as you can. In addition to "official" documents such as birth, death and marriage certificates, wills etc, the following may provide valuable information to aid research:

A family bible – a great find, as it usually records dates of events as they happened. Memorial cards, obituaries and grave papers. School reports, apprenticeship papers, graduation certificates, occupational pensions. Military service records, medals or other awards. Society/club membership cards or trade union subscription cards. Diaries, scrapbooks, letters, newspaper cuttings, old address or birthday books.

Photograph albums are particularly helpful as "memory joggers" when talking to older members of the family, and if possible, make a recording of any interviews. Whilst there are certain questions you need to ask, take care not to be too demanding - several short interviews may be more productive than one long one. This is also a good time to ensure that you have recorded on your own photos "who, when and where". Future generations will thank you for it!

Don't discount the family myth or legend – every family has at least one. They are usually firmly based on the truth, but like Chinese whispers, they tend to become embellished or distorted as they are passed on from generation to generation. Set out to verify the information with documentary evidence and share your findings with other family members. You may find out that someone is already researching your family's history, or is interested in joining in with you. This is an excellent way of sharing the workload – and the costs. There are numerous books about genealogical research available – and you may be able to borrow some of these from your library. Monthly family history magazines usually contain a "Readers Interests" section in which people submit details of the surname, period, and area of their research, and you may find a possible entry for your family. If you do respond to any of these, please remember to enclose a stamped address envelope or international reply coupon.

Joining your local family history society will bring you into contact with individuals with the same interest – see the addresses of members of the Federation of Family History Societies in this directory. As well as regular meetings, you'll receive newsletters containing details of their publications and a "members interest" section. As you progress with your research, you may also want to join the society covering the area where your ancestors lived.

Attend a family history class. There is a whole range available, ranging from one-off workshops to academic courses leading to formal qualifications. Your local Education Authority will be able to advise you of locally run courses and look out for information at libraries and family history journals.

In this electronic age, more and more information is becoming available through the Internet. This is a great way of finding out about resources held in the area you are interested in and there are some excellent genealogical websites. However, don't expect to be able to compile your family tree solely from the world wide web. Whilst there are many indexes and resources accessible in this way, you will need to carry out research in numerous repositories – and this is part of the fun of family history. Nothing is more rewarding than seeing a 150 year old signature of one of your ancestors in a parish register, or visiting the church where family events were celebrated!

YOU are the most important person in your family tree, because you must always work from the known back to the unknown, generation by generation - yourself, parents, grandparents, great grandparents and so on. Never try to come forwards with your research – you may end up with an impressive family tree, but not necessarily your own. For most of us the first major national source we encounter is the General Register Office (GRO) Index, which includes every birth, death and marriage registered in England and Wales since the introduction of civil registration on 1 July 1837. Scotland and Ireland have their own registration systems which commenced in 1855 and 1864 respectively. The index has separate volumes for birth, death and marriage and until 1984, when it became an annual cumulative index, it is split into four quarters:

March - events registered in January, February and March; **June** - events registered in April, May and June; **September** - events registered in July, August and September; **December** - events registered in October, November and December
Each index is arranged alphabetically by surname, then by forename(s) and shows the district where the event was registered, the volume and page number. As a period of up to 42 days is allowed between the birth and its registration, check the quarter following the birth.

Your birth certificate shows your parents names and mothers maiden name THEN
Your parents marriage certificate shows the names of both grandfathers THEN
Your parents birth certificates show your grandparents names and grandmothers maiden name THEN Your grandparents marriage certificates show the names of both greatgrandfathers.......and so on.......

The General Register Office Index is now available in many libraries and other repositories. The Office of National Statistics (ONS) at Smedley Hydro, Trafalgar Road, Birkdale, Southport, Merseyside, PR8 2HH can provide details of local holdings. Once you have traced the entry you require, the full copy certificate can be purchased by post from the above address, from the register office at which the event was registered or by personal visit to the Family Records Centre at Myddleton Place, Myddleton Street, London EC1R 1UW. In the latter case, the certificate can either be collected a few days later or posted to you.

Before the establishment of civil registration, it was the responsibility of the Church to record baptisms, marriages and burials, and in order to utilise the church registers, you will need to know the parish where the events took place. A census – a count of

the population – has been taken every 10 years since 1801 with the exception of 1941. The census of 1841 is the earliest to contain information about individuals and as there is a 100 year closure on public access to the census enumerator's books, the latest that is currently available (for England and Wales) is the 1901 census – which was released VERY recently - in January 2002. Its availability in electronic format means that household entries can be downloaded and printed directly using a system of pre-payment. More recent returns for Scotland and Ireland are already available.

Census returns contain lists of all inhabited buildings, showing the names, ages, occupations, marital status, birth places and relationship to the head of household of everyone resident on the night the census was taken – but with less detail on the 1841 return. It is usually necessary to know an address – or at least a street to "find" a household as the returns are arranged by enumeration district, but there is a surname index to the 1881 census of the whole of England and Wales. Many local family history societies have produced indices for their own locality in respect of other returns. The census enumerators books for the whole of England and Wales are available at the Family Records Centre, whilst county record offices and main libraries usually hold copies covering their locality.

The Church of Jesus Christ of Latter Day Saints (the Mormon Church) has produced the International Genealogical Index (IGI) which is a worldwide resource and regularly expanded in its on-line form as *FamilySearch* on the Internet. Much of the information has been taken from original parish registers and complemented by family histories submitted by Church members. In its microfiche format, it is arranged by country then region/county and within these, alphabetically by surname, then forename and chronologically by event. For England and Wales, the majority of entries cover baptisms and marriages in the Established Church and may go back to the introduction of parish registers in the mid sixteenth century. The IGI can be found at major libraries, county record offices and at Church of Jesus Christ of Latter Day Saints Family History Centres. Their addresses can be found in telephone directories. Once an entry has been found on the IGI/*FamilySearch* always obtain a copy of the entry from the relevant repository as this will, in most

gravestones in church burial grounds. You can "browse" the catalogue of the Public Record Office (PRO) on-line prior to paying a visit and so organise your time effectively. The series of information leaflets is also available on the Internet at *http:www.pro.gov.uk* and these cover a wide range of topics for family history.

Since 1858 it has been the responsibility of the Government to administer wills and grant probates. The national, annual indexes (*Index of Wills and Letters of Administration*) can be found in major libraries and other record offices and the extracts include sufficient information to enable a full copy will to be purchased. They are arranged in alphabetical order by surname, then forename, and appear in the index covering the year in which the probate was granted - which may be several years after the date of death. Don't assume that only the rich or gentry left wills – a glance at the above indexes shows how many "ordinary" people made wills – and whilst the monetary value may be negligible, the amount of genealogical information can be enormous.

Do keep an open mind as you carry out research – whilst official documents provide evidence of names, dates, occupations and addresses, there are many other sources that will help to put your ancestors in their contemporary setting. Maps and photographs of the area in which the family lived will show how much (or how little) it has changed over time, whilst local newspapers give an account of what was going on. National and global events – such as the world wars of the twentieth century – affected our families and the demise of a local industry/employer might have instigated migration or a complete change of occupation for family members.

You may have thought that your family was "Brummie born and bred" but as you progress back in time, you will probably find that your ancestors came from all over the British Isles – and maybe beyond. The search will take you far afield in geographical terms as well as in time, adding to the fascination that is family history.

cases, provide additional information, including the signatures of the bride groom and witnesses at marriages. Whilst some churches still hold their parish registers, the majority will be found in the Diocesan Record Office – which is often based at the County Record Office. As well as registers of baptism, marriage and burial, the "Parish Chest" contains numerous other records relating to the Church, its officers and its parishioners. You may find that one of your ancestors was a prominent member of the church and appears as a Churchwarden or other parish official. Alternatively, an ancestor may have hit hard times and appear in the Overseers of the Poor's accounts as being in receipt of parish relief.

More and more "finding aids" and indexes are being produced for family history. One of these was the National Burials Index which became available on CD during 2000 to complement the published books of monumental inscriptions transcribed from (legible)

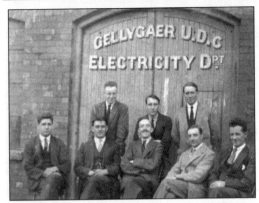

Your "Todays' are 'Tomorrows' Family History.

Elizabeth Blatchford

with a different aspect on writing a history

If, like many amateur family historians, you have spent hours on research, drawing up family trees, and travelling to various repositories – and have begun to run out of fresh avenues to explore, why not start again. This time, write a fresh history – the one about 'You'.

We are all living our own histories. Our childhood experiences, living conditions, thoughts and opinions can be recorded now, and, hopefully these records could provide future generations with comprehensive details they could never glean from any official sources.

Many of us have long charts showing family trees with dates of Births, Marriages and Deaths, and – if you are lucky, occupations: but what were your ancestors really like in appearance and personality ? – what thoughts did they have on national events, and how did their social surroundings and status affect them ?

Those of us who are lucky enough to be the descendants of the famous, or indeed, infamous, can find wonderful cameo descriptions in contemporary writings and newspapers of the time. For example, when Lord Nelson died at the Battle of Trafalgar in 1805, reports at the time mention personal details about him including the fact that he suffered dreadfully at the start of every voyage from seasickness. When Captain Scott died with his companions at the Antarctic in February 1913, his diary was found by his side. From this, we gain so much insight into their feelings at the time. Recorded during her lifetime, are details about Queen Elizabeth I who suffered greatly from black and decaying teeth (hidden from the artists who portrayed her) stating that she was terrified at the thought of having extractions.

For the vast majority of us there are no such biographies to which we can refer. Occasionally, someone is lucky and finds a day-to-day diary of life in earlier times, or possesses a bundle of letters, perhaps sent home by an emigrant family, telling of the trauma of long sea voyages and the privations endured in their new homelands. These diaries and letters which survive were often written at a time when very few of our ancestors were literate. Perhaps we no longer write as many letters as our

grandparents did, but we really have no excuse not to keep some small record of our own lives.

There are many choices in the way you write your history. Why not select a number of photos and explain the detail behind them. I was a child in the 1950's. I have a small photo of a group of us taken on an annual Sunday School trip to Whitby. This photo reminds me of the excitement we felt as we piled into carriages on the steam train for our day out at the seaside. Not many families owned their own cars so the day trip was really special. We were cautioned against sticking our heads out of the carriage windows, which dropped down by the use of a strong leather strap with holes in. If you looked out in to the steam from the engine it was likely that you would get a cinder in your eye.
Everyone took sandwiches and flasks, and our entertainment was primarily self-made – sea, sand, Punch and Judy Shows, donkey rides and beach cricket. I've many wistful memories of these days out – all rekindled from looking again at a tiny black and white Box Brownie photo.

Another photo, this time in fading colour, shows me as a gauche teenager, mini-skirted, and with a Cilla Black style hairdo. Many of us blush when we remember those teenage years. If you shared this period of history why not jot down the reactions from your parents to the "teenage" phenomenon. Were you part of the 'swinging 60's' ?, or, like me, did you live in an area where the old, small-community taboos were prevalent. We dabbled on the edge of this culture shock copying the latest fashions and playing the pop music of the time

Do you have photos when you were a Teddy Boy, or a flapper in the 1920's ? Did you enter a profession where you wore a uniform, and some proud relative took a snap of you as a rookie nurse, fireman or as you entered the Forces. These long forgotten photos, many without any indication on the back as to who the subject matter is or when they were taken, have such tales to tell and only you can record the stories behind the picture.

What about writing your memories of your schooldays. My generation of post-war 'baby boomers' will probably share recollections of some of the following:- compulsory school assemblies, small bottles of school milk with cardboard tops; seasons for marbles,skipping, collecting frog spawn and hula-hoops; inkwells and leather satchels; lace-up shoes in winter, and crepe-soled sandals with white socks in summer; liberty bodices and gaberdine macs; plaits and multicoloured hair ribbons. Now this is obviously from a girl's perspective – you boys must recall your side of things !

Maybe you were a child during one of the World Wars. Make a note of the impact on you as a child. Only you can write your feelings, fears and aspirations as affected by local and wider social conditions of the time. How thrilled we would all be had our forebears kept diaries or simple notebooks recalling the minutiae of their daily lives.

There are so many other titles under which you could tell your own story. Here are a few suggestions :-

My Hobbies — Our Family Celebrations
Family Holidays — Freedoms and Restrictions
Houses in which I have lived — My Family
First Romance — National Service
My life as a — Miner, Policeman, Docker, Student …..etc
My favourite books, films, music etc
Experiences in Hospital .. in an orphanage...In prison etc
My First job.

History is as recent as yesterday. In 1953, one month before the coronation, over one million black and white television sets were sold in Britain. Like so many other families, we did not own a T.V. and we crowded into a friend's house to watch this occasion. Now most households own one if not two colour T.V.'s, along with video recorders, satellite dishes and computers. So many changes we all experience, creeping upon us day by day.

So don't delay. Write something about yourself straightaway. You do not need a computer, there will be no charges for certificates, or travel expenses to Record Offices.
The essential equipment is one notebook, one pen/pencil, and a comfortable chair.
This is your chance to have your say, and your history is unique.

One little piece of advice. Once you get started, do ensure your story is kept somewhere safe, and do tell someone what you are doing. If not, all your efforts may disappear as you will eventually, and you'll just become another anonymous face on a fading photograph, or a series of dates on someone else's family history chart in years to come.

The Institute
of Heraldic and
Genealogical Studies

The Institute of Heraldic and Genealogical Studies is a charitable educational trust that was established in Canterbury, Kent in 1961 to promote the study of the history and structure of the family. To fulfil this aim a series of day, residential, evening and correspondence courses are run throughout the year for the benefit of family historians and genealogists. The courses range from those suitable for complete beginners to the subject, to those aimed at individuals wishing to pursue genealogical research as an income earning profession.

The day and residential courses offered in 2002 are —

Tudor & Stuart Ancestry	Residential Course	**15-17 March**
Introduction to Family History	Day School	**6 April**
Help I'm Stuck	Day School	**11 May**
My Ancestor was a British Soldier	Day School	**15 June**
Tracing Your Family History	Residential Course	**22-26 July**
Tracing Your Family History	Residential Course	**5-9 August**
Palaeography	Day School	**21 September**
Heraldy fo Family Historians	Day School	**12 October**
Tracing the History of a House	Residential Course	**15-17 November**

Accommodation for the residential courses is provided at one of the historic hotels or guesthouses in the delightful medieval city of Canterbury, close to the Institute's comprehensive library.

The Institute also runs an evening course that encompasses the whole of its syllabus required for qualification in genealogical research. This course, Family History, is held each year in central London at the London School of Economics, as well as at our premises in Canterbury. The course leads to graded assessments and examinations for certificates and diploma.

Family History	35 week evening course at the LSE	**4 September**
Family History	35 week evening course at the IHGS	**5 September**

For those students not able to study in Canterbury or London, the Institute runs a very popular correspondence course that is accredited by the Open and Distance Learning Quality Council. This is composed of a series of 24 in-depth assignments, each requiring written answers to questions on the particular topic. Individual tutorial guidance is given. The course is also open to students from abroad with an interest in British genealogical research and takes two or three years to complete, studying on a parttime basis.

Full details of the courses can be obtained from the Registrar on receipt of a large SAE.
Please send your enquiry to IHGS, 79-82 Northgate, Canterbury, Kent, CT 1 1BA
Tel 01227 768664   Fax 01227 765617   registrar@ihgs.ac.uk   http://www.ihgs.ac.uk

Family & Local History Courses

Angela Petyt

Who are my ancestors? What does my surname mean? Why did my forebears move so far away from their homeland? Who built those houses? How did that road get its name? Why is there a church standing alone in that field?

A visit to Wakefield's Chantry Chapel

There has been an increasing fascination in recent years with all things historical. Books, magazines, television and radio programmes, and the growing number of museums illustrate this *need* to know more about our heritage. History is all around us. In every village, town and city in every part of the world there is a story. Whether of ancient origin or modern, each locality is a testament to the families who lived there and the community they built. Generation after generation has added more history, as we will do in our lifetimes.

Let us find out more about ourselves by investigating the past.

Why join a course?
I have been teaching adult education classes in family and local history for the past seven years, in and around the Wakefield and Leeds districts of Yorkshire. Family history courses cover beginners, intermediate and advanced levels; the local history courses focus on the history of the city of Wakefield and the history of the village of Sandal Magna. I have also acted as an advisor to community groups in Allerton Bywater (near Castleford, Yorkshire) and Lupset (near Wakefield, Yorkshire) who wished to research and write books about the history of their area. Most classes meet once a week for two hours, the courses lasting for a ten-week term, although I have also taught more intensive one-day courses. I have travelled to and taught in many towns and villages and in many venues - ranging from portakabins to stately homes!

The abundance of resources available to research family and local history means that it is easier than ever before to work on our own, at our own pace, collecting and recording information. However, there are a lot of advantages to joining a family or local history course -

Learning with like-minded people
The social aspect is a major factor. Forming friendships, swapping memories and research tips. In my experience groups have ranged from six to almost forty students, and in all of them, a bond is formed. Many of those attending these classes are retired, particularly if they are held during the daytime, but younger people do enrol too. Married couples, in-laws, and neighbours often join together, sharing a common interest. The most popular classes are those that are informal, with plenty of opportunity for questions and discussion. If there is a friendly, welcoming atmosphere, people enjoy learning all the more.

The knowledge and skills of the tutor
Family history is a complex subject, involving many aspects of historical study as well as various research techniques to get the most out of available resources. In a beginners class, many of the students will be just starting out, although others may be more experienced and wish to take a 'refresher course'. A tutor will guide their class, showing step-by-step the logical route, covering the vital sources such as civil registration, census, the IGI and parish registers. Each topic will be clearly explained, both its historical context and relevance for genealogical research. Examples of the document will be shown and discussed, as well as samples of books on the subject. It is a great help if students receive a weekly guidance sheet to keep, detailing the main points of the topic. These can then build up into a useful work of reference. More advanced family history courses will usually follow the same format, introducing lesser used sources such as records of schools, manor court rolls, dating old photographs and reading old handwriting, both English and Latin. Tuition will also be given in how to compile research information and draw family tree charts, both by hand or using a computer.

Local history courses may be general, focussing on similar documents and research strategies as covered in a family history class, to assist students in undertaking a particular project. Other courses may look in detail at a community, be it a district, town or village. In such courses, the tutor will share the knowledge and research they have done themselves with the class, taking them back through the centuries in the weekly sessions, unfolding the story. Again, it is very helpful if guidance sheets are provided and collections of documents, photographs, maps and books brought to the class for the students to look at and discuss. Students attending such classes might be interested in the history of the community where they live, or have ancestors living in the area and want to find out more to 'flesh out the bones' of their family tree.

Very often those attending family history classes go on to enrol on a local history class, or vice-versa. The subjects are very much intertwined.

Visits to archives, libraries, LDS family history centres
In both family and local history courses, the tutor will usually arrange group visits to repositories - perhaps the Local Studies Library, County Record Office and the Latter Day Saints (Mormon) Family History Centre. These visits might involve guided tours around the building, showing storage areas and document repair workshops, special access to documents, or guest speakers. Group visits help students to get a

In Class

'feel' of how such places operate. Beginners in particular can be nervous about going to a record office for the first time. Attending as a group, with the staff explaining all the regulations and procedures, helping and advising in an informal atmosphere, can assist greatly.

Visits to local places of interest and guided walks
Particularly in local history courses, the tutor may arrange guided walks around the locality. For example in my History of Wakefield class, I take my students around hidden corners of the city, pointing out features of landscape and architecture. Such walks are informal yet informative (and good exercise!), adding to the social aspect. As well as outdoor activities, tutors might also book special tours to local churches, castles, stately homes, museums and important civic buildings - often where the public don't normally have access.

Such tours and walks, when combined with classroom sessions, will provide a good mixture of learning experiences.

Gain a qualification
In some courses you can gain a qualification, which can be satisfying in itself or be a springboard to undertaking other accredited courses. Some examples of awarding bodies are the Institute of Heraldic and Genealogical Studies, the Open University, and the Open College Network.

Who runs courses?
Many different organisations now offer courses in family and local history, and the list is growing all the time. They can range from one session per week (either in the daytime or evening), to one-day workshops, to correspondence courses or residential courses. Some may be free of charge, for others, a fee will be payable. Those organisations running such courses include -
Further Education Colleges
Worker's Educational Association (WEA)
Local Education Authorities
Family/Local History Societies
Institute of Heraldic and Genealogical Studies
Society of Genealogists
Public Record Office
Community groups

Open University
Libraries and Archives
'Virtual classes' delivered via the Internet

If there are no family and local history classes offered in the area where you live, do contact some of the above - if there is sufficient demand and a suitable tutor, these classes may be arranged.

What happens after the course finishes?
When the course is over, hopefully students will then possess the knowledge and confidence to carry out their own research. They may wish to join a family/local history society, which can extend the social and educational aspect. Forming a study group with friends made on the course is another way of keeping in touch and developing experience and skills.

Or you might wish to enrol on another course!

Angela Petyt lives in Wakefield, Yorkshire. She has a BA (Hons) in History and Language Studies from the University College of Ripon and York St. John, and (DA301) Studying Family and Community History from the Open University. Angela works as a lecturer in family and local history and is currently Director of Publications for the Federation of Family History Societies.

The Castle that didn't Exist ....
Robert Blatchford
advises a cautionary approach to research

A news report in The Times newspaper on Tuesday 3rd April 2001 reminded me of the need for accuracy and to verify the sources of information upon which we rely in our family history research. Without that firm principle we are likely to go astray and create a false family history. It is essential for our descendants to be able to rely upon the accuracy of our researches because if we go wrong in those endeavours the result is really not worth the paper it is written on.

According to Alan Hamilton in his report in TheTimes, American tourists have fallen for an ancestral castle spoof and have swallowed a myth which has sent a steady stream of transatlantic visitors in search of their ancestral home at Brancaster Castle.

"Battlemented on top of its high Norfolk cliff, this ancient English bulwark has withstood Norsemen, Danes and French invaders. Sometimes its hundred dungeons have brimmed with prisoners, sometimes it has been a refuge for the Christian oppressed. It is a place of such romantic history that it is really quite a shame it does not exist. The giveaway is its clifftop location. Brancaster, site of a fine golf course and bird sanctuary, is far from cliff-girt; at that point north of King's Lynn, Norfolk, surrenders itself almost imperceptibly to the waters of The Wash in a low and lazy succession of dunes and mudflats. They don't know that in Des Moines, Iowa, and other landlocked Midwest habitations. They come in person, they make phone calls to the local vicar and they bombard the village website with e-mails. They are all called Rix."

They are all basing their connection with Brancaster on a book in the Library of Congress. Published in 1906 the book, The History and Genealogy of the Rix Family of America, was written by a Guy S. Rix,. He wrote "an accurate and scholarly work, of how the Rix family emigrated from England in the 17th century" but included a letter apparently written in 1894 telling of the family's glorious past in a Norfolk castle with "12ft thick walls, which had been visited by Henry VIII". He presumably inserted the letter in the belief "that more namesakes would buy his book if they thought they were descended from English castle-owning nobility."

Nowadays the local Rector of Brancaster, Rev Lawrence Campbell, has become involved and said lots of Americans turn up on his doorstep asking for information about the castle becoming angry and upset when he tells them the truth. Mr Campbell thought they wanted to visit the area as soon as "they get an inkling they are from a famous family with a castle."

During 2000, the keeper of the tower at Brancaster church, Bernard Lock, said that he had encountered four American couples hunting for the castle. One lady and her husband had photocopied pages from the book and in an attempt to put the record straight Mr Lock has written to the Library of Congress in Washington, who have agreed to put a note in its copy of the book explaining that Brancaster Castle does not, and never has, existed. He has also persuaded an American publisher to add a correction when it issues a reprint.

This example of a false family history shows how too easily we can be led astray in our researches. It reminded me of an incident in my own research. I had found an elderly cousin and he had been a great help. I was able to show him our great grandparents' grave which was in the local churchyard. He had walked past this gravestone on a weekly basis when visiting his wife's grave.

On one of my visits to see my cousin I had given him a copy of the drop line chart as it stood at that time. Sadly, shortly after this he died, and the chart passed to one of his nephews. Some time later I was told that a lot of the information on the chart had been 'published' on the internet. Out of curiosity I looked at the site and discovered many inaccuracies – people who had died were still living, names were incorrect as was much of the detail. More worrying for me was the fact I had died over 30 years previously. After a quick check with my wife she assured me that I was truly alive and well.

The problem for researchers arises when we rely too heavily upon third party information which invariably contains inaccurate or wrong information, or has been incorrectly transcribed. As I travel about the country at Family and Local History Fairs or when I am talking to groups I am quite often told that a person has 'done' their family tree and that they 'got it all off the internet'. If this is symptomatic of a lot of research today then there will be many families relying upon false information.

Unless you verify the source of your information it is always advisable to check and confirm that information with the original or a photocopy/film of that material.

When I decided to put pen to paper – this is still accurate even if it is keyboard and computer! – I made a search of the internet. It was surprising to discover that there was so much material on the web dealing with false family histories.

The Jaznuary/February 2001 issue of the North American family history magazine , *Family Chronicle*, carried an article by Ron Wild " *Beware of Fraudulent Genealogies*" in which Ron warned that not all genealogists were interested in finding the truth.

Ron said that never before in the history of genealogy have researchers been able to access such a vast assortment of genealogical records with 'the ease and speed that we have come to accept as the normal state of affairs.' He ascribes this phenomenon to two reasons. Firstly that many family history researchers in their enthusiasm to go 'on record' have *published* family histories that contain much detail that is unconfirmed. These have then become incorporated into the huge databases on the internet and form the record pool that many hundreds of thousands of researches extract material from every day. They have probably submitted these details with the best of intentions wishing to share their research with everyone but by and large they lack the source verification that would allow the information to be accepted accurately. However it is Ron Wild's second reason that is the more ominous in that like Guy S Rix many internet databases contain fraudulent genealogies created by 'forgers'. Ron continues his article by discussing the master forger Gustave Anjou who created hundreds of genealogies in the late 19th and early 20th centuries. It seems that Anjou has created over 2000 common surname genealogies which can only be regarded as tainted.

The list of forgeries grows each day and the Genealogy Frauds website estimates that up to 55% of online genealogies contain serious errors. www.linkline.com/personal/xymox/fraud/fraud223.htm The number of occasions that I hear people say I can do all my research on the 'net' or on 'my computer' could mean that your research is being done in isolation or via internet chat rooms. There is no way that these methods can replace the excitement of examining original records or facimilies amongst fellow researchers or archivists. To handle or look at material that is many generations old can be inspirational. I once looked at a parish register from the early 18th century and was able to see the doodles and comments written by the Curate more than 200 years previously. Did he realize that his comments would be examined and digested in their original hand towards the end of the 20th century. I do not think he would have given it a thought. Likewise it is incumbent upon ourselves to ensure that what we have written today about our family history stands as an accurate and verified record which can be relied upon in 200 years time.

Not only is this a plea to every researcher to ensure accuracy in their research but it also aims to encourage you to visit the Record Offices, Archives and all other repositories to view and examine original records to verify and ensure accuracy in your family history. It would be a great disappointment if after years of searching, the truth is exposed and that family history of which you are so proud is literally *not worth the paper it is written on.*

Further Reading
The Times , Tuesday 3rd May 2001 page 3
Beware of Fraudulent Genealogies by Ron Wild
   Family Chronicle January February 2001
   Volume 5 Number 3 ISSN 1209-4617
Fraudulent Lineages
www.linkline.com/personal/xymox/fraud/fraud223.htm
Watch Out for Fake Family Trees by James Pylant
www.genealogymagazine.com/watoutforfak.html
Fraudulent Genealogies
   www.rideau-info.com/genealogy/revmir-15.html
Heraldry Lecture by Joseph C Wolf
   www.digiserve.com/heraldry/lecture.htm

India and Family History
Simon Fowler
discusses Anglo-India ancestry

Since the seventeenth century there has always been close links with the Indian sub-continent. Initially this relationship was based on trade. During the nineteenth century this was increasingly replaced by imperial considerations, particularly after the Mutiny of 1857. Finally after independence and partition in 1947 a number of Indians and Anglo-Indians made their home in Britain, although it should be stressed that this was not a new phenomena – the first MPs of Indian origins were elected in the 1890s.

Until 1857, British relations with India were largely handled by the East India Company (EIC) – 'John Company' as it was sometimes known. The Company was founded in December 1600, as one of a number of European ventures trading with the Moghul emperors and other Indian princely states, importing silks and spices in return for guns and other metal goods. By the mid-eighteenth century the EIC had become the dominant player in Indian affairs, having largely seen off European rivals, although small French and Portuguese enclaves remained until the 1960s.

In contrast to their nineteenth century successors the Company initially encouraged relationships between European employees and local people. In 1687, for example, the EIC promoted Christian marriages between European soldiers and the Indian women of Fort St George in Madras, by giving the mother of each child a small grant on the day the child was baptised. Later the Company encouraged "their humbler servants to make their permanent abode in India" by introducing a five-rupee monthly allowance for every child born to a soldier in the ranks.

During the 18th century it was not uncommon for British soldiers and officials of all ranks to form liaisons with Indian women. Indeed it is now thought that at least a third of these men took Indian wives and mistresses. Sir Eyre Coote, who had fought at the Battle of Plassey in 1757 and later became commander in chief of British forces, married a local woman. David Ochterlony, the general who first fought and then befriended the Gurkhas, provided one of the sights of 1820s Calcutta, when he and his thirteen wives made their daily progress across the Maidan, mounted on the backs of elephants.

However this changed towards the end of the century, partly out of fears that the Anglo-Indian community had other loyalties than to Britain and would ferment revolt against the Company. In 1789 Eurasians were prevented from serving as soldiers in the Indian Army, and later excluded from senior employment within the EIC. The exclusion was based upon "the injuries which could accrue to the discipline and reputation of His Majesty's troops employed in India, from the admission of persons as officers, or even soldiers, who are born of black women, natives of the Country". However, they were still recruited as bandsmen, surveyors and apothecaries. The Anglo-Indians, however, saw themselves as Europeans, and were resentful of official prejudice against them. One historian of the community, Frederick Anthony, wrote that in "certain periods of our history, our treatment by the British was not only deliberately, but advisedly repressive and unnaturally cruel".

During the first half of the 19th century the Eurasian community entered a period of decline as they faced discrimination from both the Indian and European communities. They began to face competition for jobs from Western-educated Indians and the increasing numbers of British people living in India. Between 1830 and 1859, the unofficial British population in the sub-continent rose from 2,000 to 10,000. Anglo-Indians increasingly took jobs in the Posts and Telegraphs and Customs departments and on the railways, eventually forming the majority of drivers, guards and stationmasters.

The Indian Mutiny of 1857 is undoubtedly the most important event in British-Indian relations. The spark was the distribution of fat to native soldiers to grease their guns, which rumour said contained pork – the use of which was against the beliefs of Muslim sepoys. But it was based on a variety of grievances and grumbles against the British rulers. It took six-months for the Mutiny to be crushed – and crushed it was with determination. *The Times* demanded that: "every tree and gable-end in the place should have its burden in the shape of a mutineer's carcass."
The consequences were profound. The East India Company was disbanded. In its place came the Government of India – the Raj - under a Viceroy appointed by the British government. Relations between the British and Indians became more formal.

The British formed a distinct self-contained community, who distrusted Indian and Anglo-Indian alike. The Raj now regarded itself as a ruling enclave, different in kind from the people it rules – an institution rather than a community, whose best intentions and most useful works were ever after tinged with distrust, disapproval or superiority.
Over the next ninety years, the British worked diligently to modernise the sub-continent. The greatest memorial

remains the railway system, but great areas were irrigated for the first time, a legal system offering equality for all, and perhaps the most lasting of all – cricket - were also introduced. Indians were initially employed at the lowest levels, but by the time of partition in 1947 occupied virtually every position in the government.

It cannot be said that the British were much loved in India. The imposition of the conventions and beliefs of mid-Victorian England on native customs grated, as did the petty racism and slights against local people. Only the maharajahs and the rulers of the Princely states seemed immune, but even here they often became more English than the English. There were of course Brits who immersed them in local tradition or treated Indians as equals, but they were rare birds indeed.

The movement towards Indian independence began in the 1880s with the formation of the Congress Party. By the 1920s the vast majority of Indians - of every religious belief - supported independence. Two decades of violence and increasing lawlessness followed as the British dithered about what to do. After the Second World War it was clear that unless independence was granted quickly the country would slide into communal violence which the Imperial authorities could not control. Viscount Mountbatten, the last Viceroy, was given the job of partitioning the sub-continent into mainly Hindu India and Moslem East and West Pakistan. Hundreds of thousands of lives were lost in the months after independence. After a short civil war in 1972, East Pakistan seceded to become Bangladesh.

The records
Before the Indian Mutiny of 1857 British India was controlled and administered by the private East India Company. In 1859, control was placed in the hands of the Government of India under a Viceroy. Under the Company India was divided into three presidencies: Bengal. Bombay and Madras, each with their own army. This division continued to a degree even after 1859, so if you are looking for British soldiers, administrators or clerks it is important to know which presidency he served with. There was also a patchwork of native or princely states, nominally independent in which power usually lay with a British resident.

If you are tracing soldiers who served in India it is important that you know whether they served with the British Army or the Indian Army – as the records are very different. This is usually clear from the names of the regiments they were with. If you are not sure staff at the PRO or British Library (BL) should be able to help you.

Very few records about British residents remain in India itself – the major source is probably monumental inscriptions for men and their families who died while on service there. These MIs may have been transcribed and published by the British Association for Cemeteries in South Asia (BACSA) and are available at the Society of Genealogists.

The vast majority of records are with the British Library's Oriental and Indian Office Collections. Other places with records include the Public Record Office (PRO) and the Society of Genealogists (SoG). The PRO's holdings are almost entirely for men who served in the British Army in India, rather than were directly employed by the East India Company or the Government

of India. The PRO library however does have an incomplete set of the *East India Register*, *India Office List* and other official publications listing officials, and army and navy officers. The List, for example, includes brief biographical details for senior civil servants. Other sets can be found at the SoG (also incomplete) and British Library.

The India Office and Oriental Collections at the BL is a unique source of information on the history of British involvement in South Asia and neighbouring areas. These records are described in a free leaflet *Sources for Family History* (Oriental and Indian Office Collections Guide No 4) which is available from the Library.

Probably the first port of call however is the biographical index, which contains nearly 300, 000 entries for civil and military servants and their families, as well as for non-official Europeans living in India. The bulk of the archival material consists of original documentation usually arranged in regular series of original letters received, drafts or copies of letters sent, registered files of correspondence, minutes of proceedings of committees and other corporate bodies, lists of personnel and nominal returns, wills and other legal documents, books of account, reports, memoranda, and ships' journals. They include Ecclesiastical Returns, which comprise copies of registers of baptisms, marriages and burials of European and Eurasian Christians resident in South Asia from the early-eighteenth century to 1948, although there are Catholic registers only for the early-Victorian period. There are also service records for men who served in the East India Company and the Indian Army for the period up to the First World War. Another useful source are entry papers for people wishing to join the EIC between 1749 and 1856, as well as personnel records for the 'Uncovenanted Civil Service', that is the junior or technical grades between 1818 and 1947.

The Society of Genealogists also has some useful collections. As well as official lists there are some unofficial lists of Europeans who served in India during the eighteenth century and a set of correspondence in 1948 and 1949 with a number of Anglo-Indians seeking to prove British nationality.

Useful addresses
British Empire and Commonwealth Museum, Clock Tower Yard, Temple Meads, Bristol BS1 6QH Tel: 0117-925 4980
E-mail: staff@empiremuseum.co.uk
www.empiremuseum.co.uk
The museum has a number of collections, including many MIs for Indian cemeteries
Oriental and India Office Collections
British Library, 96 Euston Rd, London NW1 2D
Tel: (020) 7412 7641 E-mail: oioc-enquiries@bl.uk
WWW: www.bl.uk
To use these collections you will need to obtain a reader's ticket on your first visit to the Library, which is to be found next to St Pancras Station. You will need two passport photographs as well as some form of identity. The collections themselves are on the third floor. The Library has some of the most expensive catering (it's not very good either), I've ever come across so bring sandwiches or lots of money!

Further reading
Ian Baxter, *India Office Library and Records: A Brief Guide to Biographical Sources* (British Library,1990)
A. Gabb, *The Anglo-Indian Legacy 1600-1947: A Brief Guide to British Raj India History* (2nd edition, 2001 available from the author, Church Farm Bungalow, Overton, York YO39 1YL, price £8.10). This is a very useful guide.
Sources for Anglo-Indian Genealogy in the Library of the

Society of Genealogists.(Society of Genealogists, 1990)
Geraldine Charles, 'Anglo-Indian Ancestry' *Family History Monthly* (June 2001) is a good introduction for people with Eurasians in their family tree

The Indiaman, 2 South Farm Avenue, Harthill, Sheffield S26 7WY, Tel: 01909-774416
www.Indiaman.com claims to be 'the only genealogical and history magazine in the world for people researching their ancestry of British and European origin in India and Southern Asia from 1600 to the 20th century.'
Websites
By far the best website is the Family History in India site:
www.ozemail.com.au/~clday/
www.anglo-indians.com also has lots of very interesting material.
Societies
British Association for Cemeteries in South Asia (BACSA)
Families in British India Society
Society of Genealogists

In Defence of the Realm
Barbara Chambers

From 1793 - 1802 Britain was at war with France and during this period known as the 'French Revolutionary War', had seen her allies disappear and France occupy many countries in Europe and further afield. It had also seen the rise to power of Napoleon Bonaparte, who had become First Consul. By 1801 both countries were weary, and wanted peace, though for very different reasons. Britain in order to reduce the starvation and heavy taxation that the war had produced and settle down to trading, and building her Empire. The French to build up her power in order to enlarge her conquest in Europe and elsewhere and build up her forces to destroy Britain. During this period of this war there had been invasions scares and on 5th April 1798 'The Defence of the Realm Act, was given the Royal Assent. Many men joined the fencibles and volunteer forces raised during this period, at one time the volunteers totalled 10,000, the army strength was 380,000 in addition the Navy at its' height had 133,000 men. Although the Navy had many successes against France and her allies, and was able to prevent supplies reaching the French army by carrying out blockades and also prevent the invasion of Britain, the Army struggled during this period. However the peace signed on 27th March 1802 brought relief to Britain and a massive reduction in her Navy and Army.

Britain entered whole-heartily into the celebration of peace and resumed her trading and visits to the continent including France .

The peace was however to be short lived and 16th May 1803 saw a resumption of hostilities with France. By January 1803 the strength of the British Army abroad was 50,304 and at home was 45,071 this included Militia, but not the Royal Artillery and Engineers. The realisation that war was unavoidable saw Britain begin a massive mobilisation of her people to defend the country from the threat of invasion by Napoleon. A flurry of Acts of Parliament were passed raising Militia and Volunteer forces to defend Britain and the strength of the Army was also increased. The Militia in May 1803 had 51,128 men and the Army at home had risen to 150,839 men, by the end of the year the numbers were 84,697 for the Militia and 172,286 in the Army, the numbers abroad stayed fairly static during this time.

With the ever growing threat of invasion further Acts were passed to increase the number of men available to defend Britain, These Acts of Parliament were to enable an 'additional Military force to be raised for the better Defence of the United Kingdom and for the more vigorous prosecution of the war '. The first two acts passed on 6th July 1803 applied to England & Wales, with a separate Act for Scotland. These were followed on 11th July 1803 an Act 'to raise and assemble, in Ireland, an additional Military Force' for the same reasons as the earlier Acts and also on 27th July 1803, an Act for raising in the City of London, 'a certain Number of Men as an Addition to the Military Force'.

This separate Act for the City of London was needed because, despite the City through various charters being exempted from raising men for military service they volunteered to raise men and offered 800, nominating the numbers of men to be raised from each ward of the City.

All these men were to be put into an Army of Reserve and each county was given a specific number of men it had to raise, either from volunteers or by ballot, these men were then to be sent either as reserves to specific regiments or to specified reserve battalions raised for this purpose. The men raised in England, Wales, Scotland and the City of London were only required to serve in Great Britain, Ireland and the Islands of Guernsey, Jersey and Alderney. Those raised in Ireland initially were required only to serve in Ireland, however as a result of officers and men indicating that 'they wished to volunteer their services for the interest and security of the United Kingdom' in May 1804 an Act was passed allowing any Irish Militia Forces who voluntarily offered themselves, to be allowed to be employed anywhere in Great Britain. From the start the Government encountered difficulties in raising and later in maintaining the numbers, partly because there were many exemptions and partly because there was an ever increasing need to maintain the Army and Navy as well as keeping up numbers in the County Militia regiments. In June and July 1804 the rules were change and Acts were passed 'for establishing and maintaining a permanent additional force for the Defence of the Realm and to provided for augmenting His Majesty's Regular Forces, and for the gradual reduction of Militia'. Quotas required to be supplied by each county or ward were again specified.

The manpower of the Army increasingly became the priority and in April 1805, Acts allowing a certain proportion of the Militia in Great Britain and Ireland voluntarily to enlist into His Majesty's Regular Forces and Royal Marines, were passed. Manpower by August 1805 was 66,034 abroad, 182,293 at home and 74,426 Militia.

The Acts to recruit an Army of Reserve which were passed in 1803, laid out the procedures for recruiting the men, the organisation of the ballot's and those exempted from these ballot. Initially each parish had to draw up a list of all men liable to be balloted and those exempt from ballot, which included those who had left the parish before 22nd June 1803. This list was affixed to doors of churches. Among those exempted were any men already serving in the military, militia or volunteer forces, clergymen, licensed teachers, constables, justices of the peace, articled clerks and apprentices under 21yrs. Professional seamen, and other seafarers, dockyard, and ordinance employees. Poor man having one child under 10yrs, in Scotland two under 10yrs. Those who had already served in Militia unless their turn had come round again, were also excluded. Of the men selected by ballot those under 5'2" but otherwise fit were deemed to be unfit.

The procedure once a man was selected was that a notice was served at his place of abode five days before the time he was required to assemble at the meeting which was to be called within 14 days of the ballot. They were to be enrolled to serve as a Private in the Army to be raised. If the notice was left with his wife or member of family or servant at his usual or last place of abode this shall be deemed to have been served. Those failing to appear were subject to fine. The men balloted were permitted to find suitable substitutes, and from records checked so far it would appear many did. Although Quakers were not exempted from the ballot, it was recognised that they would refuse to serve, so were as others refusing to serve fined £20 and remained on the lists, substitutes were to be provided for any Quakers balloted and a levy of £20 raised from sale of their goods and chattels. Balloted men were to received a bounty of 2 guineas marching money on joining and substitutes 1 guinea.

All those balloted or substituted were to be examined by a surgeon before enrolling. Their conditions of service were for 5 years in the United Kingdom of Great Britain and Ireland, and the Islands of Jersey, Guernsey and Alderney. The men could not be compelled to serve abroad unless they freely and voluntarily enlisted for general service in any Regiment. It would appear that many took up this option throughout the period this Reserve was in being.

Wives and families of men raised were entitled to relief under the same circumstance as the Militia.

Details of many of the men so raised for England & Wales are to be found in the documents- Public Record Office E182 - 'Exchequer. King's Remembrance: Particulars of Account or Land & Assessed Taxes' Included with the land tax documents for the years 1803 and 1804, among other items some of which are detailed below, are numerous pieces of paper listing details of marching money awarded to men of that county. The payment was made by the exchequer from the Land Tax funds for each county, and details of the men together with the regiment or reserve battalion that they entered and sometimes the Regiment they transferred to is included. Some men are recorded by companies, some give details of the place of birth or parish they represent, the two need not necessarily be the same, all give details of the county they represent.

The lists also show some of the early volunteers to Army Regiments or the Royal Artillery, where the claim has been made by that Unit, although all these men would initially have been in either the appropriate Regiment or Reserve Battalion. However those who went on to volunteer for Regiments of the line or Artillery are by no means all listed as such and many more later joined for unlimited service in the regiment they were initially sent to or another regiment. Their information would be found in the Regimental muster rolls of the battalion they were in. Also contained in these boxes in addition to the details of the land taxes, are 'Payments made to Wives and Families of reserve men' in some case naming the wife and listing the number of children. These payments were again made from the Land Tax Revenue rather than the parish; various other payments relating to the organisation of the balloting for the Army of Reserve are also including, by way of payments made to various

officials. In addition the boxes contain details of marching money paid for Militia companies naming the men, but not their parishes; and payments made for the apprehension of deserters naming the deserter and his Regiment and the person apprehending him.

Maintaining the numbers in the Army of Reserve proved to be an impossible task, the 16 Reserve battalions were finally disbanded and merged on 24th February 1805 NCO's & Private men being sent to the 3 Garrison Battalions, under the same conditions of service. Finally in December 1806 the last remaining men serving in the Reserves of various Regiments were transferred to additional newly formed Garrison Battalions. By this time the threat of invasion had gone and Britain had now begun to send out troops to aid various countries not yet invaded by the French, beginning the next stage of the war and an ever increasing build up of men under arms.

Army of Reserve
I have begun to index the men recruited for the Army of Reserve who appear in E182, for the years 1803 and 1804, the indexes are being compiled by county and the way the counties are selected is by including all those counties sending to the same regiment or reserve battalion.

Additional information
I have a full list of the make up of each of the 16 reserve battalions in relation to where the men came from. Including details on which of the Garrison battalions those left would have finally gone into.

Of those men sent to reserve battalions of regular regiments I also have details of which Regiments the men from England, Scotland and Wales were sent. Men who served in the Army of Reserve or the Militia and who later went on to join the regular army, and receive a pension, do not always have their service in the reserve or militia mentioned on the discharge documents. A couple of pointers which could indicated service in the reserve is if the men joined in late 1803 early 1804 and were not near their homes at the time of enlistment, then it is possible that they may have served in the reserve. With regards Militia service from 1805 onwards if the place of enlistment is unusual and from 1811 onwards more increasingly in Ireland then the likelihood is that they were a volunteer from the militia.

Those men still serving in the reserves of regular regiments in June 1806, would not have been included in the musters which were required to be completed at this time showing details of men 'fit for overseas service as at June 1806'. As they were still only required to serve in Britain. These musters are found in Public Record Office references WO25/871-1120, and I am also indexing these at present.

INDEXES
The indexes for Army of Reserve 1803 contain:
Surname, forename, parish*, county, balloted/substitute, Regiment/reserve battalion
*Parish is not always included, this is place of birth or parish they represent they need not necessarily be the same thing.
Regimental Indexes for number one service returns 1806 contain:
Surname, forename, rank, year of enlistment; Regiment.

For up to date information see
http://members.aol.co./BJCham2809/homepage.html

Nurses & Midwives Records
Audrey Daykin

discusses another research area

Audrey Walker-Smith 1958

Nursing records from the mediaeval period are sketchy and of more interest to the nursing historian than the family historian. Worth noting is that at that time both sexes were involved in the care of the sick. It was only after the Dissolution of the Monasteries that nursing became predominently female, a situation which prevailed up until the 20th century. The religious orders set very high standards but since then nursing has been like a barometer peaks and troughs until an attempt at a national equilibrium was made in the first quarter of the 20th century.

Midwives have always been important members of a healthy, well ordered society. By an Act of Parliament dated 1511 midwives needed a licence from either a bishop or an archbishop before they could practise and they were required to show their licence at each Episcopal Visitation. Many of these licences have survived and they are held by Diocesan Record Offices. The greatest numbers are held by the Provinces of York and Canterbury. The Borthwick Institute in York holds 300 and Lambeth Palace Library holds 100. The latest example at The Borthwick is 1772. The midwife had to petition for registration supported by a group of experienced midwives with whom she had served an apprenticeship.

They are an interesting group and given that occupations tend to run in families are well worth exploring if a 19th century nurse is found in the family. Because of the nature of their work they feature quite often in the records of ecclesiastical courts and the entries can be informative. In 1753 a case of adultery was heard in the Consistory Court of St.Paul's Cathedral. One witness was Hannah Chattin, midwife, wife of a lighterman called William Chattin.

When King Henry VIII suppressed the religious houses there was nowhere for the poor and sick to go. Six years after the Dissolution of the Monasteries the King responded to petitions from the Lord Mayor and Citizens of London and re established St.Bartholomew's Hospital as a secular foundation. There is evidence that Lay Sisters were appointed to care for the sick. It was a slow uncertain start to nursing as a secular occupation and gradually the Lay Sisters disappeared as nursing entered its' own Dark Ages.

Throughout the late 17th-18th centuries hospitals sprang up all around the country mostly financed by voluntary contributions. In many instances minutes of management committee meetings have survived and they are heavily peppered with the misdeeds of nurses.

A few examples from around the country are; - Nurse Lewis discharged for misbehaviour; Susannah Woodbridge for misdeneanour; Mary Paul guilty of mistakes when giving patients their physick; Nurse Stevens and Phoebe Burnham were drunk! These were the days of Hogarth's "Gin Lane", drunk for 1d. dead drunk for 2d. Nurse Squibbs was lucky in that she got away with calling a patient "Bitch!" Records from this time can be found and it is worth noting that they do exist, that is - if you want to own her!

Hogarth's "Gin Lane" in the 18th century became Dickens' Sarah Gamp in the 19th century. Although the incidence of Sarah Gamp types is currently being looked at again it is a fact that the names of nurses continue to appear in hospital minutes and the records are becoming more numerous ; - Ann Duncombe was noisy and disruptive, Elizabeth Langston supplied patients with strong liquor but poor Nurse Grubb was reprimanded for drinking tea with a patient at 11pm. However change was on the way.

300yrs after the Reformation the religious houses came to the rescue. In 1840 Elizabeth Fry started an Institute of Nursing Deaconesses. The Anglican Church was quick to follow suit and established many Nursing Sisterhoods. But still murmurings continued. At The London Hospital there is a minute to the effect that youngish literate women were hard to find. Such were the experiences of Doncaster Royal Infirmary that it says in their minutes "The inexperienced and ignorant care of any honest woman was preferred where attainable" In 1868 that same hospital was in such difficulty it hired a nurse from Liverpool at a fee of £1—1s per week. Interestingly the two hospitals discussed who should pay her superannuation which was very forward thinking for the time. In 1767 Leeds General Infirmary appointed Mrs Mary Turner aged over 50yrs Matron and Elizabeth Atkinson, aged, over 43yrs as the nurse, By 1869 the hospital had a staff of 14 qualified nurses. These facts put the situation into context; locally we are researching rather small numbers, the vast majority of nurses were domestics rather than carers.

As the 19th century moved on the cry for change became an outcry and the outcry was heard. There was a pool of educated spinsters with no escape from boredom except into good works. Also there were gentle caring women denied their vocation since the reign of Henry VIII. Ladies like Miss Nightingale were organisational geniuses, articulate and forceful. My favourite quote from Miss Nightingale is "The hospital should do the patient no harm" (taken from her 'Notes on Hospitals 1857') Thanks to Miss Nightingale organised nurse training began at St Thomas 's and then fanned out across the country. Nursing had become respectable. The movement for reform did not confine itself to the voluntary hospitals; it extended into workhouse infirmaries and slowly the destitute became recipients of care. Sisters were recruited separately and were usually from a higher social class, as were the matrons. In 1888 The Royal National Pension Fund for

Minnie West
Died South Africa 1901

Nurses was established to care for the carers: the records of The Leeds Trained Nurses Association contain many references to that excellent organisation. It is true to say that nursing played a large part in the emancipation of women.

In his book Gary Swann mentions the research into the 1851 census, viz. 25,466 nurses by profession.; 39,139 nurses in domestic service.; 2,822 midwives. These figures illustrate how rapidly nursing was growing but also how much still needed to be done.

In the censuses are references to "Wet Nurses". A nurse was a carer and a wet nurse cared for the needs of the newborn. A wet nurse fed someone else's baby. These were invariably decent working class women and it was a useful source of income for her family. Furthermore she would receive several months of good food which could only be of benefit to herself and her family.

The censuses also contain references to "Monthly Nurses". These were trained specialist nurses who moved into a home when the midwife had delivered the baby. They were employed in a private capacity. In 1903 a fee was in the region of £6-6s per month, payable to the institution which had provided her. I found many references to these ladies in the annual reports of The Trained Nurses Institution of Leeds. Dating from 1878 they are in the Local Studies section of Leeds Library and I am sure other cities will have something similar. I read details of their training given by a combination of midwives and district nurses; their duties and conditions of service. Their job was to care for a mother and her baby during the first month after the birth. The incidence of monthly nurses increased steadily over the 19th century and this must have been a drain on the services to the poor.

People often come to me with a photograph of a woman in uniform and ask if I can identify the hospital. The short answer is no, I cannot. Uniforms did not follow fashion, they were practical and unchanging for many years. Some hospitals did keep their individuality. A spotted dress with leg o'mutton sleeves is instantly recognisable as The London Hospital; army nurses, district nurses are clearly identifiable. With many though what I suggest is to date it through its photography and then narrow down the geographical area to which it could relate. Then research the hospitals within that area.

In the 1970's the winds of change blew through the National Health Service and in some parts of the country reached storm force. Many old ledgers, registers and photographs were lost at that time. Fortunately for us some well motivated people accessed their hospital archives and wrote a history. We owe

them a debt of gratitude. These accounts of individual hospitals are a valuable source of information about nurses. They contain some names of nurses appointed, length of service and reason for leaving where appropriate. The books are to be found in Local Studies Libraries, - but not always in their own town. I found Doncaster in York. Original hospital archives which survived the 1970's are in record offices and museums. Some hospitals have excellent museums; the Nightingale Museum at St Thomas's is outstanding but I also saw some interesting nurses registers at The Thackray Medical Museum in Leeds. It is a case of just looking.

Traditionally, as far as is possible, a family has cared for its own, with the help of the local 'nurse'. All very well in the villages perhaps but the inner cities were in great need during the 19th century. In England the system of district nurses, trained in their specialty began in 1859 in Liverpool, followed in 1868 by The East London Nursing Society. From then on it snowballed nationwide until in 1887 it coalesced into The Queen Victoria Jubilee Institute for Nurses, now known as The Queens Nursing Institute.

The Queens Nursing Institute is still going strong and has excellent detailed records of nurses. My Gt.. Gt, Aunt was a Queens Nurse and the QNI was able to give me the following information. "Rhoda Elizabeth Harper, born in 1857, completed her general training at the Royal Infirmary in Hull 1883-1889 (6yrs!) She commenced district nurse training in October 1901 in Leeds, qualified as a Queens Nurse in July 1904, resigned from her position in 1918." I followed up this information to see what else I could find out about her. The Annual Reports of the Leeds District Nursing Association are in Leeds Local Studies Library and from those I learned her conditions of service, the nursing rules which applied, and in that she lived in Lovell Street Nurses Home, her probable area of work. Quite moving is the knowledge that she was one of a band of only 20 highly qualified nurses who had chosen to care for the poorest members of society as opposed to 86 working out from The Trained Nurses Institution at the same time - private nurses to those who could afford to pay.

I have used Rhoda Elizabeth Harper as an example of just how much information can be gleaned about one provincial nurse; not well documented like the Nightingale nurses, not heroic like the military nurses, just an ordinary woman doing her duty.

When The Queens Nursing Institute was formed it incorporated earlier domiciliary nursing orders and so its archive actually goes back to 1840, to Elizabeth Fry and her Protestant Sisters of Charity. These have recently been catalogued.

Qualified nurses do not have a long history in the Armed Forces. The Crimean War was a turning point but it was not until the Boer War that large numbers became involved and they have been researched by Sheila Gray in New Zealand. Her book 'The South African War 1899-1902 is available directly from her. As with everything to do with the Services the records of Military Nurses are held by The Public Record Office in Kew. By World War 1 the nursing archive is extensive and the Public Record Office have a very good guide titled "Military Nurses and Nursing Services". It is number 55 in the Military Records Information. Lastly, do not forget War Memorials, I

Rhoda Harper 1857 -1936

found my kinswoman on the one outside York Minster; and do not forget the Medal Rolls - she was there too.

In the 20th century, amidst much opposition from within the profession, nursing finally became organised on a national basis. The Midwives Act 1902 led to the formation of The Central Midwives Board which granted the qualification State Certified Midwife. The Nurses Act 1919 established The General Nursing Council for England and Wales which granted the qualification State Registered Nurse. The Midwives Roll was always said to be "LIVE" which meant that it only contained the names of practising midwives. This can present problems to the researcher with a photograph clearly concerned with midwifery and perhaps a known qualification; there is no way of verifying the facts.

By contrast The Register of Nurses contained the names of every nurse who had passed the State Examinations. Criticised in its lifetime it is now very much alive so far as family historians are concerned.

All these records are in The Public Record office in Kew. Nursing is a major source and the class reference for general nurses is DV1O and for midwives DV7. There is a very good Domestic Records Information handout, number 79, called 'Civilian Nurses and Nursing Services' which is essential preparatory reading before going to search this source.

An important point to note is that these records have been indexed and the printed index for the General Register runs from 1921-1968. The indexes are in the form of year books in alphabetical order and are easy to work from. They are not as detailed as the actual Register but they lead one to it. Without a known date the Register itself is very difficult to sort out.

Each entry in the General Register gives a name, home address, date of registration and training hospital with dates. The early registers are fascinating to read in that some of the training dates are very early. These were primarily maiden ladies often coming to the end of their professional life having been hard at work for many years. I saw training dates as far back as 1885. To have a home address for 1919 and a working address for the 1880's is useful knowledge. Also of use is that a change of name on marriage was recorded.

The Register for Nurses set up in 1919 was female only. There were supplementary registers for male nurses, fever nurses, paediatric nurses and mental/mental subnormality (NB old terminology not acceptable today) This was the situation until 1949 when male nurses were merged into the female register; the need for nurses who specialised in infectious diseases dwindled as antibiotics brought the epidemics

under control but paediatrics and psychiatry continued to be important registers.

Within this archive in the PRO there is another class. DVll is a Roll of General Nurses as opposed to the Register. The Roll came into being in 1944 and the names on it have the qualification State Enrolled Nurse. An SEN had undertaken a shorter training than an SRN and she was, so to speak, a junior partner in the firm.

A final word from Kew, in the tradition of their mediaeval forebears the midwives have left us a bit extra. DV7 contains details of midwives back to 1872, listed with The Obstetical Society of London.

In 1973 nursing records were computerised and it is the records from before then which are in the PRO. The General Nursing Council and The Central Midwives Board were dissolved in 1979,

Nursing is less well documented than medicine and also when records were being made no one had family historians in mind. Although the location of many nursing archives is known many more are still coming to light and I am certain many more will be found in attics, cellers or simply misfiled. The whereabouts of some are known but await the attention of an archivist. The book "Nursing History and the Politics of Welfare" (see bibliography) has a chapter called 'Archival Sources for Nursing History' which contains some useful addresses.

Those readers with a knowledge of nursing will appreciate that I have only skimmed the surface of the history of nursing but this article is not aimed at nurses. It is for those who have found a nurse in their family and have become curious about her.

I started nursing in 1952. I know where my records are but I have not looked; I leave that to future researchers into the history of my family. I promise you though, I was never drunk, I did not steal, but I did drink tea with patients at all hours of the night!

BIBLIOGRAPHY
1 1997 M. Baly. Florence Nightingale & the Nursing Legacy.
2. 1979 A.E,Clark-Kennedy. London Pride
3. Sheila Gray. The South African War 1899-1902
4. 1997 Rafferty Robinson & Elkan. Nursing History & Politics of Welfare
5. 1999 M.E.Snodgrass. An Historical Encyclopaedia of Nursing
6. 1972 G.Swann. Doncaster Royal Infirmary 1792-1972
7. 1995 A.Tarver. Church Court Records

ADDITIONAL READING - just in case anybody is interested.
1960 Brian Abel Smith. A History of the Nursing Profession
1746 An account of the public hospital for the diseased poor in the County of York
1966 Eric Sigsworth. A provincial hospital in the 18th—19th centuries
1809 York County Hospital a short report on the state of the hospital
1936 The historical development & activities of York County Hospital
1977 M.Bottomly. The development of the District Nursing Service in Leeds.
From 1888 Leeds District Nursing Association Annual reports
From 1888 Leeds & District Workpeoples Hospital Fund
1917 Banes. Historical sketch of Leeds General Infirmary
From 1878 Leeds Trained Nurses Institution Annual Reports
1988 Dingwall Rafferty Webster. An Introduction to the Social History of Nursing
1987 C.Maggs. A Century of Change (RNPFN centenary)
Sept 2000 Journal of the City of York & District FHS

Bishops' Transcripts

Pauline M. Litton BA FSG(Assoc)
Vice President
Federation of Family History Societies

York, All Saints' Church, Pavement.

What are Bishops' Transcripts?

Bishops' Transcripts (BTs) - generally listed in the Diocese of York as Parish Register Transcripts, in East Anglia (and sometimes in Lincolnshire and Kent) as Archdeacon's Transcripts, or occasionally as Register Bills (see that for Harpham in Yorkshire page 29) but usually referred to generically as BTs - are contemporary 'copies' of Anglican parish registers (PRs), made principally during the seventeenth to nineteenth centuries. They exist only for England and Wales. There are none for other parts of the British Isles; documents in Ireland and the Isle of Man sometimes referred to as Bishops' Transcripts are nineteenth century copies of earlier registers.

The making of such annual copies of entries contained in the parish register was first ordered in 1597 and confirmed in an Ecclesiastical Mandate of 1603 which said *the churchwardens shall once every year, within one month after the five and twentieth day of March, transmit unto the Bishop of the diocese, or his Chancellor, a true copy of the names of all persons christened, married or buried in their parish, in the year before (ended the said five and twentieth day of March), and the certain days and months in which every such christening, marriage, and burial was had.*

The transcript was to be on parchment, signed by the minister and the churchwardens, and, in theory, forwarded to the relevant diocesan registry where it was to be "faithfully preserved" and available for consultation. Its use was envisaged if the parish register was damaged or destroyed or for purposes of comparison if it appeared that the register had been subject to *alteration, erasure or forgery.* Parchment (which the parish had to provide and pay for) was too expensive to waste so transcripts for small parishes may be found written on a piece about three inches square, whereas those for large ones may cover a piece the size of a large table cloth, or consist of several strips, either rolled or sewn together as a book.

What is the survival rate of Bishops' Transcripts?

This varies widely from diocese to diocese. Once the transcripts had been sent to the bishop, there were few guidelines as to how they should be preserved and in some dioceses they were badly stored, often suffering damage from damp or vermin, so that many have been lost altogether or are at best partly legible. Some dioceses have a high percentage of documents surviving from 1597 (and, in a few dioceses, even earlier as some churchmen had encouraged the keeping of duplicate copies before the 1597 order) to the mid, or late, nineteenth century. In others virtually none survive before the nineteenth century. *Bishops' Transcripts and Marriage Licences, Bonds and Allegations: a Guide to their Location and Indexes,* compiled by Jeremy Gibson and published by the Federation of Family History Societies (Publications) Ltd. (5th edition 2001) gives brief details of the dates covered by BTs for each diocese and county. County volumes of the *National Index of Parish Registers* normally include dates of existing BTs and many record repositories publish guides which include this information or have lists available for consultation.

You are advised to check these sources before visiting a repository to look at BTs. If you are accustomed to studying BTs in, say, Yorkshire or Cheshire, which both have many documents dating from around 1600, it can come as a shock to find that, for example, for Cumberland and Westmorland, there are very few before 1660; Durham and Northumberland before 1760; the Diocese of Winchester before 1780 and the Diocese of London (which included the City, Middlesex, most of Essex and some parishes in Hertfordshire) before 1800. Those for Wales begin in 1660 or later (depending on the individual diocese).

In dioceses where they do exist, the survival rate of BTs tends to be patchy for the first half of the seventeenth century and they were not kept between the mid-1640s and 1660 (the period of the Civil War and Interregnum) although a few were compiled from memory and sent in after 1660. From 1660 onwards their numbers increase markedly but complete runs are rare and almost all parishes have at least the odd year missing before 1812. From 1813 many parishes have complete sets, with the exception of marriages after 1837 which were generally omitted, until BTs cease to be returned usually at some point in the second half of the nineteenth century.

You will often find that there are no BTs for historic Cathedrals and those for Peculiars can vary dramatically between a complete absence of BTs, partial coverage, or almost complete runs. Peculiars were areas which were not subject to normal ecclesiastical jurisdiction. Some dioceses, including Chester and Durham, had none; others, like York and Salisbury, had large numbers spread across several counties which can make locating their records difficult.

Where will I find Bishops' Transcripts?

Most will be kept in either a county record or archive office, or in a diocesan registry. It is important to remember that a diocese often did not coincide with a county. At least until 1836 (when a major re-organisation of the whole diocesan system began and some new ones were created) a diocese could cover part of a county (the diocese of Rochester covered 91 out of some 400 parishes in Kent); a whole county (the diocese of Chichester and the county of Sussex coincided); or extend over several counties (the diocese of Lincoln included five counties and a few parishes in two further ones; that of Lichfield two counties and a substantial part of two others).

The establishment of county record or archive offices, and the effects of the Parochial Registers and Records Measure, which came into force in 1979, have seen most parish registers deposited in these offices but for BTs the situation is less clear-cut. In some cases, such offices have also become diocesan registries, and are responsible for both parish registers and bishops' transcripts, but, in others, the diocesan registry remains separate (sometimes associated with a university department) and continues to hold BTs and other classes of diocesan records (such as marriage bonds & allegations and probate documents).

Never assume that PRs and BTs will necessarily be held in the same repository; it pays to read one of the publications previously mentioned, or check with the likely record repository, before setting out on a journey. In Cheshire, for example, both types of record are at the record office in Chester but, for Durham, the PRs are largely in Durham County Record Office whilst the BTs are in Durham University Library Archives and Special Collections. BTs for the five counties included in the Diocese of Lincoln have been sorted and dispersed to the relevant county repositories but those for the four counties in Lichfield Diocese are all still held at Lichfield Record Office. Yorkshire has one principal repository for each historic Riding, between them holding a large proportion of the county's original PRs, but none of these holds any BTs, the bulk of which are at the Borthwick Institute of Historical Research (part of the University) in York, with most of the remainder at the West Yorkshire Archive Service office in Leeds. Those for Wales are all at the National Library of Wales in Aberystwyth with the exception of a few border parishes whose records are in Chester and Hereford.

If you want to look at BTs for a parish both before and after the mid-nineteenth century you may find that you have to visit two repositories. The re-structuring of many dioceses which began in 1836 resulted, in some cases, in a division of the records. Berkshire, for instance, previously an Archdeaconry in the diocese of Salisbury, was transferred in that year to the Diocese of Oxford but its BTs were not, so its pre-1836 BTs are in Trowbridge Record Office in Wiltshire and post-1836 BTs are in Oxford (as are those for Buckinghamshire after about 1845).

Fortunately, many BTs have been microfilmed, microfiched or published, making them much more widely available, so you may find that, although you cannot view the original records (many repositories, in any case, no longer produce these for family history researchers), copies are available elsewhere and a county record office may well have microform copies of BTs: held by a diocesan record office in another county; for Peculiars; or for parishes close to county boundaries which were geographically in one county but ecclesiastically in another. The Church of Jesus Christ of Latter-day Saints has filmed the BTs for many counties. Microfilms of these, for researchers to study, can usually be ordered through their Family History Centres and entries for baptisms and marriages, at least to 1837, will normally be included in the International Genealogical Index. The Society of Genealogists also holds copies of many BTs.

What information should Bishops' Transcripts contain?

BTs are commonly described as copies of the parish registers but in many cases before 1813 this is not strictly accurate. Sometimes they *are* duplicates, copied directly from the register; often they contain an abbreviated form of the register entry; occasionally they include more information than is in the register. The two documents may also differ markedly, with variations in names, spellings, and dates.

As with PRs, the amount of information included and the format used depended very much on the individual churchwarden, parish clerk or minister who wrote them out. The full date should be given, but in some parishes only the year appears. The 1603 mandate required only the names of those baptised, married or buried so a busy scribe could omit: parents from baptisms; from marriages such details as place of residence, occupation and whether it took place following banns or licence; and, from burials, relationships and ages. In a few parishes marriages are omitted altogether between 1754 and 1812, which can lead you to assume incorrectly that none took place following Hardwicke's Marriage Act of 1753. In others they are not included for several years at a time, with no reason apparent for their omission. Using BTs as a substitute for the parish register may, therefore, lead to your missing vital information and, where possible, it is highly advisable to check both sets of records.

Rose's Act of 1812 introduced a standard printed format to be used in parish registers and from 1813 duplicate forms were used for BTs so from this date they become, with very few exceptions, exact copies of the register entries except that marriages are rarely included after 1837 (it being generally thought that the keeping of two marriage registers as ordered in the 1836 Act meant a further copy was unnecessary). Returns from Peculiars, and a few Cathedrals, are also made with more regularity from this date.

Pitfalls to watch out for:
Do not fall into the trap of thinking that a BT, before 1813, will cover a period of twelve months from January to December. Rose's Act specified that the transcript for the previous year should be compiled by the end of February and submitted by 1 June but, before this date, the situation was much less straightforward.
The original instruction in 1597 had ordered that the transcripts be sent to the relevant authority within a month after Easter; in 1603 this was amended to a month after Lady Day (25 March and, until 1752, the beginning of the new year) and this date was not officially altered until 1812 so some parishes continued, until the early nineteenth century, to submit BTs which covered a period of twelve months from 25 March. In 1752, when the beginning of the year switched to 1 January, a number of parishes began to submit BTs which ran from January to December and, in the course of the succeeding 60 years, many others switched to this system.

Always check exactly which months are covered by a BT. It is easy not to realise that a BT, which appears to cover a given year, in fact covers only the last nine months of that year (and the first three of the succeeding one) and that you need to check the previous year's document for January to March entries. In many dioceses it became customary to hand in the BT when a Bishop, or his representative, made his annual 'visitation' to an area (as being easier than despatching it to the diocesan registry). This visit could take place at any time of the year (most

Harpham Bishop's Transcript 1694
Reproduced by kind permission of the
Borthwick Institute for Historical Research in York

Yapham cum Meltonby
Bishop's Transcript 1729
Reproduced by kind permission of the
Borthwick Institute for Historical Research in York

commonly in summer). In some parishes the scribe would end his BT on 25 March but not begin the new one until after the visitation so that entries for weeks or even months (particularly in April and May) may not be recorded in the BT - and remember that the IGI entries for a number of counties are taken from the BTs!

If you are working in a repository where original BTs are still produced, be aware that the year written on the outside of the document (and which is commonly the one listed in a record office's calendar) is often the year it was filed in the registry, which will frequently be the year following most of the events listed in it. Thus, a BT labelled 1749 is likely to include events for 1748; that for 1750 will include most of those for 1749; and if the 1750 BT is listed as missing it is the 1749 events which are lost.

BT s tend to have their covering dates written at the top of the piece of parchment but as the edges are the areas most likely to be damaged, or faded, by poor storage conditions or careless folding it can be exceedingly difficult to ascertain to which year the document refers and occasionally a 'best guess' has to be made. The same may apply to names and dates close to an edge (see the BT for Yapham in Yorkshire page 30).

To save parchment, some scribes copied their entries as a solid block of text, running entries on one after the other rather than putting each one on a separate line. It pays to check for this practice before running your eye down the left-hand side of a column looking for a particular name and missing it because it is actually near the end of the previous line. Watch also for the copier who broke off in the middle of an entry and, on picking up his quill, finished it with details from the line above or below.

In most record offices BTs are sorted and filmed by parish but in a few they are stored and filmed in annual batches by archdeaconry. Looking through archdeaconry-sorted records for those of a single parish can be very time-consuming so it will pay you to ascertain in advance of a visit which system applies.

Table cloth-size BTs are notoriously difficult to search accurately on microfilm. When being filmed some required ten or more frames to cover a single year, with parts of frames overlapping and sometimes no indication of month or year on a frame. It is perilously easy to think you have searched the entire sheet when, in fact, you have

missed a column or part of one. There may be the added complication of entries from chapelries being listed separately but on the same BT as the mother church and, when several chapelries are involved, their entries can be very difficult to locate.

Advantages of Bishops' Transcripts

BT s are most useful when the PR does not survive or is damaged, is still held at the church, or is in a different record office to the one you are visiting. In a number of counties they pre-date PRs, often starting about 1600 with the earliest surviving register not beginning until around 1660. Sometimes they are in a better condition, and easier to read, than the PR. Before 1733, when many PRs are in Latin, the BT will often be written in English. This can help you decide, for instance, whether the name 'Jacobus' in the PR should be interpreted as Jacob or James and whether the abbreviated entry 'Fran: fil.' stands for Francis, son of, or Frances, daughter of. In some instances the BT will contain information not given in the PR - in one Yorkshire parish, for example, in the early eighteenth century, the PR includes only the father's name in baptism entries but the BT gives the mother's Christian name as well - although the reverse is more often true.

Bishops' Transcripts and Parish Registers are both invaluable to family history researchers but remember that the two are complementary. If possible, don't rely on one source but compare the two - you may be surprised how many differences there are between the PR and its supposed copy.

Bibliography
Bishops' Transcripts & Marriages Licences... JSW Gibson. (FFHS: 5th edition 2001)
National Index of Parish Registers series (Society of Genealogists: 1967 to date).
© Pauline Litton

Palaeography made easy

Kate Thompson

For the family or local historian who wishes to go back in time beyond the nineteenth century the ability to read old handwriting is essential. It is actually easier to read a document written in, for example, what is known as Secretary Hand (roughly in the sixteenth century); because only a limited number of people could write, everyone used the same style and it is therefore less of a problem than something written in the last century when individual styles of handwriting emerge.

Most people can acquire the necessary skills quite easily and in my many years of teaching palaeography I only recall one person who failed to 'crack the code'. The sense of satisfaction felt by those able to read older hands is out of all proportion to the amount of effort required. By far the best way is to go to an evening class where the tutor is on hand to help, but if this is not possible it is feasible to learn from one of the several books on the subject. The key to palaeography, like so much else, is practice. The more you read, the better you will become; the old adage of riding bicycles comes to mind!

I understand that we learn palaeography in a similar way to how we learnt to read as children, that is we recognise certain letters and gradually build up our knowledge. Another analogy one can use is with a crossword: most of us start with a few clues but quite a few gaps, and gradually fill in the missing words. One way of deciphering letters is to find another example of the same shape which you can identify. In palaeography there are certain 'key' letters, such as 'e', 'h', 'r' and 'w' which are often very distinctive. Capital letters present special problems, especially the less common ones; they are often illustrated in books on palaeography

Early documents may not be written in English (or Welsh in the principality). Latin was the language used for formal documents although the vernacular became common after about 1500. The use of Latin was not brought to an end until an Act of Parliament in 1733, which also stopped the use of abbreviations; these had been necessary when writing materials – principally parchment and vellum – were in short supply. In the early medieval period Anglo-Norman French was used for official documents but most family and local historians will rarely, if ever, need to use documents written in this language. Some Latin words will be encountered occasionally, such as 'ibidem' ('first of all') and 'item' (obvious!) in inventories.

It will be necessary to be aware of some common abbreviations, even after 1733. Most of them will be obvious and will take the form of a superior letter, contraction or a special sign. A horizontal line above the abbreviation will indicate where a word has been shortened. A common example of the use of a superior letter is the word 'with' which is often written w^th – this seems rather odd when the letter 'i' takes up so little space! A common contraction is the phrase 'Your Majesty' which is often written as Yo[ur] Ma[jes]^ty. (When transcribing a document any letters added to the text to make sense of the meaning should be enclosed in square brackets as shown above.)

Some words beginning with 'p' are commonly abbreviated, of which the most obvious example is parish. The abbreviation symbol is written through the tail in one of two ways: a horizontal line denotes that the 'p' is followed by a vowel and then by 'r'; a looped

Inventory of
Edward Dislington 1582
Reproduced with permission of
Leicestershire Record Office

line through the tail stands for 'pr' + vowel; the word 'proper' uses both these forms! An ampersand (&) can confuse readers; it stands for the Latin word 'et' ('and') and therefore &c = etc.

Three Saxon letters crept into the Latin alphabet but only one is likely to be encountered regularly; this is 'thorn' which stands for 'th'. It looks a bit like a 'y' but should be transcribed as 'th', eg thorn + 'e' = 'the', not 'ye'!

Roman numerals were in general use until the sixteenth century and will occasionally be found after that time. Most family and local historians will come across them in inventories. They are:

I or i = 1	V or v = 5	X or x = 10
L or l = 50	C or c = 100	D or d = 500
M or m = 1,000		

You can practise by looking at the dates in film and television credits, which for some reason are always given in Roman numerals! The figure '4' is usually written as iiij rather than iv, with the last letter given as a 'j'.

For those family and local historians who rarely use documents earlier than the sixteenth century the most difficult items to interpret will be personal and place names, as most other words will be decipherable with some patience. For those living in the locality to which the documents relate place names will rarely present a problem and for unfamiliar places there are a number of sources of assistance. Even the humble road atlas can help! The English Place Name Society has published a number of volumes on individual counties which include names below that of the parish or village.

In the past there were a limited number of personal forenames, although some strange ones often turn up. Virtues were used as personal names, such as Patience and Charity. Some clergy Latinised names in the parish registers but most of them are easily recognisable, such as Willelmus, Henricus, Ricardus, etc. However beware of Jacobus – it means James, not Jacob. In the future family and local history may present more of a problem when dealing with personal names, as the range today is very large. Surnames will be more difficult but the method of comparing letters, referred to above, will invariably solve the dilemma.

The moral of this article is – don't panic if faced with an apparently indecipherable document. You can acquire the skill with a bit of a help and a lot of practice and it will be worth the effort. Although there is a lot of material in print it is much more satisfying to work from the original document!

© Kate Thompson

Shops in Regency Yorkshire
1811~1820

Prudence Bebb
describes shopping in Regency times

A Bow-windowed
shop in
Whitby,
Yorkshire

Regency streets were bordered with small shops; a few were ancient timbered buildings but most had 'modern' brick facades with bow windows. Very charming those windows were but you couldn't see much through them. No one had invented plate glass, these were much more beautiful but they were divided by glazing bars into small sections and some of the glass was unevenly thick so you got a distorted view of the contents. You needed to go up the steps, holding the wrought-iron rail if you required it, and through the door under the fanlight.

Inside was a high counter with weighing scales, a ledger, some quill pens and a big pewter inkpot; nobody had a cash register. The goods were stacked on shelves unless they needed to be kept in drawers. In Knaresborough, the oldest chemist's shop in England still has its drawers, each painted with the name of its contents such as Ichthyocolla, Gentian, Alloes Spice and Plumbox Rub (which was red lead).

At apothecary's shops throughout Yorkshire the apprehensive patient might see a jar perforated with air holes which was the home of the green- striped leech. This slimy- looking creature could be placed upon an arm where it would obligingly suck the blood of someone who was thought to need bleeding.

It was more cheerful to look at the bookshelves for many chemists had food for the mind as well as potions for the body. You could buy a book about ancient Rome when you purchased your Cornwell's Oriental Cordial, which was recommended '... when Debility of the Stomach and Intestines are severe and alarming.'

If you were unfortunate enough to need 'Itch Ointment', you could procure it from Mr Pierson, Mr Todd or Mr Gillet in Sheffield, Mr Crookes in Rotherham, Mr Wright in Doncaster or Mr Justice in Howden. Customers in the West Riding could get it from Woods in Wakefield, Osbornes in Pontefract or Mr Brooke in Huddersfield.

The customer might decide to try one of the apothecary's own preparations. The York chemist grew herbs behind his shop and could grind his own remedies to a fine powder with the pestle and mortar on his wooden counter. He was John Palmer and his old shop is still in Stonegate on the corner of Coffee Yard.
Passers-by, gazing through the little window-panes,

might see a row of heads; these belonged to the unfortunates who sat on a bench awaiting the services of a leech or, worse still, the apothecary himself with his bleeding bowl.

It was more cheerful to press your nose to the bow window of the draper and try to see the bolts of cloth on his shelves. But the only fabrics you could see really well were the ones festooned across the doorway. These draped cloths, which could be viewed and touched, gave the drapers their name.

Many of these shops sold a wide variety of fabrics. In Harrogate Mr Frankland sold silk, velvet, lace, muslin and poplin for fashionable ladies to wear. In Sheffield High Street, Mr J Morton sold linen and woollen materials. In Scarborough John Rowntree was both a draper and a grocer

Drapers were in great demand for it was nearly impossible to get ready-to-wear clothes. Either you had to make up your own or employ a dressmaker. Some dressmakers had shops where you could see the latest fabrics brought from London and give your orders for gowns pictured in the fashion magazines. Some, like Miss Couldwell in Rotherham, made hats as well as dresses which was very useful if you wanted your bonnet to be trimmed with material matching your gown.

Mrs Peacock, who had a shop in York, sent her daughters to London on the stage-coach to buy the latest fabrics and bonnet shapes after which she announced in the local paper that '...the ladies of York and its Vicinity' were invited to come and view the new season's designs which she could make for them.

Presumably there was a steady stream of customers being measured for gowns there because she was affluent enough to take a house in Scarborough on St Nicholas Cliff (the best part of the town) where she made high-waisted gowns and decorated bonnets for the noble and genteel ladies who came in summer to try the benefits of seawater.

Of course, some shops dealt exclusively in hats. They were the real milliners whose weary apprentices stitched and ruched for long hours. They decorated straw shapes with ribbons and silk flowers and their employers had a stock of beaver, wool and fur. Some would have bought feathers from Mr Haden at number 18, The Market Place, Sheffield. He sold off his stock in 1812 and members of the trade were glad to acquire his ostrich and other feathers to adorn glamorous bonnets.

Not that all bonnets were glamorous. When Lydia Bennet bought hers, she confessed that: "There were two or three much uglier in the shop".

After 1815 the crowns of bonnets became much higher

The Old Chemist's Shop, Knaresborough

to accommodate the new hair styles and the hairdressers were busy piling flaxen, brunette and even grey locks on top of their customers heads. John Parsons was York's best hairdresser, at least he thought he was. His customers, he said, were "The Nobility and Gentry" which naturally made everyone else want to go to him as well. His premises were in an élite situation next door to the Mansion House. He even sold French perfumes and he could provide bald gentlemen with wigs. Other hairdressers were jealous of him and someone bribed his apprentice to be rude to the customers. Breathing fire and slaughter, Mr Parsons sacked the apprentice and wrote a very irate letter to the newspaper.

 The life of an apprentice could be drudgery. The girls, who stitched whalebone into "stays" for the larger Yorkshire ladies, would get sore fingers; although anyone working for Mrs Kelsall (who once made corsets for George III's daughter, Elizabeth) at least got to the seaside. Mrs Kelsall travelled to York and to Scarborough each year to make these corsets for her clients.

Apprentices (sometimes orphans) were at the mercy of their employer, to whom they were legally bound until they came of age. Some were well-treated by men who considered themselves in loco parentis. Others were inadequately housed and fed yet overworked.

The apprentice in the fairy tale, who married his employer' s daughter and inherited the business,was quite often a real life character. However, the apprentice, who ran away to sea, was often a true person as well.

Many shopkeepers sold goods which were made at the back of the premises. Shoes, for instance, and riding boots, were usually made to measure by the journeymen and apprentices. If an apprentice had learnt to make the wares well enough to satisfy his master's guild, he became a journeyman - that is a paid worker.

Sometimes a shopkeeper was desperate to get an extra apprentice. Mr Whitehead, a York draper, put a plea in the York Herald in 1814 saying he was 'In immediate want of an apprentice'. The next month one of York's grocers was advertising for 'Journeymen grocers and an apprentice in a shop. None need apply who have not been in a respectable situation and can bring a good character for Honesty, Sobriety and Industry. Application (post paid) may be made to Mr John Bleckly of York who has room for a clever lad from the country as an apprentice'.

Advertising was very discreet for there were no

telephones and no TV transmissions. Shopkeepers often had a printed card with a neat little picture and beautifully engraved lettering which could be handed to prospective customers.

 Some sent advertisements to the newspapers. As the local papers were weekly ones and confined to one double page, all the printing was very small. What the advertisement lacked in size was compensated by most obsequious wording. In 1816 this typical notice appeared:
 Mrs Cooke
Begs permission most respectfully to inform the Ladies of York and her friends in general, that Mr Cooke has just returned from London, having selected an Extensive, Elegant, and Fashionable Assortment of STRAW, CHIP and WILLOW hats and bonnets; also OSTRICH FEATHERS, ARTIFICIAL FLOWERS, RIBBONS, &,&, of the most Fashionable Kinds. Mrs C's showrooms will be fitted up and opened on Monday 27th instant, when the honour of a call will be highly esteemed.

Coney Street, York May 22
Scarborough had its own method of obtaining custom. When a carriage brought a visitor to the town, it was met by the 'Tooters'. As the visitors alighted at their hotel or lodgings, the Tooters surrounded them offering to show where the best shops were.

When a shopkeeper decided to give up his trade, he was said to be 'declining business' and then he might advertise his entire shop for sale, though he might call it a warehouse. One such advertisement described: 'An old - accustomed and well established shop .... with the dwelling house and other conveniences, situate near the Butter Cross (the centre of the town of Doncaster) in the County of York' The dwelling house and the warehouse were often combined.

In most towns there was a 'chinaman' who was not an oriental gentleman. York's chinaman was Mr Pomfret. He had to hire an extra room in Lop Lane, York, when his stock of porcelain, bronze and crystal was too large for his shop. There wasn't much you couldn't buy from his 'China and Glass Repository'. If you wanted the popular blue and white tableware with chinoiserie designs on it or the latest oil lamps or even elegant chandeliers, William Pomfret was your man.

Not only yours. Besides his prestigious shop in Stonegate, York, he also had a warehouse in Lowgate, Hull, where he kept beautiful porcelain ready packed to be transported to the docks and loaded on merchant ships to sail with the tide. W. Pomfret and Co. were purveyors of fine china for both the home and export markets. At this time when Spode, Minton and Wedgwood were producing some of their most beautiful work, William Pomfret was ready to send it overseas.

Some of Yorkshire's merchandise travelled on carrier's carts, waggons and even stage-coaches to other parts of the country. In November 1811 Miss Ringrose's Goose and Game Pies were sending delicious odours down Feasegate and John Ringrose assured the public that these Christmas pies could be '...sent with safety to any part of the kingdom on the shortest notice'.

No one had ever heard of convenience foods but a few readymade sauces were available. Elliott's shop in Spurriergate, York, sold Purkiss's Essence of Lobsters. 'By using it according to the directions given, a superior sauce is obtained in a few minutes with half the usual trouble, at any period, when lobsters are out of season or where they cannot be procured'. But one feels that Mr Elliott's own pies might be more tasty.

Perhaps the most appetising smells in York came from Castlegate where Tukes made chocolates behind their grocery store. It was a smell that was to become part of York for a descendant of William Tuke married a Rowntree. In the Regency, however,William Tuke's shop sold various groceries and he was described as a Tea Dealer. This was a superior title as it indicated someone who attended the sales of tea on London Docks when East India Company ships brought their wares from the Far East.

If a shopkeeper died, those owing money to him had to pay their debt to the executors. When James Furness a Sheffield grocer, died, the local newspaper published a request from Septimus and Matthias Furness, his executors, that all debts should be paid to them. If anyone was owed money from the estate, they had to send in accounts to the same gentlemen.

Shopping streets often rang with the metallic clopping of hooves on cobbles. A solitary farmer might ride down the street needing to buy something which could not be produced at home. A flashy young man might drive a curricle, which was a two-wheeled sporting carriage pulled by a pair of horses. Gentlemen walked on the outside of ladies to protect them from mud splashes. Fortunately some shops sold a preparation to get the dirt off buff dresses. You had to pick your way carefully when you wanted to cross a road frequented by horses. It was unwise to gaze at the bow window opposite, much safer to keep your eyes on the ground.

Of course, the horses themselves brought trade. There were shops devoted to saddles and harness; in the back journeymen and apprentices stitched leather. Brearey and Morley of York sold carriages and gigs. You could even hire a hearse from them ready to be pulled by horses wearing black mourning plumes.

You might be in need of a hearse yourself if you tried to visit some shops after they were shut. Shopkeepers could buy the Patent Burglary Pistol. This would be loaded and concealed in a corner. If an intruder entered by a window, or even opened the door, it rang a bell and fired at him at the same time.

Doubtless silversmiths and jewellers were particularly anxious to avoid theft.

People were literally short of money because there was not enough metal during the Napoleonic Wars to make as many coins as the country needed. Consequently, shopkeepers who had security, were allowed to make tokens which were used as currency locally. Gold and silversmiths were able to do this; Cattle and Barber, York jewellers, made their own shillings. In Whitby tokens had the town's coat-of-arms engraved on them. People were happy to accept them because they were silver and of real value.

Wise shopkeepers kept buckets handy in case of fire, which was a worrying hazard. Most properties contained wooden beams, floorboards and furniture. Buildings were close together and some contained inflammable stock. Alderman Spencer lived in an elegant villa in the village of Nether Poppleton but his shop was in York where he sold paints. One June night in 1816 whilst Isaac Spencer was asleep at home, his shop caught fire at three in the morning. Fortunately folk living nearby saw the fire and soon a crowd gathered and, according to the

Stonegate, York

newspaper, '...by the exertions of the neighbours it was extinguished without much loss being sustained. It is, however, highly probable, from the combustible nature of the goods in the warehouse, that if it had remained undiscovered a little longer the whole of the neighbourhood would have fallen a sacrifice to that consuming element'.

It might indeed. Fire-engines were horse drawn and their tanks only contained a limited amount of water which had to be pumped by hand to send it up a leather hose. In a world lit by candles and oil lamps the fear was always there that a shopkeeper's stock, painstakingly made on the premises, might disappear in a rush of orange flame and choking smoke.

BIBLIOGRAPHY
Newspapers:
Sheffield Iris 1811 - 1812
York Chronicle 1811 - 1820
York Courant 1811 - 1820
York Herald 1811 - 1820
Trade Directories
York 1818-1819
Secondary Sources
Aldburgham, Alison: Shops and Shopping (1981)
Arlott, John: The Snuff Shop (Michael Joseph, 1974)
Austen, Jane: Pride and Prejudice
Bebb, Prudence: Shopping in Regency York. Butcher, Baker, Candlestick Maker (Sessions of York, 1994)
Chandler, George: Four Centuries of Banking (Batsford,1964)
Davis, Dorothy: History of Shopping (1966)
Sturt, George: The Wheelwright's Shop (Cambridge University Press, 1948)

Prudence Bebb taught History in the East Riding at Howden before taking early retirement to concentrate on her writing. She now lives in a village outside York and gives talks on the Regency period which she has studied for over thirty years. She has written four novels which have all been republished in large print for the visually handicapped and two of them have been translated into Italian. She has written six local history books so far.
Her publications are:

The Eleventh Emerald	(Robert Hale, 1981)
The Ridgeway Ruby	(Robert Hale, 1983)
The White Swan	(Robert Hale, 1984)
The Nabob's Nephew	(Robert Hale, 1985)
Life in Regency York	(Sessions of York, 1992)
Butcher, Baker, Candlestick Maker.	(Sessions 1994)
Georgian Poppleton	(Sessions1994)
Life in Regency Harrogate	(Sessions, 1995)
Life in Regency Scarborough	(Sessions, 1997)
Life in Regency Whitby	(Sessions,2000)

Past Times and Leisure Pursuits

Doreen Hopwood

Nowadays there is a club or society catering for every leisure pursuit and many have a monthly magazine full of news and ideas for specialist interests – including family history!

Membership of clubs and societies is by no means a 20th century phenomenon. At the turn of the century, the inhabitants of Birmingham had a huge choice of organisations competing for their membership. They ranged from the elitist, like the Arnold Club for Headmasters to the Bean Club (political not horticultural) with a wide variety of musical and sporting societies as well.

The earliest appearance of the word 'hobby', taken in its current usage, can be found in the 1816 New English Dictionary, and the term '*pottering* ' is uniquely English with no equivalent in any other language. It can mean any hobby or home-based leisure activity.

The introduction of the shorter working week - 5? days – in the 1850s gave workers free time to pursue leisure activities, and, by 1910, the standard weekly working hours had been reduced from 60-70 hours to 53 hours. The Bank Holiday Acts of 1871 and 1875 gave workers extra days off, and the combination of fewer working hours and higher wages provided both the time and the money for organised activities and the pursuit of hobby crafts. By 1900, sports had become regulated with the introduction of universal rules, such as those of the Football Association, and people were both playing and watching a wider variety of sporting activities. In *Tom Brown's Schooldays* Tom cried 'Cricket is more than a game. It is an institution!' Initially a middle-class sport, working class boys could recite the names of county players and the number of runs scored in matches, even if they didn't know how to play the game. It formed part of the gentlemanly code and the term 'not cricket' came to characterise anything that was underhand or dishonest.

Despite the proliferation of gardening and DIY programmes on television today, these are by no means new hobbies. As early as the 1850s it was noted how the English, of all classes, decorated their homes and were fond of making improvements to them. Some thirty years earlier it was said of Northumberland miners 'Their spare time impels them to continue things to smarten their homes'. Peeking at other peoples' homes and visiting exhibitions is not new either. The Great Exhibition of 1851 attracted visitors of all classes, especially on "shilling days" and on October 13 1851, The *Times* reported that the greatest number of people in the Crystal Palace at one time "…was at 2 o'clock on Tuesday last when 92,000 persons were present"

Various acts enabled local government to provide municipal amenities which included museums, art galleries, parks, libraries and public baths, among other facilities. "Going to the baths" did not necessarily mean swimming – Birmingham's first baths, opened in 1851, and offered "sixty-nine private hot and cold water baths, two large swimming pools, three plunge baths and a public wash-house with laundry fitted up with twenty five washing stalls and two sets of seventeen drying horses". Later many of the swimming baths were covered with floors in the winter and used for dancing, gymnastics and even as bowling greens. As levels of literacy increased, public libraries provided both educational and leisure reading material, and advances in printing technology made newspapers and other reading material cheaper. The last half of the 19th century saw a growth in the numbers of magazines being published and many of the Victorian classics (such as Dickens' *Hard Times*) appeared in instalments.

The coming of the railways brought the country and seaside within reach of the town dweller and whole communities would take an excursion. In 1842 nearly two and a half thousand Sunday School children and their teachers left Preston for a day trip to Fleetwood in a train consisting of 27 coaches.

By the end of the 19th century, hobbies were being systematised, organised and commercially exploited. The first edition of '*Hobbies*' magazine was published in October 1895, and this included instruction in fretwork and laying in wood, photography for amateurs, stamp collecting, magic lanterns, bazaars and how to decorate them.

Most societies, movements and clubs of a voluntary nature fall into broad categories of sport, hobby/craft, philanthropic, social service, mutual aid and occupational. Each share most of the following characteristics:

Have a formal name or title
Membership is voluntary
Have some kind of constitution, hold regular-minuted meetings, and elect officers who take responsibility for the societies affairs.
The members decide membership qualifications
It is not an '*ad hoc*' association (convened only for a specific occasion or purpose)

Many may have been in existence for over a hundred years and the Secretary may still hold their annual reports, minutes and programmes. It is more likely that annual reports can be found in major libraries, or county record offices, and whilst these may not contain biographical articles, an ancestor's name and address may appear in the list of subscribers, or as an officer of the organisation. Football and other professional sporting programmes may be found in larger libraries, or at the club itself.

Contemporary town and county directories and local newspapers give an indication of what was going on in a particular area at a particular point in time, and these, too, can be found in libraries and record offices. Most local newspapers carried results of the local sports matches as well as reports of social/club activities, and by the twentieth century, special sporting editions of newspapers began to appear on Saturday evenings. Larger towns had their own suburban weekly papers, like the Handsworth Herald in Birmingham, which carried news of a very localised nature.

The sheer numbers of entries under the headings of 'Innkeeper' and 'Publican' in directories indicate just how many such establishments existed at any given point in time. An estimate for the late 19th century suggests that on average there was one drinking establishment for every 186 inhabitants in England and Wales. However, public houses were not just a place in which to imbibe alcohol. They were the meeting places for all types of clubs, watering holes for ramblers, cyclists and hikers and, until the beginning of the 20th century, the place where coroner's inquests were held, or even doctor's surgeries. In times of poor living conditions – damp, overcrowded houses – the public house was a welcome alternative. The separation of the public sphere of activity for men and the private sphere of home and family for women was echoed in the types of leisure each of the sexes could enjoy. Needless to say, the choice for females was far more limited than that of their male counterparts. Temperance societies advocating teetotalism and decrying the evils of drink grew up in large towns and cities. The Band of Hope was the junior branch which urged children to 'sign the pledge', and their Temperance Halls were used by other community groups for all kinds of events.

Large scale urbanisation and the concentration of people in inner cities put a strain on existing facilities and local councils feared unrest unless some recreational provision was made. Employers too were concerned about the observance of 'St Monday' by their workforce, and also sought to provide alternative leisure pursuits to compete with the public houses, bare-knuckle fighting, and cockfighting. The mechanical age took people away from the harmonious holidays of rural England, attuned to the seasons, and replaced them with 'improving' clubs and organisations. In 1892, Collings Smallholding Bill enacted the provision of allotments for city and town dwellers.

Allotment, Horticultural and Tenants Associations were encouraged as council estates developed during the inter-war years, and community halls were built on these estates, which could be used for all sorts of recreational activities. Government support was provided as associations were seen as fostering a sense of pride in the new environment, and as a means of reducing crime and social unrest.

Group organisation of specialist hobbies led to regular local meetings – often in public house function rooms, and these eventually developed into national organisations for the control and administration of the activity. This is particularly evident in animal-based hobbies, such as dog breeding (Crufts), canary breeding and pigeon racing. Many of today's famous football clubs started off as pub or works teams, such as West Bromwich Albion which was founded at Salters Springs Works and had employees on the team until the 20th century

The difference in 'popular amusements' between the 1830s and the 1880s was summed up in 1885 by reference to a contemporary newspaper:

> "One would now look in vain for the announcements of pugilistic encounters … cockfighting and performances of terrier dogs. One would have then looked in vain for accounts of cricket matches which now occupy whole pages … for the notices to excursionists … for the miscellaneous programmes of picture exhibitions, lectures, music halls."

Mass production techniques made the manufacture of bicycles cheaper and therefore more accessible. 'Cycling Clubs' swept the country in the years leading to the First World War, and, as early as the 1880s, special maps were being produced to indicate routes and showing 'dangerous' hills. Specialist clubs and societies proliferated and their reports may be found in main libraries, as may the 'Cyclos' magazine, which includes maps.

Hobbies were often an extension of work itself – many carpenters built their own furniture and later car workers 'tinkered' with engines. Before the First World War, the tools of a trade were generally the personal possessions of the craftsman and could also be used to practise their hobby-craft. Unskilled workers would have been unable to afford the necessary tools for many hobbies and more often than not followed sports, or hobbies with little capital outlay.

Paternalistic employers (like Cadbury's at Bournville, and Lever's at Port Sunlight) built almost self-contained communities for their workforce to meet all of their housing, educational, recreational and spiritual needs. Like many employers, Cadbury's had a regular staff magazine, which carried announcements of births, engagements, marriages, retirements and obituaries of employees, together with news and reviews. Club and works societies reports appeared a well as competitions, such as 'The Housewife of the Year'. Large and small employers alike organised social events for their workers – ranging from outings to the theatre or

focus, such as the YMCA (The Young Men's Christian Association). This was founded in London on 6 June 1844 for "the improvement of the religious condition of young men". Just a few years later, the ecclesiastical census of 1851 indicated that less then half of the country's population attended a church service on the census day, but by 1900, there were over 950 YMCAs within Britain and her dependencies.

In 1891, facilities in Birmingham included an 'admirable reading room, well stocked with current newspapers and magazines, and a library of 1030 volumes'. Art, shorthand and language classes were available and a 'thoroughly equipped gymnasium, lighted at night by electric light' was much used. There were also sporting societies for cricket, cycling, football, harriers, rambling and swimming available to members.

Voluntary uniformed organisations, such as the St John Ambulance Brigade and Red Cross, may have their own archive – but it is unlikely that records of individual members have been kept. However, there may be photographs or newspaper cuttings in which an ancestor appears.

Uniformed organisations for young people – boy scouts, girl guides, the Boys Brigade and Girls Brigade were formed in the early 20th century and initially catered for the children of the middle classes, artisans and skilled workers. Over 80% of children in Britain were of the working class, but the cost of the uniforms and weekly "subs" were prohibitive to families on a tight budget. Nevertheless, there were over 2000 members of the Boys Brigade in Manchester in 1917, each of whom paid 6d to join, 6d for the cap and a weekly subscription of a penny. As well as drill and discipline, the boys (aged between 12 and 17) were taught first aid, religion and how to play a brass instrument. Segregation of the sexes occurred in these organisations too, although initially girls joined in with their scouting brothers. This was frowned upon by their parents and a letter appeared in the *Spectator* in 1909 complaining that the "The Girl Scouts and Boy Scouts roam the countryside on what I can only describe as glorified larking expeditions, from which they have been known to return as late as ten p.m." Lord Baden-Powell's sister, Agnes, came to the rescue and the Girl Guide Movement was founded in 1910.

After the First World War, commercial activities were replacing many of the church based recreations as professional sport, dance halls and cinemas became established. There was also a growing move to private and home based leisure pursuits with the increasing availability of the wireless (radio), gramophone, cheaper books, the private car and later, computer games and television. Houses were no longer overcrowded or damp and cold, thus helping to foster the popularity of home based leisure activities. In many areas the use of buildings has come almost full circle – non-conformist chapels have a particularly chequered history, moving from religious use to secular (cinemas, dance or bingo halls) and back to religious in the form of temples or other non-Christian places of worship.

seaside, to providing sporting facilities or educational programmes. Copies of the magazines may be found in major libraries, or the company may have its own archive.

Amateur Dramatic societies and dance classes were popular and posters and/or programmes may well have survived. Advertisements often appeared in the local press – or the parish magazine, especially if the event was to take place in the Parish Hall. Local institutes like the Moseley and Balsall Heath Institute in Birmingham were the venues for a whole range of activities, from political meetings, debates, and lectures to flower shows and amateur theatrical productions. Surviving programmes usually give a full list of characters/actors and, in some cases, a brief biography of the 'stars'. Many large towns also had weekly newspapers – such as 'The Dart' in Birmingham –, which carried advertisements for forthcoming entertainments, as well as reviews of plays and concerts. Most date from the late 19th century and ceased production in the early 20th century. Some larger libraries also have 'ephemera' collections, which include posters.

Local theatrical societies may still be in existence today, and these generally maintain their own archive, complete with photographs of the plays they have produced. Whilst minutes of clubs and societies usually deal with the administration of the organisation, surviving records may contain some information of genealogical use – if only to confirm an address at a given point in time.

Many organisations for young people had a religious

The range of leisure pursuits available to us today seems infinite, but many of them owe their origins to the pioneers of the clubs and societies formed a hundred or more years ago, and through them our traditions are being kept alive.

Barmaids & Publicans
Simon Fowler
tells us how to find out
more about them

The public house has been an
important social institution
since medieval times. As the
authorities have always
looked on pubs with some
degree of suspicion,
regarding them as potential
centres for dissension,
drunkenness, and disorder,
there are documents going
back until Tudor times which
list publicans. In addition
there are other records which
can shed light on publicans,
the people they employed,
and their lives.

The public house as we know it today is really an
invention of the 18th century, before then there were
alehouses that sold beer brewed on the premises often
by women, known as alewives or brewsters. More
salubrious were inns, much larger establishments,
which might offer food, stabling for horses, and a
variety of dining and meeting rooms.

The 18th and 19th centuries saw a massive rebuilding
of pubs in reaction to changing tastes and the opening
of new establishments to meet new demand in
industrial and suburban areas. Meanwhile more and
more pubs were being bought by breweries with the
object of selling the company's products. At the same
time the authorities sought to close pubs as a way of
reducing drunkenness, which was endemic among
sections of the working classes. In addition increasing
restrictions were placed on pubs, particularly with
regard to opening and closing hours and the games
which might be played there.

Since the Second World War a further revolution has
taken place as pubs have had to compete with an
increasing range of leisure pursuits. Many started
selling food, while others became theme pubs in the
hope of attracting young people. Their problems were
compounded by immense changes in the brewing
industry itself, which first saw rationalisation into a
few large companies and then the decision of many
breweries to stop brewing altogether.

Over the centuries hundreds of thousands of people
have run pubs. Indeed it stills remains an ambition for
many a drinker, although few realise how hard the
work is. There is no clear rule about who became
publicans, alewives or innkeepers, but the following
suggestions may help you in your search.
A number of publicans were former sportsmen or
servants (such as butlers and footmen) who often saw
a pub as a way of providing for their retirement.
Many children followed their parents into running

pubs. Girls started as barmaids or working in the
kitchen, while boys became potboys or ostlers.
It was extremely common for publicans, particularly
in smaller establishments, to work only part-time,
combining run a bar with other work. During the day
running the pub was left in the hands of his wife and
other members of the family.
A number of women also ran pubs, often taking over
on the death of their husbands or fathers.

A number of different people were involved with
pubs. Your ancestor may have undertaken one or
more of these tasks.

The publican, sometimes known as the landlord,
licensee, licensed victualler, 'the gaffer', 'gov'nor' or
'mine host'. It is he (sometimes she) who holds the
license to run the pub and it is his job to ensure the
financial success of the premises. Many licensees are
tenants of a brewery, that is they run the pub on an
agreement with the brewery which owns it, and pay
the brewery an agreed amount every year in rent.
Over the past thirty years or so salaried managers, put
in by the company, have begun to run an increasing
number of pubs.

Barmaids – female bar staff were often the wives
and daughters of publicans, although by the end of
the nineteenth century barmaids were being hired in
the larger and more popular establishments. Victorian
sensibilities ensured that barmaids only worked in the
more expensive saloon or lounge bars, where a better
class of customer was served. Pay was low and hours
long, although it was the custom for accommodation
and meals to be included.

Barmen – tended to be young. They were better paid
than barmaids, although hours were as long. Most
only remained as barmen for a few years, before
seeking other work.

Cellarmen – are employed to look after the barrels of
beer. They tend to be employed in the larger or busier
establishments. Elsewhere the publican or barstaff

usually managed the cellars.

Ostlers – were men and boys who looked after the horses in coaching inns. This was important work as dozens of coaches might pass through an inn everyday.

Potmen or potboys – potmen were originally employed to keep pewter drinking mugs clean and shiny. As glassware replaced pewter during the nineteenth century, these people were increasingly used to collect glass from tables in the bar and to act as a general servant to the pub. They were less well paid than the barstaff.

The Records
Licenses
From 1552 onwards, anyone who wanted to sell ale had to apply for a licence at the Quarter Sessions or the Petty Sessions. In addition alehouse keepers had to declare that they would not keep a 'disorderly house' and prohibit games of bowls, dice, football and tennis. These declarations were called recognizances or bonds. Although the requirements have changed over the years, landlords still have to get a licence, renewed yearly, and which can be revoked if the magistrates, meeting in the annual brewster session, feel that the individual has been running a disorderly pub.
In 1617 the requirement for licences was extended to inns. In addition between 1570 and 1792 licences could be obtained directly from the Crown (from 1757 the Stamp Office) rather than from local magistrates, although few records now survive of these licences.

The system was overhauled in 1828 with a new Alehouses Act that provided a framework for granting licences to sell beer, wine and spirits and for regulating inns.

Records of these licences can generally be found in Quarter and Petty Session records at local record offices. Quarter sessions were originally meetings of magistrates (JPs) who met together four times a year to dispense justice and discuss the administrative needs of the county, hence the term. Petty sessions were summary meetings of two or more magistrates to deal with less important matters.

You should look out for registers of recognizances and licences granted to licensed victuallers. Few records however survive from the seventeenth century, but an act of 1753 enforced the keeping of such registers, so most counties have some material from the late-eighteenth century. Again the system fell into abeyance, particularly after 1828, but detailed registers have been kept since 1871. The most detailed registers give the name of the licensee, the parish in which he lived, the inn sign (i.e. name of the pub), and the names of occupations of two guarantors who vouched for the applicant's probity. However, you are more likely to find just the name or names of individuals and possibly the parish they came from, with no indication of which pub he ran. Within the records there may also be correspondence, copies of bonds and notes that might contain other information.

The most useful introduction to these records is Jeremy Gibson and Judith Hunter, Victuallers' Licences (Federation of Family History Societies, 1997). The Access to Archives project is making indexes to all these records, including those relating to licensed victuallers, available on the internet at www.pro.gov.uk/a2a/

Records of breweries
From the late eighteenth century breweries increasingly bought pubs which would then only sell their beer. These pubs were known as tied houses, those which remained free of any tie were free houses. By the 1980s, about 90% of public houses were tied to one brewery or another.
The recent turbulent changes in the brewing industry can make it difficult to track down which brewery originally owned the pub. If you don't know or have this information, it is worth trying to track down an old photograph of it which may include signs indicating who owned it. Local studies libraries (see below).often have large, and well indexed, collections of local photos. If the pub is still trading the locals may be able to help.

Once you have tracked down the right brewery, their records may tell you from whom the pub was bought or when the land it was built on was acquired. Estate records are usually held in alphabetical order by premises, and may include title deeds, mortgages, maps and plans, pub lists and books containing lease and conveyance details, In addition there may also be records of beer sold (known as barrelage in the trade) by the pub, although here too the records are arranged by property rather than by the publican.
Some breweries keep their own records, but many have been deposited at local record offices. Because of the great changes taking place in the brewing industry at present it is not always clear where the records of the larger brewers are. The Brewery History Society (see below) is keeping an eye on the situation to ensure the brewery archives are maintained by their new owners or transferred to the appropriate archival repository. The National Register of Archives (also see below) should be able to advise you where these records are at present. Another useful source is Lesley Richmond and Alison Turton, The Brewing Industry: a Guide to the Historical Records (Manchester University Press, 1990).

A few breweries have published histories, which often describe their pubs. Unfortunately these books can be hard to track down. The best place to start is probably the local history library.

Other record sources
Census records – will list everybody sleeping on the premises on census night

Directories – the landlords of pubs should appear in trade or street directories.

Land records - Even quite small public houses in rural areas are likely to have a plot of land attached. Descriptions of this land will appear in tithe and enclosure maps and accompanying documents, which are roughly for the period between about 1750 and 1850. Sets of these records are at both the Public

Record Office and at local record offices. Valuation Office returns, between 1911 and 1915, (at the PRO) describe individual pubs and the land they occupied in both urban and rural areas, although the records are difficult to use. Ordnance survey and fire insurance maps will show pubs and the land they occupied in towns – sets of these maps are normally at local record offices. Local record offices may also have records about the sale of properties.

Newspapers – may well record the arrival and retirement of landlords, as well as notable events at the pub.

Ratebooks - Rates have long been levied on property, normally of the reasonably well to do. Before the twentieth century separate highway and poor rates were levied but they were normally collected together, and details recorded in rate books, which are normally to be found at local record offices. They list the householder, landlord if appropriate, rate levied, with a brief description of the premises. Pubs will be included, although it can sometimes difficult to identify individual properties

Wills - Publicans may well have made wills.

Further reading

Norman Barber *A Century of British Brewers* (Brewery History Society, 1994). The BHS is also publishing a number of more detailed county guides to breweries, including home-brew pubs. Counties covered so far are South Yorkshire, Leicestershire and Rutland, Northamptonshire and Norfolk. The volume for Oxfordshire and Buckinghamshire is due out shortly.

Peter Clark, *The English Ale House*, 1200-1830 (Longman, 1983)

Mark Girouard, *Victorian Pubs* (Studio Vista, 1975)

Peter Haydon, *The English Pub*: A History (Robert Hale, 1994) – the best introduction!

See also entries for alehouses and inns in David Hey (ed), The Oxford Companion to Local and Family History (Oxford UP, 1996) and sections in Andrew Barr, Drink: A Social History (Pimlico, 1995). In addition, there are several useful articles in Family History Monthly. Issue 34 contains an article on Publicans, Helen Osborn looked at 'Brewers and their records' in issue 56. Copies cost £3 each and can be obtained from Family History Monthly, 45 St Mary's Rd, London W5 5RQ (020-8579 1082).

A number of local history societies and individuals have published histories of public houses in their areas, which can often be very hard to track down. The local study librarian or archivist should be able to tell you what exists for their district. Copies should have been deposited with the British Library, although this is rarely the case. The Society of Genealogists (see below) also has a small collection.

Websites

The Pubs, Inns and Taverns Index, 1801-1901 is building an index to the public houses of the 19th century and the people who worked in them: www.pubsindex.freeserve.co.uk

The excellent National Pubs and Breweries website, which has a bulletin board and links to other sites around the country.
www.btinternet.com/~steven.williams1/pubpgintro.htm

Also useful, there are pages on tracing the history of pubs on my web site at www.sfowler.force9.co.uk And, of course, don't forget the Pub History Society's own website www.uk-history.co.uk/phs.htm

There are several sites devoted to pubs of particular counties. Essex is covered at www.essexpubs.co.uk while on the other side of England the pubs of Gloucestershire can be visited at www.gloucestershirepubs.co.uk

Other useful addresses
Pub History Society, 15 Hawthorn Rd, Peterborough PE1 4PA www.uk-history.co.uk/phs.htm exists to encourage research into pubs, the architecture, what took place there and the people who worked behind the bar.
Brewery History Society, Manor Side East, Mill Lane, Byfleet, West Byfleet KT14 7RS www.breweryhistory.co.uk
A large variety of books on inns and breweries is sold by Paul Travis, BeerInn Print, Long High Top, Heptonstall, Hebden Bridge HX7 7PE.

Simon Fowler is the Editor of Family History Monthly and worked for many years at The Public Record Office. Prior to becoming editor of Family History Monthly he was at the Society of Genealogists.

Transcription of the 1851 unfilmed census for Manchester and district

Ray Hulley Project Co-ordinator

The 1851 census is a vital source of evidence for family and social historians, being one of the earliest data banks covering all persons on a single date. It is the first census that shows full details of family relationships, exact ages and occupations of all employed persons. Most importantly, it shows for the first time the birth town or village of all English-born people. This enables the researcher to go back into the pre-census period with a definite location for further work. Most of the returns have been microfilmed, surname and location indexed and analysed by researchers and family history societies. Their efforts have made the searching of the records a comparatively easy task and many of us are greatly indebted to them for their hard work.

In 1983, the Manchester and Lancashire Family History Society decided to surname index all the returns for Manchester and district and John Coupe, the society's project officer, set up a programme of work. A team of volunteers was recruited and the first volume of surnames was published in March 1984.

The initial exercise immediately drew attention to a major problem with the Manchester returns. The microfilms used to index the details were, in many cases, extremely difficult to read, mainly because of water damage to the original returns that had been suffered whilst the returns were still under the jurisdiction of the Home Office. This water damage was reproduced on the film as large, ghost-like areas of white with the text being completely obliterated from the same area. Further enquiries at the Public Record Office revealed that in many instances the original returns were so badly damaged that it was not even worth filming them. Indeed, it was once believed that these returns had been completely destroyed, much to the disappointment of hundreds of family historians.

The work of indexing the filmed returns continued between 1983 and 1989 and it was decided to seek clarification from the PRO about the fate of the unfilmed returns. Although badly damaged - those affected were covered in a brown stain, caused by the water-based ink used by the enumerator having been washed all over the paper - they were all extant and stored with their companion returns in piece number order. A number of them were extremely fragile, some were in tatters and many appeared impossibly difficult to read. In late 1990, an analysis of all the unfilmed returns gave an indication of the extent of the problem, which was much greater than at first envisaged.

A later comparison with the population tables of the district indicated that over 120,000 people were missing from the filmed returns and the areas affected included parts of Manchester - London Road, Deansgate, Hulme, Chorlton on Medlock and St George's sub-districts, as well as most of Salford - Greengate, Regent Road, Pendleton and Pendlebury sub-districts. Outlying areas also had large swathes of population unaccounted for - Ashton under Lyne, Oldham, Harpurhey, Blackley and Prestwich all had missing population amounting to over 50% of the total. This was a serious omission for historians and one that could not be replaced by other sources.

In early 1991, the Society sought volunteers from amongst their London-based members to transcribe the unfilmed returns and the work started in April at Chancery Lane. Susan Lumas of the Editorial Services Department was appointed as liaison officer between the PRO and the volunteers and kept an eagle eye on us. The work had to be carried on without the use of any form of artificial light and although an ultra violet light source was tried initially, the results were unsatisfactory, mainly because of the poor quality of the rather outdated apparatus available. Great reliance was placed on natural daylight and the team's successes in those days were almost entirely dependent on the vagaries of London's weather.

Two volunteers transcribed the returns independently and their results were matched by a third, who arbitrated on any differences. A complete transcription of all readable text was made, including obvious errors, spelling mistakes and side notes. At one time, there were as many as fifteen volunteers working on the returns from a large table in the middle of the room either on a Wednesday or Thursday. Later, the work was transferred to a 'turret' room on the southwestern corner of the building, thus increasing significantly the amount of natural daylight available to the team who usually attended on one day each week, either Tuesdays or Thursdays.

After transcription the results were delivered to the Society's office in Manchester where another team of volunteers input the results into a computer prior to their preparation and eventual production on microfiche. The finished result contained a surname index, a location index and a full transcription of all recaptured data. A copy of each microfiche was deposited at the Census Room for public use.

In 1995, it came to my attention that the problem of reading very damaged documents had appeared to be solved by the authorities in Spain. A computer software package which incorporated the use of a document scanner and imaging camera had given very positive results from fifteenth-century documents that appeared at first sight to have the same type of damage as shown on the Manchester returns. Examples of "before" and "after" images from the Spanish documents gave a boost to the chances of an easier and more effective system being employed on the returns at the PRO and I wrote to the Keeper with details of and examples from the Spanish work. Unfortunately the PRO decided that the Spanish system was rather slow and labour-intensive and was unlikely to be of major benefit to our work. This was a disappointing setback, especially now that we had reached the stage in our transcription work where the returns were even more difficult to transcribe, the easier ones having been tackled first.

The Chancery Lane operation of the PRO closed in December 1996 and all functions except the Census Room and other small areas were transferred to Kew. It was important to maintain the continuity of our work at Kew, especially now that we could just about see the light at the end of a six-year tunnel. Realising that the availability of natural daylight was a prerequisite to the success of our work, my first venture into the dim area of the Editorial Services Department (facing due north!) filled me with trepidation and dismay. In fact, Kew One, where the ESD was located, was deliberately designed to reduce the amount of natural light available in order to protect the original documents. In spite of this setback, the PRO authorities had an alternative option for the work.

The transcription work was now made the responsibility of the Conservation Department, whose head, Mario Aleppo, initially introduced me to a location with no windows!! Ironically this was known as the Disaster Room and was normally used whenever documents were in need of special recovery treatment. This room eventually proved to be absolutely ideal for our work and we are most grateful to Mario Aleppo for his foresight. He demonstrated on the unfilmed returns the use of the latest in ultra-violet light aids - a hand-held scanner - and convinced me beyond doubt that reliance on natural daylight to read the unreal was a thing of the past. In addition to these facilities, we were allowed to use artificial light for those occasions when UV couldn't pierce the gloom of washed-out ink. Our experience over the past 4 years working in the Disaster Room has confirmed that a combination of UV and artificial light sources have usually uncovered those parts of the returns that can be read.

Our technique on the returns now being worked on consists of the following:
1. The returns are checked page-by-page using a strong artificial light source and a magnifying glass. Each column is checked vertically rather than checking each line horizontally. In this way, we are able to identify family names, relationships, ages and birthplaces with more accuracy.
2. If there are areas that have not been transcribed by the above method, then a UV hand-held light source is used to scan the appropriate area of the page. We have to don protective eye cover when using the UV light and the room is in complete darkness to ensure the maximum contrast conditions. A powerful magnifying glass is again used at this stage.
3. The results are checked by a second team member. Particular attention is given to missing surnames,

especially where all other details of the household have been found.
4. A Xerox copy is made of the completed transcription sheets and is held by myself as security in case of loss of the top copy.
5. The top copy is delivered to Manchester for the next stage - computer inputting. The final results are published by the society on microfiche.

The results of our work to date are set out below.

Further details of all the above transcribed returns are available from the Manchester and Lancashire Family History Society, Clayton House, 59 Piccadilly, Manchester M1 2AQ or from their website at http://www.mlfhs.demon.co.uk.

What about our future work? We have learnt from our experience of using both artificial and UV light sources that it has been possible to decipher some of the most difficult returns. We therefore intend to complete a recheck of the originals of the earlier results from Salford Greengate, Salford Regent Road and Hulme using our current techniques. This will further increase the overall recapture rate, hopefully towards 75%.

This project has been long and arduous and I would like to pay tribute to those members of the Manchester and Lancashire Family History Society who have assisted me with the work. Some have found the going rather tough and have only managed to stay with us for a few weeks; others, like Kath Arkwright and Jeanne Bryan have lasted the pace almost from the start and special thanks are due to both of them. We shall never know the full benefits of our work over the past ten years but, judging from the kind comments already given to us by those researchers who have discovered their previously 'lost' ancestors in the unfilmed returns, then these benefits will increase over the coming years.

PRO ref HO 107/	District	Unfilmed population Original	Recaptured	%
2220	Chorlton on Medlock, Ardwick * (being transcribed 2001)	51,300	33,900(est)	66
222	Hulme	20,800	12,400	60
2222	Pendleton and Pendlebury	16,900	7,000	41
2223	Salford Greengate	34,700	20,800	60
2224	Salford Regent Road	11,100	9,700	87
2227	Deansgate* (to be transcribed in 2002)	33,200	24,900(est)	70
2230	Manchester St George's	11,600	10,400	90
2232	Harpurhey, Blackley & Prestwich	9,000	8,000	89
2233	Ashton-u-Lyne & Knott Lanes	18,800	18,000	96
2240	Oldham-below-Town	5,700	5,500	97
	Totals	213,100	150,600	71

*these originals were mostly filmed but are very badly damaged

RESTING AFTER A DAY'S WORK ON BANANA FIELD.

British West Indian Genealogy: an overview

Guy Grannum

The West Indies are a chain of volcanic and coral islands, stretching from Florida to Venezuela. During the 16th century although the Spanish nominally held the West Indies they did not settle on most of the islands. During the 17th and 18th centuries other European powers, predominately the French, British, Dutch, and to a lesser extent the Danes and Swedes, challenged Spanish claims to the West Indies and settled on many islands. Indigenous Amerindians originally inhabited most of the larger islands, but their numbers dwindled until by the mid-17th century only Jamaica, St Lucia, St Vincent, Tobago and Dominica held substantial populations. Indeed, the Caribs of St Vincent, St Lucia and Tobago managed to restrict European expansion to those islands until the late 18th century.

By 1800 the population of the West Indian islands was a mixture of indigenous Amerindians, Spanish, Portuguese, Sephardic Jews, British, French, Dutch, Danes, Swedes, Germans, and most significantly Africans. The populations were mobile with merchants and planters of all nations settling on islands of other powers. The region was also extremely unstable as European wars were also fought in the West Indies which caused the migrations of the populations of the victors and losers. During the Spanish, French and American republican wars in the 18th and 19th centuries royalist populations migrated to friendly islands.

In the 19th century the ethnic population of the West Indies began to change. The most significant new group were East Indian indentured labourers, recruited from the 1840s to help overcome the severe labour problems experienced by many British colonies following the abolition of slavery in 1834. Other groups of labourers included Chinese, who first settled in Trinidad in 1806, Portuguese from Madeira, and liberated Africans freed from illegal slavers.

The British took their social, legal and ecclesiastical systems with them to the West Indies. The colonies were divided into parishes with vestries and parish churches, a poor law, and justices of the peace with petty and quarter sessions. The types of records created by these colonies will be familiar to those who have undertaken genealogical research in Britain. For example, parish registers of baptisms, marriages and burials, electoral registers, poor law records, registers of deeds, marriage licences, and wills. Differences will be experienced in those colonies which had previously been held by another European power, such as Trinidad, St Lucia, and Grenada where the British authorities retained the previous social and legal systems. For example documents were often written in English and the second language. The Church of England is not the dominant religion and the records of the earlier administration may be in other European archives.

Britain does not hold the domestic (locally created) records of her dependencies and former colonies. There are no unified records and most records, if they survive, are to be found in the archives and other depositories in the relevant country. Unfortunately, the survival rate of records in many of the islands is poor partly because of poor record keeping practices, neglect and fire, fates so familiar to researchers in Britain. Most of the losses, however, are due to two major factors which will not be experienced by researchers in Britain.

War and invasion. This often led to the destruction of public and private buildings, estates and personal property and the migration of victors and the defeated. Tropical climate. High humidity, tropical insects and tropical storms especially hurricanes are a significant cause for the loss of records. In addition, many of the West Indian islands experience earthquakes and volcanic eruptions.

In order to undertake family history research in the British West Indies you need to know which country the family was from and approximate dates. Family history research in the British West Indies is very similar to researching in Britain, as the records and the information recorded are very similar. Although most of the more important family history sources are to be found on the individual islands, many sources are available in the Public Record Office (PRO); some of which will be described later. Also, many sources have been

---

British West Indian Colonies in 1815

List of British West Indian colonies in 1815, with dates they became British colonies and the name of the former colonial power. The British government included British Honduras (now Belize), British Guiana (now Guyana) and the Bermudas as part of the West Indies.

Anguilla (1650)
Antigua and Barbuda (1632)
Bahamas (from 1629)
Barbados (1625)
Bermudas (1612)
British Guiana (1814)   Dutch
British Honduras (1638)
British Virgin Islands (from 1666)   Dutch
Cayman Islands (1670)   Spanish
Dominica (1763)   French
Grenada (1763)   French
Jamaica (1655)   Spanish
Montserrat (1632)
Nevis (1628)
St Christopher (1623) joint French and British
St Lucia (1814)   French
St Vincent and the Grenadines (1763)   French
Tobago (1814)   Courlanders/Dutch/French
Trinidad (1797)   Spanish
Turks and Caicos Islands (1678)

Trinity Cathedral, Trinidad.

microfilmed by the Church of Jesus Christ of Latter-Day Saints (LDS) and can be seen at their Family History Centres. The most important records for researchers are:

Parish registers: the dominant denomination of most of the British islands was Church of England. On the French and Spanish islands ceded to Britain the Roman Catholic Church is more important. The records of baptisms, marriages, burials, vestries and the administration of the poor law are arranged by parish as in Britain. Until this century none of the islands had large urban areas and therefore researching the records of several parishes should not be too onerous. Parish records are usually to be found in the country's archives or registration offices, and many have been microfilmed by the LDS. However, some are still with the incumbent. Some returns for the early 1700s were copied to the British government and can be found in Colonial Office records in the PRO.

Census returns: from the 1670s the colonial governors were encouraged to send regular returns on the population, the numbers of adults and children, the numbers of slaves, the growth (or decrease) in the population, and the military strength. Most of this information was statistical, but some returns list the head of household with the numbers of free whites, free blacks or coloured, and numbers of slaves that made up the household. Many of these early statistical and nominal censuses are to be found in the Colonial Office records in the PRO. The colonies continued taking regular censuses during the 19th and 20th centuries and if the returns survive they will be found in the islands.

Wills and administrations: most wills and administrations of persons dying in the West Indies would have been handled locally and survive locally. However, British subjects dying abroad who either resided in Britain or who had estates in England and Wales had their wills proved until 1857 by the Prerogative Court of Canterbury (PCC), the records of which are held by the PRO. In 1858 the PCC's role in probate administration was abolished and the responsibility went to the Principal Probate Registry. Bequeathed slaves may be named in wills, and associated inventories may include lists of slaves.

Civil registration: this is the recording of births, marriages and deaths by the state rather than by individual churches. The starting dates for registration varied from county to country, for example Jamaican returned started in 1878, Trinidad in 1848 and Tobago in 1868. Also, the registration of different events sometimes started at different times, for example, in Barbados

registration of births started in 1890, and of deaths in 1925. The returns are usually to be found in the country's registration offices, and again many are available from the LDS.

Newspapers: early West Indian newspapers describe British, European and local news and for genealogists include notices for sale of property, birth, marriage and death notices, and information on runaway servants, apprentices and slaves. Some early West Indian newspapers can be found among the governors' despatches in the PRO, while for the period 1830s to 1850s survive as separate collections in Colonial Office 'miscellanea' series. Good collections of West Indian newspapers are to be found in the British Library, Newspaper Library.

Estate records: these are private papers and are commonly known as plantation records. The West Indies were an agricultural economy with most of the land owned and managed by a few landholders. Plantation records comprise such material as mortgages, deeds, accounts, journals, correspondence, duty ledgers, estate maps and inventories of property. In addition to information on the estate, the owner and his or her family, genealogists may find accounts of payments to contract labourers and merchants, wage lists of household servants and labourers and lists of slaves. If these records have survived they may be found amongst the family papers in British and West Indian archives under the name of the plantation or the owner. The Historical Manuscripts Commission may be able to advise on surviving papers in Britain.

Although these are private papers some are to be found in the PRO under three main headings. The equity side of the Court of Chancery dealt with a wide variety of disputes such as debt, inheritance, bankruptcy, legitimacy and marriage settlements. Many plantation deeds, correspondence, mortgages and journals were provided as evidence and those which were not collected or returned survive as **Chancery Masters Exhibits** (C 103 - C 114, J 90). Following insurrections in Jamaica and hurricanes in Barbados, St Lucia, St Vincent and Dominica in the 1830s the **West Indian Hurricane Relief Commission**, 1832-1881 (PWLB 11), issued loans to governors for general relief and to individual plantation owners to rebuild estates. The records of this commission include mortgages made out to the crown as security for the loans, inventories, lists of slaves and evidence of ownership. The **West Indian Encumbered Estates Commission**, 1854-1886 (CO 441), investigated estates which had become overburdened by mortgages and in some cases to sell them. The records include transfer mortgages, accounts, deeds, plans and inventories of property including slaves.

The following types of records are uniquely colonial in origin and format. They are to be found in the Public Record Office but copies may survive locally. With the exception of the records of the slave registry and Slave Compensation Commission (T 71) the records are to be found among the records of the Colonial Office (departmental code CO). For the most part the records are arranged under the colony or administrative unit.

Colonial Office, original correspondence: these are the official correspondence from the governors, together with letters from other colonial officials and British government departments relating to economic, military and social matters of the colonies. Although the records tend to be of an administrative nature they contain much information which is useful to family historians. Some sources for genealogists have already been described and others include returns of the sale or rent of government lands. Between 1820 and 1834 there are many slave returns, including the number of slave marriages, manumissions (grants of freedom) and government owned slaves. Some of this is statistical but others give names, for example, records of manumissions provide the name of the slave and usually the name of the owner. Other material to be found includes petitions to the governor, the British government and the monarchy, applications for colonial appointments, pensions, newspapers and tax lists etc.

Government gazettes: these were the colonial equivalent to the *London Gazette* and are a most important source from the mid-1800s, although gazettes for some colonies do not start until after 1900. Many early newspapers are the predecessors to the government gazettes and contain similar information. The information in the gazettes varies from colony to colony but can include tax lists, electoral registers, grants of government lands, arrears of rent on government land, letters at the post offices, licences (for example, for guns, dogs, boats, chemists, oil, and alcohol), changes of name, first class passengers, lists of jurors, midwives, constables, nurses and militia officers, appointments and resignations of government officials, notices relating to cases of intestacy, guardianship and wills, notices of applications for naturalization, and the transfer and mortgage of property etc.

Sessional Papers: these are the proceedings of the local government and are the colonial equivalent of the British Parliamentary Papers and Hansard. They comprise minutes and reports of the legislative, executive and privy councils, and departmental reports and include material such as petitions to the assembly, manumissions granted by the legislature, and details of local appointments.

Acts: these are copies of local acts and ordinances. For family historians they can include private acts of naturalization in the colony, sales of land to recover debt, grants of manumission, appointments of office holders, and names of persons transported or deported from the colony.

Blue Books of Statistics: annual books which begin in 1821 and continue until the mid-1940s. They contain statistical information about the colony, such as population, education, religion and economy. They also include names and employment details of public employees and pensioners.

Slave registry and the **Slave Compensation Commission**: this is the most important series of records for family historians for the period 1817-1834. The slave trade to British colonies was abolished in 1807 but the trade between West Indian colonies was restricted from 1805. In order to prevent the illegal importation of slaves the colonies established slave registers whereby owners of slaves had to record the names of their slaves, their ages, countries of origin and occupations, and whether they were black, mulatto, quadroon or coloured etc (the titles for the degrees of colour varied from colony to colony). The registers were kept up to date by re-registration; for some this was annual, and for others triennial. The period of the registers is roughly 1817 to 1834 when slavery as an institution was abolished and replaced by apprenticeship, a form of indentured labour. These registers were used to calculate the amount of compensation to be paid to slave owners on emancipation and as evidence of ownership.

These registers are important to both the slave owning and the slave communities. Most free people of modest means would have owned at least one slave and therefore the registers can be used as a census of almost every householder. Slaves were chattel (moveable property) and therefore could be gifted, purchased, sold, inherited and given as a dowry etc. The registers record such changes of ownership, for example they can be used to show deaths of owners as family members could inherit slaves. Also slaves were often given to children when they reached adulthood or following marriage.

Personal information regarding slaves is usually very limited. Slaves did not officially have surnames, they could not own property, and they are not usually listed in family units, although for St Lucia and Trinidad the registers record families (mother and children) and surnames if any. For people with slave ancestors the registers are usually the earliest records to be found. These registers will help identify owners who may have left private papers which may contain additional information.

The original registers should survive in the islands. The duplicate registers and the records of the Slave Compensation Commission are held by the PRO in the series T 71.

I have given a very brief overview of the history of the British West Indies and the types of records available for genealogists. The most useful records are to be found, assuming they survive, in the relevant West Indian archives, but much information, especially for the period 1817-1834, can be found among the holdings in the PRO. Research will not be easy unless you have a probable country and a date. It may mean that you have to undertake some research in other European archives. Next time you visit the island of your ancestors consider spending some time in the record office!

Useful addresses and websites
Public Record Office, Kew, Surrey, TW9 4DU
        Tel: 020 8392 5200, Internet: www.pro.gov.uk
British Library, Newspaper Library, Colindale
        London NW9 5HE, Internet: prodigi.bl.uk/nlcat/
Church of Jesus Christ of Latter-Day Saints
        British Isles Family History Service, 185 Penns
        Lanes, Sutton Coldfield, Birmingham B76 1JU,
        Internet: www.familysearch.com
Historical Manuscripts Commission
        Quality House, Quality Court, London
        WC1A IHP, Internet: www.hmc.gov.uk
Caribbean Genealogical Web Project:
        www.rootsweb.com/~caribgw/
Cyndi Howell's online gateway to resources for Hispanic,
South American and Caribbean family history:
        www.cyndislist.com/hispanic.htm

Antigua and Barbuda
Antigua National Archives, Rappaport Centre, Victoria Park, St John's, Antigua
Registrar General, High Street, St John's, Antigua
Bahamas
Public Records Office, Department of Archives, PO Box SS-6341, Nassau, Bahamas
Registrar General's Office, PO Box N532, Nassau, Bahamas
Barbados
Department of Archives, Lazaretto Building, Black Rock, St Michael, Barbados

Registration Department, Supreme Court of Barbados, Law Courts, Colleridge St, Bridgetown, Barbados
Belize
Belize Archives Department, 26/28 Unity Boulevard, Belmopan, Belize
Bermuda
Bermuda National Archives, Government Administration Building, 30 Parliament St, Hamilton HM 12, Bermuda
British Virgin Islands
Library Services Department, Flemming St, Road Town, Tortola, British Virgin Islands
Cayman Islands
Cayman Islands National Archive, Government Administration Building, George Town, Grand Cayman
Registrar General, Tower Building, George Town, Grand Cayman
Dominica
National Documentation Centre, Government Headquarters, Roseau, Commonwealth of Dominica
General Registrar, Bay Front, Roseau, Commonwealth of Dominica
Grenada
National Museum, Young St, St George's, Grenada
Registrar General, Church St, St George's, Grenada
Guyana
National Archives of Guyana, River Police Building, Stabroek Square, Georgetown, Guyana
General Register Office, GPO Building, Robb St, Georgetown, Guyana
Jamaica
Jamaica Archives, Spanish Town, Jamaica
The Registrar General, Vital Records Information, Twickenham Park, Spanish Town, Jamaica
Montserrat
Montserrat Public Library, Government Headquarters, Plymouth, Montserrat
Registrar General, PO Box 22, Plymouth, Montserrat
St Christopher and Nevis
National Archives, Government Headquarters, Church St, Box 186, Basseterre, St Kitts
Registrar General, PO Box 236, Basseterre, St Kitts
St Lucia
St Lucia National Archives, PO Box 3060, Clarke St, Vigie, Castries, St Lucia
St Vincent and the Grenadines
Archives Department, Cotton Ginnery Compound, Frenches, Kingstown, St Vincent
Registrar General, Kingstown, St Vincent
Trinidad and Tobago
National Archives, PO Box 763, 105 St Vincent St, Port-of-Spain, Trinidad
Registrar General's Office, Registration House, South Quay, Port-of-Spain, Trinidad

Further reading:
Herbert C Bell and David W

Parker, *Guide to British West Indian archive materials in London and in the islands for the history of the United States* (Carnegie Institution of Washington, 1926).
Bryan Edwards, *The History of the British West Indies*, 5th edition, 5 vols (London, 1819)
Calendar of State Papers, Colonial, America and West Indies, 1574-1739, 40 volumes (1860-1993), published on CD-ROM by Routledge (2000)
Family Tree Magazine, contains many articles on sources for West Indian genealogical research
General Register Office, *Abstract of arrangements respecting registration of birth, marriages and deaths in the United Kingdom and the other countries of the British Commonwealth and in the Republic of Ireland* (London: HMSO, 1952)
Guy Grannum, *Tracing Your West Indian Ancestors. Sources in the Public Record Office* (PRO Publications, 1995)
Arthur E Gropp, *Guide to libraries and archives in Central America and the West Indies, Panama, Bermuda and British Guiana* (New Orleans, 1941)
Kenneth EN Ingram, *Manuscript sources for the history of the West Indies* (University of the West Indies, 2000)
Journal of the Board of Trade and Plantations, 1704-1782, 14 volumes (1920-1938)
Thomas Jay Kemp, *International vital records handbook*, 4th edn (Genealogical Publishing Co Inc, 2000)
Madeleine E Mitchell, *Jamaican Ancestry: How to find out More* (Heritage Books, 1998)
Vere Langford Oliver, ed, *Caribbeana*, 6 vols (1910-1919)
Stephen D Porter, *Jamaican Records. A Research Manual: a Two Part Guide to Genealogical & Historical Research using repositories in Jamaica & England* (1999)
Anne Thurston, *Records of the Colonial Office, Dominions Office, Commonwealth Relations Office and Commonwealth Office* (The Stationery Office, 1997)
George F Tyson, jnr, *A guide to manuscript sources in United States and West Indian depositories relating to the British West Indies during the era of the American Revolution* (Scholarly Resources Inc, 1978)
Peter Walne, ed, *A Guide to Manuscript Sources for the History of Latin America and the Caribbean in the British Isles* (Oxford University Press, 1973)

Guy Grannum, has worked in the Public Record office since 1988. He is the author of Tracing your West Indian Ancestor - sources in the Public record office (PRO Publications 1995) and is currently writing a second edition.

ON THE RIO COBRE RIVER, JAMAICA

Work and Occupational Sources

Doreen Hopwood

Brass Foundary, Messrs. Vickers, Ltd., Barrow-in-Furness

Have you ever wondered what a 'sagger makers bottom knocker' actually did in his daily working life, or how a 'grayman' earned his living? Many trades and occupations have long since disappeared, but descriptions of these live on in primary and published material held in various repositories, and you may be able to see crafts and trade demonstrations at working museums, such as The Black Country Museum, Beamish and Ironbridge. Archaic terms and types of occupation appear in many books, but need to be understood in their contemporary setting if we are able to make sense of them. My grandmother was described as a 'hooker' in the 1891 census (her father was a bootmaker), but, some hundred years later, this term has a very different meaning!

Most trades and crafts required some kind of training, either by formal apprenticeship or by 'on the job' instruction. The term 'journeyman' often appears after the father's name on a birth certificate and this officially referred to a person who hired himself to a master of the trade on a daily basis (from the French *jour* (day)). However, by the early 20th century this was generally used to describe any worker who was carrying out a trade for which he had received training, but had not served an apprenticeship. During the 13th and 14th centuries craft guilds were formed to regulate crafts and trades – such as weavers, tailors etc. There were usually three grades of skill, the master (or craftsman), the apprentice (trainee) and journeyman. The Guilds were able to control their trade or craft by obtaining exclusive rights to practise their trade, and by a strict method of entry into the guild – usually by the requirement of completing a seven-year apprenticeship. Some towns had numerous guilds in existence simultaneously – such as London, whilst others had just one or two. In order for a man to practise in the leather/tanning industry in Walsall he was required to fulfil the stringent conditions set out in a 15th century ordinance. Only men born or apprenticed in the Parish of Walsall could practise his trade there. They were also obliged to pay an annual sum of 6s 8d to maintain the Chapel of St Katherine and the Light of St Anne in the Parish Church, which ends with the warning 'If any man works contrary to this ordinance the warden shall ask him to leave'.

The Guilds of London were known as Livery Companies because of the distinctive uniform (livery) worn by the senior members of each company. By obtaining royal grants and charters they had monopolies within the jurisdiction of the City of London, which prevented non-members from practising their trade. By the 19th century London had 77 Livery Companies still effectively regulating trade, although the influence of guilds outside London had dramatically declined by the 18th century. Restrictions and strict controls in guild towns often meant a decrease in trade at the expense of the newly emerging non-guild towns, such as Birmingham. The records of most livery companies can be found at the Guildhall Library, and the Society of Genealogists has 'Crisps Apprentices' Indentures', which contains some 15,000 entries, indexed by name, covering the 17th to the 19th centuries. These include the name of the apprentice, his father's name and occupation, the name of the master and his trade, and may include the apprentice's date and place of birth. During the period 1710 to 1804 a stamp duty was levied on apprenticeship indentures, and there is a central register covering England and Wales – Apprenticeship Books at Class IR1 at the Public Record Office. Those covering the years 1710 to 1774 have been indexed by the name of the apprentice, and may be found at the Public Record Office and the Society of Genealogists. Later apprenticeships may have been indexed by local societies and may be found at County Record Offices – usually under trade, name of the master and apprentice.

Members of professions, such as the law, clergy, medicine and officers in the navy, army or airforce, are relatively easy to research as comprehensive records have been maintained by their professional bodies. The General Law List was established in 1775 and superseded by the Law List of 1797, which is still published annually detailing attorneys and solicitors. Until the 19th century solicitors were required to swear an oath before being allowed to practise, and these can be found in the Courts of Common Pleas or Kings Bench at the Public Record Office. Barristers were appointed through the Inns of Court and many admission registers have been indexed with copies at the Society of Genealogists. The appointment/promotion of senior civil servants, high ranking clergy, Justices of the Peace and military personnel were announced in the London Gazette, and this is also an excellent source for tracing information about any companies that went into liquidation, insolvencies and persons declared bankrupt. Records relating to doctors prior to 1745 can be found in material of The Worshipful Company of Barbers and Surgeons, and the Medical List and Medical Register have been published since 1845 and 1859 respectively. Doctors were required to hold a university degree, so you may find further information in lists of graduates (alumni). Those of both Oxford and Cambridge Universities have been published (in alphabetical order of graduates) up to c1900, and you are likely to find members of the Anglican clergy in these. There are annual directories for Catholic, Anglican and Methodist clergy, and these, along with the Law List/Register and

Army, Navy and Air Force List, can be usually be found in main reference libraries. The latter resource lists army officers, but records relating to 'other ranks' can be found at the Public Record Office, and '*Tracing your ancestors in the PRO*' includes a comprehensive guide to these sources.

'Ag labs' and domestic servants probably feature in most of our family histories, and you may find information in estate or family papers if you know the name of the land-owning family for whom he/she worked. Many of these have been deposited in County Record Offices, and may include wages, references and possibly a 'biopic' of the person. Pamela Horns' *The Rise and Fall of the Victorian Servant*' includes a comprehensive guide to primary and published sources about this huge body of individuals.

Before the nineteenth century there are few occupational statistics until the introduction of the census, which, among other things, aimed to obtain a reliable record of the economic geography of Britain at ten-yearly intervals. The census enumerators' books themselves are helpful in showing the distribution of a particular occupation in a given area and observing occupational trends in families and communities. In certain districts of any large town, you will find that almost everyone living on the same street was involved in the same trade, and by reference to contemporary maps you are likely to be able to identify the manufactory or business at which they worked. Proximity of home and workplace was vital until the development of trams (or other public transport systems), so most people worked within walking distance of their homes. Similarly, many smaller towns and villages relied on a single trade or employer for their livelihood so when this declined, people were often forced to move to larger towns to find work. The introduction of steam and other forms of power meant the demise of the cottage industries, such as nail and chain making, but some factories were able to adapt in order to meet new demands. This occurred in the Black Country where wagon and carriage makers redeployed themselves to make rail rolling stock and suchlike.

Do be aware of potential aggrandisement of occupational status on the census returns. I recently found an individual described as a merchant in 1871, but the birth certificate of his son a few months later indicated that he was a hawker! "Shopkeeper" could mean anything from the owner of an emporium to person selling second-hand clothes in her front room. Many women were in paid employment outside their homes, but this is rarely shown on the census returns or on their marriage certificates.

Parliamentary reports and the lists of occupations compiled by the Registrar General can give a good idea of types of occupation and working conditions. Factory inspectors regularly interviewed employees as well as employers, so your ancestor may feature in these. During the 19th century Henry Mayhew interviewed people from all walks of life and *The Unknown Mayhew* edited by EP Thompson and Eileen Yeo in 1973, includes comprehensive contemporary descriptions of the pay, living and working conditions of people involved in "everyday" occupations, such as joiners, boot and shoemakers, coopers, tailors and dressmakers.

There are plenty of publications about single occupations, including the "Shire" series and the *Victoria County History* volumes include brief histories of major trades and industries in the relevant county. Stuart Raymonds' *Londoners' Occupations : a genealogical guide* includes histories of the Livery Companies and has a detailed bibliography of published material for most trades and occupations. There are also numerous published accounts about the processes involved in certain types of manufacture and working conditions in local trades, and you should find these in main reference libraries and county record offices. In 1866, Samuel Timmins edited a series of reports which had been collected by the Local Industries Committee and covers all Midland industries from ribbon making to the iron bedstead trade. Local Studies departments of main libraries may also hold ephemera collections which may include strike notices and posters advertising job vacancies. Many family history societies, individuals and repositories have compiled indexes to local trades and businesses, and Jeremy Gibsons' *Guide to Marriage, Census and Other Indexes* provides information about what is available county by county. There is an index of pipers at the Northumberland County Record Office, whilst Northampton Museum holds an index of shoemakers. Local museums often have a collection of tools used in local trades and in areas where a particular trade or craft was prevalent there may be a working museum demonstrating how the work was done. There is a lock museum in Willenhall, a leather museum at Walsall and in Birmingham the Museum of the Jewellery Quarter is housed in a 19th century workshop. Details of the opening hours and the location of such museums can be found on the website for the town or can be obtained from the relevant Tourist Information Office.

Biographies and autobiographies can also provide us with an insight into working conditions in a given trade and *Useful Toil : autobiographies of working people from the 1820s to the 1920s*, edited by John Burnett is both interesting and informative. Types of occupation and work processes changed dramatically during the 20th century, so it is well worth interviewing older friends and relatives to get an account of a typical working day in their line of employment. My mother trained as a shorthand typist in the 1920s and is amazed by the "new" office skills of today.

Surname indexes have often been compiled from trade directories. The earliest for London date back to the early 18th

century with those of the provinces and counties from the mid 18th century, so those covering a specific trade can span almost 200 years. The "commercial" sections of trade directories consist of an alphabetical list of individuals and companies in business, showing the name and address of the business, and may include the residential address of the proprietor. By examining directories covering a large number of years it is possible to ascertain any changes in ownership or location. Surviving rates books show the name of the owner and the type of premises as well as the name of the person responsible for paying the rates on the property. Directories are also a good indication of the economic activity of the area and sometimes include a synopsis of the main trades at the beginning of the entry for the town. Where there is a significant single trade, the precise nature of the business is often shown. For example, the manufacture of buttons was very important in Birmingham and in the "Trades" section of directories, there are entries under the headings of different types of buttons, such as pearl, horn, Florentine, glass etc. The iron trades are covered by national directories such as Rylands, so if you are trying to find where an anchor maker may have moved to in the 19th century, this publication lists the major manufacturers of these.

Trade directories include advertisements, so you may find these in respect of the business for whom an ancestor worked – sometimes showing an illustration of the factory or works. In the same way, trade cards and catalogues were important in marketing goods and many businesses have deposited these in the local county record office, library or in their own archives. Where a company has been taken over, records can generally be found in the repository covering the location of the new companys' head or registered office. Although these are unlikely to provide genealogical information, they paint a picture of the type of work carried out by an ancestor,

and show the finished goods in which he played a role. Where collections of cards and catalogues are held, they are generally indexed by trade and by the name of the company and you will find that most date from the mid 19th century.

The Parish relied heavily on local trades and craftsmen, both to maintain the fabric of the church and its lands and to provide the Overseers of the Poor with grain, bread, clothing and even coffins. Therefore, you may find a mention of an ancestor who was a tailor, slater, miller or glazier in the accounts held in the parish chest. By the beginning of the 18th century, the Overseers of the Poor had come to realise that it was cheaper to apprentice pauper children and orphans to a master outside of the parish, who would then take on responsibility for future relief. A century later, Quarry Bank Mill, a textile mill, owned by Samuel Gregg had 90 parish apprentices, whom he had acquired through advertisements in national newspapers, and most of the children, aged between 10 and 12 years had come from London. Gregg saw himself as a paternalistic employer, believing that if he looked afther his operatives he would be rewarded with a more efficient workforce. During the 19th and early 20th centuries, other employers built not only houses for their workers, but a whole community around their manufactories. Titus Salt created Saltaire in the West Riding of Yorkshire, Rowntrees at York and Lever Brothers at Port Sunlight on the Wirral. Cadburys' Bournville estate was designed to cater for the educational, spiritual and recreational needs of his employees who lived in quality houses with gardens. A vast improvement on the back to back houses of Birmingham. Material relating to the Bournville Village Trust, including a large collection of photographs, is deposited at Birmingham Central Library.

Larger employers usually provided sports and social facilities for their workforce and often published regular newsletters and magazines. These generally included birth, marriage and retirement news as well as obituaries and reports of the fortunes of the firms sports teams and any outings. Many professional football teams started as works teams – such as West Bromwich Albion, formed at Salters Springs Works. Personnel and staff records are less likely to have been retained and where they do exist, there is usually a closure period of 75 years. However, if you have a postal worker among your ancestors, the Post Office has its own extensive archive at Freeling House, Mount Pleasant, Farringdon Road, London EC1A 1BB and there is a guide to holdings by J Farrugia.

Until the railways were nationalised, each of the railway companies kept its own staff records, most of which have been deposited at the Public Record Office. However, you do need to know the company for which an ancestor worked and the type of job he did in order to access these. D T Hawkings' *Railway Ancestors : a guide to the staff records of railway companies of England and Wales, 1822 to 1947* indicates which companies operated in different parts of the country. Most major reference libraries and record offices have copies of maps of their area covering a large time span, and may have maps showing railway networks. There are similar ones plotting the development of the canal system, so if you have boat or barge keepers in your familys' history, such maps can be of help. Boats and barges using navigable inland waters were regularly inspected and issued with certificates by the Quarter or Petty Sessions. You may find information in the records of these courts, along with those relating to persons in other trades who were required to hold a licence or certificate. These include wig powder makers, woolwinders, gamekeepers and victuallers. Material relating to the latter appears in the minutes of the Licensing Judges, and may even include a physical description of the applicant. Publicans and innkeepers usually appear in trade directories both by surname of the licensee (in the commercial section) and by name of the public house in the trades section.

Local newspapers carried job advertisements and if you have professional theatrical or musical ancestors, theatrical journals date back to the early 19th century. Local theatre programmes, posters and photographs of the *artistes* may be held in main libraries or record offices, together with other business ephemera such as share prospectuses, building plans of factories and photographs. The latter were generally taken to show the manufactory, but often include workers carrying out their day to day tasks.

The Business Archives Council and the Royal Commission on Historical Manuscripts have extensive holdings of business records, but rarely include any information about individual workers. Similarly, the Modern Archives Centre at Warwick University holds a substantial amount of material relating to trade unions, but these generally relate to national conferences and policies.

You are most likely to find material relating to specific occupations in the areas where they were most common, so try the main library and record office initially. If you have a surname which has derived from an occupation, you may find that your Fletcher or Cooper ancestors were indeed arrow makers or barrel makers.

Illegitimacy
Angela Petyt

If the parents of a child are not married at the time of birth, then that child is illegitimate in the eyes of the law. In the course of research most family historians discover illegitimate forebears. 'It's a wise man who knows his own father' so the old saying goes. Nowadays, blood tests and DNA profiling can prove this beyond reasonable doubt, but our ancestors were often skilled in the art of concealment. This article will discuss how the truth can be revealed, by investigating various documents. I will say now that I can't guarantee you will find out exactly who the errant father was. Sometimes it's just plain impossible. However, a combination of detective work, logic, intuition and luck can work wonders, as I shall illustrate with a couple of case studies. Never say never!

History and Background
Illegitimacy is nothing new. It has always been a fact of life. Attitudes to illegitimacy have varied throughout periods in history and amongst differing social classes. Royal and gentry families are well known for siring offspring out of wedlock and being proud of it - King Charles II is an excellent example. Indeed, the surname prefix *Fitz-* can often indicate a family's illegitimate descent from nobility. Even in agricultural labouring villages, illegitimacy was tolerated to a certain degree by the community and not particularly frowned upon. It has to be said that it was mainly the Victorians who stigmatised illegitimacy and this hardening of attitudes lasted well into the 20th century.

Studies have been made of illegitimacy rates. In the Tudor and Stuart periods, the highest point was 3% (in many years it was only 1-2%). From 1750, the number of births out of wedlock began to rise, and by the early Victorian period, this rate had more than doubled to 7%. Moreover, a third of women at this time were already pregnant at the time of marriage. Why? Population growth coupled with the Industrial Revolution; massive social and economic change; unprecedented migration. All these factors may play a part. However, by the 1890s, the rate had fallen to 4%, *officially*. This figure may be suspect as the turn of the 20th century is known to be the most difficult period to discover paternity of illegitimate children, due to very strict moral values at the time. Today, in the year 2002, illegitimate births account for over 30% of all children born in England and Wales.

The most commonly used term for an illegitimate child is *bastard*. The dictionary definition states that this word is from the Old French *bastart*, perhaps from *bast* in the phrase *fils de bast* son of the packsaddle, i.e. not of the marriage bed. However, there are many other English words and phrases used in the records to describe an illegitimate child, for example - base, baseborn, begotten in fornication, by-blow, child of shame, lovechild, merrybegot, misbegotten, whoreson, wrong side of the blanket. 'Reputed son' means that there is some certainty as to the identity of the father stated, 'imputed son' means there may be some doubt. In Latin there are - filius nullius (son of none - the girl didn't know or want to say), filius populi (son of the people - anyone's guess!), filius meretricis (son of a prostitute). For the mother, such terms as in trouble, in a certain condition, fallen, broken-winged, ruined, and sinned were used,

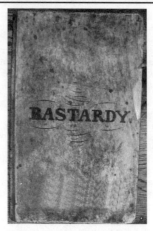

Horbury Bastardy Book 1834-1846 Reproduced with permission of West Yorkshire Archive Service Ref; D135/9/1

particularly by the prudish Victorians.

The Records
Civil registration - this is the first stumbling block and some researchers give up hope as soon as they receive the birth certificate of their ancestor with 'name of father' *blank* 'occupation of father' *blank*. I know very well that crestfallen feeling! The child will be registered under the mother's surname, and her occupation (if she has one) will be given. After 1875, a man had to give his consent before he was recorded as the natural father of the child and he had to attend the register office if he wished his name to go on the certificate.

Parish Registers - a vital source for family history generally, these can reveal paternity in several different ways. Baptism registers are the main point of reference. Before 1813, clergymen had free rein to write whatever they wished. In small country parishes, where most of our ancestors were living in the 16th-early 19th centuries, the vicar would know all his parishioners personally, and would no doubt be made aware of any pre-marital or extra-marital goings-on. If he has a good idea as to the identity of the father, this may well be written in the register, in particular to avoid the spectre of incest raising its head in the future (e.g. the legitimate son wishing to marry the illegitimate daughter of the same man) -
July 19th 1634 - Rachel, the reputed daughter of William Tomlinson of Thwaite House unlawfully begotten of the body of Elizabeth Young (baptism register, Bolton Abbey, Yorkshire)
After 1813, when printed forms were introduced; this somewhat hampered our vicars' scope for fascinating comments. Nevertheless, the terms base, illegitimate, and bastard son/daughter of may appear, although the name of the father might be included less and less as the Victorian age wears on, due to moral values and the growth of towns with the anonymity they offered. Nevertheless, the mother of the child might give you a helping hand. In Yorkshire, Lancashire, London and amongst nonconformists, a family surname might be used by a married couple as a middle name for their child. If, however, a single woman gives her child a surname as a middle name, investigate further. It could well be the surname of the father -
2nd August 1818, Sarah Lowcock, daughter of Ann Procter, single woman of Halton (baptism register, Bolton Abbey, Yorkshire)
Marriage registers can be useful, particularly after 1837 when the fathers of the bride and groom were stated. A blank in this space may indicate illegitimacy, although it could also mean that the father was dead or that the vicar didn't bother asking! A step-father's name might be

stated instead. However, you might find a strange man's name in this space. Quite often, upon reaching adulthood, an illegitimate child might be told the identity of their biological father, and therefore his name is included on the marriage certificate.

Burial registers must not be overlooked, as, like baptism registers, the early ones can reveal paternity, particularly at the death of a child -

November 24th 1764 - Thomas, son of Wm Shaw of Little Cropwell by Elizabeth Robinson (burial register, Long Clawson, Leicestershire)

Other Parish Records and Quarter Sessions - Under the terms of the Old Poor Law the parish was responsible for caring and providing for its own paupers. A pregnant single woman with no means of supporting herself presented an economic problem, and one which needed to be solved. A bastard belonged to the parish where it was born, so any woman who did not have a right of settlement in the parish was swiftly moved on before she gave birth. Various laws were passed to deal with illegitimacy (see below) and the documents which result from this are some of the most fascinating items in the 'parish chest.' If no marriage looked like taking place and the mother-to-be looked likely to 'fall on the parish' then the Overseers of the Poor and the Churchwardens began to make enquiries as to the identity of the father. If a name was forthcoming from the girl after this Examination then they would interview the man. He was then required to enter into a bond to pay for the birth expenses and regular maintenance thereafter to support the child. This was called a Bastardy Bond (the Child Support Agency is nothing new!) If he refused to sign the bond, the alleged father could be taken before Quarter Sessions, where a significant amount of pressure would be brought to bear. Some men evaded their responsibilities by absconding or joining the armed forces. Gentry often paid a lump sum to the girl or the Overseers for the matter to be dealt with 'on the quiet.' Any Bastardy Bonds which survive are full of interesting information, not least the name of the father. In addition, do check Overseer's Account Books and Churchwardens' Accounts for details of maintenance payments, where the father's name will also be stated. Some parishes kept special Bastardy Books.

The New Poor Law of 1834 brought many changes. The poor were no longer the sole responsibility of the parish, but rather a 'union' or group of parishes under the control of a Board of Guardians. 'Outdoor' relief (paid to people in their own homes) was to be replaced with 'indoor' relief in purpose-built workhouses. Cases of illegitimacy were no longer investigated in as great detail as before and the unfortunate woman was now often 'on her own'. Shame was heaped on her head. Unless her family could support her, then she had to go into the workhouse and give birth there. The other option was to be brave and sue the alleged father for maintenance at Petty Sessions. The Bastardy Order which was awarded in a successful case has very similar wording and stipulations as the old Bastardy Bond. However, outdoor relief never really stopped in practice and out relief lists can be very informative -

Hannah Hodgson, aged 42 of Eastwood Row, Keighley; calling - bakes bread; cause of requiring relief - 6 bastard children; amount of relief out of the workhouse given during the last quarter - £1 6s 0d. (List of paupers receiving relief in the quarter ending September 1843, Keighley, Yorkshire)

The main laws relating to illegitimacy -
1575-6 - Justices have the power to investigate cases of illegitimacy and issue Bastardy Orders to the alleged father.

1609-10 - Any 'lewd' woman with an illegitimate child who was being paid for by the parish could be sent to the county House of Correction for a year. The public whipping of the parents of the child was a common occurrence in this period, or doing penance wearing a white sheet at the church porch. However, most blame was placed on the mother.

1732-3 - A Pregnant single woman had to declare herself as such and name the father under oath. Any man convicted of being the father was to be jailed unless he promised the parish that he would pay maintenance.

1743-4 - An illegitimate child was now to have the parish of settlement of his or her mother, rather than the parish of its birth as before.

1834 - New Poor Law Act. Many births of illegitimate children take place in workhouses. Women could apply to Petty Sessions and obtain a Bastardy Order against the father.

1926 - where a couple were free to marry when an illegitimate child was born, then that child was legitimated on subsequent marriage. The child had to be re-registered.

1969 - illegitimate children are legitimated on subsequent marriage even if the parents were married to someone else at the time.

Census returns - useful from 1851 - 1901 when family relationships are stated. Who is the head of household? Remember, many couples had their first child (or more) before marrying. The child may keep the name it was registered with (usually the mother's) or may take his father's name as he grows up. However, census returns can also conceal all kinds of falsehoods - for example, step-children from a previous relationship being passed off as natural children of the head, or a baby of an unmarried daughter being brought up in the family home by its grandmother. Do investigate censuses carefully.

Wills - illegitimate children needed to be clearly stated as such to gain anything from the father's will i.e. 'I bequeath to my reputed son William John Smith…' Since 1969, all children are treated as equal in a will.

Newspaper reports - if the case was particularly bitter or salacious, it might be recorded in the local or even national press. However, a rich man might pay off the editor to avoid a scandal. Things never change!

Case studies
Here follow two case studies. Both examples are from my own family and I hope they will show various stages and strategies in researching illegitimate ancestors, producing often surprising results.

Case 1
A birth certificate dated 1917. No father's name. The mother is a single woman and her occupation is 'Music Hall Artist.' No other documentation, nothing discussed in the family…until…found tucked inside an old Bible is a sheet of paper. A Bastardy Order. The details are an absolute mine of information. The mother, a girl of nineteen, sues for maintenance one month after the birth, applying to the Petty Sessions. The case is held at the Police Court in a town in County Durham. The father of the child is named, together with his address. He is summoned at his lodgings but does not appear at the hearing. The court agrees with the case of the girl and orders that maintenance be paid - ten shillings for lying-in expenses, £1 5s 6d for obtaining the Order, and five shillings per week thereafter until the child reaches the ages of sixteen. So, a name! Moreover, two forenames and an unusual surname. I would never have found out if this document had not survived. I have been told since that the maintenance was faithfully paid and that many solicitors' letters and other papers relating to this case were deliberately burnt. Have I found this errant father? Who was he? A fellow actor? A 'stage-door Johnny'? Why was he not

fighting - this was the period of World War I after all. Was he in a reserved occupation? Why wouldn't he marry her? Well, a thorough search through 25 years of births in the GRO indexes has produced no-one with that combination of names. Could it have been his stage name? Perhaps. I did find a birth entry with nearly the right name, the middle forename is very similar to the one on the Bastardy Order - Edmund instead of Edward - and this might well be him. In addition, are there any police records relating to this case? I will investigate further…

Case 2

A birth certificate dated 1923. No father's name. The mother is a married woman, with no occupation. The child is *not* her husband's. In contrast to Case 1, many facts are already known in the family, which have assisted me in delving more deeply. The mother has left her husband but has not divorced him. She has moved to a small mining village in Yorkshire with some of her children and is openly living with another man, the father of the child. He does not go with her to register the birth. However, he does attend the baptism as his name is written in the parish register, then crossed out by the vicar, but not crossed out *well enough* - the name can be clearly seen. So to the father…through family knowledge I could search and obtain his death certificate. The age at death then led me to his birth certificate. When this arrived anticipation turned to dismay - he was also illegitimate. Born in a nearby village. What next? Search the nearest census after the birth, 1871. Fortunately they were still living in the street named on the birth certificate, but a few doors up. What a revelation the census was. The mother had married and the three year-old child has the husband's surname instead of hers. So this is why I never found him in the 1881 census index! Therefore this ancestor could be listed in records under two different surnames (alias names can be a good indicator of illegitimacy). But is the child his? The little boy has an unusual forename for the Victorian period. A search through the village reveals a brother of the alleged father, with the same forename as the boy. This looks like firm evidence.

The places of birth for both mother and father are small villages in the High Peak of Derbyshire. This is interesting as family tradition states that there was a Derbyshire connection but no-one knew quite what or where. I have now been able to trace this family back to 1841 so far and also recently visited the villages in Derbyshire.

And Finally

Don't forget to talk to relatives. Family tales of descent from the Lord of the Manor might be the stuff of fairy tales, but one of the golden rules of family history is don't dismiss anything out of hand. You just never know, and through delving into some of the records listed above, all sorts of things might be revealed - it might be Lord X, it might be the footman. Illegitimacy is one of the proverbial 'skeletons in the closet' and it could be something which certain members of the family do not want to be reminded of. Please be tactful, this is a subject which still raises strong emotions.

Warrant for disobeying Order of Bastardy Sandal Magna 1800

Reproduced with permission of West Yorkshire Archive Service

Ref: D20/9/10/1

Biographical Index for North-East Cheshire 1600~1760

Jill Groves

What is it?

'Index' is perhaps a misnomer. It is more of a listing or record of all the written information on people living in the townships of Altrincham, Ashton-on-Mersey (not to be confused with the Lancashire towns of Ashton-in-Makerfield or Ashton-under-Lyne), Baguley, Bowdon, Dunham Massey, Etchells (townships of Stockport and Northern), Hale, Northenden, Sale, and Timperley, in the parishes of Bowdon, Ashton-on-Mersey and Northenden, between c.1600 and c.1760. The bulk of the information comes from Wills and probate documents. Other sources include *Chester Marriage Licences 1606-1700* (published by the Lancashire and Cheshire Record Society); 1667 Poll Tax Roll for Bucklow East; 1664 Hearth Tax for the whole area; 1673 Hearth Tax for Ashton-on-Mersey and Sale; odd published extracts for Bowdon and Ashton parishes in *A History of Altrincham and Memorials of the Ancient Parish of Ashton*; the registers for Northenden, 1560-1640; Bertram Merrell for Marriage Index 1700-1837 (Family History Society of Cheshire); St. Martin, Ashton-on-Mersey, Burials 1730-1890; St. Martin, Ashton-on-Mersey, Monumental Inscriptions and Commemorative Inscriptions; Northenden Court Leet/Court Baron Records, Etchells Court Leet/Court Baron Records, Northenden and Etchells leases (in the Tatton Family Papers, John Rylands Library), the Rental Surveys for Dunham Massey estate (transcribed by Joyce Littler), the 1642 Grand Remonstrance for the parish of Bowdon and 1723 Oath of Allegiance for the Parish of Bowdon (both transcribed by Peter Kemp), the history of the Leather families in Hale, Bowdon and Altrincham, lists of alehouse keeps, rectors, vicars, curates, dissenting ministers, schoolmasters and lawyers from various sources, plus other odd sources such as title deeds.

The information listed for each person can range from as little as the witnessing of someone else's will, to a full-blown life to death biography complete with a bit of scandal thrown in along the way.

MARGARET LAMB OF BOWDON, 1631

Date: 21st February, 1630/31
Residence: Bowdon
Marriage status: by licence on 21st February, 1630/31 at Bowdon or Northenden. Bondsman Ralph Heaton
Spouse: Thomas Astbury of Bowdon
Documents: *Chester Marriage Licences Index 1624-32, Part 3*

THOMAS HALL OF ASHTON-ON-MERSEY, 1689, 1714, 1717, 1732, 1733, 1742, 1771

Date: 1689; 7th July, 1714; 11th October, 1717; 3rd March, 1731/32; 19th April, 1732; 11th May, 1732; 19th January, 1739/40; 1742, 27th October, 1771
Residence: Ashton-on-Mersey
Parents: Joshua and Jane Hall of Ashton-on-Mersey
Brothers: Joshua the younger and Samuel
Other kin: James Kay, son-in-law; Hannah Hall (née Darbishire), daughter-in-law; Jared Birmingham, son-in-law; Thomas Hall of Failsworth, uncle.
Marriage status: married. 2nd marriage by banns at Ashton on 19th April, 1732
1st Spouse: Jane (d.1732)
2nd spouse: Margaret Heyward of Sale (d.1740)
Children of 1st spouse: Joshua, Susannah Birmingham and Jonathan (d.1732)
Children of 2nd spouse: Thomasin Kay (1734-1806)
Illegitimate children by 2nd spouse: 1 child born by Margaret Heyward of Sale in 1717
Landholding: farm in Ashton-on-Mersey and in Failsworth
Witness: Will of William Moss of Ashton-on-Mersey, linen weaver, 1742
Date of birth: 1689
Date of death: 27th October, 1771
Legacy: He was given 1s to buy a pair of mourning gloves by Samuel Renshawe of Ashton-on-Mersey, 1714 Thomas was given the farm in Ashton-on-Mersey and one in Failsworth by his father.
1s from Joseph Artinstall of Ashton-on-Mersey in 1742
Documents: Will of Samuel Renshawe of Ashton-on-Mersey, 1714; Will of Joshua Hall of Ashton-on-Mersey, yeoman, 1718; St. Martin, Ashton-on-Mersey, Monumental and Commemorative Inscriptions; Parish of St. Martin, Ashton-on-Mersey, County of Cheshire, Burials 26 April 1731 to 8 February 1890, North Cheshire FHS microfiche; Will of Joseph Artinstall of Ashton-on-Mersey, 1742; Will of William Moss of Ashton-on-Mersey, linen weaver, 1742.

HUGH HOBSON OF ASHTON-ON-MERSEY, 1664, 1665, 1667, 1669

Date: 15th December, 1663; 11th October, 1665; February 1667; 20th November, 1669
Residence: Ashton-on-Mersey Rectory, Glebelands Road, Ashton-on-Mersey.
Occupation/status: Rector of Ashton-on-Mersey
Brother: Jonathan
Other kin: Richard Massey of Sale, esquire, father-in-law (died 1667); Barbara Massey of Sale, later Manchester, mother-in-law (died 1684); Richard Massey of Sale, gentleman, brother-in-law (died 1685); William Massey of Sale, brother-in-law (died 1706); Anne Prescott (née Massey) of Liverpool, sister-in-law; Jane Leech (née Massey) of Manchester, sister-in-law; Robert Massey, brother-in-law (died 1666); Barbara Leech (née Massey) of Manchester, sister-in-law; Elizabeth Massey (née Massey) of Mosse, sister-in-law
Marriage Status: Married
Spouse: Mary Massey of Sale
Occupation/status of spouse: Gentlewoman
Children: Theodosia, born c.1665, and Elizabeth born after 1667, but died March, 1672
Servants: He had two servants, James Arstall who was not paid a £1 for his wages, and Elizabeth Roylands, wages £1 10s.
Hearth Tax: 4 heaths, taxed in 1664. Living in the 'Old House' in 1673.
Landholding: Glebelands of Ashton: In Ashton township, The Marna (3 Cheshire Acres); Two Reaches near the parsonage, meadow land, 1.5 Cheshire Acres, arable; The Little Reach, arable land; Churchland, 10 perches; Little Scholes, 60 perches; The Bett, 60 perches, meadow land; Loom Furlong. In Sale township, The Parson's Acre, 1 Cheshire acre; Great Barrow (1 dole - 30 perches); Little Barrow (1 dole - 20 perches).

Total 16.73 acres statute acres.
Date of death: 1679
Notes: Hugh Hobson's courtship and marriage to Mary Massey of Sale seems to have been fraut. Her family, especially her father, are reputed to have objected to the marriage. Hugh was a Presbyterian or at least close to being one. He was presented to the Rectorship of Ashton-on-Mersey by George Booth, Lord Delamer, of Dunham Massey, a Presbyterian. Richard Massey was a high Anglican, nearly Roman Catholic.
Mary was very much in love with Hugh. She threatened to drown herself in the Mersey if she was not allowed to marry him. Her parents sent her to her uncle John Gleave of Pulford, near Chester, a day's ride away. When they thought she was over her infatuation, she was allowed home.
However, Mary couldn't help but meet Hugh Hobson again. Hugh got a marriage licence and they married in Chester, although, according to Barbara Massey, the mother-in-law, Richard Massey wanted the wedding at Bowdon. Even so Richard was so reconciled to the marriage that he sent a servant with Mary to Chester and gave her all the money she was owed from the wills of her Gleave grandparents. However, Mary said she hadn't received all the money she was owed and started an action against her mother and uncle after the death of her father, in the Consistory Court at Chester, saying that her father's will was illegal. The court, however, agreed with her mother.
In 1665 Hugh Hobson administered the oath to the administratrix of George Ravald's estate, his widow, Anne.
In 1669 young Thomas Renshaw had made a bargain with Hugh Hobson to use the hay tithe on two tenements (his own and that of Richard Renshaw, his cousin), to which Thomas was entitled to be used, for the upkeep of Thomas's illegitimate child. Hugh Hobson succeeded the Presbyterian minister John Ford in 1662.
Documents: Will of Richard Massey of Sale, esquire, 1663; 1664 Hearth Tax; Inventory of George Ravald of Ashton-on-Mersey, husbandman, 1665; 1667 Poll Tax Roll for Ashton-on-Mersey; Will of Thomas Renshaw of Sale, yeoman, 1669; 1673 Hearth Tax for Ashton-on-Mersey, quoted in *Memorials of the Ancient Parish of Ashton-on-Mersey*.

As you can see, it is a form of record-linkage. However, compared with more academic record-linkage projects reported in the *Local Historian* over the last few years, it is not very high-tech. In fact, it is medium to low tech since it uses a word-processing database and not a spreadsheet database. This makes it easier to copy and paste entries into another word-processed document, such as an article or as notes to wills published in the 'Between the Mersey and the Bollin' series [see below]. There are nearly 5,000 people listed in fifteen files covering 650 A4 pages - and it is growing larger every day it sometimes seems. Not all of these people lived in the ten townships listed above. For example, many people living in Stretford, Lancashire had family connections in Ashton-on-Mersey and Sale. So they are mentioned in wills, they married in Ashton church by licence because it was nearer than their official parish church, St. Mary's in Manchester, and they had themselves buried in St. Martin's churchyard. The same is true of people in Ashley and Mobberley with Hale and Bowdon, Dunham Massey with Lymm, and Stockport with Northenden and Etchells.

Why was it set up?
There are two reasons for the setting up the Biographical Index.
1. To record details of the lives of people who left no extant wills and sometimes were not even recorded in parish records, such as 'Poor Daniel's wife'. Even such well-to-do people as the Altrincham schoolmaster Francis Newton did not leave wills themselves, although he wrote and witnessed many for others from 1680 to 1710.
2. To provide background information on people mentioned in wills and inventory for notes on the wills published in 'Between the Mersey and the Bollin' series.

Because the Biographical Index is used as background material, it means that as the wills are transcribed townsship by towns, so the Index contains more on the townships whose wills have been already published or are in preparation for publication. As the Index stands at the moment, Bowdon, Ashton and Sale have been published and Hale Wills are in preparation.

What uses has it?
Apart from the already mentioned background notes to the published wills, the Index is also very good at sorting out complicated local families, such as the Renshaws of Ashton-on-Mersey, Sale and Timperley. So far, the Biographical Index says that the Renshaws of Ashton-on-Mersey kept dying in 1641 and again in 1714 and were replaced by Renshaws from Sale and (in the nineteenth century) by the Renshaw medical doctors (father and several sons) from Timperley and Altrincham.
The Index has also sorted out the two lines of two Moores families in Sale, one from a farm called Birchen Roe and the other from a farm called Wall Bank or Well Bank for one hundred years. It has even established that the Moores of Birchen Roe where all four brothers were shoemakers in the early to mid-eighteenth century. It also helped to established that the John Moores of Sale, shoemaker, who died in 1759 and wrote a will, was a member of the Birchen Roe branch and that he was separate from the other John Moores, who died in the same year and who left only an inventory. The latter John Moores was a member of the Wall Bank family. Another of the Index's important uses is an aid to family historians. Up to three surnames can be pulled out of the Index for the cost of a 31p A4 sae. It can be the luck of the draw and tends to be a mixture of different branches of families from different townships. However, most were connected at sometime. For example, the Whiteleggs were well established in Northenden in the seventeenth century and a branch was established in the late seventeenth century in Ashton-on-Mersey. Probably Whiteleggs from Northenden moved westwards into Ashton-on-Mersey, possibly in the 1630s when there was land hunger.
The Goulden family had branches in Bowdon, Hale, Northenden, Baguley and Timperley. Possibly through their connection with the Eatons (a Goulden widow married an Eaton man) who came from Great Budworth originally, one branch moved there too. Three Goulden brothers lived in three different townships with their families in the latter half of the seventeenth century - Richard the whitesmith and gunsmith in Northern Moor, Northenden, Edward the carpenter in Timperley and Robert in Baguley.

The Future of the Biographical Index
Getting much larger, possibly as much as over 2,600 A4 pages listing as many as 19,000 people.
When the whole index is finished and the last will of the last township has been published (sometime in the next ten to fifteen years), then the whole Index will be available on CD or DVD or whatever cheap-to-produce, easy-to-use piece of technology has appeared by then. In the meantime, as pointed out above, the Index is searchable for surnames for an A4 sae. Contact Mrs Jill Groves, 77 Marford Crescent, Sale, Cheshire M33 4DN.

To the King's Most excellent Majesty
Criminal Petitions 1819-1854
Jill Chambers

At the beginning of the 19th century there were over 100 crimes for which the death sentence could be imposed. In many cases this sentence would automatically be reduced to a term of transportation, or, in some cases during the early part of the century, service in the army or navy. During this period the Home Office was inundated with petitions, or appeals, sent on behalf of people who had been sentenced to death, transportation and various terms of imprisonment, from as little as two or three weeks. Some of these petitions were successful, with sentences reduced or pardons recorded, but most were ineffective and have the word 'nil' scribbled on them, or even worse, 'the law to take its course'. There are some eighteenth century petitions to be found at the Public Record Office. Before 1782 they were kept in State Papers Domestic, SP36 (1727-60) and SP37 (1760-82), some survive in Home Office papers HO42 and HO44. Others, covering the years 1819-1844, survive in the Privy Council papers, PC1. There is also a series covering 1784-1830 in HO47. These are bound in annual volumes, 75 in all, entitled 'Judges' Reports'. The vast majority of appeals, the documents referred to in this article, are to be found among the Home Office papers, in HO17 (1819-39) and HO18 (1839-54).

I became aware of these petitions when I was carrying out research for my first book on the 'Swing Riots', the machine breaking and rioting in 1830/31, involving the agricultural labourers, mainly in southern England. These documents gave a wonderful insight into the lives of these men and their families. One thing that struck me about the bundles of documents I was looking at was that many of them did not appear to have been opened for many years and I began to think that there were an under used source of information on criminals and convicts. There are indexes to these documents in HO19, they are arranged annually by the year they were received, and by the first letter of the surname. Whilst looking for petitions sent on behalf of the Swing Rioters I soon noticed that although most petitions were sent at the time of the convictions, in a number of cases they had been sent many years after sentencing, as in the case of a letter written by a Mr Philips in August 1833 on behalf of Joseph Turner, one of the 'Pentridge Rebels', who had been tried at Derby in 1817. So in order to check if a particular person had a petition it would be necessary to check all the existing Indexes in HO19. It was with this in mind that I began indexing the boxes as I worked through them. I am not sure just how many individual petitions are contained in these two sets of documents but if I say that there are 381 separate bundles in HO18, each bundle containing between 60 and 80 appeals, there are 131 piece numbers in HO17, and I have indexed thirty of these (HO17/40-69), and the index now contains 7,516 names, this might give you an idea of the vast number of appeals to be found.

The offences mentioned in these appeals are as varied as the characters that committed them. There are sheep and horse stealers, poachers and common thieves, machine breakers and Chartists, highwaymen, coiners, forgers, pickpockets, murderers and bigamists, smugglers and pirates, alongside the simple 'rogue and vagabond'. Men women and children of all ages are represented, and they are from all walks of life. There are labourers, clerks and housemaids, together with ex-soldiers and sailors, with wounds from Waterloo and Trafalgar.

The majority of these documents were directed to the Judge, or the Home Secretary or Monarch of the day, begging for a mitigation of the sentence, but there are a few which advise against any such reprieve. One such case is that of Noel Chapman, 16 years old, who was tried at the Surrey Assizes in the winter of 1825, and sentenced to seven years transportation. His father, Benjamin, asked that his son be sent to New South Wales where he has friends, in order to remove him from the bad influence of his associates at home. (HO17/57 K129) A few of those committing crimes were judged to be insane and were committed to Lunatic Asylums. The details are generally written on printed forms, and can include age, date and place of trial, offence, date of committal and behaviour. Some also record death or release from the asylum.

Occasionally the name on the outside of the bundle will differ from that given on the petition. In more than one of the cases where I have noted this as being the case it was because the person on trial had hoped to spare his family the upset of being related to a criminal, and had used a false name at his trial. There will of course be many others who have used a false name and did not record the fact.

The petitions themselves vary in length and presentation. Some of the documents simply list those who were on the Hulks, who 'have served more than half the Term of their respective Sentence on board the said Hulk (and on account of their Quiet, Orderly and Uniform good Behaviour since they came here) are now selected by the Captain with the approbation of the Chaplin as the Ten best behaved Men in the Hulk and therefore are Recommended by Captain ...... (who is ready to make oaths of his impartiality in the choice of them) to the Inspector, as fit objects for Mercy.' These lists often give brief details of the behaviour of the men, and how they have been employed whilst on board. An example is the case of John Hindry, aged 29, who was found guilty of Grand Larceny at Norwich on 14th January 1824, and sentenced to seven years transportation. In July 1828, whilst serving his time on board the *Leviathan* Hulk, he was one of those listed to receive a Free Pardon. He is described as, 'Teaching in the Prisoner's School – received a hurt in the Dockyard. (HO17/50 Part 2 Hh25) There are similar lists sent in on behalf of prisoners held in the General Penitentiary at Millbank.

There are short, simple letters, written by an anxious husband, wife, parent, or child, on behalf of their convicted relative, such as the following written by John Collett on behalf of his thirteen year old son, George.

The Humble Petition of John Collett of Stoke Newington in the Co. of Middlesex – Labourer.

Prayeth
That the Petitioner's son, who is 13 years of age, while in company with another lad, some years older than himself, was detected by the Police in stealing 13 Pears from the Garden of an uninhabited House. They underwent an Examination at Worship Street Police Office where the elder lad was discharged upon payment of 10/- fine & 6d the value of the Pears. Your humble Petitioner (with the consent & advise of … Twyford Esq., the Magistrate who committed him) therefore prayeth that your Gracious Lordship will in consideration of the child's tender years and it being his first offence, be graciously pleased to permit him to be liberated from a situation so heart rending to his Family, and your Humble Petitioner as in duty bound will ever Pray.
John Collett (HO17/41 Fs18)

There are similar letters from friends of the convicted, as in the case of Harry Elkins from Shaftsbury, in Dorset, vouching for his former character.

To the Right Honourable the Secretary of State for the Home Department
May it please your Lordship
We the undersigned, having known Harry Elkins convicted of Machine Breaking at the Special Commission held at Dorchester in and for the County of Dorset, and sentenced to Seven Years Transportation, do most humbly represent, that we have always known him to be of irreproachable character, and hope, that on consideration of his case, his sentence will be remitted, if not wholly, at least from transportation to imprisonment.
Harry Elkins has hitherto supported himself by honest industry, and we believe that if he were permitted to return to his home again he would continue to do so. (HO17/50 Part 1 Hp9)

Other petitions are large documents on parchment, written in elaborate scripts and signed by virtually all the local landowners and tradesmen in the prisoners' home area. Some, like those on behalf of the 'Tolpuddle Martyrs', who were sentenced to transportation in 1834, fill a whole box. (HO17/42 Ft1) There are others that are so detailed that it is possible to build up a very detailed picture of the person on whose behalf the petition was sent. One such case is detailed below.

The Case of Elias John
Elias John, together with John Rosser, was tried for sheep stealing at the Glamorgan Spring Sessions, in 1828. Both men had a sentence of death recorded against them, but this was commuted to transportation for life. Their characters from the gaol have been written on the petition, it says, 'Bad, have attempted to break prison'. The first correspondence on their behalf appears to be the petition sent the 'The Right Honourable Robert Peel', from 'The Principal Inhabitants of St Maryhill Parish, in the County of Glamorgan', dated 5th May 1828 and signed by William Leigh, Minister, Anthony Griffiths and Morgan William, Churchwardens, amongst others. The petition describes the two men as, 'belonging to this parish', and states that 'previous to this affair the men brought up each of their large family by their industry as daily labourers', and asks for a mitigation of their sentence. The petition was forwarded to Sir Robert Peel by Sir Christopher Cole (Cote), MP for the County of Glamorgan, together with a note from him dated, United Services Club, May 9th 1828. A letter quickly followed this from the Vicar of Maryhill to Sir Christopher, begging to request him not to intervene on behalf of the two men as, 'they are persons of notoriously bad character and it is desirable that they should be sent out of the Country'. On the 22nd May 1828 Sir Christopher wrote to Mr Phillips, enclosing this letter, and stating that he now believed the petition sent on behalf of Rosser and John to be 'not worthy of the lest consideration'. Elias John and John Rosser both sailed from New South Wales on board the *Mellish*, arriving in Sydney Cove on

the 18th April 1828. Elias John was 55 years old when he arrived in Australia, a married man with three children, and he could 'plough and milk' according to his Convict Indent. A note on the Indent to say that he received a Royal Free Pardon, dated at the Court of St James, 1st June 1852, 24 years after his arrival in Australia, and if it were not for the petitions and accompanying letter that might have been the end of Elias John's story.

A letter dated Government House, 30th December 1851, was sent by Charles A Fitzroy to the Right Honourable Earl Grey, enclosing a Petition from Elias John, praying ' the indulgence of an Absolute Pardon'. Mr Fitzroy begs to recommend John, saying that he had 'formerly served as a private in the old 95th Regiment'. In his petition Elias John lists his service with the 95th during the Peninsular War as follows:-
At the Battle of Vimiera in 1808
In the retreat with Sir John Moore from Madrid to Corunna in 1809
At the Battle of Corunna 1809
At the Battle of Palaveia 1809
At Busaco 1810
At Albulera 1811
At Fuentes d'Onor 1811
At the siege of Cuidad Rodrigo and Badajoz 1812
At the Battle of Salamanca 1812
At Vittoria 1813
At the storming of St Sebastian 1813
At the Pyrenees 1814
And finally at the Battle of Toulouse.

He also lists the wounds he had received in the various battles:-
Wounded in the left arm by a Bayonet at the Battle of Vimiera
Also received a sword cut on the head and ear from a French Dragoon during he retreat from Caleabala
Also received a musket ball above the hip at the Battle of Busaco
Also received a musket ball in the right leg above the ankle at the battle of Toulouse. (HO17/40 Part 2 Fn24)

In 1838 Elias John received a ticket of Leave, a Conditional Pardon followed this in July 1846, but he was 'desirous of returning home to his Native Country', and for that he needed an Absolute Pardon. This was granted on the 30th September 1851. Sadly Elias never returned home, he died in the Liverpool District of New South Wales in 1858, at the age of 80.

I am still working on Indexing these fascinating documents, and hopefully when complete the Index will make searching for a petition a little easier.

Tracing Railway Ancestors
Simon Fowler

Until September 1829 – the date of the famous Rainhill railway trials - nobody had travelled as fast as 30 miles an hour. Yet this would change rapidly with the arrival of the railway. Its impact is still being felt nearly two centuries later.

Background
The major period of the expansion of the railways took place in the 1830s and 1840s, particularly the mid-1840s. By 1850 the system we know it today was largely complete. The last major new line to be built was the Great Central Railway, linking London and Sheffield completed in 1896. The period before the First World War also saw the construction of many branch lines and light railways which linked even quite small communities to the network. The greatest period of the railways prosperity was before 1914. There was little or no competition – stage coach services had all but disappeared, and the railway companies had bought up the canals and largely transferred traffic onto the rails. Passenger numbers rose in ever greater numbers, attracted in part by improved comfort in first class and cheaper fares in third class. There was considerable rivalry between the various companies, for example the great railway races of the 1890s, was all about cutting the journey time between London and Edinburgh. The railways transformed almost every aspect of Victorian life. It was now possible for middle-class women to come 'to town' to do their shopping in the new department stores, which themselves benefited from cheap goods brought by train from factories and ports. The railway conveyed working class families to holidays by the sea in resorts such as Blackpool, Scarborough and Southend. These towns were largely the creation of railways. And of course railway companies employed hundreds of thousands of men and, a surprising number of, women.

The First World War proved to be a traumatic experience for the railways – the strain of transporting troops and munitions almost bankrupted the companies. In 1923 they were merged (or grouped as the phrase went) into four companies – the 'Big Four' as they were known: the Great Western (GWR), London Midland and Scottish (LMS), London and North Eastern (LNER) and Southern (SR). Although this amalgamation made economic sense, the inter-war period was still very difficult for the new companies. Although we remember today the crack expresses – The Flying Scotsman or the Coronation Scot – the railways found themselves unable to invest in modern equipment and techniques and faced increasing competition from coaches and lorries. The damage suffered during the Second World War, not just in terms of bomb damage, but also stress and strain to elderly engines and rolling stock, brought the railways to their knees. There were few protests when they were nationalised on April 1947. The 1950s and 1960s saw considerable modernisation of the railways. The Beeching Report axed a third of the network: a decision that is still controversial. Diesels and a modest amount of electrification replaced steam – the last mainline steam locomotive left service in 1968. Even so passengers and freight continued to drift away. During the 1970s and 1980s the railways gentle decline continued aided by a lack of investment or political direction. And when privatisation during the 1990s is discussed your author becomes very angry!

Railway workers
From the start railways were very labour intensive, employing many hundreds of thousands of men and women. Even the smallest country station had a stationmaster, ticket clerks and porters. In part this was due to the relative lack of mechanisation – particularly in track maintenance ('the permanent way') and clerical work, together with the cheapness of labour. At the time of Queen Victoria's Diamond Jubilee, the London and North Western Railway claimed it had 70,000 employees. When the railways were nationalised in 1948, British Railways employed 641,00 people. The current figure is little more than 10% of this number. The railway, and here all the companies were alike, was very grade conscious. There were a clear divide between the salaried white collared staff and the weekly paid manual workers. At the top of the salaried staff were the managers and clerical workers of the General Manager's Office. Engine drivers, particularly those entrusted with the crack passenger trains, were at the pinnacle of the manual staff. In general the men and women who worked on the railways were generally of a much higher calibre than their equivalents outside the industry. Even so wages were in general low and it was difficult to rise through promotion. It might take twenty years or so to become a train driver. Men worked their way up starting as a cleaner in the works or engine sheds, becoming a fireman, and beating stiff competition to become a driver. There were many compensations. By the standard of the times companies were generally benevolent employers and provided sick benefits and pensions. There was often time to develop outside interests – in particular signalmen were known for their bookish pursuits and industrial militancy. Many local Labour Parties, particularly in rural and suburban areas, for example were formed by members of the National Union of Railwaymen. This led to great feelings of loyalty and pride in their work. Many people spent their whole careers working for just one company.

Surprising numbers of women were also employed. Initially women ran station restaurants and bars and laundries. By the First World War they were also undertaking clerical tasks. With the conscription of tens of thousands of railway men during the two world wars, women undertook work from cleaning engines to running lost-luggage offices, which previously would have been unthinkable.

The Records
The types of records you might use
Although each railway company kept details of its staff in different ways, the types of documents described below may give you an idea of what to look out for. In addition the survival of records is somewhat patchy.
Staff registers – these records are most often found among the records of the larger companies, although their survival is rather patchy particularly for the early period. They generally provide a rather basic record often noting no more than how much a person was paid, their grade and any promotions or transfers. Sometimes dates of entry, resignation or death are also given. The format and contents varies from company to company. If you can't find an individual in a register he may appear in registers of a predecessor or successor company.
Pay records – some companies have left records of wages and salaries paid to staff. They may take the form of wages lists giving names and job titles or vouchers recording wages paid.
Minutes – a neglected source are company minute books, which may record the appointment, promotion and dismissal or resignation of individual members of staff. In smaller companies these matters may be recorded in the minutes of the board itself, but it was more usual for minute books for the various committees to record this sort of information. Thus if an ancestor worked as an engineer, his appointment might be recorded in the minutes of the Engineering Committee.
Pensions and benefits – many companies operated superannuation and benefit schemes, whose records may survive. They are likely to record date of resignation, pension paid, next of kin (where appropriate) and date of death.
Accidents – railways particularly during the nineteenth century were dangerous places to work. Fatal accidents were thoroughly investigated by the Railway Inspectorate and full reports published.
Staff magazines – by the First World War most of the larger railway companies published monthly staff magazines, which contain a lot about individual members of staff – often with photographs.

Public Record Office
By far the largest collection of staff and records can be found at the Public Record Office (PRO). On nationalisation of the railways in 1947, the records of the former railway and canal companies passed to the British Railways Board, who eventually gave them to the PRO in 1977. This BTHR Collection, as it was known, was assigned the lettercode or prefix RAIL. Each railway company was assigned one or more series (or class) number. The records of the North Sunderland Railway are in RAIL 533, while the Great Western Railway (GWR) can be found in a number of series between RAIL 236 and RAIL 254. However, it is not unusual to find material in other places particular in records of successor companies and there are a number of general series of material. Thus if you have an ancestor who worked for the Eastern Counties Railway, you should also look in the records of the Great Eastern Railway (GER) which absorbed it in the 1850s, or even the LNER into which the GER was merged in 1923.
There is a card index to the BTHR material in the Research Enquiries Room. This has largely been superseded by PROCAT, the computerised catalogue to the PRO's holdings, which is also available on the Office's website.
The amount of material for each company varies

considerably. In general the smaller and older the company the less is likely to survive. The most complete records by far are for the Great Western Railway and the various companies it took over during the 110 years of its existence. Why this is so is not clear. The PRO also has records of the British Railways Board and associated bodies have also been transferred under the provisions of the Public Records Act 1958 and are generally available thirty years after the files have been finished with. The lettercode here is AN. Few staff records are to be found here, largely because personal records are normally closed for 75 years.
A little used source at the Office is the various runs of railway journals, which are to be found under the ZPER lettercode. Of particular interest to family historians are the company staff magazines, which begin about 1900 and continue into the 1960s, as they may contain details of postings, retirements and the social activities which railwaymen (and sometimes their families) engaged in. Copies of magazines may also be found at the National Railway Museum and sometimes in the larger local libraries.

If your ancestor was involved in a railway accident, particularly a fatal one, the Railway Inspectors would almost certainly have been involved. Their reports, between 1840 and 1964 are in series MT 29, with some indexes in MT 30. Other reports are in MT 114.
Accidents were also covered at some length in local (and occasionally national) newspapers, so it is worth trying to track down the relevant issues. Local studies libraries or record offices often have sets of local newspapers usually on microfilm.
Cliff Edward's *Railway Records* describes most of the other series of records containing material relating to railways at the PRO, although it should be stressed that it rarely contains anything about individuals.

Other repositories
Apart from the PRO, the major repository of railway records is the National Railway Museum at York. Their holdings however are largely technical, including such things as plans of locomotives and rolling stock and track layouts. They do however have some runs of staff magazines, which, as explained above, can be a useful source.
Records of the former Scottish railway companies were in general passed to the Scottish Record Office (now the National Archives of Scotland) in Edinburgh, although a little material is at the PRO. The format of this material is very similar to those found at Kew.
Records of many of the London Underground railways and London Transport, which took them over in 1933, are at the London Metropolitan Archive (formerly the Greater London Record Office). Sets of staff magazines and some other records are also held by London Transport Museum, Covent Garden Plaza, London WC1, Tel: 020 7379 6344 Email: library@ltmuseum.co.uk WWW: *www.ltmuseum.co.uk*
Some records of the former London Underground companies are also in the BTHR material at the PRO.

Many local record offices, railway museums and preserved railways have collections of material relating to their areas. For example the Cheshire Record Office in Chester, has some records of the works at Crewe. The Society of Genealogists has very little about railway workers, although it has a set of GWR share registers for the Inter-war period which is being indexed at present. If you are interested in how the railways were built – perhaps your ancestor had land on which a line was constructed – then you may need to use the House of Lords Record Office Record Office (sometimes called the Parliamentary Archives). Before a line was built a bill had to be passed by Parliament. Particularly in the early days of the railway the planned route was often contested by landowners and others who did not want the line to pass through their estates. The route of the London and Birmingham Railway through Watford, for example, was diverted through a mile-long tunnel to avoid the land of powerful local landowners.

Further information
The following archives have major collections of railway records or can help you find records.
Public Record Office, Kew, Richmond Surrey TW9 4DU Tel: 020-8392 5200 WWW: www.pro.gov.uk
National Railway Museum, Leeman Rd York YO2 4XJ Tel: 01904-621261 WWW: www.nmsi.ac.uk/nrm/
National Archives of Scotland, HM General Register House Edinburgh EH1 3YY 0131-535 1314 WWW: www.nas.gov.uk
House of Lords Record Office, House of Lords, London SW1A 0PW Tel: 020-7219 3074 WWW: www.parliament.uk
London Metropolitan Archives 40 Northampton Rd London EC1R 0HB Tel: 020-7332 3820 WWW: www.cityoflondon.gov.uk/
Historical Manuscripts Commission, Quality House, Quality Court, Chancery Lane London WC2A 1HP Tel: 020-7242 1198 WWW: archives/lma www.hmc.gov.uk
If you have railway ancestors it is worth joining the **Railway Ancestors Family History Centre**, who also offer a research service. They can be contacted at: Lundy Guest House, King Edward St, Barmouth Gwynedd e-mail: jim@railwayancestors.org.uk WWW: www.railwayancestors.fsnet.co.uk/
A profile of the Society appeared in issue 66 (March 2001) of *Family History Monthly*.

Further reading:
Cliff Edwards, *Railway Records: A Guide to Sources* (PRO, 2001)

David Hawkins, *Railway Ancestors: A Guide to Staff Records* (Sutton, 1996)
Tom Richards, *Was Your Grandfather a Railwayman* (Federation of Family History Societies, 1995) This book is temporarily out of print, but a new edition is in preparation. An article about tracing railway ancestors appeared in issue 61 (October 2000) of *Family History Monthly*. The PRO also has a free leaflet *Railway Staff Records*, which is available from the Office or can be downloaded from the Office's website.
There are a huge number of books on all aspects of the railway history. Of particularly interest are the very many histories of companies and individual lines, which although they may not mention your ancestor by name give an idea of why lines were built, the level of traffic, important incidents (such as accidents) and where appropriate why they closed. Large bookshops often have selections. In addition there are a number of specialist outlets. One of the best is Motor Books, to be found in Cecil Court near Leicester Square in London

What's in a Surname
John Titford

* BLAIR : From one of several places of this name in Scotland
* HAGUE : From a place called Haigh (Lancashire, West Riding of Yorkshire) or `dweller by the enclosure'.
* KENNEDY : `Ugly head'

What Are Surnames ?

It's a fact of life that each of us responds to a number of different names which others choose to call us by. Mr.Thomas Smith might respond to being called "Mr.Smith", "T.Smith Esquire", "Thomas", "Tom", "Dad", "Grandad", "Darling", "Pet" - or even, "Oi, YOU!".

In most of the English-speaking world, a surname is passed on by a father to his male and female children; he, in turn, got it from his father - and so on, usually back to the fourteenth century or so, when surnames, "add-on names", were first being widely adopted in order to distinguish individuals of the same Christian name one from the other. The village was full of "Richard"s, so why not separate them by calling one "Richard Williams", another "Richard Selby" and another - of dark compexion - "Richard Black"? And so it was.

It is the very existence of surnames that allows family historians to trace pedigrees back through several centuries (with a bit of luck!), and the surname you bear tells you at least something about that far-distant mediaeval ancestor - that he came from Cornwall, that he had red hair, that he was a smith by trade, that his baptismal name was William - and so on.

Most surnames can conveniently be classified into various groups of names of similar origins, and that is what we'll do here. Are your friends and relations amongst them?

Surnames classified according to origin:

* Surnames based upon a father's baptismal name.
The practice of sons and daughters adding their father's name to their own is the oldest method used to distinguish individuals one from the other. There are many variations on this theme: Russians will commonly bear three names - a first name, a second name which is patronymic (i.e., the father's name with "vich" added for men and "evna" for women) and a surname. Characters in novels like *War and Peace* will commonly refer to each other by both the first and the patronymic name, and Victor Komarovsky in *Dr.Zhivago*, hoping to endear himself to a young lady, says: "Don't call me `Mr.Komarovsky', my dear - call me `Victor Ippolotovich'." How romantic!

Most Welsh surnames are patronymic in origin, and many in centuries past were not hereditary surnames at all. Hugh, son of William, would be called "Hugh Williams"; his son David would be called "David Hughes", while David's son Evan would be called "Evan Davies" - and so on. This can sometimes make the tracing of Welsh pedigrees a difficult if not impossible task! The Welsh prefix "ap" (or "ab" before a vowel) means "son of". This might be shortened so that Hugh the son of Richard would be "Hugh ap Richard", but eventually "Hugh Pritchard". Surnames with this origin include Probert, Pumphrey, Pugh, Powell (ap Howell), Pryce (ap Rhys), Bowen and Bevan.

KINNOCK, otherwise spelt KINNOCH, KINNACH or KYNOCH, is a variation on the Gaelic personal name "Coinneach" (now "Kenneth"). The best-known recent bearer of this name, Neil Kinnock, is the descendant of a Scotsman who emigrated to the Welsh valleys.

Surnames (that is, 'proper' hereditary surnames) based upon the Christian name of the father are very common in amongst English-speaking peoples. The surname might take the Christian name with no modification - so a person might be called Thomas JOHN or John THOMAS; an "s" might be added, giving WILLIAMS, PHILLIPS or RICHARDS (i.e., "William's son, Richard's son"); the ending "son" might be used, giving us RICHARDSON, THOMPSON or ANDERSON (son of Andrew). TENNYSON was the son of Dennis. Equally, a nick-name version of the Christian name might be used, so we have DICKSON (son of Richard), WATSON (son of Walter), or HOBSON (son of Hob, a nickname for Robert). Hundreds of surnames are formed in this way. In Scotland and in Ireland "MAC" or "Mc" means "son of", while many families which had settled in Ireland soon after the Norman Conquest have a surname beginning with "Fitz" (from the French "fils", son). "Fitz" as used in England often indicates illegitimacy - so the surname FITZROY means the illegitimate son of the King (from the French, FILS du ROI). The Irish "O'", as in "O'Brien", means the grandson of Brien. The suffix "kin" can be used in surnames as a diminutive - so TOMKIN is "Little Thomas", WILKIN is "Little William" and PERKIN is "Little Peter". Similarly, BARTLETT is Little Bartholemew, DICKENS is the son of Little Dick, PHILPOTT is Little Philip.

The permutations can roll on and on - so William as a Christian name has led to the following surnames : WILLIAMS; WILLIAMSON; WILSON; WILCOX WILCOXSON; WILKINS; WILKINSON

The Christian name David (the most popular of all Old Testament names) has given us:
DAVEY; DAVIDS; DOWELL; DAVIDSON; DAVIDGE; DAVIE; DAVIES; DAVIS; DAVISON; DAYSON DAVY; DAVYS; DAW; DAWE; DAWES; DAWKES; DAWKINS; DAWS; DAWSON; DAY; DAVITT; DOWSON; DOWD; DOWDEN; DOWLING

The baptismal name "Richard" has been modified to give us a bewilderingly large range of surnames :
DICK; DICKENS; RICKSON; DICKENSON; DICKSON; RITCHIE; DIXON; HEACOCK; RITCHARD; HICK; HICKIN; HICKMAN; HICKMOT; HICKOX; HICKS; HICKSON; HIGGINS; HIGGINSON; HIGGS; HIGMAN;

HISCOCK; HITCH; HITCHCOCK; HITCHISON; HITCHMOUGH; HIX; RECKETT; RICARD; RICH; RICHARD; RICHARDS; RICHE; RICHER; RICHETT ; RICHEY; RICHIE; RICHMAN; RICK; RICKARD; RICKEARD; RICKETT; RICKETTS; RICKMAN; RICKS; RIX

* Surnames from countries, towns and lands:
"Locative" surnames, based upon place names, are the commonest of all. You can usually spot them by their suffixes or endings, such as : - LEY, - TON, - DON, - FORD, - BY, - HAM.

Watch out for Scottish surnames which are not pronounced in accordance with their spelling : DALZIEL (think of the former Member of Parliament, Tam Dalziel) is a place name in origin, and is pronounced "Deeyell", just as MENZIES is often pronounced "Mingis". This is a subject in its own right, of course: how do you pronounce the following English and Scottish surnames : GROSVENOR; MARJORIBANKS; FIENNES; WALDEGRAVE; BEAUCHAMP; FEATHERSTONEHAUGH, VILLIERS (answer: "Grovenor", "Marchbanks", "Fines", "Waldgrave", "Beecham", "Fanshaw", "Villers").

LYLE (or L'ISLE) is "the island"; INNES (from the Gaelic "Inis") also means "an island". GLADSTONE comes from lands in Teviotdale called "Gledstanes". MAXWELL comes from possessions of that name on the Tweed. Surnames can be derived from counties (DERBYSHIRE, WESTMORLAND, CORNWALL, MONTGOMERY), from towns (CHESTER, YORK, or BRISTOW from Bristol), or from villages (RUSHBY, FLOCKTON, SMALLEY, CLIFFORD). Less obvious is ARMYTAGE (a man who lived at or near a hermitage).

Many surnames have overseas origins, hardly surprisingly in view of the fact that large numbers of immigrants arrived in Britain over the years from France, the Low Countries and elsewhere. For some odd reason there are people who are proud of the fact that they believe (rightly or wrongly) that their French-sounding surname was brought over in 1066 by that bunch of marauding savages known as the Normans, led by the man called variously William, Earl of Normandy or William the Bastard. Can you spot surnames with a French origin? Why not start off with the name PICKARD - a person from Picardy? And if your surname is DEATH, why not at least pretend that it's French (and, indeed, it may well be) by spelling it D'EATH?

* Surnames from trades, offices or occupations:
This is a numerous class of surnames. Many surnames come from trades : CARPENTER ("Zimmermann" in German), FISHER, COOK, SADDLER, FORESTER, ROPER, SPOONER (a spoon maker), MERCER, GLOVER, MILLER (also MILLAR, MILLS, MILNER), PAINTER, COLLIER, COOPER (or COWPER), CHAPMAN (a travelling dealer in wares), MASON, SKINNER, BARBER, THATCHER (who would thatch both houses and haystacks), SMITH, ARKWRIGHT (a meal chest maker), WAINWRIGHT (he made "wains" or waggons, as in the John Constable painting, "The Hay Wain"), BUTCHER, BAKER ... but no candlestick-makers, alas. A PARKER and a FORESTER would look after the manorial parks and forests respectively; a WOODWARD would tend the woods, a wood reeve (giving us WOODRUFF) was responsible for policing such areas, while a WARNER (or WARRENER) would be responsible for the rabbit warrens. Note that the surname TAYLOR is always spelt with a "y", while the person plying this trade is a "tailor" with an "i". Odd, really, why this should have been so. "Taylor/Tailor" would simply have been alternative spellings of the same word at one time. A "herd" was a man responsible for

tending animals, so we have a SHEPHERD (sheep), a COWARD or COWHERD (cows), a GODDARD (goats), STODDARD (in charge of a stud of horses).

The wool trade upon which England's wealth was once based gives us the surnames FULLER (he would clean cloth), TUCKER, WALKER, BARKER (a tanner) and DYER.

SMITH (from a person who would "smite" or strike with a hammer) is not only the commonest surname in England - it is also the commonest in Scotland and in the United States. The Latin for a smith is "Faber", so in German we have the surname FABER (as well as SCHMIDT), and in French there is the very common surname LEFEVRE or LEFEBVRE. The Celtic name for a Smith gives us GOVAN, GOWAN, COWAN and GOW, while the Polish equivalent is KOVACS or KOWALSKI. SMYTHE, of course, is simply an alternative spelling for SMITH, and there would seem to be no good reason for not pronouncing the name as if it were spelt SMITH. Meanwhile a SICKMITH made sickles.

Some surnames come from a female version of a occupational name. A BAXTER was a female baker, a BREWSTER was a female brewer and a WEBSTER was a female weaver. A "Spinster", of course, stayed at home spinning while her contemporaries upped and got married.

Less obvious trade names include LORIMER (a harness maker), CHAUCER (a shoe maker, from the French "Chaussures"), POTTICARY (an apothecary). The name FARMER ("Ackermann" in German) is not as common as you might suppose, considering how many English people farmed for a living. In fact the name FARMER usually derives from a person who collected ("farmed") taxes and revenues, and paid for the privilege. Surnames may be derived from the office a person held: CHAMBERLAINE (and thus CHAMBERS and CHALMERS), BUTLER, MARSHALL.
Surnames which sound so fine, like KNIGHT, BISHOP, KING etc. probably came from individuals who played these roles in pageants or in mediaeval miracle or mystery plays. A person named "King" is unlikely to be descended from a real King, alas!
The Church has given us surnames like: BISHOP, CLERK, PRIEST, DEAN, POPE, DEACON, CHAPLIN, PARSONS, ABBOT, PRIOR, MONK, FRIAR, VICARS, CHURCH. Again, not all BISHOPs or POPEs are descended from Popes. Most Popes (not all!) were childless. A summoner (surname SUMNER) would summon parishioners to attend the dreaded ecclesiastical court, while a PALMER had returned from a pilgrimage to the Holy Land, bearing palm leaves.

* Surnames from animals:
An English person may be called FOX, while in Scotland the surname TOD means the same thing (a TODHUNTER would have chased foxes), as does FUCHS in German. A sixteenth-century German botanist of this name gave his name to the flower, the FUCHSIA. People called COWE are named after a cow, and the Scottish name VEITCH has the same meaning, (compare the French, "Vache"). The famous Scottish border family of TURNBULL may have once been strong enough to turn a strong bull around - or they may have "turned" English bulls into their own Scottish fields, a common enough practice at one time. Birds have given us the names DUCK and DUCKWORTH, FALKNER (a falconer), WOODCOCK, WREN, PEACOCK (or PEABODY), CROW(E) and CORBET (a crow, from the French "Corbeau"). East Anglia in particular abounds in surnames like PARTRIDGE, PHEASANT and the rest. Fishy names include PIKE, SALMON, SPRATT.

* Surnames from trees, plants, rivers, etc.
A rose by any other name would smell as sweet... unless your surname is ROSE, in which case you may well feel attached to the name, which was probably given to a distant ancestor who was as sweet as a rose, was fond of roses, cultivated roses, looked like a rose, even? There's no evidence of anyone being surnamed "Cauliflower" because of a cauliflower ear, however...

Other plant or flower names include LILLY, FLOWER(S), BRIER(S), BROOM, HOLLYHOCK, FERN. The original bearer of the surname WOOD might have dwelt in or near a wood; similarly we have ATWOOD, BYWOOD, UNDERWOOD. A SHAW was a small wood; FOREST, HEATH and MOOR speak for themselves. Similar names include ASH, and NASH (the dweller "atten-ash", i.e., by the ash, shortened to NASH).

Jenny LIND's surname comes from the Swedish word for a lime tree (as in "Unterdenlinden" in Germany). The Scottish name LINDSAY means "isle of limetrees".

Surnames from water include BROOK, BURN(S), WATERS, WELLS, RIVERS. WELLESLEY (and its variant WESLEY), the surname of the family of the Duke of Wellington, means "the field of wells". The dramatist John DRINKWATER probably had a teetotal ancestor!

* Surnames from weapons of war :
A MARTEL was a battle-axe - something to think about next time you buy a bottle of brandy. A FORTESCUE was a strong shield. A BOWYER made bows to which a STRINGFELLOW would add the bow-string; then the ARROWSMITH or the FLETCHER (from the French word "Flèche"), made arrows for an ARCHER to shoot.

The trick with surnames is never to let one pass you by. Think about the surnames of those around you; can you guess or intuit what they mean, or what the origin could be? Every time you encounter a new surname, give it the treatment: try guessing its meaning first, if you like, then look it up in a surname dictionary. There are several of these on the market, those by C W Bardsley, P H Reaney, H Harrison, C L'E Ewen and P Hanks and F Hodges being the best known. At their best, such dictionaries reveal fine scholarship, but even the best can be prone to guess-work on occasions - so beware!

For a further in-depth look at the fact, fiction and humour of surnames (and much else) see Succeeding in Family History: helpful hints and time-saving tips by John Titford, published by Countryside Books (ISBN 1-85306-691-5) at £6.95.

Ron in Clacton

Ron's Story
Richard Ratcliffe F.S.G

Every September my adrenalin level starts to rise as I prepare to start another series of 10 week adult classes in family History. What will the new classes be like ? Will all the students get on well together? Will the new classes really be complete beginners or will there be some students who have dabbled with their Family History and expect me to sort out their muddled research? Do the new group of students realise that tracing their ancestry quickly becomes addictive and that once the course has started their lives will be changed forever? Am I as their tutor fully aware of the impact the course will have on the daily lives of the students, their families and the relations that they are likely to discover in the coming weeks, months and years? Are they prepared to find out stories of family quarrels, bastardy, murder and intrigue, as well as stories of achievement, bravery and links with the rich and famous?

This is the story of how joining a Family History class has changed Ron's life.

Ron joined my Beginners' Class in September 1998. He had just celebrated his 50th birthday and had recently lost his job as a result of contacting Multiple Sclerosis. He had tried to start tracing his family history by writing to the Office for National Statistics[ONS] at Southport for his Grandfather's Birth Certificate only to receive a reply that they could not find an entry in their indexes that agreed with the details provided and so could not supply a certificate. Ron had told the ONS that his grandfather's name was Stephen Richard SILVERBACK who was born in 1900. [This was based on the age shown on Stephen's Marriage Certificate of 1919].So he came to my class feeling very depressed and wondering if there was any hope of ever tracing his family history.

As most of my students are Senior Citizens, I offer to go to the Family Records Centre and locate and order certificates to get them started, often taking some of the fitter students with me. After spending the first two sessions discussing family sources and looking through Directories such as the Genealogical Research Directory[GRD], BIG R and back numbers of Family Tree Magazine, and the Essex Society for Family History Members' Directory, I usually go to the FRC before the third session with a list of 20-30 requests for certificates. Off I went with Ron's request for his grandfather's Birth

Certificate. At first I failed to find it in1900 but as I always do a 5 year search the event of not finding a birth in the given year [people were not always truthful on their Marriage Certificates] I looked before and after 1900.In 1902 I spotted the entry for a Charles William SILBERBACH March Quarter, Hackney 1b 575 - could this be a connection? Back to the 1900 indexes and there in the June Quarter I found the entry that the ONS and I had overlooked - Stephen Richard SILBERBACH St Albans 3a 693. After ordering this certificate I then carried out a 20 year search in the Birth indexes form 1895-1915 finding only 7 Silberbach/Silverback entries mostly in Hackney and West Ham Registration Districts. Could they be connected?

The birth certificate showed that Stephen was the son of Richard SILBERBACH and his wife Alice Maud formerly PARKES. Using this information, I then found the Marriage Certificate of Richard SILBERBACH son of Alexander Frederick SILBERBACH, Artist and Alice Maud PARKES, Widow, Daughter of Silas WALLIS, schoolmaster at St Augustine's Parish Church, South Hackney.This led to the Birth Certificate of Richard SILVERBACK in 1871 in Mile End Old Town, son of Charles Frederick Alexander SILVERBACK, Portrait Painter and his wife Charlotte, formerly GLOCKLER That certificate led to the Marriage Certificate of Charles Frederick Alexander SILBERBACH and Charlotte GLOCKLER, daughter of John GLOCKLER . When I found the 1851 Census entry of the SILBERBACH family courtesy of the surname index of Mile End Old Town compiled by the East of London FHS which showed that Charles was born in Koenigsberg, East Prussia while Charlotte was born in Charlbury, Oxfordshire, Ron was hooked. He wanted to know if it was possible to check records in East Prussia

Richard Pether Silberbach
Ron's great grandfather who is the son of
Carl Silberbach and Charlotte Glocker

and also to find out if there were any other descendants of Charles apart from himself and his family living in England today. While I went to the FRC and carried out a complete search of the BMD Indexes, Ron wrote to Peter Towey, Chairman of the Anglo-German FHS to enquire about membership and also went to the local library to check all the Telephone Directories for Silberbach/Silverback entries.

My searches revealed that between 1837 and 1999 there were 53 SILBERBACH/SILVERBACK Births registered, 36 Marriages and 36 Deaths. Over the next few months, Ron purchased the lot.

Ron's searches through the Telephone Directories drew a complete blank, but Peter Towey gave him a number of useful suggestions on tracing ancestors in Germany. Ron also took up my suggestion of subscribing to at least one monthly Family History magazine. In Family History Monthly, he spotted an advertisement by Rosie Ritchie offering to look up surnames in directories in USA, Canada and Australia. For a small fee , Rosie supplied Ron with 5 telephone numbers in Australia. Imagine his delight when he phoned them up to find that all 5 families were descended from Stephen Richard Silverback's brother Leonard who had "emigrated" in the 1920s. Leonard and his Australian wife Nellie [nee KINGSTON] had 2 sons who between them had produced 11 cousins. One of them, another Ron, said that his son Luke and daughter Kate were working in London and had been trying to locate English relations without success. Ron rang them immediately and invited them to Clacton just days before they were due to return to Australia. If Ron had been dubious about tracing his family history this visit dispelled all worries! Ron is now in regular contact with all his Australian cousins.

To find out more about his German origins, I suggested that he should write to the Family History Library in Salt Lake City where from my own experiences on a visit organised by Family Tree Magazine in 1998, I knew the Library held a considerable amount of European Records. The Library sent him a list of professional researchers who were experienced in searching German records. Ron wrote to Ruth Froelke who sent him transcripts and photocopies of Silberbach entries in Koenigsberg Parish Registers from which he was able to trace his ancestry back to 1720 [or 7 generations].

Sadly, only a few months after starting on his family history, Ron's father died and was buried in Manor Park Cemetery. At the family get together after the funeral, Ron talked to many relatives, most of whom he had little or no previous knowledge. Several of them promised to look out certificates and photographs and soon Ron had a sizeable collection of family photographs to go with those of his mother and father - the only ones he had to start with. Now he has family photographs going back to the 1870s.

The funeral also started him wondering where other members of the Silverback family might be buried. I got him a copy of " London Cemeteries" [SOG,1999] which has proved invaluable. He has found wonderful help from Cemetery Superintendents and Official of London Boroughs who have supplied details and maps of burial plots.

To date, Ron has located over 100 graves and has got details of relatives who are buried in each plot.

Ron is now researching several kindred families. He is collecting information about the GLOCKLER, ROMACK and MEHL families from Germany; the

Alice Maud Silberbach
nee Parkes
Ron's greatgrandmother with his grandfather Stephen and great aunt
Florence Walthamstow, London

HUX, CARPENTER and GONDOUX families from Charlbury and Shipton under Wychwood in Oxfordshire; BEEVOR/BEVIS from Upwell in Cambridgeshire; BUNDOCK from Epping in Essex and WINES from Stepney in Middlesex.

For Christmas 1999, Ron treated himself and his wife Sharon, who had also caught the Family History bug, to a Personal Computer, purchased Family Tree Maker and got connected to the Internet. They are now both inveterate communicators, both by Snail mail and Email. Among the surprising discoveries that he has made, Ron has found an uncle living only 10 miles away from his Clacton home at Great Oakley: that his Great/ great grandfather Charles Alexander Frederick Silberbach died in Colney Hatch Asylum in 1907and that his 5 x great grandfather John Gondoux was murdered at Charlbury in Oxfordshire in 1811, but the truth about his death only came out in 1888 in an old lady's death bed confession. Tracing his family history has transformed Ron's life. The transformation started when he joined a Family History Class 3 years ago - he still keeps signing up each year - but due to his persistence to get answers and the helpful assistance of newly discovered relatives, archivists, librarians, fellow students and many other people, he has now traced over 700 ancestors and kindred relations in spite of largely having to work from home. It's no wonder I nominate Ron as my star pupil. Cheers Ron!

Christmas Card, Knockaloe Camp
© Peter Towey

Internment of German Civilians and other Aliens in the UK.

Peter Towey
Chairman
Anglo-German Family History Society

on as the most secure place to intern men and the first camp opened there in a former holiday camp in Douglas in September 1914. A farm on the other side of the island, near Peel, was prepared as another larger camp and opened in 1915 in time for the May 1915 flood of internees: this was Knockaloe. It was first designed for 5,000 men but soon nearly 30,000 were housed there in wooden huts. There were also other camps at Stratford in east London; in a former workhouse in Islington; on 9 liners off Ryde, Gosport and Southend; a disused wagon works in Lancaster, and Libury Hall in Hertfordshire was used to house elderly and infirm internees. There were hundreds of other camps all over the UK. Conditions were usually bad and when protests were made about the food at Douglas camp on 19th November 1914 five internees were shot and killed in the "riot". The inquest blamed overcrowding and the poor food but no-one in the camp administration was held to account.

The internees were a wide cross-section of German society in UK. It must be stressed that they were all civilians and not military POWs though they were normally called "Civilian POWs" as if they had been captured under arms! Some were long-term residents with families in England; these probably suffered worse as they felt they were being punished unfairly just for being born German; their businesses had been confiscated; their wives and families were often without resources while the breadwinner was interned, and their families were often on the receiving end of anti-German violence and hatred. During the First World War there were many riots where German-owned businesses and homes were attacked by mobs and, in many cases, the police were not able or willing to protect them. Not knowing how your loved ones were doing must have been difficult. There are also documented cases where an internee's wife died and he was not allowed out to attend her funeral. This kind of thing must have felt even worse when their English-born sons were fighting and dying in the British Army and they, the father, was still treated as an enemy. The camps also included those who were on holiday in UK at the outbreak of war; seamen off captured German merchant navy and fishing vessels and, no doubt, some German military reservists. The problem was that no attempt was made at first to differentiate. By 1917, however, some internees with families in London were being moved to Islington and Alexandra Palace where they could keep in touch more easily with their families.

Until 1914 there was little control over immigration into the United Kingdom and people of any nationality could settle and live and work in England, Scotland, Ireland or Wales without needing prior permission or needing to naturalise. During the 19th century one of the largest groups of foreigners living in UK was the Germans. Germans had been settling in UK for generations and many individuals had moved to Great Britain or Ireland while young, married a British wife and had children who were born in UK and so were British Subjects. It probably never crossed anyone's mind that there was a need or duty for the immigrant (or his wife!) to naturalise. People had always lived in UK without needing to so why should anything change?

The change came with the international crisis that led up to the outbreak of war in August 1914. All over Europe the people were being stirred up by the Press and politicians to hate the potential enemy. This had been happening gradually over the previous generation and, at the outbreak of war, all enemy aliens were required to register with the local police. Men of fighting age, say 18 to 50, were to be interned in hastily prepared Internment Camps across the UK. Women and children and old men were not interned but still had to register. The main camps in London were at Olympia (a transit camp which closed by December 1914) and Alexandra Palace. The conditions in the camps were bad principally because arrangements had not been properly planned and, indeed, the Government quietly released some of the men, and failed to intern others, because there was nowhere to put them.

In May 1915, however, the SS "Lusitania" was sunk by a German submarine with considerable loss of life. The public outcry was such that all Enemy Alien men of fighting age were interned again and this time it was for the duration.

The British government identified the Isle of Man early

There was an intent at first to repatriate to Germany all men over fighting age. They were generally moved to transit camps like Spalding in Lincolnshire before being shipped from one of the East Coast ports and transferred to neutral Dutch ships in the North Sea. When landed in Holland they were taken by train to the German frontier where they were welcomed and sent to their homes (if they still had one in Germany!). . As the war proceeded, however, and it was found that the Germans were calling up older age groups to man their Armies, the qualifying

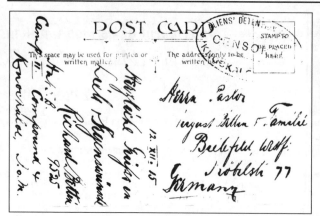

Christmas Card, Knockaloe Camp (Reverse)
© Peter Towey

age for repatriation was increased.

Wives and children were also liable to be repatriated (if that is the right word where they were English-born and spoke no German!). It was seen as a punishment for remaining loyal to their husbands and fathers and there was official encouragement for wives to divorce their German husbands – there was a fast route to get their English nationality back if they did. Imagine their situation, deposited in Germany with no resources and seen by the Germans as enemy British, without any knowledge of the language or anyone or any place to call home! The legality of the British Government's actions is questionable even in wartime as the children born in UK were legally British Subjects – not German.

To balance the black picture painted above, the Germans treated British civilians in much the same way and the conditions in the Camps were very similar. Indeed, both Governments treated the civilian internees as "hostages" for the treatment of their own nationals in the enemy Country and there were several instances where "privileges" were withdrawn because of real or imagined bad-treatment of their fellow countrymen. In several cases these appear to be due to Governments believing their own propaganda!

Overall, though, the main enemy in the camps was boredom; being locked up for months at a time with nothing useful to do. As time went by the internees organised their own employment and entertainment. The Quakers were at the forefront in organising manufacturing of carvings and flat-packed furniture (!) that could be sold abroad for the benefit of the internees and their dependants. Bone carvings are quite common and do sometimes turn up at auction sales: these were meat bones from the Camp kitchen. The camp at Knockaloe even had its own printing press and printed newspapers, adverts, calendars and even Christmas cards [see picture]. "Living with the Wire" illustrates a large number of examples of this and the other activities in the camps. There is in the Manx Museum a set of thousands of glass plate photographs of the internees: group and single portraits. Unfortunately, while the plates are numbered, the photographer's key to the identity of each person is lost and the photos remain anonymous.

At the end of the war, the great majority of the internees were deported to Germany though it seems to be well into 1919 before that happened. There was even an Act passed enabling the Government to remove British

nationality from naturalised former-Germans, though I do not know to what extent that Act was used. There was legislation earlier in the war preventing enemy aliens from being naturalised without first getting the permission of the Secretary of State for Home Affairs. The legislation preventing naturalisation was not repealed until the 1960s. In many cases applicants had paid their naturalisation fee to their solicitors and I recall seeing a newspaper report of a Court case where the internee tried to recover his fee. He lost because the Courts refused to allow Enemy Aliens to sue in British Courts until after the war!

Many people with German-looking surnames, whether Germans or British (or Dutch or Danish!) tried to change their surnames to avoid the day-to-day annoyance of being treated as an enemy. This had been going on for many years but there was a feeling in some quarters that this was to hide their fifth column activities! So similar legislation was passed requiring people with German names to get Home Office approval before changing their names. Again this stayed on the Statute Book until relatively recently.

Many members of the Anglo-German FHS are the descendants of men who were interned in the First World War. Many had their childhood blighted by the anti-German feeling rife during much of the early and mid 20th century; so much so that some even asked that their name be left off any published list of members. Fortunately this is less common today and people are even changing their surnames back to the original German form. We also noticed that there was little evidence of where internment had taken place and we were in danger of forgetting what had happened. The site of Knockaloe Camp in the Isle of Man is now an experimental farm run by the Manx Ministry of Agriculture and the Society arranged in 1998 to have a plaque put on one of the surviving buildings there. A large number of members attended on the day and the plaque was unveiled by the Minister of Agriculture, Mrs Hannam. Fortunately the Manx Museum sees the camp as part of the island's history and had put on a very interesting exhibition about internment on the island in both World Wars. The catalogue of the exhibition is well illustrated and copies of it are still available for sale there and from the Anglo-German FHS.

Internment in England is much less well-known and one of our members, whose grandfather had been interned in Alexandra Palace, was incensed when he went on a tour of the Palace and was told that only military POWs had been there. We were able to up-date the Palace's information and were eventually allowed to unveil a plaque there in June 2000 to all the civilian enemy alien POWs held there in the First World War. Appropriately the mother of the member who had first complained was the person who unveiled the plaque. She remembered as a child visiting her father there. Again, a large group of people with family memories of internment there were present and were all very moved. Many felt that being allowed to erect the plaque symbolised the acceptance by British authorities that the internees had been unfairly treated and this enabled many to feel that a measure of justice had been done.

The experience of internment during the Second World War was different. Refugees from Nazi Germany, Jewish and Gentile, had been coming to UK from the early 1930s. It was evident to most people that being at war with Nazi Germany did not mean that all people who were legally German citizens were automatically enemies of the UK and its allies. A tribunal system was set up to review the cases of all enemy aliens and consider which should be interned. This time it affected both women and men, Germans, Austrians and Italians, and the tribunals' card index is now available in the PRO in HO396. Refugees and anti-Nazi aliens were not interned as a rule.

Records:

The British Government kept very detailed records of all civilian internees and their confiscated property. These records were kept in the Prisoners of War Information Bureau in Covent Garden in London. Unfortunately these records were all lost when the building was destroyed by bombing in the Second World War. Each week the British Government sent to the Red Cross details of all men newly interned in the previous week. The Red Cross then sent copies to the relevant enemy Government – these were Germany, Austria-Hungary, Bulgaria and Turkey. A set also went to the Protecting Power (the neutral Government selected to keep an eye on the internees and ensure that they were not too badly treated) – up to 1917 that was USA but after they joined the Allies it was Switzerland. There do not appear to be any copies of the weekly lists of internees in USA but they could well have passed them over to the Swiss. Unfortunately I have not been able to find them in Switzerland. The Germans have some copies of the lists from 1916 to 1919 but these only record those newly interned in that period and changes of circumstances for others (ie deaths, movement to other camps, illnesses, etc). The Anglo-German FHS has copied and indexed those German records and can search them for names but the information available is not usually all that helpful. One useful list found with them in Germany was a list of the internees for whom the POW information Bureau held property; it was produced by the British authorities to serve as a finding aid if claims for compensation were to be made after the war – it just lists the names but it might set you looking for property that might have been confiscated such as houses, shops, or factories. I have also noticed that, after the First World War, the POW Information Bureau acted as executor of wills

presumably where the person concerned had been interned as an enemy alien and the compensation had not been sorted out after the war.

The International Committee of the Red Cross, (ICRC Archives, 19 Avenue de la Paix, CH-1212 Geneva, Switzerland) does hold a complete set of the weekly lists and will search them for you. You can write and they will reply in English. It does take some months normally but they do have other responsibilities! They charge 80 Swiss Francs an hour for searching but you should not send any money when you write; they will let you know when to send the money. Unfortunately, however, their records appear to work from the wrong end! You really need to tell them the age and place of birth of the prisoner and when and where he was interned before they can get you whatever else they have. You can see that this is sensible if you are trying to track down what happened to a POW. However, the reason we are using their archives normally is to find out where a prisoner came from; this they do not appear to be able to do.

The Anglo-German FHS is constantly looking for other sources that can substitute for the lost records. The wives and young children of internees could have been entitled to Poor Law relief while their breadwinner was interned. Some instances have been discovered in the Poor Law records at the London Metropolitan Archives and there are probably more out there. Where aliens registered with the police in 1914 and subsequently, the records have usually been destroyed though there are one or two examples (like Salford) where records have survived. Naturalisation records do not generally help as naturalised British Subjects were not interned but, where former internees naturalised after the First World War, the records may be with their Home Office files which you can see either at the Public Record Office in Kew or by getting permission from the Departmental Record Officer at the Home Office.

As changing your surname from a German name to a more English-looking one was banned in 1914, there are no records. In most cases, people just started using the preferred surname (perfectly legally because English law does not require you to take legal steps to change your name unless you want to!).

Bibliography:
"An Insight into Civilian Internment in Britain during WWI; from the diary of Richard Noschke and a short essay by Rudolf Rocker", published by Anglo-German FHS, 1998. ISBN 0 9514133 7 6. Richard Noschke was a Londoner who was interned at Stratford Camp & Alexandra Palace before being repatriated via Spalding and Holland. Rudolf Rocker was a well-known socialist internee who was asked by the Camp Commandant to write a report on Alexandra Palace.
"Germans in Britain Since 1500", edited by Panikos Panayi, published by The Hambledon Press, 1996. ISBN 1 85285 126 0. A series of articles on the way Germans were treated at various times but with special emphasis on the last 150 years.
"Living with the Wire. Civilian Internment in the Isle of Man during the two World Wars", edited by Yvonne M. Cresswell, published by Manx National Heritage. ISBN 0 901 106 35 6. Well illustrated with photographs, drawings and extracts from memories. Available by post from the Anglo-German FHS.
"Immigrants and Aliens. A guide to sources on UK immigration and citizenship", by Roger Kershaw and Mark Pearsall. PRO Readers Guide No 22. Published by the PRO, Kew, Richmond, Surrey, TW9 4DU. ISBN 1 873162 94 4. Excellent background to the surviving records of internment in UK; mainly useful for the Second World War.
"Prisoners of War Information Bureau. List of Places of Internment", reprinted by the Imperial War Museum, London. The British official listing of all internment camps in the British Empire during WWI. It also includes the codes used in official records for the camps.

Commemerative Plaque, Alexander Palace June 2000 © Mrs Lilian Stone

National Maritime Museum Caird library

Hellen Pethers
Library & Information assistant

©National Maritime Museum

The National Maritime Museum Library was founded in 1934 and is now the largest and most significant reference library of its kind in the world. The library is named after the museum's principal founder and benefactor Sir James Caird (1864-1954). The Library collection includes over 100,000 books, 20,000 pamphlets, 20,000 bound periodicals including 200 current titles and 8,000 rare books dating from 1474 to 1850. A computerised catalogue of the books is available via the Museum's web site. The Library is staffed by a team of professional librarians and subjects specialists who are available to help and advise readers at all times.

The Caird Library's contents range over every aspect of maritime history, including emigration, navigation, piracy, astronomy, shipping companies, shipwrecks, biographies, the two world wars, horology, merchant and Royal navy, and special collections for researching family history, merchant shipping and warships. Sources which may be particularly useful for researching the merchant navy include:
Lloyd's Captains' Register, 1851 – 1947 (microfilm) : A register of masters and mates of merchant ships with their certificate numbers. Summary of service provided. The Library holds office copies of Masters' Certificates (1845-1927).
Lloyd's Register: 1764-1833 lists all ships surveyed, *1834-1838* all British ships over 50 tons, *1839-1875* all ships surveyed, *1876* onwards lists all ocean going ships world wide over 100 tons. They provide an alphabetical listing by ship name, published annually, giving information such as master's name, type of vessel, when and where built and name of owner.
Mercantile Navy List 1857-1977 : A list of all British registered merchant ships with their official number, plus a list of masters and mates with certificate number (1857-1864 only).
Lloyd's Register of Yachts 1879-1980
Lloyd's List 1741 to date (1933 onwards on microfilm) : Reports shipping movements for ocean going vessels and casualties to shipping of all types. An annual index by ship is available on microfilm for the period 1838-1927.
Merchant Navy cards regarding deaths at sea during World War II.

Sources which may be particularly useful for researching the Royal Navy include:
Colledge, JJ Ships of the Royal Navy: the complete record of all fighting ships of the Royal Navy from the fifteenth century to the present. 1987
Commissioned Sea Officers of the Royal Navy 1660-1815. An alphabetical list of naval officers annotated with warships in which they served.
Admiralty Movement Books 1939-1945
Conway's all the World's Fighting Ships 1860-1982
Jane's Fighting Ships 1898 to date.
Lyon, David The Sailing Navy List: all the ships of the Royal Navy built, purchased and captured 1688-1860. 1993.
Navy Lists 1814 to date : *provides details of stations of warships and contains seniority lists of officers. Regulations for rank, rate and pay rates are included.*
Warship Histories (microfiche)

Manuscripts collection
The National Maritime Museum's manuscripts collection spans approximately four and half miles of shelving. A diverse range of subjects are covered including personal papers, lieutenants logs, masters certificates, crew lists (1861, 1862 and years ending in 5 up to 1955) and shipping company records, including the P&O archive. The catalogue can be accessed online via the museum web site. There are set retrieval times throughout the day, and not all manuscripts are on site, so it is advisable to contact the Manuscripts department prior to your visit, 020 8312 6691/6669.

Charts and Atlases
The Library and hydrographic collections contain over 100,000 maps and charts covering most areas of the world. Dating from the fifteenth to the twenty-first centuries they illustrate the work of the leading cartographers and hydrographers throughout the history of mapmaking and charting. Charts are stored at an outstation and are not available on demand. If you wish to consult items from this collection please contact the Library, prior to your visit.

Prints, Drawings and Oil Paintings.
The National Maritime Museum has one of the world's largest collections of maritime art. This includes over 4,000 oil paintings encompassing four hundred years of art and a fine collection of over 60,000 watercolours, etchings, engravings, aquatints and lithographs. An online prints and drawings catalogue is available via the web site. Images of items in the collections are available for the general public to purchase as prints, as well as prints on canvas. For further details contact the Picture Library, 020 8312 6631/6704.

Historic Photographs

©National Maritime Museum

©National Maritime Museum

The National Maritime Museum holds the country's finest collection of historic maritime photographs, with prints and negatives dating back to the beginnings of photography in the 1840's. The collection comprises of approximately 270,000 negatives including glass, nitrate and safety film negatives, one million prints and 1463 albums. Copies are available to the public of all photographs for which there is a negative or where copyright permission can be obtained. The collection is housed at an outstation and visits must be by prior arrangement. An online catalogue is available via the web site or enquiries can be made through the Historic Photographs department 020 8855 1647.

Ship Plans
The Ship Plans archive at the National Maritime Museum maintains the largest single collection of original drawings in the world. The one million plans date from the early 18th century to the present day and are broadly divided into 'Admiralty' and 'Merchant'. This collection is housed at an outstation and visits must be by prior arrangement, please contact the Ship Plans department, 020 8855 1647.

Search Station
The Museum has over 2 million artefacts in its collection, making it the largest maritime museum in the world. The Search Station is a multi media resource providing access to selected highlights from the collection. Using the latest touch-screen technology you can view hidden treasures with computer graphics, sound and moving images. You can access the Search Station online at www.nmm.ac.uk/searchstation The Search Station is located outside the Caird Library and is open seven days a week 10.00 – 16.45.

PORT Port is an online catalogue of high quality maritime related Internet resources. Every resource has been selected and described by a librarian or subject specialist from the National Maritime Museum. The service is freely available to search from the PORT website: www.port.nmm.ac.uk

Research
Museum staff cannot undertake research on behalf of the public. It is necessary to visit the library in person bringing some form of identification. If a visit is not possible, a list of independent professional researchers can be provided. To help you carry out your own research, a set of research guides and answers to frequently asked questions are also available on the Museum's website. Highly specialised enquiries that relate to the Museum's collections may be answered by the curatorial specialists. There is a charge for this service.

Reading room
Anyone over 18 years of age with a relevant research enquiry can gain access to the reading room. Entry is obtained by applying for either a day pass or annual readers ticket, both are free although formal identification is required. Readers are asked to observe basic rules such as no bags/coats, photography or food in the reading room and pencils only. A fee-paid photocopying and microfilming facility is available.

The Caird Library
National Maritime Museum, Greenwich, London SE10 9NF
Tel: 020 8312 6673/6528 Fax: 020 8312 6599
Library E-mail: library@nmm.ac.uk
Manuscripts E-mail: manuscripts@nmm.ac.uk
Website: www.nmm.ac.uk
Opening Hours
Monday to Saturday 10.00 – 16.45 (Saturdays by appointment only) Sundays, Bank Holidays, and the third week in February – Closed

Comings and Goings ~
To~ings & Fro~ings
Doreen Hopwood

discusses migratory ancestors

We all dream of finding our ancestors buried in a beautifully inscribed family grave under the shade of a yew tree in a picturesque country churchyard. However, for most of us, the reality is that after the 19th century it is unlikely that more than one generation lived out their lives in the place where they were born. Migration may not have necessarily involved long distances, but, as Britain changed from a rural nation into a country of town dwellers, our 'ag-labs' left the countryside to adapt their skills to industrial work. During the reign of Queen Victoria, Britain was the world's leading manufacturer and the demands of industry brought people into the towns, attracted by the prospect of higher wages at same time as agricultural work was decreasing. Routes of local migration can often be followed by changes in employment opportunities in a particular area – such as the iron trades. Miners from Wales and Shropshire migrated to the Black Country industrial areas in South Staffordshire and North Worcestershire, working in the heavy metal trades before finding themselves in Birmingham and involved in lighter manufactory. Town and Country directories list the carriers and their routes, and maps showing the railway, canal and road networks from the mid-19th century are helpful in ascertaining how migration was affected. Inter-generational migration is known as 'Step-migration' and can be particularly identified with certain types of worker – such as railway employees, boatmen and miners.

Chain-migration generally involves longer-distance movement and occurs when a person (usually a male 'pioneer') leaves his home to settle in a new place. Once established, he sends for other members of his family and may return 'home' to marry, bringing his bride to his place of settlement. This process often sparks of further chains of migration as members of the extended family comes to join them, and stories of success filter back to their place of origin, encouraging further migration. In this way, areas of certain towns become known as 'Little Italy', 'Little Germany' etc. Once settled, the new communities inter-married and established their own clubs and organisations, some of which still exist. The main library of the town should have listings of all local organisations with contact names and addresses.

There are usually strong 'pull and push' factors connected with any decision to migrate, and these may have been political, economic or religious. The persecution of the Puritans led to the migration of large numbers to New England in the early 17th century, and Huguenots and other Protestant groups fled to Britain from France to avoid persecution. The

Huguenots established their own churches and the Huguenot Society has published many of their registers. Economic factors were instrumental in the migration of the Irish, especially during the potato famines of the 19th century. The 1861 census of England and Wales includes about 52,000 Irish-born residents. Political and religious persecution made thousands flock from Eastern Europe in the 19th and 20th centuries, and sources which may help identify their places of origin include the census returns from 1851. Unfortunately, these sometimes give only the country of birth, or possibly the province, and where the actual place of birth is shown this may have been 'anglicised' and written down as it sounded by the enumerator. In these cases, a gazetteer of the country can be helpful, as it is not only foreign place names that get misspelt! You should find gazetteers in your main reference library, along with both historical and contemporary maps and atlases.

Ships passenger list are helpful for both immigration and emigration, but you need to have some basic information, such as the name of the ship, the port and approximate date of entry/departure in order to access the records, which are not indexed. These are held at the Public Record Office, and cover ships arriving from outside Europe from 1890 to 1960 at Class BT 32, whilst those of emigrants are at Class BT 27 for the same period. Immigrants (or aliens) may have become British Subjects through the process of denization or naturalisation. There is a published index to persons granted naturalisation certificates at the Public Record Office covering the period 1844 to 1900, and, after 1886, the names are included in the London Gazette. Many immigrants did not go through the process of naturalisation, especially if they married a British subject because any children of the marriage acquired British nationality. Various Aliens Acts have been passed since the late 18th century and under these all foreigners were required to register with a Justice of the Peace. Similarly, lodging house keepers were required to provide their parish constable with details of any aliens lodging in their property. Where such records have survived they are deposited at the relevant County Record Office. During the First World War all aliens, however temporary their visit to Britain, were required to register with the police who kept track of their movements. The Aliens Registers for Birmingham contain several thousand entries and are held at the Police Museum. Each entry gives a brief physical description of the person, their address, occupation, marital status, names of spouse and children (with ages), date and place of birth and date of arrival in Britain. It also details any military service in the country of origin and movements within Britain during the period of the register. One such register includes almost of the '*artistes*' appearing with the Turner's Opera Company, and the complete crew list of a ship from Hong Kong.

Most emigration from Britain in the 19th century was for economic reasons, and a Public Record Office Information Leaflet lists the sources available there for emigration. This, and other leaflets in the series, can be found on the website at familyrecords.gov.uk and can be printed off for reference. Although emigration on a large-scale occurred in the 19th century, the idea of a new life in another country was by no means a Victorian phenomenon. In the 300 years between 1551 and 1851, it is estimated that almost 2? million people left England, the most popular destinations being the Americas, Australia and other colonies. Prior to 1914, passports were not a legal requirement, but you may find details of those issued (mainly to diplomats or merchants) from 1794. In the late 16th and 17th centuries, soldiers going to the Low Countries, or civilians travelling to New England, may have been issued with a 'licence to pass beyond the seas'. Surviving records are held at the Public Record Office and there are some published lists of British emigrants. Further information can be found in the Public Record Office Leaflet No.69.

Copies of the Calendar of State Papers, Colonial, America and West Indies 1547-1738 can be found in main reference libraries, and these are indexed, including names of individuals. One of the major sources for emigration to the United States of America are the volumes of *Passenger and Immigration Lists Index* by Filby and Meyer, first published in 1981 with further annual supplements. These give details of families and individuals, and their port of embarkation in America, with the source for further information.

The Guildhall Library and the Public Record Office hold copies of some of the indentures of people who went out to work on the plantations in the colonies. In exchange for payment of passage and board they agreed to work for a certain period of time for a master, and on completion they received a cash payment and grant of land. Following the passing of the Poor Law Amendment Act in 1834, the Boards of Guardians of Poor Law Unions soon realised that it was more economical for them to send poor families to the New World or Australia than to support them at home. Parish assisted emigration continued until 1890, and lists of names of pauper emigrants can be found in the Public Record Office (in class MH 12). These are arranged by county and poor law union and often detail the occupation and destination. You may

also find information in the poor law minutes/accounts held at the relevant County Record Office. However, less than 10% of emigrants left England and Wales under this scheme.

Various 17th century Acts empowered the Overseers of the Poor of a parish to remove any strangers if they became chargeable to the parish. From 1697, the Overseers of the new parish were able to ask the newcomer for a certificate from his own parish confirming that he would be received back if he became a pauper. These Settlement Certificates were kept by the Overseers as authority and can be found in the Diocesan or County Record Offices. When a settlement claim was disputed, Justices of the Peace heard the case so further details may be found in the Quarter Sessions Records. Some County Record Offices and family history societies have indexed settlement papers for their area.

The Poor Law Amendment Act of 1850 allowed Boards of Guardians to send children aged 16+ overseas, and child migration schemes were soon established in Britain. However, as early as 1617, the City of London sent over 100 poor or orphaned children to America at the request of the Virginia Company. Vagrant children were also being shipped there as slave labour.

Philanthropic Societies, such as Dr Barnardo's, began to organise the migration of poor or orphaned children to Canada, Australia, New Zealand and South Africa on a large scale from the late 19th century, and the schemes continued until 1965. It is estimated that over 100,000 children were sent to Canada between 1869 and 1948. Some schemes were organised on a national basis, but most were local philanthropic organisations, such as Middlemore's in Birmingham and the Manchester and Salford Boys and Girls Refuges. Once they reached their new homes, the children were visited on a regular basis, and reports sent to the organisations' headquarters in England. These reports can usually be found in the county record office of main library, possibly with the records relating to individuals. However, in many cases these have a closure period of 100 years (or even 125 years), but may be consulted by permission from the Archivist or Officer of the Emigration Home

– usually granted to direct descendants only. The records of Dr Barnardo's are held at Liverpool University (in special collections and archives), and the website at www.liv.ac.uk/archives provides short histories of other child emigration schemes and how to find their records.

Local and National newspapers published advertisements for migrants, so you may find that people from one particular area in England moved *en bloc* to a new destination. This is particularly true of groups coming to England from Europe and Ireland. Irish communities grew around a Catholic Church, and migrants from other Catholic countries soon joined them. Italians from the Lazzio area settled in and around Birmingham, whilst most of the Italian settlers in the Manchester area originated from Frosinone. In 1829, William Cobbett published *The Emigrants Guide in Ten Letters*, and a supplement *to The Illustrated London News* detailed 'opportunities for emigrants' in 1850. and includes an excellent description of the emigration process.

Over 200,000 people migrated in the 1920s and 1930s to Canada, Australia and New Zealand, many of whom received assisted passages under the 1922 Settlement of the Dominions Act. Emigration was seen as a way of alleviating the huge unemployment problem in this country whilst helping to develop new dominions, summed up by a telegram from the Governor General of Australia as 'We have not enough people you have too many. This interest you, as much as us'

Immigrants arriving in their new home often had a photograph taken, to be sent to the loved ones they had left behind. Photographic studios specialising in such photographs could be found in the main ports and towns where immigrants settled. The Dyche Collection of photographs is held at Birmingham Central Library and contains portraits of immigrant families, as well as individuals.

The Waterloo Dock at Liverpool was the main place of departure for the majority of people emigrating to North America, and the Merseyside Maritime

Museum, at the Pier Head, Liverpool L3 1DN, gives a graphic visual insight into the process of immigration, with a reconstruction of an emigrant vessels' steerage quarters and a lodging house at their destination.

Not all emigration was voluntary, and records of convicts transported to America (up to 1775) and Australia can be found both at the location where the sentence was carried out and in the Assize and Quarter Session covering the trial. In 1778 the first convicts were transported to Van Diemans Land, and, by 1868, it is estimated that about 162,000 men and women were sent to Australia in this way. Records can be found at the Public Record Office, including convict transportation registers, and a census of 1828 for New South Wales and Tasmania giving the names of 35,000 individuals, both convicts and free settlers. David T Hawkins book 'Criminal Ancestors' explains transportation records in depth. Many Family History Libraries of the Church of Jesus Christ and Latter Day Saints hold copies of Emigrant lists on microfilm, and the new Ellis Island website at www.ellisislandrecords.org covers over 70% of all passengers arriving in the United States between 1892 and 1924 – some 22 million individuals.

Whether your ancestors moved a few, or a thousand, miles from their place of birth, there are now numerous sources available to trace them, both in their place of origin and in their new home. You may think that you are 'Brummie born and bred', but as you conduct research into your family's history, you will probably find yourself travelling geographically as well as back in time.

A Jewish Doctor at the Court of Queen Elizabeth

Doreen Berger

Officially there was no Jewish presence in England in Tudor times. The small Jewish population had been expelled by Edward I in 1290 and had fled to the Continent. So the Jews were not here. Or were they? It is known very small numbers of Jews resided in England in Tudor times and traded as merchants. Henry VIII consulted with Jewish scholars during negotiations for his divorce from Catherine of Aragon. Queen Elizabeth I consulted with Jewish doctors. Jewish merchants were considered useful by Elizabeth's ministers because of their international connections. It is even thought that The Merchant of Venice may have been inspired by an Elizabethan scandal involving them.

Roderigo or Ruy Lopez, a native of Portugal, settled in England in 1559. He is described in the census of foreigners living in London in 1571 as earning his living as a physician, and was the first house physician at St. Bartholomew's Hospital. During this time he was criticised for not giving enough care to the poor, but was also recommended as skilful in dieting, purging and bleeding, amongst other attributes. He became a member of the College of Physicians and chief physician in the household of the Earl of Leicester. Lopez was further credited with skill in poisoning, no doubt a useful attribute. At one time he lived in Wood Street. He had a house in Holborn called Mount Joy's Inn, given to him, it is said, by a grateful patient, and also rented property belonging to Winchester College. Although known as a Jew, he lived on the surface as a Christian. In 1586 Roderigo became chief physician to the Queen and in 1589 she granted him a monopoly for the importation of aniseed and sumach. It was said at this time that he was one of the best physicians in the court, and had grown in wealth and reputation with the Queen and the highest in the land. He was a linguist and his connections in Spain were considered useful. However, Roderigo had made an enemy - the powerful Earl of Essex, bitter rival of the Earl of Leicester, the patron of Roderigo. This was to prove his undoing.

An agent of the King of Spain was introduced by Roderigo to important personages, including Lord Burghley and his son, Sir Robert Cecil. Don Antonio, pretender to the Portuguese throne, was in London and Roderigo became involved in his affairs. Don Antonio's attendant, De Gama, was arrested at Roderigo's house. Essex accused the good doctor of involvement in a plot against the Queen. It was suggested Lopez had been offered promises of affluent husbands for his daughters. No incriminating evidence was found against him and Elizabeth at first did not believe this story, telling Essex he was a rash and temarious youth to enter into a matter against the poor man which he could not prove. However, torture was used against Don Antonio's attendants and Lopez was eventually imprisoned in the Tower. He was tried at the Guildhall, together with De Gama and others. During the trial Roderigo was described as a perjured and murdering villain, a Jewish doctor, worse than Judas himself. On the 28th February, 1594 he was found guilty and sentenced to death. Sir Robert Cecil commented Lopez had been found guilty with the applause of the world. Where were his aristocratic friends now? The Queen, with her famous procrastination, waited for

three months before signing his death warrant, and on the 7th June Roderigo was taken to the Queen's Bench to plead for mercy. He declared he had never thought to harm the Queen, but a few hours later he was taken to Tyburn and executed by being hanged and quartered, still insisting he loved the Queen as well as he loved Jesus Christ. Was there an irony in this? A statement regarding Roderigo's guilt was immediately made available to the public, written by Francis Bacon. Queen Elizabeth, however, did not deal too harshly with the family. His son, Anthony, was a student at Winchester in 1594, and was granted by the Queen a parsonage of £30 a year for his maintenance at the school.

The following is an extract from the State Papers:
"March 6, 1595. Grant to Sarah, widow of Dr. Lopez, attainted of high treason, and her children, of the right and term of years which the Queen has by attainder, to Mountjoy's Inn and other adjoining tenements in London, which he held by lease from Winchester College; also of the goods and chattels, not exceeding £100, forfeit by the attainder, excepting a jewel set with a diamond and a ruby, sent by some minister of the King of Spain to Dr. Lopez."

Was this jewel a bribe by the King of Spain to rid himself of Don Antonio and Elizabeth? Queen Elizabeth is said to have worn this jewel at her girdle until her death. Did the Queen's leniency, even partiality, towards the family mean she did not believe in the guilt of her Portuguese doctor? It has even been hinted that the Queen felt a personal interest towards her flamboyant doctor.

The execution of Dr. Roderigo Lopez led to the dispersion of the Jewish merchants living in Tudor England, most of whom chose to move to the Jewish community of Amsterdam. Nowadays, it is believed Roderigo was an innocent victim of political intrigue at the Court of Queen Elizabeth I. However, there would be no official Jewish presence in this country until the Re-admittance under Oliver Cromwell in 1656.

Many years later, another Portuguese Jewish doctor proved more fortunate than Dr. Lopez. Fernando Mendes was appointed Physician-in-Ordinary to Queen Catherine of Braganza, Consort of Charles II, attended the King in his last illness and was even a signatory to the certificate of his death. His grandson, Moses Mendes, married the daughter of Rev. Sir Francis Head, and in 1770 his great-grandsons assumed the surname of Head. Famous descendants of this Portuguese doctor include Sir George Head, Assistant Commissary-General and Deputy Knight Marshal, and Sir Francis Bond Head, Bart., PC., Lieutenant-Governor of Upper Canada, both of whom had distinguished careers.

Interesting articles on this Elizabethan scandal can be found in The Jewish World of January, 1880 (newspaper) and The Dictionary of National Biography.

This year of the second Elizabeth is the tenth anniversary of The Jewish Genealogical Society of Great Britain. Membership has risen to over 800 world wide. The Society can be contacted at PO Box 27061, London N2 OGT.
Doreen is award winning author of: The Jewish Victorian: Genealogical Information from the Jewish Newspapers 1871-80. Essential 600 page reference book.
Available from Robert Boyd Publications (600 pages), 260 Colwell Drive, Witney, Oxfordshire OX8 7LW, England. £34.95, postage £4.60 UK, overseas surface mail £6. Order form on www.ort.org/jgsgb/book1.htm

Bringing the past to light

We all know that researching Family and Local History can quickly become an all-consuming passion. Who has not experienced the "thrill of the chase" when long hours of painstaking research turn up gems in the form of documents, certificates, photographs and drawings? Or what about theatre tickets, post cards, stamps and even video recordings? A picture of the past through archival evidence is gradually built up, and the older and more obscure that evidence, the more rewarding it is to uncover it.

However, the very act of bringing objects from the past into present view for handling and display can sadly hasten their degradation. For example, old photographs which have lain untouched for years can quickly start to fade when left out in the harmful Ultra Violet rays of natural light, and regular handling and inspection of old documents and maps can soon cause tearing and breakdown.

Today, many treasured and irreplaceable documents are on materials which are mass-produced but not necessarily durable, and where material is unique one only gets one chance to look after it effectively. The following guidelines give some general pointers to preserving the physical past:

Photographs
By their very nature, photographs are unstable and difficult to preserve for long periods, with particular problems presented by light, temperature, humidity, poor processing, pollution and mishandling. However, a few basic approaches to storage and display can greatly enhance their effective life:

2. Extreme temperature and humidity can cause fading, curling or mould growth. Recommended levels of temperature are 58°-68° F (15°-20° C) , and 30-50% relative humidity, and fluctuations in temperature and humidity of more than 5% should be avoided where possible. Do not store them in attics or basements; cracked image surfaces and mould are among the possible consequences.

3. Most Black & White photographic images are composed of silver particles and therefore prone to degradation through metallic corrosion. The same chemical pollutants that cause silver to tarnish can cause the degradation of photographic images : rubber and leather contact with photographs should be avoided, as they contain harmful sulphur.

4. When it is necessary to write on prints, use pencil along borders or on the reverse, and press lightly to avoid embossing the surface.

5. Do not touch negatives, transparencies or plates other than by the edges, and avoid touching the face of prints. The acids in human skin oils will cause damage : Cotton Gloves are most useful in any case.

6. The best protection for prints and negatives is polyester sleeves or pockets. This material is glass clear, very strong and chemically inert, whereas other plastics such as PVC contain plasticizers which can degrade the image very quickly. Do not use brown kraft paper, glassine, or coloured paper envelopes.

7. Avoid the use of ordinary "magnetic" style albums, and ensure that your album is from a reputable manufacturer and archival in construction. Use Secol V-Mount to mount photos in albums; do not use adhesives.

8. Ensure that outer containers are acid-free. A drop-spine compilation ring-binder unit with clam-shell construction is particularly helpful in keeping out light and pollutants.

9. When framing antique photographs, always use acid-free, lignin-free rag mat board and a window mat to ensure the print does not touch the glass. Use of Ultra Violet filtering glass will be of great benefit. Only archival-quality adhesive tapes should be used for framing.

10. Surface dirt should be removed using a soft brush. More extensive cleaning and repair should be left to a professional conservator since photographs are easily damaged by moisture and solvents.

Printed Materials
Ironically, Centuries ago the problems of archival permanence were less significant, as papers were cotton rather than wood based and inherently much more stable. However, the wood based mass-produced papers which emerged in the 19th Century contained lignin, which can degrade to form acidic compounds which in turn become yellow, brittle and weak. Modern Newspapers use wood-based paper, and after a few weeks in sunlight will visibly start to degrade.

1. The most common cause of damage to paper based material is by far careless handling. Clean white cotton gloves should always be worn, or at least care should be taken to wash hands frequently to reduce salts and oils. Never eat, smoke or drink in the vicinity of archival collections, and use only pencils. Don't use pens, markers, Paper clips, binder clips or post-it notes.

2. When moving a paper or parchment document always support it from below : the safest method is to slide a piece of stiff paper or matboard underneath the material to support it, particularly for brittle paper or parchment. Never lift a piece of paper by its edges, particularly if there are any tears present.

3. The storage of documents within a clear polyester sleeve or pocket provides an ideal method of protection from handling, dirt, dust and tearing, also allowing viewing of both sides of the document. These glass-clear enclosures can be pockets (open 1 side), sleeves (open two parallel sides) or folders (open two adjacent sides), and for extra ease of access or for particularly fragile items Secol Trantec© lock-down sleeves can be opened on three sides and closed with a special flap.

4. The size of polyester sleeve should in general be as close to the overall document size as possible. For smaller items such as postcards or tickets, a larger divided sleeve with individual pockets such as the Secol A-S Filing page system provides a practical solution.

5. Encapsulated documents should be placed into acid free boxes, folders or ring-binders for long term storage. All storage boxes, paper folders and tissue paper should be acid-free, lignin free and have a neutral pH.

6. Severely degraded paper should be stored in *buffered* boxes that contain an alkaline reserve. Alkaline reserve buffers are chemicals that absorb acids that are generated by the degraded paper. Regular inspection and cleaning of boxes and folders will aid in extending the life of collections.

7. Extensive photo-copying of books and documents should be avoided as it can lead to damage in the form of

fading, and regular compression of books in photo-copiers can also break the binding and spine of the book. Documents can be effectively photocopied without removing their polyester sleeve for additional protection.

8. Atmospheric pollution in the form of sulphuric acid, nitric acid, ozone, formaldehyde and others causes fading of dyes and pigments. Air filtration can help eliminate such pollution, but sleeves and boxes can also help keep it at bay. Good housekeeping and regular inspection should also guard against insect infestation in books or documents.

9. In the home, damage should be minimized by avoiding extremes in temperature and humidity. This can be done by ensuring that objects are kept away from heat sources such as heaters, fire places, lights and direct sunlight. Recommended conditions for the storage and display of archival material are 68° F (15°-20° C) , and 30-50% relative humidity.

10. Light, and in particular ultra-violet light, can lead to fading of inks and discoloration. All documents should be stored in light-proof containers and displayed or viewed away from direct sunlight. Coloured inks are far more susceptible to light damage and should be displayed in dim areas, free from bright light sources : media such as black ink can tolerate somewhat higher exposure levels.

Uncovering history, or literally "bringing the past to light" can present preservation problems, in the same way that ancient archaeological sites can remain intact for thousands of years but when uncovered become eroded by air pollution or trampled by visitors. The very act of bringing the past to light can be destructive.

However, providing one is aware of the main potential dangers it can be relatively simple to alleviate them and enjoy the enormous satisfaction of linking the present to the past without endangering its future.

No fixed abode:
sources for ancestors who worked and lived on the move
Sharon Floate
Chairman Romany & Traveller Family History Society

Many people coming new to family history fondly imagine the past as a slow-paced, rural idyll where their forebears spent generations in the same small village.

But as they quickly discover, the reality is that our ancestors were remarkably mobile. Many would be on the move from as young as 14: the age at which it was the convention for most children to start their working lives by leaving home to become apprentices, house or farm servants with other families in other places.

And for some, the very act of being on the road was as natural as drawing breath. These were the people who were nomads by culture - the Gypsies - or whose livelihoods depended on them travelling from place to place to perform their jobs or find customers. Among this number - those often with no permanent place to call home - are included fairground people and circus performers, travelling actors and other entertainers, hawkers, bargees and brushmakers.

Because they often lived on the outskirts of settled society and therefore sometimes also outside the conventions and regulations that governed the majority of the population, ancestors of this kind may often be missing from the conventional sources for family history or may be included in them in a different way. But - fortunately for us - they are also likely to appear in other more specialist sets of records.

The aim of this article is to highlight what and where those specialist records are, as well as suggesting a more focussed approach to familiar family history sources, concentrating particularly on tracing ancestors who worked and lived on the move in Britain in the 19th century.

The sources are presented by record *type* rather than by occupation, as in certain cases the same sources are valid for more than one kind of itinerant. It also has to be considered that there was a certain degree of 'cross-over' between the different occupations - sometimes as a result of marriage - with Gypsies becoming showmen and bargees, showmen moving into the world of the circus or the travelling menagerie and pedlars entertaining with waxworks and puppet shows. So it's always useful to remain aware of the full range of material available in case you find your ancestor changing direction at some point.

Specialist sources
Online sources
There's a growing number of specialist sites on the Internet for those researching itinerant ancestors. Many contain not only useful background reading and links but searchable databases too, such as extracts from newspapers and census returns. Make visits to these your priority and then take advantage of the links they offer to other relevant sites:

Websites
itinerantroots
www.users.globalnet.co.uk/~paulln/index.htm
This site provides information, historical data and links for all kinds of travelling ancestors: actors, Gypsies, circus and fairground people. The site host Paul Newman also runs an e-mailing list that you can subscribe to here.
National Fairground Archive
http://www.shef.ac.uk/uni/projects/nfa
The University of Sheffield is the home of a massive collection relating to the history of British fairgrounds and their people. This site is a useful introduction to it and also provides useful links to other relevant sites, plus extracts from the showmen's newspaper, *World's Fair*.
Gypsy Collections, Liverpool
http://sca.lib.liv.ac.uk/collections/gypsy/intro.htm
This is one of the three principal Gypsy archives in Britain, housed in the Library of the University of Liverpool. The site includes general information about both British and Continental Gypsies, plus pages dedicated to a number of individual families, including photographs.

e-mailing lists
itinerantroots@yahoogroups.com
Subscribe to this list by visiting the itinerantroots Website (see above) and try posting an enquiry on it about your Gypsy, circus, fairground or theatrical ancestor for good results.

THEATRE-UK-L-request@rootsweb.com
For those with theatrical ancestors or an interest in theatre history. Subscribe by sending an e-mail to this address with 'Subscribe' as the subject.

Circus Historical Society of Great Britain
To subscribe visit the Website at:
http://communities.msn.co.uk/CIRCUSHISTORICALSOCIETYOFG REATBRITAIN/_whatsnew.msnw

Family History Societies
Romany & Traveller FHS
This is the Society to join if you have British Gypsy or travelling show people in your family tree. Established in 1994 the R&TFHS now has over 500 members worldwide. An active publications programme has seen the production of specialist research guides, books of census extracts, document transcripts, oral history accounts and reprints of classic Gypsy titles. For membership information, visit the Website or contact The Membership Secretary, 27 Conyers Close, Hersham, Surrey KT14 4NG, UK, enclosing a stamped addressed envelope or 2 IRCs.
http://website.lineone.net/~rtfhs

Romani Association of Australia Incorporated
Founded in 1990, the Association helps people in
Australia with Romany Gypsy ancestry to learn more
about their culture. A key aspect of this is family
history research and the Association has a specialist to
give help and guidance. Contact Ruth MacDonald,
Family History Adviser, 9 Melaleuca Place, Alfords
Point, New South Wales 2234, Australia.

The Society of Brushmakers' Descendants
A specialist society for those with brushmaking
ancestors, traditionally a 'travelling trade'.
Membership information from the Website or from 13
Ashworth Place, Church Langley, Essex CM17 9PU,
UK. www.brushmakers.com

Barge people
As far as the writer is aware, there isn't yet a specialist
family history society for descendants of barge people,
although the creation of one has been in discussion for
some time. At least two individuals in the UK are
compiling databases of barge families and welcome
contributions. They are: John Roberts, 52 St Andrews
Road, Sutton Coldfield, Warwickshire B75 6UH, UK;
and Judy Berry, 5 Hambling Close, Nottingham,
Nottinghamshire NG6 7DX, UK.
judyberry@ukonline.co.uk

Historical Societies
Fairground Association of Great Britain
Information from www.fun-fairs.co.uk or from Chris
Gibson, 157 Field Lane, Horninglow, Burton upon
Trent, Derbyshire DE13 ONJ, UK. (Please enclose a
stamped addressed envelope or 2 IRCs with your
enquiry.)

British Music Hall Society
Information from
:www.musichall.bigwig.net/Homex.html or from the
Society's historian, Max Tyler, 76 Royal Close,
Chichester, West Sussex PO19 2FL, UK. (Please
enclose a stamped addressed envelope or 2 IRCs with
your enquiry.)

The Waxworks Society
For those interested in the history of travelling and
permanent waxworks shows. Information from Paul
Braithwaite, 65 Sandown Road, Brislington,

Bristol BS4 3PL, UK. (Please enclose a stamped
addressed envelope or 2 IRCs with your enquiry.) Or
via the itinerantroots Website, above.

Printed sources
Specialist research guides - Gypsy families
**'On the Gypsy Trail: sources for the family history
of Gypsies'**
by Alan McGowan (published 1998 and available from
the Romany & Traveller Family History Society -
address for publications sales, below).

'My Ancestors were Gypsies'
by Sharon Sillers Floate (published by the Society of
Genealogists, 1999)

Census extracts
The Romany & Traveller Family History Society is
publishing a series of books of extracts from the 1891
census that include Gypsies, travelling
showmen and other itinerants in locations throughout
England and Wales. Three volumes have already
appeared. Visit the Society's Website for details or
write for a publications list with a stamped addressed
envelope or two IRCs to: R&TFHS Publications, 6 St
James Walk, South Chailey,
East Sussex BN8 4BU, UK.

Directories - circus
'The Victorian Arena' Vols 1 and 2
This is the *Who's Who* of 19th century British circus
performers and therefore essential reading for those
with circus ancestors. Available from
the author - John Turner - at: Lingdales Press, 15
Lingdales, Formby,
Liverpool L37 7HA, UK.

Specialist Indexes
Census
The Romany & Traveller Family History Society holds
an index of census returns featuring Gypsies and show
people, searchable on a fee basis. For details contact
Pat White at 61 Springford Gardens, Lordswood,
Southampton, Hampshire SO16 5SW, UK, with a
stamped addressed envelope or two IRCs.

Libraries
These are the UK's principal archive collections for the

'travelling professions'. All are open to family history researchers but most by prior arrangement only. For some a letter of introduction may be necessary.

Fairground History
National Fairground Archive, University Library, Sheffield S10 2TN, UK.

Gypsy History
The Gypsy Collections, Sydney Jones Library, University of Liverpool, PO Box 229, Liverpool L69 3DA, UK.
The Romany Collections, Brotherton Library, University of Leeds, Leeds LS2 9JT, UK.
The Robert Dawson Romany Collection, Rural History Centre, University of Reading, Whiteknights, PO Box 229, Reading, Berkshire RG6 6AG, UK.

Theatre History
The Theatre Museum, 1e Tavistock Street, London WC2E 7PA, UK. (Holds over 1 million theatre playbills and circus posters but unfortunately not name indexed.)
Westminster Reference Library, 35 St Martin's Street, London WC2H 7FP, UK. (Specialist collection of books and newspapers relating to the theatre.)
The Guildhall Library, Aldermanbury, London EC2P 2EJ, UK (Collection of playbills.)

Circus History
The Fenwick Collection, Tyne & Wear Archives Service, Blandford House, Blandford Square, Newcastle-upon-Tyne NE1 4JA, UK.
Circus Friends Association Archives, Mellor House, Primrose Lane, Mellor,
Blackburn, Lancashire BB1 9DN, UK.

Newspapers and Journals
This is a brief summary of the main specialist newspapers and journals written for or relating to the travelling professions. (A more extensive list can be found on the itinerantroots Website, above.) Any references or events relating to your ancestors discovered in these can obviously then be cross-checked in local and regional newspapers.

Gypsy Research
Journal of the Gypsy Lore Society, 1888-1973
The most important of the sources for Gypsy research, the *Journal* first appeared in 1888 and has been published to the present day in five series. Those of greatest value to family historians are the Old Series (1888-1892), New Series (1907-1916) and Third Series (1922-1973), which contain articles, family trees and anecdotes about and from many British Gypsy families. Good runs of the *Journal* can be found at the British Library, the National Libraries of Scotland and Wales, the three University libraries listed under Libraries above, plus a number of major public reference libraries. See also *World's Fair*.

Showmen
World's Fair, 1904-present
This is the weekly newspaper for fairground people and contains valuable biographical information in the form of birth, marriage and death notices and obituaries, provides useful pointers to when and where fairs were held plus 'business' news in the shape of articles and advertisements. Gypsy families who were associated with fairgrounds are often included. Runs of the newspaper can be found at the Newspaper Library, Colindale, London NW9 5HE, UK, and at the National Fairground Archive (see above.)

Music Hall and Theatre Review, 1889-1912
This included a Showman Page in issues before c1910.
The Era, 1838-1939
Although principally for the performing professions, this newspaper also carried a column for showmen and is most useful in the late 19th century before the advent of *World's Fair*.

Acting Profession
The Era, 1838-1939
One of the prime newspapers for performers. The editorial provides reviews and circuit theatre 'calls' that give valuable information on the routes taken by travelling theatre groups. Advertisements can also be a useful tracking device.
The Era Almanac, 1868-1919
This annual digest of *The Era* is useful for finding notices of the deaths and obituaries of performers from the theatre, music hall and circus. In the earlier issues, it also contained a consolidated list of the deaths of performers dating back to the late 18th century.

Circus People
The Era, 1838-1939
This gives good accounts of circus people and performances as well as being an excellent source for circus advertising, particularly before 1900.

Conventional Family History Sources
Census returns
Through the nature of their work, itinerant ancestors were often not living in houses on census night. This fact has a direct impact on whether or not they were likely to be enumerated, and if they were, *where* in the returns they are to be found.

In 1841 and 1851 – for example - enumerators were instructed only to record those found 'not living in houses' by number rather than by name. However, you do sometimes find that they went beyond their brief and recorded itinerants in full: the entries may be crossed through but still legible. In 1861 any people found living in the open air, in tents, caravans or barns should be enumerated at the end of each enumeration district under the heading 'Persons not in houses'. In the censuses from 1871 onwards, they should be enumerated in the street or field where they were found, in sequence with the house-dwellers.

It's always worth scanning through the returns for public houses and lodging houses in locations where there were fairs, theatres and circuses as the showmen and performers sometimes lodged here rather than in their own travelling wagons.

Trade directories
The editorial section that precedes the list of residents and tradespeople for each town in a 19th century trade directory usually also gives details of what pleasure and trading fairs and markets were held there and their dates in the calendar. These events formed an important business opportunity for many itinerants and so knowing when they occurred can give a useful pointer to what weeks or months to look at in other sources: for example, coverage in local newspapers or marriages or baptisms taking place in neighbouring churches.

Poor Law records
Under the provisions of the Settlement Act of 1662

people who arrived in a location without visible means of support (or without having a 'passport' in the shape of a Settlement Certificate) could be subjected to a Settlement Examination and sent back to their last legal parish of settlement by means of a Removal Order. This could be their place of birth, place of marriage to a settled parishioner, apprenticeship, residence in a property with an annual rental value of £10+ or where they had held an official parish role such as churchwarden or overseer of the poor.

As itinerant ancestors were rarely able to offer evidence of most of these, you may find their names included in these Examination and Removal Order documents which are to be found among the Poor Law papers of individual parishes. They can be particularly valuable in that - before the era of the census - they are one of the few means of getting biographical information about ancestors as complete family groups, including names, relationships, ages and birthplaces. These records are generally found in County Record Offices – and in a growing number of counties they have been name-indexed by the Record Office itself or by the local family history society.

Vagrancy records
The Poor Law regulations also had provisions for incarcerating 'rogues and vagabonds' in the local gaol or House of Correction and putting them on trial for vagrancy, usually at Quarter Session courts. Because of their size,

Quarter Session records can be notoriously difficult to plough through unless you have a specific trial date to go for, gained from a newspaper report or gaol/House of Correction registers, for example. However, in counties where the Quarter Session records have been name- or subject- indexed, they are always worth consulting.

Licensing
In the 19th century some 'travelling trades' were regulated by licence. Before 1870, these licences were issued by Quarter Sessions to pedlars (who travelled on foot), hawkers (who travelled by horse) and chimney sweeps - among others. From 1870, this licensing became the responsibility of local police forces. Most of the records relating to the licences are now held in County Record Offices. The information contained in them typically includes name, place of abode, age and date of issue.

Local government records
Fairs, shows and circuses needed permission to set up and perform in each town. This had to be formally sought from the local authority's Street Market and Fairs Committees. So as a way of tracking the route your ancestors took or placing them in a certain location at a certain date, it can be useful to consult the minutes of these Committees. These records are usually to be found in County Record Offices or in the Local Studies collections of major public libraries in the area.

The Phoenix Line

Gabriel Alington

Deep in the Carmarthanshire countryside you come upon a vast transparent tortoise - or so it appears. This massive structure, made up of 1,000 panes of glass, is the Great Glasshouse, the centrepiece of the National Botanic Garden of Wales, first opened to the public in May, 2000. With its numerous climate zones - the temperature of each is computer-controlled to suit certain species of plants and trees - the world's largest single-span greenhouse is state-of-the-art as well as being a botanical treasurehouse. No wonder it draws visitors from round the world.

In a sense it is an echo of another great glasshouse, an earlier phenomenom, which in its day was seen as equally innovative and probably rather more spectacular, for it was built in Hyde Park, in the heart of London, to house the Great Exhibition of 1851.

It was Chrystal Palace. Its designer was Sir Joseph Paxton.

And now, like a pheonix rising from the past, the Great Glasshouse has been sited at Middleton Hall, once the home of another member of the family, Sir William Paxton, who was born sixty years before Sir Joseph.

Strangely, and most appropriately, for Chrystal Palace was destroyed by fire, the coat of arms of the Paxton family features a pheonix rising from the ashes.

Sir William and Sir Joseph were two of the more distinguished Paxtons, a family who can trace their history back beyond the point where records began.

Misleadingly the name Paxton has nothing to do with either the latin word for 'peace', 'pax', or an abbreviated version of 'town', 'ton'. It is Saxon in origin and is almost certainly derived from the tribal name Pacingas. Each syllable has a separate meaning; 'pac', or 'pacc', which identifies the family, is a typically short, sharp, Saxon word similar to many of the single-syllable names found on the Scottish Borders; Hogg, Rigg, Gabb, for example. Following 'pacc' 'in' simply refers to the immediate family, and 'gas' to the descendants. The Pacingas, a branch of the more prominent Bernicians, were a Saxon tribe from the north German plain, who, during the 5th and 6th centuries, after the Roman occupation, set out across the North Sea to discover new farming and hunting grounds. It seems likely they made landfall in the region of Berwick-on-Tweed in the Saxon kingdom of Northumbria, then, pressing on upstream, established their settlement where they found soil that was rich and moist. Naturally this is speculation; no records exist of early Northumbrian settlements. There is however a village of Paxton near Berwick-on-Tweed in what is now the county of Berwickshire.

Colonel Llewellyn Paxton
in retirement at Lavant

There is also a village of Paxton in Huntingdonshire, indeed their are a pair of villages, Great and Little Paxton; they lie in a fertile valley on the east bank of the Ouse between St Neots and Godmanchester. So it may be - and again it's speculation - that at some point in the second half of the first millenium a number of the Pacingas broke away from their Northumbrian kin and made their way south. At a guess they went by sea following the coastline then paddled up river from the Wash in search of favourable land. It is possible that by this time the Pacingas had been converted from their Celtic beliefs to Christianity. This new faith had been gradually spreading throughout Britain during the latter part of the first millenium. Missionaries had arrived from all directions and one of the most notable, Aidan, had founded a monastery on Lindisfarne, the island off the Northumbrian coast, from which missionaries set out to preach and convert. It was here on this holy island, as Lindisfarne became known, that at the end of the 7th century the great St Cuthbert became abbot of the monastery and also the Bishop of Lindisfarne.

And if the Hutingdonshire Pacingas were not already Christian when they moved south, their conversion must have happened within a century or two, certainly during the Saxon age. Evidence for this is the church at Great Paxton, which is indisputedly late Saxon; it is, in fact, one of the largest and finest of its period. With its magnificent arches, its feeling of light and space, Holy Trinity, Great Paxton, can only be compared to certain 10th and 11th century churches on the Continent Research has shown that it was one of the early medieval 'Minster' churches which, before the existance of parishes, had control over a number of surrounding dependant churches.

The earliest reference to the village of Great Paxton is in the Domesday Book, 1086. The first known record of the Paxton family, however, is two centuries later in 1240. It refers to one of the Northumbrian Paxtons, David de Pakestun, who served as a witness to a land claim by the 1st Earl of Dundee. The spelling of Paxton varies, as all spelling did then, and for long afterwards; for example the next mention of the family is of Walter and Andrew, who spell their name de Paxtun; they also acted as witnesses at a deed of sale.

References to de Paxtons, and de Paxtuns, crop up here and there throughout the late 13th century. There was John de Paxtun who, in 1273, refused to contribute a tithe of his benefice to the crusades, then in 1296, Robert de Paxton, who was Prior to the Hospital of St John of Jerusalem in Berwickshire, a more creditable citizen than John perhaps, went to Berwick with his kinsman, Nicol de Paxton to swear fealty to Edward I. Robert's loyalty was rewarded with the gift of lands in Wiltshire but sadly, in 1322, records show he was in trouble for harbouring Adam de Paxton, who, with others had been denounced as rebel and traitor to the English crown. Adam had presumably sworn fealty to the Scottish king, who at the time had fallen out with Edward III.

Being located on the borders between two realms, where, during the Middle Ages the boundaries were a constant matter of dispute was an ongoing problem for the Northumbrian Paxtons, who were often caught in the cross-fire. Nonetheless records show that they managed to grow increasingly prosperous. There were, of course, troubles from time to time, mainly due to the geography. For instance when Berwick surrendered to the Scots, William de Paxtun found his large estate of Aldencrowe, as well as his fishery on the Tweed, seized by the Sheriff. Later a charter was issued by Edward III restoring both the land and the fishery to Lucia, the wife of Roger de Paxton. What relation Roger was to William de Paxton is unclear. And why was the property restored to his wife rather than to him? Chances are we shall never know. Again during the reign of Edward III - the year was 1333 - there is mention of another Roger de Paxton. This time it occurs in Hungtingdonshire and again it sets one wondering. This Roger was a priest, the incumbent of Holy Trinity at the village of Great Paxton and according to the board which lists the priests of the parish, he was excommunicated; the abbreviation 'excom.' is written after his name. Why should this have happened? What had he done? Again, who knows? But it was certainly the case in the Middle Ages that excommunication was pronounced, if not frequently, considerably more often than in later times, and for crimes undeserving of such punishment.

Through the ensuing centuries families of de Paxtons broke away spreading further south; the name occurs frequently in records of the counties of Oxfordshire, Bedfordshire and Buckinghamshire.

In the Civil War between Cromwell and Charles I the Paxtons were Parliamentarians, very firmly so. Indeed a member of the family, James Paxton, is said to have officiatd at the execution of the King. However, while everything went well for James and his kinsmen during the years of the Commonwealth, when the Restoration came James took flight. He at once sailed to Ireland with his family. They settled in Antrim changing their name to Paxon, presumably to avoid detection. It was not enough. Soon the Ulster Stuarts discovered them. Some stuck it out, enduring persecution; their names are recorded on a memorial in the churchyard of the Presbyterian church at Ballycashone in County Down. Others, a branch of the family who had by then become Quakers, perhaps to distance themselves further from Catholicism, decided to leave Ireland, to take ship to the New World and find a better life.

Although from about 1350 for the next two centuries the line is rather tenuous, the Northumbrian Paxtons, the long established clans who had first settled there, continued to thrive, to multiply and grow prosperous. There was, for example, William Paxton who died at Coldingham in 1595. His descendants, for several generations, had numerous sons, all solid, law-abiding citizens; at least there are no records to the contrary. It was during the 18th century that one John Paxton experienced serious trouble. With his partner, Archibald Stewart, John ran a wine business in Edinburgh, an extremely successful business - until 1745, when the Jacobite Rebellion threw life into turmoil. The army of the Pretender marched on Edinburgh, where Archibald Stewart then happened to be Provost. Records show that the defence of the city was poorly organised; there were delays, muddles and inefficiencies - it was said that Archie Stewart had secret sympathy for the Pretender. How big a part John Paxton played in this is not clear. Certainly the wine business was badly disrupted so the following year, John with Archie Stewart, their fortunes still in tact, left the repercussions of the failed Rebellion and moved their business to London. Soon afterwards, however, Archie was arrested for pro-Pretender sympathies and sent to the Tower. Meanwhile John Paxton, who had managed to steer clear of trouble, carried on the business from his newly acquired London house. Number 11 Buckingham Street is a substantial mansion with room for the family as well as the business. As it happened Samuel Pepys.had once lived next door. John Paxton had three sons; Archibald, the eldest, who took on the family business, next John, whose success as a portrait painter won him membership of the Scottish Royal Academy, and lastly William, who, in 1756, at the age of 12, joined the King's Navy. His journal, penned in the finest copperplate, reveals, uncomplainingly, the cramped and spartan conditions he endured for three months on board HMS Devonshire, one of the ships supporting General Wolfe during the seige of Quebec. Tedium was a problem; there was little action; his journal makes note of weather conditions, punishment floggings, the number of lashes adinistered, the arrival on board of consignments of fresh meat - the diet was atrocious. Equally tough was the seven years he served in HMS Thunderor, spent mainly patrolling the Straits of Gibraltar to keep the French out of the Mediterranean

Mary Paxton with her sons Charlie (standing) and Llewellyn. But where is Archie?Probably he has recently died, which is why she, (though still youthful, and with her own hair), is already in mourning

After thirteen years William had had his fill of seatime; he had other ideas. So resigning from the King's Navy and, having pulled a few strings, he acquired both a letter of recommendation and an introduction to Lord Clive. The outcome; William was accepted into the East India Company. He clearly did well, for fourteen years later, at the age of only 31, he was appointed Master of the Mint in Calcutta. In 1785 he decided to relinquish this exalted position and return to England. Perhaps, aged 41, he thought it time to find a wife who would produce an heir. He found Anne Dawney; she was less than half his age. They married the following year and she proceeded to bear him 11 children.. By 1794 it was clear they were going to need a larger house. It was then that William bought Middleton Hall with its surrounding estate, deep in the heart of Carmarthanshire. The house was old and inadequate; the Paxtons wanted something grander and more fashionable. Their highly distinguished architect, S.P.Cockerell, designed them a Palladian mansion. It was extremely grand - possibly rather too much so for his Carmarthanshire neighbours, for William was not popular in Wales. Despite giving a piped water supply to both Carmarthan and Tenby, as well as building a fine bath-house for Tenby, when, he stood as a Whig candidate in the general election of 1803, the response was lukewarm. Even Whig supporters failed to back him and he had to resort to tossing them bucketfuls of silver coins as well as buying quantities of free drinks, in order to win his seat.

It may well have been that the Welsh distrust of 'The

Scottish Kipper', as Sir William was known locally, went deeper than the fact he was a 'foreigner', a rich incomer, who had vaunted his wealth right under their noses. Somehow, perhaps, word had reached Carmarthan that Sir William had once been involved in corruption. It had happened while he was in India and concerned his friendship, an extremely close friendship plus business connections, with the Governor of Bengal, Warren Hastings. Hastings, accused of corruption and irregular dealings, had been called back to England to face impeachment. Hastings' trial was a sensation, a long drawn out affair - it lasted seven years - and though finally he was acquitted, his costs were £70,000 and his reputation never recovered. William Paxton got away with it entirely. In fact, there is no evidence that he was involved. And yet there were rumours, a murmur of gossip that would not go away. The honour of a knighthood the same year as the election must have been, therefore, particularly pleasing. Added to which, after his death in 1824, he was buried in St Martin-in-the Fields. If only he had known. Perhaps he did.

Sir William's 11 sons and daughters, inheriting his wealth, lived comfortably; they were conventional and highly respectable, leading citizen types; for instance one was a general, another a colonel, one became a distinguished doctor as well as an eminent biologist. And, being Victorians, they were patriarchs with large families. In the next generation it was the son of a Miss Paxton, who had married a Wavell, who became one of outstanding figures of his time. Archibald Percival Wavell rose to be Field Marshall, Earl Wavell, who eventually became the penultimate viceroy of India.

It was, however, the Paxton responsible for Chrystal Palace who achieved recognition for the family name. Joseph, born at Woburn, Bedfordshire in 1801, began life as a gardener and, under the patronage of the Duke of Devonshire, whose garden at Chatsworth he landscaped and supervised, he experimented with a new technique for constructing greenhouses using iron and glass. It was this technique he used later to build Chrystal Palace for the Great Exhibition of 1851. Chrystal Palace made Joseph's name. It was a sensation, renowned throughout the world. Even after the fire that reduced it to ashes, its fame lived on.

Recent generations of Paxtons have produced a predominance of daughters but, though the number of males has dwindled, the line has by no means died out. The eldest living Paxton, a sprightly 90 year old who enjoys life to the full, maintains that the family have tenacious genes; they are by nature survivors, she believes.

Five years before Chrystal Palace burned down, on 10th November, 1931, Middleton Hall, William Paxton's fine mansion in Carmarthanshire, was destroyed by fire. And now the Great Glasshouse, the centrepiece of the Welsh Botanic Gardens, has like an echo of Chrsytal Palace, risen in its place.

But then with its connection to the family whose crest is a pheonix rising from the ashes, what else could you expect?

The Picture Postcard

Remember there are two sides to the story

Colin Buck

We live in an age of instant communication. Press a few buttons and we can instantly speak with anyone, virtually anywhere in the world. This is, of course, progress and generally to be welcomed. However, there is a drawback from a social and family historian viewpoint. Once you have passed or received that message it is, of course, gone forever. With the written word there is at least has a chance of the content surviving. Of course letters have always been sent but seldom treasured or retained. But there was one method of communicating that has had a good survival rate. **THE PICTURE POSTCARD.**

The story of postcard development over the past century is an interesting one. Prior to 1902 there were postcards but there were comparatively few of them. Then the Post Office made the decision that was to lead to a huge explosion in postcard sending. They allowed the back of the card to be divided so that as well as the address the card could contain a lengthy message. In the early part of the century telephones were the preserve of the very privileged. Can you imagine now life without the phone? People still needed to make contact as we do today. So they used postcards then as we do the telephone today. Some three million cards a day were going through the mailing system.In many areas there were three collections and deliveries a day and it was possible to rely on same day communication, Nellie wrote to Miss E Hemsley of Tottenham in September 1907 "Look out for a parcel today…". Mabel wrote to Emmie Ivy of East St London by the 12.30 p.m. post of July 22nd 1906 "Could you come tonight about 8pm as I am going back tonight?".

There were no class barriers, from the pauper to the prince, people were busily writing and receiving postcards. The biggest hobby of the day was postcard collecting. Virtually every household had someone with an album collecting cards sent by friends and relatives from all over the United Kingdom and abroad. Many were sent just to add to the collection and contained little by way of a message. Many others however were sent with the purpose of giving information about family matters or impending visits, about illness, deaths, and births. Many were messages of love and show the heartache of separation especially during the Great War when they were used as a vital line of communication between the men at the front and their loved ones at home. As today, everyone going on holiday sent cards to loved ones and friends speaking of the weather, the lodgings and the bracing sea air. The sending of postcards began to decline around 1918 when the postal cost was doubled to one penny.

Where have all the old cards gone?
Well, some families are lucky and the collections have been passed down and are now valued for their family connections. But most disappeared.
In the mid 1940s a new type of postcard collector began to appear. These collectors became interested in the picture content of the 'old' cards and with this many families sold off the cards collected years before by their ancestors. Thus millions of cards have fallen into the hands of collectors in the past fifty years. Many are now very valuable for the picture content but many are of little monetary value. It is these cards that make up the POSTCARD INDEX. They are of great value but probably only a family historian would appreciate the joy of possessing something once "in the hands" of their ancestors so many years ago. Many of us at fairs have searched through the postcard dealers' boxes for pictures of streets, churches, villages and the like of some relevance to our own family history. Some are lucky and for a "small" fee we can add something to the bare bones

of our research. I am sure many of us have also read the other side of the card in the often forlorn hope that the recipient may be someone connected to us.

If you have a feeling for both social and family history you will share my feelings when reading information. which is a small snapshot of a moment in the lives of those families, the times they lived in and the effect the events of the day were having on them. The information is interesting and indeed fascinating BUT can you imagine how I, and perhaps you, would feel if the recipients were OUR family. Surely out there is someone who would cherish this information for what it is, a prized piece of family history. From such thoughts THE POSTCARD INDEX was born.

At the time of writing I have 80,000 cards covering 60,000 names. Cards have been indexed by the recipient's name and address at the rate of 1,000 a month for the past 5 years and the Index continues to increase at that rate. Many of them have short simple messages, indeed some only have a signature and are obviously sent to add to the collection. But nevertheless they are family history, they were in the hands of our ancestors regardless of content.

What information is on the back of the cards.
Britains have always been fascinated by the weather. A large percentage of the cards actually mention the weather somewhere in the text. (I probably know what the weather was like on most days between 1900 and 1950) Fortunately they talk of other things as well. Often the tittle tattle of family activity either at home or on holiday. George wrote to Alf Dredge of Shepherds Bush in July 1907 "….Sorry I shall not be down on Sunday, I'm taking the wife to Ryde….". (Did he bring her back I wonder.) Someone's health features on many cards. Lily wrote to Ethel Humphrys of Streatham in 1903 "…how is your cold and have you any chilblains?, if so let me know Mrs Howe has some lotion and I will bring some bottles with me". F Gay wrote to Mrs Howard of Acocks Green in 1906 "...You will be glad when father's affairs are all settled, so sorry you are so poorly, I am no worse than when I last saw you and Francis has had a bad time with her face, its not right yet and she has been to the doctor and the dentist...". Someone sent a card to Eileen Gunn of Seymour Street London in 1914 "...I am waiting impatiently for you my cherie as it is a month since I heard from you, I am in bed since Monday with an attack of appendicitis!!...". Bad news was common. Edith wrote to Lizzie Fenwick at Kirkman Hall Knaresboro in November 1911 "...to tell you Mrs Foxton is dead, they found her in bed, my auntie is coming to visit soon and Mrs Turnbull was buried on Thursday...". Also many mysteries, Fred Jackson of New Barnett was sent a

card by his mother c1910 "…It is rather a bad job you cannot find a girl, I cannot wonder at it if you pinch them...". An appeal from the heart from Buster to Mr Garton of manor Park in June 1923 "….Please ask E not to cook any tapioca or rhubarb for me...". Miss Nelly Kemp of Diamond Cottage Ripe SO was in bother in April 1906 when brother George wrote "…now you are away from school you must work and help mother and leave off all your little fits of temper and listen to what mother tells you. I am looking for a great improvement when I next come home". Some cards have mysterious messages that we will probably never know the answer to. Charlie wrote to Mrs A Coyne of Hadley Wood in 1925 "Do not worry I will take NO risks, father is A1 and up to now all going swimmingly, no eggs for lunch!..". A rather worried Johnny wrote to Sgt Cranston of Eccles in 1906 "My dear Sgt Please don't for goodness sake tell Dorothy what happened at the school last night. You saw the worst, nothing passed between us after leaving the schoolroom and the hand shake wasn't even cordial…". What a relief for K in 1948 when she wrote to Jon Whatson at Plendennis Hotel Buxton "The emeralds have been found, I had taken the green bobble fringe from the velvet cloth on the mantlepiece of the servants hall and put it round the hem of my petticoat. However the necklace must have slipped down and lodged there and our new third chaffeur found it , quite by chance! when I asked him to stop the car in the lower woods yesterday but that's another story. I gave him a big reward! I must get Percy to promote him to 2nd chaffeur…".

The "Passed by Censor" stamp appears on many of the cards. Goodness knows how many cards of France were sent home in the Great War. Because of the censor they tend to all be upbeat and really just sent with a few word to the effect that all was well and hoping family are well. From Will Poole to his parents at the Tailors shop in St James Barton in 1915 "My dear dad and ma, I have arrived and quite safe so far, hope you are both well". From 'Dearest wife Olive' to Private 22790 George J Brown "I saw this card in Lunns and had to buy it as I hope the words will give you comfort…". From Loving cousin Jack, Reserve Battalion Boscombe to Edith Clarke Stoke Holy Cross in March 1918 "….As you can see I am at Boscombe but expect to be sent to France shortly…". I do sit and wonder how many of the soldiers on my cards survived the conflict, I wish I had time to find out! Many cards talk of airships, of motor cars and watching aeroplanes flying over, all new and then worthy of mention on a postcard. Cycling was clearly very popular. One of

many like ones, Reg to Miss D Gibson of Milton in 1914 "…Came today from Chester by cycle, 68 miles so am rather fagged, there are 6,000 of us Manchester Terriers here…". Many cards were used for business matters . From Maggie Wildash to Mrs Cottee of Tottenham in 1907 "Dear Madam shall not be down for any eggs this week but will call next Tuesday". A minor complaint from Alice May Heeley to her mother in Sheffield in 1907 "… received cake this morning, it was very nice but rather underdone in the middle anyway I can't eat cake as I have had indegestion for a fortnight…".

Of the 2,500 so far "housed" with interested parties I have had many letters of appreciation but only one, I know of so far, of a 'live' interest is one where it was discovered that the card was sent to a small boy nearly 70 years ago who is still with us. He was apparently 'astounded' to see the card again after so many years.

Some senders went to extraordinary lengths to keep the content private. I have messages written in mathematical formula, symbols clearly made up by the writer and presumambly only decipherable by the receiver, morse code, Egyptian hieroglyphics (I think). Mirror image writing was common as was shorthand. Some of the writing is so bad it takes an age to decipher (too long for the postman to read perhaps). A lot of cards are actually photographs of people. It was common practice to be sent a photo of the sender and/or family with the back in the form of a postcard with a message often indicating that the photo is of the sender "….you'll recognise this lady I hope…". Whilst it will not always be possible to identify the people on the photograph anyone researching the family who received it may have enough clues to have a chance of identification. I have one card with a lovely photograph of a family group. it was sent by Pollie (I suspect the lady in the photo) to Mrs Alice Mellor of Heaton Norris Stockport. This card was sent on the 6th August 1914 and is a good example of events affecting people, "Dear Alice. It is very bad about the war. I hope it will soon be over, it seems to upset everything. I expect my brother is amongst it somewhere, Love Pollie".

Many of the one name groups and societies are delighted by my project. It allows them to fit many of the cards receivers into their trees by reference to the addresses. Often the messages talk of third parties which do make sense to the people who have done much research into that family and associates.

What a rich source of trivia from a bygone age are contained in the collection, (80,000 at time of writing) but I don't want them. They should all belong to someone somewhere who would treasure them as a small part of their family history. All I have to do is find them!!!!

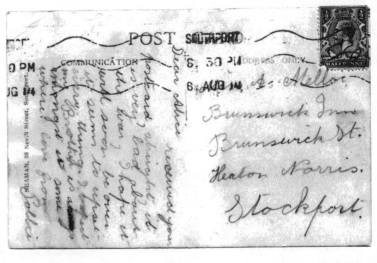

The Public Record Office

John Wood
Public Services Development Team

The Public Record Office is the national archive of England, Wales and the United Kingdom. The PRO, as it is commonly known, is based at Kew. It houses one of the most definitive archive collections in the world representing the events and people of the past thousand years. The 100 miles of records are stored at Kew were created in the course of government and dispensing of justice. Although the PRO is recognised as a major international research institution in fact around 80% of the visitors use the records for family or local history research. Recently, the PRO has:

Made available ³/₄ of a million Merchant seamen's records
Increased the number of WW1 soldiers records available to over 3.5m
Completed the Navy and RAF (RFC) personnel records for WW1
Enlarged the range of services to callers via the PRO contact centre
Expanded the modern Education and Visitor Centre featuring icons from British History including the Domesday Book and Magna Carta
Established the onsite and online bookshop as a major attraction for all
Launched 'Ancestors' a new magazine for today's family historian
Brought in an integrated document ordering and tracking system

The gateway to the PRO is the website at www.pro.gov.uk where you will find
The complete PRO catalogue online including a keyword search facility
Hundreds of information leaflets on the PRO's holdings
Step by step guide to researching at the PRO
Advance document ordering details
Online bookshop and ordering facility
Award winning interactive education and museum galleries.
Details of all the PRO services and events.

Opening hours
The PRO is open 6 days a week throughout the year except bank and public holiday weekends and the annual stocktaking week - usually in December. Up to date details are on the website or can be checked through the Contact centre. Late night openings are Tuesdays and Thursdays. It is always advisable to call the PRO contact centre before visiting for the latest information on opening times, records availability, travel conditions and events.

Transport and Access
The PRO is 200 yards level walk from Kew Gardens station, served by the District underground line and the Silverlink Metro rail service. Kew Bridge station is half a mile away. Local bus services run nearby. Road access to the motorway system is good. Free parking is available on site. Easy access facilities for those with disabilities, including a lift to all floors.

Services and facilities for visitors
Admission is free and, other than for coach parties and large groups, **no** advance booking is required. Researchers need to obtain a readers ticket at Reception

to gain admission to the reading rooms. The website has full details on the registration process or call the contact centre for individual information. All new readers are given an orientation tour to familiarise newcomers with PRO's vast range of research facilities.

The most popular records have made available in the self-service Microfilm Reading room There are always staff on hand to help you make the most of your research and to advise on the different avenues that you can follow.

The ground floor and public access areas are open to all and contain::
An extensive modern bookshop
The Museum and visitor centre featuring important landmarks in world history
Comprehensive restaurant facilities
Cyber café.

Coach parties and groups
Coach parties are welcome to visit the PRO. As space is limited for coaches all parties **must** be pre-booked. Bookings are taken up to 18 months in advance. All coach parties receive a dedicated orientation tour for newcomers in their party and are provided with an advance reader ticket registration scheme. To enquire about available dates and reserve your coach group booking telephone the contact centre or use the email facility listed below. There is no access to the site for coaches that have not pre - booked.

Essential contacts and information
The Public Record Office
Ruskin Avenue, Kew, Richmond, Surrey TW9 4DU

Website: www.pro.gov.uk
Contact centre:
Tel (020) 8392 5200   Fax: (020) 8392 5286
Email: enquiry@pro.gov.uk
Coach party bookings: Tel: (020) 8392 5200
Or email: coaches@pro.gov.uk
Events: Tel: (020) 8392 5202
Publications or bookshop enquiries:
Tel: (020) 8392 5271

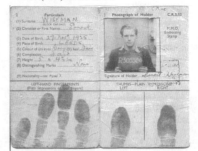

Ernie Wise's
Seamens Ticket
- one of
³/₄ million
recently made
available in
Record Series
BT372

Public Record Office Census Online

Our vision at the Public Record Office is to make our services and records available electronically on-site and remotely via the Internet. The result will be widely available services both in the UK and world-wide. A key project for achieving our vision was the digitization of the 1901 Census returns for England and Wales. From January 2002 you can access this key resource over the Internet at www.census.pro.gov.uk.

The census returns are our most popular historical records, being a key source for those researching their family trees, local areas or the history of a house. They also provide the raw data for local, social and economic historians.

Why are we doing this?
If you want to look at census returns for the nineteenth century you currently have two options. The first is to visit your local record office or library which usually house the returns for the locality. The second is to travel to the Family Records Centre in London which houses the census returns for England and Wales from 1841 to 1891.

However, many users find it expensive to travel to the south-east and many are simply unable to get to our reading rooms because of domestic or work commitments. We also feel that as we are the National Archive for England and Wales, we have a duty to serve all citizens and we should make our services more widely available. We see the Internet as an ideal medium to meet the needs of our ever-growing group of users, and more and more researchers are using the Internet to access information to further their research.

Exciting new plans
Throughout the 1901 Census Online Project we were asked about our plans for digitising the earlier censuses and making them available over the Internet. The 1901 Census Project has paved the way for digitising the earlier censuses and we decided to go forward with the 1881 and 1891 censuses even before the 1901 was released. Our aim is to have both the 1881 and 1891 censuses available over the Internet by the end of 2002.

How are we achieving this?
1901 Census Online
The 1901 Census for England and Wales was taken on 31 March 1901. The population at the time was over 32 million and these 32 million entries will be available on-line for the very first time from the first working day of January 2002. Never before will it have been so easy to learn of those who lived in Edwardian times; to understand their work; to trace the homes they lived in and to speculate on the lives they led. In order to make this happen there are many people working busily behind the scenes on the three elements of the digitisation project. Firstly we have had to create electronic images of the census returns themselves. The images have been scanned from the archival microfilm copy of the returns and a high quality digitized image produced.
Secondly, we have created a database of information transcribed from the census returns. This will allow us to provide you with a means of accessing and navigating the data more flexibly and readily than by traditional means. You will be able to conduct a number of searches and, having found an individual, you can go directly to the images of the returns.
Thirdly the database was linked to the digital images and

the whole service was put on the Internet.

1891 Census Online
Work began on scanning the 1891 returns in the summer of 2001 and the first county (London) should be available in the Spring of 2002. Other counties will soon follow (probably those with large cities as a first priority). Initially users will be able to access the 1891 returns through a basic name index. Once all the counties are complete the index will be enhanced with more searchable fields.

1881 Census Online
Work began on scanning the 1881 returns in the summer of 2001 and these will be linked to the GSU (Genealogical Society of Utah) database. The aim is to have the full 1881 index, transcription and original images all available over the Internet by the end of 2002.

A wonderful resource for the future
The Public Record Office is pleased at the progress of Census Online and we feel we are now offering a significant service to family historians and many other researchers. Census Online is still only part of our (*PRO's Nation's Memory*) programme to make available many other record series and services over the Internet.

Using the 1901 Online Census
To provide you with the most cost-effective method of utilising these census returns we have endeavoured to ensure that all basic searches are free and you will be able to conduct a number of different types of searches; for example by name, place, address, institution or vessel. We expect that most of you will wish to search by name and a typical name search in the 1901 online service will work as follows: You can undertake a basic search using name (forenames and surnames), place and age. If a surname is double barrelled you will need to search on each element. For example for Lloyd-Gibson you would search on 'Lloyd' and 'Gibson' and if you are unsure of the age of the person you wish to locate you will be able to input a range of years. A feature of this basic search will be:

Wildcards for single or multiple characters. For example 'BR*N' which would enable you to locate all those names beginning with BR and ending in N with any combination of letters in between. Results of this search would include names such as Brown, Braun and Broughton.

If you find that your basic search results in too many returns, then you can undertake an advanced search which enables you to use a variety of other search fields with which to refine your search strategy. This is particularly useful if you are searching for a popular surname which may result in a large number of returns. Features on the advance search will include:

Soundex match which enables you to identify names with similar phonetics, for example Brown and Browne. Synonyms and abbreviations; that is where if you provide a full forename the system will return matching synonyms and abbreviations. For example, a search for John will also return references to Jon, Jack and Jno. You will also be able to search on forename only (an important facility for those looking for female ancestors without knowing their maiden name).

Once you have completed your search and found the individual you require, you have two options:

Firstly you can view a digital image of the census return. The image will be a complete page from the original enumeration book which will typically include more than one household and all the residents within. This image will cost 75p. Once you have bought the image you can save it to your own system and/or print out a copy. If you do not have printing facilities at home you will be able to place an order online and a copy will be posted to you. Secondly you can view transcribed details from the census returns relating to an individual. This will cost 50p. If you wish to view the details of all those resident in the same household you can do this for an extra 50p.

Methods of payment
We expect that most of you will wish to purchase your digital images or transcripts by credit card and we are able to accept Visa, MasterCard, American Express and Debit Cards (Switch/Delta). Unfortunately we will not be able to accept Diners Club cards. If you do not wish to use a credit card you will be able to buy vouchers to use the 1901 Census service (in units of £5, £10 and £50). Full details of the ways to pay are on the census website.

Users have a choice
We will provide free access to a set of the 1901 returns on microfiche along with the standard finding aids in our reading rooms at Kew (on a similar basis to our other microform records). In addition, many local record offices and libraries have bought microform copies of the 1901 returns for their own areas.

Consultation and communication
We have kept in regular contact with those interested in our work throughout the 1901 Census Online project and will continue to do so as the next censuses are underway. If you have access to the Internet you can visit our census web site at <www.census.pro.gov.uk> for regular updates on Census Online.

We have also established a special panel to advise us on the development of Census Online. The following organisations are represented: Federation of Family History Societies; Society of Genealogists; Guild of One-Name Studies; Association of Genealogists and Record Agents; British Association for Local History; University of Essex Minutes of the meetings of this Advisory Panel are posted on the website and displayed on the 1901 notice board at the FRC.

Future Events
Members of the 1901 Team will be attending a range of events to promote Census Online and will include some of the larger genealogical fairs Keep an eye on the website for up-to-date details.

Regular information
Regular information is available on the census web site <www.census.pro.gov.uk>. If you wish to speak to someone about Census Online please telephone: 020 8392 5200.

The
Family Records
Centre

Family Records Centre

1 Myddelton Street, London, EC1R 1UW

www.familyrecords.gov.uk

A service provided by The Public Record Office &
The Office for National Statistics (General Register Office)

The Family Records Centre provides access to the following:

Ground Floor
Indexes of births, marriages and deaths in England and Wales from 1837
Indexes of legal adoptions in England and Wales from 1927
Indexes of births, marriages and deaths of some British citizens abroad from the late 18th century, including deaths in the two World Wars
Certificates can be purchased of any entry in the above. If you need a certificate but cannot visit the Family Records Centre in person, you can place an order by post, fax or telephone. Please ring 0870 243 7788 for further information and details of fees.

First Floor
Census returns for England and Wales (1841-1891)
Wills and administrations from the PCC up to 1858
Death Duty registers (1796-1858) and indexes (1796-1903)
Records of nonconformist births, baptisms and burials (mainly pre-1837) and marriages (mainly pre-1754)
Miscellaneous foreign returns of births, deaths and marriages (1627-1960)
These records are seen on microfilm

From January 2002: online access to the 1901 census returns for England and Wales

The Family Records Centre also offers the following services:
Bookshop and information point, selling publications on family history
Advice on family and local history research
Family history reference area, including books and maps
FamilySearch including the International Genealogical Index (IGI)
On-line indexes to Scottish registration and census records via Scot Link
Self-service or staffed photocopying service for census and wills
Regular users' consultations
Refreshment area with vending machines
Good facilities for customers with disabilities
Baby changing room

Contact Details
Births, Marriages, Deaths, Adoptions and Overseas enquiries:
Telephone: 0870 243 7788 Fax: 01704 550013

E-mail: certificate.services@ons.gov.uk
Census and general enquiries
Telephone: 0208 392 5300 Fax: 0208392 5307
E-mail: enquiry@pro.gov.uk
Minicom: 020 8392 9198

Planning Your Visit
Opening Hours
Monday 9:00 am - 5:00 pm Tuesday 10:00 am - 7:00 pm Wednesday 9:00 am - 5:00 pm Thursday * 9:00 am - 7:00 pm Friday 9:00 am - 5:00 pm Saturday 9:30 am - 5:00 pm * On Thursday mornings the tills on the ground floor do not open until 10:00 am
The Centre is closed on Sundays, Public and Bank Holidays
Please check closure dates for Easter and Christmas (020 8392 5300)
There is no need to book.

Group Visits
You are welcome to bring a group/coach party to the FRC at any time during our normal opening hours. However, we would advise you to plan your visits to avoid our busiest times - e.g. school holidays (particularly half-term weeks). We also tend to be busy on Tuesdays, Thursdays and Saturdays. On our busy days the lockers are often all in use so try to bring no more than you need for your research. Please let us know if you are planning to bring a large group to the FRC. We can then publicise this information for the benefit of other users.

How to get here
By rail
Angel – Northern Line (City Branch)
Farringdon – Hammersmith and City, Metropolitan, Circle Lines and Thameslink
King's Cross – Victoria, Northern, Piccadilly, Circle, Metropolitan, Hammersmith and City Lines and mainline services
By bus 19, 38 and 341 along Rosebery Avenue
63 along Farringdon Road
By Car There are NCP car parks in Bowling Green Lane (off Farringdon Road) and Skinner Street, both of which are within easy walking distance of the Centre. There is limited Pay & Display parking in the surrounding streets. **There is reserved parking for visitors with disabilities at the Centre, but spaces must be booked in advance. Please ring 020 7533 6436 before you visit.**

Census Returns

A Census has been taken every 10 years since 1801 except in 1941 during the Second World War. The census returns for 1801, 1811, 1821, 1831 were not preserved. However there are some areas where returns for these years have been found. The first census that is useful to researchers is the one taken in 1841.
The Census returns were taken on:

1841	7th June 1841	1851	30th March 1851	1861	7th April 1861
1871	2nd April 1871	1881	3rd April 1881	1891	5th April 1891

These census returns can be consulted. They were subject to public closure for 100 years because of the sensitive personal information they contained. At the present time the 1901 census is subject to that closure until 2nd January 2002.

Emily of the short Petticoat..

Anne Batchelor

Have you ever looked at school log-books? They can be a wonderful window into the past.

JULY 4 1870
" An indecent note was passed through the curtain from the boys school to Mary Ann Wilson during the dinner-hour. Several children read it and gave it to me when I came. I talked to all the children concerned in it. I have forbidden Mary Ann Wilson to have her dinner at school again, as she is constantly getting into mischief."

Poor Mary Ann What about the blessed boy who <u>wrote</u> the note? And what would an indecent note say in 1870? "Show us your ankles, Mary Ann!" What a gift for any researcher of the Wilson family of Rickmansworth.

It was in these same log - books of St. Mary's that Rickmansworth's local historian, Wilf Broughton, came across Mary Emily Batchelor. Knowing of my interest in the Rickmansworth Batchelors of 1690, he wondered whether Emily was a later one of mine. He picked out more entries about her, including this clash with her headmistress, Martha Smith, in July 1871 -"I told Emily Batchelor that I disliked to see her dress festooned over a short petticoat as she was wearing it and told her to let it down. She came this morning with it in the same style and on being told again to let it down she answered very impertinently and for some time refused to do so. I reasoned with her about the impropriety of her conduct and told her that I should expect an apology. This she refused to give and was very disrespectful in her manner."

Emily continued to get into trouble at school, for "dressing up too much", "walking about the town in such a manner as to cause remarks to be made about her", as well as her behaviour in the choir and wildness of hair! When she became a pupil teacher at St. Mary's she was told to wear a hat "more becoming a school - teacher." Did she, I wonder, wear one of those exhuberant creations of feathers and flowers so loved by ladies of those days? I wouldn't be surprised!

Emily Batchelor's Schoolhouse - Great Gaddesden

Wilf followed her progress, via a scholarship, to Hockerill Teacher Training College and thence to the village school at Great Gaddesden, Herts., where she eventually became Headmistress. In July, 1882, she wrote in the log-book of that school, "Today I sent in my resignation." She was only thirty years old. Rather early for retirement! Wilf thought I might like to take up the challenge and try to find out why she left and what became of her. He knows my love of a good mystery. I do so enjoy playing Miss Marple.

The first step was simple enough - look for her on a census return. I went for 1871, when I knew she was teaching at Great Gaddesden. There, on the census was the schoolhouse - empty! "Miss Batchelor temporarily absent", wrote the enumerator. Blow! Where could she be? Perhaps it was the Easter holiday and she had gone home to Rickmansworth to visit her parents? Bingo! There she was, in Rickmansworth High Street, with her father, John Batchelor, mother Maria and brother John Joseph.

Emily was aged eighteen, "a teacher in a National School," so I was able to calculate her birth year and obtain her birth certificate for 23 July, 1852. So far, so good. Now for the records of Hockerill College, Bishop Stortford, where she had trained as a teacher. I heard that they were at Hertford Record Office, so being a cautious researcher I rang up to check. I was assured that they had received the records when the college closed, so off I went to Hertford to see them.

That sounds so easy. What it entailed was - getting up at 4a.m. for a taxi at 5 a.m., to catch a coach to London at 6.a.m , to connect with a train to Hertford at 11.a.m., which brought me to Hertford in the early afternoon. "Oh yes," said the archivist, "We do have the Hockerill records, boxes and boxes of them, but we have not had time to sort and classify them, so I'm afraid they are not available yet!"

She must have seen my bottom lip trembling as I thought of that 4a.m. start, so she added hastily that there was a box of unsorted photographs which I could see. Imagine my delight when

"Miss Emma" (Ethel Mary) Flint in her first teaching post Cannock Grammar School (seated left)

I found a group picture taken in 1873 - the year my Emily was there, in her second year.

I studied the faces of the young ladies, trying to spot one who looked as though she might be the extrovert Emily. I did notice one young girl with a pert expression , rather like the young Elizabeth Taylor, but I had no way of knowing whether this was, indeed, Emily Batchelor. How frustrating! Never mind, on with the hunt for the rest of her story.

I felt that I wanted to visit the school at Great Gaddesden where she became Headmistress, so I wrote to the present Head, explaining my interest in the school and asking permission to visit. I was welcomed with open arms because, the Head told me, she had been teaching the children maypole dancing and they needed a special visitor to dance for. So I arrived at the gate of Emily's school, in the pretty village of Great Gaddesden. I noticed the path up to the church, where she would have taken her children to services, and the beautiful brick and flint house beside the school where she had lived. A magic moment!

The children were gathered in the hall of the tiny village school, which was Emily's original classroom. I explained the reason for my visit, telling the children that my name was Miss Batchelor and I was a teacher, and that in this very hall, over a hundred years ago, another Miss Batchelor had taught the children of Great Gaddesden. Having studied the log-books of this school, written in Emily's own hand, I was able to tell them the names of some of the children she had taught. I mentioned one family with the unusual name of Ginger. "Please Miss," said a tiny girl on the front row, "My name is Mary Ginger!" How lovely to have found a living link with my Emily.

I was still puzzling over Emily's reason for leaving this little school at such an early age. She had her own school, excellent reports from the school inspectors, a lovely house in beautiful surroundings - why ever did she leave? Isn't that the sort of question which makes family historians tear out their hair? We can become quite skilled in finding the when? and where? of our family stories, but it is the why? which always frustrates us.

I decided to consult the St. Catherine's Indexes to see whether they could help me. In her Great Gaddesden log-book for 1882, Emily quite often wrote, "The assistant opened the school. I went to the doctor." Perhaps she was very ill and died soon after? So I spent fruitless weeks trawling through the index of deaths No Emily Batchelor died within the next few years. Then I wondered, could the headstrong young woman be suffering from morning sickness? If she were still wearing her short petticoats and unsuitable hats, perhaps she had got "into trouble"? No, there was no baby Batchelor born in her area in the next nine months, so I apologised to her.

That only left marriage. I had discovered, in conversation with a very old lady, that on marriage ladies used to have to leave teaching. I wound my way through the St. Catherine's index of marriages (- no wonder I have problems with the tendons of my wrist!) and found only one Mary Emily Batchelor getting married, just one month after she left Great Gaddesden. But was it my Emily? Sometimes, in this game, you just have to gamble your money on an unseen certificate, so I did just that.

The Flint Home Walsall

Back it came - "Mary Emily Batchelor, aged 27 (she was 30) Jesse Flint, an organist, aged 27 (he was 25!)

They were married at Camberwell, Surrey, a long way from Great Gaddesden and from her family home in Rickmansworth, where I had expected her to marry. The bridegroom lived in Woodhouse Eaves, Leicestershire. I needed proof that this was indeed my Emily. It was there in the names of the witnesses - John Joseph Batchelor (her brother mentioned in the 1871 census) and Maria (either her mother or her sister, both of whom had that name.)

Now I got a touch of the Catherine Cooksons, imagining Jesse playing the organ at the church, seeing the bright-faced young schoolteacher bringing her pupils into church. Their eyes meet in his organ's rear view mirror. Love at first sight". Let me take you away from all this!" Perhaps it was something like that. Certainly she must have loved Jesse to leave everything for him. They settled in Woodhouse Eaves, where their only child, Ethel Mary Flint, was born.

Then they disappeared completely. No sign of them anywhere. Anyone with any sense would give up and end the story there, but of course family historians don't have any sense, do they? So I batted on and found nothing at all for months. Perhaps they had volunteered for the mission field and were now in India or Africa!

Then one wonderful day, when I was taking my family history class on a visit to the Society of Genealogists in London, I had the breakthrough I needed. On a shelf marked "MUSICIANS" I found the annual report of the Royal College of Organists dated 1922-3. Too late for Jesse, I thought, but I opened it up and had a quick look. To my delight it listed Fellows and Associates of the college long before 1922. I could hardly believe my luck when I found, on a list of Associates for 1890, "FLINT, J."

An eager letter to the Royal College brought a wonderfully detailed reply which gave me details of

Jesse's membership. Not only that but it gave me no fewer than nine addresses at which Jesse and my Emily had lived between 1883 and 1904. They had lived in Leicestershire, Surrey and Hertfordshire before finally settling in Walsall, West Midlands. According to their records, Jesse held an appointment at the Girls' High School, Walsall. Now the hunt was up.

Off went one of my famous grovelling letters to the High School. "Dear Sir or Madam," I wrote, "I know you must be awfully busy, and letters like mine must be a great nuisance, but I would be so very grateful if you could possibly find the time, when you are not too busy-" Eagerly I awaited their reply. My heart sank when they denied all knowledge of Jesse. "However," they wrote, "there was a famous Miss Emma Flint (whose real name was Ethel Mary Flint) who was mayor of Walsall-"

Jesse and Emily's daughter was called Ethel Mary, so off went a grovelling letter to Walsall Town Hall, asking for more information on their "Miss Emma." They sent me a bundle of newspaper cuttings about her, including her obituary, for she had died in January, 1968 at the age of 84. Exactly the right age for Emily's daughter but I needed more proof than this.

Her obituary revealed an amazingly talented and eccentric woman. She was a teacher and later became principal of Lichfield College of Art. As a watercolour artist herself, she fought Walsall Council for fifty years for an Art Gallery. Many of her old pupils remembered her with affection and gratitude, not unmixed with awe! This remarkable woman became a Town Councillor at the age of 67 and Mayor of Walsall when she was 82. She was also the first woman in Walsall to own a motorbike!

I uncovered such a lot of information about "Miss Emma" that I became quite fond of her. But the object of my research was to discover whether she was the daughter of Emily of the short petticoat. I felt it in my bones she was, but that was not enough.

When stuck at the genealogical "brick wall" my advice is

EMMA BRINGS EMILY HOME !

always to go back and reread your notes. Her newspaper obituary gave her place of burial - Ryecroft Cemetery. Could she perhaps be in a family grave? A grovelling letter to Mr. Billings, Principal Cemeteries and Crematoria Officer, produced a wonderful list of grave occupants
Grave no. 35-3-714
Jesse Flint aged 61yrs. buried on 11 July 1918
Mary Emily Flint aged 80yrs. buried on 1 Sept. 1932

Ethel Mary Flint aged 84 yrs. buried on 25 January 1968
I wanted to hang out the flags! She was buried with her parents, Jesse and Emily of the short petticoat!

Just to confirm her relationship with my Emily, I found "Miss Emma" on a list of exhibitors at the Royal Academy where she gives her name as Ethel Mary Batchelor-Flint! What a buzz that gave me. Now most people would have accepted this as the end of the story, but not me. I was greedy for more.

"Wonder what I can discover about Jesse's death?" I pondered. "Perhaps there was something in the local newspaper?" There was indeed, a fine obituary to my church organist. He had been taken ill at church on Sunday evening, carried home and died shortly afterwards.

The obituary described him as - of modest, retiring, unselfish nature" and said that he endeared himself to a wide circle of friends. No wonder Emily loved him and left her little village school for him. It also told me that he was a composer of hymn tunes. A friend of mine found three of his tunes, including one called "Walsall", in a book at the bottom of her piano-stool!
He was often guest organist at leading London churches and (here was another goodie for me) he was a member of Wednesbury Lodge of Freemasons. A grovelling letter to Freemasons' Hall in London produced a list of offices held by Jesse. Beware - there is now a £30 research charge to non-members. Jesse reached the impressive rank of Past Provincial Grand Deacon the year before his death.

Now for Emily. The cemetery records gave me her death date, so I wrote at once to Walsall Register Office for her death certificate. I couldn't believe it when my cheque was returned. Her death had not been registered in Walsall, though presumably she was dead when they buried her there! I searched the St. Catherine's Index for her, but no Mary Emily Flint died in the Walsall or Rickmansworth areas. What to do next?

Then I remembered helpful Mr. Billings, Walsall's Cemetery Officer, and sent him a cry for help. He wrote, "It appears from the burial records that Mrs. Flint died at Carhampton, Somerset." Emily was running true to form. As soon as I thought I had her, she would slip through my fingers and lead me a merry dance. It took me ages to track down the Carhampton registration, via Williton and Taunton.

At last I held her death certificate. She died on holiday at "The Ramblers", a B+B where she was staying on her own, of heart disease and senile decay. When Miss Emma, in Walsall, heard the news she leapt on her motorbike and drove down to Carhampton. She brought her mother home in the side-car! Not for her the coffin in the guardsvan. Her mother came home in style.

So my lovely Emily's story was over. She really played hard to get, and led me round in circles, but her research brought me so much fun and satisfaction that I forgive her.

And what lessons are to be learnt from her story? Firstly, remember that it is not true that "people didn't move around much in those days, did they?" Look again at Emily's life. - She was born in Rickmansworth, Hertfordshire taught in Great Gaddesden, Hertfordshire married in Camberwell, Surrey gave birth in Woodhouse Eaves, Leicestershire lived with Jesse in Loughborough, Leicestershire and Bexley Heath, Greater London and Hendon, Greater London and Berkhamsted, Hertfordshire and Walsall, West Midlands died at Carhampton, Somerset and is buried in Walsall, West Midlands.

Secondly, it is important to remember that the place of burial is not always the place of death. Carhampton is over a hundred miles away from Walsall. Neither is the place of birth always the place of registration. Ethel Mary Flint was born at Woodhouse Eaves, some distance from her registration at Barrow Upon Soar. As for marriage - Emily from Hertfordshire married Jesse from Leicestershire in Camberwell, Surrey!

I'm sure you are asking yourself, - but was Emily one of Anne's Batchelors?" That, after all, was the object of this exercise when I began to chase Emily of the short petticoat all that long time ago. My mother is convinced Emily is one of my family, for she says I am just like her daughter, Miss Emma - an unmarried ex-school teacher, stubborn and eccentric. I never had a motorbike, but I did drive three-wheelers for 28 years, so perhaps I am eccentric!

But yes, when I traced Emily's Batchelors of Rickmansworth back through the generations I found that she was descended from William Batchelor, Parish Clerk in the early 18th century. Me? I'm descended from his brother Edward, labourer and pauper. So Emily has the last laugh after all!

Anne's three books are still available from

34 Bancroft Heights, Leeds LS14 1HP

A Batchelor's Delight £9.10 including p & p
My Gallant Hussar £4.25 including p & p
My Name is Frances £10.10 including p & p

Archives to go!

David Tippey

discusses Home computer based genealogy research..

Courtesy of Apple Computers

Computers and family history research are becoming inextricably linked, as more and more data becomes accessible via your keyboard and mouse, and even traditionalists see the advantages of using them. One day perhaps, it will no longer be necessary to drag yourself out of your cosy armchair to go to the library or record office. In the meantime, research is increasingly using a blend of the two resources.

Early Days

The purchase of my first computer coincided with a family funeral at which I watched my brother and cousin, rather unsuccessfully trying to construct a family tree on the back of an envelope. I knew just as little about our family as they did, but that event sparked my interest in the subject. I'd just acquired the ideal tool for storing and sorting information, here was something I could do with it, which, hopefully would be a little more enjoyable than the work I had bought it to perform. That was the beginning and as you will know, once bitten by the genealogy bug, this is a voyage of discovery that never ends.

I was pretty sure I could do a better job than my siblings had attempted, but unfortunately the funeral was for my aunt, the last surviving member of my father's generation, leading to many other problems along the way, but that's another story.

Knowing nothing of family history research I raided the library, buying the first of seemingly hundreds of family history magazines and those ever useful little booklets. Programs were not as sophisticated as they are today, but after some searching, a suitable shareware genealogy program, GENE, was found for my Mac Classic and that was the start of my obsession with the past.

Like most people, I found that my research wasn't particularly local and virtually every hard won fact or date required at least a 70+ mile round trip to the nearest LDS Family History Library in Leeds or to a suitable library. The travelling was time consuming and costly, but seemed worthwhile when you came home with a few more facts or dates to add to your database that evening. The computer helped me record and order that data, and now the easy availability of family history software is luring many new people to look at their roots, who wouldn't have done before. Since I started, even though it is less than 10 years ago, the task has been eased a little by the arrival of new programs and data, and in the last couple of years, resources that you can buy on disk or access via the Internet have boomed, making at least some parts of the research process much easier.

Pitfalls

One drawback that is emerging, is that an increasing number of people are trying to research their family history without leaving their computer keyboard, expecting everything they need to be either on CD or the Internet. This situation isn't helped by the claims made by some suppliers on their packaging. Well it hasn't happened yet, you still need plenty of legwork and many hours toiling over a film reader or dusty volume. While having a quiet pint in my local, someone who had just learned that I wrote for various family history publications and ran a course at the local college, came up to me. He proudly announced that this family history research was easy, and that he had just "researched" his family tree back to the 1500s and it had only taken him 3 days using his computer!

Choking on my beer, I resisted giving him a lecture on research and the pitfalls of the available Internet resources. Fortunately having now "done" his family tree, he's lost interest and I can enjoy my quiet pint again.

Software

Record keeping and the presentation of all those accumulated records in an easily usable form, are the main strengths of the computer program over traditional paper based systems. Family history programs have progressed greatly and the better ones have now added just about every feature required by the serious researcher, whilst retaining ease of use for beginners and those who just want to dabble. My personal favourite is Generations, or Reunion if you own a Mac, both are very flexible and powerful tools which you can use to organise your research. However you don't even need to buy a program, as you can download the very capable PAF 5 from the LDS church for free, or buy it on CD for a nominal charge.

The one area which lets most family history programs down is the drawing of dropline pedigree charts. All the popular programs produce US style box charts, which aren't very good at showing complex relationships. The editable charts such as those created by Generations and Reunion can be annotated to make things clearer, but you can overcome the problem better by drawing your own or using a charting program such as TreeDraw, which creates truly editable trees with UK style charting conventions, over which you have complete control.

Not everyone uses linked family history database programs, One-name studies and researchers who don't want to clutter up their linked family database with all those odd items which you turn up when researching, can use an ordinary database to store all the information. You could write your own, but Custodian was designed for the job, and probably the program you would come up with if you had the time and expertise.

Many other useful software tools are available to aid your research and these include:

LDS Companion, a conversion facility for processing data from various LDS Church sources.

RTF Wizard, another LDS data conversion program for the 1881 census data.

GenMap, an event database with mapping facilities.

Armed with your own selection from the range of available computer research utilities, you can collect, sort and manage vast quantities of data, whilst presenting it in a variety of useful formats, all with great ease. It certainly beats the shoe box full of file cards and roll of wallpaper school of record keeping, when it comes to flexibility and presentation.

CD Data sources

Advances haven't only taken place on the record keeping side of family history, there has been something of a revolution on the data front over the last few years too. Starting with just a trickle of floppy disks and CDs, covering odd transcriptions and indexes; a real pot luck mix which never seemed to apply to my research, we now have some very useful, widely applicable resources available.

Trade Directories seemed to be the first area to receive major attention from publishers. These are fairly rare in their printed form and aren't widely available outside the areas to which they refer. Despite the fact that only a small proportion of the population is reflected in their content, they have proved very popular and you can now find CD versions of directories for most parts of the country.

Scarce and expensive books are an obvious target for digitising and republishing cheaply on disk, and old gazetteers, local histories and atlases which would normally be too expensive for most researchers to buy, are now readily available on CD. They are not always as convenient or aesthetically pleasing to use as the originals, but they do provide an excellent resource for historians at a reasonable cost. Old maps and gazetteers are especially useful when working with census material, which will soon be more widely available.

The publication of the LDS 1881 census Index was the first major milestone in data availability and showed that large and seriously useful collections of data could be made widely available to the public and not just to institutions. The LDS church have led the way in making genealogy information widely available to computer users. Their tri-county index from the 1851 census and the British Vital Records CDs were two further large scale UK data collections that appeared, and they have produced several major collections of records for other parts of the World too.

However resources such as these still only scratch the surface, and serendipity plays a very important part in just how useful they are to the individual researcher. What we really require are many more complete resources like the 1881 census index. One small, data publisher has decide to take on this challenge and having progressed from trade directories, to the Phillimore's Marriage extract series and various other published Parish Record transcripts, S&N are now digitising the entire 1891 census and publishing it on CD and DVD, with pricing not too dissimilar to the LDS data. This project is already up and running and 1891 census for the London area is being followed by the enumeration books for Yorkshire then Lancashire. They are also to start work on the other census years shortly, and as this requires different equipment to the 1891 census, the projects will run alongside each other. Major projects like this will encourage other publishers and should have a serious impact on researching your ancestors back into the early 19th century, making it a much easier and cheaper experience for most people.

Family History societies have started publishing their Indexing, MI and Transcription projects in computer usable form. Many of them have collaborated with the Federation of Family History Societies to create the new National Burial Index, a project which will amongst other things, provide some of the essential information which is missing from the IGI.

Sources on the Web

Publication on CD may be the commercial route, but now that many people have access to the Internet from home, anyone can easily and cheaply become their own publisher. This has recently led to a wealth of small websites carrying various databases, transcriptions and to special interest sites for individual families, one-name and one-place studies. Previously, the Internet contained very little in the way of searchable data, and was mainly a source of information detailing resources and research methods. GENUKI became well established as the starting point for UK research, a mine of information organised in a hierarchical manner, starting with general UK resources and working its way down through county, to parish level information. This has steadily grown and now contains links to many databases, photographs and other useful resources.

The LDS church have again been up with the leaders, launching their superb FamilySearch website, which includes amongst it's many resources, the ever useful, though fallible, IGI and Ancestral File.

The Rootsweb co-operative have provided free web resources and genealogy project support for a long time and even though they have now become part of a commercial organisation, their resources are still free. They host many of those extremely useful genealogy mailing lists, which now cover most areas of the UK. These are excellent forums for seeking and sharing information and prove extremely useful to many researchers. Rootsweb also support many surname and other allied lists, plus some major transcription projects. Two of the most advanced transcription projects hosted by them are the Immigrant Ships Transcribers Guild and the Free BMD project. Although nowhere near completion, both of these now have large scale, useful databases containing many transcriptions of the GRO birth marriage and death indexes and passenger lists of ships travelling to various parts of the world.

Immigration to the US accounts for many people slipping off our family trees and the excellent new Ellis Island site is an good place to look for elusive branches of the family. The database is well presented, easy to use and provides quite detailed information.

The publication of the entire 6 inch first series OS mapping online, has enabled us to look in detail at the towns and villages our ancestors lived in during the latter part of the 19th century. Whilst modern mapping, and up-to-date telephone and address information allows us to readily locate and contact living relatives.

The year 2002 will bring the next major, complete data set to your computer, when the PRO publish the 1901 census online. We have already had a chance to see how it will work, using the pilot 1891 census for Norfolk, which will hopefully make a reappearance on the web and not disappear forever. I understand that the 1901 census is to be followed very rapidly by the 1881 census, by using the existing LDS index linked to the scanned enumerators book images and the software developed for the 1901.

The future looks good for both the online and digital media publishing of genealogy data. Some will mourn the loss of "free" access to some of these resources, but in reality, the time and cost of travel and possibly accommodation, meant that for most people they were anything but free anyway, and access on a "pay to view" basis will be cheaper and available at any time. The day when you can sit down at your computer and research all your family history is still a long way off, but it's getting nearer. The bare bones of research are getting easier and quicker all the time and much more convenient too, but even when all the basic resources become available on your computer, visits to the Library or Record Office are still going to be essential to flesh them out and will remain so in the foreseeable future.

© David Tippey

Wakefield Manor Court Roll 1590
Reproduced with permission of
West Yorkshire Archive Service Ref: MD225/1/316

Manorial Records

Angela Petyt

We might have heard of the words 'Manor House' and 'Lord of the Manor'. We might also have heard of the phrases 'to the manor born', often used to indicate high social status, or 'keep off our manor', a term often used by the gangster fraternity! But what does all this actually *mean*? In fact, gaining an understanding of the manor and the records generated by it, from the 13th century up until 1925, can add real richness to the history of families and communities. One of the most under-used classes of document, I hope to show what a treasure-chest awaits the researcher...

What is a manor?

The manor was the ancient unit of land tenure, dating from Anglo-Saxon times. The Normans built upon this and created a complex network. It was based upon the estate of the Lord of the Manor, who held the land by the grace of the monarch, under the feudal system. Feudalism in its simplest form can be likened to a triangle, with the monarch at the top, who owns all land in England. Under him are the barons who are called tenants-in-chief. The monarch divides blocks of land amongst them as long as they swear to be loyal. Their rent was in the form of taxes and provision of soldiers. Under them is a larger group made up mainly of knights. The tenants-in-chief sub-let portions of their land to them as long as they swear to be loyal. These tenants paid rent through taxes and providing soldiers for the barons. At the bottom of the triangle is by far the largest group - the peasants. They were allowed to live and work on the land provided that they also worked for their Lord of the Manor and paid him taxes.

It is uncertain how many manors there actually were - estimates range widely from 25,000 to 65,000. However, there were only 11,000 parishes, so this means that there might have been several manors in one parish. On the other hand, there might be a number of parishes, or parts of parishes, in a single manor.

Geographical, political and economic unit - a manor was all of this and more.

Life on the Manor

There is no such thing as a 'typical' manor, but in a basic sense it can be laid out thus - at the heart is the Manor House, headquarters of the Lord of the Manor, and his reserved grounds called demesne. Nearby is the church. Clustered around a central green or market place are the peasants' cottages. There is some common pasture and perhaps a few enclosed fields called closes. Some land is left as waste ground and there will be a good deal of woodland close at hand. The rest is made up of three large arable fields. The crops grown in these fields will be decided annually by the peasants, who divide the fields into long narrow strips in such a way that all had a share

in the best and worst land. This is called ridge-and-furrow.

It could be assumed that all the peasants or serfs were the same, however, there was a 'class system' amongst the residents of the manor. At the top level were the freemen, called franklins or sokemen. Some of them might be dispossessed Saxon noblemen. Below them were the villeins, a kind of 'middle-class' peasant, then came the cottars, who were entitled to less strips of land in the fields than the villeins, and at the bottom of the pile were the bordars, who lived on the waste ground. All serfs except freemen were not allowed to leave the manor without the lord's permission. They were tied to the lord by a special system of customary duties and obligations, for example, they had to work for part of the week on the lord's demesne and had to grind their corn at the manor mill, paying the lord for the privilege. Although this might paint a harsh picture, the peasants had all sorts of perks called customs of the manor. These varied from place to place but usually included the right to graze animals on the common, to take wood for building houses and making fires, to take fodder for their pigs, to take turf and to take fish from the river. They also had the protection of the Lord of the Manor in hard times.

The Records

Manorial administration developed and became increasingly sophisticated. Many lords did not actually live on or even visit their manor, particularly the major landholders who had many manors to control. Most of the lord's work was carried out by his deputy, called the steward. The bailiff ran the day to day business of the manor, collecting rents, overseeing demesne farming and liaising with the Saxon farm foremen, called a reeve (in the south) or grave (in the north). There were several other officials - the affeeror fixed payment of fines, the constable maintained the peace, the hayward looked after hedges and fences and the ale-tester made sure brewing was up to strength (this was the job no-one refused to take!)

The lord's juristiction was enforced by the manor court. There were two courts - court baron (which dealt with land tenure and the lord's and tenants' rights and duties - the customs of the manor) and court leet (which dealt with crimes and misdemeanours). The former met on average every three weeks depending on the size of the manor; the latter met every six months. All tenants had to attend, give an excuse for absence (essoin) or else be fined (amerced). The main business of the court baron was transfer of copyhold land. When a peasant died his land reverted back to the lord of the manor. His heir then had to apply to the court to take the land back into that family, and after paying a fee to the lord or giving him his best beast, he was granted the tenancy and given a copy of the entry in the court roll to keep as proof. This entry would record the surrender and admission of the copyhold land, and the relationship between the old and new tenant, sometimes with an extract from the deceased's will. Thus it can be seen that families with the same plot of copyhold land can

Wakefield Manor Court Roll 1596
Reproduced with permission of
West Yorkshire Archive Service Ref: MD225/1/322

be traced back through several generations, to the time before parish registers. Court leet dealt with minor crime such as theft and public order offences, though in the middle ages the lord had the power to hang the guilty. This was often accompanied by the view of frankpledge, an Anglo-Saxon system of lawkeeping taken over by the Normans. Householders formed into groups of ten or twelve called tithings - a kind of neighbourhood watch system. They were responsible for the good behaviour of one another and had a duty to report on misdeeds committed by their members. The court also had a jury of twelve respected local men. The powers of court leet were diminished by the 17th century when quarter sessions took over much of their business.

One of the main duties of the steward was to keep written records of the manor. The most important were the court rolls, so called because originally they were on sheets of parchment stitched together at the top edge and rolled up, but later they developed into book format. Manor court rolls and other documents, such as surveys, rent rolls and maps make up the single most important record of local government and community life, particularly in the medieval period. The earliest manor court rolls start in the 13th century and end in 1925 when the Law of Property Acts converted all copyhold land into freehold.

Accessing the Records
Because of their legal significance, there is an official listing of all known manorial records in England and Wales. Their whereabouts are recorded by the Historical Manuscripts Commission in a Manorial Documents Register (MDR). There are two card indexes, one arranged by parish and the other arranged by manor. They list the surviving types of records for each manor, covering dates and location. These can range from the Public Record Office and County Record Offices to private individuals. Limited enquiries can be dealt with by post (i.e. a request for one or two manors, or one parish) but wider research can be done by visiting the searchroom. The address is - Historical Manuscripts Commission, Quality House, Quality Court, Chancery Lane, London WC2A 1HP. There is also an ongoing programme to put the Manorial Documents Register on the internet - www.hmc.gov.uk Currently, Yorkshire, Hampshire, the Isle of Wight and Wales are online and the database can be searched in a number of ways. For example, a search for the parish of Wragby, Yorkshire, brings up nine documents referring to three manors in the parish, the records being held in three different repositories. A search for the manor of Badsworth, Yorkshire, results in nine documents dating from 1313-1826, stored in three different record offices.

Unfortunately, many manorial records no longer exist. Only about 4% of manors have records from before 1500

and 20% have records from 1500-1700. Around half of the manors have records surviving from 1700-1925. Up to 1733 (apart from the Commonwealth period 1653-1660) most manorial documents will be written in Latin. Practice in reading later English court rolls can help enormously in understanding the earlier Latin documents as the format and phrasing are basically the same. A number of court rolls and other manorial records have been transcribed and published. For information about manors and their lords, the Victoria County History volumes can be of great use, as can the topographical descriptions in trade directories.

Examples of Court Roll entries
All of the following examples are taken from the Wakefield Manor Court Rolls of the late 13th century. The Manor of Wakefield in Yorkshire is unusual in that it was so large - stretching twenty-one miles north to south and thirty miles east to west, encompassing many towns and villages. It also has one of the best surviving series of court rolls, dating from 1274-1925. They are held at the Yorkshire Archaeological Society in Leeds. Many of the rolls have been painstakingly repaired and there is an ongoing project to transcribe and publish the records. I have selected these entries to give a flavour of the riches to be found in manorial documents. All human life is here!

Administration
Court held at Wakefield on the Friday in the eve of S. Margaret the Virgin Edward I 1275 in the time of the said [Steward]
Essoigns John de Byrstal essoigned himself the second time as to suit [of Court] by Alan the servant of John de Ravenesfeud pledge Peter de Walton. [1275]

Birton - Tourn held…twelve jurors: Willaim de Thorniceley Robert de Wlvewro William de Birton Adam de Helay Richard de Brocholis Adam de Wodehuses Thomas son of John de Fouleston Adam the Forester of Eppewrth Richard the Grave of Scholes John son of Mary de Wlvedale Hugh de Litelwode and John son of Robert de Holne. [1275]

Land and Customs of the Manor
Sandal - Adam son of Henry Tubbing gives 12d. for licence to take four acres of land from Robert Nyrp the smith, in Crigeliston, for a term of fifteen years. Robert shall do the services and customs for the last three years, and Adam for twelve years. Pledge Richard the Grave. [1274]

Sandale - The land of Adam son of William de Sandale is still in the Earl's hands because he is dead. [1275]

Halifax - That Bate son of Hugh del Bothes is the Earl's villein, and has gone from the Earl's land without licence. He is to be arrested if found within the Earl's liberty. He is living at Haldewrth. [1275]

Sandal - William de Ossete gives 12d. for licence to marry Ybotta de Overhalle of Sandale. [1297]

Crimes and Misdemeanours
Soureby - Jordan de Schakeltonstall and his accomplices charged with taking a stag in the Forest of Soureby, have respite until the Earl's coming. [1274]

Wakefeud - John Graffard, 12d. because his dog chased the Earl's game in the forest. [1274]

Sourby - Jordan de Werloweley fined 6d. for chattering in Court. [1274]

Sandale - Order to distrain the whole township of Walton on account of a stray bullock which remained there from Saint Giles Day until Christmas which they concealed and would not present to the Earls bailiff. They must make fine. [1275]

Wakefield - That Richard Pykard was killed in the town of Normanton at Christmas last they know not by whom but as Robert son of Adam Wynes of Staynford was standing near Richard at the time he ought to answer it. Therefore let him be arrested. [1275]

Ravenesfeud - They say also that Juliana wife of Richard Pykard brewed contrary to the assize and that when the ale-tasters appointed to look after the assize of ale came Juliana said that she would sell ale against the will of them and of the bailiffs, in despite of the Earl. In mercy fine 12d. The township of Normanton is in mercy for concealing that she [and several others] brewed contrary to the assize, fine 4s. [1275]

Alverthorpe - They also say that Agnes Kaynel has a key made to open and shut the doors of the neighbours and that she deceives the neighbours children and takes from them wholes loaves barley and oats to their serious damage. Therefore let her be arrested. She was not found. [1275]

Hyperum - Thomas [the servant of Thomas de Coppley] offers himself against the said Peter [son of Alice de Hyperum], and says that on Friday before Saint Barnabas' Day, he was in Wakefield Market, where many person were laying at throwing the stone and a quarrel arose between himself and Peter, and Peter came running with a drawn knife, and wounded Thomas in the jaw,against the

peace, etc., to his damage and affront of 13s. 4d. Peter denies it, word by word. Therefore let him wage his law; pledges, William son of Hugh de Schipeden and Robert de Soureby. [1275]

Rastrick - Isabella wife of Adam le Blomer against Eda de Blahomner, says she stole a super-tunic of blue cloth, value 18d., and a hood of the same cloth, value 6d., at the forge in the great wood of Wakefued, last Wednesday night. Eda was found with goods and confessed. Therefore let her be hanged. [1286]

Wakefeud - Walter the Chaplain, for the escape of 6 pigs in the Earl's pannage. 12d. [1297]

Sandal - Richard the Smith of Sandale v. Henry the Chaplain of Sandale for assaulting him in John Bestes curtilage and breaking his head with a stone he held in his fist, he claims 20s. damages. [1297]

Recommended reading
Using Manorial Records - Mary Ellis (Public Record Office, 1997)
Manorial Records - Eve McLaughlin (The Author, 1996)
A Guide to the Medieval Manor - Eric Overton (Local History Publications, 1994)
My Ancestors were Manorial Tenants - Peter Park (Society of Genealogists, 2nd ed. 1994)
Manorial Records - Denis Stuart (Phillimore, 1992)

Research in Europe ~
Roger Leslie (Dmitrevsky)
recounts his personal experience

Emigration whether voluntary or enforced by persecution or some other cause has been a constant feature of human history. The result is that many people continue their lives elsewhere than in their homeland and there is a tendency as one generation succeeds another for the homeland to become but a distant memory. Quite often descendants may have no knowledge whatsoever of this part of their family history. In many cases sooner or later an interest will be awakened and a desire to delve into this aspect will develop. Additionally a category of people having a potential interest in foreign research are descendants of people who at some stage of their lives spent time abroad for example artisans, nannies and governesses and service personnel. In this article I intend in the main to confine myself to the first group. In passing I would say that as regards the second category there is material to be researched in this country. For example records of a benevolent society for retired governesses are lodged at the London Metropolitan Archives. Also it would be useful to read Alan Bird's "Tracing your Ancestors in Russia," in the February issue of Family Tree Magazine.

Those who know of their foreign connections and those who discover them will at once be confronted by two questions, how and where to start? I found myself in this situation and quickly realised that I was entering virtually uncharted territory. I made some tentative enquiries and with the best of intentions no doubt, was advised that it was virtually impossible and I should give up the idea. However one academic did offer advice and encouragement sufficient to decide me to embark upon the task.

From what I have said already it's clear I am not professing to be an expert. Inevitably however one learns by one's experiences and it's just possible that an account of my researches may be helpful in suggesting to others possible avenues of enquiry or at least to consider the challenge. As a first step I would suggest a reading of appropriate sections of Angus Baxter's "In Search of Your European Roots" published by Genealogical Publishing Co. Inc. Whilst intended for a New World public it is nevertheless useful to European researchers, including as it does sections on every European country. It's also a good idea to learn something of the particular country's history and culture; it helps for a better understanding as you research and promotes an awareness of ever shifting national boundaries. In my case I have learnt Russian sufficiently to get around and be capable of dealing with most documents

The degree of difficulty one is likely to experience depends very much upon the specific country being researched. In my case it was difficult as I was researching in the main countries of the former Soviet Union principally Russia and Ukraine. I descend from Scottish clansmen who went and settled in Russia. Over the years they prospered becoming ennobled and Russified. Their way of life came to an end as a result of the Great War, the Russian Revolutions and Civil War. Following defeat in the latter father now bearing the

name of Dmitrevsky had no option but to flee leaving behind his mother and sister. He eventually settled in this country beginning life here virtually with no more than what he stood up in.

Our parents died in the early '90s at which point a few original documents; photographs and some jottings came into my possession. In addition to this I already knew via father, where he was born, Volsk on the Volga in Saratov province and where he spent his later years, Odessa on the Black Sea as well as the related names Pligin and Khardin. I think it appropriate at this stage to make a comment regarding the rendering of names in Russian (Cyrillic script) into a Latin equivalent. Be aware that the western ear is not particularly well attuned to the pronunciation of Russian and many corruptions have resulted. Time spent mastering the Cyrillic alphabet will repay you many times over. One other thing father had mentioned was spending holidays with relations in Lausanne, Switzerland before the Great War. In the mid-1950s we were in temporary contact with some of these relations then living in France. This initial contact was via the Red Cross. This then was the material I had to begin with.

I fully utilised the resources of the Church of Latter Day Saints and came across details of the Christening of a Vladimir Dmitrevsky in Saratov in 1878. I decided to follow this up and eventually was in touch with the contributor, an Estonian lady living in Sweden. This lead to details of about a dozen more Dmitrevskys culled from the registers of Dorpat University now Tartu in Estonia. These are not necessarily related but it is my idea to create a database. Incidentally whilst in America at this time I accessed an online telephone directory and came up with four Dmitrevskys; three were related and the fourth's name had been corrupted from Dmitrovsky bearing out the point I made earlier. I am still in touch with the eldest of these Dmitrevskys who was born in a refugee camp on the Greek Island of Lemnos. Another source I tapped was bookshops. In the process I have acquired quite a respectable collection relating to the history of Russia including many accounts by emigres. One of my most helpful purchases has turned out to be a book appearing in the series People to People entitled Russia edited by Jim Haynes and published by Zephyr Press, Somerville, MA 02145 US, but available from Cannongate Books, 14, High St., Edinburgh EH1 1TE, Scotland. Other countries included in the series are The Baltic Republics i.e. Estonia, Latvia and Lithuania, Poland, Czechoslovakia, Hungary and Bulgaria. Please bear in mind that the Baltic Republics, part of Poland, Belarus, The Ukraine and Moldova fell within the Russian hegemony. With the aid of this book I was able to establish a contact in St. Petersburg whose help has been immeasurable.

I belong to an affinity group that among other things arranges foreign holidays. In November 1997 I was off with a group to Russia with a little free time in both Moscow and St. Petersburg that I hoped to make good use of. I spent a delightful evening with the academic's Russian colleague in Moscow during the course of which he showed me a huge chart of Russian Leslies. Unfortunately for me he could not find a link. Regarding my other names he suggested I began with Fond (Collection) 1343 at the Russian State Historical Archive in St. Petersburg located at Angliyskaya Naberejnaya 4, (English Embankment), 190000 St Petersburg, Russia, Telephone 7 (812) 315-54—35 and 311-09-26, Fax 7 (812) 311-22-52, adjacent to Admiralty Square. Before leaving he gave me details of some Leslies living in Moscow.

A few days later in St. Petersburg and armed with directions from my unfortunately absent contact I located the Archive. It is my recollection that most buildings whether public or commercial seem to have some sort of security quite often armed. Do not be deterred and do persevere. My limited Russian helped, as did the fact I had taken with me some of my photos. Presently I was discussing my mission with a most efficient lady. I filled in a form, left copy of some of my material, paid a deposit that had to be in Roubles and departed. One thing you will need to have arranged beforehand is method of payment and details of person to be contacted when the work is completed. In my case I nominated my contact to whom I forwarded funds via Western Union when requested. I need to make several points at this stage. It's my understanding that very little of archives' holdings are computerised and few finding aids exist; all searches are manual and to all intents and purposes for the likes of us a personal search is out of the question. Sooner or later the question of whether to pay for research will arise. Most of us prefer to do our own research but I expect on occasion have employed a record agent to do some for us for whatever reason. The stark choice one has regarding Russian research is to pay either the archive direct or a record agent for his work on your behalf or to go without.

Thoughtfully my contact had arranged someone else for me to meet and as a result I was able to spend an afternoon at the home of a member of the Russian Genealogical Society. He raised my hopes at one point by mentioning he had put on one side some references to a change of name involving Dmitrevsky but unfortunately for me had mislaid them prior to my visit.

This is the school attended by Roger's father until May 1916. It bore the name B.A.ZHUKOVSKSOVO, 26 Kherson Street, Odessa now renamed Pastera Street

Equally disappointing was the news that in recent times great damage had been caused by fire to the Kostroma archives during the course of burglary. Father had said quite a lot about his paternal grand father living there and I would have expected in due course to enjoy success there.

In due time I received a package of some hundred sheets of copied records in Russian of the Imperial period relating to my "names". One way and another I had it all translated and found some seventy sheets related to Khardin, twenty to Pligin and ten to Dmitrevsky. In effect I had asked for a blanket search and I would certainly advise making search requests as focused as possible. The result will be less but more relevant material and a lesser expense for translation. Part of the Dmitrevsky material related to awards to my great grandfather in 1900. The best part was that to ensure awards to fit and proper persons enquiries into intended recipients' backgrounds had to be reported on. As a result I received confirmation he descended from the nobility, together with extensive details of his marriage and subsequent birth of four children. Grandfather was the eldest. I was able to trace my Khardin line to the early seventeenth century and Pligins to early 1700s.

Earlier I mentioned Odessa now in the Ukraine. I am friendly with a family that periodically visits Ukraine. On one occasion they visited the local archive, one of two, and broke the ice for me. I emphasise again the need to stand one's ground and not be too easily rebuffed. Soon I was in contact with one of the archivists and again upon payment, dollars US this time received a package of material. I learnt that grandfather

Roger Leslie with the Librarian at
The Prince George Galitizine Memorial Library
St Petersburg, Russia

alongside Lake Geneva and details of his funeral at the Russian Church in Geneva.

I felt that more would be gleaned by a personal visit so later I found myself in Switzerland based in Lausanne. Further information was indeed forthcoming and in Lausanne I discovered in a copy of the local newspaper a death announcement for great grandfather in 1920. This lead to a burial register wherein was indicated the Cemetery of Montoise together with a plot number. Sadly there was nothing to indicate his grave but I was shown where his grave would have been. Part of my stay was spent visiting and photographing the addresses where he had resided apart from one where in fact he died. This had been demolished during the course modernisation work. Another day a short trip by rail brought me to the second archive. More documentation emerged relating to the accident victim. This was the report of the winding up of his estate in Switzerland and included a copy of his will made several years earlier at Montreux. Additionally the latter gave details of his two sister beneficiaries with addresses in St. Petersburg. I was able to locate his former residence in a hamlet overlooking Geneva and together with my companion visited it. It was a perfect day for driving there by car and one enquiry upon arrival located the house. Following a telephone call to the present resident, an elderly lady, we were invited to call in on her. It transpired that her husband descended from a Russian officer posted to London before the Great War to negotiate material for uniforms. We had a most enjoyable time and reluctantly left with an invitation to stay another time ringing in our ears. I struck lucky again at the third archive when it was explained why the accident victim had laid in a temporary grave for over four years. Apparently it had been intended to rebury him in Russia but subsequent events put paid to that intention. The person dealing with me accompanied me to municipal offices dealing with burial records where I was allowed to peruse the records. Unfortunately I was running short of time and had to call a halt. The assistant said she knew of someone who might be able to assist and true to her word she emailed me his details; as a result I received a copy of the Russian Church burial record.

Early summer 1999 saw me again in Russia this time cruising between St. Petersburg and Moscow. I had an escort in St. Petersburg, Oleg, who showed me a different side to the city. With his help I located the sisters' addresses, one as it would have been in her time the other since modernised. Unfortunately we ran out of time to visit the technical institute where grandfather had studied; at least I have a reason to visit St. Petersburg again. Also I met my original contact and was able to thank her personally for her assistance. Part of the tour included Kostroma and a nunnery there that had housed local records in Soviet times. I did learn that some records had been saved from the fire and were now lodged elsewhere. The highlight of the short stay in Moscow was the afternoon spent in the home of one of the Leslie sisters enjoying real Russian hospitality while looking at photos and talking of our ancestry.

was assistant engineer of the city waterworks, that he had written several technical works. Included was his application for this position. It mentioned he had graduated from the Nicholas 11 Technical Institute, St Petersburg in 1896 and that at the time of his application he was Chief Engineer at the Grodno City Waterworks, now in Belarus. I foresaw a trip to Ukraine in the then not too distant future.

In between times I had been carrying out research in Switzerland in the French speaking canton of Vaud, mainly Lausanne and Geneva. This was an area much favoured by expatriate Russians. Initially, my rather rusty school French fortunately sufficing I conducted my research by correspondence with the following archives.

1. Archives De La Ville De Lausanne, Rue de Maupas 47, Case Postale CH-1000, Lausanne 9. Telephone (international) 41 21 624 43 55, Fax (international) 41 21 624 06 01.
2. Archives Cantonales Vaudoises, Rue de La Moline 32, 1022 Chavannes-pres-Renens. Telephone (international) 41 21 316 37 11, Fax (international) 41 21 316 37 55.
3. Archives d'Etat, 1, rue de l'Hotel-de-Ville, Case Postale 164, CH-122, Geneve 3. Telephone (international) 41 22 319 33 95, Fax (international) 41 22 319 33 65.

I was more than satisfied with the material that arrived in due course by post and I feel the service was excellent and fees reasonable. Via this research I obtained the following.

Confirmation of father's visit to Switzerland in 1913. Details of several visits of other relations as recorded by passport control.
Details of issue of Permis de Sejour (Residents' Permits) to relations. This turned out to be very useful as it furnished all the addresses in Lausanne where great grandfather lived.
Some information regarding a motor accident in 1916 whereby an uncle was fatally injured whilst driving

Next I was off to Ukraine where I stayed for a week in September 2000 as guest of a family in Odessa. Perhaps it would be appropriate to say a little about travel documentation for holiday trips to these countries. UK citizens currently require visas and applications must be supported by a written invitation. This is normally taken care of by the travel agent organising the holiday however recently I have noticed that a number of brochures are emphasising that it's the client's responsibility to obtain any necessary visa. In the case of my trip to Odessa I obtained the necessary invitation and the visa was obtained by my travel agent, Bob Sopel Travel of Oldam that specialises in Ukraine. Intending a personal visit to the city Archive I took with me a copy of father's school leaving certificate that came into his possession at the time he was reunited with his step-grandmother in the 1950s. Also I wished to visit places that either through previous research or through mention by father I now knew to be relevant.

On several occasions it was necessary because of the distance involved to hire transport, driver and guide cum interpreter. This was all arranged for me by the family in whom I had every confidence at a very reasonable price. One whole day was spent some thirty kilometres outside the city at the pumping station where grandfather had been engineer. Since his time a museum had been established and the curator showed us around. Scanning the photographs displayed I did not see any of grandfather. This was not altogether surprising. When I mentioned my relationship and showed my documents and photographs the curator's eyes lit up and he was soon photocopying and taking down detail. He said he would have an exhibit mounted in time for my next visit. He was able to identify the subject matter of some of my photos. A slightly longer trip on another day took me to an ancient site on the coast near the city of Kherson. It was called Olbia and father went there several times in search of ancient Greek coins. I next visited the Odessa State Archive, at 18, Shukovskovo Street; Odessa 270001 Ukraine and in the temporary absence of the head of the Foreign Relations Department arranged to see her later in the day. In the meantime having been given directions to grandmother's town house and father's school I went to look at them and take photographs. Returning to the Archives I had a warm welcome from the department head and a promise to search further for me. From her I learnt to direct my enquiry regarding grandfather's and father's military service to the Russian State Military Historical Archive, 2 Baumanskaya, 3, 107864, Moscow, Russia, Telephone 7 (095) 261-20-70. Some time after my return home I received some more copied material originating from grandfather in which I discovered he had attended an All Russia conference on water supply in 1913 in Riga, now in Latvia. Also visited was the English Club of which grandfather had been a member; it is now the museum of the merchant marine. This was interesting also especially as I had a long conversation with a retired employee who had childhood memories of the Revolution and Civil War. One morning I had an escorted tour of the city's catacombs, these particular ones had been used as a base by Russian partisans fighting the Germans during the Patriotic War. The catacombs are all over the place and can be dangerous. Father recounted how as a young boy he had learnt his way about them. This stood him in good stead when he had to hide from the Bolsheviks.

My latest research trip has been to Paris. I wished to enquire into the part played by the French army as part of the interventionist forces in Russia following the

withdrawal from the war by the Bolsheviks and especially in South Russia after the surrender of Turkey. Additionally as part of the allied occupation of Constantinople the French had the greater responsibility for dealing with the Russian refugee problem arising from defeat of the White Russians. The archives of the three armed services are located at Chateau de Vincennes but I confined myself to the military archive the address of which is: - Service Historique De L'Armee De Terre, Fort de Vincennes Boite Postale 107, 00481 ARMEES. Telephone 01 4193 34 44, Fax 01 41 93 38 90. For the record, details of the naval archive are, Service historique de la Marine, Chateau de Vincennes BP 2 –00300 Armees. Telephone 01 43 28 81 50 Fax 01 43 28 31 60. E-mail shistorique@cedocar.fr. To gain access to these archives one needs to show proof of identity and residence and from notices it appears that research must be in person or conducted on one's behalf by an agent. I found straight away on the open access shelves two books relevant to my quest and thereby gained some more information. In correspondence prior to my visit I had indicated my area of interest and had had sent me a listing of files of possible interest. Once there it was quite a simple to order required files. It is as well that I found material in the open access section as the files I ordered took some three hours to be presented. However it was worth the delay on account of the information contained in them.

Part of my time was spent visiting the village just outside Paris where I had met the relations in the 1950s. I visited the local cemetery and noted the new additions on the family grave. The family home was a sad sight being totally derelict and boarded up. I visited the municipal offices nearby and found the staff very helpful with further detail regarding death of relations. From them I also learnt details of the current owner and that there were plans to rebuild. During the stay contact was made with these owners to discover they were not the initial buyers. At the same offices I had enquired regarding details of the vendors and I am currently waiting to hear. Wealthier Russians to avoid the rigours of their climate over wintered elsewhere in areas such as the Crimea or abroad, such as the South of France particularly Nice. On a hunch I contacted telephone enquiries and obtained details of a relation living in the Nice area. I have sent a letter and hopefully there will be a response. Finally I paid a visit to another cemetery. This was the Russian Cemetery at Sainte Genevievre des Bois about an hour's travel outside Paris. There after a search aided by reference to the available hard copy of a database of memorial inscriptions I found great grandmother's grave. The database is dated 1995 so later burials go unrecorded here. These records are distinct from municipal records where in appropriate cases enquiry should be directed.

At the present time I have in mind further trips, to Vol'sk, on the Volga and to the Burgundy region of France in the latter case to endeavour to track down information about father's former governess by the name of Falcognet last heard of in Neuville-les-Dames, Ain.

During the course of my researches I have used various means of communication with people in Russia. I have not found it necessary to send in Russian, although I believe more people there speak German as a second language than English. I have always found it best when using "snail mail" to use the special delivery service to ensure delivery. Computers are fine for email; most computer users in Russia seem to be able to accept Latin script. The web has been useful, but mainly as a tool to identify possible lines of enquiry rather than a source of specific genealogical information. However recently I have made contact with a French lady bearing one of our "names". Her grandfather's experiences as a refugee mirrored those of father.

Web sites I would mention are http://www.genforum.com, http://www.people.adicom.ru www.distantcousin.com and http://www.mtu-net.ru/rrr . The first has a country selection option and accessing a country of your choice a message display reveals a list of those seeking or giving information or advice. Some messages generate quite a bit of activity, the more general the greater chance of a response. One item, from Ludmilla, was an offer to accept requests and convert them to Russian for inclusion on the second site I mention. All you need to do is add /english.htm. The second site is in Russian albeit with English options. To access, it may be necessary to download a Cyrillic software package. Mikhail Kroutikhin's web site, fourth in my list too is well worth visiting containing as it does some useful advice together with details of a number of archives.

As stated at the outset my researches have been mainly concentrated upon countries forming part of the former Soviet Union. I would venture to say that my approach is equally applicable to other European countries with the prospect of even greater success. I hope I have shown that research in Russian is not a complete no-no and that with a little determination a measure of success can be achieved.

Further Reading

In Search of Your European Roots Angus Baxter Published by Genealogical Publishing Co. Inc.
People to People Series - Russia edited by Jim Haynes and published by Zephyr Press, Somerville, MA 02145 US, but available from Cannongate Books, 14, High St., Edinburgh EH1 1TE, Scotland.
Tracing your Ancestors in Russia, Alan Bird Family Tree Magazine February 2001.

Archives.

RUSSIA
Russian State Historical Archive (RGIA) Angliyskaya Naberejnaya 4, (English Embankment), 190000 St Petersburg, Russia, Telephone 7 (812) 315-54—35 and 311-09-26, Fax 7 (812) 311-22-52.
Russian State Military Historical Archive, 2 Baumanskaya, 3, 107864, Moscow, Russia, Telephone 7 (095) 261-20-70.

UKRAINE
Odessa State Archive, 18, Shukovskovo Street; Odessa 270001, Ukraine.

SWITZERLAND.
Archives De La Ville De Lausanne, Rue de Maupas 47, Case Postale CH-1000, Lausanne 9
Telephone (international) 41 21 624 43 55
Fax (international) 41 21 624 06 01.
Archives Cantonales Vaudoises, Rue de La Moline 32, 1022 Chavannes-pres-Renens. Telephone (international) 41 21 316 37 11, Fax (international) 41 21 316 37 55.
Archives d'Etat, 1, rue de l'Hotel-de-Ville, Case Postale 164, CH-122, Geneve 3
Telephone (international) 41 22 319 33 95
Fax (international) 41 22 319 33 65.

FRENCH MILITARY.
(Army).
Service Historique De L'Armee De Terre, Fort de Vincennes Boite Postale 107, 00481 ARMEES.
Telephone 01 4193 34 44, Fax 01 41 93 38 90.
(Navy).
Service Historique de la Marine, Chateau de Vincennes BP 2 –00300 Armees. Telephone 01 43 28 81 50 Fax 01 43 28 31 60. E-mail shistorique@cedocar.fr.

Russian Cemetery.
Cimetiere russe de Sainte-Genevievre-des-Bois, 8, rue Léo-Lagrange, 91700, Sainte-Genevievre-des-Bois, France.

Web-Sites.
http://www.genforum.com
http://www.people.adicom.ru
http://www.distantcousin.com
http://www.mtu-net.ru/rrr

Following retirement from the police Roger Leslie (Dmitrevsky) is kept busy with various pursuits including travel and research. His book, *The Russian Foreigner*, about the early years of the last century in Russia regarding an ancestor that he has been researching for several years is due for publication this autumn. Roger is interested in hearing from anyone with a similar interest. Whilst never having involved himself in research commissions for gain, time permitting he is willing to offer such help as he can by way of advice and suggestions. He can be contacted in the first instance via the publishers.

New Developments at The Society of Genealogists

If you haven't visited the Society of Genealogists' buildings recently then you are in for a big surprise. There have been some very major changes brought about by our recent refurbishment that we hope have achieved important improvements.

The Society was founded in 1911 by genealogists who wanted to pool their research efforts: it was the first organisation of its kind in the British Isles. Although the Society grew slowly at first, the rising interest in family history since the 1960s has seen an enormous increase in Membership and some 15,000 people belong today, including about 10% from overseas.

Briefly, our objects are to promote, encourage and foster the study of genealogy and family history by (1) setting up a library of printed works relating to genealogy and allied subjects; (2) forming a permanent safe depository for pedigrees and other manuscripts; (3) indexing, transcribing and acquiring original records; (4) supplying advice and information; (5) associating with other like bodies in the UK and elsewhere; (6) assisting in research; and (7) contributing to the expenses of special projects of research, transcription, indexing or otherwise of value to genealogy.

That's quite a mouthful but, after nearly 100 years, our collections have grown to nearly 105,000 printed works: we now have the largest genealogical library outside the USA by far. Much of our material is unique and can't be seen anywhere else. What's more, although most family historians are concerned with the past, the Society is far from old-fashioned!

For those interested in how computers can be used to help in genealogical research and recording, the Society has published since 1982 a quarterly magazine 'Computers in Genealogy', one of the first in the world on this subject! The Society also has its own Web site at: www.sog.org.uk. Here you can find free copies of a number of the Society's publications, such as articles from 'Computers in Genealogy', the leaflet Guides series, and the 'County Sources at the Society of Genealogists' series. The latter series lists what the Library holds for each English county on Parish Register, Nonconformist Register and Marriage Licence copies, transcripts and indexes. Lists of the Library's Memorial Inscription holdings will shortly be added to this series. The web site also holds the Society's on-line Bookshop that contains over 5,000 different books, maps, microfiche, floppy disks and CD-ROMs to help you with your genealogical research.

The Society of Genealogists is leading the way in publishing some of its important data bases and finding aids on line on www. englishorigins.com. This site is growing all the time and will enable researchers to access information without having to visit the Society's premises in London. The Society also maintains an on-line members' mailing list which is a great forum for advice and help with research.

A National Society
We consider that we are the national genealogical society. Our members can be found in every branch of family history in the land and there can be few family history societies that do not include at least a few of us. We are particularly concerned with outreach beyond London and endeavour to sponsor or attend events in many other locations whenever possible. We founded and continue to run annually the largest Family History Fair in the country. We have an extensive publishing programme for books on genealogical subjects and on the collections in our Library.

Although our Library is our pride and joy, we feel that our Members are our greatest assets. We run a wide range of lectures, visits, courses and conferences - this year's programme can be obtained from the Society and is, of course, on the web site. Many of our Members work on projects at home or in the Society's rooms furthering our objects. Over half of all the Society's collections have been donated - mainly from Members - although we welcome donations and bequests of money and genealogical material from anyone.

The Library
In Spring 2001 our Library re-opened to considerable acclaim after a refurbishment programme costing more than £500,000. You really must visit our bright and cheerful building to see it in all its glory! It's not just the repainting - there is new carpeting throughout with new and increased seating on every floor. With the readers' areas in bright natural light and the new purpose built adaptable shelving. It all makes research a real pleasure. If you can drag yourself away from our re-designed and well-stocked bookshop, you will find a new airy common room, an air-conditioned lecture hall and facilities for the disabled - including a lift. We have banks of film and fiche readers and many computers all in a spacious air-conditioned research suite where our unbound manuscript collections and roll pedigrees are also available for fast delivery.

Our computer facilities include not just a growing library of CD-ROMs but free on-line access to a number of Internet genealogical sites such as FamilySearch or GENUKI. This includes free access to the data normally charged for on both the English Origins (www.englishorigins.com) and the USA based Ancestry.Com World Wide Web sites. The savings made by using these facilities could mean that you recoup your membership subscription in one or two visits!

Helpful and knowledgeable staff are available throughout the building, backed up by volunteers who are happy to answer questions and point readers in the right direction. Free tours and advice sessions are regularly arranged on alternate Saturdays and there are two open days a year for newcomers to look round and see what is in the library. Our own simple-to-use, fully-computerised genealogical catalogue with easy access can be found on every floor. This lists all of the library's holdings and is an indispensable finding aid Detailed Floor Guides are also available free on request. In many ways, the Society is a one-stop research centre. Why not see most, if not all, of the records you seek in one, comfortable place? In any event we may well hold the text books, indexes or finding aids that you will need before you set off for that faraway record office.

The Collections
Our collections include a vast range of key genealogical records such as more than 30,000 register copies and transcripts for some 10,000 parishes, Boyd's Marriage Index (7 million names), 11,000 monumental inscription transcripts, some 5,000 census indexes together with films of many enumeration books and will indexes for most British probate jurisdictions. We also hold large collections for many other countries not available anywhere else in the UK. We have a colossal amount of finished work (more than 8,000 printed family histories, nearly 800 boxes of manuscripts for some 16,000 names plus nearly 300 special collections of papers and a splendid collection of over 4,000 roll pedigrees many beautifully illuminated). Then there's Bernau's Index to Chancery records (over 4 million names), some 300 biographical dictionaries, our Great Card Index of 3 million entries - the list goes on and on. Our shelves bulge with directories, poll books, county and local histories, textbooks and books on schools, universities, professions, the clergy and the armed forces. We hold most UK genealogical magazines and many from overseas as well.

Nowadays, our impressive topographical collections attract many local historians. Biographers and social historians often use our Library as well. Still, for the serious family historian, membership of the Society is a must.

That's all very impressive but what's in it for me?
Although the Library is open to non-members for a modest charge, full Membership carries many other advantages. As well as unlimited free access to the superb Library, members receive each quarter the Genealogists Magazine, a Society Newsletter and a Library Accessions list. They can attend also lectures and courses at reduced rates and receive discounts on all Society publications. Members are allowed one free access each quarter from their own computer to Society data on English Origins, plus access to an on-line Members Mailing List.

The opportunity to associate with other family historians many possessing unrivalled experience is, of course, without price. For example, although there are currently about five hundred members who subscribe to the on-line Members Mailing List, anyone who asks a genealogical question there usually gets several replies, often from experts on the particular subject! And remember, your annual subscription could cost you less than a couple of cups of tea a week.

For a free Membership Pack contact the Society at Dept BF1, 14 Charterhouse Buildings, Goswell Road, LONDON EC1M 7BA
Telephone 020-7553 3291   Fax 020 7253 5677
e-mail membership@sog.org.uk
The Society is always happy to help with enquiries and the following contacts may be of assistance

Library & shop hours:
Tuesday, Friday & Saturday, 10am to 6pm;
Wednesday & Thursday, 10am to 8pm
Administration hours: Monday to Friday, 9am to 5pm

Contacts:
Library Enquiries: Tim Lawrence Tel: 020 7702 5485
Email: library@sog.org.uk
Membership: Miss Helen Marshall Tel: 020 7553 3291
Email: membership@sog.org.uk
Genealogy Enquiries: Miss Else Churchill
Tel: 020 7702 5488 Email: genealogy@sog.org.uk
Archivist & Document Collection
Miss Sarah Henning Tel: 020 7702 5491
Email; archivist @sog.org.uk
Shop: Ken Divall tel: 020 7702 5483
Email: sales@sog.org.uk
Lectures & courses: Miss Julia English
Tel: 020 7553 3290 Email; events@sog.org.uk
General Enquiries: Mrs Sheila Marshall
Tel: 020 7702 5480
Assistant Director (Finance & Admin): Mrs June Perrin
Tel: 020 7553 3296 Email: asstdir@sog.org.uk
Library & Shop Fax: 020 7250 1800
Membership & Events Fax: 020 7251 6773
Members of the Executive Committee can be contacted via the Society.

The Police
Fred Feather
Chairman
Essex Society for Family History

I suppose it is the sign of advancing years that a simple phrase can work you into a paroxysm of bile. In my case such is the phrase which I have used for my title. Quote – "**The Police** did such and such. " Quote – "My ancestor was in **The Police**." My reply is usually "What exactly do you mean by **The Police**?" There have been a couple of hundred different organisations within that definition and there are still at least 43. Forty-one years service with the brutal and licentious constabulary have left me with an enduring impression that there is no such thing. To me the Service (politically correct term) has always had a kaleidoscope of facets which were a constant source of wonder. Often the question was posed "How can I trace my ancestor? His marriage, census or death record described him as "policeman" (and increasingly in enquiries "policewoman."). Please forgive me if, in my reply, I occasionally become subjective and refer to the county of Essex, in which I was the first and founding curator of its Police Museum.

In one force (which is the "f... word" no longer used by those who yearn to achieve higher rank) we had a shift whose members included Sage, Onions and Bacon. Our jailer at Southend was a Fellow of the Royal Microscopical Society and I cannot count all those who left to became clergymen. The modern successor to Lord Nelson was, a few years since, a Detective Constable in Hertfordshire. From 1831 there were Special Constables raised for special occasions, the most famous being the future Emperor Napoleon III. Louis-Napoleon walked the beat in Kensington ,at the time of the Chartist problem and his duty armband is currently in the care of the Chelmsford and Essex Museum at Chelmsford. I always delighted in "canteen culture," where the stories of life and derring-do made my occupation something called "The Job", alas nowadays mostly described as "a job.".

We will assume that you will set about your task in two ways, that is, with the aid of a computer, or the other way. First, with a computer. I will start by quoting Bill Wood, the list owner of a rootsweb list (POLICE-UK-D-request@rootsweb.com) for persons seeking police ancestors. He writes "There is no such thing as a

centralised record of policemen". Nothing more true will ever be circulated. Alternatively: How to do it without a computer. Exactly the same truth prevails.

Prior to 1829 there were police forces, such as those in Glasgow and on the River Thames. The grave of the founder of the latter can be found in Paglesham churchyard, to the east of Southend and the west of Belgium. From London an organisation, pursuant to Bow Street Runners and known as the Horse and Foot Patrols, spread investigations out towards surrounding counties. Lists of officers are available, but they often became members of the Metropolitan Police when it was formed in 1829. The Public Record Office at Kew is strong on records of "The Met" and the other large forces, such as the pre-1922 Royal Irish Constabulary. P.R.O. leaflets on police subjects can be downloaded from their web-site.

Forces with the title "Police".
From an Act of Parliament of 1835 small towns with a charter began to employ policemen. In Essex they were Colchester, Harwich, Maldon and Saffron Walden. The early beat book of Colchester from 1836 has survived and is the basis on which the Steele Index of officers of that town, up to a 1947 amalgamation, was produced. Minutes of the Watch Committee, controlling body of a town force, have survived. In Colchester each new officer was introduced by name to that committee, their names minuted. Harwich and Saffron Walden officers are being traced from the 1841 and 1851 censuses and newspaper reports until their demise, when they and many other small forces ceased to exist in 1857, as policing of all areas became compulsory. Maldon, officers traced in a similar fashion, lasted until made obsolete by future legislation in 1889 by amalgamation. Those large enough to survive independently used the title "Police". The largest town forces retained the title for another 130 years. The two big London services, the Metropolitan Police and City of London Police, always retained this title. My own force, Essex Police, assumed it in 1974, when their former title, The Essex and Southend on Sea Joint Constabulary, became too unwieldy for administration and cap badges. Watch Committees disappeared nearly forty years ago.

Forces called "Constabulary"
Under the provisions of an 1839 Act of Parliament, Rural Police emerged, Wiltshire late in that year, Essex and various others a few weeks later in 1840. Where a larger county force amalgamated with a smaller Police or Constabulary, the title "Constabulary" usually survived.

In Essex we believe that we have records of everyone serving since 1840 and, with the use of our Giggins Index, can nearly always produce a biography. There is also the Feather Index of everyone who served with the former Southend on Sea Constabulary (1914-1969). Constabulary records can be found in the papers of Quarter Sessions, their supervising authority, usually reported in newspapers or retained as originals in Record Offices. Later this body became the Standing Joint Committee, now Police Committee. Others, such as

Hertfordshire Constabulary (1841-2001), destroyed their records many years since, and painful reconstructions from newspapers will be required. Kent Constabulary was not formed until 1857. Many of the 43 UK forces retain the word "Constabulary", many other are still called it despite disposing of the name many years since.

Other policemen
All referred to as policemen were not necessarily in a Town Police or a County Constabulary. Within my own county I recall security men at Southend Airport (Southend on Sea Constabulary Special Constables) and later at Stansted Airport (British Airports Constabulary). On the railways we had members of the London Transport Police, Eastern Counties Railway, pre-1947 the London Midland & Scottish and London and North Eastern Railways, the London Tilbury and Southend Railway (who in Victorian times sponsored an Essex Constabulary officer). One enquiry I answered assured a lady that she was not going mad, in that successive censuses showed her target being promoted from Detective Constable to Station Master. The Metropolitan Police positioned Special Branch officers at immigration points such as the port of Harwich. Whilst working on the 1851 Devon census I discovered a pocket of Metropolitan Policemen stationed in Royal Docks, such as Portsmouth and Devonport. Royal residences also drew their men. Commercial Docks had policemen and that is what they were called, until a short time ago, when established forces such as the Royal Parks Constabulary, Docks Police, Ministry of Defence Police and British Rail Police became "agencies." In Essex we maintain a strays register, the Bayliss Index, of men and women of other forces who were temporarily in our county.

A miscellany of police museums.
Police Museums come and go, based on the whims of those who command. Bad news for the museum of the former Essex Constabulary (1840-1969), loaded onto the launch "Vigilant" and ordered dumped somewhere off Southend Pier in the early 1970s. Someone wanted a computer suite in the room it occupied. Good news; some rebellious spirit rescued most of the goodies and put them in a room where normally only dogs practising sniffing for drugs would find them. Most are now in the reconstituted museum of 1991. Other collections have been mothballed, including, I believe, Cambridgeshire, Cheshire and Cumbria though some part of these collections may be in Record Offices. Many towns such as Huntingdon and Kings Lynn have excellent police museums. Others such as Kent have placed theirs within a tourist facility, Chatham Historic Dockyard. Many respected museums, such as that of Devon and Cornwall, are on the back burner due to the loss of the services of the person with the knowledge to run them. And, these can return to the game at any time. There are also well-funded and independent museums such as that of Greater Manchester and the West Midlands services. Of the situation above the border I am ignorant but informed that there are also centres of excellence there. In London the City Police have a museum with the excellent Roger Appleby as curator. The Metropolitan Police museum is still a dream, but it has friends. Do not confuse this project with the Black Museum at New Scotland Yard. That is not about policemen, it is the world's oldest crime-museum, mainly devoted to criminality and artefacts. At Weathersfield in Essex we also have the excellent museum of the Ministry of Defence Police (its forebears, the civilian police of Army, Navy and Air Force). Military organisations such as the Royal Military Police (Chichester), the R.A.F. Police and the Navy

(Chatham Dockyard) have police museums.

How to identify a policeman from a picture.
Senior officers were most photographed, but few in number. Wiltshire and Essex had not a dozen chief constables between them in over 320 years joint service. Victorian uniforms can be sumptuous but, a word of warning, there were many ex-military senior officers that uniforms can be confusing. We have no picture of the founding Chief Constable of Essex, John Bunch Bonnemaison McHardy, (served 1841-1881), perhaps because he was a full Admiral and could have as much braid as he required.

Ranks were mostly denoted by military insignia. Constables wore numbers, a prime source for police humour; One Training Officer numbered a good friend "40 Watts." Said Brian: "Are they suggesting I am not too bright?" PC49 always provokes laughter after a 1940's radio show. PC 1001 was always described as "Clean round the bend" Essex does not issue "666" or "999" as anyone with those numbers attending a pub brawl would be under extra pressure, neither, in deference to his family, has that of a late lamented colleague, murdered on duty. Our collection of photographs, with the helmet or collar, showing a number, is a prime source for identification. Acting sergeants had stripes and numbers, full and station sergeants had crowned stripes. Inspectors wore Bath Stars, Superintendents and above, crowns, "pips" and laurels. This of course varied between forces and eras. The Essex Constabulary in 1840 had only Superintendents and Constables, later Inspectors were added, only in 1855 did the Sergeant appear. In different times there were Chief Inspectors and Chief Superintendents. In London the chiefs of both forces were Commissioners. Some smaller forces had High Constables

When first formed the police took a non-army profile, with reinforced civilian top hats, but from the 1870s the majority of working policemen wore helmets. There are three distinct shapes; A) a Roman style comb from front to back, this was, and still is, worn by the City of London Police, but the Victorian Metropolitan Police also wore it for several decades. It is presently used by Essex, Kent, Thames Valley and many others. The comb has a small filigree front, in the majority of these forces featuring a Maltese Cross, whilst Essex has the cockle-shell in honour of Southend Constabulary. B) a military looking spike & ball on the top, these include Humberside, Devon & Cornwall and Royal Parks Constabulary. C) the commonest helmet has a rose-top and is used by the present Metropolitan Police and many others. From 1970 red, blue and green insignia arrived, pioneered by Greater Manchester, Metropolitan, Essex and Kent. Kepis were the working headgear of senior officers but with the advent of the car the peaked cap became fashionable. In Scotland a cap with the black and white diced band replaced the helmet some 70 years ago, whilst in England caps were plain blue until about 1970, when diced bands were adopted (but not by Surrey for many years).

Heraldry identifies uniforms geographically, and the period can be identified by the crown used. Not all forces used a crown, some forces, including Norfolk, did not use helmet badges. There are three types of crown; A) Geulphic or Victorian - a distinct high sided shape worn until 1901. In Essex they sawed these off when the old Queen died and soldered on B) The Edward or King's crown, much heavier but with a lower profile. A good

place to learn the difference is on old postage stamps. Kings wore the Edward crown until 1952, since then we have the familiar C) or Queen's crown.

Jackets - The wearing of the arm band indicated whether an officer was on duty and can be a good ageing or identifying mark. The City of London still wear theirs in red/white vertical stripes. The Metropolitan Police wore blue/white vertical stripes. In Colchester Police the armband was horizontal blue/white.

Medals are a good dating method, their configuration and shape identify a military and police career. Those issued by the sovereign are worn on the left breast, those by other authorities on the right breast. Victorian medals are for temperance, marksmanship and for bravery awarded by local authority, by the Royal Society for the Protection of Life from Fire, the Royal Humane Society and sundry other worthy groups. Registers for some of these awards are with parent organisations and the P.R.O. Familiar Sovereign's ribbons are the blue/white/blue of the Long Service & Good Conduct Medal, issued from 1952 and the red/white/black of the Special Constabulary medal, issued since the Great War.

Decorated truncheons are a subject that follows many of the above rules but should be taken to an expert for analysis. They mostly pre-date Victoria or were issued within her reign, those special presentations continued until this day.

Memorials and diversions.
In Lancashire Sergeant Anthony Rae of Preston is charting the deaths of officers of all UK forces killed on duty. Essex Police is about to launch a web-site as a memorial to about 150 officers who died violently on duty or in the service of their country. There are Rolls of Honour in Chelmsford, Belfast, Scotland Yard and many others with such details. Another unusual source could be Coventry Cathedral, where is housed the National Register and Memorial to all special constables killed on duty, poignantly dominated by Reserve Constables of the Royal Ulster Constabulary. The earliest page is devoted to Henry Trigg, Parish Constable of Berden in Essex, murdered in the course of a robbery in 1814. At our Chelmsford Museum we also have details of the investigators of that case, Bow Street Runners Vickery, Bishop and Stafford. I know because I arranged both entries.

Now to endeavour (was that not Inspector Morse's Christian name?) to get the Freemason canard out of the way. In Victorian times senior officers often had a prominent social position within a community, but were not allowed to openly support political parties, which meant that they could not join the Liberal or Conservative clubs or frequent certain pubs. Masons provided one means of socialising with peer groups which is nowadays provided by golf clubs. Masonics were then often very open and brothers named in all newspaper reports of funerals etc. Over the years many joined, some, it is suggested, in the hope of socialising with those who could promote them. I personally think those days are past and that there are now comparatively few police Masons but many more golfers. Read all about it in "My Ancestor was a Freemason" by Pat Lewis. If you suspect a police ancestor of mixing with clergy, school teachers, soldiers, sailors, marines, firemen, solicitors and other local worthies, you could try to trace the present whereabouts of their Lodge and write to them. You may be pleased with the response.

How to contact police sources.
Here are some things you might consider:

Contact the Record Office in the area in which you suspect your target was located. Ask about local police records and if the local service has a museum.

Post your enquiry on the rootsweb above. Metropolitan enquiries get a fabulous response via Paul Rason of The Friends of the Metropolitan Police Museum and follow up by Maggie Bird the New Scotland Yard archivist.

Log on to the Internet and search for force histories (www.police.uk). Some service sites, such as Lincolnshire, Merseyside and Bradford may give you a pleasant surprise. Written histories such as East Yorkshire and Sunderland are interesting. To mark the 150th anniversary of foundation many counties produced histories in 1989/1990. Look out for the Police Vehicle Enthusiasts Club.

Write to one of the 43 UK services, perhaps the Garda Siochana in Dublin, or the various agencies. Address it to the Chief Officer, enclosing a self addressed envelope. This puts pressure on the recipient. Ask what facilities they have, who is interested in their force history and if anyone answers historical enquiries. Enclose a photocopy of your photograph and they may point you in the right direction.

Please note that the Police History Society is an academic society devoted to research on police subjects and is not usually geared to accepting enquiries about individual officers. There is no central source.

Now, I have tried to show you that **The Police** is a touch too bland a title for such a varied organisation and be assured that generalisations can often be shot down in flames. My advice is **No quick e-mailed** "do me a look-up" The information is probably there, but you will have to work for it.

Wives, mothers, sisters, daughters:
finding out about women in local and family history
Dr Jane Batchelor

Anyone who has tried to find out about their family/local area will be aware that finding simple facts about who people are and what they do can be difficult, but this is especially the case when you try to find about women in history. This article attempts to offer some useful hints about where an ordinary person may start to find about female relatives or women in local history. In doing so it aims to cast some light on the value of treating local and family history in a more creative way.

Milborne Port, glovers, 1910. Photograph (S.C.C. negative 28117): source Somerset Studies Library, Taunton. This photograph appeared as plate 34 in the Victoria County History's *Somerset VII.*

Women, families and the importance of names
To find out about somebody, you need to know who s/he is, and this means knowing her/his name. This is not as easy as it sounds, especially when finding out about women. Women can be found under a variety of names; their maiden name, their married name, another name if they are married again. Given moreover that in the past spelling of names was not standardised, and the popular tradition, which still continues, of naming girls after their mothers as boys are named after their fathers and you can see how easy it is to confuse two women from the same family, or to lose track of a female relative altogether. Thus it is always sensible to check and recheck your information, making sure names, dates and places tally, so that you know you are finding out about the right person.

Dictionaries, encyclopedias, reference books and indexes
The fact that a woman has traditionally taken a man's name when she marries underlines an important point. Women have traditionally been defined in relation to men, and this tradition is reflected in libraries, research centres and in books. In short, as far as many dictionaries and reference books are concerned, women are almost invisible. As children we are all encouraged to look up things in dictionaries and encyclopedias, as these give the "answers" to our questions. So, when we look up something in an index and cannot find it we may be discouraged. We may feel that if there is no information about something then the subject must be trivial, minor and unimportant. To overcome this challenge, it is best to play the dictionaries at their own game. There are a number of ways to do this. Firstly, if women are traditionally defined in relation to others, if they do usually have their own entry in a dictionary, then use the others as a starting point. That is, if you know your female relative is related to an important local man, family or organisation then begin with this, rather than with the woman herself. Look for the father, son, uncle, famous male literary figure if you cannot find her; details about her life may be buried in details about them. Secondly, be aware that the trivial can be important. It is

illuminating to look at the bits of reference books which you would usually ignore. For example, sections on the family and domestic life are often shunted to the back; since women have traditionally been defined by their families, this is a good place to start finding out about them, a place where subjects of "minor" importance are covered. Moreover, in many dictionaries the best place to find out about what women did is in the sections on minor literary figures. Thirdly, trust you own judgement. The trouble with dictionaries is that if ten books repeat that Mrs Brown was a minor local figure the information takes on the solidity of fact. Few people believe everything that they read in the tabloids; in the same way, it is wise not to believe everything you read in dictionaries. So, if there does not seem to be any information in a dictionary, then ask; ask a librarian, ask a researcher, look for the information hidden in footnotes or bibliographies at the back of reference books, keep an open mind. Fourthly, if the dictionaries you look at do not seem to be helping you, try a different dictionary. Today there are also an increasing amount of alternative dictionaries and reference sources available about who women are, and what they did, which attempt to think about the real women behind the myths. Your local library may not always have them, but they can be ordered through interlibrary loan, or through a subject search. Above all, do not give up; information is nearly always there, even if you cannot immediately see it.

Reading God's Word: religious books and the religious life for women
In medieval times religious life was a well established alternative to marriage for women, providing the chance of education and the opportunity to read and write. The medieval church may not always have presented women favourably, but, as with ordinary men who entered the church, it did give many of them a chance of education they might not otherwise have had. The sixteenth century likewise saw a significant number of books on the virtues of women, albeit the emphasis was increasing switched to virtuous wives and mothers and the spiritual importance of marriage. Many women naturally took the opportunity to read and write religious books, and Bible reading became a new argument for women's literacy. A woman needed to read so that she could be all society

wanted her to be: it is no accident that well into the nineteenth century religious institutions remained places where women could obtain an education. If this suited society it also suited many women who wished to portray themselves as "virtuous". So, in finding out about women and what they did then it is worth always looking at the history of convents, at religious books and pamphlets, at local church newspapers, at the family Bible held traditionally by the eldest daughter in each family in which family trees were recorded and at the records of churches and charities where women have long had an established presence: for, women and religion have never been far apart.

Virtuous wives and mothers: books on household management

As well as religious books for women there have always been books on household management, on cookery, needlework, fashions, childcare and all aspects of running a home, many of which provide a fascinating glimpse into women's everyday life which may not be recorded elsewhere. From sixteenth century herbals to Mrs Beaton, from 1950's books on keeping a perfect house to Nigella Lawson's *Domestic Goddess* this tradition is very much still alive, and has in part been perpetuated by women as a way of enhancing their image in relation to other's expectations of themselves but also a medium in which they can freely express their thoughts, ideas, and opinions. In this context too women's magazines, specifically targeted at women and often containing works by them are also worth looking at. An interesting way to find out about the world of your grandmother is look at the household books and magazines which many families have lying around; such books may also still be picked up easily in book fairs and charity shops.

"Private literature"

In writing about God and about the godly home women kept safely within the personal sphere, but these were not the only "private" means by which they could promote themselves. Letter writing, biographies of family members, prefaces and wills are all ways in which women could have space to write. But in fact none of these types of writing are necessarily as "private" as they appear, and can tell you a great deal about the society in which your relative lived. For instance, in an age before the proliferation of media and PR men and women alike recognised the opportunities for promotion not only for the author but for themselves which a flattering preface offered, whilst wills have always been a means by which private wishes are made public. Similarly, a will can tell you what mattered to a woman, how literate she was, her financial position, or simply, if she had a family Bible; which, as has been said, may provide an essential clue in finding out about your family.

Local history collections: women as local history

Another window into finding out about women is looking in local libraries, museums and records offices. This makes sense for two reasons. First, family and cultural expectations for women have meant that often although not always women have been based for long periods in one area, and so are well placed to play a pivotal role in local life. Second, whereas national history collections tend to have a broad focus, covering "major" works, local history collections are more specific and focused on one area. This means that, intentionally or not, more "domestic", "specialist", "minor" and "private" works, i.e. works that might be likely to mention women find their way into these collections.

Literature and "special" collections

Many of the things I have said so far about finding out about women in history apply to the relationship between women and literature. Firstly, it should now appear that the idea that women were not generally writing before the twentieth century is a misleading one. The problem of literacy for women as for men was a general one; nevertheless there were quite a few women writing on a variety of topics, albeit some of these have been buried and dismissed over time. Secondly, as regards fiction, it is always important to remember that fiction is generally written for enjoyment rather than for information. Nevertheless, fiction written about women and by women often provides a useful way of finding out about women's lives – sometimes, the only way. In finding out about women as writers of fiction as in finding out about women as local figures it is important to bear in mind that judgements repeated about women are not necessarily "true" or based on fact; they are just as likely to be based on repetition, a bit like a good story doing the rounds in a pub. Again, it is wise to search the minor sections of reference books and indeed poetry books; it is important not to take at face value the idea that a woman has written only one poem or only one work. In this context the more detailed focus of special collections can be invaluable. Often attached to or formed from local history special collections mean that instead of going to a library and reading the same entry or piece of information about a woman you may suddenly find a whole collection of her works which have not been reprinted.

Making something out of nothing

Finally, when there appears to be very little to go on in finding out about local women or female relatives the following suggestions may help:

a) *Make use of oral history*
If it could be argued that much of the history available to the reader is written from the premise that predominantly male privileged public lives are what count, then conversely there has been a recent trend towards the recording of oral history, the unwritten, everyday, mundane, domestic and the private, the life of the ordinary person, whether male or female, and an increasing number of television programmes and recordings have encapsulated this history. On a more basic level, it is worth simply asking your mother, aunt, or grandmother about their lives as a starting point for thinking about the past lives of women.

b) *Use alternative sources*
If you cannot find the information you need in one book, then try another. As stated, interlibrary loan and subject searches can be a useful way of tracking down a wider range of information. Domestic books can be found at book fairs, charity shops and with relatives. As many women are locally based, try the back issues of your local newspaper. I have mentioned the value of household books; household objects can be equally informative. Women have long been at the centre of the household and the things that they have and use. Samplers, hatpins, clothes, pictures, cooking pots, warming pans, ornamental fans; all these things have been an essential part of what women did, and how they defined themselves. It is also worth making use of the Internet. A relatively new and flexible information source the Internet lends itself to finding out alternative information. York University has a website on women and local history

(http://www.york.ac.uk/services/library/subjects/womeni
nt.htm) and Indiana University has a useful website on
finding information on women
(http://odin.indstate.edu/level1.dir/lio.dir.women.html)

c) *Use what you have well*
If you have a very little information about a woman, then
trust only sources which you feel to be reliable. There is
nothing wrong with using this information to build up a
picture of what you think the person you are finding out
about might have been like. For example, if a Census
return tells you a relative was a hat maker you may not
be able to find out about where she had her shop, but
you might be able to information about the lives of hat
makers in a book on the history of women's fashions.

d) *When possible, use primary sources*
Since much of the information which has come down to
us through the centuries about women and what they did
has been filtered in a particular way it is worth getting
back wherever possible to first hand accounts, especially
first hand accounts from women. These are likely to give
a better feeling for what women actual thought and did
than the truncated versions that tend to reach us now.

e) *Keep an open mind*:
Be prepared to change your mind about information in
the light of new details which you find out.

In conclusion, finding out about women in family and
local history is not always easy, but it is possible, if you
are prepared to work hard at finding and checking the
information at your disposal, and are not put off by the
people who will tell you, because they sincerely believe
it, that there is no information about women and what
they did. In this brief article I have tried to raise some
questions in your mind about assumptions in family and
local history, assumptions that say that local history and
family history only tell you about important local men
and their families, that if information is not in a

dictionary or placed at the back of a book it does not
matter, assumptions that if you read something it must be
true. The jettisoning of these ideas has implications not
only for finding out about the history of women, but
about the history of us all; believing them is like reading
a biography with half the pages ripped out. The past
makes us what we are, it forms our views, attitudes and
aspirations; if we know only half our past then we are
stumbling blindly into the future. There is information on
wives, mothers, sisters and daughters. But do not take
my word for it: find out for yourself.

Select Bibliography
Tillie Olsen, *Silences* (London, Virago, 1980) – focuses
particularly on oral history, and the need for women's voices
to be heard.
Bonnie S. Anderson and Judith P. Zinsser eds. *A History of
Their Own; Women in Europe from Prehistory to Present*
(London, Penguin 1989) – a series of essays tracing the
history of women from prehistory through to today.
Did Women Have a Renaissance? In *Women, History and
Theory: The Essays of Joan Kelly*, ed. By Catharine R.
Stimpson (Chicago: University of Chicago Press, 1984) pp.
19-50 – looks at the idea of the Renaissance in relation to
women.
Sherrin Marshall ed. *Women in Reformation and Counter-
Reformation Europe: Private and Public Worlds*
(Indianapolis: Indiana University Press, 1989) – a series of
essays looking at the relationship between women, their
domestic lives and the turbulent religious debates and
conflicts of the sixteenth and seventeenth century.
Jane Spencer, *The Rise of the Woman Novelist from Aphra
Behn to Jane Austen* (4th edn, 1st pub. 1986 (Oxford: Basil
Blackwell, 1993) – looks at the way women used the novel,
a developing new literary form, to mirror life from a female
perspective.
Moira Ferguson, *Subject to Others: British Women and
Colonial Slavery 1670 – 1834* (London, Routledge, 1992) –
examines the sometimes ambiguous relationship which
British women, subject to society's restrictions, had to
slavery and the power it gave them in relation to others.

Stanton Long harvest home. Photograph from Shropshire County Museum Service, Much Wenlock Museum, ref. MW 117,
from a postcard, 1911; reproduced with the kind permission of the family of the late Mrs Wadlow.
This photograph appeared as plate 37 in the Victoria County History's *Salop X*.

EWZ –
the best source for Eastern Europe's Germans
Dave Obee

*shows how Wartime Documents from Germany
can help researchers*

researchers.

This series includes personal information on more than 2.1 million individuals processed by the central German authority for the immigration and naturalization of qualified ethnic Germans for Reich citizenship during the period 1939-1945. These people, nominally citizens of Poland, the Baltic states, the Soviet Union, France, and the countries of southeastern Europe, became part of the National Socialist plans for Germanizing the frontiers of the future Reich. Reichsführer-SS Heinrich Himmler created the EWZ in October 1939, a few weeks after Germany invaded Poland, as a way to ease the resettlement to German territory of ethnic Germans living in Eastern Europe. The Nazis believed all ethnic Germans should be united in one state, just as they believed that non-Germans were to be removed from German soil. The more Germans in Germany, the theory went, the stronger the nation would be. The first immigration office started operations in October 1939 in Poland.

It had to process about 70,000 Baltic Germans repatriated from Estonia and Latvia. This was followed by a major movement of ethnic Germans from Galicia and western Volhynia. In the first year, the immigration headquarters was moved several times before being located on Holzstrasse in Litzmannstadt (Lodz) for the duration of the war. There were several sub-offices, such as the one used by Maria and Anna Krause in Welun, close to the camps where the new arrivals were held while they were processed. Much of the trek from the east was often accomplished on foot, although some people had help from the German troops. The first part of the great trek into German territory ended for most people at one of the temporary camps. For the most part, new arrivals were assigned to camps in groups; since these people had been travelling together from their villages in Russia, the result was that people who had been neighbors in Russia were once again neighbors in the refugee areas. And those people often went to the local EWZ office, to take care of the necessary paperwork, within days of each other. There were, of course, exceptions to the rule. Not everyone from one village ended up in the same camp; it could have been because of which camps had free space, or which camps housed relatives who had arrived earlier. In any event, most of the people who left Russian areas together ended up in a temporary camp together. These camps were widely scattered throughout German territory. Several were in the Lodz area; others were in Silesia; some were as far east as Bavaria. As the Germans arrived in EWZ offices, they were registered and photographed. Entire families were generally processed together, with separate forms for every person aged 15 years or older. An inventory was taken of their property, and compensation was often granted for non-portable items that had to be left behind. In some cases, this would have come as a shock to the refugees, who had been told by the German authorities that their move out of their Russian homes

Any family historian who still believes mobility is a recent notion should consider the case of Anton and Maria Krause. Anton and his wife, the former Maria Tutschinski, were both born in Latvia in 1881. Within a few years of their marriage they made their way to London, where their daughter Anna was born in 1910. Anton died in England, and Maria and her daughter set out again this time to the Saporoshje area of Russia. They were soon caught up in the horrors of the Russian revolution, followed by the forced collectivization of farmland, then the famine created by Josef Stalin, and then the war. In 1943, they joined the great trek of refugees out of the Soviet Union, accompanying the retreating Wehrmacht army to German territory. They were placed in a temporary camp until their applications to settle in Germany could be processed by the authorities. On April 3, 1944, they went to the Einwandererzentralstelle (literally, immigration office) in Welun to complete their paperwork. In so doing, they joined about two million other people from outside of Germany who, during the Second World War, sought permission to live in Germany. The records created by the Einwandererzentralstelle, opened to public use in the mid 1990s, represent one of the greatest resources for genealogists seeking information on any relatives who had lived in the old German colonies in Russian territory.

There is one thing that all genealogists have in common, no matter what area of the world they are working on, no matter how much work was done by others in the family, no matter when they started their research. They should have started sooner. So imagine being able to go back, and make up for lost time, by collecting information from people who have already died. Imagine discovering that your relatives had been extensively interviewed about family history, and the papers they filled out half a century ago are available to you today. That is possible with the Einwandererzentralstelle (EWZ) records from the Berlin Document Center. Available on microfilm through the National Archives in the United States and the Family History Library of the Church of Jesus Christ of Latter-day Saints, they offer great rewards to was only temporary. The screening process for eligible ethnic Germans initially took three to four hours, with examinations by six to nine people. Later, the time needed stretched to six hours, then two days. Each arrival aged six or older was given a basic health test, accompanied by an SS racial examination, which resulted in an assessment of the overall racial quality of both the individual and the family. The authorities then looked into the political activities and professions of the new arrivals. If everything checked out, the arrivals were generally assigned to new homes in German territory.

The forms completed by the new arrivals at the EWZ offices are of tremendous value to today's family historians. They contain basic information on the individuals who completed the forms, including dates of birth and marriage, as well as the names and vital information, where known, of parents and grandparents. The paperwork reveals, in many cases, much more pre-war migration than would be expected. Some people moved between the various areas of Ukraine, such as between Bessarabia and Volhynia. Some people, such as Anna Krause, were born in England, or Canada or the United States. Apparently, their parents had tried life outside of Russia, didn't like it, and returned. Sometimes, these moves within Russian territory were not voluntary. The forms reveal where the Germans were sent during the First World War, and the removal by the Russians of Germans within 100 kilometres of the border prior to the invasion by Germany in 1941.

Many of the people who arrived in German territory during the Second World War found themselves in Poland or the eastern part of Germany at the war's end. They were captured and shipped to Russia, then Kasachstan. The survivors were not allowed to return to Germany (with their children and grandchildren) until the 1990s. For those who did not live long enough to get out of the Soviet Union, the EWZ documents represent a remarkable collection. For many of these people, family historians will never be able to find any documentation other than what appears in the Berlin Document Center files. The EWZ office processed about one million ethnic Germans during the five years of its existence. The vast majority of these people came from areas which later became part of the Soviet Union.

In 1945, most of these records were seized by the Allied Forces. About 80,000 files were lost or burned before capture. Those that survived are available on 8,000 rolls of microfilm, through the U.S. National Archives II in College Park, Maryland.

The EWZ records come in three basic series. While there is a lot of duplication between the three series, each one offers something that the other two do not. And, in some cases, files for certain people appear in one series, but are not to be found in the other series. All three should be consulted when possible. The three series:

1. Anträge, or applications
More than 400,000 applications, arranged by country or region, then alphabetically by family name. Each application might include several documents; together, they represent the most comprehensive series in the set of EWZ microfilms. Documents found in a typical file might include basic family history information going back three generations, as

well as the details on children; a story written by the applicant, describing his or her life; a pedigree chart; and citizenship documents. This series includes:
EWZ50 - USSR. About 110,000 files on 843 microfilm rolls.
EWZ51 - Romania. About 82,000 files on 700 microfilm rolls.
EWZ52 - Poland. About 100,000 files on 701 microfilm rolls.
EWZ53 - Baltic. About 73,000 files on 587 microfilm rolls.
EWZ5410 - Yugoslavia. About 23,000 files on 150 microfilm rolls.
EWZ5420 - Romania. About 14,000 files on 223 microfilm rolls.
EWZ5430 - Bulgaria. About 700 files on 6 microfilm rolls.
These films are not in the FHL system; they are available only through the U.S. National Archives in College Park.

2. E/G Kartei, basic card index
The central registry for naturalization. The set includes about 2.9 million cards in phonetic order on 1,964 microfilm rolls. These cards list name, place and date of birth, religion, marital status, education, profession, citizenship, all relatives in the same group of immigrants, and information on the property left behind. The information here is not as comprehensive as for the first series, but does include details of family relationships and physical characteristics that are not found on the forms in the other two series. Also, many, many more people are included in this index than are in the other two series; part of the reason is that this set covers all of the new arrivals in Germany, no matter where they were from. These films are available through the Family History Library.

3. Stammblätter, family forms
There are about one million forms here on 742 rolls. The documents provide name, date and place of birth, citizenship, country of origin, religion, marital status, number of children, their names and dates of birth, as well as the names and dates of birth of parents. A photograph of each applicant is generally included. These forms have more information than the big card index, but less than the individual files. These files are organized by number, rather than alphabetically, so this set can't be tackled first. If a person is listed in the basic card index, but not the applications, check the family forms to get a bit of extra information. This set enables researchers to quickly find neighbours of their people of interest, and those neighbours will often offer clues that will help research the families in the direct line. That's because people from one village were often processed at roughly the same time, so their numbers would be close to each other. Once numbers are found for some relevant people, a researcher can find out who went through the system with them. This series is also available through the Family History Library. There are two ways to access the EWZ records, by starting with films from either the Anträge or E/G Kartei series. Given that one series (the E/G Kartei) is more accessible than the other, thanks to the Family History Library, the choice will usually be easy. Both of the series are in alphabetical order, but there is a knack to using the E/G Kartei. Names are not filed in strict alphabetical order; sometimes, all names with the same basic pronunciation are grouped together. If you're looking for Dalke, for example, be sure to try Dahlke instead. The file cards in the E/G Kartei series aren't the most valuable, in terms of offering information to genealogists, but be sure to check the

back of the cards (the second page on the film) for the names of the person's siblings. This is not generally recorded in the other EWZ documentation. If possible, a researcher should start with the Anträge series. It offers far more information than the other series, simply because it has copies of all of the forms that had to be filled out by the ethnic Germans who were desperately trying to prove their ancestry. On the other hand, the Anträge series does not cover as many people.

Both of these two series will offer a critical bit of information, the EWZ number, which is used to access the files in the Stammblätter. The EWZ numbers were assigned to arrivals aged 15 years or older as the arrivals were being processed by the EWZ teams. Since most people in one village went through the system at the same general time, the EWZ numbers they received are generally close to each other. It's a simple matter, once a few EWZ numbers are known, to get the Stammblätter films that include those numbers. And those films will include a large number of people of interest to your family, if not all of the people from the village. Checking all of the families from a village will probably reveal a variety of missing or unknown relatives. Most of these will be women with new surnames as a result of marriage. In many families, it's more important to search for women than for men. The reason is simple: Josef Stalin. These forms were filled out a few years after Stalin's infamous purges of the 1930s, which saw many males arrested and either murdered or sent to forced labor camps. A search of the records based strictly on known surnames may fail to find much new information. The people with that surname are often people who married into the family; they couldn't give a lot of information to the authorities, because they didn't know it. The women who would know the details are the women who married into other families, and who appear in the records under their new surnames.

The information on the forms is remarkably accurate, most of the time. That is probably because the people providing the information were well aware what fate might await them if they provided the wrong answers. Also, given the uncompromising nature of the German government during the time of war, the people providing the information had plenty of reason to have fear. That's why it's possible to find full information on illegitimate children, and on common-law marriages. The people involved did not want to take the chance of covering these things up. You will also find references to past involvement in the Russian army, and to relatives who were serving in the Russian army or living in North America at the time the forms were being filled out.

The autobiographies of the arrivals found in the Anträge files vary considerably in quality and quantity of content. In some cases, the autobiographies simply repeat the basic vital information provided in other forms. In other cases, they provide fascinating accounts of what life was like. These stories may not have been provided by the direct ancestors of a researcher, but if they were done by people who lived in the same village, it is likely the same conditions were faced by the direct ancestor. These stories can certainly add color and drama to

any family history project. While the EWZ forms offer many benefits, they are not perfect. There were plenty of people who had things they were desperate to hide. There was no point, for example, in admitting to Jewish ancestry; that would only mean a trip to the gas chamber. So, in some cases, family information has been altered.

There are forms that have errors that can be clearly identified as such. People did their best to be accurate, but it's no different than getting birth information from a death certificate today. The people were relying on what they had been told, and what had been passed down through the years. Some of the errors are in the spelling of village names. It could be that the person providing the information had no idea how to spell the name of the community where he or she had lived as a child, and it could be that the person filling out the form didn't know either, and couldn't read Cyrillic. So many, many village names are to be taken with a grain of salt. Sometimes, obvious errors were missed by the German authorities. The EWZ files identify one woman who was born in 1891. Her father had died in 1881. That 10-year discrepancy is repeated in a couple of places in the file, but nobody noticed.

Another file took a family back to 1810, one of the earliest dates possible in a three-generation chart done in the 1940s. The only problem was that the woman born in 1810 had had a son in 1886. Again, the obvious error was not caught. One more bit of caution about the forms: Sometimes, documents have been misfiled. This is especially a concern when dealing with the Anträge series, which often has large files, and a greater likelihood of an error in handling. When you find a file referring to a person of interest, always take a moment to scan through the adjacent files on the microfilm. But even with these words of caution, the value of the EWZ collection far outweighs any concerns about errors. For many people doing research into the Germans from Russia, this series is the most important source yet available.

And while it helps to know German, it's not essential. It's possible to sort out the basic family units easily, because a researcher is dealing with standardized forms, basic names and simple German words. The EWZ collection will provide solid information needed in building comprehensive histories of individual German villages in Russia. There are three basic ways to gain access to the information in the EWZ microfilms: — Two of the three basic series are available through the Family History Library of the Church of Jesus Christ of Latter-day Saints and its branches.

Researchers in the Washington area (USA) can check the films in the archives on your behalf. The microfilms are available for purchase. The cost is $34 US if you're in the States, and $39 US if you're in another country.

Dave Obee, an author and lecturer on family history research techniques, is a partner in Interlink Bookshop and Genealogical Services in Victoria, British Columbia, Canada.

One-Place Genealogy
David Hawgood

English Street, Carlisle.

Other articles in this book describe "One-Place Studies". In most of these researchers put together information about the people in a place from a variety of sources. I want to put these into the context of "One- Place Genealogy" which is a wider subject, the knowledge of a place and of its records which have lists of names. I will do this from the point of view of the person who accumulates information about one place, and from the point of view of the family historian who needs information about a place.

How did I get involved? I did start a one-place study of Warminster in Wiltshire over 20 years ago, but it was for an Open University course project and had a very limited scope, people who lived there from 1820 to 1850. I still have the box of index cards and help people who make relevant enquiries on Wiltshire email lists. But my interest in the general subject started when John Dowding and then Colin Mills collected details of a number of one-place studies, but didn't find a way of publishing the list. I have been writing and publishing books on the use of computers for genealogy for some years, and offered to extend my activity. So by the time this Family and Local History Handbook is published, I will have written and published a book "One-Place Genealogy" which will be available from Family Tree Magazine and the Federation of Family History Societies (Publications) Ltd (FFHS). I sent letters or emails to everyone on Colin Mills' list of one-place studies, and will publish the list of those replying, with details of their studies. I am always happy to hear of more - write to David Hawgood, 26 Cloister Road, Acton, London W3 0DE, England or email david@hawgood.com. I will be putting the list and the text of my book on my website at *www.hawgood.co.uk/opg* and will put additions and amendments there. My list will include one name studies which can be contacted only by letter, or where the material has been deposited in a record office or library, or published in a book. It will also include those contactable by email - such studies are also listed by Mike Fisher on John Palmer's website at www.wirksworth.org.uk/oneplace.htm and we co-operate. I have also become more interested in one-place genealogy since I started maintaining the Wiltshire pages of Genuki - see www.genuki.org.uk. Some one-place studies are also given in "Specialist Indexes" by Jeremy Gibson & Elizabeth Hampson, published by FFHS.

Isn't a one-place study just the same as local history? No, the one-place study and one-place genealogy consider all the inhabitants of a place. Sometimes local histories extend to considering who appears in the census records and parish registers, but many only mention the notable inhabitants. As examples, take two books I bought on villages where I have ancestors. "Portrait of Slindon" by Josephine Duggan Rees (Chichester, 1974) describes the village in Sussex where my Sapp ancestors were maltsters. There is useful information about houses, farms, church, schools and particular people but no lists of inhabitants. "Aspects of Brington" by Dr Stephen Mattingley (Brington, 1997) came out of "Project Parish 2000" for this Northamptonshire village where my Hawgood relatives lived. The Brington book lists the Brington platoon of the Home Guard in the Second World War, the names on the war memorial from the First World War, everyone from the 1851 census, owners and occupiers of land on the 1840 Tithe map, the 1777 militia, those contributing to an Easter offering in 1585. Of course it

also has much about the Spencers of Althorp, but it lists all the local people. Both books have been invaluable in my family history research but the Brington book mentions everyone, the Slindon book just a few.

Do all one-place studies involve transcription and indexing? To my surprise, not necessarily. Some researchers transcribe and index original sources. Some use existing transcripts and contemporary lists like trade directories to collate information about the inhabitants of one place. Others collect information about which records and indexes exist so that an enquirer can be directed to the appropriate web site, book, microfiche or search service. The answers can be quite complex, involving knowledge of which Methodist Circuit, Deanery, Hundred etc a place is in, which probate jurisdiction, where marriage licences will be found. While drawing up lists of church records and their indexes for parishes in Wiltshire, to put on the Internet in GENUKI, I have been surprised to find some parish registers indexed several times - by the LDS Church, the Wiltshire Family History Society, and various individual indexers - while for other parishes there is no index at all. I also find that some places which figure in enquiries on email lists are not the names of historic parishes.

The most frequent start point for a one-place study is history of a family using a variety of records from one place about the family, either to help a decision on which is the correct line to follow, or to add flesh to the bones of family history. Then the researcher realises that the family is connected to quite a few local families, and a "little" more effort would put together the total population of the place.

Another start point is local history, an individual starting from an interest in the general history of the place, and extending it to a study of all the people who live there. Slightly different is the community history or social history, sometimes using the past to illuminate present day social interactions, sometimes as academic research into aspects of the place, its people, occupations, social and economic history. The Open University has been particularly active in these fields with its courses D301 and later DA301; people all over the United Kingdom have studied aspects of the history of their communities, and their projects have been available on CDROM. The projects have also often led to articles in local history and family history magazines.

Rather different is the demographic study. The one used a great deal by researchers associated with the Cambridge Group for the History of Population and Social Structure and Local Population Studies Society is reconstitution from parish registers. The basic method is to take each baptism, try to find siblings, marriage of parents, the marriage and burial for that person, from this build linked families with event dates. From this derive the population, age at marriage, number of children, infant mortality, and other similar measures. The methods are rather different from those used in genealogy. In demography, it doesn't matter much which you choose from two similar candidates for the post of father of the person baptised - it won't affect the statistics. In genealogy we really do want to follow the correct line for our ancestors rather than some alternative for people who turn out to be unrelated.

Other studies are based on local groups or local courses. People get together in a class, study a local topic, maybe continue as a group.

So far I have described studies focused on one place. But these only exist for a fairly small number of places. For many more places information is held as part of a wider collection. For example Genuki holds information at country and county level, and is extending it to parish level. The county Record Office or Local Studies library will hold a mass of information about each place in a county - not in a connected way, but in an available way, usually with a place index. And there are bibliographies and guides to records of various kinds, arranged or searchable by place. For Cornwall (see www.parsons1998.freeserve.co.uk/opc.htm) and Devon (www.cs.ncl.ac.uk/genuki/DEV/OPCproject.html) there are schemes of "On-line parish clerks" where individuals act as the focal point for genealogy enquiries and collection of transcripts for a parish. For Essex, Suffolk and Hertfordshire (maybe others) there are Local History Recorder schemes, aiming to record local history as it happens now - ask the record office or library if there is a scheme for your county.

Methods of enquiry

Ways of finding about the genealogy of a place may start from one- place studies, books, the internet, and contact with local collections and organisations - these all overlap, of course. Websites and books listing one-place studies are given above.

Books

For books, I always start by looking in The Phillimore Atlas and Index of Parish Registers edited by Cecil Humphery-Smith (Phillimore, new edition 1995). This has a list of parishes with information about their registers and indexes, and for each county a map of the parishes and a topographical map from 1834. I use various gazetteers, for example A Genealogical Gazetteer of England, by Frank Smith (Genealogical Publishing Co, Baltimore, 1982). There are county gazetteers published by Family History Societies for many counties. For detailed information I use the county volumes from the National Index of Parish Registers, published by the Society of Genealogists. This series includes more than the name implies - street addresses of churches and chapels, information about municipal cemeteries, as well as information like dates and gaps in Bishop's Transcripts which may be hard to find elsewhere. For information about records and indexes the prime source is the Gibson Guides from FFHS - containing much information available nowhere on the internet. Of these "Marriage and Census Indexes for Family Historians" is essential. The series on Poor Law records includes a gazetteer which will tell you which poor law union a place came into - these may straddle county boundaries so are not at all obvious. Victuallers, Militia, Probate Jurisdictions, Coroners' Records, and many others - they are all arranged by county and place and lead to records and indexes for your ancestral village. You may find a One-Place Study included in "Specialist Indexes". If you are lucky your county of interest is

included in the British Genealogical Library Guides by Stuart Raymond, published by him and FFHS. These give extensive information on books and magazine articles, arranged by place. Family History Societies publish books, transcripts and indexes - contact the relevant society or see "Current Publications by Member Societies" and "Current Publications on Microfiche" from FFHS. There are several books listing record offices - for example one of the Gibson Guides. If you can visit the place of interest or nearest town, a look in the local bookshop may lead to you spending more money than you expected and going away with locally published books which are hard to find in catalogues.

Internet

The best places to start looking for genealogical information about a place on the internet are Cyndis List at www.cyndislist.com and GENUKI at www.genuki.org.uk. The former has a comprehensive collection of internet links, the latter is arranged by place within county and is more likely to list details of organisations without their own websites. The section within each Genuki county for "Archives and Libraries" will provide relevant addresses and in some cases links to on-line catalogues.

The Historical Manuscripts Commission may sound rather forbidding but is invaluable, for an introduction see Archives in Focus at www.hmc.gov.uk/focus and for a list of archives searchable by place see their National Register of Archives at www.hmc.gov.uk/nra/. You will probably find far more entries than you expect. However, note that it is the titles of collections, not their contents, which are indexed.

It is always worth using a general purpose search engine like "Google" or "Alta Vista" to look for the place of interest. Very often this will find a town or village web site, with details of societies and often a "history" section written by a local enthusiast. This type of search may also turn up other genealogists with interests in the place. A tip is to try adding the word "genealogy" to the search.

Most genealogists with internet will have tried the LDS website at www.familySearch.org. But not all realise that a search in the family History Library Catalog for a place of interest turns up a substantial list of holdings, many that can be seen on microfilm at any of their Family History Centres world-wide.

National Collections

Either by using the internet or by a visit, search the relevant national collections like the Public Record Office and British Library.

Local Collections

The Record Office and City or County Library are obvious places to look for material about places. But they are also the place to find out about smaller local collections. For example I was lucky enough to find all I needed to know about the local Excell families in the Wootton- under-Edge library in Gloucestershire, material indexed by a local society and made freely available in the library. The Dewey Museum in Warminster, Wiltshire started as one person's collection, was available for public use on a few days of each week when I was using it for an Open University project in 1980, and is now in the local public library. In the list of one-place studies I am preparing I have heard about similar collections in Stamford, Lincolnshire and in Horley, Surrey. And some one-place studies have been deposited in the county record office. So it is always worth contacting the library and record office to ask if there are special collections for the place you are interested in.

Llyfrgell Genedlaethol Cymru The National Library of Wales

Eirionedd A. Baskerville
Head of Readers' Services - Department of Manuscripts and Records

An interest in family history is part of the Welsh psyche. According to the Laws of Hywel Dda, it was necessary to know one's relatives to the ninth remove, and Giraldus Cambrensis on his crusading tour of Wales in 1188 noted that the humblest person was able to recite from memory his family tree, going back six or seven generations.

The National Library of Wales is the premier centre for family history research in Wales, holding as it does abundant records covering the whole of Wales. Its three main Departments all have something different to offer. The Department of Printed Books holds electoral lists, newspapers and directories, while the Department of Pictures and Maps has plans, sale catalogues, and tithe maps and schedules. However, the most important Department from the point of view of genealogical research is the Department of Manuscripts and Records, which holds a whole range of useful resources.

The Department has microform copies of the returns for the whole of Wales for each of the ten-yearly censuses 1841-91, and microfiche copies of the index to the 1881 census for the English counties as well as those for Wales. In addition, some of the returns have been transcribed and indexed by enthusiastic individuals and societies who have kindly made them available to the Library's users.

Civil registration of births, marriages and deaths was introduced in England and Wales on 1 July 1837, and microfiche copies of the General Register Office's indexes of the registration records from 1837 to 1992 are available for searching free of charge at the National Library. The Library does not issue certificates, but a search of the indexes can be undertaken for a fee.

Before the introduction of civil registration, the `rites of passage' were noted in parish registers, following the order of 5 September 1538 that a register of every baptism, marriage and burial in every parish should be kept. However, the earliest surviving registers for most Welsh parishes do not commence until after 1660, although starting dates vary greatly. Parish registers held at the National Library are available on microfilm to readers. The Library also holds transcript copies of some parish registers, which have been kindly donated by the compilers. In addition, the 1988 edition of the International Genealogical Index, while far from complete, can prove a useful starting point for tracing the parish in which a baptism or marriage was registered.

Although the ravages of weather and rodents, inept vicars and disrespectful parishioners have resulted in the disappearance of many original parish registers, the bishops transcripts (annual returns submitted by Anglican parish clergy to the bishops containing copies of all the entries recorded in their parish registers during the preceding twelve months), often come to the rescue of the family historian. Transcripts were ordered to be sent annually from 1597 onwards, but there are no transcripts before 1661 in the records of the Church inhales deposited in the Library. Even after this date

there are many gaps in the returns, only a few transcripts before 1723 being extant for parishes in the diocese of Llandaff, and hardly any for the eighteenth century for parishes in the archdeaconries of Cardigan and St David's.

The transcripts cease at dates varying from parish to parish during the middle of the nineteenth century, although there are a few examples from the early twentieth century from some parishes. Transcripts of marriage entries normally cease with the introduction of civil registration in 1837. The transcripts held by the Library are listed in schedules available in the Department of Manuscripts and Records. At present the original transcripts are available to readers, but the task of preparing microfiche copies is underway.

Marriage bonds and allegations are the next most important class of Anglican Church record of use to the genealogist. These documents were executed in order to obtain a licence to marry without having banns called publicly in Church on three Sundays before the solemnisation of the marriage. Generally speaking, these records cover the eighteenth and nineteenth centuries and the first three decades of the twentieth century. The amount and nature of the information varies with the type of document, and are particularly valuable when the approximate date of a marriage is known but not its venue. The pre-1837 bonds and allegations in the Library have been indexed and may be searched on computer in the Department's Catalogue room. Also available for the diocese of St David's are registers of marriage licences, mainly for the nineteenth century.

Another class of records of paramount interest to the genealogist is wills and administrations, and those which before the introduction of Civil Probate on 11 January 1858 were proved in the Welsh ecclesiastical courts, have been deposited in the Library. Roughly speaking, the covering dates of the surviving probate records of each of the consistory courts are: Bangor, 1635-1858; Brecon, 1543-1858; Chester (Welsh Wills), 1557-1858; Hawarden, 1554-1858; Llandaff, 1568-1857; St Asaph, 1565-1857; St David's, 1556-1858. These wills have also been indexed and may be searched on computer.

For the period after 1858 the Library has custody of register copy wills from five registries, covering all but one (Montgomeryshire) of the Welsh counties, and a full microfiche set of the annual index of all wills and administrations granted in England and Wales (the Calendar of Grants), from 1858 to 1972.

Despite the fact that they are much less comprehensive than the records of the Anglican Church in Wales, Nonconformist records are an important source of information for genealogists. Many registers of dissenting congregations were deposited with the Registrar-General after the Civil Registration Act of 1836, and the Library has microfilm copies of these. A few registers of that period which never found their way to London and some other later registers are now deposited at the Library.

Other nonconformist records of genealogical value at the Library include manuscript lists of members and contribution books of individual chapels, printed annual reports, usually including lists of members and their contributions, which have been produced by many chapels since about 1880, and denominational periodicals, which often contain notices of births, marriages and deaths.

Records of the Court of Great Sessions of Wales, the most important legal and administrative body between the Act of Union and its abolition in 1830, may also prove useful for genealogical purposes. Occasionally challenge pedigrees were filed in connection with certain actions, and other documents of considerable value are depositions, which often state the age of the deponent, jury lists and coroners' inquests.

Whereas the official Quarter Sessions records for the county of Cardigan, held by the Library comprise little more than the order books from 1739, there are also some related materials among the archives of landed estates or solicitors' firms, for example a few sessional rolls and land tax records 1780-1839 from Cardiganshire, some land tax records (the most useful class of records for the genealogist) for Montgomeryshire and Breconshire, order books 1647-75 and rolls, 1643-99 for Denbighshire, and sessions records from Montgomeryshire.

Local government at a level between county and parish was practically non-existent before the formation of Poor Law Unions under the the Poor Law Amendment Act 1834 Most Poor Law Union records are now deposited at the appropriate county record office, but there are some records at the Library, mainly from Montgomeryshire. Civil parish records are also mainly held by the appropriate county record office, although the Library holds vestry books and other parochial records for many parishes for which parish registers have been deposited.

The manorial records held by the Library are mainly to be found with the estate records and listed with them They are most comprehensive for Montgomeryshire (mainly the Powis Castle and Wynnstay estate records), with substantial holdings for Glamorgan and Monmouthshire also (mainly the Badminton, Bute and Tredegar estate records). It should be noted that in many parts of Wales the manorial system never really took root.

The Library has recently prepared a manorial database for Wales in conjunction with HMC available to readers on the Internet http://www2.hmc.gov.uk/Welsh_Manorial_Documents_R egister.htm.
Most of the estate records and personal papers held by the Department of Manuscripts and Records are detailed in typescript schedules. The estate records contain title deeds, rentals, account books, correspondence, etc. Rentals may prove particularly useful in indicating a death or change of residence when a name disappears from a series of rentals.

The Department holds many manuscript pedigrees. These vary from descents of nobility, compiled in the later Middle Ages and copied time and again with

additions by later genealogists, to charts which are the work of amateurs of modern times who have given copies of their compilations to the Library. For searchers particularly interested in the pedigrees of gentry families there are several important printed works available.

There is a general card index to most of the typescript schedules of the collections in the Department of Manuscripts and Records, and probably the most useful for the family historian are the sections devoted to wills, marriage settlements, inquisitions post mortem, and pedigrees. The index to the general collections of manuscripts (NLW MSS) may also be of use to genealogists. In addition, a basic inventory of the contents of the Library's Annual Report up to 1996 is available on-line in the Catalogue room.

For further information on sources for family history research at the National Library of Wales, it is worth consulting the Department of Manuscripts and Records' pages at the Library's web site at: http://www.llgc.org.uk/

South Wales Coalfield Collection

The South Wales Coalfield Collection (SWCC) is a unique and internationally important research collection held at University of Wales Swansea. It contains a range of material in a variety of formats, which detail the social, economic and cultural experience of the whole of the South Wales Coalfield.

While we are always happy to help family historians wherever possible, due to the nature of the SWCC, very few of the documents actually provide information about individuals, unless they were prominent figures in their community or trade union, or involved in a particular event, such as a mining disaster. The collection is more useful for finding out background information about the communities in which people lived.

If you do wish to find out whether we hold information about a particular individual, please provide at least the following information: their name, trade union lodge or branch to which they belonged, the colliery at which they were employed and the period during which they were employed.

The South Wales Coalfield Collection – its origins
The SWCC developed out of a research project, funded by the Social Science Research Council (SSRC) between 1971 and 1974. The project was conducted by the Departments of History and Economic History of the then University College Swansea and supported by the National Union of Mineworkers (South Wales Area), the Coal Industries Social Welfare Organisation (CISWO) in South Wales and the National Coal Board. The aim of the project was to preserve oral and written evidence of coal miners and mining in South Wales at a time when the industry had started to decline (over one hundred mines had been closed since nationalisation in 1947) and such records were in danger of being lost. Such was the success of the first project that it was followed by a second SSRC funded project from 1979 until 1982. This project concentrated on the post 1945 history of the Coalfield.

A very wide range of material was collected as a result of these projects, both in primary and secondary forms.

Manuscript material
The collection contains records of trade unions, notably the National Union of Mineworkers (South Wales Area) and its predecessor, the South Wales Miners' Federation. These relate to its central administration and its branches or lodges and record the concerns of the trade unions in the fields of pay, safety and conditions at work and occupational disease. The South Wales Miners' Federation Register of Fatal Accidents 1934-41 (which is indexed) is held.
There are also records of other organisations within the coalfield society, in particular the miners' institutes, which reflect their positions as focal points within their local communities with the provision of libraries, reading rooms and social facilities including games rooms and often cinemas.
Records of other organisations include the Iron and Steel Trades Confederation, South Wales Division, co-operative societies and local political parties.

There is a rich collection of documents from individuals – from individual miners to trade union leaders and members of parliament, such as Arthur Horner and S O Davies.

Records of a few collieries are also held.

Many Welsh miners fought within the British Battalion of the International Brigades, indeed Welsh miners made up one of the largest contingents. The SWCC therefore holds a variety of records relating to the Spanish Civil War, including letters sent home from Welsh miners who fought for the International Brigades in Spain, and memorial leaflets for some of the men killed in Spain.

Photograph Collection
Over 4,500 photographs are held which record events, people and landscapes from the late nineteenth century to the present day. They illustrate most aspects of life in the coalfield over the period: trade union leaders and delegations, marches and disputes, alongside recreational activities such as choirs, sports teams, Galas and the Miners' Eisteddfod. There are a substantial number of photographs of collieries and photographs associated with collieries i.e. workmen or rescue teams of a particular colliery. Examples include the official opening of Abercrave Colliery pit-head baths in 1953 and a photograph of the view of Universal Colliery (Senghenydd) pit-head after the devastating explosion in 1913 when 426 men lost their lives.

The collection includes numerous photographs relating to the Spanish Civil War, including photographs of Welsh volunteers Serving in the International Brigades in Spain in 1937; photographs of prisoners held at Burgos Penitentiary for International Brigaders in 1939; Basque children, refugees from the Spanish Civil War disembarking from a ship; South Wales miners visiting a children's home for Basque children in 1938; and several photographs of collection of food for Spain (which was carried out in many towns and villages throughout the South Wales Coalfield during the Spanish Civil War).

Oral history collection
Over 600 interviews area held with individuals from all parts of the coalfield. The interviews carried out during the first project concentrated largely on the labour and social history of the coalfield up until 1945.

The project was grouped into various studies, including village life and the Spanish Civil War. These give insights into particular communities, such as Maerdy (Little Moscow) during this period of strikes, wars, unemployment and depression. Other recorded groups include founder members of the South Wales Miners' Federation, local leaders, and Members of Parliament. There are also studies concentrating on the miners' institutes, libraries, and welfare halls, and adult education in the valleys, especially during the inter-war period. The second project concentrated more on the post-1945 period, with greater attention being given to the national profile, management, and the "decision makers" within the energy sector. This collection includes interviews with former Prime Ministers and mining constituency Members of Parliament; chairmen from the National Coal Board, British National Oil Corporation, and British Petroleum; as well as national figures of coalfield leadership. Also included is a study on members from the NUM South Wales Area, local lodge officers, and discussion groups from Maerdy, Penllergaer, and Aberdare collieries.

Video Collection
The video recordings consist mainly of interviews with groups and individuals, which concentrate on working conditions and the impact of pit closures on communities. However there are recordings of the cultural activities of the mining communities including the Miners' Eisteddfod and the Miners' Gala and recordings of conferences arranged by the South Wales Miners' Library in the 1970s and 1980s. Conference titles include 'Class and Community: the Welsh Experience'; 'The Inheritance of the South Wales Miners'; 'Mountain Ash and Deep Duffryn Colliery: a community in crisis.

Posters
The collection includes posters collected from the South Wales Miners' Federation and the National Union of Mineworkers (South Wales Area) as well as Miners' Institutes and Welfare Halls. The collection also contains a number of 'home made' posters from the 1984-85 miners' strike and an important collection dating from the Spanish Civil War.

Trade Union Banners
Of the 38 banners held in the collection, the majority are National Union of Mineworkers (South Wales Area) Lodge banners, which date from the 1950s onwards. Each banner has its own unique imagery and slogan that reflect the politics of the Lodge and the community it serves.

South Wales Miners' Federation.

AID FOR THE SPANISH PEOPLE

AN APPEAL.

The dreadful sufferings of the Spanish people, the ruthless slaughter of men, women and children, and the destruction of their homes by the rebel Franco and his FASCIST accomplices, ITALY and GERMANY, call for the active sympathy of ALL Workers.

The Fight of the SPANISH WORKERS against Fascism IS YOUR FIGHT.

The success of Fascism in Spain would endanger the liberties of the Workers in all Countries.

Fascism means the horrors of the Concentration Camps, Imprisonment and Death.

Help the Spanish People in their heroic struggle.

A Collection will be taken at your Colliery on FRIDAY NEXT, JULY 16th, to help to relieve distress caused by the Civil War.

THE SPANISH PEOPLE ARE GIVING THEIR LIVES, WE ASK YOU TO GIVE A GENEROUS CONTRIBUTION. THE EXECUTIVE COUNCIL.

Printed material
The collection includes books, periodicals, pamphlets and newspaper cuttings.
Many of the books and pamphlets were collected during the projects from over 50 Miners' Institute Libraries throughout the South Wales Coalfield. Three of the libraries (Bargoed, Tylorstown and Pontyberem) were deposited almost in their entirety. Remarkably, there is little duplication in the collection, partly because different parts of each library survived, but also because the content of each library differed; it essentially mirrored the community it served, providing for its particular educational and recreational needs. A number of personal libraries are also held, including those of ordinary miners and members of parliament, such as SO Davies, and George Daggar. The pamphlets are an important resource to researchers, and include a unique series of pamphlets dating from and about the Spanish Civil War. There is also an outstanding selection of Independent Labour Party (ILP) pamphlets.

Resources to assist family historians
Although very few of the documents held in the SWCC actually provide information about individuals, unless they were prominent figures in their community or trade union, or involved in a particular event, such as a mining disaster, the Archives and the South Wales Miners' Library between them, do hold a number of resources to assist family history enquires. These include:- books about genealogy; local history material, books, journals and local history dissertations; Inspector of Mines Reports (South Wales District) from 1889 to 1912 ; SWMF Register of Fatal Accidents, 1934 to 1941; information about collieries throughout the South Wales Coalfield; information about unions

South Wales Strikers

How to contact us

We welcome enquiries by letter, phone, fax or e-mail.
For further information about the South Wales
Coalfield Collection or to make an appointment to visit
the South Wales Miners' Library and/or Archives,
please contact:
Archives:
Elisabeth Bennett, Archivist, Library & Information
Centre, University of Wales Swansea, Singleton Park
Swansea SA2 8PP Tel: 01792 295021
E-mail: archives@swansea.ac.uk
http://www.swan.ac.uk/lis/archives/
South Wales Miners' Library:
Siân Williams
Librarian, South Wales Miners' Library
University of Wales Swansea, Hendrefoelan House,
Gower Road, Swansea SA2 7NB
Tel: 01792 518603/518693
E-mail: miners@swansea.ac.uk
http://www.swan.ac.uk/lis/swml/

Opening Hours
Archives
An appointment must be made to visit the Archives.
Monday – Friday 9.15am - 12.45pm, 2.00pm - 5.00pm
During term time, the Archives is also open on
Tuesday evenings from 6pm – 9.30pm. Appointments
for Tuesday evenings must be made by 5pm the
previous Friday.
Please note that required documents must be specified
in advance.
South Wales Miners' Library
Term time
Monday-Friday 10.30am - 1pm, 2pm - 5pm
Saturday 10am – 4.30pm
Sunday Closed
During term time, the Library is normally open until
7pm a few evenings per week. Please contact the
South Wales Miners' Library for details.
Vacation
Monday-Thursday 9am - 1pm, 2pm - 5pm
Friday–Sunday Closed
http://www.swan.ac.uk/swcc

information about working conditions and wages;
information about social and welfare facilities

Wherever possible, SWCC staff will always refer
individuals to other organisations such as local record
offices and public libraries, who may be able to assist
further.

How to view the collection
The collection is split between two locations at
University of Wales Swansea: the Archives in the
Library and Information Centre and at the South Wales
Miners' Library in Hendrefoelan House on the
Hendrefoelan campus as
follows.
The **Archives** houses the
manuscript records and the
photographic collection.
The **South Wales Miners'
Library** holds the printed
material, the oral history
collection, video collection,
posters and banners. Annual
reports and minute books of
the South Wales Miners'
Federation and NUM (South
Wales Area) are held at both
locations.
A catalogue of part of the
South Wales Coalfield
Collection is available at the
following website:
http://www.swan.ac.uk/swcc
The rest of the collection is
listed in printed guides, which
are available for consultation
at the Archives and the South
Wales Miners' Library.

Welsh Emigrants to Patagonia

Eirionedd A. Baskerville
Head of Reader Services - National Library of Wales

Reproduced with the Permission of Llyfrgell Genedlaethol Cymru   The National Library of Wales © The National Library of Wales 2001

There have been many occasions on which a group of Welsh men and women have felt the need to leave their native land and head for a new life across the Atlantic, believing that America was the land of the future and of freedom. In the seventeenth century Welsh Quakers fled religious persecution to claim land promised by William Penn, and it was because of religious and political persecution in Britain that the Baptist minister and radical, Morgan John Rhys, emigrated in 1794. The motivation behind emigration became an economic one at the end of the eighteenth century as the lure of expanded territories in the American mid-west beckoned those who had suffered as a result of a series of bad harvests. Morgan John Rhys urged his fellow countrymen to join him and in 1795 he formed the Cambrian Company of Philadelphia in order to acquire land to create a Welsh community in western Pennsylvania, so that the emigrants could retain the language and traditions of Wales in their new home. Through the words of three Welsh emigrants in documents held at the National Library of Wales we can witness the perils which they experienced on their way to 'a better life'.

Morgan John Rhys's call was heeded by a large group of settlers, mainly from the Llanbrynmair area of Montgomeryshire, who emigrated in 1795 under the leadership of a clock and watchmaker named Ezekiel Hughes. Among those was George Roberts, who, in a letter which he wrote on 1 March 1850 from Ebensburg to his nephew, the Rev. Samuel Roberts, Llanbrynmair, describes the problems which the group suffered even before they set sail for America. While Ezekiel Hughes was in Bristol arranging for the brig *Maria* to meet the group at Carmarthen, George had had the banns for his marriage to Jane Edwards called, and the marriage was solemnized on 20 May. On 11 July the group set off for Carmarthen, only to find that the *Maria* was too large to enter the port and they were directed to Bristol. As they

took their baggage to the sloop which was to take them to Bristol, they spied two members of a Press Gang in a nearby boat, so went into hiding. They were advised that they were safe while they remained in the town but that the Press Gang could catch them if they were on the river, so the men started to walk to Bristol, leaving the women to follow in the sloop. When they reached Bristol they heard that the women had sailed to Llanstephan; George wrote to tell them to stay with the boat, baggage and provisions and gave instructions as to where they should meet up. Unfortunately, the women had to wait for some three weeks for a 'fair wind', and having despaired of ever sailing they decided to follow the example of their men folk and walk to Bristol. They got as far as Swansea from where they sailed for Bristol, and upon their arrival went in search of their men folk. To their horror they were told that the men had started for America the previous morning; fortunately this was untrue and the group was eventually reunited and fifty passengers, all Welsh except for three cabin passengers, set sail on 6 August for America. But their troubles were not over; on the 27th two Men of War in pursuit, fired a cannon to make the Maria stop, and hoisted a French flag 'in disguise, for they were British'. This was during a period of hostility between Britain and France and the passengers were worried that the men 'would be taken as soldiers on board a British Man of War or as prisoners by the French', but they were allowed to proceed.

The emigrants stoically survived seasickness and heavy seas, although a tremendous storm on 17 October caused great consternation. There was an English preacher on board, 'who prayed on deck every forenoon and when the weather was favourable in the afternoon', but the Welsh expected more than this and would go into a large boat on deck and read, sing and pray, and they usually had preaching in Welsh and English on Sundays. Having 'found soundings at 22 fathoms' on 24 October, they fixed a candle in a lantern at the head of the mast in the hope that a pilot would see them, and at about 3 o'clock the next morning the news spread that a pilot was in a boat alongside. 'We then began to hope that we should once [more] have our feet on terra firma about 10 o'clock we saw land and soon saw the elegant houses in Cape May smiling upon us'. George describes entering the Delaware, passing Newcastle and Wilmington. 'A Doctor came on board to examine if there was any contagious fevers amongst us, he was pleased with our appearance and told us we might all get employment before breakfast tomorrow'. Some men landed when the boat arrived at the wharf opposite Philadelphia, but George stayed till the next morning – twelve weeks but a day since they had left Bristol. When he went up on deck on Monday morning 'little pamphlets were circulating among the passengers from the emigrant society offering instructions to all but chiefly addressed to the poor, the sick, etc. admonishing them not to be discouraged that they would render unto them all the assistance that laid *(sic)* in their power with directions where to apply'. At the beginning of his letter George states that he was unable to weep at leaving his friends and family, but when he read the little pamphlets, 'I could shed tears freely. It was a serious thing to be in a place where I did not know one person in the whole country'.

Another contingent braved the waves in 1848, and one of the passengers, Morris Peat, kept a diary of his journey to Ebensburg. With him travelled his wife Lowri and a number of Llanbrynmair folk, including Michael D. Jones, a native of Llanuwchllyn but with strong Llanbrynmair connections, for his mother was Mary Hughes, a cousin of Ezekiel Hughes who had led the 1795 group.

The diary begins with the entry for 20 April 1848 - 'I started from Tynreithin for America to live there'. They left Liverpool at 9 am on 2 May, 'A very fair day, the wind behind us, the ship in full sail travelling quite quickly'. Everyone was quite well and comfortable and cheerful, 'except little Thomas, Jack's son'. A service was held that evening, and the marriage banns of Richard Jones and Jane Peat were read, the marriage ceremony being performed the following day by Michael D. Jones. On 6 May they received an allowance from the Captain – six pounds of hard bread – and the following day Morris notes that everyone except Evan Jones was sea-sick. They felt so light-headed that they had to stay in bed all day, 'without lighting a fire or eating', and unable even to hold a service or to read. Next day, however, everyone was feeling better; Morris Peat ate a herring and his wife some tea and bread and water. Tragedy struck when, at 8 o'clock, the three year old youngest son of David and Ann Morgan died and was buried at midnight. Most of the diary is taken up with describing the weather, the sea and the contents of religious services. There was a discussion on 10 May as to whether they would be teetotal or merely temperate when they reached America. They made flummery on 31 May, a pudding on 6 June and sour-oat bread on 9 June. It was on that day, too, that they caught their first glimpse of America, Maryland, and at 6 am the Doctor came to 'look us over, he never saw a shipload of such healthy folk, about 317'. Finally, at 8 o'clock on 17 June 1848, Morris Peat and Lowri reached the house of his uncle, Thomas M. Jones, in Ebensburg.

The same motives of finding a better life in the New World were behind another emigration which took place just seventeen years after Morris Peat's voyage, namely the voyage of the *Mimosa* to Patagonia. Here again

there was a strong connection with Ezekiel Hughes, Montgomeryshire, and the Rev. Michael D. Jones. There were also other motives - the oppression of landlords and the enclosure of common land and poverty. Farmers had suffered a series of wet summers and poor crops; taxes were heavy and prices high. In a letter to George Roberts his father, Evan, writes, 'We have at the present time been sent from Dolgadfan Mill as the result of much oppression and injustice. Our landowner intended to do us much harm but thanks to Him who holds the hearts of Kings in his hand we were not turned out till half way through the Spring and paid until May 1st.'

These Welsh emigrants desired also to create a new nation across the sea, and the instigation to found a strong, independent Welsh colony came from Welsh exiles in the United States. They believed that if it were possible to persuade the thousands of people who left Wales every year to follow them to a Welsh colony, they could establish a strong nation there with its own Welsh government. The problem with previous Welsh settlements in America was that their Welsh identity became diluted by mixing with other immigrant cultures, and the children invariably became English in speech and lost their national characteristics. Michael D. Jones had come to realise this during his time as minister in Cincinnati (he was ordained as 'an evangelist' for the Welsh immigrants of the far west of America in Cincinnati in December 1848). He had established Cymdeithas y Brythoniaid in order to safeguard the rights of the poor Welsh immigrants and help them to get over linguistic difficulties and unemployment in a strange world. The struggle to keep their unique identity helps explain the emergence of various attempts to discover within north America some place where the Welsh might create a new and pure homeland. Unfortunately the Civil War and other factors thwarted their plans, and after considering Oregon, Vancouver and Wisconsin as possible sites for a Welsh Colony, Michael D. Jones finally decided on Patagonia.

The movement gained momentum with the founding of a Colonial Society in Liverpool in 1861, and members toured Wales addressing meetings, extolling the virtues of a Welsh Colony in Patagonia and trying to collect money for the venture. As Wales had no government to support them, the committee in Liverpool had to enter into an agreement with the Argentine government concerning the plan, and as they lacked money they also hoped to receive financial help from that government. Their aim was to send enough Welshmen to Patagonia to enable them to claim provincial status within the Argentine Republic, with a large measure of self-government. Towards the end of 1862 Lewis Jones, a Caernarfonshire born printer and Sir Love Jones-Parry, squire of Madryn, in Lln, were sent to inspect the country. After many setbacks they returned to Buenos Aires and signed a contract with the Argentine Government, and although they were not satisfied with the contract, which provided only land for the settlers and not self-government, Lewis Jones and other members of the Liverpool Committee went ahead with the plans.

The challenges facing potential emigrants to Patagonia were tremendous. As Rhys Gwesyn Jones pointed out in *Ddraig Goch*, January 1865, 'There are no houses there, nor railways, nor roads those things will have to be built together with many other things which are necessary in order to make a comfortable neighbourhood in our time'.

One of those who took up the challenge was Joseph Seth Jones, and it is thanks to the diary that he kept while on the voyage that we know much about that pioneering journey. From the 26th of April to the 25th of May he hung about in Liverpool, waiting for a ship to take him and the other emigrants to Patagonia. The ship originally chartered was the *Halton Castle*, which was due to sail on 25 April 1865. The charge was £12 for adults, £8 for children under 12, and babies under one year old went free. A deposit of £1 for adults, 10/- for children, was to be sent to the Treasurer, the remainder to be paid when the emigrants arrived in Liverpool. One hundred acres of land were to be given to every three emigrants, and to the first colonists, gifts of horses, oxen, sheep, wheat, furniture, etc., and it was claimed the Council had also sent representatives to build houses in readiness for their arrival. However, the *Halton Castle* was late getting back to dock so the *Mimosa* became the chosen vehicle of liberation. A former tea-clipper, she had been crudely refitted to carry passengers by the nailing of planks along the side of the hold, and placing a rickety ladder which led to the confined deck above.

In preparation for his new life Joseph Seth Jones bought a two barrelled fowling piece for £2, a jacket and linen trousers and a flat iron for 5/-, two pounds of powder, several pounds of shot and a box of caps and 50 bullets – they cost about 10/-, and a knife 2/-, a pair of nibbs 6d, shears 2/-, bed 2/9, 2 scythes 2/6, a Spanish and English vocabulary 1/6, the American Frugal Housewife, a pair of shoes 8/6, Ginco hat 2/6, slate 6d, Phrenologist 2/6, twelve carte de visites 5/-'.

Finally, around 10am on 25 May, the Mimosa started for the river, where she remained till about 4am on 28 May. The journey was a troublesome one from the very beginning. A powerful storm arose but the Captain, Captain Pepperell, refused to accept any help from the lifeboat sent to help him. There was some disagreement between the Captain and the leaders of the emigrants during the voyage – about the food, the right to hold religious services on Sunday and the general arrangements on board the Mimosa. On 1 June William Hughes and Anne Lewis were married, the Rev. Lewis Humphreys blessing the marriage and Captain Pepperell registering it. Many of the passengers, including Joseph, were often ill. On 5th June, a very hot day; four went out in a boat to swim. Late on the night of the 9th, Catherine Jane, the 2 year old daughter of Robert and Mary Thomas of Bangor died, and was buried at 10am the next morning 'by throwing her into the sea in a box built for that purpose, with stones at one end so that it would sink'. At 10 o'clock that night, Aaron and Rachel Jenkins's two year old son James died, and was buried 'in the same way as before'. The Canary Islands were sighted in the distance on June 13th, and they saw the peak of Tenerife. On June 16th the settlers were up in arms when the Captain, having heard that the emigrants, especially the girls, were dirty ordered one of the sailors to shear the girls' heads right down to the scalp and wash them clean with soap and water. The girls and their parents stood firm and the Captain eventually relented. The doctor examined every head and found them perfectly clean.

On the 20th, travelling at a speed of 12 miles an hour, they caught a flying fish, and the wind blew Joseph's notes into the sea. Some of the boys went to bathe on the 22nd; 'they tied a rope to the bowsprit, which went down almost to the water, then sat on the bottom and, as the front and back end of the ship rose and fell alternately they were soaked'. Tragedy struck another family on June 27th with the death of John, son of Robert and Catherine Davies, Llandrillo. On 5 July Joseph saw

a big bird – 'an albatross or something', and on the 9th they spied Cape Fris. The Reverend Lewis Humphreys baptised 3 children, and there was great joy when a son, Morgan, was born to John Jones and his wife, and a daughter, Rachel, to Aaron and Rachel Jenkins. Joseph describes crossing the equator on June 28th, two sailors putting on beards; setting off fireworks and throwing buckets of water over each other. They sent up rockets, and 'some of the more respectable went to drink with the captain in the cabin and some were said to be quite full'. By the 17th it was thought that they had left Rio de la Plata and were going onwards opposite the province of Buenos Aires. At 8pm Elisabeth, the daughter of Griffith and Elizabeth Solomon died, aged thirteen months. A whale was spotted on 22 July, though some thought it was a steamer 'as it was blowing up steam' and on the 26th, land was clearly spied. On the 27th Joseph woke up in New Bay; The journey had taken 65 days.

Although preparations for the emigrants' arrival had been under way for three months there were disappointments. Some of the provisions had been lost and they had landed on an unwelcoming beach in mid-winter; the day was short and heavy rain blew like a whiplash, bitterly cold. There is no doubt that the early settlers did suffer greatly, but they overcame their obstacles. Many of their descendants still remain true to the way of life which their ancestors cherished – although Argentinians they speak Welsh, hold eisteddfodau and worship in their chapels, and thus, in south America, the Welsh emigrants seem to have fulfilled a measure of the aspirations of Morgan John Rhys, in 1794, of retaining the language and traditions of Wales in their new home.

The Search for Scottish Sources –
Planning a Genealogical Journey
Rosemary Bigwood M.A. M.Litt

Planning a visit to Scotland in the quest of the ancestral past is not always an easy matter, especially if time is of the essence. A question frequently asked is "Should I go first to Edinburgh to the National Archives of Scotland and the General Register House or search in local record offices?" From a distance it is difficult to find out what source material is kept where and also to determine what records might be most fruitful to consult. There is, in fact, no easy answer to these queries, as decisions will depend on what is known about the family and the extent of research already carried out.

As with all travelling, however, some pre-journey preparations will be valuable. One of the great interests in carrying out genealogical research is that you never know with certainty where it will lead in the end but in getting ready to embark on "on-site" work, it is important to make a list of your objectives – whether these be concerned with tracing back the family further, putting flesh on the bones by viewing the old family "stamping grounds" or trying to locate living relatives. Bring with you a summary of sources already searched so that you avoid duplication and identify on a map the areas where the family are known to have lived in Scotland.

Where to start - Edinburgh
Many Scottish records are centralised in Edinburgh, concerned both with national and local administration and life. Articles in the *Handbook* outline the rich resources of New Register House, the National Archives of Scotland and the National Library of Scotland. If you have work still to be done in extracting information from statutory registers of birth, death and marriage, in searching censuses or Old Parish Registers, then time spent in New Register House (also known as the General Register Office for Scotland) will be valuable. A day's ticket for access may seem expensive (currently £17) but, thanks to the self-service system which enables a visitor to consult not only indexes but all the actual records, including copies of the statutory register pages, a great deal can be achieved within this time.

Having exhausted the resources of New Register House, it is time to assess what is now known about the family in which you are interested. What did these ancestors do - were they landlords or labourers? When did they live and where did they live? On this will depend the choice of records in which to carry out research "beyond" the parish registers. Records are made by the contact of one person with another, with a group of people (perhaps the community) or with an authority such as a legal court or the church, for example. Thus a merchant or proprietor may have owned land, have left a will, had business and family dealings which are recorded in registers of deeds, been involved in trade and have had a place in society, perhaps as a burgess in a burgh, member of

the town council or acting as a JP – all of which matters may have resulted in the making of records. A tenant farmer is less likely to have owned land but could have left a testament, have had dealings with a landlord or initiated some legal proceedings, while the labourer may be mentioned in poor law records, have appeared before a court for some misdemeanour, be listed in the local kirk session minutes or have had to serve in the militia if he lived at the time of the Napoleonic Wars – all contacts offering possible scope for research in specific classes of records.

The second evaluation must be of the records themselves. How likely are they to throw light on a particular person and their circumstances? Are there indexes or finding aids and how long will it take to search them? Will the records be in Scots or Latin and will they be readable? Many documents, particularly those concerning with the possession of land, were written in Latin till well on in the eighteenth century and before the beginning of the eighteenth century, when handwriting changed, there may be difficulties in reading the Old Scots hand. And lastly, where will these records be held – in Edinburgh or locally – and if the latter, where?

The National Archives of Scotland holds a vast and sometimes bewildering collection of material – much of it of vital interest to family historians. Testaments, deeds (both in the Books of Council and Session and in the Sheriff Courts), sasines, charters, retours, court records and a vast collection of church material, especially regarding the Established Church, are held there - as well as the muniments of many Scottish families, and these sources are likely to be of prime importance in genealogical research. The problem arises, however, in classes of records where part may be in the NAS and part still kept locally. The kirk session minutes and other material concerning the Church is an example of this. Unlike the case of Old Parochial Registers where there was a legal directive that all these records should be given into the keeping of the Registrar General, no such obligation concerned other church records – whether of the Established Church or of dissenting congregations - and therefore some may be found in the National Archives of Scotland and others in local council archives or even still held privately. Some records, previously held in the NAS, have been re-transmitted to local archives, though in a number of cases, microfilm copies are retained in Edinburgh.

To summarise - if possible, it is likely to be worth while spending some time in the National Archives at the commencement of a genealogical journey. To tackle the treasure store of a national archive does need courage and hard work. The cataloguing system (at present still in typed form – look for *The Summary Catalogue*) is not easy to master. A preliminary study of published guides to records such as Cecil

Sinclair's two books - *Tracing Your Scottish Ancestors in the Scottish Record Office* and *Tracing Scottish Local History in the Scottish Record Office* will be of assistance in helping to identify source material which may be of value, while *Tracing Scottish Ancestors* (Rosemary Bigwood) offers help in evaluating and selecting various classes of records, as well as indicating what may be found in the NAS and what is kept in local archives or to be found in libraries. A visit to the National Library Map Room will almost certainly be of value in offering opportunities to look at old printed maps of the area in which you are interested.

Local Council Archives

In the past, the main administrative units in Scotland were the parish, the burgh and the sheriffdom or county. In 1975, as the result of the reorganisation of local government, burghs and counties were abolished and Scotland was divided into nine Regional Councils with a number of District Councils in the tier below. In 1996 there was yet another change when the present system of thirty-two local councils took over in charge of Scotland local administration. These are listed below with the administrative headquarters given in brackets after each:

Aberdeen City (Aberdeen) Inverclyde (Greenock) Aberdeenshire (Aberdeen) Midlothian (Dalkeith) Angus (Forfar) Moray (Elgin) Argyll & Bute (Lochgilphead) North Ayrshire (Irvine) City of Edinburgh (Edinburgh) North Lanarkshire (Motherwell) Clackmannanshire (Alloa) Orkney Islands (Kirkwall) Dumfries & Galloway (Dumfries) Perth & Kinross (Perth) Dundee City (Dundee) Renfrewshire (Paisley) East Ayrshire (Kilmarnock) Scottish Borders (Melrose) East Dumbartonshire (Glasgow) Shetlands Islands (Lerwick) East Lothian (Haddington) South Ayrshire (Ayr) East Renfrewshire (Glasgow) South Lanarkshire (Hamilton) Falkirk (Falkirk) Stirling (Stirling) Fife (Glenrothes) West Dumbartonshire (Dumbarton) Glasgow City (Glasgow) Western Isles (Stornoway) Highland (Inverness) West Lothian (Livingstone)
It is envisaged that each council will have an archivist but lack of funding and premises has in some cases made this difficult to implement immediately. However, there are currently twenty four local council archives in place. These are as follows:

Aberdeen City Archives (also covering Aberdeenshire)
Town House, Broad Street, Aberdeen, AB10 1AQ
Tel: 01224 522521
Angus Archives
Montrose Library, 214 High Street, Montrose, DD10 8PH
Tel: 0167 671415
Argyll & Bute Council Archives
Manse Brae, Lochgilphead, Argyll, PA31 8QU
Tel: 01546 604120
Ayrshire Archives Centre (includes East, North and South Ayrshire Council records)
Craigie Estate, Ayr, KA8 0SS
Tel: 01292 287584
Clackmannanshire Council Archives
26-28 Drysdale Street, Alloa, FK10 1JL
Tel: 01259 722262
Dumfries & Galloway Archives
Archive Centre, 33 Burns Street, Dumfries DG1 2PS
Tel: 01387 269254

Dundee City Archives
Support Services, 21 City Square, Dundee, DD1 3BY
Tel: 01382 434494
Edinburgh City Council Archives
City Chambers, High Street, Edinburgh EH1 1YJ
Tel: 0131 5294291
Falkirk Council Archives
Falkirk Museums History Research Centre, Callendar House, Callendar Park, Falkirk FK1 1YR
Tel: 01324 503778
Fife Council Archive Centre
Carleton House, Balgonie Road, Markinch, Glenrothes, Fife, KY6 7AH
Tel: 01592 416504
Glasgow City Archives
Mitchell Library, North Street, Glasgow G3 7DN
Tel: 0141 2872910
Highland Council Archive
Inverness Library, Farraline Park, Inverness IV1 1NH
Tel: 01463 220330
Midlothian Council Archives
Library Headquarters, 2 Clerk Street, Loanhead, Midlothian EH20 2DR
Tel: 0131 2703976
Moray Council Heritage Centre
Grant Lodge, Cooper Park, Elgin, Moray IV30 1HS
Tel: 01343 544475
North Highland Archive
Wick Library, Sinclair Terrace, Wick, KW1 5AB
North Lanarkshire Archive
10 Kelvin Road, Lenziemill, Cumbernauld G67 2BA
Tel: 01236 737114
Orkney Archives
The Orkney Library, Laing Street, Kirkwall, KW15 1NW
Tel: 01856 873166
Perth & Kinross Council Archive
A.K. Bell Library, 2-8 York Place, Perth, PH2 8EP
Tel: 01738 477012
Renfrewshire Council Archives
Room 2.4, North Building, Cotton Street, Paisley, PA1 1TR
Tel: 0141 8403703
Scottish Borders Archive & Local History Centre
St. Mary's Mill, Selkirk TD7 5EU
Tel: 01750 20842
Shetland Archives
44 King Harald Streeet, Lerwick ZE1 0EQ
Tel: 01595 696247
South Lanarkshire Archives
Records Management Unit, 30 Hawbank Road, College Milton, East Kilbride G74 5EX
Tel: 01355 239193
Stirling Council Archives Services
Unit 6, Burghmuir Industrial Estate, Stirling, FK7 7PY
Tel: 01786 450745
West Lothian Council Archives
7 Rutherford Square, Brucefield Industrial Estate, Bellsquarry, Livingston, West Lothian EH54 9BU
Tel: 01506 460020

Records of the Local Council Archives

It is first necessary to identify the local council which covers the district in which you are interested. Appendix 6 of *Tracing Scottish Ancestors* (Bigwood) gives a list of parishes and the local authority responsible for each.

The holdings of the various local council archives vary widely. In Fife, for example, an archivist has only recently been appointed but a valuable body of material is being collected in the local council archive, including school board minutes, Commissioners of Supply books, parochial board minutes and various burgh and town council minutes. The largest collection of records for the area, however, is still held in the St. Andrews University archives – including deposits of records of a number of the Fife burghs – but other primary material is scattered in other centres – such as in the local history department of Dunfermline Library or in the Kirkcaldy Museum and Art Gallery. In other parts of the country, archives are more centralised and one local council archive may hold most of the records of the royal burghs within their areas such as deeds, town council minutes, court records, parochial board records, lists of burgesses and also a wide range of other documents concerning local administration. Records of kirk sessions (of both the Established Church and dissenting congregations), trade records, papers of associations of various kinds, collections of family papers, individuals and businesses, maps and plans may also be found in these archives.

Exploring Scottish History (2nd edition) edited by Michael Cox is a directory of resource centres for Scottish local and national history and is an invaluable guide to what is held where. It includes a broad description of the holdings of each local council. The book also notes the web-sites which can be useful to consult though the information provided on individual sites ranges from bare particulars of times of opening to quite detailed listings of holdings.

The Scottish Record Association publishes a useful set of *Datasheets* which give summaries of a number of Scottish archival holdings. These can be obtained from Robin Urquhart, SCAN, Thomas Thomson House, 99 Bankhead Crossway North, Edinburgh EH11 4DX.

The Scottish Archive Network - SCAN - is currently working on giving on-line access (by 2003) to the "top level finding aids" of participating Scottish archives, providing a single searchable access point to their catalogues. These finding aids will summarise the nature and content of each collection and show whether there are more detailed catalogues available and in what form they can be consulted. The archives contributing to the network include all Scottish university archives, most local council and health board archives, many specialist repositories and also national institutions such as the NAS and the manuscripts department of the National Library of Scotland. Details concerning surveys on private archives carried out by the National Register of Archives (Scotland) will also be incorporated. The web-site is http://www.scan.org.uk.

When planning to visit a local council or specialised archive, it is wise to contact the archivist in advance. Not all archives (Stirling, for example) are open every day and in some there is limited space for researchers. The scope of material held, amount of help given, ease of access to records and premises themselves will, however, vary from place to place. Some provide facilities for photocopying, a user friendly cataloguing system and a café in the building. In others, archivists are struggling with inadequate storage space, understaffing and old premises. A great many of the archivists compensate for any such problems with their compendious knowledge of the district and its records and their willingness to help researchers.

University Archives

Many of the Scottish Universities have extensive holdings of primary material which may include papers of local families, estates and firms and large photographic collections, as well as records relating to the university itself and its students. For an outline description of university archives, consult *Exploring Scottish History* (Cox). Eight Scottish Universities are participating in the SCAN project and their entries will be cross-referenced to the descriptions of holdings on their individual web-sites. Another web-site dealing with the holdings of British universities – at present fifteen but to be extended to thirty by next year – is Archives Hub at http://www.archiveshub.ac.uk. Some of the university holdings include specialised collections. The University of Glasgow Business Records Centre is especially valuable in having a large collection of records of businesses of various kinds.

Specialist Archives and Museums

A number of organisations and professional bodies have archives – such as the Royal College of Physicians, Regimental Museums or the Royal Highland and Agricultural Society of Scotland - to mention just a few. As well as documentary evidence, artifacts, old agricultural machinery, presentations showing how people lived in the past displayed in local or specialised museums often add an extra dimension to family history. A wide range of both specialised archives and museums are mentioned in *Exploring Scottish History.*

Libraries

Local libraries often have very useful collections of regional books and copies of old newspapers, some of which may have been indexed. Small collections of primary material and photographic material may also be held there. The local knowledge of a librarian can be invaluable in pointing a researcher in the right direction. The telephone directory for the area will list both the local council library headquarters and also the branch libraries in the section dealing with the various operations of the council concerned.

Family History Centres and Societies

Many family history centres and societies have premises which hold material of value to researchers – transcripts of monumental inscriptions, collections of published and unpublished genealogical works and reference books, as well as microfilm copies of parish registers, copies of the International Genealogical Index, and fiche indexes to census returns. Some of these centres make a small charge for non-members. Not all are open every day and it is well to check on this. Like the local libraries, these societies will provide opportunities for sharing local knowledge.

Rosemary Bigwood is a lecturer, researcher and genealogist, specialising in older Scottish records. Her handbook *Tracing Scottish Ancestors*, first published by Harper Collins in 1999, has been updated and republished in 2001. It provides detailed guidance on a wide range of sources, how to locate and use them. The book is available in the UK, America, Australia and New Zealand.

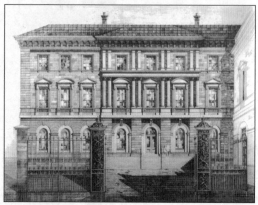

General Register Office for Scotland

Registration of births, deaths and marriages in Scotland

Registration of baptisms and proclamations of marriage was first enacted in Scotland by a Council of the Scottish clergy in 1551. The earliest recorded event - a baptism of 27 December 1553 - can be found in the register of baptisms and banns for Errol in Perthshire. Following the Reformation registration of births, deaths and marriages became the responsibility of the ministers and session clerks of the Church of Scotland. Standards of record-keeping varied greatly from parish to parish, however, and even from year to year. This together with evidence of the deterioration and loss of register volumes through neglect led to calls for the introduction of a compulsory and comprehensive civil registration system for Scotland. This came into being on 1 January 1855 with the establishment of the General Register Office for Scotland headed by the Registrar General and the setting up of 1027 registration districts. In 2001 registration districts number 331.

Records in the custody of the Registrar General The main series of vital events records of interest to genealogists are held by the Registrar General at New Register House in Edinburgh. They are as follows:

Old parish registers (1553-1854): the 3500 surviving register volumes (the OPRs) compiled by the Church of Scotland session clerks were transferred to the custody of the Registrar General after 1855. They record the births and baptisms; proclamations of banns and marriages; and deaths and burials in some 900 Scottish parishes. They are far from complete, however, and most entries contain relatively little information. Microfilm copies of these records are available world-wide and there are computerised and microfiche indexes to baptisms and marriages. A project to index the death and burial entries got under way in 1997 and is still ongoing.

Register of neglected entries (1801-1854): this register was compiled by the Registrar General and consists of births, deaths and marriages proved to have occurred in Scotland between 1801 and 1854 but which had not been recorded in the OPRs. These entries are included in the all-Scotland computerised indexes.

Statutory registers of births, deaths and marriages (from 1855): these registers are compiled by district registrars. They are despatched by the district examiners to New Register House at the end of each calendar year ready for the creation of all-Scotland computerised indexes. Microfiche copies of the register pages are available in the New Register House search rooms.

Adopted children register (from 1930): persons adopted under orders made by the Scottish courts. The earliest entry is for a birth in October 1909.

Register of divorces (from 1984): records the names of the parties, the date and place of marriage, the date and place of divorce and details of any order made by the court regarding financial provision or custody of children. Prior to May 1984 a divorce would be recorded in the RCE (formerly the Register of Corrected Entries, now the Register of Corrections Etc), and a cross-reference would be added to the marriage entry.

Births, deaths and marriages occurring outside Scotland (The Minor Records): these relate to persons who are or were usually resident in Scotland.

Marine Register of Births and Deaths (from 1855)
Air Register (from 1848)

Service Records (from 1881)
War Registers (from 1899) for the Boer War (1899-1902) and the two World Wars
Consular returns (from 1914)
High Commissioners' returns (from 1964)
Foreign Marriages (from 1947)
Register of births, deaths and marriages in foreign countries (1860-1965)

Census records (from 1841): these are the enumerators' transcript books of the decennial census of the population of Scotland. They record the name, age, marital state, occupation and birthplace of every member of a household present on census night. Census records are closed for 100 years and only the schedules for the 1841 to 1891 Censuses are open to the public. The 1901 Census records will be opened to the public in January 2002.

(To discover more details about the history of the records held by the GROS, buy a copy of our publication "Jock Tamson's Bairns: a history of the records of the General Register Office for Scotland" by Cecil Sinclair, ISBN 1 874451 591, 52 pages, cost GBP6.99 (USD10.50). See http://www.gro-scotland.gov.uk for details of how to order.)

Searching at New Register House

New Register House was opened in 1861 as a purpose-built repository for Scotland's civil registration records. Today it provides 100 search places and is open to the public from 09:00 to 16:30, Monday to Friday. Access to the indexes requires payment of a statutory fee but this also allows self-service access to microform copies of all the open records. The fee can be for a day, a week, four weeks, a quarter or a year. There are discount arrangements and a limited number of seats can be booked in advance. There is also provision for group evening visits.

Indexes to the statutory records (including overseas events), OPR baptism and marriage entries, and the 1881 and 1891 Census records are available on computer. There is self-service access to the statutory register pages on microfiche and the OPR and Census records on roll microfilm. It is also possible to order official extracts of any entry.

Since July 2000, the GROS has made available a single-step linked imaging search facility. This allows customers to search the indexes of the 1891 Census returns, and the statutory registers of births, deaths and marriages for the year 1891, which have been linked to digital images of the record pages. This facility is now also available on the Scots Origins website. From January 2002 we will also have limited images and indexes for the 1901 Scottish census available at New Register House.

Online Access to the New Register House Indexes

The all-Scotland computerised indexes can also be accessed from local registration offices which have links to the New Register House system. Some local registration offices provide search room facilities with access to microfiche copies of the statutory registers for their area The Family Records Centre in London has also been provided with online access (- the "Scotlink"); while the indexes to records over 100 years old for births and marriages, and over 75 years old for deaths, have been made available for searching over the Internet on the pay-per-view website 'Scots Origins'.

To find out more see the GROS website at **http://www.gro-scotland.gov.uk**.
Pay-per-view search website is **http://www.origins.net/**

The Scots Origins Internet Service General Register Office for Scotland

Scots Origins is the GROS's fully searchable pay-per-view database of historical indexes on the World Wide Web, and has been running since 6 April 1998. It is maintained on behalf of the department by OMS Services Ltd and provides access to the indexes of birth and marriage records over 100 years, and death records over 75 years old. To avoid raising concerns about browsing among records relating to living persons, indexes to birth and marriage entries less than 100 years old and deaths less than 75 years, are not available on the Internet.

The Indexes
Origins provides access to indexes of Scottish birth and marriage records from 1553 to 1899 and death records from 1855 to 1899. As yet, there is no all-Scotland index to the pre-1855 death and burial entries. All-Scotland indexes to the 1881 and 1891 census returns are available as well as limited digital images of the latter. The site therefore gives access to some 30 million index entries. An additional year of historical index data is added to the database at the beginning of each year, so 1900 birth and marriage data, and 1925 death data will be available by 2002.

Searching
New users can look at a demonstration version and refer to a detailed online guide to searching the indexes before they actually log on. They can also do a free search on their surname, which will tell them how many entries there are on the indexes under that name. They are then invited to register with the database and give name, postal address and credit-card details over a secure link to the *Origins* server. The complex security software has the approval of one of Britain's largest retail banks, the National Westminster, and authorisation is in real-time taking approximately 10 seconds. Card details are not stored and are transferred via an encrypted channel. Following authorisation by the bank that issued the card the server debits the card account with the GBP6 fee and gives the user a credit worth 30 pages to be viewed within a 24 hour period (allowing a customer to log off and on the Internet as required via a designated user code and password).

Those familiar with the New Register House system will find that *Origins* is slightly different in several respects. Searches can be made across the database, that is, for OPR, statutory and census indexes; for a given year plus or minus up to five years; for all or just one type of event; on more than one name; and narrowed down to a particular district name. Tables of registration district and parish names are available online with links to UK maps. A Soundex option can be used to search for similar-sounding names an important point as the spelling of names can vary considerably (Mac changing to Mc and so on) particularly in the OPRs.

The search form is easy to use being similar to those of web search-engines with check-boxes and blank data-entry fields. Search terms can be in upper or lower case and can include the standard wild-card characters '*' and '?'. The results of a search are initially displayed as an on-screen summary of the number of 'hits' found on the database and the number of pages (comprising a minimum of one and a maximum of 15 entries) it would take to display them all. It is then possible either to download the pages or to refine the search.

Once downloaded a page can be stored as a file on the user's computer (for viewing off-line or printing at a later date) or it can be consulted again gratis on the *Origins* database as often as required during the same session. The hits are displayed in a colour-coded table - there is an explanatory key at the bottom of the screen - with columns for event, sex, age, date (in the statutory index this is the year, but in the OPR index the date in full), surname, first name, parents' or spouse's name (depending on event type) and the district or parish. A miscellaneous column gives the parents or spouse and OPR microfilm frame number where appropriate. Microfilm copies of the OPR and open census records can be consulted at libraries and family history centres run by the Genealogical Society of Utah world-wide.

1891 Census images
Digital images of the record pages from the 1891 Scottish census are also available, linked to the indexes. These come in tiff file format, and browsers will require a 'plug-in' to display this non-standard image format. Images found can be downloaded for further viewing.

Looking further ahead, it is likely that further imaged records will become available as GROS continues its DIGROS programme of digitising all the historical records in its care.

Ordering extracts
Alongside each index entry is a button which can be selected to order the full register extract direct from the database. There is a charge of GBP10 per document which includes postage. Online helptext provides full details of what is contained in the different types of register extract backed up by images of sample pages from the statutory, OPR and census records. Orders are processed by staff at GROS in Edinburgh who send out the paper documents by ordinary post, aiming at a response within 15 working days.

SCOTS ORIGINS can be accessed at http://www.origins.net.

DIGROS *From Paper Page to Electronic Image*

On 6 July last year the Registrar General launched a new product that heralded a significant change to the way in which GROS presents its records. The product launched was of particular interest to family historians – namely digital images of the 250 000 pages of the 1891 Census paper records, which were linked to an existing computer index of over 4 million individual names of those people who were recorded by that Census. This product also included digital images of statutory registers of births, deaths and marriages for the year 1891. These impressively detailed images can now be viewed by customers who use our popular searching facilities at New Register House in Edinburgh, and are available also over the Internet.

The digitisation of the 1891 census served as a pilot project, allowing GROS and its contractors to look at the feasibility of using state-of-the-art technology to capture large groups of records. Following the success of this pilot, a major new programme is now under way. Known by us as the DIGROS programme (the Digital Imaging of the Genealogical Records of Scotland's people), this will make digital images of all the paper records held on the 6.5 kilometres of shelves in New Register House, which document more than 60 million individual names.

The first priority for this exciting new programme has been to scan and digitally capture the returns from the Scottish Census of 31 March 1901, which were held only in unindexed paper format, and which have remained closed to the public for a period of 100 years. To achieve this, we microfilmed the paper documents on 35mm archive film. Copies of these microfilms are available to customers in New Register House, and for commercial sale. Once captured on film, we have commissioned private-sector contractors to scan and image the films, and to undertake the indexing of the census. This will create a separate computer index of the 4.5 million individual names recorded in the 1901 returns, to be linked to the digital images and made available to the public in this form during January 2002 after the 100-year closure-period ends.

With the digitisation of 1901 census records completed, GROS and its contractors are now working on the imaging of the 1841 census and the statutory registers of births from 1855 onwards. Eventually, we plan to make **ALL** of the historical records that we hold available in the form of a searchable electronic-text index linked to high-quality electronic images of the paper pages. These consist of:
open census records (1841-1901)
the historical statutory registers (births and marriages 1855-1900 and deaths 1855-1925)
the old parish registers of baptisms, banns/marriages and deaths

These images will be available to readers in New Register House, and will replace the microfilm and microfiche formats currently used to access these records. As part of this improvement to our services, GROS search rooms have been re-equipped, with high quality flat-screen monitors.

All of these historical records could also be viewed on the Internet for a fee, essentially as an extension of our successful **'Scots Origins'** service (http://www.origins.net/GRO). Internet customers will no longer need to buy a formal paper extract certificate, though they will still be able to do so if they wish

But the **DIGROS** programme will achieve a lot more than simply digitising our historical records, because it is intended to capture current registration material as well. Once all of our records have been digitally captured, a process that is likely to take until 2004 at the earliest, customers accessing current records in New Register House will no longer need to view registers on microfiche.

Digitisation is at the heart of the GROS strategy for improving access to Scotland's historical records. In conjunction with the internet, it will enable genealogists and others to benefit from the information contained in these unique records of Scotland's people whether they are able to visit Edinburgh, or are searching from their homes.

The National Archives of Scotland

David Brown - Head of Reader Services

The National Archives of Scotland (NAS) holds one of the most varied collections of records in Britain. Occupying some 60 kilometres of shelving, the records date from the 12th century to the present day. They include the formal records of pre- and post-Union government, the law courts, the public registers of deeds and sasines (land transfers), the records of the Church of Scotland as well as those of some other denominations, estate papers of landed families, a large collection of maps and plans, the Scottish railway archives, and the records of a variety of businesses, charitable institutions and public bodies.

Two books, both by Cecil Sinclair, give much fuller information about these and other records. They are: *Tracing Your Scottish Ancestors. A Guide to Ancestry Research in the Scottish Record Office* (Stationery Office, 1997, price £9.99) and *Tracing Scottish Local History* (Stationery Office, 1994, £9.99). Both will enable family historians to assess likely sources of information before they visit us, so as to make the best use of their time in our search rooms.

Before visiting the NAS, it is advisable to start investigating Scottish ancestry in the records held by the General Register Office for Scotland (GROS). Hopefully these should provide a skeleton tree, to be fleshed out from the records held by us. As most readers of this *Handbook* will know, the GROS is located at New Register House, Edinburgh EH1 3YT. This is next door to our main building, HM General Register House. Both are at the east end of Princes Street. The GROS holds old parish registers of the Church of Scotland (up to 1854), statutory registers of births, marriages and deaths (from 1855) and census returns (from 1841- open up to 2001).

For family historians, the most popular NAS records are the registers of wills and testaments, dating from the 16th century to 1984. Testaments from 1985 are held by the Edinburgh Commissary Office, 27 Chambers Street, Edinburgh EH2 1LB. To search for a testament in NAS you need to have an idea of the date of death and - for wills recorded before 1876 - a place of residence. There are good indexes for the years before 1823, arranged by locality. Indexes for 1823-1875 are currently less satisfactory but from 1876 to 1984 there is a good annual index covering all Scotland.

Since late 1999, NAS has been a partner in a major project, the Scottish Archive Network. Financed principally by the Heritage Lottery Fund, partly by NAS itself and partly by the Genealogical Society of Utah, one object of the Network is to generate digital images of all the testaments for the years before 1876 and produce a union index for them. Progress has been good, and the first version of the index for the years 1823-1875 is almost complete. It will be tested from July 2001 and will eventually be freely available on the Internet. When the testaments are fully imaged, each image will be linked electronically to its index entry. It will then be possible to view the images in NAS, enabling readers to gain almost instant access to any testament. Website access will be to the index only, but the Archive Network will sell paper and electronic copies of images to enquirers. This imaging process will take some time, and the original testaments are being progressively withdrawn from public access between now and the end of 2001. They will be replaced by substitutes, either microfilms or digitally generated photocopies. Consequently readers intending to visit are advised to contact us to confirm whether particular records are available.

Perhaps the second most popular class of records is the **Register of Sasines**, beginning in 1617 and recording the transfer of lands and houses, together with transactions in which land was used to secure loans. Sasines contain information or clues about the individuals and families involved in these transactions, although they do not mention tenants. There are good indexes for the years after 1781, but before that the indexes are less straightforward and searching may have to be done using contemporary minute books. The Royal burghs kept separate series of their own for urban property transactions.

The **Retours** (or **Services of Heirs**) concern the inheritance of land. Although they deal only with landowners, a small proportion of the population, they can be a valuable resource. They run from 1530 until modern times, although they are of declining importance after 1868. When a vassal of the Crown died, his heir had to prove his right to inherit his ancestor's lands by obtaining an inquest by jury which delivered a return ('retour') to Chancery. The procedure could also be used by people who were not Crown vassals in order to provide evidence of their right to inherit land. Until 1847 the record was kept in Latin and the published indexes for the years before 1700 (the *Inquisitionum ad Capellam Regis Retornatarum Abbreviatio*) are also in Latin. Retours are very stylised documents, however, and a researcher will need only a minimum of instruction to understand their contents. The indexes from 1700 are in English.

The **church records** held by NAS are often consulted by family historians who have been unsuccessful in tracing an ancestor in the Old Parish Registers held by the GROS. These records, although catalogued, are not indexed. In consequence the most profitable searches tend to be those where a family has an association with a particular denomination and parish. The largest bodies of these records are those for the kirk sessions of the established Church of Scotland (minute books, communion rolls, etc) and those for the other Presbyterian churches which broke away from the Church of Scotland in the years after 1733, and which gradually reunited with it in the years after 1843. The collection is large, but not complete. Another group of church records meriting special mention is that of the Roman Catholic Church. These consist of bound sets of photocopies of Scottish Catholic parish registers for the years before 1855, particularly of baptisms and marriages. The earliest of these dates from the 18th century, but in most parishes they do not start until the 19th century. They are not indexed.

The NAS operates two search rooms in Edinburgh. One, the Historical Search Room at General Register House, Princes Street, EH1 3YY, is used mainly by family historians. The other, at West Register House, Charlotte Square, may hold relevant material and is the principal store both for judicial records and for our plans collection. Please telephone well before any visit, to check which search room is most appropriate for your work and to ask about any arrangements for consulting out-housed records. You should also make sure that your visit does not coincide with public holidays. The NAS has its annual stocktaking in November and the Historical Search Room is closed for the first two full weeks in that month, the West Search Room for the third. These arrangements may be changed after 2001.

We respond to every written or e-mailed enquiry but the pressure of correspondence is considerable and we cannot undertake research for enquirers.

The records mentioned above are described, with others, in more detail on the NAS website. The Scottish Archive Network's website also has much useful information about Scottish family history and can be viewed at www.scan.org.uk.
Enquiries: Telephone: 0131-535-1334 **E-mail**:research@nas.gov.uk enquiries@nas.gov.uk
Website: www.nas.gov.uk

The Scottish Archive Network
- Internet Access to the Written History of Scotland

Project Background
The 30 November 2000 saw the launch of a major national website (www.scan.org.uk) linking up 49 Scottish archives and opening up Scotland's rich archival heritage to the rest of the world. This website was the result of a successful bid to the Heritage Lottery Fund made in 1999 by the Scottish Archive Network (SCAN) in conjunction with the Genealogical Society of Utah (GSU) and the National Archives of Scotland (NAS). The project is worth around £4 million and is scheduled to last 3 years, finishing in December 2002. The Scottish Archive Network project is a Scotland-wide initiative, involving archives large and small, public and private, across the country. The 49 participant archives include national institutions, local authorities, universities, professional associations, health boards and several specialised archives. The project will put Scotland on the world map of archives and the Network is likely to be a prototype for others.

The initial bid to the Heritage Lottery Fund was made in response to the prevailing situation in Scotland's archives. Although every year more and more people visit archives in Scotland, access to the information held therein is often hampered because users often find it difficult to discern which archives hold what, existing catalogues prove time-consuming to search and most archives are only open on weekdays during standard working hours.

Main Aims
The project has 3 main objectives. In summary these are:-
1. **Online Catalogues** - To convert the top level catalogues of 49 participating archives to one searchable database. Where available, these may link to more detailed catalogues on the participating archives' own web-site. This service should become available from autumn 2001.
2. **Scottish Wills** - To combine the indexes to Scottish Wills and Testaments into one unified index covering the period 1500-1875. Users will be able to search this index via the SCAN web-site for free. Each individual index entry will then be linked to digital images of all of the relevant documents (some 2 million images!). This service will be available at the end of 2002.
3. **Online Resources** - Thirdly, we are providing a range of additional on-line services free to users to help them interpret the holdings of Scotland's archives. Many of these services were available from the date of the launch of the web-site.

Online Catalogues
The purpose of this part of the project is to create (if not already available) collection level descriptions for all the archives held by the 49 participating archives; and combine all these descriptions in one easily searchable database. Collection level descriptions will provide users with essential information about the nature and range of material held within Scottish archives. For example, you will find brief descriptions of the scope and content of the collections, and biographical or administrative information about the creators of the collections; and there will be information about the extent of the collections, any access restrictions and the availability of more detailed catalogues. Those more detailed catalogues, which list the contents of each archive down to the most basic unit, the item(s) that would be produced in the participating archives' search rooms, will not themselves be made available through the SCAN web-site. Too many of the catalogues are not in a good enough state to be made available as yet in this form, perhaps because some re-cataloguing is required to bring them up to acceptable modern standards. But by providing some information about the scope of the collections, which will be available for all the participating archives in one place for

the first time ever, SCAN hopes to give potential users a fair idea of what is held in Scottish archives.

Because the information which will be available in SCAN's database is general rather than specific, there may be thoughts that this data will have only limited use for genealogical enquiries, as in many cases family historians want to know if there are documents available about one particular person, which would seem to require detailed catalogues to be available. But remember that quite often archivists, when asked if they have any documents about John Smith, who was perhaps a tailor in Edinburgh or a farm worker in Angus, will not then go to consult some massive index of all the personal names in the collections of documents they hold (because they don't exist), but they will think that they know of collections of records which refer to tailors in Edinburgh or farm workers in a particular area of Angus. Therefore, when using the SCAN database, family historians will be able to do some of that work themselves, and establish in advance of a visit to a particular archive that there is/are collection(s) which will help them.

Users may well also find that they are not the only people who have been researching a particular family, and that certain archives have deposited with them someone's collected notes on their research. Quite a few of the participating archives have such collections of notes, and they might save researchers time by showing what sources could be useful, or perhaps quoting from private papers not generally accessible as they are held by the descendants of 19th century emigrants from Scotland.

As matters stand at the time of writing (July 2001), the collections description database was not accessible through the SCAN site. We do hope that it will become available in the autumn of 2001, but there are some technical issues which need to be resolved first, and we are reluctant to specify a date as yet when the database will be made available.

Wills and Testaments
As previously mentioned, the SCAN website will also provide access to Scottish Wills and Testaments - a fantastic resource for genealogists and historians alike. Towards the end of 2002, site visitors will find nearly half a million index entries to the testaments (wills) of Scots from the 16th century to 1875. Users will find Scots from all walks of life, famous, infamous or unknown, rich, poor or middling and from all parts of Scotland. Once the project is complete visitors to the site will also be able to order copies of any testaments - selecting from some 2 million high-quality digital images.

Currently, access to the wills and testaments is a lengthy process, because the index before 1876 is incomplete. Readers may only see the wills in the search rooms of the National Archives of Scotland. Also, many of the documents themselves are deteriorating, due to frequent use. For these reasons the wills were chosen as the first major collection in the National Archives of Scotland to be digitised.

As a result of the Scottish Archive Network project, all Scottish wills up to 1875 will be digitally imaged in full colour and the images will be linked to an index entry giving the name, occupation and place of residence of the deceased. The index will be available free of charge on the internet. The images may be seen free of charge in the National Archives of Scotland, or copies may be ordered for a charge over the internet in electronic or hard copy format.

If you have not used wills as a resource before, you may find them a valuable resource for both family and local history. For instance, they contain hundreds of thousands of personal and place names, all of which will be searchable using our index. They also contain a wealth of information about the way people lived in the past, and can provide details about the furnishing of people's homes, the tools they used for work, the contents of shops, the clothes they owned, the books they read, who owed them money and who they owed money to, the livestock they kept, the crops they grew and the names of their children or other relatives.

You will also be able to search the index for specific occupations and find information relating to, say, all the bakers in Scotland, or search for all the wills and testaments relating to a particular place. It may be possible to find hitherto unknown ancestors, or more information about those you already know of. In short, we hope that the SCAN project will open up the wills of Scots to searchers all over the world with an interest in Scottish local or social history, or Scottish ancestry.

Online Resources
The project website at www.scan.org.uk is the main means of accessing the key resources produced by the SCAN project - namely the Scottish Wills and the Online Catalogues. However, the web-site provides a great deal of supporting information to help users interpret these and other key archival sources. These include the following:-
Knowledge Base providing 1000 answers to questions frequently asked in Scottish archives.
Research Tools such as a guide to Scottish handwriting, a glossary of unusual words and a 'Virtual Strongroom' where images of original documents are displayed
Exhibitions - highlighting some of the riches held by Scotland's archives. These currently include exhibitions on trade cards, herbal remedies, the women of Angus through the ages, and the Highland Railway
Bookshop - displaying publications from Scottish archives and associations
Family history pages providing a basic guide to tracing your Scottish ancestors
Discussion forum on Scottish history and archives
Featured documents - highlighting topical or interesting documents from SCAN's participating archives
Directory of contact information for Scottish archives and associations

The web-site also includes supplementary information relating to the Online Catalogues and Scottish Wills projects to increase understanding of the project's key aims.

Perhaps the most important of these facilities is the Knowledge Base. In compiling the Knowledge Base, the Scottish Archive Network has tapped into the experience of Scotland's archivists to answer frequently asked questions about the historical records they look after. Between them Scotland's archivists answer thousands of enquiries each year from family historians, and many of these are repetitive or very similar, for example:
my ancestor was a shoemaker: where will I find his apprenticeship records?
why can't I find where my great-great grandmother was buried?
where can I find the passenger list for an emigrant ancestor?

Very few archives in Scotland have the resources to answer each enquiry as fully as the enquirer would like, and a vague enquiry typically requires a further exchange of letters or emails clarifying what the researcher requires and, often, redirecting the enquirer to a more appropriate archive or agency. The Knowledge Base aims to make researchers (and archivists) better informed about the location and limitations of historical records in Scotland and help ensure that archives are not flooded with repetitive or vague enquiries. Knowledge Base entries on, for example, School Registers (under 'Types of Records'), Emigration (under 'Subjects'), and Burghs (under 'Places') give a minimum of historical background along with guidance on where relevant records may be found and how to carry out research in them.

Because a large proportion of enquiries to Scottish archives come from family historians the SCAN website contains a separate way into the Knowledge Base for genealogists, via the Family History section. This gives general guidance for family historians and, in the section called 'My Ancestor Was . . .', links to relevant parts of the Knowledge Base. For example 'My ancestor Was a school pupil', 'My ancestor was an emigrant' and 'My ancestor was a burgess' link, respectively, to the three Knowledge Base entries mentioned above. Although this is a handy way in to the Knowledge Base for those with specific enquiries, it is worth getting to know the Knowledge Base proper, as it might explain why you have been having difficulty finding out something or suggest an avenue of research you had not considered.

Project Progress
At the time of writing this article (July 2001), the following progress had been made with SCAN's major objectives :-
Some 6000 online catalogue entries had been compiled from 20 participating archives
Over 100, 000 digital images of wills and testaments had been created.
Over 550 Knowledge Base entries had been completed plus 6 exhibitions. Another 5 exhibitions were in development.

Project Updates
The best way to find out about major new additions to the Scottish Archive Network website is to "register for updates" by following the link from the SCAN home page. This will guarantee that you are emailed notification when the Network's major facilities become available. If you just want to find out about project progress, then read the 'News Roundup' (linked from the home page).

Any enquiries about the SCAN project should be directed to *enquiries@scan.org.uk.*

RCAHMS

The National Monuments Record of Scotland

The National Monuments Record of Scotland (NMRS) is one of the main sources of information for researchers interested in Scotland's archaeology, buildings and maritime heritage. Within the NMRS there is a vast collection of material: over 3 million photographs, including over 1 million vertical air photographs, some 1 million drawings and c. 50,000 books. Included in the collections are antiquarian drawings, architects' drawings and plans, modern survey drawings, manuscript material, sketch books, topographical engravings, historic and modern photographs, aerial photographs from the 1940s to the present day and a wide range of reference books and other textual information.

The NMRS is a primary contact for members of the public carrying out local or family history research, for architects, archaeologists, students, publishers and many other researchers. Over 14,000 enquiries are made by researchers each year. Enquiries can be made in person by visiting the NMRS library; this is open to the public from Monday to Friday 9:30am to 4:30pm. You can also telephone, fax, email or write to the NMRS directly where specialised members of staff are able to help with topics of research.

Photographs, slides, digital images, photocopies, lasercopies and computer print-outs can be obtained from the NMRS for personal research, publications and exhibitions. Publications are also available for sale.

The collections can sometimes be useful for family history research: for example, directories held in the library give the names and addresses of residents in areas around Scotland dating back to 1837; a selection of geneaology and historical reference books can be consulted, including books on Scottish Family History, clans and the origins of Scottish names; files are held on architects, craftsmen, designers and others related to these fields, containing biographies and lists of their works.

Enquiries regularly relate to a person or clan and these can often be traced back to an ancestral home, building, castle or site; the NMRS can often source and supply relevant images of these locations. Maps dating back to the mid-19th century can also be a useful source of information, as are the Name Books which detail the origins of the names of buildings,

Alexander N. Paterson, Architect as a student (seated second left) with his class at the Ecole des Beaux-Arts, Paris. Crown Copyright: RCAHMS

villages and towns on Ordnance Survey maps from the 1850s. There are also numerous graveyard surveys held in the collections.

The NMRS is an integral part of the Royal Commission on the Ancient and Historical Monuments of Scotland (RCAHMS) who are responsible for recording and interpreting the buildings, archaeology and maritime heritage of Scotland. All information gathered from the detailed surveys is available through the NMRS.

Website

Modern technology is increasingly being used to improve public access to all the information and collections held in the NMRS. CANMORE, the NMRS database, is accessible worldwide on the Internet through the RCAHMS website at www.rcahms.gov.uk. For each site or building, location details, bibliographical references and reports are available, with details of the items held in the NMRS Collections. This serves as an invaluable resource of information for all manner of research purposes. There are currently over half a million entries in CANMORE and information is added on a daily basis.

CANMORE gives the ability to search for information relating to sites and buildings around Scotland by a variety of search parameters, including site name, area, building type or by a more general keyword search. Recent developments have increased the depth of available queries to include searches by person, collection and type of collection item.

In addition, the website simply and clearly describes the history and aims of RCAHMS and details the services available from the NMRS. A regularly updated What's New page informs visitors of work in progress, current events and exhibitions as well as giving a full list of RCAHMS publications available to buy direct.

NMRS is just one of several sources of information for global users researching their ancestry in Scotland. Visit Edinburgh to consult the NMRS, or make contact by email, telephone, fax or letter. Staff will be pleased to help or, if there is nothing relevant in the NMRS, to direct you to other organisations.

View of gardeners at The Glen, Tweedale.
Second from right, standing - Mr MacIntyre, Head Gardener. Third from right, standing -Alexander Black (father of Miss Black) who became head gardener from 1907 to 1921, and was then head gardener at Ancrum House until 1930. He left The Glen because the tenants could not afford to keep up the staff of twenty one gardeners, and he would have had to work below his station. He trained at Hutton Castle (1902-4) and later married Mr MacIntyre's daughter. Date c.1900.
Crown Copyright: RCAHMS

Enquiries:
National Monuments Record of Scotland, John Sinclair House, 16 Bernard Terrace, Edinburgh EH8 9NX Scotland
Telephone: +44 (0)131 662 1456 Fax: +44 (0)131 662 1499
Email: nmrs@rcahms.gov.uk Website: www.rcahms.gov.uk

Scottish Brewing Archive
Alma Topen

The Scottish Brewing Archive [SBA] was officially opened in 1982 at Heriot-Watt University, Edinburgh due to the efforts of Alec Anderson, the late librarian, and the staff of the Brewing Department. They gathered in the archives from surviving Scottish breweries, including records for long - established breweries that had been taken over and closed during the rationalisations of the 1950s to 1980s. Further deposits have been received from breweries, collectors, ex-employees and by SBA purchase. The largest deposits of archives originated from the brewing groups of Scottish & Newcastle plc, Tennent Caledonian Breweries, Usher Vaux and Allied Breweries, and include firms like J & R Tennent Ltd, John Jeffrey & Co Ltd, Wm Younger & Co Ltd, Wm McEwan & Co Ltd, T & J Bernard Ltd, Maclachlans Ltd, James Aitken & Co (Falkirk) Ltd, John Fowler & Co Ltd of Prestonpans, George Younger & Son of Alloa, Drybrough & Co Ltd, Ushers Brewery Ltd, Lorimer & Clark Ltd, the Devanha Brewery Co in Aberdeen, McLennan & Urquhart Ltd of Dalkeith. The archive is funded by the industry and is administered by a Board of Trustees. It is open to the public and is used by the industry for heritage and marketing projects, by academics, students, brewing enthusiasts and family historians. In 1991 the archive relocated to Glasgow University Archives[GUA].

Research opportunities
Primary and secondary sources in the SBA offer opportunities for research into all aspects of Scottish brewing from the eighteenth century to the present day, but most records date from the 1850s to the 1970s. However, some commercial and personnel material is closed to the public. The SBA holds the archives of 120 companies and associations, such as the Brewers' Association of Scotland and the Institute of Brewing (Scottish Section). The collections are diverse, covering not only brewing, but also malting, coopering, bottlers, soft drinks, label manufacturers, hotels, a vintner and a vinegar brewer. There is a library of technical and historical books and a large collection of artefacts such as cans and bottles. While this article will highlight sources for family historians, there is also scope for research into brewery architecture, the brewing process, products, technology, distribution, staff, advertising and the threat of the temperance movement.

It is worth noting that we do not have records for every brewery in Scotland nor do we have a list of every brewer there has ever been in Scotland. Compiling such a list would be a major research project. The majority of the companies represented in the SBA are from Edinburgh, Glasgow, Alloa and Falkirk, which were the main centres of the commercial and export trade in the nineteenth and twentieth centuries. Breweries that disappeared before 1920 are poorly represented as are firms outwith the central belt. We are building up files of notes on breweries throughout Scotland - notes gleaned from local history books, the trade press and passed on from local historians.

Types of records
In general, the companies' archives have the following types of records: corporate, administrative, financial, production, distribution, staff, publicity, advertising, photographs and historical notes. Each company is catalogued separately, but due to differential survival rates the quantity and quality of the records can vary widely from company to company. The collection for William Younger of Edinburgh is the best one as there is something of everything in it, as you will see from the number of examples used in this article.
A major re-listing programme is nearing completion. A list of all the collections, together with summaries, can be found on the SBA website. More detailed summaries, along with short company histories, are in preparation and should be

Blair's of Alloa

available in 2002. The web site also has a number of Frequently Asked Questions as well as source lists such as temperance and general books on brewing history. More are being compiled.

People
Family historians use the SBA collections to supplement information already gathered from statutory and census records. Proof of an ancestor having worked at a particular brewery, a photograph of him/her, a history and photograph of the brewery are the usual requests. Workers in a brewery or maltings would have included brewers, maltsters, coopers, bottlers, packers, deliverymen, labourers, apprentices, office staff, travellers. There were also agents in other towns and abroad. It is possible to find information about individual workers, but it is not always easy, especially if the request is for a labourer in a brewery somewhere in Edinburgh in the nineteenth century! (There were 25-30 breweries in Edinburgh before 1900). Material about brewery workers is often patchy as wages books do not survive for every company. Access to wages, salaries books and personnel material is restricted and is closed for 75 years.
It is easier to find out about senior staff and directors than general labourers as they have left more documentary evidence behind. But you won't find a big, fat personnel file for your ancestor. You will have to search through minute books, ledgers, salaries and wages books (if they exist) and other documents and may only end up with a few references, or you could be lucky and find lots of information.

Brewers before 1800.
The SBA does not have primary material for brewers before 1725. Local record offices and the National Archives of Scotland [NAS] should be consulted for Burgh and Town Council records (a good source for information about women brewers pre 1700), business and personal papers of brewers and maltsters. Local taxation records exist. For example, Edinburgh City Archives hold the Ale Impost Ledgers for the eighteenth century. They list annually all the brewers in Edinburgh and Leith paying the 2d per pint tax on ale and beer. Dundee City Archives have the records of the Maltmen Incorporation of Dundee.
Sequestration (bankruptcy) papers at the NAS often have business papers included. A database of all sequestrations from 1781-1913 is available at GUA. There are over two hundred entries for brewers, maltsters and coopers and several hundred more for inn keepers, tavern keepers, wine & spirit merchants and porter sellers. It was difficult to find individual case papers but the NAS have solved this problem by compiling an electronic index to the sequestrations between 1838-1913 which links the original reference number with its modern reference number.
The printed Acts of Parliament of Scotland have regulations relating to brewers, maltsters, ale sellers and related trades and they are indexed

One of the earliest documents in the SBA is a 1725 printed petition to the Lords of Council and Session against an increase in beer duty. This was signed by 62 Edinburgh brewers, including 2 women. Another printed document –a court case to settle whether brewers in Dalkeith were obliged to grind all their malt at the Duke of Buccleugh's mill – lists all the brewers in Dalkeith in 1763.

Other eighteenth century records are customer ledgers or journals which give the names of customers, but not always the addresses. If your ancestor was a publican in Edinburgh or Glasgow there might be an entry for him/her. Examples survive for Drybrough of Edinburgh, 1784-1793 and for J & R Tennent, 1782-84. This latter volume has names, but no addresses. Another Tennent's ledger from 1806-10 is much better as it has addresses of customers and has an index. Mr Drybrough had a very impressive list of clients among the Edinburgh aristocracy and included James Boswell, Dukes & Duchesses and also the Governor of Edinburgh Castle. It is also possible to work out which of the customers were publicans by the amount of ale bought. They bought hogsheads while private households tended to buy a few gallons at a time.

Partnerships and employment contracts
There are a number of partnership agreements in the collections for breweries and licensed premises, dating from the 1800s to the 1970s. These detail the names of partners, sometimes with information about previous partners in the firm, and the financial arrangements. A good example is for Gilcomston Brewery, Aberdeenshire in 1819. This mentions the partners, the buildings and the nature of the business. There is also a series of partnership agreements in the William Younger collection, the earliest one being 1818. Gilcomston brewery also has a series of agreements and correspondence relating to appointing agents in Dundee and London in the 1830s.

Minute Books
Directors' minute books are the first place to try for references to directors and senior management such as brewers, chemists, office workers, travellers and agents. They are usually indexed. They are available for most companies from the 1880s or 1890s onwards but there are notable absences. For instance, there are no minute books for George Younger of Alloa before 1960 and none at all for G & J Maclachlan. Minute books record appointments, retirals, deaths, salaries, dismissals for misdemeanours, long-term illnesses, accidents, pensions for widows, granting of loans and even allocation of company cars to travellers. The minute books and board papers of J & R Tennent are very useful for information about the German workers employed in their German-designed lager brewery from 1891 to 1914. There is also information about them being interned during World War 1 and not being re-employed afterwards because of adverse public feeling.

Salaries and Wages books
Salaries[S] and wages books [W] exist but only for some companies but are incomplete: they include: John Aitchison (1936-49 S & 1955-60 W), T & J Bernard (1889-1912 S &1932-46 W), Cairns and Rawson Ltd (1961-62 S & W), Drybrough (1912 –22 S & 1922-61 W), John Jeffrey (1958-59 W), Lorimer and Clark, (1934-65 W), Wm McEwan

McEwan Draymen

(1873-1938 S & 1896-1939 W), J & J Morison (1948-60 S &1912-60 W & time books), Robert Younger (1956-59 W), William Younger (1864-1940 S). Information in these books normally give dates of payment (monthly for senior staff and weekly for coopers, labourers, apprentices etc), name of staff member (sometimes, but not always, with job designation) and amount paid. Time off for holidays and sickness is sometimes recorded.

The names of female employees hired during the First World War are in a William Younger salary book, but only for a few months. A separate book of female employees is referred to but has not survived. The salary books also record the names of men in the forces in red ink as 'OHMS'. There is also a list from 1941 of all Wm Younger men who served in the forces, civil defence or other war work.

The William McEwan records include wages books of all those employed at the Slateford Road maltings from 1897 to 1939, a cooper's apprenticeship contract from 1886 for John McAra and a wages book for coopers and apprentices from 1896-98.

Names of draymen appear in the horse stocks lists for William Younger & Co Ltd from 1919 to 1943. These give the names of the horses, ages, valuations and names of handlers. There is also a series of photographs taken in 1871 of the horses and handlers. While the horses, like Bob and Captain, are all identified, the handlers are not.

Ledgers
Ledgers can also be useful for tracing people. They have names of suppliers, customers, commission paid to agents and the private ledgers have salaries of directors.

At the end of the William Younger ledgers for 1805-39 is a list of all the tenants and rents of his properties in the Abbey precincts of Holyrood Palace in Edinburgh.

Ledgers can also contain owners' private expenditure. Alexander Hutchison, a farmer and maltster near Kirkcaldy, had private expenditure entries in the private ledger of Robert Hutchison & Co Ltd in the 1890s. These included school fees for his children at St Andrews schools. He also kept little diaries recording farming, business and personal items, 1855-1903.

Wm McEwan, the Edinburgh brewer, recorded his personal expenditure in the brewery private ledgers, including about £15,000 on building and furnishing his house in Palmerston Place from 1880-1885 and the first instalment on the McEwan Hall for Edinburgh University, a project that cost him over £100,000.

Press cuttings/scrap books
These can be an excellent source of information about the industry in general and about the particular company, especially for news of senior management. Thee include appointments, retirals or obituaries, staff outings, the provision of recreational facilities such as bowling greens, industrial relations, accidents, war time incidents. Press cuttings books survive for George Younger of Alloa ,1898-1949, William Younger, 1922-48 and Scottish & Newcastle plc, 1960s & 1970s.

There are also presscuttings for Meiklejohn's Bass Crest Brewery centenary celebrations in 1874.

House magazines
These are extremely useful and have features on staff, the work of different departments, regional breweries, staff news -promotions, retirals, obituaries, opening of new hotels and pubs and photographs and reports of staff sports clubs. Magazines are available for Scottish & Newcastle from 1965 to the present, although the series is not complete, for the Vaux group for 1965-75 and Tennent Caledonian Breweries for the 1960s –1980s.

Collections with family papers
There are a few collections with historical material relating to the owners of companies.

Tennent Caledonian Breweries employed a professional genealogist in the early 1980s to gather together copies of birth, marriage, death certificates, wills, title deeds, census

Wrights of Perth

records, and references in Glasgow history books relating to the Tennent family. These documents are in forty filing boxes and cover the period from the 1550s to the 1970s.

The family history of the Younger family of Abbey and Holyrood breweries in Edinburgh was researched for the book *The Younger Centuries*, by David Keir, 1949 to coincide with the 200th anniversary of the founding of the company. There are copies of title deeds, wills and biographical material on family members. Theses notes have been supplemented by research done for the latest book, published in 1999, *Good Company, The History of Scottish & Newcastle plc*, Berry Ritchie.

The Younger letter books survive from the 1840s to around 1920 and have business and personal letters. The series for Henry Johnston Younger in the 1860s and 1870s are particularly useful. He seemed to have been an arrogant spendthrift who nearly brought the firm to a state of collapse in the 1870s. There are angry letters with his partners and brothers, letters about him buying personal possessions such as horses, a carriage, furniture, a house and even a golden flute. There is also interesting material about a sojourn in Australia in the 1850s where he invested in a cattle and sheep station and did a spot of gold-mining. His cattle station ledger for 1856-60 have accounts for buying and selling livestock.

There are also some personal papers for William McEwan who built Fountain Brewery in 1856. Before that he was a clerk in Glasgow, then in charge of the office of a spinning mill in Honley, Yorkshire and then went to his uncles' brewery to learn the trade. There is a collection of letters from family and friends which give an interesting insight into his life style in the 1840s and 1850s. There are notebooks where he recorded every half-penny he spent on food, lodgings, books, evening classes and outings with friends.

A few family papers survive for Mr James Drybrough regarding employing Allan Masterton to teach his children writing, arithmetic and book-keeping between 1795-1797.

Public houses

We are often asked about the history of individual public houses and publicans. If you want to research the history of a pub, you would be best to start with other sources such as title deeds, Licensing Court records and Valuation Rolls. If you discover the pub was bought by a brewery, then contact us and we can see if any records survive to help you. Because of different licensing laws in Scotland, pubs were generally owned or rented by publicans and not by breweries, although there were exceptions. Scottish breweries did not build up large tied house estates in Scotland until the 1940s and 1950s and were often operated by subsidiary companies. For example we have records for West of Scotland Taverns and Stag Inns (Edinburgh)Ltd. Files on currently- owned pubs are still with the relevant breweries.

The purchase and sale of pubs and hotels can be found in company minute books and property records and we have

financial records for some pubs, but they are not very helpful for family historians.

There is a particularly good series of managed-house files for the Edinburgh brewers, T & J Bernard for the 1930s - 1950s which mainly deal with staff, repairs and stock Breweries did loan money to publicans to improve public houses and they bought the brewery's beer for the term of the loan. Loan ledgers are extant from the 1880s onwards for a number of companies. The T & J Bernard collection also has documents pledged in security for loans from the 1890s to 1950s. These often have copies of title deeds, correspondence, sometimes notes about the publican and his family-whether a good or bad risk for the loan.

Photographs

There is a variety of workers' photographs and photographic portraits of management dating from the 1870s to the 1960s, however they are not always identified. There are photographs dating from the 1870s onwards that show building exteriors, interiors, people at work and the evolution of mechanised equipment, particularly bottling and canning lines. The Drybrough, William Younger and Tennent collections have the best range of brewery photographs, with views of buildings and staff. Tennent's has a unique collection of photographs of women workers in 1916. William Younger's has photographs of staff from the 1870s onwards, including group photographs of workers in different departments of the breweries and maltings in the 1930s and 1949. Many of the 1949 workers have been identified.

The William Younger collection also has 2 photograph albums from the 1860s to 1870s belonging to H J Younger. There are photographs of family, friends, holiday snapshots in Britain and Europe, country house parties, horses, dogs, the brewery, views of Australia, annual camps of the London and Scottish Regiment on Wimbledon Common.

Library

In addition to the archive material there is the Alec Anderson Memorial Library which contains an important collection of historical and technical books, some dating to the eighteenth century.

There are periodicals such as *The Brewers' Guardian* (1871-96 & 1937-93) and *The Brewer's Almanack* (1895-1971) and directories of brewers such as *The Incorporated Brewers' Directory*, 1947-1991. A full list of periodicals we have is on the website.

There are also copies of *The National Guardian* from 1889-1913, although in a fragile state, which were donated by the Mitchell Library after they had been microfilmed. This was a strong anti-temperance trade newspaper for the industry in Scotland and is an invaluable source for information on national issues, breweries and distilleries (especially openings, refurbishments, fires), features on and photographs of personalities in the licensed trade, accidents to workers, court cases (especially thefts and running illicit drinking shops), obituaries, licensing court news, annual brewery outings and brewery soirées.

Contact details

If you have any enquiries regarding the resources or work of the SBA, or want to visit, please contact us.
The Archivist works three days a week -Tuesday, Thursday and Friday - and therefore an appointment is advisable before visiting.
Email: A.Topen@archives.gla.ac.uk
Telephone: 0141 330 6079
Address: 13 Thurso Street, Glasgow G11 6PE
Web page: www.archives.gla.ac.uk

Alma Topen is the Archivist for The Scottish Brewing ArchiveCurrently undetaking research into the development of Partickhill in the West End of Glasgow from the 1790s and the life of William McEwan, the Edinburgh brewer. She is a keen gardener, a member of the Embroiders Guild and is married with two cats

The Public Record Office of Northern Ireland
Anne McVeigh & Stephen Scarth

Refurbishment has been the key word this year as we continue to strive to improve our service to our readers. Of major significance has been the transformation of the old Exhibition Hall into the new Self-Service Microfilm Reading Room and Library.

NEW SELF-SERVICE MICROFILM READING ROOM
From comments made by our customers, we were aware that the self-service facility, though popular as a service, was not housed in a room conducive to study nor was it large enough to accommodate the increasing number of users. Moreover, the accommodation arrangements for the library meant that we could only offer a limited service. After a 'think tank' - commissioned to report on possible improvements to the public areas - came up with the idea of turning the under-utilized Exhibition Hall into the Microfilm Reading Room, feasibility plans were drawn up. It emerged that, not only could we fit in more microfilm reading machines, and make it more accessible to those with walking disabilities, but it would also open up the library to the public for the whole of our opening hours. We now have twenty-four machines - eight of them brand new - and a much improved ambience. Those who used the old self-service room - either over in the red-brick building or upstairs in the main building - agree that the present arrangement is a vast improvement.

COPY WILL BOOKS
And to improve the service even more, we can now offer more films on a self-service basis. In addition to the church records and the 1901 census we have added the copy will books (1858- c.1900) to the self-service range. These are available on MIC/15C.

PRONI LIBRARY BOOKS
The PRONI library books, some of which are comparatively rare, are now available for consultation during normal opening hours instead of two hours in the afternoon as was the case previously. The library was initially opened to the public in 1998, the idea being to give readers the opportunity to combine research into primary and secondary sources under one roof. The library holds many items of general interest to researchers as well as many rare books that may be difficult to find elsewhere. These include: an almost complete set of Thom's Directories; the best set of land law and legal books outside a law library; histories of the various regiments within the British Army and the Police Force; books on every conceivable form of transport; and biographies, many of which were compiled using primary sources found in PRONI, for example, Lord Castlereagh, Lord Carson, the Marquess of Dufferin and Ava, and Earl Macartney. There are church histories, books on emigration, on family history, Irish history, local history and economic history. As expected, works on the major industries feature strongly, with the linen industry particularly well represented. There is a full set of the Dictionary of National Biography. Often abbreviated to the DNB, the Dictionary of National Biography contains short biographical notes on all the prominent people of the British Isles. This is an extremely valuable source for checking information on famous people. And finally, there is the Beck Collection. While out of print and difficult to source books are to be found throughout the library, the Beck collection is a particularly rich source. Here you will find books about old Belfast, its history, its industries and its places of interest as well as local histories of various places.

PHILLIMORE PRIZE
On the subject of books, let me take the opportunity to blow our own trumpet just a little. At the Annual General Meeting of the Society of Archivists, it was announced that PRONI's *Guide to Local History Sources in the Public Record Office of Northern Ireland* was the winner of the Phillimore Prize.

Awarded annually by the publishing company, Phillimore, who specialise in books on local history, the prize goes to the best archival publication on a themed topic, this year's being for material that supports life-long learning. This little book (£9.99 at all good bookshops!) was compiled and edited by Jonathan Bardon, under contract to PRONI. We are delighted that this prestigious prize has been conferred on our publication - and by the way, you can consult a copy in our library!

NEW LECTURE THEATRE
Having moved the microfilm readers downstairs this left us with an empty room upstairs but nowhere to hold our popular talks and lectures. It was decided to turn the old microfilm room into a new lecture theatre and exhibition area. Repainted and re-carpeted, the room appears nothing like its former self. It can now hold up to forty people comfortably (fifty at a pinch) and has new subdued lighting - perfect for those wishing to take notes during the 'PRONI Made Easy', 'Tracing your Family Tree' or 'Sources for Local History' talks. These talks are continuing to prove popular and, apart from a break in July, will be offered on a three-month rotational basis for the foreseeable future.

OPEN DAY
The new lecture theatre coped admirably with the Open Day that PRONI held under the aegis of Adult Learners Week, promoted by the Educational Guidance Service for Adults (EGSA). Forty people attended the event held in May. Staff from the various sections within PRONI made themselves available to answer questions from the public, and offer advice on caring for their own precious documents. There were talks on using the sources for tracing a family tree and for discovering the history of a particular locality, as well as tours of both the public areas and behind the scenes in the record storage areas and in conservation.

OUTREACH CENTRES
The official opening of our latest outreach centre, to be based at Armagh Ancestry in the St Patrick's Trian, Armagh, had to be postponed as a precautionary measure against the spread of foot and mouth disease. Meanwhile, Morrow's Shop Museum, which hosted our Ballymena outreach centre, finally closed down. The museum and centre were relocated in new, purpose-built premises at 3 Wellington Court, Ballymena, and renamed the Ballymena Museum. It opens for business in June 2001. Our other outreach centres, at the Harbour Museum in Londonderry and at the Border Counties History Collective at Blacklion, Co. Cavan, continue to flourish.

OTHER CHANGES
Other changes introduced this year include the provision of a web-enabled computer in the waiting area that allows access to the PRONI website and to other selected archival sites. We hope this will be an addition that will be welcomed by our readers.
We have placed signs in the public areas that we hope will allow new readers to locate places and items more readily, as well as benefiting those with vision difficulties.
Staff now wear badges to distinguish them from members of the public (look for the gold and blue 'PRONI' symbol and the word 'Staff').

NEW ACCQUISITIONS
As ever, PRONI acquired important accessions of historical documents that we hope will be of interest to our readers.

CHURCH RECORDS:
Church of Ireland
Microfilm copies were made of the records of Armoy Parish, 1750-1982, of Loughguile Parish, 1801-1992, and of

Drumtullagh Parish, 1871-1946, all in Co. Antrim. They comprise baptism, marriage and burial registers, vestry minutes, preachers' books, account books, and a Sunday School roll book. Original records were received from St Patrick's, Ballymena, Co Antrim (**CR/1/78-79**), and include baptisms, marriages, burials, vestry minute books and preachers' books, 1778-1923. In Co. Down the baptism register for St. Paul's Parish Church, Castlewellan, 1872-1950 was copied (**CR/1/80**), while for Co. Londonderry the following records were microfilmed: Kildollagh Parish (**MIC/1/337**), which consist of baptisms, 1879-1956, marriages, 1858–1958, and burials, 1888-1951; and Ballyrashane Parish (**MIC/1/338**), comprising baptisms, 1877-1903, marriages, 1845-1947, and burials, 1877-1958.
Presbyterian Church
Presbyterian Church records microfilmed include First and Second Donagheady, Co. Tyrone and consist of baptisms, marriages, and communicants' roll books, 1838-1932. (**MIC/1P/458-459**)
Congregational Church
PRONI microfilmed three volumes of minute books of Coleraine Congregational Church, Co. Londonderry 1844-98, which include baptisms, 1837-50 and 1859-81, marriages, 1847-8 and 1855, burials, 1844-9, lists of members, c.1840-1850, and accounts, 1854-59 and 1880-98 (**MIC/1G/1**). An addition to the records of York Street Congregational Church, Dublin, was a marriage register, 1863-81. (**CR/7/3 add**)
Baptist Church
Baptist Church records microfilmed include a membership register for Coleraine Baptist Church, Co. Londonderry, c.1860-1993, containing baptisms, 1905-46. (**MIC/1H/1**)
Reformed Presbyterian Church
Records received from Baillies Mills Reformed Presbyterian Church, Co. Down, 1866-1937, include financial records, 1934-83, a communicants' roll book, 1898-c.1970, marriage registers, 1866-1906, and baptism registers, 1844-1974. (**CR/5/19**). Also received was an additional marriage register, 1863-1937 from Knockbracken Reformed Presbyterian Church, Co. Down. (**CR/5/16**)

BUSINESS RECORDS:
The records of Moygashel Mills, Co. Tyrone which incorporates, amongst others, the records of Braid Water Spinning Mill, Ballymena, Co. Antrim, include c.200 volumes comprising minute books, order-books, accounts and annual reports, c.1860-1970. (**D/4256**)
The records of *Barbour Threads, Hilden, Co Antrim,* late 19th to the mid 20th century, comprise correspondence, financial records and an intriguing range of registered trademarks amassed from literally all around the world, a visual legacy of the global involvement of the mill. (**D/4272**)
The *E.T. Green Ltd* records (Belfast Mills and Animal Feedstuffs Manufacturer) contain plans for a proposed extension, 1959. (**D/4259**)
The *Denis Rebbeck* papers, former chairman of Harland & Wolff consist of correspondence, photographs, accounts, financial records and pamphlets, c.1950-1980. (**D/4266**)
Architectural records of *H.A. Patton & Partners*, Belfast, contain elevations, plans and photographs of: Castlecoole, Co. Fermanagh; St. Angelo House, Ballycassidy, Co.Fermanagh; the Crown Bar, Belfast; the Elmwood Hall, Belfast; Enniskillen Town Hall, Co. Fermanagh; and Lisnamallard House, Co. Fermanagh, 1972-88. (**D/4257**)

ESTATE PAPERS:
Additional Ely patents include two extremely important letters patent, the first creating Charles, Earl of Ely, the 1st Marquess of Ely on 1 January, 1801, and the second creating the same individual as the 1st Baron Loftus in the peerage of the UK on the same date. The earl was being rewarded by the British government for his willingness to throw his influence behind the legislative union between Great Britain and Ireland. (**D/3130 add**)
Additional *Lord Lurgan* papers include maps of the Londonderry estate, 1751-1832, and maps of the Richmond estate, Co.Armagh, 1830-1841. (**D/1928 add**)

Added to the *Earl of Antrim* papers was one 1820 map of the Earl's estate in the barony of Glenarm, Co. Antrim, that includes a coloured depiction of Glenarm Castle, village and harbour. (**D/2977 add**)
We also received eleven deeds relating to the *Scullion* and *Agnew* families of Ballynease, Co.Londonderry, 1863-1922 (**D/4273**) and two title deeds relating to William Eccles of Gortnadarragh, Co. Fermanagh, 1713. (**D/4265**)

SENTRY HILL
In conjunction with Newtownabbey Borough Council, PRONI accepted as a temporary deposit, the papers of the McKinney family of Sentry Hill, Co. Antrim, comprising diaries, letters and photographs relating to William Dee McKinney (1832-1917). This is a collection of outstanding significance which has already been the subject of a book by Brian Walker – *Sentry Hill, An Ulster Farm And Family* (Blackstaff, 1981). However, the real importance derives from the provenance of the archive: whilst major landlords were scrupulous about record keeping, the papers relating to middle ranking Ulster farmers were frequently not preserved.

SOCIAL HISTORY:
Belfast Rotary Club donated their records that include 26 volumes of minute books, 1917-52 (**D/4264**), and the Ulster Local History Trust donated their papers consisting of minutes, letters and reports, 1989-92. (**D/4267**)

HEALTH RECORDS:
The Pharmaceutical Society of Northern Ireland donated their papers consisting of 15 volumes of minute books, 11 correspondence files, three photographs and one volume of newspaper cuttings, 1925-1992. (**D/4275**)

PHOTOGRAPHIC MATERIAL:
The papers of Joseph Toner of Belfast were augmented by a further 32 photographs of the Ulster Home Guard, 1942-44. (**D/3803 add**)

POLITICAL RELATED PAPERS:
The papers of Joseph O'Dolan of Belcoo, Co Fermanagh, were donated by his niece. They consist of an autograph book and the associated correspondence of O'Dolan who was an internee on the prison ship, 'Argenta' from 1922 to 24. (**T/3873**)

AND FINALLY ...
From the 2nd August, 2001, the Public Record Office of Northern Ireland will open at 10 am on the first Thursday of each month. This is 45 minutes later than our normal opening time. As the office is open late every Thursday it was felt that this would be least disruptive to our customers. The reason for the later opening is to allow those members of staff who interface with the public time to have staff briefings and training sessions together.

We hope to continue to offer the best service possible and to live up to our vision: 'leading best practice in archives'.

National Archives of Ireland

Aideen M Ireland National Archives of Ireland

The National Archives comprises the holdings of the former Public Record Office of Ireland and of the State Paper Office. The combined holdings date from medieval times to the present day.

The holdings comprise the records of the former Chief Secretary's Office in Dublin Castle, including papers relating to the Rebellion of 1798, the Fenian movement of the 1860s, and crimes and convictions throughout the nineteenth century. The Transportation Records are of particular importance to Australians whose ancestors were transported from Ireland to Australia as convicts in the period 1788 to 1868. Microfilms and a computerised index of the most important records relating to transportation have been deposited in the Australian National Library in Canberra and copies of the microfilms are available at state libraries throughout Australia. Record collections include those relating to the employment of Resident magistrates and other local government officials. There are also excellent prison records.

The national Archives collections also comprise the records of the former Public Record Office of Ireland. This office suffered in 1922 during the Civil War and many of the records were destroyed. However, in many cases there are copies, transcripts, précis and indexes of this material. Many other records of genealogical and historical interest have been acquired since 1922.

Among other records which are available in the National Archives are the census returns of 1901 and 1911 (and nineteenth century census returns for the decades 1821 - 1851, if extant), which list all persons living in Ireland on the nights on which the census were compiled. There are also some eighteenth century census collections.

For the nineteenth century Griffith's Primary Valuation of Ireland of 1846 - 1863 lists all immediate house and land occupiers except those living in tenements. This is a return of the head of the family only. The Tithe Applotment Books of 1823 - 1837 list all those holding over one acre of (agricultural) land who were obliged to pay a tithe for the maintenance of the local Church of Ireland clergyman. This also is a return of the head of the family only. The Tithe Applotment Books are least satisfactory for urban areas. The census returns and the records of the Primary Valuation and of the Tithe Applotment are available in microform and there are comprehensive finding aids.

Wills, grants of probate, grants of administration, and schedules of assets survive for the twentieth century and are available for consultation if older than twenty years. Many of the records also survive for the nineteenth century and earlier - either in copy or precis form. Much of the testamentary material has been abstracted by professional genealogists in the period before 1922 or by the Commissioners for Charitable Donations and Bequests and is available for research. Some Inland Revenue returns of wills, grants of probate and grants of administration survive for the first half of the nineteenth century. The testamentary collection is a particularly rich and important source for genealogists. There are comprehensive finding aids to all these testamentary collections.

Records for the Church of Ireland survive in original, copy or extract form. The records in local custody have, in many instances, been copied on microfilm and are also available for research. There is a comprehensive finding-aid to all known surviving records.

Many other collections will also be of interest to the genealogist. These include the records of the National School system up to modern times (especially regarding the employment of National School teachers), admission registers to workhouses (where they survive), estate collections (including leases and tenants' agreements), Voters' registers (where they survive) and the records of local administration in Ireland throughout the nineteenth century.

The National Archives is open to the public, Monday to Friday from 10.00 a.m. to 5.00 p.m. Documents are not produced after 4.30 p.m. However, the reading room does not close over lunchtime. The office is closed for periods at Christmas and Easter and on Public Holidays. Staff are always available in the reading room to give advice and help researchers. There are comprehensive finding aids in the Reading Room and printed leaflets, which are updated regularly, are available to assist the researcher.

Bishop Street is easily accessible on foot from both St Stephen's Green and St Patrick's Cathedral.
From O'Connell Street via Trinity College - O'Connell Street O'Connell Bridge, Westmorland Street College Green (passing the Front Gate of Trinity College on your left), Grafton Street, St Stephen's Green West, Cuffe Street Kevin Street Lower, Bride Street Bishop Street (West end).
From the Four Courts via St Patrick's Cathedral - Inns Quay, O'Donovan Rossa Bridge, Winetavern Street (passing under the arch of Christ Church),Nicholas Street, Patrick Street (passing St Patrick's Cathedral on your left) Kevin Street Upper, Bishop Street (West end).
From the National Library and Genealogical Office - Kildare Street, St Stephen's Green North, St Stephen's Green West, Cuffe Street, Kevin Street Lower, Bride Street, Bishop Street (West end).
From the General Register Office -
Either Lombard Street East, Pearse Street, College Street and get the number 83 or 155 bus. - Or, Lombard Street East, Westland Row, Lincoln Place, Leinster Street, Kildare Street and continue walking as from the National Library.

The best bus routes from the City Centre to Bishop Street are the number 83 to Kimmage and the number 155 to Greenhills Get of at the stop on Redmond's Hill cross the road at the next traffic lights, walk along Kevin Street Lower, turn right onto Bride Street and almost immediately again onto Bishop Street and cross the street . The National Archives is the building in front of you as you cross Bishop Street.

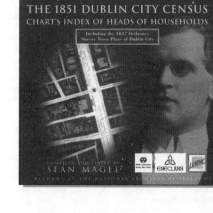

The Church Of Ireland –
Genealogy and Family History

Christ Church, Kilbrogan, Bandon, Cork, Ireland
now Bandon Heritage Centre
© Robert Blatchford 1994

The archives of the Church of Ireland, and particularly parochial registers of baptisms, marriages, and burials, are a primary source for genealogists and family historians. Although many registers were destroyed in the past, especially in the fire in the Public Record Office of Ireland in 1922, many others have survived in a number of custodies and are available to researchers.

Survival of Parish Registers
Almost half of the surviving registers were destroyed in 1922 and others have been lost at earlier periods. However, much of the lost information survives in transcripts and abstracts. The most recent published listing of parish registers is Noel Reid (ed) A table of Church of Ireland parochial records and copies (Irish Family History Society, Naas, 1994). In addition useful genealogical information may be had from other parish records especially vestry minute books, churchwardens' account books and cess applotment books.

Location of Parish Records
The Representative Church Body Library is the Church of Ireland's principal repository for its archives and manuscripts, and holds records from some 600 parishes in the Republic of Ireland. Records from a small number of parishes in the Republic are in the National Archives, and the remainder are in the custody of local clergy.

In Northern Ireland most parish registers are available in copy form in the Public Record Office of Northern Ireland (PRONI), while original parish records are either in the custody of the local clergy or in PRONI.

Names and addresses of local clergy may be had from the Church of Ireland Directory, published annually, which is available from the Religious Education Resource Centre, Holy Trinity Church, Church Avenue, Rathmines, Dublin 6 and the APCK Bookcentres at 61 Donegal Street, Belfast, BT1 2QH and St Ann's Church, Dawson Street, Dublin 2.

Access to Parish Records
Access to records in the RCB Library, National Archives and PRONI is straightforward but it is mutually beneficial if potential researchers contact the repository in advance to check on opening hours and conditions of admittance. However, repositories will not usually undertake genealogical research on behalf of enquirers.

Records in the custody of local clergy may be more difficult to see and the following procedure is recommended:
1. Write to the clergyman detailing the information which you need and ask if he will perform a search. If the clergyman agrees to perform a search there will be a fee of £5 per hour and it would be prudent to offer some payment in advance.

2. Clergy are not required to conduct searches on behalf of researchers, but they are required to make the registers available to researchers or their agents: this is a statutory requirement under the terms of the Constitution of the Church of Ireland, and relevant national archives and public records legislation in the Republic of Ireland and Northern Ireland.

If you are making the search yourself you should write to the clergyman to make an appointment and confirm that appointment by telephone before travelling. However, many clergy work alone and occasionally pastoral emergencies may cause the last minute cancellation of your appointment. The clergy are required to supervise your search and there is a fee of £5 per hour for this activity.

Reprography
Certified copies of entries in parish registers can be issued by local clergy or by the certifying officers in the repositories. Certified copies of entries of all baptisms and burials and marriages before 1845 cost £5 each. The cost of copies from civil marriage registers from 1845 is set by the respective governments and varies from time to time. Photocopying of parish records is forbidden on all occasions. Photography from parish records may only be undertaken with the written permission of the owner of the copyright. Further information on copyright matters may be had from the RCB Library.

Preparing for Searches
Most Church of Ireland parish registers do not have indexes and there is no single comprehensive index to all their contents. In general, in order to prosecute a successful search in parish registers you need a name, a date and a place name. However, there are a number of ongoing projects to index genealogical material on a county basis and some of these projects have included Church of Ireland records: details may be had from the Irish Family History Society.

The following publications and agencies can help with your preparations:
* Donal Begley (ed) Irish genealogy. A record finder (Heraldic Artists, Dublin, 1981)
* John Grenham Tracing your Irish ancestors (Gill & Macmillan, Dublin, 1992)
* Maire Mac Conghail & Paul Gorry Tracing Irish ancestors (Harper Collins, Glasgow, 1997)
* Brian Mitchell A new genealogical atlas of Ireland (Genealogical Publishing Co, Baltimore, 1988)
* Raymond Refaussé Handlist of Church of Ireland parish registers in the Representative Church Body Library (copies of this list, which is updated regularly, are available from the RCB Library at IR£2.50 including postage)
* Association of Professional Genealogists, c/o Genealogical Office, 2 Kildare Street, Dublin 2
* Irish Family History Society, PO Box 36, Naas, Co Kildare
* Irish Genealogical Research Society, The Irish Club, 82 Eaton Square, London SW1W 9AL
* National Archives, Bishop Street, Dublin 8
* Public Records Office of Northern Ireland, 66 Balmoral Avenue, Belfast, BT9 6NY
* Ulster Historical Foundation, Balmoral Buildings, 12 College Square East, Belfast, BT1 6DD

It may be helpful to visit the Directory of Irish Websites at http://doras.eircom.net/ and search for sites using the keyword "genealogy".

Other Genealogical Sources in the RCB Library
Apart from Church of Ireland archives, the RCB Library holds a number of collections with obvious attraction to genealogists. Among the more important are the biographical succession lists of Church of Ireland clergy, compiled by J B Leslie; collections of copy wills; extracts from the destroyed 1766 religious census; and collections of pedigrees.

New Book on Church of Ireland Records

One of the more remarkable of phenomena in Irish historiography in recent years has been the upsurge in interest in local history. Often this is spontaneous and arises from the curiosity of people who have moved to a new locality, but increasingly it is structured either through local historical societies or in schools, colleges and universities.

Central to most local historical endeavours in Ireland is the Church, which is the only institution to have survived from the earliest times to the present day. Its longevity combined with its sustained presence in almost every corner of the country suggests that it is, or has been, the most profound influence on the development of Irish society.

The Church of Ireland as the lineal descendant, legally at least, of the Church in Ireland following the Reformation, and, subsequently as the established Church until the late nineteenth century, has inherited responsibility for many of the sources which are fundamental to Irish local history. Records of parishes, dioceses and cathedrals, church buildings and graveyards, memorials in stone, glass and silver contain much valuable information not only about local Church of Ireland people but also the wider communities in which they lived and worked.

In order to make such resources better known a new series of guides entitled "Maynooth Research Guides for Irish Local History" is being developed under the general editorship of Dr Mary Anne Lyons from the history department of St Patrick's College, Drumcondra. The first guide in this series Church of Ireland Records, which has been written by the Librarian and Archivist of the Church of Ireland, Dr Raymond Refaussé, has just appeared.

Church of Ireland Records offers an introduction to the archives and manuscripts of the Church of Ireland and to the

administrative structures which produced these records. Access to the records, both intellectually and physically, is discussed, as are problems of interpretation. Church of Ireland Records is published by Irish Academic Press at IR£9.95 and is available through bookshops.

St Peter's Church, Ballymodan, Bandon, Cork, Ireland
©Robert Blatchford 1994

The staff of the RCB Library will be glad to offer advice on all queries concerning Church of Ireland archives and manuscripts and related printed and reference works. It should be stressed, however, that they will not undertake genealogical research on behalf of readers.

If you have any queries, please contact the RCB Library library@ireland.anglican.org - in the first instance.

National Library of Ireland
Colette O'Flaherty

The National Library of Ireland derives its origins from the Library of the Royal Dublin Society, founded in 1731. In 1877 a substantial portion of the Royal Dublin Society library was purchased by the State and the new National Library of Ireland was established.

Situated in Kildare Street, Dublin, the Library aims to collect, preserve and make accessible materials on or relating to Ireland, whether published in Ireland or abroad, together with a supporting reference collection. The Library's current collection of some six million items constitutes probably the most outstanding collection of Irish documentary material in the world, an invaluable representation of Irish history and heritage. Books, serial publications, newspapers, manuscripts, maps, photographs, official publications, prints, drawings and ephemera make up the bulk of the collections.

The National Library has long been one of the key centres for family history research in Ireland. In recognition of this the Library's Genealogy Service - an expert service staffed by a panel of professional genealogists, together with experienced Library staff - is designed with the specific needs of family history researchers in mind. The Service, which is freely available to all visitors to the Library, offers the opportunity to consult with expert researchers who will advise on specific records and research procedure. Visitors to the Genealogy Service are offered expert advice on their research together with access to reference material and finding aids. Information leaflets, including a series on family history research in the Library, are readily available.

While the Genealogy Service is of particular value to first-time researchers, the Library also encourages more experienced family history researchers to continue to use the facilities for next-step advice from the genealogists and Library staff there.

The records most used by family history researchers in the National Library fall under the following headings:

(a) Parish Records

For most family history researchers parish registers are the earliest direct source of family information, providing clear evidence of links between one generation and another (via baptismal registers) and one family and another (via marriage registers). They are particularly important for any information they provide for the period before the commencement of civil or State registration of all births, marriages and deaths in 1864.

The National Library holds microfilm copies of almost all Roman Catholic parish registers up to circa 1880. Most of the registers begin in the period 1810-1830 but some - particularly in counties along the western seaboard - begin somewhat later. In a number of counties in the province of Leinster registers begin in the 1780-1790s, while in the cities the start dates may be as early as 1760. In the case of three dioceses - Kerry, Limerick and Cashel and Emly - formal written permission to consult registers must be obtained in advance from the relevant diocese. Contact addresses and telephone numbers for these dioceses are listed in National Library Family History leaflet no. 2 (Parish registers), a copy of which may be obtained from the Library.

The Library's parish register microfilming programme is ongoing, with gaps in the collection being steadily reduced. A comprehensive listing, by diocese, of the Library's holdings may be consulted in the Genealogy Service and in the main

Reading Room.

(b) 19th Century Valuation Records
The Library holds copies of Griffith's Valuation (on microfiche) and of the Tithe Applotment Books (on microfilm). A CD-ROM index to Griffith's Valuation is also available for consultation.

The county by county Index of Surnames, a listing of the surnames recorded in Griffith's Valuation and the Tithe Books, continues to be a much-used source. The Index of Surnames acts as a valuable aid to pinpointing relevant parishes and parish records, and to understanding the distribution of particular surnames in parishes throughout the country.

(c) Trade and Social Directories
The National Library has extensive holdings of Dublin, provincial and countrywide trade and social directories. The first of the Dublin directories dates from 1751. Dublin directories, which steadily expanded in scope over the years, continue in publication up to the present time. While the earliest of the provincial directories - Ferrar's Directory of Limerick - dates from 1769, the nineteenth century saw the widespread publication of such directories. The nineteenth-century also saw the publication of countrywide directories such as Pigot's Commercial Directory of Ireland (1820 and 1824) and Slater's Directories (1846, 1856, 1870, 1881 and 1894), all of which may be consulted in the Library.

(d) Newspapers
The National Library has the largest newspaper collection in Ireland, with complete files of many local as well as national newspapers. In newspapers, the bulk of information relevant to genealogical research occurs in the form of advertisements and biographical notices (of birth, death or marriage). As there are few indexes available, relevant family information can be difficult to locate. As with the trade and social directories, newspaper information tends to be exclusive of the majority of the population: most births, marriages and deaths went unannounced and daily life continued without advertisement or report. Nonetheless, while direct family information may not be available, newspapers are rich in context and provide a sense of the community and times in which particular ancestors lived.

A comprehensive listing of Irish newspapers, including the National Library's holdings, may be found in the publication NEWSPLAN - Report of the NEWSPLAN Project in Ireland (Revised edition, 1998. Edited by Sara Smyth). The Report includes a town and county index of places of publication, subdivided chronologically. The updated NEWSPLAN database may be consulted on the National Library of Ireland website.

(e) Manuscripts Records
The main components of the Library's manuscripts collections are Gaelic manuscripts, landed estates archives, maps, political material and literary papers. Of these, it is the archives of the former landed estates that are of particular interest to family history researchers. Among the more notable of these archives held by the Library are Castletown (Co. Laois), Clements (Cos. Leitrim and Donegal), Clonbrock (Co. Galway), Coolattin (Co. Wicklow), De Vesci (Co. Laois), Doneraile (Co. Cork), Headford (Co. Meath), Inchiquin (Co. Clare), Lismore (Co. Waterford), Monteagle (Co. Limerick), O'Hara (Co. Sligo), Ormond (Cos. Tipperary and Kilkenny), Powerscourt (Co. Wicklow), Prior-Wandesforde (Co. Kilkenny), Sarsfield (Co. Cork) and Wicklow (Co. Wicklow). Estate archives contain the records of the administration of estates by landlords and their agents, and generally include leases, rentals, accounts, correspondence and maps, mostly dating from the eighteenth and nineteenth centuries.

Also of interest to family history researchers in the Department of Manuscripts are a number of collections of wills and will abstracts.

Information on Department of Manuscripts catalogues and guides is readily available from the National Library. For those intent on searching for relevant estate material, the expert advice from the Library's Genealogy Service will be of assistance in pinpointing who the relevant landowner might have been.

(f) Maps
The Library's map collections comprise some 150,000 maps and include cartographic materials ranging from a 12th century coloured sketch map of Europe to the most recent Ordnance Survey maps. Special collections include the Down Survey maps (18th century copies of 17th century originals), 18th century estate maps - including the collection of surveyors Brownrigg, Longfield and Murray, maps commissioned by the County Grand Juries (late 18th -19th century) and Ordnance Survey maps (1830s onwards).

Both printed and manuscript maps are listed in a card catalogue. Manuscripts maps are also listed in the various manuscripts catalogues.

(g) Other Sources
Other sources regularly consulted by family history researchers in the National Library include many printed family histories, often compiled and published for private circulation by individuals who have researched their own family history. It should also be noted that publications of local history societies from around the country often contain valuable transcripts of local sources, including gravestone inscriptions, freeholders lists, etc. Other relevant material in the Library's collections include the annual printed Army Lists, Navy Lists, Royal Irish Constabulary (RIC) publications including the annual RIC Directories, the 1796 Spinning Wheel Premium Entitlement List (microfiche) and various other records of trades and professions, as well as a comprehensive series of Registers of Electors. Also, as research progresses, the appendices to nineteenth-century Parliamentary reports may prove useful.

The Library's photographic collections - held at the National Photographic Archive in Meeting House Square, Dublin 2 - may also be of interest. Collections acquired from various commercial photographic studios such as Poole (Waterford and surrounding counties) and Wynne (Castlebar) include studio portraits and an unparalleled collection of topographical images of Ireland.

There are comprehensive finding aids to Library collections available in the Library Reading Rooms. Regularly updated information leaflets - with information on various Library collections and services - are readily available.

Exhibitions and publications: Exhibitions are held in both the main Library building and in the National Photographic Archive. The Library publishes a wide range of materials including books and guides, reports, booklets, document facsimile folders, CD-ROMS, calendars and postcards. These are available in the Library shop.

Admission to the National Library of Ireland: For Genealogy (microfilms) and Newspaper research, passes - which may be obtained in the main Library building - are required. Other readers must apply for a Readers Ticket (for which proof of identity and two passport photos are necessary). To view manuscripts, a supplementary Manuscripts Readers Ticket, issued by the Duty Librarian, is required.

The Readers Ticket Office is open during the following hours: Mon-Wed 1000-1230, 1400-1700; Thu-Fri 1000-1230, 1400-1630; Sat 1000-1230.
Library Opening Hours:
Main Reading Room/ Microform Reading Room Mon-Wed 1000-2100 Thu-Fri 1000-1700 Sat 1000-1300
Manuscripts Reading Room
Mon-Wed 1000-2030 Thu-Fri 1000-1630 Sat 1000-1230
National Photographic Archive Reading Room
Mon-Fri 1000-1700
Contact details:
National Library of Ireland, Kildare Street, Dublin 2
Tel: +353-1-6030 200 Fax: +353-1-6766 690
Email: info@nli.ie Internet: http://www.nli.ie/

Dublin Archives

Dublin City Archives comprise the historic records of the municipal government of Dublin from the twelfth century to the present. The City Archives contain a significant number of medieval documents, including two important bound manuscripts written on vellum: the White Book of Dublin (also known as the 'Liber Albus' and the Chain Book of Dublin. The City Archives also include a series of Assembly Rolls, written on parchment, which record the minutes of the Dublin City Assembly (a forerunner of today's City Council) from 1447 to 1841. The Assembly Rolls, together with the White Book and Chain Book, were transcribed and translated by Sir John T. and Lady Gilbert and published as Calendar of Ancient Records of Dublin (19 vols, Dublin, 1889-1944).

In addition to these published materials, the Dublin City Archives contain a wealth of records which have not been published and are available for research. These records include City Council and committee minutes, account books, correspondence, reports, court records, charity petitions, title deeds, maps and plans, photographs and drawings, all of which document the development of Dublin over eight centuries. The Archives hold the magnificent series of 102 charters granted to the city by successive English monarchs. The earliest was issued by King Henry II in 1171/2, giving the men of Bristol the right to live in the city of Dublin. Later charters contain grants to Dublin of rights, privileges and property, and taken together they form the basis of municipal law in Ireland.

The Ancient Freedom of the City of Dublin
The Dublin City Archives holds lists of citizens who received the Freedom of Dublin between 1468 and 1918. It is possible to trace several generations of old Dublin families through these lists, which are a useful source for genealogical research. The ancient Freedom of Dublin was instituted at the time of the Norman Invasion in the late 12th century, Holders of the Freedom were known as "Free Citizens" and were entitled to significant trading privileges and the right to vote in municipal and parliamentary elections . Admission to the Freedom of Dublin was granted by the Dublin City Assembly at the great feasts of Christmas, Easter, Midsummer and Michaelmas. In order to qualify for the Freedom, it was usually necessary to have been born within the city boundaries, or "franchises", and to be a member of one of the Trade Guilds of Dublin. Members of "the Irish Nation" were excluded, but in practice many people with Irish surnames succeeded in obtaining the Freedom. Under the Penal Laws, Roman Catholics were excluded from the Freedom of Dublin from 1691 until 1793.
There were six main categories of admission:
1.Admission by Service was granted to those who completed an apprenticeship in one of the Trade Guilds of Dublin.
2. Admission by Birth was granted to sons, and sometimes daughters, of Free Citizens. Several generations of one family could hold the Freedom of Dublin.
3. Admission by Marriage was granted to sons-in-law of Free Citizens.
4. Admission by Fine was confined to prosperous professional men who were required to pay a substantial sum of money into the city treasury. Sometimes the Fine consisted of the presentation of a pair of gloves to the Lady Mayoress.
5. Admission by Grace Especial also known as Special Grace was the equivalent of the modern Honorary Freedom, and was reserved for dignitaries and for craftsmen who were not in a trade guild.
6. Admission by an Act of Parliament to "Encourage Protestant Strangers to Settle in Ireland" was granted to French Huguenots and Quakers from England.

Lists of those admitted to the ancient Freedom of Dublin survive for the period 1225-1250, 1468-1512 and 1575-1918. These lists may be consulted at Dublin Corporation Archives, City Hall, Dublin 2. A computerised index to the lists is being prepared by the Dublin Heritage Group. The lists are of interest to students of social and economic history and are also important for genealogical research.

Honorary Freedom of the City of Dublin
The Honorary Freedom of Dublin was instituted under the Municipal Privileges Act, 1876 and is presently conferred under the provisions of the Local Government Act 1991. The founder of the Home Rule Party, Isaac Butt, was the first person to receive the Honorary Freedom of Dublin. Other illustrious recipients include Charles Stewart Parnell, George Bernard Shaw, John Count McCormack and John Fitzgerald Kennedy, President of the United States of America. In recent years, it has been conferred on Pope John Paul II;Mother Teresa of Calcutta; the world champion cyclist Stephen Roche; and the former President of Ireland, Dr. Patrick Hillery. Nelson Mandela received the Freedom in 1988, whilst still a political prisoner. It has also been conferred on Jack Charlton, manager of the Republic of Ireland football team; & Bill Clinton, President U.S.A.

Wide Streets Commission
The Wide Streets Commission was established in 1757 to develop wide and convenient streets through the city of Dublin. Among its other achievements, the Commission built Parliament St., Westmoreland St. and D'Olier St. as well as Carlisle Bridge (now O'Connell Bridge). The minute books, maps, title deeds and architecttral drawings produced for the Commission before it was abolished in 1849 are all held in the Dublin City Archives. These important records tell the story of the lay-out and development of much of Georgian Dublin.

Mansion House Fund for Relief of Distress
Ireland was beset by harvest failure during the 1870's and in 1880 famine threatened the country. To prevent this, the Mansion House Fund was set up to collect money from Irish emigrants all over the world. The records of the Fund are held in the Dublin City Archives and are important for local history because they contain reports from 800 local committees which distributed relief in every county in Ireland. Records of other relief committees are also available for inspection.

Records of Urban District Councils
The areas of Rathmines and Rathgar and of Pembroke each had their own local government until 1930, and their records are preserved in the Dublin City Archives, describing the development of these suburbs from the mid 19th century. The records of the Howth Urban District Council are also available, from 1318 to 1940.

Dublin City Archives are housed in the City Assembly House (beside the Powerscourt Town House Centre) where a Reading Room is provided for members of the public who wish to consult the Archives. An advance appointment is essential. Some records, because of their antiquity or fragile condition, may be withdrawn for conservation treatment and may not always be available for research.The City Archives are for reference and research and may not be borrowed; access to the storage area is not permitted. The Archivist will be pleased to answer any queries relating to the records. Photocopying, photography and microfilm services are provided as appropriate. The Archivist can advise on costs and conditions of copyright.
Dublin City Archives, City Assembly House,
58 South William Street, Dublin 2.
Tel: (01) 677 5877 Fax: (01) 677 954 Opening Hours: Monday-Friday, 10.00- 13.00; 14.15- 17.00

Banbridge Genealogy Services
Jason Diamond

Banbridge Genealogy Services came about thanks to a circular received in 1987 by the local historical society from the North West Centre for Learning and Development, explaining how The Derry Journal was being indexed. The committee of Banbridge & District Historical Society decided a similar project would be suitable for Banbridge and in respect of this an approach was made to Banbridge Combined Community Services to see if it would be possible to get help with such a project. This resulted in two people being employed for a year under the Action for Community Employment (ACE) scheme and they began indexing old Banbridge Chronicles in August.

Working with one hundred year old newspapers proved to be rather tricky as the pages were brittle and tore easily. As well as this, many had faded considerably due to the passage of time, which made reading them a somewhat tedious task. For these reasons the indexing was very slow and laborious. After the year was up, the historical society approached the Department of Economic Development with the view of funding a larger project. The application was successful and the project commenced in August 1988. Due to legal complications the indexing scheme had to be formed into a limited company under the name Banbridge Heritage Development Ltd. Eleven local people were employed and housed in the Old Technical Building (which had originally started life as a Carnegie Free Library), Downshire Road, Banbridge.

At the beginning of the project everything was done by hand ie everything was filed alphabetically with approximately seven hundred headings to identify the material, which was copied onto slips of paper and given a reference, pinpointing its exact location in the old newspaper. However, in 1991 grant aid of some £30 000 was awarded from the Department of Finance based at Stormont. This grant was awarded under the European Regional Development Fund (ERDF).

As well as indexing newspapers, it was decided to undertake a programme of computerisation of Marriage, Baptismal and Death records for the South Down Area prior to 1900. As time went on, it was noticed that there were more people interested in these records rather than the old newspapers and so the emphasis was shifted from the indexing of newspapers to the computerisation of marriage, baptismal and death records. The database software package for this was developed in the Republic of Ireland.

Unfortunately, a few years ago the premises from which Banbridge Heritage Services Ltd operated were badly damaged in a flood. The database was not damaged, but it meant that the whole operation had to move from the Old Technical College to The Bleachgreen Centre. This had been an old mill where linen was bleached and dyed for the once extensive linen industry that was concentrated around the Bann Valley area.

Due to Government cutbacks, funding was gradually withdrawn and hence the number of staff was reduced until only two full time and two part-time people were employed. Eventually, the ACE scheme ceased altogether and as Banbridge Heritage Development Ltd had been set up more as a service to the general public (there was a nominal charge of £5 for the initial search plus £1 per record printed out), it could not sustain itself.

The BHD Ltd committee then decided that an approach should be made to Banbridge District Council offering them the database and any other relevant documents and equipment on the proviso that they kept one employee. This went before Council who decided that, going from the number of enquiries and visitors from afar afield as America, Canada, Australia etc, it would be a useful addition to their Tourist Information Centre, providing an extra incentive for tourists with ancestors from South Down to visit the area. However, this would be on a year's trial basis to see just how much of a need there was for such a service.

Once again Banbridge Heritage Services Ltd found itself on the move, only this time with a name change to Banbridge Genealogy Services. It returned to its original home, the Old Technical College. After the year's trial period, it was decided to move the whole operation to the council's purpose built Tourist Information Centre situated on the Newry Road, Banbridge, where it has now been for this last year and a half.

Over the years Banbridge Genealogy Services have helped hundreds of people in tracing their ancestors. Recently, they were involved in helping an American by the name of Dave Appleby trace a connection to Banbridge's most famous son, Captain Francis Rawdon Moira Crozier, an explorer who set out to discover the Northwest Passage. Dave's time in Banbridge was filmed for a local television programme, which will go out sometime next year under the title Blood Ties.

The whole thing came about a year ago when an e-mail arrived at the Tourist Information Centre. Dave's grandmother and grandfather were born in Banbridge and after a visit in 1999 he gave a copy of a family tree he had drawn up to his cousin Cathy Dumont who put it on various genealogy websites. This was picked up by Alex Noddings from Glasgow who also had a family tree, but up until that point had no idea what had happened to the branch of the family that had gone to America. He then e-mailed Cathy and they discovered that they were cousins. Alex explained to Cathy that he had found the Noddings connection and the Savage connection in Northern Ireland. Later, he and Dave met up in Glasgow.

Dave, his cousin Cathy and Alex, along with their respective spouses, arrived in Northern Ireland on the 28th September, holding a family reunion in The Downshire Hotel on the Saturday night. During their time here they were shadowed by the film crew, the pivotal moment in the whole experience being when the connection to the Crozier family was established.

At the minute Banbridge Genealogy Services have just launched a new website at HYPERLINK "http://www.banbridgegenealogy.com" www.banbridgegenealogy.com and are developing new software to make searching the database more efficient and user friendly. All being well, Banbridge Genealogy Services, which also hold copies of Griffith's valuation for the Banbridge and Newry areas, will continue to help people find their roots in South Down for many years to come.

County & Country Codes
(Pre 1974 counties)

England	ENG	Wales	WLS	Ireland (Eire)	IRL	Canada	CAN
All Counties	ALL	Anglesey	AGY	Antrim	ANT	Alberta	ALB
Bedfordshire	BDF	Brecknockshire	BRE	Armagh	ARM	British Columbia	BC
Berkshire	BRK	Caernarvonshire	CAE	Carlow	CAR	Manitoba	MAN
Buckinghamshire	BKM	Cardiganshire	CGN	Cavan	CAV	New Brunswick	NB
Cambridgeshire	CAM	Carmarthenshire	CMN	Clare	CLA	Newfoundland	NFD
Cheshire	CHS	Denbighshire	DEN	Cork	COR	North West Terr	NWT
Cornwall	CON	Flintshire	FLN	Donegal	DON	Nova Scotia	NS
Cumberland	CUL	Glamorgan	GLA	Down	DOW	Ontario	ONT
Derbyshire	DBY	Merionethshire	MER	Dublin	DUB	Prince Edward Is	PEI
Devonshire	DEV	Monmouthshire	MON	Fermanagh	FER	Quebec	QUE
Dorsetshire	DOR	Montgomershire	MGY	Galway	GAL	Saskatchewan	SAS
Durham	DUR	Pembrokeshire	PEM	Kerry	KER	Yukon Territory	YUK
Essex	ESS	Radnorshire	RAD	Kildare	KID		
Gloucestershire	GLS			Kilkenny	KIK	Austria	OES
Hampshire	HAM	**Scotland**	**SCT**	Leitrim	LEI	Belarus	BRS
Herefordshire	HEF	Aberdeenshire	ABD	Leix(Queens)	LEX	Belgium	BEL
Hertfordshire	HRT	Angus	ANS	Limerick	LIM	Croatia	CRO
Huntingdonshire	HUN	Argyllshire	ARL	Londonderry	LDY	Czechoslovakia	CS
Isle of Wight	IOW	Ayrshire	AYR	Longford	LOG	Czech Republic	CZR
Kent	KEN	Banffshire	BAN	Louth	LOU	Denmark	DEN
Lancashire	LAN	Berwickshire	BEW	Mayo	MAY	Estonia	EST
Leicestershire	LEI	Bute	BUT	Meath	MEA	Finland	FIN
Lincolnshire	LIN	Caithness-shire	CAI	Monaghan	MOG	France	FRA
London (city)	LND	Clackmannanshire	CLK	Offaly(Kings)	OFF	Germany (1991)	BRD
Middlesex	MDX	Dumfriesshire	DFS	Roscommon	ROS	German Old Emp	GER
Norfolk	NFK	Dunbartonshire	DNB	Sligo	SLI	Greece	GR
Northamptonshire	NTH	East Lothian	ELN	Tipperary	TIP	Hungary	HU
Northumberland	NBL	Fifeshire	FIF	Tyrone	TYR	Italy	ITL
Nottinghamshire	NTT	Forfarshire	ANS	Waterford	WAT	Latvia	LAT
Oxfordshire	OXF	Invernessshire	INV	Westmeath	WES	Liechtenstein	LIE
Rutland	RUT	Kincardineshire	KCD	Wexford	WEX	Lithguania	LIT
Shropshire	SAL	Kinrossshire	KRS	Wicklow	WIC	Luxembourg	LUX
Somerset	SOM	Kirkcudbrightshire	KKD			Netherlands	NL
Staffordshire	STS	Lanarkshire	LKS	**Channel Islands**	**CHI**	New Zealand	NZ
Suffolk	SFK	Midlothian	MLN	Alderney	ALD	Norway	NOR
Surrey	SRY	Moray	MOR	Guernsey	GSY	Poland	POL
Sussex	SSX	Nairnshire	NAI	Jersey	JSY	Romania	RO
Warwickshire	WAR	Orkney Isles	OKI	Sark	SRK	Russia	RUS
Westmorland	WES	Peebleshire	PEE	**Isle of Man**	**IOM**	Slovakia	SLK
Wiltshire	WIL	Perthshire	PER			Slovinia	SLO
Worcestershire	WOR	Reffrewshire	RFW	**Australia**	**AUS**	Spain (Espagne)	ESP
Yorkshire	YKS	Ross & cromarty	ROC	Capital Territory	ACT	Sweden	SWE
YKS E Riding	ERY	Roxburghshire	ROX	New South Wales	NSW	Switzerland	CH
YKS N Riding	NRY	Selkirkshire	SEL	Northern Territory	NT	Ukraine	UKR
YKS W Riding	WRY	Shetland Isles	SHI	Queensland	QLD	United Kingdom	UK
		Stirlingshire	STI	South Australia	SA	United States	USA
		Sutherland	SUT	Tasmania	TAS	USSR	SU
		West Lothian	WLN	Victoria	VIC	Yugoslavia	YU
		Wigtownshire	WIG	Western Australia	WA		
						Papua New Guinea	PNG
						Rep South Africa	RSA

These codes are used to avoid confusion in the use of abbreviations for countries and counties.
Created by Dr Colin Chapman they are universally recognised and should always be used.

Lochin Publishing
6 Holywell Road, Dursley GL11 5RS England

FEDERATION OF FAMILY HISTORY SOCIETIES (PUBLICATIONS) LIMITED

Publishers and Suppliers of a wide range of books on Family History (and related subjects) to Family History Societies, individual Family Historians, Libraries, Record Offices and Booksellers, etc.

- *Well over 100 titles commissioned by the Federation of Family Historians and produced at attractive prices, plus a fine selection of titles from other publishers.*

- *A wide range of **'Basic Series'** and **'Introduction to'** books with detailed guidance on most aspects of family history research.*

- ***Gibson Guides** giving explicit advice on the precise extent and whereabouts of major record sources*

- ***Stuart Raymond's** extensive listings of published family history reference material at national and local level*

Titles available from your local Family History Society and by post from:-

**FFHS (Publications) Limited,
Units 15 and 16 Chesham Industrial Centre,
Oram Street, Bury, Lancashire, BL9 6EN**

Visit our 'On-line bookshop' and Catalogue at

www.familyhistorybooks.co.uk

Tel: 0161 797 3843 Fax: 0161 797 3846

Email enquiries to: sales@ffhs.org.uk

INDISPENSABLE BOOKS ON GENEALOGY

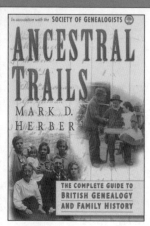

Ancestral Trails

The Complete Guide to British Genealogy and Family History

Mark D. Herber

Forward by John Titford, Institute of Heraldic and Genealogical studies

• The Most comprehensive and up to date reference work available
• Winner of the Library Association's McColvin Medal for outstanding work of reference.

' a defining work...I confidently predict that in future years, the phrase "according to Herber" will be used to confer authority on deliberations about family history research' Family Tree Magazine

"enormously impressed by the breadth and depth of coverage"
Anthony Camp, Director, society of Genealogists

£19.99
paperback 720pp
ISBN 07509 2484 5

The Complete Peerage

Of England Scotland Ireland Great Britain and the United Kingdom Extant Extinct or Dormant

G.E. Cockayne

'This classic work is essential to every historical library'
Hugh Trevor-Roper, The Sunday Times

'Debrett's and Burke's are mere almanacs of snobbery; G.E.C is the anatomy of a class: its politics, its wealth, its achievements, its peculiarities, its openness, its variety - all are there.'
David Starkey, History Today

Comprising a full and genealogical account of all peerages created in England, Scotland and Ireland between the Conquest and the early twentieth century, the main text includes details of every peer's birth, parents, honours, offices, marriage, death and burial while the footnotes deal with wills, incomes, royal charters, rent rolls, illegitimate children, romances, treasons, public achievements, works of art and works of literature.

£280.00
6 vols (472pp, 584pp, 408pp, 496pp, 448pp, 416pp) cased in a slip case, 244 x 172mm
ISBN 0904387828

ORDERS TO: HAYNES PUBLISHING, SPARKFORD, NR YEOVIL, SOMERSET,BA22 7JJ
TELEPHONE: 01963 440635 FAX: 01963 440001

SUTTON PUBLISHING
w w w . s u t t o n p u b l i s h i n g . c o . u k

The Family and Local History Handbook
Local History Section
produced in collaboration with the

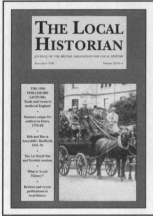

Another Comedy of Errors

Alan Crosby

Act 1 Scene 1:
An ancient house on the edge of Stratford-upon-Avon

Touristus And so they say, who know these things, that this ancient house, this venerable pile of timbers roughly hewn and plaster white, this place wherein for many a year 'twas said the mother of our famous bard did dwell, that this fair house is not all it's said to be. Can this be so? Can our journey here, from't shore of far Illyria, be in vain?

Tourista 'Tis true, husband, 'tis true, and crossing those perilous seas was all for naught. For in yon ivory-toweréd pile of ancient learning and wisdom most arcane, that place which near forty summers hath been called (it lacks poetic song) the University of Warwick, there labours as a chemist (not 'pothecary's sort, more boffin-like by far) Nat Alcock and he, with infinite guile and detection most subtle, hath revealed unto a world which spinneth now dismayed, but with some wry amusement, that Mary Arden's house was not hers, that we and all the world have been misled, and all who came from Worlds both Old and New to offer their respects in ground thus hallowed, have been fooléd most piteously.

Touristus Yet since the distant mists of time did swirl, since guides first brought encamera'd persons here, since those years long gone when that name of great Shakespeare first was famed, this house, this place, this spot hath been a shrine, for 'twas home before the marriage bed to she who—it seems like unto divinity—bore the immortal bard. So how hath Nat now laid flat those tales, those legends, that place of such repute?

Tourista Did I not say with guile and subtlety? Forsooth it was, for he did use the very rings of which those mighty timbers are composed, and with his glass which maketh all to magnify did count them, one by one, employing to himself that mystery known to some (but not to humble souls who pass their lives in unsuspecting ignorance) as

dendrochronology ('tis hard indeed to rhyme or scan that word, my lord) until patient calculation led him to bold conclusion—that house was built, by sweat of man and toil and tears, not while the grandsire of our bard was young, as had been thought, but later far than that—verily, husband, that house was built while that same bard himself was young and mewled and puked on Mary's knee. And thus it is, the books, the cards, the tales, the trinkets and the toys, the chocolate boxes and calendars of time, are all in vain and do now seem so shallow and so false. For Arden's house is Arden's house no more, and we must fast regain Illyria's shore.

Touristus But wife, stay thou thy haste! If she was not born there, where was her natal place? Which other happy spot can now lay claim to hold the shades of Ardens, progenitors of Shakespeare's fame? For if this house must now lose such great honour, can another, endowed as though by miraculous fate, now gain yet greater glory?

Tourista Husband! Hear this! All's well that endeth well! Our labour is not lost. For this paper doth report that ... quick, pick up thy lens and grab thy film, cancel the passage to Illyria's shore, for Mary Arden, strange though it might seem, was most conveniently born in't house next door!

Local History News May 2001

TECHNICALLY, YOU'RE CONTRAVENING THE TRADES DESCRIPTION ACT...

MARY ARDEN'S HOUSE

Dedication and Inspiration
Alan Crosby

This year (2001) B.A.L.H. is presenting its first Local History Awards to recognise personal achievement. These are in addition to those encouraging research and publication that have been awarded for some years. The scheme honours individuals and, in a more general sense, recognises the dedication of people who over the years have made local history what it is and have helped to extend, by their often unsung efforts, its scope, its depth and its interest. Many people have given outstanding service and have assisted and inspired others who work in the same field, but until now there has been little opportunity to make proper acknowledgment of their contribution.

I think we all know the heroines and heroes who keep local history going. Consider for a moment the tireless work of all those who compile newsletters, book speakers, man bookstalls, organise visits and outings, juggle with finances, negotiate with the council for grants, send out notices of the AGM, keep minutes and make sure the meeting room is locked up at the end of each session. Think about the dedicated teachers who inspire audiences with lectures and talks, or patiently guide students through the minefields of palaeography or census analysis or medieval Latin or the laws of settlement. And then there are the professionals in universities and colleges who, despite pressures of work and wearisome academic bureaucracy, are courageous enough to give talks in village halls, carrying the message of local history and its endless fascination to groups and demonstrating that elitism is wrong. These people perhaps embody the spirit of those extension studies teachers who, a century and more ago, sought to make the infinite wonders of knowledge available to everybody.

When today the class meets or the talk is given, how many of us remember the valiant efforts of those pioneers and give thanks not only for what they did, but also for the example they set? We should do so and we should also strive to keep alive the flame of their simple philosophy: that learning, education and expanding one's knowledge are worthy objectives for their own sake. In this age of proliferating qualifications, financial assessments and best value audits there should still be a large place for the sheer joy and enriching experience of finding out about something, understanding a process or a phenomenon not previously clear or comprehensible, or achieving an intellectual goal (whether solving the meaning of life or interpreting an obscure word in a 17th century probate inventory).

And so it is entirely right that the people who make these things possible should have the acknowledgement which is their due. We cannot give an award to everybody, though we would like to do so, but we would ask you to consider putting names forward for next year's shortlist. It doesn't have to be somebody famous, with letters after his or her name or a long list of publications. It could be an individual who has run a local history society, or organised a local research or recording project, or given inspirational talks, or produced an outstanding piece of written work for the newsletter, or ... well, think about the people you know and ask whether they deserve some recognition for their dedication and devotion, hard slog, inspirational teaching, or long years of modest service. We would love to hear from you.

Local History News May 2001

BRITISH ASSOCIATION FOR LOCAL HISTORY
AWARDS FOR LOCAL HISTORIANS

- *To encourage research and publication*
  One or more awards may be made each year for published work presenting sound original research in well-written form. To be eligible a piece of work, of any length, must appear in a journal, newsletter or similar publication produced by a local voluntary body, which is sent to the Reviews Editor of *The Local Historian* for review or listing. All relevant material sent to the Reviews Editor is automatically considered, and a short-list prepared for the Awards Panel

- *To recognise other kinds of personal achievement*
  One or more awards may be made each year as a means of publicly honouring local historians who have made outstanding and significant contributions to the subject in their own areas. No specific guidelines are laid down: the purpose of this award is to identify and publicise good practice in whatever form it appears. Nominations must be made on the form available from the Awards Secretary.

Awards are made at the Phillimore Lecture each June in London

Reviews Editor	BALH Awards Secretary
The Local Historian	59 High Street Ashwell
30 Lime Grove BIDEFORD EX39 3JL	BALDOCK SG7 5NP

THE LOCAL HISTORIAN
Journal of the British Association for Local History

Volume 29, appeared in February, May, August and December 1999, containing some 16 articles. Once again, there was a considerable range in period, from the Anglo-Saxon (a study of sources for English beekeeping) to the almost contemporary (open-air schools in Birmingham, 1911-1970). Our contributors were representative of the wide variety of people who have an interest in local history, from the full-time teachers of the subject in further and higher education, to those who work as freelance researchers and writers; from retired professionals who have developed an interest in local history, to people who work in related fields, such as archivists and librarians. The geographical spread of contributions was restricted to the British Isles this year, although an article on the effects of the First World War on Scottish tourism did allow the author to mention the overseas destinations of Scottish travellers, and there was an Irish dimension in the discussion of the Irish in two London boroughs in 1851.

The nineteenth century still exercises a strong influence over the choice of research topics for local history, and this is reflected in two articles discussing aspects of enclosure (in Yorkshire and in Buckinghamshire), two making use of census material (the Irish in Hammersmith and Fulham, 1851; kinship ties in Sheffield, 1841–91), and another analysing retailing patterns (using Wolverhampton as a case study, and ranging in period from 1800 to 1950).

One very pleasing feature of the year was the use made of hitherto unrecognised forms of 'documentary' evidence. Scraps of clothing accompanying registration papers for foundlings led to a breakthrough in costume and textile history (infant fashion in the eighteenth century). An exploration and recording of those mysterious marks on the outside of letters, rather than the content of the letters themselves, gave an insight into postal routes and postal practice in Berkshire in the eighteenth century.

On a more traditional note, the potential of friendly society records for research was fully revealed, and we were challenged to think about the very nature and methodology of local history in an article which will probably continue to stir up debate well into the next year. The third Phillimore Lecture, published in November's issue, gave a masterly exposition of the current state of research and thinking into the patterns of trade and the role of towns in medieval England. We reviewed 27 books in some depth, and in his annual Round-up, the Reviews Editor surveyed some of the many publications issued to commemorate the 80th anniversary of the First World War.

www.thelocalhistorian.org
or details from BALH PO BOX 1576 SALISBURY SP2 8SY

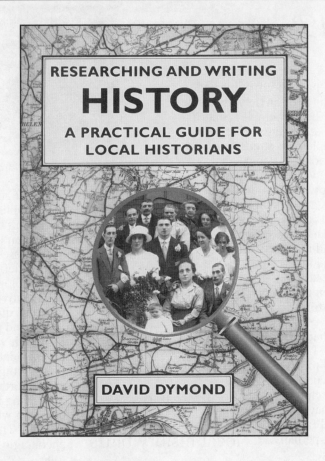

This book is essential reading for anybody who has written, is writing or might one day write local history. The earlier version of the book, Writing Local History, was first published in 1981 and became an instant classic. Now it has been totally rewritten, extended and updated so that local historians in the early 21st century, will have an even better reference book to help them produce work of the highest quality. David Dymond has spent most of a lifetime as a professional local historian, and he writes from that personal knowledge and experience. The contents of the book include an assessment of the present state of local history; the challenge of writing; choosing a subject; the search for sources; transcribing; analysing and assembling evidence; interpreting the evidence; writing techniques; the final draft; and numerous appendices which illustrate sample styles of local historians, show how to present information, and demonstrate good and bad practice in writing. It is, in short, an invaluable, stimulating and often entertaining exposition of how we should approach our subject.

180 pages   £12.00 (£10.00 for members)
from BALH (P) PO BOX 1576 SALISBURY SP2 8SY

Reviews and Reviewers
Alan Crosby

Anybody who has had a book published will know the feelings of anxiety about the reviews. Will they be favourable? Snide? Flattering? Go off at tangents? Expose weaknesses? Complement strengths? In 1999 one of my books was somewhat unfavourably reviewed by an internationally-known historian who thought that it was a 'wasted opportunity', and that I failed to address various complex issues, had made absurdly subjective judgments, and had reached some very superficial conclusions. Seemingly my greatest sin was to have written the book for 'local history buffs', an offence presumably punishable by eternal damnation. I was, of course, devastated to have my scholarship so publicly condemned. The main consolation was that the same reviewer had fairly recently shredded, perhaps literally as well as metaphorically, a widely used book written by two well-respected regional historians—at least they suffered more than I did. But I wonder, should I have accepted the condemnation with humility and due academic modesty, or issued a furious riposte, or tried to find one of the reviewer's own books to review with equal savagery and thus started a vendetta? I recently read the book reviews in a certain county history newsletter. There was a particularly glowing account of a new village history, lauding the approach, content, fascinating detail and splendid illustrations, and urging that all those interested in local history should buy the book. Heavens, I thought, who has published this prodigy? It turned out to be the author. All well and good (pace my review in the November 2000 issue of The Local Historian) but where could I obtain a copy? By contacting an individual who ... oh dear, there's the rub ... an individual who probably not by coincidence was also the writer of the fulsomely glowing review.

> **Seemingly my greatest sin was to have written the book for 'local history buffs'**

What price objectivity there? In contrast, another review in the same newsletter gave a careful and measured assessment of a work published by a local history society, discussing the content and main themes and then gently but firmly pointing out the weaknesses of the work—deficiencies in its methodology, a lack of comparative analysis, practical questions of layout and production quality. It was a commendable attempt to be fair, highlighting praiseworthy features while not shying away from criticism where it was merited. The review was encouraging and positive in tone.

Let us review the reviewers, then. Condemn those who simply summarise the content of the book and make no effort to judge its merit—we might as well read the publisher's blurb. Give no credence to those who, with axes of their own to grind, make little attempt to conceal their prejudice. Be not one of those who feel that to praise is to display softness or weakness. Reject those who seek to blind the reader with their own esoteric learning, by demonstrating that the writer of the book manifestly lacks such erudition. Have no truck with those who gloat over minor errors and sneer in the 'didn't he know that ...' fashion. Instead, may we have reviewers who are thoughtful, generous in their praise and judicious in their criticism, informative, and understanding of the needs of those who read the review. All reviewers in The Local Historian naturally fall into this latter category!

Local History News February 2001

It's good to talk
Alan Crosby

When giving talks to local societies, which I do regularly and enjoy very much, I am always intrigued by their different ways of Coping with The Speaker. Most organisations are highly competent, with an efficient and friendly 'welcoming service' and effective administrative arrangements. Very occasionally, though, things are not quite as they should be. Such times are very rare indeed but, dear reader, picture the following. You drive, tired after a day's work, 35 miles along country roads on a wet late autumn night, having crammed down a quick meal. Arriving in the village, you find the meeting hall in darkness even though it is 7.20 and the meeting starts at 7.30. It transpires that you aren't actually wanted until 8.00 but you weren't told that—you need not have gobbled down the beans on toast. People drift in, eye you suspiciously, and then ignore you completely. Eventually somebody detaches himself from a lively conversation, says, 'Oh, are you the speaker? I'll be with you in a minute', then goes back to the important chat with committee members. When he returns he asks 'How long do you talk for? An hour? I'm not sure if our members will like that, it's a bit long for the older ones. Do you have slides?' 'What, you mean you just talk, no pictures? I hope they stay awake for you'.

The dingy hall has no heating, appalling acoustics, and rows of chairs have to be set out. You are shown to the front of a decaying and very draughty stage on which are piled mountains of jumble ready for next week's sale. You are given an insubstantial folding table, apparently about to collapse. You shuffle your papers, gaze at the regrettable pictures of poodles and lopsided vases of flowers which are hung on the walls,

> People drift in, eye you suspiciously, and then ignore you completely.

products of the Tuesday morning art class (beginners' section) and then stare at the audience—who are not in the slightest bit agog to hear what you are going to say. You overhear a couple of them ask 'Who is this Dr Crosby, have we had him before' and 'I really liked that talk by that lady who'd been on the Rhine Cruise that we had last month, didn't you' and 'What a funny subject he's going to talk about—how can anyone keep on for an hour about that I wonder'.

Requests for a glass of water are met with bemusement, followed by protracted delvings in the unsavoury recesses of a dusty cupboard. You wipe the rim of the glass surreptitiously on your hankie. The chairman, after announcing the Christmas dinner, arrangements for the coach trip, and the latest circular leaflets from B.A.L.H., and begging for somebody please to be chairman next year, says, 'And now here's our speaker, Mr. er ... [looks hastily at scrap of paper] Crosby [or some approximation to my name] who's going to talk to us on ... [looks again at tattered scrap and utters something like title of lecture] ... and I expect it'll be quite interesting'.

The talk over, the chairman asks if anyone has questions and immediately launches into irrelevant and rambling anecdote of his own. Afterwards, having stood around for a few minutes waiting for the cheque or used fivers, you are told that the treasurer is unfortunately on holiday and you can't be paid for another three weeks. You are expected to consider this a sensible and civilised arrangement. And, inevitably, it is then suggested that 'We're sure you'd like to come to talk to us again next year'. Fortunately, of course, the Hell & District Local History Society does not really exist. Does it?

Local History News February 2001

By his postcode ye shall know him

Alan Crosby

Woodbridge Post Office & Staff c1912 ©Crown Copyright

My local paper recently carried a series of articles highlighting the Great Preston Postcode Debate. The PR area has too many addresses and too few postcode divisions, so the Post Office wants to subdivide some of these. This has provoked an outburst from those who live over the river, in the Borough of South Ribble (which you will know from its title, is a spurious administrative area created by the 1974 local government reforms). South Ribble Council, ever anxious to deny that its area is merely suburban Preston under a different name, began a campaign to have a new SR postcode of its own. The Council had not done its homework. Sunderland already has an SR postcode, and postcodes have nothing at all to do with administrative areas anyway, but the issue emphasised the way in which postcodes have worked their way into public consciousness in many different ways.

'Are you PR1 or PR2?' is a question, loaded with all sorts of social, economic and political weight, which could be repeated with letters suitably altered almost anywhere.

This subject came to mind after reading about a new local history society which, very innovatively I felt, chose not a conventional name, defined by parish, town, or county, but has called itself The RH7 History Group. To those of you, surely few in number, who don't know it, RH is Redhill, Surrey, which in the late 20th century became a postcode area largely because, 150 years before, the London and Brighton railway was built through that place rather than through nearby Reigate. RH7 covers that attractive, prosperous area of green fields, woodland, large Wealden houses and giant overflow car parks for Gatwick airport which extends around Lingfield, in south-east Surrey (whenever I fly into Gatwick, I notice one of the most distinctive features of the south-east English landscape—the jewel-like turquoise squares and rectangles of countless swimming pools). The RH7 Group was set up as a support organisation for the New Lingfield Guest House Local History Centre—the 'guest house' is a medieval hall house which houses the county library and local history centre. The Group intends to man the centre, raise funds to augment its collections, and develop interest and activity in the local history of this corner of Surrey.

The RH7 group set me thinking, further, about the perpetual debate in local history about where to draw the boundaries. Should our area of research be an administrative unit—a history of my parish, town, or county—or should it be a region, or a group of parishes, or several towns, or an indefinable and ill-defined unit which simply fades away at the edges or ... well, why not a postcode area. Those who argue that parishes have never meant much in reality, that administrative boundaries are quite artificial, and that we should look instead at regions or units with which people identify, might like to ponder the place of postcode areas in their scheme of things. Do we identify with a postcode area, I wonder? Do we feel loyalties to or loathing of PR1 or GU22 or NR2? Do we see in our minds a pattern of postcode boundaries which falls like a net over another mental landscape of streets, buildings and open countryside. For many years the old London postal subdivisions (NW1 and its like) have had just such an identity, setting apart those who have arrived from those who aspire to do so and those who never stood a chance. Postcodes have become a basic identification code in most modern business and commercial activity, in social attitudes, in prejudices and in pressure group campaigning—perhaps history defined by postcodes is a logical next step.

Local History News November 2000

> The RH7 group set me thinking, further, about the perpetual debate in local history about where to draw the boundaries.

'See you down The Local Historian at half-eight then'?
Alan Crosby

In Borsetshire they don't have any problem with pub names—all true Ambridge folk frequent *The Bull*, where they not only enjoy a pint of Shires but also relish the complex marital circumstances of mine host. Those of a less savoury nature go instead to *The Cat and Fiddle*, while those who want a rather more respectable but slightly more distant venue choose *The Feathers*. So far, so normal. But what about that extraordinary and mysterious place, *The Goat and Nightgown*? We know little of its decor, clientele, or the beer and food which it serves, but its name is one to set the pulse of the local historian racing. Heraldic emblem? Local legend? Spectral happening recorded in Victorian folklore? 1960s hippy theme? Who knows? But we can say for certain that it is an authentic and historically noteworthy example of the naming patterns of the English hostelry.

Here in another county, Lancashire, I am from time to time to be found (always in a respectably decorous fashion) within the hallowed and time-honoured precincts of the *Derby Arms* (named, like many others throughout the North West, after our most illustrious aristocratic family), *The Plough* (source of name obvious), or *The Bushells* (named from benefactor of adjacent almshouses). But when in Preston town centre I am very reluctant indeed to cross the threshold of *The Flax and Firkin*. There are several reasons for this, some associated with the fare on offer,

> I am very reluctant indeed to cross the threshold of *The Flax and Firkin.*

but most important is that it was until recently known as *The Corn Exchange* (until about ten years ago it was the public hall, Preston's favourite meeting-place and venue for romance during the 1930s and 1940s; a century and a half ago it actually was the corn exchange). But then it underwent what CAMRA, the Campaign for Real Ale, terms 'firkinisation' and was given a silly name, particularly absurd in what was one of the half dozen greatest cotton towns in the western world. There were letters to the paper, public protests and local outrage, not just because of the principle of renaming a much-loved landmark (the pub itself was only a few years old), but because of the pathetic and infantile nature of the marketing man's gimmick. One concession was made: the name *Corn Exchange* was allowed to stay on the building, even though the fascia signs were all changed. So kind. Thanks.

In July the Culture Secretary, Chris Smith, discussed pub names in the House of Commons (I expect he was glad to return to the theme of The Dome, uncontroversial by comparison). He suggested that changing the names 'destroyed the public houses' links with local history' and that 'we are surely in danger of losing an important part of local history and local folk memory'. He may be overstating the case, for most names are not in reality notably ancient and have changed constantly in the past, while in the late 17th century many drinking-places were known only by the name of the owner. But their historical interest is nonetheless clear. Several articles in *The Local Historian* over the years have noted how 19th century pub names, like street names, reflect the personalities who were 'in the news' at the time of their opening, such as General Gordon and Queen Victoria. Older sources often indicate names which would be equally familiar and comfortable now—for example, *The Crown, The Lion, The Key,* and *The Castle* appear in one diarist's list of places visited on a Manchester pub crawl in 1712. Today, in contrast, we suffer the 'themed' names which make the heart sink.

Local History News November 2000

The quarry in sight
Alan Crosby

The title above is that of an article in The Amateur Historian in the mid-l950s, concerning the genealogical hunt for ancestors. Now a different quarry is in sight. I am approaching the end of a project to prepare a full index and abstracts of all articles in volumes 1-29 of *The Amateur Historian* and *The Local Historian* (covering the period 1952-1999 inclusive). Although at times I felt that picking oakum or sewing mailbags would be a blissful alternative, it has been a very interesting if lengthy undertaking. What has seemed most remarkable is the extraordinary diversity of subject matter which the journal has dealt with over 47 years—from the history of horseshoes to local history in Japan, from medieval bee-keeping to Christian cricket teams in the 1930s. from wife-selling to bus services. Surely nothing in the entire world of local history has not been at least mentioned in passing somewhere in the pages of the journal.

It is unusual, maybe even unknown, for anybody to begin reading a journal such as this at page 1 of volume I and to work steadily through it, but I think I have probably now read every page published before December last year. I looked at reviews of books long-since consigned to top shelves or library throw-out piles (some, no doubt, deservedly); I looked at news of events now forgotten which seemed so urgent and vital at the time; I read comments and queries which were, in the 1950s, redolent of the antiquarian era in local history and whose sentiments were indeed Victorian; and I read articles which even decades later were fresh and sharp, and in which the excitement of new discovery and radical new interpretation was palpable. I read again the sometimes vitriolic debates about what local history meant, how it should be taught and practised, and I noted how from the beginning, right up to the final issue of 1999, the same themes were evident. Plus ça change, plus c'est la meme chose.

One of the most interesting aspects was the onward march of technology. When I was in

> nothing in the entire world of local history has not been at least mentioned in passing somewhere in the pages of the journal

the first year of my postgraduate research I started a computing course, since we were all told that the future lay in computing and we certainly needed to know about it. I went to two sessions before deciding that endlessly punching cards was not for me. *The Local Historian* for 1974-1975 recaptured that time, as I read the first references to how the new technology might be employed—the new President of BALH, Joe Bettey, was the author, in those distant days of the pioneering article, which was about the computer analysis of Dorset probate inventories. This, and others over the next few years, told us how to use punched cards, but by the mid-1980s a new theme was emerging. Punched cards were out, software was in, And now, of course, the methodologies of computing are almost universally familiar, punched cards are found in museums, and these articles are themselves of historical interest.

So, the journal is a wonderful quarry. It is full of riches and represents a vast resource of accumulated knowledge and opinion. The list of authors is remarkable, for among the contributors are great and famous historians (Christopher Hill wrote an article in the first issue) and people whose work is unsung and known only to a few—apart from their appearance in these pages. The detailed index and abstracts should, for the first time, unlock these resources in their entirety: this is BALH's 'millennium project' (carefully timed to satisfy both the 2000 and the 2001 millennium lobbies!), and we feel sure that it will be welcomed by local historians everywhere.

Alan Crosby is the BALH General Editor
The Index and Abstracts were published in 2001.
Local History News August 2000

Resource ...
or should it be re:source
Alan Crosby

A new Resource has appeared, to come to our aid. The capital letter is deliberate, for this isn't just any resource (small 'r'). This is what was briefly known as MLAC (not a purgative or digestion remedy, though might give indigestion to some). You may not know much about MLAC, but be thankful that it didn't end up, as it might have done, as CAML (as we all know, a horse designed by a committee). No, MLAC is transmogrified into Resource, and this is the new name for (fanfare of trumpets as explanation is at last forthcoming) The Council for Museums, Archives and Libraries. It is the successor to the Museums and Galleries Commission (MGC) and the Library and Information Commission (LIC): we live in a world of acronyms and initials.

Resource, according to its chief executive, is a name which 'captures effectively the main elements of commonality between museums, libraries and archives and which we hope reflects some of the dynamism within the sector'. In fact, the letter which announces the name spells it re:source on the headed notepaper but Resource in the text, so the precise spelling is not absolutely clear. Perhaps a little commonality between top of paper and middle of letter would have been a good idea. And a little dynamism in the proof reading sector?

What we are witnessing is the creation of what in the old days was called a quango. This is the 'strategically focussed body' (I quote) which will develop and implement government policy towards ML and A. And, naturally, will decide how the money will be spent. It has ambitious plans, and its consultation document speaks of 'promotion of access', 'pursuit of excellence and innovation', 'nurturing of educational opportunity', and 'fostering of the creative

> ## That the language of Shakespeare should fall so far!

industries' (whatever that might mean). It also says that among the 'three broad aspects of its work' will be 'synergy—identifying issues and initiatives of a cross-sectoral nature', That the language of Shakespeare should fall so far.

To cut a long and sometimes tedious document short, this new and strategically focussed body is going to be responsible in the future, or until the names change again, for much of what happens in the institutions on which local historians depend so heavily (or perhaps, following the phraseology of the consultation material, which are in an ongoing interface situation with the local history community). We should all be deeply concerned with what is happening, and seriously motivated to try to influence the actions of those who run re:source (aka Resource). But the problem—I speak as one who sits on the North West Regional Archives Council, the work of which is closely connected with resource/re: source—is that the documentation is so ineffably dull and so laden with fashionable jargon, and takes so many pages of dreary sub-prose to say what is often fairly obvious, that most people with any imagination might simply go home and make the cocoa.

That would be a pity, for the new body, once the burden of management-speak is stripped away, is serious in its intention to transform the relationships between museums, archives and libraries, which historically are contentious, and may have the power and will to make real improvements. The constitution and the staffing levels of Resource (re:source) are only now being finalised, so we must wait to see what practical results flow from its endeavours. But at last a broad-minded policy is being developed, and we may yet see the emergence of long-term strategies rather than ad hoc expedients, So, please, Resource (or re:source), try to write in good clear English about the real world, and (a final plea) spend some real money on the real needs of M, L and A.

Local History News August 2000

Amateurs

Alan Crosby

Of the controversies which have generated debate in local history in the last 50 years, the most persistent is the relationship between the amateur and the professional. The renaming of *The Amateur Historian* as *The Local Historian* in the mid-1960s reflected the fact that many who were amateur, in that they were retired or were employed in other work so that local history was their 'leisure pursuit', were professional in their impressive skills in research, analysis and writing. By that time 'amateur', like 'antiquary' a hundred years before, was fast-becoming a term of abuse or disdain. In the first chapter of *Researching and Writing Local History: a practical guide for local historians* (BALH, 1999 - buy it if you haven't already done so) David Dymond usefully summarises some of these issues, as they have been debated over the last thirty years.

These debates have been conducted almost exclusively by professional regional and local historians. For the great majority of those who work in local history the issues are unknown or are regarded as irrelevant or tedious. Most 'amateur' local historians undertake their work for pleasure, not for remuneration, and if they work in a way which offends the academic judgments of certain professionals, they are rightly unconcerned as long as they achieve satisfaction from doing the work in their way. But many who have contributed to the debate seem to imply that the professional should not only encourage and inform the amateur, but should also seek to impose an orthodoxy of method and approach, an intellectually-approved way of doing local history research. Amateurs, they hint, cannot be trusted to do the work in the 'right' way and so should be discouraged from embarking upon such tasks until they have received the correct wisdom.

A quick look at the occupations of those who have written articles in The Local Historian in the last couple of years reveals a high proportion of 'academics' (just over 50% of all authors, though quite a few of these worked not in history but in associated disciplines). The occupations of the other 50% demonstrate the broadness of the church which is local history. One contributor was proud to call himself an 'amateur local historian', and we also had, among others, two archivists, an economist, a couple of civil servants, several administrators of charities and

'interest groups', a freelance social services project director, a management consultant, a retired tropical entomologist and a consultant physician specialising in endocrinology. This broad range of backgrounds characterises our subject and represents one of its greatest strengths. Local history is one of the comparatively few areas in which non-professionals can compete on roughly equal terms with those who hold paid or salaried posts in the field.

Some are apprehensive about or downright condemnatory of this very fact - the ubiquitous presence of 'non-professionals' is, after all, one of the justifications for the low status which local history has in the eyes of a significant number of mainstream historians. We must have academic debate but nobody should seek to impose his or her views on others and if local historians choose not to go along with the debate, so be it. Everybody else is free to accept or reject their methods and findings - and that, of course, is equally true of the work of professional historians. The presence of 'amateurs' is not a weakness but an abiding strength, for it is one of our safeguards against elitism - indeed, against that intellectual totalitarianism which says that not only should all researchers follow the prescribed frameworks and paths of study laid down by the professionals, but that <u>only</u> the professionals may fruitfully follow those paths.

> Most 'amateur' local historians undertake their work for pleasure

The Index of One-Place Studies

Colin Mills

What is a one-place study? As the name suggests, there is an analogy with one-name studies. The difference is that rather than trace all instances of a surname, or a related group of surnames, world-wide, one-placers deal with the inhabitants of a particular locality. One-placers are volunteers actively working to compile complete transcriptions or name indexes of the major extant sets of primary records of genealogical or historical relevance for a given parish, ideally in its entirety, or at least for particular places, such as villages or hamlets within the parish.

There are a number of different reasons for starting a one-place study. Some start as a local history. Some start with a family interest in a place, and compile or search lists of everyone in the place to help in identifying people in the family tree. Others start from demography and parish reconstitution, listing everyone in a place to deduce statistics about their lives. Related to these are social and community history, listing people and studying their occupations, class, religion, politics, etc.

Because one-place studies deal with larger numbers of people, indexing is more important, and because they deal with a single locality, one-placers have local knowledge, being more familiar with local history and local industries.

John Dowding first embarked on the Index of One-Place Studies in 1994. He found that one-place studies often comprised an index of historical events, parish registers, tithe apportionments, census returns and sometime local newspapers. These were of little interest to other local historians, who tended to be interested only in their own parishes, but are of vital interest to family historians, who usually find their family roots are in faraway parts of the country. After three decades' work on compiling information on Burnham and Creeksea in Essex where he was born, John began work on his own family history, where he almost immediately traced the family back to Wessex, where Dorset, Wiltshire and Somerset meet. He then wished that someone had done for the Dorset town of Gillingham, what he had done for Burnham.
The difficulty is to make available the work done by local historians for family historians, two sub-types of the species *Homo historicus* who normally do not mix, as they have separate organizations, separate journals and separate meetings. Although there are 15 – 20,000 parishes in Britain, it is difficult to trace one-place studies or local histories. An index of those working or having worked on one-place studies would help to bridge the gap between local historians and family historians, to their mutual benefit.

Colin Mills took over the Index from John Dowding in 1999, and managed to arouse some interest in the index. John Palmer has added to his Wirksworth web-site a list, maintained by Mike Fisher, of the e-mail addresses of those conducting one-place studies with

their web-sites at www.wirksworth.org.uk/oneplace.htm. There are lists of online parish clerks, which is a very similar scheme, for Cornwall at www.parsons1998.freeserve.co.uk/opc.htm and for Devon at www.cs.ncl.ac.uk/genuki/DEV/OPCproject.html

The criteria for a one-place study would be
- willingness to answer queries when the search fee (if there is one) is paid, and including a large stamped addressed envelope or International Reply Coupons; or a reference to a published or deposited study.
- the study must include more than one type of record – e.g. including both parish registers and censuses – or else covers a complete run of one type of record: 1841-1901 censuses, trade directories over a period, parish registers.
- the researcher must have indexes to all names within the records in the study; that is, not a one-name study for the place, nor a local history merely picking out the most significant people from limited material.

The criteria are not designed to exclude but to encourage: if one is working towards achieving them, there must have been reasonable progress made towards becoming a one-place study. After all, you can't index a book before the first volume has been completed.

David Hawgood is writing a book on one-place genealogy, including a directory of those conducting one-place studies, giving the parishes or localities, with names and postal addresses, and e-mail addresses and web-sites where they apply. The book will also include several articles on one-place studies. The main criteria for an entry would be:
study one place (or a group of places) in Great Britain and Ireland;
have available information useful to family historians;
provide access in some way, and answer e-mail or pre-paid queries.

An e-mailing list exists for anyone who is actively involved in studying a single parish or group of parishes in the United Kingdom, as well as those who are about to embark on such a project.
To subscribe send "subscribe" to one-place-study-l-request@rootsweb.com (mail mode) or one-place-study-d-request@rootsweb.com (digest mode).

Online parish clerks, local history recorders and local historians, might also find this e-list useful.
Mike Fisher: address – Numey Cottage Farm, Westwood Park, Droitwich, Worcs WR9 0AE; e-mail m.j.fisher@btinternet.com.
David Hawgood: address – 26 Cloister Road, Acton, London W3 0DE; e-mail David_Hawgood@compuserve.com or david@hawgood.com.
Colin Mills: address – 70 Chestnut Lane, Amersham, Bucks HP6 6EH; e-mail cdjmills@hotmail.com.
John Palmer: address – 29 Sutherland Avenue, Broadstone, Dorset BH18 9EB; e-mail john.palmer@wirksworth.org.uk.

Local History Week 4 -12 May 2002

A Celebration of Local and Family History organised by
The Historical Association
in conjunction with BBC History magazine.

Suzanne Cawsey

The good news on everyone's lips at the moment is that history's popularity as a subject seems to be at an all time high. Ratings for television history are soaring and the BBC's History magazine recruited tens of thousands of subscribers in just one month. On the high street, too, sales of history books are only exceeded by those of fiction. History's real success story, however, often lies hidden behind these dramatic national figures and that is the huge popularity, and exciting and diverse activities of hundreds of local and family history organisations across the country. However, local history and its historians are often not receiving the recognition they deserve or the resources to publicise and further their work.

Local History Week 2002
Local History Week is a way of combining the diverse activities which already exist at a local level and to give them more widespread publicity and appreciation. Local history, after all, is a historical theme which can involve everyone, from professionals to enthusiasts and from the biggest organisations right down to individuals who have an interest in their communities. It is also an increasingly important area of the National Curriculum and access to local historical resources is relatively easy for teachers and students

The Events
Hundreds of events will be taking place across England, Wales and Scotland, everywhere from Cornwall to The Orkneys and will include things like:
Local and Family History Fairs,
History adventure walks
Museum and archive discovery days
Special exhibitions   Talks and debates
Conferences and events   History projects
Online activities   Re-enactments and demonstrations
Competitions and prizes

Just some of the highlights for the week are The National Trust's evacuation project at Lanhydrock House and special workshops for schools at The Lizard and Bottallack in Cornwall, as well as lots of other exciting events at other National Trust properties throughout the country. The National Museums and Galleries of Wales have a very wide range of ideas for the week, including adventure walks, museums and archive discovery days and themed displays, and there will be special local history exhibitions at lots of other museums throughout Britain linked to Museums and Galleries Month. Many places are holding local and family history fairs with talks and information stands run by local organisations. Competitions include a history

THE HISTORICAL ASSOCIATION
THE VOICE FOR HISTORY

of science competition run by the British Society for the History of Science with Adam Hart-Davies and a competition for the publication of the best local history manuscript by Sutton Publishing. The Victoria County History Project, a major source for local historians, will be holding a number of events around the country linked to its new development scheme and the Historical Manuscripts Commission, along with many regional archives, will have staff on hand throughout the week to give expert advice on local history research.

The Historical Association itself has around 70 branches throughout England, Wales, Scotland and Northern Ireland and many of these will be putting on special events for the day, often in conjunction with other local organisations. To discover your nearest branch of the Historical Association visit our website at **www.history.org.uk** or phone (020) 7735 3901 for more information about the work we do to promote history nationally. There will also be special editions of our magazines, The Historian, Teaching History and Primary History for the week, offering teaching resources and in-depth historical articles.

The Society of Genealogists **Family History Fair**, will launch Local History Week on the weekend of 4th and 5th May at the Royal Horticultural Society conference centre in Westminster. As usual, this promises to be very lively event with local and family historians from all over the country coming together to visit the exhibition, pick up advice and share information. For more details about this event visit the Local History Week website from the autumn or contact the Society of Genealogists on (020) 7553 3290 or e-mail: **events@sog.org.uk**.

The climax of Local History Week will be the event at the Beveridge Hall in London on Saturday 11 May 2002, where speakers from a huge range of organisations will discuss current issues in local history and and give a behind-the-scenes view of some fascinating local projects. It will also be a chance to meet other people with a passion for history.
The programme for the Keynote Event (provisional) willinclude
The Local History of Minorities
Black, Asian and Jewish Histories
Landscape and Buildings
Urban and Rural Spaces
Individuals and Communities
Local History Now
For more information about this conference, organised jointly by The Historical Association, The Institute of Historical Research and The Victoria County History Project, please contact Debra Birch,The Institute of Historical Research. Fax: (020) 7862 8745. E-mail: d.birch@sas.ac.uk
The Website
The programme of events and lots more information

about Local History Week will be accessible online from October 2002 and will be updated regularly. Visit The Historical Association homepage at www.history.org.uk and click on the Local History Week logo. This will take you through to the main Local History Week Menu. To find out about events going on in your local area click on Events and choose a county or select from national events for more details about the Keynote Event and the Family History Fair. Local History activities and competitions for schools will run from January 2002. The website will include details of these, together with lots of resources and ideas for teachers. For members of the Historical Association the special editions of our magazines will also be available online. If you are a local society, library, archive or other organisation, however small, and would like to take part in Local History Week 2002, we would love to hear from you. Details of how to join in and a copy of the form to register local events are available in the 'How to get involved' section. Also on the Local History Week site are useful contacts for organisations in your area and lots of important links to other history related websites.If you have difficulty accessing the website then please contact The Historical Association direct on (020) 7735 3901 or e-mail us at **enquiry@history.org.uk** and we will be delighted to help.

Local History and Resources
During my work in setting up the event I have come across so many interesting and amazing projects. The deprived communities which have had such enthusiasm for their history that they have set up their own community archives. The village societies which have worked tirelessly to restore their historic buildings and monuments. The local history societies who have organised archaeological excavations of ancient sites in the area. The individual researchers who are working on their fourth or fifth local history book. It has been such a pleasure to work with other people who have so much energy and enthusiasm for exploring the past.

These same people are often trying to achieve a very high standard but on very limited resources. Obtaining funding for heritage and historical projects is a problem faced by both national and local organisations. The future for local projects is improving, however, thanks to the 'Awards for All' scheme financed by the National Lottery. This programme was specifically set up to provide grants of between £500 and £5000 to community projects and many local history societies and community archive groups have already benefited from the scheme to publish books, buy computers, fund exhibitions and many other activities. The scheme is relativey simple to apply for and you don't have to find any matching funds, which can so often be an obstacle to fundraising activity. If you would like to find out more about this scheme to finance projects connected with Local History Week or independent of it, then visit the Awards for All website at www.awardsforall.org.uk or phone 0845 600 2040.

As for Local History Week itself, The Historical Association must thank a whole range of sponsors and other historical organisations who have responded so enthusiastically to support the plans. BBC History magazine has generously agreed to sponsor publicity

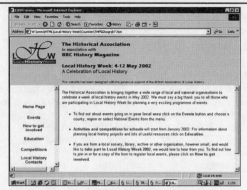

for the week and will be producing a special Local History Week edition. Channel 4 Learning are sponsoring the Keynote Event on 11 May with Channel 4 itself screening a number of exciting local history related programmes before and during the week. The British Association for Local History, who support local historians and publish The Local Historian and Local History News, is sponsoring the website and many other organisations are involved in putting on events and publicising the week.

The Future
While a local history week cannot hope to completely reform political attitudes and instantly solve the problems of funding and resources faced by historical societies, raising the profile of history nationally is a move in the right direction. The long-term benefits of local history week will be valuable: highlighting the importance of history both as an academic subject in schools and as a way of encouraging people to take pride in their communities, providing encouragement to local historians to undertake research and publish their findings, encouraging the use of IT and multimedia in researching and presenting findings, and above all enjoying history and the diversity which its study entails. In the short-term, the immediate aim of the week is to encourage wider active participation in local history by helping everyone find out just how much is going on in their area and how they can join in. As to the future, if Local History Week 2002 is a success we hope that National History Weeks might be held regularly.

If you would like more details or are interested in becoming involved, please contact Suzanne Cawsey at The Historical Association, 59A Kennington Park Road, London SE11 4JH. Telephone: 0207 735 2021. E-mail: suzanne.cawsey@history.org.uk

Devon On~Line Parish Clerks
Deborah O'Brien

Following the initiative of David Stick and Michael McCormick from the Cornish-Gen Mailing list where an On-Line Parish Clerk [OPC] project is in operation for Cornwall, I asked and received their permission to use a similar idea, and, together with the co-operation of Brian Randell, the Devon Mailing List and GENUKI/Devon, an OPC project for Devon was established.

A volunteer (OPC) for each Parish acts as a focus or co-ordinator for gathering together Parish Register Transcriptions, Indexes, Censuses, Land Tax Assessments and similar genealogical related data for the individual Ancient Parishes of Devon.

Many OPCs have websites that identify their holdings, and all are willing to assist others with their research using the resources available to them. All queries are generated via e-mail, and the answers sent in the same format.

We are always looking for further donations of material – odd Parish Register entries are hard to co-ordinate, but transcriptions of whole pages of a Parish Register or similar resource are very welcome additions. These should preferably be submitted in electronic form via e-mail, or traditional mail by prior arrangement. The submitter has the responsibility to ensure that the appropriate permissions have been given for the transcripts to be made. For material originally obtained from them, the Devon Record Office will provide advice on this matter, on a case by case basis. The Archivist can be e-mailed at: DevRec@devon.gov.uk

However, in general, there is no need to seek such prior permission to transcribe or index material held by the Public Record Office – see their rules concerning copyright at http://www.pro.gov.uk/about/copyright.htm

To date 65 Devon Parishes have an OPC who either has an extensive collection of transcripts, indexes etc., or who is willing to receive copies of same and make them available to other researchers in the form of look-ups. Seventy-four Cornish Parishes have OPCs. We also would welcome any others willing to become an OPC. A website is not necessary, but an e-mail address is.

A full explanation of the project and Parishes covered to date is available at the OPC website: http://www.cs.ncl.ac.uk/genuki/DEV/OPCproject.html The Cornwall project is described at: http://www.parsons1998.freeserve.co.uk/opc.htm

As well as being OPC Co-Ordinator and OPC for Meavy & Sheepstor Deborah O'Brien is a member of the Devon and Cornwall Family History Societies Email: deborah.obrien5@gte.net

Glamorgan History Society

The Glamorgan History Society, founded in 1950 as the Glamorgan Local History Society, aims to promote the study of the history of Glamorgan through its annual journal **Morgannwg** as well as its twice-yearly meetings, when members and their friends are treated to lively and entertaining addresses by guest speakers expert in their respective fields. These meetings have latterly been fixed as the second Saturday in May at The Rest, Porthcawl for the Annual General Meeting (which is followed by an address from a guest speaker) and the second Saturday in November, at Margam Orangery, Margam Park for the Autumn Day School.

Autumn Day School themes in recent years have included Margam Abbey, music in Glamorgan, maritime Glamorgan, the Glamorganshire Canal, castles in Glamorgan, the life and work of G.T. Clark, Glamorgan landscapes, Welsh cathedrals and garden history. The theme for this year will explore various aspects of Welsh nonconformity. The Day School programme affords not only the opportunity to listen to eminent speakers, but to lunch in pleasant surroundings and to browse, and perhaps purchase, from bookstalls staffed by representatives of the county's local history societies.

Membership of the Society, which is a registered charity, is open to all those with an interest in the history of Glamorgan and of Wales. The annual subscription is currently £6 (with special rates for students and institutions) and entitles a member to receive the current edition of **Morgannwg**.

The journal **Morgannwg** has achieved a reputation for consistently high standards of scholarship, publishing the latest research and attracting contributions from many well-known local and national historians. Each volume carries three or four main articles which, over the years since 1957, have dealt with almost every aspect and period of the history of the old county. The journal is of interest to all with a commitment to local history, to teachers of Welsh history and to genealogists with Glamorgan ancestry.

One-Place Studies in Genealogy and Family History
Dr Diane Brook

Is there really such a place as the 'ancestral home'? Family historians soon find that our ancestors moved from place to place more often than we were taught to think, in the traditional historical view of a rural population well-rooted in small settlements. Indeed, if our ancestors had never moved, we would all be from separate local kindreds and be very inbred! And yet, there is some truth in the idea, especially for families before the nineteenth century. In some places, we find a family line remaining for several generations with many and wide links in one village or parish as well as the surrounding area. This can lead to a different type of exploration of family history, the one-place study.

Colin Mills of Amersham wrote to *Family Tree Magazine* in December 2000 suggesting there should be a register of one-place studies and suggested some ground rules. One-place studies would be those where all the evidence is collected for the inhabitants in a particular place, whether parish, hamlet, town or even city. Mr Mills' suggested rules included collecting all families in the chosen place, collecting strays for only one generation before or after living in the place, at least one major source be transcribed and indexed, and enquirers to be expected to provide return postage for all enquiries. Also suggested were a few protective rules; the one-placer would be under no expectation to answer queries about any other place in the locality of their study nor to index all available sources of information. Mr Mills further suggested publishing a register, either in this volume, the BIGR, the Genealogical Research Directory (GRD), or the members' interests of the local family history society journal. This writer, having put a one-place interest in the GRD some years ago and having received no responses, suggested an Internet guide to such studies provided through the parish headings within the GENUKI web sites. It would also be useful if such a register indicated which core source had been indexed, such as the available census records or the parish register, and, whether a coverage list were available. Only those with extensive coverage of the major sources would be listed as having a wide or comprehensive study.

What should a one-place study cover and how should such studies be managed? One could argue that the idea is merely a new name for one aspect of local history, a subject already well established and with well developed groups, overall managing groups and published journals. In one sense, this is a fair point. Many local history studies cover many of the same topics as genealogy; parish register and census studies, studies of manorial and tax records. Indeed, exactly this point was made by Michael Browning in an article titled 'Local Historian' in the Somerset & Dorset FHS Journal, 1997, where he described the benefits to family history of detailed local studies. Both local history and family history can include demography, the study of family groups and populations.

The difference is one of aim and emphasis. A one-place family history study would be concentrated on the people in a place and their family relationships. It might include but would not focus on the events, buildings, land, industries, and all the other topics rightly in the centre of local history studies. Although Michael Browning is both a family and local historian, other local historians may not view family history with the same positive attitude. More importantly, local historians may not organise their records in a way suitable for providing answers to family history queries.

Records
The holder of a one-place study, as Mr Mills implied, would be primarily a family historian, with the information organised in such a way as to assist other family historians. Such studies would also address many of the questions we have about the nature of family history in the United Kingdom through time. There are many topics which would both assist in pedigree creation and general family history.

The first is the most obvious and often a cross-over with local history, the transcribing and indexing of major local genealogical sources such as the parish registers, bishops' transcripts (BT's) and any non-conformist registers, the available census years and monumental inscriptions. There are also many other sources that may survive such as other parish documents, the Tithe Plan and apportionment, the Land Tax Assessments and manorial records. Less well known and considered records are more likely to be collected by the one-placer. Peter Talbot-Ashby writes that one researcher records not only the parish registers and the census details but also details of everything from local businesses, services (i.e. electricity, gas, water and telephones); transport from early stage coaches; local organisations from the Girls Guides and Scouts to the Over 50's Club!! He has pamphlets and leaflets about local events in the village over the years, and much, more. Others collect local maps, newspaper cuttings, war records and local involvement in civil defence, local customs, etc.

The local entries from other types of indexes can also be extracted such as wills, hearth taxes and lay subsidies. County historical, archaeological and local record society publications can be checked for relevant entries. The local family history society may have covered the place in a county census index or monumental inscriptions recording; the one-place study adds the extraction or indexing of all the entries in a county marriage or census index for the particular place. The county indexes assume the individual researcher will use the indexes to find a particular family event. Strays indexes attempt to address the movement of people between counties but again arrange them for the individual researcher, by surname and not by individual place.

Surnames

Surname studies focus on the origins of a particular surname across geographical boundaries. Although they obviously include any bearers of the name who remain in one place for more than one generation, the studies are not specifically organised by place. A one-place study can examine the length of time a surname, indeed groups of surnames, have been present in the selected place. The increase or ramification of the name can be examined and how many separate kindreds with the surname in the place are found. The writer's work on Queen Camel, Somerset, shows that only 23 surnames listed in the 1673-4 Hearth Tax returns are also found in the census records from 1841 to 1891. On the other hand, some surnames such as RAYMOND appear to have been in the village from at least the late 1500's when the manorial records begin and others, such as MORRIS, well before that. Other names appear for centuries but die out. Further study may show that the descendants remain but in the female line only. At Queen Camel, the surnames OLDAYES, GAPPER and SNOW, for example, appear regularly throughout the seventeenth century and into the eighteenth but have disappeared by the nineteenth. Oldayes or OLDHAYES also appeared as 'alias WATTS' and probably survives as the Watts family. An even earlier example is the evocative name, MIDWYNTER, recorded in the earliest detailed local list, the Lay Subsidy of 1327. The date is so early that the name could have been a nickname, not an inherited surname, for someone born in mid-winter or perhaps of a gloomy disposition. The Lay Subsidy of 1546/7 lists a 'John Mydwynter', hence the name was or became a surname. The surname does not occur anywhere in Britain in 1881.

Spelling variants and alias names can be evaluated against family structures and otherwise unlinkable ancestries discovered as names fluctuate over time. This is something not usually possible through indexes of one source type, such as marriage indexes.

Detailed studies of local people should provide evidence for the origins of local place-names formed from personal names. In Queen Camel, there is a 'Grace Martin's Lane'. The 'bridge by Grace Martin's' is mentioned as early as 1695 but there are several Grace Martins in the records to choose from. In fact, one-place studies could help show when and how such place-names were formed and in what parts of the country and for what types of local features.

Forenames

Forenames clearly run in families and assist in linking families together. The tradition that some names are used in every generation, especially for men, has only recently died out and may be being revived. One-place studies of pedigrees can help show how long this pattern has been in place and in what social groups. For example, in Queen Camel, there was a Cuthbert Raymond in most generations from at least 1601 to 1881. Other families such as the Brook/Brooks did not develop such a distinctive pattern although many branches used Benjamin after the first known Benjamin baptised in 1737. The contribution of new male names from the female side of families could also be investigated.

Female forenames may also run in families and can help suggest links, although women's name fashions change more quickly than men's. For example, there were several women named Dorothy Langdon and Dinah Reeves in Queen Camel. Some were so named at birth and others gained the surname at marriage. Whether these patterns were family traditions or just forename fashions needs to be investigated.

There can be other influences in name fashions. The forename Edith appears about 1750 in Queen Camel. This would seem to arise from the fact that the lady of the manor at the time was Edith Mildmay. Other patterns to look for are royal names such as George which became much more popular after it became the royal name from about 1720 to 1830. The Brook/s of Queen Camel affected Biblical names for a generation or two: Isaac was probably the great-uncle of Jacob, Elisha and Benjamin. There is an Abraham Brook from the next parish who may also be a relative. The Biblical genealogy is Abraham, father of Isaac, father of Jacob. Is the fashion for Biblical names a reflection of the religious leanings of families or incidental? In fact, there is no evidence that any branch of the Brook/s had non-conformist tendencies until the nineteenth century.

Demography

Demography, as noted above, is the formal study of patterns in a population. Academic historians often use one place such as a parish to investigate a manageable-sized population through time. There are many features of a population to study. For family historians, the results, which give typical rates such as age at marriage or distance of between marriage partners' birthplaces, also help suggest further research strategies for family tracing.

The whole life span of the individuals in the population can be studied. Birth rates can be worked out over time if the parish register baptisms survive. How many children do most families have? What are the rates of infant and child mortality?

The usual age at first marriage is remarkably standard although it varies over time. For the men in rural Somerset in many families, age twenty-five is very typical and has actually produced quick results when searching for a marriage as late as 1889. Once enough evidence for occupations is available, one can also work out who married whom, the selection of partners by class, and how often men and women married 'up' or 'down'.

The combined forces of the county marriage indexes and a one-place study provide the evidence for the distance away for the marriage partners from other places and how many of the local population married elsewhere. It is now thought that the underlying pattern in Europe is 'virilocal', residence where the man already lives, rather than the woman. This is surprising as it is men who are thought of as the invaders and migrants and there is also some evidence of this at the wider historical level. At the local level, although marriages may typically take place at the bride's parish, something to review in a one-place study, it seems likely that many couples actually lived in the man's home village or town. In Queen Camel in 1851, of the 112 married or widowed adults, nearly two-thirds (61%) of the men were born in the village but less than half of the women (39%). Amongst the couples with children, both partners were born elsewhere in only a quarter of couples. A series of one-place studies would show if such patterns hold in general or vary from place to place and over time.

Once both baptisms and burials registers survive in detail, ages at death can be calculated for many of the population. Combined with evidence of occupation, one can look at the relationship of social class with age at death. There has been a very strong correlation between higher social class and longer life recorded since the beginning of civil registration in 1837.

Migration
One of the family historian's constant problems is migration. As suggested above, the one-place family history study would keep a record of at least one generation before and after the family was living in the selected place. This would provide a link to any other one-place study and assist researchers linking families. It would also add to the overall knowledge of migration patterns already mentioned in relation to marriages. The places and distances people came from and moved to can be calculated and mapped. These patterns can be looked at in terms of types of destinations, whether village, town or city, what actual places people migrated to and from, and by age, class, gender, and occupation and through time.

Temporary migration is also of interest. The settlement laws made sure our ancestors were often sent 'home' if they became too poor to maintain themselves in their new place of residence. Settlement papers, orders for removal to or from the place and depositions about the circumstances can indicate failed attempts at migration and also indicate where to look for missing family records.

For example, Nicholas Brook, baptised 1740 in Queen Camel, has a settlement deposition from Sherborne in Dorset where he had gone, working for an apothecary. He had married and had a child when his employment ended. The whole family was sent back to Queen Camel where two further children were born. In fact, the Sherborne registers record Nicholas' first marriage, the death of his first wife, his second marriage and the baptism of his first child.

More exciting travels were found when reviewing the census occupations of some of the old men of the Queen Camel in 1851, four army pensioners and one former navy man. The army careers were looked up on the computerised index to the WO97 returns at the Public Record Office, Kew. Elias WILLIS had been born to an ordinary family in Queen Camel in 1789 and joined the 13th Regiment of Foot. He served in Lower Canada and was wounded in the action at La Cole Mill and was discharged in 1814. His wife was born in St. John's, Upper Canada. The old soldiers had all served in different regiments and enlisted in different years, so had not been recruited or press-ganged at the same time. A military career can explain missing records for marriages and births of children that took place far from home, even outside Britain.

Other Aspects
Once the one-place study is well developed, one can look at inheritance patterns. Each family can be looked at in terms of occupations, the inheritance of land, changes in social class, patterns of forenames, religion adherence and many other categories. Each class of record can not only help with such studies but also add to the pedigrees themselves. A detailed knowledge of the families in the place can also suggest further links. For example, the pedigree of the Brook family in Queen Camel cannot be completely linked before 1734 as the baptismal registers are defective from 1703 to 1733 and lost before that, except for the intermittent bishop's transcripts. There are numerous references to the surname in the BT's and also in leases and the manorial records. The lands mentioned in the manor rolls strongly suggest the holder in 1607, Thomas, son of Thomas Brook, who took over the land from his widowed mother, Florence, is the ancestor of the husband of Mary Brook, widow, who died about 1698. The field names mentioned in 1607 and 1698 are mostly the same or very similar.

Another feature of the one-place studied can be looked at for many families in turn. What proportion of the population of the chosen place are related to each other at any one time? For example, the descendants of Peter and Elizabeth Brook of Queen Camel, married by 1734, formed at least 15% of the population of the village recorded on the 1851 census. Linking the families will also show when relatives were working together or supporting each other. Only 5% of households in Queen Camel in 1851 included a parent or parent-in-law to a head of household but 32% included relatives other than couples and their children, including grandchildren, siblings, other in-laws, nephews, nieces and a cousin.

Finding One-Place Studies
Who is doing one-place studies and how do you find them? This publication will list such studies in future and Peter Talbot-Ashby has offered to keep a register. There is some indication of one-place studies in the subject sections of the GRD volumes. A search on the internet for the place-name may provide references to local history studies but as noted above, these may not be designed for family historians.

There are some UK studies available which approach being true one-place studies. The work on the Essex parish of Earl's Colne is a long-standing social history project with a name index fully cross-indexed to all the transcribed documents including a parish register transcript to 1851, and 1841 and 1851 census indexes, accessible on the internet at
http://www-earlscolne.socanth.cam.ac.uk/index.html. Some of the early, pre-1550, names are not indexed.

The Genuki web site has pages for each county in the UK and within each county a places and parishes section. A small sample of a few places in several counties showed no one-place studies listed. This may be a result of a policy not to include local links which can quickly go out of date. For example, the Earl's Colne study web site address is not shown on the Genuki page for that parish.

No doubt there are very many local and family historians with one-place studies already in progress. Colin Mills is working on Chesham Bois, Buckinghamshire whilst his wife is working on Amersham in the same county. The writer is working on Queen Camel in south-east Somerset, Michael Browning on High Littleton and Hallatrow in north Somerset. Two contributors to the June 2001 issue of Family Tree Magazine pointed out that the Essex and Sussex Family History Societies already keep registers of local historians. The idea has caught on so quickly that a classified advert appeared in the same issue for a 'one-place study' of Feckenham, Worcestershire. Those

with knowledge of other such studies should pass them to the editor of this volume, Robert Blatchford, Family and Local History Handbook, 33 Nursery Road, Nether Poppleton, York YO26 6NN and to Peter Talbot-Ashby at Conifer House, George Street, Hintlesham, Suffolk IP8 3NH. Email: aroco@tesco.net

Family historians tend to start one-place studies once they have traced a family in one location and found that place and its people to be of interest. The one-placer will tailor their approach to their own interests. Some will only want to record and index sources, others will want to undertake some of the analyses suggested here, whilst others will address still other topics.

This writer enjoys the reconstruction of the family histories of all the people in the one-place study as it extends the hobby from just one's own lines to the wider group of the ancestor's local relatives, neighbours, and work mates, and their employers, doctors, midwives, teachers and religious leaders. The researcher is pulled deeper into many types of records. And, the pleasure of finding new ancestors and connections becomes a much more frequent event as the whole population of the chosen place becomes part of the 'family'.

Queen Camel one-place study; main source indexed - 1841 to 1891 census records, some other records indexed, coverage list available. Dr Diane Brook, 7 Werfa Street, Roath Park, Cardiff CF23 5EW U K . Email: dd.brook@ntlworld.com

Earlsdon ~
The Growth of a Suburb of the City of Coventry
Mary Montes

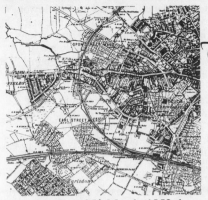

Earlsdon 1889 showing original six streets & relationship to Coventry City Centre

On Lady Day, 25th March, 1852 the conveyance for the sale of about 30 acres of land was signed by the Trustees of the Coventry Branch of the Freehold Land Society.[1] The site was an area of open farm land, lying about three quarters of a mile from the city centre, and although the area had been known for generations as Elsdon, it was now to be known as the Earlsdon Estate.

The Freehold Land Society[2] basically had the same political motive as similar societies backed by the Anti-Corn Law League – that of enlarging the electorate by enabling working men without sufficient capital to qualify for a vote by the ownership of property. The scheme, masterminded by a Birmingham man, James Taylor, (1814-1887) , himself a hard working artisan of modest means, was nationwide in concept, Liberal backed and aimed at breaking the political hold of the Tory Party. Individual societies were formed in areas where, due to high urban growth, there was a need for substantial housing development. These included, after the success of the Birmingham Society (certified on 27th December, 1847), Wolverhampton, Derby, Coventry, Stourbridge, Dudley and then beyond the Midlands to Sheffield, Bradford and London among others.

Taylor's plan for the operation of the scheme was simple: by payment of a small weekly subscription intending purchasers of building plots became automatic members of the local Society. From these members, Trustees were appointed who would select a suitable site, purchase it under mortgage to the Society and divide it into plots for the erection of individual dwelling houses. Each member could then either select his own plot or it was selected for him by ballot, and with money advanced to him by the Society, purchase it from the Trustees. With further help from a Building Society he could then build his house, whereby he not only provided a decent home for himself and his family, but also secured his right to a vote, preferably for the Liberal Party. As a means of providing working men with decent housing by an easy financial arrangement, the scheme was a success,

but politically it failed: only a comparatively small number of electors was added to the register, and of these certainly not all voted Liberal.

Earlsdon was one of the six estates purchased by the Coventry Branch of the Society and ideally should have yielded upwards of 200 votes. However, this hope was dashed. According to the 1865 County Electoral register, only 120 electors qualified because of property they owned in Earlsdon, only six of whom actually occupied such property. Also, in the 1863 By-election caused by the death of the Rt. Hon. E. Ellice, only 46 out of a possible 100 or so Earlsdon names appear on the Borough Poll list, of whom only 26 voted Liberal, 15 voted Tory and five did not use their votes.

However, although the estate was politically disappointing, it is interesting to consider its success socially as a residential area and to consider whether the community spirit associated with Earlsdon by today's residents was there from its beginnings.

A 'community' will mean different things to different people, but for Earlsdon the definition formulated by Butterworth and Weir has been used. In 'The Sociology of Modern Britain'[3], they define it succinctly as containing 'some or all of the following: a territorial area, a complex of institutions within an area and a sense of "belonging"'.

Territorially then, Earlsdon was in an ideal situation. It lay about three quarters of a mile south west of Coventry, in pleasant, open country, between the two commons, Hearsall to the north, with its scrub and gorse and Stivichall, a pleasant wooded area to the south. To the east and west of the estate was open farm land. It stood on high, well drained land and had been laid out into eight 36ft wide[4] gravel surfaced streets, which had been divided into 251 building plots large enough to ensure against over crowding. It had its own water supply laid on from the artesian well at Spon End, which also supplied the city[5], and a drainage system to take away the sink waste and surface water to keep the streets clean and free from mud.[6] Admittedly there was no piped sewage disposal system, but nor was there at this time in the city itself and at least each Earlsdon family would be supplied with an individual privy – there was to be no sharing with four or five other families as was usual in some other local districts.

In fact conditions on the little estate were in direct, very welcome contrast to the poor conditions prevailing in the city. There was open space, light and air in the rural setting, whereas in the city there was appalling overcrowding, filthy streets, a smoky, murky atmosphere and an ever present threat of cholera and other diseases.[7]

By 1861, the year of the first relevant census, 112 houses had been built, scattered at random throughout the eight streets, with 107 of them actually occupied. The scene seemed to be set for the development of a small, stable community; however, from the evidence of the census returns available there is little sign of that population stability which would indicate that the estate was developing its own identity as a community. The population movement of the first 30 years of its life was extraordinarily high.

From the names in the census returns we find that of the 110 heads of household in the 1861 census, 59.1% had moved away and had largely been replaced by 1871. Of those named in 1871, 57% had been replaced by 1881, and a further 48% had been replaced by 1891.

The 30 year period covered by this survey was one of high population movement country-wide, and an equivalent survey carried out in three other Coventry districts highlights an even greater rate of mobility than that of Earlsdon. This survey, of Chapelfields, Hillfields and Gosford Street[8] however, only covers the ten years 1851 to 1861, a period which as far as Earlsdon is concerned is ten years too early to be really relevant, but it does illustrate that Earlsdon was not unique in the unsettled nature of its residents.

The four areas together, moreover, were each unique in that they had their own problems and advantages. Gosford Street, with a population movement of 79% in the ten years 1851-1861, was an ancient Coventry main road with very old houses subdivided and extended into courts and seems to have had the sole merit of providing very cheap accommodation. Hillfields, quite recently developed, providing much better, and therefore much more expensive housing, had a movement of 85% during the same period. But, as the residents in both districts were mainly engaged in silk ribbon weaving, they were equally affected by the disastrous slump in the trade at that period.[9]

Chapelfields, in contrast, was a newly established watchmaking centre. Geographically it could be seen as an extension of the Spon Street/Spon End watchmaking district, which had become too overcrowded for comfort, particularly to the highly skilled watchmaking fraternity. It is significant that Chapelfields had a much lower rate of movement of only 59% during the same ten years, and, although there were fluctuations in the watch industry, it was not nearly as drastically affected at this time as the ribbon industry and was much more stable.

These figures, however, do not include removal by death, which, judging by the death rate for salubrious Earlsdon, would have made a significant difference. The death rate for Earlsdon of the heads of household[10] ran at the surprisingly high rate of 8.2% in the ten year period 1861-71, 16% for 1871-81 and 12% for 1881-1891. In only a few cases did the widow or family stay on in the district.

A striking fact when considering the high population movement is the apparent ease with which families moved from one area to another, and this reinforces the fact of the failure of the Freehold Land Society's intention – that of helping artisans to qualify for enfranchisement by the easy purchase of their own property. If out of the 10 7 heads of household named in the census of 1861 as residents of Earlsdon, only 46 apparently qualified to vote in the Borough[11] (most of whom qualified because of being Freemen of the city anyway), and six qualified for the County elections[12], then clearly the presumption proved mistaken that individuals would actually buy land on which to build homes for themselves and their families. Also, although we do not have the Freehold Land Society's list of purchasers, there is in existence a Petition made to the Water Board for a supply of water to be laid on to the area prior to the laying out of the streets.[13] This contains the signatures of 87 purchasers who stated that they intended to build, and of these 87 names, only 19 appear on the census returns as actual residents there.

It would seem, therefore, that the majority of plots had been bought rather for speculative purposes. A purchaser would have a house or houses built on his land as an investment[14], renting them out, as did John Jones, living in Spon Street, but leasing his houses in Warwick Street, Earlsdon. In other cases, two adjoining houses would be built, one for the occupation of the owner and one to be let; an example for which is James Dillon, with his two houses in Moor Street. In both cases a steady return was to be expected on the initial investment. A further example is that of an employer building a number of small houses for his employees, as John Flinn, a watch manufacturer, did when he built a row of thirteen cottages in Arden Street, but this would have been more for convenience than speculation. There seems to have been no restriction on the number of plots, if available, which could be bought.

As the only means readily available for assessing owner-occupier status is by reference to the electoral registers, it is obviously impossible to be precise, although the few title deeds which have been examined do confirm this premise. As the area was not incorporated into the city until 1890, no city rates were payable at this time, merely a small levy to the Rural Sanitary Authority for which no relevant information is available. Hence the majority of residents had no great problem when considering leaving Earlsdon for another area – a week's notice to their landlord and they were free to pack up their belongings and go. They were under no great pressure to stay and try to make the best of what they apparently felt was a bad job. Any motivation to encourage them to settle was lacking.

The principal trade carried on in Earlsdon, as in Chapelfields, was watchmaking[15], with 112 men and boys engaged in the trade in 1861, 98 in 1871, a period of trade depression, 110 in 1881 and 123 in 1891, showing that, although many watchmakers left the area, others came to take their places. Clearly the general fluctuations in the trade during the period had very little bearing on the population movement. Economic considerations on the whole do not seem to have been a major factor; the number of lodgers taken in remained very little changed, as did the

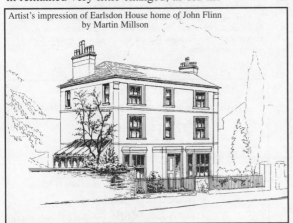

Artist's impression of Earlsdon House home of John Flinn by Martin Millson

number of servants, dropping only slightly in 1871, but recovering again by the end of the period.

One of the main reasons for the dissatisfaction of many would-be residents was purely social. In some respects the estate was in an ideal position, but it had the disadvantage that, although only a fairly short distance from the city, it was not easy to get to, involving a long trek by country lanes if one had a dog cart or carriage of some sort, or for foot travellers down a pathway to the Butts. This pathway appears quite pleasant from photographs of the period, but in reality it was notoriously bad.[16] In other words the city was not easily accessible, making trade intercourse difficult for

1930

the men and social intercourse difficult for all, giving Earlsdon residents a sense of a certain amount of isolation.

Watchmaking was also essentially an urban occupation; the worker and his family were used to the amenities of the town, with plenty of choice in the many grocers' shops, cookshops and bakehouses. The capacity for self-sufficiency by the village or country dweller, with his vegetable plot and his pig had been largely lost. This was a distinct disadvantage in the rural, garden suburb of Earlsdon with its one small shop and many residents obviously found it difficult to adapt.

The women probably found life most difficult. In 1861 a little over half of the heads of household had been born in Coventry, so we can assume that they at least had families and friends in the city and retained some contact with them. The rest had left their families and friends further afield, in areas such as other parts of Warwickshire, in Berkshire, Leicestershire, Cheshire and the other watchmaking centres of Clerkenwell, Liverpool and Prescott, consequently having much less contact with them. Of the 100 or so families named in the 1861 census there is evidence of shared kinship in the case of only four – the Abbotts with the Hulmes and the Fletchers with the Tranters. This fact of little or no local kinship contact would naturally have affected the women more than the men. Normally in those days a young married woman (and there were many in Earlsdon) would have relied heavily on the advice and help of her mother or other close relative at times of childbirth, family illness and for information on the myriad aspects of maintaining a comfortable home for her family.

Of the eleven heads or members of the household who stayed for the whole of the period of the survey and in some cases much longer, ten were employed in the watchmaking industry; they had served seven years apprenticeship and were highly skilled craftsmen. Joined later by other watchmakers (in 1891 there were still 123 of them), at least some of whom settled for a considerable period, they formed the nucleus of the gradually developing Earlsdon community.

Many of them were devout Methodists,[17] and apart from the kinship formed by their shared employment, they also developed their sense of belonging by founding in 1871, the first church on the estate. The successor to that embryo church still serves the community today and plays an important role in Earlsdon's life, as does the school, founded in 1881,[18] also by those early settlers. These early institutions, naturally joined by others over the years – for instance the shopping centre, the parish church, the Social Club and so on, (although the watchmaking industry no longer exists), have served the Earlsdon community well, making the suburb one of the most popular, and, according to the Property Agents, one of the 'most desirable' of all the Coventry suburbs. Those early pioneers would surely be extremely interested to see how the seeds they sowed 150 years ago have developed into the Earlsdon community of today.

NOTES

1. Coventry Freehold Land Society Committee Report, 3rd July, 1852.
2. John Prest *Politics in the Age of Cobden*, Macmillan, 1977, Chapter on Freehold Land Societies
3. Butterworth & Weir, *The Sociology of Modern Britain* Fontana 1980
4. Coventry City Record Office Acc 202/27 Indenture of Release between William Pickering and John Warden and William Henry Marston dated 25th March 1852.
5. Frederick Smith, Six Hundred years of Municipal Life, Coventry 1945, p 126
6. Petition by members of the Freehold Land Society of the

Earlsdon Estate to the Coventry Water Works Committee of the City Council, 6th May 1852.
7. For a full description of the sanitary conditions in Coventry in the middle of the nineteenth century, see Mr Ranger's report to the Coventry Local Board of Health, 1853, Coventry Pamphlets, Coventry and Warwickshire Collection.
8. *Population Movement in Coventry*, 1851-1861. Document produced by a Local History Research Group, Warwick University, 1982.
9. Peter Searby, Coventry in Crisis, 1858-1863, University of Warwick Open Studies, 1976.
10. Coventry Cemetery Registers, 1854-1900
11. Borough Electoral Registers, 1858 and 1863.
12. County Electoral Registers, 1865
13 Petition by the Earlsdon Estate F.L.S. as above.
14 Evidence for this and following statements has been gathered from the   County Electoral Registers, 1854-1865, Title Deeds for property in Moor Street, Warwick Street and Earlsdon Street, together with local Press advertisements for property to let in the area.
15. For further information on the local watchmaking industry see Mary Montes *Brown Boots in Earlsdon,* Coventry Branch of the Historical Association and publications by the Coventry Watch Museum Project Ltd.
16. The main problem with this path was the open sewer which ran beside it, and which carried the drainage from Earlsdon to the river Sherbourne in the city. See Coventry General Works Committee minutes, 1874-1890 for an account of the sanitation problems in Earlsdon.
17. Arthur Pearson, *How Methodism came to Earlsdon,* booklet published by the Church, 1930 and Mary Montes *The Church on the Corner,* also published by the Church, 1999.
18. David Barnett, *A Hundred Years of Education in Earlsdon,* booklet published by the author, 1982, Victoria County History, VIII, pp301, 308, Earlsdon School Log Book, 1882-1890.

Born and bred in Earlsdon Mary Montes naturally has always taken an interest in the area and began seriously researching its history over 20 years ago. She has written 8 books reflecting aspects of Earlsdon its social, religious and industrial history. She is the historical consultant for the Earlsdon Society and an active member of other various local groups.

History Societies & Organisations

British Isles National Organisations & Specialist Subject Societies

The Anglo-Zulu War Historical Society, Woodbury House, Woodchurch Road, Tenterden, TN30 7AE Tel: 01580-764189 Fax: 01580-766648
WWW: www.web-marketing.co.uk/anglozuluwar
Records & Documentation of Zulu War
Association of Local History Tutors
47 Ramsbury Drive, Earley, Reading, RG6 7RT
Tel: 0118 926 4729
Association of Friends of Waterloo Committee
2 Coburn Drive, Four Oaks, Sutton Coldfield, B75 5NT
Tel: 0121-308-4103 Email: jwhite02@globalnet.co.uk
Baptist Historical Society, 60 Strathmore Avenue, Hitchin, SG5 1ST Tel: 01462-431816 Tel: 01462-442548
Email: slcopson@dial.pipex.com WWW: www.baptisthistory.org.uk
British Association for Local History, PO Box 1576, Salisbury, SP2 8SY Tel: 01722-332158 Fax: 01722-413242
WWW: www.balh.co.uk The BALH each year commissions a distinguished academic figure to deliver the Phillimore Lecture, in London, based on current research by the presentation of The Local History Awards. There is also a Regional Conference each year, Seminars with University
British Deaf History Society
288 Bedfont Lane, Feltham, TW14 9NU
Email: bdhs@iconic.demon.co.uk
Brewery History Society
Manor Side East, Mill Lane, Byfleet, West Byfleet, KT14 7RS
Email: jsechiari@rmcbp.co.uk WWW: www.breweryhistory.com
Do not have information on publicans. Contact Pub History Society
British Records Association
40 Northampton Road, London, EC1R 0HB Tel: (020) 7833 0428 Fax: (020) 7833 0416 Email: britrecassoc@hotmail.com
WWW: www.hmc.gov.uk/bra, The BRA brings together everyone interested in archives;owners, custodians, users. It publishes, informs, lobbies and plays an active part in the work of preserving records.
British Records Society,
Stone Barn Farm, Sutherland Road, Longsdon, ST9 9QD Tel: 01782 385446 Tel: 01538 385024
Email: carolyn@cs.keele.ac.uk britishrecordsociety@hotmail.com
WWW: www.britishrecordsociety.org.uk
British Society for Sports History
Dept of Sports & Science, John Moore's University, Byrom Street, Liverpool, L3 3AF
Congregational History Circle
The Flat, Trinity Congregational Church, St Matthew's Road, London, SW2 1NF
The Costume Society
St Paul's House, 8 Warwick Road, London EC4P 4BN
Cross & Cockade International - The First World War Aviation Historical Society, 5 Cave Drive, Downend, Bristol, BS16 2TL WWW: www.crossandcockade.com
Current Archaeology, 9 Nassington Road, London, NW3 2TX
Tel: (020) 7435-7517 Fax: (020) 7916-2405
Email: editor@archaeology.co.uk WWW: http://www.archaeology.co.uk
The English Place Name Society
c/o School of English Studies, University of Nottingham, Nottingham, NG7 2RD Tel: 0115 951 5919 Fax: 0115 951 5924
Email: janet.rudkin@nottingham.ac.uk
WWW: www.nottingham.ac.uk/english/
Family & Community Historical Society
73 Derby Road, Cromford, Matlock, DE4 3RP
WWW: www.fachrs.com
Friends Historical Society
Friends House, 173-177 Euston Road, London, NW1 2BJ
Historical Fellowship
69 Leyspring Road, Leytonstone, London, E11 3BP
The Historical Association (Local History)
59A Kennington Park Road, London, SE11 4JH Tel: (020) 7735-3901 Fax: (020) 7582 4989 Email: enquiry@history.org.uk
WWW: http://www..history.org.uk
Historical Medical Equipment Society, 8 Albion Mews, Apsley, HP3 9QZ Email: hmes@antiageing.freeserve.co.uk,
The Hugenot Society of Great Britain & Ireland
Hugenot Library University College, Gower Street, London, WC1E 6BT Tel: 020 7679 7094 Fax: 020 8993 4835
Email: s.massil@ucl.ac.uk
WWW: www.ucl.ac.uk/ucl-info/divisions/library/huguenot.htm
Labour Heritage
18 Ridge Road, Mitcham, CR4 2EY Tel: 020 86402019
Email: agenda870@aol.com:

Legion of Frontiersmen of Commonwealth
4 Edwards Road, Belvedere, DA17 5AL
Local Studies Group of the Library Association
25 Bromford Gardens, Edgbaston, Birmingham, B15 3XD Tel: 0121 454 0935 Fax: 0121 454 7330
Email: prthomaspdt@aol.com
Local Population Studies Society
78 Harlow Terrace, Harrogate, HG2 0PN Tel: 01423-560429
Fax: 01423-560429 Email: sir_david_cooke@compuserve.com
WWW: home.att.net/~jkbfa
Mercia Cinema Society
5 Arcadia Avenue, Chester le Street, DH3 3UH
Military Historical Society
Court Hill Farm, Potterne, Devizes, SN10 5PN Tel: 01980 615689 Tel: 01380 723371 Evenings Fax: 01980 618746
Museum of the Royal Pharmaceutical Society
Museum of the Royal Pharmaceutical Society, 1 Lambeth High Street, London, SE1 7JN Tel: (020) 7572 2210 Email: museum@rpsgb.org.uk WWW: http://www.rpsgb.org.uk, Records of pharmacists from 1841 Research fee charged £20 per person or premises researched to Non members of the Society, £10 per person or premises researched for members(Genealogical Enquiries) Enquirers may visit and undertake research themselves by
Open University History Society
111 Coleshill Drive, Chapel End, Nuneaton, CV10 0PG
Tel: (024) 76397668
Society of Antiquaries
Burlington House, Piccadilly, London, W1J 0BE Tel: (020) 7479 7080 Fax: (020) 7287 6967 Email: admin£sal.org.uk
WWW: www.sal.org.uk
Society of Brushmakers Descendants Family History Society
13 Ashworth Place, Church Langley, CM17 9PU
Tel: 01279-629392 Email: s.b.d@lineone.net
WWW: http://www.brushmakers.com
Social History of Learning Disability Research Group,
School of Health & Social Welfare, Open University, Milton Keynes, MK7 6AA
Society of Jewellery Historians
Department of Scientific Research, The British Museum, Great Russell St, London, WC1B 3DG Tel: (020) 7323 8768 Tel: (020) 7323 8224 Fax: (020) 7323 8118
Email: jwallace@thebritishmuseum.ac.uk
WWW: www.thebritishmuseum.ac.uk
Society for Name Studies in Britain & Ireland
22 Peel Park Avenue, Clitheroe, BB7 1ET Tel: 01200-423771
Fax: 01200-423771
Strict Baptist Historical Society
38 Frenchs Avenue, Dunstable, LU6 1BH Tel: 01582 602242
Email: kdix@sbhs.freeserve.co.uk
WWW: www.strictbaptisthistory.org.uk
Royal Geographical Society
1 Kensington Gore, London, SW7 2AR Tel: 020 7291 3001
Fax: 020 7591 3001
Royal Photographic Society Historical Group
7A Cotswold Road, Belmont, Sutton, SM2 5NG
Tel: (020) 8643 2743
Royal Society, 6 Carlton House Terrace, London, SW1Y 5AG
Tel: 020 7451 2606 Fax: 020 7930 2170
Email: library@royalsoc.ac.uk WWW: www.royalsoc.ac.uk
Tennyson Society
Central Library, Free School Lane, Lincoln, LN2 1EZ Tel: 01522-552862 Fax: 01522-552858
Email: linnet@lincolnshire.gov.uk,
Unitarian Historical Society
6 Ventnor Terrace, Edinburgh, EH9 2BL
Upholstery Old and New
7 Selly Avenue, Selly Park, Birmingham, B29 7PE
Vernacular Architecture Group
Ashley, Willows Green, Chelmsford, CM3 1QD
Tel: 01245 361408
Victorian Military Society
PO Box 5837, Newbury, RG14 7JF Tel: 01635 48628 Email: beverley20@tesco.net WWW: www.vms.org.uk, The leading Society covering military history of all nations and races from 1837 to 1914
Volunteer Corps of Frontiersmen
Archangels' Rest, 26 Dark Lane, Witney, OX8 5LE
The Veterinary History Society
608 Warwick Road, Solihull, B91 1AA
The Waterways Trust
The National Waterways Museum, Llanthony Warehouse, Gloucester Docks, Gloucester, GL1 2EH Tel: 01452 318053

Avon
Avon Local History Association
4 Dalkeith Avenue, Kingswood, Bristol, BS15 1HH
Tel: 0117 967 1362
Bristol & Avon Archaeological Society
3 Priory Avenue, Westbury on Trym, Bristol, BS9 4DA
Tel: 0117 9620161 (evenings)

Bath & NE Somerset
Avon Local History Association
4 Dalkeith Avenue, Kingswood, Bristol, BS15 1HH
Tel: 0117 967 1362

Bedfordshire
Ampthill & District Archaeological and Local History
14 Glebe Avenue, Flitwick, Bedford, MK45 1HS Tel: 01525
712778 Email: petwood@waitrose.com
WWW: www.museums.bedfordshire.gov.uk/localgroups/ampthill2/html
Ampthill & District Preservation Society
Seventh House, 43 Park Hill, Ampthill, MK45 2LP
Ampthill History Forum
10 Mendham Way, Clophill, Bedford, MK45 4AL
Email: forum@ampthillhistory.co.uk
WWW: www.ampthillhistory.co.uk
Bedfordshire Archaeological and Local History Society
7 Lely Close, Bedford, MK41 7LS Tel: 01234 365095
WWW: www.museums.bedfordshire.gov.uk/localgroups
Bedfordshire Local History Association
29 George Street, Maulden, Bedford, MK45 2DF Tel:
1525633029
Bedfordshire Local History Soiciety
14 Glebe Avenue, Flitwick, MK45 1HS
Bedfordshire Historical Record Society
50 Shefford Road, Meppershall, SG17 5LL Tel: 01462 813363
Biggleswade History Society
6 Pine Close, Biggleswade, SG18 QEF
Caddington Local History Group
98 Mancroft Road, Caddington, Nr. Luton, LUL 4EN
Carlton & Chellington Historical Society
3 High Street, Carlton, MK43 7JX
Dunstable & District Local History Society
12 Friars Walk, Dunstable, LU6 3JA Tel: 01525 659955
Dunstable Historic and Heritage Studies
184 West Street, Dunstable, LU6 1 NX Tel: 01582 609018
Harlington Heritage Trust
2 Shepherds Close, Harlington, Near Dunstable, LU5 6NR
Knoll History Projext
32 Ashburnham Road, Ampthill, MK45 2RH
Leighton-Linslade Heritage Display Society
25 Rothschild Road, Linslade, Leighton Buzzard, LU7 7SY
Luton & District Historical Society
22 Homerton Rd, Luton, LU3 2UL Tel: 01582 584367
Toddington Historical Society
17 Alma Farm Road, Toddington, Dunstable, LU5 6BG Tel:
01525 873825 Email: dgwhitfield@netscape.co.uk
Wrestlingworth History Society
Memorial Hall, Church Lane, Wrestlingworth, SG19 2EJ

Berkshire
Berkshire Industrial Archaeological Group
6 Harefield Close, Winnersh, Wokingham, RG41 5NP
Tel: 0118 978 5234
Berkshire Local History Association
37 Heron Island, Caversham, Reading, RG4 8DQ Tel: 0118 947
7345 Fax: 0118 947 7345
Email: heronisland@netscapeonline.co.uk
Bracknell & District Historical Society
16 Harcourt Road, East Hampstead, Bracknell, RG12 7JD
Tel: 01344 640341
Berkshire Record Society
Berkshire Record Office, 9 Coley Avenue, Reading, RG1 6AF
Tel: 0118-901-5130 Fax: 0118-901-5131
Email: peter.durrant@reading.gov.uk, Berkshire Record Society publishes
editions of historic documents (including many with family history interest) relating to the
ancient County of Berkshire
Chiltern Heraldry Group
Magpie Cottage, Pondwood Lane, Shottesbrooke, SL6 3SS Tel:
0118 934 3698
Cox Green Local History Group
29 Bissley Drive, Maidenhead, SL6 3UX Tel: 01628 823890
Goring & Streatley Local History Society
45 Springhill Road, Goring On Thames, Reading, RG8 OBY
Tel: 01491 872625

Heraldry Society
PO Box 32, Maidenhead, SL6 3FD Tel: 0118-932-0210
Fax: 0118 932 0210 Email: heraldry-society@cwcom.net
Hungerford Historical Association
Hungerford, RG17
Maidenhead Archealogical & Historical Society
70 Lambourne Drive, Maidenhead, SL6 3HG
Middle Thames Archaeological & Historical Society
1 Saffron Close, Datchet, Slough, SL3 9DU Tel: 01753 543636
Newbury District Field Club
Glenwood, 30 Monkswood Close, Newbury, RG14 6NS
Tel: 01635 43554
Thatcham Historical Society, Hope Cottage, Stoney Lane,
Ashmore Green, Thatcham, RG18 9HD
Wargrave Local History Society
6 East View Close, Wargrave, RG10 8BJ Tel: 0118 940 3121
Email: Email:history@wargrave.net
WWW: www.wargrave.net/history

Bristol
Alveston Local History Society
6 Hazel Gardens, Alveston, BS35 3RD Tel: 01454 43881
Avon Local History Association
4 Dalkeith Avenue, Kingswood, Bristol, BS15 1HH
Tel: 0117 967 1362
Bristol & Avon Archaeological Society
3 Priory Avenue, Westbury on Trym, Bristol, BS9 4DA
Tel: 0117 9620161 (evenings)
Bristol and Gloucestershire Archaeological Society
22 Beaumont Road, Gloucester, GL2 0EJ Tel: 01452 302610
Email: david_j_h.smith@virgin.net
WWW: http://www.bgas.org.uk,
Calandar of Apprentice Registers of City of Gloucester 1595-1700 published October 2001
Bristol Records Society
Department of Historical Studies, University of Bristol, 13-15
Woodland Road, Bristol, BS8 1TB
Congresbury History Group
Venusmead, 36 Venus Street, Congresbury, Bristol, BS49 5EZ
Tel: 01934 834780
Email: rogerhards-venusmead.breathemail.net
Downend Local History Society
141 Overndale Road, Downend, Bristol, B516 2RN
Keynsham & Saltford Local History Society
Keynsham, Bristol, BS31 Full address not provided
The West of England Costume Society
4 Church Lane, Long Aston, Nr. Bristol, BS41 9LU Tel: 01275-
543564 Fax: 01275-543564
Whitchurch Local History Society
62 Nailsea Park, Nailsea, Bristol, B519 1BB
Yatton Local History Society
27 Henley Park, Yatton, Bristol, BS49 4JH Tel: 01934 832575

Birmingham
Alvechurch Historical Society
Bearhill House, Alvechurch, Birmingham, B48 7JX
Tel: 0121 445 2222
Birmingham & District Local History Association
112 Brandwood Road, Kings Heath, Birmingham, B14 6BX
Tel: 0121-444-7470
Birmingham Canal Navigation's Society
37 Chestnut Close, Handsacre, Rugeley, WS15 4TH
Birmingham War Research Society
43 Norfolk Place, Kings Norton, Birmingham, B30 3LB
Tel: 0121-459-9008 Fax: 0121 459 8128
Quinton Local History Society
15 Worlds End Avenue, Quinton, Birmingham, B32 1JF
Tel: 0121-422-1792 Fax: 0121 422 1792
Email: qlhs@bjtaylor.fsnet.co.uk WWW: www.qlhs.org.uk
Small Heath Local History Society
381 St Benedicts Road, Small Heath, Birmingham, B10 9ND
Wythall Local History Society
64 Meadow Road, Wythall, Birmingham, B47 6EQ
Email: val@wythallhistory.co.uk WWW: www.wythallhistory.co.uk

Buckinghamshire
Buckinghamshire Archaeological Society
County Museum, Church Street, Aylesbury, HP20 2QP
Tel: 01269 678114
Buckinghamshire Record Society
County Record Office, County Hall, Aylesbury, HP20 1UU Tel:
01296-303013 Fax: 01296-382274
Chesham Bois One-Place Study
70 Chestnut Lane, Amersham, HP6 6EH Tel: 01494 726103 Fax:
01494 729358 Email: cdjmills@hotmail.com

Chesham Society
54 Church Street, Chesham, HP5 IHY
Chess Valley Archealogical & Historical Society
16 Chapmans Crescent, Chesham, NP5 2QU
Pitstone Local History Society
Vicarage Road, Pitstone, Nr Ivinghoe Tel: 01582 605464
WWW: http://website.lineone.net/~pitstonemus
Princes Risborough Area Heritage Society
Martin's Close, 11 Wycombe Road, Princes Risborough, HP27
0EE Tel: 01844 343004 Fax: 01844 273142
Email: sandymac@risboro35.freeserve.co.uk

Cambridgeshire
Cambridgeshire Local History Society
1A Archers Close, Swaffham Bulbeck, Cambridge, CB5 0NG
Cambridge Antiquarian Society
PO Box 376, 96 Mill Lane, Impington, Cambridge , CB4 9HS
Tel: 01223 502974 Email: liz-allan@hotmail.com
Cambridgeshire Archaeology
Castle Court, Shire Hall, Cambridge, CB3 0AP
Tel: 01223 717312 Fax: 01223 362425
Cambridgeshire Record Society
5 Bateman Street, Cambridge, CB2 1NB Tel: 01223 364706
Email: francesca@bateman5.demon.co.uk
Cambridge Group for History of Population and Social History
27 Trumpington Street, Cambridge, CB2 1QA
Hemingfords Local History Society
8 Weir Close, Hemingford Grey, Huntingdon, PE28 9EJ
Tel: 01480 464843 Email: hemlocks@hotmail.com
Huntingdonshire Local History Society
2 Croftfield Road, Godmanchester, PE29 2ED
Tel: 01480 411202
Houghton & Wyton Local History Society
Church View, Chapel Lane, Houghton, Huntingdon, PE28 2AY
Tel: 01480 469376 Email: gerry.feake@one-name.org
Oundle Historical Society, 13 Lime Avenue, Oundle,
Peterborough, PE8 4PT Tel: Tel:
Sawston Village History Society
21 Westmoor Avenue, Sawston, Cambridge, CB2 4BU
Tel: 01223 833475
Upwood & Raveley History Group
The Old Post Office, 71-73 High Street, Upwood, Huntingdon,
PE17 1QE

Cheshire
Altrincham History Society
10 Willoughby Close, Sale, M33 6PJ
Ashton & Sale History Society
Tralawney House, 78 School Road, Sale, M33 7XB
Tel: 0161 9692795
Bowdon History Society
5 Pinewood, Bowdon, Altrincham, WA14 3JQ
Tel: 0161 928 8975
Chester Archaeological Society
Grosvenor Museum, 27 Grosvenor Street, Chester, CH1 2DD
Tel: 01244 402028 Fax: 01244 347522
Email: p.carrington@chestercc.gov.uk
WWW: http://www.morpork.u-net.com
Cheshire Heraldry Society
24 Malvern Close, Congleton, CW12 4PD
Cheshire Local History Association
Cheshire Record Office, Duke Street, Chester, CH1 1RL
Tel: 01224 602559 Tel: 01244 603812
Email;recordoffice@cheshire.gov.uk
Christleton Local History Society
25 Croft Close, Rowton, CH3 7QQ Tel: 01244 332410
Congleton History Society
48 Harvey Road Road, Congleton, CWI2 2DH
Tel: 01260 278757 Email: awill0909@aol.com
County Palatine of Chester Local History Committee,
Department of History, University College Chester, Cheveney
Road, Chester, CH1 4BJ
Disley Local History Society
5 Hilton Road, Disley, SK12 2JU Fax: 01663 764910
Historic Society of Lancashire & Cheshire
East Wing Flat, Arley Hall, Northwich, CW9 6NA
Tel: 01565 777231 Fax: 01565 777465
Lancashire & Cheshire Antiquarian Society
59 Malmesbury Road, Cheadle Hulme, SK8 7QL Tel: 0161 439
7202 Email: morris.garrett@lineone.net
Lawton Heritage Society
9 Woodgate Avenue, Church Lawton, Stoke on Trent, ST7 3EF
Tel: 01270-878386 Email: dmcall12280@aol.com
Lymm Local History Society
2 Statham Drive, Lymm, WA13 9NW

Macclesfield Historical Society
42 Tytherington Drive, Macclesfield, SK10 2HJ
Tel: 01625 420250
Northwich & District Heritage Society
13 Woodlands Road, Hartford, Northwich, CW8 1NS
Poynton Local History Society
6 Easby Close, Poynton, SK12 1YG
South Cheshire Family History Society incorporating S E Cheshire Local Studies Group
PO Box 1990, Crewe, CW2 6FF WWW: www.scfhs.org.uk
Stockport Historical Society
59 Malmesbury Road, Cheadle Hulme, Stockport, SK8 7QL
Tel: 0161 439 7202
Weaverham History Society
Ashdown, Sandy Lane, Weaverham, Northwich, CW8 3PX
Tel: 01606 852252 Email: jg-davies@lineone.net
Wilmslow Historical Society
4 Campden Way, Handforth, Wilmslow, SK9 3JA
Tel: 01625 529381

Cleveland
Cleveland & Teesside Local History Society
150 Oxford Road, Linthorpe, Middlesbrough, TS5 5EL, ,
Membership Secretary: 14 Oldford Crescent, Acklam,
Middlesbrough TS5 7EH
North-East England History Institute (NEEHI)
Department of History University of Durham, 43 North Bailey,
Durham, DH1 3EX Tel: 0191-374-2004 Fax: 0191-374-4754
Email: m.a.mcallister@durham.ac.uk
WWW: http://www.durham.ac.uk/eehi.history/homepage.htm
The Steel Bonnets - Re-enactment Society
12 Marske Road, Saltburn by the Sea, TS12 1PZ Tel: 01287
625744

Cornwall
Bodmin Local History Group
1 Lanhydrock View, Bodmin, PL31 1BG
Cornwall Association of Local Historians
St Clement's Cottage, Coldrinnick Drive, Duloe, Liskeard, TR19
6SJ Tel: 01503 220947Email: anne@coldrinnic.freeserve.co.uk,
Cornwall Family History Society
5 Victoria Square, Truro, TR1 2RS Tel: 01872-264044 Fax:
Email: secretary@cornwallfhs.com WWW: http://www.cornwallfhs.com
The Devon & Cornwall Record Society
7 The Close, Exeter, EX1 1EZ
Fal Family History Group
4 Downside Close, Treloggan, Newquay, TR7 2TD
Courtney Library & Cornish History Research Centre
Royal Cornwall Museum, River Street, Truro, TR1 2SJ Tel:
01872 272205 Fax: 01872 240514
Email: RIC@royal-cornwall-museum.freeserve.co.uk
WWW: www.cornwall-online.co.uk/ric

County Durham
Architectural & Archaeological Society of Durham & Northumberland
Brancepeth Castle, Brancepeth, DH7 8DF Tel: 0191-378 3383
Email: Email: steve_cousins@yahoo.co.uk
The Derwentdale Local History Society
36 Roger Street, Blackhill, Consett, DH8 5SX
Durham County Local History Society
3 Briardene, Margery Lane, Durham, DH1 4QU Tel: 0191 386 1500
Durham Victoria County History Trust
Redesdale, The Oval, North Crescent, Durham, DH1 4NE
Tel: 0191 384 8305 WWW: www.durhampast.net, The Victoria History
of the Counties of England c/o Institute of Historical Research, University of London
Elvet Local & Family History Groups
37 Hallgarth Street, Durham, DH1 3AT Tel: 0191-386-
4098Email: Turnstone-Ventures@durham-city.freeserve.co.uk
Monkwearmouth Local History Group
75 Escallond Drive, Dalton Heights, Seaham, SR7 8JZ
Tow Law History Society, 27 Attleee Estate, Tow Law, DL13
4LG Tel: 01388-730056 Email: RonaldStorey@btinternet.co.uk
WWW: www.historysociety.org.uk
Teesdale Heritage Group
Teesdale Historical Research, The Plains, Aukside, Middleton in
Teesdale, DL12 0QY Tel: 01833 640450
Lanchester Local History Society, 11 St Margaret's Drive,
Tanfield Village, Stanley, DH9 9QW Tel: 01207-236634
Email: jstl@supanet.com
Wheatley Hill History Club
Broadmeadows, Durham Road, Wheatley Hill, DH6 3LJ Tel:
01429 820813 Tel: Mobile 0781 112387
Email: wheathistory@onet.co.uk
WWW: http://www.members.home.net/wheathill/HISTORY/index.htm

Cumbria

Appleby-In-Westmorland Society
67 Glebe Road, Appleby-In-Westmorland, CA16 6EU
Cartmel Peninsula Local History Society
Fairfield, Cartmel, Grange Over Sands, LA11 6PY Tel: 015395 36503
Cumberland and Westmorland Antiquarian and Archaeological Society
2 High Tenterfell, Kendal, LA9 4PG Tel: 01539 773542
Email: info@cwaas.org.uk WWW: www.cwaas.org.uk
Cumbria Industrial History Society
Coomara, Carleton, Carlisle, CA4 0BU Tel: 01228-537379
Fax: 01228-596986 Email: gbrooksvet@netscapeonline.co.uk,
Cumbria Local History Federation
10 Mill Cottages, Distington, Workington, CA14 5SR
Tel: 01946 833060 Fax: 01946 833060
Email: gillyfoster@cumbrialocalhistory.org.uk
WWW: www.cumbrialocalhistory.org.uk
Cartmel & District Local History Society
1 Barton House, Kents Bank Road, Grange-Over-Sands, LA11 7HD
Distington Family & Loacl History Society
10 Mill Cottages, Distington, Workington, CA14 5SR Tel: 01946
833060Email: gillyfoster@distington.idps.co.uk
WWW: www.distington.idps.co.uk
Friends of Cumbria Archives
The Barn, Parsonby, Aspatria, Wigton, CA7 2DE Tel: 01697
320053 Email: john@jounmary.freeserve.co.uk
Staveley and District History Society
1 Oakland, Staveley, Kendal, LA8 9JE Tel: 01539 821194
Email: Jpatdball@aol.com
Sedbergh & District History Society
c/o 27a Main Street, Sedbergh, LA10 5AD Tel: 015396 20504
Email: history@sedberghcomoff.force9.co.uk
Upper Eden History Society
Yew Tree House, Winton, Kirby Stephen, CA17 4HS

Derbyshire

Allestree Local Studies Group
30 Kingsley Road, Allestree, Derby, DE22 2JH
Arkwright Society
Cromford Mill, Mill Lane, Cromford, DE4 3RQ Tel: 01629
823256 Fax: 01629 823256 Email: info@cromfordmill.co.uk
WWW: www.cromfordmill.co.uk
Chesterfield & District Local History Society
Melbourne House, 130 Station Road, Bimington, Chesterfield,
S43 1LU Tel: 01246 620266
Derbyshire Archaeological Society
2 The Watermeadows, Swarkestone, Derby, DE73 1JA
Tel: 01332 704148 Email: barbarafoster@talk21.com
WWW: www.DerbyshireAS.org.uk
Derby & District Local History Forum
230 Woodbridge Close, Chellaston, Derby, DE73 1QW
Derbyshire Local History Societies Network
Derbyshire Record Office, Libraries & Heritage Dept, County
Hall, Matlock, DE4 3AG Tel: 01629-580000-ext-3520-1
Fax: 01629-57611 Email: recordoffice@derbyshire.gov.uk
WWW: www.derbyshire.gov.uk
Derbyshire Record Society
57 New Road, Wingerworth, Chesterfield, S42 6UJ Tel: 01246
231024 Email: neapen@aol.com
WWW: www.merton.dircon.co.uk/drshome.htm
Holymoorside and District History Society
Mrs Margaret Richmond, 12 Brook Close, Holymoorside,
Chesterfield, S42 7HB Tel: 01246 566799
WWW: www.holymoorsidehistsoc.org.uk
Ilkeston & District Local History Society
c/o 28 Kensington, Ilkeston, DE7 5NZ
New Mills Local History Society
High Point, Cote Lane, Hayfield, High Peak, SK23
Tel: 01663-742814 Fax: 01663 742814
Old Dronfield Society
2 Gosforth Close, Dronfield, S18 INT

Devon

Chagford Local History Society
Footaway, Westcott, Chagford, Newton Abbott, TQ13 8JF
Tel: 01647 433698 Email: cjbaker@jetdash.freeserve.co.uk
The Devon & Cornwall Record Society
7 The Close, Exeter, EX1 1EZ
WWW: www.gendex.com/users/branscombe/genuki/devon.htm
The Devon History Society
c/o 82 Hawkins Avenue, Torquay, TQ2 6ES Tel: 01803 613336
Holbeton Yealmpton Brixton Society
32 Cherry Tree Drive, Brixton, Plymouth, PL8 2DD

Lashbrook One-Place Study
70 Chestnut Lane, Amersham, HP6 6EH Tel: 01494 726103 Fax:
01494 729358 Email: cdjmills@hotmail.com, Covers Bradford,
Talaton, Thornbury in Devon and Shiplake, Oxfordshire see also
Lashbrook One-Name Study (Under Family History Societies)
Modbury Local History Society
Cawte Cottage, Brounston Street, Modbury, PL21 0RH
Moretonhampstead History Society
School House, Moreton, Hampstead, TQ13 8NX
Newton Tracey & District Local History Society
Home Park, Lovacott , Newton Tracey, Barnstaple, EX31 3PY
Ogwell History Society
East Ogwell, Newton Abbott, TQI2 6AR
The Old Plymouth Society
625 Budshead Road, Whiteleigh, Plymouth, PL5 4DW
Tavistock & District Local History Society
18 Heather Close, Tavistock, PL19 9QS Tel: 01822 615211
Thorverton & District History Society
Ferndale, Thorverton, Exeter, EX5 5NG Tel: 01392 860932
Wembury Amenity Society
5 Cross Park Road, Wembury, Plymouth, PL9 0EU
Yelverton & District Local History Society
4 The Coach House, Grenofen, Tavistock, PL19 9ES

Dorset

Bournemouth Local Studies Group
6 Sunningdale, Fairway Drive, Christchurch, BH23 1JY Tel:
01202 485903 Fax: Email: mbhall@tinyonline.co.uk
Dorchester Association For Research into Local History
68 Maiden Castle Road, Dorchester, DT1 2ES
Dorset Natural History & Archaeological Society
Dorset County Museum, High West Street, Dorchester, DT1
1XA Tel: 01305 262735 Fax: 01305 257180
Dorset Record Society
Dorset County Museum, High West Street, Dorchester, DT1
1XA Tel: 01305-262735
William Barnes Society
Pippins, Winterborne Zelston, Blandford Forum, DT1 1 9EU,
William Barnes is primarily (but not exclusively) a Dorest Dialect Poet

Durham - see County Durham

Essex

Barking Historical Society
11 Coulson Close, Dagenham, RM8 1TY Tel: (020) 8590 9694
Email: pgibbs9@tesco.net
Billericay Archaeological and Historical Society
24 Belgrave Road, Billericay, CM12 1TX Tel: 01277 658989,
Group within Society recording MIs at Churches in Essex
Brentwood & District Historical Society
51 Hartswood Road, Brentwood, CM14 5AG
Tel: 01277 221637
Burnham & District Local History & Archealogical Society
The Museum, The Quay, Burnham On Crouch, CM0 8AS
Colchester Archaeological Group
172 Lexden Road, Colchester, CO3 4BZ Tel: 01206 575081
The Colne Smack Preservation Society
76 New Street, Brightlingsea, CO7 0DD Tel: 01206 304768
WWW: www.colne-smack-preservation.rest.org.uk
Dunmow & District Historical and Literary Society
18 The Poplars, Great Dunmow, CM6 2JA Tel: 01371 872496
East London History Society
13 Three Crowns Road, Colchester, CO4 5AD
Essex Archaeological & Historical Congress
1 Church Cottages, Witham Road, Longford, Maldon, CM9 4JT
Tel: 01621 853175 Email: essexahc@aol.com
Essex Historic Buildings Group
2 Eton Walk, North Shoebury, SS3 8TB Tel: 01702 216586
Email: challett@barclays.net WWW: www.hadfield.demon.co.uk
Essex Society for Archeaology & History
2 Landview Gardens, Ongar, CM5 9EQ Tel: 1277363106
Email: family@leachies.freeserve.co.uk
WWW: www.leachies.freeserve.co.uk
Friends of Historic Essex
11 Milligans Chase, Galleywood, Chelmsford, CM2 8QD Tel:
01245 431113 Fax: 01245 257365 Email:
geraldine.willden@essexcc.gov.uk
Friends of The Hospital Chapel
174 Aldborough Road South, Seven Kings, Ilford, IG3 8HF Tel:
(020) 8590 9972 Fax: (020) 8590 0366
Friends of Thomas Plume's Library
The Old Vicarage, Great Totham, Maldon, CM9 8NP Tel: 01621
892261, No facilities for enquiries and no material relevant to
Genealogists

Halstead & District Local History Society
Magnolia, 3 Monklands Court, Halstead, C09 1AB
(HEARS) Herts & Essex Architectural Research Society
4 Nelmes Way, Hornchurch, RM11 2QZ Tel: 01708 473646
Email: kpolrm11@aol.com
High Country History Group
Repentance Cottage, Drapers Corner, Greensted, Ongar, CM5
9LS Tel: 01277 364305 Email: rob.brooks@virgin.net, Covers
the rural area of S W Ongar being the parishes of Greensted,
Stanford Rivers, Stapleford Tawney and Theydon Mount
Ingatestone & Fryerning Historical and Archaeological Soc
36 Pine Close, Ingatestone, CM4 9EG Tel: 01277 354001
Loughton & District Historical Society
97 Staples Road, Loughton, IG10 1HR Tel: (020) 8508 0776,
This Society keeps no records of Genealogical interest - any
material given to the Society is passed to Essex Record Office
Maldon Society
15 Regency Court, Heybridge, Maldon, CM9 4EJ
Nazeing History Workshop
16 Shooters Drive, Nazeing, EN9 2QD Tel: 01992 893264
Newham History Society
52 Eastbourne Road, East Ham, London E4 6AT
Romford & District Historical
5 Rosemary Avenue, Romford, RM1 4HB Tel: 01708 730150
Fax: 01708 730150,
Thurrock Local History Society
13 Rosedale Road, Little Thurrock, Grays, RM17 6AD Tel:
01375 377746 Email: tcvs.tc@gtnet.gov.uk
Thurrock Heritage Forum
c/o Thurrock Museum, Ossett Road, Grays, RM17 5DX
Waltham Abbey Historical Society
29 Hanover Court, Quaker Lane, Waltham Abbey, EN9 1HR
Tel: 01992 716830
Walthamstow Historical Society
173 Brettenham Road, Walthamstow, London, E17 5AX Tel:
(020) 8523 2399 Fax: (020) 8523 2399
Wanstead Historical Society
28 Howard Road, Ilford, IG1 2EX
Westcliff High School for Girls Society
Kenilworth Gardens, Westcliff on Sea, SS0 0BS
Witham History Group
35 The Avenue, Witham, CM8 2DN Tel: 01376 512566
Woodford Historical Society
2 Glen Rise, Woodford Green, IG8 0AN

Gloucestershire
Gloucestershire County Local History Committee
Gloucestershire RCC, Community House, 15 College Green,
Gloucester, GL1 2LZ Tel: 01452-309783 Fax: 01452-528493
Email: glosrcc@grcc.org.uk
Blakeney Area Historical Society
Hillside, Morston Road, Blakeney, NR25 7BG
Tel: 01263-740589
Bristol and Gloucestershire Archaeological Society
22 Beaumont Road, Gloucester, GL2 0EJ Tel: 01452 302610
Email: david_j_h.smith@virgin.net
WWW: http://www.bgas.org.uk, Calandar of Apprentice Registers
of City of Gloucester 1595-1700 (October 2001)
Campden and District Hiostorical & Archaeological Society
14 Pear Tree Close, Chipping Campden, GL55 6DB
Charlton Kings Local History Society
19 Lyefield Road West, Charlton Kings, Cheltenham, GL53 8EZ
Tel: 01242 524258
Cheltenham Local History Society
39 Tivoli Road, Cheltenham, GL50 2TD
Cirencester Archaeological and Historical Society
Corinium Museum, Park Street, Cirencester, GL7 2BX
Forest of Dean Local History Society
120 Farmers Close, Witney, OX28 1NR Tel: 01993 773927
Email: iapope@waitrose.com WWW: www.forestofdeanhistory.co.uk
Frenchay Tuckett Society and Local History Museum
247 Frenchay Park Road, Frenchay, BS16 ILG Tel: 0117 956
9324 Email: Email: raybulmer@compuserve.com
WWW: http://ourworld.compuserve.com/homepages/raybutler
Friends of Gloucestershire Archives
17 Estcourt Road, Gloucester, GL13LU Tel: 01452 528930
Email: patricia.bath@talk21.com
Leckhampton Local History Society
15 Arden Road, Leckhampton, Cheltenham, GL53 OHG
WWW: www.geocities.com/llhsgl53
Moreton-In-Marsh & District Local History Society
Chapel Place, Longborough, Moreton-In-Marsh, GL56 OQR
Tel: 01451 830531
Newent Local History Society, Arron, Ross Road, Newent,
GL18 1BE Tel: 01531 821398

Painswick Local History Society
Canton House, New Street, Painswick, GL6 6XH Tel: 01452
812419 Fax: 01452 812419
Stroud Civic Society
Blakeford House, Broad Street, Kings Stanley, Stonehouse,
GL10 3PN Tel: Tel:
Stroud Local History Society
Stonehatch, Oakridge Lynch, Stroud, GL6 7NR Tel: 01285
760460 Email: john@loosleyj.freeserve.co.uk
Swindon Village Society
3 Swindon Hall, Swindon Village, Cheltenham, GL51 9QR Tel:
01242 521723
Tewkesbury Historical Society
20 Moulder Road, Tewkesbury, GL20 8ED Tel: 01684 297871

Gloucestershire - South
Avon Local History Association
4 Dalkeith Avenue, Kingswood, Bristol, BS15 1HH Tel: 0117
967 1362
Marshfield & District Local History Society
Garth Cottage, Weir Lane, Marshfield, Chippenham, SN14 8NB
Tel: 01225 891 829

Hampshire
Aldershot Historical and Archaeological Society
10 Brockenhurst Road, Aldershot, GU11 3HH Tel: 01252 26589
Andover History and Archaeology Society
140 Weyhill Road, Andover, SPIO 3BG Tel: 01264 324926
Basingstoke Archaeological and Historical Society
16 Scotney Road, Basingstoke, RG21 5SR Tel: 01256 322090
Email: JTHerring@aol.com
Bishops Waltham Museum Trust
8 Folly Field, Bishop's Waltham, Southampton, S032 1EB
Tel: 01489 894970
Bitterne Local History Society
Heritage Centre, 225 Peartree Avenue, Bitterne, Southampton
Tel: (023) 80444837 Fax: (023) 80444837
Email: sheaf@sheafrs.freeserve.co.uk WWW: www.bitterne.net
Botley & Curdridge Local History Society
38 Bryony Gardens, Horton Heath, Eastleigh, SO50 7PT
Farnham and District Museum Society
Tanyard House, 13a Bridge Square, Farnham, GU9 7QR
Fareham Local History Group
Wood End Lodge, Wood End, Wickham, Fareham, PO17 6JZ
Fleet & Crookham Local History Group
33 Knoll Road, Fleet, GU51 4PT
Fordingbridge Historical Society, 26 Lyster Road, Manor
Park, Fordingbridge, SP6 IQY Tel: 01425 655417
Hampshire Field Club & Archaelogical Soc(Local History),
c/o Hampshire Record Office, Sussex Street, Winchester, SO23 8TH
Or 8 Lynch Hill Park, Whitchurch, RG28 7NF Tel: 01256
893241 Email: jhamdeveson@compuserve.com
WWW: www.fieldclub.hants.org.uk/
Havant Museum
Havant Museum, 56 East Street, Havant, P09 1BS Tel: 023 9245
1155 Fax: 023 9249 8707 Email: musmcp@hants.gov.uk
WWW: www.hants.gov.uk/museums, Also Friends of Havant
Museum - Local History Section Collection open
Tuesday to Saturday 10.00.a.m. to 5.00.p.m.
History of Thursley Society
50 Wyke Lane, Ash, Aldershot, GU12 6EA
Email: norman.ratcliffe@ntlworld.com
WWW: http://home.clara.net/old.norm/Thurslay
Lymington & District Historical Society
Larks Lee, Coxhill Boldre, Near Lymington, 5041 8PS
Lyndhurst Historical Society
13 Northerwood Avenue, Lyndhurst, SO43 7DU
Milford-on-Sea Historical Record Society
New House, New Road, Keyhaven, Lymington, S041 OTN
North East Hampshire Historical and Archaeological Society
36 High View Road, Farnborough, GU14 7PT
Tel: 01252-543023, Email: nehhas@netscape.net
WWW: www.hants.org.uk/nehhas
Parish Register Transcription Society
50 Silvester Road, Waterlooville, PO8 5TL
Email: mail@prtsoc.org.uk WWW: www.prtsoc.org.uk
Somborne & District Society
Forge House, Winchester Road, Kings Somborne, Stockbridge,
S020 6NY Tel: 01794 388742
South of England Costume Society
Borough House, 101 The Borough, Downtown, Salisbury, SP5
3LX Tel: 01725 511649 Fax: 01725 511649 Email:
user@boroughhouse.m2home.co.uk, Enquiries: c/o Sarah
Howard, Hampshire County Museum Service, Chilcomb House,
Chilcomb Lane, Winchester SO23 8RD

Southern Counties Costume Society
173 Abbotstone, Alresford, SO24 9TE
Southampton Local History Forum
Special Collections Library, Civic Centre, Southampton, England
Stubbington & Hillhead History Society
34 Anker Lane, Stubbington, Fareham, PO14 3HE
Tel: 01329 664554
West End Local History Society
20 Orchards Way, West End, Southampton, S030 3FB Tel: 023
8057 5244, Museum at Old Fire Station, High Street, West End
Winchester Historical Association
66 St Cross Road, Winchester, SO23 9PS

Herefordshire
Council for British Archeology - West Midlands
c/o Rowley's House Museum, Barker Street, Shrewsbury, SY1
1QH Tel: 01743 361196 Tel: 01743 358411 Fax: Email:
museums@shrewsbury-atcham.gov.uk WWW:
www.shrewsburymuseums.com www.darwincountry.org
Eardisland Oral History Group
Eardisland, Leominster, HR
Ewyas Harold & District Wea
C/O Hillside, Ewyas Harold, Hereford, HR2 0HA
Tel: 01981 240529
Kington History Society
Kington Library, 64 Bridge Street, Kington, HR5 3BD Tel:
01544 230427 Email: vee.harrison@virgin.net
Leominster Historical Society
Fircroft, Hereford Road, Leominster, HR6 8JU
Tel: 01568 612874
Weobley & District Local History Society and Museum
Weobley Museum, Back Lane, Weobley, HR4 8SG Tel: 01544 340292

Hertfordshire
Abbots Langley Local History Society
80 Abbots Road, Abbots Langley, WD5 0BH
WWW: http://www.allhs.btinternet.co.uk
Black Sheep Research (Machine Breakers, Rioters & Protesters)
4 Quills, Letchworth Garden City, SG6 2RJ Tel: 01462-483706
Email: J_M_Chambers@compuserve.com
Braughing Local History Society
Pantiles, Braughing Friars, Ware, SG11 2NS
Codicote Local History Society
34 Harkness Way, Hitchin, SG4 0QL Tel: 01462 622953
East Herts Archaeological Society
1 Marsh Lane, Stanstead Abbots, Ware, SG12 8HH
Tel: 01920 870664
1st or Grenadier Foot Guards 1803 -1823
39 Chatterton, Letchworth, SG6 2JY Tel: 01462-670918
Email: BJCham2809@aol.com
WWW: http://members.aol.com/BJCham2809/homepage.html
Hertfordshire Archaeological Trust
The Seed Warehouse, Maidenhead Yard, The Wash, Hertford,
SG14 1PX Tel: 01992 558 170 Fax: 01992 553359
Hertfordshire Association for Local History
c/o 64 Marshals Drive, St Albans, AL1 4RF Tel: 01727 856250
Fax: 01727 856250 Email: ClareEllis@compuserve.com
The Harpenden & District Local History Society
The History Centre, 19 Arden Grove, Harpenden, AL5 4SJ
Tel: 01582 713539
Hertfordshire Record Society
119 Winton Drive, Croxley Green, Rickmansworth, WD3 3QS
Tel: 01923-248581 Email: info@hrsociety.org.uk
WWW: www.hrsociety.org.uk
Hertford & Ware Local History Society
10 Hawthorn Close, Hertford, SG14 2DT
Hitchin Historical Society
c/o Hitchin Museum, Paynes Park, Hitchin, SG5 2EQ
Kings Langley Local History & Museum Society
Kings Langley Library, The Nap, Kings Langley, WD4 8ET
Tel: 01923 263205 Tel: 01923 264109
Email: frankdavies4@hotmail.com alan@penwardens.freeserve.co.uk
London Colney Local History Society
51A St Annes Road, London Colney, Nr. St. Albans, AL2 1 PD
North Mymms Local History Society
89 Peplins Way, Brookmans Park, Hatfield, AL9 7UT
Tel: 01707 655970 WWW: www.brookmans.com
Potters Bar and District Historical Society
9 Hill Rise, Potters Bar, EN6 2RX Tel: 01707 657586
Rickmansworth Historical Society
20 West Way, Rickmansworth, WD3 7EN Tel: 01923 774998
Email: geoff@gmsaul.freeserve.co.uk, Search service for
Rickmansworth (old Parish area) - census, baptisms, marriage & burials up to late 1800s

Royston & District Local History Society
8 Chilcourt, Royston, SG8 9DD Tel: 01763 242677
Email: david.allard@ntlworld.com
St. Albans & Herts Architectural & Archaeological Society
24 Rose Walk, St Albans, AL4 9AF Tel: 01727 853204
South West Hertfordshire Archaeological and Historical Soc
29 Horseshoe Lane, Garston, Watford, WD25 0LN
Tel: 01923 672482
Watford and District Industrial History Society
79 Kingswood Road, Garston, Watford, WD25 0EF Tel: 01923
673253
Welwyn Archaeological Society
The Old Rectory, 23 Mill Lane, Welyn, AL6 9EU
Tel: 01438 715300 Fax: 01438 715300
Welwyn & District Local History Society
9 York Way, Welwyn, AL6 9LB Tel: 01438 716415

Hull
Hull Central Library Family and Local History Club
Central Library, Albion Street, Kingston upon Hull, HU1 3TF
Tel: 01482 616828 Fax: 01482 616827
Email: gareth2ukorigins.co.uk WWW: http://www.hullcc.gov.uk/genealogy
Free membership. Meets second Tuesday of every month

Isle of Wight
Isle of Wight Natural History & Archaeological Society
Salisbury Gardens, Dudley Road, Ventnor, PO38 1EJ Tel: 01983
855385
Newchurch Parish History Society
1 Mount Pleasant, Newport Road, Sandown, P036 OLS
ROOTS Family & Parish History
San Fernando, Burnt House Lane, Alverstone, Sandown, P036
0HB Tel: 01983 403060 Email: peters.sanfernando@tesco.net
St. Helens Hist Soc
c/o The Castle, Duver Road, St Helens, Ryde, P033 1XY
Tel: 01983 872164
St Helens Historical Society
Gloddaeth, Westfield Road, St. Helens, Ryde , P033 LUZ

Kent
Ashford Archaeological and Historical Society
9 Wainwright Place, Newtown, Ashford, TN24 0PF
Tel: 01233 631017
Bromley Borough Local History Society
62 Harvest Bak Road, West Wickham, BR4 9DJ
Tel: 020 8462 5002
Canterbury Archaeology Society
Dane Court, Adisham, Canterbury, CT3 3LA
Crayford Manor House Historical and Archaeological Soc
17 Swanton Road, Erith, DA8 1LP Tel: 01322 433480
Croydon Natural History & Scientific Society Ltd
96a Brighton Road, South Croydon, CR2 6AD Tel: (020) 8688
4539 WWW: http://www.croydon.gov.uk/cnhss/
Council for Kentish Archaeology
3 Westholme, Orpington, BR6 0AN
Gravesend Historical Society
58 Vicarage Lane, Chalk, Gravesend, DA12 4TE Tel: 01474 363998
Faversham Society
10-13 Preston St, Faversham, ME13 8NS Tel: 01795 534542
Fax: 01795 533261 Email: faversham@btinternet.com
WWW: http://www.faversham.org
Fawkham & District Historical Society
6 Nuthatch, New Barn, Longfield, DA3 7NS
The Kent Archaeological Society
Three Elms, Woodlands Lane, Shorne, Gravesend, DA12 3HH
Tel: 01474 822280 Email: secretary@kentarchaeology.org.uk
WWW: www.kentarchaeology.org.uk
Kent History Federation
48 Beverley Avenue, Sidcup, DA15 8HE
Maidstone Area Archaeological Group
14 The Quarter, Cranbrook Road, Staplehurst, TN12 0EP
Maidstone Historical Society, 37 Bower Mount Road,
Maidstone, ME16 8AX Tel: 01622 676472
Romney Marsh Research Trust
11 Caledon Terrace, Canterbury, CT1 3JS Tel: 01227 472490
Email: s.m.sweetinburgh@ukc.ac.uk
WWW: www.ukc.ac.uk/mts/rmrt/
Sandwich Local History Society
Clover Rise, 14 Stone Cross Lees, Sandwich, CT13 OBZ Tel:
01304 613476 Email: frankandrews@FreeNet.co.uk
Tonbridge History Society
8 Woodview Crescent, Hildenborough, Tonbridge, TN11 9HD
Tel: 01732 838698 Email: s.broomfield@dial.pipex.com
Wealden Buildings Study Group

64 Pilgrims Way, East Otford, Sevenoaks, TN14 5QW

Lancashire
Aspull and Haigh Historical Society
3 Pennington Close, Aspull, Wigan, WN2 2SP
Tel: 01942 256145
Birkdale & Ainsdale Historical Research Society
20 Blundell Drive, Birkdale, Southport, PR8 4RG
WWW: www.harrop.co.uk/bandahrs
Blackburn Civic Society
20 Tower Road, Blackburn, BB2 5LE Tel: 01254 201399
Burnley Historical Society
66 Langdale Road, Blackburn, BB2 5DW Tel: 01254 201162
Chadderton Historical Society
18 Moreton Street, Chadderton, 0L9 OLP Tel: 0161 652 3930
WWW: http://www.chadderton-hs.freeuk.com
Ewecross History Society
Gruskholme, Bentham, Lancaster, LA2 7AX Tel: 015242 61420
Fleetwood & District Historical
54 The Esplanade, Fleetwood, FY7 6QE
Garstang Historical & Archealogical Society
7 Rivermead Drive, Garstang, PR3 1JJ Tel: 01995 604913
Email: marian.fish@btinternet.com:
Historic Society of Lancashire & Cheshire
East Wing Flat, Arley Hall, Northwich, CW9 6NA Tel: 01565
777231 Fax: 01565 777465
Hyndburn Local History Society
20 Royds Avenue, Accrington, BB5 2LE Tel: 01254 235511
Lancashire Family History and Heraldry Society
15 ChristChurch Street, Accrington, BB5 2LZ
Email: jehuntingdon@08002go.com
WWW: www.lancashire-fhhs.org.uk
Lancashire History
4 Cork Road, Lancaster, LAl 4AJ
Lancashire Local History Federation
298 Blackpool Road, Poulton le Fylde, FY6 7QU
Email: secretary@lancashirehistory.co.uk
WWW: www.lancashirehistory.co.uk
Lancashire Parish Register Society
188 Greenwood Drive, Houghton Green, Warrington, WA2 0EG
Email: tom_obrien@bigfoot.com
WWW: http://www.genuki:org.uk/big/eng/LAN/lprs
Leyland Historical Society
172 Stanifield Lane, Farington; Leyland, Preston, PR5 2QT
Littleborough Historical and Archaeological Society
8 Springfield Avenue, Littleborough, LA15 9JR Tel: 01706 377685
Maghull and Lydiate Local History Society
15 Brendale Avenue, Maghull, Liverpool, L31 7AX
Mourholme Local History Society
173a Main Street, Warton, Carnforth, LA5 9QF Tel: 01524
724110 Email: nt.stobbs@virgin.net
Nelson Local History Society
5 Langholme Street, Nelson, BB9 0RW Tel: 01282 699475
North West Sound Archive
Old Steward's Office, Clitheroe Castle, Clitheroe, BB7 1AZ Tel:
01200-427897 Fax: 01200-427897
Email: nwsa@ed.lancscc.gov.uk
WWW: www.lancashire.gov.uk/education/lifelong/ro
Saddleworth Historical Society
7 Slackcote, Delph, Oldham, OL3 5TW Tel: 01457 874530
Friends of Smithills Hall Museum
19 Leighton Avenue, Heaton, Bolton, BL1 4EH
Tel: 01204 840506
Urmston District Local History Society
26 Grangethorpe Road, Urmston, Manchester, M41 9HT

Leicestershire
Desford & District Local History Group
Lindridge House, Lindridge Lane, Desford, LE9 9FD
East Leake & District Local History Society
8 West Leake Road, East Leake, Loughborough, LE12 6LJ
Tel: 01509 852390
Glenfield and Western Archaeological and Historical Group
50 Chadwell Road, Leicester, LE3 6LF Tel: 1162873220
Leicestershire Archaeological and Historical Society,
The Guildhall, Leicester, LE1 5FQ Tel: 0116 2703031 WWW:
http://www.le.ac.uk/archaeology/lahs/lahs.html or
37 Dovedale Road, Leicester, LE2 2DN Tel: 0116 270 3031
Email: alan@dovedale2.demon.co.uk
WWW: www.le.ac.uk/archaeology/lahs/lahs.html
Sutton Bonington Local History Society
6 Charnwood Fields, Sutton Bonington, Loughborough, LE12
5NP Tel: 01509 673107
Vaughan Archaeological and Historical Society

c/o Vaughan College, St Nicholas Circle, Leicester, LEl 4LB
Willoughby on the Wolds Heritage Group
Group Archive & Village History Enquiries, 1 Church Lane,
Willoughby on the Wolds, Nr Loughborough, LE12 6SS
Tel: 01509 880077

Lincolnshire
Chapels Society
18 Dickens Drive, Stamford, PE9 2GS
Lincoln Record Society
Lincoln Cathedral Library, The Cathedral, Lincoln, LN2 1PZ
Tel: 01522 544544
Society for Lincolnshire History & Archaeology
Jews' Court, Steep Hill, Lincoln, LN2 1LS Tel: 01522-521337
Stamford Historical Society
Meadowcroft, 14 Castle Rise, Belmesthorpe, Stamford, PE9 4JL
Tel: 01780 764213
South Holland Family & Local History Group
6 Brendon Walk, Spalding , PE11 3AG Tel: 01775 714781
Tennyson Society
Central Library, Free School Lane, Lincoln, LN2 1EZ Tel:
01522-552862 Fax: 01522-552858 Email:
linnet@lincolnshire.gov.uk, WWW:

London
Acton History Group
30 Highlands Avenue, London, W3 6EU Tel: (020) 8992 8698
Birkbeck College
Birkbeck College, Malet Street, London, WC1E 7HU Tel: (020)
7631 6633 Fax: (020) 7631 6688 Email: info@bbk.ac.uk
WWW: www.bbl.ac.uk
Brixton Society
82 Mayall Road, London, SE24 0PJ Tel: (020) 7207 0347
Email: apiperbrix@aol.com WWW: www.brixtonsociety.org.uk
Brentford & Chiswick Local History Society
25 Hartington Road, London, W4 3TL
Bromley Borough Local History Society
62 Harvest Bank Road, West Wickham, BR4 9DJ
Tel: 020 8462 5002
Centre for Metropolitan History
Institute of Historical Research, Senate House, Malet Street,
London, WC1E 7HU Tel: (020) 7862 8790 Fax: (020) 7862 8793
Email: o-myhill@sas.ac.uk WWW: www.history.ac.uk/cmh/cmh.main.html
Croydon Local Studies Forum
208 Turnpike Lane, London, CR0 5NZ
Croydon Natural History & Scientific Society Ltd
96a Brighton Road, South Croydon, CR2 6AD Tel: (020) 8688
4539 WWW: http://www.croydon.gov.uk/cnhss/
East London History Society
13 Three Crowns Road, Colchester, CO4 5AD
Edmonton Hundred Historical Society
7 Park Crescent, Enfield, EN2 6HT Tel: (020) 8367 2211
Friends of Historic Essex
11 Milligans Chase, Galleywood, Chelmsford, CM2 8QD
Tel: 01245 431113 Email: geraldine.willden@essexcc.gov.uk
Fulham & Hammersmith History Society
85 Rannoch Road, Hammersmith, London, W6 9SX
Fulham and Hammersmith Historical Soceity
Flat 12, 43 Peterborough Road, Fulham, London, SW6 3BT
Tel: (020) 7731 0363 Email: mail@fhhs.org.uk
WWW: www.fhhs.org.uk
Hornsey Historical Society, The Old Schoolhouse, 136
Tottenham Lane, London, N8 7EL Tel: (020) 8348 8429
WWW: www.hornseyhistorical.org.uk
Hendon & District Archaeological Society, 13 Reynolds Close,
London, NW11 7EA Tel: (020) 8458 1352 Fax: (020) 8731 9882
Email: denis@netmatters.co.uk
London & Middlesex Archaeological Society
Placements Office, University of North London, 62-66 Highbury
Grove, London, N5 2AD
London Record Society
c/o Institute of Historical Research, Senate House, Malet Street,
London, WC1E 7HU Tel: (020) 7862-8798
Fax: (020) 7862 8793 Email: creaton@sas.ac.uk
WWW: http://www.ihr.sas.ac.uk/ihr/associnstits/lrsmnu.html
Mill Hill Historical Society
41 Victoria Road, Mill Hill, London, NW7 4SA
Tel: (020) 8959 7126
Newham History Society
52 Eastbourne Road, East Ham, London, E6 6AT
Tel: (020) 8471 1171 WWW: www.pewsey.net/newhamhistory.htm
Paddington Waterways and Maida Vale Soc(Local History)
19a Randolph Road, Maida Vale, London, W9 1AN Tel: 020 7289 0950
The Peckham Society

6 Everthorpe Road, Peckham, London, SE15 4DA Tel: (020) 8693 9412 Fax: (020) 8693 9412Secretary: 67 Gordon Road, London SE15 2AF
Richmond Local History Society
9 Bridge Road, St Margarets, Twickenham, TWI IRE
The Vauxhall Society
20 Albert Square, London, SW8 1BS
Walthamstow Historical Society
173 Brettenham Road, Walthamstow, London, E17 5AX
Tel: (020) 8523 2399 Fax: (020) 8523 2399
Wandsworth Historical Society
31 Hill Court, Putney Hill, London, SW15 6BB Covers the areas of Balham, Southfields, Tooting, Wandsworth, Roehampton, Earlsfield, Putney, Battersea
West London Local History Conference
25 Hartington Road, London, W4 3TL This is a group of various Family and Local History Societies who organise a conference each Spring with a West London context. It is an organising body only and does not have a membership. No local or family history enquiries undertaken
Willesden Local History Society (London Borough of Brent)
9 Benningfield Gardens, Berkhamstead, HP4 2GW
Tel: 01442 878477, Covers the parishes of Cricklewood, Willesden, Kilburn, Park Royal, Harlesden, Neasden, Park Royal & Kensal Rise
Woolwich Arsenal Historical Society
Room 132 Building 22, Royal Arsenal West, Woolwich, London, SE18 6ST

Manchester
Denton Local History Society
94 Edward Street, Denton, Manchester, M34 3BR
Stretford Local History Society
26 Sandy Lane, Stretford, Manchester, M32 9DA
Tel: 0161 283 9434 Email: mjdawson@cwcom.net
WWW: www.stretfordlhs.cwc.net
Urmston District Local History Society
26 Grangethorpe Road, Urmston, Manchester, M41 9HT

Merseyside
Birkdale & Ainsdale Historical Research Society
20 Blundell Drive, Birkdale, Southport, PR8 4RG
WWW: www.harrop.co.uk/bandahrs
Friends of Williamson's Tunnels
15-17 Chatham Place, Edge Hill, Liverpool, L7 3HD
Tel: 0151 722 3363 Tel: 0151 287 1167 Fax: 0151 722 3363
WWW: www.williamsontunnels.com The Society works to excavate and renovate the Williamson Tunnels under Liverpool as well as to research the life and times of their creator, Joseph Williamson (1769-1840). Visits to tunnels by arrangement
Historic Society of Lancashire & Cheshire
East Wing Flat, Arley Hall, Northwich, CW9 6NA
Tel: 01565 777231 Fax: 01565 777465
Maghull and Lydiate Local History Society
15 Brendale Avenue, Maghull, Liverpool, L31 7AX
Merseyside Archaeological Society
20 Osborne Road, Formby, Liverpool, L37 6AR
Tel: 01704 871802

Middlesex
Edmonton Hundred Historical Society
7 Park Crescent, Enfield, EN2 6HT Tel: (020) 8367 2211
Borough of Twickenham Local History Society
258 Hanworth Road, Hounslow, TW3 3TY
Email: pbarnfield@post.com
Hounslow & District History Society
16 Orchard Avenue, Heston, TW5 0DU Tel: (020) 8570 4264
London & Middlesex Archaeological Society
Placements Office, University of North London, 62-66 Highbury Grove, London, N5 2AD
Middlesex Heraldry Society
4 Croftwell, Harpenden, AL5 1JG Tel: 01582 766372
Northwood & Eastcote Local History Society
7 The Greenway, Ickenham, Uxbridge, Ruislip, UBLO 8LS
Ruislip Northwood & Eastcote Local History Society
3 Elmbridge Close, Ruislip, HA4 7XA Tel: 01895 637134
Pinner Local History Society
8 The Dell, Pinner, HA5 3EW Tel: (020) 8866 1918
Email: mwg@pinnerlhs.freeserve.co.uk
WWW: www.pinnerlhs.freeserve.co.uk/index.html
Sunbury And Shepperton Local
30 Lindsay Drive, Shepperton, TW17 88JU
Email: H.L.Brooking@eggconnect.net

Norfolk
Federation of Norfolk Historical and Archaeological Orgs
14 Beck Lane, Horsham St Faith, Norwich, NR10 3LD
Feltwell (Historical and Archaeological) Society
16 High Street, Feltwell, Thetford, IP26 Tel: 01842 828448
Email: peterfeltwell@tinyworld.co.uk The Museum is at The Beck, Feltwell Open Tuesday & Saturday April to September 2.00.p.m. to 4.00.p.m.
Holt History Group
6 Kelling Close, Holt, NR23 6RU
Narborough Local History Society
101 Westfields, Narborough, Kings Lynn, PE32 ISY WWW: www.narboroughaerodrome.org.uk Narborough Aerodrome 1915-1919 ongoing research - Narborough Airfield Research group. Over 1000 names of Officers Men & Women who served at Narborough. 15 Military graves
Norfolk Archaeological and Historical Research Group
50 Cotman Road, Norwich, NR1 4AH Tel: 01603 435470
Norfolk Heraldry Society
22 Cintra Road, Norwich, NR1 4AE Tel: 01603 436149 WWW: http://norfolk-heraldrey.get-the-web.com/
Norfolk and Norwich Archaeological Society
30 Brettingham Ave, Cringleford, Norwich, NR4 6XG Tel: 01603 455913
Richard III Society - Norfolk Group
20 Rowington Road, Norwich, NR1 3RR

Northumberland
Architectural & Archaeological Soc of Durham & Northumberland
Brancepeth Castle, Brancepeth, DH7 8DF Tel: 0191-378 3383
Email: steve_cousins@yahoo.co.uk
Association of Northumberland Local History Societies
Centre for Lifelong Learning, King George VI Building, University of Newcastle upon Tyne, Newcastle upon Tyne, NE1 7RU Tel: 0191-222-7458 Tel: 0191-222-5680
Felton & Swarland Local History Society
23 Benlaw Grove, Felton, Morpeth, NE65 9NG Tel: 01670 787476
Hexham Local History Society
Dilstone, Burswell Villas, Hexham, NE46 3LD Tel: 01434 603216
Morpeth Antiquarian Society
14 Southgate Wood, Morpeth, NE61 2EN
Morpeth Nothumbrian Gathering
Westgate House, Dogger Bank, Morpeth, NE61 1RF
National Inventory of War Memorials (North East England)
Bilsdale, Ulgham, Morpeth, NE61 3AR Tel: 01670 790465
Email: gjb@bilsdale.freeserve.co.uk, WWW:
North-East England History Institute (NEEHI)
Department of History University of Durham, 43 North Bailey, Durham, DH1 3EX Tel: 0191-374-2004 Fax: 0191-374-4754
Email: m.a.mcallister@durham.ac.uk
WWW: http://www.durham.ac.uk/eehi.history/homepage.htm
The Ponteland Local History Society
Woodlands, Prestwick Village, Ponteland, NE20 9TX Tel: 01661 824017 Fax: 01661 824017 Email: jmichaeltaylor@talk21.com
WWW: www.ponthistsoc.freeuk.com
Prudhoe & District Local History Society
Prudhoe Community Enterprise Office, 82 Front Street, Prudhoe, NR42 5PU
Stannington Local History Society
Glencar House, 1 Moor Lane, Stannnington, Morpeth, NE61 6EA

Northamptonshire
Bozeat Historical and Archaeological Society
44 Mile Street, Bozeat, NN9 7NB Tel: 01933 663647
Brackley & District History Society
32 Church Lane, Evenley, Brackley, NN13 5SG Tel: 01280 703508
Higham Chichele Society
3 Bramley Close, Rushden, NN10 6RL
Houghtons & Brafield History
5 Lodge Road, Little Houghton, NN7 IAE
Historical Medical Equipment Society
8 Albion Mews, Apsley, HP3 9QZ
Email: hmes@antiageing.freeserve.co.uk
Irchester Parish Historical Society, 80 Northampton Road, Wellingborough, NN8 3HT Tel: 01933 274880
Fax: 01933 274488 WWW: www.irchester.org www.iphs.org.uk
Northamptonshire Association for Local History
Copthorne Cottages, 2 Bridle Road, Old Northampton, NN6 9QY Email: enquiries@northants-history.org.uk WWW: www.northants-history.org.uk
Northamptonshire Record Society
Wootton Park Hall, Northampton, NN4 8BQ Tel: 01604 762297
Rushden & District History Society
25 Byron Crescent, Rushden, NN10 6BL
Email: rdhs.rushden@virgin.net WWW: www.rdhs.org.uk
Weedon Bec History Society
35 Oak Street, Weedon, Northampton, NN7 4RR

West Haddon Local History Group
Bramley House, 12 Guilsborough Road, West Haddon, NN6 7AD

Nottinghamshire

Basford & District Local History Society
16 Harcourt Crescent, Nuthall, Nottingham, NG16 1AT Tel: 0115 927 2370
Beeston & District Local History Society
16 Cumberland Avenue, Beeston, NG9 4DH Tel: 0115 922 3008
Bingham & District Local History Society
56 Nottingham Road, Bingham, NG13 8AT Tel: 01949 875866
Bleasby Local History Society
5 Sycamore Lane, Bleasby, NG14 7GJ Tel: 01636 830094
Bulwell Historical Society
21 Rowe Gardens, Bulwell, Nottingham, NG6 9ER
Burton Joyce and Bulcote Local History Society
9 Carnarvon Drive, Burton Joyce, Nottingham, NG14 5ER Tel: 0115 931 3669
Caunton Local History Society
Beech House, Caunton, Newark, NG23 6AF Tel: 01636 636564
Chinemarelian Society
3 Main Street, Kimberley, NG16 2NL Tel: 0115 945 9306,
Cotgrave Local History Society
81 Owthorpe Road, Cotgrave, NG Tel: 0115 989 2115
Eastwood Historical Society
18 Park Crescent, Eastwood , NG16 3DU Tel: 01773 712080
East Leake & District Local History Society
8 West Leake Road, East Leake, Loughborough, LE12 6LJ
Tel: 01509 852390
Edwalton Local History Society
The Croft, Main Street, Edingley, Nottingham, NG22 8BE
Tel: 01623 882507
Edwinstowe Historical Society
12 Church Street, Edwinstowe, NG21 9QA Tel: 01623 824455
Epperstone History Society
Sunny Mead, Main Street, Epperstone, NG14 6AG
Farndon & District Local History Society
Chinley Chine, 7a Wyke Lane, Farndon, Newark, NG24 3SP Tel: 01636 673900
Flintham Local History Society
Flintham Museum, Inholms Road, Flintham, NG23 5LF Tel:
0163.6 525111 Email: flintham.museum@lineone.net
WWW: www.flintham-museum.org.uk
Gotham & District Local History Society
108A Leake Road, Gotham, NG11 0JN Tel: 0115 983 0494
Fax: 0115 983 0494
Hucknall Heritage Society
68 Papplewick Lane, Hucknall, Nottingham, NG15 8EF
Lambley Historical Society
11 Steeles Way, Lambley, Nottingham, NG4 4QN Tel: 0115 931 2588
Lenton Local History Society
53 Arnesby Road, Lenton, Nottingham, NG7 2EA Tel: 0115 970 3981
Long Bennington Local History Society
8 The Meadows, Long Bennington, Newark, NG23 5EL
Lowdham Local History Society
3 Red Lane, Lowdham, NG14 7AU Tel: 0115 966 3891
Fax: 0115 966 3891 Email: gloriarees@ukonline.co.uk
Keyworth & District Local History Society
Innisfree, Thelda Avenue, Keyworth, Nottingham, NG12 5HU
Tel: 0115 937908 Fax: 0115 9372908
Email: info@keyworth-history.org.uk WWW: www.keyworth-history.org.uk
Newark Archaeological & Local History Society
13 Main Street, Sutton on Trent, Newark, NG23 6PF
Tel: 01636 821781 (Evenings) Email: jill.campbell@ic24.net
North Muskham History Group
Roseacre, Village Lane, North Muskham, NG23 6ES Tel: 01636 705566
Nottingham Civic Society
57 Woodhedge Drive, Nottingham, NG3 6LW Tel: 0115 958 8247
Nottingham Historical and Archaeological Society
9 Churchill Drive, Stapleford, Nottingham, NG9 8PE Tel: 0115 937 7140
Nottinghamshire Industrial Archaeology Society
18 Queens Avenue, Ilkeston, DE7 4DL Tel: 0115 932 2228
Nottinghamshire Local History Association
128 Sandhill Street, Worksop, S80 1SY Tel: 01909 488878
Tel: Mobile: 07773887803
Nuthall & District Local History Society
14 Temple Drive, Nuthall, Nottingham, NG16 1BE
Tel: 0115 927 1118 Email: tony.horton@world.com
Old Mansfield Society
7 Barn Close, Mansfield, NG18 3JX Tel: 01623 654815
Email: dcrut@yahoo.com WWW: www.old-mansfield.org.uk
Old Mansfield Woodhouse Society
Newboundmill Lane, Pleasley, Mansfield, NG19 7QA Tel: 01623 810396
Old Warsop Society
1 Bracken Close, Market Warsop, NG20 0QQ
Pentagon Society
Dellary, Mill Road, Elston, Newark, NG23 5NR Tel: 01636
525278 Covers Elston, Shelton, Sibthorpe, East Stoke & Syerston

Pleasley History Group
8 Cambria Road, Pleasley, Mansfield, NG19 7RL Tel: 01623 810201
Radford Memories Project
25 Manston Mews, Alfreton Road, Radford, Nottingham
NG7 3QY Tel: 0115 970 1256
Retford & District Historical & Archaeological Society
Cambridge House, 36 Alma Road, Retford, DN22 6LW Tel:
01777 701902 Email: joan@j-a-e-sewell.demon.co.uk
Ruddington Local History Society
St Peter's Rooms, Church Street, Ruddington, Nottingham,
NG11 6HA Tel: 0115 914 6645
Sherwood Archaeological Society
32 Mapperley Hall Drive, Nottingham, NG3 5EY
Tel: 0115 960 3032 Email: pjneale@aol.com
Sneinton Environmental Society
248 Greenwood Road, Nottingham, NG3 7FY Tel: 0115 987 5035
Southwell & District Local History Society
Fern Cottage, 70 Kirklington Road, Southwell, NG25 0AX Tel: 01636 812220
Stapleford & District Local History Society
25 Westerlands, Stapleford, Nottingham, NG9 7JE Tel: 0115 939 2573
Sutton Heritage Society
8 Sheepbridge Lane, Mansfield, NG18 5EA Tel: 01623 451179
Email: lildawes@yahoo.co.uk
Sutton on Trent Local History Society
14 Grassthorpe Road, Sutton on Trent, Newark, NG23 6QD
Tel: 01636 821228
Thoroton Society of Nottinghamshire
59 Briar Gate, Long Eaton, Nottingham, NG10 4BQ Tel: 0115-
972-6590 Email: thoroton@keithgoodman.com
WWW: www.thorotonsociety.org.uk
Tuxford Heritage Society
140 Lincoln Road, Tuxford, Newark, NG22 0HS
West Bridgford & DistrictLocal History Society
30 Repton Road, West Bridgford, NG2 7EJ Tel: 0115 923 3901
Wilford History Society
10 St Austell Drive, Wilford, Nottingham, NG11 7BP Tel: 0115 981 7061
Whitwell Local History Group
34 Shepherds Avenue, Worksop, S81 0JB
Woodborough Local History Society
The Woodpatch, 19 Sunningdale Drive, Woodborough, NG14
6EQ Tel: 0115 965 3103
WWW: www.woodborough-heritage.org.uk
Worksop Archaeological & Local History Society
17 Highfield Avenue, Mansfield, NG19 7DD Tel: 01623 631893

Oxfordshire

Abingdon Area Archaeological and Historical Society
17 Fitzharrys Road, Abingdon, OX14 1EL Tel: 01235 531566
Asbury Local History Society
Claremont , Asbury, Swindon, SN6 8LN
Banbury History Society
c/o Banbury Museum, 8 Horsefair, Banbury, OX16 OAA
Blewbury Local History Group
Spring Cottage, Church Road, Blewbury, Didcot, OX11 9PY
Tel: 01235 850427 Email: audrey@blewburey427.freeserve.co.uk
Chinnor Historical & Archaelogical Society
7 Cherry Tree Road, Chinnor, 0X9 4QY
Cumnor History Society
4 Kenilworth Road, Cumnor, Nr Oxford, OX2 9QP Tel: 01865 862965
Faringdon Archaeological & Historical Society
1 Orchard Hill, Faringdon, SN7 7EH Email: fdahs@bigfoot.com
Longworth Local History Society
7 Norwood Avenue, Southmoor, OX13 5AD Tel: 01865 820522
Fax: 01865 820522 Email: keene@thematictrails.u-net.com
Oxfordshire Architectural and Historical Society
c/o Centre for Oxfordshire Studies, Westgate, Oxford, OX1 1DJ
Email: tony@oahs.org.uk WWW: www.oahs.org.uk
Oxfordshire Local History Society
3 The Square, Aynho, Nr Banbury, 0X17 3BL
Oxfordshire Local History Association
12 Meadow View, Witney, OX28 6TY Tel: 01993 778345
Oxfordshire Record Society
Bodleian Library, Oxford, OX1 3BG Tel: 01865 277164
Email: srt@bodley.ox.ac.uk
Wallingford Historical and Archaeological Society
Wallingford Museum, Flint House, 52a High Street,
Wallingford, OX1O 0DB Tel: 01491 837720
Witney & District Historical & Archaeological Society
16 Church Green, Witney, OX28 4AW Tel: 01993 703289
Wychwood's Local History Society
Littlecott, Honeydale Farm, Shipton-Under-Wychwood,
Chipping Norton, 0X7 6BJ Enquiry letters should be accompanied by an
SAE or 2 IRCs if from abroad
Yarnton & Begbroke History Society
1 The Garth, Yarnton, Kidlington, OX5 1LZ

Oxfordshire (South), Berkshire Local History Association
37 Heron Island, Caversham, Reading, RG4 8DQ Tel: 0118 947
7345 Email: heronisland@netscapeonline.co.uk

Rutland
Rutland Local History & Record Society
c/o Rutland County Museum, Catmos Street, Oakham, LE15
6HW Tel: 01572 758440 Email: rutlandhistory@rutnet.co.uk
WWW: www.rutnet.co.uk/rlhrs

Shropshire
Cleobury Mortimer Historical Society
The Old Schoolhouse, Nee Savage, Cleobury Mortimer,
Kidderminster, DY14 8JU Tel: 01299 270319
Council for British Archaeology - West Midlands
c/o Rowley's House Museum, Barker Street, Shrewsbury, SY1
1QH Tel: 01743 361196 Email: museums@shrewsbury-atcham.gov.uk
WWW: www.shrewsburymuseums.com www.darwincountry.org
Field Studies Council
Preston Montford, Montford Bridge, Shrewsbury, SY4 1HW
Tel: 01743 852100 Email: fsc.headoffice@ukonline.co.uk
WWW: www.field-studies-council.org
Shropshire Archaeological and Historical Society
Lower Wallop Farm, Westbury, Shrewsbury, SY5 9RT
Tel: 01743 891215 Tel: 01743 891805 Fax: 01743 891805
Email: walloparch@farming.co.uk WWW: www.shropshirearchaeology.com
Whitchurch History and Archaeology Group
The Field House, Wirswall, Whitchurch, SY13 4LA Tel: 01948 662623

Somerset
Axbridge Archaeological and Local History Society
King John's Hunting Lodge, The Square, Axbridge, BS26 2AR
Tel: 01934 732012
Bathford Society
36 Bathford Hill, Bathford, BA1 7SL
Bristol Records Society
Department of Historical Studies, University of Bristol, 13-15
Woodland Road, Bristol, BS8 1TB
Castle Cary & District Museum & Preservation Society
1 Fir Tree Cottages, Lower Ansford, Castle Cary, BA7 7JY
Freshford & District Local History Society
Quince Tree House, Pipehouse Lane, Freshford, Bath, BA2 7UH
Tel: 01225 722339
Oakhill & Ashwick Local History Society
Bramley Farm, Bath Road, Oakhill, BA3 5AF Tel: 01749 840241
Somerset Archaeological & Natural History Society
Taunton Castle, Taunton, TA1 4AD Tel: 01823 272429
Fax: 01823 272429 Email: secretary@sanhs.freeserve.co.uk
Somerset Record Society
Somerset Studies Library, Paul Street, Taunton, TA1 3XZ Tel:
01823-340300 Fax: 01823-340301

South East Somerset Archaeological and Historical Society,
Abbascombe Barn, Lilly Lane, Templecombe, BA8 OHN Tel:
01963 371163
South Petherton Local History, Cobbetts Droveway, South
Petherton, TAI3 5DA Tel: 01460 240252
South Petherton Local History, Crossbow, Hele Lane, South
Petherton, TA13 5DY
The West of England Costume Society
4 Church Lane, Long Aston, Nr. Bristol, BS41 9LU Tel: 01275-543564
Yeovil Archaeological and Local History Society
Plantagenet Chase, Yeovil, YO1 01935 78258

Somerset - North
Avon Local History Association
4 Dalkeith Avenue, Kingswood, Bristol, BS15 1HH Tel: 0117 967 1362
Congresbury History Group
Venusmead, 36 Venus Street, Congresbury, Bristol, BS49 5EZ
Tel: 01934 834780 Email: rogerhards-venusmead.breathemail.net
Nailsea & District Local History Society
PO Box 1089, Nailsea, BS48 2YP

North East Somerset
Avon Local History Association
4 Dalkeith Avenue, Kingswood, Bristol, BS15 1HH Tel: 0117
967 1362

Staffordshire
Berkswich Local History Group
1 Greenfield Road, Stafford, ST17 OPU
Council for British Archaeology - West Midlands
c/o Rowley's House Museum, Barker Street, Shrewsbury, SY1
1QH Tel: 01743 361196 Tel: 01743 358411

Landor Society
38 Fortescue Lane, Rugeley, WS15 2AE Tel: 01889 582709
Lawton Heritage Society
9 Woodgate Avenue, Church Lawton, Stoke on Trent, ST7 3EF
Tel: 01270-878386 Email: dmcall12280@aol.com
Birmingham Canal Navigation's Society
37 Chestnut Close, Handsacre, Rugeley, WS15 4TH
North Staffordshire Local History Guild
14 Berne Avenue, Newcastle under Lyme, ST5 2QJ
Ridware History Society
Priory Farm, Blithbury, Nr. Rugeley, WSI5 3JA Tel: 01889 504269
Staffordshire Archaeological and Historical Society
6 Lawson Close, Aldridge, Walsall, WS9 0RX Tel: 01922 452230
Stafford Historical & Civic Society
86 Bodmin Avenue, Weeping Cross, Stafford, ST17 OEQ
Tel: 01785 612194 Email: esj@supanet.com
Staffordshire Local Studies Forum - No contact address at present
based in Stafford

Suffolk
Brett Valley History Society
17 Manor Road, Bildeston, Ipswich, IP7 7BG
Elmswell Millennium History Group
Hill Court, Church Road, Elmswell, P30 9DY Tel: 01359 240390
Essex Archealogical and Historical Congress
Lowe Hill House, Stratford St Mary, C07 6JX
Framlingham & District Local History & Preservation Soc
43 College Road, Framlingham, IP13 9HA Tel: 01728 723214
Lowestoft Archaeological and Local History Society
1 Cranfield Close, Pakefield, Lowestoft, NR33 7EL Tel: 01502 586143
Suffolk Local History Council
Resource Centre, 2 Wharfedale Road, Ipswich, IP1 4JP
Suffolk Institute of Archaeology and History
Roots, Church Lane, Playford, Ipswich, IP6 9DS Tel: 01473-624556

Surrey
Addlestone History Society
53 Liberty Lane, Addlestone, Weybridge, KT15 1NQ
Beddington & Carshalton Historical Society
57 Brambledown Road, Wallington, SM6 0TF
Beddington Carshalton & Wallington History Society
57 Brambledown Road, Wallington, SM6 0TF Tel: (020) 8647 8540
Bourne Society
54 Whyteleafe Road, Caterham, CR3 5EF Tel: 018833 492287
Tel: 01883 347143 Fax: 01883 341638
Email: robert@friday-house.freeserve.co.uk WWW: www.bournesociety.org.uk
Covers the districts of Caterham, Chaldon, Chelsham, Chipstead, Coulsdon,
Farleigh, Godstone, Kenley, Old Coulsdon, Parley, Sanderstead, Whyteleafe,
Warlingham and Woldingham.
Carshalton Society
43 Denmark Road, Carshalton, SM5 2JE
Centre for Local History Studies
Faculty of Human Sciences, Kingston University, Penrhyn Road,
Kingston, KT1 2EE Tel: (020) 8547 7359
Email: localhistory@kingston.ac.uk WWW: http://localhistory.kingston.ac.uk
Croydon Local Studies Forum
Flat 2, 30 Howard Road, South Norwood, London, SE25 5BY
Tel: (020) 8654-6454
Croydon Natural History & Scientific Society Ltd
96a Brighton Road, South Croydon, CR2 6AD Tel: (020) 8688
4539 WWW: http://www.croydon.gov.uk/cnhss/
Danehill Parish Historical Society - contact not known RH17
Domestic Buildings Research Group (Surrey)
The Ridings, Lynx Hill, East Horsley, KT24 5AX Tel: 01483 283917
Farnham and District Museum Society
Tanyard House, 13a Bridge Square, Farnham, GU9 7QR
Friends of Public Record Office
The Public Record Office, Ruskin Avenue, Kew, Richmond,
TW9 4DU Tel: (020) 8876 3444 ext 2226
Email: friends-pro@pro.gov.uk WWW: www.pro.gov.uk/friends/default.htm
Guildford Archaeology and Local History Group
6 St Omer Road, Guildford, GU1 2DB Tel: 01483 532201
Email: H.E.Davies@surrey.ac.uk
Leatherhead District Local History Society
Leatherhead Museum, 64 Church Street, Leatherhead, KT22
8DP Tel: 01372 386348
Nonsuch Antiquarian Society
17 Seymour Avenue, Ewell, KT17 2RP Tel: (020) 8393 0531
Richmond Local History Society
9 Bridge Road, St Margarets, Twickenham, TWI IRE
The RH7 History Group
Bidbury House, Hollow Lane, East Grinstead, RH19 3PS
Send and Ripley History Society
St Georges Farm House, Ripley, GU23 6AF Tel: 01483 222107
Fax: 01483 222107 Email: slatford@johnone.freeserve.co.uk

Surrey Archaeological Society
Castle Arch, Guildford, GU1 3SX Tel: 01483 532454 Fax:
01483 532454 Email: surreyarch@compuserve.com
WWW: www.ourworld.compuserve.com/homepages/surreyarch,
Covers the Historic County of Surrey
Surrey Local History Council
Guildford Institute Ward Street, Guildford, GU1 4LH
Surrey Record Society
c/o Surrey History Centre, 130 Goldsworth Road, Woking,
GU21 1ND Tel: 01483 594603 This is a publishing society only.
No research can be undertaken by the honorary officers.
Walton On The Hill District Local History Society
5 Russell Close, Walton On The Hill, Tadworth, KT2O 7QH Tel: 01737 812013
Walton & Weybridge Local History Society
67 York Gardens, Walton on Thames, KT12 3EN
Westcott Local History Group
6 Heath Rise, Westcott, Dorking, RH4 3NN Tel: 01306 882624
Email: dubois@unforgettable.com
Shere Gomshall & Peaslake Local History Society
Twiga Lodge, Wonham Way, Gomshall, Guildford, GUS 9NZ
Tel: 01483 202112 Email: twiga@gomshall.freeserve.co.uk
WWW: www.gomshall.freeserve.co.uk/sglshhp.htm
Puttenham & Wanborough History Society
Sunnyway Cottage, Seale Lane, Puttenham, Guildford, GU3 1AX

Sussex
Danehill Parish Historical Society
Butchers Barn, Freshfield Lane, Danehill, RH17 7HQ Tel: 01825 790292
Lewes Archaeological Group
Rosemary Cottage, High Street, Barcombe, near Lewes
BN8 5DM Tel: 01273 400878
Sussex Archaeological Society
Barbican House, 169 High Street, Lewes, BN7 1YE
Tel: 01273 405738 Email: library@sussexpast.co.uk
WWW: sussexpast.co.uk
Sussex History Study Group
Colstock, 43 High Street, Ditchling, BN5 8SY
Sussex Local History Forum and
Sussex Past
Anne of Cleves House, 52 Southover High Street, Lewes, BN7
1JA Tel: 01273 405738 Fax: 01273 486990
Email: library@sussexpast.co.uk WWW: www.sussexpast.co.uk

Sussex - East
Sussex, Blackboys & District Historical Society
6 Palehouse Common, Framfield, Nr Uckfield, TN22 5QY
Brighton & Hove Archealogical Society
115 Braeside Avenue, Patcham, Brighton, BN1 8SQ
Eastbourne Natural History and Archaeological Society
11 Brown Jack Avenue, Polegate, BN26 5HN Tel: 01323 486014
Family & Community Historical Research Society, 56 South
Way, Lewes, BN7 1LY Tel: 01273 471897
Forest Row Local History Group - Society Disbanded
Friends of East Sussex Record Office
The Maltings, Castle Precincts, Lewes, BN7 1YT Tel: 01273-
482349 Fax: 01273-482341 WWW: www.esrole.fsnet.co.uk
Peacehaven & Telscombe Historical Society
2 The Compts, Peacehaven, BN1O 75Q Tel: 01273 588874 Fax:
01273 589881 Email: paths@openlink.org
WWW: www.history-peacehaven-telscombe.org.uk
Maresfield Historical Society
Hockridge House, London Road, Maresfield, TN22 2EH
Tel: 01825 765386
Sussex History Forum
Barbican House, 169 High Street, Lewes, BN7 1YE Tel: 01273-
405736 Email: research@sussexpast.co.uk WWW: www.sussexpast.co.uk
Uckfield & District Preservation Society
89 Lashbrooks Road, Uckfield, TN22 2AZ
Warbleton & District History Group
Hillside Cottage, North Road, Bodle Street Green, Hailsham,
BN27 4RG Tel: 01323 832339
Email: junegeoff.hillside@tinyonline.co.uk

Sussex - West Sussex
The Angmering Society
Holly Lodge, Rectory Lane, Angmering, BNI6 4JU Tel: 01903-
775811 Fax: 01903-775811
Beeding & Bramber Local History Society
19 Roman Road, Steyning, BN44 3FN Tel: 01903 814083
Bolney Local History Society
Leacroft, The Street, Bolney, Haywards, RH17 5PG Tel: 01444
881550 Email: constable@lespres.freeserve.co.uk
Billingshurst Local History Society
2 Cleve Way, Billingshurst, RH14 9RW Tel: 01403 782472
Email: jane.lecluse@wsatkins.com

Chichester Local History Society
20 Cavendish Street, Chichester, P019 3BS
Horsham Museum Society
9 The Causeway, Horsham, RH12 1HE Tel: 01403 254959
Mid Sussex Local History Group
Woodborough, Stockcroft Road, Balcombe, RH17 6LH
Tel: 01444 811275
Steyning Society
30 St Cuthmans Road, Steyning, BN44 3RN
Sussex History Forum
Barbican House, 169 High Street, Lewes, BN7 1YE Tel: 01273-405736
Sussex Record Society
West Sussex Record Office, County Hall, Chichester, PO19 1RN
Tel: 01243 753600 Fax: 01243-533959
Email: peter.wilkinson@westsussex.gov.uk
West Sussex Archives Society
c/o West Sussex Record Office, County Hall, Orchard Street,
Chichester, PO19 1RN Tel: 01243 753600 Fax: 01243 533959
Email: Records.Office@westsussex.gov.uk
WWW: www.westsussex.gov.uk/CS/RO/rohome.htm
Wivelsfield Historical Society
Middlefield Cottage, Fox Hill, Haywards Heath, RH16 4QY

Tyne and Wear
Association of Northumberland Local History Societies
Centre for Lifelong Learning, King George VI Building,
University of Newcastle upon Tyne, Newcastle upon Tyne, NE1
7RU Tel: 0191-222-7458 Tel: 0191-222-5680
Cullercoats Local History Society
33 St Georges Road, Cullercoats, North Shields, NE30 3JZ Tel:
0191 252 7042
North Eastern Police History Society
Brinkburn Cottage, 28 Brinkburn Street, High Barnes,
Sunderland, SR4 7RG Tel: 0191-565-7215
Email: harry.wynnne@virgin.net WWW: http://nepolicehistory.homestead.com
North East Labour History Society
Department of Historical & Critical Studies, University of
Northumbria, Newcastle upon Tyne, NE1 8ST Tel: 0191-227-
3193 Fax: 0191-227-4630 Email: joan.hugman@unn.ac.uk
North East England Local and Family History
University of Newcastle, Newcastle Upon Tyne, NEl 7RL Tel:
0191 222 6546 WWW: www.ncl.ac.uk/lifelong-learning/
National Inventory of War Memorials (North East England)
Bilsdale, Ulgham, Morpeth, NE61 3AR Tel: 01670 790465
Email: gjb@bilsdale.freeserve.co.uk
North-East England History Institute (NEEHI)
Department of History University of Durham, 43 North Bailey,
Durham, DH1 3EX Tel: 0191-374-2004 Fax: 0191-374-4754
Email: m.a.mcallister@durham.ac.uk
WWW: http://www.durham.ac.uk/eehi.history/homepage.htm
Northumbria Historic Churches Trust
The Vicarage, South Hylton, Sunderland, SR4 0QB
Society of Antiquaries of Newcastle upon Tyne
Black Gate, Castle Garth, Newcastle upon Tyne, NE1 1RQ Tel:
1912615390 Tel: 0771 216 0431 Email: socantiqs@ncl.ac.uk
WWW: http://museums.ncl.ac.uk/socantiqs
South Hylton Local History Society
6 North View, South Hylton, Sunderland, SR4 0LH Tel: 0191
552 6587 Tel: 0191 534 4251 Email:
douglas.scrafton@virgin.net
The 68th (Durham) Regiment of Light Infantry Display Team
23 Neville Court, Marlborough Park, Washington, NE37 3DY
Tel: 0191 415 7952 Email: jeff@23peacock.freeserve.co.uk
WWW: www.68dli.com

Warwickshire
Alcester & District Local History Society
Applecross, Worcester Road, Inkberrow, Worcester, WR7 4ET
Email: cjjohnson@care4free.net
Council for British Archaeology - West Midlands
c/o Rowley's House Museum, Barker Street, Shrewsbury, SY1 1QH
Tel: 01743 361196 Email: museums@shrewsbury-atcham.gov.uk
WWW: www.shrewsburymuseums.com www.darwincountry.org
Kineton and District Local History Group
The Glebe House, Lighthorne Road, Kineton, CV35 0JL
Tel: 01926 690298 Email: p.holdsworth@virgin.net
Warwickshire Local History Society
9 Willes Terrace, Leamington Spa, CV31 1DL Tel: 01926 429671
Watford, Watford and District Industrial History Society
79 Kingswood Road, Garston, Watford, WD25 0EF Tel: 01923 673253
West Dorset, Bridport History Society
c/o 22 Fox Close, Bradpole, Bridport, DT6 3JF Tel: 01308
456876 (Home) Email: celia@cgulls.fsnet.co.uk

West Midlands

Aldridge Local History Society
45 Erdington Road, Walsall, WS9 8UU
Barr & Aston Local History
17 Booths Farm Road, Great Barr, Birmingham, 642 2NJ
Black Country Society
PO Box 71, Kingswinford, DY6 9YN
Black Country Local History Consortium
Canal St, Tipton Rd, Dudley, DY1 4SQ Tel: 0121 522 9643
Email: info@bclm.co.uk WWW: ww.bclm.co.uk
Local History Consortium
The Black Country Living Museum, Tipton Road, Dudley
DY1 4SQ Tel: 0121 557 9643
Midland Railway Society
4 Canal Road, Yapton, BN18 0HA Tel: 01243-553401
Email: BeeFitch@aol.com WWW: www.derby.org/midland
Romsley & Hunnington History Society
Port Erin, Green Lane, Chapmans Hill, Romsley, Halesowen, B62
0HB Tel: 01562 710295 Email: ejhumphreys@mail.com
Smethwick Local History Society
47 Talbot Road, Smethwick, Warley, B66 4DX
War Research Society
27 Courtway Avenue, Birmingham, B14 4PP Tel: 0121 430 5348
Fax: 0121 436 7401 Email: battletour@aol.com
WWW: www.battlefieldtours.co.uk
Wesley Historical Society
34 Spiceland Road, Northfield, Birmingham, B31 1NJ Email:
106364.3456@compuserve.com Genealogical research is NOT
undertaken. The Society holds no genealogical records. Methodist Records should
be deposited in the Local Record Office or local recognised repository. Advice on
Methodist sources given where possible. SAE required
Wythall Local History Society
64 Meadow Road, Wythall, Birmingham, B47 6EQ Email:
val@wythallhistory.co.uk WWW: www.wythallhistory.co.uk

Westmoreland see also Cumbria

Cumberland & Westmorland Antiquarian & Archaeological Soc
2 High Tenterfell, Kendal, LA9 4PG Tel: 01539 773542
Email: info@cwaas.org.uk WWW: www.cwaas.org.uk or

Wiltshire

Amesbury Society
14 Stonehenge Road, Amesbury, SP4 7BA Tel: 01980 623123
Atworth History Group
41 Dovers Park, Bathford, Bath, BA1 7UD Tel: 01225 852160
Chiseldon Local History Group
24 Carisbrook Terrace, Chiseldon, SN4 0LW Tel: 01793 7400473
Devizes Local History Group
9 Hartfield, Devizes, SN10 5JH Tel: 01380 727369
Freshford & District Local History Society
Quince Tree House, Pipehouse Lane, Freshford, Bath, BA2 7UH
Tel: 01225 722339
The Hatcher Society
11 Turner Close, Harnham, Salisbury, SP2 8NX
Highworth Historical Society
2 The Dormers, Highworth, Swindon, SN6 7NY Tel: 01793
765079 Email: bryanelk@aol.com
The Historical Association (West Wiltshire Branch)
24 Meadowfield, Bradford on Avon, BA15 1PL Tel: 01225 862722
Marshfield & District Local History Society
150 High Street, Marshfield, Chippenham, SN14 8LU
Melksham & District Historial Association
13 Sandridge Lane, Melksham Tel: 01225 703644
Mere Historical Society
Bristow House, Castle Street, Mere, BA12 6JF Tel: 01747 860643
Mid Thorngate Society
Yewcroft, Stoney Batter, West Tytherley, Salisbury, SP5 ILD
Pewsey Vale Local History Society
6 Tinkers Mead, Pewsey, SN6 5HS Tel: 01672 563028
Purton Historical Society
1 Church Street, Purton, SN5 4DS Tel: 01793 770331
Redlynch & District Local History Society
Hawkstone, Church Hill, Redlynch, Salisbury, SP5 2PL
Email: pat.mill@btinternet.com
Salisbury Civic Society
4 Chestnut Close, Laverstock, Salisbury, SP1 1SL
Salisbury Local History Group
67 St Edmunds Church Street, Salisbury, SP1 1EF Tel: 01722 338346
South Wiltshire Industrial Archaeology Society
34 Countess Road, Amesbury, SP4 7AS Tel: 01980 622092
Email: goodhugh@btinternet.com

Swindon Society
4 Lakeside, Swindon, SN3 1QE Tel: 01793-521910
Tisbury Local History Society

Suzay House, Court Street, Tisbury, SP3 6NF
Trowbridge Civic Society
43 Victoria Road, Trowbridge, BA14 7LD
Warminster History Society
13 The Downlands, Warminster, BA12 0BD Tel: 01985 216022
Wiltshire Local History Forum
Tanglewood, Laverstock Park, Salisbury, SP1 1QJ Tel: 01722-328922
Wiltshire Record Society
County Record Office, County Libraries Hq, Trowbridge, BA14
8BS Tel: 01225 713136 Fax: 01225 713515
Wiltshire Archaeology & Natural History Society
41 Long Street, Devizes, SN1O INS Tel: 01380 727369 Fax:
01380 722150 Email: wanhs@wiltshireheritage.org.uk, WWW:
Wiltshire Archaeological and Natural History Society,
Wiltshire Heritage Library, 41 Long Street, Devizes, SN10 1NS
Tel: 01380 727369 Fax: 01380 722150 Email:
wanhs@wiltshireheritage.org.uk
Wiltshire Buildings Record Society
Libraries & Heritage HQ, Bythesea Road, Trowbridge, BA14 8BS
Wilton Historical Society
3 Wiley Terrace, North Street, Wilton, SP2 0HN Tel: 01722 742856, Small
local history Society with no genealogical information.
Wootton Bassett Historical Society
20 The Broadway, Rodbourne Cheney, Swindon, SP25 3BT

Worcestershire

Alvechurch Historical Society
Bearhill House, Alvechurch, Birmingham, B48 7JX Tel: 0121 445 2222
Bewdley Historical Research 8 Ironside Close, Bewdley, DY12
2HX Tel: 01299 403582 Email: angela.ironside@bigfoot.com
Council for British Archeaology - West Midlands
c/o Rowley's House Museum, Barker Street, Shrewsbury, SY1
1QH Tel: 01743 361196 Tel: 01743 358411
Dodderhill Parish History Project - Discovering Wychbol's Past
9 Laurelwood Close, Droitwich Spa, WR9 7SF
Droitwich History and Archaeology Society
45 Moreland Road, Droitwich, WR9 8RN Tel: 01905-773420
Feckenham Forest History Society
Lower Grinsty Farmhouse, Callow Hill, Redditch, B97 5PJ Tel:
01527-542063 Fax: 01527-542063
Feckenham Parish, Worcestershire One Place Study
33c Castle Street, Astwood Park, Worcester, B96 6DP
Email: benwright3@hotmail.com
Kidderminster and District Archaeological and Historical Soc
178 Birmingham Road, Kidderminster, DYlO 2SJ or 39 Cardinal
Drive, Kidderminster, DY104RZ Email: bob.millward@virgin.net
Kidderminster Field Club
7 Holmwood Avenue, Kidderminster, DYL 1 6DA
Pershore Heritage & History Society
6 Abbey Croft, Pershore, WR10 1JQ Tel: 01386 552482
Wolverley & Cookley History Society
The Elms, Drakelow Lane, Wolverley, Kidderminster, DY11 5RU
Tel: 01562 850215, History of parishes of Wolverley & Caskley.
Annual journal contact John Pearsall 01562 850915
Worcestershire Archaeological Service
Woodbury Hall, University College of Worcester, Henwick
Grove, Worcester, WR2 6AJ Tel: 01905 855455 Fax: 01905
29054 Email: archaeology@worcestershire.gov.uk
WWW: http://worcestershire.gov.uk/archaeology
Worcestershire Archaeological Society
The Greyfriars, Friar Street, Worcester, WR1 2LZ Tel: 01905
23571
Worcestershire Industrial Archeaology & Local History Soc
99 Feckenham Road, Headless Cross, Redditch, B97 5AM
Worcestershire Local History Forum
45 Moreland Road, Droitwich, WR9 8RN Tel: 01905-773420
Wythall Local History Society
64 Meadow Road, Wythall, Birmingham, B47 6EQ Email:
val@wythallhistory.co.uk WWW: www.wythallhistory.co.uk

Yorkshire

Yorkshire Archaeological Society
Claremont, 23 Clarendon Rd, Leeds, LS2 9NZ Tel: 0113-245-
6342 Tel: 0113 245 7910 Fax: 0113-244-1979
Email: j.heron@sheffield.ac.uk WWW: www.yas.org.uk
Opening Hours: Tues,Wed 2.00 to 8.30pm; Thurs, Fri 10.00 to 5.30; Sat
9.30 to 5.00 Appointment necessary for use of archival material.
Yorkshire Architectural & York Archaeological Society
c/o York Archaeological Trust, Cromwell House, 13 Ogleforth,
York, YO1 7FG
Email: www.homepages.tesco.net/~hugh.murray/yayas/
The Yorkshire Buildings Preservation Trust
c/o Elmhirst & Maxton Solicitors, 17-19 Regent St Barnsley, S70 2HP
Yorkshire Dialect Society
51 Stepney Avenue, Scarborough, YO12 5BW

Yorkshire Philosophical Society
The Lodge, Museum Gardens, Museum Street, York, YO1 7DR
Tel: 01904 656713 Email: yps@yorkphil.fsnet.co.uk
The Yorkshire Heraldry Society
35 Holmes Carr Road, West Bessacarr, Doncaster, DN4 7HJ Tel: 01302-539993
Yorkshire Vernacular Buildings Study Group
18 Sycamore Terrace, Bootham, York, YO30 7DN
Victorian Revival
Sugar Hill Farm, Knayton, Thirsk, YO7 4BP

Yorkshire - East
East Riding Archaeological Society
455 Chanterland Avenue, Hull, HU5 4AY Tel: 01482 445232
East Yorkshire Local History Society
13 Oaktree Drive, Molescroft, Beverley, HU17 7BB
Hull Central Library Family and Local History Club
Central Library, Albion Street, Kingston upon Hull, HU1 3TF Tel:
01482 616828 Fax: 01482 616827 Email: gareth2ukorigins.co.uk
WWW: http://www.hullcc.gov.uk/genealogy

Yorkshire - North
Forest of Galtres Society
Crawford House, Long Street, Easingwold, YO61 3JB Tel: 01347 821685
Local Population Studies Society
78 Harlow Terrace, Harrogate, HG2 0PN Tel: 01423-560429
Email: sir_david_cooke@compuserve.com WWW: home.att.net/~jkbfa
Northallerton and District Local History Society
17 Thistle Close, Romanby Park, Northallerton, DL7 8FF
Tel: 01609 771878
Poppleton History Society
Russett House, The Green, Upper Poppleton, York, YO26 6DR
Tel: 01904 798868 Fax: 01904 613330 Email: susan.major@virgin.net
WWW: www.onwards.to/poppleton-history
Scarborough Archaeological and Historical Society
10 Westbourne Park, Scarborough, YO12 4AT Tel: 01723 354237
Email: archaeology@scarborough.co.uk
Snape Local History Group
Garthland, Snape, Bedale, DL8 2TF Tel: 01677 470769 Email:
debbie.fiona@ukgateway.net, WWW:
Stokesley & District Local History Study Group, 21 Cleveland
Avenue, Stokesley, TS9 5EZ
Upper Dales Family History Group - affiliated to Cleveland FHS
Croft House, Newbiggin in Bishopdale, Nr Leyburn, DL8 3TD
Tel: 01969 663738 Email: glenys@bishopdale.demon.co.uk
WWW: www.bishopdale.demon.co.uk
Upper Wharfedale Museum Society & Folk Museum
The Square, Grassington, BD23 5AU
Upper Wharfedale Field Society (Local History Section)
Brookfield, Hebden Hall Park, Grassington, Skipton, BD23 5DX
Tel: 01756-752012

Yorkshire - South
Barnscan - The Barnsdale Local History Group
23 Rushymoor Lane, Askern, Doncaster, DN6 0NH
Tel: 01302 700083 Email: barnscan@btinternet.com
WWW: www.barnscan.btinternet.co.uk
Bentley with Arksey Heritage Society
45 Finkle Street, Bentley, Doncaster, DN5 0RP
Chapeltown & High Green Archives
The Grange, 4 Kirkstead Abbey Mews, Thorpe Hesley,
Rotherham, S61 2UZ
Doncaster Archaeological Society (Group of the Yorkshire Archaeological Soc)
Merrylees, 1b Ellers Road, Bessacarr, Doncaster, DN4 7BE
Tel: 01302 531581 Email: acruse@globalnet.co.uk
Greneside & District Local History Group
50 St Michael's Road, Ecclesfield, Sheffield, S35 9YN
South Yorkshire Archaeology Unit and Museum
Ellin Street, Sheffield Tel: 0114 2734230
Wombwell Heritage Group
9 Queens Gardens, Wombwell, Barnsley, S73 0EE

Yorkshire - York
York Archaeological Trust
11 - 13 Ogleforth, York, YO1 2JG
York Georgian Society
King's Manor, York, YO1 7EW

Yorkshire - West
Beeston Local History Society, 30 Sunnyview Avenue, Leeds,
LS11 8QY Tel: 0113 271 7095, This is Beeston, Leeds and should
not be confused with Beeston, Nottinghamshire

East Leeds Historical Society
10 Thornfield Drive, Cross Gates, Leeds, LS15 7LS, Also East
Leeds Heritage Centre
Halifax Antiquarian Society

13 Russell Avenue, Queensbury, Bradford, BD13 2AL Tel: 01274 880268
Kippax & District History Society
8 Hall Park Croft, Kippax, Leeds, West Yorkshire Tel: 0113 286
4785 Email: mdlbrumwell@tinyworld.co.uk
WWW: www.kippaxhistoricalsoc.leedsnet.org
Lowertown Old Burial Ground Trust
16 South Close, Guisley, Leeds, LS20 8TD
Olicana Historical Society
23 Clifton Road, Ben Rhydding, Ilkley, LS29 8TU Tel: 01943 430798
Ossett & District Historical Society
29 Prospect Road, Ossett Tel: 01924 279449
Northern Society of Costume and Textiles
43 Gledhow Lane, Leeds, LS8 1RT
Thoresby Society
23 Clarendon Road, Leeds, LS2 9NZ Tel: 0113 245 7910
Wakefield History Society
18 South Drive, Sandal, Wakefield, WF2 7ND
Wetherby & District Historical Society
73 Aire Road, Wetherby, LS22 7UE
Yorkshire Archaeological Society - Local History Study Section
Claremont, 23 Clarendon Road, Leeds, LS2 9NZ Tel: 0113-245-
7910 Fax: 0113-244-1979 Email: blong@historydb.force9.co.uk
The Yorkshire Heraldry Society
35 Holmes Carr Road, West Bessacarr, Doncaster, DN4 7HJ Tel: 01302-539993

Wales
Federation of History Societies in Caernarfonshire, Melin Pant
yr Ynn, Bethania, Blaenau Ffestiniog, LL41 3LZ Tel: 01766
830540

Anglesey
The Anglesey Antiquarian Society & Field Club
1 Fronheulog, Sling, Tregarth, Bangor, LL57 4RD Tel: 01248 600083

Cardiff
Pentyrch & District Local History Society
34 Castell Coch View, Tongwynlais, Cardiff, CF15 7LA
South Wales Record Society, 12 The Green, Radyr, Cardiff,
CF15 8BR

Carmarthenshire
Gwendraeth Val History Society, 19 Grugos Avenue,
Pontyberem, Llanelli, SA15 5AF
Carmarthenshire Antiquarian Society
Ty Picton, Llansteffan, SA33 5JG Tel: 01267 241 727
Email: arfon.rees@btinternet.com
Gwendraeth Valley Hist Society
19 Grugos Avenue, Pontyberem, Llanelli, SA14 5AF

Caernarfonshire
Federation of History Societies in Caernarfonshire
Melin Pant yr Ynn, Bethania, Blaenau Ffestiniog, LL41 3LZ Tel: 01766 830540

Ceredigion
Ceredigion Antiquarian Society, Henllys, Lôn Tyllwyd,
Llanfarian, Aberystwyth, SY23 4UH

Clwyd
Friends of The Clwyd Archives
16 Bryntirion Avenue, Rhyl, LL18 3NP Tel: 01745 342168

Conwy
Abergele Field Club and Historical Society
Rhyd y Felin, 47 Bryn Twr, Abergele, LL22 8DD Tel: 01745 832497

Denbighshire
Flintshire Historical Society
69 Pen y Maes Avenue, Rhyl, LL18 4ED Tel: 01745 332220

Flintshire
Flintshire Historical Society
69 Pen y Maes Avenue, Rhyl, LL18 4ED Tel: 01745 332220
Ruthin Local History Group
27 Tan y Bryn, Llanbedr D.C., Ruthin, LL15 1AQ Tel: 01824
702632 Email: gwynnemorris@btinternet.com

Glamorgan
Kenfig Society, 6 Locks Lane, Porthcawl, CF36 3HY Tel: 01656
782351 Email: terry.robbins@virgin.net WWW:
http://freespace.virgin.net/terry.robbins/
South Wales Record Society
12 The Green, Radyr, Cardiff, CF15 8BR
Llantrisant & District Local History Society
Cerrig Llwyd, Lisvane Road, Lisvane, Cardiff, CF14 0SG Tel:
029 2075 6173 Fax: Email: BDavies203@aol.com

Mid Glamorgan

Glamorgan History Society
7 Gifford Close, Two Locks, NP44 7NX Tel: 01633 489725
(Evenings Only) Email: rosemary_hewlett@yahoo.co.uk
Merthyr Tydfil Historical Society
Ronamar, Ashlea Drive, Twynyrodyn, Merthyr Tydfil, CF47
0NY Tel: 01685 385871
Pentyrch & District Local History Society
34 Castell Coch View, Tongwynlais, Cardiff, CF15 7LA

Gwent
Gwent Local History Council
8 Pentonville, Newport, NP9 5XH Tel: 01633 213229 Fax:
01633 221812 Email: byron.grubb@gavowales.org.uk
Abertillery & District Museum Society
5 Harcourt Terrace, Glandwr Street, Abertillery, NP3 1TS
Pontypool Local History Society
24 Longhouse Grove, Henllys, Cwmbran, NP44 6HQ Tel: 01633 865662
Abertillery & District Museum
5 Harcourt Terrace, Glandwr Street, Abertillery, NP3 ITS

Gwynedd
Abergele Field Club and Historical Society
Rhyd y Felin, 47 Bryn Twr, Abergele, LL22 8DD Tel: 01745 832497
**Cymdeithas Hanes a Chofnodion Sir Feirionnydd Meirioneth
Historicial and Record Society**
Archifdy Meirion Cae Penarlag, Dolgellau, LL40 2YB Tel:
01341 424444 Fax: 01341 424505
Cymdeithas Hanes Beddgelert - Beddgelert History Society
Creua, Llanfrothen, Penrhyndeudraeth, LL48 6SH Tel: 1766770534
Caernarvonshire Historical Society
Gwynedd Archives, County offices, Caernarfon, LL555 1SH
Tel: 01286 679088 Email: caernarvonshirehistoricalsociety@btinternet.com
WWW: www.caernarvonshirehistoricalsociety.btinternet.co.uk,
Membership details from; The Membership Secretary, Hyfrydle,
Caernarfon Road, Y Felinheli LL56 4NJ
Llandudno & District Historical Society
Springfield, 97 Queen's Road, Llandudno, LL30 1TY Tel: 01492 876337

Pembrokeshire
The Pembrokeshire Historical Society
The Castle, Haeverford West, SA61 2EF Tel: 01348 873316

Powys
Radnorshire Society
Pool House, Discoed, Presteigne, LD8 2NW Email:
sadie@cole.kc3ltd.co.uk

Wrexham County Borough
Flintshire Historical Society
69 Pen y Maes Avenue, Rhyl, LL18 4ED Tel: 01745 332220
Wrexham Maelor History Society
37 Park Avenue, Wrexham, LL12 7AL

Isle of Man
Isle of Man Natural History & Antiquarian Society
Ballacrye Stream Cottage, Ballaugh, IM7 5EB Tel: 01624-897306
Isle of Man Natural History & Local History Society
Stream Cottage, Ballacrye, Ballaugh, IM7 5JF

Channel Islands
Jersey
Societe Jersiaise, 7 Pier Road, St Helier, JE2 4XW Tel: 01534
730538 Fax: 01534 888262 Email: societe@societe-jersiaise.org
WWW: http://www.societe-jersiaise.org

Scotland
Society of Antiquaries of Scotland
Royal Museum of Scotland, Chambers Street, Edinburgh, EH1
1JF Tel: 0131 247 4115 Tel: 0131 247 4133 and 0131 247 4145
Fax: 0131 247 4163
Scottish Records Association
National Archives of Scotland, H M General Register House,
Edinburgh, EH1 3YY Tel: 0141 287 2914 Fax: 0141 226 8452,
Publsher of journal, Scottish Archives and datasheets on holdings
of Scottish Archives and libraries

Airdrie
Monklands Heritage Society
141 Cromarty Road, Cairnhill, Airdrie, ML6 9RZ Tel: 01236 764192

Angus
Abertay Historical Society
27 Pitcairn Road, Downfield, Dundee, DD3 9EE Tel: 01382 858701 Email:
abertay@dmcsoft.com WWW: www.dcmsoft.com/abertay

Ayrshire
Ayrshire Federation of Historical Societies
11 Chalmers Road, Ayr, KA7 2RQ

Dundee
Abertay Historical Society
27 Pitcairn Road, Downfield, Dundee, DD3 9EE Tel: 01382 858701 Email:
abertay@dmcsoft.com WWW: www.dcmsoft.com/abertay
Friends of Dundee City Archives
21 City Square, Dundee, DD1 3BY Tel: 01382 434494 Fax: 01382 434666
Email: richard.cullen@dundeecity.gov.uk WWW: http://www.dundeecity.gov.uk/archives

East Ayrshire
Stewarton Library
Cunningham Institute, Stewarton, KA3 5AB Tel: 01560 484385

Falkirk
Falkirk Local History Society
11 Neilson Street, Falkirk, FK1 5AQ The Society produces a local
history journal twice a year called "Calatria" and has a limited archive of
material related to the Falkirk Council Area

Fife
Abertay Historical Society
27 Pitcairn Road, Downfield, Dundee, DD3 9EE Tel: 01382 858701 Email:
abertay@dmcsoft.com WWW: www.dcmsoft.com/abertay

Glasgow
Glasgow Hebrew Burial Society
222 Fenwick Road, Griffnock, Glasgow, G46 6UE Tel: 0141 577 8226

Perthshire
Abertay Historical Society
27 Pitcairn Road, Downfield, Dundee, DD3 9EE Tel: 01382 858701 Email:
abertay@dmcsoft.com WWW: www.dcmsoft.com/abertay
Dunning Parish Historical Society
The Old Schoolhouse, Newtown-Of-Pitcairns, Dunning, Perth,
PH2 0SL Tel: 01764 684448 WWW: www.dunning.uk.net

Renfrewshire
Bridge of Weir History Society
41 Houston Road, Bridge Of Weir, PA11 3QR Local Society providing
monthly lecvture meetings and an outing once a year. No archive material available
Paisley Philosophical Institution
14 Newton Avenue, Elderslie, PA5 9BE
Renfrewshire Local History Forum
Museum & Art Galleries, High Street, Paisley, PA1 2BA
Tel: 0141 889 3151 WWW: www.rlhfas.org.uk

Stirling
Drymen Library
The Square, Drymen, G63 0BL Tel: 01360 660751
Email: drymenlibrary@stirling.gov.uk

West Lothian
Scottish Local History Forum
45 High Street, Linlithgow, EH54 6EW Tel: 01506 844649 Fax:
0131 260 6610 Email: chantal.hamill@dial.pipex.com
Linlithgow Union Canal Society
Manse Road Basin, Linlithgow, EH49 6AJ Tel: 01506-671215
(Answering Machine) Email: info@lucs.org.uk WWW:
www.lucs.org.uk, No genealogical information held

Northern Ireland
Federation of Ulster Local Studies
18 May Street, Belfast, BT1 4NL Tel: (028) 90235254
Presbyterian Historical Society of Ireland
Church House, Fisherwick Place, Belfast, BT1 6DW Tel: (028)
9032 2284 Opening hours: Mon to Fri 10am to 12.30pm. Wed afternoons 1.30pm to 3.30pm

Co Tyrone
Centre for Migration Studies
Ulster American Folk Park, Mellon Road, Castletown, Omagh,
BT78 5QY Tel: 028 82 256315 Email: uafp@iol.ie

County Londonderry
Roe Valley Historical Society
36 Drumachose Park, Limavady, BT49 0NZ

Ireland
Federation of Local History Societies
Rothe House, Kilkenny

County Dublin
Raheny Heritage Society
4 Thorndale Drive, Artane, Dublin 5 Tel: 01 831 9028 Lists of
individuals interests supplied on request to Hon Secretary with International Reply Coupon

County Mayo
Mayo North Family Heritage Centre
Enniscoe, Castlehill, Ballina Tel: 00 44 096 31809
Email: normayo@iol.ie WWW: www.mayo-ireland.ie/motm.htm
South Mayo Family Research Centre
Main Street, Ballinrobe Tel: 353 92 41214
Email: soumayo@iol.ie WWW: http:/mayo.irish-roots.net/

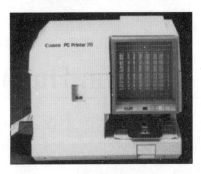

Where can you …

- *Access over 100,000 items on local & family history?*
- *Use the largest collection of parish register & census index copies in Britain?*
- *Get immediate, valuable advice from experienced genealogists?*
- *Attend informative lectures presented by experts?*
- *Browse the best-stocked genealogical bookshop in the country?*
- *Surf a growing range of online records?*

You get all these and more from …

The Society of Genealogists

The One-Stop resource for everyone in Family & Local History

Take advantage of our unique, newly refurbished **Library** with over 9000 Parish Register copies and wide-ranging material on Civil Registration, Censuses, County Records, Poll Books, Heraldry & Family Histories - on microfilm, fiche & PC.

Visit our **Bookshop** for an impressive range of books, microfiche, CDs, disks & IT genealogy programs at very competitive prices. Surf over 7000 items online at www.sog.org.uk via our secure server. Contact us at sales@sog.org.uk.

Join the Society - **Membership** gives you:

- Free access to the library & borrowing rights
- a 20% discount on all Society publications, lectures and courses
- free copies of the highly respected *Genealogists' Magazine*
- free access to an increasing range of online records

and all for **just £30 a year** *

For an information pack, simply email the Membership Secretary on

membership@sog.org.uk,
tel: 020-7553 3291

Make the most of your research with:

**The Society of Genealogists
14 Charterhouse Buildings, Goswell Road
London EC1M 7BA**

Tel: 020-7251 8799; Fax: 020-7250 1800

* special Direct Debit offer

The Records of the British Army 1660-1920

I S Swinnerton

If you possess a soldier ancestor in your family tree, you may well be able to discover more about him and his life and travels in the British Army than you could ever hope to achieve in the case of a civilian forbear. This applies particularly to soldiers who served in the ranks. There is a considerable amount of misunderstanding and confusion regarding the whereabouts of the principal holdings of British Army records.

The records of soldiers who served in the British Army on regular engagements between its birth in 1660 and 1913 are housed at the Public Record Office (PRO) at Kew, together with other old War Office records of various kinds. So too are those of men of the British and Irish militias, although some of these may occasionally be found in county record offices. The collection occupies nearly seven miles of shelf space and may be seen and researched by anyone. Unfortunately, contrary to what seems to be the popular belief, records relating to individual soldiers are not in named, neat little bundles to be easily picked from a shelf but in most cases, require detailed research. Unfortunately, for the overseas family historian, the PRO does not undertake research for members of the public, so you will need either to visit Kew yourself or engage a professional researcher to act on your behalf. It should go without saying that it is advisable to engage someone on personal recommendation or to employ a suitably qualified member of AGRA or ISRA.

As a general rule, the records of all British soldiers will be found at Kew and includes those belonging to Scottish, Irish and Welsh regiments. The documents are fully described in PRO Leaflet No.9 - 'British Military Records as Sources for Biography and Genealogy'. In addition, the three oldest regiments of Foot Guards - the Grenadier, Coldstream and Scots Guards – also possess some very good records of their own including lists of names. However, many of these are simply copies of the documents at Kew but if you know that your ancestor was a guardsman who served, for instance, at the battle of Waterloo or during the Crimean War, and you have been unable to find any personal information about him at Kew, you could try asking the appropriate regiment whether it has any record of him and his service. You should write to the Regimental Adjutant, RHQ Grenadier, Coldstream or Scots Guards, Wellington Barracks, Birdcage Walk, London SW 1 E 6HQ. For the rest of the army, regimental museums as a general rule do not have records of individual soldiers but they may have lists of officers.

The principal records are the soldier's Discharge Papers for those soldiers discharged with a pension. They are classified under WO.97. Sadly, the papers for those discharged without a pension before 1883 were destroyed by fire many years ago. So - to find the papers for your ancestor, you must search in the period of his discharge. The records are grouped by date:
1760-1854: 1855-1872: 1873-1882: 1883-1900: 1900-1913
From 1760 to 1872 they are arranged by regiment; from 1873 to 1882 alphabetically by name within the arms of service i.e. cavalry, infantry, artillery and corps and from 1883 to 1913 alphabetically by name for the whole army.

For the period before 1882, therefore, you need to know whether your soldier served in the Cavalry, Infantry, Artillery, Engineers etc. and, in the case of the first two his regiment. There were over 100 Infantry Regiments of the Line and 28 Cavalry Regiments so, although possible, it would be a mammoth task to search them all.

In the documents you should find his attestation papers (the forms he completed when he joined the army), which give his place of birth, age on joining, trade or occupation before joining, and a physical description. There will be an account of his army career - promotions, demotions, medals awarded, places where he served etc. and, finally, the place and date of discharge and an address where he intended to live. In later documents, you will often find details of next of kin and brothers and sisters and a medical history. You will certainly find his signature, often several times. Not all the records are by any means complete and the Medal Rolls (classified under WO100) can be useful in filling in gaps.

The other main records are the Pay Lists and Muster Rolls which sometimes, particularly for those soldiers who were not discharged to pension because they took an early discharge or died in service, are the only source of information about a soldier. The early series are Muster Rolls, which start about 1760 and end in the 1880s. They will be found under: WO10 (Royal Artillery): WO11 (Royal Engineers): WO12 (Cavalry, Guards and Infantry) and WO13 Yeomanry, Militia and Volunteers. They are continued for all arms in WO.16 for the post-1881 reorganisation Muster Rolls which includes all the district depots.

Pension Records are to be found under WO116 (Medical Pensions) and WO117 (Service Pensions). There are also records of soldiers who took deferred pensions and who purchased their discharges. Do not despair if you cannot find him under these records, there are many other records which can be consulted such as the special files and Description Books for Royal Artillery and Engineers - the general Description Books are under WO25/2666-2688. There are records of Courts Martial, Prisoners of War and of the effects of soldiers who died in service to name but a few. An Index to all soldiers (no officers) discharged to pension between 1760 and 1854 has been compiled on computer by volunteers from the Friends of the PRO.

There is also the Soldiers Index 1792-1838 (no officers or Militia) compiled from sources outside the PRO such as Barracks Census Returns, parish records, regimental journals and histories. Details of this may be obtained, on receipt of an SAE, from J.D.Beckett, 34 Eastwood Avenue, Droylsden, Manchester M35 6BJ. For a list of other useful indexes to soldiers see 'Marriage, Census and Other Indexes' by J.S.W.Gibson published by the Federation of Family History Societies, PO Box 8684, Shirley, Solihull, B90 4JU.

ARMY RECORDS OF THE GREAT WAR
Microfilm copies of service records for soldiers of the British Army who enlisted or were conscripted to fight in

the First World War and for pre-war regular soldiers whose service ended between 1914 and 1920 have now been transferred from the custody of the Ministry of Defence to the Public Record Office, Kew. **The actual documents, however, remain at the MOD Depot at Hayes.** The records were originally kept so that the War Office (as it then was) could answer queries about pensions, medals and allowances for disablement. Sadly, during the last war about 60% of them were destroyed in the bombing of London. Most of those that survived were badly damaged either by fire or from the water that was used to put out the flames. They have become known as the *Burnt Collection* and contain the service records of roughly 25-30% of the estimated 5 million men who served in the British Army in the Great War. They are stored in a staggering 33,000 boxes on nearly 2 miles of shelving but are in such a fragile condition that **they will never be open to public inspection**.

The Public Record Office, Kew has received a grant from the National Lottery Fund to finance a project to conserve and microfilm them. The letters A,B,C,D,E,F,I,J,K,L,M,N,O,P, Q, R, S,T,U,V,W,X,Y & Z have been filmed and are available for inspection with a forecast for H – April 2002 and G – June 2002. They are classified as record class WO (War Office) 363 but in many cases, only fragments of pages have survived. For a fee of £20 the Ministry of Defence will search the records not yet filmed and still at Hayes and the search can now be done for anyone, not just the next-of-kin as previously. Write to MOD CS(RM)2, Bourne Avenue, Hayes, Middlesex UB3 1RF.

There is another collection of records known as *the Unburnt Collection* which are already available for searching. These were compiled from duplicate records held by the Ministry of Pensions and comprise the records of another 8-10% of the soldiers. These have been microfilmed by the Genealogical Society of Utah and were released for public consumption at a special conference held at the PRO on Armistice Day 1996. It is hoped to have copies of these in other locations in due course and they are, of course, available through LDS Family History Libraries. They have been classified as WO 364.

Both the Burnt and Unburnt Collections include service records not only for regular soldiers (which can date back to the 1880s) but also for members of the Territorial Force and Special Reserve who had enlisted pre-war and for members of the Royal Flying Corps.

In the case of Officers, some 85% of records have survived: in this case they have not been filmed because the original records have been transferred to the PRO and are available for searching in Class WO338. They will also appear in the Medal Rolls and in the printed Army Lists. All officers and soldiers who served in a Theatre of War were entitled to some of the medals that were issued to commemorate the war. The important point here is that they had to have served in a Theatre of War – there was no equivalent of the Second World War Defence Medal which was awarded to home based forces as well as the fighting troops overseas. There were three principal awards for the Great War – the 1914 Star (also issued in a 1914-15 version), the British War Medal and the Victory Medal. There were also special medals for pre-war Territorials who served in the war and for members of the Merchant Navy. There is a microfiche index to these at the PRO in record class WO372 (the actual medal rolls are in class WO329) and also to Gallantry Awards and to Mentions in Despatches. So - even if you are unlucky and your ancestor's records have not survived, he will most certainly be listed on the medal rolls provided that he served in a War Zone.

The Imperial War Museum, Lambeth Road, London SE1

6HZ has a photographic archive at its All Saints Annexe, Austral Street, London, (0171-416-5333, open by appointment Monday – Friday, 10.00am – 5.00pm.) or you can write to them. They have over 5 million WWI, WW2 and post-war photographs.

The Jervis World War I Photographic Index has been compiled to ensure that photographs and ephemera relating to service personnel who fought in the First World War found in bookshops and at fairs which would otherwise have been lost, are preserved and made accessible. The compiler is particularly concerned with ensuring that the part played by the common man in the tumultuous events of the Great War does not go unmarked by posterity and that there is more than just a name on a war memorial to record the passing of men who fought and often died for King and Country. The index, compiled by Simon Jervis and consisting of photographs of World War I servicemen and officers (mainly soldiers, but it does include some sailors, marines and airmen) is open for searches. Every photograph has been carefully researched and identified from the Medal Rolls and other records.

The number, rank and name is given together with the regiment or unit and details of any decorations. Details of regiment(s) and corps in which the man served are also recorded together with any subsequent renumbering. Many men served with several regiments and many who were wounded were not sent back to the trenches after convalescence, but transferred to the Labour Corps. The index also includes other ephemera such as postcards and letters to and from the man, discharge documents, photographs of graves (often the original field grave), medal slips, Christmas cards, memorial cards and pay books.

The index has been computerised by Imperial Soldier Searches and on receipt of a cheque or postal order for £3 and a stamped, addressed, envelope (UK) or an International Money Order for £3 in sterling, self addressed envelope and two Inter-national Reply Coupons (overseas) a search will be made. If nothing is found, the enquiry will be included in the database and checked against future additions as new material is coming in all the while. If an entry is found the enquiry will be passed to Simon Jervis who will negotiate with the enquirer direct for copies of the relevant material. Because of the archival nature of the material, he will retain copyright of all photographs and will offer laser or photographic copies and negatives. Remittances, payable to I.S.Swinnerton, should be sent to Cobwebs, Long Burton, Sherborne, Dorset DT9 5PD, UK.

Bibliography.
An Introduction to the British Army: Its History, Traditions & Records
Iain Swinnerton, FFHS (as above) 2nd Edition 1998.
Army Records for Family Historians
Simon Fowler and William Spencer. Public Record Office Reader's Guide No.2 published by the PRO, Ruskin Avenue, Kew, Surrey TW9 4DU.
My Ancestor was in the British Army
M.J. & C.T.Watts, Society of Genealogists 1992
A Guide to the regiments and corps of the British army on the regular establishment
J.M.Brereton, Bodley Head 1985
In search of the "Forlorn Hope: a comprehensive guide to locating British regiments and their records (1640-WW1)
John M.KitzmullerII, Manuscript Publishing Foundation, Salt Lake City 1988.
World War One Army Ancestry by Norman Holding
The Location of British Army WWI Records by Norman Holding and Iain Swinnerton
More Sources for WWI Ancestry by Norman Holding
Identifying Your World War One Soldier from Badges and Photographs by Iain Swinnerton
All published by the Federation of Family History Societies, PO Box 8684, Shirley, Solihull B90 4JU.
Army Service Records of the First World War by Simon Fowler, William Spencer and Stuart Tamblin. Public Record Office Readers' Guide No.19. published by the PRO, Ruskin Avenue, Kew, Surrey TW9 4DU England.

Family History in the Department of Printed Books – Imperial War Museum

Sarah Paterson

Many of you will already have read our previous articles relating to family history research at the Imperial War Museum, so rather than simply repeating them we thought it a much better idea to give you some idea of what has been happening here and news about forthcoming developments. The text of our family history notes leaflets for the Army and Prisoners of War (the most recent of these leaflets) is also included in this entry. We also have leaflets for the Royal Air Force, the Royal Navy and the Merchant Navy. These can be consulted on the Museum's website, the address of which is www.iwm.org.uk

Other items on the website include some of our recommended reading lists. These are on topics as diverse as The Royal Marines, Second World War air raid shelters and Changi Civilian Internment Camp. As well as suggesting books that can be consulted in our Reading Room (or alternative copies may be available through your local library's inter-library loan scheme) these often include relevant addresses, website addresses or other useful information. You are welcome to contact the address below to see whether we might have a reading list on a subject of interest to you, and even if we don't, we should be able to make some suggestions that should help you find out more about your area of interest.

Our Reading Room – shared by the Department of Printed Books and the Department of Documents – is located in the Dome, at the very top of the Museum. It is a striking and attractive room, with features of the old chapel that it used to be still prominent (the building had a former incarnation as the Bethlem Mental Hospital). However, for some of our readers it can be difficult to reach because it involves climbing a set of steep and twisty stairs. We are delighted to announce that we now have better facilities for disabled readers or for those who find the stairs difficult to negotiate. Room "D12" has been refitted with a wide door, wheelchair friendly carpet, four new purpose-built workstations and a cord-pull emergency alarm system. A grant from the Friends of the Imperial War Museum also enabled us to purchase special closed circuit television and computerised equipment for blind and visually impaired readers. It is necessary to have booked an appointment, and if you are registered disabled you will be able to book a car parking space – it is best to book several days before you intend visiting. Appointments can be made on (020) 7416 5342 if you wish to use Printed Books materials or (020) 7416 5222 if you will be using Documents (please note that these are private and personal papers, such as letters and diaries, and not official documents, which are held at the Public Record Office).

Trench maps are very frequently asked about, and in order to make these more readily available, the Museum has been involved in a project with Naval and Military Press. This has resulted in a CD-Rom called **The Imperial War Museum Trench Map Archive on CD-Rom**. This can be viewed in our Reading Room, or it may be purchased directly from Naval and Military Press or large reference libraries may have copies of this. It consists of 175 large scale 1:10,000 maps providing a near complete coverage of the British section of the Western Front from the North Sea at Nieuport in Belgium southwards to St Quentin. All the battles of the First World War are represented

here, with the maps showing the trench systems developing over the months and years. Different editions of the same sheet enable the operations to be followed, British trenches in blue and German trenches in red (until mid-1918 when the colours were reversed to follow French practice). For security reasons, although the trench maps show all the German trenches and tactical features, they mostly only show the British front line, until 1917-18 when this policy was gradually relaxed.

Other projects underway at the moment include a select bibliography on the Spanish Civil War, to coincide with the exhibition opening at the Museum in October 2001. This will be in the same style as our 184 page **Select Catalogue of English-Language Material on the Holocaust held in the Department of Printed Books** (priced at £20) and our 57 page **Select Catalogue of English-Language Material on the Korean War, 1950-1953** (priced at £12). A similar publication relating to women will be launched to coincide with the exhibition **Women in Uniform** opening in late Spring 2002. We plan to produce some more of our family history leaflets relating to women in the Armed Services, and also intend to publish more in our **Tracing Your Family History** series on female involvement in both World Wars.

Many of you may not be aware of our best-selling **Tracing Your Family History** series. This set of books consists of volumes on the **Army**, **Royal Air Force**, **Royal Navy** and **Merchant Navy** and these sell for £5.50 each. They are ideal introductions to the subject of tracing ancestors in each of these services from 1914 onwards, and have been compiled in response to the many questions we get asked regularly. As well as providing information about where records can be found, they include information about the structure and organisation of the branch of service, medals, numbering, and suggestions for further research. Useful book titles, addresses and websites are also included.

If you wish to make an appointment to visit our Reading Room, or have a question you would like to ask (bearing in mind that we cannot embark on detailed research for you), please contact us in one of the following ways:

Telephone (enquiries): (020) 7416 5342
Post: Imperial War Museum, Department of Printed Books
Lambeth Road, London SE1 6HZ
Email: books@iwm.org.uk Website: www.iwm.org.uk

© Robert Blatchford

Tracing Army Ancestry
Family History notes from the Imperial War Museum

The most important piece of information is the unit that an individual served with (it is a sad fact that those who died during the World Wars will be easier to trace than those who survived, and this information is readily obtainable from the **Commonwealth War Graves Commission**). The personal service record should be the starting point, but not all of these records for the First World War survived Second World War bombing. Records are located according to an individual's date of discharge.

The Imperial War Museum only covers the period from the First World War War onwards. Military history from 1485 to date is covered by the **National Army Museum, Royal Hospital Road, Chelsea, London SW3 4HT (Tel: 020 7730 0717 Website: http://www.national-army-museum.ac.uk)**. Pre-1914 service records are held at the **Public Record Office, Ruskin Avenue, Kew, Richmond, Surrey TW9 4DU (Tel: 020 8392 5200; Website: http://www.pro.gov.uk)**. The PRO also holds all surviving First World War service records for officers who left the Army before 1922. Surviving First World War Service records for other ranks who ceased service before 1920 are slowly being released to the PRO where they can be consulted on microfilm. It is hoped that this process will be complete by autumn 2002. The records of any First World War soldier who saw service after these cut-off dates or who rejoined the Army will still be held by the **Ministry of Defence, Army Records Centre, DR2B Bourne Avenue, Hayes, Middlesex UB3 1RF**. The publication *Army service records of the First World War* by William Spencer, 3rd edition, (Richmond, Surrey: PRO, 2001) is essential reading for those interested in the released First World War records, and *Army records for family historians* by Simon Fowler and William Spencer, 2nd edition, (Richmond, Surrey: PRO, 1998) will also prove helpful.

The **Army Records Centre** holds the records for those soldiers who served after 1920, and officers who served after 1922 until the mid 1990s (immediately after a soldier's discharge they are held by the **Army Personnel Centre** in Glasgow). The ARC will release records to proven next of kin for a £25 fee, but there may be a lengthy wait for this service.

The Brigade of Guards and Household Cavalry form an exception to this, and generally speaking retain their own records. The addresses to apply to for these are:
Regimental Headquarters Grenadier/Coldstream/Scots/Irish/Welsh Guards, Wellington Barracks, Birdcage Walk, London SW1E 6HQ and **Household Cavalry Museum, Combermere Barracks, Windsor, Berkshire SL4 3DN**.

The careers of Army officers can be traced using the regular official publication *The Army List*, and the Department of Printed Books holds an almost complete set of these from 1914 to date.

Casualty Records
The **Commonwealth War Graves Commission, 2 Marlow Road, Maidenhead, Berkshire SL6 7DX (Tel: 01628 634221)** has details of all service personnel who died between the dates 4 August 1914-31 August 1921 and 3 September 1939-31 December 1947. The CWGC may charge a fee for postal enquiries, but the website containing their computerised database, *Debt of Honour* can be consulted at **http://www.cwgc.org**

Details about the burial places of soldiers who died outside the dates covered by the CWGC are held by the **Ministry of Defence, PS4 (A) (Cas/Comp), Building 43, Trenchard Lines, Upavon, Pewsey, Wiltshire SN9 6BE**. They also have some details relating to soldiers' wives or children who may have died outside the UK.

Sources held by Department of Printed Books include a complete set of the CWGC's memorial and cemetery registers and the 80 volume *Soldiers died in the Great War, 1914-19*. This was originally published in 1921 by HMSO but was republished by J B Hayward in 1989. It is also now available on a CD-ROM produced by Naval and Military Press. *Officers died in the Great War, 1914-19* is less detailed and has probably been superseded by *Officers who died in the service of British, Indian and East African Regiments and Corps, 1914-1919* by S D and D B Jarvis (Reading: Roberts Medals, 1993).

For the Second World War there is a computer coded roll of honour, which can be quite difficult to use in its present form. This is held by both the Department of Printed Books and the PRO, but Promenade Publications are in the process of publishing a ten volume set of this. Rolls of honour for other later conflicts are also held, and in addition the DPB has a large collection of published rolls of honour for localities, schools, institutions etc. Regimental histories and journals often contain rolls of honour.

The soldiers' own home area should not be forgotten when researching an individual's service - there may be local war memorial records, a local account of war service may have been published, and contemporary local newspapers can prove very helpful. It is also possible that school, church or workplace records may still exist.

Medal Records
Campaign medals are those given to soldiers who are eligible for them because they were in a particular theatre of war within given dates. The PRO holds the First World War Medal Roll which provides a listing of all those who qualified for the 1914 Star, 1914/15 Star, British War Medal, Victory Medal, Territorial Force War Medal and/or the Silver War Badge. If a First World War record was destroyed some basic information about a soldier's service may be found in this.

Gallantry medals are those medals awarded for an especially heroic deed or action. Records for these are held at the PRO, but may not be very detailed. Notifications and citations (if published, which was not the case for awards such as the Military Medal and Mentions in Despatches) appeared in the official journal *London Gazette*. A complete set of this, and the all important indexes, is held at the PRO. The Department of Printed Books has some published listings of medal awards for decorations such as the Victoria Cross or

Distinguished Conduct Medal. Usually you will need to go either to the official unit war diary (held at the PRO) or to a published unit history to see whether you can find out more about the action for which the decoration was awarded.

Regimental histories
The Department of Printed Books has an excellent collection of regimental histories. For those unable to visit our reading room (open 10am-5pm, Monday to Saturday), *A bibliography of regimental histories of the British Army* compiled by Arthur S White (London: London Stamp Exchange, 1988) provides details of published histories that may be available through your local library's inter-library loan scheme. Regimental journals and forces newspapers should not be overlooked.

A useful title for locating regimental museums (although these are very unlikely to hold information about individuals) is *A guide to military museums: and other places of military interest* by Terence and Shirley Wise (Knighton, Powys: Terence Wise, 1999).

We can also advise on the addresses of Old Comrades Associations. The internet has made it easier to establish contact with people who may have served in the Forces, or who may be conducting research similar to your own. The British Legion website at **www.britishlegion.org.uk** is a good place to start. Other websites of interest include The Western Front Association at **www.westernfront.co.uk** and Land Forces of Britain, the Empire and Commonwealth at **www.regiments.org/milhist/**

Tracing Prisoners of War
Family History notes from the Imperial War Museum

© Robert Blatchford

Records of prisoners of war were compiled by each national branch of the Red Cross and are now all held centrally by the **Archives Division and Research Service, International Committee of the Red Cross, 19 Avenue de la Paix, Geneva CH-1202, Switzerland**. Because of their personal nature, these records are not accessible to the general public but paid searches can be conducted (currently 80 Swiss Francs an hour) – please be patient as this may take some time. You will need to know the **full name** and **nationality** of the individual you are researching. Additional details such as regiment, number, place and date of birth, date of capture and name of father are likely to aid your enquiry.

Some details about those who died in captivity during both World Wars will be held by the **Commonwealth War Graves Commission**. The computerised database *Debt of Honour* can be accessed on the website at http://www.cwgc.org The Commission can be contacted at **2 Marlow Road, Maidenhead, Berkshire SL6 7DX (Tel: 01628 634221)**.

Any official documentation relating to British POWs is held by the **Public Record Office, Ruskin Avenue, Kew, Richmond, Surrey TW9 4DU (Tel: 020 8392 5200)**. More information about these records can be found in *Military Records Information Leaflet 12 (British Prisoners of War, c1760-1919)* and *Military Records Information Leaflet 20 (British Prisoners of War, 1939-1953)*. These leaflets can be found on the PRO website at http://www.pro.gov.uk/leaflets/

Sources at the Department of Printed Books of the Imperial War Museum include autobiographies and camp journals, although inevitably some locations are better documented than others. Please contact us to find out more about the particular camps you are interested in. Items can be viewed by appointment in the Reading Room (shared with the Department of Documents and anyone visiting should also check their holdings). The following items may be helpful for starting your research.

First World War
The *List of British Officers taken Prisoner in the Various Theatres of War between August 1914 and November 1918* compiled by the military agents Cox and Co in 1919 will prove helpful if you are seeking an individual who was commissioned. Another useful source is the monthly *Enquiry Lists* issued by the **Enquiry for the Wounded and Missing Department of the British Red Cross and Order of St John**. Our holdings of this are not complete, with better coverage

for some periods than others.

The Department of Printed Books also holds a set of *War Office Weekly Casualty Lists* from December 1917 to February 1919 that contain references to killed, wounded and captured servicemen. This is a difficult source to use and does not yield much information for those seeking prisoners.

The Department of Printed Books' *Women's Work Collection* (on microfilm) contains some information about soldiers and non commissioned officers who were taken prisoner before Christmas 1914, and were therefore eligible to receive Princess Mary's Gift Box. These lists are arranged by regiment in sections B.O.2 1/11 – B.O.2 1/328 (you will need to use the inventory to work out which precise part of the microfilm you need to look at).

We also have for sale (£5.00) a reprint of *Map of the main Prison Camps in Germany and Austria*, a map gazetteer showing the principal Central Powers prisoner of war camps in Germany and Austria, compiled by Mrs Pope-Hennessey and published by Nisbet and Co during the First World War.

Second World War
Three useful volumes have been reprinted by John Hayward in conjunction with the Department of Printed Books. These are nominal rolls of POWs held in Germany and German occupied Territory, corrected up to the end of March 1945. Volume one is entitled *Prisoners of War: British Army 1939-1945: Alphabetical Nominal Registers (including Rank, POW Number, Regiment or Corps and Camp Location details) Listing over 107,000 British Army Prisoners of War of all Ranks held in Germany and German Occupied Territories*. Volume two covers *Armies and other Land Forces of the British Empire* and volume

© Robert Blatchford

three covers *Naval and Air Forces of Great Britain and the Empire*.

Probably the best single volume of work dealing with POWs generally is *Official History of New Zealand in the Second World War, 1939-1945: Prisoners of War* by W Wynne Mason (Wellington, New Zealand: War History Branch, Department of Internal Affairs, 1954).

Issues of *The Prisoner of War: the Official Organ of the Prisoners of War Department of the Red Cross and St John War Organisation*, contain interesting background information, particularly about activities in POW camps in Occupied Europe.

For those interested in prisoners in the Far East, *Prisoners of the Japanese in World War II: Statistical History, Personal Narratives, and Memorials concerning POWs in Camps and on Hellships, Civilian Internees, Asian Slave Laborers and Others Captured in the Pacific Theater* by Van Waterford (Jefferson, North Carolina: McFarland, 1994) provides helpful guidance, information about the camps and suggestions for further reading.

Korean War
Prisoners of War Korea, 1950-1953: the British Army compiled by Peter Gaston (London: London Stamp Exchange, 1976) lists men taken prisoner.

Useful Contacts
There are too many worthwhile organisations to list here and we would suggest that enquirers contact us for advice on addresses, including details of the various branches and regional Far East Prisoner of War associations. Meanwhile, one of the more general organisations in this field is:

The National Ex-Prisoner of War Association, Historian: P D Chinnery Esq, 10 Lambert Avenue, Langley, Berkshire SL3 7EB

The following have websites that contain helpful links to other sites as well as useful information:
Royal Air Forces Ex-POW Association
Website: http://freespace.virgin.net/frank.haslam/rafexpow.html

COFEPOW (Children (and Families) of the Far East Prisoners of War)
Website: http://www.cofepow.org.uk

The Imperial War Museum does not hold any service records, official documentation or comprehensive listings of Prisoners of War, but it does have extensive material that will be helpful for providing information and understanding about their experience. This leaflet should be used in conjunction with the relevant leaflet for the individual's branch of service – Army, Royal Air Force, Royal Navy or Merchant Marine.

The Department of Printed Books welcomes visitors by appointment (Monday to Saturday, from 10am to 5pm). Other reference departments in the Museum – Art, Documents, Exhibits and Firearms, Film and Video Archive, Photograph Archive, and the Sound Archive – may also be able to assist. Advance appointments are required.

Department of Printed Books
Imperial War Museum, Lambeth Road, London SE1 6HZ
Tel: (+44) 020 7416 5342 Fax: (+44) 020 7416 5246
Website: http://www.iwm.org.uk Email: books@iwm.org.uk

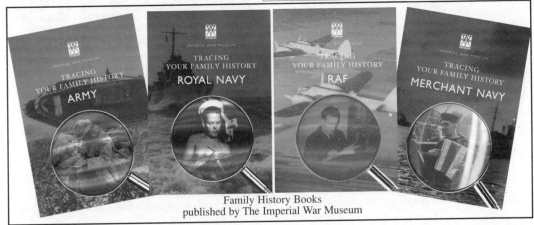

Family History Books
published by The Imperial War Museum

The Commonwealth War Graves Commission

Peter Francis
Commonwealth War Graves Commission

The Commonwealth War Graves Commission, was established by Royal Charter of 21 May 1917, the provisions of which were amended and extended by a Supplemental Charter of 8 June 1964. Its duties are to mark and maintain the graves of the forces of the Commonwealth who died during two world wars, to build and maintain memorials to the dead whose graves are unknown, and to keep records and registers. The cost is shared by the partner governments - those of Australia, Canada, India, New Zealand, South Africa and the United Kingdom - in proportions based upon the numbers of their graves.

The Commission is responsible for 1.7 million commemorations, with war graves at over 23,000 locations and in some 150 countries. The work is founded upon the principles that each of the dead should be commemorated individually by name either on the headstone on the grave or by an inscription on a memorial; that each of the headstones and memorials should be permanent; that the headstones should be uniform; and that no distinction should be made on account of military or civil rank, race or creed.

Today, the Commission's major concern is the maintenance of those graves, cemeteries and memorials, to the highest standards, in the face of exposure to the elements and the passage of time - to ensure that "Their Name Liveth For Evermore". In addition to the day to day horticultural and structural maintenance of the cemeteries and memorials, an enquiry service is on offer to the public, whereby the commemorative details for any Commonwealth casualty who died during either of the two world wars can be provided. Commemorative information for Commonwealth civilians who died as a result of enemy action during the Second World War is also available on a Roll of Honour numbering over 66,400 names.

Originally, casualty data was stored on card indexes in over 3,000 drawers. After the First World War, details were compiled into some 1,500 cemetery registers. All enquiries were handled by a wholly manual process until 1995. The work was carried out, as it had been for decades, by dedicated, knowledgeable staff, using large ledgers. The ledgers are organised by country, name of cemetery and alphabetically by surname. To overcome the challenge of an enquirer only knowing a casualty's surname and not the place of burial, there are large volumes of alphabetical lists, cross-referenced by code numbers to the appropriate cemetery register. In late autumn 1995 the Commission's vast resource of information was computerised, allowing for a more efficient service to be offered to the public. The information for each entry was broken down into searchable 'fields' - For example, Surname, Age, Regiment, Cemetery Name, Date of Death e.t.c.

Not only do the computerised records allow for better access to the casualty details and place of commemoration, it also allows the operator to trace single casualties more quickly, from less information, and offer services like casualty-listing reports. This has become increasingly important as the value of the database for educational purposes is recognised and

enquiries become more complex. Some of the most popular criteria for casualty listings include a same surname search, a regimental search and a home town search. It is even possible to trace, for example, how many Captains were killed on the first day of the Battle of the Somme.

In line with this public access policy, the Commission took the initiative to use the Internet to further promote access to the records. In November 1998, to coincide with the eightieth anniversary of the Armistice that brought to an end the First World War, the Debt of Honour Register was launched. The Register, a search by surname database, is available to the public via the Commission's web site at www.cwgc.org. The database provides known details of the casualty as well as the name of the cemetery or memorial, directions on how to find it and the exact plot, row, grave or memorial panel reference to enable the enquirer to locate the place of burial or commemoration should they make a pilgrimage to the cemetery or memorial. A second page on the web site prints the casualty details in the form of a commemorative certificate for the enquirer.

The launch of the Debt of Honour Register on the Internet has been an incredible success - the site averages 500,000 hits a week. The Register has widened public knowledge and interest in commemoration, reunited families with the records of their long-fallen loved ones, assisted the historian, researcher and the student and most importantly, proved a highly effective way of keeping the names of those the Commission commemorates alive in the hearts and minds of a new generation. Enhancements to the site since it was launched have reduced down time and increased the accessibility of the site still further. The Commission anticipates further enhancements to the site in the near future.

In 1926, the Commission's founder, Fabian Ware, said the cemeteries and memorials built and maintained by the Commonwealth War Graves Commission, 'will bear a message to future generations as long as the stone of which they are constructed endures.' With the launch of the Debt of Honour Register, names once kept alive only in stone are now readily available to be carried in the hearts and minds of a new generation. As we move further away from the two world wars the Commission will ensure the stone, the gardens, the records, the memory and the message endure - that 'Their Name Liveth for Evermore".

Further Information
The Commission welcomes enquiries from the public. We request that you supply the Commission's enquiries department with as much information as possible. This will enhance the chances of a positive trace.

A full list of the Commission's services and publications on offer to the public is available from:

The Records & Enquiries Section
The Commonwealth War Graves Commission
2 Marlow Road, Maidenhead, Berkshire, SL6 7DX
Tel: 01628 634221 Fax: 01628 771208
E-mail: casualty.enq@cwgc.org Web Site: www.cwgc.org

The Commonwealth War Graves Commission Civilian Roll of Honour

Peter Francis
Commonwealth War Graves Commission

In 1938, the Imperial, now Commonwealth, War Graves Commission unveiled the Australian Memorial at Villers-Bretonneux. It was the last of the Great War memorials to be completed from the war that was to end all wars and yet within a year the Second World War had started and the Commission was called upon to prepare for a new harvest of death. This second catastrophe of the twentieth century was a very different conflict to the one that had taken place only twenty or so years previously. The war was one of quick movement - the German Blitzkrieg sweeping all before it and forcing the Commission to temporarily relinquish control of the cemeteries and memorials in occupied Europe.

With the conquest of mainland Europe complete, Hitler's forces concentrated their efforts on the invasion of the United Kingdom. In order to invade, Germany had first to achieve total air superiority and so began the Battle of Britain and the large-scale bombing of airfields, factories and later in an attempt to smash the morale of the British people, cities. Distinctions between soldiers and non-combatants were non-existent. The phrase Total War was coined to represent the fact that civilian populations as well as front line troops were now considered targets.

On 7 September 1940 the first major air raid on a British city was carried out by the Luftwaffe. The Commission's founder, Fabian Ware, witnessed first hand the deaths of women, children, firemen and air-raid wardens. This new and horrifying war was impacting on communities like never before. Surely, he reasoned, each casualty deserved a fitting commemoration? Soon London itself was a target of the Blitz. Ware decided to act and wrote to the Prime Minister, Winston Churchill, on 18 September, urging the commemoration of those civilians killed by enemy action. In his words, "The deliberate slaughter of civilians was creating a new category of normal war casualties. Theirs should be counted an equal sacrifice".

Churchill, who had so successfully argued for the Commission's principle of equality of treatment for the war dead while Chairman of the Commission during the parliamentary debates on commemoration of the early 1920s, had no objection. In fact, he believed that civilian deaths might well outnumber military casualties - fortunately, he was not proved correct.

In January 1941, the Commission began to keep records of all civilian deaths caused by enemy action and its Royal Charters were adjusted to give it the necessary powers to do so. The biggest single obstacle to this task was obtaining the names and addresses of those killed. The information provided by the authorities, like the Registrar General, was not always complete and often did not include the addresses of next of kin. In February 1941, to encourage a greater flow of information and further publicise the commemoration of civilians, Ware decided to make a tour of the hard-hit areas. During his tour he enlisted the help of mayors and local authorities and the information provided to the Commission greatly improved. In November 1941, he made a further appeal on national radio and in the press for help and the records began to take shape - the Commission already had over 18,000 individuals recorded.

However, Ware was not satisfied with the mere recording of names at the Commission's headquarters. As the Commission would have no responsibility for the graves of civilians, Ware suggested to the Dean of Westminster in January 1942 that the names should be inscribed on a Roll of Honour which might be placed in the Warrior's Chapel of the Abbey. "The symbolic significance of ...the admission of these civilian dead to the adjacency and companionship with the Unknown Soldier would...give a right inspiration." The Dean readily agreed.

In December 1942 the first typed lists, leather bound in three volumes, were deposited for safekeeping at Westminster. The volumes were not put on display until after the war because it was believed that if the extent of civilian casualties were known, it might damage the morale of the nation. It was not until 1956 that the completed volumes of the Civilian Roll of Honour were handed to the Dean of Westminster by the Duke of Gloucester. Today, there are six volumes with over 66,000 names recorded. In a fitting tribute to those commemorated, the books are still on display to the public at the Abbey. A new page of the Civilian Roll of Honour is turned every day and so unfolds 66,000 tragic stories - the sudden death of a pensioner aged one hundred or of an infant a few hours old, of 163 people killed in an instant when a V2 rocket fell on Woolworth's at New Cross, and of the 1,500 dead of Malta.

What information does the Civilian Roll of Honour have? The casualty details available include the person's name, age, date of death, last known address and the particulars of the next of kin. The entries are structured along the lines of the old Borough system and then alphabetically by surname. Just one moving example reads: Betty Francis, Civilian War Dead. Died 9 April 1941, Aged 2. Daughter of Emily and the late Tom Francis of Clevedon Road, Balsall Heath. County Borough of Birmingham. The civilian records, like the military records, are still updated to this day. Amendments made on the computerised system are later added to the leather bound volumes at the Abbey twice a year by a member of the Commission's records department. In this way, that 'equal sacrifice' is preserved for future generations.

For the family historian, all of this information is available from the Commission's enquiries department in Maidenhead and the Debt of Honour Register at www.cwgc.org The Civilian Roll of Honour is a highly moving tribute not only to the many innocents who had their lives brutally cut short by war but to the bravery of services like the Fire Brigade and Ambulance crews who risked their lives to save others. The Commonwealth War Graves Commission keeps faith with them all, ensuring that

Their Name Liveth For Evermore.

R.F.C. R.N.A.S and R.A.F. Register 1914 - 1919
David J Barnes

Background

The main aim of this research project, which started in October 1983, is to try to provide a central source of service and biographical information of all those who served in the British and Commonwealth Aerial Forces during the First World War, which would be of benefit to Aviation Enthusiasts, Family History Researchers, Medal Collectors, etc.

I decided to take on this mammoth project because although material was available about early war flying, 'aces' and the types of aircraft flown, there was very little information that was available about the men who had actually served. This is particularly true of the ground crew and men in supporting roles, who are generally overlooked

There was a book published in 1917, 'Royal Flying Corps (Military Wing), Casualties and Honours during the War 1914-17', compiled by Captain G L Campbell, R.F.A., assisted by R H Blinkhorn, [Reprinted 1987] and covers some of the Casualties and Honours up to June/July 1917, unfortunately there are a number of errors and omissions, and consequently cannot be relied upon. Information regarding 'Other Ranks' is very brief

The 'Official' Records

The most complete records should be those held by the Ministry of Defence, however some of these were destroyed during the Blitz in 1940, and other files were accidentally destroyed.
The information that is available was only released to next of kin after payment of a £20 search fee, though the next of kin requirement has since been waived, searches will only be done for a fee, if the material is still held by the Ministry of Defence
During 1997/98 some of these records were released to the Public Record Office.
It should be remembered that Army Officers Records of Service (including the R.F.C.) which were released to the Public Record Office in 1998, are only 60-70% complete, and are found under P.R.O. reference WO339.

For the 'Record of Service' with the Army and the Royal Flying Corps contact; Ministry of Defence, Army Records Office CS(R)2b, Bourne Avenue, Hayes, Middlesex UB3 1RF

For Commissioned Service (i.e. Officers) in the Royal Air Force, the Ministry of Defence files were released to the Public Record Office in October 1997 and are held in AIR 76 RAF Officers Records files. However if the Officer continued to serve in the Royal Air Force after the war, the Ministry of Defence have usually retained these files and the address you would have to contact is; Ministry of Defence, R.A.F. Personnel Management Centre, Eastern Avenue, Barnwood, Gloucester GL4 7PN

The Airmen's Documents for R.A.F. Enlistment's were released by the Public Record Office in September 1998 under reference Air 79 and are arranged in R.A.F. Service Number order, and will cover numbers up to 329,000. This does not include all airmen who served in the First World War. An index to R.A.F. service numbers is available in AIR 78 and is held on 190 reels of microfilm. This index was filmed by the R.A.F. in the early 1980's and covers all R.A.F. enlistment's up to 1975. However the Public Record Office admit that *'it is of doubtful quality in terms of comprehensiveness and legibility of some of the entries.'*

Numbers	Allocated to	Date Allocated
329001 to 335000	RAF - Civilians	Mar/Aug 1919
336001 to 338000	RAF - Civilians	Aug-Sep 1919
360001 to 360200	RAF - Canadians in UK. June 1918
360201 to 361200	RAF - Canadian Cadets in UK June 1918
	[Used up to 360665 only]
400000 to 410432	RAF - Army Transfers in	1918

A large amount of numbers from the above block 400,000 - 409095 appear on the R.A.F. Muster Roll for April 1918. There is no available information on other ranks in any of the blocks of numbers allocated to Canadian Other Ranks;

70,000 - 75,000	150,001 - 155,000	170,001 - 175,000
270,000 - 275,000	360,001 - 360,200	360,201 -361,200

'Other Ranks' R.A.F. service after April 1918 might be verified. There are some files which are not available, including those men who continued to serve in the Royal Air Force after the war, for these 'Other Ranks' Records of Service in the R.A.F. contact; Ministry of Defence , R.A.F. Personnel Management Centre, Innsworth, Gloucester GL3 1EZ

Records for Officers in the Royal Naval Air Service are held in ADM/273 at the Public Record Office and 'Other Ranks' in the Royal Naval Air Service were made available by the Public Record Office on 1 April 1998.
This latter category is in their original form, covering service numbers F1 - F55000 which are held in 86 volumes in the Alphabetically Prefixed numbers series in ADM 188 class. These records provide the date and place of birth, physical description, date of enlistment, rating, descriptions of ships or stations served upon, assessment of character & conduct and date of discharge The Naval Wing of the Royal Flying Corps, later the Royal Naval Air Service had numbers usually prefixed by 'F', though there are examples with 'G', 'J' & 'M' (Sick Berth Attendant's). The RAF Muster Roll shows that RNAS Numbers had reached F54121 by 1st April 1918, and on formation of the RAF all their numbers were prefixed by 200,000. For example; F12 became 200,012 and F23199 became 223,199

Numbers	Allocated to	Date Allocated
200001 to 202902	RAF - RNAS Enlistments	1914 -1 April 1918
202903 to 210316	RAF - RNAS Enlistments	1915 - 1 April 1918
210317 to 225060	RAF - RNAS Enlistments	1916 - 1 April 1918
225061 to 244710	RAF - RNAS Enlistments	1917 - 1 April 1918
244711 to 260000	RAF - RNAS Enlistments	1918 - 1 April 1918
	[Used up to 254574 only]	
313001 to 316000	RAF - Royal Naval Personnel attached to RNAS	1 April 1918
	[Used up to 315179 only]	

I have not traced any central records for Medical Discharges or transfers out of the RNAS, though I know that approximately 420 men of the RNAS Armoured Car Division transferred in 1917 to the Motor Branch of the Machine Gun Corps, given the rank of Sergeant and allocated an Army service number in the range 79600 - 80100. Some of these are listed in the Public Record Office file ADM 116/17171-e, Record of Ratings Service with Russian Armoured Cars, sadly there is no cross reference to their Machine Gun Corps Service Number.

The **Fleet Air Arm Museum,** RNAS Yeovilton, Ilchester,

Somerset BA22 8HT also hold the following documents ;

Officers: Records of service held on a series of aperture cards, filed in alphabetical order. Also on a series of alphabetical aperture cards are Records of service for officers who formed the RAF on 1 April 1918, which included those former member of RNAS and RFC

Ratings: 15 volumes of enlistment papers, amounting to approximately 6,600 records. These are for ratings who did not join the RAF on 1 April 1918, or those who joined as ratings and were subsequently commissioned. These are not service records, and are filed in service number order

The research costs are £15 per day for personal visitors and £20 per postal enquiry on one individual

Other Records

In the course of my research I learned of the **RAF Muster Roll** which was compiled to show all the 'Other Ranks' who were serving in the Royal Air Force on it's formation on 1 April 1918, and is arranged in RAF Service Number order. This listing includes Service Number, Name & Initials, Date & Terms of Enlistment, Trade, Rank and Date of Last Promotion, **it does not give Squadrons or Units attached to.** (Volume 1 covers service numbers SR 1 - SR 25)(1 - 102940) (Volume 2 covers service numbers 102941 - 186817)(200001 - 223200) (Volume 3 covers service numbers 223201 - 254121) (401001 - 409095) **Note**: There are gaps of unallocated numbers in both Volumes 2 and 3

The Service Numbers were allocated in the following manner; when the Military Wing, Royal Flying Corps was formed in April 1912, it absorbed personnel who had been serving with the Air Battalion, Royal Engineers but these men did not retain their original numbers. New numbers from 1 onwards were issued, with further enlistments and transfers into the Corps were in numerical order. A useful book, 'A Contemptible Little Flying Corps' by Ian McInnes & Jack V Webb, was published by The London Stamp Exchange in 1991, and this lists all the early RFC Enlistments, with some biographical detail, up to Number 1400 (14 August 1914). A lot of work was put in by a number of people, including myself, to fill in the missing numbers, i.e. those early numbers that are not on the 1918 Muster Roll.

As the size of the RFC was increased from June 1916 there were batches of transfers into the Corps, these appear within the normal batches of enlistments, these transfers usually being gathered in a group each month.

There are instances were a straight-forward RFC enlistments was assigned a four figure 'P' Number, which was later changed to a five figure number, which bore no relation to the earlier number, so caution must be taken

The RAF Muster Roll, compiled for 1st April 1918, shows that RFC enlistments had reached 186,817. However there were many gaps of unallocated numbers between 134,721 and 186,807.

So for over the last ten years I have been single handedly and without funding, been in the process of transposing this Muster Roll into an alphabetical card index listing. I have currently Royal Flying Corps enlistment details up to the end of May 1917. I believe my own files will be complementary to those held by the Public Record Office. As any additional

information comes to hand this is added on to the records, there are several sources of information that can be consulted to expand the details I have, these can include the following.

Useful secondary Sources

Absent Voters Lists. An act of Parliament passed on the 6th February 1918 allowed service men to register in order to obtain a vote in the constituency of their home address. The first lists were published on the 15 October 1918 from applications received up to 18 August 1918. The second list was published on the 15 April 1919. The details that appear were those supplied by the men themselves, and not by their dependants. Men had to be over 21 years of age to vote, therefore men under 21 in the armed forces were not included in this source. Town / District / Trade**Rolls of Honour** and **Records of Service**, **School Registers**, Rolls of Honour and Records of Service, Contemporary **Local Newspapers**, Back Issues of **'Flight'** & **'The Aeroplane'**, Journals of Cross & Cockade Society, Extracts from **Who's Who**, Memoirs etc.

Although there are missing numbers on the RAF Muster Roll and I have kept a log of these, some can be for casualties, transfers out, discharges or commissions Some of the gaps in the 'missing' numbers extracted from the R.A.F. Muster Roll have now been filled in.

Army 'Other Ranks' Casualties were listed in the 80 volumes of the officially produced 'Soldiers Died in the Great War 1914-19'. There was not a separate volume for the Royal Flying Corps, which had been a part of the Army up to 1 April 1918, when it merged with the Royal Naval Air Service, to form the Royal Air Force. However this problem was partly corrected in 1995 when 'Airmen Died in the Great War 1914-1918', compiled by Chris Hobson was published. This book covers both Officer and 'Other Rank' casualties up to 11 November 1918 and records information from the Commonwealth War Graves Registers and includes useful appendices, including details about the aircraft in which the aircrew were flying.

Officers in the Royal Flying Corps and Army Officers attached to the R.F.C. and R.A.F. appear in the HMSO publication 'Officers Died in the Great War', but this is not a comprehensive listing, since Officers who joined the R.A.F. directly are not included, nor are Colonial Officers on attachment. However some of the latter are included in the up-dated version of 'Officers Died...' which was published in 1988. With the help of a colleague, Peter Bilbrough, who volunteered to search the Commonwealth War Grave Registers, an alphabetical list has been put together of all the fatal casualties in the British aerial forces from 4 August 1914 to 31 August 1921 I have been through 'Soldiers Died in the Great War' and extracted lists of all those noted 'formerly RFC'.

For members of the ranks from the Royal Flying Corps who were medically discharged and awarded the 'For Services Rendered' Silver War Badge I have listings of 1,962 men granted each badge and details of the number stamped on the reverse. It is interesting to note that this number did not relate to their service number, but was based upon batches of badges allocated by the War Office. The vast majority of claims were made against discharges due to sickness. Sometimes the type of sickness is specified and very occasionally, more detail is given, e.g.;

2806 Deakin, John, Sergeant   Enlisted RFC 7 January 1915
Did not serve overseas
Discharged 10 January 1917 following the amputation of the right arm, in an aircraft accident, whilst on duty
Granted Silver War Badge No.55266

Currently there are no available records of the 13,000 Silver War Badges issued by the Royal Air Force, all of which have an RAF prefix on the number stamped on the reverse of the badge

I have yet to find a single source which specifically lists the men who transferred to or from the Royal Flying Corps. Some of these details can be found from the individual index cards in the Index to the Medal Rolls of the British Army Soldiers and RFC/RAF Airmen who received service medals, this master microfiche index is arranged in alphabetical order is held at the Public Record Office under their reference number WO/329.

In addition to the files on Other Ranks, I have compiled a good deal of information on Officers, which, on the whole, are much easier to find, i.e. Copies of Army, Navy and Air Force Lists.

I have compiled Record of Service Sheets for all Royal Naval Air Service Officers and Officers attached to the R.N.A.S., and I have also completed a biographical card index of Casualties to the Royal Naval Air Service.

Clive Maitland WATERLOW

Born 9 September 1885, eldest son of Mr David Sydney Waterlow, former M.P. for Islington,& Mrs Edith Waterlow of 38 Cornwall Gardens, London SW. Grandson of late Sir Sydney Waterlow.Educated Rugby 1899 - December 1902 Royal Military Academy, Woolwich Commissioned 2nd Lieutenant, Royal Engineers 21 March 1905 Served at Chatham, then went to the Balloon Factory at Farnborough, under Colonel John Edward Capper 2nd Lieutenant, Balloon School, Royal Engineers 18 October 1906 A member of the Ground Party (in Samuel Franklin Cody's Car) when Colonel J E Capper & Mr S F Cody flew the Airship 'Nulli Secundus' round London in October 1907 Promoted Lieutenant, Royal Engineers 23 December 1907 Held the third Airship Pilot's Licence(Aeronaut Certificate 18) issued by the Royal Aero. Club 14 February 1911 With Airship Company, Air Battalion, Royal Engineers on it's formation 1 April 1911 Appointed to No 1 Squadron, Military Wing, Royal Flying Corps on it's formation 13 May 1912 Piloted Airship 'Beta' when King George V made a visit to the Headquarters of the RFC and the Royal Aircraft Factory May 1912 Appointed Flight Commander and Temp. Captain 1 July 1912 Seconded for Airship Work to Naval Wing, Royal Naval Air Service 1 July 1914 when the Admiralty took over all the Army Airships. One of the most enthusiastic and active Airship Pioneers in Great Britain. He began a history of British Military Airships in 1916, but he had not got much further than 'Nulli Secundus II' when he was killed. His notes , which had been made at the time the events had occurred and with access to Airship log books were subsequently collected by Air Commodore E D Masterman and his account was published in 'The Airship' Volume 7 Nos 3 -6 Appointed Wing Commander R.N.A.S. August 1916. He was still gazetted to the Royal Engineers, holding the rank of Lieutenant Colonel at the time of his death, when he was the Commanding Officer of the Airship Training Wing at Cranwell Killed on 20 July 1917 in assisting the landing/take off of H.M. Airship SS 39, he failed to release a handling guy rope and was lifted high up into the air before he fell to his death. The crew could do nothing to save him. In June 1917 he had married Winifred Joan , daughter of John Henry Clare, of Farlands Croft, Farnham, who later remarried and became Mrs Waller and lived at Willetts, Loxwood, Sussex

A Portrait of C M Waterlow appears in Vol 5 of Memorials to Old Rugbeians who fell in the Great War

A partial listing of Officer P.O.W.'s appears in the book *'List of British Officers taken prisoner in various Theatres of War between August 1914 and November 1918'* which was compiled from records kept by Messrs. Cox & Co. I have compiled more comprehensive listings of R.F.C., R.N.A.S., R.A.F. Prisoners of War and Interned Prisoners, covering both Officers & Other Ranks. For example

Richard (Dick) CALROW Born: Bury, Lancashire Educated: Bury Grammar School, Bury, Lancashire Joined R.F.C. as 2nd Lieutenant 2 August 1917 Posted to School of

Instruction, Reading 11 September 1917 17 Training Squadron, Oxford 24 October 1917 Graduated 16 March 1918, flying a R.E. 8 Lieutenant R.A.F. Pilot 1 April 1918 66 Training Squadron,Yatesbury 9 April 1918 Flew 34 hours solo since graduation, flying D.H. 6, B.E. 2e and R.E. 8 aircraft. Wounded on a Corps Reconnaissance, France with 59 Squadron 24 August 1918 Shot down and made prisoner of war, whilst piloting R.E. 8 D4687 on a Corps Reconnaissance Mission, on 6 October 1918, serving with 59 Squadron. Held at Charlottenberg November 1918 Arrived back in England (Dover) 29 November 1918 Granted 2 months sick-leave until 29 January 1919. After the war he joined the County Bank, which later became part of the District Bank, now the National Westminster Bank.

I have also extracted names from the following War Office Weekly Casualty and Air Ministry Casualty listings

WAR OFFICE DAILY CASUALTY LISTS

Weekly List War Office	Daily No.	Date
1	5324	30 July 1917
83	5810	28 Feb 1919

AIR MINISTRY DAILY CASUALTY LISTS

Air Ministry List No:	Date	Comment
1	26 April 1918	Appeared at end
252	28 February 1919	P.O.W Repatriations

I have not been able to trace the earlier daily listings which should run from August 1914 to the end of July 1917 or any later weekly listings, and would be interested if any reader knows of any in existence.

I always welcome any information, no matter how trivial it might seem. The loan of documents or photographs is also useful, and any material loaned to me would receive great care and would be returned as soon as details had been copied .

As I am still in the process of compiling a master biographical index of all those who served, you will appreciate that sometimes the details I can supply may only be minimal, but they are the starting point for further research.

If you would like me to advise you on avenues of research, to check my records, or would like to pass information on to me, for inclusion in the register, please write to;

David J. Barnes, R.F.C., R.N.A.S., R.A.F. Register
c/o 148 Parkinson Street, Burnley, Lancashire, England,
BB11 3LL

[Web site address : www.rfc-rnas-raf-register.org.uk]

48 Suqdron France

The nation's lost sons

As First World War battlefields yield up their dead in rising numbers, experts and historians still strive to identify the men who are found, and to trace relatives

MARTIN FLETCHER reports

© Robert Blatchford

One morning, 75-year-old Keith Clarke, a retired brewery drayman from Newport in Gwent, arrived home after taking his wife to the physiotherapist to find a letter from the Ministry of Defence on the hallway floor.

"I said 'Hello! What does the MoD want with me? Are they calling me up?'," he recalls. Then he started reading. The letter was from PS4, the ministry's "casualty and compassionate cell".

"Dear Mr Clarke," it began. "This department is trying to trace the next of kin of Private Richard Thomas Clarke who served with the 2nd Battalion Royal Welch Fusiliers during the First World War and who was killed in action in France on June 22, 1916. We believe from our research that you may be related to the soldier."

Clarke was astounded. The soldier was his uncle, killed ten years before he was born, whose remains had evidently been dug up in a field on the old Western Front. Clarke was apparently the only surviving relative.

"I knew of him, but to me he was a figment of history," he says. He has no photographs, no scribbled letters from the trenches, no knowledge of what his uncle did before the war or what he was like. "My father never talked about him. He only mentioned that he was killed in the First World War."

The letter arrived in March. Now, 85 years after his death, Private Clarke is to be reburied this month with full military honours — a 19-year-old soldier of whose brief life there would soon have been no trace left at all, had a French souvenir-hunter not gone exploring with his metal detector in a newly ploughed field one day last year.

So many men were lost in action during the First World War that half the families in Britain could potentially receive the sort of letter that the MoD sent to Clarke. The bodies of nearly

370,000 Commonwealth troops are still concealed in the rich soil of northeastern France and western Belgium. In the past half-century a mere 2,010 have been recovered. But the rate is accelerating as land is developed and ever more people use metal detectors to search, sometimes illegally, for memorabilia.

For example, more than 113 sets of remains have been found since 1999 in a single field near Ypres where a frozen vegetable factory is to be built.

Before that the remains of 27 Royal Fusiliers were recovered from what was probably an unmarked mass grave during construction of an industrial site at Monchy-le-Preux in France.

Of those 2,010 disinterred remains, only 65 have been identified. Many soldiers were literally blown apart, or their bones scattered in subsequent battles. Dog tags have either perished (most were made of fibre or compressed carboard) or were removed by comrades in the heat of battle so that relations could be informed. Other clues, such as regimental insignia, were taken by wartime souvenir hunters.

In Belgium, no British remains had been identified for 20 years before an amateur historian discovered a rusted dog tag alongside the bones of Private Harry Wilkinson in a field near Ploegsteert Wood last year. The 29-year-old Lancashire millworker is to be buried this autumn.

In France, the remains identified most recently were those of 2nd Lieutenant Marcel Simon, buried last September, and Private George Nugent, buried last July. Simon was found with his Royal Berkshires cap badge, his officer's shoulder pip, and a flask that still contained water. Nugent, killed on the first day of the Battle of the Somme, was found by two British tourists who spotted his bones protruding from the edge of a crater, and identified by a cut-throat razor

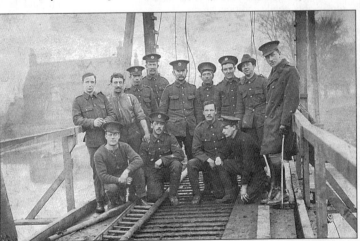

© Robert Blatchford

© Robert Blatchford

mobile and asked him to trace Clarke on the Commission's website. Within five minutes the friend had called back to confirm that a 19-year-old soldier of that name had indeed been killed at that spot on June 22, 1916.

Hancart showed me the spot on a damp and misty day, the flatness of the surrounding land broken only by distant rows of poplars, the occasional church spire and a solitary water tower. Amid the lines of vivid green spring wheat you could still discern the probable cause of Private Clarke's death in the contours of what was once a crater.

bearing his name and number.

The man who found Private Clarke's remains was Olivier Hancart, a burly 30-year-old welder from Lens. Like many others, Hancart goes out with his metal detector most weekends, scavenging in the fields for First World War memorabilia. In a back room of his bungalow he showed me a breathtaking collection of helmets, mortars, regimental badges, bayonets and other battlefield debris he had dug from the mud over the years.

One Saturday last year, Hancart went to a field on the edge of the village of Givenchy-lès-la Bassée, overlooked by a squat stone memorial to the 55th West Lancashire Division, where he knew there had once been trenches.

Beneath the freshly tilled soil he soon detected a sheet of corrugated iron. Beneath that were a British helmet and a skull.

He began digging and unearthed the complete upper half of a skeleton, lying face up and sloping downwards. He came across scraps of jacket bearing the insignia of the Royal Welch Fusiliers — Siegfried Sassoon's and Robert Graves's old regiment. He found a flask, a bayonet, a leather purse containing a set of false teeth, and half a comb. Thanks to their corrugated iron shelter, the artefacts were in remarkably good condition.

Hancart realised that this was something special. He telephoned the Commonwealth War Graves Commission in Arras, which sent an official to help him to dig. Together they found the jumbled bones of two more soldiers lying below Clarke, along with razors, shovels, a scabbard, twisted forks and spoons, two broken toothbrushes, buckles, the remains of a rucksack, more false teeth, and a Royal Welch Fusilier badge still bearing traces of the brown paint that soldiers used to prevent reflected sunlight from making them a target for German snipers.

But the most exciting discovery was a small oval mirror, cracked and bent, with a casing made of tortoiseshell or bakelite. Inside the folding cover they found, written in blue ink, the words "Pte R.Clarke, 1115 B Coy, RWF Aug 14, British Expeditionary Force France." Hancart telephoned a friend on his

The regimental history records that his battalion had moved up to the front line on June 20. On the evening of the following day his commanding officer was worried by "the uncanny peace and stillness of a beautiful summer night in a part of the line noted for its ferocity".

At 2.05am on June 22 there was a vast explosion caused by 36,000lb of explosives that German tunnellers had placed under the British trenches. Eighty yards of the British front line were wrecked and nearly 50 soldiers killed. If Private Clarke did not die instantly, he was killed soon afterwards as the German troops attacked. The crater, caused by the largest mine the Western Front had seen, is still known as the "Red Dragon Crater" after the regiment's symbol.Private Clarke's remains were not the first that Hancart had found.

About seven years ago he dug up those of a German soldier. Shortly after that he found another set of remains which he assumed to be British because he found a corned beef tin close by. But Private Clarke's were the first with an apparent identity.

"I was really surprised and happy. My first thought was to find the family of this soldier," he says. However, the mirror alone was not sufficient proof for the MoD. It could have been borrowed by one of the three dead soldiers, or hurled into their midst by the explosion, or deposited there by the farmer's plough. PS4 began searching its sparse records on Private Clarke and the regiment's movements, and then called in Margaret Cox, a professor of forensic archaeology and anthropology at Bournemouth University.

Cox is the "human bones expert" on the Channel 4 archaeology programme *Time Team*, has exhumed genocide victims from mass graves in Kosovo for the international war crimes tribunal, and was taken on by PS4 last December to help out in cases such as Private Clarke's. Her brief is to determine a soldier's race, age, height and other distinguishing features from his remains, and her report can provide the MoD with the final corroboration it requires.

That does not always happen. One set of remains was found recently near Ploegsteert Wood in Belgium with a regimental cap badge and a spoon bearing the final digits of a service number. PS4 knew that the soldier to whom they probably belonged had been wounded earlier in the war and hoped that Cox's examination would confirm his identity. In the event she was presented with several lumps of blackened, bony material from which she could tell nothing, and no identification was made.

"If we are not almost 100 per cent certain, we would say 'No, we can't name that person'," says Sue Woolford, PS4's head.

At the War Graves Commission offices in Arras, Cox was presented with a box full of the muddied, mixed-up bones of all the three soldiers found by Hancart. There was a boot with a foot inside, bits of ammunition and shreds of clothing. It was a "nightmare", she said, but from the three sets of femurs she managed to determine each soldier's approximate height, and from the respective pelvises their ages. One set of measurements matched Private Clarke's military records, but Cox noticed something else that helped to clinch the case.

The clavicles were pitted where the ligaments joined the bone. That suggested heavy manual labour using the upper body, and PS4 knew that Private Clarke had enlisted in the Welsh town of Blaengarw, where coalmining was almost the only occupation. "It did sort of fit it all together," says Janet Thompson, the PS4 desk officer who then had to track down his family.

That is never an easy task because families move, 60 per cent of the War Office's First World War service records were destroyed during the Blitz, and so many of the casualties were young, single men with no direct descendants. Private Clarke was a case in point — and of his four siblings, two died childless and another disappeared to Canada in the 1920s. The fourth, Keith Clarke's father, died in 1967.

Thompson spent six weeks trawling through voluminous records in Wales and London before she finally tracked down the lone nephew. There were times, she admits, when she thought despairingly: "This is not going to work. We haven't found anything."

Until recently Private Clarke was, in Rudyard Kipling's famous words, known only unto God. Now he is to be buried in a blaze of publicity on May 26 in the Gorre Cemetery, not far from the Red Dragon Crater, where 15 comrades killed in the same explosion already lie.

He will be buried in the same coffin as his two unidentified companions because not even Cox could tell exactly which bones were which. Hundreds will attend the funeral, including the British military attaché from Paris, the Colonel of the Regiment, scores of past and present members of the Royal Welch Fusiliers, and many French veterans. Hancart and Thompson will also attend, and Cox would have done had she been free, because it is almost impossible not to become emotionally involved in such a poignant story.

The regiment will provide a band, pallbearers, a guard of honour and a firing party. "This is one of our family we have found and are honouring," said Major Bob Lake, the regimental secretary.

The service will include a laying of wreaths, a minute's silence, and the playing of the Last Post, the Reveille and the National Anthem. "It will be an experience," says Clarke, who has chosen to have the epitaph "Died For Our Tomorrows" inscribed on his uncle's headstone. The other artefacts will be inside the coffin, but the regiment will mount the mirror and present it to the nephew.

Later, Private Clarke's name will be removed from the Loos Memorial in the Dud Corner Cemetery near Lens which commemorates 20,000 officers and men with no known grave.

Out of sentimentality, perhaps, I visited the memorial last week and realised that I had been there once before.

Not far from Private Clarke's name is that of Lieutenant Harold Sanderson of the Black Watch, killed in 1915 at the age of 22. He was my great-uncle, and it was with a jolt that I realised that it could just as easily have been his remains that Hancart found last year.

© Robert Blatchford

Identification and Dating
British Military Uniforms
David J Barnes

It is quite common when researching family history to come across photographs of members of the armed forces, particularly the army. How can these pictures be made to yield their clues? It is necessary to study the detail minutely; not just the uniform itself, but any cap, collar, trade or qualification badges, rank insignia, medals, shoulder titles or wound stripes. To do this you may need to enlarge the photograph, or at the very least employ a magnifying glass powerful enough to enable an identification of a badge to be made.

Such a study may help in two ways. Firstly, knowing that an ancestor or relative was in a particular regiment, you may suspect that he is the soldier portrayed in an uncaptioned military photograph. If a careful examination of the uniform confirms that the soldier portrayed belonged to the regiment concerned, you may consider this evidence as sufficient to make a presumed identification. However, it is always important to remember that the picture could show a 'pal' in the same regiment; if there are several photographs of the same soldier, it is much more likely that the person shown is your ancestor.

Secondly, what if you know the identity of the ancestor in the picture but have found out relatively little about him? A military photograph may be the sole means of identifying the regiment or unit in which he served. Once you know this, you can try and pinpoint the Battalion or sub-unit to which he belonged; and if you succeed, you can often fill out the background with details of the actions in which that unit took part, places it was stationed and so on. The National Army Museum, the appropriate Regimental Museum and, for the period after 1914, the Imperial War Museum, may be able to supply information about the unit, to add interest to your family history.

Army Service Records for (apart from Royal Artillery and of the Royal Engineers) are in the Public Record Office at Kew. The most useful source material as follows:

WO100/1-397	Campaign Medals 1793-1912.
WO101/1-7	Meritorious Service Awards 1846-191.
WO102/1-16	Long Service & Good Conduct 1831-1902

If discharged to pension:

WO97/1722-2170	Soldiers Documents 1873-1882
WO1722-1762	Cavalry
WO1763-1848	Royal Artillery
WO1849-1857	Royal Engineers
WO1858-1870	Foot Guards
WO1871-2147	Infantry
WO2147-2170	Corps & Misc Units

If soldier has not been killed on service:
WO97/2171-6322 Soldiers Documents 1883-1913.

All the surviving Officer records for the period 1914-1921 have been transferred from the Army Records Centre (ARC) to the Public Record Office, and it is estimated that about 86% of these are still in existence. WO339 has the records of over 140,000 men who were mainly Regular, Special Reserve, and Emergency Officers; WO374 contains over 70,000 officers' records mainly for those commissioned into the territorial force. The records of soldiers discharged after 1913 are held at the Army

Records Centre. It should however be understood that more than two thirds of the records covering the period 1914-1920 were destroyed or damaged by enemy bombing during the Second World War. Most of the surviving First World War records are being moved from the Army Records Centre to the Public Record Office at Kew, although the project will not be complete until 2003. There are two Public Record Office sequences containing First World War service records.

The 'unburnt documents' (WO364) consist of about 4,000 microfilm reels, and it has been estimated that there is a 10% chance of finding the soldier being sought.

The 'burnt documents' (WO363) are being transferred alphabetically. If your ancestor claimed a war disability pension, the relative papers will probably have been removed and be filed with the PIN71 records at the Public Record Office.

Identifying a relative

A good example of the value of military uniforms in identifying a relative is provided by photographs provided by a distant family member of the former ITN Newsreader Gordon Honeycombe. There were three photographs of soldiers in an album in Salt Lake City, Utah, U.S.A., by the grandson of Thomas Le Breton and his wife Margaret *nee* Honeycombe, who had emigrated from Jersey, in the Channel Islands to Utah, U.S.A. in 1894. It was known, from family sources that John Honeycombe, the brother of Margaret Le Breton, who was baptised as St. Helier, Jersey in 1868 was later a soldier who had died of enteric fever in India. Research into the military records at the Public Record Office at Kew showed that John Honeycombe was a Private in the Hampshire Regiment. He had been a member of 'C' Company since 1 October 1888, and was on the Monthly Muster Roll for the year ending 31 March 1889 , at Chatham. He was recorded as 'Absent on duty' on the Monthly Muster Roll taken at Chatham 1 April 1890. His burial, on 12 October 1896, was found in the return of burials at Mooltan, Punjab.

Two of the three photographs were taken in India, one was marked *Lucknow, Naini Tal, G.W. Laurie & Co., Mussoorie and Allahabad* and the other, *Jno Burke, Artiste Photographer, Punjab.* But which, if any, was John Honeycombe? John's niece, Mrs Florence Fones, aged 85, and living in Tuuele, Utah, U.S.A. had suggested it was the first photograph, but was she correct?

At the time of examination of the photographs I had no prior knowledge of the family history behind the photographs.

Photograph 1 was marked *Lucknow, Naini Tal, G.W. Laurie & Co., Mussoorie and Allahabad* and was of a soldier in white tropical uniform taken in India towards the end of the 19th Century.

The badge worn on the front of the white colonial pattern helmet was that of the Hampshire Regiment. It is of a design worn from the formation of that regiment in 1881, following the Cardwell reforms, when the 37th and 67th Regiments of Foot were amalgamated and given a county title.

A collar badge is worn, again these were introduced in 1881, and whilst the details are not clear, the distinct shape, helped with identification. The badge was a Hampshire rose, within a wreath of oak leaves.

There are two inverted chevrons worn on the lower left tunic sleeve, these are good conduct stripes indicating six years service, and were worn in this position from 1 March 1881.

The absence of any medal for the Burmese Expedition of 1887, in which the Hampshire Regiment took part, suggests the earliest date the photograph was taken could be 1887. The absence of any campaign medal for the Niger Expedition 1897-1898 or the South African War (Anglo-Boer War) 1899-1902 suggests 1897 as the latest date for the photograph.

A further check on the Regimental Rolls or station returns could find exactly when and where he was in India.

Photograph 2, taken by *Jno Burke, Artiste Photographer, Punjab*, was of an infantry officer, taken in India towards the end of the 19th Century.

His rank can be found by examination of the cuff insignia, introduced in 1868. The more elaborate the design, the higher was the officer's rank. Between 1855 and 1880 rank badges had been worn on the collar, the ranks being shown in stars and crowns. A special Army Order in October 1880 introduced a new system of rank badges, worn on the shoulder, with a regimental badge to be worn on the collar.

The officer in the photograph has a very ornate cuff, and a rank badge appears on this right shoulder cord. In addition, a row of loops is to be seen on the collar. These were a distinction of field officers (i.e. Majors and senior ranks); his cuff insignia confirms the rank of Major. Although an infantry officer, being of field rank, he would have ridden a horse on parade.

Normally his regiment could be identified from the waist belt buckle, which unfortunately is obscured in this case, nor can the badge on his helmet be seen. However his

regimental collar badge appeared to be a shield with a scroll below, and as the shape of this shied is uncommon in military insignia, it was easy to trace, it is the arms of Nassau. According to Dress Regulations the collar badge of the Royal Irish Regiment was an escutcheon of the arms of Nassau, with a silver scroll inscribed *Virtutis Namurcensis Praemium* ('The reward for valour at Namur').

The facing colour worn on the collar and cuffs below the insignia should also be borne in mind. Care should be taken here, as some colours in old photographs cannot be identified with certainty, and a number of them, e.g. buff, primrose yellow and white may all look very similar in monochrome. Remember too that some light colours often appear dark in old photographs - a major point to keep in mind when trying to identify a medal ribbon or cloth badge etc.

In this photograph the facing colour seems to be the same dark shade as the uniform trousers, and Dress Regulations confirm that dark blue was the facing colour of the Royal Irish Regiment. If the cap badge, collar badge and helmet plate are obscured or missing, you may have to try to identify the regiment, or draw up a short-list of possible regiments, based upon this colour alone. If so, try to check out the period. New facing colours were introduced in the Cardwell Army Reforms of 1881, when a large number of the old regiments of foot were merged to form 'new' Country Regiments, but by 1914 some regiments had received permission to revert to their old facing colours.

This photograph is, therefore, that of a Major in the Royal Irish Regiment. He is wearing the uniform described in Dress Regulations of 1900 - though this particular dress would have been worn some years before that date. However the photograph must have been taken before 1902, when the sash was taken from the shoulder and worn around the waist. An examination of the Army Lists between 1896-1900 will confirm which Battalion of the Royal Irish Regiment were in India, where they were stationed and the names of Major's in the regiment.

Had it not been possible to identify the uniform by the badges or facings, you would have had to bear in mind two possibilities;

Firstly, that he may have been a British officer serving with an Indian Army Regiment. Whilst the Indian Army used a similar system of ranks and regimental devices, its units operated independently, with separate regulations covering dress, badges and training, which you would have to consult.

Secondly, that he was on Staff duties. He would usually have had an aiguillette (loops of plaited cords) worn on the right shoulder by officers on the Headquarters Staff, and on the left shoulder by other staff officers.

Pinpointing a Unit

Using family papers , archival sources, or the insignia shown in photographs, you may have successfully identified the regiment in which your ancestor served, but most regiments had a number of battalions, especially during the First World War 1914-1918, when some had nearly fifty, and unless you can pinpoint the correct one, you cannot follow up this important lead. The photograph, and any caption or inscription should, of course, be meticulously examined first. Next come family sources. Where photographs survive, there are likely to be other items as well. Medals, often inscribed on the reverse or the rim with the Number, Rank, Names and Unit, identity tags, discharge papers, pay books, odd bits of military equipment such as cap badges or shoulder titles. Is there a tarnished military button lurking in someone's button box? Even if you have nothing of this kind in your possession, such bric-a-brac may have come down another branch of the family, so do the rounds of your relatives before resorting to more complex procedures.

Portraits of Individuals

You may be able to identify the battalion from an individual photograph if this is signed with the soldier's name. In such a case it is worth searching the casualty rolls of the regiment, which are often found in battalion order. First and Second World War Army casualty searches are fairly straight forward to do with the data being available on CD ROM. A photograph with a fairly distinctive first name can also provide a strong lead.

Example 1. A First World War photograph of a soldier wearing a cap badge of the Lancashire Fusiliers, signed 'Your best pal, Ezra C', would lead to the the discovery of the following entry in the Regimental Casualty Rolls:

LANCASHIRE FUSILIERS - 2nd Battalion
Crooks, Ezra. B[orn] Blackburn, Lancs. E[nlisted]
Rochdale, Lancs.
6003 Lance-Corporal
Died F[rance] & F[landers] 26 August 1916

Sometimes, though unfortunately not in this example, after the place of enlistment, his home town or place of residence was included. Lance-Corporal Crooks' name appears on Blackburn's Roll of Honour, and it should be possible to seek further information about him in copies of local newspapers of the period.

The Commonwealth War Graves Commission records show that Lance-Corporal E Crooks is buried in Woods Cemetery, Zillebeke, Belgium (Plot 3, Row A, Grave7). You can also investigate the history of the battalion around this period. The regimental history showed that the 2nd Battalion, Lancashire Fusiliers were in trenches at Verbrandenmolen, near Ypres, from 23 to 28 August 1916. The commanding officer at that time was Major R R Willis, who had won the Victoria Cross at Gallipoli. A further rich vein of material could be the Battalion War Diary, if it survives, though this will not usually name individual soldiers, but will provide information about what the unit were doing.

Example 2. An Officer casualty record from the First World War does not provide information about the area they were born and lived. For example;

THE QUEEN'S OWN (ROYAL WEST KENT
REGIMENT)
Serving with 6th Battalion
Ashton, Cyril James. Temp. Lieutenant (Acting Captain)
D[ied] of W[ounds] 12 March 1918

By referring to the Army List, you would be able to check the date he was appointed to that rank, and also see who his fellow officers were.

It is more likely that information on an officer casualty will be found in a regimental history. A request for information about Captain Ashton was sent to the curator of the appropriate Regimental Museum, who found the following entry in the Regimental History;

"In the half-light of dawn on 9 March 1918, a party of 200 men, commanded by Captain Ashton, raided German trenches, after forming up in water filled trenches and crossing 'No-man's Land' without being detected.
The German's were taken completely by surprise, a machine gun and nine prisoners were taken and heavy losses were inflicted on the enemy. Some 25 of our men were killed and Captain Ashton was mortally wounded. Command was taken over by Lieutenant Elliot, who stormed a German pill box."

A more detailed report of the action appeared in the unit's War Diary and a copy of Captain Ashton's service record is held amongst Officers Records held in the Public Record Office.

Captain Ashton is buried in Merville Communal Cemetery, France (Plot 7, Row A, Grave 42)

Group Photographs

If you have a signed photograph of a military group, use the same identification procedure as for an individual portrait, try to pick out your relative from the group, by comparison with photographs of him of the same period

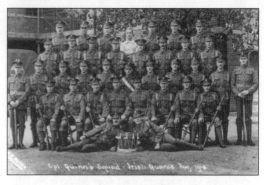

or later. Also remember that the picture may show a friend's unit, and not that of your relative at all. If you have an unsigned or uncaptioned group photograph, the odds are that it *is* a picture of your ancestor's unit - but it may not prove easy to identify!

Occasionally you find that a group photograph has been captioned by the photographer, particularly where troops have been training in the United Kingdom, e.g. *'C' Company, 17th Battalion, Lancashire Fusiliers, 32nd Field Company, Royal Engineers.* This practice of captioning groups was particularly common with Guards Regiments, during the First World War, where captions such as *Cpl Quinn's Squad, Irish Guards, Aug. 1918* are not uncommon.

It should be remember that some photographs may record groups formed for a small duration, for example men from mixed units attending courses of instruction. Often these are not captioned and it is often difficult to ascertain where they were and what they were doing. In instances where such photographs are captioned, there is often little chance of records surviving listing men attending a particular course etc/ I have a large framed photograph captioned *No.40 Course, Army Signals School, Dunstable Signal Depot, May 1918*, but the records for this course have vanished.

A posed studio photograph of individual or groups of soldiers were often taken in a garrison town, or at or near a camp where the soldiers were based. Occasionally you can find an item marked *'On the Veldt in South Africa'* or *'Somewhere in France'*, and as slight as such a clue may be, it can prove invaluable in making up a list of possible units. Casualty records are particularly useful for locating the units serving in a particular area at a given time.

In the space available it has been possible only to look at a few examples and outline some useful procedures, most of which are readily applicable not only to military photographs but also to sailors, airmen and other uniformed personnel such as police, fire brigade, railwaymen etc.

The guiding principle is always the same: Examine each photograph with meticulous care and follow up every clue it provides. To do this you may have to track down specific reference books, either through specialist book dealers or through inter-library loan. Do not be diffident about seeking specialist help, but remember that there is no reason whey they should give time and expertise for nothing. Send a good copy of the photograph, for the specialist to retain for reference, preferably do not send a photocopy or scanned image, as these disintegrate into a series of dots when magnified. Be as specific as possible in your enquiries, give details of sources you have already consulted (in order to save time and money) and include a stamped, self addressed envelope and express a willingness to pay a reasonable fee

United Kingdom National Inventory of War Memorials

Nick Hewitt Project Co-ordinator

Fig

For readers of the *Family & Local History Handbooky* who have not come across UKNIWM before, the project was jointly initiated in 1989 by the Imperial War Museum and the Royal Commission on the Historic Monuments of England (which has been part of English Heritage since 1999). The *ad hoc* nature of memorial building by British communities led to a lack of any centralised information about them, and the project was founded on the premise that the key to successful preservation lay first in the creation of accurate records. Recording sheets are sent out to parish councils, veterans' organisations including the Royal British Legion, historical research groups like the Western Front Association, as well as local and family history societies.

Anyone who is already familiar with us will notice our slight change in title. Since devolution, we have been aware that the project was in danger of being seen as over-dependent on 'English' or 'metropolitan' organisations, in a way that it was not at its inception in 1989. At a meeting of the Supervisory Committee on 31 January 2001, therefore, it was decided that approaches would be made to appropriate heritage organisations in Scotland, Wales and Northern Ireland to invite them to become involved with the Inventory. It was also decided that the name of the project would be changed from the "National Inventory of War Memorials" to the cumbersome but more explicit "United Kingdom National Inventory of War Memorials".

The project is now going through what is arguably the most exciting period of its history since 1989, as we move towards a public launch of the database on 8 November this year. This marks the end of the first phase of the project, which has concentrated almost entirely on field work and cataloguing. Although no project of this nature can ever be truly described as "complete" – quite apart from anything else, people are still erecting new memorials – the archive now contains around 45,000 individual memorial records, of which over 40,000 have been computerised at time of writing, and we all felt that it was time to move forward.

We will also be launching the long-awaited second edition of our *Conservation of War Memorials* guidance notes on the 8th. Revised, enlarged and updated, the new edition has been renamed the *War Memorials Handbook*.

Following the launch, the database will be immediately available to the public at IWM as one of the research facilities offered by the Museum's Department of Printed Books. In addition, the Project Office will still offer the opportunity for researchers to submit more complex inquiries and view original files. At present, the database does not contain the Inventory's extensive collection of photographs or our transcribed lists of names, as neither the staff nor the resources have been available for the enormous task of adding them. However, this material would again be available to visitors in the Project Office, by appointment.

It is important to realise that field work will still continue, but from 8 November the main priority of the Inventory will change from gathering information to public service i.e. making information available. We will also be looking at ways in which the process of information gathering can be made more efficient, as it is now clear that the size of the archive and the number of active field workers (around 500) has made the risk of duplicated information and wasted effort unacceptably high.

After the launch and the advent of public access within the Museum, we will start looking at ways in which the archive and database can be further developed and disseminated. Most importantly for genealogists, we will be examining the possibility of computerising names and photographs, and the possibility of making the entire database available over the Internet. However, funding for these expensive and time consuming operations are not yet in place, so unfortunately no firm commitment to them can be made.

The scope of the collection has grown enormously since 1989. The Inventory began as an essentially art historical project aimed primarily at recording sculptural work associated with the First World War, but over the years the terms of reference have expanded to include a multitude of other wars, both preceding and following 1914 – 1918. Some of the more unusual examples include, from before 1914, the Ashanti Wars, the Boxer Rebellion and the Maori Wars, and from after 1918, the Falklands War and the conflicts in Borneo and Cyprus, as well as the Second World War.

The project has also moved well beyond sculptural work alone, part of the reason why the collection has almost doubled from the original estimated total of around 25,000. The archive now contains records relating to rolls of honour inscribed on parchment, simple boards, plaques and tablets mounted on the walls of churches and other public buildings; church fittings including bells, pews, lecterns, stained glass windows and font covers; memorial buildings including chapels, civic halls and hospitals; and public open spaces like playing fields, parks or gardens. We have small groups of sundials, clock towers, fountains and paintings. Possibly the most unusual recorded examples are Piel Island in Barrow in Furness, presented to the town by the Duke of Buccleuth as a war memorial in 1920, a number of bus shelters, several examples of church heating or lighting, and two decommissioned warships, HMS *Plymouth*, a memorial to the Falklands War, and HMS *Cavalier*, a memorial to those killed serving aboard Royal Navy destroyers during the Second World War.

Of course, outdoor monuments are still an important part of the collection, even though numerically they now comprise only around 20% of the total. By far the most common are crosses, but we also have fine examples of sculptural groups and single figures, cenotaphs modelled on Lutyen's Whitehall original, simple classical models like obelisks,

Fig 2

THE NEW CASUALTY DEPARTMENT which is THE BOROUGH OF ISLINGTON WAR MEMORIAL

Fig 3

pillars or columns and elaborate architectural schemes like the triumphal arches in Leicester and Nottingham.

I have chosen illustrations which I hope will show the variety of memorials which have been recorded. *(Fig1)* The first is the magnificent and complex sculptural group at Oldham, Lancashire, one of the first memorials to be recorded on behalf of the Inventory **(NIWM 10).** The memorial was the work of the sculptor Albert Toft and the architect Thomas Taylor. It was unveiled by General Sir Ian Hamilton on 28 April 1923. The names of the fallen – over 2,000 for the First World War – are inscribed on bronze panels mounted on the churchyard wall, forming a background to the memorial. Toft's sculpture depicts five soldiers clambering from a trench or dugout, surrounded by the debris of war and is remarkable for its graphic depiction of trench warfare - most First World War figurative memorials shy away from this kind of gritty realism, preferring more idealised depictions of soldiers.

(Fig 2) The second example is the casualty department at the Royal Northern Hospital in Holloway, north London, which was unveiled by HRH the

Prince of Wales (the future King Edward VIII) on 27 November 1923. **(NIWM 12057)** Although the hospital itself was demolished in 1997 and replaced by housing, the arched gateway recording the names of 1,337 Islington men who lost their lives in the First World War was retained *(Fig 3)* and sympathetically integrated into the new development. *(Fig 4)*

(Fig 5) The final example is one of the simplest war memorials in the archive, a hand-written roll of honour in St Mary's Church, Luxborough, Somerset, listing only the names of the fallen **(NIWM 24625)**

Fig 5

Fig 4

To conclude, we are all aware that genealogists and family historians have been at the forefront of recording work over the last thirteen years, and have made an enormous contribution to the collection – without your help we would have no database to launch on 8 November. Although we will be closing the office to researchers over the summer, so that our small team can concentrate on adding as much new material to the database as possible, we will be open for "business as usual" from 9 November and look forward to welcoming visitors.

Friends of War Memorials
Maggie Goodall Conservation Officer

Friends of War Memorials is the national organisation concerned with war memorials of all dates and types, from the Crimean to the Gulf and beyond. It is unique in being the only society of its type solely concerned with war memorials (as opposed to war graves or other types of public monument).

Founded in 1995 in an attempt to combat vandalism, theft and neglect of war memorials, FoWM is now a registered charity and fast becoming the first port of call for those with an interest in or query about war memorials. It has a growing membership and anenthusiastic team of nearly 200 Regional Volunteers in England, Scotland and Wales. They help to carry out research, assist local groups with restoration projects and keep a vigilant eye on memorials "at risk" and on the skips and antiques markets where so many displaced plaques and Rolls of Honour end up.

Friends of War Memorials aims firstly to act as a focal point for reports on the condition of war memorials, and point of liaison between local people and the relevant bodies and secular and ecclesiastical authorities, to encourage them to take responsibility for remedial action and on-going regular maintenance. In offering advice on conservation, sources of grant funding and practicalities, FoWM can also act as a facilitator for a diverse range of war memorial projects. Secondly, FoWM aims to educate and inform the general public, particularly young people, about the spiritual, historical and architectural significance of war memorials. It has been especially anxious to have war memorials recognised as an important and distinct aspect of the national heritage, and is working with the national heritage bodies English

Heritage, Historic Scotland and, in Wales, Cadw to this end.

The diversity of war memorial types encountered on a day-to-day basis is fascinating and astounding – from the nineteenth century plaques recording casualties in the Crimea, to the sword-bearing angels and drummer boys of the 1899-1902 South African War. From the soldier figures, obelisks and crosses so familiar in our towns and villages to the memorial books and Rolls of Honour (some with photographs or painted allegories), and salutary fragments of tank, fieldgun and aeroplane, of WWI and II.

Swanland, East Yorkshire
A well maintained War Memorial

Many are remarkable works of architecture, sculpture and craft, for example Lutyens' cenotaphs, Blomfield and Coates Carter's memorial crosses, the poignant sculpted figures by Jagger, Toft, Ledward and Goscombe John, and more recent abstract forms. Others are the work of (often anonymous), local masons and craftspeople, which take a utilitarian form – bus shelters, footbridges, drinking fountains, memorial rooms or

Rededication North Wales 1998

parks, hospital wards and village halls. The National Inventory of War Memorials currently being compiled at the Imperial War Museum estimates that there are some 50,000 war memorials in the UK. By virtue of the names and actions the record of all these are in a sense unique, and of historical importance. The threats and problems encountered by war memorials are equally diverse. In particular First World War memorials were frequently constructed by public subscription on donated land, with no long-term provision being made for their routine maintenance. Though local secular authorities are empowered to care for memorials, and church authorities or local groups are often ready to take action, in many cases ownership or actual responsibility are difficult to establish. This, combined with a lack of funds, can make arranging for essential maintenance, or repairs following vandalism or accidental damage (lightning strikes and vehicle collision being unfortunately common) frustratingly complicated.

Where ownership is uncertain, or changes in demography and infrastructure have altered an area's character, problems can arise of neglect and displacement from redundant and demolished buildings or to make way for development. In spite of many communities' concern for their war memorial, deliberate damage remains disappointingly common – from opportunist casual vandalism of the type seen at the Cenotaph earlier this year, to purposeful attacks such as that at Fenton in Staffordshire which left the memorial's soldier figure with its arms broken off at the elbow.

Sadly also, a growing interest in war memorials has gone hand in hand with a rise in architectural theft and commercial sale of plaques, Rolls of Honour and sculpture as architectural curios. FoWM works with Salvo, the organisation concerned with ethical practice in architectural salvage, to publicise and hopefully recover stolen items, such as a figure of St Michael taken recently from a Bedfordshire churchyard and now recovered after being recognised from Salvo's "Theft Alert" internet site.

With many war memorials now reaching an age when conservation and repair work becomes necessary, and in recognition of their special character, English Heritage has allocated £100,000 to a grant scheme administered by Friends of War Memorials, for war memorial conservation and repair in England. To be eligible, a war memorial must be independently listed Grade II and situated in a Conservation Area. Information and application packs are available from FoWM along with an advice sheet on "Getting a War Memorial Listed".

With the current interest in war time events, even as these conflicts retreat into past centuries the future of the memorials which commemorate them appears brighter. The release of historical documents into the public domain, the decommissioning of military sites and the inevitable diminution of generations with direct experience of large-scale conflict all contribute to the growing concern for war memorials, appreciation of their significance and a willingness to act to ensure their survival into the future.

If you would like further information on Friends of War Memorials or the grant scheme, or wish to become a Friend or Regional Volunteer please contact:

Maggie Goodall – Conservation Officer or Amy Louise Flint – Membership Secretary at:

Friends of War Memorials (Registered Charity No 1062255) 4 Lower Belgrave Street, London, SW1W 0LA Tel (020) 7259 0403 Fax (020) 7259 0296 e-mail: fowm@eidosnet.co.uk website: www.war-memorials.com

Annual membership £20 Life membership £100 (includes events programme and quarterly 12 page Newsletter)

A damaged War Memorial
Audenshaw, Greater Manchester

The British Army in the Anglo-Boer War, South Africa 11 October 1899 - 31 May 1902

David J Barnes

The crisis in South Africa which caused the war was the culmination of 250 years of expansion and conflict between the Boers and British settlers. The original colony was founded in 1652 at the Cape of Good Hope by the Dutch East India Company. Settlers were mainly Dutch Calvinists who brought with them a tradition of dissent and resentment against Europe, and farmers soon began to move deeper into African territory in search of good land. In 1806 Britain took control of the colony, and when slavery was abolished in 1834 the Great Trek began. 5,000 Boers (and their slaves) crossed the Orange and Vaal rivers to establish the Transvaal and Orange Free States where blacks and coloureds were denied political rights, while Cape Colony and Natal remained British.

In 1877 Britain annexed the Transvaal, but this was reversed following the Transvaal Revolt (the First Boer War), which took place between 1880 and 1881. The Boers were led by Paul Kruger, Petrus Jacobus Joubert, and Marthinus Pretorius. On 28 January 1881, some 2,000 Boers, invaded Natal. British General Sir George Colley with 1,400 troops were defeated at Laing's Nek in the Drakensberg Mountains. One month later, at the Battle of Majuba Hill, Colley was overwhelmed by the Boer riflemen, he and 91 others were killed. On 5 April 1881, the Treaty of Pretoria was signed, granting independence to the South African Republic.

The discovery of gold at Kimberley in 1870 and diamonds in the Transvaal in 1886 upset the existing balance of power. It made Cecil Rhodes and Alfred Beit into millionaires who wanted to take over the Transvaal, led to the foundation of Rhodesia, and a rush of British settlers into Boer territory

In December 1895, Leander Starr Jameson, a friend of Cecil Rhodes, led a band of 500 British armed men in an unauthorised attempt to support the rebellious Uitlanders in the South African Republic. Rhodes organised the raid, and Beit and Phillips financed it, although the raid failed, it convinced the Boers that the British were determined to take away their hard-won independence. The angered Boers, led by their new president, Paul Kruger, began to arm themselves. Paul Kruger was an elegant, stubborn and deeply religious man and was beloved by his people, who often referred to him as "Oom Paul" (Uncle Paul). He was described as a "natural orator; rugged in speech, lacking in measured phrase and in logical balance; but passionate and convincing in the unaffected pleading of his earnestness." Kruger was uncompromising in his opposition to the Uitlanders.

In 1899, the recently appointed British governor of Cape Colony, Sir Alfred Milner, who strongly resented the Afrikaners' treatment of the British, with the help of Wernher and Beit , secretly began to incite a full-scale war that would bring the wealth of the Boer lands completely into the Empire. To hide his plans, the British Commissioner agreed to "negotiate" with Kruger over the status of the "Uitlanders." Milner demanded citizenship rights for the flood of immigrants who had poured into the Boer republics. President Paul Kruger responded with bitterness and anger, "It is our country you want!" The talks finally broke down, as Milner had

53rd Coy Imperial Yeomanry

intended. While the "negotiations" were underway, Wernher and Beit were secretly financing an "outlander" army of 1,500 that eventually grew to 10,000.

England had to send troops to South Africa in preparation for war, it had only about 10,000 troops in the Cape and Natal. It augmented the force by another ten thousand before delivering an ultimatum to President Kruger, asking the Government of India to provide more than six thousand. The military authorities in India were very prompt. The initial force sent from India composed of 5,635 British officers and men, 1,078 Indians, 2,334 horses, and 611 mules and ponies. A majority of Indians were assigned to field hospitals or used as stretcher-bearers; the rest were transport drivers, grooms and private servants.

The troops arrived in Natal between 3 and 8 October 1899, and were moved to the Transvaal border. Kruger demanded their withdrawal, but as this was refused, the Transvaal declared war on Britain on 9 October 1899 followed by the Orange Free State on 11 October 1899.

In October of 1899 the Boers, starting the war with the maxim *'the key to a good defence is a good offence'*, invaded Natal and Cape Province, attacked the British forces and by the end of the month had besieged Mafeking, Kimberley and Ladysmith.

• The troops of Colonel Robert S. S. Baden-Powell were surrounded by Boer General Piet A. Cronje's troops in the northern town of Mafeking. Colonel Baden-Powell, armed some blacks, prompting a Boer commander to accuse him of "an enormous act of wickedness".

• Orange Free State forces besieged Kimberley.

• 15,000 Boer troops, under Boer General Joubert, pushed through General Sir George White's Natal Defence Force at Laing's Nek. After battles at Talana Hill, Elandslaagte, and Nicholson's Nek, General Joubert bottled up White's troops at Ladysmith in Natal. Constant shelling meant that the occupants of Ladysmith could not move openly during the day and had to live in insanitary dug-outs rather than in the open, which accelerated the spread of disease. Attempts were made to improve morale by producing siege newspapers such as the "Ladysmith Lyre". While the Ladysmith garrison waited for General Redvers Buller to break through Boer lines, conditions grew worse. General White had initially believed that they could still fight their way out and therefore did not treat the situation as a siege, despite the lack of food. It was not until Buller was defeated at Spioen Kop in January 1900 that White agree to reduce rations, give horses' meal to the men and slaughter the horses for food. The conditions in the hospitals were generally poor, the rate of death from disease was 10 to 20 per day - Ladysmith had a high rate of typhoid even before the siege.

City Imperial Volunteers

The British were taking heavy losses, in the Battle of Stormberg, General Sir William Gatacre and his troops got lost between a Boer camp and Queenstown and were ambushed. General Paul Methuen's 10,000 men with 16 guns moved to relieve Kimberley. After the 70,000 Boer troops under Generals Cronje and Jacobus H. De La Rey delayed Methuen, he finally broke through to the Modder River, losing 72 men with 396 wounded. At the Battle of Colenso, Cronje occupied a fortified hill near the Modder River with about 8,000 troops. Methuen attacked at dawn in the rain, and was defeated with 210 men dead, 675 wounded, and 63 missing.

In December 1899, the British commander-in-chief, Sir Redvers H. Buller, led 21,000 men to relieve Ladysmith. Buller attempted to break through the troops of Boer General Louis Botha and his 6,000 men. The British, in difficult terrain, were hit by small-arms fire, then a concealed force of Boers attacked. The British were driven back with 143 dead, 756 wounded, and 220 men and 11 guns captured. The Boers lost less than 50 men. Buller was so badly beaten, he approved the surrender of Ladysmith. Buller sent in fresh reinforcements from Canada, Australia, and New Zealand, but he foolishly divided the relieving forces as he tried to check the Boers everywhere at once. Within a week, referred to as "Black Week" , each of the reinforcements had been defeated by the Afrikaner forces. Buller resigned his post as commander-in-chief.

On 10 January 1900, the popular British General Frederick Sleigh 'Bobs' Roberts, was sent to replace Buller as commander-in-chief. Buller remained to fight throughout the war, he was defeated in the battles of Spion Kop and Vaal Kranz with 408 killed, 1,390 wounded, and 311 missing. In February 1900 General Roberts ordered the British commander, John D. P. French, north to relieve the city of Kimberley from Boer Generals De La Rey and Christiaan R. De Wet. French completed this task four days later. During this time, Roberts undertook a march from Cape Colony into the Orange Free State. Gen. Cronje retreated across the Modder where he was blocked by the French.

Roberts, temporarily sick, turned his command over to his chief of staff, Horatio Herbert Kitchener, who made a disastrous attack on the Boer's wagon train in the Battle of Paardeberg. Attacked by Cronje on 27 February 1900, Roberts fought back successfully and forced the surrender of Cronje and his troops of about 4000 men in the Siege of Paardeberg. Cronje had the option of breaking out with 4,000 men, but he stubbornly refused to abandon his wounded and was starved into surrender. On 28 February 1900, Buller advanced towards Ladysmith and the Boers withdrew. On 13 March 1900,

Roberts captured Bloemfontein, the capital of the Orange Free State. Roberts captured Kroonstad on 12 May , and on 15 May 1900 he captured Glencoe and Dundee. The British had annexed Orange Free State. On 17 May 1900, Major General Bryan T. Mahon relieved the troops of Robert Baden-Powell in the besieged city of Mafeking. Roberts captured the city of Johannesburg on 31 May and Pretoria, the capital of the South African Republic, on 5 June 1900. Roberts and Buller joined forces at Vlakfontein on 4 July , ending all formal resistance. The tide seemed to have turned, after achieving overwhelming superiority in the field the British managed to lift the sieges and capture the capital cities of the two Boer republics. The British annexed the South African Republic and President Kruger fled to Europe. Roberts, believing the war to be won, returned to England in January 1901, leaving Kitchener in command.

However the war was far from over, De Wet, De La Rey, Botha, and some minor leaders rallied some disbanded Boer commando units, the 'bitter-enders', escaped into the vast bush country and, for some eighteen months, continue to wage unconventional guerilla warfare by blowing up trains, and ambushing British troops and garrisons, defying all attempts to corner them. The British Army, unable to defeat the Boers using conventional tactics, had to adopt many of the Boer methods, and the war degenerated into a devastating and cruel struggle between Britain and Boer. The British criss-crossed the countryside constructing a line of iron blockhouses to protect the railroad and other communication lines and to flush the Boers into the open. Kitchener then copied Spanish tactics in Cuba , British mounted infantry swept through Southern Africa and a 'scorched earth' policy was adopted.

The last of the Boer commandos, left without food, clothing, ammunition or hope, surrendered in May, 1902 accepting British rule and the Treaty of Vereeniging was signed on 31 May 1902. The British granted the Boers £3 million in compensation for the destroyed farms and gave amnesty to Boer soldiers who pledged loyalty to Britain. The Orange Free State and the South African Republic became British colonies. Dutch and English were made official languages. The Union of South Africa became a self-governing nation in 1910, and the first Prime Minister was the former Boer general, Louis Botha.

The Boer War was a watershed event for the British Army, the Boers employed hit-and-run tactics that not only caused losses the British can't afford, they did not conform to the usual "gentlemanly" rules of war. It became clear to the British that they needed to adopt new tactics to defeat the Boers. They needed to fight a series of battles over a long period of time covering wide areas of ground, this involved marching in long columns for days at a time across the vast plains or "veldt", often without proper uniforms or rations. The weather caused problems, with freezing temperatures and storms in the winter and very hot summers.

The British started off with less than 25,000 men in South Africa, but before the war was ended about 500,000 men were in the field. As costs and casualties mounted, over 20,000 British Troops were laid to rest in the heat and dust of the South African veldt, with 22,829 being wounded. The Boer War, according to Rudyard Kipling, taught the British "no end of a lesson". Thomas Pakenham, author of The Boer War has called it the longest, costliest, bloodiest and most humiliating war for

British Army: Records 1899-1902	
British Army	
Regular/ Regular Reservists	256,340
Regulars (including Reservists)	256,000
Cavalry	27,000
Artillery	21,000
Infantry	175,000
Staffs and Others	33,000
Militia	45,556
Yeomanry	36,553
Volunteers	19,856

Some 126,274 new recruits, without any military experience joined the Army during the war

Blockhouse used during the Boer War

Recruitment in the British Regular Army 1899-1902

	Recruits with no previous military experience	Recruits from the Militia	Recruits from the Volunteers	Imperial Yeomanry	Total
1899	23,259	16,396	3,045	---------	42,700
1900	43,992	23,165	20,962*	10,242	98,361
1901	28,516	15,662	14,221**	17,252	75,651
1902	30,507	18,994	8,300	7,239	65,040
Total:	126,274	74,217	46,528	34,733	281,752

* of which 14,559 on one-year engagements, including 1,664 City Imperial Volunteers
** of which 6,776 on one-year engagements
Source: *General Annual Return of the British Army*, 1902 and 1903

Britain between 1815 and 1914.

The Reservists
These were men liable to be recalled from civilian life for up to nine years and their fitness for military service varied. There were around 83,000 reservists.

Militia
These were attached to Regular battalions as reinforcements. Their engagement was for six years and they had to attend an initial six weeks' training period and a 28 day camp each year. Over half the Militia were youths under 19 who intended joining the Regulars when they had reached the required medical standards. About 105,000 joined the Militia in the South African War.

Yeomanry and Volunteers
The Volunteers and the Yeomanry were formed to be employed only for home defence, but in January, 1900, to circumvent this restriction, new units were formed out of existing ones, being known as *Imperial Yeomanry*. These troops were usually keen amateurs and had little or no proper training. About 92,000 enlisted in these formations.
Minimum Official Age for Service Overseas was 20
The Colonies Australia 16,000 New Zealand 6,600 Canada 6,000 South Africa 52,414
Constabulary Britain 7,723 Canada 1,258
British Forces Grand Total 448,435
(Figures from *Official History*)

Service Records
Service records for men who served in the Boer War are in several sources in the Public Record Office.
Army: Officers Records It is fairly easy to trace the career of an officer from the Army Lists. Service records of officers are for the most part in WO 76 with some records, especially for men who saw action in the First World War, in WO 339 and WO 374 (with indexes in WO 338). Embarkation returns for officers are in WO 25/3520-3522.
Army: Soldiers' Discharge Papers
The best starting point for records of a soldier's career is the incomplete collection of Soldiers' Documents (attestation and discharge papers) in WO 97. They cover discharges from the army for the period 1760 to 1913, and are often an excellent source, providing place of birth, age on enlistment, details of appearance and, from 1883 next of kin. However, please remember that if a soldier died whilst serving, his record will not usually be found in WO97.

From 1883 to 1913 the series includes soldiers who were discharged to pension and those who were discharged for other reasons, such as termination of limited engagements or discharge by purchase. If nothing can be found in this class, the basic framework of a soldier's career can often be established through Muster Rolls and Pay Lists.
Royal Hospital Chelsea, Soldiers' Documents
The soldiers' documents are arranged by date of discharge, in WO 97 as follows:
Soldiers Discharged 1882-1900
All discharge papers were filed alphabetically by name, for the whole army (WO 97/2172-4231). Some discharge papers are now in a second alphabetic sequence in WO 97/6355-6383.
Soldiers Discharged 1900-1913
All discharge papers were filed alphabetically by name, for the whole army (WO 97/4232-6322). Some discharge papers are now in a second alphabetic sequence in WO 97/6323-6354.
Artillery Records
WO 69 contains some useful material, up to 1913.
Auxiliary Army Forces: Volunteers, Yeomanry
The Volunteers were originally raised in 1794, and the Yeomanry (cavalry) in 1804, as support against a possible invasion of Great Britain by the French, but by 1816 the Volunteers had been dissolved. The Yeomanry continued and following the revival of the Volunteer Force (or Rifle Volunteers) in 1859 they combined in 1907 to form the Territorial Force. Many Volunteer and Yeomanry Units saw service in the Boer War
The Volunteers
The main sources for information on the Volunteers are; Officers appear in the Army List and their commissions were gazetted in the London Gazette - ZJ1.
Records of pensions paid to Volunteers for some of the years between 1817-1927 may be found in PMG 13/4-50
Registers of the Volunteers Officers' Decoration, 1892-1932, are in WO 330/3, WO 330/4.

The Yeomanry
The Yeomanry were mounted volunteers, introduced in 1804 for home service only. Very few records are held at the PRO, most being in private collections or regimental museums. Records of pensions paid to the Yeomanry for some years between 1817-1927 may be found in PMG 13/4-50.
The Imperial Yeomanry
The Imperial Yeomanry was raised in 1899 specifically for the South African War, and general records of its administration can be found in WO 108. Records of officers in the Imperial Yeomanry do not seem to have survived, although the 1901-2 Army Lists can give an outline of service, together with the roll of officers in WO 129/12. Commissions were announced in the London Gazette - ZJ1.

Spion Kop after the battle

A roll of officers and NCO's in the Imperial Yeomanry is in WO 108/93-95 with casualty books and a nominal roll of officers in the Yeomanry awarded the Queen's South Africa Medal in WO 129/8-12.

Attestation and discharge papers are in WO 128, arranged by service number. Service numbers can be found by using the registers in WO 129. If a man went on to serve in the regular army, and was discharged before 1914, his record should be in WO 97.

Casualty Books for this period may be found in WO 129/8, WO 129/9, WO 129/10, WO 129/11, and WO 108/338. Awards of the Imperial Yeomanry Long Service and Good Conduct Medal were announced in Army Orders, now in WO 123.

Pensions

There are several series of records relating to subsequent pension claims. The two most useful sources are WO 148, for claims made between 1901 and 1904, and PMG 9/48-50 for later claims. Occasionally, individual claims can be found in the selected war pensions award files in PIN 71.

Casualties

Death by disease was the far more likely cause than death on the battlefield and, of the roughly 22,000 British and colonial fatalities, only 6,000 were killed in action; typhoid or enteric fevers claimed the other 18,000. Virtually all those killed were buried where they fell, leaving their graves to indicate the line of battle. Unfortunately, many of the battlefield graves were later exhumed and the dead reburied in centralised cemeteries.

Graves of Victims of Conflict

This division of the National Monument Council is responsible for the maintenance and recording of graves of those who died in wars in South Africa from 1795. A record of graves has been established along with a computerised database of casualties. The database includes information such as the names of the casualty, the place where the individual was killed or mortally wounded, the date of death and the final burial place. Enquiries regarding the burial site of individuals are processed at a fee of R100-00 (one hundred South African Rand). An additional charge is made if a photograph of the graves is requested. The current photographic collection of individual grave sites is incomplete

Postal address is: P.O. Box 87552, Houghton, 2041, South Africa

Telephone number is: 27-11-482 8365/6 (international code is 27)

Fax number is: 27-11-482 8196

E-mail address is: jbeater@jhb.sahra.org.za

You can search an online index to the Anglo Boer War Database on http://www.nationalmonuments.co.za/search.htm Searches can be made using the following categories; Surname, Initials, Rank or Regiment. However be wary of how the names of British Regiments have been entered, *for example* the East Lancashire Regiment, is entered as Lancashire Regiment, with East being entered into the Rank category. There are no listings for the Loyal North Lancashire Regiment. There are no service numbers given, no Battalions are listed and there are no proper identification of cavalry regiments, they are merely grouped as 'Dragoon Guards', 'Dragoons', 'Hussars' or 'Lancers'. However it can be a way of identifying casualties

There are discrepancies in Casualty figures between the *Official History* **and** *The Times* **Vol VII, whose figures are shown in brackets.**

British Forces

Killed in Action or Died of Wounds 7,582 including 712 officers   (7,894; 706 officers).

Died of Disease 13,139 including 406 officers   (13,250; 339 officers).

Total Deaths 20,721 (21,942, includes 800 accidental).

Total Casualties from all Causes including Wounded: 52,150 (of which 41,551 were British).

A complete list of casualties is WO 108/360 at the Public Record Office and in WO 108/89-91, 338 and WO 25. Naval losses are recorded in ADM 116/529.

A list of soldiers buried in Cape Province is in DO 119/1479.

Medal rolls Most of the empire's soldiers who served in South Africa were eligible for one or both of two campaign medals for the War:

• Queen's South Africa Medal (QSA) awarded to men who served in the campaign and served between October 1899 until the Queen's death on 22 January 1901.On the ribbon of the medal could be up to nine metal bars for the Army or eight for the Navy, awarded for 26 campaigns and major actions in which the wearer had fought.

• King's South Africa Medal (KSA) for men who served on or after January 1902. On the ribbon of the medal could be up to two metal bars for South Africa 1901 and South Africa 1902 and this medal was never issued without the Queen's South Africa Medal.

Recipients of the Queens (and King's) South Africa Medal are listed in the medal rolls, WO 100/120-130, and WO 100/356, WO 100/357 respectively. If you are not sure which unit a man was serving with, you may be able to get this information from the medal roll.

Gallantry awards can be found in several places. Correspondence can be found in WO 32 (CODE 50). Registers of awards of the Victoria Cross is in WO 98/4,7

Distinguished Conduct Medal 1855-1909 WO 146

Meritorious Service Awards 1846-1923 WO 101

Long Service and Good Conduct Medal 1831-1902 WO 102

Submission papers 1803-1914 WO 103

Recommendations- South African War 1899-1902 WO 108/135-179

Royal Red Cross Medal 1883-1928 WO 145

Awards to men who served in the Royal Navy during this period are in ADM 171/52-54, including awards to Marines and members of the Naval Division.

Cross & Cockade International
The First World War
Aviation Historical Society
www.crossandcockade.com

This article is divided into three parts: part one introduces you to Cross & Cockade International, and we hope you will find our broader subject interesting; while part two is a summary of the first few months of WWI from an aviation perspective. This includes information on the three British air services, along with a look at some of the early operations, training and the personalities who were well known at the time or would become well known leaders during WWII. Finally, in part three we have tried to help those of you who are involved in researching relatives who served with the air forces of the British Empire.

This group of officer pilots and observers shows a variety of uniforms and cap badges, indicating the regiments with which the officers had served before secondment to the RFC.

1. A Brief Introduction

Cross and Cockade International is the world's foremost World War One Aviation Historical Society. Now in our 32nd year, our members are constantly researching all aspects of the first major conflict in the air. The results of this research are published in our colour quarterly journal. Most of the articles are the outcome of many years research and are often illustrated with rare and previously unpublished photographs from private family collections.

Our articles cover British, German, Austrian, American, French, Italian, and Turkish forces and all theatres of operations. Squadron and biographical articles are frequently published. Indexes to the first 25 volumes of the journal are now available on diskette to make research easier (see advertisement on page 240). There are over 8000 names listed, not only from the British and Commonwealth forces, but also from the other combatant nations. So if one of your relatives served with any of the flying services, why not check us out, they may feature in an article or a photograph; you might wish to know more about their squadron and where it was deployed, or the aircraft with which they were equipped.

Visit our web site and view our on-line index to articles, which may whet your appetite to join the on-line discussion group, where you can post questions and requests.

If you wish to know the exact location of an aerodrome in Northern France, we have recently produced our Gazetteer of Northern France on diskette. At the end of this article are some useful tips on researching the RFC and RAF in WWI.

For further details on Cross & Cockade International, the Society and its quarterly journal, contact the Membership Secretary, Roger Tisdale, 5 Cave Drive, Downend, Bristol BS16 2TL; email: rmmt@zetnet.co.uk.

2. The First Great War in the Air

The First World War saw many new developments take place during the 20th century's most devastating world conflict. Amongst the carnage of the battlefield, new weapons were developed and deployed – not least amongst these was the military aeroplane. The fledgling aviation services of the combatants took to the field of battle alongside the deployed armies. Great Britain sent the Royal Flying Corps to France with the British Expeditionary Force and although it may be fair to say that the Army High Command did not know exactly, other than for reconnaissance, the capabilities of the RFC, they were soon to find out the value of the aeroplane. On 19 August 1914, just 15 days after war was declared and six days after the deployment of the

first four squadrons of the RFC to France, Lt G. Mapplebeck and Capt P. Joubert de la Ferté from 4 Squadron carried out the first reconnaissance over the German positions. On 22 August many aircraft were sent out to try and locate the German army under General A. von Kluck in the Mons area, and one report late in the day was so important that the commanding officer of the RFC in the field Brigadier-General Sir David Henderson personally took it to the army General Headquarters. This day's reports saved the BEF from being outflanked by the Germans. The 22nd was also the first day on which a British machine failed to return from a patrol. The crew, Lt C.G.G. Bayly and V. Waterfall, were both killed, the first of many to die in the air.

The Royal Naval Air Service had broken away from the RFC on 1 July 1914 and pursued aviation with a naval eye. The RNAS developed British airships which were deployed around the coast and were mainly used for anti-submarine work, coastal and convoy protection patrols. The fixed wing force took part in naval campaigns, in France alongside the RFC, in the Dardanelles and Italy and others less well known. The RNAS also played an important part in the development of the British aircraft industry, with orders for the Sopwith Triplane and Camel (among others) for its fighting squadrons. The navy along with the RNAS would later develop seaplane carriers and the first true aircraft carrier HMS *Argus*, capable of launching and recovering aircraft on the same deck, rather than having them ditch alongside the ship for recovery. *Argus* was later equipped for carrying aircraft to enable it to strike at the German High Seas Fleet. It was the RNAS who struck the first British blow against Germany when on 22 September 1914 four aircraft attacked the Zeppelin sheds at Düsseldorf, one of a number of raids the service was to carry out against the feared Zeppelin airships. Although the aircraft reached and bombed the target, only one bomb hit a Zeppelin shed and that did not explode. However, another attack, on 8 October against the sheds at Düsseldorf and the railway station at Cologne, was more successful, with Flt Lt R.L.G. Marix destroying Zeppelin LZ 25 during the attack on Düsseldorf. He was shot down on the way back to his base at Antwerp, but managed to return safely. On 21 November three aircraft raided the Zeppelin sheds at Friedrichshafen destroying one airship. Another notable event for the navy occurred on 25 December, when flying from the seaplane carriers HMS *Empress*, *Engadine* and *Riviera*, the RNAS attacked the Zeppelin sheds at Cuxhaven. These are some of the notable early actions that were to typify the spirit and determination of the services throughout the war.

Sgt Cyril Trevett, MSM
– later promoted to Warrant Officer.

Men, Training & the Future

The airmen who flew with the RFC and the RNAS (They amalgamated as the Royal Air Force on 1 April 1918) were drawn from two sources: the RFC men were recruited either from the regiments of the army or direct entry, whilst the RNAS drew their personnel either from serving Royal Navy officers and men seconded or through direct recruiting.

At first these men had to pay for their own basic flying instruction and once they obtained their 'Ticket', the all-important Royal Aero Club certificate, the government reimbursed the cost. They then progressed to more advanced training at a military school and eventual posting to an operational squadron. At first these squadrons were involved with army reconnaissance, but later in 1915 when the lines were more static, they became involved in artillery spotting, counter battery work, and also aerial fighting.

In the earlier days of combat, squadrons were mixed with a flight of reconnaissance aircraft and a few aircraft to act as scouts (fighters). Later they developed into specialist squadrons with specific roles: reconnaissance, bombing, ground attack and scout (fighter) squadrons, each usually equipped with only one type of aircraft. These aircraft would become as well known as some of their pilots: the Vickers Gunbus, the RE8 (known as the Harry Tate, after the music hall star) and perhaps the most famous British scout of the war, the Sopwith Camel. The scout pilots included Englishmen Major Lanoe Hawker of 24 Squadron, who was killed by Manfred von Richthofen on 23 November 1916, and Captain Albert Ball from Nottingham, who flew with 56 Squadron, who was also killed, on 7 May 1917; Canadians Major William Bishop of 60 Squadron, who rose to high rank within the RCAF, and George Barker, who died in an air crash in Canada on 12 March 1930; Anthony Beauchamp-Proctor, a South African, would die in the peacetime RAF, when he crashed while performing aerobatics on 21 June 1921; Englishman Alan Jerrard served in the RAF after the war and died at Weston-super-Mare on 14 May 1968; Edward 'Mick' Mannock the socialist Irishman, died in combat on 26 July 1918, and Australian Frank McNamara, who died in England on 2 November 1961: all had been decorated with the Victoria Cross.

These were some of the men who set the example for the future of the Royal Air Force. Others would go on to be leaders and fight the next war from high office: Arthur 'Bomber' Harris who commanded 45 Squadron in France during 1917, would later lead Bomber Command in WWII; Hugh Dowding was at Fighter Command during the Battle of Britain, and Chief of the Air Staff Sir Charles Portal would command the RAF through the final part of WWII. Other well known names from the first war in the air include Air Marshal Gerald Gibbs, Air Chief Marshal Trafford Leigh-Mallory, Marshal of the R.A.F Lord Tedder, Sholto Douglas, Arthur Coningham, Keith Park and Philip Joubert de la Ferté, who would all lead their later commands with distinction.

3. WWI Research Sources for Family Historians

The Public Record Office, Kew, West London is the prime source of original documents relating to the RFC and RNAS from 1912 to March 1918 and the RAF from April 1918 to about the middle of 1919. These documents are in Class AIR 1.

To trace a pilot or observer through the squadron record books you will need to know the dates they were serving with the squadron and also, as some of the record books are held by the controlling Wing, the Wing number. This is because squadrons were not static, but moved along the front and also between theatres. An example might be 66 Squadron, who went to France in March 1917 under the control of 9 Wing, in November 1917 they were redeployed to Italy under the control of 14 Wing. The same applies to combat reports; whilst there is a section in AIR 1 devoted to combat reports, if your squadrons are 'missing', check the Wing records as they may found amongst these.

Service Records

To look up an officer's service record, first check Class AIR 76 where the records are available on microfilm. However, you should be aware that in some cases these records were written up retrospectively and there can be large gaps in the information. This is especially true in the case of naval officers transferring to the RAF. That said, many of the records do have a considerable amount of detail to do with postings, promotions, periods of sickness and other personal details. Finally, if the officer you are looking for was retained in the peace time RAF, his record will not be available. If the officer was seconded from the army, you could try and consult the records in class WO363 'the burnt series' or WO364. For those discharged before the foundation of the RAF look in class WO338 which is the index to class WO339 and WO374. RNAS officers' service records are in class ADM 273.

Studio portrait of Cadet Pte 50971 King

Reginald Liddon Alderson
a Major in the RAF and formerly Lt Cdr RNVR who died of influenza on 30 July 1918. His pilot's wings can be seen above the uniform cuff lace.

RFC/RAF airmen's records are in class AIR 79, and you will need to consult the index in Class AIR 78. This is a difficult class to view and it will help with common surnames to know the airman's service number and his initials to identify the correct file. The RNAS enlisted airmen's records are in ADM 188.

There is a limited number of Women's Royal Air Force records in Class AIR 80.

Another rich source of information for people who would like to know when officers or airmen were given leave, transferred from an army regiment to the RFC, RAF or posted to other units are the 'Wing Standing Orders' - where they are available.

A useful source to look at is the medal cards available on microfiche for the RFC and RAF in class WO329, and for the RNAS in class ADM 17. The army cards can be very helpful in filling in details of service number changes if transferred between regiments or corps; date of entry in theatre, medal entitlement, name and rank. The PRO also has copies of the *London Gazette* in class ZJ1; the *Gazette* contains the dates of promotions and medal citations when published, but note that not every medal has a published citation. On the shelves of the reading room are comprehensive collections of Navy, Army and Air Force Lists.

Other Sources
The Royal Air Force Museum at Hendon holds the original Royal Aero Club Cards, which contain some details of pilots who obtained their 'ticket': there may also be an accompanying photograph, although some of these are missing. The museum also holds thousands of casualty cards for WWI in two series, and these can be very informative, giving dates and type of injury, aircraft type, serial number and squadron. The accidents include non-flying accidents as well, so you may be surprised to find that granddad was injured playing rugby! The museum has an extensive collection of logbooks, photographs and other documents. Other places to consider are the Fleet Air Arm Museum at Yeovilton, The Museum of Army Flying at Middle Wallop and the Imperial War Museum at Lambeth, London.

For information on where a soldier is buried contact the Commonwealth War Graves Commission, 2 Marlow Road, Maidenhead, Berks or visit the web site at www.cwgc.org/. But a word of warning, some of the details held are not correct as the information for many entries appear to have been collected from the families or next of kin, so some dates may be wrong and indeed there are some men who are listed as unmarried although they had wives!

Other sources to consider are contemporary local newspapers, which should be available at the British Library Newspaper Library, Colindale Avenue, London NW9 5HE. Their catalogue is viewable on-line at www.bl.uk/collections/newspaper/. Local libraries usually hold copies of the local publications.

Education and professional records can be helpful. If you know where someone was educated or employed, it can be worth exploring if there was a school magazine, university record, an educational or professional year book. Investigations at the local record office will sometimes turn up useful information, photographs and rolls of honour.

There are many very good reference books available, and to recommend a reading list would be impossible, but consider *The Sky their Battlefield* by T. Henshaw and *Airmen Died in the Great War 1914-1918* by C. Hobson. Air Britain publish some very authoritative monographs on WWI subjects, their volume *Royal Air Force Flying Training and Support Units* being very useful for tracing the hundreds of miscellaneous unit name changes, dates, wing and command changes. Their web site is at www.air-britain.org.uk.

Imperial Forces
For records of men who served in the Australian Imperial Forces prior to transferring to the British flying services, contact Australian Archives at WW1 Personnel Records Service, PO Box 7425, ACT Mail Centre, Fyshwick ACT 2610, Australia. It will help if you know the regiment, regimental number and full name. The files are very comprehensive and list personal details, date and place of enlistment, regiments, promotions, wounds, if wounded which hospitals they were in and the dates and also names of ships involved. There is a charge but the service is excellent. They are also on the web at www.aa.gov.au/

For those who served in the Canadian Imperial Forces, contact the National Archives of Canada, Client Services and Communications Branch, Ottawa, Canada, K1A 0N3, or visit their web site at www.archives.ca/. Once they agree to release the document concerned, they have an excellent scheme, whereby you can have up to 25 pages of photocopy free if you specify the type of information you require, (enlistment papers etc) and they will also copy whole documents at a reasonable charge.

Cabinet War Rooms © Imperial War Museum

Cabinet War Rooms
Phil Reed
Director

Shortly after Winston Churchill had been appointed Prime Minister in May 1940, in succession to Neville Chamberlain, he visited the Cabinet War Rooms and proudly proclaimed in the bunker's War Cabinet meeting room that 'this is the room from which I will lead the war'. Well, fine words, noble sentiments and perhaps a pretty sensible idea, with the ruling expectation of that time being the imminence of devastating air raids. But Churchill was no 'ducker' and he proceeded to 'run the war' from the prime ministerial base of Number 10. Despite the consternation of his staff, this was not as absurd an idea as it might sound.

The Cabinet War Rooms had been developed as a result of studies being made throughout the 1930s as to how best to prepare the country - and in particular its military and civil command – for a war which the RAF in particular predicted would involve air raids of such a magnitude and intensity that the nation's hospitals and mortuaries would be deluged with the dead and the dying. After much deliberation, it was decided in 1938 to create a 'war room' which could function as a central information source for detail about all aspects of the course of the war and which might double up to provide sheltered working accommodation for the Prime Minister and the War Cabinet. However, the solution created by the adaptation of the storage basement of the so-called 'New Public Offices' underneath the Board of Trade for us as the Cabinet War Rooms was not only a makeshift one, it was based on the mistaken belief – or deliberate deception, as the structure of the building above was no secret - that the building above embodied new construction technology in the shape of a steel frame structure. Such a structure, it was thought, might better withstand blast (though not the actual penetration) from enemy bombs. Sadly, the building did not contain such a structure and would probably have offered little better resistance to bombs than any other Whitehall basement.

Although the CWR became fully operational on 28 August 1939, the country enjoyed several months of the 'phoney war', when life in the capital and elsewhere, while wearing many of the trappings of war, saw the return of many of the routines and pastimes of peacetime. Even after the war became more threatening and personal, as the Nazi scythe cut through Europe, and as British troops were sent to France and Belgium to meet Britain's treaty obligations, the country's ebullient new Prime Minister and his War Cabinet saw little reason (and still less comfort) in meeting in the CWR's cramped and stuffy surroundings. That was until the rear of Number 10 was badly damaged by a German bomb on 14/15 October 1940 (and Churchill famously rescued his cook, Mrs Landemar). At that point Churchill's advisers seem to have finally won their own battle to reduce his obduracy and persuaded him, still reluctant, to meet below ground in the stronghold adapted for that purpose.

Even then, however, Churchill refused to make it his principal living and sleeping quarters and insisted on having a series of offices directly above the CWR adapted to provide living, working and sleeping accommodation for himself and his wife (concern for his wife's safety and proximity was a regular feature of the man throughout the war, though there are many examples of his obduracy in the face of her parallel concern for his safety). This 'Number 10 Annexe', as it became known, provided a base for him and his wife for the rest of the war, and though its anti-bomb protection consisted principally of steel shutters on the windows, it was within a couple of minutes' saunter of his underground CWR fortress.

It is astonishing to find how few War cabinet Meetings were actually held in the underground bunker, even during the Blitz and after real efforts to render the site bomb proof had finally been taken in late 1940. We know he addressed the nation from down there on four separate occasions and today the site resonates to recordings of those rhythmic, often virulent, and always inspiring speeches which gave people across the free and the enslaved world alike a belief in their ability to achieve victory, at a time when, based on experience, they had little reason to credit such an idea. It still thrills today to experience that same passion with which his words bolstered our recent ancestors' self-belief and sense of common cause. It is scarcely surprising to find his voice, his persona and his words being dusted off at each major crisis not only in this country, but by nations across the globe. The power of the man and his oratory speaks across generations and probably always will.

The War Rooms today could not be said to pay homage to the man, though, as one wanders through this site preserved just as it was in wartime, one cannot avoid the central, dominating figure of Churchill at every turn. Until recently, however, the Rooms tended to resonate almost exclusively to the sound of this one titanic figure. Certainly, the fabric of the site, its fittings, its quaint equipment and dreary government-finish paintwork provide a sense of time

Cabinet War Rooms © Imperial War Museum

and of walking through history that few other sites could rival. But it was in danger of becoming the dead Roman Forum of its age, with few signs of how people – from the lowliest to the loftiest – lived their daily (diurnal and nocturnal) lives, and how they felt about these 'lifestyles'. Having relied for years on the 'Marie Celeste approach' – the Map Room kept empty and abandoned as it was so suddenly the day after VJ Day – an attempt was made in the mid-1990s to restore life to the place in which several hundred people of all ranks and all walks of life worked and slept, but, above all, socialised, muddled through, complained, compared tales of daily woes and good fortunes, and, sacrilege, lost patience with their great leader.

The change of approach began with a simple change. The PM's chamber pot, for so long displayed like some ancient relic, was placed, where a 'gozzunder' belongs, at the bottom of his bed, indicating at a stroke how he – and he was far from alone - loathed the miserable chemical toilet facilities of the site. Life-like figures in concentrated or just routine postures were added to the rooms, with one particular middle ranking naval officer robbed of his rank by the standard winceyette, striped pyjamas of the time. Just a few doors down from him, young, female civilian staff produce unbelievably perfect copy from their leaden typewriters, or do the best they can to prepare themselves for their evening date at the Covent Garden palais de danse. While down below in the sub-basement, as the new sound guide tells the visitor, something resembling revolt against the primitive conditions down there stirs among the otherwise loyal, unstinting subjects. Where once we might have been happy to think of the war as a period of unreserved patriotic fervour, where communal song allayed any discomfort, and great leaders lived like the rest of us, we now see how people did indeed maintain a belief in victory at any cost – but also suffered, complained and railed against their lot, as humankind will whatever the cause.

And now the War Rooms are about to make the lives of their many and varied occupants even more open to inspection than ever, by opening up rooms that have been inaccessible to the public for well over fifty years. The first phase of expansion will show another side of the life of the 'roaring lion', with aspects of his family and domestic life on

show: Mrs Churchill's cell-like bedroom, the couple's cramped windowless dining room and their ample kitchen that could keep the Prime Minister sustained, as he was accustomed to be in peace and war alike – and as this most crucial figurehead needed to be. Here too will be a greatly expanded Education Centre offering more insights than ever into people's daily lives as well as the ways of the country's higher echelons. Beyond these, in a now deserted expanse of wartime upright steel girders and splintered parquet floor, a museum dedicated to telling the story of the life of the man considered by many here and across the globe to be this country's greatest leader and one of the world's most inspiring figures. It seems only right and not at all hero worship to mount a permanent exhibition, dedicated to the man whom American Presidents revere, the man in whom Palestinian and Israeli leaders alike find a source of fascination, the man whose recorded voice and written words find a relevance for every generation, nationality and age-group as easily as Shakespeare.

It will not be hagiography, it will not hide the man's faults or glance over the criticisms, it will not put him on a pedestal. It will show how he developed politically, personally and historically to become the figure he is for so many people today. It will place him in the context of his War Rooms and the whole extension will show better than ever how it was not simply this 'Caesar' who won the war, but also the countless foot soldiers and civilians who followed him, who laboured below ground in a wide variety of functions and who rarely gave the slightest hint to their loved ones of the secret nature of their toil.

'It is part of your family's history' is the slogan of the Imperial War Museum. At the Cabinet War Rooms the visitor will always be able to gain that rare, first-hand, unalloyed experience of the original atmosphere of that age. Soon they will be able to see more closely still how great men and women and the multitudes whose fates they command live in times of war. In times of peace this will always be a source of fascination and even puzzlement for us. In times of crisis this will provide us with reason and self-belief.

Cabinet War Rooms
© Imperial War Museum

Across the world and through the Centuries
Ian Passingham

Founded in 1976, Holts have become the leading Battlefields and History Tours Company with an international reputation for providing a range of subjects that take our travellers worldwide and which span 2,000 years of history. Formed by Major Tonie Holt and his wife Valmai, the Company began with visits to well-known sites such as the Somme, Ypres, (or "Wipers" as it was popularly known by the British "Tommy" of the First World War), Normandy, Arnhem and Waterloo amongst others.

It now has a portfolio of over 200 tours, which concentrate on the First and Second World Wars, but also cover ancient history, the medieval and Napoleonic eras, the American War of Independence and American Civil War, the Franco-Prussian War, British Colonial conflict, including the Zulu and Boer Wars, and post-1945 campaigns such as Vietnam and the Falkland Islands.

Knowledgeable and friendly guides help you to enjoy an informal, friendly atmosphere amongst the tour group. Each trip provides an objective, well-researched and interesting account of the historical facts, and a fascinating glimpse of the individual experience of the personalities who fought on either side, from the Generals to the soldiers at the rough end of the trench.

Our tours reflect the fact that no matter how intricate or brilliant a plan may be, a battle can only be won or lost by the soldiers, sailors or aircrews involved. Whether in the front line, at the gun line, or serving in a support role in war, every individual has a story to tell.

Our travellers are constantly moved by these stories of courage, sacrifice and the grim realities of war, as well as some tales of the lighter side of life in the front line. As an example, a British soldier, wounded during the First World War, wrote to his mother:

'I have no pain, oh mother dear, but oh! I am so dry. So hitch me to a brewery and leave me there to die!'

The sense of humour of British servicemen and women across the years has undoubtedly sustained them in their darkest hours and is unique amongst the armed forces of the world.

One of the most important aspects of the tour is "being there". Seeing the ground on the Somme for the first time is an extraordinary experience. Only then do you begin to fully understand the enormity of the task which faced the British Army in attempting to overcome apparently rock-solid German defences with all the advantages of the high ground dominating no man's land.

To be there with veterans of the battles on the Somme, or veterans of the many other campaigns that Holts cover, is the icing on the cake. We have been privileged to share the company of many veterans of both World Wars over the years. Seeing the battleground and hearing from men and women who were there are remarkable and humbling experiences.

Many of our first-time travellers come for a very personal reason – less to do with the detail of the history than a sense that they too must "be there" to make special, poignant visits to the graves or memorials of loved ones who gave their lives for their country.

In each case, the discussion of grand strategies and descriptions of a battle are swept away. We see the reality of war through the eyes of a family affected, sometimes generations later, by their loss and who wish to spend an intimate, silent moment where a father, grandfather or other relation rests, or is commemorated.

Occasionally, the veteran and the family remembrance are brought together in a unique way. In 1991, Holts conducted a major visit to the Somme to commemorate the 75th Anniversary of the campaign of 1916. One of the many groups associated with the visit was a contingent of officers of the Royal Hampshire Regiment, (the Hampshire Regiment in the First World War).

Amongst the group were two veterans of the Hampshire Regiment, then in their mid-90s, who had fought on the Somme in 1916 - Ernie Billet and George Louth.

One of the other travellers was a Mrs Renate Farley, whose father and two uncles had all also fought on the Somme. The difference was that her relations had served in the German Army. Renate's father, Albert Mühmelt, had survived the War. Her uncles, Alois and Robert, did not.

The three brothers, born in Breslau (in what is now Wroclaw in Poland), were from a family of nine children. Alois, a Gefreiter, or Lance-Corporal in the 5th Battalion of Infantry Regiment Number 66 by 1916, had been in the front line in the final week of June 1916 during the preliminary artillery bombardment of the German defences before the British Fourth Army's "Big Push" began.

Though he withstood this infernal barrage, Alois was killed in action on the 1st of July, aged 24. He was one of over 8,000 German casualties on that fateful day -

light when compared with the nearly 60,000 British casualties – but no less tragic for his grieving brothers at the front and the rest of his family in Breslau. His elder brother Robert was listed as Missing in Action on the 17th of September during the continued bloody struggle on the Somme. His remains were never found. Renate's father Albert was to be taken prisoner on the 14th of October 1918, shortly before the Armistice.

Renate had contacted the German equivalent of the Commonwealth War Graves Commission - Volksbund Deutsche Kriegsgräberfürsorge (the German War Graves Association) – to find out where her uncle Alois was buried. They confirmed that he was laid to rest in the German Military Cemetery at Achiet-le-Petit on the north-eastern edge of the former Somme battlefield. Alois had been billeted at Achiet-le-Petit before moving into the front line and it was here that he wrote his last letters home. 75 years on, Renate proved that a family's love can transcend the passage of time – She had returned on behalf of her family to pay her respects at her uncle's grave.

There was a simple ceremony at the graveside, which included the laying of a wreath, a brief, silent reflection and a rendition of Captain Charles Hamilton Sorley's poem: "To Germany".

'You are blind like us. Your hurt no man designed,
And no man claimed the conquest of your land.
But gropers both through fields of thought confined
We stumble and we do not understand.
You only saw your future bigly planned,
And we, the tapering paths of our own mind,
And in each other's dearest ways we stand,
And hiss and hate. And the blind fight the blind.

When it is peace, then we may view again
With new-won eyes each other's truer form
And wonder. Grown more loving-kind and warm
We'll grasp firm hands and laugh at the old pain,
When it is peace. But until the peace, the storm,
The darkness and the thunder and the rain.

Sorley, in common with other British people before 1914, had lived in Germany and had many friends there. But at the outbreak of war in August 1914 he had joined the British Army. He was killed in action just over a year later during the Battle of Loos. The Victorian and Edwardian eras had encouraged an easy alliance of kinship between the two countries before the War. Renate, too, had married an Englishman, Oliver, who was with her at her uncle's grave.

Nevertheless, some would assume that our two Hampshire Regiment veterans, having witnessed the horrors of trench warfare and the blood-letting in 1916, would have balked at the idea of attending this personal commemoration for one of the enemy – but not a bit of it.

George Louth and Ernie Billet stepped forward to accompany Renate to her uncle's final resting-place and after the laying of a wreath, saluted their former foe as a mark of respect for him, his family, and in reconciliation.

For all who witnessed it, there was no better way to acknowledge that tours of this type are not about the glory of war, but a shared desire to understand our history, so that we are not doomed to repeat it through collective ignorance and political arrogance.

Above all, it reminds us that soldiers on either side of no man's land were ordinary men forced into extraordinary circumstances who had anxious families praying that they would one-day return. Those on either side who did not must be remembered and their sacrifice commemorated in perpetuity.

For further information on Holts' 2002 programme and any general enquiries, please contact us via:
Holts Tours Limited, Battlefields & History, The Plough, High St, Eastry, Nr Sandwich, Kent CT13 0HF
Freephone: 0800 731 1914 Telephone: 01304 612248
Fax: 01304 614930 e-mail address: info@holts.co.uk
Or visit our Website at: www.battletours.co.uk

The South Africa War 1899 - 1902
Service Records of British & Colonial Women
Sheila Gray

This register contains the service records of over 1,700 military and civilian nurses, laywomen and civilian volunteers from throughout the British Empire who were rewarded for their service in the South African (Anglo-Boer) War, 1899 - 1902.

At the end of the nineteenth century, nursing in Britain's military hospitals was performed by trained male medical orderlies, with the female members of the Army Nursing Service (A.N.S.) acting in a supervisory role only. In 1897, the Princess Christian Army Nursing Service Reserve (A.N.S.R.) was established for the express purpose of supplementing the A.N.S. in time of war. Reservists were unpaid in peacetime and continued to work in civilian hospitals, but in wartime they could be mobilised for service in the military hospitals in England to replace members of the A.N.S. who volunteered for service overseas; the reservists could also volunteer for overseas service. In 1899, the total establishment of the Army Nursing Service was 84 Nursing Sisters and Superintendents, and there were 101 civilian nurses on the Reserve roll.

The Anglo-Boer War was the first major military campaign for which female nurses in civil hospitals in Britain who volunteered were accepted for service with the Army overseas. By great good fortune, peace-time arrangements were completed in July 1899 for bringing the principal voluntary aid societies - the Army Nursing Reserve, the Order of St John and the National Aid Society under one central authority for the provision of auxiliaries to the A.N.S. in time of war. Consequently, when war broke out three months later the credentials of hundreds of nursing volunteers were screened by the Central Committee of the British Red Cross in London, and by District Committees in military districts further afield. Those accepted for army service were enlisted in the A.N.S.R.

In addition, some socially prominent men and women in England, Scotland, Ireland and Wales set about raising money to equip tented civil hospitals for use in the field in South Africa. Nine of these superbly equipped "private" hospitals with their full complement of civilian doctors and nurses were shipped out to South Africa , where each was placed under the overall authority of an officer of the Royal Army Medical Corps (R.A.M.C.).
Nurses in South Africa and other countries of the Empire - and even in America, volunteered their services. The Governments of Canada and New South Wales sent contingents of nurses, whilst nurses from the other Australian colonies and from New Zealand travelled there independently. Some were supported financially by friends and local well-wishers, others were equipped and financed by public donations to funds set up for the purpose by public spirited citizens. On arrival in South Africa, those accepted for service in the military hospitals were attached to the A.N.S.R

All these women were later rewarded with medals for their Army service, and yet no official records of their service were kept. Similarly, no formal service records were kept of the members of South African religious orders who cared for the sick and wounded, or the many laywomen who were rewarded for their service - the cooks and maidservants who accompanied contingents of British nurses, and the local women engaged in South Africa for the same purpose, all of whom suffered the same privations under canvas as the nurses they cared for. Many women were also awarded medals for their voluntary service in organisations such as the British Red Cross and various aid societies in South Africa, which collected and distributed comforts for the troops and provided facilities and entertainment for convalescents and men on leave.

The officer in charge of a military hospital was required to send in a regular return of all the staff on the hospital's payroll to the HQ in Capetown. At the end of the war, these registers provided the evidence on which the award of medals for service in South Africa was based. For the first time, a British miltary war service decoration was awarded to large numbers of women on the same basis of service as the men. All categories of nurses and female support staff were awarded the Queen's South Africa medal (Q.S.A.) without bars, and 587 nurses were also awarded the King's South Africa medal (K.S.A.). Instances are also recorded of medals awarded to women being witheld or later withdrawn because of "bad behaviour"! The surviving military hospital registers on which these awards were based are held in the Public Records Office, London.

Using these registers, and many additional informal resources such as newspapers, personal letters, ship's passenger lists, civil hospital nursing bulletins and troopship newssheets, this book brings together a great deal of scattered and previously unpublished data, and sets out in detail the individual service records of each woman in all these disparate categories.
However, owing to the sparse and fragmentary nature of information available the records are not, and never can be, complete.

A feature of the South African War was its fluid nature. The army's medical services, structured to support the set-battle format, struggled to adapt to this new, highly mobile and scattered type of warfare which ebbed and flowed over the mainly high-altitude territory encompassing the two Boer republics of the Transvaal and the Orange Free State, and the British colonies of the Cape and Natal.

General Hospitals were extended again and again by the addition of marquees, tents and prefabricated huts, and sometimes had to be packed up and moved hundreds of miles nearer to the action. Initially they were equipped with standard iron hospital beds for 500 men and 20 officers and delivered the full range of surgical and medical services, including X-rays. In a letter dated 20 November 1900, Staff-Sergeant Prins of the R.A.M.C. commented that No 9 General Hospital at Bloemfontein (which had been moved up from Capetown in March as the army advanced), was originally equipped with 86 marquees and 40 bell tents but in May 1900 (at the height of a typhoid epidemic) it had been extended to 100 marquees and 200 bell tents to accommodate no less than 1850 sick and wounded, and a further 40 bell tents housed the R.A.M.C. contingent. Stationary Hospitals established along the Lines of Communication (the railways), were equipped with 100 camp stretchers instead of proper beds. In spite of their name, they were intended to be light-weight mobile hospitals for the temporary accommodation of the injured while they were prepared for evacuation by Hospital Train to the Base Hospitals on the coast. In fact they often accommodated many times more than that number and for long periods.

Most of the nurses accepted for service in South Africa, stayed for twelve months. They nursed in both the General and Stationary Hospitals in purpose-built and requisitioned buildings, and in pre-fabricated huts, marquees and tents in the field. They were moved frequently as demand dictated at very short notice - sometimes no more than an hour or two.Nurses also staffed the Hospital Trains that evacuated patients from the Stationary Hospitals to the coast, journeys that were usually of two or three days duration. Sister Laura Wollcombe, a New Zealand nurse on the staff of St Bartholomew's Hospital, London, was a member of the A.N.S.R. and was mobilised a few days after the outbreak of hostilities for service on one of the two new Hospital Trains under construction in Capetown. Her contingent of nurses arrived there in November 1899 and she served for two and a half years on No.2 Hospital Train. Other nurses worked on the fleet of Hospital Ships that repatriated the sick and wounded from Durban and Capetown to Southampton. Some served continuosly on these ships, whilst others were posted to a Hospital Ship - or a passenger ship carrying sick or wounded officers, for one round trip as a "holiday" after a particularly arduous time in the field!

The mortality rate from disease was twice that from the fighting itself. Apart from the inevitable gunshot wounds and horse-riding accidents from riding over the rough terrain of the veldt, the climate and harsh conditions in the field contributed to the high death rate.Typhoid, then called "enteric fever", was endemic in South Africa and clean water supplies few and far between. A dead horse might be pushed into a muddy stream or lie unburied beside a water-hole from which water-bottles were refilled; a temperature of 100F during the day might drop to below freezing at night; troops equipped lightly during a rapid advance frequently slept out with only a blanket for protection from the cold; severe sunburn - especially among the kilted highlanders and insect bites took their toll. Doctors, overworked male medical orderlies and

nurses also died from such diseases as typhoid, pneumonia, measles or scarlet fever during their service in South Africa.

Separate chapters in the book, each with an explanatory introduction, detail the service of each woman in the different categories of nursing and support staffs: The Army Nursing Service; Army Nursing Service Reserve; civilian nurses engaged locally in South Africa; the nursing staff of wards in civil hospitals in South Africa who nursed sick and wounded troops; the nursing staffs of the privately organised Field Hospitals; nurses of the Natal Volunteer Medical Corps; Canadian nurses; Australian nurses; New Zealand nurses; cooks, maidservants and wardmaids and civilian volunteers rewarded for service in South Africa. The book also includes Rolls of the nurses and other volunteers who were Mentioned-in-Despatches, and of the women awarded the Royal Red Cross for services to the sick and wounded.

The large number of individuals involved, and their frequent movement between the different types of hospital or transport units, has necessitated the use of cryptic abbreviations to detail their service records. The abbreviations themselves are listed in information categories and follow a set sequence, and readers report that they quickly become familiar with the format, and are surprised and delighted at the detailed information revealed. The following example is an extract from p.15 of the book:

ARMY NURSING SERVICE RESERVE
BOWLES, A.A.

ARR CT	EX ENG	9.03.00 E
TO	8GH BFT	19.03.00 E
8GH BFT	TO CT	20.08.00 E
	TO 2GH PRE	27.08.01

This entry can be interpreted as follows: Nursing Sister A.A.Bowles (A.N.S.R.) arrived in Capetown from England on 9 March 1900. On 19 March she was posted to No.8 General Hospital at Bloemfontein (capital of the former Boer Republic of the Orange Free State). She left No.8 General Hospital for Capetown on 20 August 1900. On 27 August of the following year, 1901, she was reported as being on the staff of No.2 General Hospital at Pretoria, in the Transvaal. However, there is no record of where she was in Capetown between the 9 - 19 March 1900, nor how long she was at 2GH in Capetown from the end of August 1900 before being posted to Pretoria, nor when she returned to England. A letter "E" in the right-hand margin indicates the **exact** date, otherwise the date is that of the military hospital return in which her name appears as a member of the nursing staff employed.

This book is intended as a tool for further research, and readers are invited to share information with the author that will add to or amend the service records of the more than 1,700 women recorded. They were courageous, determined women, many of them in their 30s and 40s who gave extraordinary service in the best traditions of nursing; twenty-five of them lost their lives in South Africa. The hope is that one day the stories of all of them will be more widely known.

Military Museums

The Battlefields Trust
33 High Green, Brooke, Norwich, NR15 1HR
Tel: 01508 558145 Fax: 01508 558145
Email: Battlefield.trust@aol.com
WWW: www.battlefieldstrust.com
Commonwealth War Graves Commission
2 Marlow Road Maidenhead, SL6 7DX
Tel: 01628-634221 Fax: 01628-771208
Coldstream Guards Record Office
Wellington Barracks, Birdcage Walk London, SW1E 6HQ Access is
by appointment made in advance. Search fee of £25.00 per search
Fleet Air Arm Museum Records Research Centre
Box D61, RNAS Yeovilton Nr Ilchester, BA22 8HT Tel:
01935-840565 Fax: 01935-840181
Grenadier Guards Record Office
Wellington Barracks, Birdcage Walk London, SW1E 6HQ, Access is
by appointment made in advance. Search fee of £25.00 per search
Guards Museum
Wellington Barracks, Birdcage Walk London, SW1E 6HQ
Tel: (020) 7414 3271/3428 Fax: (020) 7414 3429
Imperial War Museum
Lambeth Road London, SE1 6HZ
Tel: (020) 7416-5000 Fax: (020) 7416 5374
Email: books@iwm.org.uk WWW: www.iwm.org.uk
Irish Guards Record Office
Wellington Barracks, Birdcage Walk London, SW1E 6HQAccess is
by appointment made in advance. Search fee of £25.00 per search
Museum of Army Flying
Middle Wallop, Stockbridge, SO20 8DY
Tel: 01980 674421 Email: daa@flying-museum.org.uk
WWW: www.flying-museum.org.uk
Museum of Coldstream Guards
Coldstream, Scotland
Royal Air Force Museum
Grahame Park Way, Hendon, London, NW9 5LL Tel: (020)
8205-2266 Email: info@refmuseum.org.uk
WWW: http://www.rafmuseum.org.uk
Scots Guards Record Office
Wellington Barracks, Birdcage Walk London, SW1E 6HQ, Access is
by appointment made in advance. Search fee of £25.00 per search
Welsh Guards Record Office
Wellington Barracks, Birdcage Walk London, SW1E 6HQ, Access is
by appointment made in advance. Search fee of £25.00 per search

England

Bedfordshire
Bedford Museum Bedfordshire Yeomanry
Castle Lane, Bedford, MK40 3XD
Tel: 01234 353323 Fax: 01234 273401
Bedfordshire & Hertfordshire Regimental Museum
Luton Museum, Wardown Park Luton, LU2 7HA Tel: 01582
546719
Berkshire
Commonwealth War Graves Commission
2 Marlow Road Maidenhead, SL6 7DX
Tel: 01628-634221 Fax: 01628-771208
R.E.M.E. Museum of Technology
Isaac Newton Road, Arborfield, Reading, RG2 9NJ Tel: 0118-
976-3567 Email: reme-museum@gtnet.gov.uk
WWW: http://www.eldred.demon.co.uk/reme-museum/index.htm
Royal Berkshire Yeomanry Cavalry Museum
T A Centre, Bolton Road Windsor, SL4 3JG
Tel: 01753-860600
The Household Cavalry Museum
Combermere Barracks, Windsor
Tel: 01753 755112 Fax: 01753 755112
Royal Army Education Corps Museum
HQ Beaconsfield Station, Wilton Park Beaconsfield, HP9
2RP Tel: 01494 683232

Cambridgeshire
Cambridgeshire Regimental Collection
Ely Museum, The Old Goal, Market Street Ely, CB7 4LS
Tel: 01353-666655

Cornwall
Duke of Cornwall's Light Infantry Museum
The Keep Bodmin, PL31 1EG Tel: 01206-72610

County Durham
Durham Light Infantry Museum
Aykley Heads Durham, DH1 5TU
Tel: 0191-384-2214 Email: dli@durham.gov.uk

Cumbria
Border Regiment & Kings Own Royal Border Regiment Museum
Queen Mary's Tower, The Castle Carlisle, CA3 8UR Tel:
01228-532774 Fax: 01228-521275 Email:
rhq@kingsownborder.demon.co.uk Museum devoted to the
history of Cumbria's County Infantry Regiment 1702 to
date, with information on Regular, Territorial Volunteer and
Militia units associated with the Regiments
Regimental Museum of the 9th/12th Royal Lancers
The Strand Derby, DE1 1BS Tel: 01332 716656
Fax: 01332 716670 Email: akelsall@derbymuseum.co.uk
WWW: www.derby.gov.uk/museums

Devon
Museum of Barnstaple & North Devon incorporating Royal Devon Yeomanry Museum
Peter A Boyd, The Square Barnstaple, EX32 8LN
Tel: 01271 346 747 Email: admin@sal.org.uk

Dorset
Royal Signals Museum
Blandford Camp Nr Blandford Forum, DT11 8RH Tel:
01258-48224
WWW: www.royalsignalsarmy.org.uk/museum/
Tank Museum
Bovington, BH20 6JG Tel: 01929 405096
Email: admin@tankmuseum.co.uk
WWW: www.tankmuseum.co.uk
The Keep Military Museum
The Keep, Bridport Road Dorchester, DT1 1RN Tel: 01305
264066 Email: keep.museum@talk21.com
WWW: www.keepmilitarymuseum.orguk

East Yorkshire
Museum of Army Transport
 Flemingate Beverley, HU17 0NG Tel: 01482-860445

Essex
England's Secret Nuclear Bunker
Kelvedon Hall Lane, Kelvedon Common, Kelvedon Hatch,
Brentwood, CM15 0LB Tel: 01277 364883
Essex Regiment Museum
Oaklands Park, Moulsham Street Chelmsford, CM2 9AQ
Tel: 01245 615101Email: pompadour@chelsfordbc.gov.uk
WWW: http://www.chelmsfordbc.gov.uk
Gloucestershire
Soldiers of Gloucestershire Museum
Gloucester Docks, Commercial Road Gloucester, GL1 2EH
Tel: 01452 522682 Fax: 01452 311116

Hampshire
Aldershot Military Museum
Queens Avenue Aldershot, GU11 2LG
Tel: 01252-314598 Email: musim@hants.gov.uk
Army Medical Services Museum
Keogh Barracks Ash Vale, Aldershot, GU12 5RQ
Tel: 01252 340212 Email: museum@keogh72.freeserve.co.uk

Army Physical Training Corps Museum
ASPT, Fox Line, Queen's Avenue, Aldershot, GU11 2LB
Tel: 01252 347168 Fax: 01252 340785
Museum of Army Flying
Middle Wallop, Stockbridge, SO20 8DY Tel: 01980 674421
Email: daa@flying-museum.org.uk
WWW: www.flying-museum.org.uk
Queen Alexandra's Royal Army Nursing Corps Museum
Regimental Headquarters Army Medica, Keogh Barracks,
Ash Vale, Aldershot, GU12 5RQ
Royal Marines Museum
Eastney Southsea, PO4 9PX Tel: (023) 92 819385-Exts-224
Fax: (023) 92 838420
Email: matthewlittle@royalmarinesmuseum.co.uk
WWW: www.royalmarinesmuseum.co.uk
No charges for research other than material costs. Donations
welcome. Visits by appointment Mon to Fri 10am to 4.30pm
Royal Naval Museum
H M Naval Base (PP66), Portsmouth, PO1 3NU Tel: (023)
9272 7562 Fax: (023) 9272 7575
Royal Navy Submarine Museum
Haslar Jetty Road Gosport, PO12 2AS Tel: (023) 92510354
The Gurkha Museum
Peninsula Barracks, Romsey Road Winchester, SO23 8TS
Tel: 01962 842832 Fax: 01962 877597
The King's Royal Hussars Museum (10th Royal Hussars PWO 11th Hussars PAO & Royal Hussars PWO)
Peninsula Barracks, Winchester, SO23 8TS
Tel: 01962 828540 Email:
beresford@krhmuseum.freeserve.co.uk
WWW: www.hants.gov.uk/leisure/museum/royalhus/index.html
The Light Infantry Museum
Peninsula Barracks, Romsey Road Winchester, SO23 8TS
Tel: 01962 868550
The Royal Green Jackets Museum (Oxford and Bucks Light Infantry King's Royal Rifle Corps and The Rifle Brigade)
Peninsula Barracks, Romsey Road Winchester, SO23 8TS
Tel: 01962 828549 Fax: 01962 828500

Hertfordshire
Hertford Museum (Hertford Regiment)
18 Bull Plain Hertford, SG14 1DT Tel: 01992 582686

Kent
Buffs Regimental Museum
The Royal Museum & Art Gallery, 18 High Street
Canterbury, CT1 2RA Tel: 01227-452747
Princess of Wales and Queen's Regiment Museum
Inner Bailey, Dover Castle, Dover, CT16 1HU
Tel: 01304-240121
Princess of Wales's Royal Regt & Queen's Regt Museum
Howe Barracks, Canterbury, CT1 1JY
Tel: 01227-818056 Fax: 01227-818057
Royal Engineers Library
Brompton Barracks, Chatham, ME4 4UG
Tel: 01634-822416 Fax: 01634-822419
Royal Engineers Museum of Military Engineering
Prince Arthur Road Gillingham, ME4 4UG
Tel: 01634 406397 Fax: 01634 822371
Email: remuseum.rhgre@gtnet.gov.uk
WWW: http://www.army.mod.uk/armymuseums
The Queen's Own Royal West Kent Regiment Museum
Maidstone Museum and Art Gallery, St. Faith's Street
Maidstone, ME14 1LH Tel: 01622 754497 Fax: 01622
602193
West Kent Regimental Museum
Maidstone

Lancashire
South Lancashire Regiment Prince of Wales Volunteers Museum
Peninsula Barracks Warrington

King's Own Royal Regimental Museum
The City Museum Market Square, Lancaster, LA1 1HT Tel:
01524 64637 Fax: 01524 841692
Email: kingsownmuseum@iname.com
Museum of Lancashire (Queen's Lancashire Regiment Duke of Lancaster's Own Yeomanry Lancashire Hussars 14th/20th King's Hussars)
Stanley Street, Preston, PR1 4YP Tel: 01772 264075
Museum of the Manchesters
Ashton Town Hall, Market Place Ashton-u-Lyne, OL6 6DL
Tel:0161 342 3078/3710
Museum of the Queen's Lancashire Regiment (East South and Loyal North LancashireRegiments)
Fulwood Barracks, Preston, PR2 8AA
Tel: 01772 260362 Email: rhqqlr@aol.com
The Fusiliers Museum (Lancashire)
Wellington Barracks, Bolton Road Bury, BL8 2PL Tel: 0161
764 2208

Leicestershire
Royal Leicestershire Regiment Museum
Newark Museum, 53 New Walk Leicester, LE1 7AE Tel:
0116 2470403 Postal enquiries: Newarke Houses Museum,
The Newarke, Leicester LE2 7BY
The Queen's Royal Lancers Regimental Museum (16th/5th and 17th/21st Lancers)
Belvoir Castle, nr Grantham , NG32 1PD
Tel: 0115 957 3295 Fax: 0115 957 3195

London
Guards Museum
Wellington Barracks, Birdcage Walk London, SW1E 6HQ
Tel: (020) 7414 3271/3428
Imperial War Museum
Lambeth Road London, SE1 6HZ Tel: (020) 7416-5000 Tel:
(020) 7416 5348 Fax: (020) 7416 5374 Email:
books@iwm.org.uk WWW: www.iwm.org.uk
National Army Museum
Royal Hospital Road London, SW3 4HT Tel: (020) 7730-
0717 Fax: (020) 7823-6573
Email: info@national-army-museum.ac.uk WWW:
http://www.national-army-museum.ac.uk
National Maritime Museum
Romney Road, Greenwich, London, SE10 9NF Tel: (020)
8858-4422 Fax: (020) 8312-6632 WWW:
http://www.nmm.ac.uk
Royal Air Force Museum
Grahame Park Way, Hendon, London, NW9 5LL Tel: (020)
8205-2266 Fax: (020) 8200 1751
Email: info@refmuseum.org.uk
WWW: http://www.rafmuseum.org.uk
Royal Artillery Regimental Museum
Old Royal Military Academy, Red Lion Lane, Woolwich,
London, SE18 4DN
Tel: (020) 8781 5628 ext 3128
The Royal Regiment of Fusiliers
H M Tower of London, London, EC3N 4AB
Tel: (020) 7488 5610

Liverpool
King's Regiment Collection
Museum of Liverpool Life, Pier Head Liverpool, L3 1PZ
Tel: 0151-478-4062

Norfolk
Royal Norfolk Regimental Museum
Shirehall, Market Avenue Norwich, NR1 3JQ
Tel: 01603 493649 Fax: 01603 765651
The Battlefields Trust
33 High Green, Brooke, Norwich, NR15 1HR
Tel: 01508 558145 Fax: 01508 558145 Email:
Battlefield.trust@aol.com
WWW: www.battlefieldstrust.com

The Muckleburgh Collection
Weybourne, Holt, NR25 7EG Tel: 01263 588210 Email:
jenny@muckleburgh.demon.co.uk

North Yorkshire
Eden Camp Museum Malton, YO17 6RT Tel: 01653-
697777Email: admin@edencamp.co.uk
 WWW: http://www.edencamp.co.uk
Green Howards Regimental Museum
Trinity Church Square Richmond, DL10 4QN Tel: 01748-
822133 Fax: 01748-826561
**Royal Dragoon Guards Military Museum (4th/7th Royal
Dragoon Guards & 5th Royal Inniskilling Dragoons)**
3A Tower Street York, YO1 9SB
Tel: 01904-662790 Tel: 01904 662310 Fax: 01904 662310
WWW: www.rdg.co.uk
co-located with Prince of Wales' Own Regiment of Yorkshire
Military Museum (West & East Yorkshire Regiments)
Yorkshire Air Museum
Halifax Way, Elvington, York, YO41 5AU
Tel: 01904-608595

Northamptonshire
**Abington Museum and Museum of The
Northamptonshire Regiment**
Abington Park Museum, Abington, NN1 5LW
Tel: 01604 635412

Northumberland
**A Soldier's Life 15th/19th The King's Royal Hussars
Northumberland Hussars and Light Dragoons**
Discovery Museum, Blandford Square Newcastle-upon-
Tyne, NE1 4JA Tel: 0191 232 6789
Email: ralph.thompson@tyne-wear-museums.org.uk
Fusiliers Museum of Northumberland
The Abbot's Tower, Alnwick Castle Alnwick, NE66 1NG
Tel: 01665-602151 Email: fusmusnorthld@btinternet.com
King's Own Scottish Borderers Museum
The Barracks, The Parade Berwick upon Tweed, TD15 1DG
Tel: 01289 307426

Nottinghamshire
Sherwood Foresters Museum and Archives
RHQ WFR, Foresters House, Chetwynd Barracks, Chilwell,
Nottingham, NG9 5HA
Tel: 0115-946-5415 Fax: 0115-946-5712
Sherwood Foreters (Notts & Derbys Regt) Museum
The Castle, Nottingham, NG1 6EL
Tel: 0115 946 5415 Fax: 0115 946 9853
 Address for enquiries: RHQ WFR, Foresters House,
Chetwynd Barracks, Chilwell, Nottingham NG9 5HA

Oxfordshire
**Oxfordshire and Buckinghamshire Light Infantry
Regimental Museum**
Slade Park Headington, Oxford, OX3 7JL
Tel: 01865 780128

Shropshire
**Shropshire Regimental Museum (King's Shropshire
Light Infantry, Shropshire Yeomanry)**
The Castle, Shrewsbury, SY1 2AT
Tel: 01743-358516 Tel: 01743-262292

Somerset
Fleet Air Arm Museum Records Research Centre
Box D61, RNAS Yeovilton Nr Ilchester, BA22 8HT Tel:
01935-840565 Fax: 01935-840181
**Somerset Military Museum (Somerset Light Infantry
Yeomanry) Militia and Volunteers County Museum**
The Castle, Taunton, TA1 4AA
Tel: 01823 333434 Fax: 01823 351639

South Yorkshire
King's Own Yorkshire Light Infantry Regimental Museum
Doncaster Museum & Art Gallery, Chequer Road Doncaster,
DN1 2AE Tel: 01302 734293
Email: museum@doncaster.gov.uk
WWW: www.doncaster.gov.uk
**Regimental Museum 13th/18th Royal Hussars and The
Light Dragoons**
Cannon Hall, Cawthorne Barnsley, S75 4AT
Tel: 01226 790270
York and Lancaster Regimental Museum
Library and Arts Centre, Walker Place, Rotherham S65 1JH
Tel: 01709 823635 Fax: 01709 823631 Email:
guy.kilminster@rotherham.gov.uk
WWW: www.rotherham.gov.uk

Staffordshire
Museum of The Staffordshire Regiment
Whittington Barracks, Lichfield, WS14 9PY
Tel: 0121 311 3240
Museum of the Staffordshire Yeomanry
The Ancient High House, Greengate Street Stafford, ST16
2HS Tel: 01785 40204 (Tourist Info. Office)

Suffolk
Suffolk Regiment Museum -Museum closed to the public
Suffolk Record Office, 77 Raingate Street Bury St Edmunds,
IP33 2AR Tel: 01284-352352
Email: bury.ro@libhev.suffolkcc.gov.uk
WWW: http://www.suffolkcc.gov.uk/sro/
Museum closed to the public but archives available for inspection

Surrey
**Queen's Royal Surrey Regiment Museum (Queen's
Royal Surrey East Surrey & Queen's Royal Surrey
Regiments)**
Clandon Park, West Clandon, Guildford, GU4 7RQ Tel:
01483 223419 Fax: 01483 224636
Email: queenssurreys@caree4free.net
WWW: www.surrey-on;line.co.uk/queenssurreys
Regimental Museum Royal Logistical Corps
Deepcut, Camberley, GU16 6RW
Tel: 01252 340871 Tel: 01252 340984
Royal Military Police Museum
Roussillon Barracks, Chichester PO19 4BN Tel: 01243
534225 Email: museum@rhqrmp.freeserve.co.uk
WWW: www.rhqrmp.freeserve.co.uk

Sussex
**Sussex Combined Services Museum (Royal Sussex
Regiment and Queen's Royal Irish Hussars)**
Redoubt Fortress, Royal Parade Eastbourne, BN22 7AQ Tel:
01323 410300

Warwickshire
**Regimental Museum of The Queen's Own Hussars (3rd
King's Own and 7th Queen's Own Hussars)**
The Lord Leycester Hospital, High Street Warwick, CV34
4EW Tel: Tel:01926 492035
Royal Warwickshire Regimental Museum,
St. John's House, Warwick , CV34 4NF
Tel: Tel:01926 491653
Warwickshire Yeomanry Museum
The Court House, Jury Street Warwick, CV34 4EW Tel:
01926 492212 Fax: 01926 494837

West Yorkshire
Duke of Wellington's Regimental Museum
Bankfield Museum, Akroyd Park, Boothtown Road, Halifax,
HX3 6HG Tel: 01422 354823
Fax: 01422 249020

Wiltshire
Duke of Edinburgh's Royal Regiment (Berks & Wilts) Museum
The Wardrobe, 58 The Close, Salisbury, SP1 2EX Tel: 01722-414536 Fax: 01722 421626
Royal Army Chaplains Department Museum
Netheravon House, Salisbury Road Netheravon, SP4 9SY
Tel: 01980-604911 Fax: 01980-604908

Worcestershire
The Worcestershire Regiment Museum
Worcester City Museum , Foregate Street Worcester, WR1 1DT Tel: 01905-25371 Museum Tel: 01905 354359 Office
Email: rhq_wfr@lineone.net
Postal Address: The Curator, The Worcestershire Regimental Museum Trust, RHQ WFR, Norton Barracks, Worcester WR5 2PA
Worcestershire Regiment Archives (Worcester and Sherwood Forester's Regiment)
RHQ WFR Norton Barracks, Worcester, WRS 2PA Tel: 01905-354359

Wales
The Royal Welch Fusiliers Regimental Museum
The Queen's Tower, The Castle Caernarfon, LL55 2AY Tel: 01286 673362 Fax: 01286 677042
Email: rwfusiliers@callnetuk.com
1st The Queen's Dragoon Guards Regimental Museum
Cardiff Castle, Cardiff, CF1 2RB Tel: (029) 2022 2253 Tel: (029) 2078 1232 Fax: (029) 2078 1384 Email:
morris602.hhq@netscapeonline
WWW: www.QdDG.org.uk
Monmouthshire Royal Engineers (Militia)
Castle and Regimental Museum, The Castle Monmouth, NP5 3BS Tel: 01600-712935

Monmouth
Nelson Museum & Local History Centre
Priory St Monmouth, NP5 3XA Tel: 01600 713519
Email: nelsonmuseum@monmouthshire.gov.uk

Powys
South Wales Borderers & Monmouthshire Regimental Museum of the Royal Regt of Wales (24th/41st Foot)
The Barracks, Brecon, LD3 7EB
Tel: 01874-613310 Email: rrw@ukonline.co.uk
WWW: http://www.ukonline.co.uk/rrw/index.htm

Scotland
Museum of The Royal Highland Fusilers (Royal Scots Fusilers and Highland Light Infantry)
518 Sauchiehall Street Glasgow, G2 3L
 Tel: 0141 332 0961 Fax: 0141 332 5439
Royal Scots Regimental Museum
The Castle, Edinburgh, EH1 2YT
Tel: 0131-310-5014 Fax: 0131-310-5019
Gordon Highlanders Museum
St Lukes, Viewfield Road Aberdeen, AB15 7XH
Tel: 01224 311200 Fax: 01224 319323
 Email: museum@gordonhighlanders.com
WWW: www.gordonhighlanders.com
Ayrshire Yeomanry Museum
Rozelle House, Monument Road Alloway by Ayr, KA7 4NQ
Tel: 01292 445400 (Museum)
Tel: 01292 264091
Museum of Coldstream Guards
Coldstream
Queen's Own Highlanders (Seaforths & Camerons) Regimental Museum Archives
Fort George Ardersier, Inverness, IV1 2TD
Tel: 01463-224380

The Cameronians (Scottish Rifles) Museum
c/o Low Parks Museum, 129 Muir Street Hamilton, ML3 6BJ Tel: 01698 455714
Tel: 01698 328232 Fax: 01698 328232
Perthshire, Regimental Museum and Archives of Black Watch
Balhousie Castle, Hay Street, Perth, PH1 5HS
Tel: 0131-3108530 Tel: 01738 621281 ext 8530 Fax: 01738-643245
Email: bwarchivist@btclick.com
WWW: www.theblackwatch.co.uk
Scottish Horse Regimental Museum
The Cross Dunkeld, PH8 0AN
Regimental Museum Argyll and Sutherland Highlanders
Stirling Castle, Stirling, FK8 1EH
Tel: 01786 475165 Fax: 01786 446038

Northern Ireland
Royal Irish Fusiliers Museum
Sovereign's House, Mall East Armagh, BT61 9DL Tel: (028) 3752 2911 Tel: (028) 3752 2911
Royal Ulster Rifles Regimental Museum
RHQ Royal Irish Rifles, 5 Waring Street Belfast, BT1 2EW
Tel: (028) 90232086
Royal Inniskilling Fusiliers Regimental Museum
The Castle, Enniskillen, BT74 7BB
 Tel: (028) 66323142 Tel: (028) 66320359

Belgium
In Flanders Fields Museum
Lakenhallen, Grote Markt, Ieper B-8900
Tel: 00-32-(0)-57-22-85-84
Fax: 00-32-(0)-57-22-85-89
WWW: www.inflandersfield.be

The Anglo-German Family History Society
Peter Towey Chairman

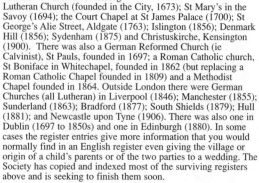

It all grew out of an advert Roy Bernard placed in the East of London Family History Society magazine "Cockney Ancestor" in 1987 asking if there was anyone else out there interested in German family history. The response was much larger than he expected and before long the Anglo-German FHS was formed at a meeting in Cookham, Berkshire, where Roy lives. Roy was the first Chairman, Jenny Rushton (now my wife!) was the first (and still is the) Secretary and I was the Treasurer. Since 1987 we have achieved a lot: indexing many records, publishing several research guides and forming a Names Index of over half a million names of Germans in UK. Most of all though we have helped each other with our research and surmounted those obstacles that then seemed to loom so large! We must be doing something right as we have over 1,500 members mainly in UK, especially South-east England, but from all over the World including USA, Australia,New Zealand and even Germany itself.

You may think that having German or other Central or East European ancestry in UK is unusual. Not a bit of it! Germany is just over the North Sea from the British Isles and, not surprisingly, there has always been a lot of migration both ways. Obviously you cannot trace your ancestry back to the Angles, Saxons and Jutes who came here after the Romans in the Dark Ages but from the 16th century onwards you have a better chance! There were Germans here in the 16th century; brought over as miners from Augsburg and the Tyrol to open up mining in Cornwall, South Wales and Cumberland; in the 17th century as mercenaries in the Civil War and as religious refugees; in the 18th century as religious refugees (the poor Palatines of 1709 many of whom ended up in Ireland and New York) and as Court officials, craftsmen and merchants who followed in the train of King George I when he came over from Hanover; in the Napoleonic Wars as soldiers and seamen; and in the 19th century as craftsmen looking for a better life: sugar bakers, bakers, pork butchers, hairdressers, to mention but a few. This largely came to an end with the anti-German hysteria of the First World War when many men were interned as enemy aliens and many men, women and children were deported to Germany during and after the War. This broke up the earlier German community in UK but in the 1930s other (Jewish and Gentile) Germans came as political refugees from Nazi Europe.

If you are just starting out on your German research (or indeed research into immigrants from East and Central Europe) we can help you. It is important to realise that the records you need for this research are not necessarily the same as you would use in UK but the first requirement is to identify who your immigrant ancestor was and where they came from. There are no nation-wide records, like birth marriage and death indexes or will indexes, in Germany, Poland, Austria, or any of the other successor States where you ancestor may have come from so you need to use the British records to identify where to start looking.

You need records that give you the immigrant's date and place of birth and the Society aims to help you find those records. You do not need to read or speak German (or Polish or Czech!) but we can advise you on how to get those important letters and documents translated either way. Many Americans have ancestry in East and Central Europe too and so many books and sources are now available in English. The Anglo-German FHS saw this early on and joined the US-based Federation of Eastern European Family History Societies enabling us to keep in touch with over 200 Societies that cover many modern Countries that used to be in the German, Austrian or Russian Empires. It is useful to remember that there was no State called "Germany" until 1871 and that the boundaries of that State changed again radically in 1919 and again during and after WWII. Similarly the Austrian and Russian Empires changed radically at the same times. Trying to identify the State a town or village was in at any particular time in the last few centuries is not always easy but the Society has maps and textbooks that enable us to help you.

As there were so many German-speakers in UK from an early time, there were several Protestant churches, especially in London, where services were given in the German language. These were mainly Lutheran as most of the Germans who came

here were from North Germany where that was the principal religion. The main such churches in London were: the Hamburg Lutheran Church (founded in the City, 1673); St Mary's in the Savoy (1694); the Court Chapel at St James Palace (1700); St George's Alie Street, Aldgate (1763); Islington (1856); Denmark Hill (1856); Sydenham (1875) and Christuskirche, Kensington (1900). There was also a German Reformed Church (ie Calvinist), St Pauls, founded in 1697; a Roman Catholic church, St Boniface in Whitechapel, founded in 1862 (but replacing a Roman Catholic Chapel founded in 1809) and a Methodist Chapel founded in 1864. Outside London there were German Churches (all Lutheran) in Liverpool (1846); Manchester (1855); Sunderland (1863); Bradford (1877); South Shields (1879); Hull (1881); and Newcastle upon Tyne (1906). There was also one in Dublin (1697 to 1850s) and one in Edinburgh (1880). In some cases the register entries give more information that you would normally find in an English register even giving the village or origin of a child's parents or of the two parties to a wedding. The Society has copied and indexed most of the surviving registers above and is seeking to finish them soon.

Some trades and occupations seem to have a large proportion of Germans : hairdressing; sugar baking or refining; (bread) baking; confectionery; soldiers, marines and sailors (Royal Navy and Merchant Navy); street musicians (as well as major composers like Handel and C P E Bach) and fur traders. I have even found a substantial group of "Spanish leather workers" in the parish registers of Bermondsey in South London at the end of the 18th century all of whom had German surnames (I think it was the leather that was Spanish not the workers!). I have not been able to discover why they were there. Bermondsey was the centre of London's leather trade but why German workers? We do not know all the answers but we will have a good try!

While we are a national, indeed an international, Society we still try to organise meetings where members can get together, chat and exchange information, and listen to talks. We meet six times a year in London near St Pancras on Saturday afternoons and we also organise occasional meetings in other parts of the Country: in South Wales, in Devon and in Manchester. We also arrange occasional visits by coach to Germany; while these are more of a social nature members often learn quite a bit in discussions on the coach and in the hotel!

One of the joys of the Society is helping members find their roots even when they started off with no information other than a German surname or a family story. Once you have brought your German ancestor "home" to Germany or Austria or wherever, you will often be surprised how much information there is in the local records. German records normally provide a great deal more background information on the individuals concerned and there are very informative German records that have no equivalent in the UK. You can often trace your family back for several more centuries on the Continent.

For details of how the Society can help you and an application form write with a self-addressed, stamped envelope to Mrs Jenny Towey, Secretary, Anglo-German FHS, 20 Skylark Rise, Plymouth, Devon, PL6 7SN. Membership in UK is £10.00 a year; in the rest of the EU £11.50 a year and in the rest of the World £13.50. In addition there is a one-off joining fee of £5 payable when you join. Don't send any money until you have the form to fill in. When you join you will be sent a Welcome Booklet which details the various facilities we offer including searches in the Society's Names Index, the German & Austrian telephone Directories on CD-ROM and many other searchable sources we have obtained, our postal bookshop and library and our German translation and place-identification service.

THE DERBYSHIRE FAMILY HISTORY SOCIETY

www.dfhs.org.uk

For all your
Family History Research in Derbyshire
Visit our Website
or our
HEADQUARTERS AND RESEARCH CENTRE
at
THE HISTORIC BRIDGE CHAPEL HOUSE
ST MARY'S BRIDGE, DERBY

**We are open every
Tuesday, Thursday and Saturday
From 10.00a.m. until 4.00.p.m.
Or contact our Secretary**

Mr G Wells
76 Elms Avenue, Littleover, Derby DE23 6FD

We have Club Meetings every month at
Derby, Glossop and Shirland

Plus exhibitions and Open Days

Our Quarterly Magazine is packed with information

Come and Talk to us. We can Help

Gypsy/Traveller ancestors? Track them down here.

Join the Romany and Traveller Family History Society and you'll join forces with a group of keen family historians with a special interest in their British Gypsy and Traveller Roots.

For membership details and growing publications list, visit our Website: http://website.lineone.net/~rtfhs

Or sent an SAE or two IRCs to: Membership Sec., Romany & Traveller FHS, 27 Conyers Close, Hersham, Surrey KT12 4NG UK

KEIGHLEY & DISTRICT FAMILY HISTORY SOCIETY

Publications available for sale include:

MI's Utley Cemetery Vols 1-9
Keighley News Indexes Marriages & Deaths 1862-1901
1851 Census Index for Keighley area
Kildwick Baptisms 1572-1778

Full list of publications and Membership details send sae to: Mrs S Daynes, 2 The Hallows, Shann Park, Keighley, West Yorkshire BD20 6HY

BMSGH

TRACING YOUR ANCESTORS IN
STAFFORDSHIRE, WARWICKSHIRE OR WORCESTERSHIRE?
THEN CONTACT
THE BIRMINGHAM AND MIDLAND SOCIETY FOR GENEALOGY AND HERALDRY
BMSGH

THE BMSGH COVERS THE THREE COUNTIES, WAS FOUNDED IN 1963 AND ASSISTS MEMBERS TO TRACE THEIR OWN ANCESTORS. MEMBERSHIP INCLUDES A QUARTERLY JOURNAL, A COMPREHENSIVE LIST OF PUBLICATIONS, A LIBRARY AND REGULAR MEETINGS AT BRANCHES IN BIRMINGHAM, BURTON ON TRENT, STOKE ON TRENT, WOLVERHAMPTON, KENILWORTH, BROMSGROVE, STOURBRIDGE, WORCESTER AND LONDON.

FOR FURTHER DETAILS CONTACT

MRS OLIVE PRICE (GENERAL SECRETARY)
AT
9 CLAYDON GROVE, YARDLEY WOOD, BIRMINGHAM B14 4NB

OR CONSULT OUR WEBSITE

STAFFORDSHIRE ▼

WARWICKSHIRE ▼

WORCESTERSHIRE ▼

www.bmsgh.org

Registered as a Charity No. 505916-R

City of York and District Family History Society

The society was formed in 1975 to further the study of family history within the area covered by the ancient Archdeaconry of York. This spans an area, which stretches from Coxwold in the North to Carlton in the South, and Weaverthorpe in the East to Bramham in the West, thus taking in part of all three historic Ridings of Yorkshire. At its centre is the beautiful and ancient city of York, and around are many pretty villages and charming small towns, each with a proud and fascinating past. In its 26 years of existence the society has twice outgrown its meeting places and the regular monthly meetings at the Priory Street Centre in York are full to capacity. The society president is Sir Marcus Worsley, Bt. of Hovingham, who takes a supportive interest in the society and candidly tells of his family's origins on the other side of the Pennines, but as the members interests cover all corners of the British Isles and beyond, no one minds, and anyway the family have been Yorkshire for three hundred years!

The origin of the society, as with many others, lies in an evening class on the topic of Family History. That was some 28 years ago, and the course rejoiced in the title of 'Dig up your Family Tree', and was one of the first such courses in the country organised under the auspices of a Local Authority. The shared experience of the course drew the participants together and led to the formation of the 'York Family History Group', with its initial formal meeting on Monday 17th March 1975. Recording and transcribing records useful to genealogists began early in the society's history, with the first publication, the Parish Registers for the parish of St Martin-le-Grand, York (1813-1837), hitting the streets in 1978. This was followed by the York City Marriage Index (1701-1837), which has recently been transferred to CD ROM as a searchable database.

Our area overlaps with neighbouring societies with whom we seek to maintain good relations, and undertake joint ventures where appropriate, for example in the recording and publication of Monumental Inscriptions (MIs) for an increasing number of parishes. Over a period of 20 years, starting in 1979, society members have worked with the Friends of York Cemetery in recording and publishing the MIs of this very large cemetery, which has been renovated and now forms a significant green space on the edge of the city. The society is active in publishing indexes of the 1851 and 1891 censuses for the society's area: Burial Indexes, which also appear as part of the National Burial Index: Parish Registers for York churches, and specialised lists, such as the 1914-18 Roll of Honour for employees of the North Eastern Railway. Whilst in the past most of the societies publications have been available on microfiche, the switch is being made to CD ROM format.

For several years we have held an open day each March to publicise the work of the society and provide access to other local family history societies and local and national organisations who supply products and services for the genealogist. At the special open day to commemorate the 25th anniversary of the society, we welcomed the Public Record Office and the Commonwealth War Graves Commission, as well as regulars such as the locally based City of York Library Service and York Minster Library and Archives. With these, the City Archives and the Borthwick Institute for Historical Research, York is an ideal base for research into one's Yorkshire roots and local history.

In addition to holding our own open days, the society attends other local and family history events across the North of England, with the main event being the Yorkshire Family History Fair. This is held on the last Saturday in June at the York Racecourse, being one of the largest of such events in Britain with approximately 100 stands, taken by societies and businesses from across the country.

In the furtherance of family history on a wider scale, the society is affiliated to the Federation of Family History Societies and is also involved with the North East group of Family History Societies. The society's website www.yorkfamilyhistory.org.uk publicises our activities and publications, and members are encouraged to join the society's 'eGroup', which acts as bulletin board and occasional chatroom, and allows members throughout the world to be actively involved in exchanging information and helpful tips. In addition we are also involved with the Yorkshire Evening Press, a local newspaper, with their 'Communigate' website in providing access to family history expertise. To encourage the growth of interest in family history and to recruit new members, exhibitions have been held in local libraries across the society's area, and other exhibitions are planned.

With the exception of August, the society runs a full programme of meetings on the first Wednesday of the month in the Main Hall of the Priory Street Centre at 7pm for 7.30, with access to our library, bookstall, help desk and search facilities, as well as offering opportunities to listen to interesting speakers; visitors are welcome. Our speakers have covered such diverse topics as, finding Quaker ancestors, the history of the hospitals of York before the NHS, and the wartime evacuation from northern cities. The society Journal is published three times per year and contains relevant articles, and requests for assistance as well as keeping members informed of society activities.

The society is not content to rest on its laurels and seeks to develop its activities and facilities for members and the wider circle of family historians. To this end it has become a Registered Charity (No. 1085228) and plans to establish a research room in the city for use of members and visitors.

The Federation of Family History Societies

The Federation
- was formed in 1974 and granted charitable status in 1982
- membership has grown to around 200 societies throughout the world, including national, regional and one-name groups
- its principal aims are to co-ordinate and assist the work of societies or other bodies interested in family history, genealogy and heraldry; and to foster mutual co-operation and regional projects in these subjects.

Membership
- is open to any society or body specialising in family history or an associated discipline
- full membership is open to properly constituted organisations in the British Isles
- associate membership is available to overseas family history, genealogical and heraldic groups as well as to other bodies within the British Isles for whom family history is a secondary interest.

The Federation Council
- comprises representatives of the member societies
- defines policy, which is implemented by an elected executive committee
- meets in Britain twice a year
- provides societies with an opportunity to exchange views and debate matters of importance to family historians.

Family History News & Digest
- the Federation's journal is published twice a year, in April and September
- contains news of the activities of all member societies
- contains a digest section which carries over 400 abstracts of articles appearing in family history, genealogical and heraldic journals or other publications of interest to its readers; being classified, it is an effective cumulative index to current literature for family history
- each issue carries an up-to-date list of member societies with contact addresses
- copies of Family History News and Digest are sent to individual subscribers and institutions
- *Family History News and Digest* is supplemented every other month with *Newsflash*, which is available only to committees of member societies and gives the latest information from officers of the Federation, changes of address and up-to-the minute news items.

Federation Handbook
Many societies exchange their journals with fellow members which ensures the maximum amount of publicity and interchange of information throughout the world. The Federation publishes every other year a Handbook listing vital statistics of all member societies (e.g. subscription rates, officers' names and addresses, and meeting places and dates). This is issued free to member societies.

National Projects
- are co-ordinated by the Federation
- a considerable contribution is being made to the National Inventory of War Memorials, established by the Imperial War Museum in 1988
- the 1881 census was the object of a national indexing project, completed in 1996
- the first edition of the *National Burial Index* was published in 2001

Education
Is a vital element within the Federation. This is achieved informally through the regular meetings and discussions conducted by its member societies; also formally through the many courses on family history organised around the world. A list of speakers prepared to talk on family history, heraldry or allied topics is available.

Conferences
are organised on a national basis both by the Federation and by member societies in conjunction with the Federation. These draw the attention of the general public to the study of family history, thereby encouraging new members to join family history societies. Those attending conferences meet others with similar interests and, quite apart from the formal proceedings, many ideas are exchanged during informal discussion and social events.

Representations
The Federation:
- makes representations to official bodies on matters affecting the study of family history and related topics
- has a seat on the Record Users Group
- is represented on the British Association for Local History
- has established regular liaison with the Society of Antiquaries, the Society of Archivists, the Historical Association, the British Records Association and the British Records Society.

The Federation provides an authentic, audible, and respected voice for the many thousands of individual family historians.

Publications
covering aspects of family history research and the whereabouts of relevant records are commissioned by the Federation, with a view to assisting member societies and individuals with their research. These are available at a discount to societies for sale to their members and to the general public.

Co-operation
between family historians, heraldists, archivists, archaeologists and many others is essential as more and more people become involved in the study of their roots and heritage. The Federation is the ideal vehicle for such co-operation.

For further details and a list of member societies , visit the Federation of Family History Societies' website, **www.ffhs.org.uk** or e-mail **info@ffhs.org.uk** or write to:

The Administrator
FFHS, PO Box 2425, Coventry CV5 6YX
All correspondence to the Federation or its member societies must be accompanied by a self-addressed envelope and two International Reply Coupons, or the appropriate UK postage stamps, to ensure a reply.

The Society of Indexers Genealogical Group (SIGG)

Origins and Aims
Many family historians are used to working through masses of unindexed or poorly indexed
source material. The Society of Indexers Genealogical Group (SIGG) exists to ease their task by promoting good practice in the indexing of family and local history source material and publications. SIGG was founded in 1993 by Tony Rydings, a retired librarian and long standing member of the Society of Indexers (SI). The SI, founded in 1958, is the professional body for paid indexers, but also encourages special interest groups, membership of which is not confined to SI members. SIGG is such a group and is open to anyone interested.

SIGG's aim is still as Tony Rydings expressed it in 1993: " ... to bring together those indexers who have specialist knowledge, and those who are embarking on family history or local history projects in which indexing is an important part, so that a body of expertise may be formed, which may then be shared with others."

Scope and activities
Tony Rydings provisionally suggested that SIGG should focus on the techniques used to index the following material: general books on genealogy; registers of births, deaths and marriages; court rolls; collections of historical documents; catalogues of books on genealogy and related subjects; works on local history; family histories including individual biographies; periodicals on family history, including publications of family history societies; bibliography of works on family history; works on the use of computers in family history; wills and administrations; ecclesiastical records, including tithes; monumental inscriptions; land records; possibly heraldry, royalty, nobility, gentry, trades and occupations. SIGG's purpose is to encourage good indexing practice rather than to produce indexes.

Organisation and finance
Membership is too small and scattered for meetings to be practical. SIGG consequently holds no AGM and has no formal constitution. Its "officials" are thus unelected volunteers to whom Tony Rydings has progressively handed over the running of the group. Colin Mills (70 Chestnut Lane, Amersham, Buckinghamshire HP6 6EH) is the convenor and SIGGNL editor, Andrew Warren (35 Bank Crest, Baildon, Shipley, West Yorkshire BD17 5HB) is membership secretary, treasurer and SIGGNL distributor and David Squire (david@squireuk.com) is the webmaster. To meet newsletter production costs and related expenses members pay an annual subscription which is currently £5.00 for UK members and £8.50 for others. SIGG has also had generous support from SI in the form of grants.

The Newsletter (SIGGNL)
SIGGNL remains, for the present, the hub of our activities. It is published as a single-section, A5 booklet; it has ranged in size up to 48 pages and appears three or four times a year. As well as an editorial and administrative information it typically includes a range of articles, news items, enquiries, reviews and abstracts.

Topics covered by SIGGNL
The topics covered by SIGGNL have included:
general methods - including the principles of indexing and the particular difficulties encountered with the treatment of personal names;
indexing of familiar material - such as parish registers, census returns, marriage licences, local newspapers and the records arising from one-name studies;
comprehensive indexes of local material - covering the varied records which relate to a particular locality;
indexes of specialist material - such as those related to a particular trade or occupation, diaries and journals, institutions or collective groups such as emigrants or travellers;
use of computers and the internet - including the relative merits of different software packages.

SIGG projects
SIGG does not undertake the preparation of indexes although many of its members are personally involved with such projects. However it has initiated several projects which share in common the goal of producing genealogical aids for genealogical indexers.

Website
The society's website can be found at www.sigg.org.uk. As well as general information about the group it includes a selection of articles in earlier newsletters.

Summary
In its eight years, SIGG has made contributions, through its newsletter and activities, to good indexing practice in many of the areas originally listed by its founder. Through increased membership, wider distribution of SIGGNL, and greater use of its website we now hope to add to the specialist knowledge already shared and disseminate it more widely throughout the family and local history fraternities. Membership enquiries are warmly welcomed by Andrew Warren at 35 Bank Crest, Baildon, Shipley, West Yorkshire BD17 5HB.

Herefordshire Family History Society
Registered Charity No 517785

Publications. Cheques payable to: *Herefordshire Family History Society*

Mrs Jean Istance, 13 Harald Street, Hereford HR1 2QU
1851 Census by Registration District. **Full list available on request.**
Countywide Index (R.D. plus areas which overlap into surrounding counties) £13.00

Monumental Inscriptions   Index of Published MI's on CD **£5.00**

Burial Index Currently being compiled - available from Mr Alec Whitfield
E-mail: alecwhitfield@lineone.net
1 Castle Barn, Dilwyn, Herefordshire HR4 8HZ   S.A.E.

Marriage Index 1538 -1837   *Details from the Secretary*

Meetings are held every 3rd Friday in the Month at 7.30.p.m.
Venue; St Thomas Cantilupe School, Coningsby Street, Hereford

Secretary
Mr Brian Prosser
6 Birch Meadow, Gosmore Road, Clehonger, HerefordHR2 9RH
E-Mail: prosser_brian@hotmail.com

Home Page: **www.rootsweb.com~ukhfhs**

Researching Ancestors in Cumberland,
Westmoreland or North Lancashire?
Then you need the

Cumbria Family History Society

Send a SAE to the Secretary:
Mrs M. Russell,
"Ulpha", 32 Granada Road, Denton,
Manchester. M34 2LJ

Web site:
http://www.genuki.org.uk/big/eng/CUL/
cumbFHS/membership.html

Registered Charity 518393

MANCHESTER & LANCASHIRE
FAMILY HISTORY SOCIETY

Bolton & District
FHS

Oldham & District
FHS

Anglo - Scottish
FHS

Irish Ancestry
Branch

Family History in the Greater Manchester Area

Our research library, located in central Manchester, is
convenient for all of the City's major archives.

We hold copies of GRO indexes, IGI and many other
basic sources and a large collection of local material.

The Society publishes many indexes and transcripts to
assist in local research. This includes indexed
transcripts of the water-damaged 1851 census returns.
All our publications can either be consulted in the
library or purchased from our bookshop which also
offers a mail order service.

Our e-mail forum brings the Society to members
across the globe.
New members are warmly welcomed.

Membership enquiries to:
Clayton House, 59 Piccadilly, Manchester M1 2AQ
Tel:0161 236 9750 Fax; 0161 237 3812
E-mail; office@mlfhs.demon.co.uk
Or visit our website www.mlfhs.demon.co.uk

Huddersfield & District Family History Society

Registered Charity No. 702199

The Huddersfield & District Family History Society caters for those researching and with interests in the Kirklees Metropolitan area which covers about 160 square miles. Within our boundaries lie the ancient parishes of Almondbury, Batley, Birstall, Dewsbury, Emley, Hartshead, Huddersfield, Kirkburton, Kirkheaton, Mirfield and Thornhill.

We have a research room and library at Meltham, which houses our transcriptions of the 1841 & 1851 census for our area, the 1881 census for England & Wales plus the 1992 edition of the IGI for the whole of Britain and the National Probate Calenders 1858 - 1943.

The Society has about 300 publications for sale of Parish Registers and the 1841 and 1851 censuses. We are also participating in the National Burial Index. Search Services on these and other databases are also available.

For further details please contact our
Secretary Mrs. E. Bass at
292, Thornhills Lane, Clifton, Brighouse, W. Yorkshire, HD6 4JQ
or visit
our website at www.hdfhs.org.uk

Aberdeen & NE Scotland
Family History Society

The Society exists to assist and promote the study of genealogy and family history based on the North East corner of Scotland.
This area covers the old counties of Aberdeenshire, Banffshire, Kincardineshire and Morayshire.
The Society holds regular meetings.
Meetings are held in Aberdeen, Glasgow, Elgin and in the West Midlands of England.
The Society publishes a quarterly journal, which is issued free to members.
Extensive publication list covering all Scotland
Articles of interest are published; also reports of meetings and lectures, and information and enquiries from members.
Members may advertise, free of charge, their Members' Interests (family names) and Help Wanted.

Membership from £15
Our centre is open Mon-Fri, 10-4, Sat 9-1
plus Tues & Fri 7-10pm

**Aberdeen & NE Scotland FH Society,
164 King Street, Aberdeen. AB24 5BD**.
Or see our website: www.anesfhs.org.uk
E-mail: enquiries@anesfhs.org.uk

GLASGOW
& WEST OF
SCOTLAND
FAMILY HISTORY
SOCIETY

2002
25th Anniversary Year

The Society, was formed in 1977
for those with interests in Glasgow City, Argyll, Ayrshire, Bute, Dunbartonshire, Lanarkshire, Renfrewshire
and Stirlingshire (part)

Facilities and resources for members at
Unit 5, 22 Mansfield Street,
Glasgow G11 5QP

Send s.a.e. for membership details, publications list and further information.

Tel: 0141 339 8303
Website: www.gwsfhs.org.uk

Hosts of the
Scottish Association of
Family History Societies
Conference April 2002

Doncaster & District Family History Society

The Society meets on the last Wednesday of each month (except December) - 7.00 pm for 7.30 pm
at Doncaster College for the Deaf, Leger Way, Doncaster

PUBLICATIONS - A5 Books

Burial Indexes – taken from *commencement* of parish registers to at least 1900
for all the parishes within the Archdeaconry of Doncaster

1851 Census Index and Marriage Indexes – for all parishes covered by the Society

MICROFICHE

Cemetery Registers – for Bentley with Arksey, Conisbrough, Goole Hook Road,
Mexborough (New), Mexborough (Old) and Doncaster Hyde Park

Monumental Inscriptions – All churches and churchyards within the Archdeaconry of Doncaster,
and Doncaster Hyde Park Cemetery

1891 Census – A complete transcription of most parishes covered by the Society

Doncaster Health Authority Death Registers – for deaths in Doncaster from 1875 to 1928

NAME SEARCH AND PRINTOUT SERVICE

On various records covering Doncaster and District: 1851, 1871 and 1891 Censuses on data base for
most of the Archdeaconry of Doncaster; 1881 Census Index for the whole country
Surname Index on MIs in all the churches and churchyards in the Archdeaconry of Doncaster; Bawtry and
Doncaster Cemetery MIs, and Vital Records Index for the British Isles.

Dedicated Research Room
Our Research Room at the Doncaster College for the Deaf is open on
Monday, Tuesday and Friday 10 am to 4 pm , Wednesday 10 am to 2 pm
Tuesday and Wednesday 7 pm to 9 pm
It contains all our publications, microfiche, and CDs, also
GRO – births/marriages/deaths 1837 to 1950 **Parish Registers** from 1754, and **IGI**.

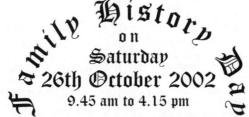

Family History on Saturday 26th October 2002
9.45 am to 4.15 pm

at Yorkshire College for the Deaf, Leger Way, Doncaster
Speakers: Audrey Collins, Joan Grundy and Peter Park

Society resources and various databases available during early morning, coffee breaks and lunchtime

Ample free parking   -   Disabled facilities   -   Optional lunch

Send SAE for further details and leaflets for any of the above to:

**Mrs June Staniforth, 125 The Grove, Wheatley Hills, Doncaster DN2 5SN
Tel: 01302 367257 Email: TonyJune@aol.com**

Website: http://www.doncasterfhs.freeserve.co.uk

Clwyd Family History Society

The Clwyd Family History Society was founded on the 19th May 1980 with an inaugural meeting at the Shire Hall, Mold where over 90 people attended. The Society which now numbers over 1200 members celebrated its 21st anniversary in December 2001 with a special anniversary meeting and celebration cake.

The name of the Society was taken from the county of Clwyd, which was formed in 1974 from the ancient counties of Denbighshire, Flintshire and the Edeirnion district of Merionethshire. In 1996 the county was abolished and replaced by the four unitary authorities of Conwy, Denbighshire, Flintshire and Wrexham. The Society has retained its original name and area of coverage.

The Society's aims are to encourage the study of genealogy and family history in North-East Wales; to provide a forum for people who are interested in these subjects to meet and to help each other; to provide guidance in family history research to those who have family connections in North-East Wales, but who now live elsewhere; to seek out, transcribe, index, and wherever possible, publish or make available material relevant to the interests of the Society. The Society publishes a quarterly journal, which is published in January, April, July and October and is free to members. Members can publish their research interests and request help with their research problems. It is also a forum to have their research published and articles are accepted in English and Welsh.

Since its formation the Society has had an active transcription, indexing and publication programme. The first project undertaken in 1981 was the transcription and indexing of the Non-conformist registers for Clwyd. Prints-outs were presented to the Denbighshire and Flintshire Record Offices. Once this project was completed work began on the transcription, indexing and publication of all the ancient parish registers of Clwyd from the earliest register to 1812. The project was started in 1984 with the Wrexham parish registers and to date nearly 500 volumes have been published. Although the project as first envisaged is nearing completion many transcribers working on the project have continued several parishes beyond 1812 and with more volunteers it is hoped to continue all the parishes further than 1812. The Society took part in the transcription of the counties of Denbighshire and Flintshire for the 1881 Census Project and had the distinction to be the first Welsh Society to complete their area. Another project has been monumental inscription recording programme. Unfortunately progress on the project has been limited due to lack of volunteers but it is hoped to encourage more of our members to take part in this project. It is encouraging that several graveyard recordings have been published recently. Another new project, which is about to get underway, is the transcription and indexing of the 1851 Census for Denbighshire and Flintshire. It has yet to be decided how this project will be published.

The Society has a programme of meetings every month throughout the year except in August. Meetings are generally held on the 2nd Saturday of the month from October to April and on the 2nd Monday of the month from May to September and there is an annual outing in July. The monthly meetings are held at various venues in the following areas Colwyn Bay, Denbigh, Hawarden, Ruthin, Rhyl and Wrexham. Our recent outings have included visits to St Deiniol's Library, Hawarden, Bodrhyddan Hall, and Llangar Church and Rhog Chapel.

The Society opened a research centre for members at Ruthin in 1988. The Centre is normally open on Saturdays from 10.00 a.m. to 4.00 p.m. throughout the year (except for those winter Saturdays when the Society holds its monthly meeting) and also on alternate Tuesday afternoons and/or evenings during the summer months. The Centre, which is well equipped with microfiche readers, holds a considerable amount of material, including the GRO indexes (England and Wales) from 1837 to 1950; the 1881 census index for England and Wales on microfiche; the 1891 census for the area of the former county of Clwyd; calendars of probate for England and Wales from 1858 to 1943; marriage indexes - for all Anglican marriages in Denbighshire and Flintshire (in most cases up to the mid-Twentieth century); Clwyd parish register transcriptions for north-east Wales; monumental inscriptions; indexes of wills proved pre 1858 in the four ancient dioceses of Wales (Bangor, St. Asaph, St. David's and Llandaff); the 1992 edition of the IGI on microfiche; many reference books and files on family history and local history; an extensive collection of exchange journals from most of the Family History Societies of Wales and England and some from overseas, dating back over a number of years. New material is added regularly.

The Society is represented at a number of family history fairs and open days during the year including Preston, York, Llandrindod Wells and Northwich. In 2001 we had a successful Society stand at the National Eisteddfod at Denbigh where we also represented the Association of Family History Societies in Wales. Since 2000 the Society has organised jointly with the Gwynedd Family History Society the North Wales Family History Fair at the North Wales Theatre and Conference Centre, Llandudno and which is held on the first Saturday of September.

New members are always welcome. Our annual subscription rates are: Individual £9 (UK or EU); Family (two members living at the same address, UK or EU) £9; Overseas Surface Mail £11; Overseas Airmail £15. Subscriptions are due on 1st September. Enquiries regarding membership should be addressed to Mrs Hilda Robson, Membership Registrar, 1 Coed y Bryn, Flint Mountain, Flintshire CH6 5QP. General enquiries should be addressed to Mrs Alison Anderson, Secretary, The Laurels, Dolydd Road, Cefn Mawr, Wrexham LL14 3NH. Further information is available on the Society's website at www.clwydfhs.org.uk. The Society also administers the CLWYD mailing list, which is hosted by RootsWeb.com, Inc. The Society is a member of the Federation of Family History Societies and the Association of Family History Societies in Wales.

Cymdeithas Hanes Teuluoedd Dyfed Family History Society

The Society was formed in April 1982 by a group of enthusiasts who were interested in researching their ancestors in the three old counties of Cardiganshire, Carmarthenshire, and Pembrokeshire, which at that time formed the county of Dyfed, one of the ancient Principalities of Wales. Since that time the Counties have reverted to their original names with the exception of Cardigan which has become Ceredigion.

The aim of the Society was to foster and help the study of Family History through out the then County of Dyfed. In order to achieve this, steps were taken to record Parish Registers, Monumental Inscriptions, and Census Returns. These have all been published on Microfiche. Recently Mr and Mrs David Treharne Lewis have donated to the Society a series of Records indexed and produced by the Merlin Index Group under the direction of Mr Treharne Lewis. This Index are Records of Baptism, Marriages, and Burials in a large number of Parishes in Carmarthenshire not previously recorded, also included are the Vaccination Records around the Carmarthen area. The Vaccination Records give the Childs Name, Date of Birth, Address, Fathers Name, and Occupation, a valuable source for "lost" ancestors.

The Society has five Branches in Wales namely, Cardigan, Carmarthen, Haverfordwest, Llandovery (Upper Towy), and Llanelli, and an interest in a London Branch which is also linked to other Welsh Societies. Each Branch organises it's own programme of talks an events on a monthly basis. Visitors are welcome at all meetings.

Membership of the Society is open to all, Individuals, Overseas, and Institutions at £8 per annum, and Family Membership at £12 per annum. The Society send out a very helpful Starter Pack to all new Members together with all Journals for the current year. Members joining after the first of October are current for the following year and only receive the December Journal. All subscriptions are due on 1st January each year, a reminder is in the December Journal. Subscriptions can now be paid by Credit Card direct to the Society Secretary.

The Society hope to produce their first CD in time for Christmas 2001. The subject will be the Churches and Chapels of Dyfed. It will Index over 1000 places of worship and have over 600 Photographs. This will be an useful addition to the Family History File. The CD will contain maps showing where each Church and Chapel is giving an OS position. This is an ideal opportunity to see the place Baptism, Marriage, or Burial of you ancestor. The CD will also state where the Records of the Church or Chapel are held, saving time and money in wasted journeys to Record Offices.

The Scottish Genealogy Society

The Scottish Genealogy Society was founded in Edinburgh in 1953 to promote research into Scottish family history and to advance and encourage the collection, exchange and publication of material relating to genealogy and family history. In accordance with the wishes of the original founding members, the Society is purely consultative and does not undertake professional record searching. Volunteer members will answer general queries from the library resources but will not undertake detailed searches. A list of professional searchers can be provided for members to contact.

The Library and Family History Centre book and microform collection

The Library and Family History Centre contains a wealth of material for the genealogist, both professional and amateur. Over the years the Society has amassed a diverse and fascinating collection of books and manuscripts covering general subjects such as reference books and directories, biographies, topographies, gazeteers, trades and profession lists, general Scottish history, peerage, heraldry, school and university rolls, to individual family collections both published and unpublished. Books and manuscripts relating to families in other countries round the world have been donated to the Library. There is also a large and ever expanding collection of microfiche, microfilm and CD Roms. This ranges from The Mormon microfiche and census microfiche collection to a wide collection of Old Parish Register and census microfilm. This last is incomplete but is continually being expanded. There are viewing facilities for these available in the Library. Over the years members and friends have sent and been encouraged to contribute copies of their pedigrees, family histories, research notes, etc. and these have all been meticulously indexed by surname in the Family History Index. Members are encouraged to donate items to this collection, on paper or computer disk, as the larger it becomes, the more effective it is.

The Scottish Genealogy Society also publishes its own quarterly journal. Members can contribute articles for publication in this and there is also a queries section to encourage liaison with other members researching particular surnames or subject matter. The Society also sends its journal to other Family History Societies in return for a copy of their journal. There are also monthly lectures, held from September to April at The Royal College of Physicians in Queen Street on a wide variety of topics.

Gravestone Inscriptions

Since its foundation the Society has been actively engaged in transcribing gravestone inscriptions and has built up the largest collection of Scottish Monumental Inscriptions in the world. It was started in the 1950s by John and Sheila Mitchell and has been continued by their children Angus and Alison Mitchell. Society and other members have also assisted and added to this growing, valuable source for family historians. This collection is available in published volumes, for sale or research, and also in manuscript form if unpublished. The work on this collection is ongoing and people wishing to transcribe are encouraged to contact the Society to avoid duplication.

Sales & Publishing programme

The Society has an extensive and increasing list of titles for sale. The Sales List is available at the Library, is regularly updated and included in the Journal twice a year. It can also be viewed on our web page. The Publications Committee is more than willing to consider publishing works of general interest.

The Library and Family History Centre is situated in Victoria Terrace, a raised terrace running along the top of the shops in Victoria Street, in the heart of Edinburgh's Old Town. It is a haven for historians and researchers being ideally situated for easy access to The National and Central Reference Libraries, The National Archives of Scotland, New Register House, West Register House and the many museums and art galleries in the city. For visitors from further afield it is a short walk from Waverley Station and St Andrews Bus Station. Buses from various parts of Princes Street come up The Mound and The Bridges to George IV Bridge and the Lawnmarket.

The Genealogical Society of Victoria Inc

During 2001 the Genealogical Society of Victoria (GSV) celebrated its Diamond Jubilee. In 1941 a small group of Victorian genealogists, who were members of the Sydney based Society of Australian Genealogists, recognised that their research interests lay with local Victorian records. Today the GSV is a vibrant family history organisation of some 6500 members

Prior to Federation in 1901 what is now known as Australia was a number of separate colonies, each maintaining its own government records for matters such as births, marriages and deaths, immigration, naturalisation, land grants and sales, government employment, police, railways and education. Apart from military records since federation, naturalisation from 1904 and immigration from the 1920s, these records remain the responsibility of the individual states.

Australia is a nation of immigrants. While a proportion of Australians can trace their roots to the original inhabitants of this continent the vast majority of us can readily trace our family trees back to ancestors living overseas. Some GSV members have one or more ancestors who arrived on the First Fleet in 1788 either as convicts or gaolers. Many of us have ancestors who arrived in Australia in the gold rush period of the 1850s. Perhaps a long-lost brother or cousin on your family tree was a convict or gold-rush immigrant. Others came in the post-war immigration influx of the 1950s and 60s and more recently. Whenever our ancestors arrived in Australia sooner or later most will research records of the country of origin.

Finding our ancestors on passenger lists of immigrants is an important goal for Australian family history researchers. Most of us want to know when and where our ancestors arrived in Australia and where they came from. Governments kept detailed records of assisted immigrants for whom money was outlaid. For these immigrants information may include names of family members remaining in Britain or relatives already in Australia. Occupation, literacy and religion were also recorded. When immigrants paid for their own passage much less information was recorded. Indexes to passenger lists have been prepared by government agencies and volunteers and made available for researchers. Our library holdings include published indexes from all Australian states and microform copies of many original passenger lists.

Several generations of Australians denied their convict ancestry. Now we are proud to find one or more convicts on our family trees. Those with convict forebears from the mid 1820s on can even find details of their physical appearance - height, hair and eye colour and complexion. Date and place of trial, length of sentence, ship of transportation, details of voyage, employment after arrival, applications to marry, petitions to bring family to Australia, tickets of leave and certificates of freedom may all be found amongst the records of the GSV library.

Our library holdings include an ever increasing list of overseas material, particularly records of the British Isles. This has been aided by members' donations towards large items such as the GRO indexes of England and Wales and 1851 London census films and individual items such as microform copies of British parish registers purchased through our 'Wish List' scheme.

Migration within Australia has also been extensive over the years, between rural and metropolitan areas, between states, and between Australia and New Zealand. Indexing of records important to genealogists has been carried out by government organisations, often with the help of volunteer family historians, by individuals and by genealogical organisations. The GSV library contains copies of published indexes to births, marriages and deaths and immigration records for all the Australian states and New Zealand. We also hold many cemetery, probate and other indexes for Victoria and the rest of Australia.

GSV volunteers have assisted the Victorian registry with preparation of consolidated indexes to births, marriages and deaths. We now have the Pioneer Index, a single alphabetical index to births marriages and deaths for the whole of Victoria 1836-1888, the Federation Index for 1889-1901, the Edwardian Index 1902-1913, and the Great War Index 1914-1920. The series of consolidated indexes continues with all Victorian deaths 1921-1985 in a single index. These Victorian indexes provide a wealth of information for the researcher which can be increased by purchase of a copy of the relevant certificate. Birth indexes provide surname and given name of child, father and mother (with maiden surname) place of birth, year and registration number. The birth certificate also includes birth places and ages of both parents, date of marriage and names and ages of previous children. Marriage indexes provide names of both bride and groom while the certificates give the names of both sets of parents with mother's maiden surname. Death indexes give the names of mother and father, when known, while the certificates also give names of spouse and all children, with ages of those still living. These indexes are available in the GSV library in both microfiche an CD-ROM format. Consolidated indexes have also been produced by the other Australian states. The information given and time period covered varies from state to state. Not all states provide as much information on their certificates as does Victoria. All these indexes can be consulted in the Society library.

Our library is equipped with thirty-four microfiche readers and five printers, eight microfilm readers and one printer and sixteen data search computers, five catalogue computer terminals and one internet connection. The catalogue of library holdings is available on computer throughout our library and online via our internet site at www.gsv.org.au. As well as books, microform and CDs the catalogue includes items of interest from the more than 800 periodical titles we receive regularly from throughout the English speaking world.

Ancestor, the official journal of the GSV is published quarterly. This publication, which is distributed free to members, includes many articles to aid local and overseas research as well as news of forthcoming events, members' queries, book reviews, new acquisitions in the library and new bookshop items for sale.

From a small collection of books housed in one mid-city room and staffed by volunteers the Society has grown to occupy one floor of a modern office building in the commercial heart of Melbourne. Our premises comprise a large library, a meeting room which can seat 100 people, offices, workrooms and a bookshop stocked with books, magazines, charts, CDs, computer software and microfiche. We have a volunteer Council, one full-time and four part-time employees plus an army of voluntary workers who assist with maintenance and use of the library collection, carry out professional research on behalf of members and others, assist with administration and work on transcribing and indexing projects. Regular training sessions ensure that our library research assistants can guide the progress of members and visitors as they consult the vast amount of information available in our library. Through our bookshop researchers can purchase items for background reading, frequently consulted indexes and records and software and materials for organising and preserving information and records. We also provide services to facilitate purchase of British wills and certificates, and a research service to search specific records or more generalised family history research.

For many years the GSV had branch groups throughout the state of Victoria whose members transcribed local burial registers and headstone inscriptions from a large number of cemeteries. In 1991 the country groups and several Melbourne based special interest groups became separate incorporated bodies but most still maintain a link to the GSV as Member Societies. There are now three formal special interest groups catering for members with Irish, Scottish and Non-British interests. Each of these three groups meets quarterly, produces a quarterly newsletter for subscribers and has contributed extensively to our library collection with items to assist researchers in these areas. These include a complete set of tithe applotment books for Ireland on microfilm and complete sets of 1841 and 1851 census films for Scotland. Several informal groups or discussion circles meet monthly or bi-monthly for mutual assistance with research problems in a particular region of England.

Within the GSV library collection are copies of burial registers and/or headstone transcriptions for more than 550 Victorian cemeteries, representing metropolitan Melbourne, major regional cities and small rural townships. During 2001 the Society published indexes to and transcriptions of memorial inscriptions at Melbourne General Cemetery. Burials at this cemetery commenced in 1856 and the index includes more than 110,000 names and 40,000 memorials.

Indexing for publication by the Society has included the convict indents for New South Wales and the convict records of Tasmania, the latter a joint venture with the Archives Office of Tasmania. We have also indexed admission registers for several hospitals, particularly for the goldfields areas of central Victoria from the 1850s. Current indexing includes the ward books for the Royal Melbourne Hospital from 1856. Early hospital records usually contain the place of origin of the patient and often the name of the immigrant ship. The advent of the computer has greatly enhanced the ease of collecting, sorting and accessing data. The aim of these indexing projects is to make the information widely available within our library and to a wider population by publication on CD..

The library is open Monday 1.00-6.00, Tuesday-Thursday 10.00-3.00, Friday 10.00-8.00, Saturday 10.00-3.00 and one Sunday per month 10.00-3.00. We are closed on Public holidays, Easter Saturday, Christmas Eve and New Year's Eve. The office is open Monday-Friday 8.45-4.00. The bookshop is open whenever the library or the office is open.

We hold weekly lunchtime meetings from February to November with speakers from within the Society and elsewhere. Talks cover a wide range of topics, particularly focussing on our library holdings and how to use them. We also conduct several seminars throughout the year on a variety of topics including beginning family history.

The GSV is a member of the Federation of Family History Societies, the Australasian Federation of Family History Organisations, and the Victorian Association of Family History Organisations. In April 2003 the GSV will host the triennial Australasian convention on genealogy and heraldry.

For membership, research inquiries and bookshop contact:
The Genealogical Society of Victoria Inc.
Level 6, 179 Queen Street,
Melbourne, Victoria, 3108
Australia
Ph: +61 3 9670 7033
Fax: +61 3 9670 4490
Email: gsv@gsv.org.au
Web page: www.gsv.org.au

Family History & Genealogical Societies

All Family History & Genealogical Societies were circulated to confirm the information is correct and up to date. Some Societies did not responded (January 2002)

National

Ancestral Rescue Club
Briar Rose House, 109 Furness, Glascote, Tamworth, B77 2QH
Tel: 01827-65322 Email: ancestral@rescue.fsnet.co.uk
WWW: www.rootsweb.com/~engarc/index.html
British Association for Local History
PO Box 1576, Salisbury, SP2 8SY Tel: 01722-332158
Fax: 01722-413242, WWW: www.balh.co.uk
East Anglian Group of Family History Societies
2 Burleigh Road, St Ives, Huntington, PE17 6DF
Email: 114040.3430@compuserve.com
Federation of Family History Societies
PO Box 2425, Coventry, CV5 6YX Tel: 070 41 492032
Fax: 01564 703100 Email: admin@ffhs.org.uk
Institute of Heraldic & Genealogical Studies
79 - 82 Northgate, Canterbury, CT1 1BA Fax: 01227-765617
Email: ihgs@ihgs.ac.uk WWW: www.ihgs.ac.uk
North West Group of FHS Family History Fairs, North West
Group of Family History Societies, 4 Lawrence Avenue,
Simonstone, Burnley, BB12 7HX Tel: 01282-771999
Email: ed@gull66.freeserve.co.uk
Society of Genealogists - Library
14 Charterhouse Buildings, Goswell Road, London, EC1M 7BA
Tel: 020-7251-8799 Tel: 020-7250-0291 Fax: 020-7250-1800
Email: library@sog.org.uk - Sales at sales@sog.org.uk
WWW: http://www.sog.org.uk
South West Group of Family History Societies
55 Osborne Road, Weston Super Mare, BS23 3EJ
Tel: 01934 627053,
The North East Group of Family History Societies
11 Colins Street, Great Horton, Bradford, BD7 4HF

England

Avon
Bristol & Avon Family History Society
784 Muller Road, Eastville, Bristol, BS5 6XA Tel: 0117 951
8838 Email: secretary@bafhs.org.uk WWW: www.bafhs.org.uk

Bedfordshire
Bedfordshire Family History Society, P0 Box 214, Bedford,
MK42 9RX Tel: Email: bfhs@bfhs.org.uk
WWW: http://www.bfhs.org.uk

Berkshire
Berkshire Family History Society, 5 Wren Close, Burghfield
Common, Reading, RG7 3PF Tel: 0118-983 6523 Email:
john.gurnett@btinternet.com WWW: www.berksfhs.org.uk

Birmingham
Birmingham & Midland Society for Genealogy & Heraldry
2 Castle Croft, Oldbury, B68 9BQ Tel: 0121 429 9712 Email:
birmingham@terrymorter.fsnet.co.uk WWW: www.bmsgh.org

Buckinghamshire
Buckinghamshire Family History Society
PO Box 4003, Aylesbury, HP21 7GU Tel: 01494-712258 Email:
society@bucksfhs.org.uk WWW: http://www.bucksfhs.org.uk

Cambridgeshire
Cambridge University H&GS
c/o Crossfield House, Dale Road, Stanton, Bury St Edmunds,
IP31 2DY Tel: 01359 25105 Email: president@one-name.org
WWW: www.cam.ac.uk/societies/cuhags/
Cambridgeshire Family History Society,
49 Mill Lane, Ramsey, CB17 2EF, WWW: www.cfhs.org.uk
East Anglian Group of Family History Societies
2 Burleigh Road, St Ives, Huntington, PE17 6DF, Email:
114040.3430@compuserve.com

Fenland Family History Society, 7 Churchfield Way, Wisbech St Mary, PE13 4SY Tel: 01945 410755 Brian Payne Tel: 01945 587723 Bridget Hunter, Email: paynewsm@btinternet.com & peter.hunter3@btinternet.com

Huntingdonshire Family History Society
42 Crowhill, Godmanchester, Huntingdon, PE29 2NR
Tel: 01480 390476 Email: huntsec@ckesseler.freeserve.co.uk
WWW: http://www.genuki.org.uk/big/eng/HUN/HFHS

Peterborough & District Family History Society
33 Farleigh Fields, Orton Wistow, Peterborough, PE2 6YB
Tel: 01733 235956,

Cheshire
Family History Society of Cheshire
Mayfield, 101 Irby Road, Heswall, Wirral, CH61 6UZ
Email: h2@massey48.freeserve.co.uk

North Cheshire Family History Society
2 Denham Drive, Bramhall, Stockport, SK7 2AT
Tel: 0161-439-9270 Email: roger@demercado.demon.co.uk
WWW: http://www.genuki.org.uk/big/eng/CHS/NorthChesFHS

South Cheshire Family History Society incorporating S E Cheshire Local Studies Group
PO Box 1990, Crewe, CW2 6FF, WWW: www.scfhs.org.uk

Cleveland
Cleveland Family History Society
1 Oxgang Close, Redcar, TS10 4ND Tel: 01642 486615

Cornwall
Cornwall Family History Society
5 Victoria Square, Truro, TR1 2RS Tel: 01872-264044 Email:
secretary@cornwallfhs.com WWW: http://www.cornwallfhs.com

Cornish Forefathers Society
Credville, Quakers Road, Perranwell, Truro, TR3 7PJ, ,

Fal Worldwide Family History Group
57 Huntersfield, South Tehidy, Camborne, TR14 0HW Tel:
01209-711557, 01209-711557 Email: cfdell@clara.net
WWW: http://beehive.thisiscornwall.co.uk/falwwfhg

Coventry
Coventry Family History Society
61 Drayton Crescent, Eastern Green, Coventry, CV5 7EL
Tel: (024) 7646 4256 Email: enquiries@covfhs.demon.co.uk

Cumbria /Cumberland
Cumbria Family History Society
"Ulpha", 32 Granada Road, Denton, M34 2LJ
WWW: http://www.genuki/big/eng/CUL/cumbFHS/membership.html

Cumbria
Distington Family & Local History Society
10 Mill Cottages, Distington, Workington, CA14 5SR Tel: 01946
833060, 01946 833060 Email: gillyfoster@distington.idps.co.uk
WWW: www.distington.idps.co.uk

Furness Family History Society
64 Cowlarns Road, Hawcoat, Barrow-in-Furness, LA14 4HJ Tel:
01229-830942 Email: julia.fairbairn@virgin.net
WWW: www.members.aol.com/furnessfhs/fpw.htm

Derbyshire
Chesterfield & District Family History Society
Skerries, 485 Newbold Road, Chesterfield, S41 8AE
Tel: 01246-471983 Email: cadfhs@chesterfield24.fsnet.co.uk

Derbyshire Ancestral Research Group
86 High Street, Loscoe, Heanor, DE75 7LF Tel: 01773-604916

Derbyshire Family History Society
Bridge Chapel House, St Mary's Bridge, Sowter Road, Derby,
DE1 3AT Tel: 01332 608101 WWW: www.dfhs.org.uk

Devon
Devon Family History Society
PO Box 9, Exeter, EX2 6YP Tel: 01392-275917 Email:
members@devonfhs.org.uk WWW: www.deveonfhs.org.uk

Thorverton & District History Society
Ferndale, Thorverton, Exeter, EX5 5NG Tel: 01392 860932,

Dorset
Dorset Family History Society
131 Lynwood Drive, Merley, Wimborne, BH21 1UU Tel: 01202
842838 Email: shirley@dfhs.freeserve.co.uk
WWW: www.dfhs.freeserve.co.uk/index.html

Somerset & Dorset Family History Society
PO Box 4052, Sherborne, DH9 6YL Tel: 01935 389611, 01935
389611 Email: society@sdfhs.org WWW: www.sdfhs.org

Durham
Cleveland Family History Society
1 Oxgang Close, Redcar, TS10 4ND Tel: 01642 486615

Elvet Local & Family History Groups
37 Hallgarth Street, Durham, DH1 3AT Tel: 0191-386-4098
Email: Turnstone-Ventures@durham-city.freeserve.co.uk

Newton Aycliffe Family History Society
25 Anne Swyft Road, Newton Aycliffe, DL5 5HD
Tel: 01325-315538,

Northumberland & Durham Family History Society
2nd Floor, Bolbec Hall, Westgate Road, Newcastle-on-Tyne,
NE1 1SE Tel: 0191-261-2159
WWW: http://www.geocities.com/athens/6549/

East Sussex
Family Roots Family History Society (Eastbourne & District)
94 Northbourne Road, Eastbourne, BN22 8QP
Email: sarahslaughter@madasafish.com

Hastings & Rother Family History Society
Flat 22 The Cloisters, St Johns Road, St Leonards on Sea, TN37
6JT Tel: 01424-422139, WWW: www.hrfhs.org.uk

Essex
Essex Society for Family History
Research Centre, Essex Record Office, Wharf Road,
Chelmsford, CM2 6YT Tel: 01245 244670
Email: secretary@esfh.org.uk WWW: www.esfh.org.uk

Waltham Forest Family History Society,
49 Sky Peals Road, Woodford Green, IG8 9NE

Gloucestershire
Gloucestershire Family History Society
4 Twyver Close, Upton St Leonards, GL4 8EF Tel: 01452-52344
(RESOURCE CENTRE) Email: glosearch@hotmail.com
WWW: http://www.cix.co.uk/~rd/genuki/gfhs.htm

Gloucestershire - South
Sodbury Vale Family History Group
36 Westcourt Drive, Oldland Common, Bristol, BS30 9RU
Tel: 0117 932 4133 Email: sladekf@supanet.com

Hampshire
Hampshire Genealogical Society
PO Box 48, Cosham, PO6 3UN Email: society@hgs-online.org.uk
WWW: www.hgs-online.org.uk

Herefordshire
Herefordshire Family History Society
6 Birch Meadow, Gosmore Road, Clehonger, Hereford, HR2
9RH Tel: 01981-250974 Email: prosser_brian@hotmail.com
WWW: www.roortsweb.com~ukhfhs

Hertfordshire
Codicote Local History Society
34 Harkness Way, Hitchin, SG4 0QL Tel: 01462 622953 Tel:

Hertfordshire Family & Population History Society
2 Mayfair Close, St Albans, AL4 9TN Email: hfphs@btinternet.com
WWW: http://www.btinternet.com/~hfphs/index.htm

Letchworth & District Family History Group
84 Kings Hedges, Hitchin, SG5 2QE

Royston & District Family History Society
60 Heathfield, Royston, SG8 5BN Tel: 01763 241462
Email: joyce3Atoptalise.co.uk

St. Albans & Herts Architectural & Archaeological Society
24 Rose Walk, St Albans, AL4 9AF Tel: 01727 853204

Welwyn & District Local History Society
9 York Way, Welwyn, AL6 9LB Tel: 01438 716415

Hull
Hull Central Library Family & Local History Club
Central Library, Albion Street, Kingston upon Hull, HU1 3TF
Tel: 01482 616828 Fax: 01482 616827
Email: gareth2ukorigins.co.uk
WWW: http://www.hullcc.gov.uk/genealogy

Isle of Wight
Isle of Wight Family History Society
Spindrift, 3 Milne Way, Newport, PO30 1YF Tel: 01983 524469,

ROOTS Family & Parish History
San Fernando, Burnt House Lane, Alverstone, Sandown, P036
0HB Tel: 01983 403060 Email: peters.sanfernando@tesco.net

Kent
Folkestone & District Family History Society
Brickwall Farmhouse, Dengemarsh Road, Lydd, TN29 9JH
Email: levina.jones@virgin.net WWW:
www.freespace.virgin.net/jennifer.killick/folkestone&districtfhs
Kent Family History Society
Two Ways, Salisbury Road, St Margarets Bay, CT15 6DP,
Email: dickbarton@aol.com WWW: http://www.canterhill.co.uk/kfhs
Tunbridge Wells Family History Society
The Old Cottage, Langton Road, Langton Green, Tunbridge
Wells, TN3 0BA Tel: 01892-521495
Email: s.oxenbury@virgin.net WWW: www.tunwells-fhs.co.uk
Woolwich & District Family History Society
132 Belvedere Road, Bexleyheath, DA7 4PF
North West Kent Family History Society
6 Windermere Road, Bexleyheath, DA7 6PW
WWW: http://www.users.ox.ac.uk/~malcolm/nwkfhs

Lancashire
Bolton & District Family History Society
205 Crompton Way, Bolton, BL2 2RU Tel: 01204 525472
Email: bolton@mlfhs.demon.co.uk
WWW: www.mlfhs.demon.co.uk
Cumbria Family History Society
"Ulpha", 32 Granada Road, Denton, M34 2LJ WWW:
http://www.genuki.big/eng/CUL/cumbFHS/membership.html
Lancashire Family History & Historical Society
15 Christ Church Street, Accrington, BB5 2LZ
Tel: 01254 398579 Email: jhunt@christchurch92.freeserve.co.uk
WWW: http://www.lfhhs.mcmail.com
Lancaster Family History Group
94 Croston Road, Garstang, Preston, PR3 1HR
WWW: http://www.fhgroup.freeserve.co.uk
Liverpool & S W Lancashire Family History Society
11 Bushbys Lane, Formby, L37 2DX
WWW: www.lswlfhs.freeserve.co.uk
Manchester & Lancashire Family History Society
Clayton House, 59 Piccadilly, Manchester, M1 2AQ
Tel: 0161-236-9750 Email: office@mlfhs.demon.co.uk
 WWW: www.mlfhs.demon.co.uk
North Meols Family History Society
9 The Paddock, Ainsdale, Southport, PR8 3PT Tel: 01704
578797 Email: nadine@xplorasia.freeserve.co.uk
WWW: www.users.zetnet.co.uk/nmfhs
Oldham & District Branch of Manchester & Lancashire FHS
Clayton House, 59 Piccadilly, Manchester, M1 2QA Tel: 0161
236 9750 Email: office@mlfhs.demon.co.uk
WWW: www.mlfhs.demon.co.uk
Ormskirk & District Family History Society
c/o Ormskirk College, Hants Lane, Ormskirk, L39 1PX
Tel: 01695-578604 Email: petert@skelmersdale.ac.uk
WWW: www.odfhs.freeserve.co.uk
Wigan Family History Society
464 Warrington Road, Goose Green, Wigan, WN3 6QF

Leicestershire
Leicestershire & Rutland Family History Society
11 Spring Lane, Wymondham, Leicester, LE14 2AY
Tel: 01572 787331 Email: ray.broad@ntlworld.com
WWW: www.lrfdhs.org.uk

Lincolnshire
Lincolnshire Family History Society
1 Pennygate Gardens, Spalding, PE11 1XJ
WWW: www.genuki.org.uk/big/eng/LIN/lfhs
South Holland Family & Local History Group
6 Brendon Walk, Spalding , PE11 3AG Tel: 01775 714781,

London
East of London Family History Society
37 Medopra Road, Romford, RM7 7EP
WWW: http://eolfhs.rootsweb.com
Hillingdon Family History Society
20 Moreland Drive, Gerrards Cross, SL9 8BB Tel: 01753
885602 Email: gillmay@dial.pipex.com WWW: www.hfhs.co.uk
London & North Middlesex Family History Society
7 Mount Pleasant Road, New Malden, KT3 3JZ
Tel: (020) 8949-6765,
Waltham Forest Family History Society
49 Sky Peals Road, Woodford Green, IG8 9NE
Westminster & Central Middlesex Family History Society
1d Uplands Park Road, Enfield, EN27PS Amalgamated with
London & North Middlesex Family History Society

London (South East)
North West Kent Family History Society

Liverpool
Liverpool & S W Lancashire Family History Society
11 Bushbys Lane, Formby, L37 2DX
WWW: www.lswlfhs.freeserve.co.uk

Manchester
Manchester & Lancashire Family History Society
Clayton House, 59 Piccadilly, Manchester, M1 2AQ
Tel: 0161-236-9750 Email: office@mlfhs.demon.co.uk
WWW: www.mlfhs.demon.co.uk

Merseyside
Liverpool & S W Lancashire Family History Society
11 Bushbys Lane, Formby, L37 2DX
WWW: www.lswlfhs.freeserve.co.uk

Middlesex
Hillingdon Family History Society
20 Moreland Drive, Gerrards Cross, SL9 8BB Tel: 01753
885602 Email: gillmay@dial.pipex.com WWW: www.hfhs.co.uk
London & North Middlesex Family History Society
7 Mount Pleasant Road, New Malden, KT3 3JZ Tel: (020) 8949-6765
West Middlesex Family History Society
10 West Way, Houslow, TW5 0JF
Westminster & Central Middlesex Family History Society
1d Uplands Park Road, Enfield, EN27PS Amalgamated with
London & North Middlesex Family History Society

Norfolk
Mid-Norfolk Family History Society
Codgers Cottage, 6 Hale Road, Bradenham, Thetford, IP25 7RA,
Email: melaniedonnelly@codgerscottage.fsnet.co.uk WWW:
http://www.uea.ac.uk/~s300/genuki/NFK/organisations/midnfhs
Norfolk Family History Society
Kirby Hall, 70 St Giles Street, Norwich, NR2 1LS
Tel: 01603-763718 Email: nfhs@paston.co.uk
WWW: www.uea.ac.uk/~s300/genuki/NFK/organisations/nfhs/

Northamptonshire
Northamptonshire Family History Society
2 Yewtree Court, Boothville, Peterborough, NN3 6SF
Email: northamptonshire_fhs@tesco.net
WWW: http://www.fugazi.demon.co.uk

Northumberland
Northumberland & Durham Family History Society,
2nd Floor, Bolbec Hall, Westgate Road, Newcastle-on-Tyne
NE1 1SE Tel: 0191-261-2159
WWW: http://www.geocities.com/athens/6549/

Nottinghamshire
Mansfield & District Family History Society
15 Cranmer Grove, Mansfield, NG19 7JR, Email:
flinthambe@aol.com
Nottinghamshire Family History Society
15 Holme Close, Woodborough, Nottingham, NG14 6EX
WWW: http://www..nottsfhs.org.uk

Oxfordshire
Oxfordshire Family History Society
19 Mavor Close, Woodstock, Oxford, OX20 1YL
 Tel: 1993812258 Email: julie@kennedy91.fsnet.co.uk
WWW: www.ofhs.org.uk

Rutland
Leicestershire & Rutland Family History Society
11 Spring Lane, Wymondham, Leicester, LE14 2AY
Tel: 01572 787331 Email: ray.broad@ntlworld.com
WWW: www.lrfdhs.org.uk

Shropshire
Cleobury Mortimer Historical Society
The Old Schoolhouse, Nee Savage, Cleobury Mortimer,
Kidderminster, DY14 8JU Tel: 01299 270319,
Shropshire Family History Society
Redhillside, Ludlow Road, Church Stretton, SY6 6AD
Email: secretary@sfhs.org.uk WWW: www.sfhs.org.uk

Somerset
Burnham & Highbridge FHS - Disbanded April 1998
Somerset & Dorset Family History Society
PO Box 4052, Sherborne, DH9 6YL Tel: 01935 389611 Fax:
01935 389611 Email: society@sdfhs.org WWW: www.sdfhs.org

South West Group of Family History Societies
55 Osborne Road, Weston Super Mare, BS23 3EJ Tel: 01934 627053,
Weston-Super-Mare Family History Society
55 Osbourne Road, Weston Super Mare, BS23 3EJ Tel: 01934 627053 Email: kes.jack@virgin.co.uk

Staffordshire
Birmingham & Midland Society for Genealogy & Heraldry
2 Castle Croft, Oldbury, B68 9BQ Tel: 0121 429 9712 Email: birmingham@terrymorter.fsnet.co.uk WWW: www.bmsgh.org
Ancestral Rescue Club
Briar Rose House, 109 Furness, Glascote, Tamworth, B77 2QH Tel: 01827-65322 Email: ancestral@rescue.fsnet.co.uk WWW: www.rootsweb.com/~engarc/index.html
Audley & District Family History Society
20 Hillside Avenue, Endon, Stoke on Trent, ST9 9HH

Suffolk
Felixstowe Family History Society
Drenagh, 7 Victoria Road, Felixstowe, IP11 7PT Tel: 01394-275631, Fax: 01394-275631
WWW: http://www.btinternet.com/~woodsbj/tths
Suffolk Family History Society
Willow House, Church Road, Little Waldingfield, Sudbury, CO10 0SP Tel: 01473-748677, Fax: 01473-744854 Email: barfield@cedarcroft.fsnet.com WWW: http://www.genuki.org.uk/big/eng/SFK/Sfhs/Sfhs.htm

Surrey
East Surrey Family History Society
27 Burley Close, London, SW16 4QQ
Email: stephenturner1@compuserve.com
WWW: www.eastsurreyfhs.org.uk
West Surrey Family History Society
Deer Dell, Botany Hill, Sands, Farnham, GU10 1LZ Tel: 01252 783485 Email: sylviamcq@onetel.co.uk
WWW: http://www.surreyweb.org.uk/wsfhs/index.html

Sussex
Sussex Family History Group
7 Tower View, Uckfield, TN22 1SB Tel: 01825 765561 Email: secretary@sfhg.org.uk WWW: http://www.sfhg.org.uk

Tyne & Wear
Northumberland & Durham Family History Society
2nd Floor, Bolbec Hall, Westgate Road, Newcastle-on-Tyne, NE1 1SE Tel: 0191-261-2159, WWW: http://www.geocities.com/athens/6549/

Waltham Forest
Waltham Forest Family History Society, 49 Sky Peals Road, Woodford Green, IG8 9NE

Warwickshire
Birmingham & Midland Society for Genealogy & Heraldry
2 Castle Croft, Oldbury, B68 9BQ Tel: 0121 429 9712 Email: birmingham@terrymorter.fsnet.co.uk WWW: www.bmsgh.org
Coventry Family History Society
61 Drayton Crescent, Eastern Green, Coventry, CV5 7EL Tel: (024) 7646 4256 Email: enquiries@covfhs.demon.co.uk
Nuneaton & North Warwickshire Family History Society
14 Amos Avenue, Nuneaton, CV10 7BD
WWW: www.nnwfhs.org.uyk
Rugby Family History Group
17 St Mary's Close, Southam, Leamington Spa, CV33 0EW
Tel: 01926-817667
Email: durnomitchell@Jamesdurno.swinternet.co.uk
Warwickshire Family History Society
7 Mersey Road, Bulkington, CV12 9QB
Email: n.wetton.@virgin.net WWW: www.wfhs.org.uk

Westmorland
Cumbria Family History Society
"Ulpha", 32 Granada Road, Denton, M34 2LJ
WWW: http://www.genuki.org.uk/big/eng/CUL/cumbFHS/membership.html

Wiltshire
Wiltshire Family History Society
10 Castle Lane, Devizes, SN10 1HJ Tel: 01380 722893
Email: wfhs@devizes39.freeserve.co.uk

Worcestershire
Birmingham & Midland Society for Genealogy & Heraldry,
2 Castle Croft, Oldbury, B68 9BQ Tel: 0121 429 9712

Email: birmingham@terrymorter.fsnet.co.uk
WWW: www.bmsgh.org
Malvern Family History Group
22 Jasmine Road, Malvern Wells, WR14 4XD

Yorkshire
Yorkshire Archaeological Society - Family History Section
Claremont, 23 Clarendon Road, Leeds, LS2 9NZ, WWW: http://www.users.globalnet.co.uk/~gdl/yasfhs.htm
Yorkshire Consortium of Family History Societies - London Group
20 Avon Close, Watford, WD25 0DN Tel: 01923 672691,

Yorkshire - East Yorkshire
City of York & District Family History Society, 4 Orchard Close, Dringhouses, York, YO24 2NX
WWW: www.yorkfamilyhistory.org.uk
East Yorkshire Family History Society
12 Carlton Drive, Aldbrough, HU11 4SF
WWW: www.eyfhs.org.uk
Hull Central Library Family & Local History Club
Central Library, Albion Street, Kingston upon Hull, HU1 3TF
Tel: 01482 616828, Fax: 01482 616827 Email: gareth2ukorigins.co.uk WWW: http://www.hullcc.gov.uk/genealogy

Yorkshire - North
City of York & District Family History Society
4 Orchard Close, Dringhouses, York, YO24 2NX
WWW: www.yorkfamilyhistory.org.uk
Cleveland Family History Society
1 Oxgang Close, Redcar, TS10 4ND Tel: 01642 486615
Ripon Historical Society-Ripon, Harrogate & District Family History Group
29 Kingsley Drive, Harrogate, HG1 4TJ
Email: gdl@globalnet.co.uk WWW: www.users.globalnet.co.uk/~gdl/index.htm
Upper Dales Family History Group - affiliated to Cleveland Family History Society
Croft House, Newbiggin in Bishopdale, Nr Leyburn, DL8 3TD
Tel: 01969 663738 Email: glenys@bishopdale.demon.co.uk
WWW: www.bishopdale.demon.co.uk
Wharfedale Family History Group
1 West View Court, Yeadon, Leeds, LS19 7HX
Tel: 0113 258 5597 Email: wfhg@yorksgen.org.uk
WWW: http://www.yorksgen.org.uk

Yorkshire - South
Barnsley Family History Society
58A High Street, Royston, Barnsley, S71 4RN
Email: kath@barnsleyfhs.freeserve.co.uk
WWW: http://www.barnsleyfhs.freeserve.co.uk
Boothferry Family & Local History Group
17 Airmyn Avenue, Goole, DN14 6PF
Email: howardrj@madasafish.com
Doncaster & District Family History Society
'Marton House', 125 The Grove, Wheatley Hills, Doncaster, DN2 5SN Tel: 01302-367257 Email: tonyjunes@aol.com
WWW: http://www.doncasterfhs.freeserve.co.uk
Isle of Axholme Family History Society
Alwinton, 51 Mill Road, Crowle, Isle of Axholme, DN17 4LW
Tel: 01302 350849 WWW: www.linktop.demon.co.uk/axholme/
Rotherham Family History Society
12 Hall Grove, Moorgate, Rotherham, S60 2BS
WWW: www.rotherhamfhs.f9.co.uk
Sheffield & District Family History Society
10 Hallam Grange Road, Sheffield, S10 4BJ, Email: secretary@sheffieldfhs.org.uk WWW: www.sheffieldfhs.org.uk

Yorkshire - West
Bradford Family History Society
2 Leaventhorpe Grove, Thornton, Bradford, BD13 3BN, Email: DFlax@aol.com WWW: http://www.genuki.org.uk/big/eng/YKS/bfhs/
Calderdale Family History Society inc Halifax & District
61 Gleanings Avenue, Norton Tower, Halifax, HX2 0NU Tel: 01422-360756, WWW: www.users.globalnet.co.uk/~cfhs/
Huddersfield & District Family History Society
292 Thornhills Lane, Clifton, Brighouse, HD6 4JQ
WWW: http://www.hdfhs.or.uk
Keighley & District Family History Society
2 The Hallows, Shann Park, Keighley, BD20 6HY
Tel: 01535-672144

Morley & District Family History Group
26 Wynyard Drive, Morley, Leeds, LS27 9NA
WWW: www.morleyfhg.co.uk
Pontefract & District Family History Society
62 Wheatfield Avenue, Oakes, Huddersfield, HD3 4FR
Tel: 01977 643358 WWW: www.genfair.com
http://.freespace.virgin.net/richard.lockwood
Wakefield & District Family History Society
11 Waterton Close, Walton, Wakefield, WF2 6TT Tel: 01924
258163 Tel: 01924 250882 (Membership Secretary)
  Email: ronaldpullan@hotmail.com
WWW: http://homepage.virgin.net/wakefield.fhs
Wharfedale Family History Group
1 West View Court, Yeadon, Leeds, LS19 7HX
Tel: 0113 258 5597 Email: wfhg@yorksgen.org.uk
WWW: http://www.yorksgen.org.uk

Yorkshire - York
City of York & District Family History Society
4 Orchard Close, Dringhouses, York, YO24 2NX
WWW: www.yorkfamilyhistory.org.uk

Isle of Man
Isle of Man Family History Society
5 Serlborne Drive, Douglas, IM Tel: 01624-862088
WWW: www.isle-of-man.com/interests/genealogy/fhs

Channel Islands
Guernsey
Family History Section of La Société Guernesiaise, P0 Box
314, Candie, St Peter Port, GY1 3TG
Jersey
Channel Islands Family History Society, P0 Box 507, St
Helier, JE4 5TN, Email: cifhs@localdial.com
WWW: www.user.itl.net/~glen/AbouttheChannelIslandsFHS.html

Wales
London Branch of the Welsh Family History Societies
27 Princes Avenue, Carshalton Beeches, SM5 4NZ
  Email: regandpaddy@btinternet.com WWW:

Brecknockshire
Powys Family History Society
Oaker's Lodge, The Vineyards, Winforton, HR3 6EA Tel: 01544
327103 Email: 114251.2276@compuserve.com WWW:
http://ourworld.compuserve.com/homepages/michaelmacsorley/p
owys1.htm & also via Genuki

Cardiganshire
Cardiganshire Family History Society
Trebrysg, Tregaron, SY25 6LH Tel: 01974-298 884, WWW:
http://www.heaton.celtic.co.uk/cgnfhs

Carmarthenshire
Dyfed Family History Society
38 Brynmelyn Avenue, Llanelli, SA15 3RT Tel: 01554 774545
Email: johnhtjames@lineone.net WWW:
http://www.westwales.co.uk/dfhs/dfhs.htm

Ceredigion
Dyfed Family History Society
38 Brynmelyn Avenue, Llanelli, SA15 3RT Tel: 01554 774545
Email: johnhtjames@lineone.net
WWW: http://www.westwales.co.uk/dfhs/dfhs.htm

Clwyd
Clwyd Family History Society
The Laurels, Dolydd Road, Cefn Mawr, Wrexham, LL14 3NH
Tel: 01978-822218, WWW: www.clwydfhs.org.uk

Denbighshire
Clwyd Family History Society
The Laurels, Dolydd Road, Cefn Mawr, Wrexham, LL14 3NH
Tel: 01978-822218, WWW: www.clwydfhs.org.uk

Dyfed
Dyfed Family History Society
38 Brynmelyn Avenue, Llanelli, SA15 3RT Tel: 01554 774545
Email: johnhtjames@lineone.net
WWW: http://www.westwales.co.uk/dfhs/dfhs.htm

Flintshire
Clwyd Family History Society
The Laurels, Dolydd Road, Cefn Mawr, Wrexham, LL14 3NH
Tel: 01978-822218, WWW: www.clwydfhs.org.uk

Glamorgan
Glamorgan Family History Society
Hampton House, 86 Penprysg Road, Pencoed, Bridgend, CF35
6SF Tel: 01685 877086Email: thomasje@btinternet.com
WWW: http://website.lineone.net/~glamfhsoc

Gwent
Gwent Family History Society
11 Rosser Street, Wainfelin, Pontypool, NP4 6EA, Email:
secretary@gwentfhs.org.uk WWW: http://welcome.to/gwent.fhs

Gwynedd
Gwynedd Family History Society
36 Y Wern, Y Felinheli, LL56 4TX Tel: 01286 871838 Email:
Gwynedd.Roots@tesco.net WWW:
http://www.gwynedd.fsbusiness.co.uk

Monmouthshire
Gwent Family History Society
11 Rosser Street, Wainfelin, Pontypool, NP4 6EA, Email:
secretary@gwentfhs.org.uk WWW: http://welcome.to/gwent.fhs

Montgomeryshire
Montgomeryshire Genealogical Society
1 Moreton Road, South Croydon, CR2 7DN
Email: montgensoc@freeuk.com
WWW: http://home.freeuk.net/montgensoc
Powys Family History Society
Oaker's Lodge, The Vineyards, Winforton, HR3 6EA Tel: 01544
327103Email: 114251.2276@compuserve.com

Pembrokeshire
Dyfed Family History Society, 38 Brynmelyn Avenue, Llanelli,
SA15 3RT Tel: 01554 774545 Email: johnhtjames@lineone.net
WWW: http://www.westwales.co.uk/dfhs/dfhs.htm

Powys,
Powys Family History Society, Oaker's Lodge, The Vineyards,
Winforton, HR3 6EA Tel: 01544 327103
  Email: 114251.2276@compuserve.com WWW:
http://ourworld.compuserve.com/homepages/michaelmacsorley/powys1.htm
& also via Genuki

Radnorshire
Powys Family History Society
Oaker's Lodge, The Vineyards, Winforton, HR3 6EA Tel: 01544
327103Email: 114251.2276@compuserve.com WWW:
http://ourworld.compuserve.com/homepages/michaelmacsorley/powys1.htm

Scotland
Scottish Genealogy Society, 15 Victoria Terrace, Edinburgh,
EH1 2JL Tel: 0131-220-3677, Fax: 0131-220-3677 Email:
info@scotsgenealogy.com WWW: www.scotsgenealogy.com

Aberdeen
Aberdeen & North East Scotland Family History Society
164 King Street, Aberdeen, AB24 5BD Tel: 01224-646323
Fax: 01224-639096 Email: enquiries@anefhs.org.uk
WWW: http://www.anesfhs.org.uk

Angus
Tay Valley Family History Society & Research Centre
Family History Research Centre, 179–181 Princes Street,
Dundee, DD4 6DQ Tel: 01382-461845, Fax: 01382 455532
Email: tvfhs@tayvalleyfhs.org.uk
WWW: http://www.tayvalleyfhs.org.uk

Argyll
Glasgow & West of Scotland Family History Society
Unit 5, 22 Mansfield Street, Partick, Glasgow, G11 5QP Tel:
0141-339-8303, Fax: 0141-339-8303, WWW:
http://www.gwsfhs.org.uk

Ayrshire
Alloway & Southern Ayrshire Family History Society
c/o Alloway Public Library, Doonholm Road, Alloway, Ayr, KA7 4QQ
East Ayrshire Family History Society
c/o Dick Institute, Elmbank Avenue, Kilmarnock, KA1 3BU,
Email: enquiries@eastayrshirefhs.org.uk WWW:
www.eastayrshirefhs.org.uk

Glasgow & West of Scotland Family History Society
Unit 5, 22 Mansfield Street, Partick, Glasgow, G11 5QP Tel: 0141-339-8303 Fax: 0141-339-8303 WWW: http://www.gwsfhs.org.uk

Largs & North Ayrshire Family History Society
28 Walkerston Avenue, Largs, KA30 8ER WWW: http://www.freeyellow.com/members7/lnafhs/index.html
Troon & District Family History Society, c/o M.E.R.C., Troon Public Library, South Beach, Troon, KA10 6EF

Berwickshire
Borders Family History Society
Pentennen, 15 Edinburgh Road, Greenlaw, TD10 6XF

Borders
Borders Family History Society
Pentennen, 15 Edinburgh Road, Greenlaw, TD10 6XF

Bute
Glasgow & West of Scotland Family History Society
Unit 5, 22 Mansfield Street, Partick, Glasgow, G11 5QP Tel: 0141-339-8303 Fax: 0141-339-8303
WWW: http://www.gwsfhs.org.uk

Caithness
Caithness Family History Society
Belmont, Willowbank, Wick, KW1 4NZ

Central Scotland
Central Scotland Family History Society
11 Springbank Gardens, Dunblane, FK15 9JX
Tel: 01786 823937 Email: mturner200@hotmail.com
WWW: www.csfhs.org.uk

Dunbartonshire
Glasgow & West of Scotland Family History Society
Unit 5, 22 Mansfield Street, Partick, Glasgow, G11 5QP
Tel: 0141-339-8303 Fax: 0141-339-8303
WWW: http://www.gwsfhs.org.uk

Dundee
Tay Valley Family History Society & Research Centre
179–181 Princes Street, Dundee, DD4 6DQ Tel: 01382-461845, Fax: 01382 455532 Email: tvfhs@tayvalleyfhs.org.uk
WWW: http://www.tayvalleyfhs.org.uk

Dumfries
Dumfries & Galloway Family History Society
Family History Research Centre, 9 Glasgow Street, Dumfries, DG2 9AF Tel: 01387-248093 Email: shop@dgfhs.org.uk
WWW: www.dgfhs.org.uk

East Lothian,
Lothians Family History Society
c/o Lasswade High School Centre, Eskdale Drive, Bonnyrigg, EH19 2LA Tel: 0131-660-1933 Fax: 0131-663-6634
Email: anne_agnew@online.rednet.co.uk

Edinburgh
Lothians Family History Society
c/o Lasswade High School Centre, Eskdale Drive, Bonnyrigg, EH19 2LA Tel: 0131-660-1933 Fax: 0131-663-6634
Email: anne_agnew@online.rednet.co.uk

Fife
Fife Family History Society
Glenmoriston, Durie Street, Leven, KY8 4HF Tel: 013333 425321 Email: fife@ffhoc.freeserve.co.uk
WWW: http://www.fifefhs.pwp.bluyonder.co.uk
Tay Valley Family History Society &Research Centre
179–181 Princes Street, Dundee, DD4 6DQ Tel: 01382-461845 Tel: Fax: 01382 455532 Email: tvfhs@tayvalleyfhs.org.uk
WWW: http://www.tayvalleyfhs.org.uk

Glasgow
Glasgow & West of Scotland Family History Society
Unit 5, 22 Mansfield Street, Partick, Glasgow, G11 5QP
Tel: 0141-339-8303 Fax: 0141-339-8303
WWW: http://www.gwsfhs.org.uk

Kinross-shire
Tay Valley Family History Society & Research Centre
179–181 Princes Street, Dundee, DD4 6DQ Tel: 01382-461845 Email: tvfhs@tayvalleyfhs.org.uk
WWW: http://www.tayvalleyfhs.org.uk

Highlands
Highland Family History Society
c/o Reference Room, Inverness Public Library, Farraline Park, Inverness, IV1 1NH
Invernesshire
Highland Family History Society
c/o Reference Room, Inverness Public Library, Farraline Park, Inverness, IV1 1NH

Lanarkshire
Glasgow & West of Scotland Family History Society
Unit 5, 22 Mansfield Street, Partick, Glasgow, G11 5QP
Tel: 0141-339-8303 Fax: 0141-339-8303
WWW: http://www.gwsfhs.org.uk

Lanarkshire
Lanarkshire Family History Society
c/o Ref Department, Hamilton Central Library, 98 Cadzow Street, Hamilton, ML3 6HQ
Midlothian
Lothians Family History Society
c/o Lasswade High School Centre, Eskdale Drive, Bonnyrigg, EH19 2LA Tel: 0131-660-1933 Email: anne_agnew@online.rednet.co.uk

North East Scotland,
Aberdeen & North East Scotland Family History Society
164 King Street, Aberdeen, AB24 5BD Tel: 01224-646323 Fax: 01224-639096 Email: enquiries@anefhs.org.uk
WWW: http://www.anesfhs.org.uk

Orkney
Orkney Family History Society
Community Room, The Strynd, Kirkwall, KW15 1HG Tel: 01856 761582 (Home) Email: daf.mooney@virgin.net

Peebleshire
Borders Family History Society
Pentennen, 15 Edinburgh Road, Greenlaw, TD10 6XF

Perthshire
Tay Valley Family History Society & Research Centre
Family History Research Centre, 179–181 Princes Street, Dundee, DD4 6DQ Tel: 01382-461845, Fax: 01382 455532 Email: tvfhs@tayvalleyfhs.org.uk
WWW: http://www.tayvalleyfhs.org.uk

Renfrewshire
Glasgow & West of Scotland Family History Society
Unit 5, 22 Mansfield Street, Partick, Glasgow, G11 5QP
Tel: 0141-339-8303, Fax: 0141-339-8303
WWW: http://www.gwsfhs.org.uk

Renfrewshire
Renfrewshire Family History Society, c/o Museum & Art Galleries, High Street, Paisley, PA1 2BA
WWW: www.renfrewshire.org.uk

Roxburghshire
Borders Family History Society
Pentennen, 15 Edinburgh Road, Greenlaw, TD10 6XF

Selkirkshire
Borders Family History Society
Pentennen, 15 Edinburgh Road, Greenlaw, TD10 6XF

Shetland
Shetland Family History Society
6 Hillhead, Lerwick, ZE1 0EJ, Email: shetland.fhs@zetnet.co.uk WWW: www.users.zetnet.co.uk/shetland-fhs

Stirling
Central Scotland Family History Society
11 Springbank Gardens, Dunblane, FK15 9JX Tel: 01786 823937 Email: mturner200@hotmail.com WWW: www.csfhs.org.uk

Stirlingshire
Glasgow & West of Scotland Family History Society
Unit 5, 22 Mansfield Street, Partick, Glasgow, G11 5QP
Tel: 0141-339-8303 Fax: 0141-339-8303
WWW: http://www.gwsfhs.org.uk

Northern Ireland

Irish Heritage Association
A.204 Portview, 310 Newtownards Road, Belfast, BT4 1HE
Tel: (028) 90455325,
North of Ireland Family History Society
c/o Graduate School of Education, 69 University Street, Belfast,
BT7 1HL, Email: R.Sibbett@tesco.net
WWW: http://www.nifhs.org
Ulster Historical Foundation
Balmoral Buildings, 12 College Square East, Belfast, BT1 6DD
Tel: (028) 9033 2288 Fax: 028 9023 9885
Email: enquiry@uhf.org.uk
WWW: http://www.uhf.org.uk & www.ancestryireland.com

Ireland

Council of Irish Genealogical Organisations
186 Ashcroft, Raheny, Dublin 5,
Genealogical Society of Ireland
11 Desmond Avenue, Dun Laoghaire Tel: 353 1 284 2711
Email: dlgs@iol.ie & GenSocIreland@iol.ie
WWW: http://welcome.to/genealogyireland
Irish Ancestry Group
Clayton House, 59 Piccadilly, Manchester, M1 2AQ
Tel: 0161-236-9750 Email: mlfhs.demon.co.uk
Irish Family History Society
PO Box 36, Naas, Email: ifhs@eircom.net
WWW: http://homepage.eircom.net/~ifhs/
Ballinteer FHS
29 The View, Woodpark, Ballinteer, Dundrum, 16
Tel: 01-298-8082 Email: ryanc@iol.ie
Cork Genealogical Society
c/o 4 Evergreen Villas, Evergreen Road, Cork City Tel: 086
8198359 Email: micaconl@eircon.ie
WWW: http://homepage.eircon.net/~adcolemen
Irish Genealogical Research Society
c/o 82 Eaton Square, London, SW1W 9AJ
WWW: www.igrsoc.org
Flannery Clan
81 Woodford Drive, Clondakin, Dublin, 22
Raheny Heritage Society
4 Thorndale Drive, Artane, Dublin 5 Tel: 01 831 9028,
Wexford Family History Society
24 Parklands, Wexford Tel: 053-42273 Email: murphyh@tinet.ie
Wicklow County Genealogical Society
1 Summerhill, Wicklow Town,

Specialist Family History Societies

Anglo-French Family History Society
31 Collingwood Walk, Andover, SP10 1PU
WWW: www.anglo-french-fhs.org
Anglo-German Family History Society
20 Skylark Rise, Plymouth, PL6 7SN Tel: 01752 310852
Fax: 01752 310852 Email: jt@toweyj.fsnet.co.uk
WWW: www.agfhs.org.uk
Anglo-Scottish Family History Society
Clayton House, 59 Piccadilly, Manchester, M1 2AQ Tel: 0161-
236-9750, Fax: 0161-237-3512 Email: mlfhs.demon.co.uk
Australian Society of the Lace Makers of Calais Inc
PO Box 946, Batemans Bay, 2536 Tel: 0244-718168 Tel: 0244-
723421, Email: carolynb@acr.net.au
British Ancestors in India Society
2 South Farm Avenue, Harthill, Sheffield, S26 7WY Tel: +44 (0)
1909 774416, Fax: +44 (0) 1909 774416 Email:
editorial@indiaman.com WWW: www.indiaman.com
British Assn for Cemeteries in S.Asia
76 1/2 Chartfield Avenue, London, SW15 6HQ Tel: (020) 8788-6953
Catholic Family History Society
45 Gates Green Road, West Wickham, BR4 9DE
WWW: www.catholic-history.org.uk
Cawdor Heritage Group
Family & Local History Room, Nairn Museum, Viewfield Drive,
Nairn, IV12 4EE Tel: 01667 456791 Fax: 01667 455399
Email: manager@nairnmuseum.freeserve.co.uk
Clans of Ireland Ltd (Charity No 11585)
Grange Clare, Kilmeague, Naas, Ireland Tel: 01365-322353
Email: coolavin@indigo.ie WWW: http://www.irishclans.com
Descendants of Convicts Group
PO Box 12224, A'Beckett Street, Melbourne 3000,

Families in British India Society
Sentosa, Godolphin Road, Weybridge, KT13 0PT
Email: peter@sentosa.swinternet.co.uk
Genealogical Society of Utah (UK)
185 Penns Lane, Sutton Coldfield, B76 1JU Tel: 0121-384-2028
Fax: 0121-382-5948
Heraldry Society
PO Box 32, Maidenhead, SL6 3FD Tel: 0118-932-0210, Fax:
0118 932 0210 Email: heraldry-society@cwcom.net
Historical Medical Equipment Society
8 Albion Mews, Apsley, HP3 9QZ, Email:
hmes@antiageing.freeserve.co.uk
Hugenot & Walloon Research Association
Malmaison, Church St, Great Bedwyn, SN8 3PE
**International Police Association - British Section - Genealogy
Group**
Thornholm, Church Lane, South Muskham, Newark, NG23 6EQ
Tel: 01636 676997 Email: ipagenuk@thornholm.freeserve.co.uk
**International Society for British Genealogy & Family
History**
PO Box 3115, Salt Lake City, 84110-3115 Tel: 801-272-2178,
WWW: http://www.homestart.com/isbgfh/
Irish Ancestry Group
Clayton House, 59 Piccadilly, Manchester, M1 2AQ Tel: 0161-
236-9750, Fax: 0161-237-3512 Email: mlfhs.demon.co.uk
Irish Genealogical Research Society
c/o 82 Eaton Square, London, SW1W 9AJ WWW: www.igrsoc.org
Jewish Genealogical Society of Great Britain
Finchley Synagogue, Kinloss Gardens, London, N3 3DU Tel:
01923 825197, Fax: 01923 820323, WWW: www.ort.org/jgsgb
Lancashire Parish Register Society
188 Greenwood Drive, Houghton Green, Warrington, WA2 0EG,
Email: tom_obrien@bigfoot.com WWW:
http://www.genuki:org.uk/big/eng/LAN/lprs
Lighthouse Society of Great Britain
Gravesend Cottage, Gravesend, Torpoint, PL11 2LX, Email:
k.trethewey@btinternet.com WWW: http://www.lsgb.co.uk
Local Population Studies Society
78 Harlow Terrace, Harrogate, HG2 0PN Tel: 01423-560429,
Fax: 01423-560429 Email: sir_david_cooke@compuserve.com
WWW: home.att.net/~jkbfa
London & North Western Railway Society - Staff History Group
34 Falmouth Close, Nuneaton, CV11 6GB Tel: 024 76 381090,
Fax: 024 76 373577 Email: nuneatonral@compuserve.com
North East England Family History Club
5 Tree Court, Doxford Park, Sunderland, SR3 2HR Tel: 0191-522-8344
Quaker Family History Society
1 Ormond Crescent, Hampton, TW12 2TJ
Email: info@qfhs.co.uk WWW: www.qfhs.co.uk
Railway Ancestors Family History Society
Lundy, 31 Tennyson Road, Eastleigh, SO50 9FS Tel: (023) 8049
7465 Tel: (023) 8090 0923 Fax: (023) 8049 7465 Email:
jim@railwayancestors.org.uk WWW:
www.railwayancestors.org.uk
Rolls Royce Family History Society
25 Gisburn Road, Barnoldswick, Colne, BB18 5HB Tel: 01282
815778 Email: ken@ranson.org.uk
Romany & Traveller Family History Society
6 St James Walk, South Chailey, BN8 4BU, WWW:
http://website.lineone.net/~rtfhs
Scottish Association of Family History Societies
51/3 Mortonhall Road, Edinburgh, EH9 2HN Tel: 0131-667-
0437, Fax: 0131 667 0437 Email: scots@safhs.org.uk
Society for Name Studies in Britain & Ireland
22 Peel Park Avenue, Clitheroe, BB7 1ET Tel: 01200-423771,
Fax: 01200-423771,
Society of Brushmakers Descendants Family History Society
13 Ashworth Place, Church Langley, CM17 9PU Tel: 01279-
629392 Email: s.b.d@lineone.net
WWW: http://www.brushmakers.com
Tennyson Society
Central Library, Free School Lane, Lincoln, LN2 1EZ Tel:
01522-552862, Fax: 01522-552858 Email:
linnet@lincolnshire.gov.uk
The Chapels Heritage Society
2 Sandy Way, Wood Lane, Hawarden, CH5 3JJ
Victorian Military Society
PO Box 5837, Newbury, RG14 7JF Tel: 01635 48628 Email:
beverley20@tesco.net WWW: www.vms.org.uk

One Name Societies

Guild of One Name Studies
14 Charterhouse Buildings, Goswell Road, London, EC1M 7BA
Tel: 01293-411136   Email: guild@one-name.org
WWW: www.one-name.org

Alabaster Society
No 1 Manor Farm Cottages, Bradenham, Thetford, IP25 7QE
Tel: 01362-821243 Email: Laraine_Hake@compuserve.com
WWW: www.alabaster.org.uk

Alderson Family History Society
13 Spring Grove, Harrogate, HG1 2HS Tel: 01423-565871,

Allsop Family Group
86 High Street, Loscoe, Heanor, DE75 7LF

Armstrong Clan Association
Thyme, 7 Riverside Park, Hollows, Canonbie, DG14 0UY Tel:
013873 71876 Email: ted.armclan@aol.com

Beresford Family Society
2 Malatia, 78 St Augustines Avenue, South Croydon, CR2 6JH
Tel: (020) 8686 3507, Fax: (020) 8681 3740 Email:
beresford@atlas.co.uk
WWW: www.beresfordfamilyhistory.freeserve.co.uk

Blanchard Family History Society
Mill Farm, Church Street, Bainton, YO25 9NJ

Bliss Family History Society
Spellowgrove Farm, Station Road, Clenchwarton, Kings Lynn,
PE34 4DH Tel: 01553-772953 Email: bliss@one-name.org
WWW: http://www.members.aol.com/keithbliss/fhs/main.htm

Braund Society
12 Ranelagh Road, Lake, Sandown, PO36 8NX
Email: braundsociety@fewiow.freeserve.co.uk

Brooking Family History Society
37 Church Mead, Keymer, Hassocks, BN6 8BW Tel: 01273
842560 Email: bob@rbrooking.fsnet.co.uk
WWW: www.brookingsociety.org.uk

Bunting Society
'Firgrove', Horseshoe Lane, Ash Vale, GU12 5LL Tel: 01252-
325644, Fax: 01252-325644 Email: firgrove@compuserve.com
WWW: http://homepage.virgin.net/teebe.axeminster/BuntingSociety.htm

Burntwood Family History Group
71 Lawnswood Avenue, Hammerwich, Burntwood, WS7 8FZ,
Email: manlaw@freeuk.co.uk

Caraher Family History Society
142 Rexford Street, Sistersville, VA 26175

Cave Society,
5 Wisbech Road, Thorney, Peterborough, PE6 0SA

Clan Davidson Association
Aisling, 67 Shore Road, Kircubbin, Newtownards, BT22 2RP
Tel: 028 427-38402 Email: RCDavison@msn.com

Clan Gregor Society
2 Braehead, Alloa, FK10 2EW Tel: 01259-212076
Fax: 01259-720274 Email: clangregor@sol.co.uk
WWW: http://www.clangregor.com/macgregor

Cobbing Family History Society
89a Petherton Road, London, N5 2QT Tel: (020) 7226-2657,

Cory Society
2 Pankhurst Close, Bexhill on Sea, TN39 5DL

Courtenay Society
Powderham Castle, Kenton, Exeter, EX6 8JQ Tel: 01626-891554
Email: courtenay@courtsoc.demon.co.uk

Dalton Genealogical Society
11 Jordan Close, Leavesden, Watford, WD25 7AF Tel: 01923
661139 Email: pam-lynam@lineone.net
WWW: http://members.aol.com/daltongene/index.html

East Family History Society
64 Bearsdown Road, Eggbuckland, Plymouth, PL6 5TR Tel:
01752-771157

Family History Society of Martin
PO Box 9, Rosanna, Victoria 3084 Australia

Family History Society of Martin (UK)
5 Otlinge Road, St Mary Cray, Orepington, BR5 3SH
Tel: 01689 816114

Geoghegan/McGeoghegan One Name Study
330 Dereham Road, Norwich, NR2 4DL
Email: josi@geoghegan18.fsnet.co.uk
WWW: www.jgeoghegan.org.uk

The Goddard Association of Europe
2 Lowergate Road, Huncoat, Accrington, BB5 6LN Tel: 01254-
235135 Email: johnc.goddard@virgin.net
WWW: www.eese.qut.edu.au/~goddard/gae01.htm

Hamley, Hambly & Hamlyn Family History Society (International)
59 Eylewood Road, West Norwood, London, SE27 9LZ Tel:
(020) 8670-0683 Fax: (020) 8670-0683
Email: hamley@one-name.org
WWW: http://www.freespace.virgin.net/ham.famis/

Hards Family Society
Venusmead, 36 Venus Street, Congresbury, Bristol, BS49 5EZ
Tel: 01934 834780 Email: rogerhards-venusmead@breathemail.net
WWW: www.hards.freewire.co.uk

Haskell Family History Society
36 Hedley Davis Court, Cherry Orchard Lane, Salisbury, SP2
7UE Tel: 01722 332873
Email: suzyfli@salisbury5.freeserve.co.uk

Holdich Family History Society
19 Park Crescent, Elstree, WD6 3PT Tel: (020) 8953 7195
Email: apogee@tesco.net

International Relf Society
Chatsworth House, Sutton Road, Haselbury Plucknett,
Somerton, TA11 6QL Tel: 01458-274015
Email: chris.relf@bucklebury.demon.co.uk

Krans-Buckland Family Association
PO Box 1025, North Highlands, 95660-1025 Tel: (916)-332-4359
Email: jkbfa@worldnet.att.net

Lashbrook One-Name Study
70 Chestnut Lane, Amersham, HP6 6EH Tel: 01494 726103,

Leather Family History Society
134 Holbeck, Great Hollands, Bracknell, RG12 8XG
Tel: 01344-425092 Email: s.leather@ic.ac.uk

Lin(d)field One Name Group
Southview, Maplehurst, Horsham, RH13 6QY
Tel: 01403-864389 Email: lindfield@one-name.org
WWW: http://www.lindfield.force9.co.uk/long

Mackman Family History Society
Chawton Cottage, 22a Long Ridge Lane, Nether Poppleton,
York, YO26 6LX Tel: +44-(0)1904-781752
Email: mackman@one-name.org

Mayhew Ancestry Research
28 Windmill Road, West Croydon, CR0 2XN

The Metcalfe Society
29 Farriers Close, Bramley, RG26 5AX Tel: 01256 883633
Fax: 01256 883633 Email: diane_howarth@uk.ibm.com
WWW: http://www.metcalfe.org.uk

Morbey Family History Group
23 Cowper Crescent, Bengeo, Hertford, SG14 3DZ

Morgan Society of England & Wales
11 Arden Drive, Dorridge, Solihull, B93 8LP Tel: 01564 774020,
Fax: 01564 774020 Email: morgansociety@tesco.net
WWW: http://freepages.genealogy.rootsweb.com/~morgansociety
WWW: http://homepages.tesco.net/n.morganpublications/morganpu.htm

Moxon Family Research Trust
1 Pine Tree Close, Cowes, PO31 8DX Tel: 01983 296921 Email:
john@j.c.moxon.freeserve.co.uk WWW: www.moxon.org.uk

Moxon Society
59 Grantham Road, Sleaford., NG34 7NG Tel: 01529 304426,

Offley Family Society
2 The Green, Codicote, Hitchin, SG4 8UR Tel: 01438-820006
Email: joffley.htg@care4free.net
WWW: http://homepages.ntlworld.com/kevin.offley/

Orton Family History Society
25a Longwood Avenue, Bingley, BD16 2RX
Email: derek@beckd.freeserve.co.uk
WWW: www.redflag.co.uk/ortonfhs.htm

Palgrave Society
Crossfield House, Dale Road, Stanton, Bury St Edmunds, IP31
2DY Tel: 01359-251050, Fax: 01359-251050
Email: DerekPalgrave@btinternet.com
WWW: www.ffhs.org.uk/members/palgrave.htm

Penty Family Name Society
Kymbelin, 30 Lych Way, Horsell Village, GU21 4QG Tel:
01483-764904 Email: PENTYTREE@AOL.COM

Percy-Piercy Family History Society
32 Ravensdale Avenue, North Finchley, London, N12 9HT

Pomerology
The Keep, 3 Stokehouse Street, Poundbury, Dorchester, DT1
3GP Tel: 01305 257570 Tel: 01305 257912
Email: pomerology@compuserve.com,

Rose Family Society
62 Olive Street, Grimsby, L3M 2C4 Tel: **-905-945-3352
Email: gordrose@vaxxine.com,

Serman, Surman Family History Society
24 Monks Walk, Bridge Street, Evesham, WR11 4SL Tel: 01386 49967 Fax: 01386 49967 Email: design@johnsermon.demon.co.uk WWW: www.johnsermon.demon.co.uk
Silverthorne Family Association
1 Cambridge Close, Lawn, Swindon, SN3 1JQ
Tel: 01793 537103,
Society of Cornishes
1 Maple Close, Tavistock, PL19 9LL Tel: 01822 614613
Fax: 01822 614613 Email: cornish@one-name.org
Sole Society
49 Kennel Ride, North Ascot, SL5 7NJ Tel: 01344 883700
Email: info@sole.org.uk
WWW: www.solesociety.freeserve.co.uk
Spencer Family
1303 Azalea Lane, Dekalb, 60115
Stockdill Family History Society
6 First Avenue, Garston, Watford, WD2 6PZ Tel: 01923-675292,
Fax: 01923-675292 Email: roystock@compuserve.com
WWW: http://ourworld.compuserve.com/homepages/roystock
The Stockton Society
The Leas, 28 North Road, Builth Wells, LD2 3BU Tel: 01982 551667 Email: cestrienne@aol.com
Swinnerton Society
30 Coleridge Walk, London, NW11 6AT Tel: (020) 8458-3443
Email: roger.swynnerton@whichnet
Talbot Research Organisation
142 Albemarle Avenue, Elson, Gosport., PO12 4HY Tel: 023 92589785 WWW: http://www.kiamara.demon.co.uk/index.html
Toseland Clan Society
40 Moresdale Lane, Seacroft, Leeds, LS14 5SY
Fax: 0113-225-9954
Tyrrell Family History Society
16 The Crescent, Solihull, B91 7PE
Watkins Family History Society
PO Box 1698, Douglas, 31534-1698 Tel: 912-383-0839
Email: watkinsfhs@alltel.net
buzzwatk@aol.com WWW:
http://www.iinet.net.au/~davwat/wfhs/
Witheridge Family History Society
6 Nore Close, Gillingham., ME7 3DG

AUSTRALIA

Society of Australian Genealogists
Richmond Villa, 120 Kent Street, Observatory Hill, Sydney 2000 Tel: 61-02-92473953 Fax: 61-02-92414872
Email: socgenes@ozemail.com.au

NEW SOUTH WALES
1788-1820 Pioneer Association
PO Box 57, Croydon, New South Wales, 2132
Tel: (02)-9797-8107
Australian Society of the Lace Makers of Calais Inc
PO Box 946, Batemans Bay, New South Wales, 2536
Tel: 0244-718168, 0244-723421 Email: carolynb@acr.net.au
Bega Valley Genealogical Society Inc
PO Box 19, Pambula, New South Wales, 2549
Berrima District Historical & Family History Society Inc
PO Box 851, Bowral, New South Wales, 2576
Blayney Shire Local & Family History Society Group Inc
c/o The Library, 48 Adelaide Street, Blayney, New South Wales, 2799 Email: blayney.library@cww.octec.org.au
Botany Bay Family History Society Inc
PO Box 1006, Sutherland, New South Wales, 2232
Broken Hill Family History Group
PO Box 779, 75 Pell Street, Broken Hill, New South Wales, 2880 Tel: 08-80-881321
Burwood Drummoyne & District Family History Group
c/o Burwood Central Library, 4 Marmaduke Street, Burwood, New South Wales, 2134
Cape Banks Family History Society
PO Box 67, Maroubra, New South Wales, NSW 2035
Email: hazelb@compassnet.com.au
Web: www.ozemail.com.au/mhazelb/capebank
Capital Territory Historical & Genealogical Society of Canberra
GPO Box 585, Canberra, ACT 2601
Casino & District Family History Group Inc
PO Box 586, Casino, New South Wales, 2470
Email: hughsie@nor.com

Central Coast FHG Inc
PO Box 4090 East Gosford NSW 2250
Coffs Harbour District Family History Society Inc
PO Box 2057, Coffs Harbour, New South Wales, 2450
Cowra FHG Inc
PO Box 495, Cowra, New South Wales, 2794
Deniliquin Family History Group Inc
PO Box 144, Multi Arts Hall, Cressy Street, Denilquin, New South Wales, 2710 Tel: (03)-5881-3980 Fax: (03)-5881-1270
Dubbo & District FHS Inc
PO Box 868 Dubbo NSW 2830
Family History Society - Singleton Inc
PO Box 422, Singleton, New South Wales, 2330
Fellowship of First Fleeters
First Fleet House, 105 Cathedral Street, Woolloomooloo, New South Wales, 2000 Tel: (02)-9360-3988
Forbes Family History Group Inc
PO Box 574, Forbes, New South Wales, 2871
Tel: 0411-095311-(mobile)
Goulburn District Family History Society Inc
PO Box 611, Goulburn, New South Wales, 2580
Griffith Genealogical & Historical Society Inc
PO Box 270, Griffith, New South Wales, 2680
Gwydir Family History Society Inc
PO Box EM61, East Moree, New South Wales, 2400
Tel: (02)-67549235-(President)
Hastings Valley Family History Group Inc
PO Box 1359, Port Macquarie, New South Wales, 2444
Hawkesbury FHG
C/o Hawkesbury City Council Library, Dight Street, Windsor, New South Wales, 2756
Hill End Family History Group
Sarnia, Hill End, New South Wales, 2850
Hornsbury Kuring-Gai FHS Inc
PO Box 680, Hornsby, New South Wales, 2077
Illawarra FHG
PO Box 1652 South Coast Mail Centre, Wollongong 2521
Inverell District FHG Inc
PO Box 367, Inverell, New South Wales, 2360
Leeton Family History Society
PO Box 475, Centre Point, Pine Avenue, Leeton, New South Wales, 2705 Tel: 02-6955-7199, 02-6953-2301
Little Forest Family History Research Group
PO Box 87, 192 Little Forest Road, Milton, New South Wales, 2538 Tel: 02-4455-4780, 02-4456-4223
Email: cathyd@shoalhaven.net.au
Web: www.shoalhaven.net.au/~cathyd/groups.html
Liverpool & District Family History Society
PO Box 830, Liverpool, New South Wales, 2170
Manning Wallamba FHS
c/o Greater Taree City Library, Pulteney Street, Taree, New South Wales, 2430
Milton Ulladulla Genealogical Society Inc
PO Box 619, Ulladulla, New South Wales, 2539
Tel: 02-4455-4206
Nepean Family History Society
PO Box 81, Emu Plains, New South Wales, 2750
Tel: (02)-47-353-798 Email: istack@penrithcity.nsw.gov.au
Web: www.penrithcity.nsw.gov.au/nfhs/nfhshome.htm
New South Wales Association of Family History Societies
PO Box 48, Waratah, New South Wales, 2298
Newcastle Family History Society
PO Box 189, Adamstown, New South Wales, 2289
Orange Family History Society
PO Box 930, Orange, New South Wales, 2800
Port Stephens-Tilligerry & Districts FHS
PO Box 32, Tanilba Bay, New South Wales, 2319
Richmond River Historical Society Inc
PO Box 467, 165 Molesworth Street, Lismore, New South Wales, 2480 Tel: 02-6621-9993
Richmond-Tweed Family History Society
PO Box 817, Ballina, New South Wales, 2478
Email: warmer@nor.com.au
Ryde District Historical Society Inc
770 Victoria Road, Ryde, New South Wales, 2112
Tel: (02)-9807-7137
Scone & Upper Hunter Historical Society Inc
PO Box 339, Kingdon Street, Upper Hunter, Scone, New South Wales, 2337 Tel: 02-654-51218
Shoalhaven Family History Society Inc
PO Box 591, Nowra, New South Wales, 2541 Tel: 02-44221253
Fax: 02-44212462 Email: jmoorley@shoal.net.au

Snowy Mountains Family History Group
PO Box 153, Cooma, New South Wales, 2630
Wagga Wagga & District Family History Society Inc
PO Box 307, Wagga Wagga, New South Wales, 2650
Wingham FHG
PO Box 72, Wingham, New South Wales, 2429
Young & District FHG Inc
PO Box 586, Young, New South Wales, 2594
Blue Mountains Family History Society
PO Box 97, Springwood, NSW, NSW 2777 Fax: 02-4751-2746
Dubbo & District Family History Society Inc
PO Box 868, Dubbo, NSW, 2830 Tel: 068-818635
Illawara Family History Group
The Secretary, PO Box 1652, South Coast Mail Centre,
Wollongong, NSW, 2521 Tel: (02)-42622212
Web: www.magna.com.au/~vivienne/ifhg.htm
Lithgow & District Family History Society
PO Box 516, Lithgow, NSW, 2790

NORTHERN TERRITORY
Genealogical Society of the Northern Territory
PO Box 37212, Winnellie, Northern Territory, 0821
Tel: 08-898-17363

QUEENSLAND
Queensland Family History Society
PO Box 171, Indooroonilly, Brisbane, Oueensland, 4O68
Beaudesert Branch
Genealogical Soc of Queensland Inc
PO Box 664, Beaudesert, Queensland, 4285
Bundaberg Genealocical association Inc
PO Box 103, Bundaberg, Queensland, 4670
Burdekin Contact Group Family Hist Assn of N Qld Inc
PO Box 393, Home Hill, Queensland, 4806
Caboolture FH Research Group Inc
PO Box 837, Caboolture, Queensland, 4510
Cairns & District Family History Society Inc
PO Box 5069, Cairns, Queensland, 4870 Tel: 07-40537113
Central Queensland Family History Asociation
PO Box 8423, Woolloongabba Queensland 4102
Charters Towers & Dalrymple F H Association Inc
PO Box 783, 54 Towers Street, Charters Towers, Queensland,
4820 Tel: 07-4787-2124
Cooroy Noosa Genealogical & Historical Research Group Inc
PO Box 792, Cooroy, Queensland, 4563
Email: wefielder@bigpond.com.au
Dalby FHS inc
PO Box 962, Dalby, Queensland, 4405
Darling Downs Family History Society
PO Box 2229, Toowoomba, Queensland, 4350
Genealogical Society of Queensland Inc
PO Box 8423, Woolloongabba, Queensland, 4102
Gladstone Branch G.S.Q.
PO Box 1778, Gladstone, Queensland, 4680
Gold Coast & Albert Genealogical Society
PO Box 2763, Southport, Queensland, 4215
Gold Coast Family History Research Group
PO Box 1126, Southport, Gold Coast, Queensland, 4215
Goondiwindi & District Family History Society
PO Box 190, Goondiwindi, Queensland, 4390 Tel: 0746712156
Fax: 0746713019 Email: pez@bigpond.com
Gympie Ancestral Research Society Inc
PO Box 767, Gympie, Queensland, 4570
Ipswich Genealogical Society Inc.
PO Box 323, 1st Floor, Ipswich Campus Tafe, cnr. Limestone &
Ellenborough Streets, Ipswich, Queensland, 4305
Tel: (07)-3201-8770
Kingaroy Family History Centre
PO Box 629, James Street, Kingaroy, Queensland, 4610
Mackay Branch Genealogical Society of Queensland Inc
PO Box 882, Mackay, Queensland, 4740 Tel: (07)-49426266
Maryborough District Family History Society
PO Box 408, Maryborough, Queensland, 4650
Mount Isa Family History Society Inc
PO Box 1832, Mount Isa, Queensland, 4825
Email: krp8@+opend.com.au
North Brisbane Branch - Genealogical Soc of Queensland Inc
PO Box 353, Chermside South, Queensland, 4032
Queensland FHS Inc
PO Box 171, Indooroophilly, Queensland, 4068
Rockhampton Genealogical Society of Queensland Inc
PO Box 992, Rockhampton, Queensland, 4700

Roma & District Local & Family History Society
PO Box 877, Roma, Queensland, 4455
South Burnett Genealogical & Family History Society
PO Box 598, Kingaroy, Queensland, 4610
Southern Suburbs Branch - G.S.Q. Inc
PO Box 844, Mount Gravatt, Queensland, 4122
Sunshine Coast Historical & Genealogical Resource Centre Inc
PO Box 1051, Nambour, Queensland, 4560
Toowoomba Family History Centre
c/o South Town Post Office, South Street, Toowoomba,
Queensland, 4350 Tel: 0746-355895
Townsville - Fam Hist Assoc of North Queensland Inc
PO Box 6120, Townsville M.C., Queensland, 4810
Whitsunday Branch - Genealogical Soc of Queensland Inc
PO Box 15, Prosperpine, Queensland, 4800

SOUTH AUSTRALIA
South Australian Genealogical & Heraldic Society
GPO Box 592, Adelaide 5001, South Australia
Tel: (08)-8272-4222 Fax: (08)-8272-4910
Email: saghs@dove.net.au Web: dove.net.au/~saghs
South East FHG Inc
PO Box 758, Millicent, South Australia, 5280
Southern Eyre Peninsula FHG
26 Cranston Street, Port Lincoln, South Australia, 5606
Whyalla FHG
PO Box 2190, Whyalla Norrie, South Australia, 5608
Yorke Peninsula Family History Group - 1st Branch SAGHS
PO Box 260, Kadina, South Australia, 5554

TASMANIA
Genealogical Society of Tasmania
PO Box 60, Prospect, Tasmania, 7250
Tasmanian FHS Inc
PO Box 161 Lanceston 7250
VICTORIA
Ararat Genealogical Society inc
PO Box 361, Ararat, Victoria, 3377
Australian Institute of Genealogical Studies
PO Box 339, Blackburn, Victoria, 3130
Email: aigs@alphalink.com.all
Web: www.alphalink.com.au/~aigs/index.htm
Benalla & District Family History Group Inc
PO Box 268, St Andrews Church Hall, Church Street, Benalla,
Victoria, 3672 Tel: (03)-57-644258
Bendigo Regional Genealogical Society Inc
PO Box 1049, Bendigo, Victoria, 3552
Cobram Genealogical Group
PO Box 75, Cobram, Victoria, 3643
East Gippsland Family History Group Inc
PO Box 1104, Bairnsdale, Victoria, 3875
Echuca/Moama Family History Group Inc
PO Box 707, Echuca, Victoria, 3564
Emerald Genealogy Group
62 Monbulk Road, Emerald, Victoria, 3782
Euroa Genealogical Group
43 Anderson Street, Euroa, Victoria, 3666
First Fleet Fellowship Victoria Inc
Cnr Phayer & Barnet Streets, South Melbourne, Victoria, 3205
Geelong Family History Group Inc
PO Box 1187, Geelong, Victoria, 3220
Email: flw@deakin.edu.au
Web: www.home.vicnet.net.au/wgfamhist/index.htm
Genealogical Society of Victoria
Ancestor House, 179 Queen Street, Melbourne, Victoria, 3000
Tel: +61-3-9670-7033 Fax: +61-3-9670-4490
Email: gsv@gsv.org.au Web: www.gsv.org.au
Hamilton Family & Local History Group
PO Box 816, Hamilton, Victoria, 3300 Tel: 61-3-55-724933
Fax: 61-3-55-724933 Email: ham19.@mail.vicnet.net.au
Web: www.freenet.com.au/hamilton
Italian Historical Society
185 Faraday Street, Carlton, Victoria, 3053
Kerang & District Family History Group
PO Box 325, Kerang, Victoria, 3579
Mid Gippsland Family History Society Inc
PO Box 767, Morwell, Victoria, 3840
Mildura & District Genealogical Society Inc
PO Box 2895, Mildura, Victoria, 3502
Narre Warren & District Family History Group
PO Box 149, Narre Warren, Victoria, 3805
Web: www.ozemail.com.au/~narre/fam-hist.html

Nathalia Genealogical Group Inc
R.M.B. 1003, Picola, Victoria, 3639
Port Genealogical Society of Victoria Inc
PO Box 1070, Warrambool, Victoria, 3280
Email: joyceaustin@start.co.au
Sale & District Family History Group Inc
PO Box 773, Sale, Victoria, 3850
Stawell Biarri Group for Genealogy Inc
PO Box 417, Stawell, Victoria, 3380
Swam Hill Genealogical & Historical Society Inc
PO Box 1232, Swan Hill, Victoria, 3585
Toora & District Family History Group Inc
PO Box 41, Toora, Victoria, 3962
Wangaratta Genealogical Soc Inc
PO Box 683, Wangaratta, Victoria, 3676
West Gippsland Genealogical Society Inc
PO Box 225, Old Shire Hall, Queen Street, Warragul, Victoria,
3820 Tel: 03-56252743 Email: watts@dcsi.net.au
Web: www.vicnet.net.au/~wggs/
Wimmera Association for Genealogy
PO Box 880, Horsham, Victoria, 3402
Wodonga FHS Inc
PO Box 289, Wodonga, Victoria, 3689
Yarram Genealogical Group Inc
PO Box 42, 161 Commercial Road, Yarram, Victoria, 3971

WESTERN AUSTRALIA
**Australasian Federation of Family History Organisations
(AFFHO)**
c/o 6/48 May Street, Bayswater, Western Australia, 6053
Geraldton FHS
PO Box 2502, Geralton 6531, Western Australia
Web: www.com.au/gol/genealogy/gfhs/gfhsmain.htm
Goldfields Branch
West Australian Genealogical Society Inc
PO Box 1462, Kalgoorlie, Western Australia, 6430
Melville Family History Centre
PO Box 108 (Rear of Church of Jesus Christ Latter Day Saints,
308 Preston Point Road, Attadale, Melville, Western Australia,
6156
Western Australia Genealogical Society Inc
6/48 May Street, Bayswater, Western Australia 6053
Tel: 08-9271-4311 Fax: 08-9271-4311
Email: wags@cleo.murdoch.edu.au
Web: www.cleo.murdoch.edu.au/~wags

NEW ZEALAND
Bishopdale Branch NZ Society of Genealogists Inc.
c/o 19a Resolution Place, Christchurch, 8005 Tel: 03 351 0625
Cromwell Family History Group
3 Porcell Court, Cromwell, 9191
Fairlie Genealogy Group
c/o 38 Gray Street, Fairlie, 8771
General Research Institute of New Zealand
PO Box 12531, Thorndon, Wellington, 6038
Hawkes Bay Branch NZ Society of Genealogists Inc.
P O Box 7375, Taradale, Hawkes Bay
Kapiti Branch NZ Society of Genealogists Inc.
P O Box 6, Paraparaumu, Kapiti Coast, 6450
Mercury Bay Branch NZ Society of Genealogists Inc.
31 Catherine Crescent, Whitianga, 2856 Tel: 0 7 866 2355
Morrinsville Branch NZ Society of Genealogists Inc.
1 David St., Morrinsville, 2251
N.Z. Fencible Society
P O Box 8415, Symonds Street, Auckland, 1003
New Zealand Family History Society
P O Box13,301, Armagh, Christchurch Tel: 03 352 4506
Email: ranz@xtra.co.nz
New Zealand Family History Society Inc
PO Box 13301, Armagh, Christchurch Email: ranz@extra.co.nz
New Zealand Society of Genealogists Inc
PO Box 8795, Symonds Street, AUCKLAND, 1035
Tel: 09-525—0625 Fax: 09-525-0620

Northern Wairoa Branch NZ Society of Genealogists Inc.
60 Gordon Street, Dargaville, 300
NZ Society of Genealogists Inc. - Alexandra Branch
21 Gregg Street, Alexandra, 9181
Palmerston North Genealogy Group
P O Box 1992, Palmerston North, 5301
Panmure Branch NZ Society of Genealogists Inc.
29 Mirrabooka Ave, Howick, Auckland, 1705

Papakura Branch NZ Society of Genealogists Inc.
P O Box 993, Papakura, Auckland
Polish Genealogical Society of New Zealand
Box 88, Urenui, Taranaki Tel: 06 754 4551
Email: pgs.newzealand@clear.net.nz
Rotorua Branch NZ Society of Genealogists Inc.
17 Sophia Street, Rotorua, 3201 Tel: 0 7 347 9122
Scottish Interest Group NZ Society of Genealogists Inc.
P O Box 8164, Symonds Street, Auckland, 1003
South Canterbury Branch NZ Society of Genealogists Inc.
9 Burnett Street, Timaru, 8601
Tairua Branch NZ Society of Genealogists Inc.
c/o 10 Pepe Road, Tairua, 2853
Te Awamutu Branch NZ Society of Genealogists Inc.
Hairini, RD1, Te Awamutu, 2400
Te Puke Branch NZ Society of Genealogists Inc.
20 Valley Road, Te Puke, 3071
Waimate Branch NZ Society of Genealogists Inc.
4 Saul Shrives Place, Waimate, 8791
Wairarapa Branch NZ Society of Genealogists Inc.
34 Rugby Street, Masterton, 5901
Whakatane Branch NZ Society of Genealogists Inc.
P O Box 203, Whakatane, 3080
Whangamata Genealogy Group
116 Hetherington Road, Whangamata, 3062
Whangarei Branch NZ Society of Genealogists Inc.
P O Box 758, Whangarei, 115 Tel: 09 434 6508

SOUTH AFRICA
Genealogical Institute of South Africa
115 Banheok Road, Stellenbosch, Western Cape, South Africa
Tel: 021-887-5070 Email: GISA@RENET.SUN.AC.ZA
Genealogical Society of South Africa
Suite 143, Postnet X2600, Houghton, 2041, South Africa
Human Sciences Research Council
Genealogy Information, HSRC Library & Information Service,
Private Bag X41, Pretoria 0001, South Africa
Tel: (012)-302-2636 Fax: (012)-302-2933
Email: ig@legii.hsrc.ac.za
West Rand Family History Society
The Secretary, PO Box 760, Florida 1710, South Africa

ZIMBABWE
Heraldry & Genealogy Society of Zimbabwe
Harare Branch, 8 Renfrew Road, Eastlea, Harare, Zimbabwe

NORTH AMERICA

CANADA

ALBERTA
Alberta Family Histories Society
PO Box 30270, Station B, Calgary, Alberta, T2M 4P1
Alberta Genealogical Society (Edmonton Branch)
Room 116, Prince of Wales Armouries, 10440-108 Avenue,
Edmonton, Alberta, T5H 3Z9 Tel: (403)-424-4429
Fax: (403)-423-8980 Email: agsedm@compusmart.ab.ca
Web: www.compusmart.ab.ca/abgensoc/branches.html
Alberta Genealogical Society Drayton Valley Branch
PO Box 6358, Drayton Valley, Alberta, T7A 1R8
Tel: 403-542-2787 Email: c_or_c@telusplanet.net
Alberta Genealogical Society Fort McMurray Branch
PO Box 6253, Fort McMurray, Alberta, T9H 4W1
Alberta Gene Soc Grande Prairie & District Branch
PO Box 1257, Grande Prairie, Alberta, T8V 4Z1
Alberta Gen Society Medicine Hat & District Branch
PO Box 971, Medicine Hat, Alberta, T1A 7G8
Alberta Gen Society Red Deer & District Branch
PO Box 922, Red Deer, Alberta, T4N 5H3
Email: evwes@telusplanet.net
Brooks & District Branch Alberta Genealogical Society
PO Box 1538, Brooks, Alberta, T1R 1C4
Ukrainian Genealogical & Historical Society of Canada
R.R.2, Cochrane, Alberta, T0L 0W0 Tel: (403)-932-6811

BRITISH COLUMBIA
British Columbia Genealogical Society
PO Box 88054, Lansdowne Mall, Richmond V6X 3T6
Campbell River Genealogy Club
PO Box 884, Campbell River, British Columbia, V9W 6Y4
Email: rcase@connected.bc.ca WWW: www.connected.bc.ca/~genealogy/

Comox Valley Family History Research Group
c/o Courtenay & District Museum & Archives, 360 Cliffe Street, Courtenay, British Columbia, V9N 2H9
Kamloops Genealogical Society
Box 1162, Kamloops, British Columbia, V2C 6H3
Kelowna & District Genealogical Society
PO Box 501, Station A, Kelowna, British Columbia, V1Y 7P1
Tel: 1-250-763-7159 Email: doug.ablett@bc.sympatico.ca
Nanaimo FHS
PO Box 1027, Nanaimo, British Columbia, V9R 5Z2
Port Alberni Genealogy Club
Site 322, Comp. 6, R.R.3, Port Alberni V9Y 7L7
Powell River Genealogy Club
PO Box 446, Powell River, British Columbia, V8A 5C2
Prince George Genealogical Society
PO Box 1056, Prince George, British Columbia, V2L 4V2
Revelstoke Genealogy Group
PO Box 2613, Revelstoke, British Columbia, V0E 2S0
Shuswap Lake Genealogical Society
R.R.1, Site 4, Com 4, Sorrento, British Columbia, V0E 2W0
South Okanagan Genealogical Society
c/o Museum, 785 Main Street, Penticton V2A 5E3
Vernon & District FHS
PO Box 1447, Vernon, British Columbia, V1T 6N7
Victoria Genealogical Society
PO Box 45031, Mayfair Place, Victoria V8Z 7G9

MANITOBA
Canadian Federation of Gen & Family History Societies
227 Parkville Bay, Winnipeg, Manitoba, R2M 2J6
WWW: www.geocities.com/athens/troy/2274/index.html
East European Genealogical Society
PO Box 2536, Winnipeg, Manitoba, R3C 4A7
La Societe Historique de Saint Boniface
220 Ave de la Cathedral, Saint Boniface, Manitoba, R2H 0H7
Manitoba Genealogical Society
Unit A, 1045 St James Street, Winnipeg, Manitoba, R3H 1BI
South West Branch of Manitoba Genealogical Society
53 Almond Crescent, Brandon, Manitoba, R7B 1A2
Tel: 204-728-2857 Email: mla@access.tkm.mb.ca
Winnipeg Branch of Manitoba Genealogical Society
PO Box 1244, Winnipeg, Manitoba, R3C 2Y4

NEW BRUNSWICK
Centre d'Etudes Acadiennes
Universite de Moncton, Moncton, New Brunswick, E1A 3E9
New Brunswick Genealogical Society
PO Box 3235, Station B, Fredericton E3A 5G9

NEWFOUNDLAND & LABRADOR
Newfoundland & Labrador Genealogical Society
Colonial Building, Military Road, St John's A1C 2C9

NOVA SCOTIA
Archelaus Smith Historical Society
PO Box 291, Clarks Harbour, Nova Scotia, B0W 1P0
Email: timkins@atcon.com
Cape Breton Genealogical Society
PO Box 53, Sydney, Nova Scotia, B1P 6G9
Genealogical Association of Nova Scotia
PO Box 641, Station Central, Halifax, Nova Scotia, B3J 2T3
Queens County Historical Society
PO Box 1078, Liverpool, Nova Scotia, B0T 1K0
Shelburne County Genealogical Society
PO Box 248 Town Hall, 168 Water St, Shelburne B0T 1W0

ONTARIO
British Isles Family History Society of Greater Ottowa
Box 38026, Ottawa, Ontario, K2C 1N0
Bruce & Grey Branch - Ontario Genealogical Society
PO Box 66, Owen Sound, Ontario, N4K 5P1
Bruce County Genealogical Society
PO Box 1083, Port Elgin, Ontario, N0H 2C0
Elgin County Branch Ontario Genealogical Society
PO Box 20060, St Thomas, Ontario, N5P 4H4

Essex County Branch Ontario Genealogical Society
PO Box 2, Station A, Windsor, Ontario, N9A 6J5
Halton-Peel Branch Ontario Genealogical Society
PO Box 70030, 2441 Lakeshore Road West, Oakville, Ontario, L6L 6M9 Email: jwatt@ica.net
WWW: www.hhpl.on.c9/sigs/ogshp/ogshp.htm

Hamilton Branch Ontario Genealogical Society
PO Box 904, LCD 1, Hamilton, Ontario, L8N 3P6
Huron County Branch Ontario Genealogical Society
PO Box 469, Goderich, Ontario, N7A 4C7
Jewish Genealogical Society of Canada
PO Box 446, Station A, Willowdale, Ontario, M2N 5T1
Email: henry_wellisch@tvo.org
Kawartha Branch Ontario Genealogical Society
PO Box 861, Peterborough, Ontario, K9J 7AZ
Kent County Branch Ontario Genealogical Society
PO Box 964, Chatham, Ontario, N7M 5L3
Kingston Branch Ontario Genealogical Society
PO Box 1394, Kingston, Ontario, K7L 5C6
Lambton County Branch Ontario Genealogical Society
PO Box 2857, Sarnia, Ontario, N7T 7W1
Lanark County Genealogical Society
PO Box 512, Perth, Ontario, K7H 3K4
Email: gjbyron@magma.ca
WWW: www.globalgenealogy.com/LCGs
Marilyn Adams Genealogical Research Centre
PO Box 35, Ameliasburgh, Ontario, K0K 1A0
Tel: 613-967-6291
Niagara Peninsula Branch Ontario Genealogical Society
PO Box 2224, St Catharines, Ontario, L2R 7R8
Nipissing District Branch Ontario Genealogical Society
PO Box 93, North Bay, Ontario, P1B 8G8
Norfolk County Branch Ontario Genealogical Society
PO Box 145, Delhi, Ontario, N4B 2W9
Email: oxford.net/~mihaley/ogsnb/main.htm
Nor-West Genealogy & History Society
PO Box 35, Vermilion Bay, Ontario, P0V 2V0 Tel: 807-227-5293
Norwich & District Historical Society
c/o Archives, R.R. #3, Norwich, Ontario, N0J 1P0 Tel: (519)-863-3638
Ontario Genealogical Society
Suite 102, 40 Orchard View Boulevard, Toronto, Ontario, M4R 1B9 Web: www.ogs.on.ca
Ontario Genealogical Society (Toronto Branch)
Box 513, Station Z, Toronto, Ontario, M4P 2GP
Ottawa Branch Ontario Genealogical Society
PO Box 8346, Ottawa, Ontario, K1G 3H8
Perth County Branch Ontario Genealogical Society
PO Box 9, Stratford, Ontario, N5A 6S8 Tel: 519-273-0399
Simcoe County Branch Ontario Genealogical Society
PO Box 892, Barrie, Ontario, L4M 4Y6
Sioux Lookout Genealogical Club
PO Box 1561, Sioux Lookout, Ontario, P8T 1C3
Societe Franco-Ontarienne DHistoire et de Genealogie
C.P.720, succursale B, Ottawa, Ontario, K1P 5P8
Stormont Dundas & Glengarry Genealogical Society
PO Box 1522, Cornwall, Ontario, K6H 5V5
Sudbury District Branch Ontario Genealogical Society
c/o Sudbury Public Library, 74 MacKenzie Street, Sudbury, Ontario, P3C 4X8 Tel: (705)-674-9991 Email: fredie@isys.ca
Thunder Bay District Branch Ontario Genealogical Soc
PO Box 10373, Thunder Bay, Ontario, P7B 6T8
Upper Ottawa Genealogical Group
PO Box 972, Pembroke, Ontario, K8A 7M5
Waterdown East Flamborough Heritage Society
PO Box 1044, Waterdown, Ontario, L0R 2H0 Tel: 905-689-4074
Waterloo-Wellington Branch Ontario Genealogical Soc
153 Frederick Street, Ste 102, Kitchener, Ontario, N2H 2M2
Email: lestrome@library.uwaterloo.ca
Web: www.dos.iwaterloo.ca/~marj/genealogy/ww.html
West Elgin Genealogical & Historical Society
22552 Talbot Line, R.R.#3, Rodney, Ontario, N0L 2C0
Whitby - Oshawa Branch Ontario Genealogical Society
PO Box 174, Whitby, Ontario, L1N 5S1

QUEBEC
Brome County Historical Society
PO Box 690, 130 Lakeside, Knowlton, Quebec, J0E 1V0
Tel: 450-243-6782
Federation Quebecoise des Societies de Genealogie
C.P. 9454, Sainte Foy, Quebec, G1V 4B8
Les Patriotes Inc
105 Prince, Sorel, Quebec, J3P 4J9
Missisquoi Historical Society
PO Box 186, Stanbridge East, Quebec, J0J 2H0
Tel: (450)-248-3153 Email: sochm@globetrotter.com
Quebec Family History Society
PO Box 1026, Postal Station, Pointe Claire, Quebec, H9S 4H9

Societ de Genealogie de la Maurice et des Bois Francs
C.P. 901, Trois Rivieres, Quebec, G9A 5K2
Societe de Conservation du Patrimoine de St Fracois de la Riviere du Sud
C P 306, 534 Boul St Francois Ouest, St Francois, Quebec, G0R 3A0
Societe de Genealogie de Drummondville
545 des Ecoles, Drummondville, Quebec, J2B 8P3
Societe de Genealogie de Quebec
C.P. 9066, Sainte Foy, Quebec, G1V 4A8
Societe de Genealogie des Laurentides
C.P. 131, 185 Rue Du Palais, St Jerome, Quebec, J7Z 5T7
Tel: (450)-438-8158
Web: www.societe-genealogie-laurentides.gc.ca
Societe de Genealogie et d'Histoire de Chetford Mines
671 boul. Smith Sud, Thetford Mines, Quebec, G6G 1N1
Societe d'Histoire d'Amos
222 1ere Avenue Est, Amos, Quebec, J9T 1H3
Societe d'Histoire et d'Archeologie des Monts
C.P. 1192, 675 Chemin du Roy, Sainte Anne des Monts, Quebec, G0E 2G0
Societe d'Histoire et de Genealogie de Matane
145 Soucy, Matane, Quebec, G4W 2E1
Societe d'Histoire et de Genealogie de Riviere du Loup
300 rue St Pierre, Riviere du Loup, Quebec, G5R 3V3
Tel: (418)-867-4245 Email: shgrd@icrdl.net
Web: www.icrdl.net/shgrdl/index.html
Societe d'Histoire et de Genealogie de Verdun
198 chemin de lAnce, Vaudreuil, Quebec, J7V 8P3
Societe d'histoire et de genealogie du Centre-du-Quebec
34-A, rue Laurier est, Victoriaville, Quebec, G6P 6P7
Tel: (819)-357-4029 Fax: (819)-357-9668
Email: geneatique@netscape.net Web: www.geneatique.qc.ca
Societe d'Histoire et de Genealogie Maria Chapdeleine
1024 Place des Copains, C.P. 201, Dolbeau, Quebec, G8L 3N5
Societe d'Histoire et Genealogie de Salaberry de Valley Field
75 rue St Jean Baptiste, Valleyfield, Quebec, J6T 1Z6
Societe Genealogie d'Argenteuil
378 Principale, Lachute, Quebec, J8H 1Y2
Societe Genealogique Canadienne-Francaise
Case Postale 335, Place d Armes, Montreal, Quebec, H2Y 2H1
Societie de Genealogie de L'Outaouaid Inc
C.P. 2025, Succ. B , Hull, Quebec, J8X 3Z2

SASKATCHEWAN
Battleford's Branch Saskatchewan Genealogical Society
8925 Gregory Drive, North Battleford, Saskatchewan, S9A 2W6
Central Butte Branch Saskatchewan Genealogical Society
P.O. Box 224, Central Butte, Saskatchewan, S0H 0T0
Grasslands Branch Saskatchewan Genealogical Society
P.O. Box 272, Mankota, Saskatchewan, S0H 2W0
Tel: 306-264-5149
Grenfell Branch Saskatchewan Genealogical Society
P.O. Box 61, Grenfell, Saskatchewan, S0G 2B0
Tel: (306)-697-3176
Moose Jaw Branch Saskatchewan Genealogical Society
1037 Henry Street, Moose Jaw, Saskatchewan, S6H 3H3
Pangman Branch Saskatchewan Genealogical Society
P.O. Box 23, Pangman, Saskatchewan, S0C 2C0
Radville Branch Saskatchewan Genealogical Society
P.O. Box 27, Radville, Saskatchewan, S0C 2G0
Regina Branch Saskatchewan Genealogical Society
95 Hammond Road, Regina, Saskatchewan, S4R 3C8
Saskatchewan Genealogical Society
1870 Lorne Street, Regina, Saskatchewan, S4P 3E1
South East Branch Saskatchewan Genealogical Society
P.O. Box 460, Carnduff, Saskatchewan, S0C 0S0
West Central Branch Saskatchewan Genealogical Society
P.O. Box 1147, Eston, Saskatchewan, S0L 1A0
Yorkton Branch Saskatchewan Genealogical Society
28 Dalewood Crescent, Yorkton, Saskatchewan, S3N 2P7

YUKON
Dawson City Museum & Historical Society
P.O. Box 303, Dawson City, Yukon, Y0B 1G0
Tel: 867-993-5291 Fax: 867-993-5839
Email: dcmuseum@yknet.yk.ca

FAMILY HISTORY SOCIETIES EUROPE

AUSTRIA
Heraldisch-Genealogische Gesellschaft 'Adler'
Universitatsstrasse 6, Wien, A-1096, Austria

BELGIUM
Cercle de Genealogie Juive de Belgique
74 Avenue Stalingrad, Bruxelles, B-1000, Belgium Tel: 32 0 2 512 19 63 Fax: 32 0 513 48 59
Email: mjb<d.dratwa@mjb-jmb.org>
Federation des Associations de Famille
Bruyeres Marion 10, Biez, B-1390, Belgium
Federation Genealogique et Heraldique de Belgique
Avenue Parmentier 117, Bruxelles, B-1150, Belgium
Office Genealogique et Heraldique de Belgique
Avenue C Thielemans 93, Brussels, B-1150, Belgium

CROATIA
Croatian Genealogical Society
2527 San Carlos Ave, San Carlos, CA, 94070, USA

CZECHOSLOVAKIA
Czechoslovak Genealogical Society International
PO Box 16225, St Paul, MN, 55116-0225, USA

DENMARK
Danish Soc. for Local History
Colbjornsensvej 8, Naerum, DK-2850, Denmark
Sammenslutningen af Slaegtshistoriske Foreninger
Klostermarker 13, Aalborg, DK-9000, Denmark
Email: ulla@silkeborg.bib.dk
Society for Danish Genealogy & Biography
Grysgardsvej 2, Copenhagen NV, DK-2400, Denmark
Web: www.genealogi.dk

ESTONIA
Estonia Genealogical Society
Sopruse puiestec 214-88, Tallin, EE-0034, Estland

FINLAND
Genealogiska Samfundet i Finland
Fredsgatan 15 B, Helsingfors, SF-00170, Finland
Helsingfors Slaktforskare R.F.
Dragonvagen 10, Helsingfors, FIN-00330, Finland

FRANCE
Amicale des Familles d'alliance Canadiennne-Francaise
BP10, Les Ormes, 86220, France
Amities Genealogiques Bordelaises
2 rue Paul Bert, Bordeaux, Aquitaine, 33000, France Tel: 05 5644 8199 Fax: 05 5644 8199
Assoc. Genealogique et Historique des Yvelines Nord
Hotel de Ville, Meulan, 78250, France
Association Catalane de Genealogie
BP 1024, Perpignan Cedex, Languedoc Rousillon, 66101,
Association de la Bourgeoisie Ancienne Francaise
74 Avenue Kleber, Paris, 75116, France
Association Genealogique de la Charente
Archives Departementales, 24 avenue Gambetta, Angouleme, Poitou Charentes, 16000, France
Association Genealogique de l'Anjou
75 rue Bressigny, Angers, Pays de la Loire, 49100, France
Association Genealogique de l'Oise
BP 626, Compiegne Cedex, Picardie, 60206, France
Association Genealogique des Bouches-du-Rhone
BP 22, Marseilles Cedex, Provence Alpes Cote d'Azur, 1,
Association Genealogique des Hautes Alpes
Archives Departementales, route de Rambaud, Gap, Provence Alpes Cote d'Azur, 5000, France
Association Genealogique du Pas de Calais
BP 471, Arras Cedex, Nord-Pas de Calais, 62028
Association Genealogique du Pays de Bray
BP 62, Serqueux, Normandie, 76440 Fax: 02 3509 8756
Association Genealogique du Var
BP 1022, Toulon Cedex, Provence Alpes Cote d'Azur, 83051
Association Genealogique Flandre-Hainaut
BP493, Valenciennes Cedex, Nord-Pas de Calais, 59321,
Association Recherches Genealogiques Historique d'Auvergne
Maison des Consuls, Place Poly, Clermont Ferrand, Auvergne, 63100, France
Bibliotheque Genealogique
3 Rue de Turbigo, Paris, 75001, France Tel: 01 4233 5821
Brive-Genealogie
Maison des Associations, 11 place J M Dauaier, Brive, Limousin, 19100, France

Centre de Recherches Genealogiques Flandre-Artois
BP 76, Bailleul, Nord-Pas de Calais, 59270, France
Centre d'Entraide Genealogique de France
3 Rue de Turbigo, Paris, 75001, France Tel: 33 4041 9909
Fax: 33 4041 9963 Email: cegf@usa.net
Web: www.mygale.org/04cabrigol/cegf/
Centre Departemental d'Histoire des Familles
5 place Saint Leger, Guebwiller, Alsace, 68500, France
Email: cdhf@telmat-net.fr Web: web.telemat-net-fr~cdhf
Centre Entraide Genealogique Franche Comte
35 rue du Polygone, Besancon, Franche Comte, 25000
Centre Genealogique de la Marne
BP 20, Chalons-en-Champagne, Champagne Ardennes, 51005
Centre Genealogique de Savoie
BP1727, Chambery Cedex, Rhone Alpes, 73017, France
Centre Genealogique de Touraine
BP 5951, Tours Cedex, Centre, 37059, France
Centre Genealogique des Cotes d'Armor
3bis rue Bel Orient, Saint Brieuc, Bretagne, 22000, France
Fax: 02 9662 8900
Centre Genealogique des Landes
Societe de Borda, 27 rue de Cazarde, Dax, Aquitaine, 40100,
Centre Genealogique des Pyrenees Atlantique
BP 1115, Pau Cedex, Aquitaine, 64011, France
Centre Genealogique du Perche
9 rue Ville Close, Bellame, Normandie, 61130, France Tel: 02
3383 3789
Centre Genealogique du Sud Ouest
Hotel des Societes Savantes, 1 Place Bardineau, Bordeaux,
Aquitaine, 33000, France
Centre Genealogique et Heraldique des Ardennes
Hotel de Ville, Charleville Mezieres, Champagne Ardennes, 8000
Centre Genealogique Protestant
54 rue des Saints-Peres, Paris, 75007, France
Cercle de Genealogie du Calvados
Archives Departementales, 61 route de Lion-sur-Mer, Caen,
Normandie, 14000, France
Cercle de Genealogie et d'Heraldique de Seine et Marne
BP 113, Melun Cedex, 77002, France
Cercle de Genealogie Juive (Jewish)
14 rue St Lazare, Paris, 75009, France Tel: 01 4023 0490
Fax: 01 4023 0490 Email: cgjgeniefr@aol.com
Cercle d'Etudes Genealogiques et Heraldique d'Ile-de-France
46 Route de Croissy, Le Vesinet, 78110, France
Cercle d'Histoire et Genealogique du Perigord
2 rue Roletrou, Perigueux, Aquitaine, 24000, France
Cercle Genealogique Bull
rue Jean Jaures, BP 53, Les-Clayes-sous-Bois, 78340, **Cercle
Genealogique d'Alsace**
Archives du Bas-Rhin, 5 rue Fischart, Strasbourg, Alsace, 67000
Cercle Genealogique d'Aunis et Saintonge
c/o Mr Provost, 10 ave de Metz, La Rochelle, Poitou Charentes,
17000, France
Cercle Genealogique de la Manche
BP 410, Cherbourg Cedex, Normandie, 50104, France
Cercle Genealogique de la Meurthe et Moselle
4 rue Emile Gentil, Briey, Lorraine, 54150, France
Cercle Genealogique de la Region de Belfort
c/o F Werlen, 4 ave Charles de Gaulle, Valdoie, Franche Comte, 90300
Cercle Genealogique de l'Eure
Archives Departementales, 2 rue de Verdun, Evreux Cedex,
Normandie, 27025, France
Cercle Genealogique de Saintonge
8 rue Mauny, Saintes, Poitou Charentes, 17100, France
Cercle Genealogique de Vaucluse
Ecole Sixte Isnard, 31 ter Avenue de la Trillade, Avignon,
Provence Alpes Cote d'Azur, 84000, France
Cercle Genealogique des Deux-Sevres
26 rue de la Blauderie, Niort, Poitou Charentes, 79000, **Cercle
Genealogique des P.T.T.**
BP33, Paris Cedex 15, 75721, France
Cercle Genealogique d'Ille-et-Vilaine
6 rue Frederic Mistral, Rennes, Bretagne, 35200, France Tel: 02
9953 6363
**Cercle Genealogique du C.E. de la Caisse d'Epargne Ile de
France-Paris**
19 rue du Louvre, Paris, 75001, France
Cercle Genealogique du Finistere
Salle Municipale, rue du Commandant Tissot, Brest, Bretagne,
29000, France Fax: 02 9843 0176 Email: cgf@eurobretagne.fr
Web: www.karolus.org/membres/cgf.htm

Cercle Genealogique du Haut-Berry
place Martin Luther King, Bourges, Centre, 18000, France
Fax: 02 4821 0483 Email: cgh-b@wanadoo.fr
Cercle Genealogique du Languedoc
18 rue de la Tannerie, Toulouse, Languedoc Rousillon, 31400,
France Tel: 05 6226 1530
Cercle Genealogique du Loir-et-Cher
11 rue du Bourg Neuf, Blois, Centre, 41000 Tel: 02 5456 0711
Cercle Genealogique d'Yvetot et du Pays de Caux
Pavillion des Fetes, Yvetot, Normandie, 76190, France
Cercle Genealogique et Historique du Lot et Garonne
13 rue Etienne Marcel, Villeneuve sur Lot, Aquitaine, 47340
Cercle Genealogique Poitevin
22bis rue Arsene Orillard, Poitiiers, Poitou Charentes, 86000
Cercle Genealogique Rouen Seine-Maritime
Archives Departementales, Cours Clemenceau, Normandie, 76101
Cercle Genealogique Saone-et-Loire
115 rue des Cordiers, Macon, Bourgogne, 71000, France
Cercle Genealogique Vendeen
Bat.H, 307bis, Cite de la Vigne aux Roses, La Roche-sur-Yon,
Pays de la Loire, 85000, France
Cercle Genealogique Versailles et Yvelines
Archives Departementales, 1 avenue de Paris, Versailles, 78000,
France Tel: 01 3952 7239 Fax: 01 3952 7239
Cercle Genelogique du Rouergue
Archives Departementales, 25 av Victor Hugo, Rodez,
Midi-Pyrenees, 12000, France
Club Genealogique Air France
CE Air France Roissy Exploitation, BP 10201, Roissy CDG
Cedex, 95703, France Fax: 01 4864 3220
Club Genealogique Group IBM France
CE IBM St Jean de Braye-Ste Marie, 50-56 ave Pierre Curie, St
Jean de Braye Cedex, 45807, France
Confederation Internationale de Genealogie et d'Heraldique
Maison de la Genealogie, 3 rue Turbigo, Paris, F - 75001,
Etudes Genealogiques Drome-Ardeche
14 rue de la Manutention, Valence, Rhone Alpes, 26000,
Federation Francaise de Genealogie
3 Rue de Turbigo, Paris, 75001, France Tel: 01 4013 0088
Fax: 01 4013 0089 Web: www.karolus.org
France-Louisuane/Franco-Americanie
Commission Retrouvailles, Centre CommercialeGatie, 80 avenue
du Maine, Paris, Overseas, 75014 Fax: 01 4047 8321
Web: www.noconnet.com:80/forms/cajunews.htm
Genealogie Algerie Maroc Tunisie
Maison Marechal Alphonse, Juin 28 Av. de Tubingen, Aix en
Provence, 13090, France
Genealogie Entraide Recherche en Cote d'Or
97 rue d'Estienne d'Orves, Clarmart, Bourgogne, 92140,
Genealogie et Histoire de la Caraibe
Pavillion 23, 12 avenue Charles de Gaulle, Le Pecq, Overseas,
78230, France Email: ghcaraibe@aol.com
Web: //members.aol.com/ghcaraibe
Groupement Genealogique de la Region dy Nord
BP 62, Wambrechies, Nord-Pas de Calais, 59118, France
Groupement Genealogique du Havre et de Seine Maritime
BP 80, Le Havre Cedex, Normandie, 76050 Tel: 02 3522 7633
Institut Francophone de Genealogie et d'Histoire
5 rue de l'Aimable Nanette, le Gabut, La Rochelle, Overseas,
17000 Tel: 05 4641 9032 Fax: 05 4641 9032
Institut Genealogique de Bourgogne
237 rue Vendome, BP 7076, Lyon, Bourgogne, 69301
Loiret Genealogique
BP 9, Orleans Cedex, Centre, 45016, France
Salon Genealogique de Vichy et du Centre
48 Boulevard de Sichon, Vichy, Auvergne, 3200, France
Web: www.genea.com
Section Genealogique de l'Assoc. Artistique-Banque de France
2 rue Chabanais, Paris, 75002, France
Societe Genealogique du Bas-Berry
Maison des Associations, 30 Espace Mendez France,
Chateauroux, Centre, 36000, France
Societe Genealogique du Lyonnais
7 rue Major Martin, Lyon, Rhone Alpes, 69001, France

GERMANY
Arbeirkreis fur Familienforschung e.V
Muhlentorturm, Muhlentortplatz 2, Lubeck, Schleswig-Holstein,
D - 23552, Germany
Bayerischer Landesverein fur Familienkunde
Ludwigstrasse 14/1, Munchen, Bayern, D - 80539, Germany
Tel: 089 28638 398 Email: blf@rusch.m.shuttle.de
Web: www.genealogy.com/gene/reg/BAY/BLF-d.html
Deutsche Zentalstelle fur Genealogie
Schongaver str. 1, Leipzig, D - 04329, Germany
Dusseldorfer Verein fur Familienkunde e.V
Krummenweger Strasse 26, Ratingen, Nordrhein Westfalen, D -
40885, Germany
**Herold - Verein fur Genealogie Heraldik und Reiwandte
Wissen-Scaaften**
Archiv Str. 12-14, Berlin, D -14195, Germany
Niedersachsischer Gesellschaft fur Familienkunde e.V
Stadtarchiv, Am Bokemahle 14 - 16, Hannover, Niedersachsen,
D - 30171, Germany
Oldenburgische Gesellschaft fur Familienkunde
Lerigauweg 14, Oldenurg, Niedersachsen, D - 26131, Germany
**Verein fur Familien-U. Wappenkunde in Wurttemberg und
Baden**
Postfach 105441, Stuttgart, Baden-Wuerttemberg, D - 70047,
Germany
Westdeutsche Gesellschaft fur Familienkunde e.V Sitz Koln
Unter Gottes Gnaden 34, Koln-Widdersdorf, Nordrhein
Westfalen, D - 50859, Germany Tel: 49 221 50 48 88
Zentralstelle fur Personnen und Familiengeschichte
Birkenweg 13, Friedrichsdorf, D - 61381, Germany

GREECE
Heraldic-Genealogical Society of Greece
56 3rd Septemvriou Str., Athens, GR - 10433, Greece

HOLLAND
Centraal Bureau voor Genealogie
P O Box 11755, The Hague, NL - 2502 AT, Netherlands
Tel: 070 315 0500 Fax: 070 347 8394 Web: www.cbg.nl

HUNGARY
Historical Society of Hungary
University of Eoetveos Lorand, Pesti Barnabas utca 1, Budapest,
H - 1052, Hungary Tel: 267 0966

ICELAND
The Genealogical Society
P O Box 829, Reykjavick, 121, Iceland Fax: 354 1 679840

ITALY
Ancetres Italien
3 Rue de Turbigo, Paris, 75001, France Tel: 01 4664 2722
Web: //members.aol.com/geneaita/

NETHERLANDS
Centraal Bureau voor Genealogie
P O Box 11755, The Hague, NL - 2502 AT, Netherlands
Tel: 070 315 0500 Fax: 070 347 8394 Web: www.cbg.nl
Central Bureau Voor Genealogie
PO Box 11755, 2502, The Hague, Netherland
**Koninklijk Nederlandsch Genootschap voor Geslacht-en
Wapen-Kunde**
P O Box 85630, Den Haag, 2508 CH, Netherlands
**Koninklijk Nederlandsch Genootschap voor Geslacht-en
Wapen-Kunde**
P O Box 85630, Den Haag, 2508 CH, Netherlands
Nederlandse Genealogische Vereniging
Postbus 976, Amsterdam, NL - 1000 AZ, Netherlands
Email: info@ngu.nl Web: www.ngu.nl
Nederlandse Genealogische Vereniging
Postbus 976, Amsterdam, NL - 1000 AZ, Netherlands
Email: info@ngu.nl Web: www.ngu.nl
Stichting 'Genealogisch Centrum Zeeland'
Wijnaardstraat, Goes, 4416DA Tel: 0113 232 895
Stichting 'Genealogisch Centrum Zeeland'
Wijnaardstraat, Goes, 4416DA Tel: 0113 232 895
The Caledonian Society
Zuiderweg 50, Noordwolde, NL 8391 KH Tel: 0561 431580
The Caledonian Society
Zuiderweg 50, Noordwolde, NL 8391 KH Tel: 0561 431580

NORWAY
Norsk Slektshistorik Forening
Sentrum Postboks 59, Oslo, N - 0101, Norway Tel: 2242 2204
Fax: 2242 2204

POLAND
Polish Genealogical Society of America
984 N. Milwaukee Ave, Chicago, IL, 60622, USA
Polish Genealogical Society of New Zealand
Box 88, Urenui, Taranaki, New Zealand Tel: 06 754 4551
Email: pgs.newzealand@clear.net.nz
SLOVAKIA
Slovak GHS At Matica Slovenska
Novomeskeho, 32, 036 52 Martin, Slovakia

SPAIN
Asociacion de Diplomados en Genealogia y Nobilaria
Alcala 20, 2 Piso, Madrid, 28014, Spain Tel: 34 522 3822
Fax: 34 532 6674
Asociacion de Hidalgos a Fuerto de Espana
Aniceto Marinas 114, Madrid, 28008, Spain
Cercle Genealogic del Valles
Roca 29, 5 2, Sabadell, Barcelona, 8208, Spain
Circulo de Estudios Genealogicos Familiares
Prado 21, Ateneo de Madrid, Madrid, 28014, Spain
Instituto Aragones de Investigaciones Historiograficas
Madre Sacremento 33, 1', Zaragoza, 50004, Spain
**Instituto de Estudios Heraldicos y Genealogicos de
Extremadura**
Lucio Cornelio Balbo 6, Caceres, 1004, Spain
Real Academia Matritense de Heraldica y Genealogia
Quintana 28, Madrid, 28008, Spain
Sociedad Toledana de Estudios Heraldicos y Genealogicos
Apartado de Correos No. 373, Toledo, Spain
**Societat Catalana de Genealogia Heraldica Sigillografia
Vexillologia**
P O Box 2830, Barcelona, 8080, Spain
**Societat Valenciana de Genealogia Heraldica Sigillografia
Vexillologia**
Les Tendes 22, Oliva, 46780, Spain
SWEDEN
Sveriges Slaktforskarforbund
Box 30222, Stockholm, 104 25, Sweden Tel: 08 695 0890
Fax: 08 695 0824 Email: genealog@genealogi.se

SWITZERLAND
Genealogical & Heraldry Association of Zurich
Dammbodenstrasse 1, Volketswil, CH-8604, Switzerland
Swiss Genealogical Society
Eggstr 46, Oberengstringen, CH 8102, Switzerland
Web: www.eye.ch/swissgen/SGFF.html
Swiss Society for Jewish Genealogy
P O Box 876, Zurich, CH-8021, Switzerland
Zentralstelle fur Genealogie
Vogelaustrasse 34, CH-8953, Switzerland
Fax: 44 1 742 20 84 Email: aicher@eyekon.ch

Registrars of Births, Marriages & Deaths
England, Wales and Scotland

Following is a list of Superintendent Registrars of Births, Marriages and Deaths in alphabetical order by County. We have also included details of Registration Sub Districts. **Note:** Many of the Registration Officers listed here share Office accommodation with other parties. When using the addresses given they should be prefixed "Superintendent Registrar, Register Office ...."

We offer the following advice to help readers and Superintendent Registrars
The volume and page number references which are found on the microfiche and film indexes of the General Register Office must only be used when applying for certificates from the GRO. These reference numbers are not a reference to the filing system used at local register offices and do not assist Superintendent Registrars in any way to find the entry. The General Register Office hold the records for the whole of England and Wales and therefore have their own filing system, whereas the majority of register offices are still manually searching handwritten index books which is extremely time consuming. Most offices only became computerised in the early 1990s and do not hold records before this date on computer and will never have the staff time to backlog 150 years of records. Finally, many offices are only part time, some just open a few hours per week. Unlike the larger offices they do not have receptionists or staff employed specifically to assist people researching their family history, and have to devote the majority of their time to providing certificates urgently required for passport applications, marriage bookings and pension applications.

Once the applicant has carried out their research fully using all the records and data widely available to them at no cost, they can apply to their local office with sufficient information for the Registrar to trace the entry within minutes instead of hours.

The General Register Office
Trafalgar Road, Birkdale, Southport, PR8 2HH Tel: 0151 471 4200 Tel: 0870 243 7788

England
Bath & North East Somerset, 12 Charlotte Street, Bath, BA1 2NF Tel: 01225-312032 Fax: 01225-334812
(Norton Radstock Sub-district), The Library, 119 High Street, Midsomer Norton, Bath, BA3 2DA Tel: 01761-418768

Bedfordshire
Ampthill Court House, Woburn Street, Ampthill, MK45 2HX Tel: 01525-403430 Fax: 01525-841984 Email: denmanm@csd.bedfordshire.gov.uk
Bedford, Pilgrim House 20 Brickhill Drive, MK41 7PZ Tel: 01234 290450 Fax: 01234 290454
Biggleswade, 142 London Road, Biggleswade, SG18 8EL Tel: 01767-312511 Fax: 01767-315033
Dunstable, Grove House, 76 High Street North, Dunstable, LU6 1NF Tel: 01582-660191 Fax: 01582-471004
Leighton Buzzard, Bossard House, West Street, Leighton Buzzard, LU7 7DA Tel: 01525-851486 Fax: 01525-381483
Luton, 6 George Street West, Luton, LU1 2BJ Tel: 01582-722603 Fax: 01582-429522

Berkshire
Bracknell Forest Easthampstead House, Town Square, Bracknell, RG12 1AQ Tel: 01344-35202 Fax: 01344-352010
Newbury, Peake House, 112 Newtown Road, Newbury, RG14 7EB Tel: 01635-48133 Fax: 01635-524694
Reading and Wokingham, Yeomanry House, 131 Castle Hill, RG1 7TA Tel: 0118 901 5120 Tel: 0118 901 5194 Fax: 0118 9510212
Slough, Slough Register Office, The Centre, Farnham Road, Slough, SL1 4UT Tel: 01753 787601 Fax: 01753 787605
Wokingham The Old School, Reading Road, Reading, RG41 1RJ Tel: 0118 978 2514 Fax: 0118 978 2813
(Wokingham Sub-district) see Wokingham
Windsor & Maidenhead, Town Hall, St Ives Road, Maidenhead, SL6 1RF Tel: 01628 796422 Fax: 01628 796625
(Ascot Sub-district), Bridge House, 18 Brockenhurst Road, Ascot, SL5 9DL Tel: 01344 628135 Fax: 01344 628135
(Maidenhead Sub-district), Town Hall, St Ives Road, Maidenhead, SL6 1RF Tel: 01628 796422 Fax: 01628 796625
(Windsor Sub-district), York House, Sheet Street, Windsor, SL4 1DD Tel: 01628 683652 Fax: 01682 683629

Birmingham MD
Birmingham, 300 Broad Street Birmingham, B1 2DE Tel: 0121-235-3421 Fax: 0121-303-1396

Bournemouth
159 Old Christchurch Road Bournemouth, BH1 1JS Tel: 01202 551668

Brighton and Hove
Brighton Town Hall, Bartholomews Brighton, BN1 1JA Tel: 01273-292016 Fax: 01273-292019
Hove Transferred to Brighton & Hove RD wef November 1998

City of Bristol, Quakers Friars Bristol, BS1 3AR Tel: 0117 903 8888 Fax: 0117 903 8877

Buckinghamshire
Aylesbury Vale, County Ofices, Walton Street, Aylesbury, HP20 1XF Tel: 01296-382581 Tel: 01296-395000 Fax: 01296-382675
Chiltern Hills, Wycombe Area Offices, Easton Street High Wycombe, HP11 1NH: 01494 475200 Tel: 01494 475205 Fax: 01494-475040
Chiltern & South Bucks Transferred to Chiltern Hills RD wef November 1998

Cambridgeshire
Cambridge Castle Lodge, Shire Hall, Castle Hill, Cambridge, CB3 0AP Tel: 01223 717401 Fax: 01223 717888, Email: Adrian.Wright@finance.camcnty.gov.uk
Ely, Old School House, 74 Market Street, Ely, CB7 4LS Tel: 01353-663824
Fenland, The Old Vicarage, Church Terrace, Wisbech, PE13 1BW Tel: 01945 467950 Fax: 01945 467950
Huntingdon Wykeham House, Market Hill, Huntingdon, PE29 3NN Tel: 01480 375821 Tel: 01480 375822 Fax: 01480 375725
Peterborough, The Lawns, 33 Thorpe Road, Peterborough, PE3 6AB Tel: 01733-566323 Fax: 01733-566049

Cheshire
Cheshire East Park Green Macclesfield, SK11 6TW Tel: 01625-423463 Fax: 01625-619225
Vale Royal Transferred to Cheshire Central wef April 1998
Chester West, Goldsmith House, Goss Street Chester, CH1 2BG Tel: 01244-602668 Fax: 01244-602934
Halton Heath Road Runcorn, WA7 5TN Tel: 01928-576797 Fax: 01928-573616
Cheshire Central Delamere House Chester Street, CW1 2LL Tel: 01270-505106 Fax: 01270 505107

Warrington Museum Street Warrington, WA1 1JX Tel: 01925-442762 Fax: 01925-442739

Stockport MD
Stockport, Greenhale House, Piccadilly Stockport, SK1 3DY Tel: 0161-474-3399 Fax: 0161-474-3390

Tameside MD
Tameside, Town Hall, King Street Dukinfield, SK16 4LA Tel: 0161-330-1177 Fax: 0161 342 2625

Trafford MD
Trafford, Town Hall, Tatton Road Sale, M33 1ZF Tel: 0161-912-3025 Fax: 0161 912 3031

Cleveland
Middlesbrough Corporation Road Middlesbrough, TS1 2DA Tel: 01642-262078 Fax: 01642 262091, Email: Available late 1998, Available late 1998
Redcar and Cleveland Westgate Guisborough, TS14 6AP Tel: 01287-632564 Fax: 01287 630768
Stockton-on-Tees, Nightingale House, Balaclava Street Stockton-on-Tees, TS18 2AL Tel: 01642-393156 Fax: 01642-393159

Cornwall
Bodmin, Lyndhurst, 66 Nicholas Street Bodmin, PL31 1AG Tel: 01208-73677 Fax: 01208-73677
Camborne-Redruth Roskear Camborne, TR14 8DN Tel: 01209-612924 Fax: 01209-612924
Falmouth, Berkeley House, 12-14 Berkeley Vale Falmouth, TR11 3PH Tel: 01326-312606 Fax: 01326-312606
Kerrier, The Willows, Church Street Helston, TR13 8NJ Tel: 01326-562848 Fax: 01326-562848
Launceston, 'Hendra', Dunheved Road Launceston, PL15 9JG Tel: 01566-772464 Fax: 01566-772464
Liskeard, 'Graylands', Dean Street Liskeard, PL14 4AH Tel: 01579-343442 Fax: 01579-343442
Penzance Apphington House, Alverton Place, Penzance, TR18 4JJ Tel: 01736 330093 Fax: 01736 330067
Stratton, The Parkhouse Centre, Ergue Gaberic Way Bude, EX23 8LD Tel: 01288-353209 Fax: 01288-353209
St. Austell 12 Carlyon Road St. Austell, PL25 4LD Tel: 01726-68974 Fax: 01726-67048
St. Germans Plougastel Drive, St Germans, Saltash, PL12 6DL Tel: 01752-842624 Fax: 01752-848556
Truro, Dalvenie House, New County Hall Truro, TR1 3AY Tel: 01872 322241 Fax: 01872 323891

Darlington
Darlington Central House Gladstone Street, DL3 6JX Tel: 01325-346600 Fax: 01325-346605

County Durham
Durham Central 40 Old Elvet Durham, DH1 3HN Tel: 0191-3864077 Fax: 0191383 9961
Durham Eastern, Acre Rigg, York Road Peterlee, SR8 2DP Tel: 0191-5866147 Fax: 0191 5184607
Durham Northern 7 Thorneyholme Terrace Stanley, DH9 0BJ Tel: 01207-235849 Fax: 01207-235334
(Chester le Street Sub-district), Civic Centre, Chester le Street, DH3 3UT Tel: 0191-388-3240
(Consett Sub-district), 39 Medomsley Road , Consett, DH8 5HE Tel: 01207-502797
(Stanley Sub-district), 7 Thorneyholme TerraceStanley, DH9 0BJ Tel: 01207-235849
Durham South Western 30 Galgate Barnard Castle, DL12 8BH Tel: 01833-637997 Tel: 01833-637336
Durham Western, Cockton House, 35 Cockton Hill Road Bishop Auckland, DL14 6HS Tel: 01388 607277 Fax: 01388 664388
(Bishop Auckland Sub-district), Cockton House, 35 Cockton Hill Bishop Auckland, DL14 6HS Tel: 01388 603404
(Crook Sub-district), The Community Health Clinic, Hope

Street Crook, DL15 9HU Tel: 01388-767630
(Weardale Sub-district), The Health Centre, Dales Street, Stanhope, Bishop Auckland, DL13 2XD Tel: 01388 527074

Hartlepool
Hartlepool Raby Road Hartlepool, TS24 8AF Tel: 01429-236369 Fax: 01429-236373 Email: registrar@hartlepool.gov.uk

Coventry MD
Coventry Cheylesmore Manor House Manor House Drive, CV1 2ND Tel: (024) 7683 3137 Fax: (024) 7683 3110

Cumbria
Barrow-in-Furness 74 Abbey Road Barrow-in-Furness, LA14 5UB Tel: 01229-894511 Fax: 01229-894513
Carlisle 23 Portland Square Carlisle, CA1 1PE Tel: 01228-607432 Fax: 01228-607434
Cockermouth Fairfield, Station Road, Maryport, CA13 9PT Tel: 01900 325960 Fax: 01900 325962
(Maryport Sub-district) 67 Wood Street Maryport, CA15 6LD Tel: 01900 812637 Fax: 01900 815079
(Workington Sub-district), Hill Park, Ramsay Brow Workington, CA14 4AR Tel: 01900 325160 Fax: 01900 325161
Kendal County offices Kendal, LA9 4RQ Tel: 01539 773567 Fax: 01539 773565
(Kirkby Lonsdale Sub-district) 15 Market Square, Kirkby Lonsdale, Carnforth, LA6 2AN Tel: 01542-71222
(Lakes Sub-district), Windermere Library Ellerthwaite, Windermere, LA23 2AJ Tel: 015394-62420
Millom, The Millom Council Centre, St Georges Road Millom, LA14 4DD Tel: 01229-772357 Fax: 01229-773412
Penrith Friargate Penrith, CA11 7XR Tel: 01768-242120 Fax: 01768-242122
(Alston Sub-district), Alston Register Office, Townhead Alston, CA9 3SL Tel: 01434-381784 Fax: 01434-381784
(Appleby Sub-district), Shire Hall, The Sands Appleby in Westmorland, CA16 6XN Tel: 017683-52976
Ulverston, Town Hall, Queen Street Ulverston, LA12 7AR Tel: 01229-894170 Fax: 01229-894172
Whitehaven, College House, Flatt Walks Whitehaven, CA28 7RW Tel: 01946 852690 Fax: 01946 852673
Wigton, Council Offices, South End Wigton, CA7 9QD Tel: 016973-42155 Fax: 016973-49967

Derbyshire
Amber Valley Market Place Ripley, DE5 3BT Tel: 01773-841380 Fax: 01773-841382
Ashbourne, Town Hall, Market Place Ashbourne, DE6 1ES Tel: 01335-300575 Fax: 01335-345252
Bakewell Town Hall Bakewell, DE45 1BW Tel: 0162-981-2261
(Matlock Sub-district) Firs Parade Matlock, DE4 3AS Tel: 01629-582870
Chesterfield New Beetwell Street Chesterfield, S40 1QJ Tel: 01246-234754 Fax: 01246-274493
Derby 9 Traffic Street Derby, DE1 2NL Tel: 01332 716030 Fax: 01332 716021
Erewash 87 Lord Haddon Road Ilkeston, DE7 8AX Tel: 0115-932-1014 Fax: 0115-932-6450
High Peak, Council Offices, Hayfield Road, Chapel-en-le-Frith,, High Peak, SK23 0QJ Tel: 01663-750473
High Peak , The Registrar's Office, Hardwick Square West Buxton, SK17 6PX Tel: 01298-25075
(Chapel en le Frith Sub-district), The Town Hall, Chapel en le Frith, SK23 0HB Tel: 01298-813559
(Glossop Sub-district), 46-50 High Street West, Glossop, SK13 8BH Tel: 01457-852425
South Derbyshire, Traffic Street, Derby, DE1 2NL Tel: 01332 716020 Tel: 01332 716025 Fax: 01332 716021
(South Derbyshire Sub-district), The Registrars Office, Civic Way, Swadlincote, DE11 0AB Tel: 01283 213976 Fax: 01283 213976

Devon
North Devon, Civic Centre, Barnstaple, EX31 1ED Tel: 01271-388456
Torridge, Council Offices, Windmill Lane, Northam,, Bideford, EX39 1BY Tel: 01237-474978 Fax: 01237-473385
Exeter, 1 Lower Summerlands, Heavitree Road, Exeter, EX1 2LL Tel: 01392 686260 Fax: 01392 686262
Holsworthy, 8 Fore Street, Holsworthy, EX22 6ED Tel: 01409-253262
East Devon, Dowell Street, Honiton, EX14 8LZ Tel: 01404-42531 Fax: 01404-41475,
South Hams, Follaton House, Plymouth road, Totnes, TQ9 5NE Tel: 01803-861234 Fax: 01803-868965, http://www.devon-cc.gov.uk
Mid Devon, The Great House, 1 St Peter Street, Tiverton, EX16 6NY Tel: 01884 255255 Fax: 01884 258852
Okehampton Transferred to West Devon wef July 1997
Teignbridge, 15 Devon Square, Newton Abbot, TQ12 2HR Tel: 01626 206341 Tel: 01626 206340 Fax: 01626 206346,
Plymouth, Lockyer Street, Plymouth, PL1 2QD Tel: 01752-268331 Fax: 01752-256046
West Devon, Town Council Offices, Drake Road, Tavistock, PL19 8AU Tel: 01822-612137 Fax: 01822-618935
Torbay, Oldway Mansion, Paignton, TQ3 2TU Tel: 01803-207130 Fax: 01803-525388

Dorset
East Dorset, King George V Pavillion, Peter Grant Way, Ferndown, BH22 9EN Tel: 01202-892325
North Dorset, Salisbury Road, Blandford Forum, DT11 7LN Tel: 01258-484096 Fax: 01258-484095
South Dorset, The Guildhall, St Edmund Street, Weymouth, DT4 8AS Tel: 01305-760899 Fax: 01305-772611
West Dorset, Mountfield Offices, Rax Lane, Bridport, DT6 3JL Tel: 01308 456047
Poole, Civic Centre Annexe, Park Road, Poole, BH15 2RN Tel: 01202-633744 Fax: 01202 633725

East Riding of Yorkshire
Beverley, 34 Lairgate, Beverley, HU17 8ES Tel: 01482-864205 Fax: 01482-679155
(Beverley B Sub-district), The Council Offices, Market Green, Cottingham, HU16 5QG Tel: 01482 393565 Fax: 01482 393567
(Hornsea Sub-district), The Court House, off Railway Street, Hornsea, HU18 1PS Tel: 01964 534111 Fax: 01964 534111
(Withernsea Sub-district), 243 Queen Street, Withernsea, HU19 2HH Tel: 01964-612344 Fax: 01964-612344
Goole, Council Offices, Church Street, Goole, DN14 5BG Tel: 01482 393580 Tel: 01482 393581 Fax: 01482 393582
Bridlington, Town Hall, Quay Road, Bridlington, YO16 4LP Tel: 01482 393570 Fax: 01482 393572
(Driffield Sub-district), 51 Manorfield Road, Driffield, YO25 5JE Tel: 01377-254051 Fax: 01377-254051
Pocklington, Burnby Hall, Pocklington, YO4 2QQ Tel: 01759-303614 Fax: 01759-306722

East Sussex
Eastbourne, Town Hall, Grove Road, Eastbourne, BN21 4UG Tel: 01323 410000 Tel: 01323 415051 Fax: 01323 431386
Hastings & Rother, Bohemia Road, Hastings, TN34 1EX Tel: 01424-721722 Fax: 01424-465296
Lewes, Southover Grange, Southover Road, Lewes, BN7 1TP Tel: 01273-475916 Fax: 01273-488073
Uckfield, Beaconwood, Beacon Road, Crowborough, TN6 1AR Tel: 01892-653803 Fax: 01892-669884

Essex
Braintree, John Ray House, Bocking End, Braintree, CM7 9RW Tel: 01376-323463 Fax: 01376-342423
Brentwood, 1 Seven Arches Road, Brentwood, CM14 4JG Tel: 01277-233565 Fax: 01277-262712

(Basildon Sub-district), Burghstead Lodge, 143 High Street, Billericay, CM12 9AB Tel: 01277-623939 Fax: 01277-636162
Castle Point and Rochford, Civic Centre, Victoria Avenue, Southend-on-Sea, SS2 6ER Tel: 01702-343728
(Sub-district), District Council Offices, Hockley Road, Rayleigh, SS6 8EB Tel: 01268-776362 Fax: 01268-776362
Chelmsford, 17 Market Road, Chelmsford, CM1 1GF Tel: 01245-430701 Fax: 01245-430707
Colchester, Stanwell House, Stanwell Street, Colchester, CO2 7DL Tel: 01206-572926 Fax: 01206-540626
Epping Forest, St Johns Road, Epping, CM16 5DN Tel: 01992-572789 Fax: 01992-571236
Harlow, Watergarden Ofices, College Square, The High,, Harlow, CM20 1AG Tel: 01279-427674 Fax: 01279-444594
Southend-on-Sea, Civic Centre, Victoria Avenue, Southend-on-Sea, SS2 6ER Tel: 01702-343728 Fax: 01702-612610
Thurrock, 2 Quarry Hill, Grays, RM17 5BT Tel: 01375-375245 Fax: 01375-392649
Uttlesford, Council Offices, London Road, Saffron Walden, CB11 4ER Tel: 01799-510319 Fax: 01799-510332

Barking & Dagenham
Barking & Dagenham, Arden House, 198 Longbridge Road, Barking, IG11 8SY Tel: (020) 8270-4742 Fax: (020) 8270-4745
Havering LB, Havering, 'Langtons', Billet Lane, Hornchurch, RM11 1XL Tel: 01708 433481 Tel: 01708 433403 Fax: 01708 433413
Redbridge LB, Redbridge, Queen Victoria House, 794 Cranbrook Road, Barkingside,, Ilford, IG6 1JS Tel: (020) 8708 7160 Fax: (020) 8708 7161

Gloucestershire
Cheltenham, St. Georges Road, Cheltenham, GL50 3EW Tel: 01242-532455 Fax: 01242-254600
Cirencester, Old Memorial Hospital, Sheep Street, Cirencester, GL7 1QW Tel: 01285-650455 Fax: 01285-640253
Gloucester, Maitland House, Spa Road, Gloucester, GL1 1UY Tel: 01452-425275 Fax: 01452-385385
North Cotswold, North Cotswold Register Office, High Street, Moreton-in-Marsh, GL56 0AZ Tel: 01608-651230 Fax: 01608-651226
Stroud, Parliament Street, Stroud, GL5 1DY Tel: 01453-766049 Fax: 01453-752961
Forest of Dean, Belle Vue Centre, 6 Belle Vue Road, Cinderford, GL14 2AB Tel: 01594-822113 Fax: 01594-826352

South Gloucestershire
South Gloucestershire, Poole Court, Poole Court Drive, Yate, BS37 5PY Tel: 01454-863140 Fax: 01454-863145

Hampshire
Alton, 4 Queens Road, Alton, GU34 1HU Tel: 01420-85410
Andover, Wessex Chambers, South Street, Andover, SP10 2BN Tel: 01264-352513 Fax: 01264-366849
Droxford, Bank House, Bank Street, Bishop's Waltham, SO32 1GP Tel: 01489 894044 Fax: 01489 892219
Hampshire North, Hampshire North Register Office, Goldings, London Road, Basingstoke, RG21 4AN Tel: 01256 322188 Fax: 01256 350745
Kingsclere & Whitchurch, Council Offices, Swan Street, Kingsclere,, Nr Newbury, RG15 8PM Tel: 01635-298714
New Forest, Public Offices, 65 Christchurch Road, Ringwood, BH24 1DH Tel: 01425 470150, Fax: 01425 471732
(Lymington Sub-district), Public Offices, 65 Christchurch Road, Ringwood, BH24 1DH Tel: 01425 470150 Fax: 01425 471732
(New Forest Sub-district), Totton an Eling Community CentreCivic Centre Building, Library Road, Totton, Southampton, SO4 3AP Tel: (023) 8066 9251 Fax: (023) 80863168

North-East Hampshire, 30 Grosvenor Road, Aldershot, GU11 3EB Tel: 01252-322066 Fax: 01252-338004
Petersfield, The Old College, College Street, Petersfield, GU31 4AG Tel: 01730-265372 Fax: 01730-265396
Romsey, Hayter House, Hayter Gardens, Romsey, SO51 7QU Tel: 01794-513846 Fax: 01794-830491
South-East Hampshire, 4-8 Osborn Road South, Fareham, PO16 7DG Tel: 01329-280493 Fax: 01329-823184
(Fareham Sub-district), 4 8 Osborn Road South, Fareham, PO16 7DG Tel: 01329-280493
(Gosport Sub-district), 3 Thorngate Way, Gosport, PO12 1DX Tel: (023) 92580629 Fax: (023) 92580629
(Havant Sub-district), Fernglen, Town Hall Road, Havant, PO9 1AN Tel: (023) 92482533 Fax: (023) 92482533
Winchester, Station Hill, Winchester, SO23 8TJ Tel: 01962 869608 Tel: 01962 869594 Fax: 01962 851912
(Eastleigh Sub-district), 101 Leigh Road, Eastleigh, SO50 9Dr Tel: (023) 8061 2058 Fax: (023) 8061 2058

Portsmouth, Milldam House, Burnaby Road, PO1 3AF Tel: (023) 9282 9041 Tel: (023) 9282 9042 Fax: (023) 9283 1996

Southampton
Southampton, 6A Bugle Street, Southampton, SO14 2LX Tel: (023) 8063 1422 Fax: (023) 8063 3431

Hereford and Worcester
Bromyard Council Offices, 1 Rowberry Street, Bromyard, Hereford, HR7 4DU Tel: 01432 260258 Fax: 01432 260259
Hereford County Offices, Bath Street, Hereford, HR1 2HQ Tel: 01432 260565 Tel: 01432 261720 Fax: 01432 260565
Kington Market Hall Street, Kington, HR5 3DP Tel: 01544-230156 Fax: 01544-231385
Ledbury Town Council Offices, Church Street, Ledbury, HR8 1DH Tel: 01531-632306
Leominster The Old Priory, Leominster, HR6 8EQ Tel: 01568-610131
Ross The Old Chapel, Cantilupe Road, Ross on Wye, HR9 7AN Tel: 01989-562795 Fax: 01989 564869

Hertfordshire
Barnet, 182 Burnt Oak Broadway, Edgware, HA8 0AU Tel: (020) 8731-1100 Fax: (020) 8731-1111
Bishops Stortford, 2 Hockerill Street, Bishops Stortford, CM23 2DL Tel: 01279-652273 Fax: 01279-461492, gill.wenzer@hertscc.gov.uk
Broxbourne, Borough Offices, Churchgate, Cheshunt, EN8 9XQ Tel: 01992-623107
Dacorum, The Bury, Queensway, Hemel Hemstead, HP1 1HR Tel: 01442-228600 Fax: 01442-243974
Hatfield, 19b St Albans Road East, Hatfield, AL10 0NG Tel: 01707-283920
Hertford & Ware, County Hall, Pegs Lane, Hertford, SG13 8DE Tel: 01992-555590 Fax: 01992 555493
Hitchen & Stevenage, Danesgate, Stevenage, SG1 1WW Tel: 01438-316579 Fax: 01438-357197
St Albans, Hertfordshire House, Civic Close, St. Albans, AL1 3JZ Tel: 01727-816806 Fax: 01727-816804
Watford, 36 Clarendon Road, Watford, WD1 1JP Tel: 01923-231302 Fax: 01923 246852

Hull
Municipal Offices, 181-191 George Street, Hull, HU1 3BY Tel: 01482 615401 Fax: 01482 615411

Isle of Wight
County Hall, High Street, PO30 1UD Tel: 01983-823230, Fax: 01983-823227

Kent
Ashford with Shepway, Elwick House, Elwick Road, Ashford, TN23 1NR Tel: 01233-62466 Fax: 01233-642962
Canterbury with Swale, Wellington House, 4 StStephen's Road, Canterbury, CT2 7RD Tel: 01227-470480 Fax: 01227-780176

Medway, Ingleside, 114 Maidstone Road, Chatham, ME4 6DJ Tel: 01634-844073 Fax: 01634-840165
Gravesend, 132 Windmill Street, Gravesend, DA12 1BE Tel: 01474-333451 Fax: 01474-564428
Maidstone, The Archbishop's Palace, Palace Gardens, Mill Street,, Maidstone, ME15 6YE Tel: 01622-752891 Fax: 01622 663690
Thanet with Dover, Aberdeen House, 68 Ellington Road, Ramsgate, CT11 9ST Tel: 01843-591417
Tunbridge Wells, Divisional County Offices, 39 Grove Hill Road, Tunbridge Wells, TN1 1SL Tel: 01892-527332 Fax: 01892 528518

Bexley LB
Bexley, Manor House, The Green, Sidcup, DA14 6BW Tel: (020) 83004537 Fax: (020) 8308 4967

Lancashire
Blackburn, Jubilee Street, Blackburn, BB1 1EP Tel: 01254-57602 Tel: 01254 587524 Fax: 01254 587538
Blackpool , South King Street, Blackpool, FY1 4AX Tel: 01253-477177 Fax: 01253-477176
Burnley and Pendle, 12 Nicholas Street, Burnley, BB11 2AQ Tel: 01282 436116 Fax: 01282 412221
Chorley, 16 St. George's Street, Chorley, PR7 2AA Tel: 012572-63143 Fax: 01257-263808
Fleetwood and Fylde, South King Street, Blackpool, FY1 4AX Tel: 01253-477177 Fax: 01253-477170
(Fleetwood Sub-district), Fleetwood Central Library, North Albert Street, Fleetwood, FY7 6AJ Tel: 01253-874580
(Fylde Sub-district), The Library, Clifton Street, Lytham, FY8 5ED Tel: 01253-737530
Hyndburn & Rossendale, The Mechanics Institute, Willow Street, Accrington, BB5 1LP Tel: 01254-871360 Fax: 01254 239391
(Rossendale Sub-district), 1 Grange Street, Rawtenstall, Rossendale, BB4 7RT Tel: 01706-215496
Lancaster, 4 Queen Street, Lancaster, LA1 1RS Tel: 01524-65673 Fax: 01524-842285
(Garstang Sub-district), Old Posthouse, Market Place, Garstang, PR3 1ZA Tel: 01995 603330 Fax: 01995 603330
(Preesall Sub-district), The Over Wyre Medical Centre, Pilling Lane, Preesall, FY6 0FA Tel: 01253-810722
Preston and South Ribble, PO Box 24, Bow Lane, Preston, PR1 8SE Tel: 01772 263800 Tel: 01772 263808 Fax: 01772 261012
Ribble Valley, Off Pimlico Road, Clitheroe, BB7 2BW Tel: 01200-425786 Fax: 01200-425786
West Lancashire, Greetby Buildings, Derby Street, Ormskirk, L39 2BS Tel: 01695-576009 Fax: 01695 585819
Blackburn with Darwen
Blackburn with Darwen (Darwen & Turton Sub-district), Town Hall, Croft Street, Darwen, BB3 2RN Tel: 01254-702443
Bolton MD
Bolton, Mere Hall, Merehall Street, Bolton, BL1 2QT Tel: 01204-525165 Fax: 01204-525125
Bury MD
Bury, Town Hall, Manchester Road, Bury, BL9 0SW Tel: 0161-253-6027 Fax: 0161-253-6028
Calderdale MD
Todmorden, Municipal Offices, Rise Lane, Todmorden, OL14 7AB Tel: 01706 814811 Ext 208 Fax: 01706 814811 Ext 208
Oldham MD
Oldham, Metropolitan House, Hobson Street, Oldham, OL1 1PY Tel: 0161-678-0137 Fax: 0161 911 3729
Rochdale MD
Rochdale, Town Hall, The Esplanade, Rochdale, OL16 1AB Tel: 01706-864779 Fax: 01706-864786
Wigan MD
Wigan & Leigh, New Town Hall, Library Street, Wigan, WN1 1NN Tel: 01942-705000 Fax: 01942-705013

Leicester

Leicester, 5 Pocklington's Walk, Leicester, LE1 6BQ Tel: 0116-253-6326 Fax: 0116 253 3008

Leicestershire, Coalville, 41 Ravenstone Road, Coalville, LE67 3NB Tel: 01530-832007 Fax: 01530-815802

Loughborough, 202 Ashby Road, Loughborough, LE11 3AG Tel: 01509-611954 Fax: 01509 264675

Market Harborough, 42 Coventry Road, Market Harborough, LE16 9BZ Tel: 01858 462091 Fax: 01858 432955

Melton Mowbray, County Council Area Offices, Leicester Road, Melton Mowbray, LE13 0DG Tel: 01664 562751 Fax: 01664 481910

South Wigston, Social Services Offices, Bassett Street, South Wigston, LE18 4 Tel: 0116 278 3461

Hinckley, The Chestnuts, 25 Mount Road, Hinckley, LE10 1AD Tel: 01455-637259 Fax: 01455-612817

Rutland

Rutland, Catmose, Oakham, Rutland, E15 6JU Tel: 01572 758370 Tel: 01572 758371 Fax: 01572 758380

Lincolnshire

Bourne, Saxonhurst, 35 West Street, Bourne, PE10 9NE Tel: 01778-422269 Fax: 01778-421081

Boston, County Hall, Boston, PE21 6LX Tel: 01205-310010 Fax: 01205-356690

Caistor, Council Offices, Caistor, LN7 6LX Tel: 01472-851153 Fax: 01472-852678

East Elloe, 25 West Street, Long Sutton, PE12 9BN Tel: 01406-363874 Fax: 01406 365325

(Holbeach Sub-district), 33 Boston Road, Holbeach, Spalding, PE12 7LR Tel: 01406-423166 Fax: 01406-422812

(Long Sutton Sub-district), 25 West Street, Long Sutton, PE12 9BN Tel: 01406-363874

Gainsborough, 156 Trinity Street, Gainsborough, DN21 1JP Tel: 01427-612312 Fax: 01427-678185

Grantham, The Priory, Market Place, Grantham, NG31 6LJ Tel: 01476-561061 Fax: 01476 562235

Horncastle, Holmeleigh, Foundry Street, Horncastle, LN9 6AQ Tel: 01507-522576 Fax: 01507 524849

Lincoln, 4 Lindum Road, Lincoln, LN2 1NN Tel: 01522-552501/2 Fax: 01522-589524

Louth, Louth Town Hall, Eastgate, Louth, LN11 9NH Tel: 01507-603529 Fax: 01507-608346

Sleaford, PO Box 2, Council Offices, Eastgate,, Sleaford, NG34 7EB Tel: 01529-414144-Ext.-2520 Fax: 01529 413728

Spalding, linden House, 1 Bath Lane, Spalding, PE11 1XP Tel: 01775 769064 Fax: 01775 714392

Spilsby, Offord House, Church Street, Spilsby, PE23 5EF Tel: 01790-752550 Fax: 01790-752162

(Skegness Sub-district), 30 Roman Bank, Skegness, PE25 2SG Tel:

Stamford, 2 St Mary's Hill, Stamford, PE9 2DR Tel: 01780-756004 Fax: 01780 752659

North-East Lincolnshire, Town Hall Square, Grimsby, DN31 1HX Tel: 01472-324860 Fax: 01472-324867

North Lincolnshire, 92 Oswald Road, Scunthorpe, DN15 7PA Tel: 01724-843915 Fax: 01724 872668

London

Barnet, 182 Burnt Oak Broadway, Edgware, HA8 0AU Tel: (020) 8731-1100 Fax: (020) 8731-1111

Bromley LB, Room S101Bromley Civic Centre, Stockwell Close, Bromley, BR1 3UH Tel: (020) 8313-4666 Fax: (020) 8313-4699

Brent, Brent Town Hall, Forty Lane, Wembley, HA9 9EZ Tel: (020) 8937-1010 Fax: (020) 8937-1021, "name"@brent.gov.uk

Camden LB, Camden Register Office, Camden Town Hall, Judd Street, WC1H 9JE Tel: (020) 7974 5600 Tel: (020) 7974 1900 Fax: (020) 7974 5792

City of London, Finsbury Town Hall, Roseberry Avenue, EC1R 4QT Tel: (020) 7527 6347 Tel: (020) 7527 6357 Fax: (020) 7527 6308

City of Westminster, Westminster Council House, Marylebone Road, NW1 5PT Tel: (020) 7641-1161/2/3 Fax: (020) 7641-1246

Croydon LB, Mint Walk, Croydon, CR0 1EA Tel: (020) 8760-5617 Fax: (020) 8760-5633

Ealing LB, Ealing Town Hall, New Broadway, Ealing, W5 2BY Tel: (020) 8758-8946 Fax: (020) 8758-8722

Enfield, Public Offices, Gentlemen's Row, Enfield, EN2 6PS Tel: (020) 8367-5757 Fax: (020) 8379-8562

Greenwich LB, Town Hall, Wellington Street, SE18 6PW Tel: (020) 8854-8888 Fax: (020) 8317-5747

Hackney LB, Town Hall, Mare Street, E8 1EA Tel: (020) 8356-3376 Fax: (020) 8356-3552

Hammersmith and Fulham, Hammersmith & Fulham Register Office, Fulham Town Hall, Harwood Road, London, SW6 1ET Tel: (020) 8576 5032 Tel: (020) 8576 5217 Fax: (020) 8576 5072

Hammersmith, Nigel Playfair Avenue, London, W6 9JY Tel: (020) 8748-3020 Tel: (020) 8576-5032 Fax: (020) 8748-6619

Haringey LB, Civic Centre, High Road, Wood Green, Haringey, N22 4LE Tel: (020) 8489 2605 Tel: (020) 8489 2601 Fax: (020) 8862 2912

Harrow, The Civic Centre, Station Road, Harrow, HA1 2UX Tel: (020) 8424-1618 Fax: (020) 8424-1414

Hendon see Barnet, 182 Burnt Oak, Broadway,, Edgware, HA8 0AU Tel: (020) 8952-0876 Tel: (020) 8952-0024 Fax: (020) 8381-2346, Transferred to Barnet wef April 1999

Hillingdon, Hillingdon Civic Centre, Uxbridge, UB8 1UW Tel: 01895-250418 Fax: 01895-250678

Hounslow, 88 Lampton Road, Hounslow, TW3 4DW Tel: (020) 8583 2090 Tel: (020) 8583 2086 Fax: (020) 8577 8798

Islington LB, Finsbury Town Hall, Roseberry Avenue, EC1R 4QT Tel: (020) 7527 6347 Tel: (020) 7527 6350 Fax: (020) 7527 6308

Kensington & Chelsea, The Kensington & Chelsea Register Office, Chelsea Old Town Hall, Kings Road, London, SW3 5EE Tel: (020) 7361-4100 Fax: (020) 7361-4054

Kingston upon Thames, 35 Coombe Road, Kingston upon Thames, KT2 7BA Tel: (020) 8546 7993 Tel: (020) 8546 7993 ext 203 Fax: (020) 8287 2888

Lambeth, 357-361 Brixton Road, London, SW9 7DA Tel: (020) 7926-9420 Fax: (020) 7926 9426

Lewisham, 368 Lewisham High Street, London, SE13 6LQ Tel: (020) 8690-2128 Fax: (020) 8690 1078

Merton, Morden Cottage, Morden Hall Road, Morden, SM4 5JA Tel: (020) 8540-5011 Fax: (020) 8543-2906

Newham, Passmore Edwards Building, 207 Plashet Grove, East Ham, London, E6 1BT Tel: (020) 8430 2000 Tel: (020) 8430 3616 Fax: (020) 8430 3127

Richmond upon Thames, 1 Spring Terrace, Richmond, TW9 1LW Tel: (020) 8940-2853 Fax: (020) 8940-8226

Southwark, 34 Peckham Road, London, SE5 8QA Tel: (020) 7525 7651 Tel: (020) 7525 7652 Fax: (020) 7525 7670

Sutton, Russettings, 25 Worcester Road, Sutton, SM2 6PR Tel: (020) 8770-6790 Fax: (020) 8770-6772

Tower Hamlets, Bromley Public Hall, Bow Road, E3 3AA Tel: (020) 7364 7891 Tel: (020) 7364 7898 Fax: (020) 7364 7885, This office holds the records of the former RDS of StepneyWhitechapelBethnal GreenPoplar Mile end of Old Town and St George in the East. Please note records of the former East London RD are hel

Waltham Forest, 106 Grove Road, Walthamstow, E17 9BY Tel: (020) 8520-8617 Fax: (020) 8509 1388

Wandsworth, The Town Hall, Wandsworth High Street, SW18 2PU Tel: (020) 8871 6120 Fax: (020) 8871 8100

Manchester MD
Manchester, Cumberland House, Spinningfield, Off Deansgate, M60 3RG Tel: 0161-234-7878 Fax: 0161-234-7888, register-office@manchester.gov.uk

Salford MD
Salford, 'Kingslea', Barton Road, Swinton, M27 5WH Tel: 0161-793-0077 Fax: 0161-794-4797

Merseyside
Knowsley, District Council Offices, High Street, Prescot, L34 3LH Tel: 0151-443-5210 Fax: 0151-443-5216
Liverpool MD
Liverpool, Liverpool Register Office, The Cotton Exchange, Old Hall Street, Liverpool, L3 9UF Tel: 0151 233 4973 Tel: 0151 233 4975 Fax: 0151 225 4944
Sefton MD
Sefton North, Town Hall, Corporation Street, Southport, PR8 1DA Tel: 01704-533133 Fax: 0151-934-2014
Sefton South, Crosby Town Hall, Great Georges Road, Waterloo, Liverpool, L22 1RB Tel: 0151-934 3045 Fax: 0151 934 3044
St Helens MD
St. Helens, Central Street, St Helens, WA10 1UJ Tel: 01744-23524 Tel: 01744-732012 Fax: 01744 23524
Wirral MD
Wirral, Town Hall, Mortimer Street, Birkenhead, L41 5EU Tel: 0151-666-3953 Fax: 0151-666-3955 This office now holds the records formerly held at the Wallasey officewhich has been closed and amalgamated with Birkenhead. Registration District now named "Wirral"
Wallasey The Wallasey Register Office is now closed having been amalgamated with Birkenhead Register Office. All records for Birkenhead and Wallasey (ie the whole of the Wirral peninsula) are now held at Birkenhead)

Milton Keynes
Milton Keynes, Bracknell House, Aylesbury Street, Bletchley, MK2 2BE Tel: 01908-372101 Fax: 01908 645103

Norfolk
Depwade, Council Offices, 11-12 Market Hill, Diss, IP22 3JX Tel: 01379-643915 Fax: 01379 643915
Downham, 15 Paradise Road, Downham Market, PE38 9HS Tel: 01366-388080 Fax: 01366 387105
East Dereham, 59 High Street, Dereham, NR19 1DZ Tel: 01362-698021 Fax: 01362 698021
Fakenham, Fakenham Connecrt, Oak Street, Fakenham, NR21 9SR Tel: 01328 850122 Fax: 01328 850150
Great Yarmouth, 'Ferryside', High Road, Southtown,, Great Yarmouth, NR31 0PH Tel: 01493-662313 Fax: 01493-602107
King's Lynn, St Margaret's House, St Margaret's Place, King's Lynn, PE30 5DW Tel: 01553-669251 Fax: 01553 669251
North Walsham, 18 Kings Arms Street, North Walsham, NR28 9JX Tel: 01692 406220 Fax: 01692 406220
(Erpingham Sub-district), Council Offices, North Lodge Park, Overstrand Road, Cromer, NR27 0AH Tel: 01263-513078
(Smallburgh Sub-district), 18 Kings Arms Street, North Walsham, NR28 9JX Tel: 01692-403075
Norwich, Churchman House, 71 Bethel Street, Norwich, NR2 1NR Tel: 01603-767600 Fax: 01603 632677
Wayland, Kings House, Kings Street, Thetford, IP24 2AP Tel: 01842 766848 Fax: 01842 765996

Northamptonshire
Brackley, Brackley Lodge, High Street, Brackley, NN13 5BD Tel: 01280-702949
Corby, The Old Stables, Cottingham Road, Corby, NN17 1TD Tel: 01536-203141
Cundle and Thrapston, The Old Courthouse, 17 Mill Road, Oundle, PE8 4BW Tel: 01832 273413

Daventry, Council Offices, Lodge Road, Daventry, NN11 5AF Tel: 01327-302209 Fax: 01327-300011
Kettering, 75 London Road, Kettering, NN15 7PQ Tel: 01536-514792 Fax: 01536 411359
Northampton, The Guildhall, St Giles Square, Northampton, NN1 1DE Tel: 01604-233500 Fax: 01604 238507
Towcester, Sunnybanks, 55Brackley Road, Towcester, NN12 6DH Tel: 01327-350774
Wellinborough, Council Offices, Swanspool, Wellingborough, NN8 1BP Tel: 01933 231549 Fax: 01933 231548

Northumberland
Northumberland Central, 94 Newgate Street, Morpeth, NE61 1BU Tel: 01670-513232
(Blyth Valley Sub-district), 107a Waterloo Road, Blyth, NE24 1AD Tel: 01670-352450
(Morpeth Sub-district), 94 Newgate Street, Morpeth, NE61 1BU Tel: 01670 513232
Northumberland North First, 5 Palace Street East, Berwick upon Tweed, TD15 1HT Tel: 01289 307373
(Belford Sub-district), Linhope, 29 King Street, Seahouses, NE68 7XW Tel: 01665 721631
(Berwick Sub-district), 5 Palace Street East, Berwick on Tweed, TD15 1HT Tel: 01289 307373
(Wooler Sub-district), 33 Glendale Road, Wooler, NE71 6DN Tel: 01668-281656
Northumberland North Second, 6 Market Place, Alnwick, NE66 1HP Tel: 01665-602363 Fax: 01665 510079
(Alnwick Sub-division) 6 Market Place, Alnwick, NE66 1HP
(Rothbury Sub-district), Court House, Front Street, Rothbury, NE65 2TZ Tel:
(Warkworth Sub-district), 73 Queen Street, Amble, Morpeth, NE65 0DA Tel: 01665-710744/5
Northumberland West, Abbey Gate House, Market Street, Hexham, NE46 3LX Tel: 01434 602355 Tel: 01434 602605 Fax: 01434 604957
(Bellingham Sub-district), Sutherland House, 3 St Cuthbert's Terrace, Bellingham, Hexham, NE48 2JR Tel: 01434-220321
(Haltwhistle Sub-district), Haltwhistle Library, Westgate, Haltwhistle, NE49 0AX Tel: 01434 320263
(Hexham Sub-district), Abbey Gate House, Market Street, Hexham, NE46 3LX Tel: 01434-602355 Tel: 01434-602605

Nottinghamshire
Basford, Highbury Road, Bulwell, NG6 9DA Tel: 0115-927-1294 Fax: 0115 977 1845
(Beeston & Stapleford Sub-district), Register Office, Marvin Road, off Station Road, Beeston, NG9 2AP Tel: 0115-925-5530
(Carlton Sub-district), County Council Offices, Carlton Square, Carlton, NG4 3BP Tel: 0115-961-9663
(Eastwood Sub-district), Eastwood Health Clinic, Nottingham Road, Eastwood, NG16 3GL Tel: 01773-712449
East Retford, Notts County Council Offices, Chancery Lane, Retford, DN22 6DG Tel: 01777-708631 Fax: 01777 860667
Mansfield, Notts CC Offices, St John Street, Mansfield, NG18 1QH Tel: 01623-476564 Fax: 01623 636284
Newark, County Offices, Balderton Gate, Newark, NG24 1UW Tel: 01636-705455 Fax: 01636 705455
(Southwell Sub-district), North Muskham Prebend, Church Street, Southwell, NG25 0HG Tel: 01636-814200
Nottingham, 50 Shakespeare Street, Nottingham, NG1 4FP Tel: 0115-947-5665 Fax: 0115-941-5773
Rushcliffe, The Hall, Bridgford Road, West Bridgford, NG2 6AQ Tel: 0115-981-5307 Fax: 0115-969-6189
Worksop, Queens Buildings, Potter Street, Worksop, S80 2AH Tel: 01909-535534 Fax: 01909 501067

Oxfordshire

Abingdon, Roysse Court, Bridge Street, Abingdon, OX14 3HU Tel: 01235-520156

Banbury, Bodicote House, Bodicote, Near Banbury, OX15 4AA Tel: 01295-263268 Fax: 01295-263268

Bullingdon, Littleworth Road, Wheatley, OX33 1NR Tel: 01865-874702

Henley, Easby House Site, Northfield End, Henley-on-Thames, RG9 2JW, Tel 01491-573047 Fax: 01491 573047

Oxford, Tidmarsh Lane, Oxford, OX1 1NS Tel: 01865 815900 Tel: 01865 815167 Fax: 01865 815632

Ploughley, Waverley House, Queen's Avenue, Bicester, OX6 8PY Tel: 01869-252917

Wallingford, 197 The Broadway, Didcot, OX11 8RU Tel: 01235-818706

Wantage, The Civic Centre, Portway, Wantage, OX12 9BX Tel: 012357-65796

West Oxfordshire, West Oxfordshire District Council Offices, Woodgreen, Witney, OX8 7HH Tel: 01993-703062

Shropshire

Bridgnorth, 12 West Castle Street, Bridgnorth, WV16 4AB Tel: 01746-762589 Fax: 01746 764270

Clun, The Pines, Colebatch Road, Bishop's Castle, SY9 5JZ Tel: 01588-638588,

Ludlow, Stone House, Corve Street,, Ludlow, SY8 1DG Tel: 01584 813208 Fax: 01584 813122

(Craven Arms Sub-district), The Library, School Road, Craven Arms, SY7 9PE Tel: 01588-673455

(Ludlow Sub-district), The Red Cross Centre, The Smithfield, Lower Galdeford, Ludlow, SY8 1SB Tel: 01584-874422

North Shropshire, Edinburgh House, New Street, Wem, Shrewsbury, SY4 5DB Tel: 01939-238418

(Market Drayton Sub-district), Health Centre, Cheshire Street, Market Drayton, TF9 3AA Tel:

(Wem Sub-district), Edinburgh House, New Street, Wem, Shrewsbury, SY4 5DB Tel: 01939-238418

(Whitchurch Sub-district), 29 St Mary's Street, Whitchurch, SY13 1RA Tel: 01948-663402

Oswestry, Holbache Road, Oswestry, Tel: 01691-652086

Shrewsbury, The Shirehall, Abbey Foregate, Shrewsbury, SY2 6LY Tel: 01743-259921 Fax: 01743 252922

Telford and Wrekin, The Beeches, 29 Vineyard Road, Wellinton,, Telford, TF1 1HB Tel: 01952-248292,

Somerset

North Somerset, 41 The Boulevard, Weston-super-Mare, BS23 1PG Tel: 01934-627552 Fax: 01934-412014

(Weston Super Mare Sub-district), 41 The Boulevard, Weston Super Mare, BS23 1PG Tel:

Mendip, 19b Commercial Road, Shepton Mallet, BA4 5BU Tel: 01749-343928 Fax: 01749 343928

(Frome Sub-district), West Hill House, West End, Frome, BA11 3AD Tel: 01373-462887,

(Shepton Mallet Sub-district), 19 Commercial Road, Shepton Mallet, BA4 5BU Tel: 01749-342268

(Wells Sub-district), Town Hall, Market Place, Wells, BA5 2RB Tel: 01749-675355

Sedgemoor, Morgan House, Mount Street, Bridgwater, TA6 3ER Tel: 01278-422527

Taunton, Flook House, Belvedere Road, Taunton, TA1 1BT Tel: 01823-282251 Fax: 01823 351173

West Somerset, 2 Long Street, Williton, Taunton, TA4 4QN Tel: 01984-633116

Yeovil, Maltravers House, Petters Way, Yeovil, BA20 1SP Tel: 01935 411230 Fax: 01935 413993

(Chard Sub-district), Holyrood Lace Mill, Holyrood Street, Chard, TA20 2YA Tel: 146063139 Fax: 01460 260402

(Wincanton Sub-district), Council Offices, Churchfield, Wincanton, BA9 9AG Tel: 01963-435008 Fax: 01963-34182

Staffordshire

Cannock Chase, 5 Victoria Street, Cannock, WS11 1AG Tel: 01543 512345 Fax: 01543 512347

(Rugeley Sub-district), Council Offices, Anson Street, Rugeley, WS15 2BH Tel: 01889-585322 Fax:

East Staffordshire, Rangemore House, 22 Rangemore Street, Burton-upon-Trent, DE14 2ED Tel: 01283-538701 Fax: 01283 547338

(Burton on Trent Sub-district), Rangemore House, 22 Rangemore Street, Burton on Trent, DE14 2ED Tel: 01283-538701 Fax: 01283-547338

(Uttoxeter Sub-district), 63 High Street, Uttoxeter, ST14 7JD Tel: 01889-562168 Fax: 01889-569935

Lichfield, The Old Library Buildings, Bird Street, Lichfield, WS13 6PN Tel: 01543-510771 Fax: 01543-510773

(Tamworth Sub-district), 26 Albert Road, Tamworth, B79 7JS Tel: 01827-62295 Fax: 01827-62295

Newcastle-under-Lyme, 20 Sidmouth Avenue, The Brampton,, Newcastle-under-Lyme, ST5 0QN Tel: 01782-297581 Fax: 01782-297582

(Kidsgrove Sub-district), The Town Hall, Liverpool Road, Kidsgrove, ST7 4EH Tel:

Stafford, Eastgate House, 79 Eastgate Street, Stafford, ST16 2NG Tel: 01785-277880 Fax: 01785 277884

(Stone Sub-district), 15 Station Road, Stone, ST15 8JR Tel: 01785-812087 Fax: 01785-286123

Staffordshire Moorlands, High Street, Leek, ST13 5EA Tel: 01538-373166 Fax: 01538-386985

(Biddulph Sub-district), Town Hall, High Streeet, Biddulph, ST8 6AR Tel: 01782 297939 Fax: 01782 297815

(Cheadle & Alton Sub-district), Council Offices, Leek Road, Cheadle, ST10 1JF Tel: 01538-752435 Fax: 01538-752435

(Leek & Cheddleton Sub-district), High Street, Leek, ST13 5EA Tel: 01538-373191

South Staffordshire, Civic Centre, Gravel Hill, Wombourne, Wolverhampton, WV5 9HA Tel: 01902-895829 Fax: 01902-326779

(Seisdon Sub-district), Civic Centre, Gravel Hill, Wombourne, Wolverhampton, WV5 9HA Tel: 01902-895829 Fax: 01902-326779

(Penkridge Sub-district), Haling Dene Centre, Cannock Road, Penkridge, ST19 5DT Tel: 01785-715260 Fax: 01785-715260

Stoke-on-Trent

Stoke-on-Trent, Town Hall, Albion Street, Hanley, Stoke on Trent, ST1 1QQ Tel: 01782-295640 Fax: 01782-295648

Suffolk

Bury St. Edmunds, St. Margarets, Shire Hall, Bury StEdmunds, IP33 1RX Tel: 01284-352373 Fax: 01284 352376

Deben, Council Offices, Melton Hill, Woodbridge, IP12 1AU Tel: 01394-444331 Tel: 01394-444682 Fax: 01394-383171

Gipping & Hartismere, Milton House, 3 Milton Road South, Stowmarket, IP14 1EZ Tel: 01449 612060 Fax: 01449 612054

Ipswich, St Peters House, 16 Grimwade Street,, Ipswich, IP4 1LP Tel: 01473-583050 Fax: 01473-584331

Sudbury, 14 Cornard Road, Sudbury, CO10 6XA Tel: 01787-372904

Waveney, St Margarets House, Gordon Road, Lowestoft, NR32 1JQ Tel: 01502-405325 Fax: 01502-508170

Surrey

East Surrey, East Surrey Register office, The Mansion, 70 Church Street, Leatherhead, KT22 8DA Tel: 01372 373668 Fax: 01372 376811

North Surrey, 'Rylston', 81 Oatlands Drive, Weybridge, KT13 9LN Tel: 01932-254360, Fax: 01932 227139

South-East Surrey, 44 Reigate Hill, Reigate, RH2 9NG Tel: 01737-243359 Fax: 01737 223163
West Surrey, Artington House, Portsmouth Road, Guildford, GU2 5DZ Tel: 01483-562841 Fax: 01483-573232

Tyne & Wear
Gateshead MD, Gateshaed, Civic Centre, Regent Street, Gateshead, NE8 1HH Tel: 0191 433 3000 Tel: 0191 433 2000 Fax: 0191 477 9948
Newcastle-upon-Tyne MD, Newcastle-upon-Tyne, Civic Centre, Barras Bridge, Newcastle-upon-Tyne, NE1 8PS Tel: 0191 232 8520 Fax: 0191 211 4970
North Tyneside MD, North Tyneside, Maritime Chambers, Howard Street, North Shields, NE30 1LZ Tel: 0191-2006164
South Tyneside
Jarrow District abolished 2001 records transferred to South Tyneside

South Tyneside MD
South Shields, 18 Barrington Street, South Shields, NE33 1AH Tel: 0191-455-3915 Fax: 0191-427-7564, Records from Jarrow on abolition 2001 transferred here

Sunderland MD
Sunderland, Town Hall & Civic Centre, PO Box 108, Sunderland, SR2 7DN Tel: 0191-553-1760 Fax: 0191 553 1769

Warwickshire
Mid Warwickshire, Pageant House, 2 Jury Street, Warwick, CV34 4EW Tel: 01926-494269 Fax: 01926 496287
(Leamington Spa Sub-district), 1 Euston Square, Leamington Spa, CV32 4NE Tel: 01962-428807 Fax: 01962-339923
(Southam Sub-district), The Grange, Coventry Road, Southam, CV33 0ED Tel: 01926-812636
North Warwickshire, Warwick House, Ratcliffe Street, Atherstone, CV9 1JP Tel: 01827-713241 Fax: 01827 720467
Nuneaton and Bedworth, Riversley Park, Coton Road, Nuneaton, CV11 5HA Tel: (024) 7634 8944 Tel: (024) 7634 8948 Fax: (024) 7635 0988
Rugby, 5 Bloxam Place, Rugby, CV21 3DS Tel: 01788-571233 Fax: 01788-542024
South Warwickshire, 7 Rother Street, Stratford-on-Avon, CV37 6LU Tel: 01789-293711 Fax: 01789 261423
(Alcester Sub-district), Temporary Council Offices, Kinwarten Road, Alcester, B49 6PX Tel: 01789 765441
(Shipston on Stour Sub-district), Clark House, West Street, Shipston on Stour, CV36 4HD Tel: 01608 662839
(Stratford on Avon Sub-district), Register Office, 7 Rother Street, Stratford on Avon, CV37 6LU Tel: 01789-293397 Fax: 01789-261423

West Midlands
Birmingham MD, 300 Broad Street, Birmingham, B1 2DE Tel: 0121-235-3421 Fax: 0121-303-1396
Dudley MD
Dudley, Priory Hall, Priory Park, Dudley, DY1 4EU Tel: 01384-815373 Fax: 01384-815339
Stourbridge, Crown Centre, Crown Lane, Stourbridge, DY8 1YA Tel: 01384-815384 Fax: 01384-815397
Sandwell MD
Sandwell, Highfields, High Street, Sandwell, B70 8RJ Tel: 0121-569-2480 Fax: 0121-569-2473
Solihull MD
Solihull North, The Library, Stephenson Drive, Chelmsley Wood, Birmingham, B37 5TA Tel: 0121-788-4376 Fax: 0121 788 4379
Solihull South, Homer Road, Solihull, B9 3QZ Tel: 0121-704-6100 Fax: 0121 704 6123
Walsall MD
Walsall, Hatherton Road, Walsall, WS1 1TN Tel: 01922-652260

Wolverhampton
Wolverhampton, Civic Centre, St Peters Square, Wolverhampton, WV1 1RU Tel: 01902-554989 Fax: 01902-554987

West Sussex
Crawley, Town Hall, The Boulevard, Crawley, RH10 1UZ Tel: 01293-438341 Fax: 01293-526454
(Sub-district), County Buildings, Northgate Avenue, Crawley, RH10 1XB Tel: 01293-514545 Fax: 01293-553832
Chichester, Greyfriars, 61 North Street, Chichester, PO19 1NB Tel: 01243-782307 Fax: 01243-773671
(Bognor Sub-district), Health Centre, West Street, Bognor Regis, PO21 1UT Tel: 01243-823453 Fax: 01243-823453
(Midhurst Sub-district), Capron House, North Street, Midhurst, GU29 9XX Tel: 01730-813245 Fax: 01730-813245
Haywards Heath, West Sussex County Council Offices, Oaklands Road, Haywards Heath, RH16 1SU Tel: 01444-452157 Fax: 01444-410128
Horsham, Town Hall, Market Square, Horsham, RH12 1EU Tel: 01403-265368 Fax: 01403-2170778
Worthing, Centenary House, Durrington Lane, Worthing, BN13 2QB Tel: 01903 839350 Fax: 01903 839356
(Chanctonbury Sub-district), 26 West Street, Storrington, RH20 4EE Tel: 01903 744275
(Littlehampton Sub-district), County Buildings, East Street, Littlehampton, BN17 6AP Tel: 01903 715460 Fax: 01903 715460
(Shoreham by the Sea Sub-district), Shoreham Health Centre, Pond Road, Shoreham by the Sea, BN4 5US Tel: 01273 453023

Wiltshire
Chippenham, 4 Timber Street, Chippenham, SN15 3BZ Tel: 01249 654361 Tel: , Fax: 01249 658850
Devizes & Marlborough, The Beeches, Bath Road, Devizes, SN10 2AL Tel: 01380-722162 Fax: 01380-728933
Marlborough, 1 The Green, Marlborough, SN8 1AL Tel: 01672-512483 From 5/10/98 Devizes and Marlborough Districts merged all records will be kept at Devises.
Salisbury, The Laburnums, 50 Bedwin Street, Salisbury, SP1 3UW Tel: 01722-335340 Fax: 01722 326806
Swindon, 1st Floor Aspen House, Temple Street, Swindon, SN1 1SQ Tel: 01793-521734 Fax: 01793 433887
Trowbridge, East Wing Block, County Hall, Trowbridge, BA14 8EZ Tel: 01225 713000 Fax: 01225 713097
Warminster, 3 The Avenue, Warminster, BA12 9AB Tel: 01985-213435 Fax: 01985 217688

Worcestershire
Bromsgrove, School Drive, Bromsgrove, B60 1AY Tel: 01527-578759 Fax: 01527-578750
Droitwich, Council Offices, Ombersley Street, Droitwich, WR9 8QX Tel: 01905-772280 Fax: 01905-776841
Evesham, County Offices, Swan Lane, Evesham, WR11 4TZ Tel: 01386-443945 Fax: 01386-448745
Kidderminster, Council Offices, Bewdley Road, Kidderminster, DY11 6RL Tel: 01562-829100 Fax: 01562-60192
Malvern, Hatherton Lodge, Avenue Road, Malvern, WR14 3AG Tel: 01684-573000 Fax: 01684-892378
Pershore, Civic Centre, Queen Elizabeth Drive, Pershore, WR10 1PT Tel: 01386-565610 Fax: 01386-553656
Redditch, 29 Easmore Road, Redditch, B98 8ER Tel: 01527-60647
Tenbury, Council Buildings, Teme Street, Tenbury Wells, Tel: 01584-810588
Worcester
29-30 Foregate Street, Worcester, WR1 1DS Tel: 01905-765350 Fax: 01905-765355

Yorkshire
City of York
York, 56 Bootham, York, YO30 7DA Tel: 01904-654477 Fax: 01904-638090
Yorkshire - North
North Yorkshire Registration Service North Yorkshire (Headquarters), Bilton House, 31 Park Parade, Harrogate, HG1 5AG Tel: 01423-506949 Fax: 01423-502105   Holds all historical records for the County of North Yorkshire (except the City of York)

Yorkshire - South
Barnsley
Barnsley, Town Hall, Church Street, Barnsley, S70 2TA Tel: 01226-773085 Tel: 01226 773080
Doncaster
Doncaster (Mexborough Sub-district), Council Offices, Main Street, Mexborough, S64 9LU Tel: 01302-735705
Doncaster MD
Doncaster, Elmfield ParkSouth Parade, Doncaster, DN1 2EB Tel: 01302-364922 Fax: 01302-364922
Sheffield MD
Sheffield, Surrey Place, Sheffield, S1 1YA Tel: 0114-203-9423 Fax: 0114-203-9424
Rotherham MD
Rotherham, Bailey House, Rawmarsh Road, Rotherham, S60 1TX Tel: 01709-382121

Yorkshire - West
Bradford MD
Bradford, 22 Manor Row, Bradford, BD1 4QR Tel: 01274-752151 Fax: 01274-305139
Keighley, Town Hall, Bow Street, Keighley, BD21 3PA Tel: 01535-618060
Calderdale MD
Halifax, 4 Carlton Street, Halifax, HX1 2AH Tel: 01422-353993 Fax: 01422-252370
Todmorden, Municipal Offices, Rise Lane, Todmorden, OL14 7AB Tel: 01706 814811 Ext 208 Fax: 01706 814811 Ext 208
Kirklees MD
Dewsbury, Wellington Street, Dewsbury, WF13 1LY Tel: 01924-324880 Fax: 01924 324882
Kirklees MD
Huddersfield, Civic Centre, 11 High Street, Huddersfield, HD1 2PL Tel: 01484-221030
Wakefield MD
Pontefract, Town Hall, Pontefract, WF8 1PG Tel: 01977-722670 Fax: 01977-722676
Wakefield, 71 Northgate, Wakefield, WF1 3BS Tel: 01924 361635 Tel: 01924 304130 Fax: 01924 371859
Leeds MD
Leeds, Belgrave House, Belgrave Street, Leeds, LS2 8DQ Tel: 0113 247 6711 Fax: 0113 247 6708

Wales
Anglesey
Ynys Môn, Shire Hall, Glanhwfa Road, Llangefni, LL77 7TW Tel: 01248-725264

Blaenau Gwent
Council Offices, Mitre Street, Abertilley, NP3 1AE Tel: 01495-216082
The Grove, Church Street, Tredegar, NP2 3DS Tel: 01495-72269

Bridgend
Bridgend, County Borough Offices, Sunnyside, Bridgend, CF31 4AR Tel: 01656 642391 Fax: 01656 667521

Caerphilly
The Council Offices, Ystrad Fawr, Ystrad Mynach, CF82 7SF Tel: 01443-863478 Fax: 01443-863385
(Bargoed Sub-district), Hanbury Square, Bargoed, CF8

8QQ Tel: 01443-875560 Fax: 01443-822535
(Islwyn Sub-district), Council Offices, Pontllanfraith, Blackwood, NP2 2YW Tel: 01495 235188 Fax: 01495 235298

Cardiff
Cardiff, The Register Office, 48 Park Place, Cardiff, CF1 3LU Tel: (029) 2087 1690 Tel: (029) 2087 1680 Fax: (029) 2087 1682

Carmarthenshire
Carmarthen, Carmarthen Register Office, Parc Myrddin, Richmond Terrace, Carmarthen, SA31 1DS Tel: 01267 228210 Tel: 01267 228212 Fax: 01267 228215
Llanelli, County Council Offices, Swansea Road, Llanelli, SA15 3DJ Tel: 01554-774088 Fax: 01554-749424
Ceredigion
Cardiganshire Central, The Register Office, 21 High Street, Lampeter, SA48 7BG Tel: 01570-422558 Fax: 01570-422558
Cardiganshire North, Swyddfar Sir, Marine Terrace, Aberystwyth, SY33 2DE Tel: 01970-633580
Cardiganshire South, Glyncoed Chambers, Priory Street, Cardigan, SA43 1BX Tel: 01239-612684 Fax: 01239-612684

Conwy
Colwyn, New Clinic and Offices, 67 Market Street, Abergele, LL22 7BP Tel: 01745-823976 Fax: 01745-823976
(Sub-district), Bod Alaw, Rivieres Avenue, Colwyn Bay, LL29 7DP Tel: 01492-530430
Aberconwy, Muriau Buildings, Rose Hill Street, Conwy, LL32 8LD Tel: 01492-592407 Fax: 01492-2315

Gwynedd
Conwy CB
Conwy County Borough Council, Civic Offices, Colwyn Bay, LL29 8AR Tel: 01492 575183 Fax: 01492 575204
Gwynedd
Aberconwy, Muriau Buildings, Rose Hill Street, Conwy, LL32 8LD Tel: 01492-592407 Fax: 01492-2315
Ardudwy, Bryn Marian, Church Street, Blaenau Ffestiniog, LL41 3HD Tel: 01766-830217
Bangor, The Register Office, Town Hall, Bangor, LL57 2RE Tel: 01248-362418
Caernarfon, Swyddfa Arfon, Pennrallt, Caernarfon, LL55 1BN Tel: 01286-682661
De Meirionndd, The Register Office, Bridge Street, Dolgellau, LL40 1AU Tel: 01341-424341
Denbighshire, Denbighshire North, Morfa Hall, Church Street, Rhyl, LL18 3AA Tel: 01745 708368 Fax: 01745 361424
Denbighshire South, The Register Office, Station Road, Ruthin, LL15 1BS Tel: 01824-703782 Fax: 01824-704399
Dwyfor, The Register Office, 35 High Street, Pwllheli, LL53 5RT Tel: 01758-612546 Fax: 01758-701373
Penllyn, Penllyn Register Office, Fron Faire, High Street, Bala, LL23 7AD Tel: 01678 521220 Tel: 01678 520893 Fax: 01678 521243

Flintshire
Flintshire East, The Old Rectory, Rectory Lane, Hawarden, CH5 3NN Tel: 01244-531512 Fax: 01244-534628
Flintshire West, The Register Office, Park Lane, Holywell, CH8 7UR Tel: 01352-711813 Fax: 01352-713292

Gwent
Blaenau Gwent, The Grove, Church Street, Tredegar, NP2 3DS Tel: 01495-722305

Merthyr Tydfil
Merthyr Tydfil, The Register Office, Ground Floopr, Castle House, Glebeland Street, Merthyr Tydfil, CF47 8AT Tel: 01685-723318 Fax: 01685 721849

Glamorgan
Merthyr Tydfil, The Register Office, Ground Floopr, Castle House, Glebeland Street, Merthyr Tydfil, CF47 8AT Tel: 01685-723318 Fax: 01685 721849
Neath Port Talbot, The Register Office, 119 London Road, Neath, Port Talbot, SA11 1HL Tel: 01639-643696 Tel: 01639 760020 Fax: 01639 760023

Monmouthshire
Monmouth, Coed Glas, Firs Road, Abergavenny, NP7 5LE Tel: 01873 735435 Fax: 01837 735841
(Abergavenny Sub-district), Coed Glas, Firs Road, Abergavenny, NP7 5LE Tel: 01873 735435 Tel: 01873 735468 Fax: 01873 735429
(Chepstow Sub-district), High Trees, Steep Street, Chepstow, NP6 6RL Tel: 01291 635725

Neath Port Talbot
Neath Port Talbot, The Register Office, 119 London Road, Neath, Port Talbot, SA11 1HL Tel: 01639-643696 Tel: 01639 760020 Fax: 01639 760023

Newport
Newport, The Register Office, 8 Gold Tops, Newport, NP9 4PH Tel: 01633-265547 Fax: 01633 220913

Pembrokeshire
South Pembroke, The Register Office, East Back, Pembroke, SA71 4HL Tel: 01646-682432 Fax: 01646 621433
Haverfordwest, The Register Office, Tower Hill, Haverfordwest, SA61 1SS Tel: 01437 762579 Fax: 01437 779357
(Fishguard & Cemaes Sub-district), Town Hall, Fishguard, SA65 9HE Tel: 01348-872875 Fax: 01348-872875
(Haverfordwest & Milford Haven Sub-district), Tower Hill, Haverfordwest, SA61 1SS Tel: 01437-762579

Powys
Brecknock, Neuadd Brycheiniog, Cambrian Way, Brecon, LD3 7HR Tel: 01874-624334, 01874 625781
Hay, The Borough Council Offices, Broad Street, Hay-on-Wye, HR3 5BX Tel: 01479-821371 Fax: 01479 821540
Machynlleth, The Register Office, 11 Penrallt Street, Machynlleth, SY20 8AG Tel: 01654-702335 Fax: 01654-703742
Mid Powys, Powys County Hall, Llandrindod Wells, LD1 5LG Tel: 01597-826386 Fax: 01597-826220
(Radnorshire West Sub-district), Register Office, Powys County Hall, Llandrindod Wells, LD1 5LG Tel: 01597-826382
Newtown, Room 4, Council Offices, The Park,, Newtown, SY16 2NZ Tel: 01686-627862
Newtown (Llanidloes Sub-district), Town Hall, Llanidloes, SY18 6BN Tel: 01686-412353
Radnorshire East, The Register Office, 2 Station Road, Knighton, LD7 1DU Tel: 01547 520758
Welshpool & Llanfyllllin, Neuadd Maldwyn, Severn Road, Welshpool, SY21 7AS Tel: 01938 552828 Ext 228 Fax: 01938 551233
(Builth Sub-district), The Strand hall, Strand Street, Builth Wells, LD2 3AA Tel: 01982-552134
Welshpool & Llanfyllin (Llanfyllin Sub-district), Room 8 First Floor, Powys County Council Area Offices, Youth & Community Centre, Llanfyllin, SY22 5DB Tel: 07811 315393
Ystradgynlais, County Council Offices, Trawsffordd, Ystradgynlais, SA9 1BS Tel: 01639-843104

Rhonda Cynon Taff
Pontypridd, The Register Office, Court House Street, Pontypridd, CF37 1JS Tel: 01443-486869 Fax: 01443

406587
(Cynon Valley Sub-district), The Annexe, Rock Grounds, Aberdare, CF44 7AE Tel: 01685-871008
(Rhondda No 2 Sub-district), Crown Buildings, 69 High Street, Ferndale, Rhondda, CF43 4RR Tel: 01443-730369
(Taff Ely Sub-district), The Register Office, Courthouse Street, Pontypridd, CF37 1LJ Tel: 01443-486870 Fax: 01443-406587
(Rhondda No1 Sub-district), De Winton Field, Tonypandy, CF40 2NJ

Swansea
Swansea, The Swansea Register Office, County Hall, Swansea, SA1 3SN Tel: 01792-636188 Fax: 01792-636909
Torfaen
Torfaen, The Register Office, Hanbury Road, Pontypool, NP4 6YG Tel: 01495-762937 Fax: 01495 769049

Vale of Glamorgan
Vale of Glamorgan, The Register Office, 2-6 Holton Road, Barry, CF63 4HD Tel: 01446 709490 Fax: 01446 709502

Wrexham
Wrexham, The Register Office, 2 Grosvenor Road, Wrexham, LL11 1DL, Tel:, 01978-265786, Fax: 01978-262061

Northern Ireland
General Register Office of Northern Ireland Oxford House, 49 - 55 Chichester St, Belfast, BT1 4HL
Tel: 028 90 252033 Fax: 028 90 252044
Email: gro.nisral@dfpni.gov.uk WWW: www.groni.gov.uk

Superintendent Registars Scotland
ABERCHIRDER 91 Main Street, Aberchirder, AB54 5TB Tel: 01466-780735
ABERDEEN St Nicholas House Upperkirkgate, Aberdeen, AB10 1EY Tel: 01224-522616, Fax: 01224-522616
ABERFELDY, DULL & WEEM Municipal Buildings Crieff Road, Aberfeldy, PH15 2BJ Tel: 01887-820773
ABERFOYLE + MENTHEITH 4 Montrose Road, Aberfoyle, FK8 3UL Tel: 01877-382311
ABERLOUR 46 High Street, Aberlour, AB38 9QD Tel: 01340-871635
ABOYNE District Council Offices Bellwood Road, Aboyne, AB34 5HQ Tel: 01339-886109, Fax: 01339-86798
AIRDRIE Area Registration Office 37 Alexander Street, Airdrie, ML6 0BA Tel: 01236-763322
AIRTH 100 South Green Drive Airth Falkirk, FK8 8JR Tel: 01324-831538
ALFORD Council Office School Road, Alford, AB33 8PY Tel: 01975-652421, Fax: 01975-563286
ALLOA Marshill House, Marshill Alloa, FK10 1 AD Tel: 01259-123850 Email:clack.lib@mail.easynet.co.uk
ANNAN Moat House Bruce Street, Annan, DG12 5DE Tel: 01461-204914
APPLECROSS Coire-ringeal Applecross, Kyle Ross-shire IV54 8LU Tel: 01520-744248
ARBROATH Academy Lane, Arbroath, DD11 1EJ Tel: 01241-873752
ARDGOUR 9 Clovullin Ardgour by Fort William, PH33 7AB Tel: 01855-841261
ARROCHAR 1 Cobbler View, Arrochar, G83 1 AD Tel: 01301-702289
ASSYNT Post Office House, Lochinvar by Lairg, IV27 4JY Tel: 01571-844201
AUCHINLECK 154 Main Street Auchlinleck Cummock, KA18 2AS Tel: 01290-420582
AUCHTERARDER 187 High Street, Auchterarder PH3 1AF Tel: 01764-663581
AUCHTERDERRAN 145 Station Road, Cardenden, KY5 0BN Tel: 01592-414800

AUCHTERMUCHTY Town House High Street, Auchtermuchty, KY14 7AP Tel: 01337-828329 Fax: 01337-821166

AVIEMORE Tremayne Dalfaber Road, Aviemore PH22 1PU Tel: 01479-810694

AYR Sandgate House 43 Sandgate, Ayr, KY7 1JW Tel: 01292-284988, Fax: 01292-885643

BAILLIESTON Council Office 89 Main Street, Baillieston, G69 6AB Tel: 0141-771-1901

BALLACHULISH 5 Wades Rood Kinlochleven, Argyll, PA4O 4QX Tel: 01855-831350

BALLATER An Creagan S Queens Road., Ballater AB35 5RJ Tel: 01339-755535

BANCHORY Aberdeenshire Council The Square High Street Banchory, AB3 1 Tel: 01330-822878

BANFF Seafield House 37 Castle Street, Banff, AB4S DQ Tel: 01261-812001

BARRA Council Offices, Castlebay Dana, HS9 5XD Tel: 01871-810431

BARRHEAD Council Office 13 Lowndes Street, Barrhead, 078 2QX Tel: 0141-8813551/2, Fax: 0141-5773553

BATHGATE 76 Mid Street, Bathgate, EH48 1QD Tel: 01506-653162

BEAULY 7 Viewfield Avenue, Beauly, 1V4 7BW Tel: 01463-782264

BELLSHILL 20/22 Motherwelt Road, Bellshill, ML4 1RB Tel: 01698-747145

BENBECULA Council Offices Balivanich Benbecula South Uist, HS7 5LA Tel: 01870-602425

BIGGAR 4 Ross Square, Biggar, MLI2 6DHT Tel: 01899-220997

BIRSAY Sandveien Dounby, Orkney, KW15 2118 Tel: 01856-771226

BISHOPBRIGGS Council Office 1 Balmuildy Road, Bishopbriggs, G64 2RR Tel: 0141-772-1154/5

BLACK ISLE (NORTH) Operating from Dingwall Tel: 01349-863113, Fax: 01349-866164

BLACK ISLE (SOUTH) Black Isles Centre, Service Point Office Deans Road, Fortrose, IV10 8TJ Tel: 01381-620797/8, Fax: 01381-621085

BLAIR ATHOLL Lauchope The Terrace, Blair Atholl, PH15 5SZ Tel: 01796-481242

BLAIRGOWRIE Council Buildings 46 Leslie Street, Blairgowrie, PH10 6AW Tel: 01250-872051 Fax: 01250-876029

BO'NESS + CARRIDEN 12 Corbiehail, Bo'ness EH51 0AP Tel: 01506-778990

BOISDALE Post Office Hse Daliburgh, South Uist PA81 5SS Tel: 01878-700300

BONAR + KINCARDINE Post Office Bonar Bridge, Ardgay, IV24 3EA Tel: 01863-766219

BONNYBRIDGE Operating from Denny Tel: 01324-504280

BRAEMAR Piedmont 9 Auchendryne Square, Eraemar, AB35 5YS Tel: 01339-741501

BRECHIN 32 Panmure Street, Brechin, DD9 6AP Tel: 01356-622107

BRESSAY No 2 Roadside Bressay, Lerwick Shetland ZE2 9BL Tel: 01595-820356

BROADFORD Fairwinds, Broadford Skye 1V49 9AB Tel: 01471-822270

BUCKIE 1 West Church Street, Buckie, AB56 1UN Tel: 01542-832691

BUCKHAVEN Council Office 96 Wellesley Road, Buckhaven, KY8 1HT Tel: 01592-414444 Fax: 01592-414490

BUCKSBURN Nea Office 23 Inverurie Rd., Bucksburn, AB2 9LJ Tel: 01224-712866

BURRA ISLES Roadside Hannavoe, Lerwick Shetland ZEZ 9LA Tel: 01595-859201

CALLANDER 1 South Church Street, Callander FKI7 B2N Tel: 01877-330166

CAMBUSLANG Council Office 6 Glasgow Rd, Cambuslang, G72 7BW Tel: 0141-641-8178

CAMPBELTOWN Council Office Witchburn Road, Campbeltown, PA28 6313 Tel: 01586-555253

CARLOWAY The Registry, Carloway Lewis PA86 9AU Tel: 01851-643264

CARLUKE 25 High Street., Carluke, MLB 4A3 Tel: 01555-772273

CARNOCH Bridgend, Strathconon Muir Of Ord 1V6 7QQ Tel: 01997-477254

CARNOUSTIE Council Chambers, Carnoustie DDV 6AP Tel: 01241-853335/6

CASTLE DOUGLAS District Council 5 Street Andrew Street, Castle Douglas, D07 1DE Tel: 01557-330291

CASTLETON Dalkeith House 13 Douglas Square, Newcastleton, TD9 OQD Tel: 01387-375835

CATRINE 9 Co-operative Aye, Catrine, KA5 6SG Tel: 01290-551638

CHIRNSIDE White House, Chirnside Duns, TD11 3XL Tel: 01890-818339

CHRYSTON Lindsaybeg Road Muirhead Glasgow G69 9HW Tel: 0141-779-1714

CLYNE Gower Lane, Brora, KW9 6NT Tel: 01408-621233

COALBURN 'Pretoria 200 Coalburn Road, Coolburn, ML11 0LT Tel: 01555-820664

COATBRIDGE 183 Main Street, Coatbridge, ML5 3HH Tel: 01236-422133

COIGACH The Stores, Achilibuie Ullapool, IV26 2Y0 Tel: 01854-622256

COLDSTREAM Operating from Duns Tel: 01361-882600

COLL 9 Carnan Road, Isle Of Coll PA78 6TA Tel: 01879-230329

COLONSAY & ORONSAY Scalasaig Farm, Colonsay, PA6 1 7YW Tel: 01951-200357

COUPAR-ANGUS Union Bank Buildings, Coupar- Angus, PH13 9AJ Tel: 01828-628395

COWDENBEATH 320 High Street, Cowdenbeath KY4 9QX Tel: 01383-313131

CRAWFORD 76 Carlisle Road Crawford Biggar ML12 6TW Tel: 01864-502633

CRIEFF 14 Comrie Street, Crieff, PH7 4AZ Tel: 01764-655151

CUMBERNAULD Fleming House Tryst Road, Cumbernauld, G67 1JW Tel: 01236-616390 Fax: 01236-616386

CUMBRAE 49 Stuart Street, Millport, KMS GAG Tel: 01475-53074112, Fax: 01475-530891

CUPAR County Buildings St Catherine Street, Cupar KYI5 4TA Tel: 01334-412200, Fax: 01334-412110

CURRIE 133 Lanark Road West, Currie, EH14 5NY Tel: 0131-449-5318

DALBEATTIE Town Hall Buildings Water Street, Dalbeattie, DG5 '41X Tel: 01557-330291-Ext323

DALKEITH 2-4 Buccieuch Street, Dalkeith, EH22 IHA Tel: 0131-660-7570/1

DALMELLINGTON Area Office 1 New Street, Dalmellington, KA6 7QX Tel: 01292-550229 Fax: 01292-550229

DALRY 42 Main Street Daly, Castle Douglas, DG7 3UW Tel: 01644-430310

DARVEL Operating from Galston. Tel: 01563-820218

DELTING Soibakkan, Mossbank Shetland ZE2 9R13 Tel: 01806-242209

DENNY Carronbank House Carronbank Crescent, Denny, PK4 2DE Tel: 01324-504280

DINGWALL Council Offices Ferry Road, Dingwall IV15 Tel: 01349-863113, Fax: 01349-866164

DORNOCH Cathedral Square, Dornoch, 1V25 3SW Tel: 01862-810202, Fax: 01862-810166

DOUGLAS Post Office Ayr Road, Douglas, ML1 I OPU Tel: 01555-851227

DUFFTOWN Brentwood Villa Albert Place, Dufftown, AB55 4AY Tel: 01340-820663

DUMBARTON 18 College Way, Dumbarton, G82 1LJ Tel: 01389-767515

DUMFRIES Municipal Chambers Buccleuch Street, Dumfries, DO 1 2AD Tel: 01387-260000 Fax: 01387-269605

DUNBAR Town House 79/85 High Street, Dunbar, EH42 IER Tel: 01368-863434, Fax: 01368-865728

DUNBLANE Municipal Buildings, Dunblane, FK15 OAG Tel: 01786-822214, Fax: 01786-822214

DUNDEE 89 Commercial Street, Dundee, DD1 2AO Tel: 01382-435222/3, Fax: 01382-435224 Email: grant.law@dundeecity.gov.uk WWW: dundeecity.gov.uk/dcchtml/sservices/genealogy.html

DUNFERMLINE 34 Viewfield Terrace, Dunfermline, KY12 7HZ Tel: 01383-3-12121

DUNKELD Buchanans Bridge Street, Dunkeld, P118 OAR Tel: 01350-727268

DUNOON Council Offices Hill Street, Dunoon, PA23 7AP Tel: 01369-704374, Fax: 01369-705948

DUNROSSNESS Wiltrow, Dunrossness Shetland 2E2 930 Tel: 01950-460792

DUNS 8 Newtown Street, Duns, TD11 3AS Tel: 01361-882600

DUNVEGAN Tigh-na- Bruaich, Dunvegan Isle Of Skye IV55 8WA Tel: 01470-521296

DURNESS Mid Villa Durine, Durness by Lairg, 1W7 4PN Tel: 01971-511340

EAST CALDER East Calder Library 200 Main Street, East Calder, EH53 0EJ Tel: 01506-884680, Fax: 01506-883944

EAST KILBRIDE Civic Centre Cornwall Street East Kilbride Glasgow, G74 1AF Tel: 01355-220841

EAST NEUK Municipal Office Ladywalk, Anstruther, KYID 3EY Tel: 01333-31227R

EASTWOOD + MEARNS Council Offices Easiwood Park Roukenglen Rd Giffnock, G46 7JS Tel: 0141-638-7588

EDAY + PHARAY Redbanks, Eday Orkney, KW1 2AA Tel: 01857-622239

EDINBURGH 2 India Buildings Victoria Street, Edinburgh, EH1 2EX Tel: 0131-220-0349 Fax: 0131-220-0351

EDINBURGH (L) 30 Ferry Road, Edinburgh, EH6 4AE Tel: 0131-554-8452

ELGIN 240 High Street, Elgin, IV30 1BA Tel: 01343-541202, Fax: 01343-541202

ELLON Area Office Schoolhill Road, Ellon, AB41 9AN Tel: 01358-720295

EYEMOUTH Community Centre Albert Road, EyemouTh, TD14 5DE Tel: 01890-750690

FAIR ISLE Field, Fair Isle Shetland ZE2 9JU Tel: 01595-760224

FALKIRK Old Burgh Buildings Newmarket Street, Falkirk, FK1 IIE Tel: 01324-506580, Fax: 01324-506581

FETLAR Lower Toft Funzie, Fetlar Shetland 7E2 9DJ Tel: 01957-733273

FIRTH & STENNESS Langbigging, Stenness Orkney KWI6 3LB Tel: 01856-850320

FLOTTA Post Office, Flotta Kirkwall Orkney KWI6 3NP Tel: 01856-701252

FORFAR The Cross, Forfar, DD8 1BX Tel: 01307-464973

FORRES Forres House High Street, Fortes, 1V36 0BU Tel: 01309-672792

FORT AUGUSTUS Cich Collage, Fort Augustus PH32 4DH Tel: 01320-366245

FORT WILLIAM Tweeddale Buildings High Street, Fort William, PH33 EEU Tel: 01397-704583,Fax: 01397-702757

FORTH 4 Cloglands, Forth, ML11 8ED Tel: 01535-811631

FOULA Magdala Foula, Shetland 7E2 9PN Tel: 01595-753236

FRASERBURGH 14 Saltoun Square, Fraserburgh AB43 5DB Tel: 01346-513281

GAIRLOCH (NORTH) 12 Bualnaluib, Aultbea, IV22 2JH Tel: 01445-731320

GAIRLOCH (SOUTH) District Office Poolewe, Achnasheen Ross-shire IV22 2JU Tel: 01445-781243 Fax: 01445-781315

GALASHIELS Library Buildings Lawyers Brac, Galashiels, TU1 3JQ Tel: 01896-752822

GALSTON 11 Cross Streel, Galston, KA4 8AA Tel: 02563-820218

GIGHA The Post Office, Gigha, PA4 17AA Tel: 01583-505251

GIRTHON & ANWOTH Bleachfield Birtwhistle Street, Gatehouse Of Fleet, DG7 2JJ Tel: 01557-814046

GIRVAN 22 Dalrymple Street, Girvan, KA26 9AE Tel: 01465-712894, Fax: 01465-715576

GLASGOW 1 Martha Street, Glasgow, G1 1JJ Tel: 0141-287-7677, Fax: 0141-225-7666

GLASGOW (PC) - Genealogy Unit 22 Park Circus, Glasgow, G3 6BE Tel: 0141-287-8350, Fax: 0141-225-8357

GLENELG Taobl Na Mara, Glenelg Kyle Ross-shire IV40 8JT Fax: 01599-522310

GLENROTHES Albany House Albany Gate Kingdom Centre, Glenrothes, KY7 5NX Tel: 01592-414141-Ext-4900

GOLSPIE Murrayfield Main Street, Golspie, KW10 6TG Tel: 01408-633150

GORDON Operating from Kelso, , Tel: 01573-225659

GRANGEMOUTH Municipal Chambers Bo'ness Road, Grangemouth, FK3 3AY Tel: 01324-504499

GRANTOWN-ON-SPEY Council Offices The Square, Grangetown On Spey, PH26 3HP Tel: 01479-872539

GREENOCK 40 West Stewart St., Greenock, PA15 1YA Tel: 01475-720084, Fax: 01415-781647

GRETNA Central Avenue, Orcina, DG16 5AQ Tel: 01461-337648, Fax: 01461-338459

HADDINGTON 25 Court Street, Haddington, EH41 3HA Tel: 01620-827308/368

HAMILTON 21 Beckford Street, Hamilton, ML3 0BT Tel: 01698-454211

HARRAY New Breckan, Harray Orkney KW17 2JR Tel: 01856-771233

HARRIS Council Offices, Tarbert Harris HS3 3DJ Tel: 01859-502367, Fax: 01859-502283

HAWICK Council Offices 12 High Street, Hawick, TD9 9EF Tel: 01450-364710, Fax: 01450-364720

HELENSBURGH Council Offices 25 West King Street, Helensburgh, G84 8UW Tel: 01436-673909

HELMSDALE 12 Dunrobin Street, Helmsdale, KW8 6LA Tel: 01431-821751

HOLM & PAPLAY The Register Office, Netherbreck Holm Orkney KWI7 2RX Tel: 01856-382130

HOY Laundry House Melsetter, Longhope Orkney KWI6 3NZ Tel: 01856-791337

HUNTLY 25 Gordon Street, Huntly, AB54 5AN Tel: 01466-794488

INSCH Marbert George Street, lnsch, AB52 6JL Tel: 01464-820964

INVERARAY Municipal Office, Inveraray, PA32 8UZ Tel: 01499-302124

INVERBERVIE Area Office Church Street, Inverbervie, DD10 0RU Tel: 01561-361255, Fax: 01561-362802

INVERESK Brunton Hall Ladywell Way, Musselburgh, EH21 6AF Tel: 0131-665-3711

INVERKEITHING 6 Fleriot Street, Inverkeithing, KY11 1ND Tel: 01383-411742

INVERNESS Farraline Park, Inverness, IV1 1NH Tel: 01463-239798

INVERURIE Gordon House Blackhall Road, Inverurie, AB51 3WA Tel: 01467-620981, Fax: 01467-628012

IRVINE 106-108 Bridgegate Hse, Irvine, KA12 8BD Tel: 01294-279333, Fax: 01294-312879

ISLAY Council Office Jamieson Street Bowmore Islay, PA43 7HL Tel: 01496-810332

ISLE OF BUTE Council Office Mount Pleasant Road, Rothesay, PA20 9HH Tel: 01700-50331/551

JEDBURGH Library Building Castlegate, Jedburgh, TD8 6AS Tel: 01835-863670

JOHNSTONE 16-18 Mc Dowall Street, Johnstone, PA5 8QL Tel: 01505-320012, Fax: 01505-382130

JURA Forestry Cottage Craighouse, Jura, PA60 7AY Tel: 01496-820326

KEITH Area Office Mid Street, Keith, AE55 5DY Tel: 01542-882166-Ext-39, Fax: 01542-882014

KELSO Rose Lane, Kelso, TD5 7AP Tel: 01573-225659

KELTY Kelly Local Services Sanjana Court 51 Main Street Kelty, KY4 0AA Tel: 01383-839999

KENMORE The Old Schoolhouse, Acharn by Aberfeldy, PH15 2HS Tel: 01887-830307 Fax: Same-as-tel-no

KENNOWAY Sandybrae Community Centre, Kennoway Fife, KY8 5JW Tel: 01333-351721

KILBIRNIE, BEITH & DALRY 19 School Wynd, Kilbirnie, KA25 7AY Tel: 01505-682416 Fax: 01505-684334

KILBRANDON + KILCHATTAN Cnoc Groin Isle Of Seil by Oban PA34 4RF Tel: 01852-300380

KILFINICHEN & KILVICKEON The Anchorage, Fionnphori Isle Of Mull PA66 6BL Tel: 01681-700241

KILLIN Ardlun 17 Monemore, Killin, FK21 8XD Tel: 01567-820618

KILMARNOCK Civic Centre John Dickie Street, Kilnianock, KA1 1HW Tel: 01563-576695/6

KILSYTH Health Centre Burngreen Park, Kilsyth G65 0HU Tel: 01236-822151

KILWINNING 32 Howgale, Kilwinning Ayrshire KAI3 6EJ Tel: 01294-55226112

KINGUSSIE Town Hall Spey Street, Kingussie, PH21 1EH Tel: 01540-661867

KINLOCHBERVIE 114 Inshegra, Rhiconich Lairg, IV27 4RH Tel: 01971-521388

KINLOCHLUICHART The Old Manse, Garve Ross-shire IV23 2PX Tel: 01997-414201

KINROSS 40 High Street, Kinross, KY13 7AN Tel: 01577-862405

KIRKCALDY 7 East Fergus Place, Kirkcaldy, KY1 1XT Tel: 0I592-412121, Fax: 01592-412123

KIRKCONNEL Nith Buildings Greystone Avenue Kelloholm Kirkconnel, DG4 6RX Tel: 01659-67206, Fax: 01659-66052

KIRKCUDBRIGHT District Council Offices, Kirkcudbrigbt, DG6 4JG Tel: 01557-330291-Ext-234

KIRKINTILLOCH Council Office 21 Southbank Road, Kirkintilloch, G66 1NH Tel: 0141-776-2109

KIRKLISTON 19 Station Road, Kirkliston, EH29 9BB Tel: 0131-333-3210

KIRKMABRECK The Bogxie Creetowm, Newton Stewart, DG8 73W Tel: 01671-820266

KIRKTON (FARR) 47 Crask, Bettyhill by Thurso, KW14 7SZ Tel: 01641-521335

KIRKWALL Council Offices School Place, Kirkwall Orkney KW15 1NY Tel: 01856-873535-Ext-2109

KIRRIEMUIR CouncilChambers, Kirriemuir, DD8 8BJ Tel: 01575-572845

KNOYDART Knoydari Estate Office, Inverie Knoydart by Mallaig, PH41 4PL Tel: 01681-462331, Fax: 01687-462243

LAIRG 4 Lochside, Lairg Sutherland IV27 4EG Tel: 01549-402424

LAMLASH District Council Office, LamLash Isle Of Arran KA27 8LB Tel: 01770-600338, Fax: 01770-600028

LANARK 25 Hope Streel, Lanark, ML11 7NN Tel: 01555-664679

LANGHOLM Town Hall, Langholm, DG13 0JQ Tel: 01387-380255

LARBERT 318 Main Street, Lathert, FK5 3BE Tel: 01324-503580

LARGS Macturn 24 Greenock Road, Largs, KA30 8NE Tel: 01475-674521, Fax: 01475-689227

LARKHALL Council Office 55 Victoria Street, Larkhall, ML9 2BN Tel: 01698-882454/5

LATHERON Post Office, Latheron, KW5 6DG Tel: 01593-741201

LAUDER Session House Old Causeway East High St Lauder, TD2 6FX Tel: 01578-722795

LAURENCEKIRK Royal Bank Buildings, Laurencekirk, AB30 1AF Tel: 01561-377245, Fax: 01561-378020

LEADHILLS Violet Bank 30 Station Road, Leadhills, ML12 6XS Tel: 01659-74260

LENNOXTOWN Council Office 132 Main Street, Lennoxtown, 065 7DA Tel: 01360-311362

LERWICK County Buildings, Lerwick Shetland ZE1 OHD Tel: 01595-693535-Ext-368

LESMAHAGOW 40/42 Abbeygreen, Lesmahagow, ML11 0DE Tel: 01555-893314

LEVEN 12 Station Road, Leven, KYS 4NH Tel: 01333-592538

LINLITHGOW 29 The Vennel, Linlithgow, EH49 7EX Tel: 01506-775373, Fax: 01506-775374

LISMORE Bachuil, Lismore Oban PA34 5UL Tel: 01631-760256

LIVINGSTON Lammermuir House Owen Sq, Almondvale S. Livingston, EH54 6PW Tel: 01506-414218, Fax: 01506-462575

LOCH DUICH Aird View Dornie, Kyle Of Lochalsh, IV40 8EZ Tel: 01599-555201

LOCHALSH Hamilton House Plock Road, Kyle of Lochalsh IV40 8BL Tel: 01599-534270

LOCHCARRON Curaig Lochcarron, Strathcarron IV54 8YD Tel: 01520-722390

LOCHGELLY Lochgelly Local Office Town House Hall Street Lochgelly, KY5 911 Tel: 01592-782614

LOCHGILPHEAD Dairiada House Lochnell Street, Lochgilphead, PA31 8ST Tel: 01546-604511

LOCHGOILHEAD The Register Office, Creiganiver Lochgoilhead, PA14 8AJ Tel: 01301-703222

LOCHBROOM Locality Office 29 Market Street, Ullapool, 1V26 2XE Tel: 01854-612426, Fax: 01854-612717

LOCHORE The Register Office, Rosewell Lochore by Lochgelly, KY5 SDA Tel: 01592-860237

LOCHRANZA Operating from LarnlashTel: 01770-600338 Tel: 01770-600028

LOCKERBIE Town Hall High Street, Lockerbie DG11 2ES Tel: 01576-204267/8

LOGIERAIT Operating from Pitlochry Tel: 01796-472409

LONGFORGAN 8 Norval Place Longforgan Dundee DD2 5ER Tel: 01382-360283

LUNNASTING Vidlin Farm, Vidlin Shetland, 7E2 9QB Tel: 01806-577204

MALLAIG Golden Sands Morar, Mallaig Inverness-shire PH40 4PA Tel: 01687-462383

MAUCHLINE 2 The Cross, Mauchline Ayrshire KA5 5DA Tel: 01290-550231, Fax: 01290-551991

MAUD County Offices, Maud Aberdeenshire AB4 SND Tel: 01771-613667

MAYBOLE Council Office 64 High Street, Maybole KAI9 713Z Tel: 01655-882124

MELROSE Public Library Market Square, Melrose T06 9PN Tel: 01896-823114

MEY Operating from Thurso Tel: 01847-892786 Fax: 01847-894611

MID + SOUTH YELL Schoolhouse, Ulsia Yell, ZE2 98D Tel: 01957-722260

MILNATHORT Rowallan' 21 Church Street, Milnathort, KY13 7XE Tel: 01577-862536

MOCHRUM Granite House 85 Main Street, Fort William, DG8 9HR Tel: 01988-700265

MOFFAT Town Hall High Street., Moffat, DG10 9HF Tel: 01683-220536

MONTROSE 51 John Street, Montrose Angus DD10 8LZ Tel: 01674-672351

MORVERN Dungrianach, Morvern by Oban PA34 5XW Tel: 01961-421662

MOTHERWELL & WISHAW Civic Centre Windmillhill Street, Motherwell, ML1 1TW Tel: 01698-302222

MUCKHART + GLENDEVON Operating from Alloa Tel: 01259-723850

MUIRKIRK 33 Main Street, Muirkirk, KA18 39R Tel: 01290-661227

NAIRN The Court House, Nairn, IV12 4AU Tel: 01667-458510

NESTING Laxfirth Brettabister, Lerwick Shetland ZE2 9PR Tel: 01595-694737

NETHYBRIDGE Operating from Grantown-on-Spey Tel: 01479-872539

NEW ABBEY 1 Ingleston View New Abbey Dumfries, DG2 8BZ Tel: 01387-850343

NEW CUMNOCK Town Hall The Castle, New Cumnock, KA18 4AN Tel: / Fax: 01290-338214

NEW KILPATRICK Council Office 38 Roman Road, Bearsden, G61 2SH Tel: 0141-942-2352/3

NEW MILN S Operating from Galston Tel: 01563-820218/9

NEWBURGH Tayside Institute High Street, Newburgh, KY4 6DA Tel: 01337-840917

NEWPORT-ON-TAY Blyth Hall Blyth Street, Newport On Tay, DD6 8BJ Tel: 01382-542839

NEWTON STEWART AREA The Old Town Hall 79 Victoria Street, Newton Stewart, DG8 6NL Tel: 01671-404187

NORTH BERWICK 2 Quality Street, North Berwick, EH39 4HW Tel: 01620-893957

NORTH RONALDSAY Waterhouse, North Ronaldsay Orkney KW17 2BE Tel: 01857-633263

NORTH UIST Fairview' Lochmaddy, North Uist HS6 5AW Tel: 01876-500239

NORTH YELL Breckon, Cullivoe Yell, ZE2 9D Tel: 01957-744244

NORTHMAVEN Uradell, Eshaness Shetland ZEZ 9RS Tel: 01806-503362

OBAN Council Office Albany Street, Oban, PA34 4AR Tel: 01631-562137

OLD CUMNOCK Council Office Millbank 14 Lugar Street., Cummock, KA18 1AB Tel: 01290-420666 Fax: 01290-426164

OLD KILPATRICK 57 Kilbowie Road, Clydebank G81 1BL Tel: 0141-952-1330

OLD MELDRUM Gordon Cottage Urquhart Road, Oldmeldrum, AB51 0EX Tel: 01651-873028 Fax: 01651-872060

ORPHIR The Bu, Orphir Kirkwall, KW17 2RD Tel: 01856-811319

PAISLEY Registration Ornce Cotton Street, Paisley PA1 1BU Tel: 0141-889-1030

PAPA STOUR North House Papa Stout, Lerwick Shetland ZE2 9PW Tel: 01595-873238

PAPA WESTRAY Backaskaill, Papa Westray Kirkwall, KW17 2BU Tel: 01857-644221

PEEBLES Chambers Institute High Street., Peebles, EH45 8AF Tel: 01721-720123

PENICUIK & GLENCORSE 33 High Street, Penicuik, EH26 8HS Tel: 01963-672281

PERTH Rose Terrace, Perth, PH1 5HA Tel: 01738-632486, Fax: 01738-444133

PETERCULTER Lilydale 102 North Deeside Road, Peterculter, AB1 0QB Tel: 01224-732648/9

PETERHEAD County Offices 88 King Street, Peterhead, AB42 6UH Tel: 01779-472761/2, Fax: 01779-476435

PITLOCHRY District Area Office 21 Atholl Road, Pitlochry, PH16 5BX Tel: 01796-472409

POLMONT + MUIRAVONSIDE Council Offices Redding Road Brightons Falkirk, FK2 0HG Tel: 01324-712745

PORT GLASGOW Scarlow Street., Port Glasgow PA14 5EY Tel: 01475-742140

PORTREE Registrars Office King's House The Green Portree, IV51 9BS Tel: 01478-613277, Fax: 01478-613277

PORTSOY 2 Main Street, Portsoy Banffshire AB45 2RT Tel: 01261-843843

PRESTONPANS Aldhammer House High Street, Prestonpans, EH32 9SE Tel: 01875-810232

PRESTWICK 2 The Cross, Prestwick, KA9 1AJ Tel: 01292-671666

QUEENSFERRY Council Office 53 High Street, South Queensferry, EH30 9HN Tel: 0131-331-1590

RAASAY Operating from Portee, , Tel: 01478-613217 Fax: 01478-613277

RANNOCH + FOSS Bridgend Cottages, Kinloch-rannoch Pitlochry, PH16 5PX Tel: 01882-632359

RATHO Operating from India Buildings, Ratho Tel: 0131-220-0349, Fax: 0131-2200351

RENFREW Town Hall, Renfrew, PA4 8PF Tel: 0141-886-3589

ROSNEATH Willowburn Clynder by Helensburgh, G84 0QQ Tel: 01436-831212, Fax: 01436-831212

ROSSKEEN Invergordon Service Point 62 High St, Invergordon, IV18 0DH Tel: 01349-853139

ROUSAY + EGILSAY Braehead Rousay, Kirkwall KW17 2PT Tel: 01856-821222

RUTHERGLEN Town Hall Buildings King Street, Rutherglen, G73 1BD Tel: 0141-647-1072

SALTCOATS 45 ARoadrossan Road, Saltcoats, KA21 5BS Tel: 01294-463312/604868

SANDAY 2 Lettan, Sanday Kirkwall KWI7 2BP Tel: 01857-600280

SANDNESS 13 Melby, Sandness Shetland ZE2 9PL Tel: 01595-870257

SANDSTING + AITHSTING Modesty, West Burrafirth Aithsting ZE2 9NT Tel: 01595-809428

SANDWICK Yeldabreck, Sandwick Stromness KWI6 3LP Tel: 01856-841596

SANDWICK+CUNNINGSBUR Pytaslee Leebitton, Sandwick Shetland ZE2 9HP Tel: 01950-431367

SANQUHAR Council Offices 100 High Street, Sanquhar, DG4 6DZ Tel: 01659-50347

SAUCHEN Fresta Cottage 6 Main Street, Sauchen AB51 7JP Tel: 01330-833254

SCOURIE 12 Park Terrace, Scourie by Lairg IV27 4TD Tel: 01971-502425

SELKIRK Municipal Buildings High Street, Selkirk TD7 4JX Tel: 01750-23104

SHAPINSAY Girnigoe, Shapinsay Orkney KWI7 2EB Tel: 01856-711256

SHIELDAIG The Register Office, Baramore Shieldaig Strathcarron IV54 8XN Tel: 01520-755296

SHOTTS Council Ornee 106 Station Road, Shottss ML7 8BH Tel: 01501-823349

SKENE & ECHT 25 Glebe Land Kirkion Of Skene, Westhill Aberdeenshire AB32 6XX Tel: 01224-743371

SLAMANNAN Operating from Falkirk Tel: 01324-506580

SMALL ISLES Kildonan House, Isle Of Eigg PH42 4RL Tel: 01687-482446

SOUTH COWAL Copeswood Auchenlochan High Rd, Tighnabruaich, PA21 2BE Tel: 01700-811601

SOUTH LOCHS 7 Kershader, South Lochs Isle Of Lewis PA86 9QA Tel: 01851-880339

SOUTH RONALDSAY West Cara Grimness South Ronaldsay, KWI7 2TH Tel: 01856-831509

ST ANDREWS Area Office St Man's Place, St Andrews, KY16 9UY Tel: 01334-412525

STIRLING Municipal Buildings Corn Exchange Road, Stirling, FK8 2HU Tel: 01786-432343

STONEHAVEN Viewrnount Arduthie Road, Stonehaven, AB39 2DQ Tel: 01569-762001:-EXT:-8360

STORNOWAY Town Hall 2 Cromwell Street, Stornoway, HS1 2BW Tel: 01851-709438

STRACHUR Memorial Hall, Strachur Argyll PA27 8DG Tel: 01369-8603I6

STRANRAER AREA 23 Lewis Street, Stranraer DG9 7AB Tel: 01776-702151-Ext-254

STRATHAVEN R Bank Of Scot Blds 36 Common Green, Strathaven, ML10 6AF Tel: 01357-520316

STRATHDON Old Engine House Candacraie Nursery Garden, Strathdon, AB36 8XT Tel: 01975-651226

STRATHENDRICK District Office 32 Buchanan St., Balfron, G63 0TR Tel: 01360-440315

STRATHY Hillside Portskerra Melvich Thurso, KWI4 7YL Tel: 01641-531231

STROMNESS 5 Whitehouse Lane, Stromness Orkney KW16 3EY Tel: 01856-850854

STRONSAY Strynie Stronsay Kirkwall, KWI7 2AR Tel: 01857-616239

STRONTIAN Easgadail Longrigg Road, Strontian Acharacle Argyll PH36 4HY Tel: 01967-402037

TAIN Operating from Rosskeen Tel: 01862-853139

TARBAT The Bungalow Chaplehill Portmahomack Portmathom Tain, IV20 1XJ Tel: 01862-871328

TARBERT Argyll House School Road, Tarbert, PA29 6UJ Tel: 01880-820374

TARRADALE Service Point Office Seaforth Road, Muir Of Ord, IV6 7TA Tel: 01463-870201

TARVES Post Office Udny, Ellon Aberdeenshire AB4 I 0PQ Tel: 01651-842253

TAYINLOAN Bridge House, Tayinloan Tarbert, PA29 6XG Tel: 01583-441239

TAYPORT Burgh Chambers, Tayport, DD6 9JY Tel: 01382-552544

THORNHILL 15 Dalgarnock Road, Thornhill Dumfriesshire DG3 4JW Tel: 01848-330108

THURSO District Office Davidson's Lane, Thurso KW14 7AF Tel: 01847-892786, Fax: 01847-894611

TINGWALL 20 Meadowfleld Road Scalloway Lerwick Shetland ZEI 0UT Tel: 01595-880732

TOBERMORY Council Offices Breadalbane Street, Tobernory, PA75 6PX Tel: 01688-302051

TOMINTOUL Jubilee Cottage 51 Main Street, Tomintoul, AB37 9HA Tel: 01807-580207

TONGUE The Kyle Centre, Tongue Lairg, IV27 4XB Tel: 01847-601330

TORPHINS Willowbank, Kincardine O' NeilI, AB34 5AX Tel: 01339-884308

TRANENT 8 Civic Square, Tranent, EH33 1LH Tel: 01875-610278

TROON Municipal Buildings 8 South Beach, Troon, KA10 6EF Tel: 01292-313555, Fax: 01292-318009

TURRIFF Towie House Manse Road, Turiff, AB53 7AY Tel: 01888-562427, Fax: 01888-568559

TYREE The Register Office, Crossapol Isle Of Tyree PA77 6UP Tel: 01879-220349

UIG(LEWIS) 10 VaItos Uig Lewis, PA86 9HR Tel: 01851-672213

UIG(SKYE)(INVERNESS) 3 Ellishadder Staffin Portree, IV51 9JE Tel: 01410-562303

UNST New Noose, Ballsound Unst, ZE2 9DX Tel: 01957-711348

UPHALL 99 East Main Street, Broxburn, EH52 5JA Tel: 01506-775500, Fax: 01506-775505

VALE OF LEVEN 77 Bank Street, Alexandria, G83 0LE, Fax: 01389-752413

WALLS Victoria Cottage, Walls Lerwick Shetland ZE2 9PD Tel: 01595-809384

WANLOCKHEAD Operating from Sanquhar Tel: 01659-74287

WEST CALDER 1 East End, West Calder, EH55 8AB Tel: 01506-871763

WEST FIFE The Health Centre Chapel St High Valleyfield, Dunferrnline, KY12 8SJ Tel: 01383-880682

WEST KILBRIDE Kirktonhall 1 Glen Road, West Kilbride, KA23 9BL Tel: / Fax: 01294-823569

WEST LINTON Council Office, West Linton, EH46 7ED Tel: 01968-660267

WESTERN ARDNAMURCHAN Post Office, Kilchoan Acharacle, PH36 4LL Tel: 01972-510209

WESTRAY Myrtle Cottage, Pierowall Westray Orkney KW1 2DH Tel: 01857-677278

WHALSAY Conamore Brough, Whalsay Shetland ZE2 9AL Tel: 01806-566544

WHALSAY-SKERRIES Fairview, East Isle Skerries Lerwick ZE2 9AS Tel: 01806-515224

WHITBURN 5 East Main Street, Whitburn, EH47 0RA Tel: 01501-678000, Fax: 01506-678026

WHITENESS & WEISDALE Vista, Whiteness Shetland ZE2 9LJ Tel: 01595-830332

WHITHORN AREA 75 George Street, Whithorn DG8 8NU Tel: 01988-500458

WICK Town Hall Bridge Street, Wick, KW1 4AN Tel: 01955-605713

WIGTOWN AREA Council Sub-office County Buildings, Wigtown, DG8 9HR Tel: 01988-402624

Registration Records in The Republic of Ireland
Oifig An Ard-Chlaraitheora (General Register Office)
Joyce House, 8/11 Lombard Street East, Dublin, 2.

The General Register Office and Research Room are open Monday to Friday, (excluding public holidays) from 9.30 a.m. to 12.30 p.m. and from 2.15 p.m. to 4.30 p.m. for the purpose of searching the indexes to birth, death and marriage records and obtaining certificates. Joyce House is near the junction of Pearse Street and Westland Row Dublin

The following records are deposited in the General Register Office:-
1. Registers of all Births registered in the whole of Ireland from 1st January, 1864, to 31 December, 1921, and in Ireland (excluding the six north-eastern counties of Derry, Antrim, Down, Armagh, Fermanagh and Tyrone know as Northern Ireland) from that date.
2. Registers of all Deaths registered in the whole of Ireland from 1st January, 1864, to 31st December 1921, and in Ireland (excluding Northern Ireland) from that date.
3. Registers of all Marriages registered in the whole of Ireland from 1st April 1845, to 31st December 1863, except those celebrated by the Roman Catholic clergy.
4. Registers of all Marriages registered in the whole of Ireland from 1st January, 1864, to 31st December, 1921, and in Ireland (excluding Northern Ireland) from that date.
5. Registers of Births at Sea of children, one of whose parents was Irish, registered from 1st January, 1864, to 31st December, 1921. Register of Births at Sea of Children one of whose parents was born in the Republic of Ireland, registered after 1921.
6. Register of Deaths at Sea of Irish-born persons, registered from 1st January, 1864, to 31st December, 1921, and after 1921 of Irish born persons other than those born in Northern Ireland.
7. Registers of Births of children of Irish parents, certified by British Consuls abroad, from 1st January, 1864 to 31st December, 1921.
8. Registers of Deaths of Irish-born persons, certified by British Consuls abroad, from 1st January, 1864, to 31st December, 1921.
9. Register of Marriages celebrated in Dublin by the late Rev. J F G Schulze, Minister of the German Protestant Church, Poolbeg Street, Dublin, from 1806 to 1837, inclusive.
10. Registers under the Births, Deaths and Marriages (Army) Act, 1879.
11. Adopted Children Register – legal adoptions registered in the Republic of Ireland on or after 10th July, 1953. Note: Cost of certificates issued from the Adopted Children Register: £5.50 for full certificate: £3.50 for short certificate: £0.70 for certificate for Social Welfare purposes.
12. Birth and Death Registers under the Defence (Amendment) (No. 2) Act, 1960.
13. Registers of certain births and deaths occurring outside the State (The Births, Deaths and Marriages Registration Act, 1972, Sec. 4).
14. Register of Certain Lourdes Marriages (Marriages Act, 1972, Sec.2).
15. Registers of Stillbirths registered in Republic of Ireland from 1st January 1995 (certified copies available to parents only).

Reading Room Searches.
There are two types of searches available to the public. A search for a maximum of 5 years costs £1.50 whilst a general search for one day covering all years costs £12. Both are payable in advance. A photocopy of an identified entry can be purchased for £1.50.

Records for births, deaths and Catholic marriages commenced in 1864. Records for non-Catholic marriages date from 1845. Information prior to this (1864) may be available from parish records which are kept in the Genealogical Office in the National Library, Kildare Street, Dublin, 2. Records of births, deaths and marriages for Northern Ireland are only available up to 1921.

The indexes are complied on a yearly/quarterly basis in alphabetical order in the same manner as a telephone directory. Records for the years 1878 to 1903 and 1928 to 1965 are divided into four quarters ending March (which includes January, February and March), June, September and December, therefore it is necessary to check the index for each quarter in any one year. Births which were registered late are at the back of the Index for each year.

Marriages are indexed under both the maiden name of the bride and the grooms surname, therefore, if you check under each name you find a cross reference which will indicate it is the correct entry relating to the marriage.

Getting the best from your local Record Office

Kate Thompson

As an archivist of over 25 years' experience, working mainly in two county record offices, it never ceases to amaze me that our users view a visit to the record office with awe or even fear! This may have been understandable thirty years ago when CROs were largely visited by academics, but not now that they are used by so many 'ordinary' people, a large proportion of whom are family historians.

The world today is of course very different from the 1960s and, while some may regret the days when six people in a searchroom made it busy, most archivists are only too pleased that more and more people want to use their service. Being pragmatic, we live in an era of 'use it or lose it' and the battle today is to convince those who hold the purse-strings that our work is valuable and should be supported at a level commensurate with the service our customers want and need.

The record office network in England and Wales, outside the major national institutions such as the Public Record Office and the British Library, is based on historic counties. Before the major reorganisation of local government in 1974 nearly all the historic counties had a record office and some of the larger ones, such as Suffolk and Yorkshire, had more than one. Where there was no CRO, as in Rutland for example, arrangements were made with a neighbouring office. In addition some of the major cities had a record office - Birmingham, Bristol, Leicester and Nottingham to name but a few. In Scotland, local record offices have developed slowly but most regions are now served, and in Northern Ireland the Public Record Office of Northern Ireland covers the whole province.

Experienced family historians need no help in making the most of their visit to the local record office but newcomers to the subject could save themselves a lot of time by some advance preparation. Those who get least out of their visit are the ones who turn up on a whim and imagine that all the information they require will be readily available. **Family history research is time-consuming!** Although the increasing amount of material available on CD-Rom or the Internet is a tremendous boon to the family historian, it does not take away the fact that the vast majority of material is still in manuscript (or microform) and unindexed.

So, a visit to the record office should **not** be your first step. The best advice is to attend an adult education class where you will be taught how to use the sources and what they can - and, more importantly, **cannot** tell you. If there is not one running near you why not approach your local provider (university, college, WEA, local authority, etc) and ask for one to be organised? Some record offices run day schools and your local family history society is also a useful source. There are many books on how to do family history and at the very least you should read the chapter on using original sources before visiting the record office.

Record office staff have tried hard to make the reading room environment welcoming and pleasant and, above all, non-threatening. However, a record office is not a library and you may find the routines strange; the most obvious difference is that the sources you require are not on the open shelves but stored in strongrooms designed to protect the documents against their natural 'enemies'. There are rules which have been drawn up to ensure that the material you are consulting will still be available in

the next millennium. Although you are unlikely to be consulting documents dating from the tenth century - not on your first visit at least! - the material you will look at will be unique and irreplaceable. It is for this reason that many heavily used sources - parish registers, wills, census returns - are only available in facsimile form, traditionally microfilm or microfiche but increasingly in a digitised version.

The first thing you will encounter is the requirement to have a reader's ticket. Unfortunately, there are unscrupulous individuals who will try to steal documents and a serious case of theft from county record offices in the early 1980s led to the establishment of the County Archive Research Network [CARN]. A CARN ticket can be used in a number of record offices although some have their own, separate system. **Please look after your CARN ticket - without it you will not be able to consult original archives**.

You will be almost certainly be asked to put any bags, including handbags, in a locker, and some offices will not allow you to take your coat into the reading room. Only pencils can be used anywhere near original documents as other writing instruments will leave indelible marks if an accident occurs. You will observe that the staff rarely use a pen and never if they have documents on their desk. Smoking is not allowed and food and drink are similarly banned; this includes sweets and chewing gum. If all this sounds draconian it is important to remember the archivist's first duty - to protect the documents in his or her care.

Having dealt with the office routines - and it is surprising how long it all takes - you will want to get at the documents. The staff will do their best to help but they are often run off their feet and you need to think carefully about what to ask. 'I am tracing my family tree; they were called Thompson and came from this county' will lead to a glazed look from the member of staff, and please resist the urge to detail everything you already know about your family! Decide *before* your visit what questions you want answered and be specific, eg find the baptism of John Thompson c 1750 in the Letchworth area, check the family of William Smith on the 1851 census in Norton. Expect to spend a lot of time finding nothing!

Much of the material used by family historians will be easy to track down, such as parish registers, probate material, poor law records and census returns, but documents do turn up in the most unlikely places. County Quarter Sessions rolls contain considerable material relating to poor law removals but these are rarely indexed even if the parish poor law material is. Wills and other probate material can be found in estate collections and elsewhere and may be the only copy if the probate records are deficient. Once you have gained experience you may wish to consult other types of material, such as title deeds, letters and diaries, to put flesh on the bare bones of the information you have gleaned. Although we have the richest archives in the western world, many documents do not survive and you should be prepared for failing to find what you are looking for.

Having consulted the indexes and archive catalogues, you can order the documents you want to use. You will be asked to fill in a document request slip - usually in duplicate or triplicate - and there will be a limit to the amount of material you can consult at any one time. You should not usually have to wait more than about 15 to 20 minutes but there will be exceptions. Not all the material cared for by the record office may be on site and less frequently consulted material may be kept in an out-store, sometimes some miles away from the office. Although systems are in place to prevent documents from being put back in the wrong place, it does happen, and there will be occasions - fortunately very few in number - when documents are misplaced. They are not lost but finding them quickly could be a problem.

Because of the need to protect records, some items may be so fragile that they cannot be produced until they have been repaired by a trained archive conservator. Some offices only have one conservator and others have to send documents away for repair. Efforts are made to minimise the amount of material classed as unfit for production but this is one area where available resources will never be adequate to meet demand. It is important to handle documents carefully and replace any packing materials when you have finished. Keep documents in bundles in the order in which you found them and report any damage to a member of staff. Use any aids provided, such as book rests, to support the documents so as to minimise further wear and tear. You should not lean on the documents or place anything on top of them, such as a notebook - unless you need lead weights to hold them flat.

It is essential to make a careful record of what you have consulted so as not to go over the same ground again. It is best to use record sheets - one for each event - on which you can note the sources used. For example, using the first example given above, record the parish registers consulted, their covering dates and the reference number for each volume. When you find the relevant entry record it carefully, noting any inconsistencies, and make sure you have quoted the document reference. It is a matter of personal choice whether to modernise spellings.

You may want to have a copy of relevant entries or whole documents. This is normally possible provided the document is sufficiently robust to be copied, there is no embargo on copying and you comply with copyright legislation. Those documents that are already in facsimile form can be copied easily and many record offices allow self-service from microform reader-printers. Original documents can be damaged by being copied, especially if you are dealing with outsize material, books with tight bindings or fragile papers. In these circumstances there is little alternative to copying out the information, but it may be possible - although of course more expensive - to have a photograph. Most documents are still owned by an individual or institution and are only on loan to the record office. It may be the case that the owner will not allow copies to be taken, although this is unlikely with most material used by family historians. Copyright legislation is a minefield and deserves an article all on its own! The relevant Act of Parliament is the Copyright Designs and Patents Act 1988, which has recently been superseded in some of its clauses by EC legislation. (The most obvious practical effect of this has been the lengthening of the time before which certain photographs can be copied, from 50 years to 70 years.) Libraries and archives have certain rights to make copies *for private research only* and this is why you will be asked to sign a copyright declaration form. Because the law is so complex, most record offices will ask you to sign a form even if you know the material is out of copyright, as no one wants to be the first test case! Some organisations are fiercer than others in protecting their copyright, such as music publishers and the Ordnance Survey, and they will prosecute. If you wish to

reproduce a document in a publication you will require permission from the chief archivist and may have to pay a fee, but unless you are a major publisher this is unlikely to be prohibitive. (For a useful guide to copyright, see *Copyright for Archivists* by Tim Padfield, published by the Public Record Office in 2001.)

There may be a charge for 'value-added' services, such as photocopying, use of the Internet and so on; a few offices also charge for all or part of their core service. No archivist likes to charge for what they feel should be provided free but unfortunately they sometimes have little choice. Many local authorities have had their budgets reduced in the last few years and it is difficult to argue that providing an archive service should have a higher priority than educating children, caring for the vulnerable in our society or the myriad other responsibilities of county, district and unitary authorities. Despite these funding problems, the progress made by record offices in the last quarter of a century has been impressive. There are some splendid new buildings such as Surrey, Hampshire and Shropshire and some imaginative refurbishments (eg Leicestershire, Suffolk and London Metropolitan Archives). The Heritage Lottery Fund has helped to finance exciting new projects, many of them in the area of new technology, and there are imaginative plans to link record offices in a way not possible before. Once could argue that one of the joys of using record offices is that they are all different but this can also be frustrating for the researcher in a hurry. There are many ways of getting involved with your local record office, such as joining its Friends if it has one, or volunteering to help with an indexing project.

As well as publicly-funded record offices, there are private ones which may contain material of interest to you; a good example is a stately home or business archive with records of former employees who may have been your ancestors. Private record offices have no obligation to allow you access but most will make the necessary arrangements if approached politely. The appropriate local record office will have information on material held elsewhere and the procedures for access.

Recent surveys have shown that most users of record offices are satisfied with the service provided but there are of course exceptions. Expectations have risen so that today's users expect such luxuries as toilets, parking and coffee machines! Archivists are proud of their services and want to provide the best they can within their resources. They cannot work miracles but are always pleased to hear suggestions for improvements. Above all, the message is 'if in doubt, ask' - archivists don't bite and would much prefer you not to suffer in silence.
© Kate Thompson

The Middlesex Sessions Vagrancy Records:

a gold mine for the Family Historian
Daniel Beagles Assistant Archivist

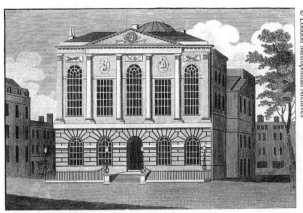

© London Metropolitan Archives

A View of the SESSIONS HOUSE for the COUNTY of MIDDLESEX on Clerkenwell Green

Since October 2000, staff at London Metropolitan Archives, with funding from the Heritage Lottery Fund have been sorting and cataloguing in detail the records of the Middlesex Sessions. This is a large and important collection of more than 4000 feet of papers. When the project finishes in April 2002 it will have generated over 100,000 database records all of which will be searchable by the public.

The Middlesex Sessions archive comprises the records of four separate courts: the Middlesex Sessions of the Peace (1549-1971); Sessions of 'Oyer and Terminer'; the Westminster Sessions (1620-1844) and the Middlesex side of the Gaol Delivery of Newgate in the Old Bailey (1549-1834). These bodies not only dealt with judicial and criminal issues, but also dealt with administrative matters such as taxation; the maintenance of roads and bridges; electoral registration; vagrancy; poor law; the regulation of prices and wages; licensing of places of entertainment; the care of the insane; the registration of aliens and the inspection of slaughterhouses. As a result Sessions Papers offer many tantalising glimpses into the ordinary (and extraordinary) lives of the people of London.

Detailed cataloguing has so far revealed many records in the Middlesex Sessions archive that are of high quality and potentially of great interest to genealogists. The papers relating to vagrancy are one such group. There are more than 4500 vagrancy settlement examinations and removal orders, which date from the mid seventeenth to the late nineteenth century.

Vagrancy and Poor Law

The Elizabethan Poor Law of 1601, like all previous statutes showed no sympathy towards vagrants. Technically it was no crime to be destitute but any paupers found outside the parish that was responsible for them could be in serious trouble. Newcomers thought likely to become chargeable to a parish could be removed by two justices of the peace. If paupers were found to be destitute and claiming poor relief elsewhere, they would be returned to their place of 'last legal settlement'. By an act of 1598 there were three possible places they could be returned to - the parish where they were born, a parish where they had lived for one year, or a parish 'through which they had last passed without punishment'. These options left plenty of scope for disputes between parishes over who was responsible.

The 1662 Act of Settlement tightened the law and redefined the meaning of settlement. In practice someone could be considered as legally settled in a parish if they had rented a tenement worth £10 a year or more, or if no complaint had been made against them for 40 days. An act of 1685 decreed that the 40 days was to run from the day that written notice was given to overseers. This would perhaps have only served to warn the overseers of the need to take prompt action. From 1692 settlement could be earned by paying local rates, by being bound apprentice, or by being hired as a servant and working for a full year. One could argue that the idea of 'settlement' was actually of benefit to the poor, as the law recognised that they had settlement somewhere, and whichever parish it was could be compelled to support them.

Wives, widows, dependent children and other family members would be considered to have the same legal settlement as the head of the family. Settlement however, could change - people constantly moved to find work, children could be born in one parish then move with their parents to another, and being apprenticed in a parish conferred right of settlement there. Complications and ambiguities still led parish officers to go to court to attempt to rid themselves of unwanted financial burdens.

The reason why it mattered so much, was that from Elizabethan times it had been the responsibility of the parish to levy a poor rate on its inhabitants in order to provide money to relieve the poor of the parish. Strenuous efforts were made to keep the rate down and ensure that payments were only made to those who were eligible. It is apparent from the records that churchwardens and overseers were keen to remove paupers back to their parish of origin, or at least get someone else to pay for their upkeep. A huge amount of paperwork was generated in the courts as a result of all their efforts and it is these documents that we are concerned with here.

These papers are of great interest both to historians and those researching their family history. It is not simply that they contain lists of names, but particular types of document provide a great deal of useful information about the lives of the people involved and their families. They can not only tell you the names and relationships of the people involved, provide clues to where people have come from, but often give details of their profession and recent 'life history'.

© London Metropolitan Archives

It would be a mistake to assume that these records are only of interest to those researching London families. Vagrancy records in the Middlesex Sessions archive relate to people who migrate surprisingly long distances, fall on hard times and are returned to where the court decides they have come from. Many of the cases heard by the Middlesex Sessions relate to people from outside London. There are many Irish and Scots for example, but also individuals from much further afield such as Sarah Levi from Strasbourg; John Shepherd who was born in Kingston, Jamaica; Lorentzo De Durattoa, a thirteen year old boy from Parma, Italy; Christopher Kitts, who was born in Guinea, 'Affrica' and brought to England, presumably as a slave; Henry Johnson, who was born in Gothenburg, Sweden, and was apprenticed to a Liverpool ship owner, before being 'impressed' into the navy. And many others, all of whom were at one time or another found destitute on the streets of London.

Types of 'vagrancy record'
There are various documents, each created for different purposes, which we can consider to be 'vagrancy records'. There may be warrants for the arrest of vagrants. Or petitions from the contractors who undertook to move the vagrants asking the court to compel the overseers of the parish to reimburse them for their costs. The money would normally be for feeding and transporting the vagrants, but sometimes they appealed for extra to pay for burying those unfortunate enough to die on the way. There are also some lists of vagrants, with the name and place of settlement given, that were submitted as part of contractors' accounts. There are even documents from people tendering for vagrancy removal contracts. An example is that of James Sturges Adams who petitioned the court in May 1705 that he might be allowed to convey vagrants out of the county for £120 per year with an extra 6 pence per day payable for the maintenance of each vagrant he might pass. The court agreed to his proposal. (MJ/SP/1757/05)

However, the most common type of documents are:

Settlement examinations
These were documents drawn up after the pauper had been questioned with the intention of discovering where they had come from. They are, in a sense, the evidence that one parish presents to prove its case that the vagrant should be somewhere else. They can be quite short, or go into a great deal of interesting detail about the vagrant, his or her family, their occupations, and where they lived. They often clearly establish the family relationships of those being moved. An example is Sarah Danks, who was found wandering destitute in the parish of Saint Giles in the Fields in

July 1776 and confirmed that she was the widow of Joseph Danks, who was born in the parish of Answorth, Staffordshire. Her settlement examination records the care that was taken to check her background thoroughly to see where she might have been able to claim legal settlement:

"Middlesex: Sarah Danks aged about Forty one years widow of Joseph Danks maketh oath that she was married to her said husband about twenty one years ago in the Parish church of St. Paul Shadwell in the County of Middlesex That her said Husband informed her he was born in the Parish of Answorth in the County of Stafford and that he never did any Act whereby he could obtain a settlement but was legally settled in the last named parish at the time of his decease which happened about Eleven years ago since which she this deponent hath not been a hired yearly servant nor rented any place of the yearly value of Ten Pounds or upwards nor paid any kind of tax
That being reduced to great want she hath been obliged to wander abroad and lodge in the open air in the streets within the Parish of St. Giles in the fields in the s(ai)d County of Middlesex" (MJ/SP/V/01/021/152)

Another typical example is that of Margaret Meanes, wife of Abraham Meanes, who was apprehended in 1772 by the overseer of Finchley, when she was found wandering and begging with her four children:

"Mary aged upwards of four years Martha upwards of Two years - And William upwards of Seven Weeks - And a daughter of her s(ai)d Husband by a former Wife named Ann aged upwards of Ten years"

When questioned, she states that her estranged husband was a yearly hired servant to the collector of tolls at Sawtrey turnpike, in Sawtrey, Huntingdon. This is enough for the churchwardens and overseers of the parish of Finchley to press the court to decide that she should be removed there. (MJ/SP/V/01/017/10)

Examinations often give the names, occupations and addresses of masters of apprentices and employers of yearly hired servants. For example the examination of George Evans on the 2nd of May 1820 confirms that he was bound apprentice to a Mr. Bailey, of Park Row, Bristol, a 'West Indies Merchant'. (MJ/SP/V/01/054/039)

The earliest surviving statements from 1740 to around 1770 contain the most information about the vagrants and people connected in some way to them. Later statements record only the bare minimum of information about why and where people are being moved, or about apprenticeships or service. This is particularly noticeable for Irish and Scottish vagrants and those born at sea. This may reflect a social trend - are there fewer people in service? Or do brief notes reflect a change in the law - courts perhaps needing less

© London Metropolitan Archives

information to make a decision? Perhaps it simply reflects an increase in the numbers of vagrants - the magistrate or court clerks may not have had the time to keep detailed records.

The examination of Henry Hamilton Mahoney on the 27th of February 1797, for example, does little more than confirm he was born in Ireland:

"The Examination of Henry Hamilton Mahoney a Rogue and vagabond. Who being upon oath saith that he was born in the County of Kerry and came thence about four months ago, and hath done no Act whereby to gain a Legal settlement in a Parish or Place in England" (MJ/SP/V/01/040/06)

Removal orders
Removal orders are the next stage in the legal process - a court document giving authority for the removal of vagrants. They can tell us which parish wishes to remove them, the name of the vagrant and sometimes that of the magistrate. They also say which parish it is intended to return the vagrant to. In addition they sometimes give details of the route - which parishes the vagrants are to go through to get there. It is clear from the documents that certain parishes were used as 'transfer of authority' points, regular stops on the route, or embarkation points. Examples include the parish of Ridge, Hertfordshire, which was a regular stop for vagrants being sent back north, or Chester, which received Irish migrants on their way back to Liverpool and Dublin.

Where an examination has not survived, the removal order can be of use as they also normally restate the reason why someone is to be moved to a particular place.

It can happen that parishes disagree about the settlement of a vagrant. As the parish and its inhabitants have to pay for the upkeep of any paupers within their area, they quite clearly do their best to discourage vagrants from settling within their bounds. There are many cases in the archive where the overseers and parish officials have appeared in court or compelled the officials of another parish to attend to explain why named individuals should not be placed with them. An example, from July 1694, is a case concerning Philip Bishop and his family. The overseers of the Hamlet of Wapping were intending to remove them to Saint Giles in the Fields and to that end, petition the court to make the

© London Metropolitan Archives

churchwardens of Saint Giles appear in court and explain why the family should not be returned to them:

"... Wherefore your petition(ers) most truly Pray That you will be pleased to Grant an order ffor the s(ai)d Churchwardens and Overseers of the poor of St Giles affores(ai)d To appeare and shewe cause to this Hono(ra)ble Bench, why the said Phillip Bishop Elizabeth his wife And the said three children shall not be repassed to the parish of St Giles..." (MJ/SP/1694/07/011)

In another case, three months later, the Hamlet of Wapping themselves are the subject of a petition, as the overseers of the parish of Saint Paul, Shadwell ask the court to make the Hamlet of Wapping explain why they won't accept the vagrant Sarah Budd. (MJ/SP/1694/10/004).

From 1820 onwards, annotations appear on many of the removal orders confirming the arrival of vagrants at their place of settlement. Payment of expenses is also recorded in some cases.

Records that deal with the poor can provide vital clues to family historians. But these records can also give us insights into social and economic conditions. It would be possible to find out where the majority of vagrants come from, or we could discover which parts of the capital are associated with particular professions. Sometimes, however, we are tantalised with more questions. Consider the case of Berry James Rowswell who on the 26th of December 1798 was removed from Saint Paul, Shadwell, a riverside parish on the Thames, to All Saints, Newcastle upon Tyne. The reason given was that he was bound apprentice there to a Roger Alderson, master mariner. Three years later on the 27th of January 1792, Berry appears in court again, as the overseers of Saint Paul, Shadwell, have again found him 'wandering abroad and begging' and remove him to Newcastle upon Tyne for the second time. (MJ/SP/V/01/032/05 and MJ/SP/V/01/035/05) Did he come to London on one of his master's ships, carrying coal perhaps? Was he left behind in London to avoid paying him wages? Or did he simply run away? Sadly, it is unlikely that we will ever know.

Other related records -Where next?
Other records relating to vagrants and the Poor Law can be found in the archives of individual parishes and Boards of Guardians. The records of more than 750 Anglican parishes in the Greater London area have been deposited at the London Metropolitan Archives. Here too, can be found the records of many of the larger Boards of Guardians and Poor Law Unions. In these collections you can not only find more removal orders and settlement examinations, but in addition, admission and discharge registers for those who were admitted to workhouses, lists of those receiving poor relief, and apprenticeship indentures. And finally, this is also where you will find the rate books that list those residents who were made to pay for all this activity.

London Metropolitan Archives
40 Northampton Road London EC1R 0HB
Telephone 020 7332 3820
Fax: 020 7833 9136
Minicom: 020 7278 8703
Email: ask.lma@corpoflondon.gov.uk

LONDON
METROPOLITAN
ARCHIVES

The place for documents, books, maps, prints and photographs about London and Londoners

Most family trees have the odd root in London and descendants of Londoners are widely spread throughout the United Kingdom and far beyond. London Metropolitan Archives (LMA) holds a vast amount of information about the capital and its citizens. Our records cover a period of nearly 900 years and over 31 miles of shelving, making LMA the largest local authority archive in the United Kingdom. If you are researching your family's history, you can visit us to search:

- 15,500 parish registers from more than 700 Anglican churches
- Non-conformist registers from over 300 churches and congregations.
- Electoral registers dating from 1832 to the present day.
- Over 8000 volumes of Land Tax records dating from 1767 to the 1840's.
- 5700 school registers for more than 800 schools in the County of London, dating from the 1840's to the 1980's.
- Admission and discharge records for hospitals, workhouses and asylums.
- The International Genealogical Index (I.G.I.)

You can also access a wide range of other collections including the records of businesses, charities, associations, families and estates. There are in addition large collections of architects' plans; one of the three largest map collections in London and almost half a million photographs. We also have a reference library of over 100,000 volumes.

If you cannot visit us in person, our Family History Research may be able to help you. The service is not designed to compile complete family trees or undertake lengthy research projects, but a whole range of relatively short searches can be made, checking individual facts for specific queries, such as the details of a marriage.

Find out about all our sources and services by contacting us at the address below, or, by checking our pages on the Corporation of London's website (www.cityoflondon.gov.uk). As part of our commitment to making finding aids available over the internet, the new site, '*London Generations*', includes a searchable database of the most popular family history sources, such as parish and school registers. You can now pay for Family History Research online through a secure internet connection.

London Metropolitan Archives
40 Northampton Road
London
EC1R 0HB

Telephone	020 7332 2820
Fax	020 7833 9136
Minicom	020 7278 8703
Email	ask.lma@corpoflondon.gov.uk

DIRIGE
CORPORATION
OF LONDON

Introducing the Rainer Archive

Shani Cassady Researcher

Frederick Rainer
© Rainer Archive

Institutions and Organisations
A great many organisations, homes and schools are represented within the archive, and in fact are too numerous to mention here, however examples can be given.

The Association for the Protection of Women and Children (ASPWC) was established in 1857 initially under the presidentship of the Marquis of Townsend, and provided a diverse range of legal and advisory services (principally) to women and children, offering assistance in cases of bigamy, seduction, abduction, sexual assaults, violence, neglect, cruelty, desertion, incest and infection. The only method of prosecution during that time was by private litigation and therefore the caseload of the society also encompassed applications to courts for affiliation and separation orders, negotiating and handling payments upon separation and in cases of illegitimacy and maintenance. Furthermore the society was called upon to assist in cases of defamation, injury, compensation, protection, property disputes, and in instances of unfair dismissal. However the society was not involved exclusively with prosecutions, nor was it the case that every application received legal funding for prosecution, indeed cases were often declined or (less frequently), passed on to the Public Prosecutor. Furthermore some applicants did not wish for a summons to be issued preferring the matter to be negotiated by the society, which in situations such as this, became a mediator (if not judge and jury), frequently imposing financial terms on the other party, against whom some threat would be levelled should they fail to comply with the conditions.

Applications for assistance or pleas for investigation

Many criminal justice agencies are able to trace their origins back to the growth of philanthropy in the nineteenth century. The modern Probation Service for example is said to have been founded in 1876 when a journeyman printer named Frederic Rainer donated 5/- to the Church of England Temperance Society (CETS) to arrest the inevitable downward spiral of those "..whose foot has once slipped". By all accounts the CETS responded admirably and appointed missionaries and mission women to the Police Courts who would befriend and assist those in need. By the end of the century every Police Court in London and Middlesex were so served, and in 1907 the first Probation Act was inaugurated, formally creating the modern day Probation Service.

The founding society continued, however in 1923 the London Police Court Mission separated from the CETS, and by 1961 it was clear that the terms Police Court and missionary were no longer appropriate and so the society changed its name to the Rainer Foundation. Today it is still concerned with the welfare of those in need, however its remit has changed, and during the latter part of the twentieth century the charity began to concentrate its efforts on projects for young people. Fortunately the evolution of this foundation (and others associated with it) has been preserved, and the collection has come to be known as the Rainer Archive.

The archive is held at the Galleries of Justice in Nottingham, and is presently undergoing an extensive research and cataloguing process, made possible by the partnership that has been developed between the Galleries and Nottingham Trent University. The collection is at first glance merely a set of boxes containing an apparently disparate set of notes, books, photographs and records between the periods 1820 to 1997, however it has quickly become evident that the archive is not only extensive but also exceptional, and once the research and cataloguing process is complete it will be a new and highly significant resource with national appeal and widespread accessibility (possibly as an internet resource). It should be noted though that the development of the Probation Service is only one facet of the archive, although it appears that all of the organisations represented in the collection have in some way contributed to the evolution of philanthropic endeavour.

A MORNING AT THE Open-all-Night Refuge.

LONDON FEMALE PREVENTIVE AND REFORMATORY HOME.
OFFICE: 200 EUSTON ROAD, N.W.

© Rainer Archive

© Rainer Archive

FRIENDLESS and FALLEN.

A Few Interesting Particulars respecting the

London Female Preventive and Reformatory Institution.

Office—200, Euston Road, N.W.

THIS Institution, founded in 1857, under the Presidency of the late Canon Dale, then Vicar of St. Pancras, is one of the pioneer works of Home Missionary enterprise for the protection and rescue of young women and girls. The Mission from which it grew was the first systematic effort made to seek out, rescue and reclaim the erring and the outcast, and to place them in "Homes" conducted on the family principle.

The objects of the Institution are threefold—

   1.—To Train destitute, friendless girls for Domestic Service.
   2.—To Shelter virtuous young women in circumstances of moral peril.
   3.—To Seek and to Reclaim the Fallen and Outcast.

came from a variety of sources, for example, from clergymen, 'Ladies Correspondents', police officers and private applications. (The society advertised in newspapers and journals on a regular basis - their services and also for subscriptions) The decision to take up a case was decided by the council on advice from their solicitor (who worked to the guidelines laid down by the council), and also from their prosecuting officer (who attended the Police Courts and other sessions on the society's behalf).

Despite its prominence during the 19th century, little has been written about the scope and effect of this society, possibly as much of the material has been unavailable, nevertheless it has been argued that its influence and impact was in fact minimal. However in the first two years of its operation 1006 cases came before the society. The majority only sought advice, nonetheless there were a substantial proportion requiring a greater depth of intervention. 238 assault cases, 105 indecent or criminal assaults, 25 rapes, 41 seductions, 437 cases of neglect, cruelty or desertion, 22 cases disputing custody of children, 17 attempts to inveigle young girls for immoral purposes and 12 miscellaneous charges.

The society suffered financial hardship on more than one occasion, nonetheless it continued attracting donations and bequests, and was never without support from the more influential in society. The philanthropic efforts of the association were not confined to the metropolis though, and eventually they began granting permission for satellite groups throughout the country. At this point the organisation changed its name to the Associated Societies for the Protection of Women and Children, however their work with children was curtailed to some degree with the inauguration of the Royal Society for the Prevention of Cruelty to Children, and eventually the ASPWC became assimilated into the London Police Court Mission.

The London Female Preventive and Reformatory Institution (LFPRI) later known as the London Haven for Women and Girls, is also well represented within the archive. This was created in 1857 by Thomas Raikes and friends following a disagreement

and separation of interests with Lieutenant Blackmore of the London Dormitory. The Thomas's, a couple well known to the group of friends, were appointed to managed the day to day running of the home and so the institution began what was to become a major source of support for thousands of women. Mr E. W. Thomas was no stranger to the work undertaken by the organisation as he had close associations with the Midnight Meeting Movement and frequently preached on their behalf at gatherings, taking the repentant to homes and reformatories to begin their life 'anew'. With this level of commitment and expertise the institution quickly grew from a small mission aimed at assisting the friendless and fallen to work in the areas of industrial schools, convalescent homes and training schools, and in 1917 they also absorbed the work of the Midnight Meeting Movement.

Admissions to the homes came principally through their night shelter, via the Midnight Meeting Movement, the Police Courts and the Refuge and Reformatory Union, and the institute regularly published accounts of their work in leaflets, reports and pamphlets.

Obviously much of this documentation regaled the reader on how much their donation was appreciated and how successful the home had been in their rescue work, however this type of literature can also provide the researcher with a greater insight into the operations and ideologies of the institute, and also of the period it covers. The first annual report states the ethos of the institute by quoting Luke xix.10 "The Son of Man is come to seek and to save that which was lost." and, Luke xiv.23 "And the Lord said unto the servant, Go out into the highways and hedges, and compel them to come in." The objectives were stated as being:

   • To seek the destitute and fallen by voluntary missionary effort.
   • To afford temporary protection to friendless young women, whose circumstances expose them to danger; also to effect the rescue of fallen females, especially those decoyed from the country, by admitting them to the benefits of the above Institution, which will be conducted as far as possible on the principles of a

© Rainer Archive

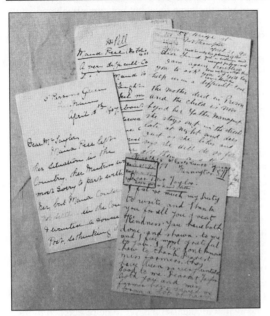

private family, under the care of a Matron…
• To restore, when practicable, the wanderer to her family and friends, whether in town or country.
• To qualify those admitted into the Institution for various departments of domestic service, to obtain suitable situations for them, and provide them with clothing.
• To aid such as for approved reasons wish to emigrate.
• Above all the seek the spiritual welfare of the inmates.

At the height of their mission the LFPRI were responsible for the management of 7 homes:
• Central home on Euston Road (probation)
• Milton House West Brompton
• Eden Grove Holloway
• Parsons Green (2 homes, one being for convalescents, viz friendless young women of good character on their discharge from hospital)
• Hampstead Road (for friendless young women and servants of good character)
• Manchester Street (night reception house)

Eventually though the need for their particular services declined as the state began to absorb the work traditionally undertaken by voluntary agencies, and in 1945 the LFPRI was assimilated by the London Police Court Mission (although one home, Newhaven, retained its own management committee).

Mary

Throughout its long and industrious career, the institution professed to many successes. One of these being the rehabilitation of Mary C. who, in 1875 was convicted of infanticide and sentenced to death. Mary came from a poor family and had fallen into an ill-advised association with a wealthy, albeit married man who abandoned her when she became pregnant.

Her parents disowned her and Mary was eventually admitted to Clerkenwell Workhouse on the 22nd March. She gave birth to a daughter on the same day and discharged herself and her child some two weeks later. On the evening of her discharge the body of a child was found in a nearby canal, and as soon as she was confronted, Mary admitted to taking the life of her newborn child. It was said at the trial that Mary was of low intelligence and possibly suffered from some mental instability brought about by the recent trauma of childbirth and abandonment. In finding her guilty, the jury asked for mercy, nevertheless the judge pronounced the ultimate penalty and Mary was taken to Newgate Gaol to await her fate. Mr Thomas of the LFPRI intervened with letters, petitions and newspaper articles urging people to write and plead on behalf of Mary. He was successful and the sentence was consequently commuted to penal servitude for life, however 7 years later Mr Thomas again contacted the Home Secretary and asked that Mary be sent to the LFPRI for rehabilitation. This was granted and Mary was taken and trained as a domestic servant at one of the homes in Parson's Green, after which she found employment and eventually married. This case was it should be said, rather unusual, and their more traditional work can be illustrated by the story of Alice L.

Alice

Alice

Alice L. was born in 1833 in Warwickshire, the daughter of Frederick a farm foreman. At the age of 15 she seems, albeit accidentally, to have set fire to some property that formed part of the farm on which her father was employed. Consequently Frederick lost his job and Alice was taken to the county police courts where she was found in the cells by a representative of the London Female Preventive and Reformatory Institution. Projecting such an air of misery and helplessness she inspired pity amongst any who came across her, which proved especially fruitful at her trial. She stood accused of arson, yet the case itself was shrouded in mystery and it could not be proved whether the crime was wilful or not. At the trial, the circumstances of Alice's background and the strong ties of her community were used to defend her, along with the sympathy her demeanour evoked. The environment she grew up in did not afford her much opportunity and being the eldest child of a large family in a small rural community she was pushed

© Rainer Archive

A **Mission of Mercy.**

Brief account of Work in London among Young Women and Girls.

"He beheld the city and wept over it."

into domestic service at a very early age. Undoubtedly this was achieved without her having received proper training and she was likely to have been completely unprepared for it. Her father was well known and respected in the locality and Alice's predicament brought disgrace on him and the family's good name. All this combined to excite pity amongst magistrates hearing the case and led one to ask, "What will become of her?"

Fortunately Alice was saved the further humiliation of prison and was given the chance to reform her character. She was discharged to the care of the LFPRI to train in domestic service and to be 'morally educated', and was admitted to the Jubilee Training Home at 7 Parson's Green in Fulham in November 1899, where she resided for 14 months and was described as 'a very good girl' by the Matron of the establishment. Morally and vocationally the training she received was rewarded for 14 months later Alice was found a situation. After a variety of lower positions she found work as a cook for a mayor in a provincial town and according to the records of the LFPRI was still working there in 1905.

The institution like any other organisation, wanted people to know of their good works, particularly in a time where numerous other foundations were doing similar philanthropic work. Case studies highlighting examples of young women like Alice were essential for the credibility and integrity of the foundation, and many such examples of their publicity material has been discovered within the archive. Many stories are illustrated by means of small pocket sized books charting the degradation and subsequent reclamation of the woman in question. One entitled 'Excelsior' was found along with a photograph of a woman and some of her letters, and it appears that the lady in question is Alice L. The book is in perfect condition so it can be argued that it was placed with the photograph and letters to be used for publicity purposes as opposed to being a keepsake for Alice. The author remarks "Really I cannot recognise her...

yes it was the same face, but how greatly altered and improved since I last looked upon it!" Letters from Alice were full of gratitude, "so you see I am getting on now, thanks to you, dear Matron, for if I had not gone into the Home when I did I should not be able to take a place like this", and signed "one of your grateful girls". One former employer is quoted as saying " I find her a very good girl...She seems very grateful to you for all your kindliness to her in the Home; and from all she tells me of her former life, I am sure it has been the means of making her a steady, sensible girl". Inside the front cover of Excelsior it states that since the publication, Alice had written to say she was about to be married '...to a steady and respectable young man and a total abstainer'.

On November 15th 1906 in Edwinstowe parish church Alice married John K. of Kirkby, Nottinghamshire, the son of George K. farm foreman with her parents as witnesses. It is thought that she subsequently had at least 2 children, a girl, Ivy in the December quarter of 1911 (registered in Basford) and a boy, Frederick (registered in Shardlow, Derby) in the December quarter of 1914.

Development of the Archive

The available material has yet to be researched more completely, nevertheless the Rainer archive is already yielding a substantial amount of interesting and invaluable material, and therefore it is expected that given the appropriate level of investment it will indeed become a highly significant national resource in the not too distant future. In parts the archive is able to reveal some personal stories and this is an area that will be developed more fully. It is possible though that families of those associated with these societies have retained some of the letters, diaries, photographs and personal reminiscences and these would certainly add a personal dimension to this unique collection. Therefore any assistance in locating these important 'pieces of the jigsaw' would be most gratefully received. In addition it may be of interest to learn that the Galleries is able to offer excellent storage facilitates for many types of historical material, either on a permanent (accession) or temporary (loan) basis. Further information may be obtained from Shani Cassady, researcher at the Galleries of Justice, High Pavement, The Lace Market, Nottingham, telephone 0115 9520555 or email at shani.cassady@ntu.ac.uk

Areas Served by The District Land Registries for England & Wales

HM Land Registry
HM Land Registry, Lincoln's Inn Fields, London, WC2A 3PH

England
Birkenhead District Land Registry
Rosebrae Court, Woodside Ferry Approach, Birkenhead,
Merseyside, L41 6DU Tel: 0151 473 1110
Tel: 0151 473 1106 Enquiries Fax: 0151 473 0366
Cheshire; London Boroughs of Kensington, Chelsea,
Hammersmith, Fulham
Birkenhead District Land Registry
Old Market House, Hamilton Street, Birkenhead, Merseyside,
L41 5FL Tel: 0151 473 1110
Tel: 0151 473 1106 Enquiries, Fax: 0151 473 0251
Merseyside; Staffordshire; Stoke on Trent
Coventry District Land Registry
Leigh Court, Torrington Ave, Tile Hill, Coventry, CV4 9XZ,
Tel: 01203 860860 Tel: 01203 860864
Enquiries Fax: 01203 860021
West Midlands
Croydon District Land Registry
Sunley House, Bedford Park, Croydon, CR9 3LE
Tel: 0181 781 9100 Tel: 0181 781 9103 Enquiries
Fax: 0181 781 9110
London Boroughs of Croydon, Sutton, Bromley, Bexley
Durham (Boldon House) District Land Registry
Boldon House, Wheatlands Way, Pity Me, Durham, County
Durham, DH1 5GJ, Tel: 0191 301 2345 Fax: 0191 301 2300
Cumbria; Surrey
Durham (Southfield House) District Land Registry
Southfield House, Southfield Way, Durham, County Durham,
England Tel: 0191 301 3500 Tel: 0191 301 0020
Darlington; Durham; Hartlepool; Middlesbrough;
Northumberland; Redcar & Cleveland; Stockton on Tees
Tyne & Wear
Gloucester District Land Registry
Twyver House, Bruton Way, Gloucester, Gloucestershire, GL1
1DQ Tel: 01452 511111 Fax: 01452 510050
Berkshire; Bristol; Gloucestershire; Oxfordshire; South
Gloucestershire; Warwickshire
Harrow District Land Registry
Lyon House, Lyon Road, Harrow, Middlesex, HA1 2EU
Tel: (020) 8235 1181 Fax: (020) 8862 0176
London Boroughs of Barnet, Brent, Camden, Islington, City of
London; City of Westminster; Harrow, Inner & Middle Temples
Kingston Upon Hull District Land Registry
Earle House, Portland Street, Hull, HU2 8JN
Tel: 01482 223244 Fax: 01482 224278
East Riding of York; Kingston Upon Hull; Lincolnshire
Norfolk; N E Lincolnshire; North Lincolnshire; Suffolk
Leicester District Land Registry
Westbridge Place, Leicester, Leicestershire, LE3 5DR
Tel: 0116 265 4000, Tel: 0116 265 4001 Enquiries
Fax: 0116 265 4008
Buckinghamshire; Leicester; Leicestershire; Milton Keynes,
Rutland
Lytham District Land Registry
Birkenhead House, East Beach, Lytham St Annes FY8 5AB
Tel: 01253 849 849 Tel: 01253 840012 Enquiries
Fax: 01253 840001 (Manchester, Salford, Stockport, Tameside
& Trafford)
Fax: 01253 840002 (Bolton, Bury, Oldham, Rochdale & Wigan)
Fax: 01253 840013 (Lancashire)
Greater Manchester; Lancashire
Nottingham District Land Registry
Chalfont Drive, Nottingham, Nottinghamshire, NG8 3RN
Tel: 0115 935 1166 Fax: 0115 936 0036 for Nottinghamshire,
Derby; Derbyshire, Nottinghamshire; South Yorkshire West
Yorkshire
Peterborough District Land Registry
Touthill Close, City Road, Peterborough, PE1 1XN
Tel: 01733 288288 Fax: 01733 280022
Bedfordshire; Cambridgeshire; Essex; Luton; Northamptonshire
Plymouth District Land Registry
Plumer House, Tailyour Road, Crownhill, Plymouth, Devon,
PL6 5HY, Tel: 01752 636000, Tel: 01752 636123 Enquiries,
Fax: 01752 636161
Bath; North Somerset; Cornwall; Isles of Scilly; North Somerset;
Somerset
Portsmouth District Land Registry

St Andrews Court, St Michael's Road, Portsmouth, Hampshire,
PO1 2JH, Tel: 01705 768888
Tel: 01705 768880 Enquiries, Fax: 01705 768768
Brighton & Hove; East Sussex; Isle of Wight; West Sussex
Stevenage District Land Registry
Brickdale House, Swingate, Stevenage, Hertfordshire, SG1 1XG,
Tel: 01438 788888, Tel: 01438 788889 Enquiries
Fax: 01438 780107
Hertfordshire
London Boroughs of Barking & Dagenham, Enfield, Hackney,
Haringey, Havering, Newham, Redbridge, Tower Hamlets,
Waltham Forest
Swansea District Land Registry
Ty Bryn Glas, High Street, Swansea, SA1 1PW
Tel: 01792 458877 Fax: 01792 473236
London Boroughs of Ealing, Hillingdon, Hounslow
Telford District Land Registry
Parkside Court, Hall Park Way, Telford TF3 4LR
Tel: 01952 290355 Fax: 01952 290356
Hereford; Worcester; Shropshire; Greenwich Kingston upon
Thames London Boroughs of Lambeth, Lewsiham, Merton,
Richmond upon Thames, Southwark, Wandsworth
Tunbridge Wells District Land Registry
Curtis House, Forest Road, Tunbridge Wells TN2 5AQ
Tel: 01892 510015 Fax: 01892 510032 Kent
Weymouth District Land Registry
Melcombe Court, 1 Cumberland Drive, Weymouth, Dorset, DT4
9TT, Tel: 01305 363636 Fax: 01305 363646
Hampshire Poole; Portsmouth; Southampton; Swindon
Wiltshire; Dorset
York District Land Registry
James House, James Street, York, YO1 3YZ
Tel: 01904 450000 Fax: 01904 450086
North Yorkshire; York

Wales
District Land Registry for Wales
Ty Cwm Tawe, Phoenix Way, Llansamlet, Swansea
SA7 9FQ, Tel: 01792 355000, Tel: 01792 355095 Enquiries
Fax: 01792 355055
A fuller item on the Land Registry appeared in 5th Edition of the
Handbook

Probate Records

Information from Probate records can provide vital pieces of the genealogical puzzle. Although often not as useful as records of births, marriages and deaths, which can evidence crucial links to previous generations, they can provide evidence of relatedness within generations, and often contain fascinating insights into the financial affairs of people in times past.

Probate is a process whereby some person or persons, usually the executor(s) of a Will if there was one, or one or more of the next-of-kin if there was no Will, are appointed in law to administer the estate of someone who has died. This is usually only necessary if the deceased person left fairly substantial assets, so don't expect to find any Probate record relating to the estate of a person who had little or no estate of their own. The Probate concept of 'estate' refers just to assets held in the sole name of the person who has died, and so Probate isn't necessary for the release of assets held jointly with another person. When an application for Probate is made, any Will that the deceased person left must be submitted to the Probate Registry. The Will, if judged to be valid, is thereafter kept on file, and it is normally possible for anyone to obtain a copy of it. There are exceptions, however, such as the Wills of members of the Royal family. The important point is that Wills are available from the Probate Registries only as a by-product of the Probate process: if Probate wasn't needed, then the Probate Registries have no record of the estate at all.

You should bear in mind that the Probate record, if any, will be dated some time after the date of death of the person concerned, so start searching from the year of death, or the year in which you think the person died. You should normally expect to find the Probate record within the first year or two after the date of death, and, if you have not found it within three, you can usually assume that Probate wasn't necessary. However, in a very small number of cases, Probate is granted many years after the person in question died. Take a tip from the professionals: if you don't find a probate record within the first few years, the next most likely time to search is the year in which their heir(s) died. This is because unadministered estate is most likely to come to light at that time. How far you want to go with the search will probably depend on how crucial the person in question is to your research, but there is as yet no shortcut: you will have to search the index for each year separately.

Control of Probate record-keeping passed from the Church to the state in 1858, at which point the records were unified into one Calendar index. These indexes, which summarise all Probate grants for England and Wales during a given year, act as a table of contents for the vast store of records held by the Probate Registries. If the subject of your research died before

Reading the Will

1858, it will be more difficult to trace their Will. However, if they were very wealthy or owned a lot of land, consult the indexes of the Prerogative Court of Canterbury (PCC) first, and then those of the lesser ecclesiastical courts of the region in which they lived. PCC records are held by the Family Records Centre in London (Tel: (020) 8392 5300), but records of the lesser ecclesiastical Probate courts are highly dispersed. Try the local authority archives, such as public libraries and County Record Offices of the appropriate region, and also any local historical research institutes. Major ecclesiastical centres are also likely to have their own archives.

The table below lists the Calendar indexes held by the various Probate Registries in England and Wales. You can usually call in to consult the indexes, but check with the Registry concerned first, especially if you intend to travel any distance. Probate grants for each year are listed alphabetically by surname. The crucial parts of the Probate record are the Grant type, which is usually 'Probate', 'Administration' or 'Administration with Will', the issuing Registry, and the grant issue date. They are normally written in sequence towards the end of the index entry, but the older books give the grant date first and highlight the issuing Registry in the text of the entry. The grant type can be inferred from the text, but note that the indexes prior to 1871 listed the 'Administration' grants in a separate part of the book from the 'Probate' and 'Administration with Will' grants, so be sure to search in both places for years prior to this. In addition, there may be a handwritten number next to entries for Wills proved in the Principal Probate Registry (London) between 1858 and 1930. This is the Folio number, which is used by the Probate Registries when obtaining copies of the Will. Always make a note of this if applicable.

If the grant type is 'Administration', this tells you that the person in question did not leave a valid Will. However, the Probate Registries can still supply a copy of the grant, which is the document naming the person appointed in law as the administrator of the estate. This can provide genealogical information, especially in older grants where the relationship of the applicant to the deceased was stated. It also gives the value of the estate, although in most cases this is stated as 'not exceeding' a certain figure rather than quoting an exact amount. In fact, the Probate record contains very little information about the estate at all, and no information about its composition. Don't expect to find inventories on file for records after 1858, although they sometimes form part of the Probate record prior to this.

In many cases you can save a lot of time and money by making the search yourself, but there is a postal service by which a search is made on your behalf for a period of four years. There is a fee of £5 for this, but this includes copies of the Will and/or grant if a record is found. It also gives you the benefit of the experience of Probate staff, for instance in knowing when to search and judging under which name the record is likely to be listed. If you want the Probate Registry to conduct a search for a period longer than the standard four years, there is an additional fee of £3 for each 4-year period after the first four. Thus, an 8-year search will cost £8, a 12-year search £11, and so on.

If you want to make a postal search, contact **The Postal Searches and Copies Department,** The Probate Registry, Duncombe Place, York YO1 7EA UK
Tel: +44 (1904) 624210   Fax: +44 (1904) 671782.

Applications for searches must be made in writing, and give the full name, last known address and date of death of the person concerned. A search can normally be made using less detail, but if the date of death is not known, you must state the year from which you want the search to be made, or give some other evidence that might indicate when the person died. If you have information about legal actions related to Probate or the disposition of assets, include that on your application. Many people find it convenient to order copies in this way even if they have already made a search of the Probate indexes and located a record relating to the subject of their research, but if this is the case, please include the grant type, issuing Registry and grant issue date on your application, as well as the Folio number if applicable (see above) as this can speed up the supply of copies considerably. The fee should be payable to "H.M.Paymaster General", and if it is paid from abroad, must be made by International Money Order or bank draft, payable through a United Kingdom bank and made out in £ sterling. If you are applying for a search as well, you can request a search of any length, and fees for this are outlined above.

The records referred to here relate only to estates in England and Wales.

The list overleaf shows what indexes the various Probate Registries hold. Most Registries will have had indexes dating back to 1858, but are not required to keep them for more than fifty years. Usually, the older indexes will have been donated to local authority archives. Contact your local public library or County/City Record Office to see what Probate records they have. If you know of any historical research institute in your area, find out if they have any Probate records. Please note that, since the York Probate Registry serves as a national centre for postal requests for searches and copies, it is not possible to inspect the Probate indexes in person there.

Probate Registries & Sub-Registries

REGISTRY	RECORDS	TELEPHONE
Bangor Probate Sub-Registry Council Offices, FFord, Bangor LL57 1DT	1946 to 1966 and 1973 to 1998	(01248) 362410
Birmingham District Probate Registry The Priory Courts, 33 Bull Street, Birmingham B4 6DU	1948 to date	(0121) 681 3400
Bodmin Probate Sub-Registry Market Street, Bodmin PL31 2JW	1858 to 1966 and 1973 to 1998	(01208) 72279
Brighton District Probate Registry William Street, Brighton BN2 2LG	1935 to date	(01273) 684071
Bristol District Probate Registry Ground Floor, The Crescent Centre, Temple Back, Bristol BS1 6EP	1901 to date	(0117) 927 3915
Carmarthen Probate Sub-Registry 14 King Street, Carmarthen SA31 1BL	1973 to 1998	(01267) 236238
Chester Probate Sub-Registry 5th Floor, Hamilton House, Hamilton Place, Chester CH1 2DA	1948 to 1966	(01244) 345082
Exeter Probate Sub-Registry Finance House, Barnfield Road, Exeter EX1 1QR	1858 to 1966 and 1973 to 1998	(01392) 274515
Gloucester Probate Sub-Registry 2nd Floor, Combined Court Building, Kimbrose Way, Gloucester GL1 2DG	1947 to 1966	(01452) 522585
Ipswich District Probate Registry Level 3, Haven House, 17 Lower Brook Street, Ipswich IP4 1DN	1936 to date	(01473) 253724
Leeds District Probate Registry 3rd Floor, Coronet House, Queen Street, Leeds LS1 2BA	1949 to date	(0113) 243 1505
Leicester Probate Sub-Registry 5th Floor, Leicester House, Lee Circle, Leicester LE1 3RE	1890 to 1966 and 1973 to date	(0116) 253 8558
Lincoln Probate Sub-Registry Mill House, Brayford Side North, Lincoln LN1 1YW	1936 to 1966 and 1973 to 1998	(01522) 523648
Liverpool District Probate Registry Queen Elizabeth II Law Courts, Derby Square, Liverpool L2 1XA	1946 to date	(0151) 236 8264
Manchester District Probate Registry 9th Floor, Astley House, 23 Quay Street, Manchester M3 4AT	1947 to date	(0161) 834 4319
Middlesbrough Probate Sub-Registry Teesside Combined Court Centre, Russell Street, Middlesbrough TS1 2AE	1973 to 1998	(01642) 340001
Newcastle-upon-Tyne District Probate Registry 2nd Floor, Plummer House, Croft Street, Newcastle-upon-Tyne NE1 6NP	1929 to date	(0191) 261 8383
Nottingham Probate Sub-Registry Butt Dyke House, Park Row, Nottingham NG1 6GR	1973 to 1998	(0115) 941 4288
Oxford District Probate Registry Combined Court Building, St.Aldates, Oxford OX1 1LY	1940 to date	(01865) 793050
Sheffield Probate Sub-Registry PO Box 832, The Law Courts, 50 West Bar Sheffield S3 8YR	1935 to 1966 and 1973 to 1998	(0114) 281 2596
Stoke-on-Trent Probate Sub-Registry Combined Court Centre, Bethesda Street, Hanley, Stoke-on-Trent ST1 3BP	1973 to 1998	(01782) 854065
Winchester District Probate Registry 4th Floor, Cromwell House, Andover Road, Winchester SO23 7EW	1944 to date	(01962) 863771
Probate Registry of Wales PO Box 474, 2 Park Street, Cardiff CF1 1ET	1951 to date	(029) 2037 6479
Principal Probate Registry First Avenue House, 42-49 High Holborn, London WC1	1858 to date	(020) 7947 6000

The Service has undergone a process of computerisation, but as yet this covers only recently-issued grants, which will be of limited interest to genealogists. However, anyone who is interested in checking up on grants since 1996 can search the Probate Service database themselves. To date, workstations for public use have been installed at the Principal Probate Registry and Manchester District Probate Registry. The Postal Searches and Copies Department at York is also completing a long period of computerisation, which should see a much-improved service to family history researchers, with clearer and more comprehensive information and quicker supply of documents.

This information is based on details supplied by the Probate Service. The details are liable to change without notice. Always telephone the Registry before visiting, to check opening times and the availability of records. While every effort is made to ensure the accuracy of these details, the Probate Service cannot be held responsible for any consequence of errors.

Please check our website at www.courtservice.gov.uk before applying for searches or copy documents by post.

The Pavement
York

Probate Records in the Borthwick Institute
Professor D M Smith MA PhD FSA

The Borthwick Institute of the University of York houses the probate records of the Archbishop of York both as diocesan and as head of the northern province, so as such is a really valuable source for family history. The diocesan probate court was known as the Exchequer; that of the province as the Prerogative Court. Since the Church authorities were chiefly responsible for the administration of the probate jurisdiction before 1858 then it follows that the location of a particular will depends upon a familiarity with the jurisdictional structure of the Church from province through diocese, archdeaconry, rural deanery, to parish.

The Exchequer Court exercised probate jurisdiction in respect of the laity and (after the middle ages) unbeneficed clergy having goods solely in the diocese of York. The post Reformation diocese covered the whole of Yorkshire (except for the north western part of the county which formed part of the Richmond archdeaconry in Chester diocese) and Nottinghamshire and the Archbishop also possessed the liberties of Ripon and Hexhamshire (the latter being in Northumberland). The original wills are arranged chronologically by month of probate in rural deanery bundles. The series of original probate material begins in 1427 but before 1591 there are only one or two items for the years when wills survive. From 1591 there are some wills extant for most years but the series is not generally complete until the 1630s onwards. Between 1653 and 1660 when the Commonwealth authorities established their own central probate court system, probate records of Yorkshire and the north of England are at the Public Record Office, London. From about 1688 the bundles generally include inventories, probate and administration bonds, declarations, renunciations etc. The inventories do not survive much after the mid 18th century and are replaced by simple declarations of the value of the estate. The original probate records of the Exchequer Court from the Nottinghamshire rural deaneries of the diocese have been transferred to the Nottingham County Record Office. As well as the original records (which are contained in some 3,000 archive boxes, in itself an indication of the size of the collection), there is a more complete series of probate registers running from 1389 to January 1858, when the Church authorities ceased to exercise probate jurisdiction. These registers contain contemporaneous registered copies of wills proved in both the Exchequer and the Prerogative Courts. From 1502 grants of probate and administration of intestates were entered into act books arranged by individual rural deanery.

The Prerogative Court of the Archbishop has its origin in the late 16th century and exercised jurisdiction in respect of probate or administration of persons with bona notabilia that is, goods etc. to the value of £5 and over either in more than one jurisdiction within the diocesan boundaries of York, or in more than one diocese in the northern province (until the 19th century the dioceses of

York, Carlisle, Chester and Durham, covering the counties of Cheshire, Cumberland, Durham, Lancashire, Northumberland, Nottinghamshire, Westmorland and Yorkshire), or in both northern and southern provinces. In such as the last case, the Prerogative Court of Canterbury was also usually resorted to in the first instance (its records are at the Public Record Office, London). The original records of the Prerogative Court of York are also arranged chronologically by month of probate and are stored with the Exchequer material. The registered copies of wills proved in the Prerogative Court are entered in the same series of volumes as described above for the Exchequer Court. A separate series of act books for the Prerogative Court (containing probate acts and grants of administration) survive from 1587.

A third York probate court is found from the middle ages onwards the **Chancery Court of the Archbishop**. Originally used for wills proved before the Archbishop in person rather than before his probate officials in the Exchequer, the Chancery came to have jurisdiction over the probate and administration of the goods of beneficed clergy in the York diocese and probate by reason of the Archbishop's periodic visitations of an inferior ecclesiastical jurisdiction. The original records survive from 1535 onwards (although rather sparsely until the late 16th century) but copies of wills have been registered in the Archbishops' registers from 1316 to 1857.

In addition to the diocesan and provincial probate jurisdictions there were a whole series of what were known as peculiar jurisdictions small ecclesiastical enclaves comprising several parishes or perhaps just one, linked to an ecclesiastical corporation such as a cathedral or monastery, or to a manor which exercised probate jurisdiction over laity having goods just in these enclaves. The Institute houses an extensive collection of the probate records of some 53 Yorkshire peculiars.

Most of the categories of probate jurisdictions described above have some kind of name index, whether printed, typescript, or manuscript. The indexes to the Exchequer and Prerogative Courts records have been published from 1359 to 1688 by the Yorkshire Archaeological Society Record Series (vols. 4, 6, 11, 14, 19, 22, 24, 26, 28, 32, 35, 49, 60, 68, 78, 89). Between 1688 and 1731 there are typescript indexes and from 1731 to 1858 there are 29 contemporaneous manuscript volumes of indexes arranged within short chronological probate periods by person. In respect of the Chancery Court there are two printed indexes published in the Yorkshire Archaeological Society Record Series under the erroneous title of Consistory Wills (vols. 73, 93). Details of these indexes are given in the *Guide to the Archive Collections in the Borthwick Institute of Historical Research* (1973), pp.155 - 180. A typescript Parish Index at the Borthwick Institute details which parishes were in which ecclesiastical jurisdiction.

(This article first appeared in the 1998 Edition)

Record Offices & Archives

National

BBC Written Archives Centre
Caversham Park, Reading , RG4 8TZ Tel: 0118 948 6281 Fax:
0118 946 1145 Email: wac.enquiries@bbc.co.uk WWW:
www.bbc.co.uk/thenandnowAccess by appointment only. Brief
enquiries can be answered by post or telephone
Birmingham University Information Services - Special Collections
Main Library, University of Birmingham, Edgbaston B15 2TT
Tel: 0121 414 5838 Email: special-collections@bham.ac.uk
WWW: www.is.bham.ac.uk
Black Cultural Archives
378 Coldharbour Lane, London, SW9 8LF Tel: (020) 7738 4591
Bristol University Library - Special Collections
Tyndall Avenue, Bristol, BS8 1TJ Tel: 0117 928 8014 Email:
library@bris.ac.uk WWW: www.bris.ac.uk/depts/library
British Coal Corporation Records & Archive
Provincial House, Solly Street, Sheffield, S1 4BA Tel: 0114 279 9643
British Genealogical Survey Library
Kingsley Dunham Centre, Keyworth, Nottingham, NG12 5GG
Tel: 0115 939 3205 Fax: 0115 936 3200 Email: info@bgs.ac.uk
WWW: www.bgs.ac.uk
British Medical Association Archive
BMA House, Tavistock Square, London, WC1H 9JP Tel: 020
7383 6588 Fax: 020 7383 6717 Email: WWW: www.bma.org.uk
British Waterways Archives and The Waterways Trust
Llanthony Warehouse, Gloucester Docks, Gloucester, GL1 2EJ
Tel: 01452 318041 Email: roy.jamieson@britishwaterways.co.uk
WWW: http://www.britishwaterways.org.uk Records relating to
the management, maintenance and operation of inland waterways in
England, Scotland and Wales for which British Waterways is the
statutory undertaker. Date range: late 17th to 20th
**Cambridge University Library - Department of Manuscripts
& University Archives**
West Road, Cambridge, CB3 9DR Tel: 01223 333000 ext 33143
(Manuscripts) Tel: 01223 333000 ext 33148 (University
Archives) Fax: 01223 333160 Email: mss@ula.cam.ac.uk
WWW: www.lib.cam.ac.uk/MSS/
Deed Poll Records Section
Room E 15 Royal Courts of Justice, Strand, London, WC2A
2LL Tel: (020) 7947 6528 Fax: (020) 7947 6807
Department of Special Collections and Western Manuscripts
Bodleian Library, Oxford, OX1 3BG Tel: 01865-277152
Institute of Heraldic and Genealogical Studies
79 - 82 Northgate, Canterbury, CT1 1BA Fax: 01227-765617
Email: ihgs@ihgs.ac.uk WWW: www.ihgs.ac.uk
National Gallery Library and Archive
Trafalgar Square, London, WC2N 5DN Tel: 020 7747 2542
Email: iad@ng-london.org.uk WWW: http://www.nationalgallery.org.uk
National Monuments Record Centre - English Heritage
National Monuments Record Centre, Great Western Village,
Kemble Drive, Swindon, SN2 2GZ Tel: 01793-414600 Email:
info@rchme.gov.uk WWW: www.english-heritage.org.uk
National Monuments Record Enquiry and Research Services
55 Blandford Street, London, W1H 3AF Tel: 020 7208 8200
WWW: www.english-heritage.org.uk/knowledge/nmr
National Portrait Gallery
Heinz Archive & library, 2 St. Martins Place, London, WC2H 0HE Tel:
(020) 7306 0055 WWW: www.npg.org.uk
National Railway Museum
Leeman Road, York, YO26 4XJ Tel: 01904 621261 Fax: 01904
611112 Email: nrm@nmsi.ac.uk WWW: www.nrm.org.uk Does
not hold Railway Company staff records generally at PRO and NAS.
Public Record Office
Public Record Office, Ruskin Avenue, Kew, Richmond, TW9
4DU Tel: (020) 8876 3444 WWW: http://www.pro.gov.uk
Royal Air Force Museum - Department of Research & Infor Services
Grahame Park Way, Hendon, London, NW9 5LL Tel: (020)
83584873 Email: info@rafmuseum.com WWW:
http://www.rafmuseum.com
Royal Commonwealth Society Library
West Road, Cambridge, CB3 9DR Tel: 01223 333198 Fax:
01223 333160 Email: tab@ula.cam.ac.uk WWW:
www.lib.cam.ac.uk/MSS/
Royal Greenwich Observatory Archives
West Road, Cambridge, CB3 9DR Tel: 01223 333056
Email: ajp@ula.cam.ac.uk WWW: www.lib.cam.ac.uk/MSS/

Royal Society
6 Carlton House Terrace, London, SW1Y 5AG Tel: 020 7451
2606 Fax: 020 7930 2170 Email: library@royalsoc.ac.uk
WWW: www.royalsoc.ac.uk
Shakespeare Birthplace Trust - Records Office
Henley Street, Stratford Upon Avon, CV37 6QW Tel: 01789
201816 Tel: 01789 204016 Fax: 01789 296083
Email: records@sharespeare.org.uk WWW: www.shakespeare.org.uk
Society of Antiquaries of London
Burlington House, Piccadilly, London, W1J 0BE Tel: 020 7479
7084 Email: library@sal.org.uk WWW: www.sal.org.uk
Society of Genealogists - Library
14 Charterhouse Buildings, Goswell Road, London, EC1M 7BA
Tel: 020-7251-8799 Tel: 020-7250-0291 Fax: 020-7250-1800
Email: library@sog.org.uk - Sales at sales@sog.org.uk WWW:
http://www.sog.org.uk
Traceline
PO Box 106, Southport, PR8 2HH Tel: 0151 471 4811 Fax:
01704-563354 Email: traceline@ons.gov.uk To be put in touch
with lost relatives and acquaintances. The ONS must be satisfied that
contact would be in the best interests of the person being sought.
The Boat Museum & David Owen Waterways Archive
South Pier Road, Ellesmere Port, CH65 4FW Tel: 0151-355-
5017 Fax: 0151-355-4079 Email: boatmuseum@easynet.co.uk
Records relating to the management, maintenance and operation of inland
waterways in ngland, Scotland and Wales. Substantial Waterways library. Date
range: late 17th century to 20th century.
Trinity College Library
Cambridge University, Trinity College, Cambridge, CB1 1TQ
Tel: 01223 338488 Fax: 01223 338532 Email: trin-
lib@lists.cam.ac.uk WWW: http://rabbit.trin.cam.ac.uk
**Victoria & Albert Museum - National Art Library - Archive
of Art and Design**
Blythe House, 23 Blythe Road, London, W14 0QF Tel: (020)
7603 1514 Fax: (020) 7602 0980 Email: archive@vam.ac.uk
WWW: www.nal.vam.ac.uk

Specialist Records & Indexes
Bass Museum
Horninglow Street, Burton on Trent, DE14 1YQ Tel: 0845
6000598 Fax: 01283 513509 WWW: www.bass-museum.com
British Waterways Archives and The Waterways Trust
Llanthony Warehouse, Gloucester Docks, Gloucester, GL1 2EJ
Tel: 01452 318041 Fax: 01452 318076 Email:
roy.jamieson@britishwaterways.co.uk WWW:
http://www.britishwaterways.org.uk, Records relating to the
management, maintenance and operation of inland waterways in
England, Scotland and Wales for which British Waterways is the
statutory undertaker. Date range: late 17th to 20th
Church of England Record Centre
15 Galleywall Road, South Bermondsey, London, SE16 3PB
Tel: 020 7898 1030 Fax: 020 7898 1031
WWW: www.church-of-england.org
Department of Manuscripts and Special Collections
Hallward Library, Nottingham University , University Park,
Nottingham, NG7 2RD Tel: 0115 951 4565 Fax: 0115 951 4558
Email: mss-library@nottingham.ac.uk WWW:
www.mss.library.nottingham.ac.uk
Guiness Archive
Park Royal Brewery, London, NW10 7RR Fax:
Lambeth Palace Library
Lambeth Palace Road, London, SE1 7JU Tel: (020) 7898 1400
Fax: (020) 7928-7932 WWW: www.lambethpalacelibrary.org
Library of the Religious Society of Friends (Quakers)
Friends House, 173 - 177 Euston Rd, London, NW1 2BJ Tel:
0207 663 1135 Tel: 0207 663 1001 Fax: Email:
library@quaker.org.uk WWW: http://www.quaker.org.uk/library,
Limited opening hours. Letter of introduction required. Please
send SAE for details or enclose IRCs
Metropolitan Police Archives
Room 517, Wellington House, 67-73 Buckingham Gate,
London, SW1E 6BE The Metropolitan Police do not hold any
records. All records that have survived are in the PRO. Do not hold
records for City of London Police or other police forces or
constabularies.
National Railway Museum
Leeman Road, York, YO26 4XJ Tel: 01904 621261 Fax: 01904
611112 Email: nrm@nmsi.ac.uk WWW: www.nrm.org.uk

Southern Courage Archives
Southern Accounting Centre, PO Box 85, Counterslip, Bristrol, BS99 7BT
Thames Valley Police Museum
Sulhamstead, Nr Reading, RG7 4DX Tel: 0118 932 5748 Fax: 0118 932 5751 Email: ken.wells@thamesvalley.police.uk Thames Valley Police formed April 1968 from Berkshire, Oxfordshire, Oxford City and Reading Borough constabularies. Only records of officers are those who served in Reading Borough and Oxfordshire.
The Museum of Berkshire Aviation Trust
Mohawk Way, off Bader Way, Woodley, Reading, RG5 4UE Tel: 0118 944 8089 Fax: Email: museumofberkshireaviation@fly.to WWW: http://fly.to/museumofberkshireaviation
Whitbread Archives - Permanently Closed
The Brewery, Chiswell Street, London, EC1Y 4SD
Young's & Co's Brewery Archives
Ram Brewery, High Street, Wandsworth, London, SW18 4JD

Military

Catterick Garrison Library
Gough Road, Catterick Garrison, DL9 3EL Tel: 01748 833543
Extensive collection of over 1350 military history books available for reference or loan. Open Mon 10.am to 12, 1pm to 5.30pm; Wed 10am to 12, 1pm to 5pm; Fri 10am to 12 noon.
Cheshire Military Museum
The Castle, Chester, CH1 2DN Tel: 01244 327617
Devonshire and The Devonshire& Dorset Regiment Archives
Wyvern Barracks, Barrack Road, Exeter, EX2 6AE Tel: 01392 492436 Fax: 01392 492469
Gallipoli Campaign 1915-16 Biographical Index
3966 Robin Avenue, Eugene, 97402 Email: patrickg@efn.org
Grenadier Guards Record Office
Wellington Barracks, Birdcage Walk, London, SW1E 6HQ Access is by appointment made in advance. Search fee of £25.00 per search
Liddell Hart Centre for Military Archives
King's College London, Strand, London, WC2R 2LS Tel: 020 7848 2015 Tel: 020 7848 2187 Fax: 020 7848 2760 Email: archives@kcl.ac.uk WWW: http://www.kcl.ac.uk/lhcma/top.htm
National Army Museum
Royal Hospital Road, London, SW3 4HT Tel: (020) 7730-0717 Fax: (020) 7823-6573 Email: info@national-army-museum.ac.uk WWW: http://www.national-army-museum.ac.uk
National Army Museum Department of Archives (Photographs, Film & Sound)
Royal Hospital Road, London, SW3 4HT Tel: (020) 7730-0717 Fax: (020) 7823-6573 Email: info@national-army-museum.ac.uk WWW: www.national-army-museum.ac.uk
Regimental Museum and Archives of Black Watch
Balhousie Castle, Hay Street, Perth, PH1 5HS Tel: 0131-3108530 Tel: 01738 621281 ext 8530 Fax: 01738-643245 Email: bwarchivist@btclick.com WWW: www.theblackwatch.co.uk
Royal Air Force Museum
Grahame Park Way, Hendon, London, NW9 5LL Tel: (020) 8205-2266 Fax: (020) 8200 1751 Email: info@refmuseum.org.uk WWW: http://www.rafmuseum.org.uk
Royal Dragoon Guards Military Museum (4th/7th Royal Dragoon Guards & 5th Royal Inniskilling Dragoons)
3A Tower Street, York, YO1 9SB Tel: 01904-662790 Tel: 01904 662310 Fax: 01904 662310 WWW: www.rdg.co.uk, co located with Prince of Wales' Own Regiment of Yorkshire Military Museum (West & East Yorkshire Regiments)
Royal Marines Museum
Eastney, Southsea, PO4 9PX Tel: (023) 92 819385-Exts-224 Email:matthewlittle@royalmarinesmuseum.co.uk WWW: www.royalmarinesmuseum.co.uk No charges for research other than material costs. Donations welcome. Visits by appointment Mon to Fri 10am to 4.30pm
U.K. National Inventory of War Memorials
Imperial War Museum, Lambeth Road, London, SE1 6HZ Tel: (020) 7416-5353 Tel: (020) 7416 5281 : (020) 7416 5445 Fax: (020) 7416-5379 Email: memorials@iwm.org.uk WWW: www.iwm.org.uk, Only holds records for memorials within the UK. The archive is not computerised index as yet. Aims to be online by end o 2002. The archive holds 50,000 memorials to the fallen of all conflicts
Probate Service
Probate Sub Registry, Duncombe Place, York, YO1 7EA Tel: 01904-624210

England by County

Bedfordshire
Bedfordshire & Luton Archives & Record Service
County Hall, Cauldwell Street, Bedford, MK42 9AP Tel: 01234-228833 Tel: 01234-228777 Fax: 01234-228854 Email: archive@csd.bedfordshire.gov.uk WWW: http://www.bedfordshire.gov.uk

Berkshire
Berkshire Record Office
9 Coley Avenue, Reading, RG1 6AF Tel: 0118-901-5132 Fax: 0118-901-5131 Email: arch@reading.gov.uk WWW: www.reading.gov.uk/berkshirerecordoffice
Commonwealth War Graves Commission
2 Marlow Road, Maidenhead, SL6 7DX Tel: 01628-634221 Fax: 01628-771208 Email: General Enquiries: General.enq@cwgc.org Casulaty & Cemetery Enquiries: casualty.enq@cwgc.org WWW: www.cwgc.org
Rural History Centre
University of Reading, Whiteknights PO Box 229, Reading, RG6 6AG Tel: 0118-931-8664 Fax: 0118-975-1264 Email: j.s.creasey@reading.ac.uk WWW: www.ruralhistory.org/index.html, Appointments required
The Museum of Berkshire Aviation Trust
Mohawk Way, off Bader Way, Woodley, Reading, RG5 4UE Tel: 0118 944 8089 Email: museumofberkshireaviation@fly.to WWW: http://fly.to/museumofberkshireaviation

Bristol
Bristol Record Office
"B" Bond Warehouse, Smeaton Road, Bristol, BS1 6XN Tel: 0117-922-4224 Fax: 0117-922-4236 Email: bro@bristol-city.gov.uk WWW: www.bristol-city.gov.uk/recordoffice
British Empire & Commonwealth Museum
Clock Tower Yard, Temple Meads, Bristol, BS1 6QH Tel: 0117 925 4980 Fax: 0117 925 4983 Email: staff@empiremuseum.co.uk WWW: www.empiremuseum.co.uk
Bristol University Library - Special Collections
Tyndall Avenue, Bristol, BS8 1TJ Tel: 0117 928 8014 Fax: 0117 925 5334 Email: library@bris.ac.uk WWW: www.bris.ac.uk/depts/library

Buckinghamshire
Buckinghamshire Record Office
County Offices, Walton Street, Aylesbury, HP20 1UU Tel: 01296-382587 Fax: 01296-382274 Email: archives@buckscc.gov.uk WWW: www.buckscc.gov.uk/leisure/libraries/archives, Advance booking. CARN ticket required. Open Mon to Thurs 9am to 5.15pm and Fri 9am to 4.45pm

Cambridgeshire
Cambridge University Library - Department of Manuscripts & University Archives
West Road, Cambridge, CB3 9DR Tel: 01223 333000 ext 33143 (Manuscripts) Tel: 01223 333000 ext 33148 (University Archives) Fax: 01223 333160 Email: mss@ula.cam.ac.uk WWW: www.lib.cam.ac.uk/MSS/
Cambridgeshire Archive Service (Huntingdon)
County Record Office Huntingdon, Grammar School Walk, Huntingdon, PE29 3LF Tel: 01480-375842 Fax: 01480 375842 Email: county.records.hunts@cambridgeshire.gov.uk WWW: www.cambridgeshire.gov.uk
Cambridgeshire Archives Service County Record Office
Shire Hall, Castle Hill, Cambridge, CB3 0AP Tel: 01223-717281 Fax: 01223-717201 Email: County.Records.Cambridge@cambridgeshire.gov.uk WWW: http://www.cambridgeshire.gov.uk/
Centre for Regional Studies
Anglia Polytechnic University, East Road, Cambridge, CB1 1PT Tel: 01223-363271 ext 2030 Fax: 01223-352973 Email: t.kirby@anglia.ac.uk APU also offers a degree course (BA Combined Honours) in family and Community History

Cheshire
Cheshire & Chester Archives & Local Studies
Duke Street, Chester, CH1 1RL Tel: 01244-602574 Fax: 01244-603812 Email: recordoffice@cheshire.gov.uk WWW: http://www.cheshire.gov.uk/recoff/home.htm, In April 2000 management of all original archives was transferred to Cheshire & Chester Archives & Local Studies, Duke Street, Chester. All archives must be consulted there. Secondary sources such as

Cheshire Military Museum
The Castle, Chester, CH1 2DN Tel: 01244 327617 Fax:
Chester Community History & Heritage
St Michaels Church, Bridge Street Row, Chester, CH1 1NG Tel:
01244 317948 Tel: 01244 402110 Email: s.oswald.gov.uk
WWW:http://www.chestercc.gov.uk/chestercc/htmls/heritage.htm
All original archives transferred to Cheshire & Chester Archives & Local
Studies, Duke Street, Chester. All archives must be consulted there.
However, secondary sources held here
Stockport Archive Service
Central Library, Wellington Road South, Stockport, SK1 3RS
Tel: 0161-474-4530 Fax: 0161-474-7750
Email: localheritage.library@stockport.gov.uk
Tameside Local Studies Library
Stalybridge Library, Trinity Street, Stalybridge, SK15 2BN
Tel: 0161-338-2708 Fax: 0161-303-8289
Email: localstudies.library@mail.tameside.gov.uk
WWW: http://www.tameside.gov.uk
The Boat Museum & David Owen Waterways Archive
South Pier Road, Ellesmere Port, CH65 4FW Tel: 0151-355-
5017 Fax: 0151-355-4079 Email: boatmuseum@easynet.co.uk
Warrington Library & Local Studies Centre
Museum Street, Warrington, WA1 1JB Tel: 01925 442890 Fax:
01925 411395 Email: library@warrington.gov.uk WWW:
www.warrington.gov.uk

Cleveland
Teesside Archives
Exchange House, 6 Marton Road, Middlesbrough, TS1 1DB Tel:
01642-248321 Email: teeside_archives@middlesbrough.gov.uk

Cornwall
Cable & Wireless Archive & Museum of Submarine Telegraphy
Eastern House,, Porthcurno, Penzance, TR19 6JX Tel:
01736 810478 Tel: 01736 810811 Fax: 01736 810640 Email:
info@tunnels.demon.co.uk WWW: www.porthcurno.org.uk,
Housed in one of Porthcurno's former telegraph station buildings, and adjacent
to the Museum of Submarine Telegraphy, the archive is a unique resource for
learning about: the history of Porthcurno
Cornwall Record Office
County Hall, Truro, TRI 3AY Tel: 01872-323127
Email: cro@cornwall.gov.uk WWW: http://www.cornwall.gov.uk
**Royal Institution of Cornwall, Courtney Library & Cornish
History Research Centre**
Royal Cornwall Museum, River Street, Truro, TR1 2SJ Tel:
01872 272205 Email: RIC@royal-cornwall-museum.freeserve.co.uk
WWW: www.cornwall-online.co.uk/ric
The Cornwall Centre
Alma Place, Redruth, TR15 2AT Tel: 01209-216760
Email: cornishstudies@library.cornwall.gov.uk WWW: www.cornwall.gov.uk

County Durham
Centre For Local Studies
The Library, Crown Street, Darlington, DL1 1ND Tel: 01325-
349630 Email: crown.street.library@darlington.gov.uk
County Record Office
County Hall, Durham, DH1 5UL Tel: 0191-383-3474 Tel: 0191-
383-3253 Fax: 0191-383-4500 Email:
record.office@durham.gov.uk WWW:
http:www.durham.gov.uk/recordoffice

Cumbria
Cumbria Archive Service
Cumbria Record Office, The Castle, Carlisle, CA3 8UR Tel:
01228-607285 Tel: 01228-607284 Fax: 01228-607270
Email: carlisle.record.office@cumbriacc.gov.uk
WWW: www.cumbriacc.gov.uk/archives
Cumbria Record Office(Kendal) County Offices,
Stricklandgate, Kendal, LA9 4RQ Tel: 01539 773540
Email: kendal.record.office@cumbriacc.gov.uk WWW:
www.cumbria.gov.uk/archives
Cumbria Record Office & Local Studies Library (Whitehaven)
Scotch Street, Whitehaven, CA28 7BJ Tel: 01946-852920Email:
whitehaven.record.office@cumbriacc.gov.uk
 WWW: http://www.cumbria.gov.uk/archives
Cumbria Record Office & Local Studies Library (Barrow in Furness)
140 Duke St, Barrow in Furness, LA14 1XW Tel: 01229-894363
Email: barrow.record.office@cumbriacc.gov.uk WWW:
www.cumbria.gov.uk/archives
Ulverston Heritage Centre
Lower Brook St, Ulverston, LA12 7EE Tel: 01229 580820
Email: heritage@tower-house.demon.co.uk WWW:
http://www.rootsweb.com/~ukuhc/

Derbyshire & Derby City
Derby Local Studies Library
25b Irongate, Derby, DE1 3GL Tel: 01332 255393**Derby
Museum & Art Gallery**
The Strand, Derby, DE1 1BS Tel: 01332-716659 Fax: 01332-
716670 WWW: www.derby.gov.uk/museums No archive material as
such, but some local genealogical information available and numerous indices
on local trades, etc eg clock makers, gunmakers, etc
Derbyshire Record Office
County Hall, Matlock, DE4 3AG Tel: 01629-580000-ext-35207
Fax: 01629-57611 The Record Office for Derbyshire - City and County
and the Diocese of Derby. The Record Office is located New Street, Matlock,
Derbyshire DE4 3AG. The address at County Hall is for correspondence only
Erewash Museum
The Museum, High Street, Ilkeston, DE7 5JA Tel: 0115 907 1141
Email: museum@erewash.gov.uk WWW: www.erewash.gov.uk

Devon
Beaford Photograph Archive
Barnstaple, EX32 7EJ Tel: 01271-288611 Fax:
Devonshire and The Devonshire& Dorset Regiment Archives
Wyvern Barracks, Barrack Road, Exeter, EX2 6AE Tel: 01392 492436
Devon Record Office
Castle Street, Exeter, EX4 3PU Tel: 01392 384253
Email: devrec@devon.gov.uk
WWW: http://www.devon.gov.uk/dro/homepage.html
North Devon Record Office
Tuly Street, Barnstaple, EX31 1EL Tel: 01271 388607 Tel:
01271 388608 Email: ndevrec@devon.gov.uk WWW:
www.devon.gov.uk/dro/homepage Open: Mon, Tues, Thurs & Fri 9.30
to 5pm;Wed 9.30 to 1pm; 2 Sats per month 9.30 to 4pm. Admission charges £2
per day
Plymouth & West Devon Record Office
Unit 3, Clare Place, Coxside, Plymouth, PL4 0JW Tel: 01752-
305940 Email: pwdro@plymouth.gov.uk
WWW: www.plymouth.gov.uk/star/archives.htm

Dorset
Dorset Archives Service
9 Bridport Road, Dorchester, DT1 1RP Tel: 01305-250550 Fax:
01305-257184 Email: archives@dorset-cc.gov.uk WWW:
http://www.dorset-cc.gov.uk/archives Research service available.
Search fee £16 per hour. £8.00 minimum charge. The service covers the areas
served by Dorset County, Bournemouth Borough and the Borough of Poole.
Poole Central Reference Library
Dolphin Centre, Poole, BH15 1QE Tel: 01202 262424 Fax:
01202 262442 Email: centrallibrary@poole.gov.uk WWW:
www.poole.gov.uk The local studies collection was relocated to The
Waterfront Museum, Poole Some records moved to Dorset Record Office.
Retains only general local history and national family history indexes.
Waterfront Musuem and Local Studies Centre
4 High St, Poole, BH15 1BW Tel: 01202 683138Email:
museums@poole.gov.uk WWW: www.poole.gov.uk

Essex
Central Reference Library - L B of Havering
Reference Library, St Edward's Way, Romford, RM1 3AR Tel:
01708 432393 Email: romfordlib2@rmplc.co.uk
Chelmsford Library
PO Box 882, Market Road, Chelmsford, CM1 1LH Tel: 01245
492758 Email: answers.direct@essexcc.gov.uk
WWW: www.essexcc.gov.uk
Essex Record Office
Wharf Road, Chelmsford, CM2 6YT Tel: 01245 244644 Fax:
1245244655 Email: ero.enquiry@essexcc.gov.uk (General Enquiries)
ero.search@essexcc.gov.uk (Search Service)
WWW: http://www.essexcc.gov.uk/ero
Essex Record Office, Colchester & NE Essex Branch
Stanwell House, Stanwell Street, Colchester, CO2 7DL Tel:
01206-572099 WWW: www.essexcc.gov.uk/ero
Essex Record Office, Southend Branch
Central Library, Victoria Avenue, Southend on Sea, SS2 6EX
Tel: 01702-464278 WWW: www.essexcc.gov.uk/ero
L B of Barking & Dagenham Local History Studies
Valence House Museum, Becontree Avenue, Dagenham, RM8
3HT Tel: 020-822-75293 Fax: 020-822-75297 Email:
fm019@viscount.org.uk WWW: http://www.bardaglea.org.uk/4-
heritage/heritage-menu.html Heritage service includes a local history
museum, and archive section. A list of resources is available upon request.
Archives of the Essex Parishes of Barking and Dagenham and the Boroughs
L B of Barking & Dagenham Local History Studies
Central Library, Barking, Dagenham, IG11 7NB Tel: (020) 8517-8666 Local
History studies from this Library have been centralised at Valence Linbrary,

Becontree Avenue, Dagenham, Essex RM8 3HT Tel & (020) 8227 5297
Redbridge Library
Central Library, Clements Road, Ilford, IG1 1EA Tel: (020)
8708-2417 Fax: (020) 8553 3299 Email:
Local.Studies@redbridge.gov.uk WWW: www.redbridge.gov.uk

Gloucestershire
British Waterways Archives and The Waterways Trust
Llanthony Warehouse, Gloucester Docks, Gloucester, GL1 2EJ
Tel: 01452 318041WWW: http://www.britishwaterways.org.uk,
Gloucestershire Record Office
Clarence Row, Alvin Street, Gloucester, GL1 3DW Tel: 01452-
425295 Fax: 01452-426378 Email: records@gloscc.gov.uk
WWW: http://archives.gloscc.gov.uk Daily admission charge £2
(£1.50 for over 60's.) I/d required

Greater Manchester
Bury Archive Service
1st Floor, Derby Hall Annexe, Edwin Street off Crompton Street, Bury, BL9
0AS Tel: 0161-797-6697 Fax: 0161 797 6697 Telephone before faxing Email:
archives@bury.gov.uk WWW: www.bury.gov.uk/culture.htm, May be moving
to new premises in 2002 check before visiting
Greater Manchester County Record Office
56 Marshall St, New Cross, Manchester, M4 5FU Tel: 0161-832-
5284 Fax: 0161-839-3808 Email: archives@gmcro.co.uk WWW:
http://www.gmcro.co.uk
Wigan Heritage Service Museum
History Shop, Library Street, Wigan, WN1 1NU Tel: 01942
828020 Fax: 01942 827645 Email: heritage@wiganmbc.gov.uk

Hampshire
Hampshire Local Studies Library
Winchester library, Jewry Street, Winchester, SO23 8RX Tel:
01962 841408 Fax: 01962 841489 Email: clceloc@hants.gov.uk
WWW: www.hants.gov.uk/library
Hampshire Record Office
Sussex St, Winchester, SO23 8TH Tel: 01962-846154 Fax:
01962-878681 Email: enquiries.archives@hants.gov.uk WWW:
http://www.hants.gov.uk/record-office, National Indexes held:
GRO 1837-1992; 1881 Census Index; IGI; National Probate Calendars 1858-1943
Microfilm and microfiche viewers must be prior booked.
Portsmouth City Museum and Record Office
Museum Road, Portsmouth, PO1 2LJ Tel: (023) 92827261 Fax:
(023) 92875276 Email: portmus@compuserve.com
Portsmouth Roman Catholic Diocesan Archives
St Edmund House, Edinburgh Road, Portsmouth, PO1 3QA Tel: 023 9282
2166 These are private archives & prior arrangements to visit have to be agreed.
Royal Marines Museum
Eastney, Southsea, PO4 9PX Tel: (023) 92 819385-Exts-224
Email: matthewlittle@royalmarinesmuseum.co.uk WWW:
www.royalmarinesmuseum.co.uk No charges for research other than
material costs. Donations welcome Visits by appointment Mon to Fri 10 am to
4.30pm
Southampton Archive Service
Civic Centre, Southampton, Hants, SO14 7LY Tel: (023)
80832251 Email: city.archives@southampton.gov.uk
WWW: www.southampton.gov.uk
Southampton City Libraries - Special Collections
Reference Library, Civic Centre, Southampton, SO14 7LW Tel: 023
8083 2205 Email: local.studies@southampton.gov.uk WWW:
www.southampton.gov.uk Special collections include information on
Southampton and Hampshire, genealogy and maritime topics.

Herefordshire
Hereford Cathedral Archives & Library
5 College Cloisters, Cathedral Close, Hereford, HR1 2NG
Tel: 01432 374225 Email: library@herefordcathedral.co.uk
Herefordshire Record Office
The Old Barracks, Harold Street, Hereford, HR1 2QX Tel: 01432
260750 Email: shubbard@herefordshire.gov.uk
WWW: http://www.herefordshire.gov.uk

Hertfordshire
Ashwell Education Services
59 High Street, Ashwell, Baldock, SG7 5NP Tel: 01462 742385
Email: aes@ashwell-education-services.co.uk
WWW: www.ashwell-education-services.co.uk Research into the
History and family histories of Ashwell and its people
Hertfordshire Archives and Local Studies
County Hall, Pegs Lane, Hertford, SG13 8EJ Tel: 01438 737333
Fax: 01923 471333 Email: herts.direct@hertscc.gov.uk WWW:
http://hertsdirect.org/hals Hertfordshire Archives & Local Studies is
comprised of the former Herts County Record Office and Herts Local
Studies Library

Hull
Brynmor Jones Library - University of Hull
Cottingham Road, Hull, HU6 7RX Tel: 01482 465265 Fax:
01482 466205 Email: archives@acs.hull.ac.uk WWW:
www.hull.ac.uk/lib
www.hull.ac.uk/lib/archives
Hull City Archives
79 Lowgate, Kingston upon Hull, HU1 1HN Tel: 01482-615102
Tel: 01482-615110 Fax: 01482-613051 Email:
city.archives@hcc.gov.uk WWW: www.hullcc.gov.uk
Local History Unit
Hull College, Park Street Centre, Hull, HU2 8RR Tel: 01482-
598952 Fax: 01482 598989 Email: historyunit@netscape.net
WWW: www.historyofhull.co.uk

Isle of Wight
Isle of Wight Record Office
26 Hillside, Newport, PO30 2EB Tel: 01983-823820/1 Fax:
01983 823820 Email: record.office@iow.gov.uk WWW:
www.iwight.com/library/default.asp

Kent
Bexley Local Studies and Archive Centre
Central Library, Bourne Townley Road, Bexleyheath, DA6 7HJ
Tel: (020) 8301 1545 Fax: (020) 8303 7872 Email:
archives@bexleycouncil.freeserve.co.uk WWW:
www.bexley.gov.uk As well as being a designated local authority record
office the Local Studies Centre is Diocesan Record Office for all the (C of E)
Parishes within the Borough ie Rochester & Southwark Dioceses
Canterbury Cathedral Archives
The Precincts, Canterbury, CT1 2EH Tel: 01227 865330 Fax:
1227865222 Email: archives@canterbury-cathedral.org WWW:
www.canterbury-cathedral.org
Canterbury Library & Local Studies Collection
18 High Street, Canterbury, CT1 2JF Tel: 01227-463608
Centre for Kentish Studies / Kent County Archives Service
Sessions House, County Hall, Maidstone, Kent, ME141XQ Tel:
01622-694363 Fax: 01622 694379 Email: archives@kent.gov.uk
WWW: www.kent.gov.uk/e&l/artslib/ARCHIVES/archiveshome.htm
East Kent Archives Centre
Enterprise Zone, Honeywood Road, Whitfield, Dover, CT16
3EH: 01304 829306 Fax: 01304 820783 Email:
eastkentarchives@kent.gov.uk
Hythe Archives - now at East Kent Archives Centre
East Kent Archives Centre, Enterprise Zone, Honeywood Road,
Whitfield, Dover, CT16 3EH Tel: 01304 829306 Fax: 01304
820783 Email: eastkentarchives@kent.gov.uk WWW:
www.kent.gov.uk/kcc/arts/archives/kentish.html
Institute of Heraldic and Genealogical Studies
79 - 82 Northgate, Canterbury, CT1 1BA Fax: 01227-765617
Email: ihgs@ihgs.ac.uk WWW: www.ihgs.ac.uk
L B of Bromley Local Studies Library
Central Library, High Street, Bromley, BR1 1EX Tel: 020 8460
9955 Fax: 020 8313 9975 Email:
localstudies.library@bromley.gov.uk
Margate Library Local History Collection
Cecil Square, Margate, CT9 1RE Tel: 01843-223626 Fax:
01843-293015
Pembroke Lodge Family History Centre and Museum
2-6 Station Approach, Birchington on Sea, CT7 9RD Tel: 01843-
841649 Fax: Email: WWW: , Please address all mail to 4 Station
approach, Birchington on Sea
**Ramsgate Library Local Strudies Collection & Thanet
Branch Archives**
Ramsgate Library, Guildford Lawn, Ramsgate, CT11 9AY Tel:
01843-593532 Archives at this library moved to East Kent
Archives CentreEnterprise Zone, Honeywood Road, Whitfield,
Dover, Kent CT16 3EH. A Local Studies Collection will remain
Sevenoaks Archives Office
Central Library, Buckhurst Lane, Sevenoaks, TN13 1LQ Tel:
01732-453118 Tel: 01732-452384 Fax: 01732-742682

Lancashire
Blackburn Cathedral & Archives
Cathedral Close, Blackburn, BB1 5AA Tel: 01254 51491 Email:
cathedral@blackburn.anglican.org WWW: www.blackburn.anglican.org
Blackburn Central Library
Town Hall Street, Blackburn, BB2 1AG Tel: 01254 587920 Fax:
01254 690539 Email: reference.library@blackburn.gov.uk
WWW: www.blackburn.gov.uk/library
Bolton Archive & Local Studies Service
Central Library, Civic Centre, Le Mans Crescent, Bolton, BL1
1SE Tel: 01204-332185 Email: archives.library@bolton.gov.uk

Lancashire Record Office
Bow Lane, Preston, PR1 2RE Tel: 01772 263039 Fax: 01772 263050 Email: record.office@ed.lancscc.gov.uk WWW: www.lancashire.gov.uk/education/lifelong/recordindex.shtm, The Lancashire Local Studies Collection is now housed here
North West Sound Archive
Old Steward's Office, Clitheroe Castle, Clitheroe, BB7 1AZ Tel: 01200-427897 Fax: 01200-427897 Email: nwsa@ed.lancscc.gov.uk WWW: www.lancashire.gov.uk/education/lifelong/ro
Oldham Local Studies and Archives
84 Union Street, Oldham, OL1 1DN Tel: 0161-911-4654 Fax: 0161-911-4654 Email: archives@oldham.gov.uk localstudies@oldham.gov.uk WWW: http://www.oldham.gov.uk/archives http://www.oldham.gov.uk/local_studies
Rochdale Local Studies Library
Arts & Heritage Centre, The Esplanade, Rochdale, OL16 4TY Tel: 01706 864915 Temporary address until September 2002: Floor 3 Champness Hall, Drake Street, Rochdale OL16 1PB
Salford City Archives
Salford Archives Centre, 658/662 Liverpool Rd, Irlam, Manchester, M44 5AD Tel: 0161 775-5643 Fax:
Salford Local History Library
Peel Park, Salford, M5 4WU Tel: 0161 736 2649 Fax:
Tameside Local Studies Library
Stalybridge Library, Trinity Street, Stalybridge, SK15 2BN Tel: 0161-338-2708 Tel: 0161-338-3831 and 0161 303 7937 Fax: 0161-303-8289 Email: localstudies.library@mail.tameside.gov.uk WWW: http://www.tameside.gov.uk
The Documentary Photography Archive - Manchester
c/o 7 Towncroft Lane, Bolton, BL1 5EW Tel: 0161 832 5284 Tel: 01204-840439 (Home) Fax: 01204-840439
Traceline
PO Box 106, Southport, PR8 2HH Tel: 0151 471 4811 Fax: 01704-563354 Email: traceline@ons.gov.uk WWW: , To be put in touch with lost relatives and acquaintances. The ONS must be satisfied that contact would be in the best interests of the person being sought. Traceline uses the NHS Central Register. NH
Trafford Local Studies Centre
Public Library, Tatton Road, Sale, M33 1YH Tel: 0161-912-3013 Fax: 0161-912-3019 Email: traffordlocalstudies@hotmail.com The collection covers the former Lancashire and Cheshire towns of Stretford, Old Trafford, Urmston, Daveyhulme, Flixton, Altincham, Bowdon, Hale, Dunham Massey, Sale, Ashton-o-Mersey, Carrington,
Wigan Heritage Service
Town Hall, Leigh, Wigan, WN7 2DY Tel: 01942-404430 Fax: 01942-404425 Email: heritage@wiganmbc.gov.uk WWW: http://www.wiganmbc.gov.uk, Open by appointment: Mon, Tues, Thurs & Fri
Leicestershire
Melton Mowbray Library
Wilton Road, Melton Mowbray, LE13 0UJ Tel: 01664 560161 Fax: 01664 410199 WWW: www.leics.gov.uk
Record Office for Leicestershire, Leicester and Rutland
Long Street, Wigston Magna, LE18 2AH Tel: 0116-257-1080 Fax: 0116-257-1120 Email: recordoffice@leics.gov.uk
Willoughby on the Wolds Heritage Group
Group Archive & Village History Enquiries, 1 Church Lane, Willoughby on the Wolds, Nr Loughborough, LE12 6SS Tel: 01509 880077

Rutland
Record Office for Leicestershire, Leicester and Rutland
Long Street, Wigston Magna, LE18 2AH Tel: 0116-257-1080 Fax: 0116-257-1120 Email: recordoffice@leics.gov.uk

Lincolnshire
Lincolnshire Archives
St Rumbold Street, Lincoln, LN2 5AB Tel: 01522-526204 Fax: 01522-530047 Email: archive@lincolnshire.gov.uk WWW: http://www.lincolnshire.gov.uk/archives
Lincolnshire County Library
Local Studies Section, Lincoln Central Library, Free School Lane, Lincoln, LN1 1EZ Tel: 01522-510800 Fax: 01522-575011 Email: lincoln.library@lincolnshire.gov.uk WWW: www.lincolnshire.gov.uk/library/services/family.htm
North East Lincolnshire Archives
Town Hall, Town Hall Square, Grimsby, DN31 1HX Tel: 01472-323585 Fax: 01472-323582 Email: john.wilson@nelincs.gov.uk

Liverpool
Liverpool Record Office & Local History Department
Central Library, William Brown Street, Liverpool, L3 8EW Tel: 0151 233 5817 Fax: 0151-233 5886 Email: recoffice.central.library@liverpool.gov.uk WWW: http://www.liverpool.gov.uk

London
Alexander Fleming Laboratory Museum / St Mary's NHS Trust Archives
St Mary's Hospital, Praed Street, Paddington, London, W2 1NY Tel: (020) 7886 6528 Fax: (020) 7886 6739 Email: kevin.brown@st-marys.nhs.uk
Bank of England Archive
Archive Section HO-SV, The Bank of England, Threadneedle Street, London, EC2R 8AH Tel: (020) 7601-5096 Fax: (020) 7601-4356 Email: archive@bankofengland.co.uk WWW: www.bankofengland.co.uk
Bethlem Royal Hospital
Archives and Museum, Monks Orchard Road, Beckenham, BR3 3BX Tel: (020) 8776 4307 Tel: (020) 8776 4053 Fax: (020) 8776 4045 Email: museum@bethlem.freeserve.co.uk The archives of the Bethlem and Maudsley NHS Trust (the Bethlem Royal Hospital and the Maudsley Hospital). Records relating to individual patients are closed for 100 years.
Bexley Local Studies and Archive Centre
Central Library, Bourne Townley Road, Bexleyheath, DA6 7HJ Tel: (020) 8301 1545 Fax: (020) 8303 7872 Email: archives@bexleycouncil.freeserve.co.uk WWW: www.bexley.gov.uk, As well as being a designated local authority record office the Local Studies Centre is Diocesan Record Office for all the (C of E) Parishes within the Borough ie Rochester & Southwark Dioceses
Black Cultural Archives
378 Coldharbour Lane, London, SW9 8LF Tel: (020) 7738 4591 Fax: (020) 7738 7168
Brent Community History Library & Archive
152 Olive Road, London, NW2 6UY Tel: (020) 8937 3541 Fax: (020) 8450 5211 Email: archive@brent.gov.uk WWW: www.brent.gov.uk
British Library of Political and Economic Science
London School of Economics, 10 Portugal Street, London, WC2A 2HD Tel: 020 7955 7223 Fax: 020 7955 7454 Email: info@lse.ac.uk WWW: http://www.lse.ac.uk
British Library Oriental and India Collections
197 Blackfriars Rd, London, SE1 8NG Tel: (020) 7412-7873 Fax: (020) 7412-7641 Email: oioc-enquiries@bl.uk WWW: http://www.bl.uk/collections/oriental
British Library Western Manuscripts Collections
96 Euston Road, London, NW1 2DB Tel: (020) 7412-7513 Fax: (020) 7412-7745 Email: mss@bl.uk WWW: http://www.bl.uk/, Note: can only respond to enquiries related to their own collections
British Red Cross Museum and Archives
9 Grosvenor Crescent, London, SW1X 7EJ Tel: (020) 7201-5153 Email: enquiry@redcross.org.uk WWW: www.redcross.org.uk, Open by appointment 10am to 4pm Monday to Friday.
Business Archives Council
3rd & 4th Floors, 101 High Street, Whitechapel , London, E1 7RE Tel: 020 7247 0024 Fax: 020 7422 0026
Centre for Metropolitan History
Institute of Historical Research, Senate House, Malet Street, London, WC1E 7HU Tel: (020) 7862 8790 Email: o-myhill@sas.ac.uk WWW: www.history.ac.uk/cmh/cmh.main.html
Chelsea Public Library
Old Town Hall, King's Road, London, SW3 5EZ Tel: (020) 7352-6056 Tel: (020) 7361-4158 Fax: (020) 7351 1294 Local Studies Collection on Royal Borough of Kensington & Chelsea south of Fulham Road
City of Westminster Archives Centre
10 St Ann's Street, London, SW1P 2DE Tel: (020) 7641-5180 Fax: (020) 7641-5179 WWW: www.westminster.gov.uk, Holds records for whole area covered by City of Westminster incl former Metropolitan Boroughs of Paddington and St Maryleborne.
Corporation of London Records Office
PO Box 270, Guildhall, London, EC2P 2EJ Tel: (020) 7332-1251 Fax: (020) 7710-8682 Email: clro@corpoflondon.gov.uk WWW: cityoflondon.gov.uk/archives/clro
Deed Poll Records Section
Room E 15 Royal Courts of Justice, Strand, London, WC2A 2LL Tel: (020) 7947 6528 Fax: (020) 7947 6807
Documents Register
Quality House, Quality Court, Chancery Lane, London, WC2A 1HP Tel: (020) 7242-1198 Fax: (020) 7831-3550 Email: nra@hmc.gov.uk

Dr Williams's Library
14 Gordon Square, London, WC1H 0AR Tel: (020) 7387-3727
Email: 101340.2541@compuserve.com The General Registers of
Protestant Dissenters (Dr Williams's Library Registers) were
surrendered to the Registrar General and are now at The Public
Record Office (RG4/4666-4673)

Ealing Local History Centre
Central Library, 103 Broadway Centre, Ealing, London, W5 5JY
Tel: (020) 8567-3656-ext-37 Fax: (020) 8840-2351 Email:
localhistory@hotmail.com WWW: www.ealing.gov.uk/libraries,
Closed Sundays & Mondays

Family Records Centre
1 Myddleton Street, London, EC1R 1UW Tel: (020) 8392-5300
Fax: (020) 8392-5307 Email: info@familyrecords.gov.uk WWW:
www.familyrecords.gov.uk

Grenadier Guards Record Office
Wellington Barracks, Birdcage Walk, London, SW1E 6HQ Access
is by appointment made in advance. Search fee of £25.00 per search

Guildhall Library, Manuscripts Section
Aldermanbury, London, EC2P 2EJ Tel: (020) 7332-1863
 Email: manuscripts.guildhall@corpoflondon.gov.uk WWW:
http://ihr.sas.ac.uk/ihr/gh/ Opening hours Mon to Sat 9.30am to 4.45pm
(last orders for manuscripts 4.30pm: on Sat no manuscripts produced bet
12noon and 2pm. Records: City of London parish records, probate records,
City Livery

Hackney Archives Department
43 De Beauvoir Road, L B of Hackney, London, N1 5SQ Tel:
(020) 7241-2886 Email: archives@hackney.gov.uk WWW:
http://www.hackney.gov.uk/history/index.html, Covers Hackney,
Shoreditch & Stoke Newington

Hertiage Services Consignia (formerly Post Office Heritage)
Freeling House,, Phoenix Place, London, WC1X 0DL Tel: (020)
7239-2570 Fax: (020) 7239-2576 Email:
heritage@consignia.com WWW: www.consignia.com/heritage,
The National Postal Museum formerley in King Edward Street, London closed
in December 1998. The Philatelic collection is available to view by
appointment at Heritage Services Consignia

Hillingdon Local Studies & Archives
Central Library, High Street, Uxbridge, London, UB8 1HD Tel:
01895-250702 Fax: 01895-811164 Email:
ccotton@hillingdon.gov.uk WWW:
http://www.,hillingdon.gov.uk/goto/libraries

Hounslow Library (Local Studies & archives)
Centre Space, Treaty Centre, High Street, Hounslow, TW3 1ES
Tel: (020) 8583 4545 Fax: 020 8583 4595

Imperial College Archives
London University, Room 455 Sherfield Building, Imperial
College, London, SW7 2AZ Tel: 020 7594 8850 Fax: 020 7584
3763 Email: archivist@ic.ac.uk WWW: http://www.lib.ic.ac.uk

Institute of Historical Research
University of London , Senate House, Malet Street, London,
WC1E 7HU Tel: (020) 7862 8740 Fax: 020 7436 2145 Email:
ihr@sas.ac.uk WWW: http://ihr.sas.ac.uk

King's College London Archives
Kins College, Strand, London, WC2R 2LS Tel: 020 7848 2015
Tel: 020 7848 2187 Email: archives@kcl.ac.uk WWW:
http://www.kcl.ac.uk/depsta/iss/archives/top.htm Includes Student
records, staff records and hospital records for Kins College Hospital

L B of Hammersmith & Fulham Archives & Local History Centre
The Lilla Huset, 191 Talgarth Road, London, W6 8BJ Tel: 0208-
741-5159 WWW: http://www.lbhf.gov.uk

Lewisham Local Studies & Archives
Lewisham Library, 199 - 201 Lewisham High Street, Lewisham,
London, SE13 6LG Tel: (020) 8297-0682 Email:
local.studies@lewisham.gov.uk WWW: http://www.lewisham.gov.uk
Covering the Parishes of Lewisham, Lee & St Paul's, Deptford.
Appointments advisable.

Library of the Royal College of Surgeons of England
35-43 Lincoln's Inn Fields, London, WC2A 3PN Tel: (020) 7869
6520 Fax: (020) 7405 4438 Email: library@rseng.ac.uk

Liddell Hart Centre for Military Archives
King's College London, Strand, London, WC2R 2LS Tel: 020
7848 2015 Tel: 020 7848 2187 Fax: 020 7848 2760 Email:
archives@kcl.ac.uk WWW: http://www.kcl.ac.uk/lhcma/top.htm

Linnean Society of London
Burlington House, Piccadilly, London, W1J 0BF Tel: 020 7437
4479 Tel: 020 7434 4470 Fax: 020 7287 9364 Email:
gina@linnean.org WWW: http://www.linnean.org

Local Studies Collection for Chiswick & Brentford
Chiswick Public Library, Dukes Avenue, Chiswick, London, W4
2AB Tel: (020) 8994-5295 Restricted opening hours for local
history room: please telephone before visiting

L B of Barnet, Archives & Local Studies Department
Hendon Library, The Burroughs, Hendon, NW4 3BQ Tel: (020)
8359-2876 Fax: (020) 8359-2885 Email:
hendon.library@barnet.gov.uk

L B of Camden Local Studies & Archive Centre
Holborn Library, 32 - 38 Theobalds Road, London, WC1X 8PA
Tel: 020 7974 6342 Fax: 020 7974 6284 Email:
localstudies@camden.gov.uk WWW: www.camden.gov.uk,
Closed Wednesday. Open: Mon & Thurs 10 to 7pm; Tues & Fri
10 to 6pm; Sats 10 to 1pm and 2pm to 5pm

L B of Croydon Library and Archives Service
Central Library, Katharine Street, Croydon, CR9 1ET Tel: (020)
8760-5400-ext-1112 Fax: (020) 8253-1012 Email:
localstudies@croydononline.org WWW:
http://www.croydon.gov.uk/

L B of Enfield Archives & Local History Unit
Southgate Town Hall, Green Lanes, Palmers Green, London,
N13 4XD Tel: (020) 8379-2724 Fax: (020) 8379 2761 The
collections specifically relate to edmonton and Enfield (both
formerly in Middlesex)

L B of Greenwich Local History Library
Woodlands, 90 Mycenae Road, Blackheath, London, SE3 7SE
Tel: (020) 8858 4631 Email: local.history@greenwich.gov.uk
WWW: www.greenwich.gov.uk, The library will be moving to a new
Heritage Centre autumn 2002. Please contact the library for more details

L B of Haringey Archives Service
Bruce Castle Museum, Lordship Lane, Tottenham, London, N17
8NU Tel: (020) 8808-8772 Fax: (020) 8808-4118 Email:
museum.services@haringey.gov.uk

L B of Islington Central Reference Library
Central Reference Library, 2 Fieldway Crescent, London, N5
1PF Tel: (020) 7619-6931 Fax: (020) 7619-6939 Email:
local.history@islington.gov.uk WWW:
http://www.islington.gov.uk Reorganisation is imminent - planned move
to Finsbury Library, 245 St John Street, London EC1V 4NB (020) 7527 6931
(020) 7527 6937Collection covers the south of the LB of Islington.

L B of Lambeth Archives Department
Minet Library, 52 Knatchbull Road, Lambeth, London, SE5 9QY
Tel: (020) 7926 6076 Fax: (020) 7936 6080 Email:
lambetharchives@lambeth.gov.uk

L B of Newham Archives & Local Studies Library
Stratford Library, 3 The Grove, London, E5 1EL Tel: (020) 8557
8856 Fax: (020) 8503 1525

L B of Wandsworth Local studies
Local Studies ServiceBattersea Library, 265 Lavender Hill,
London, SW11 1JB Tel: (020) 8871 7753 Fax: (020) 7978-4376
Email: wandsworthmuseum@wandsworth.gov.uk WWW:
www.wandsworth.gov.uk Open Tues & Wed 10am to 88pm, Fri 10am to
5pm, Sat 9am to 1pm - Research service offerred - £7.00 per half hour (the
minimum fee) apointment advised to ensure archives, hard copy newspapers (if
not microfiched)

London Metropolitan Archives
40 Northampton Road, London, EC1R 0HB Tel: 020 7332 3820
Email: ask.lma@ms.corpoflondon.gov.uk WWW:
www.cityoflondon.gov.uk

London University - Institute of Advancéd Studies
Charles Clore House, 17 Russell Square, London, WC1B 5DR
Tel: (020) 7637 1731 Fax: (020) 7637 8224 Email:
ials.lib@sas.ac.uk WWW: http://ials.sas.ac.uk

London University - Institute of Education
20 Bedford Way, London, WC1H 0AL Tel: 020 7612 6063 Fax:
020 7612 6093 Email: lib@ioe.ac.uk WWW:
http://www.ioe.ac.uk/library/

Manorial Documents Register
Quality House, Quality Court, Chancery Lane, London, WC2A
1HP Tel: (020) 7242-1198 Fax: (020) 7831-3550 Email:
nra@hmc.gov.uk

Manuscripts Room
Library Services, University College, Gower Street, London,
WC1E 6BT Tel: (020) 7387 7050 Email: mssrb@ucl.ac.uk
WWW: http://www.ucl.ac.uk/library/special-coll/

Museum of London Library
150 London Wall, London, EC2Y 5HN Tel: 020 7814 5588
Email: info@museumoflondon.org.uk WWW: http://museumoflondon.org.uk

Museum of the Order of St John
St John's Gate, St John's Lane, Clerkenwell, London, EC1M
4DA Tel: (020) 7253-6644 Fax: (020) 7336 0587 Email: WWW:
www.sja.org.uk/history

Museum of the Royal Pharmaceutical Society
Museum of the Royal Pharmaceutical Society, 1 Lambeth High
Street, London, SE1 7JN Tel: (020) 7572 2210 Fax: Email:
museum@rpsgb.org.uk WWW: http://www.rpsgb.org.uk, Records

of pharmacists from 1841 Research fee charged
£20 per person or premises researched to Non members of the Society, £10 per person or premises researched for members(Genealogical Enquiries)
National Army Museum
Royal Hospital Road, London, SW3 4HT Tel: (020) 7730-0717
Fax: (020) 7823-6573 Email: info@national-army-museum.ac.uk
WWW: http://www.national-army-museum.ac.uk
National Army Museum Department of Archives
(Photographs, Film & Sound)
Royal Hospital Road, London, SW3 4HT Tel: (020) 7730-0717
Fax: (020) 7823-6573 Email: info@national-army-museum.ac.uk
WWW: www.national-army-museum.ac.uk
National Portrait Gallery
Heinz Archive & library, 2 St. Martins Place, London,
WC2H 0HE Tel: (020) 7306 0055 Fax: (020) 7306 0056
WWW: www.npg.org.uk
National Register of Archives
Quality House, Quality Court, Chancery Lane, London, WC2A
1HP Tel: (020) 7242 1198 Fax: (020) 7831 3550 Email:
nra@hmc.gov.uk WWW: http://www.hmc.gov.uk, The National
Register of Archives (NRA) is maintained by the Historical
Manuscripts Commission (HMC) as a central collecting point for
information concerning the location of manuscript sources for Britain
Principal Registry of the Family Division
First Avenue House, 42 - 49 High Holborn, London, WC1V 6NP
Tel: (020) 7947 7000 Fax: (020) 7947 6946
WWW: www.courtservice.gov.uk
Royal Air Force Museum - Department of Research &
information Services
Grahame Park Way, Hendon, London, NW9 5LL Tel: (020)
83584873 Fax: (020) 8200 1751 Email: info@rafmuseum.com
WWW: http://www.rafmuseum.com
Royal Air Force Museum
Grahame Park Way, Hendon, London, NW9 5LL Tel: (020)
8205-2266 Fax: (020) 8200 1751 Email:
info@refmuseum.org.uk WWW: http://www.rafmuseum.org.uk
L B of Barking & Dagenham Local History Studies
Central Library, Barking, Dagenham, IG11 7NB Tel: (020) 8517-
8666 Local History studies from this Library have been centralised at
Valence Linbrary, Becontree Avenue, Dagenham, Essex RM8 3HT
Tel & (020) 8227 5297 Email: valencelibrary@hotmail.com
R B of Kensington & Chelsea Libraries & Arts Service
Central Library, Phillimore Walk, Kensington, London, W8 7RX
Tel: (020) 7361-3036 Email: information.services@rbkc.gov.uk
WWW: www.rbkc.gov.uk
Royal Botanic Gardens
Library & Archives, Kew, Richmond, TW9 3AE Tel: 020 8332
5414 Tel: 020 8332 5417 Fax: 020 8332 5430
Royal London Hospital Archives and Museum
Royal London Hospital, Newark Whitechapel, London, E1 1BB
Tel: (020) 7377-7608 Email: r.j.evans@mds.qmw.ac.uk WWW:
www.bartsandthelondon.org.uk
Southwark Local Studies Library
211 Borough High Street, Southwark, London, SE1 1JA
Tel: 0207-403-3507 Email: local.studies.library@southwark.gov.uk
WWW: www.southwark.gov.uk
St Bartholomew's Hospital Archives & Museum
Archives and Museum, West Smithfield, London, EC1A 7BE
Tel: (020) 7601-8152 Email: marion.rea@bartsandthelondon.nhs.uk
WWW: bartsandthelondon.org.uk, Visitors to use the archive by
appointment only - Mon to Fri 9.30am to 5pm
The Archives of Worshipful Company of Brewers
Brewers' Hall, Aldermanbury Square, London, EC2V 7HR
Tel: (020) 7606 1301
The Galton Institute
19 Northfields Prospect, London, SW18 1PE
The United Grand Lodge of England
Freemasons' Hall, 60 Great Queen Street, London, WC2B 5AZ
Tel: (020) 7831 9811 WWW: www.grandlodge.org
Tower Hamlets Local History Library & Archives
Bancroft Library, 277 Bancroft Road, London, El 4DQ Tel: (020)
8980 4366 Ext 129 Fax: (020) 8983-4510
Twickenham Library
Twickenham Library, Garfield Road, Twickenham, TW1 3JS Tel:
(020) 8891-7271 Fax: (020) 8891-5934 Email:
twicklib@richmond.gov.uk WWW: http://www.richmond.gov.uk,
The Twickenham collection moved to Richmond Local Studies Library
University of London (Library - Senate House)
Palaeography Room, Senate House, Malet Street, London,
WC1E 7HU Tel: (020) 7862 8475 Fax: 020 7862 8480 Email:
library@ull.ac.uk WWW: http://www.ull.ac.uk

Waltham Forest Archives
Vestry House Museum, Vestry Road, Walthamstow, London, E17
9NH Tel: (020) 8509 1917 Email: vestry.house@al.lbwf.gov.uk
WWW: http://.www.lbwf.gov.uk/vestry/vestry.htm
Visits by prior appointment only
Westminster Abbey Library & Muniment Room
Westminster Abbey, London, SW1P 3PA Tel: (020) 7222-5152-
Ext-4830 Fax: (020) 7226-4827 Email: library@westminster-
abbey.org WWW: www.westminster-abbey.org
Westminster Diocesan Archives
16a Abingdon Road, Kensington, London, W8 6AF Tel: (020)
7938-3580 This is the private archive of the Catholic Archbishop of
Westminster and is not open to the public. Pre 1837 baptismal records have
been transcribed and copies are with the Society of Genealogists.
Westminster University Archives
Information Systems & Library Services, 4-12 Little Titchfield
Street, London, W1W 7UW Tel: 020 7911 5000 ext 2524 Fax:
020 7911 5894 Email: archive@westminster.ac.uk WWW:
www.wmin.ac.uk The archive is organisationally within the Library
but is a separate entity. The University of Westminster Libraries do
not have special collections relating to family and local history
Public Record Office - 1901 Census Records
Ruskin Avenue, Kew, TW9 4DU WWW: http://www.pro.gov.uk
Records for 1901 census opened to the public in January 2002.
Available on the internet, the Public Record office and main public
libraries.

Manchester
Manchester Archives & Local Studies
Manchester Central Library, St Peter's Square, Manchester, M2
5PD Tel: 0161-234-1979 Fax: 0161-234-1927 Email:
lsu@libraries.manchester.gov.uk WWW:
http://www..manchester.gov.uk/libraries/index.htm
Methodist Archives and Research Centre
John Rylands University Library, 150 Deansgate, Manchester,
M3 3EH Tel: 0161 834 5343 Fax: 0161 834 5574

Medway
Medway Archives and Local Studies Centre
Civic Centre, Strood, Rochester, ME2 4AU Tel: 01634-332714
Fax: 01634-297060 Email: archives@medway.gov.uk
local.studies@medway.gov.uk WWW:
http://cityark.medway.gov.uk

Merseyside
Crosby Library (South Sefton Local History Unit)
Crosby Road North, Waterloo, Liverpool, L22 0LQ Tel: 0151
257 6401 Fax: 0151 934 5770 Email: local-
history.south@leisure.sefton.gov.uk The Local History Units
serve Sefton Borough Council area. The South Sefton Unit
covers Bootle, Crosby, Maghull and other communities south of
the River Alt. The North Sefton Unit covers Southport, Fo
Huyton Central Library
Huyton Library, Civic Way, Huyton, Knowsley, L36 9GD Tel:
0151-443-3738 Fax: 0151 443 3739 Email:
eileen.hume.dlcs@knowsley.gov.uk WWW:
http://www.knowsley.gov.uk/leisure/libraries/huyton/index.html
Merseyside Maritime Museum
Maritime Archives and Library, Albert Dock, Liverpool, L3 4AQ
Tel: 0151-478-4418 Tel: 0151 478 4424 Fax: 0151-478-4590
Email: archives@nmgmarchives.demon.co.uk WWW:
www.nmgm.org.uk
Southport Library (North Sefton Local History Unit)
Lord Street, Southport, PR8 1DJ Tel: 0151 934 2119 Fax: 0151
934 2115 The Local History Units serve Sefton Borough Council
area. The North Sefton Unit covers Southport, Formby. The
South Sefton Unit covers Bootle, Crosby, Maghull and other
communities south of the River
St Helen's Local History & Archives Library
Central Library, Gamble Institute, Victoria Square, St Helens,
WA10 1DY Tel: 01744-456952 No research undertaken
Wirral Archives Service
Wirral Museum, Birkenhead Town Hall, Hamilton Street,
Birkenhead, CH41 5BR Tel: 0151-666 3903 Fax: 0151-666 3965
Email: archives@wirral-libraries.net

Middlesex
British Deaf History Society
288 Bedfont Lane, Feltham, TW14 9NU Fax: Email:
bdhs@iconic.demon.co.uk
L B of Harrow Local History Collection
Civic Centre Library, PO Box 4, Station Road, Harrow, HA1
2UU Tel: 0208 424 1055 Email: civiccentre.library@harrow.gov.uk

Norfolk
Kings Lynn Borough Archives
The Old Gaol House, Saturday Market Place, Kings Lynn, PE30 5DQ Tel: 01553-774297 Tel: 01603 761349 Fax: 01603 761885 Email: norfrec.nro@norfolk.gov.uk WWW: http://archives.norfolk.gov.uk
Norfolk Record Office
Gildengate House, Anglia Square, Upper Green Lane, Norwich, NR3 1AX Tel: 01603-761349 Fax: 01603-761885 Email: norfrec.nro@norfolk.gov.uk WWW: http://archives.norfolk.gov.uk

Northamptonshire
Northamptonshire Central Library
Abington Street, Northampton, NN1 2BA Tel: 01604-462040 Fax: 01604-462055 Email: ns-centlib@northamptonshire.gov.uk WWW: http://www.northamptonshire.gov.uk, Northamptonshire Studies Room collection includes census returns 1841 to 1891, name indexes to 1851 & 1881 census, Parish Registers on microfiche, I.G.I., trade and street directories, poll books, ele
Northamptonshire Record Office
Wootton Hall Park, Northampton, NN4 8BQ Tel: 01604-762129 Email: archivist@nro.northamtonshire.gov.uk WWW: http://www.nro.northamptonshire.gov.uk
also holds Peterborough Diocesan Record Office

Northumberland

Berwick upon Tweed Record Office
Council Offices, Wallace Green, Berwick-Upon-Tweed, TD15 1ED Tel: 01289 301865 Tel: 01289-330044-Ext-265 Fax: 01289-330540 Email: lb@berwick-upon-tweed.gov.uk WWW: www.swinhope.demon.co.uk/genuki/NBL/Northumberland RO/Berwick.html, GRO indexes 1837-1930Office open Wed & Thurs 9.30am to 1pm and 2pm to 5pm. Research service - £8 per half hour.
Northumberland Archive Service
Morpeth Records Centre, The Kylins, Loansdean, Morpeth, NE6l 2EQ Tel: 01670-504084 Fax: 01670-514815 WWW: http://www.swinhope.demon.co.uk/nro/

Nottinghamshire
Nottingham Central Library : Local Studies Centre
Angel Row, Nottingham, NG1 6HP Tel: 0115 915 2873 Fax: 0115 915 2850 Email: local-studies.library@nottinghamcity.gov.uk WWW: www.nottinghamcity.gov.uk/libraries
Nottingham R.C. Diocese Nottingham Diocesan Archives
Willson House, Derby Road, Nottingham, NG1 5AW Tel: 0115 953 9803 Fax: 0115 953 9808
Nottinghamshire Archives
Castle Meadow Road, Nottingham, NG2 1AG Tel: 0115-950-4524 Admin Tel: 0115 958 1634 Enquiries Fax: 0115-941-3997 Email: archives@nottscc.gov.uk WWW: www.nottscc.gov.uk/libraries/archives/index.htm
Southwell Minster Library
Minster Office, Trebeck Hall, Bishop's Drive, Southwell, NG25 0JP Tel: 01636-812649 Fax: 01636 815904 Email: pat@southwellminster.prestell.co.uk

Oxfordshire
Oxfordshire Archives
St Luke's Church, Temple Road, Cowley, Oxford, OX4 2EX Tel: 01865 398200 Email: archives@oxfordshire.gov.uk WWW: http://www.oxfordshire.gov.uk

Peterborough
Peterborough Local Studies Collection
Central Library, Broadway, Peterborough, PE1 1RX Tel: 01733 348343 Email: libraries@peterborough.gov.uk
The telephone number may change in 2002

Shropshire
Ironbridge Gorge Museum, Library & Archives
The Wharfage, Ironbridge, Telford, TF8 7AW Tel: 01952-432141 Email: library@ironbridge.org.uk WWW: www.ironbridge.org.uk
Shropshire Records & Research Centre
Castle Gates, Shrewsbury, SY1 2AQ Tel: 01743-255350 Fax: 01743-255355 Email: research@shropshire-cc.gov.uk WWW: www.shropshire-cc.gov.uk/research.nsf
Wrekin Local Studies Forum
Madeley Library, Russell Square, Telford, TF7 5BB Tel: 01952 586575 Fax: 01952 587105 Email: wlst@library.madeley.uk WWW: www.madeley.org.uk

Somerset
Bath & North East Somerset Record Office
Guildhall, High St, Bath, BA1 5AW Tel: 01225-477421 Fax: 01225-477439 Email: archives@bathnes.gov.uk
Bristol University Library - Special Collections
Tyndall Avenue, Bristol, BS8 1TJ Tel: 0117 928 8014 Fax: 0117 925 5334 Email: library@bris.ac.uk WWW: www.bris.ac.uk/depts/library
Somerset Archive & Record Service
Somerset Record Office, Obridge Road, Taunton, TA2 7PU Tel: 01823-337600 Appointments Tel: 01823 278805 Enquiries Fax: 01823-325402 Email: archives@somerset.gov.uk WWW: http://www.somerset.gov.uk

Staffordshire
Burton Archives
Burton Library, Riverside, High Street, Burton on Trent, DE14 1AH Tel: 01283-239556 Fax: 01283-239571 Email: burton.library@staffordshire.gov.uk
Coal Miners Records
Cannock Record Centre, Old Mid-Cannock (Closed) Colliery Site, Rumer Hill Road, Cannock, WS11 3EX Tel: 01543-570666 Employment and training records held for ex mineworkers post 1917
Keele University Special Collections & Archives
Keele, ST5 5BG Tel: 01782 583237 Fax: 01782 711553 Email: h.burton@keele.ac.uk WWW: www.keele.ac.uk/depts/li/specarc
Lichfield Record Office
Lichfield Library, The Friary, Lichfield, WS13 6QG Tel: 01543-510720 Fax: 01543-510715 Email: lichfield.record.office@staffordshire.gov.uk WWW: www.staffordshire.gov.uk/archives Advance booking required. Lichfield Records Research Service. Covers all the holdings of the office, including Lichfield Diocesan records such as wills including, bishop's transcripts and marriage bonds
Staffordshire Record Office
Eastgate Street, Stafford, ST16 2LZ Tel: 01785-278373 (Bookings) Tel: 01785 278379 (Enquiries) Fax: 01785-278384 Email: staffordshire.record.office@staffordshire.co.uk WWW: www.staffordshire.gov.uk/archives For research into all Staffordshire records including parish and nonconformist registers, census and electoral registers contact:Staffordshire Record Office, Eastgate Street, Stafford ST16 2LZ Lichfie
Staffordshire & Stoke on Trent Archive Service -Stoke on Trent City Archives
Hanley Library, Bethesda Street, Hanley, Stoke on Trent, ST1 3RS Tel: 01782-238420 Fax: 01782-238499 Email: stoke.archives@stoke.gov.uk WWW: www.staffordshire.gov.uk/archives
Tamworth Library
Corporation Street, Tamworth, B79 7DN Tel: 01827-475645 Fax: 01827-475658 Email: tamworth.library@staffordshire.gov.uk WWW: www.staffordshire.gov.uk/locgov/county/cars/tamlib.htm, IGI (Derby, Leics, Notts, Shrops, Staffs, Warks, Worcs). Parish registers for Tamworth. Census for Tamworth and District, 1841 - 91. Street directories for Staffs and Warks.
William Salt Library
Eastgate Street, Stafford, ST16 2LZ Tel: 01785-278372 Fax: 01785-278414 Email: william.salt.library@staffordshire.gov.uk WWW: http://www.staffordshire.gov.uk/archives/salt.htm

Suffolk
Suffolk Record Office - Bury St Edmunds Branch
77 Raingate Street, Bury St Edmunds, IP33 2AR Tel: 01284-352352 Fax: 01284-352355 Email: bury.ro@libher.suffolkcc.gov.uk WWW: http://www.suffolkcc.gov.uk/sro/
Suffolk Record Office Ipswich Branch
Gatacre Road, Ipswich, IP1 2LQ Tel: 01473-584541 Fax: 01473-584533 Email: ipswich.ro@libher.suffolkcc.gov.uk WWW: www.suffolkcc.gov.uk/sro/
Suffolk Record Office Lowestoft Branch
Central Library, Clapham Road, Lowestoft, NR32 1DR Tel: 01502-405357 Fax: 01502-405350 Email: lowestoft.ro@libher.suffolkcc.gov.uk. WWW: www.suffolkcc.gov.uk/sro/
Suffolk Regiment Archives
Suffolk Record Office, 77 Raingate Street, Bury St Edmunds, IP33 2AR Tel: 01284-352352 Fax: 01284-352355 Email: bury.ro@libher.suffolkcc.gov.uk WWW: http://www.suffolkcc.gov.uk/sro/
Surrey
Domestic Buildings Research Group (Surrey)
The Ridings, Lynx Hill, East Horsley, KT24 5AX Tel: 01483 283917 Fax:

Kingston Museum & Heritage Service
North Kingston Centre, Richmond Road, Kingston upon
Thames, KT2 5PE Tel: (020) 8547-6738 Fax: (020) 8547-6747
Email: local.history@rbk.kingston.gov.uk WWW:
www.kingston.gov.uk/museum/, Research service available £7.50
per half hour - max 3 hours

L B of Merton Local Studies Centre
Merton Civic Centre, London Road, Morden, SM4 5DX Tel:
(020) 8545-3239 Fax: (020) 8545-4037 Email:
mertonlibs@compuserve.com

L B of Sutton Archives
Central Library, St Nicholas Way, Sutton, SM1 1EA Tel: (020)
8770-4747 Fax: (020) 8770-4777 Email:
local.studies@sutton.gov.uk WWW: www.sutton.gov.uk, The
Central Library itself holds a large selection of genealogical
sources. The Library is fully accessible. Please phone Archivist
for opening hours and further details about holdings

Sussex
East Sussex Record Office
The Maltings, Castle Precincts, Lewes, BN7 1YT Tel: 01273-
482349 Email: archives@eastsussexcc.gov.uk
WWW: www.eastsussexcc.gov.uk/archives/main.htm

Tyne and Wear
Local Studies Centre
Central Library, Northumberland Square, North Shields, NE3O
1QU Tel: 0191-200-5424 Fax: 0191 200 6118
Email: eric.hollerton@northtyneside.gov.uk
WWW: www.northtyneside.gov.uk/libraries.html

South Tyneside Central Library
Prince Georg Square, South Shields, NE33 2PE Tel: 0191-427-
1818-Ext-7860 Fax: 0191-455-8085 Email: reference.library@s-
tyneside-mbc.gov.uk WWW: www.s-tyneside-mbc.gov.uk

Northern Region Film and Television Archive
School of Law, Arts and Humanities, Room M616
Middlesbrough Tower, University of Teeside, Middlesbrough,
TS1 3BA Tel: 01642 384022 Fax: 01642 384099 Email:
lenticknapp@tees.ac.uk Founded in 1998 to collect, preserve and make
available films and tv programmes of historical and cultural relevance to the
areas of Tyneside, Teeside, Cumbria, Northumberland and County Durham

County Record Office
Melton Park, North Gosforth, Newcastle upon Tyne, NE3 5QX
Tel: 0191-236-2680 Fax: 0191-217-0905
WWW: http://www.swinnhopc.demon.co.uk/genuki/NBL/

Gateshead Central Library & Local Studies Department
Prince Consort Road, Gateshead, NE8 4LN Tel: 0191-477-3478
Fax: 0191-477-7454 Email: a.lang@libarts.gatesheadmbc.gov.uk
WWW: http://ris.niaa.org.ukw
www.gateshead.gov.uk/ls

Newcastle Local Studies Centre
City Library, Princess Square, Newcastle upon Tyne, NE99 1DX
Tel: 0191 277 4116 Fax: 0191 277 4118 Email:
local.studies@newcastle.gov.uk WWW: www.newcastle.gov.uk

Tyne & Wear Archives Service
Blandford House, Blandford Square, Newcastle upon Tyne, NE1
4JA Tel: 0191-232-6789 Fax: 0191-230-2614 Email:
twas@dial.pipex.com WWW: www.thenortheast.com/archives/

Warwickshire
Coventry City Archives
Mandela House, Bayley Lane, Coventry, CV1 5RG Tel: (024)
7683 2418 Fax: (024) 7683 2421 Email:
coventryarchives@discover.co.uk

Modern Records Centre
University of Warwick Library, Coventry, CV4 7AL Tel: (024)
76524219 Fax: (024) 76524211 Email: archives@warwick.ac.uk
WWW: http://warwick.ac.uk/services/library/mrc/mrc.html

Rugby School Archives
Temple Reading Room, Rugby School, Barby Road, Rugby,
CV22 5DW Tel: 01788 556227 Fax: 01788 556228 Email:
dhrm@rugby-school.warwks.sch.uk WWW: www.rugby-
school.warwks.sch.uk

Sutton Coldfield Library & Local Studies Centre
43 Lower Parade, Sutton Coldfield, B72 1XX Tel: 0121-354-
2274 Tel: 0121 464 0164 Fax: 0121 464 0173 Email:
sutton.coldfield.reference.lib@birmingham.gov.uk

Warwick County Record Office
Priory Park, Cape Road, Warwick, CV34 4JS Tel: 01926-412735
Fax: 01926-412509 Email: recordoffiuce@warwickshire.gov.uk
WWW: http://www.warwickshire.gov.uk Major construction
work in 2002 to extend the record office. Visitors should contact

by telephone in advance as public services will be closed during
construction work

West Midlands
Birmingham City Archives
Floor 7, Central Library, Chamberlain Square, Birmingham, B3
3HQ Tel: 0121-303-4217Email: archives@birmingham.gov.uk
WWW: http://www.birmingham.gov.uk/libraries/archives/home.htm

Birmingham Roman Catholic Archdiocesan Archives
Cathedral House, St Chad's Queensway, Birmingham, B4 6EU
Tel: 0121-236-2251 Fax: 0121 233 9299 Email: archives@rc-
birmingham.org

Birmingham University Information Services - Special
Collections
Main Library, University of Birmingham, Edgbaston,
Birmingham, B15 2TT Tel: 0121 414 5838 Fax: 0121 471 4691
Email: special-collections@bham.ac.uk WWW:
www.is.bham.ac.uk

Dudley Archives & Local History Service
Mount Pleasant Street, Coseley, Dudley, WV14 9JR Tel: 01384-
812770 Email: archives.pls@mbc.dudley.gov.uk
WWW: www.dudley.gov.uk Family History Research Service (fee
paying) available

Sandwell Community History & Archives Service
Smethwick Library, High Street, Smethwick, B66 1AB Tel: 0121
558 2561 Fax: 0121 555 6064

Solihull Library
Homer Road, Solihull, B91 3RG Tel: 0121-704-6977 Fax: 0121-
704-6212 The library is NOT an archive repository, sceondary
sources only available for Solihull MBC area only

Walsall Local History Centre
Essex Street, Walsall, WS2 7AS Tel: 01922-721305
 Email: localhistorycentre@walsall.gov.uk WWW:
http://www.walsall.gov.uk/culturalservices/library/welcome.htm

Wolverhampton Archives & Local Studies
42 - 50 Snow Hill, Wolverhampton, WV2 4AG Tel: 01902-
552480 Fax: 01902-552481 Email:
wolverhamptonarchives@dial.pipes.com WWW:
http://www.wolverhampton.gov.uk/archives

West Sussex
West Sussex Record Office
County Hall, Chichester, PO19 1RN Tel: 01243-753600
Fax: 01243-533959 Email: records.office@westsussex.gov.uk
WWW: www.westsussex.gov.uk/cs/ro/rohome.htm

Worthing Reference Library
Worthing Library, Richmond Road, Worthing, BN11 1HD Tel:
01903-212060 Email: worthinglibrary@hotmail.com Largest
library in West Sussex and specialist centre for family history
sources.

Wiltshire
Images of England Project
National Monuments Records Centre, Kemble Drive, Swindon,
SN2 2GZ Tel: 01793 414779
WWW: www.imagesofengland.org.uk

Salisbury Reference and Local Studies Library
Market Place, Salisbury, SP1 1BL Tel: 01722 411098 Fax: 01722
413214 WWW: www.wiltshire.gov.uk

Wiltshire and Swindon Record Office
Libraries HQ, Bythesea Road, Trowbridge, BA14 8BS Tel:
01225 713709 Fax: 01225-713515 Email:
wrso@wiltshire.gov.uk WWW: www.wiltshire.gov.uk

Wiltshire Buildings Record Society
Libraries and Heritage HQ, Bythesea Road, Trowbridge, BA14
8BS

Wiltshire Studies Library
Trowbridge Reference Library, Bythesea Road, Trowbridge,
BA14 8BS Tel: 01225-713732 Tel: 01225 713727 Fax: 01225-
713715 Email: libraryenquiries@wiltshire.gov.uk WWW:
www.wiltshire.gov.uk

Worcestershire
St Helens Record Office - Worcestershire
St Helens Record Office, Fish Street, Worcester, WR1 2HN Tel:
01905-765922 Email: recordoffice@worcestershire.gov.uk
WWW: www.worcestershire.gov.uk/records

Worcesterhire Record Office
History Centre, Trinity Street, Spetchley Road, Worcester, WR1
2PW Tel: 01905 765922 Email: wlhc@worcestershire.gov.uk
WWW: www.worcestershire.gov.uk/records

Worcestershire Regimental Archives
RHQ The Worcestershire & Sherwood Foresters Regiment, Norton Barracks, Worcester, WR5 2PA Tel: 01905-354359 Email: rhq_wfr@lineone.net Records of the Regiment and predecessors from1694, some bibliographical details

Yorkshire
Borthwick Institute of Historical Research
St Anthony's Hall, Peasholme Green, York, YO1 7PW Tel: 01904-642315 WWW:www.york.ac.uk/borthwick, Appointment necessary to use Archives. Research Service Available
Yorkshire Family History - Biographical Database
York Minster Library & Archives, Dean's Park, York, YO1 7JQ Tel: 01904-625308 Library Tel: 01904-611118 Archives Fax: 01904-611119 Email: library@yorkminster.org archives@yorkminster.org WWW: www.yorkminster.org

Yorkshire - East
East Yorkshire Archives Service
County Hall, Champney Road, Beverley, HU17 9BA Tel: 01482 392790 Fax: 01482 392791 Email: archives.service@eastriding.gov.uk WWW: www.eastriding.gov.uk/learning, Correspondence to County Hall, Champney Road, Beverley, HU17 9BA . Reading Room at The Chapel, Lord Roberts Road, Beverley HU17 9BQ 01482 392790 01482 392791 Appointments necessary
Yorkshire - North
Catterick Garrison Library
Gough Road, Catterick Garrison, DL9 3EL Tel: 01748 833543
Extensive collection of over 1350 military history books available for reference or loan. Open Mon 10.am to 12, 1pm to 5.30pm; Wed 10am to 12, 1pm to 5pm; Fri 10am to 12 noon.
North Yorkshire County Record Office
County Hall, Northallerton, DL7 8AF Tel: 01609-777585
Royal Dragoon Guards Military Museum (4th/7th Royal Dragoon Guards & 5th Royal Inniskilling Dragoons)
3A Tower Street, York, YO1 9SB Tel: 01904-662790 Tel: 01904 662310 Fax: 01904 662310 WWW: www.rdg.co.uk Located with Prince of Wales' Own Regiment of Yorkshire Military Museum (West & East Yorkshire Regiments)
Whitby Pictorial Archives Trust
Whitby Archives & Heritage Centre, 17/18 Grape Lane, Whitby, YO22 4BA Tel: 01947-600170 Email: info@whitbyarchives.freeserve.co.uk WWW: www.whitbyarchives.freeserve.co.uk
Yorkshire Film Archive
The University College of Ripon and York st John, College Road, Ripon, HG4 2QX Tel: 01765 602691 Fax: 01765 600516
Yorkshire - South
Archives & Local Studies
Central Library, Walker Place, Rotherham, S65 1JH Tel: 01709-823616 Fax: 01709-823650 Email: archives@rotherham.gov.uk WWW: www.rotherha.gov.uk/pages/living/learning/islib/callib.htm
Barnsley Archives and Local Studies Department
Central Library, Shambles Street, Barnsley, S70 2JF Tel: 01226-773950 Tel: 01226-773938 Email: Archives@Barnsley.govuk & librarian@barnsley.gov.uk
Doncaster Archives
King Edward Road, Balby, Doncaster, DN4 0NA Tel: 01302-859811 Email: doncasterarchives@hotmail.com WWW: doncaster.gov.uk Diocesan Record Office for the Archdeaconry of Doncaster (Diocese of Sheffield)
Sheffield Archives
52 Shoreham Street, Sheffield, S1 4SP Tel: 0114-203-9395 Fax: 0114-203-9398 Email: sheffield.archives@dial.pipex.com WWW: http://www.earl.org.uk/earl/members/sheffield/arch.htm
Sheffield Central Library
Surrey Street, Sheffield, S1 1XZ Tel: 0114 273 4711 Fax: 0114 273 5009 Email: sheffield.libraries@dial.pipex.com

Yorkshire - West
Bradford Archives
West Yorkshire Archive Service, 15 Canal Road, Bradford, BD1 4AT Tel: 01274-731931 Fax: 01274-734013 Email: bradford@wyjs.org.uk WWW: www.archives.wyjs.org.uk
John Goodchild Collection Local History Study Centre
Central Library, Drury Lane, Wakefield, WF1 2DT Tel: 01924-298929 Primarily concerned with regional history; many tens of 000s of index cards, many tons of MSS, maps, illustrations. SAE essential for reply. No photocopying; use by prior appointment.
Local Studies Library
Leeds Central Library, Calverley Street, Leeds, LS1 3AB Tel: 0113 247 8290 Email: local.studies@leeds.gov.uk WWW: www.leeds.gov.uk/library/services/loc_reso.html

Wakefield Library Headquarters - Local Studies Department
Balne Lane, Wakefield, WF2 0DQ Tel: 01924-302224 Email: wakehist@hotmail.com WWW: www.wakefield.gov.uk
West Yorkshire Archive Service, Wakefield Headquarters
Registry of Deeds, Newstead Road, Wakefield, WF1 2DE Tel: 01924-305980 Email: wakefield@wyjs.org.uk WWW: http://www.archives.wyjs.org.uk, This Office hold county-wide records of the West Riding and West Yorkshire and records of Wakefield Metropolitan District. Appointment always required.
West Yorks Archive Service Kirklees
Central Library, Princess Alexandra Walk, Huddersfield, HD1 2SU Tel: 01484-221966 Email: kirklees@wyjs.org.uk WWW: http://www.archives.wyjs.org.uk Appointment always required
West Yorkshire Archive Service Wakefield
Registry of Deeds, Newstead Road, Wakefield, WF1 2DE Tel: 01924-305982 Email: hq@wyashq.demon.co.uk WWW: http://www.archives.wyjs.org.uk
West Yorkshire Archive Service Bradford
15 Canal Road, Bradford, BDI 4AT Tel: 01274-731931 Email: bradford@wyjs.org.uk WWW: http://www.archives.wyjs.org.uk, Appointment always required
West Yorkshire Archive Service, Calderdale
Central Library, Northgate House, Northgate, Halifax, HX1 1UN Tel: 01422-392636 Email: calderdale@wyjs.org.uk WWW: http://www.archives.wyjs.org.uk, Appointment always required
West Yorkshire Archive Service Leeds
Chapeltown Road, Sheepscar, Leeds, LS7 3AP Tel: 0113-214-5814 Email: leeds@wyjs.org.uk WWW: http://www.archives.wyjs.org.uk Also at Yorkshire Archaeological Society, Claremont, 23 Clarendon Road, Leeds LS2 9NZ (0113-245-6362)
Yorkshire Archaeological Society
Claremont, 23 Clarendon Rd, Leeds, LS2 9NZ Tel: 0113-245-6342 Tel: 0113 245 7910 Fax: 0113-244-1979 Email: j.heron@sheffield.ac.uk WWW: www.yas.org.uk, Opening Hours: Tues,Wed 2.00 to 8.30pm; Thurs, Fri 10.00 to 5.30; Sat 9.30 to 5.00 Appointment necessary for use of archival material.

Yorkshire - York
York City Archives
Exhibition Square, Bootham, York, YO1 7EW Tel: 01904-551878/9 Fax: 01904-551877 Email: archives@york.gov.uk WWW: www.york.gov.uk/heritage/museums/index
City of York Libraries - Local History & Reference Collection
York Central Library, Library Square, Museum Street, York, YO1 7DS Tel: 01904-655631 Fax: 01904-611025 Email: reference.library@york.gov.uk WWW: http://www.york.gov.uk

Isle of Wight
Portsmouth Roman Catholic Diocesan Archives
St Edmund House, Edinburgh Road, Portsmouth, PO1 3QA Tel: 023 9282 2166 These are private archives and arrangements to visit have to be agreed beforehand.
Isle of Wight Record Office
26 Hillside, Newport, PO30 2EB Tel: 01983-823820/1 Fax: 01983 823820 Email: record.office@iow.gov.uk WWW: www.iwight.com/library/default.asp

Isle of Man
Civil Registry
Registries Building, Deemster's Walk, Bucks Road, Douglas, IM1 3AR Tel: 01624-687039 Fax: 01624-687004 Email: civil@registry.gov.im
Isle of Man Public Record Office
Unit 3 Spring Valley Industrial Estate, Braddan, Douglas, IM2 2QR Tel: 01624 613383 Fax: 01624 613384
Manx National Heritage Library
Douglas, IM1 3LY Tel: 01624 648000 Fax: 01624 648001 Email: enquiries@mnh.gov.im

Isles of Scilly
Islands of Scilly Museum
Church Street, St Mary's, TR21 0JT Tel: 01720-422337 Fax: 01720-422337

Channel Islands
Guernsey Island Archives Service
29 Victoria Rd, St Peter Port, GYI 1HU Tel: 01481-724512

Jersey Archives Service
Jersey Museum, The Weybridge, St Helier, JE2 3NF Tel: 01534-633303 Fax: 01534-633301
Judicial Greffe
Morier House, Halkett Place, St Helier, JE1 1DD Tel: 01534-502300 Fax: 01534-502399/502390 Email: jgreffe@super.net.uk WWW: www.jersey.gov.uk

Wales
National Library of Wales
Penglais, Aberystwyth, SY23 3BU Tel: 01970-632800 Tel:
01970 632902 Marketing Fax: 01970-615709 Email:
holi@llgc.org.uk WWW: http://www.llgc.org.uk
Department of Manuscripts
Main Library, University of Wales, College Road, Bangor, LL57
2DG Tel: 01248-382966 Fax: 01248-382979 Email:
iss177@bangor.ac.uk
National Monuments Record of Wales
Royal Commission on the Ancient & Historical Monuments of
Wales, Crown Building, Plas Crug, Aberystwyth, Wales Tel:
01970-621200 Fax: 01970-627701 Email:
nmr.wales@rcahmw.org.uk WWW: www.rcahmw.org.uk
National Monuments Record of Wales
Royal Commission - Ancient & Historical Monuments Wales,
Crown Building, Plas Crug, Aberystwyth, SY23 1NJ Tel: 01970
621233 Fax: 01970 627701
Public Record Office - 1901 Census Records
Ruskin Avenue, Kew, TW9 4DU
WWW: http://www.pro.gov.uk Records for 1901 census opened
to the public in January 2002. Available on the internet, the
Public Record office and main public libraries.

Anglesey
Anglesey County Archives Service
Shirehall, Glanhwfa Road, Llangefni, LL77 7TW Tel: 01248-
752080 WWW: www.anglesey.gov.uk

Carmarthenshire
Carmarthenshire Archive Service
Parc Myrddin, Richmond Terrace, Carmarthen, SA31 1DS Tel:
01267 228232 Fax: 01267 228237 Email:
archives@carmarthenshire.gov.uk WWW:
www.carmarthenshire.gov.uk

Ceredigion
Archifdy Ceredigion, Ceredigion Archives
Swyddfa'r Sir, County Offices, Glan y Mor, Marine Terrace,
Aberystwyth, SY23 2DE Tel: 01970-633697 Fax: 01970 633663
Email: archives@ceredigion.gov.uk
National Library of Wales
Penglais, Aberystwyth, SY23 3BU Tel: 01970-632800 Tel:
01970 632902 Marketing Fax: 01970-615709 Email:
holi@llgc.org.uk WWW: http://www.llgc.org.uk

Denbighshire
Denbighshire Record Office
46 Clwyd Street, Ruthin, LL15 1HP Tel: 01824-708250 Fax:
01824-708258 Email: archives@denbighshire.go.uk WWW:
http://www.denbighshire.gov.uk Extensive refurbishment until
early Summer 2002 - telephone before visiting

Flintshire
Flintshire Record Office
The Old Rectory, Rectory Lane, Hawarden, CH5 3NR Tel:
01244-532364 Fax: 01244-538344 Email:
archives@flintshire.gov.uk WWW: http://www.flintshire.gov.uk

Glamorgan
Glamorgan Record Office
Glamorgan Building, King Edward VII Avenue, Cathays Park,
Cardiff, CF10 3NE Tel: (029) 2078 0282 Fax: (029) 2078 0284
Email: GlamRO@cardiff.ac.uk WWW:
http://www.llgc.org.uk/cac/
Neath Central Library (Local Studies Department)
29 Victoria Gardens, Neath, SA11 3BA Tel: 01639-620139
West Glamorgan Archive Service
County Hall, Oystermouth Road, Swansea, SA1 3SN Tel: 01792-
636589 Fax: 01792-637130 Email: archives@swansea.gov.uk
WWW: http://www.swansea.gov.uk/archives

Swansea
Swansea Reference Library
Alexandra Road, Swansea, SA1 5DX Tel: 01792-516753 Fax:
01792 516759 Email: swanlib@demon.co.uk Extensive holdings
of trade directories, local census returns, newspapers (partially
indexed)
West Glamorgan Archive Service
County Hall, Oystermouth Road, Swansea, SA1 3SN Tel: 01792-
636589 Fax: 01792-637130 Email: archives@swansea.gov.uk
WWW: http://www.swansea.gov.uk/archives

Gwent & Monmouthshire
Gwent Record Office
County Hall, Croesyceiliog, Cwmbran, NP44 2XH Tel: 01633-
644886 Fax: 01633-648382 Email:
gwent.records@torfaen.gov.uk WWW: www.llgc.org.uk/cac

Gwynedd
Archifdy Meirion Archives
Swyddfeydd y Cyngor, Cae Penarlag, Dolgellau, LL40 2YB Tel:
01341-424444 Fax: 01341-424505 Email:
EinionWynThomas@gwynedd.gov.uk WWW:
www.gwynedd.gov.uk/archives/
Gwynedd Archives
Caernarfon Area Record Office, Victoria Dock, Caernarfon,
LL55 1SH Tel: 01286-679095 Fax: 01286-679637 Email:
archifau@gwynedd.gov.uk WWW:
http://www.gwynedd.gov.uk/adrannau/addysg/archifau

Newport
Newport Library & Information Service
Newport Central Library, John Frost Square, Newport, NP20
1PA Tel: 01633-211376 Fax: 01633-222615
Email: reference.library@newport.gov.uk
WWW: http://www.earl.org.uk/partners/newport/index.html
The Local Studies Collection contains information on all aspects of
Monmouthshire and or Gwent. A fee paying postal research service is
available, which uses the library's own resources.

Pembrokeshire
Pembrokeshire Libraries
The County Library, Dew Street, Haverfordwest, SA61 1SU Tel:
01437-762070Email: anita.thomas@pembrokeshire.gov.uk The
Local Studies Library covers peoiple, places and events relating to
The County of Pembrokeshire past and present. The Library also
houses The Francis Green Genealogical Collection
Pembrokeshire Record Office
The Castle, Haverfordwest, SA61 2EF Tel: 01437-763707 Fax:
01437 768539 Email: record.office@pembrokeshire.gov.uk
Tenby Museum
Tenby Museum & Art Gallery, Castle Hill, Tenby, SA70 7BP Tel:
01834-842809 Fax: 01834-842809 Email: tenbymuseum@hotmail.com
WWW: tenbymuseum.free-online.co.uk

Powys
Powys County Archives Office
County Hall, Llandrindod Wells, LD1 5LG Tel: 01597 826088
Fax: 01597 826087 Email: archives@powys.gov.uk WWW:
http://archives.powys.gov.uk

West Glamorgan
**West Glamorgan Archive Service - Neath Archives Access
Point**
Neath Mechanics Institute, Church Place, Neath, SA11 3BA Tel:
01639-620139 WWW: www.swansea.gov.uk/archives
West Glamorgan Archive Service - Port Talbot Access Point
Port Talbot Library, Aberafan Centre, Port Talbot, SA13 1PJ Tel:
01639 763430 WWW: http://www.swansea.gov.uk/archives

Wrexham
Wrexham Archives Service
Wrexham Museum, County Buildings,, Regent Street, Wrexham,
LL11 1RB Tel: 01978-317976 Fax: 01978-317982 Email:
archives@wrexham.gov.uk

Scotland
Aberdeen Synagogue
74 Dee Street, Aberdeen, AB11 6DS Tel: 01224 582135 Fax:
Dundee Synagogue
St Mary Place, Dundee, DD1 5RB Fax:
Edinburgh Synagogue
4 Salisbury Road, Edinburgh, Scotland Fax:
Grand Lodge of Scotland
Freemasons' Hall, 96 George Street, Edinburgh, EH2 3DH Tel:
0131 225 5304
General Register Office for Scotland
New Register House, Edinburgh, EH1 3YT Tel: 0131-334-0380
Tel: Certificate Order 0131 314 4411 Fax: 0131-314-4400 Email:
records@gro-scotland.gov.uk WWW: http://www.gro-
scotland.gov.uk Pay per view search site: http://www.origins.net, A fully
searchable index of Scottish birth and marriage records from 1553 to 1901 and
death records from 1855 to 1926 can be accessed on the internet at
http://www.origins.net

Glasgow Jewish Representative Council
222 Fenwick Road, Giffnock, Glasgow, G46 6UE Tel: 0141 577
8200 Email: glasgow@j-scot.org WWW: www.j-scot.org/glasgow

Glasgow University Library & Special Collections Dept
Hillhead Street, Glasgow, G12 8QE Tel: 0141 330 6767 Fax:
0141 330 3793 Email: library@lib.gla.ac.uk WWW:
www.gla.ac.uk/library

Heriot-Watt University Archives
Coporate Communications, Heriot-Watt university, Edinburgh,
EH14 4AS Tel: 0131 451 3218 Tel: 0131 451 3219 & 0131 451
4140 Fax: 0131 451 3164 Email: a.e.jones@hw.ac.uk WWW:
www.hw.ac.uk/archive

National Archives of Scotland
HM General Register House, 2 Princes Street, Edinburgh, EH1
3YY Tel: 0131-535-1334 Fax: 0131-535-1328 Email:
enquiries@nas.gov.uk WWW: www.nas.gov.uk

National Archives of Scotland - West Search Room
West Register House, Charlotte Square, Edinburgh, EH2 4DJ
Tel: 0131-535-1413 Fax: 0131-535-1411 Email: wsr@nas.gov.uk
WWW: www.nas.gov.uk All correspondence to: National
Archives of Scotland, HM General Register House, Edinburgh
EH1 3YY

National Library of Scotland - Department of Manuscripts
National Library of Scotland, George IV Bridge, Edinburgh, EH1
1EW Tel: 0131 466 2812 Fax: 0131 466 2811 Email: mss@nls.uk
WWW: http://www.nls.uk The division will answer general
enquiries but cannot undertake detailed genealogical research

National Monuments Record of Scotland
Royal Commission on the Ancient & Historical Monuments of
Scotland, John Sinclair House, 16 Bernard terrace, Edinburgh, EH8
9NX Tel: 0131 662 1456 Fax: 0131 662 1477 or 0131 662 1499
Email: nmrs@rcahms.gov.uk WWW: www.rcahms.gov.uk Website
gives access to the searchable database of NMRS Records -
'CANMORE'

National Register of Archives (Scotland)
H M General Register House, 2 Princes Street, Edinburgh, EH1 3YY
Tel: 0131 535 1405/1428 Tel: 0131 535 1430 Email: nra@nas.gov.uk
WWW: www.nas.gov.uk The papers mentioned on the Register are not
held by the NRA(S) but are deposited elsewhere or remain in private hands.
While the NRA staff are always happy to answer limited and specific
POSTAL enquiries about the existence of papers relating to a particular
individual or subject, theytare unable to undertake research on belahf of
enquirers. Once they have advised on possible sources it is then up to
enquirers either to carry out the research themselves or to engage a record
agent to do so on their behalf. Where papers remain in private hands written
applications for access shoul;d be made in the first instance to the NRA(S)

Royal College of Physicians and Surgeons of Glasgow
232 - 242 St Vincent Street, Glasgow, G2 5RJ Tel: 0141 221
6072 Fax: 0141 221 1804 Email: library@rcpsglasg.ac.uk
WWW: www.rcpsglasg.ac.uk

Scottish Archive Network
Thomas Thomson House, 99 Bankhead Crossway North,
Edinburgh, EH11 4DX Tel: 0131 242 5800 Fax: 0131 242 5801
Email: enquiries@scan.org.uk WWW: www.scan.org.uk A
lottery funded project to open up access to Scotland's archives

Scottish Brewing Archive
13 Thurso Street, Glasgow, G11 6PE Tel: 0141 330 2640 Fax:
0141 330 4158 Email: sba@archives.gla.ac.uk WWW:
www.archives.gla.ac.uk/sba/

Scottish Catholic Archives
Columba House, 16 Drummond Place, Edinburgh, EH3 6PL Tel:
0131-5563661 These archives do not hold any genealogical material. The
Catholic parish registers are still held by the parishes. There are no
arrangements for personal callers.

Scottish Genealogy Society
15 Victoria Terrace, Edinburgh, EH1 2JL Tel: 0131-220 3677
Fax: 0131 220 3677 Email: info@scotsgenealogy.com WWW:
www.scotsgenealogy.com

Scottish Jewish Archives Centre
Garnethill Synagogue, 129 Hill Street, Garnethill, Glasgow, G3
6UB Tel: 0141 332 4911 Fax: 0141 332 4911 Email:
archives@sjac.fsbusiness.co.uk WWW: www.sjac.org.uk

**St Andrews University Library - Special Collections
Department**
North Street, St Andrews, KY16 9TR Tel: 01334 462339 Email:
speccoll@st-and.ac.uk WWW: http://specialcollections.st-and.ac.uk

Strathclyde University Archives
McCance Building, 16 Richmond Street, Glasgow, G1 1XQ Tel:
0141 548 2397 Fax: 0141 552 0775

Aberdeen
Aberdeen City Archives
Aberdeen City Council, Town House, Broad Street, Aberdeen,
AB10 1AQ Tel: 01224-522513 Fax: 01224 638556
Email: archives@legal.aberdeen.net.uk
WWW: www.aberdeencity.gov.uk Also covers Aberdeenshire

Aberdeen City Archives - Old Aberdeen House Branch
Old Aberdeen House, Dunbar Street, Aberdeen, AB24 1UE Tel:
01224-481775 Email: archives@legal.aberdeen.net.uk
WWW: www.aberdeencity.gov.uk

Angus
Angus Archives
Montrose Library, 214 High Street, Montrose, DD10 8PH Tel:
01674-671415 Fax: 01674-671810 Email:
angus.archives@angus.govuk WWW:
www.angus.gov.uk/history/history.htm Family history research
service. Archive holdings for Angus County, Arbroath, Brechin,
Carnoustie, Forfar, Montrose, Monifieth, Kittiemuir.

Argyll
Argyll & Bute District Archives
Manse Brae, Lochgilphead, PA31 8QU Tel: 01546 604120 Fax:

Ayrshire
Ayrshire Archives
Ayrshire Archives Centre, Craigie Estate, Ayr, KA8 0SS Tel:
01292-287584 Fax: 01292-284918 Email: archives@south-
ayrshire.gov.uk WWW: http://www.south-
ayrshire.gov.uk/archives/index.htm, includes North Ayrshire,
East Ayrshire and South Ayrshire.

East Ayrshire Council District History Centre & Museum
Baird Institute, 3 Lugar Street, Cumnock, KA18 1AD Tel:
01290-421701 Fax: 01290-421701 Email: Baird.institute@east-
ayrshire.gov.uk WWW: www.east-ayrshire.gov.uk

North Ayrshire Libraries
Library Headquarters, 39 - 41 Princes Street, Ardrossan, KA22
8BT Tel: 01294-469137 Fax: 01924-604236 Email:
reference@naclibhq.prestel.co.uk WWW: www.north-
ayrshire.gov.uk

Clackmannanshire
Clackmannanshire Archives
Alloa Library, 26/28 Drysdale Street, Alloa, FK10 1JL Tel:
01259-722262 Fax: 01259-219469 Email:
libraries@clacks.gov.uk WWW:
www.clacksweb.org.uk/dyna/archives

Clackmannanshire Registration Office
Marshill House, Marshill, Alloa, FK10 1AB Tel: 01259-723850
Fax: 01259-723850 Email: clack.lib@mail.easynet.co.uk

Dumfries & Galloway
Dumfries & Galloway Library and Archives
Archive Centre, 33 Burns Street, Dumfries, DG1 1PS Tel: 01387
269254 Fax: 01387 264126 Email: libsxi@dumgal.gov.uk
WWW: www.dumgal.gov.uk Open : Tues, Wed, Fri, 11am to 1pm,
2pm to 5pm and on Thurs 6pm to 9pm. Please book. Postal and
consultation genealogical service available. Details on application.

Ewart Library
Ewart Library, Catherine Street, Dumfries, DG1 1JB Tel: 01387
260285 Tel: 01387-252070 Fax: 01387-260294 Email:
ruth_airley@dumgal.gov.uk &libsxi@dumgal.gov.uk WWW:
www.dumgal.gov.ukf, Fee paid research service availble

Dundee
Dundee City Archives
21 City Square, (callers use 1 Shore Terrace), Dundee, DD1
3BY Tel: 01382-434494 Fax: 01382-434666 Email:
archives@dundeecity.gov.uk WWW:
www.dundeecity.gov.uk/archives.html

Dundee City Council - Genealogy Unit
89 Commercial Street, Dundee, DD1 2AF Tel: 01382-435222 Fax:
01382-435224 Email: grant.law@dundeecity.gov.uk WWW:
www.dundeecity.gov.uk/dcchtml/sservices/genealogy.html

East Dunbartonshire
**East Dunbartonshire Local Record Offices and Reference
Libraries**
William Patrick Library, 2 West High Street, Kirkintilloch, G66
1AD Tel: 0141-776-8090 Fax: 0141-776-0408 Email:
libraries@eastdunbarton.gov.uk WWW:
www.eastdunbarton.gov.uk

East Renfrewshire
East Renfrewshire Record Offices ????
East Renfrewshire District Council, Rouken Glen Road,
Glasgow, G46 6JF Tel: 0141-577-4976

Edinburgh
Edinburgh City Archives
City Chambers, High St, Edinburgh, EH1 1YJ Tel: 0131-529-
4616 Fax: 0131-529-4957

Falkirk
Falkirk Library
Hope Street, Falkirk, FK1 5AU Tel: 01324 503605 Fax: 01324
503606 Email: falkirk-library@falkirk-library.demon.co.uk
WWW: www.falkirk.gov.uk Holds Local Studies Collection
Falkirk Museum History Research Centre
Callendar House, Callendar Park, Falkirk, FK1 1YR Tel: 01324
503778 Fax: 01324 503771 Email:
ereid@falkirkmuseums.demon.co.ukcallandarhouse@falkirkmus
eums.demon.co.uk WWW: www.falkirkmuseums.demon.co.uk
Records held: Local Authority, business, personal and estate records, local
organmisations, trade unions, over 28,000 photographs Falkirk District

Fife
Fife Council Archive Centre
Carleton House, Balgonie Road, Markinch, Glenrothes, KY6
7AH Tel: 01592 416504
**St Andrews University Library - Special Collections
Department**
North Street, St Andrews, KY16 9TR Tel: 01334 462339 Fax:
01334 462282 Email: speccoll@st-and.ac.uk WWW:
http://specialcollections.st-and.ac.uk

Glasgow
Glasgow City Archives
Mitchell Library, North Street, Glasgow, G3 7DN Tel: 0141-287-
2913 Fax: 0141-226-8452 Email: archives@cls.glasgow.gov.uk
WWW: http://users.colloquium.co.uk/~glw_archives/src001.htm
**Glasgow University Library & Special Collections
Department**
Hillhead Street, Glasgow, G12 8QE Tel: 0141 330 6767 Fax:
0141 330 3793 Email: library@lib.gla.ac.uk WWW:
www.gla.ac.uk/library
Royal College of Physicians and Surgeons of Glasgow
232 - 242 St Vincent Street, Glasgow, G2 5RJ Tel: 0141 221
6072 Fax: 0141 221 1804 Email: library@rcpsglasg.ac.uk
WWW: www.rcpsglasg.ac.uk
Glasgow University Archive Services
13 Thurso Street, Glasgow, G11 6PE Tel: 0141 330 5515 Fax:
0141 330 4158 Email: archives@archives.gla.ac.uk WWW:
www.archives.gla.ac.uk

Invernesshire
Highland Council Genealogy Centre
Inverness Public Library, The Library, Farraline Park, Inverness,
IV1 1NH Tel: 01463-236463 : Tel: 01463 220330 ext 9 Fax:
01463 711128

Isle of Lewis
Stornoway Record Office
Town Hall, 2 CromwellStreet, Stornoway, HS1 2BD Tel: 01851-
709438 Fax: 01851 709438 Email: emacdonald@cne-siar.gov.uk

Lanarkshire
South Lanarkshire Council Archives
30 Hawbank Road, College Milton, East Kilbride, G74 5EX Tel:
01355 239193 Fax: 01355 242365

Midlothian
Midlothian Archives and Local Studies Centre
2 Clerk Street, Loanhead, EH20 9DR Tel: 0131 271 3976 Fax:
0131 440 4635 Email: local.studies@midlothian.gov.uk WWW:
www.earl.org.uk/partners/midlothian/local.html

Moray
Moray Local Heritage Centre
Grant Lodge, Cooper Park, Elgin, IV30 1HS Tel: 01343 562644
Tel: 01343 562645 Fax: 01343-549050 Email:
graeme.wilson@techleis.moray.gov.uk WWW:
www.morray.org/heritage/roots.html The Moray District Record
Office has now been combined with the Local studies section at
Grant Lodge, Cooper Park, Elgin to form the Local Heritage Centre.
North Highland Archive
Wick Library, Sinclair Terrace, Wick, KW1 5AB Tel: 01955
606432 Fax: 01955 603000

North Lanarkshire
North Lanarkshire - Lenziemill Archives
10 Kelvin Road, Cumbernauld, G67 2BA Tel: 01236 737114
Fax: 01236 781762

Orkney
Orkney Archives
The Orkney Library, Laing Street, Kirkwall, KWI5 1NW Tel:
01856-873166 Email: alison.fraser@orkney.gov.uk   Open Mon
to Fri 9am to 1pm & 2pm to 4.45pm. Appointments preferred
Orkney Library
The Orkney Library, Laing Street, Kirkwall, KWI5 1NW Tel:
01856-873166 Fax: 01856-875260 Email:
karen.walker@orkney.gov.uk

Perthshire
Perth and Kinross Council Archives
A K Bell Library, 2 - 8 York Place, Perth, PH2 8EP Tel: 01738-
477012 Tel: 01738 477022 Fax: 01738-477010 Email:
archives@pkc.gov.uk WWW:
http://www.pkc.gov.uk/library/archive.htm
Regimental Museum and Archives of Black Watch
Balhousie Castle, Hay Street, Perth, PH1 5HS Tel: 0131-
3108530 Tel: 01738 621281 ext 8530 Fax: 01738-643245 Email:
bwarchivist@btclick.com WWW: www.theblackwatch.co.uk

Renfrewshire
Renfrewshire Archives
Central Library & Museum Complex, High Street, Paisley, PA1
2BB Tel: 0141-889-2350 Fax: 0141-887-6468 Email:
local_studies.library@renfrewshire.gov.uk

Scottish Borders
Scottish Borders Archive & Local History Centre
Library Headquarters, St Mary's Mill, Selkirk, TD7 5EW Tel:
01750 20842 Tel: 01750 724903 Fax: 01750 22875 Email:
archives@scotborders.gov.uk WWW:
www.scotborders.gov.uk/libraries

Shetland
Shetland Archives
44 King Harald St, Lerwick, ZE1 0EQ Tel: 01595-696247 Fax:
01595-696533 Email: shetland.archives@zetnet.co.uk
Unst Heritage Centre
Haroldswick, Unst, ZE2 9ED Tel: 01957 711528 Tel: 01957
711387 (Home)

Stirlingshire
Stirling Council Archives
Unit 6, Burghmuir Industrial Estate, Stirling, FK7 7PY Tel:
01786-450745 Fax: 01786 473713 Email:
archive@stirling.gov.uk

Strathclyde
Strathclyde Area - Genealogy Centre
The Register Office, 22 Park Circus, Glasgow, G3 6BE Tel:
0141-287-8350 Fax: 0141-225-8357

Tayside
Dundee University Archives
Tower Building, University of Dundee, Dundee, DD1 4HN Tel:
01382-344095 Fax: 01382 345523 Email:
archives@dundee.ac.uk WWW:
http://www.dundee.ac.uk/archives/

West Lothian
West Lothian Council Archives - Archives & Records Management
7 Rutherford Square, Brucefield Industrial Estate, Livingston,
EH54 9BU Tel: 01506 460 020 Fax: 01506 416 167

Northern Ireland
Public Record Office of Northern Ireland
66 Balmoral Avenue, Belfast, BT9 6NY Tel: (028) 9025 5905
Fax: (028) 9025 5999 Email: proni@dcalni.gov.uk WWW:
http://www.proni.nics.gov.uk
General Register Office of Northern Ireland
Oxford House, 49 - 55 Chichester Street, Belfast, BT1 4HL Tel:
(028) 90 252000 Fax: (028) 90 252120 Email:
gro.nisra@dfpni.gov.uk WWW: www.groni.gov.uk
Presbyterian Historical Society of Ireland
Church House, Fisherwick Place, Belfast, BT1 6DW Tel: (028)
9032 2284 Opening hours: Mon to Fri 10am to 12.30pm. Wed
afternoons 1.30pm to 3.30pm

Belfast Central Library
Irish & Local Studies Dept, Royal Avenue, Belfast, BT1 1EA
Tel: (028) 9024 3233 Fax: (028) 9033 2819 Email:
info@libraries.belfast-elb.gov.uk WWW: www.belb.org.uk
Belfast Family History & Cultural Heritage Centre
64 Wellington Place, Belfast, BT1 6GE Tel: (028) 9023 5392
Fax: (028) 9023 9885
Derry City Council Heritage & Museum Service
Harbour Museum, Harbour Square, Derry, BT48 6AF Tel: (028)
7137 7331 Fax: (028) 7137 763 The archives of Derry City Council are
an invaluable source of information for the history of both the City and the
Council from the early seventeeth century to the present day.
Banbridge Genealogy Services
Gateway Tourist Information Centre, 200 Newry Road,
Banbridge, BT32 3NB Tel: 028 4062 6369 Fax: 028 4062 3114
Email: banbridge@nitic.net

Ireland
Church of Ireland Archives
Representative Church Body Library, Braemor Park,
Churchtown, Dublin 14, Tel: 01-492-3979 Fax: 01-492-4770
Email: library@ireland.anglican.org
WWW: http://www.ireland.anglican.org/
Genealogical Office / Office of The Chief herald
Kildare Street, Dublin 2, Tel: +353-1-6030 200 Fax: +353-1-
6621 062 Email: herald@nli.ie WWW: www.nli.ie
Grand Lodge of Ireland
Freemasons' Hall, 17 Molesworth Street, Dublin 2, Tel: 00 353
01 6760 1337 :
National Archives
Bishop Street, Dublin 8, Tel: 01-407-2300 Fax: 01-407-2333
Email: mail@nationalarchives.ie WWW:
http://www..nationalarchives.ie
Presbyterian Historical Society of Ireland
Church House, Fisherwick Place, Belfast, BT1 6DW Tel: (028)
9032 2284 Opening hours: Mon to Fri 10am to 12.30pm. Wed
afternoons 1.30pm to 3.30pm
Registrar General for Ireland
Joyce House, 8 - 11 Lombard Street East, Dublin 2, Tel: Dublin-
711000 Fax:

Dublin
Dublin City Archives
City Assembly House, 58 South William Street, Dublin, 2 Tel:
(01)-677-5877 Fax: (01)-677-5954

County Clare
Clare County Archives
Clare County Council, New Road, Ennis, Tel: 065-28525 Tel:
065 21616 WWW: www.clare.ie

County Donegal
Donegal Ancestry
Old Meeting House, Back Lane, Ramleton, Letterkenny, Tel:
00353 74 51266 Fax: 00353 74 51702 Email:
donances@indigo.ie WWW: http://www.indigo.ie/~donances
Donegal County Council Archive Centre
3 Rivers Centre, Lifford, Tel: + 00353 74 72490 Fax: + 00353
74 41367 Email: nbrennan@donegalcoco.ie WWW:
www.donegal.ie
Donegal Local Studies Centre
Central Library & Arts Centre, Oliver Plunkett Road,
Letterkenny, Tel: 00353 74 24950 Fax: 00353 74 24950 Email:
dgcolib@iol.ie WWW: donegal.ie

County Down
Banbridge Genealogy Services
Gateway Tourist Information Centre, 200 Newry Road,
Banbridge, BT32 3NB Tel: 028 4062 6369 Fax: 028 4062 3114
Email: banbridge@nitic.net

County Dublin
Dublin Heritage Group
Ballyfermot Library, Ballyfermot Road, Ballyfermot, Dublin, 10
Tel: 6269324 Email: dhgeneal@iol.ie
County Limerick
Limerick City Library Local History Collection
The Granary, Michael Street, Limerick, Tel: +353 (0)61-314668
Tel: +353 (0)61-415799 Fax: +353(0) 61 411506 Email:
noneill@citylib.limerickcorp.ie WWW:
http://www.limerickcorp.ie/librarymain.htm
Limerick Regional Archives
Limerick Ancestry, The Granary, Michael Street, Limerick, Tel:
061-415125WWW: www.mayo-ireland.ie

County Mayo
Local Record Offices
The Registration Office, New Antrim Street, Castlebar, Tel: 094-
23249 Fax: 094 23249

Australia
National Archives of Australia - Canberra
PO Box 7425, Canberra Mail Centre, Canberra, ACT, 2610
Tel: 02-6212-3600 Email: archives@naa.gov.au
WWW: www.naa.gov.au
National Archives of Australia - Hobart
4 Rosny Hill Road, Rosny Park, Tasmania, 7018 Tel: 03-62-440101
Fax: 03-62-446834 Email: reftas@naa.gov.au WWW: www.naa.gov.au
National Archives of Australia - Northern Territories
Kelsey Crescent, Nightcliffe, NT, 810 Tel: 08-8948-4577
National Archives of Australia - Queensland
996 Wynnum Road, Cannon Hill, Queensland, 4170 Tel: 07-3249-4226
Fax: 07-3399-6589WWW: www.naa.gov.au
National Archives of Australia - South Australia
11 Derlanger Avenue, Collingwood, South Australia, 5081
Tel: 08-269-0100
National Archives of Australia - Sydney
120 Miller Road, Chester Hill, Sydney, New South Wales, 2162
Tel: 02-96450-100 / Fax: 02-96450-108
Email: refnsw@naa.gov.auWWW: www.naa.gov.uk
National Archives of Australia - Victoria
PO Box 8005, Burwood Heights, Victoria, 3151 Tel: 03-9285-7900
National Archives of Australia - Western Australia
384 Berwick Street East, Victoria Park, Western Australia, 6101
Tel: 09-470-7500 Fax: 09-470-2787,
New South Wales - State Archives Office
2 Globe Street, Sydney, New South Wales, 2000 Tel: 02-9237-0254
Queensland State Archives
PO Box 1397, Sunnybanks Hills, Brisbane, Queensland, 4109
Tel: 61-7-3875-8755 Fax: 61-7-3875-8764
Email: qsa@ipd.pwh.qld.gov.auWWW: www.archives.qld.gov.au
South Australia State Archives
PO Box 1056, Blair Athol West, South Australia, 5084
Tel: 08-8226-8000 Fax: 08-8226-8002,
Tasmania State Archives
Archives Office of Tasmania, 77 Murray Street, Hobart, Tasmania, 7000
Tel: (03)-6233-7488 Email: archives.tasmania@central.tased.edu.au
WWW: www.tased.edu.au/archives
Victoria State Archives - Ballerat
State Offices, Corner of Mair & Doveton Streets, Ballarat, Victoria,
3350 Tel: 03-5333-6611 Fax: 03-5333-6609,
Victoria State Archives - Laverton North
57 Cherry Lane, Laverton North, Victoria, 3028 Tel: 03-9360-9665
Fax: 03-9360-9685,
Victoria State Archives - Melbourne
Level 2 Casselden Place, 2 Lonsdale Street, Melbourne, Victoria, 3000
Tel: 03-9285-7999 Fax: 03-9285-7953,
Western Australia - State Archives & Public Records Office
Alexander Library, Perth Cultural Centre, Perth, Western Australia,
6000 Tel: 09-427-3360 Fax: 09-427-3256,

New Zealand
National Archives of New Zealand
PO Box 10-050, 10 Mulgrave Street, Thorndon, Wellington, New
Zealand Tel: 04-499-5595 Email: national.archives@dia.govt.nz
WWW: www.archives.dia.govt.nz

Africa
South Africa
Cape Town Archives Repository
Private Bag X9025, Cape Town, 8000, South Africa Tel: 021-462-4050
Fax: 021-465-2960,
Dutch Reformed Church Archive
PO Box 398, Bloemfontein, 9301, South Africa Tel: 051-448-9546,
Dutch Reformed Church Archive of O.F.S
P O Box 398, Bloemfontein, 9301, RSA Tel: 051 448 9546,
Dutch Reformed Church Records Office
PO Box 649, Pietermaritzburg, 3200, South Africa Tel: 0331-452279
Fax: 0331-452279,
Dutch Reformed Church Synod Records Office of Kwa Zulu-Natal
P O Box 649, Pietermaritzburg , 3200, RSA Tel: 0331 452279
Fax: 0331 452279 Email: ngntlargrief@alpha.futurenet.co.za,
Free State Archives
Private Bag X20504, Bloemfontein, Free State, 9300, South Africa
Tel: 051-522-6762 Fax: 051-522-6765

Free State Archives Repository
Private Bag X20504, Bloemfontein, 9300, South Africa
Tel: 051 522 6762 Fax: 051 522 6765,
National Archives - Pretoria
Private Bag X236, Pretoria, 1, South Africa Tel: 323 5300
South Africa National Archives
Private Bag X236, Pretoria, 1, South Africa
South African Library - National Reference & Preservation
P O Box 496, Cape Town, 8000, South Africa Tel: 021 246320
Fax: 021 244848 Email: postmaster@salib.ac.za

Namibia
National Archives of Namibia
Private Bag, Windhoek, 13250, Namibia Tel: 061 293 4386
Email: Renate@natarch.mec.gov.na WWW: www.witbooi.natarch.mec.gov.na

Zimbabwe
National Archives of Zimbabwe
"Hiller Road, off Borrowdale Road", Gunhill, Harare, Zimbabwe
Tel: 792741/3 Fax: 792398

EUROPE

BELGIUM
Archives de l'Etat a Liege
79 rue du Chera, Liege, B-4000, Belgium Tel: 04-252-0393 Fax: 04-229-3350 Email: archives.liege@skynet.be
De Kerk van Jezus Christus van den Heiligen
Der Laaste Dagen, Kortrijkse Steenweg 1060, Sint-Deniss-Westrem, B-9051, Belgium Tel: 09-220-4316
Provinciebestuur Limburg
Universititslaan 1, Afdeling 623 Archief, Hasselt, B-3500, Belgium
Rijks Archief te Brugge
Academiestraat 14, Brugge, 8000, Belgium Tel: 050-33-7288 Fax: 050-33-7288 Email: rijksarchief.brugge@skynet.be
Rijksarchief
Kruibekesteenweg 39/1, Beveren, B-9210, Belgium Tel: 03-775-3839
Service de Centralisation des Etudes Genealogique et Demographiques Belgique
Chaussee de Haecht 147, Brussels, B-1030, Belgium Tel: 02-374-1492
Staatsarchiv in Eupen
Kaperberg 2-4, Eupen, B-4700, Belgium Tel: 087-55-4377
Stadsarchief te Veurne
Grote Markt 29, Veurne, B-8630, Belgium Tel: 058-31-4115 Fax: 058-31-4554

CYPRUS
Cyprus Center of Medievalism & Heraldry
P O Box 80711, Piraeus, 185 10, Greece Tel: 42-26-356

DENMARK
Association of Local History Archives
P O Box 235, Enghavevej 2, Vejle, DK-7100, Denmark Fax: 45-7583-1801 WWW: www.lokalarkiver.dk
Cadastral Archives
Rentemestervej 8, Copenhagen NV, DK-2400, Denmark Fax: 45-3587-5064 WWW: www.kms.min.dk
Danish Data Archive
Islandsgade 10, Odense C, DK-5000, Denmark
Fax: 45-6611-3060, Web: www.dda.dk
Danish Emigration Archives
P O Box 1731, Arkivstraede 1, Aalborg, DK-9100, Denmark Tel: 045 9931 4221 Fax: 45 9810 2248 Email: bfl-kultur@aalbkom.dk
WWW: www.cybercity.dk/users/ccc13656
Danish National Archives
Rigsdagsgaarden 9, Copenhagen, DK-1218 Tel: 45-3392-3310 Fax: 45-3315-3239 WWW: www.sa.dk/ra/uk/uk.htm
Det Kongelige Bibliotek
POB 2149, Copenhagen K, DK-1016 Tel: 045-3393-0111 Fax: 045-3393-2218
Frederiksberg Municipal Libraries
Solbjergvej 21-25, Frederiksberg, DK-2000, Denmark Fax: 45-3833-3677, Web: www.fkb.dk
Kobenhavns Stadsarkiv
Kobenhavns Radhus, Kobenhavn, DK01599, Denmark Tel: 3366-2374 Fax: 3366-7039
National Business Archives
Vester Alle 12, Aarhus C, DK-8000, Denmark Tel: 45-8612-8533
Email: mailbox@ea.sa.dk WWW: www.sa.dk/ea/engelsk.htm
Provincial Archives for Funen
Jernbanegade 36, Odense C, DK-5000, Denmark Tel: 6612-5885
Fax: 45-6614-7071 WWW: www.sa.dk/lao/default.htm

Provincial Archives for Nth Jutland
Lille Sct. Hansgade 5, Viborg, DK-8800, Denmar
Tel: 45-8662-1788 WWW: www.sa.dk/lav/default.htm
Provincial Archives for Southern Jutland
Haderslevvej 45, Aabenraa, DK-6200, Denmark
Tel: 45-7462-5858 WWW: www.sa.dk/laa/default.htm
Provincial Archives for Zealand etc
Jagtvej 10, Copenhagen, DK-2200, Denmark
Fax: 45-3539-0535 WWW: www.sa.dk/lak.htm
Royal Library
Christains Brygge 8, Copenhagen K, DK-1219, Denmark Fax: 45-3393-2219 WWW: www.kb.dk
State Library
Universitetsparken, Aarhus C, DK-8000, Denmark
Tel: 45-8946-2022 Fax: 45-8946-2130
WWW: www.sb.aau.dk/english

FINLAND
Institute of Migration
Piispankatu 3, Turku, 20500Tel: 2-231-7536
Fax: 2-233-3460 Email: jouni.kurkiasaaz@utu.fi
WWW: www.utu.fi/erill/instmigr/

FRANCE
Centre d'Accueil et de Recherche des Archives Nationales
60 rue des Francs Bourgeois, Paris Cedex, 75141, France Tel: 1-40-27-6000 Fax: 1-40-27-6628
Centre des Archives d'Outre-Mer
29 Chemin du Moulin de Testas, Aix-en-Provence, 13090, **Service Historique de la Marine**
Chateau de Vincennes, Vincennes Cedex, 94304, France
Service Historique de l'Armee de l'Air
Chateau de Vincennes, Vincennes Cedex, 94304, France
Service Historique de l'Armee de Terre
BP 107, Armees, 481, France

GERMANY
German Emigration Museum
Inselstrasse 6, Bremerhaven, D-2850 Tel: 0471-49096
Historic Emigration Office
Steinstr. 7, Hamburg, (D) 20095, Germany Tel: 4940-30- 51-282
Fax: 4940-300-51-220 Email: ESROKAHEA@aol.com
WWW: users.cybercity.dk/gccc13652/addr/ger_heo.htm
Research Centre Lower Saxons in the USA
Postfach 2503, Oldenburg, D-2900, Germany Tel: 0441 798 2614
Fax: 0441-970-6180
Email: holtmann@hrzl.uni-oldenburg.de
WWW: www.uni-oldenburg.de/nausa
Zentralstelle fur Personen und Familiengeschichte
Birkenweg 13, Friedrichsdorf, D-61381 Tel: 06172-78263, Web:
www.genealogy.com/gene/genealogy.html

GREECE
Cyprus Center of Medievalism & Heraldry
P O Box 80711, Piraeus, 185 10, Greece Tel: 42-26-356

LIECHENSTEIN
Major Archives Record Offices & Libraries Liechtenstein
WWW: www.genealogy.com/gene/reg/CH/lichts.html

NETHERLANDS
Amsterdam Municipal Archives
P O 51140, Amsterdam, 1007 EC, Netherlands
Brabant-Collectie
Tilburg University Library, P O Box 90153, Warandelaan, Tilburg, NL-5000 LE, Netherlands Tel: 0031-134-662127
Gemeentelijke Archiefdienst Amersfoort
P O Box 4000, Amersfoort, 3800 EA, Netherlands Tel: 033-4695017
Fax: 033-4695451
Het Utrechts Archief
Alexander Numankade 199/201, Utrecht, 3572 KW, Tel: 030-286-6611
Fax: 030-286-6600
Email: Utrecht@acl.archivel.nl
Rijksarchief in Drenthe
P O Box 595, Assen, 9400 AN, Netherlands Tel: 0031-592-313523
Fax: 0031-592-314697 Email: RADR@noord.bart.nl
WWW: obd-server.obd.nl/instel/enderarch/radz.htm
Rijksarchief in Overijssel
Eikenstraat 20, Zwolle, 8021 WX, Netherlands Tel: 038-454-0722
Fax: 038-454-4506 Email: RAO@euronet.nl, Web:
www.obd.nl/instel/arch/rkarch.htm

Zealand Documentation CTR
P O Box 8004, Middelburg, 4330 EA, Netherlands

NORWAY
Norwegian Emigration Centre
Strandkaien 31, Stavanger, 4005, Norway Tel: 47-51-53-88-63
Email: detnu@telepost.no WWW: www.emigrationcenter.com

POLAND
Head Office Polish State Archives
Ul Dluga6 Skr, Poczt, Warsaw, 1005-00-950 Fax: 0-22-831-9222

SPAIN
Archivo Historico National
Serrano 115, Madrid, 28006 Tel: 261-8003- 2618004
Instituucion Fernando el Catolico
Plaza de Espagna 2, Zaragoza, 50071, Espagn
Tel: 09-7628-8878 Email: ifc@isendanet.es.mail

SWEDEN
Harnosand Provincial Archive
Box 161, Harnosand, S-871 24, Sweden Tel: 611-835-00
Email: landsarkivet@landsarkivet-harnosand.ra.se
WWW: www.ra.se/hla
Goteborg Provincial Archive
Box 19035, Goteborg, S-400 12, Sweden Tel: 31-778-6800
House of Emigrants
Box 201, Vaxjo, S-351 04, Sweden Tel: 470-201-20
Email: info@svenskaemigrantinstitulet.g.se
Kinship Centre
Box 331, Karlstad, S-651 08, Sweden Tel: 54-107720
Lund Provincial Archive
Box 2016, Lund, S-220 02 Tel: 046-197000 Fax: 046-197070
Email: landsarkivet@landsarkivet-lund.ra.se
Orebro Stadsarkiv
Box 300, Orebro, S-701 35 Tel: 19-21-10-75 Fax: 19-21-10-50
Ostersund Provincial Archive
Arkivvagen 1, Ostersund, S-831 31, Sweden Tel: 63-10-84-85
Email: landsarkivet@landsarkivet-ostersund.ra.se
WWW: www.ra.se/ola/
Stockholm City & Provincial Archives
Box 22063, Stockholm, S-104 22 Tel: 8-508-283-00
Fax: 8-508-283-01
Swedish Military Archives
Banergatan 64, Stockholm, S-115 88 Tel: 8-782-41-00
Swedish National Archives
Box 12541, Stockholm, S-102 29, Sweden Tel: 8-737-63-50
Uppsala Provincial Archive
Box 135, Uppsala, SE-751 04, Sweden Tel: 18-65-21-00
Vadstena Provincial Archive
Box 126, Vadstena, S-592 23, Sweden Tel: 143-130-30
Visby Provincial Archive
Visborgsgatan 1, Visby, 621 57, Sweden Tel: 498-2129-55

SWITZERLAND
Achives de la Ville de Geneve
Palais Eynard, 4 rue de la Croix-Rouge, Geneve 3, 1211
Tel: 22-418-2990 Email: didier.grange@seg.ville-ge.ch
Archives Canonales Vaudoises
rue de la Mouline 32, Chavannes-pres-Renens, CH 1022, Switzerland
Tel: 021-316-37-11 Fax: 021-316-37-55
Archives de l'Ancien Eveche de Bale
10 rue des Annonciades, Porrentruy, CH-2900, Suisse
Archives d'Etat de Geneve
Casa Postale 3964, Geneve 3, 1211, Suisse
Tel: 022-319-3395 Fax: 319-3365
Staatsarchiv Appenzell Ausserhoden
Obstmarkt, Regierungsgebaede, Herisau, CH-9100, Tel: 071-353-6111
Email: Peter.Witschi@kk.ar.ch
Staatsarchiv des Kantons Basel-Landschaft
Wiedenhubstrasse 35, Liestal, 4410 Tel: 061-921-44-40
Email: baselland@lka.bl.ch WWW: www.baselland.ch
Staatsarchiv des Kantons Solothurn
Bielstrasse 41, Solothurn, CH-4509, Switzerland
Tel: 032-627-08-21 Fax: 032-622-34-87
Staatsarchiv Luzern
Postfach 7853, Luzern, 6000 Tel: 41-41-2285365
Email: archiv@staluzern.c WWW: www.staluzern.ch

NORTH AMERICA - CANADA
Archives & Special Collections
PO Box 7500, Fredericton, New Brunswick, E3B 5H5
Tel: 506-453-4748 Fax: 506-453-4595,
Archives Nationales
PO Box 10450, Sainte Foy, Quebec, G1V 4N1 Tel: 418-643-8904
Fax: 418-646-0868,
Glenbow Library & Archives
130-9th Avenue SE, Calgary, Alberta, T2G 0P3 Tel: 403-268-4197
Fax: 403-232-6569,
Hudson's Bay Company Archives
200 Vaughan Street, Winnipeg, Manitoba, R3C 1T5 Tel: 204-945-4949
Email: hbca@chc.gov.mb.ca WWW:
www.gov.mb.ca/chc/archives/hbca/index.html
Loyalist Collection & Reference Department
PO Box 7500, Fredericton, New Brunswick, E3B 5H5
Tel: 506-453-4749 Fax: 506-453-4596,
Manitoba Provincial Archives
200 Vaughan Street, Winnepeg, Manitoba, R3C 1T5 Tel: 204-945-4949
Fax: 204-948-3236,
National Archives of Canada
395 Wellington Street, Ottawa, Ontario, K1A 0N3 Tel: 613-996-7458
Email: http://www.archives.ca,
New Brunswick Provincial Archives
PO Box 6000, Fredericton, New Brunswick, E3B 5H1
Tel: 506-453-2122 Email: provarch@gov.nb.ca WWW:
www.gov.nb.ca/supply/archives
Newfoundland & Labrador Archives
Colonial Building, Military Road, St Johns, Newfoundland, A1C 2C9
Tel: 709-729-0475 Fax: 709-729-0578,
Nova Scotia State Archives
6016 University Avenue, Halifax, Nova Scotia, B3H 1W4
Tel: 902-424-6060,
Ontario Archives
Unit 300, 77 Grenville Street, Toronto, Ontario, M5S 1B3
Tel: 416-327-1582 Email: reference@archives.gov.on.ca
WWW: www.gov.on.ca/MCZCR/archives
Public Archives & Record Office
PO Box 1000, Charlottetown, Prince Edward Island, C1A 7M4
Tel: 902-368-4290 Fax: 902-368-6327 Email: archives@gov.pe.ca
WWW: www.gov.pe.ca/educ/
Saskatchewan Archives Board - Regina
3303 Hillsdale Street, Regina, Saskatchewan, S4S 0A2
Tel: 306-787-4068 Email: sabreg@sk.sympatico.ca
WWW: www.gov.sk.ca/govt/archives
Saskatchewan Archives Board - Saskatchewan
Room 91, Murray Building, University of Saskatchewan, 3 Campus
Drive, Saskatoon, Saskatchewan, S7N 5A4 Tel: 306-933-5832
Email: sabsktn@sk.sympatico.ca WWW: www.gov.sk.ca/govt/archives
Yarmouth County Museums & Archives
22 Collins Street, Yarmouth, Nova Scotia, B5A 3C8
Tel: (902)-742-5539 Email: ycn0056@ycn.library.ns.ca WWW:
www.ycn.library.ns.ca/museum/yarcomus.htm

UNITED STATES OF AMERICA
Alaska State Archives
141 Willoughby Avenue, Juneau, Alaska, 99801-1720, United States of
America, Tel: 907-465-2270
Email: sou@bham.lib.al.usarchives@educ.state.ak.us,
Arizona Department of Library
Archives & Public Records
State Capitol, 1700 West Washington, Phoenix, Arizona, 85007, United
States of America, Tel: 602-542-3942
Arizona Historical Foundation Library
Hayden Library, Arizona State Univeristy, Tempe, Arizona, 85287,
United States of America, Tel: 602-966-8331
Arkansas History Commission
OneCapitol Mall, Little Rock, Arkansas, 72201 Tel: 501-682-6900,
California State Archives
Office of the Secretary of State, 1020 O Street, Sacramento, 95814
Tel: (916)-653-7715 Email: archivesweb@ss.ca.gov WWW:
www.ss.ca.gov/archives/archives.htm
Colorado State Archives
Room 1b-20, 1313 Sherman Street, Denver, Colorado, 80203-2236,
United States of America, Tel: 303-866-2390,
Connecticut State Archives
231 Capitol Ave, Hartford, Connecticut, 6106, Tel: 0860 757 6580
Email: isref@cslib.org WWW: www. cslib.org
Daughters of the American Revolution Library
1776 D Street N W, Washington, District of Columbia, 20006-5392,
United States of America, Tel: 202-879-3229,

District of Columbia Archives
1300 Naylor Court North West, Washington, District of Columbia, 20001-4225 Tel: 203-566-3690,

Family History Library of the Church of Jesus Christ of LDS
35 N West Temple Street, Salt Lake City, Utah, 84150, USA,

Georgia State Archives
330 Capital Avenue SE, Atlanta, Georgia, 30334-9002
Tel: 404-656-2350 Email: http://www.state.ga.us/SOS/Archives/,

Hawaii State Library
478 South King Street, Honolulu, Hawaii, 96813

Indiana Archives
Room117, 140 N Senate Avenue, Indianapolis, Indiana, 46204-2296
Tel: 317-232-3660 Fax: 317-233-1085,

Kansas State Historical Society - Archives
6425 SW Sixth Street, Topeka, Kansas, 66615-1099 Tel: 913-272-8681
Fax: 913-272-8682 Email: reference@hspo.wpo.state.ks.us WWW: www.kshs.org

Maryland State Archives
Hall of Records Building, 350 Rowe Boulevard, Annapolis, Maryland, 21401 Tel: 410-974-3914,

Missouri State Archives
PO Box 778, Jefferson City, Missouri, 65102 Tel: 314-751-3280,

National Archives - California
100 Commodore Drive, San Bruno, California, 94066-2350

National Archives - Colorado
PO Box 25307, Denver, Colorado, 80225-0307 Tel: 303-866-2390,

National Archives - Georgia
1557 St Joseph Avenue, East Point, Georgia, 30344, Tel: 404-763-7477
Fax: 404-763-7059 Web: www.nara.gov

National Archives - Illinois
7358 South Pulaski Road, Chicago, Illinois, 60629

National Archives - Massachusetts
380 Trapelo Road, Waltham, Massachusetts, 2154,

National Archives - Massachusetts
100 Dan Fox Drive, Pittsfield, Massachusetts, 01201-8230

National Archives - Missouri
2306 East Bannister Road, Kansas City, Missouri, 64131

National Archives - New York
201 Varick Street, New York, New York, 10014 - 4811

National Archives - Northwest Pacific Region
6125 Sand Point Way NE, Seattle, Washington, 98115
Tel: 206-524-6501 Email: archives@seattle.nara.gov,

National Archives - Pennsylvania
Rom 1350, 900 Market Street, Philadelphia, PA 19144,

National Archives - Texas
Box 6216, 4900 Hemphill Road, Fort Worth, Texas, 76115

National Archives - Washington
Pennsylvania Avenue, Washington, District of Colombia, 20408,

National Archives - Pacific Alaska Region
654 West 3rd Avenue, Anchorage, Alaska, 99501 - 2145
Tel: 011-1-907-271-2443 Fax: 011-1-907-271-2442
Email: archives@alaska.nara.gov WWW:
www.nara.gov/regional/anchorage.html

National Archives (Pacific Region)
1st Floor East, 24000 Avila Road, Orange County, Laguna Niguel, California, 92677 Tel: (949)-360-2641 Fax: (949)-360-2624
Email: archives@laguna.nara.gov WWW:
www.nara.gov/regional/laguna.html

Nevada State Archives
Division of Archives & Records, 100 Stewart Street, Carson City, Nevada, 89710 Tel: 702-687-5210,

New Jersey State Archives
PO Box 307, 185 West State Street, Trenton, New Jersey, 08625-0307
Tel: 609-292-6260,

New Mexico State Archives
1205 Camino carlos Rey, Sante Fe, New Mexico, 87501
Tel: (505)-827-7332 Fax: (505)-476-7909
Email: cmartine@rain.state.nm.us WWW: www.state.nmus/cpr

Ohio State Archives
1982 Velma Avenue, Columbus, Ohio, 43211-2497 Tel: 614-297-2510,

Pennsylvania State Archives
PO Box 1026, 3rd & Forster Streets, Harrisburg, Pennsylvania, 17108-1026 Tel: 717-783-3281,

South Carolina Department Archives & History
8301 Parklane Road, Columbia, South Carolina, 292223
Tel: 803-896-6100,

South Carolina State Archives
PO Box 11669, 1430 Senate Street, Columbia, South Carolina, 29211-1669 Tel: 803-734-8577,

South Dakota Archives
Cultural Heritage Center, 900 Governors Drive, Pierre, South Dakota, 57501-2217 Tel: 605-773-3804,

Tennessee State Library & Archives
403 7th Avenue North, Nashville, Tennessee, 37243-0312
Tel: 615-741-2764 Email: reference@mail.state.tn.us WWW: www.state.tn.us/sos/statelib

Texas State Archives
PO Box 12927, Austin, Texas, 78711-2927 Tel: 512-463-5463,

Vermont Public Records Division
PO Drawer 33, U S Route 2, Middlesex, Montpelier, Vermont, 05633-7601 Tel: 802-828-3700 and 802-828-3286
Fax: 802-828-3710,

Vermont State Archives
Redstone Building, 26 Terrace Street, Montpelier, Vermont, 05609-1103 Tel: 802-828-2308,

Virginia State Archives
11th Street at Capitol Square, Richmond, Virginia, 23219-3491
Tel: 804-786-8929,

West Virginia State Archives
The Cultural Center, 1900 Kanawha Boulevard East, Charleston, West Virginia, 25305-0300 Tel: 304-558-0230,

Wisconsin State Archives
816 State Street, Madison, Wisconsin, 53706 Tel: 608-264-6460
Fax: 608-264-6742 Email: archives.reference@ccmail.adp.wisc.edu
WWW: www.wisc.edu/shs-archives

Wyoming State Archives
Barrett State Office Building, 2301 Central Avenue, Cheyenne, Wyoming, 82002 Tel: 307-777-7826,

Low- Hill Gedneral Cemetery Liverpool 1825
'secured by a thick brick wall 13 feet high .. For the purpose of greater security,
a watchman will at all times of the night be upon the ground.'

Necropolises of the Dead: Cemeteries and their Records

Andrew Todd

introduces an excellent category of records which includes virtually everyone's ancestors

Most of our relatives who died in the period 1830-1960 are buried in cemeteries, cities of the dead which appeared in response to that most gruesome of 19th Century social problems - what to do with urban corpses. Like many family history researchers, the first sets of records I used in research were the excellent burial registers and graves books kept by such cemeteries - these survive irrespective of whether the graves were grassed over decades ago. From these, I discovered that all eight of my great grandparents were buried in Manchester cemeteries.

How the Church of England lost its Monopoly in Burials

Before the cemetery period, virtually every body was buried in an Anglican churchyard. God's Acre was a scarce, communal resource in an agricultural economy, and had to be used in what we would now term a 'sustainable' way. It takes an average of 10-12 years for an adult corpse to reduce exclusively to skeletal remains. Since the soil in the churchyard was reserved for the burial of all past, present and future parishioners, the freehold remained with the priest. No one had exclusive rights over a specific plot, but family members were usually overburied in a single grave, if this were identifiable by a stone. Those with status were buried in a family huddle of adjacent plots. Graves were left for many generations and then the ground reused. Any resurfacing old bones were popped into the charnel house.

In the early 19th Century, Britain became the first modern state to experience mass urbanisation. Town and city churchyards were simply overwhelmed by the dead, not least because urban death rates were so high. Overcrowded burial grounds became a serious health hazard. There was pressure for 'working the ground very close', a neat, almost Thatcherite euphemism for removing human remains from graves long before they had decomposed. Early morning reopenings of graves just *one month old* were described to the Health of Towns Select Committee in 1842 - its minutes of evidence have been described as 'one of the most revolting documents of the 19th Century'! Two types of cemetery appeared in response:-

1 The General Cemetery

The very real prospect of 'resurrection men' stealing freshly buried corpses to sell on to medical schools for dissection was another factor which stirred those with means to buy a solution to the horror of the urban churchyard. Bodies might fetch up to 20 guineas, the teeth of countrywomen being especially prized by dentists. Rural churchyards near cities were also vulnerable. The remnants from the dissection table would be bucketed into the nearest river. In the 1820s and 1830s, private enterprise provided secure cemeteries on the fringes of the largest towns and cities, where land was cheaper and health hazards reduced. Nonconformists, disagreeing with the doctrines of the Church of England, were particularly likely to opt for burial there, even though fees might have to be paid to the parish church as well.

Anglicans had a natural reluctance to abandon the mother church for burial, so these companies pressed their market advantage - high walls and 'regular records'. Above all they offered the purchase of a family burial plot, complete with freehold title deed. They trumped the churchyard by guaranteeing what every middle class family man desired - family cohesion secured by burial in perpetuity in its own property. The family gravestone was the final symbol of possession. Sensibility about death became a very marketable commodity. Shares in St James Cemetery, Liverpool paid an 8% dividend in the 1830s - not bad for an ex-quarry!

Whilst elevated plots in general cemeteries were sold off to local bigwigs, the lower ground could be offered to another ready urban market, the working class. Here, mass pit graves as deep as 20 or 30 feet were simply filled up in order of death.

The perpetuity of repose offered to their customers by general cemetery companies was an illusion. Once full, they went into liquidation, leaving local councils or trusts to pick up the pieces. Many have been greened over or allowed to revert to nature, graves now inaccessible. The much vandalised Undercliffe Cemetery, Bradford, was sold in 1975 for £5.00 to a property 'developer' who joined in the process of desecration by bulldozing gravestones and using kerbstones for building material, until the site was rescued in 1985 by a trust.

Do not despair! Even if a general cemetery was cleared, its records will survive, including a copy of its gravestone inscriptions.

2 The Municipal Cemetery

General cemetery companies relied on private capital which was not always forthcoming. After 1854, a curious British institution, the local burial boards, able to raise a burial rate, could be set up to lay out public (ie municipal) cemeteries. These, now in local authority care, still operate. It is in the 1850s that the burial registers of many urban parish churches come to an abrupt end, with only the occasional reopening, by special authorisation, of a family grave for a new addition.

Where to find Cemetery Records

Responsibility for municipal cemeteries has been in

the hands of district authorities in England and Wales since 1974. These are the local authorities below the level of county councils, and have titles such as East Staffordshire District Council, Derby City Council or Scarborough Borough Council. Some rural areas, and all metropolitan district/borough councils and London boroughs have only one council. District and Island authorities have this responsibility in Scotland, and districts/boroughs in Northern Ireland. Each of these local authorities has a department which administers its cemeteries. This may be called simply *Cemeteries and Crematoria*, *Parks and Recreational Services*, or, even more ironically, *Parks and Leisure Department*! The address can be found in the local authority's block entry in the telephone directory.

If you live away from the area, you can find all the country's telephone directories in any library, or in a central post office. A list of councils in the area can be found in the 'Useful Numbers' section of the BT directory, or in the Local Government category of the Yellow Pages.

The local authority department is usually the best place to start your enquiry, since they will know the whereabouts of records of their cemeteries. Increasingly, the older records are moved away from the cemetery offices - into the department itself or into the local authority archive. Cemetery records are now rarely available for public inspection. The staff will do a search over a five year span, often for a fee, so it is crucial to have a good idea of the date of death, and if possible the religious denomination of the deceased. When making a postal enquiry, enclose an SAE.

What Records survive from General and Municipal Cemeteries?

1 The Burial Register was a **chronological record of burials**, rarely indexed, and in varying formats. Below is a 20th Century example from Philip's Park

Toxteth Park Cemetery Liverpool 1885 burial at bargain rates - this entry from a receipt book shows two day old Margarter Davies's burial in the Unconcecated Section, without any religious servce

---

The Social Hierarchy of Cemetery Burial

Freehold, or Private	Exclusive burial for one family. Title deed was evidence of purchase. Headstone common
Subscription	Common grave with communal headstone; also known as public inscription graves
Common, Public or Single	Filled by bodies in order of arrival - the cheapest type of funeral. Headstone very unlikely
Pit	Mass, common grave - pre-1850s. No headstone
Pauper's	Tramps were often buried in odd corners or verges

No	Date	Name	Age	Rank or Profession	Abode	Parish or district	Mode of burial	Section	No	Minister
103967	4th Nov1912	William Leeson	68	Watchman	140 Harold St	Bradford	Single	D	436	Edwin Jones

Cemetery, Manchester:-

Some registers may give cause of death, or father's name in the case of a child. The running number (103,967) gives some idea of this cemetery's popularity!

The Church of England fought hard to safeguard its position, insisting on separate burials for Anglicans in the best parts of the municipal cemeteries and terming its sections *Consecrated*. Other sections were reserved for Roman Catholics and Nonconformist, the umbrella term for Methodists, Baptists and the rest. (The cemetery term for the non-Anglican sections, *Unconsecrated*, quite incorrectly has connotations of midnight interments for suicides and murderers!) You must search all three registers if you aren't sure of religious denomination.

A grave usually had six occupants (four in hard ground) though more could be accommodated if children were interred.

2 The Graves Book contained a summary of the interments in each space, allowing the cemetery authorities to keep track of how full any private grave

getting. Detailed graves books for common graves are rare, since these plots would be filled quickly

3 Order books, also known as **Fee Books**, contain the administrative detail needed to process each burial the name of deceased, age, address, date and time of burial, 'reopening' and burial fee, and, usefully, name and address of who paid, often a close relative, but possibly the undertaker.

It follows that if you can locate one burial in a private grave, the graves book will give you the names of other members of the family who may have died half a century before. Details of their interments should be followed up in the burial register and order books. Remember that the whole point of buying the freehold of a private grave was to ensure that the family would stay together. So, no matter what the surnames of the occupants may be, they will be connected - somehow. You can expect to find a wife's parents, or perhaps daughters under their married names. Some but not all cemeteries allowed a transfer of ownership of private graves - this will be recorded in the graves book.

Some churches and chapels began to formalise family

grave plots in the cemetery period, and may have grave plans or grave occupancy books, but these are not common.

4 Burial Plot Deeds, issued by the cemetery to the purchaser of a private grave, acted as a receipt of payment and proof of ownership. These useful documents often lie undisturbed for decades in a drawer or cupboard. Study them carefully - they carry the name, address and often occupation of the buyer, whilst the date of first purchase usually marks a family death. Since they pinpoint the plot exactly, it is simple to write to the district authority in whose area the cemetery now lies. Ask for details from the graves books, and the burial register, of all the people buried in that plot. Burial plot deeds, of course, will be in private hands, where they survive, and not at the cemetery office. More than one family historian has discovered space in a long forgotten family grave, and booked it for themselves!

5 Monumental Inscriptions often appear on private graves, but common graves rarely have stones. Beware of subscription or public inscription graves. One researcher spent months fruitlessly tracing the names of people buried with her uncle before discovering that unrelated people could be commemorated on such gravestones. Nevertheless, once you have a grave number, it is worth asking the cemetery if there is a stone, or paying a visit. Stones at municipal cemeteries are usually hardwearing marble or granite.

A gravestone may name people buried elsewhere - war dead, or relatives who died far afield in other circumstances. Similarly, there is no guarantee that a stone will name everybody in the grave. Related families were sometimes buried in adjacent or nearby plots, perhaps on the next row, where the grave number would not suggest any proximity.

The 1906 Open Spaces Act controlled how general cemeteries were closed, insisting that gravestones could not be cleared until a record had been made of 'name and date appearing thereon . . . and other such particulars as may be necessary'. This sloppy wording has allowed ages and relationship details to be omitted from some transcripts. These, along with the cemetery's registers and graves books, can usually be found at the appropriate county record office, or local authority archive.

Set out to reflect Victorian sensitivity about death, cemeteries retain a lingering atmosphere of solemnity. Considered to be morally uplifting venues for a Sunday afternoon stroll, one 1858 Rossendale newspaper soliloquised effulgently on how the new Bacup cemetery offered 'a charming invitation to all . . . to put an early period to their existence in so quiet and sequestered a spot'! A visit to an ancestral cemetery is a must. But beware - some of the great city cemeteries contain *half a million* bodies, and stretch for hundreds of acres. There is little point in searching for great granddad's stone on the basis of directions like 'over by the gate, under a tree'. Even town cemeteries can be huge. In 1935, Blackburn Cemetery had 150,000 occupants, a figure which actually exceeded the living population of the town. The cemetery may have a graves map or key to direct you to the plot. This is a good reason for going in office hours. If you find flowers on your grave, or evidence of special care, leave a note of your name,

address and relationship to the deceased.

Which Cemetery or Graveyard?

A large city could have several general and municipal cemeteries, and some churchyards might have been in use well into the 19th Century.

How can you ascertain which one contains your ancestor? Death certificates won't tell you. So try looking for:

1 burial plot deeds - ask all the family (distant cousins included) if any survive.

2 funeral or memorial cards - note that these may also have been retained by family friends.

3 the **local newspaper** may include a death notice, or even an obituary, indicating where the funeral took place. A 1930 newspaper is more likely to carry such detailed items, even for the humbler classes, than one of 1880. So pursue the most recent known burial in the family - remember that once a family grave is identified, the graves book will lead you to earlier burials in that plot.

4 a six inch Ordnance Survey map - and this needs to be contemporary since many general cemeteries and even churchyards have been converted into open spaces. Generally speaking, people are buried in the district where they live, not least because non-ratepayers were often charged double. But there were exceptions . . .

5 earlier addresses - a family often had church loyalties, or a private cemetery plot, in a district they had left years before they died. My wife's grandparents were buried in a family grave at Burton-upon-Trent Cemetery three decades after they had retired to Scarborough, 150 miles away!

6 'overflow' arrangements - in the biggest cities, where space was at a premium, burial boards might have to use land at a distance. Anthony Camp points out that after 1854 half of the London East End poor were taken by daily funeral trains to the London Necropolis at Woking, 25 miles away. Big city workhouses, where before 1930 many working class people died, made similar contracts with cemeteries, possibly at a distance. From 1885 to 1902, when Golder's Green was opened, all London cremations took place at Woking. Golder's Green, at over 250,000, has disposed of more bodies than any other crematorium.

7 seek local knowledge - several years might have separated the closure of a town's old churchyard and the opening of its cemetery. Some obscure church or chapel might have filled this burial gap. An urban churchyard might have closed in the early 19th Century, like Manchester Cathedral's, but continued with a new burial ground some distance away. Entries would continue in the same register, despite the change of location.

8 opening dates of local churches or cemeteries can be found in the introductory historical descriptions in a town's or city's trade directories of the 19th and early 20th Centuries. Fortunately, it is rare for the many town or city centre churches opened after the 1830s to have had burial grounds.

9 . . . and don't forget to **ask relatives**. It could save you a long search. 'It was a long drive, and I remember trees,' an uncle told me of a 1930 funeral he'd attended as a 15 year old. That *could* narrow it down!

10 the **National Burial Index** will, eventually, be of particular value to those of us seeking urban dead. At the Society of Genealogists is Boyd's *London Burials*, an index of some quarter of a million adult male burials between 1538 and 1852, including many in the huge Nonconformist Bunhill Fields burial ground.

A Bleak Future for Cemeteries?

Victorian legislation in the 1850s sought to tighten up on graveyard atrocities by making it illegal to disturb human remains without Home Office approval. The resulting 'security of tenure' for the dead is creating a crisis, especially in London, where some boroughs have run out of cemetery space. Disused cemeteries, as we know from the history of general cemeteries, do not wear well. Since 1974, grave plots are often only leased for a set period of100, 50 or even 40 years, but cannot as yet be reused.

Local councils are under financial pressure, note the bizarre attempt of Westminster City Council in 1987 to sell three cemeteries to 'developers' for 5p each. Since 1977, to assist maintenance, stones can be cleared from municipal cemeteries.

Burial is becoming a luxury. Whilst all eight of my Mancunian great grandparents are in cemeteries, my four grandparents were cremated. Cemeteries could become as neglected as the Pyramids. How long will a society's future generations bear the cost of maintaining monuments to their ancestral dead?

Andrew Todd MA, MSc, BEd has written and lectured on family history for over 20 years. This article is a condensed version of a chapter from his forthcoming book, *Basic Sources for Family History: Back to the Early 1700s*, a substantial enlargement of his wellknown, *Basic Sources* guide whose cut-off date was 1800

The National Burial Index For England & Wales

Carol McLee and Peter Underwood NBI Project Co-ordinators

What it Is:
The NBI is an index of burials taken from parish, non-conformist, Roman Catholic and cemetery registers. It includes entries for England and Wales dating from the 16th century to modern times although most are for the period1813 - 1851+. This beginning to indexing work does not cover all counties, parishes within counties, or dates as yet. The first edition, with more than 5.4 million names, is published on CDRom only. It is hoped to publish a cumulative NBI every three years or so. The index does NOT contain information from monumental inscriptions nor death registers.

What it Contains:
Each entry will present the following information (if available in the original source):

Forename(s) and surname of the deceased
Date of burial   Age
Parish or cemetery where the event was recorded
The county of the parish or cemetery (pre-1974 list of counties)
The society or group which transcribed the record

Note that the decision to exclude certain useful items of information from the NBI such as relationships, abode and occupation was a demand of certain family history societies at the initial planning stage and does not necessarily reflect the wish or intention of the Federation of Family History Societies.

Simply an Index:
Clearly the NBI does not contain full transcriptions of the burial records - it is simply an abbreviated finding-aid. As with the IGI, searchers are discouraged from accepting the details of an entry and should check the original source record. Those searchers who do not live close to the necessary County Record Office or repository should contact the Family History Society or Group who transcribed the record in full.

Computer Facilities Required:
PC with Pentium processor or higher, running Windows 95/98/NT/2000 and ME should be suitable with suggested 16Mbytes RAM. For screen area 640x480 should work but SVGA (800 x 600) and above is recommended. Using the program supplied on the CDRom, the searcher can select any number of spelling variants of a surname from a list of uniquely- occurring surnames which is displayed on screen. Entering one or several forenames, date ranges, counties or parishes may refine the search.

Records:
The deadline for presenting records for inclusion in the first edition of the NBI was the end of August 2000 which allowed for the checking and correction of as many records as possible before NBI inclusion. Some records which were still unchecked at the deadline will be included in the NBI but each entry will marked as such. If errors are observed by searchers after publication, an amendment will appear in the subsequent edition of the NBI at the discretion of the Family History Society or Group and the NBI organisers.

Who's Involved:
To date, over 50 Family History Societies and Groups are involved with the project. Each appoints a co-ordinator who recruits inputters, checkers and correctors. Wherever possible, transcriptions are made from original source records but where this is not feasible other sources, such as microfiche transcriptions or printed registers, are used. The number of checked records merged into the NBI to date is but the tip of the iceberg. As everyone might have anticipated the checking and correction of computerised records is the rate limiting step for most project workers so there are thousands of records already computerised but yet to be merged.

Participating Societies and Groups have produced the following records

Burial Entries of Parishes within the 'pre-1832' Counties
(rounded to the nearest 1000)
Bedfordshire 52   Middlesex 11   Berkshire 117
Monmouthshire <1   Buckinghamshire 80   Montgomeryshire <1   Cambridge 95   Norfolk 74   Cardiganshire 11
Northamptonshire 85   Cheshire 255   Northumberland 106
Derbyshire 35   Oxfordshire 213   Dorset 1   Radnorshire 5
Durham 159   Shropshire 85   Essex 48   Somerset 2
Glamorganshire 249   Staffordshire 18   Gloucestershire 154
Suffolk 429   Hampshire <1   Surrey 120   Herefordshire 42
Warwickshire 460   Hertfordshire 84   Wiltshire 145
Huntingdonshire 76   Worcestershire 483   Kent 16
Yorkshire 19   Lancashire 29   Yorkshire East Riding 28
Leicestershire <1   Yorkshire North Riding 306
Lincolnshire 616   Yorkshire West Riding 708
(Unlisted counties did not have a participating society or group)

Shroud:
Family History Societies are generally using a computer program called Shroud to input the records. The advantage of using a dedicated program like Shroud is that the text style of entries is standardised and validation of the records is made easier before they are merged into the NBI database. This is a very 'user-friendly' program which comes with full instructions. (Some societies who had already computerised their burial records have kindly donated their records to the project).

How to Obtain a Copy of the NBI:
Distribution is through most Family History Societies and FFHS Publications Ltd: email fedpubs.rams@virgin.net or write to FFHS Publications Co., Units 15-16, Chesham Industrial Centre, Oram Street, Bury, Lancs BL9 6EN, or visit the on-line bookshop on www.familyhistorybooks.co.uk for order forms and costs. It is anticipated that access to the NBI will be available eventually through FH Societies, large libraries, genealogical institutions and Family History Centres.

For further information and an up to date listing of Family History Societies (with links to their web pages) see www.ffhs.org.uk or www.genuki.org.uk or contact the FFHS Administrator, PO Box 2425, Coventry, CV5 6YX or email admin@ffhs.org.uk

Most participating societies are providing a search /printout service of their county databases (containing FULL transcriptions of burial records) for which they may charge a small fee, or have for sale burial indexes in booklet or microfiche form.

To all Contributors:
The Federation of Family History Societies would like to convey its appreciation to all NBI county co-ordinators and the hundreds of voluntary workers at home and overseas for their enthusiasm, goodwill and hard work which has made this Index possible. Also to Steve Archer for the search programming, Carol McLee as general project co-ordinator and, in particular, Peter Underwood, for his dedication and total commitment over five years in the role of joint co-ordinator and database manager.

Would You like to Help with this Project?
The NBI Project is sponsored by the Federation of Family History Societies. We hope that the first edition of the NBI will prove to be a useful signpost to these important parish records and will greatly encourage hundreds more to continue this worthwhile work in the future. To contribute in some way, please contact <u>direct</u> your chosen society or group. (See above for addresses). If you are interested in becoming a group co-ordinator, please contact initially FFHS Administrator (address above)

In order to provide additional useful listings the next pages contain a list of Cemeteries and Crematoria. The list is not exhaustive and we would be pleased to receive details of other cemeteries & crematoria to add to our future lists.

Cemeteries & Crematoria

England

Avon
Bristol General Cemetery Co
East Lodge, Bath Rd, Arnos Vale, Bristol BS4 3EW Tel:0117 971 3294
Canford Crematorium & Cemetery
Canford Lane, Westbury On Trym, Bristol BS9 3PQ Tel:0117 950 3535
Cemetery of Holy Souls
Bath Rd, Bristol, Avon, BS4 3EW Tel:0117 977 2386
Haycombe Crematorium & Cemetery
Whiteway Rd, Bath, Avon, BA2 2RQ Tel:01225 423682
South Bristol Crematorium & Cemetery
Bridgwater Rd, Bristol, Avon, BS13 7AS Tel:0117 963 4141
Westerleigh Crematorium
Westerleigh Rd, Westerleigh, Bristol BS37 8QP Tel:0117 937 4619
Weston Super Mare Crematorium
Ebdon Rd, Worle, Weston-Super-Mare BS22 9NY Tel:01934 511717

Bedfordshire
Norse Rd Crematorium
104 Norse Rd, Bedford MK41 0RL Tel:01234 353701
Church Burial Ground
26 Crawley Green Rd, Luton LU2 0QX Tel:01582 722874
Dunstable Cemetery
West St, Dunstable, Bedfordshire, LU6 1PB Tel:01582 662772
Kempston Cemetery
2 Green End Rd, Kempston, Bedford MK43 8RJ Tel:01234 851823
Luton Crematorium
The Vale, Butterfield Green, Stopsley, Luton LU2 8DD Tel:01582 723700
Luton General Cemetery
Rothesay Rd, Luton, Bedfordshire, LU1 1QX Tel:01582 727480

Berkshire
Easthampstead Park Cemetry & Crematorium
Nine Mile Ride, Wokingham RG40 3DW Tel:01344 420314
Henley Road Cemetery & Reading Crematorium
All Hallows Rd, Caversham, Reading, RG4 5LP Tel:0118 947 2433
Larges Lane Cemetery
Larges Lane, Bracknell, Berkshire, RG12 9AL Tel:01344 450665
Newbury Cemetery
Shaw Hill Shaw, Newbury RG14 2EQ Tel:01635 40096
Slough Cemetery & Crematorium
Stoke Rd, Slough, Berkshire, SL2 5AX Tel:01753 523127 (Cemetery)
Tel:01753 520702 (Crematorium)

Buckinghamshire
Chilterns Crematorium
Whielden Lane, Winchmore Hill, Amersham HP7 0ND Tel:01494 724263
Crownhill Crematorium
Dansteed Way, Crown hill, Milton Keynes Tel: 01908 568112

Cambridgeshire
American Military Cemetery
Madingley Rd, Coton, Cambridge, CB3 7PH Tel:01954 210350
Cambridge City Crematorium
Huntingdon Rd, Girton, Cambridge, CB3 0JJ Tel:01954 780681
Ely Cemetary
Beech Lane, Ely, CB7 4QZ Tel:01353 669659
Marholm Crematorium
Mowbray Rd, Peterborough, PE6 7JE Tel:01733 262639

Cheshire
Altrincham Cemetery
Hale Rd, Altrincham, Cheshire, WA14 2EW Tel:0161 980 4441
Altrincham Crematorium
White House Lane, Dunham Massey, Altrincham WA14 5RH
Tel:0161 928 7771
Cemetery Management Ltd
Church Walk, Nantwich, Cheshire, CW5 5RG Tel:01270 626037
Chester Cemeteries & Crematorium
Blacon Avenue, Blacon, Chester CH1 5BB Tel:01244 372428
Dukinfield Crematorium
Hall Green Rd, Dukinfield SK16 4EP Tel:0161 330 1901
Macclesfield Cemetery
87 Prestbury Rd, Macclesfield SK10 3BU Tel:01625 422330

Middlewich Cemetery
12 Chester Rd, Middlewich CW10 9ET Tel:01606 737101
Overleigh Rd Cemetery
The Lodge, Overleigh Rd, Chester CH4 7HW Tel:01244 682529
Walton Lea Crematorium
Higher Walton, Warrington WA4 6TB Tel:01925 267731
Widnes Cemetery & Crematorium
Birchfield Rd, Widnes WA8 9EE Tel:0151 471 7332

Cleveland
Teesside Crematorium
Acklam Rd, Middlesbrough TS5 7HD Tel:01642 817725

Cornwall
Glynn Valley Crematorium
Fletchers Bridge, Bodmin PL30 4AU Tel:01208 73858
Penmount Crematorium
Penmount, Truro, Cornwall, TR4 9AA Tel:01872 272871

County Durham
Birtley Cemetery & Crematorium
Birtley, Chester Le Street DH3 1PQ Tel:0191 4102381
Chester Le Street Cemetery
Chester Le Street District Council Civic Centre, Newcastle Rd, Chester Le Street, County Durham, DH3 3UT Tel:0191 3872117
Horden Cemetery
Lodge, Thorpe Rd, Horden, Peterlee SR8 4TP Tel:0191 5863870
Mountsett Crematorium
Ewehurst Rd, Dipton, Stanley DH9 0HN Tel:01207 570255
Murton Cemetery
Church Lane, Murton, Seaham SR7 9RD Tel:0191 5263973
Newton Aycliffe Cemetery
Stephenson Way, Newton Aycliffe DL5 7DF Tel:01325 312861
Princess Road Cemetery
Princess Rd, Seaham SR7 7TD Tel:0191 5812943
Trimdon Foundry Cemetary
Thornley Rd, Trimdon Station TS29 6NX Tel:01429 880592
Trimdon Parish Council Cemetery
Trimdon Grange, Trimdon Station TS29 6HN Tel:01429 880538
Wear Valley Cemetery
South Church Rd, Bishop Auckland DL14 7NA Tel:01388 603396

Cumbria
Carlisle Cemetery
Richardson St, Carlisle CA2 6AL Tel:01228 625310
Penrith Cemetery
Beacon Edge, Penrith CA11 7RZ Tel:01768 862152
Wigton Burial Joint Committee
Cemetery, Station Hill, Wigton CA7 9BN Tel:016973 42442

Derbyshire
Castle Donington Parish Council
Cemetery House, The Barroon, Castle Donington, Derby, Derbyshire, DE74 2PF Tel:01332 810202
Chesterfield & District Joint Crematorium
Chesterfield Rd, Brimington S43 1AU Tel:01246 345888
Clay Cross Cemetery
Cemetery Rd, Danesmoor S45 9RL Tel:01246 863225
Glossop Cemetery
Arundel House, Cemetery Rd, Glossop, SK13 7QG Tel:01457 852269
Markeaton Crematorium
Markeaton Lane, Derby DE22 4NH Tel:01332 341012
Melbourne Cemetery
Pack Horse Rd, Melbourne, Derby DE73 1BZ Tel:01332 863369

Devon
Drake Memorial Park Ltd
Haye Rd, Plympton, Plymouth, Devon, PL7 1UQ Tel:01752 337937
Exeter & Devon Crematorium
Topsham Rd, Exeter, Devon, EX2 6EU Tel:01392 496333
Littleham Church Yard
Littleham Village, Littleham, Exmouth EX8 2RQ Tel:01395 225579
Mole Valley Green Burial Ground
Woodhouse Farm, Queens Nympton, South Molton EX36 4JH Tel:01769 574512

North Devon Crematorium
Old Torrington Rd, Barnstaple, Devon, EX31 3NW Tel:01271 345431
Plymouth Devonport & Stonehouse Cemetery Co
Ford Park Rd, Plymouth, Devon, PL4 6NT Tel:01752 665442
Tavistock Cemetery
Cemetery Lodge, Plymouth Rd, Tavistock, Devon, PL19 8BY Tel:01822 612799
Torquay Crematorium & Cemetery
Hele Rd, Torquay, Devon, TQ2 7QG Tel:01803 327768

Dorset
Dorchester Cemetery Office
31a Weymouth Avenue, Dorchester DT1 2EN Tel:01305 263900
Parkstone Cemetery
134 Pottery Rd, Parkstone, Poole BH14 8RD Tel:01202 741104
Poole Cemetery
Dorchester Rd, Oakdale, Poole, Dorset, BH15 3RZ Tel:01202 741106
Poole Crematorium
Gravel Hill, Poole, Dorset, BH17 9BQ Tel:01202 602582
Sherborne Cemetery
Lenthey Rd, Sherborne, Dorset, DT9 3 Tel:01935 812909
Weymouth Crematorium
Quibo Lane, Weymouth, Dorset, DT4 0RR Tel:01305 786984

East Sussex
Brighton Borough Mortuary
Lewes Rd, Brighton, East Sussex, BN2 3QB Tel:01273 602345
Downs Crematorium
Bear Rd, Brighton, East Sussex, BN2 3PL Tel:01273 601601
Eastbourne Cemeteries & Crematorium
Hide Hollow, Langney, Eastbourne, East Sussex, BN23 8AE Tel:01323 766536(Cemetery)Tel:01323 761093(Crematorium)
Woodvale Crematorium
Lewes Rd, Brighton, BN2 3QB Tel:01273 604020

Essex
Basildon & District Crematorium
Church Rd, Bowers Gifford, Basildon SS13 2HG Tel:01268 584411
Chadwell Heath Cemetery
Whalebone Lane, North Chadwell Heath, Romford, Essex, RM6 5QX Tel:0181 590 3280
Chelmsford Crematorium
Writtle Rd, Chelmsford, Essex, CM1 3BL Tel:01245 256946
Chigwell Cemetery
Frog Hall Lane, Manor Rd, Chigwell IG7 4JX Tel:0181 501 0419
Colchester Cemetery & Crematorium
Mersea Rd, Colchester, Essex, CO2 8RU Tel:01206 282950
Eastbrookend Cemetery
Dagenham Rd, Dagenham, Essex, RM10 7DR Tel:01708 447451
Federation of Synagogues Burial Society
416 Upminster Rd North, Rainham RM13 9SB Tel:01708 552825
Great Burstead Cemetery
Church St, Great Burstead, Billericay CM11 2TR Tel:01277 654334
Harlow Crematorium
Parndon Wood Rd, Harlow CM19 4SF Tel:01279 423800
Pitsea Cemetery
Church Rd, Pitsea, Basildon, Essex, SS13 2EZ Tel:01268 552132
Romford Cemetery
Crow Lane, Romford, Essex, RM7 0EP Tel:01708 740791
Sewardstone Road Cemetery
Sewardstone Rd, Waltham Abbey, Essex, EN9 1NX Tel:01992 712525
South Essex Crematorium
Ockendon Rd, Corbets Tey, Upminster RM14 2UY Tel:01708 222188
Sutton Road Cemetary
The Lodge, Sutton Rd, Southend-On-Sea SS2 5PX Tel:01702 355015
Weeley Crematorium
Colchester Rd, Weeley, Clacton-On-Sea CO16 9JP Tel:01255 831108
Wickford Cemetery
Park Drive, Wickford, Essex, SS12 9DH Tel:01268 733335

Gloucestershire
Cheltenham Cemetery & Crematorium
Bouncers Lane, Cheltenham GL52 5JT Tel:01242 244245
Coney Hill Crematorium
Coney Hill Rd, Gloucester GL4 4PA Tel:01452 523902
Forest of Dean Crematorium
Yew Tree Brake, Speech House Rd, Cinderford GL14 3HU Tel:01594 826624

Mile End Cemetery
Mile End, Coleford GL16 7DB Tel:01594 832848

Hampshire
Aldershot Crematorium
48 Guildford Rd, Aldershot GU12 4BP Tel:01252 321653
Anns Hill Rd Cemetery
Anns Hill Rd, Gosport, Hampshire, PO12 3JX Tel:01705 580181
Basingstoke Crematorium
Manor Farm, Stockbridge Rd, North Waltham, Basingstoke, Hampshire, RG25 2BA Tel:01256 398784
Magdalen Hill Cematary
Magdalen Hill, Arlesesford Rd, Winchester SO21 1HE Tel:01962 854135
Portchester Crematorium
Upper Cornaway Lane, Portchester, Fareham PO16 8NE Tel:01329 822533
Portsmouth Cemeteries Office
Milton Rd, Southsea, Hampshire, PO4 8 Tel:01705 732559
Southampton City Council
6 Bugle St, Southampton, Hampshire, SO14 2AJ Tel:01703 228609
Warblington Cemetery
Church Lane, Warblington, Havant PO9 2TU Tel:01705 452540
Worting Rd Cemetery
105 Worting Rd, Basingstoke RG21 8YZ Tel:01256 321737

Herefordshire
Hereford Cemetery & Crematorium
Westfaling St, Hereford, Herefordshire, HR4 0JE Tel:01432 272024

Hertfordshire
Almonds Lane Cemetery
Almonds Lane, Stevenage, Hertfordshire, SG1 3RR Tel:01438 350902
Bushey Jewish Cemetery
Little Bushey Lane, Bushey, Watford WD2 3TP Tel:0181 950 6299
Chorleywood Road Cemetery
Chorleywood Rd, Rickmansworth WD3 4EH Tel:01923 772646
Woodwells Cemetery
Buncefield Lane, Hemel Hempstead HP2 7HY Tel:01442 252856
Harwood Park Crematorium Ltd,
Watton Rd, Stevenage, Hertfordshire, SG2 8XT Tel:01438 815555
Hatfield Road Cemetery
Hatfield Rd, St. Albans, Hertfordshire, AL1 3LA Tel:01727 819362
North Watford Cemetery
North Western Avenue, Watford, WD2 6AW Tel:01923 672157
Tring Cemetery
Aylesbury Rd, Tring HP23 4DH Tel:01442 822248
Vicarage Road Cemetery
Vicarage Rd, Watford, Hertfordshire, WD1 8EJ Tel:01923 225147
Watton Rd Cemetery
Watton Rd, Ware, Hertfordshire, SG12 0AX Tel:01920 463261
West Herts Crematorium
High Elms Lane, Watford, Hertfordshire, WD2 7JS Tel:01923 673285
Western Synagogue Cemetery
Cheshunt Cemetery
Bulls Cross Ride, Waltham Cross EN7 5HT Tel:01992 717820
Weston Road Cemetery
Weston Rd, Stevenage, Hertfordshire, SG1 4DE Tel:01438 367109
Woodcock Hill Cemetery
Lodge, Woodcock Hill, Harefield Rd, Rickmansworth, Hertfordshire, WD3 1PT Tel:01923 775188

Isle Of Wight
Shanklin Cemetery
1 Cemetery Rd, Lake Sandown, Sandown PO36 9NN Tel:01983 403743

Kent
Barham Crematorium
Canterbury Rd, Barham, Canterbury CT4 6QU Tel:01227 831351
Beckenham Crematorium & Cemetery
Elmers End Rd, Beckenham, Kent, BR3 4TD Tel:0208650 0322
Chartham Cemetery Lodge
Ashford Rd, Chartham, Canterbury CT4 7NY Tel:01227 738211
Gravesham Borough Council,
Old Rd West, Gravesend, Kent, DA11 0LS Tel:01474 337491
Hawkinge Cemetery & Crematorium
Aerodrome Rd, Hawkinge, Folkestone CT18 7AG Tel:01303 892215

Cemeteries & Crematoria

Kent & Sussex Crematorium
Benhall Mill Rd., Tunbridge Wells, Kent, TN2 5JH Tel:01892 523894
Kent County Crematorium plc
Newcourt Wood, Charing, Ashford TN27 0EB Tel:01233 712443
Medway Crematorium
Robin Hood Lane, Blue Bell Hill, Chatham, ME5 9QU Tel:01634 861639
Northfleet Cemetery
Springhead Rd, Northfleet, Gravesend, DA11 8HW Tel:01474 533260
Snodland Cemetery
Cemetery Cottage, Cemetery Rd, Snodland ME6 5DN Tel:01634 240764
Thanet Crematorium
Manston Rd, Margate, Kent, CT9 4LY Tel:01843 224492
The Cremation Society
Brecon House, 16 Albion Place, Maidstone ME14 5DZ Tel:01622 688292
Vinters Park Crematorium
Bearstead Rd, Weavering, Maidstone ME14 5LG Tel:01622 738172

Lancashire, Greater Manchester & Manchester
Accrington Cemetry & Crematorium
Burnley Rd, Accrington, Lancashire, BB5 6HA Tel:01254 232933
Audenshaw Cemetery
Cemetery Rd, Audenshaw, Manchester M34 5AH Tel:0161 336 2675
Blackley Cemetery & Crematorium
Victoria Avenue, Manchester, Lancashire, M9 8 Tel:0161 740 5359
Burnley Cemetery
Rossendale Rd, Burnley BB11 5DD Tel:01282 435411
Carleton Crematorium
Stocks Lane, Carleton, Poulton-Le-Fylde FY6 7QS Tel:01253 882541
Central & North Manchester Synagogue Jewish Cemetery
Rainsough Brow, Prestwich, Manchester M25 9XW
Tel:0161 773 2641
Central & North Manchester Synagogue Jewish Cemetery
Rochdale Rd, Manchester M9 6FQ Tel:0161 740 2317
Chadderton Cemetery
Cemetery Lodge, Middleton Rd, Oldham OL9 Tel:0161 624 2301
Gidlow Cemetery
Gidlow Lane, Standish, Wigan WN6 8RT Tel:01257 424127
Greenacres Cemetery
Greenacres Rd, Oldham, Lancashire, OL4 3HT Tel:0161 624 2294
Hollinwood Cemetery
Roman Rd, Hollinwood, Oldham OL8 3LU Tel:0161 681 1312
Howe Bridge Crematorium
Lovers Lane, Atherton, Manchester M46 0PZ Tel:01942 870811
Leigh Cemetery
Manchester Rd, Leigh WN7 2 Tel:01942 671560
Lower Ince Crematorium
Warrington Rd, Lower Ince, Wigan WN3 4NH Tel:01942 866455
Lytham Park Cemetery & Cremarotium
Regent Avenue, Lytham St. Annes FY8 4AB Tel:01253 735429
Manchester Crematorium Ltd
Barlow Moor Rd, Manchester M21 7GZ Tel:0161 881 5269
Middleton New Cemetery
Boarshaw Rd, Middleton, Manchester M24 6 Tel:0161 655 3765
New Manchester Woodland Cemetery
City Rd, Ellenbrook, Worsley, Manchester M28 1BD
Tel:0161 790 1300
Overdale Crematorium
Overdale Drive, Chorley New Rd, Heaton, Bolton BL1 5BU
Tel:01204 840214
Padiham Public Cemetery
St. Johns Rd, Padiham, Burnley BB12 7BN Tel:01282 778139
Preston Cemetery
New Hall Lane, Preston, Lancashire, PR1 4SY Tel:01772 794585
Preston Crematorium
Longridge Rd, Ribbleton, Preston PR2 6RL Tel:01772 792391
Rochdale Cemetery
Bury Rd, Rochdale, Lancashire, OL11 4DG Tel:01706 645219
Southern Cemetery
Barlow Moor Rd, Manchester M21 7GL Tel:0161 881 2208
St. Mary's Catholic Cemetery
Manchester Rd, Wardley, Manchester M28 2UJ Tel:0161 794 2194
St.Joseph's Cemetery
Moston Lane, Mancheste M40 9QL Tel:0161 681 1582
United Synagogue Burial Ground
Worsley Hill Farm Whitefield, Manchester, M45 7ED
Tel:0161 766 2065

Whitworth Cemetery
Edward St, Whitworth, Rochdale OL16 2EJ Tel:01706 852352

Leicestershire
Melton Mowbray Cemetery
Cemetery Lodge, Thorpe Rd, Melton Mowbray LE13 1SH
Tel:01664 562223
Loughborough Crematorium
Leicester Rd, Loughborough LE11 2AF Tel:01743 353046
Saffron Hill Cemetery
Stonesby Avenue, Leicester LE2 6TY Tel:0116 222 1049

Lincolnshire
Boston Crematorium
Marian Rd, Boston, Lincolnshire, PE21 9HA Tel:01205 364612
Bourne Town Cemetery
South Rd, Bourne, Lincolnshire, PE10 9JB Tel:01778 422796
Grantham Cemetery & Crematorium
Harrowby Rd, Grantham, Lincolnshire, NG31 9DT Tel:01476 563083
Horncastle Cemetery
Boston Rd, Horncastle, Lincolnshire, LN9 6NF Tel:01507 527118
Stamford Cemetery
Wichendom, Little Casterton Rd, Stamford, PE9 1BB Tel:01780 762316
Tyler Landscapes, Newport Cemetery
Manor Rd, Newport, Lincoln LN4 1RT Tel:01522 525195

London & Greater London
Brockley Ladywell Hithergreen & Grove Park Cemeteries
Verdant Lane, Catford, London , SE6 1TP Tel:0181 697 2555
Brompton Cemetery
Fulham Rd, London, SW10 9UG Tel:0171 352 1201
Cemetery Management Ltd
38 Uxbridge Rd, London, W7 3PP Tel:0181 567 0913
Charlton Cemetery
Cemetery Lane, London, SE7 8DZ Tel:0181 854 0235
City of London Cemetery & Crematorium
Aldersbrook Rd, London, E12 5DQ Tel:0181 530 2151
Coroners Court
8 Ladywell Rd, Lewisham, London, SE13 7UW Tel:0208690 5138
East London Cemetery Co.Ltd
Grange Rd, London, E13 0HB Tel:0171 476 5109
Edmonton Cemetery
Church St, Edmonton, London, N9 9HP Tel:0208360 2157
Eltham Cemetery & Crematorium
Crown Woods Way, Eltham, London, SE9 2RF
Tel:0181 850 2921 (Cemetery) Tel:0181 850 7046 (Crematorium)
Gap Road Cemetery
Gap Rd, London, SW19 8JF Tel:0208879 0701
Golders Green Crematorium
62 Hoop Lane, London, NW11 7NL Tel:0208455 2374
Greenwich Cemetery
Well Hall Rd, London, SE9 6TZ Tel:0181 856 8666
London Borough of Hackney Mortuary
Lower Clapton Rd, London, E5 8EQ Tel:0181 985 2808
Abney Park Cemetery
High St, Stoke Newington, London, N16 0LH Tel:0171 275 7557
Hendon Cemetery & Crematorium
Holders Hill Rd, London, NW7 1NB Tel:0181 346 0657
Highgate Cemetery
Swains Lane, London, N6 6PJ Tel:0181 340 1834
Honor Oak Crematorium
Brenchley Gardens, London, SE23 3RB Tel:0171 639 7499
Islington Cemetery & Crematorium
High Rd, East Finchley, London, N2 9AG Tel:0208883 1230
Kensal Green Cemetery
Harrow Rd, London, W10 4RA Tel:0181 969 0152
L.B.S Cemeteries
Brenchley Gardens, London, SE23 3RD Tel:0171 639 3121
Lambeth Cemetery and Crematorium
Cemetary Lodge, Blackshaw Rd, Tooting, London, SW17 0BY Tel:0181 672 1390
Lewisham Crematorium
Verdant Lane, London, SE6 1TP Tel:0208698 4955
Liberal Jewish Cemetery
The Lodge, Pound Lane, London, NW10 2HG Tel:0181 459 1635
Manor Park Cemetery Co.Ltd
Sebert Rd, Forest Gate, London, E7 0NP Tel:0181 534 1486

New Southgate Cemetery & Crematorium Ltd
98 Brunswick Park Rd, London, N11 1JJ Tel:0181 361 1713
London Borough of Newham Cemeteries
 High St South, London, E6 6ET Tel:0181 472 9111
Plumstead Cemetery
Wickham Lane, London, SE2 0NS Tel:0181 854 0785
Putney Vale Cemetery & Crematorium
Kingston Rd, London, SW15 3SB Tel:0181 788 2113
South London Crematorium & Streatham Park Cemetery
Rowan Rd, London, SW16 5JG Tel:0181 764 2255
St. Marylebone Crematorium
East End Rd, Finchley, London, N2 0RZ Tel:0208343 2233
St. Pancras Cemetery (London Borough Of Camden)
High Rd, East Finchley, London, N2 9AG Tel:0181 883 1231
St. Patrick's Catholic Cemetery
Langthorne Rd, London, E11 4HL Tel:0181 539 2451
St.Mary's Catholic Cemetery
Harrow Rd, London, NW10 5NU Tel:0181 969 1145
Tottenham Park Cemetery
Montagu Rd, Edmonton, London, N18 2NF Tel:0181 807 1617
United Synagogue
Beaconsfield Rd, Willesden, London, NW10 2JE Tel:0208459 0394
Chingford Mount Cemetery
Old Church Rd, London, E4 6ST Tel:0181 524 5030
West End Chesed V'Ameth Burial Society
3 Rowan Rd, London, SW16 5JF Tel:0181 764 1566
West Ham Cemetery
Cemetery Rd, London, E7 9DG Tel:0208534 1566
West London Synagogue
Hoop Lane, London, NW11 7NJ Tel:0208455 2569
West Norwood Cemetery & Crematorium
Norwood Rd, London, SE27 9AJ Tel:0207926 7900
Woodgrange Park Cemetery
Romford Rd, London, E7 8AF Tel:0181 472 3433
Woolwich Cemetery
Kings Highway, London, SE18 2BJ Tel:0181 854 0740

Merseyside
Anfield Crematorium
Priory Rd, Anfield, Liverpool, Merseyside, L4 2SL Tel:0151 263 3267
Southport Cemeteries & Crematoria
Southport Rd, Scarisbrick, Southport PR8 5JQ Tel:01704 533443
St.Helens Cemetery & Crematorium
Rainford Rd, Windle, St. Helens WA10 6DF Tel:01744 26567
Thornton Garden Of Rest
Lydiate Lane, Thornton, Liverpool L23 1TP Tel:0151 924 5143

Middlesex
Adath Yisroel Synagogue & Burial Society
Carterhatch Lane, Enfield, Middlesex, EN1 4BG Tel:0181 363 3384
Breakspear Crematorium
Breakspear Rd, Ruislip, Middlesex, HA4 7SJ Tel:01895 632843
Enfield Crematorium
Great Cambridge Rd, Enfield EN1 4DS Tel:0181 363 8324
Heston & Isleworth Borough Cemetry
190 Powder Mill Lane, Twickenham, TW2 6EJ Tel:0181 894 3830
South West Middlesex Crematorium
Hounslow Rd, Hanworth, Feltham TW13 5JH Tel:0208894 9001
Spelthorne Borough Council
Green Way, Sunbury-On-Thames TW16 6NW Tel:01932 780244

Norfolk
Colney Wood Memorial Park
Colney Hall, Watton Rd, Norwich NR4 7TY Tel:01603 811556
Mintlyn Crematorium
Lynn Rd, Bawsey, King's Lynn PE32 1HB Tel:01553 630533
Norwich & Norfolk Crematoria - St. Faiths & Earlham
75 Manor Rd, Horsham St. Faith, Norwich, Norfolk, NR10 3LF Tel:01603 898264
Sprowston Cemetery
Church Lane, Sprowston, Norwich NR7 8AU Tel:01603 425354

East Yorkshire
East Riding Crematorium Ltd
Octon Cross Rd, Langtoft, Driffield, East Yorkshire YO25 3BL Tel:01377 267604

East Yorkshire Council
Cemetery Lodge, Sewerby Rd, Bridlington, East Yorkshire YO16 7DS Tel:01262 672138
Goole Cemetery
Hook Rd, Goole DN14 5LU Tel:01405 762725

North Yorkshire
Fulford New Cemetery
Cemetery Lodge, Fordlands Rd, Fulford, York YO19 4QG Tel:01904 633151
Mowthorpe Garden of Rest
Southwood Farm, Terrington, York YO60 6QB Tel:01653 648459
Stonefall Cemetery & Cremetoria
Wetherby Rd, Harrogate HG3 1DE Tel:01423 883523
Waltonwrays Cemetery
The Gatehouse, Carlton Rd, Skipton BD23 3BT Tel:01756 793168
York Cemetery
Gate House, Cemetery Rd, York YO10 5AF Tel:01904 610578

Northamptonshire
Counties Crematorium
Towcester Rd, Milton Malsor NN4 9RN Tel:01604 858280
Dallington Cemetery
Harlstone Rd, Dallington, Northampton NN5 Tel:01604 751589

Northumberland
Alnwick Cematery
Cematary Lodge, South Rd, Alnwick NE66 2PH Tel:01665 602598
Blyth Cemetery
Links Rd, Blyth NE24 3PJ Tel:01670 369623
Cowpen Cemetery
Cowpen Rd, Blyth NE24 5SZ Tel:01670 352107
Embleton Joint Burial Committee
Spitalford, Embleton, Alnwick NE66 3DW Tel:01665 576632
Haltwhistle & District Joint Burial Committee
Cemetery Lodge, Haltwhistle NE49 0LF Tel:01434 320266
Rothbury Cemetery
Cemetery Lodge, Whitton Rd , Rothbury, Morpeth, Northumberland, NE65 7RX Tel:01669 620451

Nottinghamshire
Bramcote Crematorium
Coventry Lane, Beeston, Nottingham NG9 3GJ Tel:0115 922 1837
Mansfield & District Crematorium
Derby Rd, Mansfield NG18 5BJ Tel:01623 621811
Northern Cemetery
Hempshill Lane, Bulwell NG6 8PF Tel:0115 915 3245
Shirebrook Town Council
Common Lane, Shirebrook, Mansfield,NG20 8PA Tel:01623 742509
Southern Cemetery & Crematoria
Wilford Hill, West Bridgford, Nottingham, Nottinghamshire, NG2 7FE Tel:0115 915 2340
Tithe Green Woodland Burial Ground
Salterford Lane, Calverton, Nottingham NG14 6NZ Tel:01623 882210

Oxfordshire
Oxford Crematorium Ltd
Bayswater Rd, Headington OX3 9RZ Tel:01865 351255

Shropshire
Bridgnorth Cemetery
Mill St, Bridgnorth WV15 5NG Tel:01746 762386
Emstrey Crematorium
London Rd, Shrewsbury SY2 6PS Tel:01743 359883
Hadley Cemetery
85 Hadley Park Rd, Hadley, Telford TF1 4PY Tel:01952 223418
Longden Road Cemetery
Longden Rd, Shrewsbury SY3 7HS Tel:01743 353046
Market Drayton Burial Committee
Cemetery Lodge, Cemetery Rd, Market Drayton, TF9 3BD Tel:01630 652833
Oswestry Cemetery
Cemetery Lodge, Victoria Rd, Oswestry SY11 2HU Tel:01691 652013
Whitchurch Joint Cemetery Board
The Cemetery Lodge, Mile Bank Rd, Whitchurch SY13 4JY Tel:01948 665477

Somerset

Burnham Area Burial Board
The Old Courthouse, Jaycroft Rd, Burnham-On-Sea TA8 1LE Tel:01278 795111
Chard Burial Joint Committee
The Chapel, Combe St, Chard TA20 1JH Tel:01460 62170
Minehead Cemetery
Porlock Rd, Woodcombe, Minehead TA24 8RY Tel:01643 705243
Sedgemoor District Council Cemetery
Quantock Rd, Bridgwater, Somerset, TA6 7EJ Tel:01278 423993
Taunton Deane Cemeteries & Crematorium
Wellington New Rd, Taunton TA1 5NE Tel:01823 284811
Wells Burial Joint Committee
127 Portway, Wells, Somerset, BA5 1LY Tel:01749 672049
Yeovil Cemetery
Preston Rd, Yeovil, Somerset, BA21 3AG Tel:01935 423742
Yeovil Crematorium
Bunford Lane, Yeovil BA20 2EJ Tel:01935 476718

Lincolnshire

Cleethorpes Cemetery
Trinity Rd, Cleethorpes DN35 8 Tel:01472 691685
Grimsby Crematorium
Weelsby Avenue, Grimsby DN32 0BB Tel:01472 324869
Woodlands Crematorium
Brumby Wood Lane, Scunthorpe DN17 1SP Tel:01724 280289

South Yorkshire

Barnsley Crematorium & Cemetery
Doncaster Rd, Ardsley, Barnsley S71 5EH Tel:01226 206053
City Road Cemetery
City Rd, Sheffield, South Yorkshire, S2 1GD Tel:0114 239 6068
Dronfield Cemetery
42 Cemetery Rd, Dronfield S18 1XY Tel:01246 412373
Ecclesfield Cemetery
Priory Lane, Ecclesfield, Sheffield, S35 9XZ Tel:0114 256 0583
Eckington Cemetery
Sheffield Rd, Eckington, Sheffield S21 4FP Tel:01246 432197
Grenoside Crematorium
5 Skew Hill Lane, Grenoside, Sheffield S35 8RZ Tel:0114 245 3999
Handsworth Cemetery
51 Orgreave Lane, Handsworth, Sheffield S13 9NE Tel:0114 254 0832
Hatfield Cemetery
Cemetery Rd, Hatfield, Doncaster DN7 6LX Tel:01302 840242
Mexborough Cemetery
Cemetery Rd, Mexborough S64 9PN Tel:01709 585184
Rose Hill Crematorium
Cantley Lane, Doncaster DN4 6NE Tel:01302 535191
Rotherham Cemeteries & Crematorium
Ridgeway East, Herringthorpe, Rotherham S65 3NN Tel:01709 850344
Sheffield Cemeteries
City Rd, Sheffield, South Yorkshire, S2 1GD Tel:0114 253 0614
Stainforth Town Council Cemetery
Office, Church Rd, Stainforth, Doncaster DN7 5AA Tel:01302 845158

Staffordshire

Bretby Crematorium
Geary Lane, Bretby, Burton-On-Trent, Staffordshire, DE15 0QE Tel:01283 221505
Cannock Cemetery
160 Pye Green Rd, Cannock WS11 2SJ Tel:01543 503176
Carmountside Crematorium
Leek Rd, Milton, Stoke-On-Trent ST2 7AB Tel:01782 235050
Leek Cemetery
Condlyffe Rd, Leek ST13 5PP Tel:01538 382616
Newcastle Cemetery
Lymewood Grove, Newcastle ST5 2EH Tel:01782 616379
Newcastle Crematorium
Chatterley Close, Bradwell, NewcastleST5 8LE Tel:01782 635498
Stafford Crematorium
Tixall Rd, Stafford ST18 0XZ Tel:01785 242594
Stapenhill Cemetery
38 Stapenhill Rd, Burton-On-Trent DE15 9AE Tel:01283 508572
Stilecop Cemetary
Stilecop Rd, Rugeley WS15 1ND Tel:01889 577739
Uttoxeter Town Council, Cemetery
Lodge, Stafford Rd, Uttoxeter ST14 8DS Tel:01889 563374

Suffolk

Brinkley Woodland Cemetery
147 All Saints Rd, Newmarket CB8 8HH Tel:01638 600693
Bury St. Edmunds Cemetery
91 Kings Rd, Bury St. Edmunds IP33 3DT Tel:01284 754447
Hadleigh Town Council
Friars Rd, Hadleigh, Ipswich IP7 6DF Tel:01473 822034
Haverhill Cemetery
Withersfield Rd, Haverhill CB9 9HF Tel:01440 703810
Ipswich Cemetery & Crematorium
Cemetery Rd, Ipswich, Suffolk, IP4 2HN Tel:01473 252931
Leiston Cemetery
Waterloo Avenue, Leiston IP16 4EH Tel:01728 831043
West Suffolk Crematorium
Risby, Bury St. Edmunds IP28 6RR Tel:01284 755118

Surrey

American Cemetery
Cemetery Pales, Brookwood, Woking GU24 0BL Tel:01483 473237
Bandon Hill Cemetery
Plough Lane, Wallington SM6 8JQ Tel:0181 647 1024
Brookwood Cemetery
Cemetery Pales, Brookwood, Woking GU24 0BL Tel:01483 472222
Confederation of Burial Authorities
The Gate House, Kew Meadow Path, Richmond TW9 4EN Tel:0181 392 9487
Guildford Crematorium & Cemeteries
Broadwater, New Pond Rd, Goldaming GU7 3DB Tel:01483 444711
Kingston Cemetary & Crematorium
Bonner Hill Rd, Kingston Upon Thames, Surrey, KT1 3EZ Tel:0208546 4462
London Road Cemetery
Figs Marsh, London Rd, Mitcham CR4 3 Tel:0208648 4115
Merton & Sutton Joint Cemetery
Garth Rd, Morden, Surrey, SM4 4LL Tel:0208337 4420
Mortlake Crematorium Board
Kew Meadow Path, Town Mead Rd, Richmond TW9 4EN Tel:0181 876 8056
Mount Cemetery
Weyside Rd, Guildford GU1 1HZ Tel:01483 561927
North East Surrey Crematorium
Lower Morden Lane, Morden, Surrey, SM4 4NU Tel:0181 337 4835
Randalls Park Crematorium
Randalls Rd, Leatherhead KT22 0AG Tel:01372 373813
Red Stone Cemetery
Philanthropic Rd, Redhill RH1 4DN Tel:01737 761592
Reigate Road Cemetery
Reigate Rd, Dorking, Surrey, RH4 1QF Tel:01306 883769
London Borough of Richmond Cemeteries
Sheen Rd, Richmond, Surrey, TW10 5BJ Tel:0208876 4511
Surbiton Cemetery
Lower Marsh Lane, Kingston Upon Thames, Surrey, KT1 3BN Tel:0208546 4463
Sutton & Cuddington Cemetery
Alcorn Close, Sutton Common Rd, Sutton SM3 9PX Tel:0181 644 9437
The Godalming Joint Burial Committee
New Cemetery Lodge, Ockford Ridge, Godalming GU7 2NP Tel:01483 421559
Woking Crematorium
Hermitage Rd, Woking, Surrey, GU21 1TJ Tel:01483 472197

Tyne And Wear

Byker & Heaton Cemetery
18 Benton Rd, Heaton, Newcastle Upon Tyne NE7 7DS Tel:0191 2662017
Gateshead East Cemetery
Cemetery Rd, Gateshead NE8 4HJ Tel:0191 4771819
Heworth Cemetery
Sunderland Rd, Felling, Gateshead NE10 0NT Tel:0191 4697851
Longbenton Cemetery
Longbenton, Newcastle Upon Tyne NE12 8EY Tel:0191 2661261
Whitley Bay Cemetery
Blyth Rd, Whitley Bay NE26 4NH Tel:0191 2533664
Earsdon Cemetery
Earsdon, Whitley Bay NE25 9LR Tel:0191 2529455
Preston Cemetery & Tynemouth Crematorium
Walton Avenue, North Shields NE29 9NJ Tel:0191 2005861
Saltwell Crematorium
Saltwell Rd South, Gateshead NE8 4TQ Tel:0191 4910553

St. Andrews Cemetery
1-2, Great North Rd, Jesmond, Newcastl -Upon Tyne ,NE2 3BU Tel:0191 2810953
St. Johns & Elswick Cemetery
Elswick Rd, Newcastle Upon Tyne NE4 8DL Tel:0191 2734127
St. Nicholas Cemetery
Wingrove Avenue Back, Newcastle Upon Tyne, NE4 9AP
Tel:0191 2735112
Union Hall Cemetery
Union Hall Rd, Newcastle Upon Tyne NE15 7JS Tel:0191 2674398
West Road Cemetery
West Rd, Newcastle Upon Tyne NE5 2JL Tel:0191 2744737

Warwickshire
Mid-Warwickshire Crematorium & Cemeteries
Oakley Wood, Bishops Tachbrook, Leamington Spa CV33 9QP Tel:01926 651418
Nuneaton Cemetery & Crematorium
Oaston Rd, Nuneaton, Warwickshire, CV11 6JZ Tel:01203 376120
Stratford-on-Avon Cemetery
Evesham Rd, Stratford-Upon-Avon CV37 9AA Tel:01789 292676

West Midlands
Birmingham Crematorium
389 Walsall Rd, Perry Barr, Birmingham B42 2LR Tel:0121 356 9476
Birmingham Hebrew Congregation Cemetery
The Ridgeway, Erdington, Birmingham B23 7TD Tel:0121 356 4615
Brandwood End Cemetery
Woodthorpe Rd, Kings Heath, Birmingham B14 6EQ Tel:0121 444 1328
Coventry Bereavement Services
The Cemeteries & Crematorium Office, Cannon Hill Rd, Canley, Coventry, West Midlands, CV4 7DF Tel:01203 418055
Grave Care
5 Ennersdale Close, Coleshill, Birmingham B46 1HA Tel:01675 463385
Handsworth Cemetery
Oxhill Rd, Birmingham, West Midlands, B21 8JT Tel:0121 554 0096
Lodge Hill Cemetery & Cremetorium
Weoley Park Rd, Birmingham, B29 5AA Tel:0121 472 1575
Quinton Cemetery
Halesowen Rd, Halesowen B62 9AF Tel:0121 422 2023
Stourbridge Cemetery & Crematorium
South Rd, Stourbridge, West Midlands, DY8 3RQ Tel:01384 813985
Streetly Cemetery & Crematorium
Little Hardwick Rd, Aldridge, Walsall WS9 0SG Tel:0121 353 7228
Sutton Coldfield Cemetery
Rectory Rd, Sutton Coldfield B75 7RP Tel:0121 378 0224
Sutton Coldfield Cremetorium
Tamworth Rd, Four Oaks, Sutton Coldfield B75 6LG Tel:0121 308 3812
West Bromwich Crematorium
Forge Lane, West Bromwich B71 3SX Tel:0121 588 2160
Willenhall Lawn Cemetery
Bentley Lane, Willenhall WV12 4AE Tel:01902 368621
Witton Cemetery
Moor Lane Witton, Birmingham, B6 7AE Tel:0121 356 4363
Woodlands Cemetery
Birmingham Rd, Coleshill, Birmingham, B46 2ET Tel:01675 464835

West Sussex
Chichester Crematorium
Westhampnett Rd, Chichester PO19 4UH Tel:01243 787755
Midhurst Burial Authority
Carron Lane, Midhurst GU29 9LF Tel:01730 812758
Surrey & Sussex Crematorium
Balcombe Rd, Crawley, West Sussex, RH10 3NQ Tel:01293 888930
Worthing Crematorium & Cemeteries
Horsham Rd, Findon, Worthing BN14 0RG Tel:01903 872678

West Yorkshire
Brighouse Cemetery
132 Lightcliffe Rd, Brighouse HD6 2HY Tel:01484 715183
Cottingly Hall
Elland Rd, Leeds, West Yorkshire, LS11 0 Tel:0113 271 6101
Dewsbury Moor Crematorium
Heckmondwike Rd, Dewsbury WF13 3PL Tel:01924 325180
Exley Lane Cemetery
Exley Lane, Elland, West Yorkshire, HX5 0SW Tel:01422 372449
Killingbeck Cemetery
York Rd, Killingbeck, Leeds LS14 6AB Tel:0113 264 5247

Lawnswood Cemetery & Crematorium
Otley Rd, Adel, Leeds, LS16 6AH Tel:0113 267 3188
Leeds Jewish Workers Co-Op Society
717 Whitehall Rd, New Farnley, Leeds LS12 6JL Tel:0113 285 2521
Moorthorpe Cemetery
Barnsley Rd, Moorthorpe, Pontefract WF9 2BP Tel:01977 642433
Nab Wood Crematorium
Bingley Rd, Shipley BD18 4DB Tel:01274 584109
Oakworth Crematorium
Wide Lane, Oakworth, Keighley BD22 0RJ Tel:01535 603162
Park Wood Crematorium
Park Rd, Elland HX5 9HZ Tel:01422 372293
Pontefract Crematorium
Wakefield Rd, Pontefract WF8 4HA Tel:01977 723455
Rawdon Crematorium
Leeds Rd, Rawdon, Leeds LS19 6JP Tel:0113 250 2904
Scholemoor Cemetery & Crematorium
Necropolis Rd, Bradford, West Yorkshire, BD7 2PS Tel:01274 571313
Sowerby Bridge Cemetery
Sowerby New Rd, Sowerby Bridge HX6 1LQ Tel:01422 831193
United Hebrew Congregation Leeds, Jewish Cemetery
Gelderd Rd, Leeds, West Yorkshire, LS7 4BU Tel:0113 263 8684
Wakefield Crematorium
Standbridge Lane, Crigglestone, Wakefield WF4 3JA Tel:01924 303380
Wetherby Cemetery
Sexton House, Hallfield Lane, Wetherby LS22 6JQ Tel:01937 582451

Wiltshire
Box Cemetery
Bath Rd, Box, Corsham, Wiltshire, SN13 8AA Tel:01225 742476
Devizes & Roundway Joint Burial Committee
Cemetry Lodge, Rotherstone, Devizes SN10 2DE Tel:01380 722821
Salisbury Crematorium
Barrington Rd, Salisbury, Wiltshire, SP1 3JB Tel:01722 333632
Chippenham Cemetery
London Road, Chippenham, Wiltshire, SN15 3RD Tel:01249 652728
West Wiltshire Crematorium
Devizes Rd, Semington, Trowbridge BA14 7QH Tel:01380 871101

Wirral
Landican Cemetery
Arrowe Park Rd, Birkenhead, Wirral, CH49 5LW Tel:0151 677 2361

Worcestershire
Pershore Cemetery
Defford Rd, Pershore, Worcestershire, WR10 3BX Tel:01386 552043
Redith Crematorium & Abbey Cemetary
Bordesley Lane, Redditch, Worcestershire, B97 6RR Tel:01527 62174
Westall Park Woodland Burial
Holberrow Green, Redditch B96 6JY Tel:01386 792806
Worcester Crematorium
Astwood Rd, Tintern Avenue, Worcester WR3 8HA Tel:01905 22633

Wales

Aberystwyth Crematorium
Clarach Rd, Aberystwyth SY23 3DG Tel:01970 626942

Carmarthenshire
Carmarthen Cemetery
Elim Rd, Carmarthen SA31 1TX Tel:01267 234134

Conwy
Bron-y-Nant Crematorium
Dinerth Rd, Colwyn Bay, LL28 4YN Tel:01492 544677

Gwent
Ebbw Vale Cemetery
Waun-y-Pound Rd, Ebbw Vale, Gwent, NP23 6LE Tel:01495 302187
Llanelli District Cemetery
Swansea Rd, Llanelli SA15 3EX Tel:01554 77371
Grave Tending Service
14 Kelly Rd, Newport, Gwent, NP19 7RF Tel:01633 667510
Christchurch Cemetery
Christchurch, Newport, Gwent, NP18 1JJ Tel:01633 277566
Gwent Crematorium
Treherbert Rd, Croesyceliog, Cwmbran NP44 2BZ Tel:01633 482784

Flintshire
Mold Town Cemetery
Cemetery Lodge, Alexandra Rd, Mold CH7 1HJ Tel:01352 753820

Gwynedd
Bangor Crematorium
Llandygai Rd, Bangor, Gwynedd, LL57 4HP Tel:01248 370500

Mid Glamorgan
Mid Glamorgan Cemetery Section, Monks St, Aberdare, Mid Glamorgan, CF44 7PA Tel:01685 885345
Coychurch Crematorium
Coychurch, Bridgend, Mid Glamorgan, CF35 6AB Tel:01656 656605
Ferndale Cemetery
Cemetery Lodge, Highfield, Ferndale CF43 4TD Tel:01443 730321
Llwydcoed Crematorium
Llwydcoed, Aberdare CF44 0DJ Tel:01685 874115
Maesteg Cemetery
Cemetery Rd, Maesteg CF34 0DN Tel:01656 735485
Penrhys Cemetery
Cemetery Lodge, Penrhys Rd, Tylorstown, Ferndale CF43 3PN Tel:01443 730465
Trane Cemetery
Gilfach Rd, Tonyrefail, Porth CF39 8HL Tel:01443 670280
Treorchy Cemetery
The Lodge, Cemetery Rd, Treorchy CF42 6TB Tel:01443 772336
Ynysybwl Cemetery
Heol Y Plwyf, Ynysybwl, Pontypridd, CF37 3HU Tel:01443 790159

Pembrokeshire
Milford Haven Cemetery
The Cemetery, Milford Haven SA73 2RP Tel:01646 693324

South Glamorgan
Bereavement Services, Thornhill Rd, Cardiff CF14 9UA Tel:01222 623294
Cathays Cemetery
Fairoak Rd, Cathays, Cardiff CF24 4PY Tel:01222 750433
Western Cemetery
Cowbridge Rd West, Cardiff CF5 5TF Tel:01222 593231

West Glamorgan
Goytre Cemetery
Goytre Rd, Port Talbot SA13 2YN Tel:01639 883378
Margam Crematorium
Longland Lane, Margam, Port Talbot SA13 2NR Tel:01639 883570
Oystermouth Cemetery
Oystermouth Rd, Swansea SA1 3SW Tel:01792 366302

Wrexham
Coedpoeth Cemetery
Cemetery Rd, Coedpoeth, Wrexham, LL11 3SP Tel:01978 755617
Wrexham Cemeteries & Crematorium
Pentre Bychan, Wrexham, Clwyd, LL14 4EP Tel:01978 840068
Wrexham Cemetery
Ruabon Rd, Wrexham LL13 7NY Tel:01978 263159

Scotland

Aberdeenshire
Springbank Cemetery
Countesswells Rd, Springbank, Aberdeen AB15 7YH Tel:01224 317323
St. Peter's Cemetery
King St, Aberdeen AB24 3BX Tel:01224 638490
Trinity Cemetery
Erroll St, Aberdeen AB24 5PP Tel:01224 633747

Angus
Barnhill Cemetery
27 Strathmore St, Broughty Ferry, Dundee DD5 2NY Tel:01382 477139
Dundee Crematorium
Macalpine Rd, Dundee, Angus, DD3 8 Tel:01382 825601
Park Grove Crematorium
Douglasmuir, Friocheim, Arbroath DD11 4UN Tel:01241 828959

Ayrshire
Ardrossan Cemetery
Sorbie Rd, Ardrossan KA22 8AQ Tel:01294 463133
Dreghorn Cemetery

Station Rd, Dreghorn, Irvine KA11 4AJ Tel:01294 211101
Hawkhill Cemetery
Kilwinning Rd, Saltcoats, Stevenston KA20 3DE Tel:01294 465241
Holmsford Bridge Crematorium
Dreghorn, Irvine, Ayrshire, KA11 4EF Tel:01294 214720
Kilwinning Cemetery
Bridgend, Kilwinning KA13 7LY Tel:01294 552102
Largs Cemetery
Greenock Rd, Largs KA30 8NG Tel:01475 673149
Maybole Cemetery
Crosshill Rd, Maybole, Ayrshire, KA19 7BN Tel:01655 882217
Newmilns Cemetery
Dalwhatswood Rd, Newmilns, Ayrshire, KA16 9LT Tel:01560 320191
Prestwick Cemetery
Shaw Rd, Prestwick, Ayrshire, KA9 2LP Tel:01292 477759
Stewarton Cemetery
Dalry Rd, Stewarton, Kilmarnock KA3 3DY Tel:01560 482888
West Kilbride Cemetery
Hunterston Rd, West Kilbride, Ayrshire, KA23 9EX Tel:01294 822818

Banffshire
Moray Crematorium
Clochan, Buckie, Banffshire, AB56 5HQ Tel:01542 850488

Clackmannanshire
Alva Cemetery
The Glebe, Alva, Clackmannanshire, FK12 5HR Tel:01259 760354
Sunnyside Cemetery
Sunnyside Rd, Alloa FK10 2AP Tel:01259 723575
Tillicoultry Cemetery
Dollar Rd, Tillicoultry FK13 6PF Tel:01259 750216

Dunbartonshire
Cardross Crematorium
Main Rd, Cardross, Dumbarton G82 5HD Tel:01389 841313
Dumbarton Cemetery
Stirling Rd, Dumbarton, Dunbartonshire, G82 2PF Tel:01389 762033
Vale Of Leven Cemetery
Overton Rd, Alexandria , Dunbartonshire, G83 0LJ Tel:01389 752266
West Dumbartonshire Crematorium
North Dalnottar, Clydebank G81 4SL Tel:01389 874318
West Dunbartonshire Crematorium
Roseberry Place, Clydebank G81 1TG Tel:01389 738709

Fife
Dunfermline Cemetery
Halbeath Rd, Dunfermline KY12 7RA Tel:01383 724899
Dunfermline Crematorium
Masterton Rd, Dunfermline KY11 8QR Tel:01383 724653
Kirkcaldy Crematorium
Dunnikier Way, Kirkcaldy, Fife, KY1 3PL Tel:01592 260277

Inverness-Shire
Inverness Crematorium
Kilvean Rd, Kilvean, Inverness IV3 8JN Tel:01463 717849

Isle Of Cumbrae
Millport Cemetery
Golf Rd, Millport, Isle Of Cumbrae, KA28 0HB Tel:01475 530442

Lanarkshire
Airbles Cemetery
Airbles Rd, Motherwell, Lanarkshire, ML1 3AW Tel:01698 263986
Bedlay Cemetery
Bedlay Walk, Moodiesburn, Glasgow G69 0QG Tel:01236 872446
Bothwellpark Cemetery
New Edinburgh Rd, Bellshill ML4 3HH Tel:01698 748146
Cadder Cemetery
Kirkintilloch Rd, Bishopbriggs, Glasgow G64 2QG Tel:0141 772 1977
Cambusnethan Cemetery
Kirk Rd, Wishaw, Lanarkshire, ML2 8NP Tel:01698 384481
Campsie Cemetery
High Church of Scotland, Main St, Lennoxtown, Glasgow, Lanarkshire, G66 7DA Tel:01360 311127
Cardonald Cemetery
547 Mosspark Boulevard, Glasgow G52 1SB Tel:0141 882 1059
Daldowie Crematorium
Daldowie Estate, Uddingston, Glasgow G71 7RU Tel:0141 771 1004

Glasgow Crematorium
Western Necropolis, Tresta Rd, Glasgow G23 5AA Tel:0141 946 2895
Glebe Cemetery
Vicars Rd, Stonehouse, Larkhall ML9 3EB Tel:01698 793674
Glenduffhill Cemetery
278 Hallhill Rd, Glasgow, Lanarkshire, G33 4RU Tel:0141 771 2446
Kilsyth Parish Cemetery
Howe Rd, Kirklands, Glasgow G65 0LA Tel:01236 822144
Larkhall Cemetery
The Cemetery Lodge, Duke St, Larkhall ML9 2AL Tel:01698 883049
Old Aisle Cemetery
Old Aisle Rd, Kirkintilloch, Glasgow G66 3HH Tel:0141 776 2330
St. Conval's Cemetery
Glasgow Rd, Barrhead, Glasgow G78 1TH Tel:0141 881 1058
St. Patrick's Cemetery
Kings Drive, New Stevenston, Motherwell ML1 4HY Tel:01698 732938
St. Peters Cemetery
1900 London Rd, Glasgow G32 8RD Tel:0141 778 1183
The Necropolis
50 Cathedral Square, Glasgow G4 0UZ Tel:0141 552 3145

Midlothian
Dean Cemetery
Dean Path, Edinburgh EH4 3AT Tel:0131 332 1496
Edinburgh Crematorium Ltd
3 Walker St, Edinburgh EH3 7JY Tel:0131 225 7227
Seafield Cemetery & Crematorium
Seafield Rd, Edinburgh EH6 7LQ Tel:0131 554 3496
Warriston Crematorium
36 Warriston Rd, Edinburgh EH7 4HW Tel:0131 552 3020

Perthshire
Perth Crematorium
Crieff Rd, Perth, Perthshire, PH1 2PE Tel:01738 625068
Hawkhead Cemetery
133 Hawkhead Rd, Paisley PA2 7BE Tel:0141 889 3472

Renfrewshire
Paisley Cemetery Co.Ltd
46 Broomlands St, Paisley PA1 2NP Tel:0141 889 2260

Stirlingshire
Larbert Cemetery
25 Muirhead Rd, Larbert, Stirlingshire, FK5 4HZ Tel:01324 557867

Northern Ireland

County Antrim
Ballymena Cemetery
Cushendall Rd, Ballymena BT43 6QE Tel:028 256656026
Ballymoney Cemetery
44 Knock Rd, Ballymoney BT53 6LX Tel:028 27666364
Blaris New Cemetery
25 Blaris Rd, Lisburn, County Antrim, BT27 5RA Tel:028 92607143
Carnmoney Cemetery
10 Prince Charles Way, Newtownabbey BT36 7LG Tel:029 90832428
City Cemetery
511 Falls Rd, Belfast BT12 6DE Tel:028 90323112
City of Belfast Crematorium
Roselawn Cemetery
Ballygowan Rd, Crossnacreevy, Belfast BT5 7TZ Tel:028 90448342
Greenland Cemetery
Upper Cairncastle Rd, Larne BT40 2EG Tel:01574 272543
Milltown Cemetery Office
546 Falls Rd, Belfast, County Antrim, BT12 6EQ Tel:028 90613972
Roselawn Cemetery
127 Ballygowan Rd, Crossnacreevy, Belfast BT5 7TZ Tel:028 90448288

County Armagh
Kernan Cemetery
Kernan Hill Rd, Portadown, Craigavon BT63 5YB Tel:028 38339059
Lurgan Cemetery
57 Tandragee Rd, Lurgan, Craigavon BT66 8TL Tel:028 38342853

County Down
Ballyvestry Cemetery
6 Edgewater Millisle, Newtownards BT23 5 Tel:028 91882657
Banbridge Public Cemetery
Newry Rd, Banbridge, County Down, BT32 3NB Tel:028 406 62623

Bangor Cemetery
62 Newtownards Rd, Bangor BT20 4DN Tel:028 91271909
Clandeboye Cemetery
300 Old Belfast Rd, Bangor BT19 1RH Tel:028 91853246
Comber Cemetery
31 Newtownards Rd, Comber, Newtownards BT23 5AZ Tel:028 91872529
Struell Cemetery
Old Course Rd, Downpatrick BT30 8AQ Tel:028 446613086
Lough Inch Cemetery
Riverside Rd, Ballynahinch BT24 8JB Tel:028 97562987
Kirkistown Cemetary
Main Rd, Portavogie, Newtownards, County Down, BT22 1EL
Tel:028 4271773
Movilla Cemetary
Movilla Rd, Newtownards BT23 8EY Tel:028 91812276
Redburn Cemetery
Old Holywood Rd, Holywood BT18 9QH Tel:028 90425547
Whitechurch Cemetary
19 Dunover Rd, Newtownards, County Down, BT22 2LE
Tel:028 9158659

County Londonderry
Altnagelvin Cemetery
Church Brae, Altnagelvin, Londonderry BT47 3QG
Tel:028 713 343351
City Cemetery
Lone Moor Rd, Londonderry BT48 9LA Tel:028 71362615

County Tyrone
Greenhill Cemetery
Mountjoy Rd, Omagh, County Tyrone, BT79 7BL Tel: 028 82244918
Westland Road Cemetery
Westland Rd, Cookstown, BT80 8BX Tel:028 86766087

English Heritage ~ *Services to Genealogists*

Keynon Peel Hall, Little Sutton, 1881
© Crown Copyright. National Monuments Record
From the National Monuments Record,
the public archive of English Heritage

What does English Heritage do?

Our work falls into three main categories: identifying buildings of historical interest and ancient monuments for protection; assisting their owners and other bodies with conservation responsibilities to secure the future of England's historic environment; and helping the public to appreciate, understand and enjoy their heritage.

In addition, we are responsible for the management and presentation of over 400 historic properties, monuments and war memorials in the nation's care including Stonehenge, Dover Castle, Tintagel Castle, Cornwall and Osborne House on the Isle of Wight.

We are constantly expanding our knowledge of the past through excavations and other research projects. But perhaps the most significant service we have for the genealogist is our extraordinary public archive, the National Monuments Record.

The National Monuments Record includes information on just about every town and village in the country. This includes historic photography, detailed records of individual buildings including descriptions of 360,000 listed buildings, and aerial photographs covering all of England. Between them you can use our archives to build up a picture of the places your ancestors come from: if you know the name or details of an individual building related to a family member, ask us if we hold photographs or other records about that building. Alternatively ask us what aerial photographs we hold of a place of interest in the 1940s, 1950s, or 1960s.

You can search this treasure trove of information for free: simply write to us at the address below or fill in an enquiry form on our web site at:

http://www.english-heritage.org.uk/knowledge/National Monuments Record/services
E-mail:
National Monuments Recordinfo@english-heritage.org.uk
and ask for an information pack on our services. If you already have an enquiry in mind give as much detail as possible about the address and location of your building or place of interest. Our web site gives you more detailed information on our enquiry services and collections. If we find old photographs, drawings or records for you charges are made for photocopying and photographic prints, but the initial search is free subject to limitations on the complexity of your query.

If you are in London visiting the Family Records Centre or other archives why not make some time to pop into our small London Search Room at 55 Blandford Street W1H 3AF. The Search Room holds an exciting collection of photographic images of the buildings of London. Or arrange to visit the National Monuments Record Centre, our Swindon headquarters. The National Monuments Record also runs a programme of workshops and seminars aimed at showing groups how to use its materials for local history.

With all that we have to offer, a lover of the past may want to find out more about membership of English Heritage and enjoy free entry to its magnificent collection of properties, many of them containing priceless collections of paintings and other objects. Who knows, one of your forebears may have lived or worked in one.

Contact numbers
National Monuments Record Enquiry & Research Service
National Monuments Record Centre
Kemble Drive, Swindon SN2 2GZ
Telephone: 01793 414600
Fax: 01793 414606
e-mail:
National Monuments Recordinfo@ english-heritage.org.uk
Open Tuesday to Friday, 9.30am to 5pm.

Our London Search Room in Blandford Street is open Tuesday to Friday 10am to 5pm.

Enquiries about English Heritage's other work:
English Heritage Customer Services Tel: 01793 414910
or visit

http://www.english-heritage.org.uk

Byland Abbey, N Yorks, 1994
© Crown Copyright. National Monuments RecordFrom the
National Monuments Record, the public archive of English Heritage

Aldborough Roman Town
Main Street, Boroughbridge, North Yorks. YO5 9EF
Ashby De La Zouch Castle
South Street, Ashby De La Zouch, Leics. LE6 5PR
Audley End House
Saffron Walden, Essex, CB11 4JF
Aydon Castle
Northumberland, NE45 5PJ
Barnard Castle
Castle House, Barnard Castle, Durham, DL12 9AT
Battle Abbey
Battle, East Sussex, TN33 0AD
Bayham Abbey
Bayham, Lamberhurst, Kent, TN8 8DE
Beeston Castle
Beeston, Tarporley, Cheshire, CW6 9TX
Belsay Hall
Belsay, Near Ponteland, Northumberland, NE20 0DX
Berney Arms Mill
8 Manor Road, Southtown, Great Yarmouth, Norfolk, NR31 0QA
Berry Pomeroy Castle
Totnes, Devon, TQ9 6NJ
Berwick Barracks
Berwick-upon-Tweed, Northumberland, TD15 1DF
Bishop Waltham Abbey
Bishop Waltham, Hampshire, SO32 1DH
Bolsover Castle
Castle Street, Bolsover, Derbyshire, S44 6PR
Boscobel House
Brewood, Bishops Wood, Shropshire, ST19 9AR
Brinkburn Priory
Long Framlington, Morpeth, Northumberland, NE65 8AR
Brodsworth Hall
Brodsworth, Near Doncaster, South Yorks. DN5 7XJ
Brougham Castle
Brougham, Penrith, Cumbria, CA10 2AA
Buildwas Abbey
Iron Bridge, Telford, Shropshire, TF8 7BW
Busmead Priory
Colmworth, Bedfordshire, MK44 2LD
Byland Abbey
Coxwold, North Yorks, YO6 4BD
Calshot Castle
Calshot, Hants, SO4 1BR
Carisbrooke Castles
Newport, Isle Of Wight, O32 6JY
Carlisle Castle
Carlisle, Cumbria, CA3 8UR
Castle Acre Priory
Stocks Green, Castle Acre, Kings Lynn, Norfolk, E32 2XD
Castle Rising Castle
Castle Rising, Kings Lynn, Norfolk, E31 6AH

Chapter House
East Cloisters, Westminster Abbey, London, SW1P 3PE
Chester Roman Fort
Chollerford, Hexham, Northumberland, NE46 4EP
Chiswick House
Burlington Lane, Chiswick, London, W4 2RP
Chysauster Ancient Village
Newmill, Penzance, Cornwall, TR20 8XA
Cleeve Abbey
Washford, Watchet, Somerset, TA23 0PS
Clifford Tower
Clifford Street, York, North Yorkshire, YO1 1SA
Conisburgh Castle
The Ivanhoe Trust, The Priory, High St, Conisburgh, Doncaster
Corbridge Roman Site
Corbridge, Northumberland, NE45 5NT
Dartmouth Castle
Castle Road, Dartmouth, Devon, TQ6 0JN
Deal Castle
Victoria Road, Deal, Kent, CT14 7BA
Denny Abbey
Ely Road, Chittering, Cambridgeshire, CB5 9TQ
Dorchester Castle
Dorchester, Hants, O16 9QW
Dover Castle
Dover, Kent, CT16 1HU
Down House
Luxted Road, Downe, Kent, BR6 7JT
Dunstanburgh Castle
14 Queen St., Alnwick, Northumberland, NE66 1RD
Dymchurch Martello Tower
High Street, Dymchurch, Kent, CT16 1HU
Eltham Palace
Courtyard, Eltham, London, SE9 5QE
Endennis Castle
Falmouth, Cornwall, TR11 4LP
Etal Castle
Etal Village, Berwick-upon-Tweed, Northumberland, TD12 4TN
Evensey Castle
Evensey, East Sussex, BN24 5LE
Everil Castle
Market Place, Castleton, Derbyshire, S33 8WQ
Everil Castle
Castleton, Hope Valley, Sheffield, SW33 5LE
Farleigh Hungerford Castle
Farleigh Hungerford, Near Bath, Somerset, BA3 6RS
Farnham Castle
Castle Hill, Farnham, Surrey, GU6 0AG
Finchale Priory
Brasside, Newton Hall, Co Durham, DH1 5SH
Fort Brockhurst
Gunners Way, Elson, Gosport, Hants, PO12 4DS
Fort Cumberland
Fort Cumberland Rd., Eastney, Portsmouth, PO4 9LD
Framlingham Castle
Framlingham, Suffolk, IP8 9BT
Furness Abbey
Barrow In Furness, Cumbria, LH13 0TJ
Gainsborough Hall
Arnell Road, Gainsborough, Lincolnshire, DN12 2RN
Goodrich Castle
Goodrich, Ross on Wye, Worcestershire, HR9 6HY
Grimes Graves
Lynford, Thetford, Norfolk, IP26 5DE
Hailes Abbey
Near Winchcombe, Cheltenham, Glos., GL54 5PB
Halesowen Abbey
Halesowen, Huntington, West Midlands
Hardwick Old Hall
Doe Lea, Near Chesterfield, Derbyshire, S44 5QJ
Haughmond Abbey
Upton Magna, Uffington, Shrewsbury, SY4 4RW
Helmsley Castle
Helmsley, North Yorkshire, YO6 5AB
Housesteads Roman Fort
Haydon Bridge, Hexham, Northumberland, NE46 6NN
Jewel Tower
Abingdon Street, London, SW1P 3JY

Servants, 1890
© Crown Copyright. National Monuments Record
From the National Monuments Record, the public
archive of English Heritage

Kenilworth Castle
Kenilworth, Warwickshire, CV8 INE
Kenwood House
Hampstead Lane, London, NW3 7JR
Kirby Hall
Deene, Corby, Northants, NN17 3EN
Kirby Muxloe Castle
South Quay, Great Yarmouth, Norfolk, NR30 2RQ
Kirkham Priory
Whitwell-on-the-Hill, North Yorks, YO6 7JS
Lanercost Priory
Brampton, Cumbria, CA8 2HQ
Launceston Castle
Castle Lodge, Launceston, Cornwall, L15 7DR
Lincoln Bishops Palace
Minster Yard, Lincoln, Lincs, LN2 1PU
Lindisfarne Priory
Holy Island, Northumberland, TD15 2RX
Longthorpe Tower
Thorpe Road, Longthorpe, Peterborough, PE1 1HA
Lullingstone Roman Villa
Lullingstone Lane, Eynsford, Kent, DA4 0JA
Lyddington Bede House
Blue Coat Lane, Liecestershire, LE15 9LZ
Maison Deu
Water Lane, Ospring, Kent, ME13 0DW
Marble Hill House
Richmond Road, Twickenham, Middlesex, TW1 2NL
Medieval Merchants House
58 French Street, Southampton, Hants, SO1 0AT
Middleham Castle
Middleham, Leyburn, North Yorkshire, DL8 4QG
Milton Chantry
Gravesend, Kent
Mortimers Cross Water
Leominster, Herefordshire, HR6 9PE
Mount Grace Priory
Saddle Bridge, Northallerton, North Yorks. DL6 3JG
Muchelney Abbey
Muchelney, Langport, Somerset, TA10 0DQ
Norham Castle
Berwick-upon-Tweed, Northumberland, TD15 2JY
Okehampton Castle
Castle Lodge, Okehampton, Devon, EX20 1JB
Old Merchants House
South Quay, Great Yarmouth, Norfolk, IP13 2RQ
Old Sarum Castle
Castle Roads, Salisbury, Wilts, SP1 3SD

Old Wardour Castle
Tisbury, Salisbury, Wilts, SP3 6RR
Orford Castle
Woodbridge, Suffolk, IP12 2ND
Osborne House
Royal Apartments, East Cowes, Isle of Wight, PO32 6JY
Pickering Castle
Pickering, North Yorkshire, YO18 7AX
Portland Castle
Castleton, Portland, Dorset, DT5 1AZ
Prudhoe Castle
Prudhoe, Northumberland, NE42 6NA
Rangers House
Chesterfield Walk, Blackheath, London, SE10 8QX
Restormel Castle
Lostwithiel, Cornwall, PL22 0BD
Richborough Castle
Richborough, Sandwich, Kent, CT13 9JW
Richmond Castle
Richmond, North Yorkshire, DL10 4QW
Rievaulx Abbey
Rievaulx, Near Helmsley, North Yorkshire, DL10 5LB
Roche Abbey
Maltby, Rotherham, South Yorkshire, S66 8NW
Rochester Castle
The Keep, Rochester-upon-Medway, Kent, ME1 1SW
Rushton Triangular Lodge
Rushton, Kettering, Northants, NN14 1RP
Saxtead Green Post Mill
The Mill House, Saxtead Green, Suffolk, IP13 9QQ
Scarborough Castle
Castle Road, Scarborough, North Yorks. YO11 1HY
Sherborne Old Castle
Castleton, Dorset, DT19 0SY
Sibsey Trader Mill
Sibsey, Boston, Lincolnshire, PE22 0SY
St. Augustines Abbey
Canterbury, Kent, CT1 1TF
St. Mawes Castle
St. Mawes, Cornwall, TR2 3AA
Stokesay Castle
Craven Arms, Shropshire, SY7 9AH
Stonehenge
Stone Circle, Wiltshire, SP4 7DE
Stott Park Bobbin Mill
Low Stott Park, Ulverston, Cumbria, LA12 8AR
Tilbury Fort
Fort Road, Tilbury, Essex, RN18 7NR
Tintagel Castle
Tintagel, Cornwall, DL34 0AA
Totnes Castle
Castle Street, Totnes, Devon, TQ9 5NU
Tynemouth Castle
North Shields, Tyne and Wear, NE30 4BZ
Upnor Castle
High Street, Upnor, Rochester, Kent, ME2 4XG
Wall Roman site
Watling Street, Near Litchfield, Staffs. WS14 0AW
Walmer Castle
Kingsdown Road, Deal, Kent, CT14 7LJ
Warkworth Castle
Morpeth, Northumberland, NE66 0UJ
Wenlock Priory
Much Wenlock, Shropshire, TF13 6HS
Whitby Abbey
Whitby, North Yorkshire, YO22 4JT
Wingfield Manor
South Wingfield, Alfreton, Derbyshire, DE2 7NH
Witley Court
Grest Witley, Worcestershire, WR6 6JT
Wolvesey Castle
College Street, Winchester, Hants, SO23 8NB
Wrest Park
Silsoe, Luton, Bedfordshire, MK45 4HS
Wroxeter Roman Site
Wroxeter, Shropshire, SY5 6PH
Yarmouth Castle
Quay Street, Yarmouth, Isle Of Wight, PO41 0P

CADW - Welsh Heritage Sites & Locations

Barclodiad y Gawres Burial Chamber, Anglesey
Basingwerk Abbey Flintshire
Beaumaris Castle
Beaumaris, Anglesey, LL58 8AP Tel: 01248-810361
Beaupre Castle, near Cowbridge, Vale of Glamorgan
Blaenavon Ironworks
North St, Blaenavon, Blaenau Gwent, NP4 9RN Tel: 01495-792615
Bodowyr Burial Chamber, Anglesey
Brecon Gaer Roman Fort Powys
Bronllys Castle, Bronllys, Powys
Bryn Celli Ddu Burial Chamber, Anglesey
Bryntail Lead Mine Buildings, Llanidloes, Powys
Caer Gybi Roman Fortlet, Anglesey
Caer Lêb, Anglesey
Caer y Tor Hillfort, Anglesey
Caerleon Roman Baths & Amphitheatre
High Street, Caerleon, Newport, NP18 1AE Tel: 01633-422518
Caernarfon Castle
Castle Ditch, Caernarfon LL55 2AY Tel: 01286-677617
Caerphilly Castle
Caerphilly, CF83 1JD, 029 20 883143
Caerwent Roman Town, Monmouthshire
Capel Garmon Burial Chamber
near Betws-y-Coed, Conwy
Capel Lligwy, Anglesey
Carew Cross, Carew, Pembrokeshire
Carreg Cennen Castle
Tir y Castell Farm, Trapp, near Llandeilo SA19 6TS Tel: 01558-822291
Carreg Coetan Arthur Burial Chamber
Newport, Pembrokeshire
Carswell Old House, near Tenby, Pembrokeshire
Castell Bryn Gwyn, Anglesey
Castell Coch
Tongwynlais, Cardiff, CF15 7JS Tel: 029-20-810101
Castell y Bere, near Tywyn, Gwynedd
Chepstow Bulwarks Camp, Monmouthshire
Chepstow Castle
Bridge Street, Chepstow NP16 5EZ Tel: 01291-624065
Cilgerran Castle
Castle Hse, Cilgerran, Cardigan SA43 2SF Tel: 01239-615007
Coity Castle, near Bridgend
Conwy Castle
Conwy, LL32 8AY Tel: 01492-592358
Criccieth Castle
Castle Street, Criccieth LL55 0DP Tel: 01766-522227
Cymer Abbey
c/o Vanner Farm, Llanelltyd, Dolgellau LL40 2HE Tel: 01341-422854
Denbigh Castle, Denbigh, Denbighshire
Denbigh Friary
Leicester's Church and St Hilary's Chapel, Denbighshire
Derwen Churchyard Cross, near Corwen, Denbighshire
Din Dryfol Burial Chamber, Anglesey
Din Lligwy Hut Group, Anglesey
Dinefwr Castle, Llandeilo, Carmarthenshire
Dolbadarn Castle, Llanberis, Gwynedd
Dolforwyn Castle, near Newtown, Powys
Dolwyddelan Castle
Bryn Tirion Farm, Dolwyddelan LL25 OEJ Tel: 01690 750366
Dryslwyn Castle, near Llandeilo, Carmarthenshire
Dyffryn Arddwy Burial Chamber, Gwynedd
Dyfi Furnace, near Machynlleth, Ceredigion
Eliseg's Pillar, near Llangollen, Denbighshire
Ewenny Priory, near Bridgend
Ewloe Castle, Flintshire
Flint Castle, Flintshire
Grosmont Castle, Monmouthshire
Gwydir Uchaf Chapel, near Llanrwst, Conwy
Harlech Castle
Castle Square, Harlech LL46 2YH Tel: 01766-780552
Haverfordwest Priory, Pembrokeshire
Hen Gwrt Moated Site
Llantilio Crossenny, Monmouthshire
Holyhead Mountain Hut Group, Anglesey
Kidwelly Castle
5 Castle Road, Kidwelly SA17 5BQ Tel: 01554-890104
Lamphey Bishops Palace
Lamphey, Pembroke, SA71 5NT Tel: 01646-672224
Laugharne Castle
King Street, Laugharne SA33 4SA Tel: 01994-427906

Llanmelin Wood Hillfort, Monmouthshire
Llansteffan Castle, Carmarthenshire
Llanthony Priory, Monmouthshire
Llawhaden Castle, Pembrokeshire
Lligwy Burial Chamber, Anglesey
Loughor Castle, near Swansea
Maen Achwyfan Cross, near Whitford, Flintshire
Margam Stones Museum, Port Talbot
Monmouth Castle, Monmouthshire
Montgomery Castle, Powys
Neath Abbey, Neath Port Talbot
Newcastle Castle, Bridgend
Newport Castle, Newport city centre
Ogmore Castle and Stepping Stones, near Bridgend
Oxwich Castle
c/o Oxwich Castle Farm, Oxwich, Swansea, SA3 1NG
Tel: 01792-390359
Parc le Breos Burial Chamber, Gower Peninsula
Penarth Fawr Medieval House
near Criccieth, Ll?n Peninsula
Penmon Cross & Dovecote, Anglesey
Penmon Priory, Anglesey
Penrhos Feilw Standing Stones, Anglesey
Pentre Ifan Burial Chamber,
near Newport, Pembrokeshire
Plas Mawr Elizabethan Town House
High Street, Conwy, LL32 8DE Tel: 01492-580167
Pont Minllyn, near Dinas Mawddwy, Gwynedd
Presaddfed Burial Chamber, Anglesey
Raglan Castle
Raglan, Monmouthshire, NP15 2BT Tel: 01291-690228
Rhuddlan Castle
Castle Gate, Castle Street, Rhuddlan, Rhyl LL18 5AD
Rug Chapel/Llangar Old Church
c/o Coronation Cottage, Rug, nr Corwen, Denbighshire, LL21
9BT Tel: 01490-412025
Runston Chapel, near Chepstow, Monmouthshire
Segontium Roman Fort & Museum
Llanbeblig Rd, Caernarfon LL55 2LN Tel: 01286-675625
Skenfrith Castle, Monmouthshire
St Cybi's Well, Llangybi, Ll?n Peninsula
St Davids Bishops Palace
St Davids, Pembrokeshire, SA62 6PE Tel: 01437-720517
St Dogmaels Abbey, Ceredigion
St Lythan's Burial Chamber
near St Nicholas, Vale of Glamorgan
St Non's Chapel, St Davids, Pembrokeshire
St Quentin's Castle
Llanblethian, Cowbridge, Vale of Glamorgan
St Seiriol's Well, Penmon, Anglesey
St Winifrid's Chapel and Holy Well
Holywell, Flintshire
Strata Florida Abbey
Ystrad Meurig, Ceredigion, SY25 6BT Tel: 01974-831261
Swansea Castle, Swansea City Centre
Talley Abbey, near Llandeilo, Carmarthenshire
Tinkinswood Burial Chamber
near St Nicholas, Vale of Glamorgan
Tintern Abbey
Tintern, Monmouthshire, NP16 6SE Tel: 01291 689251
Trefignath Burial Chamber, Anglesey
Tregwehelydd Standing Stone, Anglesey
Tretower Court & Castle
Tretower, Crickhowell, Powys, NP8 1RD Tel: 01874-730279
Ty Mawr Standing Stone, Anglesey
Ty Newydd Burial Chamber, Anglesey
Valle Crucis Abbey
Llangollen, Denbighshire, LL20 8DD Tel: 01978-860326
Weobley Castle
Weobley Castle Farm, Llanrhidian, Swansea, SA3 1HB
Tel: 01792-390012
White Castle
Llantilio Crosenny, nr Abergavenny NP7 8UD
Tel: 01600-780380
Wiston Castle, Pembrokeshire

About Historic Scotland *Judith Sandeman*

Historic Scotland is a government agency set up to care for the country's rich built heritage, which spans a period of over 5000 years. It is responsible for protecting ancient monuments, listing buildings and maintaining over 330 properties open to the public. The agency also gives grants to private owners for conservation and repair, and a team of experts carries out technical conservation and is at the forefront of research in this field. There are currently about 8000 scheduled monuments in Scotland, and each year about 380 new sites are added. Most of these lie on private land and Historic Scotland works with owners to help preserve these. Over 47,000 buildings are listed as being of special architectural or historic interest. These comprise dwelling houses (large and small), churches, city terraces, coalmines, factories, shipyards and the Forth Rail Bridge. Gardens and designed landscapes are also included. A few of the well-known properties open to the public are Edinburgh Castle, Stirling Castle, Fort George, Skara Brae and Iona Abbey. About 260 smaller sites, such as standing stones and cairns, are free to visitors. A diverse programme of events takes place at a number of properties throughout the year and free visits for schools offer an important educational opportunity.

For further information check out **www.historic-scotland.gov.uk** or phone **0131 668 8600**. You can also find out about becoming a Friend of Historic Scotland which allows you free entry to all properties as well as other benefits.

Aberdour Castle
Aberdour, Fife, KY3 0SL Tel: 01383-860519
Arbroath Abbey
Arbroath, Angus, DD11 1EG Tel: 01241-878756
Argylls Lodging
Castle Wynd, Stirling, FK8 1EJ Tel: 01786-431319
Balvenie Castle
Dufftown, Keith, Bannfshire, AB55 4GH Tel: 01340-820121
Bishop's and Earl's Palaces
Palace Road, Kirkwall, Orkney, KW15 1PD Tel: 01856-871918
Blackhouse
42 Arnol, Barvas, Isle of Lewis, HS2 9DB Tel: 01851-710395
Blackness Castle
Linlithgow, Lothian, EH8 8ED Tel: 01506 834807
Bonawe Iron Furnace
Taynuilt, Argyll, PA35 1JQ Tel: 01866-822432
Bothwell Castle
Uddingston, Glasgow, G4 0QZ Tel: 01698-816894
Broch of Gurness
Evie, Orkney, KW17 2NH Tel: 01856-751414
Caerlaverock Castle
Glencaple, Dumfries, DG1 4RU Tel: 01387-770244
Cairnpapple Hill
ooLinlithgow Palace, Linlithgow EH49 7AL Tel: 01506-634622
Calanais Vistors Centre
Callanish, Isle of Lewis, HS2 9DY, 01851-621422
Cardoness Castle
Gatehouse of Fleet, DG7 2EH Tel: 01557-814427
Castle Campbell
Dollar, Clackmannanshire, FK14 7PP Tel: 01259-742408
Corgarff Castle
White House, Strathdon AB36 8YL Tel: 01975-651460
Craigmillar Castle
Craigmillar Castle Road, Edinburgh, EH16 4SY Tel: 0131-661-4445
Craignethan Castle
Castle Cottage, Lesmahagow ML11 9PL Tel: 01555-860364
Crichton Castle
Crichton, Pathhead, Midlothian Tel: 01875-320017
Crossraguel Abbey
by Maybole, Ayrshire, KA19 8HQ Tel: 01655-883113
Dallas Dhu Distillery
Mannachie Road, Forres IV36 2RR Tel: 01309-676548
Dirleton Castle
Dirleton, East Lothian, EH39 5ER Tel: 01620-850330
Doune Castle
Castle Road, Doune, FK16 6EA Tel: 01786-841742
Dryburgh Abbey
Dryburgh, St Boswells, Melrose TD6 0RQ Tel: 01835-822381
Duff House
Banff, AB45 3SX Tel: 01261-818181
Dumbarton Castle
Castle Road, Dumbarton, Dunbartonshire, G82 1JJ Tel: 01389 732167
Dundonald Castle
Dundonald, nr Kilmarnock, Ayrshire, KA2 Tel: 01563-851489
Dundrennan Abbey

Dundrennan, Kirkcudbrightshire DG6 4QH Tel: 01557-500262
Dunfermline Palace and Abbey
St Margaret Street, Dunfermline KY12 7PE Tel: 01383-739026
Dunstaffnage Castle
Dunbeg, By Oban, Argyll, PA37 1PZ Tel: 01631-562465
Edinburgh Castle
Castle Hill, Edinburgh, EH1 2NG Tel: 0131 225 9846
Edzell Castle
Edzell, By Brechin, Angus, DD9 7DA Tel: 01356-648631
Elcho Castle
Rhynd, by Perth, PH2 8QQ Tel: 01738-639998
Elgin Cathedral
Elgin, Morayshire, IV30 1HU Tel: 01343-547171
Fort George
By Ardersier, Inverness, IV1 2TD Tel: 01667-462777
Glasgow Cathedral
Cathedral Square, Glasgow, G4 0QZ Tel: 0141-552-6891
Glenluce Abbey
Glenluce, Newton Stewart DG8 0AF Tel: 01581-300541
Hermitage Castle
Newcastleton, Hawick, TD9 0LU Tel: 01387-376222
Huntingtower Castle
Huntingtower, Perth, PH1 3JR Tel: 01738 627231
Huntly Castle
Huntly, Aberdeenshire, AB54 4SH Tel: 01466 793191
Inchcolm Abbey
Incholm Island, Firth of Forth, (c/o GPO Aberdour), Fife, KY3 0UA Tel: 01383-823332
Inchmahome Priory
Port of Menteith, by Kippen, Stirlingshire, FK8 3RA Tel: 01877-385294
Jarlshof Prehistoric and Norse Settlement
Sumburgh, Shetland, ZE3 9JN Tel: 01950-460112
Jedburgh Abbey
4/5 Abbey Bridgend, Jedburgh TD8 6JQ Tel: 01835-863925
Kildrummy Castle
Kildrummy by Alford, Aberdeenshire Tel: 01975-571331
Kinnaird Head Castle Lighthouse
Stevenson Road, Fraserburgh, AB43 9DU Tel: 01346-511022
Linlithgow Palace
Linlithgow, Lothian, EH49 7AL Tel: 01506-842896
Lochleven Castle
Kinross, Tayside, KY13 7AR Tel: 07778-040483
MacLellans Castle
24 High Street, Kirkcudbright, DG6 4JD Tel: 01557-331856
Maes Howe
Stenness, near Stromness, Orkney, KW16 3HA Tel: 01856-761606
Meigle Museum
Dundee Road, Meigle, Perthshire, PH12 8SB Tel: 01828-640612
Melrose Abbey
Abbey Street, Melrose, TD6 9LG Tel: 01896-822562
New Abbey Cornmill
New Abbey, Dumfries, DG2 8BX Tel: 01387-850260
Newark Castle
Castle Road, Port Glasgow, PA14 5NH Tel: 01475-741858
Rothesay Castle
Rothesay, Isle of Bute, PA20 0DA Tel: 01700-502691
Seton Collegiate Church
Longniddry, East Lothian, EH32 0BG Tel: 01875-813334
Skara Brae
Sandwick, Orkney, KW16 3LR Tel: 01856-841815
Smailholm Tower
Smailholm, Kelso, TD5 7PQ Tel: 01573-460365
Spynie Palace
near Elgin, Morayshire, IV30 5QG Tel: 01343-546358
St Andrews Castle
The Scores, St Andrews, Fife, KY16 9AR Tel: 01334-477196
St Andrews Cathedral
The Pends, St Andrews, Fife, KY16 9QL Tel: 01334-472563
Stirling Castle
Castle Wynd, Stirling, FK8 1EJ Tel: 01786-431316
Sweetheart Abbey
New Abbey, by Dumfries, DG2 8BU Tel: 01387-850397
Tantallon Castle
North Berwick, East Lothian, EH39 5PN Tel: 01620-892727
Threave Castle
Castle Douglas, Kirkcudbrightshire, DG7 1RX Tel: 0411-223101
Tolquhon Castle
Tarves, Aberdeenshire, AB4 0LP Tel: 01650-851286
Urquhart Castle
by Drumnadrochit, Inverness-shire, IV3 2XJ Tel: 01456-450551
Whithorn Priory
6 Bruce Street, Whithorn, Wigtownshire, DG8 8PY Tel: 01988-500508

A Just Measure of Pain?
Louise Connell
Curator
The Galleries of Justice, Nottingham

GALLERIES
of JUSTICE

There can be few museums where that sense of reaching out and touching the past is as intense as at the Galleries of Justice. Located in the heart of Nottingham's historic Lace Market, this award-winning museum is housed in the Shire Hall, comprising the former County Court and Gaol. Over the centuries, thousands of people would have entered this building with a deep sense of dread, uncertain of their fate. Even today, visitors are invited to 'feel the fear' as they explore the labyrinth of passages, tunnels and cells, meeting warders and prisoners who explain the chilling history of the site.

The Galleries of Justice sits high on a cliff on one of the oldest thoroughfares in Nottingham. It was here that the old Anglo-Saxon settlement of Snottingham (literally, the place of Snott, the local chieftain) grew up in the 7th and 8th centuries. Following the Norman invasion, the power base shifted to Nottingham Castle, a short distance across town. Nevertheless, the Shire Hall complex remained an important legal and political stronghold, with Assize Courts and Quarter Sessions held here since at least 1375. The judges, who symbolised the Monarch's power, would arrive from London with great pageantry, delivering swift and often merciless justice. In January 1832, following Nottingham's Reform Bill Riots, the judges were met by the High Sheriff of Nottingham with his javelin men and bailiffs in full regalia, and accompanied into town by "over 1000 gentlemen on horseback". The judges, Gazelee and Littledale, spent ten days in Nottingham, and by the end of the trial, three men had been sentenced to hang, on the flimsiest of evidence. If the people of Nottingham needed to be taught a lesson, the King had certainly succeeded. The men were hanged together on the steps of the court watched by a sympathetic crowd. Evidence of their agonising death can still be seen in the grooves cut into the steps to hold the temporary scaffold.

The earliest-known illustration of the Shire Hall from 1741 shows a ruinous medieval building, with two courts on the first floor for civil and criminal cases. In 1724, the floor of the criminal court collapsed and several people fell into the cellars below. Convinced of foul play, the Judge cried out "A plot! A plot!" The consternation soon being over, the court proceeded to business. In 1770-72, it was replaced by an elegant Neo-Classical building designed by

The Galleries of Justice
Nottingham
©Galleries of Justice

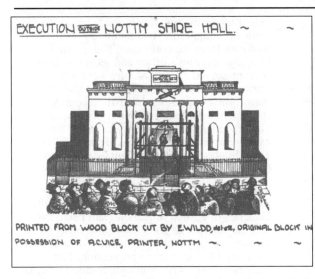

EXECUTION OUTSIDE NOTTM SHIRE HALL. ~

PRINTED FROM WOOD BLOCK CUT BY E.WILDD, detroit, ORIGINAL BLOCK IN POSSESSION OF A.C.VICE, PRINTER, NOTTM ~.

hither."

Records now held in Nottinghamshire Archives show that most of the long-term inmates held at the County Gaol were debtors, with separate living quarters and a greater degree of freedom. The remaining prisoners were those awaiting the outcome of their sentence - transportation to Australia, or execution — or petty criminals doing short stretches. Had you been a prisoner in 1828, you may have encountered John Shipley, 21, sentenced to death for stealing a sheep valued at 10 shillings. Nicholas Cousins, aged 37, was transported for life for stealing one pair of leather reins and George Dickenson, aged 22, was also transported for life for stealing a wallet worth sixpence.

London architect James Gandon. A century later, the interior was completely remodeled after a disastrous fire by Thomas Chambers Hine, the Nottingham architect also responsible for renovating Nottingham Castle. These fine oak-panelled courtrooms closed as working courts in 1986.

Seventeen steps lead from the dock in the Criminal Court to the holding cells below. The Victorian splendour of the courtroom is in complete contrast to these dark, squalid cells, which remain very much as they would have appeared to prison reformer John Howard when he visited in the 1780s. Howard was shocked at the conditions he found, with his severest criticism reserved for *"two dark and offensive dungeons, down thirty-six steps, called pits, which are never whitewashed Another dungeon in 1787 was occupied by a man sentenced to two years solitary confinement."* One can barely imagine the horrors these prisoners had to endure.

Shortly after the nationalisation of the prison service in 1878, the gaol was closed. Efforts over the years to improve conditions had left their mark, however. A new wing was built in 1833 to ease overcrowding and gas lighting in all cells was introduced in the mid-1850s. A chaplain and surgeon attended to the prisoners' spiritual and physical well-being, and efforts were made to teach prisoners to read and write. Later, following the lead from larger penal institutions, a separate system was introduced, bringing order and discipline in the spirit of mid-Victorian reform. In 1853, the Governor reported that, *"I think the system of separation and work lately introduced is much more calculated than the old system to deter prisoners from future crime, and deter their friends and companions from following them*

The stories that emerge from the history of the gaol are personal tragedies. In 1828, Susannah Watson was sentenced to 14 years transportation for stealing food and clothes. In her defence, Susannah pleaded poverty, saying she had six children to feed and her husband was serving a nine months sentence for poaching. Nevertheless, the Recorder declared *"it would be beneficial to the children to have her removed from the country "*. Whilst in gaol, Susannah's two-year old son William died. The fate of the rest of her children is not known. Stories like Susannah's, and the other unfortunates who spent time here, are not forgotten, and are now central to our understanding of the building, and how this is communicated to the visitor.

The Galleries of Justice Experience

An interactive approach to interpretation is central to the Galleries of Justice philosophy. The visitor is encouraged to imaginatively identify with those who had the misfortune to be on the wrong side of the law. What was it really like? How could I stand it if it were me? To encourage this sense of connection with the past, all visitors on the Crime and Punishment tour — the old court and gaol - are issued with a personal prisoner number, linking them with these historical characters and former inmates.

The fabric of the building holds secrets that are unlocked as the visitor explores: costumed interpreters act out the roles of cantankerous judge, turnkey, Victorian prison warder and female prisoner, the latter forever condemned to wash sheets in the prison laundry. In the prison exercise yard, scratches on the wall reveal the names of past prisoners, and marks count off the days of their sentence. The phrase 'Cast for Death' and 'Condemned for House Breaking' appear, reminders of a time where straying outside the law had serious and deadly consequences.

The authenticity of the experience is a key factor in the success of the Galleries of Justice. A year after the Galleries opened in 1995, it was awarded the prestigious Gulbenkian Prize (a European-wide award for visitor attractions), and in 2000 received a nomination for European Museum of the Year, as well as winning Visitor Attraction of the Year, English Tourist Board's "Tourism Oscars". The building was rescued from picturesque dilapidation in the early 1990s by the Lace Market Heritage Trust, who raised £3.5 million for the project. The Trust recognised the uniqueness of the site, with its magnificent 18th century façade untouched Victorian courtrooms and a hellish prison attached, complete with medieval cellars and 17th century pits. A sensitive conversion ensured that these elements were preserved in virtually their original state.

Since then, the Galleries of Justice has further developed to fully justify its role as the nation's only museum of law, with collections and study resources to match. In 1998, the museum embarked on an ambitious £5.5 million development programme, partly funded by the Heritage Lottery. This led to ambitious new developments, culminating in the creation of several new exhibition spaces, including a gallery exploring law in our everyday lives, a temporary exhibition space and the opening up of the women's wing of the Victorian prison.

The former Police Station next door, built in 1905, was transformed into the Police exhibition, providing much-needed space to show off some of the two hundred police uniforms from the collection. The original Custody Sergeant's office and reception have been preserved exactly as they were when the station closed in 1986, and old lags revisiting their former haunts would easily recognise the stark cells with their original graffiti. Modern visitors to the station literally have an 'arresting' experience as they arrive and are placed under arrest by the Custody Sergeant — one of the Galleries' team of on-site actors.

The cells and courts are excellent spaces for learning about crime and punishment, and the Galleries of Justice education team make sure that they are put to good use. Since many of our visitors are school children, education activities are geared towards crime prevention. The Galleries works with Nottinghamshire Police on Burglary Reduction initiatives for all age groups: Primary school children learn about the pitfalls of Burglar Bill, while Secondary school groups act out the trial of Robbie Hood, a young offender accused of burglary and criminal damage. RED, the Galleries' most ambitious project to date, works with young offenders on a ten-week course which aims to reform behaviour by making the young people acknowledge and understand the emotional consequence of their actions.

Role play is central to many of the activities that schools are offered. Mock Trials include

© Galleries of Justice Nottingham

Victorian Children on Trial, Long Live King Ludd, about Nottingham machine-breakers, and the trial of Darren Burton, the 1980s graffiti artist, and are acted out by pupils in an authentic courtroom environment. With the rise of Citizenship teaching in schools, in September 2001 the Galleries became the National Centre for Citizenship and the Law and launched Citizens'Zone, an interactive environment for young people to explore issues around protest, speaking out and human rights. Comparisons with the past are integral to the learning experience. The Galleries' approach is summarised in its mission statement:

"Learn about the past
Act in the present
Change the future ".

The Wolfson Resource Centre

The Galleries of Justice has a commitment to learning and historical exploration at all levels. In addition to lively and interactive interpretation and education programmes, the recently-opened Wolfson Resource Centre at the Galleries has well-equipped research facilities for anybody interested in the history of law, policing, and crime and punishment in general. Here, you can discover a wide range of historical documents, including personal letters of legal personalities and criminals, legal documents, transportation records, photographs, newspaper clippings and a significant rare book collection related to all aspects of law. As well as historical and contemporary books, CD ROMS, videos and teaching aids are available for study. Key collections include:

Probation and Reform - The Rainer Foundation Archive

This important collection dates from the 1820s to 1997 and contains a wide variety of material including letters, minute books and photographs of the London Police Court Mission, the forerunner of the probation service. The collection also contains a wealth of material related to reform institutions such as The Associated Societies for the Protection of Women and Children; the School of Discipline; and the London Female Preventive and Reformatory Institutions.

Arrests and trials

The archive holds criminal identification books of Nottinghamshire criminals from the late 1800s; material related to famous cases including Great Train Robbery photographs and forensic evidence; legal papers and personal letters of the murder case against John Lee 'the man they couldn't hang' from 1883; and unique scrapbooks with original documents and photographs from the

Nuremberg International War Tribunal. Also, material related to Sir Norman Birkett documenting his legal and political life, as an MP for East Nottingham, advocate and alternate judge at Nuremberg.

The Wolfson Resource Centre is open weekdays, 10 a.m to 4 p.m. and is a free service, by appointment only. For researchers unable to visit the Resource Centre, Galleries' staff can assist in family history and other research topics, although a fee is charged for this service. If you would like further information about our collections, information about planning a visit to the Galleries of Justice, or wish to make an appointment to use the Resource Centre, please contact the Librarian/Archivist, or visit our website at www.galleriesofjustice.org.uk.

Librarian/Archivist
Galleries of Justice
Shire Hall
High Pavement
Lace Market
Nottingham
NG1 lHN
Tel: 0115 952 0555
Fax: 0115 993 9828
email beverley.bakergalleriesofjustice.org.uk

© Galleries of Justice Nottingham

Museums

National Collections

The Battlefields Trust
33 High Green, Brooke, Norwich, NR15 1HR Tel: 01508
558145 Email: Battlefield.trust@aol.com WWW:
www.battlefieldstrust.com

The Boat Museum & David Owen Waterways Archive
South Pier Road, Ellesmere Port, CH65 4FW Tel: 0151-355-
5017 Fax: 0151-355-4079 Email:
boatmuseum@easynet.co.uk Records relating to the
management, maintenance and operation of inland
waterways in England, Scotland and Wales. Substantial
Waterways library. Date range: late 17th century to 20th
century.

British Red Cross Museum & Archives
9 Grosvenor Crescent, London, SW1X 7EJ
Tel: 020-7201-5153 Fax: 020-7235-0876
Email: enquiry@redcross.org.uk Web: www.redcross.org.uk

Cable & Wireless Archive & Museum of Submarine Telegraphy
Eastern House,, Porthcurno, Penzance, TR19 6JX Tel:
01736 810478 Tel: 01736 810811 Fax: 01736 810640 Email:
info@tunnels.demon.co.uk WWW: www.porthcurno.org.uk
Housed in one of Porthcurno's former telegraph station
buildings, and adjacent to the Museum of Submarine
Telegraphy, the archive is a unique resource for learning
about: the history of Porthcurno

Commonwealth War Graves Commission
Information Services, 2 Marlow Road, Maidenhead,
Berkshire, SL6 7DX Tel: 01628-634221 Fax: 01628-771208

Department of Manuscripts and Special Collections
Hallward Library, Nottingham University , University Park,
Nottingham, NG7 2RD Tel: 0115 951 4565 Fax: 0115 951
4558 Email: mss-library@nottingham.ac.uk WWW:
www.mss.library.nottingham.ac.uk

The Library & Museum of Freemasonry
Freemasons' Hall, 60 Great Queen Street, London, WC2B
5AZ Tel: (020) 7395 9257

Imperial War Museum
Lambeth Road, London, SE1 6HZ Tel: 020-7416-5348
Fax: 020-7416-5246 Email: books@iwm.org.uk
Web: www.iwm.org.uk

Isles of Scilly Museum
Church Street, St Mary's, Isles of Scilly, TR21 0JT
Tel: 01720-422337

Labour History Archive and Study Centre
103 Princess Street, Manchester, M1 6DD Tel: 0161-228-
7212 Fax: 0161-237-5965 Email: archives@nmlhweb.org
lhasc@fs1.li.man.ac.uk WWW: http://rylibweb.man.ac.uk

Museums Association
42 Clerkenwell Close, London, EC1R 0PA
Tel: 020-7250-1789 Fax: 020-7250-1929

The National Coal Mining Museum for England
Caphouse Colliery, New Road, Overton, Wakefield, West
Yorkshire, WF4 4RH Tel: 01924-848806
Fax: 01924-840694 Email: info@ncm.org.uk
Web: www.ncm.org.uk

National Dragonfly Museum
Ashton Mill, Ashton, Peterborough, PE8 5LB
Tel: 01832-272427 Email: ndmashton@aol.com
Web: www.natdragonflymuseum.org.uk

National Gallery
St. Vincent House, 30 Orange Street, London, WC2H 7HH
Tel: 020-7747-5950

National Maritime Museum
Romney Road, Greenwich, London, SE1O 9NF
Tel: 020-8858-4422 Fax: 020-8312-6632
Web: www.nmm.ac.uk

National Maritime Museum Memorial Index
National Maritime Museum, Greenwich, London, SE10 9NF
Tel: 020-8858-4422 Fax: 020-8312-4422
Email: manuscripts@nmm.ac.uk Web: www.nmm.ac.uk

National Museum of Photography, Film & Television
Bradford, West Yorkshire, BD1 1NQ Tel: 01274-202030
Fax: 01274-723155 Web: http:www.nmpft.org.uk

National Portrait Gallery
2 St. Martins Place, London, WC2H 0HE
Tel: 020-7306-0055 Fax: 020-7206-0058
Web: www.npg.org.uk

Natural History Museum
Cromwell Rd, London, SW7 5BD Tel: (020) 7938 9238 Fax:
020 7938 9290 WWW: http://www.nhm.ac.uk

National Railway Museum
Leeman Road, York, YO26 4XJ Tel: 01904-621261
Fax: 01904-611112 Email: nrm@nmsi.ac.uk
Web: www.nrm.org.uk

National Waterways Museum
Llanthony Warehouse, Gloucester Docks, Gloucester, GL1
2EH Tel: 01452-318054 Fax: 01452-318066
Email: curatorial1@nwm.demon.co.uk
Web: www.nwm.demon.uk

North West Sound Archive
Old Steward's Office, Clitheroe Castle, Clitheroe,
Lancashire, BB7 1AZ Tel: 01200-427897
Fax: 01200-427897 Web: www.nw-soundarchive.co.uk

Royal Armouries (Leeds)
Armouries Drive, Leeds, West Yorkshire, LS10 1LT
Tel: 0990-106666

Royal Armouries (Tower of London)
HM Tower Of London, Tower Hill, London, EC3N 4AB
Tel: (020) 7480 -6358 Ext 30 Fax: (020) 7481 2922

The Science Museum
Exhibition Road, London, SW7 2DD Tel: 0870-870-4868
Email: sciencemuseum@nms.ac.uk

Victoria & Albert Museum
Cromwell Road, South Kensington, London, SW7 2RL
Tel: 020-7942-2164 Fax: 020-7942-2162

Regional Museums Organisations

The South West Museums Council
Hestercombe House, Cheddon Fitzpaine, Taunton, Somerset,
TA2 8LQ Tel: 01823-259696 Fax: 01823-413114
Email: robinbourne@swmuseums.co.uk

West Midlands Regional Museums Council
Hanbury Road, Stoke Prior, Bromsgrove, Worcestershire,
B60 4AD Tel: 01527-872258 Fax: 01527-576960
Email: wmrmc@btinternet.com

Yorkshire & Humberside Museums Council
Farnley Hall Hall Lane, Leeds, West Yorkshire
LS12 5HA Tel: 0113-263-8909

England

Bath & North East Somerset
Roman Baths Museum
Abbey Churchyard, Bath, BA1 1LZ Tel: 01225-477773
Fax: 01225-477243

Bedfordshire
Bedford Museum
Castle Lane, Bedford MK40 3XD Tel: 01234-353323
Bedford Museum Bedfordshire Yeomanry
Castle Lane, Bedford, Bedfordshire, MK40 3XD
Tel: 01234 353323 Fax: 01234 273401
Bedfordshire and Hertfordshire Regimental Museum
Luton Museum, Wardown Park, Luton LU2 7HA
Tel: 01582 546719
Cecil Higgins Art Gallery
Castle Close, Castle Lane, Bedford MK40 3RP
Tel: 01234-211222 Fax: 01234-327149
Elstow Moot Hall
Elstow, Bedford, Bedfordshire, MK42 9XT
Tel: 01234-266889 Tel: 01234-228330 Fax: 01234-228531
Email: wilemans@deed.bedfordshire.gov.uk
Web: www.bedfordshire.gov.uk
Luton Museum & Art Gallery
Wardown Park, Old Bedford Road, Luton LU2 7HA
Tel: 01582-546725 Email: adeye@luton.gov.uk

Shuttleworth (Flying) Collection
Old Warden Aerodrome, Old Warden, Biggleswade, SG18
9ER Tel: 01767-627288 Fax: 01767-626229
Email: collection@shuttleworth.org Web: www.shuttleworth.org
John Dony Field Centre
Hancock Drive, Bushmead, Luton, Bedfordshire LU2 7SF
Tel: 01582-486983

Berkshire
The Museum of Berkshire Aviation Trust
Mohawk Way, off Bader Way, Woodley, Reading, RG5 4UE
Tel: 0118 944 8089 Email:
museumofberkshireaviation@fly.to WWW:
http://fly.to/museumofberkshireaviation
Blake's Lock Museum
Gasworks Road, Reading RG1 3DS Tel: 0118-939-0918
Duke of Edinburgh's Royal Regiment (Berks & Wilts) Museum
The Wardrobe, 58 The Close, Salisbury, SP1 2EX
Tel: 01722-414536
Household Cavalry Museum
Combermere Barracks, Windsor, Berkshire
Tel: 01753-755112 Fax: 01753-755112
Museum of Reading
Town Hall, Blagave Street, Reading, Berkshire, RG1 1OH
Tel: 0118-939-9800 Web: www.readingmuseum.org.uk
R.E.M.E. Museum of Technology
Isaac Newton Road, Arborfield, Reading, Berkshire, RG2
9NJ Tel: 0118-976-3567 Fax: 0118-976-3563
Email: reme-museum@gtnet.gov.uk
Web: www.eldred.demon.co.uk/reme-museum/index.htm
Royal Berkshire Yeomanry Cavalry Museum
T A Centre, Bolton Road, Windsor, Berkshire, SL4 3JG
Tel: 01753-860600
Slough Museum
278-286 High Street, Slough SL1 1NB Tel: 01753-526422
West Berkshire Museum
The Wharf, Newbury, Berkshire, RG14 5AS
Tel: 01635-30511

Bristol
Ashton Court Visitor Centre
Ashton Court, Long Ashton, Bristol, BS41 8JN
Tel: 0117-963-9174
Blaise Castle House Museum
Henbury, Bristol, BS10 7QS Tel:)117-950-6789
Bristol City Museum & Art Gallery
Queens Road, Bristol, BS8 1RL Tel: 0117-922-3571
Fax: 0117-922-2047
Email: general_museums@bristol-city.gov.uk
Web: www.bristol-city.gov.uk/museums
Bristol Industrial Museum
Princes Wharf, Wapping Road, Bristol, BS1 4RN
Tel: 0117-925-1470
Bristol Maritime Heritage Centre
Wapping Wharf, Gasferry Road, Bristol, BS1 6TY
Tel: 0117-926-0680
Clevedon Story Heritage Centre
Waterloo House, 4 The Beach, Clevedon, Bristol, BS21 7QU
Tel: 01275-341196
Clifton Suspension Bridge Visitor Centre
Bridge House, Sion Place, Bristol, BS8 4AP
Tel: 0117-974-4664 Fax: 0117-974-5255
Email: visitinfo@clifton-suspension-bridge.org.uk
Web: www.clifton-suspension-bridge.org.uk
Exploratory Hands on Science Centre
Bristol Old Station, Temple Meads, Bristol, BS1 6QU
Tel: 0117-907-9000
Georgian House, Bristol
7 Great George Street, Bristol, BS1 5RR
Tel: 0117-921-1362
Harveys Wine Museum
12 Denmark Street, Bristol, BS1 5DQ Tel: 0117-927-5036
Fax: 0117-927-5001 Email: alun.cox@adweu.com
Web: www.j-harvey.co.uk
Red Lodge
Park Row, Bristol, BS1 5LJ Tel: 0117-921-1360
Web: www.bristol-city.gov.uk/museums

Buckinghamshire
Amersham Local History Museum
49 High Street, Amersham, Buckinghamshire, HP7 0DP
Tel: 01494-725754 Fax: 01494-725754
Bletchley Park Trust
The Mansion, Bletchley Park, Bletchley, Milton Keynes,
MK3 6EB Tel: 01908-640404 Fax: 01908-274381
Email: jcgallehawk@bletchleypark.org.uk
Web: www.bletchleypark.org.uk
The Blue Max
Wycombe Air Park, Booker, Marlow
SL7 3DP Tel: 01494-449810
Buckinghamshire County Museum
Church Street, Aylesbury, Buckinghamshire, HP20 2QP
Tel: 01296-331441 Fax: 01296-334884
Email: museums@buckscc.gov.uk
Chesham Town Museum Project
Chesham Library, Elgiva Lane, Chesham HP5 2JD
Tel: 01494-783183
Chiltern Open Air Museum
Newland Park, Gorelands Lane, Chalfont St. Giles
HP8 4AB Tel: 01494-871117 Fax: 01494-872774
Milton Keynes Museum
Stacey Hill Farm, Southern Way, Wolverton, Milton Keynes,
MK12 5EJ Tel: 01908-316222
Royal Army Education Corps Museum
HQ Beaconsfield Station, Wilton Park, Beaconsfield,
Buckinghamshire, HP9 2RP Tel: 01494 683232
Wycombe Museum
Priory Avenue, High Wycombe HP13 6PX
Tel: 01494-421895 Fax: 01494-421897
Email: enquiries@wycombemuseum.demon.co.uk
Web: www.wycombe.gov.uk/museum

Cambridgeshire
Museum of Classical Archaeology
Sidgwick Avenue, Cambridge, CB3 9DA Tel: 01223 335153
WWW: www.classics.cam.ac.uk/ark.html/, Open 10.00.a.m.-
5.00.p.m. Mon-Fri Year round also 10.00.a.m.-1.00.p.m.
Term Time Admission Free
Cambridge Brass Rubbing
The Round Church, Bridge St, Cambridge, Cambridgeshire,
CB2 1UB Tel: 01223-871621
Cambridge Museum of Technology
Old Pumping Station, Cheddars Lane, Cambridge,
Cambridgeshire, CB5 8LD Tel: 01223-368650
Cambridgeshire Regimental Collection
Ely Museum, The Old Goal, Market Street, Ely,
Cambridgeshire, CB7 4LS Tel: 01353-666655
The Denny Farmland Museum
Denny Abbey, Ely Road, Waterbeach, Cambridge,
Cambridgeshire, CB5 9PQ Tel: 01223-860988
Fax: 01223-860988 Email: f.h.denny@tesco.net
Web: www.dennyfarmlandmuseum.org.uk
Duxford Displays Ltd
Duxford Airfield, Duxford, Cambridge, Cambridgeshire,
CB2 4QR Tel: 01223-836593
Ely Museum
The Old Gaol, Market Street, Ely CB7 4LS
Tel: 01353-666655
Fenland & West Norfolk Aviation Museum
Lynn Road, West Walton, Wisbech PE14 7
Tel: 01945-584440
Folk Museum
2 Castle Street, Cambridge CB3 0AQ Tel: 01223-355159
Imperial War Museum
Fighter Collection
Duxford Airfield, Duxford, Cambridge, CB2 4QR
Tel: 01223-834973, 01223-835000 Fax: 01223-836956
March & District Museum
March & District Museum Society, High Street, March,
Cambridgeshire, PE15 9JJ Tel: 01354-655300
Nene Valley Railway
Wansford Station, Peterborough, PE8 6LR Tel: 01780 782833
Norris Library & Museum
The Broadway, St Ives, Cambridgeshire, PE27 5BX
Tel: 01480-497314 Email: norris.st-ives-tc@co-net.com

Octavia Hill Birthplace Museum Trust
1 South Brink Place, WisbechPE13 1JE Tel: 01945-476358
Peterborough Museum & Art Gallery
Priestgate, Peterborough, Cambridgeshire, PE1 1LF
Tel: 01733-343329 Fax: 01733-341928
Email: museums@peterborough.gov.uk
Prickwillow Drainage Engine Museum
Main Street, Prickwillow, Ely CB7 4UN Tel: 01353-688360
Ramsey Rural Museum
The Woodyard, Wood Lane, Ramsey, Huntingdon,
Cambridgeshire, PE17 1XD Tel: 01487-815715
Sedgwick Museum
University of Cambridge, Downing Street, Cambridge,
CB2 3EQ Tel: 01223-333456 Email: mgd2@esc.cam.ac.uk
Wisbech & Fenland Museum
Museum Square, Wisbech PE13 1ES Tel: 01945-583817
Fax: 01945-589050 Email: wisbechmuseum.@beeb.net
Duxford Aviation Society
Duxford Airfield, Duxford CB2 4QR Tel: 01223-835594

Cheshire
Catalyst
Gossage Building, Mersey Road, Widnes, Cheshire, WA8
0DF Tel: 0151-420-1121
Cheshire Military Museum (Cheshire Regiment)
The Castle, Chester, Cheshire, CH1 2DN Tel: 01244-327617
Chester Heritage Centre - Closed August 2000
St. Michaels Church, Bridge Street, Chester CH1 1NQ
The Boat Museum & David Owen Waterways Archive
South Pier Road, Ellesmere Port, CH65 4FW Tel: 0151-355-
5017 Email: boatmuseum@easynet.co.uk Records relating
to the management, maintenance and operation of inland
waterways inE ngland, Scotland and Wales. Substantial
Waterways library. Date range: late 17th century to 20th
century
Grosvenor Museum
27 Grosvenor Street, Chester CH1 2DD Tel: 01244-402008
Fax: 01244-347587 Email: s.rogers@chestercc.gov.uk
Web: www.chestercc.gov.uk/heritage/museum
Lion Salt Works Trust
Ollershaw Lane, Marston, Northwich CW9 6ES
Tel: 01606-41823 Fax: 01606-41823
Email: afielding@lionsalt.demon.co.uk
Web: www.lionsaltworkstrust.co.uk
Macclesfield Museums
Heritage Centre, Roe Street, Macclesfield, Cheshire, SK11
6UT Tel: 01625-613210 Fax: 01625-617880
Email: postmaster@silk-macc.u-net.com
Nantwich Museum
Pillory Street, Nantwich, CW5 5BQ Tel: 01270-627104
Norton Priory Museum Trust Ltd
Tudor Road, Manor Park, Runcorn WA7 1SX
Tel: 01928-569895
On The Air
42 Bridge St Row, Chester CH1 1NN Tel: 01244-348468
Paradise Mill
Park Lane, Macclesfield SK11 6TJ Tel: 01625-618228
Warrington Museum & Art Gallery
Bold Street, Warrington WA1 1JG Tel: 01925-442392
West Park Museum
Prestbury Road, Macclesfield SK10 3BJ Tel: 01625-619831
Wirral Archives Service and Museum
Birkenhead Town Hall, Hamilton Street, Birkenhead, CH41
5BR Tel: 0151-666-4010 Fax: 0151-666-3965
Email: archives@wirral-libraries.net

Cleveland
Captain Cook & Staithes Heritage Centre
High Street, Staithes, Saltburn-by-the-Sea TS13 5BQ
Tel: 01947-841454
Captain Cook Birthplace Museum
Stewart Park, Marton, Middlesbrough TS7 8AT
Tel: 01642-311211
Dorman Musuem
Linthorpe Road, Middlesbrough TS5 6LA Tel: 01642-813781
Green Dragon Museum
Theatre Yard, High St, Stockton-on-Tees, Cleveland, TS18
1AT Tel: 01642-393938

Margrove Heritage Centre
Margrove Park, Boosbeck, Saltburn-by-the-Sea TS12 3BZ
Tel: 01287-610368 Fax: 01287-610368
North East Mills Group
Research into wind and water mills in NE England
Blackfriars, Monk Street, Newcastle upon Tyne, NE1 4XN
Tel: 0191-232-9279 Fax: 0191-230-1474
WWW: www.welcome.to/North.East.Mill.Group
Preston Hall Museum
Yarm Road, Stockton-On-Tees TS18 3RH
Tel: 01642-781184
Stockton on Tees Museums & Gallery Service
Gloucester House, Church Road Cleveland, TS18 1YB
Tel: 01642-393983 Fax: 01642-393983

Cornwall
Automobilia
The Old Mill, Terras Rd, St. Austell PL26 7RX
Tel: 01726-823092
Bodmin Museum
Mount Folly, Bodmin PL31 2DB Tel: 01208-77067
Cable & Wireless Archive & Museum of Submarine Telegraphy
Eastern House,, Porthcurno, St. Levan, Penzance, Cornwall,
TR19 6 Tel: 01736-810478/810811 Fax: 01736-810640
Email: mary.godwin@plc.cwplc.com
WWW: www.porthcurno.org.uk
Charlestown Shipwreck & Heritage Centre
Quay Road, Charlestown, St. Austell, Cornwall, PL25 3NX
Tel: 01726-69897 Fax: 01726-68025
Duke of Cornwall's Light Infantry Museum
The Keep, Bodmin, Cornwall, PL31 1EG Tel: 01208-72810
Helston Folk Museum
Market Place, Helston, Cornwall, TR13 8TH
Tel: 01326-564027 Email: enquiries@helstonmuseum.org.uk
WWW: www.helstonmuseum.org.uk
John Betjeman Centre
Southern Way, Wadebridge PL27 7BX Tel: 01208-812392
Lanreath Folk & Farm Museum
Lanreath, Nr Looe PL13 2NX Tel: 01503-220321
Lawrence House Museum
c/o Lawrence House, 9 Castle Street, Launceston, Cornwall,
PL15 8BA Tel: 01566-773277
Maritime Museum Penzance
19 Chapel Street, Penzance TR18 4AW Tel: 01736-368890
Merlin's Cave Crystal Mineral & Fossil Museum & Shop
Molesworth Street, Tintagel PL34 0BZ Tel: 01840-770023
Mevagissey Museum Society
Frazier Ho, The Quay, Mevagissey, St. Austell, Cornwall
PL26 6QU Tel: 01726-843568
National Maritime Museum (Falmouth Cornwall)
48 Arwenack Street, Falmouth TR11 3SA
Tel: 01326-313388
National Maritime Museum (Saltash Cornwall)
Cotehele Quay, Cotehele, Saltash PL12 6TA
Tel: 01579-350830
Penryn Museum
Town Hall, Higher Market Street, Penryn TR10 8LT
Tel: 01326-372158 Fax: 01326-373004
Potter's Museum of Curiosity
Jamaica Inn Courtyard, Bolventor, Launceston, Cornwall,
PL15 7TS Tel: 01566-86838 Fax: 01566-86838
Royal Cornwall Museum
River Street, Truro, Cornwall, TR1 2SJ Tel: 01872-272205

County Durham
Bowes Museum
Newgate, Barnard Castle DL12 8NP Tel: 01833-690606
Darlington Museum & Art Gallery - Closed
Collection dispersed throughout other agencies in
Darlington, Tubwell Row, Darlington DL1 1PD
Tel: 01325-463795
Darlington Railway Centre & Museum
North Road Station , Station Road, Darlington, DL3 6ST
Tel: 01325-460532
Darlington Railway Preservation Society
Station Road, Hopetown, Darlington DL3 6ST
Tel: 01325-483606

Discovery Centre
Grosvenor House, 29 Market Place, Bishop Auckland
DL14 7NP Tel: 01388-662666 Fax: 01388-661941
Email: west.durham@groundwork.org.uk
Durham Arts
Library and Museums Department, County Hall, Durham,
County Durham, DH1 5TY Tel: 0191-383-3595
Durham Heritage Centre
St Mary le Bow, North Bailey, Durham DH1 5ET
Durham Light Infantry Museum
Aykley Heads, Durham, DH1 5TU Tel: 0191-384-2214
Fax: 0191-386-1770 Email: dli@durham.gov.uk
Durham Mining Museum
Easington Colliery Welfare, Memorial Road, Easington
Tel: 07931 421709 WWW: www.dmm.org.uk
Durham University Library Archives & Special Collections
Palace Green Section, Palace Green, Durham, DH1 3RN
Tel: 0191-374-3032 Email: pg.library@durham.ac.uk
Fulling Mill Museum of Archaeology
The Banks, Durham, County Durham
Killhope Lead Mining Centre
Cowshill, Weardale, County Durham, DL13 1AR
Tel: 01388-537505 Fax: 01388-537617
Email: killhope@durham.gov.uk
 WWW: www.durham.gov.uk/killhope/index.htm
North East Mills Group
 Blackfriars, Monk Street, Newcastle upon Tyne, NE1 4XN
Tel: 0191-232-9279 Fax: 0191-230-1474
 WWW: www.welcome.to/North.East.Mill.Group
Timothy Hackworth Victorian & Railway Museum
Shildon DL4 1PQ Tel: 01388-777999 Fax: 01388-777999
Weardale Museum
South View, 2 Front Street, Ireshopeburn, County Durham,
DL13 1EY Tel: 01388-537417

Cumbria
Aspects of Motoring Western Lakes Motor Museum
The Maltings, The Maltings, Brewery Lane, Cockermouth,
Cumbria, CA13 9ND Tel: 01900-824448
Border Regiment & Kings Own Royal Border Regt Museum
Queen Mary's Tower, The Castle, Carlisle, Cumbria, CA3
8UR Tel: 01228-532774 Fax: 01228-521275
Email: rhq@kingsownborder.demon.co.uk
The Dock Museum
North Road, Barrow-In-Furness, Cumbria, LA14 2PW
Tel: 01229-894444 WWW: www.barrowbc.gov.uk
Dove Cottage & The Wordsworth Museum
Town End, Grasmere, Ambleside LA22 9SH
Tel: 015394-35544
The Guildhall Museum
Green Market, Carlisle CA3 8JE Tel: 01228-819925
Haig Colliery Mining Museum
Solway Road, Kells, Whitehaven CA28 9BG
Tel: 01946-599949 Fax: 01946-61896
WWW: www.haigpit.com
Lakeside & Haverthwaite Railway
Haverthwaite Station, Ulverston, LA12 8A
 Tel: 01539 531594
Keswick Museum & Art Gallery
Station Road, Keswick, Cumbria, CA12 4NF
Tel: 017687-73263 Fax: 017687-80390
Email: hazel.davison@allerdale.gov.uk
Lakeland Motor Museum
Holker Hall, Cark In Cartmel, Grange-Over-Sands
LA11 7PL Tel: 015395-58509
Laurel & Hardy Museum
4c Upper Brook Street, Ulverston, Cumbria, LA12 7BH
Tel: 01229-582292
Maryport Steamship Museum
Elizabeth Dock South Quay, Maryport CA15 8AB
Tel: 01900-815954
Penrith Museum
Middlegate, Penrith CA11 7PT Tel: 01768-212228
Fax: 01768-867466 Email: museum@eden.gov.uk
Roman Army Museum
Carvoran House, Greenhead, Carlisle CA6 7JB
Tel: 016977-47485

Ruskin Museum
Coniston Institute, Yewdale Road, Coniston LA21 8DU
Tel: 015394-41164 Fax: 015394-41132
WWW: www.coniston.org.uk
Senhouse Roman Museum
The Battery, Sea Brows, Maryport CA15 6JD
Tel: 01900-816168
Solway Aviation Museum
Carlisle Airport, Carlisle CA6 4NW Tel: 01228-573823
Tullie House Museum & Art Gallery
Castle Street, Carlisle CA3 8TP Tel: 01228-534781
Fax: 01228-810249
Ulverston Heritage Centre
Lower Brook Street, Ulverston LA12 7EE
Tel: 01229-580820 Fax: 01229-580820
Email: heritage@tower-house.demon.co.uk
WWW: www.rootsweb.com/~ukuhc/
William Creighton Mineral Museum & Gallery
2 Crown Street, Cockermouth CA13 0EJ Tel: 01900-828301
Fax: 01900-828001
Windermere Steamboat Museum
Rayrigg Road, Windermere LA23 1BN Tel: 015394-45565
Fax: 015394-48769 WWW: www.steamboat.co.uk

Derbyshire
Chesterfield Museum & Art Gallery
No archive or library material held., St Mary's Gate,
Chesterfield S41 7TY Tel: 01246-345727
Derby Industrial Museum
Silk Mill Lane, Derby DE1 3AR Tel: 01332-255308
Derby Museum & Art Gallery
The Strand, Derby DE1 1BS Tel: 01332-716659
Fax: 01332-716670 WWW: www.derby.gov.uk/museums
Derwent Valley Visitor Centre
Belper North Mill, Bridge Foot, Belper DE56 1YD
Tel: 01773-880474
Donington Grandprix Collection
Donington Park, Castle Donington DE74 2RP
Tel: 01332-811027
Donington Park Racing Ltd
Donington Park, Castle Donnington DE74 2RP
Tel: 01332-814697
Elvaston Castle Estate Museum
Elvaston Castle Country Park, Borrowash Road, Elvaston,
Derby DE72 3EP Tel: 01332-573799
Erewash Museum
The Museum, High Street, Ilkeston, DE7 5JA
Tel: 0115-907-1141 Email: erewashmuseum@free4all.co.uk
WWW: www.erewash.gov.uk
Eyam Museum
Eyam Museum Ltd, Hawkhill Road, Hope Valley, Eyam,
S32 5QP Tel: 01433-631371 Fax: 01433-630777
WWW: www.cressbrook.co.uk/eyam/museum
Glossop Heritage Centre
Bank House, Henry Street, Glossop SK13 8BW
Tel: 01457-869176
High Peak Junction Workshop
High Peak Junction, Cronford, Matlock DE4 5HN
Tel: 01629-822831
High Peak Trail
Middleton Top,, Rise End, Middleton, Matlock, Derbyshire,
DE4 4LS Tel: 01629-823204
Midland Railway Centre
Butterley Station, Ripley DE5 3QZ Tel: 01773-570140
Peak District Mining Museum
Pavilion, South Parade, Matlock DE4 3NR
Tel: 01629-583834
Pickford's House Museum
41 Friar Gate, Derby DE1 1DA Tel: 01332-255363
Fax: 01332-255277
Regimental Museum of the 9th/12th Royal Lancers
Derby City Museum and Art Gallery, The Strand, Derby,
DE1 1BS Tel: 01332-716656 Fax: 01332-716670
Email: akelsall@derbymuseum.co.uk
WWW: www.derby.gov.uk/museums
National Stone Centre
Porter Lane, Wirksworth, Matlock DE4 4LS Tel: 01629-824833

349

Devon
Century of Playtime
30 Winner Street, Paignton TQ3 3BJ Tel: 01803-553850
The Dartmouth Museum
The Butterwalk, Dartmouth TQ6 9PZ Tel: 01803-832923
Devon & Cornwall Constabulary Museum
Middlemoor, Exeter, Devon, EX2 7HQ Tel: 01392-203025
Devonshire & The Devonshire and Dorset Regimental Archives
Wyvern Barracks, Barrack Road, Exeter, Devon, EX2 6AE
Tel: 01392-492436 Fax: 01392-492469
Dunkeswell Memorial Museum
Dunkeswell Airfield, Dunkeswell Ind Est, Dunkeswell,
Honiton, Devon, EX14 0RA Tel: 01404-891943
Fairlynch Art Centre & Museum
27 Fore Street, Budleigh Salterton EX9 6NP
Tel: 01395-442666
Finch Foundary Museum of Rural Industry
Sticklepath, Okehampton EX20 2NW Tel: 01837-840046
Ilfracombe Museum
Wilder Road, Ilfracombe EX34 8AF Tel: 01271-863541
The Keep Military Museum
Bridport Road, Dorchester, Dorset, DT1 1RN
Tel: 01305-264066 Email: keep.museum@talk21.com
WWW: www.keepmilitarymuseum.org
**Museum of Barnstaple & Devon incorporating Royal
Devon Yeomanry Museum**
The Square, Barnstaple, Devon, EX32 8LN
Tel: 01271-346747 Email: admin@sal.org.uk
Newton Abbot Town & Great Western Railway Museum
2A St. Pauls Road, Newton Abbot TQ12 2HP
Tel: 01626-201121
North Devon Maritime Museum
Odun House, Odun Road, Appledore, Bideford, Devon,
EX39 1PT Tel: 01237-422064 Fax: 01237-422064
WWW: www.devonmuseums.net/appledore
North Devon Museum Service
St.Anne's Chapel, Paternoster Row, Barnstaple, Devon,
EX32 8LN Tel: 01271-378709
Otterton Mill Centre
Otterton, Budleigh Salterton, Devon, EX9 7HG
Tel: 01395-568521
Plymouth City Museum
Drake Circus, Plymouth, Devon, PL4 8AJ
Tel: 01752-304774
Royal Albert Memorial Museum
Queen Street, Exeter, Devon, EX4 3RX Tel: 01392-265858
Seaton Tramway
Harbour Road, Seaton EX12 7NQ Tel: 01297 20375
 Email: info@tram.co.uk WWW: www.tram.co.uk
Sidmouth Museum
Hope Cottage, Church St, Sidmouth EX10 8LY
Tel: 01395-516139
Teignmouth Museum
29 French Street, Teignmouth, Devon, TQ14 8ST
Tel: 01626-777041
Allhallows Museum of Lace & Antiquities
High Street, Honiton EX14 1PG Tel: 01404-44966
Fax: 01404-46591 Email: dyateshoniton@msn.com
WWW: www.honitonlace.com
Newhall Visitor & Equestrian Centre
Newhall, Budlake, Exeter EX5 3LW Tel: 01392-462453
Park Pharmacy Trust
Thorn Park Lodge, Thorn Park , Mannamead, Plymouth,
Devon , PL3 4TF Tel: 01752-263501

Dorset
Bournemouth Aviation Museum
Hanger 600 South East Sector, Bournemouth International
Airport Hurn, Christchurch, Dorset, BH23 6SE
Tel: 01202-580858 Fax: 01202-580858
Bridport Harbour Museum
West Bay, Bridport, Dorset, DT6 4SA Tel: 01308-420997
Cavalcade of Costume
Lime Tree House, The Plocks, Blandford Forum, Dorset,
DT11 7AA Tel: 01258-453006
Christchurch Motor Museum
Matchams Lane, Hurn, Christchurch BH23 6AW Tel: 01202-488100

Dinosaur Land
Coombe Street, Lyme Regis DT7 3PY Tel: 01297-443541
The Dinosaur Museum
Icen Way, Dorchester DT1 1EW Tel: 01305-269880
Fax: 01305-268885
Dorset County Museum and Library
66 High West Street, Dorchester DT1 1XA
Tel: 01305-262735 Fax: 01305-257180
Email: dorsetcountymuseum@dor-mus.demon.co.uk
The Keep Military Museum
Bridport Road, Dorchester DT1 1RN Tel: 01305-264066
Fax: 01305-250373 Email: keep.museum@talk21.com
WWW: www.keepmilitarymuseum.org
Lyme Regis Philpot Museum
Bridge Street, Lyme Regis DT7 3QA Tel: 01297-443370
Email: info@lymeregismuseum.co.uk
Nothe Fort
Barrack Road, Weymouth DT4 8UF Tel: 01305-787243
Portland Museum
Wakeham, Portland, Dorset, DT5 1HS Tel: 01305-821804
Priest's House Museum
23-27 High St. Wimborne BH21 1HR Tel: 01202-882533
Red House Museum & Gardens
Quay Rd, Christchurch BH23 1BU Tel: 01202-482860
Russell-Cotes Art Gallery & Museum
East Cliff, Bournemouth BH1 3AA Tel: 01202-451800
Shelley Rooms
Museum at: Shelley Park, Beechwood Ave, Bournemouth
BH5 1NE, Russell Cotes Art Gallery & Museum
(Correspondence address), (Reference Shelley Rooms), East
Cliff, Bournemouth, BH1 3AA Tel: 01202-451800
Fax: 01202-451851 Email: dedge@russell-cotes.demon.co.uk
WWW: www.russell-cotes.bournemouth.gov.uk
Sherborne Museum Association
Abbey Gate House, Church Avenue, Sherborne, Dorset, DT9
3BP Tel: 01935-812252
The Tank Museum
Bovington, Dorset, BH20 6JG Tel: 01929-405096
Fax: 01929-405360 Email: david@tankmuseum.co.uk
WWW: www.tankmuseum.co.uk
Wareham Town Museum
5 East Street, Wareham BH20 4NN Tel: 01929-553448
Waterfront Museum and Local Studies Centre
4 High Street, Poole BH15 1BW Tel: 01202-683138
Fax: 01202-660896 Email: museums@poole.gov.uk
WWW: www.poole.gov.uk
Weymouth & Portland Museum Service
The Esplanade, Weymouth DT4 8ED Tel: 01305-765206
Shaftesbury Abbey Museum & Garden
Park Walk, Shaftesbury SP7 8JR Tel: 01747-852910
Shaftesbury Town Museum
Gold Hill, Shaftesbury SP7 8JW Tel: 01747-852157

Dorset – West Dorset
West Dorset Museums Service
The Coach House, Grundy Lane, Bridport DT6 3RJ
Tel: 01308-458703 Fax: 01308-458704
Email: j.burrell@westdorset-dc.gov.uk

Essex
Barleylands Farm Museum & Visitors Centre
Barleylands Farm, Billericay CM11 2UD
Tel: 01268-282090
Battlesbridge Motorcycle Museum The
Muggeridge Farm, Maltings Road, Battlesbridge, Wickford,
SS11 7RF Tel: 01268-560866
Castle Point Transport Museum Society
105 Point Road, Canvey Island SS8 7TJ Tel: 01268-684272
East England Tank Museum
Oak Business Park, Wix Road, Beaumont, Clacton-On-Sea,
CO16 0AT Tel: 01255-871119
Englands Secret Nuclear Bunker
Visitor access via the A128. Correspondence, Kelvedon
Hall Lane, Kelvedon Common, Kelvedon Hatch, Nr
Brentwood CM15 0LB, 01277-364883, 01277-372562
Epping Forest District Museum
39-41 Sun Street, Waltham Abbey EN9 1EL Tel: 01992-716882

Essex Police Museum
Police Headquarters, PO Box 2, Springfield, Chelmsford,
Essex, CM2 6DA Tel: 01245-491491 x50771
Fax: 01245-452456
Essex Regiment Museum
Oaklands Park, Moulsham Street, Chelmsford CM2 9AQ
Tel: 01245-615101 Fax: 01245-611250
Email: pompadour@chelmsfordbc.gov.uk
WWW: www.chelmsfordbc.gov.uk
Essex Secret Bunker
Crown Building, Shrublands Road, Mistley, Essex, CO11
1HS Tel: 01206-392271 (24hr info)
Harlow Museum
Passmores House, Third Avenue, Harlow CM18 6YL
Tel: 01279-454959
Hollytrees Museum
High Street, Colchester CO1 1DN Tel: 01206-282940
Leigh Heritage Centre & Museum
c/o 13a High Street, Leigh-On-Sea, Essex, SS9 2EN
Tel: 01702-470834 Email: palmtree@northdell.demon.co.uk
LB of Barking & Dagenham Local History Studies -
Dagenham Valence Library & Museum, Becontree Avenue,
Dagenham, Essex, RM8 3HT Tel: 020-8592-6537
Fax: 020-8227-5297 Email: fm019@viscount.org.uk
WWW: www.earl.org.uk/partners/barking/index.html
Maldon District Museum
47 Mill Road, Maldon CM9 5HX Tel: 01621-842688
Mark Hall Cycle Museum
Muskham Road, Harlow CM20 2LF Tel: 01279-439680
National Motorboat Museum
Wattyler Country Park, Pitsea Hall Lane, Pitsea, Basildon,
Essex, SS16 4UH Tel: 01268-550077 Fax: 01268-581903
Saffron Walden Museum
Museum Street, Saffron Walden CB10 1JL
Tel: 01799-510333 Fax: 01799-510333
Email: museum@uttlesford.gov.uk
Southend Central Museum
Victoria Avenue, Southend-On-Sea, Essex, SS2 6EW
Tel: 01702-434449 Fax: 01702-34980
The Cater Museum
74 High Street, Billericay, Essex, CM12 9BS
Tel: 01277-622023
Valence House Museum
Becontree Avenue, Dagenham RM8 3HS
Tel: 020-8227-5293 Fax: 020-8227-5293
Email: valencehousemuseum@hotmail.com
Chelmsford & Essex Museum
Oaklands Park, Moulsham St, Chelmsford CM2 9AQ
Tel: 01245-615100 Fax: 01245-611250
Email: oaklands@chelmsford.gov.uk

Gloucestershire
Chepstow Museum
Bridge Street, Chepstow, Monmouthshire, NP16 5EZ
Tel: 01291-625981 Fax: 01291-635005
Email: chepstowmuseum@monmouthshire.gov.uk
Dean Heritage Centre
Soudley, Cinderford, Forest of Dean GL14 2UB
Tel: 01594-822170 Fax: 01594-823711
Email: deanmus@btinternet.com
Gloucester City Museum & Art Gallery
Brunswick Road, Gloucester GL1 1HP Tel: 01452-524131
Gloucester Folk Museum
99-103 Westgate Street, Gloucester GL1 2PG
Tel: 01452-526467 Fax: 01452-330495
Email: ChristopherM@glos.city.gov.uk
Guild of Handicraft Trust The
Silk Mill, Sheep St, Chipping Campden GL55 6DS
Tel: 01386-841417
Holst Birthplace Museum
4 Clarence Road, Cheltenham GL52 2AY
Tel: 01242-524846 Fax: 01242-580182
The Jenner Museum
Church Lane, Berkeley GL13 9BN Tel: 01453-810631
John Moore Countryside Museum
42 Church Street, Tewkesbury GL20 5SN Tel: 01684-297174

National Waterways Museum
Llanthony Warehouse, Gloucester Docks, Gloucester, GL1
2EH Tel: 01452-318054 Email: curatorial1@nwm.demon.co.uk
WWW: www.nwm.demon.uk
Nature In Art
Wallsworth Hall, Tewkesbury Road, Twigworth, Gloucester,
Gloucestershire, GL2 9PG Tel: 01452-731422
Email: ninart@globalnet.co.uk WWW: www.nature-in-art.org.uk
Regiments Of Gloucestershire Museum
Gloucester Docks, Gloucester GL1 2HE Tel: 01452-522682
Robert Opie Collection
Albert Warehouse, The Docks, Gloucester, Gloucestershire,
GL1 2EH Tel: 01452-302309
Shambles Museum
20 Church Street, Newent GL18 1PP Tel: 01531-822144
Soldiers of Gloucester Museum
Gloucester Docks, Commercial Road, Gloucester, GL1 2EH
Tel: 01452-522682
The Great Western Railway Museum (Coleford)
The Old Railway Station, Railway Drive, Coleford,
Gloucestershire, GL16 8RH Tel: 01594-833569,
01954-832032 Fax: 01594-832032

Gloucestershire – South Gloucestershire
Frenchay Tuckett Society & Local History Museum
247 Frenchay Park Road, Frenchay, South Gloucestershire,
BS16 1LG Tel: 0117-9569324
Email: raybulmer@compuserve.com
WWW: www.ourworld.compuserve.com/homepages/raybulmer

Hampshire
Airborne Forces Museum
Browning Barracks, Aldershot, Hampshire, GU11 2BU
Tel: 01252-349619 Fax: 01252-349203
Aldershot Military Historical Trust
Evelyn Woods Road, Aldershot, Hampshire, GU11 2LG
Tel: 01252-314598 Fax: 01252-342942
Aldershot Military Museum
Queens Avenue, Aldershot GU11 2LG Tel: 01252-314598
Fax: 01252-34294 Email: musim@hants.gov.uk
Andover Museum & Iron Age Museum
6 Church Close, Andover SP10 1DP Tel: 01264-366283
Fax: 01264-339152 Email: andover.museum@virgin.net
or musmda@hants.gov.uk WWW: www.hants.gov.uk/andoverm
Army Medical Services Museum
Keogh Barracks, Ash Vale, nr Aldershot, Hampshire, GU12
5RQ Tel: 01252-340212 Fax: 01252-340332
Email: museum@keogh72.freeserve.co.uk
Army Physical Training Corps Museum
ASPT, Fox Line, Queen's Avenue, Aldershot, Hampshire,
GU11 2LB Tel: 01252 347168 Fax: 01252 340785
The Bear Museum
38 Dragon Street, Petersfield GU31 4JJ Tel: 01730-265108
Email: judy@bearmuseum.freeserve.co.uk
WWW: www.bearmuseum.co.uk
Bishops Waltham Museum & Trust
Brook Street, Bishops Waltham SO32 1EB Trust:-
8 Folly Field, Bishop's Waltham, Southampton, SO32 1EB
Tel: 01489-894970
Eastleigh Museum
25 High Street, Eastleigh SO50 5LF Tel: 02380-643026
Email: musmst@hants.gov.uk
WWW: www.hants.gov.uk/museum/eastlmus/index.html
Eling Tide Mill Trust Ltd
The Tollbridge, Eling Hill, Totton, Southampton, Hampshire,
SO40 9HF Tel: 023-8086-9575
Gosport Museum
Walpole Road, Gosport PO12 1NS Tel: 023-9258-8035
Fax: 023-9250-1951 Email: musmie@hants.gov.uk
Gurkha Museum
Peninsula Barracks, Romsey Road, Winchester SO23 8TS
Tel: 01962 842832 Fax: 01962 877597
Hampshire County Museums Service
Chilcomb House, Chilcomb Lane, Winchester SO23 8RD
Tel: 01962-846304

Havant Museum
also Friends of Havant Museum Local History Section, 56
East Street, Havant P09 1BS Tel: 023-9245-1155
Fax: 023-9249-8707 Email: musmcp@hants.gov.uk
WWW: www.hants.gov.uk/museums
HMS Warrior (1860)
Victory Gate, HM Naval Base, Portsmouth PO1 3QX
Tel: 02392-778600 Fax: 02392-778601
Email: info@hmswarrior.org WWW: www.hmswarrior.org
Hollycombe Steam Collection
Iron Hill, Midhurst Rd, Liphook GU30 7LP Tel: 01428-724900
**King's Royal Hussars Museum (10th Royal Hussars
PWO 11th Hussars PAO and Royal Hussars PWO)**
Peninsula Barracks, Winchester SO23 8TS
Tel: 01962 828540 Fax: 01962 828538
Email: beresford@krhmuseum.freeserve.co.uk
WWW: www.hants.gov.uk/leisure/museums/royalhus/index.html
Light Infantry Museum
Peninsula Barracks, Romsey Road, Winchester, Hampshire,
SO23 8TS Tel: 01962 868550
Maritime Museum Southampton
Bugle Street, Southampton SO14 2AJ Tel: 023-8022-3941
The Mary Rose Trust
1-10 College Road, HM Naval Base, Portsmouth,
Hampshire, PO1 3LX Tel: 023-9275-0521
Museum of Army Flying
Middle Wallop, Stockbridge SO20 8DY Tel: 01980-674421
Fax: 01264-781694 Email: daa@flyingmuseum.org.uk
WWW: www.flying-museum.org.uk
New Forest Museum & Visitor Centre
High Street, Lyndhurst SO43 7NY Tel: (023)-8028-3194
Fax: (023)-8028-4236 Email: nfmuseum@lineone.net
Portsmouth City Museum & Record Office
Museum Road, Portsmouth PO1 2LJ Tel: 023-9282-7261
Fax: 023-9287-5276 Email: portmus@compuserve.com
WWW: ourworld.compuserve.com/homepages/portmus/
Priddy's Hard Armament Museum
Priory Road, Gosport PO12 4LE Tel: 023-9250-2490
Queen Alexandra's Royal Army Nursing Corps Museum
Regimental Headquarters Army Medica, Keogh Barracks,
Ash Vale, Aldershot, Hampshire, GU12 5RQ
Rockbourne Roman Villa
Rockbourne, Fordingbridge SP6 3PG Tel: 01725-518541
Royal Armouries
Fort Nelson Down End Road, Fareham PO17 6AN
Tel: 01329-233734 Fax: 01329-822092
WWW: www.armouries.org.uk
Royal Green Jackets Museum
Peninsula Barracks, Romsey Road, Winchester SO23 8TS
Tel: 01962-828549 Fax: 01962-828500
Royal Hampshire Regimental Museum
Serle's House, Southgate Street, Winchester SO23 9EG
Tel: 01962 863658
Royal Marines Museum Archives & Library
Eastney, Southsea PO4 9PX Tel: 02392-819385 Ext 224
Fax: 02392-838420
Email: mathewlittle@royalmarinesmuseum.co.uk
WWW: www.royalmarinesmuseum.co.uk
Royal Naval Museum
H M Naval Base (PP66), Main Road, Portsmouth, PO1
3NH Tel: 023-9272-3795 Fax: 023-9272-7575
Royal Navy Submarine Museum
Haslar Jetty Road, Gosport PO12 2AS Tel: 023-9251-0354
Sammy Miller Motor Cycle Museum
Bashley Manor Farm, Bashley Cross Road, New Milton,
BH25 5SZ Tel: 01425-620777
Search
50 Clarence Road, Gosport PO12 1BU Tel: 023-9250-1957
Westbury Manor Museum
West Street, Fareham PO16 0JJ Tel: 01329-824895
Fax: 01329-825917 Email: www.hants.gov.uk/museum/westbury
Whitchurch Silk Mill
28 Winchester Street, Whitchurch RG28 7AL
Tel: 01256-892065
The Willis Museum Of Basingstoke Town & Country Life
Old Town Hall, Market Place, Basingstoke, Hampshire,
RG21 7QD Tel: 01256-465902 Fax: 01256-471455

Email: willismuseum@hotmail.com
WWW: www.hants.gov.uk/leisure/museums/willis/index.html
Winchester Museums Service
75 Hyde Street, Winchester SO23 7DW Tel: 01962-848269
Fax: 01962-848299 Email: museums@winchester.gov.uk
WWW: www.winchester.gov.uk/heritage/home.htm

Herefordshire
Churchill House Museum
Venns Lane, Aylestone Hill, Hereford HR1 1DE
Tel: 01432-260693 Fax: 01432-267409
Cider Museum & King Offa Distillery
21 Ryelands Street, Hereford, HR4 0LW Tel: 01432-354007
Fax: 01432-341641 Email: thompson@cidermuseum.co.uk
WWW: www.cidermuseum.co.uk
Leominster Museum
Etnam Street, Leominster HR6 8 Tel: 01568-615186
Teddy Bears of Bromyard
12 The Square, Bromyard HR7 4BP Tel: 01885-488329
Waterworks Museum
86 Park Street, Hereford, HR1 2RE Tel: 01432-356653
Weobley & District Local History Society
Weobley Museum, Back Lane, Weobley, Herefordshire, HR4
8SG Tel: 01544-340292

Hertfordshire
First Garden City Heritage Museum
296 Norton Way South, Letchworth Garden City, SG6 1SU
Tel: 01462-482710 Fax: 01462-486056
Email: egchm@letchworth.com
Hertford Museum (Hertford Regiment)
18 Bull Plain, Hertford SG14 1DT Tel: 01992-582686
Hitchin British Schools
41-42 Queen Street, Hitchin SG4 9TS Tel: 01462-452697
Hitchin Museum
Paynes Park, Hitchin SG5 1EG Tel: 01462-434476
Fax: 01462-431316 Email: nhdc.gov.uk
Kingsbury Water Mill Museum
St. Michaels Street, St. Albans AL3 4SJ Tel: 01727-853502
Letchworth Museum & Art Gallery
Broadway, Letchworth SG6 3PF Tel: 01462-685647
Mill Green Museum & Mill
Mill Green, Hatfield AL9 5PD Tel: 01707-271362
Rhodes Memorial Museum & Commonwealth Centre
South Road, Bishop's Stortford CM23 3JG
Tel: 01279-651746 Email: rhodesmuseum@freeuk.com
WWW: www.hertsmuseums.org.uk
Royston & District Museum
5 Lower King Street, Royston SG8 5AL Tel: 01763-242587
The De Havilland Aircraft Museum Trust
P.O Box 107, Salisbury Hall, London Colney, St. Albans,
AL2 1EX Tel: 01727-822051
The Environmental Awareness Trust
23 High Street, Wheathampstead, St. Albans AL4 8BB
Tel: 01582-834580
The Forge Museum
High Street, Much Hadham SG10 6BS Tel: 01279-843301
Verulamium Museum
St. Michaels Street, St. Albans AL3 4SW
Tel: 01727-751824 Fax: 01727-836282
Email: d.thorold@stalbans.gov.uk
The Walter Rothschild Zoological Museum
Akeman Street, Tring HP23 6AP Tel: 0207-942-6156
Fax: 0207-942-6150 Email: ornlib@nhm.ac.uk
WWW: www.nhm.ac.uk
Ware Museum
Priory Lodge, 89 High Street, Ware SG12 9AD
Tel: 01920-487848
Watford Museum
194 High Street, Watford WD1 2DT Tel: 01923-232297
Welwyn Hatfield Museum Service
Welwyn Roman Baths, By-Pass-Road, Welwyn, AL6 0
Tel: 01438-716096

Huntingdonshire
Peterborough Museum & Art Gallery
Priestgate, Peterborough PE1 1LF Tel: 01733-343329
Fax: 01733-341928 Email: museums@peterborough.gov.uk

Isle of Wight
Bembridge Maritime Museum & Shipwreck Centre
Providence House, Sherborne Street, Bembridge
Isle Of Wight, PO35 5SB Tel: 01983-872223
Calbourne Water Mill
Calbourne Mill, Newport, PO30 4JN Tel: 01983-531227
Carisbrooke Castle Museum
Carisbrooke Castle, Newport PO30 1XY Tel: 01983-523112
Fax: 01983-532126 Email: carismus@lineone.net
East Cowes Heritage Centre
8 Clarence Road, East Cowes PO32 6EP Tel: 01983-280310
Front Line Britain at War Experience
Sandown Airport, Scotchells Brook Lane, Sandown, Isle Of
Wight, PO36 0JP Tel: 01983-404448
Guildhall Museum – Newport, Isle of Wight
High Street, Newport PO30 1TY Tel: 01983-823366
The Lilliput Museum of Antique Dolls & Toy
High Street, Brading, Sandown PO36 0DJ
Tel: 01983-407231 Email: lilliput.museum@btconnect.com
WWW: www.lilliputmuseum.co.uk
Natural History Centre
High Street, Godshill, Ventnor PO38 3HZ Tel: 01983-840333
The Classic Boat Museum
Seaclose Wharf, Town Quay, Newport PO30 2EF
Tel: 01983-533493
Ventnor Heritage Museum
11 Spring Hill, Ventnor PO38 1PE Tel: 01983-855407

Kent
Bethlem Royal Hospital Archives & Museum
Monks Orchard Road, Beckenham, Kent, BR3 3BX
Fax: 020-8776-4045 Email: museum@bethlem.co.uk
Buffs Regimental Museum
Royal Museum & Art Gallery, 18 High Street, Canterbury
CT1 2RA Tel: 01227-452747 Fax: 01227-455047
Canterbury Roman Museum
Butchery Lane, Canterbury CT1 2JR Tel: 01227-785575
Chatham Dockyard Historical Society Museum
Likley to move 1/2/2001 to World Naval Base, Chatham,
Cottage Row, Barrack Road, Chatham Dockyard, Chatham,
Kent, ME4 4TZ Tel: 01634-844897, 01634-250647
Cobham Hall
Cobham DA12 3BL Tel: 01474-823371 Fax: 01474-822995
Dickens House Museum - Broadstairs
2 Victoria Parade, Broadstairs CT10 1QS
Tel: 01843-861232 Fax: 01843-862853
Dolphin Sailing Barge Museum
Crown Quay Lane, Sittingbourne ME10 3SN Tel: 01795-423215
Dover Castle
Dover, Kent, CT16 1HU Tel: 01304-211067
Dover Museum
Market Square, Dover, Kent, CT16 1PB Tel: 01304-201066
Dover Transport Museum
Old Park Barracks, Whitfield, Dover CT16 2HQ
Tel: 01304-822409
Drapers Museum of Bygones
4 High Street, Rochester ME1 1PT Tel: 01634-830647
Fleur de Lis Heritage Centre &Museum
13 Preston Street, Faversham ME13 8NS
Tel: 01795-534542 Fax: 01795-533261
Email: faversham@btinternet.com
WWW: www.faversham.org
Guildhall Museum – Rochester, Kent
High Street, Rochester, Kent, ME1 1PY Tel: 01634-848717
Herne Bay Museum Centre
12 William Street, Herne Bay CT6 5EJ Tel: 01227-367368

Hever Castle
Hever, Nr Edenbridge TN8 7NG Tel: 01732-865224
Email: mail@hevercastle.co.uk WWW: www.hevercastle.co.uk
Kent Battle of Britain Museum
Aerodrome Road, Hawkinge, Folkestone CT18 7AG
Tel: 01303-893140
Leeds Castle
Maidstone, Kent, ME17 1PL Tel: 0870-600-8880 (Info line)
WWW: www.leeds-castle.co.uk

Maidstone Museum & Art Gallery
St. Faith Street, Maidstone ME14 1LH Tel: 01622-754497
Margate Old Town Hall Museum
Old Town Hall, Market Place, Margate CT9 1ER
Tel: 01843-231213
Minster Abbey Gatehouse Museum
Union Road, Minster On Sea, Sheerness, Kent, ME12 2HW
Tel: 01795-872303
Minster Museum Craft & Animal Centre
Bedlam Court Lane, Minster, Ramsgate CT12 4HQ
Tel: 01843-822312
Museum of Kent Life
Cobtree, Lock Lane, Sandling, Maidstone ME14 3AU
Tel: 01622-763936 Fax: 01622-662024
Email: enquiries@museum-kentlife.co.uk
WWW: www.museum-kentlife.co.uk
Pembroke Lodge Museum & Family History Centre
2-6 Station Approach, Birchington on Sea CT7 9RD Allmail
to: 4 Station Approach, Birchington on Sea, Kent, CT7 9RD
Tel: 01843-841649
Penshurst Place and Gardens
Penshurst, Tonbridge, Knt, TN11 8DG Tel: 01892-870307
Fax: 01892-870866 Email: enquiries@penshurstplace.com
WWW: www.penshursrtplace.com
Powell-Cotton Museum
Quex Park, Birchington, Kent, CT7 0 Tel: 01843-842168
Queen's Own Royal West Kent Regiment Museum
Maidstone Museum and Art Gallery, St. Faith's Street,
Maidstone, Kent , ME14 1LH Tel: 01622 754497
Fax: 01622 602193
Romney Toy & Model Museum
The Romney, Hythe & Dymchurch Railway
New Romney Station, Romney TN28 8PL Tel: 01797 362353
Royal Engineers Library
Brompton Barracks, Chatham, Kent, ME4 4UG
Tel: 01634-822416 Fax: 01634-822419
Royal Engineers Museum
Prince Arthur Road, Gillingham, Kent, ME4 4UG
Tel: 01634-406397 Fax: 01634-822371
Email: remuseum.rhgre@gtnet.gov.uk WWW:
www.army.mod.uk/army/museums
Royal Museum & Art Gallery
18 High Street, Canterbury, Kent, CT1 2RA
Tel: 01227-452747
Sheerness Heritage Centre
10 Rose Street, Sheerness, Kent, ME12 1AJ Tel: 01795-663317
Squerryes Court
Westerham, Kent, TN16 1SJ Tel: 01959-562345/563118
Tenterden Museum
Station Road, Tenterden, Kent, TN30 6HN
Tel: 01580-764310 Fax: 01580-766648
The C.M Booth Collection Of Historic Vehicles
63-67 High Street, Rolvenden, Cranbrook, Kent, TN17 4LP
Tel: 01580-241234
The Charles Dickens Centre
Eastgate House, High Street, Rochester, Kent, ME1 1EW
Tel: 01634-844176
Victoriana Museum The
Deal Town Hall, High Street, Deal, Kent, CT14 6BB
Tel: 01304-380546
Watts Charity Poor Travellers House,
97 High Street, Rochester ME1 1LX Tel: 01634-845609
West Kent Regimental Museum
Maidstone, Kent
Whitstable Museum & Gallery
5a Oxford Street, Whitstable CT5 1DB Tel: 01227-276998
Maritime Museum Ramsgate
Clock House, Pier Yard, Royal Harbour, RamsgateCT11 8LS
Tel: 01843-587765 Email: museum@ekmt.fsnet.co.uk
WWW: www.ekmt.fsnet.co.uk
Masonic Library & Museum
St. Peters Place, Canterbury CT1 2DA Tel: 01227-785625

Lancashire
Blackburn Museum & Art Gallery
Museum Street, Blackburn BB1 7AJ Tel: 01254-661730

Bolton Museum & Art Gallery
Le Mans Crescent, Bolton BL1 1SE Tel: 01204-332190
Fax: 01204-332241 Email: bolmg@gn.apc.org
The British in India Museum
Newtown Street, Colne Tel: 01282 613129 Tel: 0976 665320
Fax: 01282 870215
Duke of Lancaster's Own Yeomanry
Stanley Street, Preston PR1 4AT Tel: 01772-264074
East Lancashire Railway
Bolton Street Station, Bury BL9 0EY Tel: 01772 685984
Ellenroad Trust Ltd
Ellenroad Engine House, Elizabethan Way, Milnrow,
Rochdale OL16 4LG Tel: 01706-881952
Email: ellenroad@aol.com
WWW: http:\\ellenroad.homepage.com
Fleetwood Museum
Queens Terrace, Fleetwood FY7 6BT Tel: 01253-876621
The Fusiliers Museum (Lancashire)
Wellington Barracks, Bolton Road, Bury, BL8 2PL
Tel: 0161 764 2208
Gawthorpe Hall
Habergham Drive, Padiham, Burnley BB12 8UA
Tel: 01282-771004
WWW: www.lancashire.com/lcc/museums
Greater Manchester Police Museum
Newton Street, Manchester, M1 1ES Tel: 0161-856-3287,
0161-856-3288 Fax: 0161-856-3286
Hall I'Th' Wood Museum
Hall I Th Wood, Tonge Moor, Bolton BL1 8UA
Tel: 01204-301159
Heaton Park Tramway (Transport Museum)
Tram Depot, Heaton Park, Prestwich, Manchester, M25
2SW Tel: 0161-740-1919
Helmshore Textile Museums
Holcombe Road, Helmshore, Rossendal BB4 4NP
Tel: 01706-226459 Fax: 01706-218554
Heritage Trust for the North West
Pendle Heritage Centre, Colne Road, Barrowford, Nelson,
Lancashire, BB9 6JQ Tel: 01282-661704
Judge's Lodgings Museum
Church Street, Lancaster LA1 1LP Tel: 01524-32808
Keighley Bus Museum Trust
47 Brantfell Drive, Burnley BB12 8AW Tel: 01282-413179
Fax: 01282-413179 WWW: www.kbmt.freeuk.com
King's Own Royal Regimental Museum
The City Museum, Market Square, Lancaster, LA1 1HT
Tel: 01524 64637 Fax: 01524 841692
Email: kingsownmuseum@iname.com
Kippers Cats
51 Bridge Street, Ramsbottom, Bury BL0 9AD
Tel: 01706-822133
Lancashire Mining Museum - Closed wef 30/6/2000
Buile Hill Park, Eccles Old Road, Salford M6 8GL
Lancaster City Museum
Market Square, Lancaster LA1 1HT Tel: 01524-64637
Fax: 01524-841692 Email: awhite@lancaster.gov.uk
Lytham Heritage Group
2 Henry St. Lytham St. Annes FY8 5LE Tel: 01253-730767
Manchester Museum
University of Manchester, Oxford Road, Manchester
M13 9PL Tel: 0161-275-2634
Manchester Museum Education Service
University of Manchester, Oxford Rd, Manchester
M13 9PL Tel: 0161-275-2630 Fax: 0161-275-2676
Email: education@man.ac.uk
WWW: www.museum.man.ac.uk

Museum of Lancashire
Stanley Street, Preston PR1 4YP Tel: 01772-264075
Fax: 01772-264079 Email: museum@lancs.co.uk
**Museum of Lancashire (Queen's Lancashire Regiment
Duke of Lancaster's Own Yeomanry Lancashire Hussar**
Stanley Street, Preston PR1 4YP Tel: 01772 264075
The Museum of Science and Industry In Manchester
Liverpool Road, Castlefield, Manchester, M3 4JP
Tel: 0161-832-2244, 0161-832-1830 24hr Info line
Fax: 0161-833-2184 WWW: www.msim.org.uk

Museum of the Manchesters
Ashton Town Hall, Market Place, Ashton-u-Lyne, OL6 6DL
Tel: Tel:0161 342 3078/3710 or
**Museum of the Queen's Lancashire Regiment (East
South and Loyal North LancashireRegiments)**
Fulwood Barracks, Preston PR2 8AA Tel: 01772 260362
Fax: 01772 260583 Email: rhqqlr@aol.com
North West Sound Archive
Old Steward's Office, Clitheroe Castle, Clitheroe, BB7 1AZ
Tel: 01200-427897 Fax: 01200-427897 Email:
nwsa@ed.lancscc.gov.uk WWW:
www.lancashire.gov.uk/education/lifelong/ro
Oldham Museum
Greaves Street, Oldham OL1 1 Tel: 0161-911-4657
Ordsall Hall Museum
Taylorson Street, Salford M5 3HT Tel: 0161-872-0251
Pendle Heritage Centre
Park Hill, Colne Road, Barrowford, Nelson BB9 6JQ
Tel: 01282-661702 Fax: 01282-611718
Portland Basin Museum
Portland Place, Ashton-Under-Lyne OL7 0QA
Tel: 0161-343-2878
Queen St Mill
Harle Syke, Queen Street, Briercliffe, Burnley BB10 2HX
Tel: 01282-459996
Rawtenstall Museum
Whitaker Park, Haslingden Road, Rawtenstall Tel: 01706
226509, Email: rossendale_leisure@compuserve.com
Ribchester Roman Museum
Riverside, Preston PR3 3XS Tel: 01254-878261
Rochdale Museum Service
The Arts & Heritage Centre, The Esplanade, Rochdale,
Lancashire, OL16 1AQ Tel: 01706-641085
Rochdale Pioneers' Museum
31 Toad Lane, Rochdale, Lancashire Tel: 01706-524920
Saddleworth Museum & Art Gallery
High Street, Uppermill, Oldham, Lancashire, OL3 6HS
Tel: 01457-874093 Fax: 01457-870336
Salford Museum & Art Gallery
Peel Park, The Crescent, Salford M5 4WU
Tel: 0161-736-2649 Email: info@lifetimes.org.uk
WWW: www.lifetimes.org.uk
Slaidburn Heritage Centre
25 Church Street, Slaidburn, Clitheroe, BB7 3ER
Tel: 01200-446161 Fax: 01200-446161
Email: slaidburn.heritage@htnw.co.uk
WWW: www.htnw.co.uk and also www.slaidburn.org.uk
Smithills Hall Museum
Smithills, Dean Rd, Bolton BL1 7NP Tel: 01204-841265
Weaver's Cottage
Bacup Road, Rawtenstall Tel: 01706 229937 Tel: 01706
226459 Email: rossendale_leisure@compuserve.com
Whitworth Museum
North Street, Whitworth Tel: 01706 343231 Tel: 01706
853655 Email: rossendale_leisure@compuserve.com
Wigan Heritage Service - History Shop
Library Street, Wigan, Greater Manchester, WN1 1NU
Tel: 01942-828020 Email: heritage@wiganmbc.gov.uk

Leeds
Leeds City Art Gallery
The Headrow, Leeds, LS1 3AA Tel: 0113-247-8248
Leeds Museums Resource Centre
Moorfield Road, Moorfield Industrial Estate, Yeadon, Leeds,
LS19 7BN Tel: 0113-214-6526
Lotherton Hall
Lotherton Lane, Aberford, Leeds, LS25 3EB Tel: 0113-281-3259
Temple Newsham House
Temple Newsham Road, off Selby Road, Leeds, LS15 0AE
Tel: 0113-264-7321
Thwaite Mills Watermill
Thwaite Lane, Stourton, Leeds, LS10 1RP Tel: 0113-249-6453

Leicestershire
Abbey Pumping Station
Corporation Road, Abbey Lane, Leicester LE4 5PX
Tel: 0116-299-5111 Fax: 0116-299-5125
WWW: www.leicestermuseums.ac.uk

Ashby De La Zouch Museum
North Street, Ashby-De-La-Zouch LE65 1HU Tel: 01530-560090
Belgrave Hall & Gardens
Church Road, Belgrave, Leicester LE4 5PE
Tel: 0116-2666590 Fax: 0116-2613063
Email: marte001@leicester.gov.uk
WWW: www.leicestermuseums.gov.uk
Bellfoundry Museum
Freehold Street, Loughborough LE11 1AR Tel: 01509-233414
Charnwood Museum
Granby Street, Loughborough, Leicestershire, LE11 3DU
Tel: 01509-233754 Fax: 01509-268140
WWW: www.leics.gov.uk/museums/musinleics.htm#charnwood
Foxton Canal Museum
Middle Lock, Gumley Road, Foxton, Market Harborough,
Leicestershire, LE16 7RA Tel: 0116-279-2657
Harborough Museum
Council Offices, Adam and Eve Street, Market Harborough,
Leicestershire, LE16 7AG Tel: 01858-821085
Fax: 01509-268140 Email: museums@leics.gov.uk
WWW: www.leics.gov.uk/museums/musinleics.htm#harborough
Hinckley & District Museum
Framework Knitters' Cottages, Lower Bond Street, Hinckley,
Leicestershire, LE10 1QX Tel: 01455-251218
Jewry Wall Museum
St. Nicholas Circle, Leicester LE1 4LB Tel: 0116-247-3021
Leicester City Museum & Art Gallery
53 New Walk, Leicester LE1 7EA Tel: 0116-255-4100
Leicester Gas Museum
Closed mid 2001. No genealogical records. Archive material
transferred to National Gas Archive, Aylestone Road, Leicester LE2
7LF Tel: 0116-250-3190
Leicestershire Environmental Resources Centre
Holly Hayes, 216 Birstall Road, Birstall, Leicester, LE4
4DG Tel: 0116-267-1950 Email: museums@leics.gov.uk
WWW: www.leics.gov.uk
The Manor House
Manor Road, Donington Le Heath, Coalville LE67 2FW
Tel: 01530-831259 Fax: 01530-831259
Email: museums@leics.gov.uk
WWW: www.leics.gov.uk/museums/musinleics.htm#manor
Melton Carnegie Museum
Thorpe End, Melton Mowbray LE13 1RB
Tel: 01664-569946 Fax: 01664-569946
Email: museums@leics.gov.uk
WWW: www.leics.gov.uk/museums/musinleics.htm#melton
Royal Leicestershire Regiment Museum
Enquiries to: Newarke Houses Museum, The Newarke,
Leicester. LE2 7BY - New Walk Museum, 53 New Walk,
Leicester, LE1 7AE Fax: 0116-2470403
Rutland Railway Museum
Iron Ore Mine Sidings, Ashwell Road, Cottesmore, Oakham,
Leicestershire, LE15 7BX Tel: 01572-813203
Snibston Discovery Park
Ashby Road, Coalville LE67 3LN Tel: 01530-510851
Fax: 01530-813301 Email: museums@leics.gov.uk
WWW: www.leics.gov.uk/museums/musinleics.htm#snibston
The Guildhall
Guildhall Lane, Leicester LE1 5FQ Tel: 0116-253-2569

Lincolnshire
Alford Civic Trust/Manor House Museum, Alford
Manor House Museum, West Street, Alford, LN13 9DJ
Tel: 01507-463073
Ayscoughfee Hall, Museum and Gardens
Churchgate, Spalding, Lincolnshire, PE11 2RA
Tel: 01775-725468 Fax: 01775-762715
Battle of Britain Memorial Flight Visits
R.A.F Coningsby, Coningsby, Lincoln LN4 4SY
Tel: 01526-344041
Boston Guildhall Museum
South Street, Boston PE21 6HT Tel: 01205-365954
Email: heritage@originalboston.freeserve.co.uk
Church Farm Museum, Skegness
Church Road South, Skegness PE25 2HF
Tel: 01754-766658 Fax: 01754-898243
Email: willf@lincolnshire.gov.uk

Gainsborough Old Hall
Parnell Street, Gainsborough DN21 2NB Tel: 01427-612669
Gordon Boswell Romany Museum
Hawthorns Clay Lake, Spalding PE12 6BL Tel: 01775-710599
Grantham Museum
St. Peters Hill, Grantham NG31 6PY Tel: 01476-568783
Fax: 01476-592457 Email: grantham_museum@lineone.net
The Incredibly Fantastic Old Toy Show
26 Westgate, Lincoln LN1 3BD Tel: 01522-520534
Lincolnshire Aviation Heritage Centre
East Kirkby Airfield, East Kirkby, Spilsbury PE23 4DE
Tel: 01790-763207
Lincs Vintage Vehicle Society
Whisby Rd, North Hykeham, Lincoln, LN6 3QT
Tel: 01522-500566
Louth Naturalists Antiquarian & Literary Society
4 Broadbank, Louth, LN11 0EQ Tel: 01507-601211
**Museum of Lincolnshire Life & Museum of the Royal
Lincolnshire Regiment Lincolnshire Yeomanry**
Old Barracks, Burton Road, Lincoln LN1 3LY
Tel: 01522-528448 Fax: 01522-521264
Email: Finch@lincolnshire.gov.uk
National Fishing Heritage Centre
Alexandra Dock, Great Grimsby DN31 1UZ
Tel: 01472-323345 WWW: www.nelincs.gov.uk
also www.nelincsevents.co.uk
**Queen's Royal Lancers Regimental Museum (16th/5th &
17th/21st Lancers)**
Belvoir Castle, nr Grantham NG32 1PD
Tel: 01159-573295 Fax: 01159-573195
Wisbech & Fenland Museum
Museum Square, Wisbech PE13 1ES Tel: 01945-583817
Fax: 01945-589050 Email: wisbechmuseum.@beeb.net

Lincolnshire – North Lincolnshire
North Lincolnshire Museum
Oswald Road, Scunthorpe, DN15 7BD Tel: 01724-843533
Fax: 01724-270474 Email: davidwilliams@northlincs.gov.uk
WWW: www.northlincs.gov.uk/museums
Baysgarth House Museum
Caistor Road, Barton-Upon-Humber DN18 6AH
Tel: 01652-632318
Immingham Museum
Margaret St. Immingham, DN40 1LE Tel: 01469-577066

Liverpool
King's Regiment Collection
Museum of Liverpool Life, Pier Head, Liverpool, L3 1PZ
Tel: 0151-478-4062 Fax: 0151-478-4090
Maritime Museum, Liverpool
William Brown St. Liverpool, L3 8EN Tel: 0151-2070001

London
**Alexander Fleming Laboratory Museum / St Mary's
NHS Trust Archives,** St Mary's Hospital, Praed Street,
Paddington, London, W2 1NY Tel: (020) 7886 6528 Fax:
(020) 7886 6739 Email: kevin.brown@st-marys.nhs.uk
Bank of England Archive
Archive Section HO-SV, The Bank of England,
Threadneedle Street, London, EC2R 8AH Tel: (020) 7601-
5096 Fax: (020) 7601-4356 Email:
archive@bankofengland.co.uk WWW:
www.bankofengland.co.uk
Bethlem Royal Hospital Archives & Museum
Archives and Museum, Monks Orchard Road, Beckenham,
BR3 3BX Tel: (020) 8776 4307 Tel: (020) 8776 4053 Fax:
(020) 8776 4045 Email: museum@bethlem.freeserve.co.uk
The archives of the Bethlem and Maudsley NHS Trust (the Bethlem
Royal Hospital and the Maudsley Hospital). Records relating to
individual patients are closed for 100 years.
Bethnal Green Museum of Childhood
Cambridge Heath Road, London, E2 9PA
Tel: 020-8980-2415 Email: k.bones@vam.ac.uk
Black Cultural Archives
378 Coldharbour Lane, London, SW9 8LF Tel: (020)
7738 4591 Fax: (020) 7738 7168

The British Museum
Great Russell Street, London, WC1B 3DG
Tel: 020-7323-8768, 020-7323-8224 Fax: 020-7323-8118
Email: jwallace@thebritishmuseum.ac.uk

British Red Cross Museum and Archives
9 Grosvenor Crescent, London, SW1X 7EJ Tel: (020) 7201-5153 Fax: (020) 7235-0876 Email: enquiry@redcross.org.uk
WWW: www.redcross.org.uk Open by appointment 10am to 4pm Monday to Friday.

Cabaret Mechanical Theatre
Unit 33 , The Market, Covent Garden, London, WC2E 8RE
Tel: 020-7379-7961

Cabinet War Rooms
Clive Steps, King Charles Street, London, SW1A 2AQ
Tel: 020-7930-6961 Fax: 020-7839-5897
Email: cwr@iwm.org.uk Web: www.iwm.org.uk

Church Farmhouse Museum
Greyhound Hill, Hendon, London, NW4 4JR Tel: 0208-359-2666
Web: www.earl.org.uk/partners/barnet/churchf.htm

Clink Prison Museum
1 Clink Street, London, SE1 9DG Tel: 020-7403-6515

Crystal Palace Museum
Anerley Hill, London, SE19 Tel: 020 8676 0700**Cutty Sark**
Site address: King William Walk, London SE10 9HT, Cutty Sark Offices (Enquiries address), 2 Greenwich Church Street, London, SE10 9EG Tel: 020-8858-2698
Fax: 020-8858-6976 Email: info@cuttysark.org.uk
Web: www.cuttysark.org.uk

The Design Museum
Butlers Wharf 28, Shad Thames, London, SE1 2YD
Tel: 020-7403-6933, 020-7940-8791 Fax: 020-7378-6540
Email: enquiries@designmuseum.org.uk
Web: www.designmuseum.org.uk

Dickens House Museum - London
48 Doughty Street, London, WC1N 2LF
Tel: 020-7405-2127 Email: Dhmuseum@rmplc.co.uk
Web: www.dickensmuseum.com

Doctor Johnson's House
17 Gough Square, London, EC4A 3DE Tel: 020-7353-3745

The Fan Museum
12 Crooms Hill, London, SE10 8ER Tel: 020-8293-18889
Email: admin@fan-museum.org Web: www.fan-museum.org

Florence Nightingale Museum
2 Lambeth Palace Road, London, SE1 7EW
Tel: 020-7620-0374 Email: curator@florence-nightingale.co.uk
Web: www.florence-nightingale.co.uk

Freud Museum
20 Maresfield Gardens, London, NW3 5SX
Tel: 0207-435-2002, 0207-435-5167 Fax: 0207-431-5452
Email: freud@gn.apc.org Web: www.freud.org.uk

Geffrye Museum
Kingsland Road, London, E2 8EA Tel: (020) 7739 9893
WWW: www.geffrye-museum.org.uk

Geological Museum
Cromwell Road, London, SW7 5BD Tel: 020-7938-8765

Golden Hinde
St. Mary Overie Dock, Cathedral St, London, SE1 9DE
Tel: 08700-118700

Grange Museum of Community History
The Grange, Neasden Lane, Neasden, London, NW10 1QB
Tel: 020-8452-8311

Guards Museum
Wellington Barracks, Birdcage Walk, London, SW1E 6HQ
Tel: 020-7414-3271/3428 Fax: 020-7414-3429

Gunnersbury Park Museum
Gunnersbury Park, Popes Lane, London, W3 8LQ
Tel: 020-8992-1612

Hackney Museum Service
Parkside Library, Victoria Park Road, London, E9 7JL
Tel: 020-8986-6914 Email: hmuseum@hackney.gov.uk
Web: www.hackney.gov.uk/hackneymuseum

Handel House Trust Ltd
10 Stratford Place, London, W1N 9AE Tel: 020-7495-1685

H.M.S. Belfast
Morgans Lane, Tooley Street, London, SE1 2JH Tel: (020) 7940 6300 Fax: (020) 7403 0719
WWW: www.iwm.org.uk

Hogarth's House
Hogarth Lane, Chiswick, London, W4 2QN Tel: 020-8994-6757

Horniman Museum
100 London Road, Forest Hill, London, SE23 3PQ
Tel: 020-8699-1872 Email: enquiries@horniman.co.uk
Web: www.horniman.co.uk

Imperial War Museum
Lambeth Road, London, SE1 6HZ Tel: 020-7416-5348
Email: books@iwm.org.uk Web: www.iwm.org.uk

Island History Trust
St. Matthias Old Church, Woodstock Terrace, Poplar High St, London, E14 0AE Tel: 020-7987-6041

Islington Museum
Foyer Gallery, Town Hall, Upper St, London, N1 2UD
Tel: 020-7354-9442

Iveagh Bequest
Kenwood House, Hampstead Lane, London, NW3 7JR
Tel: 020-8348-1286

Jewish Museum
80 East End Road, Finchley, London, N3 2SY
Tel: 020-8349-1143 Email: jml.finchley@lineone.net

Keats House Museum
Wentworth Place, Keats Grove, London, NW3 2RR
Tel: 020-7435-2062

Kensington Palace State Apartments
Kensington Palace, London, W8 4PX Tel: 020-7937-9561

Kingston Museum & Heritage Service
North Kingston Centre, Richmond Road, Kingston upon Thames, Surrey, KT2 5PE Tel: 020-8547-6738
Fax: 020-8547-6747
Email: local.history@rbk.kingston.gov.uk
Web: www.kingston.gov.uk/museum/

Leighton House Museum & Art Gallery
12 Holland Park Road, London, W14 8LZ
Tel: 0207602-3316

Library of the Royal College of Surgeons of England
35-43 Lincoln's Inn Fields, London, WC2A 3PN
Tel: 020-7869-6520 Fax: 020-7405-4438
Email: library@rseng.ac.uk

Livesey Museumfor Children
682 Old Kent Road, London, SE15 1JF Tel: 020-7639-5604
Fax: 020-7277-5384 Email: livesey.museum@southwark.gov.uk

L B of Barking & Dagenham Local History Studies -
Dagenham Valence Library & Museum, Becontree Avenue, Dagenham, Essex, RM8 3HT Tel: 020-8592-6537
Fax: 020-8227-5297 Email: fm019@viscount.org.uk
Web: www.earl.org.uk/partners/barking/index.html

L B of Newham Museum Service
Old Town Hall, 29 The Broadway, Stratford, London, E15 4BQ Tel: 020-8534-2274

L B of Waltham Forest - Vestry House Museum
Vestry Road, Walthamstow, London, E17 9NH
Tel: 020-8509-1917 Email: vestry.house@al.lbwf.gov.uk
Web: www.lbwf.gov.uk/vestry/vestry.htm

London Canal Museum
12-13 New Wharf Road, London, N1 9RT
Tel: 020-7713-0836 Web: www.canalmuseum.org.uk

London Fire Brigade Museum
94a Southwark Bridge Road, London, SE1 0EG
Tel: 020-7587-2894 Email: esther.mann@london-fire.gov.uk

London Gas Museum
Museum Closed - Exhibits in Storage, Twelvetrees Crescent, London, E3 3JH Tel: 020-7538-4982

London Toy & Model Museum
21-23 Craven Hill, London, W2 3EN Tel: 020-7706-8000

London Transport Museum
Covent Garden Piazza, London, WC2E 7BB
Tel: 020-7379-6344 Fax: 020-7565-7250
Email: contact@ltmuseum.co.uk Web: www.ltmuseum.co.uk

Mander & Mitchenson Theatre Collection
c/o Salvation Army Headquarters, PO Box 249, 101 Queen Victoria Street, London, EC4P 4EP Tel: 020-7236-0182
Fax: 020-7236-0184

Markfield Beam Engine & Museum
Markfield Road, London, N15 4RB Tel: 020-8800-7061

Metropolitan Police Museum
c/o Room 1317, New Scotland Yard, Broadway, London,
SW1H 0BG Tel: 020-8305-2824, 020-8305-1676
Fax: 020-8293-6692

Museum of London
London Wall, London, EC2Y 5HN Fax: 020-7600-1058
Email: kstarling@museumoflondon.org.uk

Museum of the Order of St John
St John's Gate, St John's Lane, Clerkenwell, London, EC1M
4DA Tel: 020-7253-6644 Fax: 020-7336-0587
Web: www.sja.org.uk/history

Museum of the Royal Pharmaceutical Society
1 Lambeth High Street, London, SE1 7JN
Tel: 020-7735-9141-ext-354 Fax: 020-7793-0232
Email: museum@rpsgb.org.uk Web: www.rpsgb.org.uk

Museum of Women's Art
3rd Floor, 11 Northburgh Street, London, EC1V 0AN
Tel: 020-7251-4881

National Army Museum & Archives
Royal Hospital Road, London, SW3 4HT
Tel: 020-7730-0717 Fax: 020-7823-6573
Email: info@national-army-museum.ac.uk
Web: www.national-army-museum.ac.uk

National Gallery
St. Vincent House, 30 Orange Street, London, WC2H 7HH
Tel: 020-7747-5950

National Maritime Museum
Romney Road, Greenwich, London, SE1O 9NF
Tel: 020-8858-4422 Web: www.nmm.ac.uk

National Maritime Museum Memorial Index
National Maritime Museum, Greenwich, London, SE10 9NF
Tel: 020-8858-4422 Fax: 020-8312-4422
Email: manuscripts@nmm.ac.uk Web: www.nmm.ac.uk

National Portrait Gallery
2 St. Martins Place, London, WC2H 0HE
Tel: 020-7306-0055 Web: www.npg.org.uk

North Woolwich Old Station Musuem
Pier Road, North Woolwich, London, E16 2JJ
Tel: 020-7474-7244

The Old Operating Theatre Museum & Herb Garret
9a Street. Thomas's Street, London, SE1 9RY
Tel: 020-7955-4791 Fax: 020-7378-8383
Email: curator@thegarret.org.uk Web: www.thegarret.org.uk

Percival David Foundation of Chinese Art
University of London, School of Oriental & African Studies,
53 Gordon Square, London, WC1H 0PD
Tel: 020-7387-3909 Fax: 020-7383-5163

Petrie Museum of Egyptian Archaeology
University College London, Gower Street, London, WC1E
6BT Tel: 020-7679-2884 Fax: 020-7679-2886
Email: petrie.museum@ucl.ac.uk

Pitshanger Manor & Gallery
Walpole Park, Mattock Lane, Ealing, London, W5 5EQ
Tel: 020-8567-1227 Email: pitshanger@ealing.gov.uk

Polish Institute & Sikorski Museum
20 Princes Gate, London, SW7 1PT Tel: 020-7589-9249

Pollock's Toy Museum
1 Scala Street, London, W1P 1LT Tel: 020-7636-3452

Pump House Educational Museum
Lavender Pond & Nature Park, Lavender Road, Rotherhithe,
London, SE16 1DZ Tel: 020-7231-2976

Ragged School Museum Trust
46-50 Copperfield Road, London, E3 4RR
Tel: 020-8980-6405 Web: www.ics-london.co.uk/rsm

Royal Armouries (Tower of London)
HM Tower Of London, Tower Hill, London, EC3N 4AB
Tel: 020-7480-6358

Royal Artillery Regimental Museum
Old Royal Military Academy, Red Lion Lane, Woolwich,
London, SE18 4DN Tel: 0181 781 5628 ext 3128

Royal London Hospital Archives and Museum
Royal London Hospital, Newark Whitechapel, London, E1
1BB Tel: (020) 7377-7608 Email: r.j.evans@mds.qmw.ac.uk
WWW: www.bartsandthelondon.org.uk

Museum of the Royal Pharmaceutical Society
Museum of the Royal Pharmaceutical Society, 1 Lambeth
High Street, London, SE1 7JN Tel: (020) 7572 2210

museum@rpsgb.org.uk WWW: http://www.rpsgb.org.uk
Records of pharmacists from 1841 Research fee charged £20 per
person or premises researched to Non members of the Society, £10
per person or premises researched for members(Genealogical
Enquiries)

Royal Regiment of Fusiliers Museum
H M Tower of London, London, EC3N 4AB
Tel: 0171 488 5610

Sam Uriah Morris Society
136a Lower Clapton Rd, London E5 0QJ Tel: 020-8985-6449

The Science Museum
Exhibition Road, London, SW7 2DD Tel: 0870-870-4868
Email: sciencemuseum@nms.ac.uk

The Sherlock Holmes Museum
221b Baker Street, London, NW1 6XE Tel: 020-7935-8866
Email: sherlock@easynet.co.uk Web: www.sherlock-holmes.co.uk

Sir John Soane's Museum
13 Lincolns Inn Fields, London, WC2A 3BP
Tel: 020-7405-2107 Web: www.soane.org

St Bartholomew's Hospital Archives & Museum
Archives and Museum, West Smithfield, London, EC1A 7BE
Tel: (020) 7601-8152 Email:
marion.rea@bartsandthelondon.nhs.uk WWW:
bartsandthelondon.org.uk Visitors to use the archive by
appointment only - Mon to Fri 9.30am to 5pm

Theatre Museum
Russell Street, Convent Garden, London, WC2
Tel: 020 7943 4700 Email: info@theatremuseum.org
WWW: www.theatremuseum.org

Valence House Museum
Becontree Avenue, Dagenham, RM8 3HT Tel: 020-822-
75293 Fax: 020-822-75297 Email: fm019@viscount.org.uk
WWW: http://www.bardaglea.org.uk/4-heritage/heritage-menu.html

Veterinary Museum
Royal Vetinerary College, Royal College Street, London,
NW1 0TU Tel: 020-7468-5165/6 Fax: 020-7468-5162
Email: fhouston@rvc.ac.uk Web: www.rvc.ac.uk

Victoria & Albert Museum
Cromwell Road, South Kensington, London, SW7 2RL
Tel: 020-7942-2164 Fax: 020-7942-2162

Wallace Collection
Hertford House, Manchester Square, London, W1M 6BN
Tel: 020-7935-0687

Wellcome Trust Centre for the History of Medecine
183 Euston Road, London, NW1 2BE Tel: 020-7611-8888
Fax: 020-7611-8545 Email: infoserv@wellcome.ac.uk
Web: www.wellcome.ac.uk

Wellington Museum
Apsley House, 149 Piccadilly Hyde Park Corner, London,
W1V 9FA Tel: 020-7499-5676

Westminster Abbey Museum
Westminster Abbey, Deans Yard, London, SW1P 3PA
Tel: 020-7233-0019

Wimbledon Lawn Tennis Museum
Church Road, Wimbledon, London, SW19 5AE
Tel: 020-8946-6131

Wimbledon Museum of Local History
22 Ridgeway, London, SW19 4QN Tel: 020-8296-9914

Manchester & Greater Manchester
Greater Manchester Police Museum
Newton Street, Manchester, M1 1ES Tel: 0161-856-3287,
0161-856-3288 Fax: 0161-856-3286

Manchester Jewish Museum
190 Cheetham Hill Road, Manchester, M8 8LW
Tel: 0161-834-9879, 0161-832-7353 Fax: 0161-834-9801
Email: info@manchesterjewishmuseum.com
WWW: www.manchesterjewishmuseum.com

Manchester Museum Education Service
University of Manchester, Oxford Road, Manchester, M13
9PL Tel: 0161-275-2630 Fax: 0161-275-2676
Email: education@man.ac.uk
WWW: www.museum.man.ac.uk

The Museum of Science and Industry In Manchester
Liverpool Road, Castlefield, Manchester, M3 4JP
Tel: 0161-832-2244, 0161-832-1830 24hr Info line
Fax: 0161-833-2184 WWW: www.msim.org.uk

National Museum of Labour History
Labour History Archive, 103 Princess Street, Manchester,
M1 6DD Tel: 0161-228-7212 Fax: 0161-237-5965
Email: archives@nmlhweb.org WWW: www.nmlhweb.org
Wigan Heritage Service - History Shop
Library Street, Wigan, Greater Manchester, WN1 1NU
Tel: 01942-828020 Fax: 01942-827645
Email: heritage@wiganmbc.gov.uk

Merseyside
The Beatle Story Ltd
Britannia Vaults, Albert Dock, Liverpool L3 4AA
Tel: 0151-709-1963 Fax: 0151-708-0039
The Boat Museum & David Owen Waterways Archive
South Pier Road, Ellesmere Port, CH65 4FW Tel: 0151-355-
5017 Email: boatmuseum@easynet.co.uk Records relating to the
management, maintenance and operation of inland waterways in England,
Scotland and Wales. Substantial Waterways library. Date range: late 17th
century to 20th century.
King's Regiment Collection
Museum of Liverpool Life, Pier Head, Liverpool, L3 1PZ
Tel: 0151-478-4062 Fax: 0151-478-4090
Merseyside Maritime Museum
Maritime Archives and Library, Albert Dock, Liverpool, L3 4AQ
Tel: 0151-478-4418 Email: archives@nmgmarchives.demon.co.uk
WWW: www.nmgm.org.uk
National Museums & Galleries on Merseyside
127 Dale Street, Liverpool L2 2JH Tel: 0151-207-0001
Port Sunlight Village Trust
95 Greendale Road, Port Sunlight, CH62 4XE
Tel: 0151-644-6466 Fax: 0151-645-8973
Prescot Museum
34 Church Street, Prescot L34 3LA Tel: 0151-430-7787
Shore Road Pumping Station
Shore Road, Birkenhead, CH41 1AG Tel: 0151-650-1182
Western Approaches
1 Rumford Street, Liverpool L2 8SZ Tel: 0151-227-2008
Wirral Archives Service and Museum
Birkenhead Town Hall, Hamilton Street, Birkenhead, CH41
5BR Tel: 0151-666-4010 Email: archives@wirral-libraries.net
Botanic Gardens Museum
Churchtown, Southport PR9 7NB Tel: 01704-227547

Middlesex
Forty Hall Museum
Forty Hill, Enfield EN2 9HA Tel: 020-8363-8196
Hackney Museum Service
Parkside Library, Victoria Park Road, London, E9 7JL
Tel: 020-8986-6914 Fax: 020-8985-7600
Email: hmuseum@hackney.gov.uk
WWW: www.hackney.gov.uk/hackneymuseum
Harrow Museum & Heritage Centre
Headstone Manor, Pinner View, Harrow HA2 6PX
Tel: 020-8861-2626
Kew Bridge Steam Museum
Green Dragon Lane, Brentford TW8 0EN Tel: 020-8568-4757
Musical Museum
368 High Street, Brentford TW8 0BD Tel: 020-8560-8108

Midlands – West Midlands
Aston Manor-Road Transport Museum Ltd
208-216 Witton Lane, Birmingham B6 6QE
Tel: 0121-322-2298
Bantock House & Park
Bantock Park,, Finchfield Rd, Wolverhampton WV3 9LQ
Tel: 01902-552196 Fax: 01902-552196
Birmingham & Midland Museum Of Transport
Chapel Lane, Wythall, Birmingham, B47 6JX
Tel: 01564-826471 Email: enquiries@bammot.org.uk
WWW: www.bammot.org.uk
Birmingham Museum & Art Gallery
Chamberlain Square, Birmingham B3 3DH
Tel: 0121-303-2834 Fax: 0121-303-1394
WWW: www.birmingham.gov.uk/bmag
Birmingham Railway Museum Ltd
670 Warwick Road, Tyseley, Birmingham B11 2HL
Tel: 0121-707-4696

Black Country Living Museum
Tipton Road, Dudley DY1 4SQ Tel: 0121-557-9643
Email: info@bcim.co.uk WWW: www.bcim.co.uk
Blakesley Hall
Blakesley Road, Yardley, Birmingham B25 8RN
Tel: 0121-783-2193
Dudley Museum & Art Gallerey
St James's Road, Dudley, West Midlands, DY1
Haden Hall
Haden Hill Park, Barrs Road, Cradley Heath, West Midlands,
B64 7JX Tel: 01384-635846
Herbert Art Gallery & Museum
Jordan Well, Coventry CV1 5QP Tel: 024-76832381
Lock Museum
54 New Road, Willenhall WV13 2DA Tel: 01902-634542
Email: http://members.tripod.co.uk/lock_museum/
Midland Air Museum
Coventry Airport, Coventry Road, Baginton, Coventry
CV8 3AZ Tel: 024-7630-1033
Museum of the Jewellery Quarter
75-79 Vyse Street, Hockley, Birmingham, B6 6JD
Tel: 0121-554-3598 Fax: 0121-554-9700
Oak House Museum
Oak Road, West Bromwich B70 8HJ Tel: 0121-553-0759
Selly Manor Museum
Maple Road, Birmingham, B30 2AE Tel: 0121-472-0199
Walsall Leather Museum
Littleton Street West, Walsall, West Midlands, WS2 8EQ
Tel: 01922-721153 Email: leathermuseum@walsall.gov.uk
West Midlands Police Museum
Sparkhill Police Station, Stratford Road, Sparkhill,
Birmingham, West Midlands, B11 4EA Tel: 0121-626-7181
Whitefriars Gallery
London Road, Coventry CV3 4AR Tel: 024-7683-2432
Whitlocks End Farm
Bills Lane, Shirley, Solihull B90 2PL Tel: 0121-745-4891

Norfolk
Air Defence Battle Command & Control Museum The
Neatishead, Norwich, NR12 8YB Tel: 01692-633309
Bressingham Steam & Gardens
Bressingham, Diss, IP22 2AB Tel: 01379 687386 Tel: 01379
687382 (24 hour info line) Fax: 01379 688085
Bure Valley Railway
Norwich Road, Aylsham, NR11 6BW Tel: 01263 733858
EcoTech
Swaffham, PE37 7HT Tel: 01760 726100 01760 726109
Email: info@ecotech.rmplc.co.uk WWW: www.ecotech.org.uk
Castle Museum
Castle Hill, Norwich, Norfolk, NR1 3JU Tel: 01603-493624
City of Norwich Aviation Museum Ltd
Old Norwich Road, Horsham St Faith, Norwich, NR10 3JF
Tel: 01603-893080
Diss Museum
The Market Place, Diss IP22 3JT Tel: 01379-650618
Elizabethan House Museum
4 South Quay, Great Yarmouth NR30 2QH
Tel: 01493-855746
Feltwell (Historical and Archaeological) Society
16 High Street, Feltwell, Thetford, IP26 Tel: 01842 828448,
Email: peterfeltwell@tinyworld.co.uk The Museum is at The Beck,
Feltwell Open Tuesday & Saturday April to September 2.00.p.m. to 4.00.p.m.

Glandford Shell Museum
Church House, Glandford, Holt, NR25 7JR
Tel: 01263-740081
Iceni Village & Museums
Cockley Cley, Swaffham PE37 8AG Tel: 01760-721339
Lynn Museum
Old Market Street, King's Lynn, Norfolk, PE30 1NL
Tel: 01553-775001 WWW: www.norfolk.gov.uk/tourism/museums
Maritime Museum for East Anglia
25 Marine Parade, Great Yarmouth NR30 2EN Tel: 01493-842267
The Muckleburgh Collection
Weybourne, Holt NR25 7EG Tel: 01263-588210
Fax: 01263-588425 Email: jenny@muckleburgh.demon.co.uk

Norfolk Motorcycle Museum
Station Yard, Norwich Road, North Walsham, Norfolk,
NR28 0DS Tel: 01692-406266

Norfolk Rural Life Museum & Union Farm
Beech House, Gressenhall, East Dereham, Norfolk, NR20
4DR Tel: 01362-860563 Fax: 01362-860385
Email: frances.collinson.mus@norfolk.gov.uk

Royal Norfolk Regimental Museum
Shirehall, Market Avenue, Norwich, Norfolk, NR1 3JQ
Tel: 01603-493649 Fax: 01603-765651

The North Norfolk Railway
The Station, Sheringham, NR26 8RA Tel: 01263 822045
01263 823794 WWW: www.nnrailway.co.uk

Sheringham Museum
Station Road, Sheringham NR26 8RE Tel: 01263-821871

Shirehall Museum
Common Place, Walsingham, NR22 6BP
Tel: 01328-820510 Fax: 01328-820098
Email: walsingham.museum@farmline.com

Wisbech & Fenland Museum
Museum Square, Wisbech PE13 1ES Tel: 01945-583817
Fax: 01945-589050 Email: wisbechmuseum.@beeb.net

100 Bomb Group
Memorial Museum, Common Road, Dickleburgh, Diss,
Norfolk , IP21 4PH Tel: 01379-740708

Inspire Hands On Science Centre
Coslany Street, Norwich, Norfolk , NR3 3DJ
Tel: 01603-612612

Northamptonshire
Canal Museum
Stoke Bruerne, Towcester NN12 7SE Tel: 01604-862229

Museum of The Northamptonshire Regiment
Abington Park Museum, Abington NN1 5LW
Tel: 01604 635412

National Dragonfly Museum
Ashton Mill, Ashton, Peterborough, PE8 5LB
Tel: 01832-272427 Email: ndmashton@aol.com
WWW: www.natdragonflymuseum.org.uk

Northampton Iron Stone Railway Trust
Hunsbury Hill Country Park, Hunsbury Hill Road, West
Hunsbury, Northampton NN4 9UW
Tel: 01604-702031/757481, 01908-376821
Email: raf9687@aol.com also bnile98131@aol.com

Northampton & Lamport Railway Preservation Society
Pitsford & Brampton Station, Pitsford Road, Chapel
Brampton, Northampton, NN6 8BA Tel: 01604 820327

Peterborough Museum & Art Gallery
Priestgate, Peterborough PE1 1LF Tel: 01733-343329
Fax: 01733-341928 Email: museums@peterborough.gov.uk

Rushden Historical Transport Society
The Station, Station Approach, Rushden, Northamptonshire,
NN10 0AW Tel: 01933-318988

Wellingborough Heritage Centre
Croyland Hall, Burystead Place, Wellingborough,
Northamptonshire, NN8 1AH Tel: 01933-276838

Northumberland
Bellingham Heritage Centre
Front Street, Bellingham, Hexham, NE48 2DF
Tel: 01434-220050

Berwick Borough Museum
The Barracks, The Parade, Berwick-Upon-Tweed,
Northumberland, TD15 1DG Tel: 01289-330933

Bewick Studios The
Mickley Square, Mickley, Stocksfield NE43 7BL
Tel: 01661-844055

Border History Museum & Library
Moothall, Hallgate, Hexham, Northumberland, NE46 3NH
Tel: 01434-652349 Fax: 01434-652425
Email: museum@tynedale.gov.uk

Chesterholm Museum (Vindolanda Museum)
The Vindolanda Trust, Bardon Mill, Hexham, NE47 7JN
Tel: 01434-344277 Fax: 01434-344060
Email: info@vindolanda.com
WWW: www.vindolanda.com

Fusiliers Museum of Northumberland
The Abbot's Tower, Alnwick Castle, Alnwick, NE66 1NG

Tel: 01665-602152 Fax: 01665-603320
Email: fusmusnorthld@btinternet.com

King's Own Scottish Borderers Museum
The Barracks, Berwick upon Tweed, TD15 1DG
Tel: 01289-307426

Marine Life Centre & Fishing Museum
8 Main Street, Seahouses NE68 7RG Tel: 01665-721257

North East Mills Group
Blackfriars, Monk St. Newcastle upon Tyne, NE1 4XN
Tel: 0191-232-9279 Fax: 0191-230-1474
WWW: www.welcome.to/North.East.Mill.Group

Tynedale Council Museums
Department of Leisure & Tourism, Prospect House,
Hexham, Northumberland, NE46 3NH Tel: 01461-652351

Nottinghamshire
D.H Lawrence Heritage
Durban House Heritage Centre, Mansfield Road, Eastwood,
Nottingham, NG16 3DZ Tel: 01773-717353

Flintham Museum
Flintham Museum, Inholms Road, Flintham, NG23 5JF

Flintham Society
Flintham Museum, Inholms Road, Flintham, NG23 5LF Tel:
0163.6 525111, Email: flintham.museum@lineone.net
WWW: www.flintham-museum.org.uk

Galleries of Justice
Shire Hall, High Pavement, Lace Market, Nottingham, NG1
1HN Tel: 0115-952-0555 Fax: 0115-993-9828
Email: info@galleriesofjustice.org.uk
WWW: www.galleriesofjustice.org.uk

Great Central Railway
Nottingham Heritage Centre, Mere Way, Ruddington,
Nottingham, NG11 6JS Tel: 0115-940-5705

Greens Mill & Science Musuem
Windmill Lane, Sneinton, Nottingham, Nottinghamshire,
NG2 4QB Tel: 0115-915-6878

Harley Gallery
Welbeck, Worksop S80 3LW Tel: 01909-501700

Mansfield Museum & Art Gallery
Leeming Street, Mansfield, Nottinghamshire, NG18 1NG
Tel: 01623-463088 Fax: 01623-412922

Millgate Museum of Folk Life
48 Millgate, Newark NG24 4TS Tel: 01636-655730
Email: museums@newark-sherwooddc.gov.uk
WWW: www.newark-sherwooddc.go.uk

The Museum of Nottingham Lace
3-5 High Pavement, The Lace Market, Nottingham
NG1 1HF Tel: 0115-989-7365 Fax: 0115-989-7301
Email: info@nottinghamlace.org
WWW: www.nottinghamlace.org

Natural History and Industrial Museum
The Courtyard, Wollaton Park, Nottingham, NG8 2AE
Tel: 0115-9153942 Fax: 0115-9153941

Newark (Notts & Lincs) Air Museum
The Airfield, Lincoln Road, Winthorpe, Newark,
Nottinghamshire, NG24 2NY Tel: 01636-707170
Fax: 01636-707170 Email: newarkair@lineone.net

Newark Museum
Appleton Gate, Newark NG24 1JY Tel: 01636-702358

Newstead Abbey Museum
Newstead Abbey Park, Nottingham NG15 8GE
Tel: 01623-455900

Nottingham Castle Museum & Art Gallery
Castle Road, Nottingham NG1 6EL Tel: 0115-915-3700
Fax: 0115-915-3653

Nottingham Musuem Shops
Canal Street, Nottingham NG1 7HG Tel: 0115-915-6871

Ruddington Frame Work Knitter's Museum
Chapel Street, Ruddington, Nottingham NG11 6HE
Tel: 0115-984-6914

Ruddington Village Museum
St. Peters Rooms, Church Street, Ruddington, Nottingham,
NG11 6HD Tel: 0115-914-6645

Sherwood Foresters (Notts & Derbyshire Regt) Museum
The Castle, Nottingham. NG1 6EL, RHQ WFR

Sherwood Foresters Museum & Archives
RHQ WFR, Foresters House, Chetwynd Barracks, Chilwell,
Nottingham, NG9 5HA Tel: 0115-946-5415
Fax: 0115-946-5712
Whaley Thorn Heritage & Environment Centre
Portland Terrace, Langwith, Mansfield NG20 9HA
Tel: 01623-742525
Oxfordshire
Abingdon Museum
County Hall, Market Place, Abingdon, Oxfordshire, OX14
3HG Tel: 01235-523703 Fax: 01235-536814
Ashmolean Museum
University of Oxford, University of Oxford, Beaumont St,
Oxford, Oxfordshire, OX1 2PH Tel: 01865-278000
Great Western Society Ltd
Didcot Railway Centre, Station Road, Didcot OX11 7NJ
Tel: 01235-817200
Oxfordshire & Buckinghamshire Light Infantry Regt Museum
Slade Park, Headington, Oxford OX3 7JL Tel: 01865 780128
The Oxfordshire Museum
Fletchers House, Park Street, Woodstock OX20 1SN
Tel: 01993-811456, 01993-814104 Fax: 01993-813239
Email: oxonmuseum@oxfordshire.gov.uk
Pitt Rivers Museum
University Of Oxford, South Parks Road, Oxford, OX1 3PP
Tel: 01865-270927 Fax: 01865-270943
Email: prm@prm.ox.ac.uk WWW: www.prm.ox.ac.uk
River & Rowing Museum
Mill Meadows, Henley on Thames RG9 1BF
Tel: 01491-415625 Fax: 01491-415601
Email: museum@rrm.co.uk also alicia.gurney@rrm.co.uk
WWW: www.rrm.co.uk
The Vale & Downland Museum
19 Church Street, Wantage, Oxfordshire, OX12 8BL
Tel: 01235-771447 Email: museum@wantage.com
Wallingford Museum
Flint House, High Street, Wallingford, Oxfordshire, OX10
0DB Tel: 01491-835065
Witney & District Museum
Gloucester Court Mews, High Street, Witney, Oxfordshire,
OX8 6LX Tel: 01993-775915 Email: janecavell@aol.com

Rutland
Rutland County Museum
Catmose Street, Oakham, Rutland, LE15 6HW
Tel: 01572-723654 WWW: www.rutnet.co.uk

Shropshire
Acton Scott Historic Working Farm
Wenlock Lodge, Acton Scott, Church Stretton, Shropshire,
SY6 6QN Tel: 01694-781306
Blists Hill Open Air Museum
Ironbridge Gorge Museum Trust Ltd, Legges Way, Madeley,
Telford, Shropshire, TF7 5DU Tel: 01952-588016
Coalport China Museum
Ironbridge Gorge Museum Trust Ltd, High Street, Coalport,
Telford, Shropshire, TF8 7AW Tel: 01952-580650
Ironbridge Gorge Museum, Library & Archives
The Wharfage, Ironbridge, Telford, TF8 7AW
Tel: 01952-432141 Email: library@ironbridge.org.uk
WWW: www.ironbridge.org.uk
Ironbridge Gorge Museums
Ironbridge Gorge Museum Trust Ltd, Ironbridge, Telford,
TF8 7AW Tel: 01952-432141 Fax: 01952-432237
Jackfield Tile Museum
Ironbridge Gorge Museum Trust Ltd, Jackfield, Telford,
Shropshire, TF8 7AW Tel: 01952-882030
Ludlow Museum
Castle Street, Ludlow, Shropshire, SY8 1AS
Tel: 01584-875384
Midland Motor Museum
Stanmore Hall, Stourbridge Road, Stanmore, Bridgnorth,
Shropshire, WV15 6DT Tel: 01746-762992
Museum Of Iron
Ironbridge Gorge Museum Trust Ltd, Coach Road,
Coalbrookdale, Telford TF8 7EZ Tel: 01952-433418

Museum Of The River Visitor Centre
Ironbridge Gorge Museum Trust Ltd, The Wharfage,
Ironbridge, Telford TF8 7AW Tel: 01952-432405
Oswestry Transport Museum
Oswald Road, Oswestry SY11 1RE Tel: 01691-671749
Rowley's House Museum
Shrewsbury Museums Service, Barker Street, Shrewsbury,
SY1 1QH Tel: 01743-361196 Fax: 01743-358411
Royal Air Force Museum
Cosford, Shifnal, Shropshire, TF11 8UP Tel: 01902-376200
Shropshire Regimental Museum
The Castle, Shrewsbury SY1 2AT Tel: 01743-358516

Somerset
Abbey Barn - Somerset Rural Life Museum
Abbey Barn, Chilkwell Street, Glastonbury, Somerset, BA6 8DB
Tel: 01458-831197 WWW: www.somerset.giv.uk/museums
Admiral Blake Museum
Blake Street, Bridgwater, Somerset, TA6 3NB
Tel: 01278-435399 Email: Museums@sedgemoor.gov.uk
American Museum
Claverton Manor, Bath, Somerset, BA2 7BD
Tel: 01225-460503 Fax: 01225-480726
Bakelite Museum
Orchard Mill, Bridge St Williton, Taunton, Somerset, TA4
4NS Tel: 01984-632133
Bath Industrial Heritage Centre
Camden Works, Julian Road, Bath, Somerset, BA1 2RH
Tel: 01225-318348 Fax: 01225-318348
Email: bathindheritage@camdenworks.swinternet.com.uk
Bath Postal Museum
8 Broad Street, Bath, Somerset, BA1 5LJ
Tel: 01225-460333 WWW: www.bathpostalmuseum.org
Bath Royal Literary & Scientific Institution
16-18 Queen Square, Bath, Somerset, BA1 2HN
Tel: 01225-312084
Blazes Fire Museum
Sandhill Park, Bishops Lydeard, Taunton, Somerset, TA4
3DE Tel: 01823-433964
Building of Bath Museum
Countess of Huntingdon's Chapel, The Vineyards, Bath,
Somerset, BA1 5NA Tel: 01225-333-895
Fax: 01225-445-473 Email: admin@bobm.freeserve.co.uk
WWW: www.bath-preservations-trust.org.uk
Chard & District Museum
Godworthy House, High Street, Chard, Somerset, TA20 1QB
Tel: 01460-65091
Fleet Air Arm Museum
R.N.A.S Yeovilton, Yeovil, Somerset, BA22 8HT
Tel: 01935-840565
Fleet Air Arm Museum Records & Research Centre
Box D61, RNAS Yeovilton, Nr Ilchester, Somerset, BA22
8HT Tel: 01935-840565 Fax: 01935-840181
Glastonbury Lake Village Museum
The Tribunal, 9 High Street, Glastonbury, Somerset, BA6
9DP Tel: 01458-832949
The Haynes Motor Museum
Castle Cary Road, Sparkford, Yeovil, Somerset, BA22 7LH
Tel: 01963-440804 Fax: 01963-441004
Email: mike@gmpwin.demon.co.uk
WWW: www.haynesmotormuseum.co.uk
Holburne Museum & Crafts Study Centre
Great Pulteney Street, Bath, BA2 4DB Tel: 01225-466669
John Judkyn Memorial
Garden Thorpe, Freshford, Bath, BA3 6BX Tel: 01225-723312
Lambretta Scooter Museum
77 Alfred Street, Weston-Super-Mare, North Somerset, BS23
1PP Tel: 01934-614614 Fax: 01934-620120
Email: lambretta@wsparts.force9.net
Museum Of East Asian Art
12 Bennett Street, Bath, BA1 2QL Tel: 01225-464640
Email: museum@east-asian-art.freeserve.co.uk
WWW: www.east-asian-art.co.uk
No.1 Royal Crescent
1 Royal Crescent, Bath, BA1 2LR Tel: 01225-428126

Radstock, Midsomer Norton & District Museum
Waterloo Road, Radstock, Bath, Somerset, BA3 3ER
Tel: 01761-437722 Email: radstockmuseum@ukonline.co.uk
WWW: www.radstockmuseum.co.uk
Somerset & Dorset Railway Trust
Washford Station, Washford, Watchet, Somerset, TA23 0PP
Tel: 01984-640869, 01308-424630 Email: info@sdrt.org
WWW: www.sdrt.org
Somerset County Museum Service
Taunton Castle, Taunton, Somerset, TA1 4AA
Tel: 01823-320200
Somerset Military Museum (Somerset Light Infantry Yeomanry
LI Office, 14 Mount Street, Taunton, Somerset, TA1 3QE
Tel: 01823-333434 Fax: 01832-351639
Wells Museum
8 Cathedral Green, Wells, Somerset, BA5 2UE
Tel: 01749-673477
West Somerset Museum
The Old School, Allerford, Minehead, Somerset, TA24 8HN
Tel: 01643-862529
William Herschel Museum
19 New King Street, Bath, BA1 2BL Tel: 01225-311342

Somerset – North East Somerset
Roman Baths Museum
Abbey Churchyard, Bath, BA1 1LZ Tel: 01225-477773
Helicopter Museum
Locking Moor Road, Weston-Super-Mare, BS22 8PL
Tel: 01934-635227
North Somerset Museum Service
Burlington Street, Weston-Super-Mare, BS23 1PR
Tel: 01934-621028

Staffordshire
Bass Museum and Archive
Horninglow Street, Burton on Trent DE14 1JZTel: 0845 60000598
Borough Museum & Art Gallery
Brampton Park, Newcastle ST5 0QP Tel: 01782-619705
Clay Mills Pumping Engines Trust Ltd
Sewage Treatment Works, Meadow Lane, Stretton,
Burton-On-Trent DE13 0DB Tel: 01283-509929
Etruria Industrial Museum
Lower Bedford St, Etruria, Stoke-On-Trent, Staffordshire,
ST4 7AF Tel: 01782-233144
Gladstone Pottery Museum
Uttoxeter Road, Longton, Stoke-On-Trent, Staffordshire,
ST3 1PQ Tel: 01782-319232
Hanley Museum & Art Gallery
Bethesda Street, Hanley, Stoke-On-Trent, Staffordshire, ST1
3DW Tel: 01782-232323
Museum of The Staffordshire Regiment
Whittington Barracks, Lichfield, Staffordshire, WS14 9PY
Tel: 0121-311-3229/3240 Fax: 0121-311-3205
Museum of the Staffordshire Yeomanry
The Ancient High House, Greengate Street, Stafford,
Staffordshire, ST16 2HS Tel: 01785 40204 (Tourist Info
Potteries Museum & Art Gallery
Bethesda Street, Hanley, Stoke-On-Trent, ST1 3DE
Tel: 01782-232323 Email: museums@stoke.gov.uk
WWW: www.stoke,gov.uk/museums
Samuel Johnson Birthplace Museum
Breadmarket Street, Lichfield, Staffordshire, WS13 6LG
Tel: 01543-264972 WWW: www.lichfield.gov.uk
Uttoxeter Heritage Centre
34-36 Carter Street, Uttoxeter ST14 8EU Tel: 01889-567176

Suffolk
Christchurch Mansion & Wolsey Art Gallery
Christchurch Park, Soane Street, Ipswich, Suffolk, IP4 2BE
Tel: 01473-253246
East Anglia Transport Museum
Chapel Road, Carlton Colville, Lowestoft, Suffolk, NR33
8BL Tel: 01502-518459
Felixstowe Museum
Landguards Fort, Felixstowe IP11 8TW Tel: 01394-674355
Gainsborough House Society
Gainsborough Street, Sudbury CO10 2EU

Tel: 01787-372958 Email: mail@gainsborough.org
WWW: www.gainsborough.org
International Sailing Craft Assoc Maritime Museum
Caldecott Road, Oulton Broad, Lowestoft, Suffolk, NR32
3PH Tel: 01502-585606 Fax: 01502-589014
Email: admin@isca-maritimemuseum.org
Ipswich Museum & Exhibition Gallery
High Street, Ipswich, Suffolk, IP1 3QH Tel: 01473-213761
Ipswich Transport Museum Ltd
Old Trolley Bus Depot, Cobham Rd, Ipswich, Suffolk, IP3
9JD Tel: 01473-715666
Long Shop Steam Museum
Main Street, Leiston, Suffolk, IP16 4ES Tel: 01728-832189
WWW: www.suffolkcc.gov.uk/libraries_and_heritage/sro/garrett/index.html
Lowestoft Museum
Broad House, Nicholas Everitt Park, Oulton Broad,
Lowestoft, Suffolk, NR33 9JR Tel: 01502-511457,
01502-513795 Fax: 01502-513795
Maritime Museum Sparrows Nest
The Museum, Whapload Road, Lowestoft, Suffolk, NR32
1XG Tel: 01502-561963
Mid Suffolk Light Railway
Brockford Station, Wetheringsett, Stowmarket, Suffolk, IP14
5PW Tel: 01449-766899
Mildenhall & District Museum
6 King Street, Mildenhall, Bury St. Edmunds, Suffolk, IP28
7EX Tel: 01638-716970
The National Horseracing Museum & Tours
99 High Street, Newmarket CB8 8JH Tel: 01638-667333
Rougham Tower Association
Rougham Estate Office, Rougham, Bury St. Edmunds,
Suffolk, IP30 9LZ Tel: 01359-271471 Email: bplsto@aol.com
Suffolk Regiment Museum
Suffolk Record Office, 77 Raingate Street, Bury St
Edmunds, Suffolk, IP33 2AR Tel: 01284-352352
Fax: 01284-352355 Email: bury.ro@libhev.suffolkcc.gov.uk
Dunwich Museum
St. James's Street, Dunwich, Saxmundham, Suffolk , IP17
3DT Tel: 01728-648796
Norfolk & Suffolk Aviation Museum
Buckaroo Way, The Street, Flixton, Bungay, Suffolk , NR35
1NZ Tel: 01986-896644 WWW: www.aviationmuseum.net
West Stow Country Park & Anglo-Saxon Village
The Visitor Centre, Icklingham Road, West Stow, Bury St
Edmunds, IP28 6HG Tel: 01284 728718

Surrey
Bourne Hall Museum
Bourne Hall, Spring Street, Ewell, Epsom, Surrey, KT17
1UF Tel: 020-8394-1734 WWW: www.epsom.townpage.co.uk
Chertsey Museum
The Cedars, 33 Windsor Street, Chertsey, Surrey, KT16 8AT
Tel: 01932-565764 Email: enquiries@chertseymuseum.org.uk
Dorking & District Museum
The Old Foundry, 62a West St, Dorking, Surrey, RH4 1BS
Tel: 01306-876591, 01306-743821
Elmbridge Museum
Church Street, Weybridge, Surrey, KT13 8DE
Tel: 01932-843573 Email: info@elm-mus.datanet.co.uk
WWW: www.surrey-online.co.uk/elm-mus
Godalming Museum
109a High Street, Godalming, Surrey, GU7 1AQ
Tel: 01483-426510 Fax: 01483-869-495
Email: museum@godalming.ndo.co.uk
Guildford Museum
Castle Arch, Quarry St, Guildford, Surrey, GU1 3SX
Tel: 01483-444750 Email: museum@remote.guildford.gov.uk
Haslemere Educational Museum
78 High Street, Haslemere, Surrey, GU27 2LA
Tel: 01428-642112 Fax: 01428-645234
Email: haslemere_museums@compuserve.com
Kingston Museum & Heritage Service
North Kingston Centre, Richmond Road, Kingston upon
Thames, KT2 5PE Tel: (020) 8547-6738 Fax: (020) 8547-
6747 Email: local.history@rbk.kingston.gov.uk WWW:
www.kingston.gov.uk/museum/, Research service available
£7.50 per half hour - max 3 hours

Merton Heritage Centre
The Cannons, Madeira Road, Mitcham, Surrey, CR4 4HD
Tel: 020-8640-9387
Queen's Royal Surrey Regt Museum (Queen's Royal Surrey East Surrey & Queen's Royal Surrey Regiments)
Clandon Park, West Clandon, Guildford, Surrey , GU4 7RQ
Tel: 01483-223419 Email: queenssurreys@care4free.net
WWW: www.surrey-online.co.uk/queenssurreys
Regimental Museum Royal Logistical Corps
Deepcut, Camberley, Surrey, GU16 6RW
Tel: 01252-340871, 01252-340984
Reigate Priory Museum
Reigate Priory, Bell Street, Reigate, Surrey, RH2 7RL
Tel: 01737-222550
Rural Life Centre
Old Kiln Museum, The Reeds, Tilford, Farnham, Surrey, GU10
2DL Tel: 01252-795571 Email: rural.life@argonet.co.uk
Wandle Industrial Museum
Vestry Hall Annex, London Road, Mitcham, Surrey, CR4
3UD Tel: 020-8648-0127
Woking Museum & Arts & Craft Centre
The Galleries, Chobham Road, Woking , Surrey, GU21 1JF
Tel: 01483-725517 Fax: 01483-725501
Email: the.galleries@dial.pipex.com
East Surrey Museum
1 Stafford Road, Caterham, Surrey , CR3 6JG
Tel: 01883-340275

Sussex
Brighton Fishing Museum
Research Officer & Administrator, 201 Kings Road, Arches,
Brighton, Sussex, BN1 1NB Tel: 01273-723064 **Royal Military Police Museum**
Roussillon Barracks, Chichester, Sussex, PO19 4BN
Tel: 01243 534225 Email: museum@rhqrmp.freeserve.co.uk
WWW: www.rhqrmp.freeserve.co.uk
Sussex Combined Services Museum (Royal Sussex Regiment and Queen's Royal Irish Hussars)
Redoubt Fortress, Royal Parade, Eastbourne, Sussex, BN22
7AQ Tel: 01323 410300

Sussex – East Sussex
Anne of Cleves House Museum
52 Southover, High St, Lewes, East Sussex, BN7 1JA
Tel: 01273-474610
Battle Museum
Langton Memorial Hall, High Street, Battle, East Sussex,
TN33 0AQ Tel: 01424-775955
Bexhill Museum
Egerton Road, Bexhill-On-Sea, East Sussex, TN39 3HL
Tel: 01424-787950 Email: museum@rother.gov.uk
WWW: www.1066country.com
Bexhill Museum of Costume & Social History Association
Manor Gardens, Upper Sea Road, Bexhill-On-Sea, East
Sussex, TN40 1RL Tel: 01424-210045
BN1 Visual Arts Project
Brighton Media Centre, 9-12 Middle Street, Brighton, East
Sussex, BN1 1AL Tel: 01273-384242
Booth Museum
194 Dyke Road, Brighton, East Sussex, BN1 5AA
Tel: 01273-292777 Email: boothmus@pavilion.co.uk
Dave Clarke Prop Shop
Long Barn, Cross In Hand, Heathfield, East Sussex, TN21
0TP Tel: 01435-863800
Eastbourne Heritage Centre
2 Carlisle Road, Eastbourne, East Sussex, BN21 4BT
Tel: 01323-411189 and 01323-721825
The Engineerium
The Droveway, Nevill Road, Hove, East Sussex, BN3 7QA
Tel: 01273-554070 Email: info@britishengineering.com
Filching Manor Motor Museum
Filching Manor, Jevington Rd, Polegate, East Sussex, BN26
5QA Tel: 01323-487838
Fishermans Museum
Rock A Nore Road, Hastings, East Sussex, TN34 3DW
Tel: 01424-461446

Hastings Museum & Art Gallery
Johns Place, Bohemia Rd, Hastings TN34 1ET
Tel: 01424-781155
Hove Musuem & Art Gallery
19 New Church Road, Hove, East Sussex, BN3 4AB
Tel: 01273-290200 Fax: 01273-292827
Email: abigail.thomas@brighton-hove.gov.uk
WWW: www.brighton-hove.gov.uk
How We Lived Then Museum of Shops
20 Cornfield Terrace, Eastbourne, East Sussex, BN21 4NS
Tel: 01323-737143
Michelham Priory
Upper Dicker, Hailsham, East Sussex, BN27 3QS
Newhaven Local & Maritime Museum
Garden Paradise, Avis Way, Newhaven, East Sussex
BN9 0DH Tel: 01273-612530
Preston Manor Museum
Preston Drove, Brighton, East Sussex, BN1 6SD
Tel: 01273-292770 Fax: 01273-292771
Rye Castle Museum
East Street, Rye, East Sussex, TN31 7JY Tel: 01797-226728
Seaford Museum of Local History
Martello Tower, The Esplanade, Seaford, East Sussex, BN25
1JH Tel: 01323-898222
Wish Tower Puppet Museum
Tower 73, King Edwards Parade, Eastbourne, East Sussex,
BN21 4BY Tel: 01323-411620

Sussex – West Sussex
Amberley Museum
Station Road, Amberley, Arundel, West Sussex, BN18 9LT
Tel: 01798-831370 Email: office@amberleymuseum.co.uk
Chichester District Museum
29 Little London, Chichester, West Sussex, PO19 1PB
Tel: 01243-784683 Email: chicmus@breathemail.net
Ditchling Museum
Church Lane, Ditchling, Hassocks, West Sussex, BN6 8TB
Tel: 01273-844744 Email: info@ditchling-museum.com
Fishbourne Roman Palace
Roman Way, Salthill Road, Fishbourne, Chichester, West
Sussex, PO19 3QR Tel: 01243-785859
Horsham Museum
9 The Causeway, Horsham, West Sussex, RH12 1HE
Tel: 01403-254959 Fax: 01403-217581
Marlipins Museum
High Street, Shoreham-By-Sea, West Sussex, BN43 5DA
Tel: 01273-462994, 01323-441279 Fax: 01323-844030
Email: smomich@sussexpast.co.uk
The Mechanical Music & Doll Collection
Church Road, Portfield, Chichester, West Sussex, PO19
4HN Tel: 01243-372646
Petworth Cottage Museum
346 High Street, Petworth, West Sussex, GU28 0AU
Tel: 01798-342100 WWW: www.sussexlive.co.uk
The Doll House Museum
Station Road, Petworth GU28 0BF Tel: 01798-344044
Weald & Downland Open Air Museum
Singleton, Chichester, West Sussex, PO18 0EU
Tel: 01243-811363 Email: wealddown@mistral.co.uk
WWW: www.wealddown.co.uk

Tyne and Wear
A Soldier's Life 15th/19thThe King's Royal Hussars Northumberland Hussars and Light Dragoons
Discovery Museum, Blandford Square,
Newcastle-upon-Tyne, Tyne & Wear, NE1 4JA
Tel: 0191-232-6789 Fax: 0191-230-2614
Email: ralph.thompson@tyne-wear-museums.org.uk
Arbeia Roman Fort
Baring Street, South Shields, Tyne And Wear, NE33 2BB
Tel: 0191-4561369 Email: lizelliott@tyne-wear-museums.org.uk
Bede's World Museum
Church Bank, Jarrow NE32 3DY Tel: 0191-4892106
The Bowes Railway Co Ltd
Springwell Road, Springwell Village, Gateshead NE9 7QJ
Tel: 0191-4161847 Email: alison_gibson77@hotmail.com
WWW: www.bowesrailway.co.uk

Castle Keep
Castle Garth, St. Nicholas Street, Newcastle Upon Tyne,
Tyne and Wear, NE1 1RE Tel: 0191-2327938
Hancock Museum
Barras Bridge, Newcastle Upon Tyne NE2 4PT
Tel: 0191-2227418 Fax: 0191-2226753
Military Vehicles Museum
Exhibition Park Pavilion, Newcastle Upon Tyne NE2 4PZ
Tel: 0191-281-7222 Email: miltmuseum@aol.com
Newburn Motor Museum
Townfield Gardens, Newburn, Newcastle Upon Tyne NE15
8PY Tel: 0191-2642977
North East Aircraft Museum
Old Washington Road, Sunderland, SR5 3HZ
Tel: 0191-519-0662
North East Mills Group
Research into wind and water mills in NE England - promoting
public access and restoration of mills., Blackfriars, Monk Street,
Newcastle upon Tyne, NE1 4XN Tel: 0191-232-9279
WWW: www.welcome.to/North.East.Mill.Group
North East Museums
House of Recovery, Bath Lane, Newcastle Upon Tyne, Tyne
And Wear, NE4 5SQ Tel: 0191-2221661
Ryhope Engines Trust
Pumping Station, Stockton Road, Ryhope, Sunderland SR2
0ND Tel: 0191-5210235 WWW: www.g3wte.demon.co.uk/
South Shields Museum & Art Gallery
Ocean Road, South Shields, Tyne and Wear, NE33 2JA
Tel: 0191-456-8740 Fax: 0191-456-7850
Stephenson Railway Museum
Middle Engine Lane, North Shields NE29 8DX
Tel: 0191-200-7146 Fax: 0191-200-7146
Sunderland Museum & Art Gallery
Borough Road, Sunderland, Tyne and Wear, SR1 1PP
Tel: 0191-565-0723 Fax: 0191-565-0713
Email: martin.routledge@tyne-wear-museums.org.uk
Washington F Pit - Now Permanently Closed
Enquiries- Sunderland Museum & Art Gallery Tel: 0191 565 0723

Warwickshire
Leamington Spa Art Gallery & Museum
Royal Pump Rooms, The Parade, Royal Leamington Spa,
Warwickshire, CV32 4AA Tel: 01926-742700
Fax: 01926-742705 Email: prooms@warwickdc.gov.uk
WWW: www.royal-pump-rooms.co.uk
Nuneaton Museum & Art Gallery
Riversley Park, Nuneaton, Warwickshire, CV11 5TU
Tel: 024-7637-6473
**Regimental Museum of The Queen's Own Hussars (3rd
King's Own and 7th Queen's Own Hussars)**
The Lord Leycester Hospital, High Street, Warwick,
Warwickshire, CV34 4EW Tel: Tel:01926 492035
Royal Warwickshire Regimental Museum
St. John's House, Warwick CV34 4NF Tel:01926 491653
Shakespeare Birthplace Trust - Museum
Henley Street, Stratford upon Avon CV37 6QW
Tel: 01789-296083 Email: museums@shakespeare.org.uk
Warwick Castle
Warwick Tel: 01926-406600WWW: www.warwick-castle.co.uk
Warwick Doll Museum
Okens House, Castle Street, Warwick, Warwickshire, CV34
4BP Tel: 01926-495546
Warwickshire Market Hall Museum
Market Place, WarwickCV34 4SA Tel: 01926-412500
Warwickshire Yeomanry Museum
The Court House, Jury Street, Warwick, Warwickshire,
CV34 4EW Tel: 01926 492212 Fax: 01926 494837

Wiltshire
Alexander Keiller Museum
High Street, Avebury, Marlborough, Wiltshire, SN8 1RF
Tel: 01672-539250
Atwell-Wilson Motor Museum Trust
Stockley Lane, Calne, Wiltshire, SN11 0 Tel: 01249-813119
Duke of Edinburgh's Royal Regiment (Berks & Wilts) Museum
The Wardrobe, 58 The Close, Salisbury, SP1 2EX
Tel: 01722-414536 Fax: 01722 421626
Lydiard House

Lydiard Park, Lydiard Tregoze, Swindon, Wiltshire, SN5
9PA Tel: 01793-770401
Royal Army Chaplains Department Museum
Netheravon House, Salisbury Road, Netheravon, Wiltshire,
SP4 9SY Tel: 01980-604911 Fax: 01980-604908
Salisbury & South Wiltshire Museum
The King's House, 65 The Close, Salisbury, Wiltshire, SP1
2EN Tel: 01722-332151 Fax: 01722-325611
Email: museum@salisburymuseum.freeserve.co.uk
Sevington Victorian School
Sevington, Grittleton, Chippenham, Wiltshire , SN14 7LD
Tel: 01249-783070 Fax: 01249-783070
Steam: Museum of the Great Western Railway
Kemble Drive, Swindon, Wiltshire, SN2 2TA
Tel: 01793-466646 Fax: 01793-466614
Email: tbryan@swindon.gov.uk
Yelde Hall Museum
Market Place, Chippenham , Wiltshire, SN15 3HL
Tel: 01249-651488

Worcestershire
Almonry Museum
Abbey Gate, Worcestershire, WR11 4BG
Tel: 01386-446944
Avoncroft Museum of Historic Buildings
Stoke Heath, Bromsgrove B60 4JR Tel: 01527-831363
Email: avoncroft1@compuserve.com WWW: www.avoncroft.org.uk
Bewdley Museum and Research Library
Load Street, Bewdley DY12 2AE Tel: 01229-403573
The Elgar Birthplace Museum
Crown East Lane, Lower Broadheath, Worcester, WR2 6RH
Tel: 01905-333224 Fax: 01905-333224
Kidderminster Railway Museum
Station Drive, Kidderminster DY10 1QX Tel: 01562-825316
Malvern Museum
Abbey Gateway, Abbey Rd, Malvern, Worcestershire, WR14
3ES Tel: 01684-567811
The Commandery Civil War Museum
Sidbury, Worcester WR1 2HU Tel: 01905-361821
Worcester City Museum & Art Gallery
Foregate Street, Worcester WR1 1DT Tel: 01905-25371
Worcestershire City Museum
Queen Elizabeth House, Trinity Street, Worcester WR1 2PW
Worcestershire County Museum
Hartlebury Castle, Hartlebury, Worcestershire, DY11 7XZ
Tel: 01229-250416 Fax: 01299-251890
Email: museum@worcestershire.gov.uk
WWW: www.worcestershire.gov.uk/museum
Worcestershire Regiment Museum and Archives
Office address: Worcester Regiment Museum Trust, RHQ WFR,
Norton Barracks, Worcester. WR5 2PA, Worcester City Museum &
Art Gallery, Foregate Street, Worcester, Worcestershire, WR1 1DT
Tel: 01905-353871 Email: rhq_wfr@lineone.net

Yorkshire

Yorkshire – East Yorkshire
East Riding Heritage Library & Museum
East Riding Museum Service, Sewerby Hall, Bridlington,
East Yorkshire, YO15 1EA Tel: 01262-677874
Fax: 01262-674265 Email: museum@pop3.poptel.org.uk
WWW: www.bridlington.net/sew
The Hornsea Museum
Burns Farm, 11 Newbegin, Hornsea, North Humberside,
HU18 1AB Tel: 01964-533443 WWW: www.hornsea.com
Museum of Army Transport
Flemingate, Beverley, HU17 0NG Tel: 01482-860445
Withernsea Lighthouse Museum
Hull Road, Withernsea East Yorkshire HU19 2DY
Tel: 01964-614834

Yorkshire – North Yorkshire
Aysgarth Falls Carriage Museum
Yore Mill , Asgarth Falls, Leyburn DL8 3SR Tel: 01969-663399
Beck Isle Museum of Rural Life
Bridge Street, Pickering YO18 8DU Tel: 01751-473653

Captain Cook Memorial Museum
Grape Lane, Whitby, North Yorkshire, YO22 4BA
Tel: 01947-601900 Email: captcookmuseumwhitby@ukgateway.net
WWW: cookmuseumwhitby.co.uk/
Captain Cook Schoolroom Museum
Great Ayton, North Yorkshire Tel: 01642-723358
Dales Countryside Museum
Station Yard, Burtersett Road, Hawes DL8 3NT
Tel: 01969-667494 Email: dcm@yorkshiredales.org.uk
Eden Camp Museum
Malton, North Yorkshire, YO17 6RT Tel: 01653-697777
Fax: 01653-698243 Email: admin@edencamp.co.uk
WWW: www.edencamp.co.uk
Embsay Steam Railway
Embsay Railway Station, Embsay, Skipton, North Yorkshire,
BD23 6QX Tel: 01756-794727
The Forbidden Corner
Tupgill Park Estate, Coverham, Middleham, Leyburn, DL8
4TJ Tel: 01969 640638 Tel: 01969 640687
Green Howards Regimental Museum
Trinity Church Square, Richmond, North Yorkshire, DL10
4QN Tel: 01748-822133 Fax: 01748-826561
Life In Miniature
8 Sandgate, Whitby YO22 4DB Tel: 01947-601478
Malton Museum
The Old Town Hall, Market Place, Malton, North Yorkshire,
YO17 7LP Tel: 01653-695136
The North Yorkshire Moors Railway
PIckering Station, Pickering, YO18 7AJ Tel: 01751 472508,
Email: info@northyorkshiremoorsrailway.com WWW:
www.northyorkshiremoorsrailway.com
Nidderdale Museum
Council Offices, King Street, Pateley Bridge HG3 5LE
Tel: 01423-711225
Old Courthouse Museum
Castle Yard, Knaresborough Tel: 01423-556188
Richmondshire Museum
Research enquiries must be by letter, Ryder's Wynd,
Richmond, North Yorkshire, DL10 4JA Tel: 01748-825611
Ripon Prison & Police Museum
Ripon Museum Trust, St Marygate, Ripon, North Yorkshire,
HG4 1LX Tel: 01765-690799 (24hr) 01765-690799
Email: ralph.lindley@which.net
Ripon Workhouse - Museum of Poor Law
Allhallowgate, Ripon, North Yorkshire, HG4 1LE
Tel: 01765-690799
Rotunda Museum
Vernon Road, Scarborough YO11 2NN Tel: 01723-374839
**Royal Dragoon Guards & Prince of Wales' Own
Regiment of Yorkshire Military Museum**
3A Tower Street, York, North Yorkshire, YO1 9SB
Tel: 01904-662790 Tel: 01904-658051
**Royal Dragoon Guards Military Museum (4th/7th Royal
Dragoon Guards & 5th Royal Inniskilling Dragoons)**, 3A
Tower Street, York, YO1 9SB Tel: 01904-662790 Tel: 01904
662310 Fax: 01904 662310 WWW: www.rdg.co.uk co
located with Prince of Wales' Own Regiment of Yorkshire
Military Museum (West & East Yorkshire Regiments)
Royal Pump Room Museum
Crown Place, Harrogate Tel: 01423-556188
Fax: 01423-556130 Email: lg12@harrogate.gov.uk
WWW: www.harrogate.gov.uk
Ryedale Folk Museum
Hutton le Hole YO62 6UA Tel: 01751-417367
Email: library@dbc-lib.demon.co.uk
Ryedale Folk Museum
Hutton le Hole, North Yorkshire, YO62 6UA
Tel: 01751-417367 Email: library@dbc-lib.demon.co.uk
The World of James Herriot
23 Kirkgate, Thirsk YO7 1PL Tel: 01845-524234
Fax: 01845-525333 Email: anne.keville@hambleton.gov.uk
WWW: www.hambleton.gov.uk
Upper Wharfdale Museum Society & Folk Museum
The Square, Grassington, North Yorkshire, BD23 5AU
Whitby Lifeboat Museum
Pier Road, Whitby YO21 3PU Tel: 01947-602001

Whitby Museum
Pannett Park, Whitby YO21 1RE Tel: 01947-602908
Fax: 01947-897638 Email: graham@durain.demon.co.uk
WWW: www.durain.demon.co.uk
Yorkshire Air Museum
Halifax Way, Elvington, York YO41 5AU Tel: 01904-608595

Yorkshire – South Yorkshire
Abbeydale Industrial Hamlet
Abbeydale Road South, Sheffield, South Yorkshire, S7 2
Tel: 0114-236-7731
Bishops House Museum
Norton Lees Lane, Sheffield, S8 9BE Tel: 0114 278 2600
WWW: www.sheffieldgalleries.org.uk
Cannon Hall Museum
Cannon Hall, Cawthorne, Barnsley S75 4AT
Tel: 01226-790270
Clifton Park Museum
Clifton Lane, Rotherham S65 2AA Tel: 01709-823635
Email: guy.kilminster@rotherham.gov.uk
WWW: www.rotherham.gov.uk
Fire Museum (Sheffield)
Peter House, 101-109 West Bar, Sheffield S3 8PT
Tel: 0114-249-1999 Fax: 0114-249-1999
WWW: www.hedgepig.freeserve.co.uk
Kelham Island Museum
Alma Street, Kelham Island, Sheffield S3 8RY
Tel: 0114-272-2106
**King's Own Yorkshire Light Infantry Regimental
Museum**
Museum & Art Gallery, Chequer Road, Doncaster, DN1
2AE Tel: 01302-734293 Fax: 01302-735409
Email: museum@doncaster.gov.uk WWW:
www.doncaster.gov,uk
Magna
Sheffield Road, Templeborough, Rotherham, S60 1DX Tel:
01709 720002 Fax: 01709 820092 Email:
info@magnatrust.co.uk WWW: www.magnatrust.org.uk
**Regimental Museum 13th/18th Royal Hussars and The
Light Dragoons**
Cannon Hall, Cawthorne, Barnsley, South Yorkshire, S75
4AT Tel: 01226 790270
Sandtoft Transport Centre Ltd
Belton Road, Sandtoft, Doncaster, South Yorkshire, DN8
5SX Tel: 01724-711391
Sheffield City Museum
Weston Park, Sheffield, S10 2TP Tel: 0114-278-2600
York and Lancaster Regimental Museum
Library and Arts Centre, Walker Place, Rotherham, South
Yorkshire, S65 1JH Tel: 01709-823635 Fax: 01709-823631
Email: guy.kilminster@rotherham.gov.uk
WWW: www.rotherham.co.uk
Sheffield City Museum
Weston Park, Sheffield, S10 2TP Tel: 0114 278 2600 WWW:
www.sheffieldgalleries.org.uk

Yorkshire – West Yorkshire
Armley Mills
Canal Road, Leeds, West Yorkshire, LS12 2QF
Tel: 0113-263-7861 Fax: 0113-263-7861
Bankfield Museum
Boothtown Road, Halifax HX3 6HG Tel: 01422-354823
Bolling Hall Museum
Bowling Hall Road, Bradford, West Yorkshire, BD4 7
Tel: 01274-723057 Fax: 01274-726220
Bracken Hall Countryside Centre
Glen Road, Baildon, Shipley, BD17 5ED
Tel: 01274-584140
Bradford Industrial Museum & Horses at Work
Moorside Road, Eccleshill, Bradford, West Yorkshire, BD2
3HP Tel: 01274-631756
Calderdale Museums & Arts
Piece Hall, Halifax HX1 1RE Tel: 01422-358087
Castleford Museum Room
Carlton Street, Castleford WF10 1BB Tel: 01977-722085
Cliffe Castle Museum
Spring Gardens Lane, Keighley BD20 6LH Tel: 01535-618231

The Colour Museum
1 Providence Street, Bradford, West Yorkshire, BD1 2PW
Tel: 01274-390955 Fax: 01274-392888
Email: museum@sdc.org.uk WWW: www.sdc.org.uk
Duke of Wellington's Regimental Museum
Bankfield Museum, Akroyd Park, Boothtown Road, Halifax,
HX3 6HG Tel: 01422 354823 Email: Fax: 01422 249020
Eureka The Museum For Children
Discovery Road, Halifax HX1 2NE Tel: 01422-330069
Keighley Bus Museum Trust
47 Brantfell Drive, Burnley, Lancashire, BB12 8AW
Tel: 01282-413179 WWW: www.kbmt.freeuk.com
Kirkstall Abbey and Abbey House Museum
Kirkstall Road, Kirkstall, Leeds, LS5 3EH Tel: 0113 275 5821
Leeds City Art Gallery
The Headrow, Leeds, LS1 3AA Tel: 0113-247-8248
Leeds Museums Resource Centre
Moorfield Road, Moorfield Industrial Estate, Yeadon, Leeds,
LS19 7BN Tel: 0113-214-6526
Lotherton Hall
Lotherton Lane, Aberford, Leeds, LS25 3EB Tel: 0113-281-3259
Manor House Art Gallery & Museum
Castle Yard, Castle Hill, Ilkley LS29 9D Tel: 01943-600066
Middleton Railway
The Station, Moor Road, Hunslet, Leeds, LS10 2JQ Tel:
0113 271 0320, Email: howhill@globalnet.co.uk WWW:
wwww.personal.leeds.ac.uk/mph6mip/mrt/mrt.htm
The National Coal Mining Museum for England
Caphouse Colliery, New Road, Overton, Wakefield, West
Yorkshire, WF4 4RH Tel: 01924-848806
Fax: 01924-840694 Email: info@ncm.org.uk
WWW: www.ncm.org.uk
National Museum of Photography, Film &Television
Bradford, West Yorkshire, BD1 1NQ Tel: 01274-202030
Fax: 01274-723155 WWW: http:www.nmpft.org.uk
Royal Armouries (Leeds)
Armouries Drive, Leeds LS10 1LT Tel: 0990-106666
Saddleworth Museum & Art Gallery
High Street, Uppermill, Oldham, Lancashire, OL3 6HS
Tel: 01457-874093 Fax: 01457-870336
Shibden Hall
Lister Road, Shibden, Halifax HX3 6AG Tel: 01422-352246
Skopos Motor Museum
Alexandra Mills, Alexandra Road, Batley WF17 6JA
Tel: 01924-444423
Temple Newsham House
Temple Newsham Road, off Selby Road, Leeds, LS15 0AE
Tel: 0113 264 7321
Thackray Medical Museum
Beckett Street, Leeds LS9 7LN Tel: 0113-244-4343
Fax: 0113-247-0219 Email: info@thrackraymuseum.org
WWW: www.thackraymuseum.org
Thwaite Mills Watermill
Thwaite Lane, Stourton, Leeds, LS10 1RP
Tel: 0113-249-6453
Vintage Carriages Trust
Station Yard, South Street, Ingrow, Keighley, West
Yorkshire, BD21 1DB Tel: 01535-680425
Wakefield Museum
Wood Street, Wakefield, West Yorkshire, WF1 2EW
Tel: 01924-305351 Fax: 01924-305353

Yorkshire - York
Bar Convent Museum
17 Blossom Street, York, YO24 1AQ Tel: 01904-643238
Fax: 01904-631792 Email: info@bar-convent.org.uk
WWW: www.bar-convent.org.uk
Micklegate Bar Museum
Micklegate, York YO1 6JX Tel: 01904-634436
Richard III Museum
Monk Bar, York YO1 2LH Tel: 01904-634191
WWW: www.richardiiimuseum.co.uk
York Archaeological Trust
11 - 13 Ogleforth, York, YO1 2JG
York Castle Museum
The Eye of York, York, YO1 9RW Tel: 01904-653611
Fax: 01904-671078 WWW: www.york.gov.uk

Yorkshire Museum
Museum Gardens, York, YO1 7FR Tel: 01904-629745
Fax: 01904-651221
Email: yorkshire.museum@yorks.gov.uk
WWW: www.york.gov.uk or also www.yorkgateway.co.uk

WALES

Museum of Welsh Life
St Fagans, Cardiff, CF5 6XB Tel: 029-205-73437
Fax: 029-205-73490

Anglesey
Beaumaris Gaol Museum
Bunkers Hill, Beaumaris, Anglesey, LL58 8EP
Tel: 01248-810921, 01248-724444 Fax: 01248-750282
Email: BeaumarisCourtandGaol@anglesey.gov.uk
Maritime Museum
Beach Road, Newry Beach, Holyhead, Anglesey, LL65 1YD
Tel: 01407-769745 Fax: 01407-769745
Email: cave@holyhead85.freeserve.co.uk

Caerphilly
Drenewydd Museum
26-27 Lower Row, Bute Town, Nr Rhyllney, Caerphilly
County Borough, NP22 5QH Tel: 01685-843039
Email: morgacl@caerphilly.gov.uk

Cardiff
1st The Queen's Dragoon Guards Regimental Museum
Cardiff Castle, Cardiff, CF1 2RB
Tel: 02920-222253, 02920-781232 Fax: 02920-781384
Email: morris602.hhq@netscapeonline
WWW: www.qdg.org.uk
Cardiff Castle
Castle Street, Cardiff, CF10 3RB Tel: 029-2087-8100
Fax: 029-2023-1417 Email: cardiffcastle@cardiff.gov.uk
Techniquest
Stuart Street, Cardiff, CF10 5BW Tel: 02920-475475

Carmarthenshire
Kidwelly Industrial Museum
Broadford, Kidwelly, Carmarthenshire, SA17 4UF
Tel: 01554-891078
Parc Howard Museum & Art Gallery
Mansion House, Parc Howard, Llanelli, Carmarthenshire,
SA15 3LJ Tel: 01554-772029

Ceredigion
Cardigan Heritage Centre
Bridge Warehouse, Castle St, Ceredigion, Dyfed, SA43 3AA
Tel: 01239-614404
Ceredigion Museum
Coliseum, Terrace Road, Aberystwyth, Ceredigion, SY23
2AQ Tel: 01970-633088 Fax: 01970-633084
Email: museum@ceredigion.gov.uk
Llywernog Silver Mine (Mid-Wales Mining Museum Ltd)
Ponterwyd, Aberystwyth, Ceredigion, SY23 3AB
Tel: 01970-890620
Mid-Wales Mining Museum Ltd
15 Market Street, Aberaeron, Ceredigion, SA46 0AU
Tel: 01545-570823

Conwy
Betws-y-Coed Motor Museum
Museum Cottage, Betws-Y-Coed, Conwy, LL24 0AH
Tel: 01690-710760
Teapot Museum
25 Castle Street, Conwy, Gwynedd, LL32 8AY
Tel: 01492-596533

Denbigh/Denbighshire
Cae Dai Trust
Cae Dai Trust/Cae Dai Lawnt, Denbigh, LL16 4SU
Tel: 01745-817004/812107
Llangollen Motor Museum
Pentrefelin, Llangollen, Denbighshire, LL20 8EE
Tel: 01978-860324

Glamorgan
Glamorgan – Mid Glamorgan
Brecon Mountain Railway
Pant Station, Merthyr Tydfil, CF48 2UP Tel: 01685 722988,
Email: enquiries@breconmountainrailway.co.uk
WWW: www.breconmountainrailway.co.uk

Cyfarthfa Castle Museum
Cyfarthfa Park, Brecon Road, Merthyr Tydfil, CF47 8RE
Tel: 01685-723112, 01685-383704 Fax: 01685-723112
Joseph Parrys Cottage
4 Chapel Row, Merthyr Tydfil, Mid Glamorgan, CF48 1BN
Tel: 01685-383704
Pontypridd Historical & Cultural Centre
Bridge Street, Pontypridd, Mid Glamorgan, CF37 4PE
Tel: 01443-409512 Fax: 01443-485565
Ynysfach Iron Heritage Centre
Merthyr Tydfil Heritage Trust, Ynysfach Road, Merthyr
Tydfil, Mid Glamorgan, CF48 1AG Tel: 01685-721858

Glamorgan – South Glamorgan
National Museum & Galleries of Wales
Cathays Park, Cardiff, South Glamorgan, CF10 3NP
Tel: 029-2039-7951
**Welch Regiment Museum of the Royal Regiment of
Wales**
The Black & Barbican Towers, Cardiff Castle, Cardiff, CF10
3RB Tel: 029-20229367 Email: welch@rrw.org.uk
WWW: www.rrw.org.uk

Glamorgan – West Glamorgan
Cefn Coed Colliery Museum
Blaenant Colliery, Crynant, Neath, West Glamorgan, SA10
8SE Tel: 01639-750556
Glynn Vivian Art Gallery
Alexandra Road, Swansea, West Glamorgan, SA1 5DZ
Tel: 01792-655006 Fax: 01792-651713
Email: glynn.vivian.gallery@business.ntl.com
WWW: www.swansea.gov.uk
Maritime & Industrial Museum
Museum Square, Maritime Quarter, Victoria Rd, Swansea,
West Glamorgan, SA1 1SN Tel: 01792-650351
Fax: 01792-652585
Email: swansea.museum@business.ntl.com
Neath Museum
4 Church Place, Neath, West Glamorgan, SA11 3LL
Tel: 01639-645741

Gwynedd
Gwynedd Museums Service
Victoria Dock, Caernarvon, Gwynedd, LL55 1SH
Tel: 01286-679098 Fax: 01286-679637
Email: amgueddfeydd-museums@gwynedd.gov.uk
Bala Lake Railway Rheilfford Llyn Tegid
The Station Yr Orsaf, Llanuwchllyn, LL23 7DD Tel: 01678
540666 WWW: www.bala-lake-railway.co.uk
Great Orme Tramway Tramffordd Y Gogarth
Goprsaf Victoria, Church Walks, Llandudno, LL30 1AZ Tel:
01492 574003, Email: enq@greatormetramway.com WWW:
www.greatormetramway.com
Home Front Experience
New Street, Llandudno, LL30 2YF Tel: 01492 871032
WWW: www.homefront-enterprises.co.uk
Llanberis Lake Railway Rheilffordd Llyn Padarn
LLanberis, LL55 4TY Tel: 01286 870549 WWW:
www.lake-railway.co.uk
Llandudno & Conwy Valley Railway Society
Welsh Slate Museum, Llanberis Tel: 01492 874590
Porthmadog Maritime Museum
Oakley Wharf 1, The Harbour, Porthmadog, Gwynedd,
LL49 9LU Tel: 01766-513736
Royal Welch Fusiliers Regimental Museum
Caernarfon Castle, Caernarfon, Gwynedd, LL55 2AY
Tel: 01286-673362
Segontium Roman Museum
Beddgelert Road, Caernarfon, Gwynedd, LL55 2LN
Tel: 01286-675625

Sir Henry Jones Museum
Y Cwm, Llangernyw, Abergele, LL22 8PR
Tel: 01492 575371 Tel: 01754 860661
Snowdon Mountain Railway
Llanberis, LL55 4TY Tel: 0870 4580033 Fax: 01286 872518
WWW: www.snowdonrailway.co.uk
Welsh Highland Railway
Tremadog Road, Porthmadog, LL49 9DY
Welsh Slate Museum
Padarn Country Park, Llanberis, Gwynedd, Gwynedd LL55
4TY Tel: 01286-870630 Fax: 01286-871906
Email: wsmpost@btconnect.com WWW: www.nmgw.ac.uk

Merthyr Tydfil
Brecon Mountain Railway
Pant Station, Merthyr Tydfil, CF48 2UP Tel: 01685 722988,
Email: enquiries@breconmountainrailway.co.uk
WWW: www.breconmountainrailway.co.uk
Cyfarthfa Castle Museum
Cyfarthfa Park, Brecon Road, Merthyr Tydfil, CF47 8RE
Tel: 01685-723112, 01685-383704 Fax: 01685-723112
Joseph Parrys Cottage
4 Chapel Row, Merthyr Tydfil, Mid Glamorgan, CF48 1BN
Tel: 01685-383704
Ynysfach Iron Heritage Centre
Merthyr Tydfil Heritage Trust, Ynysfach Road, Merthyr
Tydfil, Mid Glamorgan, CF48 1AG Tel: 01685-721858

Monmouthshire
Abergavenny Museum
The Castle, Castle Street, Abergavenny, Monmouthshire,
NP7 5EE Tel: 01873-854282
Castle & Regimental Museum
Monmouth Castle, Monmouth NP25 3BS Tel: 01600-772175
Chepstow Museum
Bridge Street, Chepstow, Monmouthshire, NP16 5EZ
Tel: 01291-625981 Fax: 01291-635005
Email: chepstowmuseum@monmouthshire.gov.uk
Monmouthshire Royal Engineers (Militia)
Castle and Regimental Museum, The Castle, Monmouth,
NP5 3BS Tel: 01600-712935
Nelson Museum & Local History Centre
Priory Street, Monmouth, NP5 3XA Tel: 01600-713519
Fax: 01600-775001
Email: nelsonmuseum@monmouthshire.gov.uk
Usk Rural Life Museum
The Malt Barn, New Market Street, Usk, Monmouthshire,
NP15 1AU Tel: 01291-673777

Pembrokeshire
Haverfordwest Town Museum
Castle Street, Haverfordwest, SA61 2EF Tel: 01437-763087
Milford Haven Museum
Old Customs House, The Docks, Milford Haven,
Pembrokeshire, SA73 3AF Tel: 01646-694496
Newport Museum & Art Gallery
John Frost Square, Newport NP20 1PA Tel: 01633-840064
Fax: 01633-222615 Email: museum@newport.gov.uk
Pembrokeshire Motor Museum
Keeston Hill, Haverfordwest, SA62 6EH Tel: 01437-710950
Pembrokeshire Museum Service
The County Library, Dew Street, Haverfordwest, SA61 1SU
Tel: 01437-775246 Fax: 01437-769218
Pillgwenlly Heritage Community Project
within Baptist Chapel, Alexandra Road, Newport,
Pembrokeshire, NP20 2JE Tel: 01633-244893
Roman Legionary Museum
High Street, Caerleon, Newport NP18 1AE
Tel: 01633-423134
Tenby Museum, Tenby Museum & Art Gallery, Castle Hill,
Tenby, SA70 7BP Tel: 01834-842809 Fax: 01834-842809
Email: tenbymuseum@hotmail.com WWW:
tenbymuseum.free-online.co.uk
Wilson Museum of Narberth
Market Square, Narberth SA67 7AX Tel: 01834-861719

Powys
The Judge's Lodging
Broad Street, Presteigne, Powys, LD8 2AD
Tel: 01544-260650 Fax: 01544-260652
WWW: www.judgeslodging.org.uk
Llanidloes Museum
Great Oak Street, Llanidloes SY18 6BN Tel: 01686-412375
Powysland Museum & Montgomery Canal Centre
Canal Yard, Welshpool, Powys, SY21 7AQ
Tel: 01938-554656 Fax: 01938-554656
Radnorshire Museum
Temple Street, Llandrindod Wells, Powys, LD1 5DL
Tel: 01597-824513 Fax: 01597-825781
Email: radnorshire.museum@powys.gov.uk
South Wales Borderers & Monmouthshire Regimental Museum of the Royal Regt of Wales (24th/41st Foot)
The Barracks, Brecon, Powys, LD3 7EB Tel: 01874-613310
Fax: 01874-613275 Email: rrw@ukonline.co.uk
WWW: www.ukonline.co.uk/rrw/index.htm
Water Folk Canal Centre
Old Store House, Llanfrynach, Brecon, Powys, LD3 7LJ
Tel: 01874-665382

Torfaen
Big Pit Mining Museum
Blaenavon, Torfaen, NP4 9XP Tel: 01495-790311
Valley Inheritance
Park Buildings, Pontypool, NP4 6JH Tel: 01495-752036
Fax: 01495-752043

Wrexham
Wrexham Museum
County Buildings, Regent Street, Wrexham, LL11 1RB
Tel: 01978-317970 Fax: 01978-317982
Email: museum@wrexham.gov.uk

SCOTLAND

Scottish United Services Museum
The Castle, Museum Square, Edinburgh, EH1 2NG
Tel: 0131-225-7534 Fax: 0131-225-3848
Scottish Museums Council
County House, 20/22 Torphichen Street, Edinburgh, EH3
8JB Tel: 0131-229-7465 Fax: 0131-229-2728
Email: inform@scottishmuseums.org.uk
WWW: www.scottishmuseums.org.uk

Aberdeenshire
Aberdeen Maritime Museum
Shiprow, Aberdeen, AB11 5BY Tel: 01224-337700
Email: johne@arts-recreation.net.uk WWW: www.aagm.co.uk
Alford & Donside Heritage Association
Mart Road, Alford, AB33 8AA Tel: 019755-62906
Arbuthnot Museum
St. Peter Street, Peterhead, Aberdeenshire, AB42 1LA
Tel: 01779-477778 Fax: 01771-622884
Fraserburgh Heritage Society
Heritage Centre, Quarry Road, Fraserburgh, AB43 9DT
Tel: 01346-512888
Gordon Highlanders Museum
St Lukes, Viewfield Road, Aberdeen AB15 7XH
Tel: 01224-311200Email: museum@gordonhighlanders.com
 WWW: www.gordonhighlanders.com
Grampian Transport Museum
Alford, AB33 8AE Tel: 019755-62292
Hamilton T.B
Northfield Farm, New Pitsligo, Fraserburgh AB43 6PX
Tel: 01771-653504
Museum of Scottish Lighthouses
Kinnaird Head, Fraserburgh, Aberdeenshire, AB43 9DU
Tel: 01346-511022 Fax: 01346-511033
Email: enquiries@lighthousescom.co.uk
Provost Skene's House
Guestrow, Aberdeen AB10 1AS Tel: 01224-641086
Satrosphere
Moved in 2000 - new address contact, 19 Justice Mill Lane,
Aberdeen, AB11 6EQ Tel: 01224-213232
Fax: 01224-211685 Email: satrosphere@ssphere.ifb.co.uk

Angus
Arbroath Museum
Signal Tower, Ladyloan, Arbroath DD11 1PY Tel: 01241-875598
Fax: 01241-439263 Email: signal.tower@angus.gov.uk
WWW: www.angus.gov.uk/history
Glenesk Folk Museum
The Retreat, Glenesk, Brechin, Angus, DD9 7YT
Tel: 01356-670254 Email: retreat@angusglens.co.uk
WWW: www.angusglens.co.uk
The Meffan Institute
20 High Street West, Forfar, Angus, DD8 1BB
Tel: 01307-464123 Fax: 01307-468451
Email: the.meffan@angus.gov.uk

Argyll
Campbeltown Heritage Centre
Big Kiln, Witchburn Road, Campbeltown, Argyll, PA28 6JU
Tel: 01586-551400
Campbeltown Library and Museum
Hall Street, Campbeltown, Argyll, PA28 6BU
Tel: 01586-552366
Castle House Museum
Castle Gardens, Argyll Street, Dunoon, Argyll, PA23 7HH
Tel: 01369-701422
Kilmartin House Trust
Kilmartin House, Kilmartin, Lochgilphead, Argyll, PA31
8RQ Tel: 01546-510278 Fax: 01546-510330
Email: museum@kilmartin.org WWW: www.kilmartin.org
Regimental Museum Argyll and Sutherland Highlanders
Stirling Castle, Stirling, Stirlingshire, FK8 1EH
Tel: 01786 475165 Fax: 01786 446038

Ayrshire
Ayrshire Yeomanry Museum
Rozelle House, Monument Road, Alloway by Ayr, Ayrshire,
KA7 4NQ Tel: 01292-445400, 01292-264091
Dalgarven Mill, Museum of Ayrshire Country Life & Costume
Dalry Road, Dalgarven, Kilwinning, Ayrshire, KA13 6PL
Tel: 01294-552448
East Ayrshire Council District History Centre & Museum
Baird Institute, 3 Lugar Street, Cumnock, Ayrshire, KA18
1AD Tel: 01290-421701 Fax: 01290-421701
Email: Baird.institute@east-ayrshire.gov.uk
WWW: www.east-ayrshire.gov.uk
Glasgow Vennel Museum
10 Glasgow, Vennel, Irvine KA12 0BD Tel: 01294-275059
Irvine Burns Club & Burgh Museum
28 Eglinton Street, Irvine KA12 8AS Tel: 01294-274511
Largs Museum
Kirkgate House, Manse Court, Largs, Ayrshire, KA30 8AW
Tel: 01475-687081
McKechnie Institute
Dalrymple Street, Girvan, Ayrshire, KA26 9AE
Tel: 01465-713643 Email: mkigia@ukgateway.net
North Ayrshire Museum
Manse Street, Saltcoats, Ayrshire, KA21 5AA
Tel: 01294-464174 Email: namuseum@globalnet.co.uk
Rozelle House
Rozelle Park, Ayr, Ayrshire, KA7 4NQ Tel: 01292-445447

Banffshire
The Buckie Drifter Maritime Heritage Centre
Freuchny Road, Buckie AB56 1TT Tel: 01542-834646

Berwickshire
The Jim Clark Room
44 Newtown Street, Duns TD11 3DT Tel: 01361-883960
Museum of Coldstream Guards
Coldstream, Berwickshire

Caithness
Clangunn Heritage Centre & Museum
Old Parish Kirk, Latheron, Caithness, KW5 6DL
Tel: 01593-741700
Dunbeath Preservation Trust
Old School, Dunbeath KW6 6EG Tel: 01593-731233
Email: DunTrust@aol.com

The Last House
John O'Groats, Wick KW1 4YR Tel: 01955-611250
Wick Hertiage Centre
18 Bank Row, Wick KW1 5EY Tel: 01955-605393

Dumfries & Galloway/ Dumfriesshire
Dumfries Museum
The Observatory, Dumfries, DG2 7SW Tel: 01387-253374
Fax: 01387-265081 Email: info@dumgal.gov.uk
WWW: www.dumfriesmuseum.demon.co.uk
Ellisland Trust
Ellisland Farm, Dumfries DG2 0RP Tel: 01387-740426
Gretna Museum & Tourist Services
Headless Cross, Gretna Green DG16 5EA Tel: 01461-338441
Fax: 01461-338442 Email: info@gretnagreen.com
WWW: www.gretnagreen.com
John Paul Jones Birthplace Museum
Arbigland, Kirkbean, Dumfries DG2 8BQ Tel: 01387-880613
Old Bridge House Museum
Mill Road, Dumfries DG2 7BE Tel: 01387-256904
WWW: www.dumfriesmuseum.demon.co.uk
Robert Burns Centre
Mill Road, Dumfries DG2 7BE Tel: 01387-264808
Robert Burns House
Burns Street, Dumfries, DG1 2PS Tel: 01387 255297
Sanquhar Tolbooth Museum
High Street, Sanquhar DG4 6BL Tel: 01659-50186
Savings Banks Museum
Ruthwell, Dumfries DG1 4NN Tel: 01387-870640
Shambellie House Museum of Costume
New Abbey, Dumfries DG2 8HQ Tel: 01387-850375
Stranraer Museum
55 George Street, Stranraer, DG9 7JP Tel: 01776-705088
Fax: 01776-705835 Email: JohnPic@dumgal.gov.uk

Dunbartonshire
Scottish Maritime Museum
Gottries Road, Irvine, Ayrshire, KA12 8QE
Tel: 01294-278283 Fax: 01294-313211
Email: jgrant5313@aol.com

Dundee
Dundee Heritage Trust
Verdant Works, West Henderson's Wynd, Dundee, DD1 5BT
Tel: 01382-225282 Fax: 01382-221612
Email: info@dundeeheritage.sol.co.uk
WWW: www.verdant.works.co.uk
Royal Research Ship Discovery
Discovery Point, Discovery Quay, Dundee, DD1 4XA
Tel: 01382-201245 Fax: 01382-225891
Email: info@dundeeheritage.sol.co.uk
WWW: www.rrs-discovery.co.uk
Verdant Works - A Working Jute mill
West Henderson's Wynd, Dundee, DD1 5BT
Tel: 01382-225282 Fax: 01382-221612
Email: dundeeheritage@sol.co.uk
WWW: www.verdant-works.co.uk

Edinburgh
Heritage Projects (Edinburgh) Ltd
Castlehill, Royal Mile, Edinburgh, Midlothian EH1 2NE
Tel: 0131-225-7575
Huntly House Museum
142 Canongate, Edinburgh, EH8 8DD Tel: 0131-529-4143
Fax: 0131-557-3346
National Museums of Scotland - Library
Royal Museum, Chambers Street, Edinburgh, EH1 1JF
Tel: 0131-247-4137 Fax: 0131-247-4311
Email: library@nms.ac.uk WWW: www.nms.ac.uk
Royal Museum and Museum of Scotland
Chambers Street, Edinburgh, EH1 1JF Tel: 0131-225-7534,
0131-247-4027 (Text) WWW: www.nms.ac.uk
Royal Scots Regimental Museum
The Castle, Edinburgh, EH1 2YT Tel: 0131-310-5014
Fax: 0131-310-5019
Royal Yacht Britannia and Visitor Centre
Ocean Drive, Leith, Edinburgh, EH6 6JJ
Tel: 0131-555-5566, Group bookings 0131-555-8800

WWW: www.royalyachtbritannia.co.uk
Scottish United Services Museum
The Castle, Museum Square, Edinburgh, EH1 2NG
Tel: 0131-225-7534 Fax: 0131-225-3848

Scottish United Services Museum Library
The Castle, Museum Square, Edinburgh, EH1 1 2NG
Tel: 0131-225-7534-Ext-2O4 Fax: 0131-225-3848
Email: library@nms.ac.uk WWW: www.nms.ac.uk

Falkirk
Falkirk History Research Centre
Callendar House, Callendar Park, Falkirk, FK1 1YR
Tel: 01324-503778 Fax: 01324-503771
Email: ereid@falkirkmuseums.demon.co.uk
WWW: www.falkirkmuseums.demon.co.uk

Fife
Andrew Carnegie Birthplace Museum
Moodie Street, Dunfermline, Fife, KY12 7PL
Tel: 01383-724302
Dunfermline Museum
Enquiries can be made at this address for: Inverkeithing
Museum, Pittencrief House Museum and St Margaret's
Cave, Viewfield, Viewfield Terrace, Dunfermline, Fife,
KY12 7HY Tel: 01383-313838 Fax: 01383-313837
Inverkeithing Museum
Museum located at: The Friary, Queen Street, Inverkeithing,
Fife. Tel: 01383-313595, Enquiries to: Dunfermline
Museum, Viewfield, Viewfield Terrace, Dunfermline, Fife,
KY12 7HY Tel: 01383-313838 Fax: 01383-313837
John McDouall Stuart Museum
Rectory Lane, Dysart, Kirkcaldy, Fife, KY1 2TP
Tel: 01592-653118
Kirkcaldy Museum & Art Gallery
War Memorial Gardens, Abbotshall Road, Kirkcaldy, Fife,
KY1 1YG Tel: 01592-412860 Fax: 01592-412870
Methil Heritage Centre
272 High Street, Methil, Leven, Fife, KY8 3EQ
Tel: 01333-422100
Pittencrieff House Museum
Museum located at: Pittencrieff Park, Dunfermline, Fife
KY12 8QH Tel: 01383-722935, Enquiries to: Dunfermline
Museum, Viewfield, Viewfield Terrace, Dunfermline, Fife,
KY12 7HY Tel: 01383-313838 Fax: 01383-313837
Scotland's Secret Bunker
Underground Nuclear Command Centre, Crown Buildings
(Near St Andrews), Fife, KY16 8QH Tel: 01333-310301
Scottish Fisheries Museum
Scottish Fisheries Museum Trust Ltd, St. Ayles,
Harbourhead, Anstruther, Fife, KY10 3AB
Tel: 01333-310628 Fax: 01333-310628
Email: andrew@scottish-fisheries-museum.com
WWW: www.scottish-fisheries-museum.org
The Fife Folk Museum
High Street, Ceres, Cupar, Fife, KY15 5NF
Tel: 01334-828180

Glasgow
Glasgow Vennel Museum
10 Glasgow, Vennel, Irvine, Ayrshire, KA12 0BD
Tel: 01294-275059
Heatherbank Museum
Glasgow Caledonian University, Cowcaddens Road, Glasgow, G4
0BA Tel: 0141-331-8637 Email: a.ramage@gcal.ac.uk WWW:
www.lib.gcal.ac.uk/heatherbank
**Museum of The Royal Highland Fusiliers (Royal Scots
Fusilers and Highland Light Infantry)**
518 Sauchiehall Street, Glasgow, G2 3LW
Tel: 0141-332-0961 Fax: 0141-332-5439
Scotland Street School Museum & Museum of Education
225 Scotland Street, Glasgow, Lanarkshire, G5 8QB
Tel: 0141-287-0500

Inverness-Shire
Highland Folk Museum
Duke Street, Kingussie, Inverness-Shire, PH21 1JG
Tel: 01540-661307 Email: rachel.chisholm@highland.gov.uk

Highland Folk Park
Aultlarie Croft, Kingussie Road, Newtonmore,
Inverness-Shire, PH20 1AY Tel: 01540-673551
Highland Railway Museum
5 Druimlon, Drumnadrochit, Inverness, Inverness-Shire,
IV63 6TY Tel: 01456-450527
Inverness Museum & Art Gallery
Castle Wynd, Inverness V2 3ED Tel: 01463-237114
Mallaig Heritage Centre
Station Road, Mallaig PH41 4PY Tel: 01687-462085
Queen's Own Highlanders Regimental Museum
Fort George, Ardersier, Inverness, IV1 2TD Tel: 01463-224380
The Clansman Centre
Canalside, Fort Augustus PH32 4AU Tel: 01320-366444
West Highland Museum
Cameron Square, Fort William, Inverness-Shire, PH33 6AJ
Tel: 01397-702169 Fax: 01397-701927

Isle Of Arran
Arran Heritage Museum
Rosaburn House, Brodick, Isle Of Arran, KA27 8DP
Tel: 01770-302636

Isle Of Islay
Finlaggan Trust The
The Cottage, Ballygrant, Isle Of Islay, PA45 7QL
Tel: 01496-840644

Isle Of Mull
The Columba Centre
Fionnphort, Isle Of Mull, Isle Of Mull, PA66 6BN
Tel: 01681-700660

Isle Of North Uist
Taigh Chearsabhagh Trust
Taigh Chearsabhagh, Lochmaddy, Isle Of North Uist, HS6
5AE Tel: 01876-500293
Email: taighchearsabhagh@zetnet.co.uk
WWW: www.taighchearsabhagh.org.uk

Isle Of South Uist
Kildonan Museum
Kildonan, Lochboisdale, Isle Of South Uist, HS8 5RZ
Tel: 01878-710343

Kinross
Perth Museum & Art Gallery
George Street, Perth, Tayside, PHI 5LB Tel: 01738-632488
Fax: 01738-443505 Email: scpayne@pkc.gov.uk

Kirkcudbrightshire
The Stewartry Museum
St Mary Street, Kirkcudbright, DG6 4AQ Tel: 01557 331643

Lanarkshire
Auyld Kirk Museum
The Cross Kirkintilloch, Glasgow G66 1 Tel: 0141 578 0144
Barrhead Museum - Closed permanently wef 31/3/00
Main Street, Barrhead, Glasgow, Lanarkshire, G78 1SW
Biggar Museum Trust
Moat Park Kirkstyle, Biggar ML12 6DT Tel: 01899-221050
Cameronians (Scottish Rifles) Museum
c/o Low Parks Museum, 129 Muir Street, Hamilton,
Lanarkshire, ML3 6BJ Tel: 01698-455714, 01698-328232
Discover Carmichael Visitors Centre
Warrenhill Farm, Warrenhill Road, Thankerton, Biggar,
Lanarkshire, ML12 6PF Tel: 01899-308169
Fossil Grove Museum
Victoria Park, Glasgow G65 9AH Tel: 0141-950-1448
Greenhill Covenanters House Museum
Kirkstyle, Biggar ML12 6DT Tel: 01899-221572
Heritage Engineering
22 Carmyle Avenue, Glasgow G32 8HJ Tel: 0141-763-0007
Hunter House
Maxwellton Road, East Kilbride, Glasgow, Lanarkshire, G74
3LW Tel: 01355-261261
John Hastie Museum
Threestanes Road, Strathaven, Lanarkshire, ML10 6EB
Tel: 01357-521257

Lanark Museum
7 Westport, Lanark, Lanarkshire, ML11 9HD
Tel: 01555-666680 Email: paularchibald@hotmail.com
WWW: www.biggar-net.co.uk/lanarkmuseum
Low Parks Museum
129 Muir Street, Hamilton, Lanarkshire, ML3 6BJ
Tel: 01698-283981, 01698-328232
New Lanark Conservation Trust
Visitors Centre Mill No 3, New Lanark Mills, Lanark,
Lanarkshire, ML11 9DB Tel: 01555-661345
Fax: 01555-665378 Email: visit@newlanark.org
WWW: www.newlanark.org
The People's Palace
Glasgow Green, Glasgow, Lanarkshire, G40 1AT
Tel: 0141-554-0223
Scotland Street School Museum & Museum of Education
225 Scotland Street, Glasgow, Lanarkshire, G5 8QB
Tel: 0141-287-0500
The Lighthouse
11 Mitchell Lane, Glasgow, Lanarkshire, G1 3NU
Tel: 0141-221-6362
Weavers' Cottages Museum
23-25 Wellwynd, Airdrie, Lanarkshire, ML6 0BN
Tel: 01236-747712
Auld Kirk Musuem
The Cross, Kirkintilloch, Glasgow, Lanarkshire , G66 1
Tel: 0141-578-0144

Lanarkshire - North Lanarkshire
Motherwell Heritage Centre
High Road, Motherwell, North Lanarkshire, ML1 3HU
Tel: 01698-251000 Fax: 01698-253433
Email: heritage@mhc158.freeserve.co.uk

Lothian
Lothian – East Lothian
Dunbar Museum
High Street, Dunbar, East Lothian, EH42 1ER
Tel: 01368-863734
John Muir House Museum
126-128 High Street, Dunbar, East Lothian, EH42 1JJ
Tel: 01368-862585
North Berwick Museum
School Road, North Berwick, East Lothian, EH39 4JU
Tel: 01620-895457

Lothian – West Lothian
Almond Valley Heritage Trust
Livingston Mill Farm, Millfield, Livingston, West Lothian,
EH54 7AR Tel: 01506-414957
Bennie Museum
Mansfield Street, Bathgate, West Lothian, EH48 4HU
Tel: 01506-634944
Kinneil Museum
Kinneil Estate, Bo'Ness, West Lothian, EH51 0AY
Tel: 01506-778530
Linlithgow's Story
Annet House, 143 High Street, Linlithgow, West Lothian,
EH49 7EJ Tel: 01506-670677
Queensferry Museum
53 High Street, South Queensferry, West Lothian, EH30
9HP Tel: 0131-331-5545

Midlothian
History of Education Centre
East London Street, Edinburgh, Midlothian, EH7 4BW
Tel: 0131-556-4224
Lauriston Castle
2a Cramond Rd South, Edinburgh, Midlothian, EH4 5QD
Tel: 0131-336-2060
Nelson Monument
Calton Hill, Edinburgh, Midlothian, EH7 5AA
Tel: 0131-556-2716
Newhaven Heritage Museum
Pier Place, Edinburgh, Midlothian, EH6 4LP
Tel: 0131-551-4165
Scots Dragoon Guards Museum Shop
The Castle, Edinburgh, Midlothian, EH1 2YT
Tel: 0131-220-4387

Scottish Mining Museum Trust
Lady Victoria Colliery, Newtongrange, Dalkeith, Midlothian,
EH22 4QN Tel: 0131-663-7519 Fax: 0131-654-1618
WWW: www.scottishminingmuseum.com

Morayshire
Elgin Museum
1 High Street, Elgin, Morayshire, IV30 1EQ
Tel: 01343-543675 Fax: 01343-543675
Email: curator@elginmuseum.demon.co.uk
Falconer Museum
Tolbooth Street, Forres, Morayshire, IV36 1PH
Tel: 01309-673701 Fax: 01309-675863
Email: alisdair.joyce@techleis.moray.gov.uk
WWW: www.moray.gov.uk
Grantown Museum & Heritage Trust
Burnfield House, Burnfield Avenue, Grantown-On-Spey,
Morayshire, PH26 3HH Tel: 01479-872478
Fax: 01479-872478 Email: molly.duckett@btinternet.com
WWW: www.grantown-on-spey.co.uk
Lossiemouth Fisheries Museum
Pitgaveny Street, Lossiemouth, Morayshire, IV31 6TW
Tel: 01343-813772
Nairn Museum
Viewfield House, King Street, Nairn, Morayshire, IV12 4EE
Tel: 01667-456791

Orkney
Orkney Farm & Folk Museum - Birsay
Kirbister Farm, Birsay, Orkney, KW17 2LR
Tel: 01856-771268
Orkney Farm & Folk Museum - Harray
Corrigall Farm Museum, Harray, Orkney, KW17 2LQ
Tel: 01856-771411
Orkney Fossil & Vintage Centre
Viewforth Burray, Orkney, KW17 2SY Tel: 01856-731255
Orkney Museum
Tankerness House, Broad Street, Kirkwall, Orkney, KW15
1DH Tel: 01856-873191 Fax: 01856-871560
Orkney Wireless Museum
Kiln Corner, Kirkwall, Orkney, KW15 1LB Tel: 01856-871400
Scapa Flow Visitor Centre
Lyness, Stromness, Orkney, KW16 3NT Tel: 01856-791300
Stromness Museum
52 Alfred Street, Stromness, Orkney Tel: 01856-850025

Perthshire
Atholl Country Collection
The Old School, Blair Atholl, Perthshire, PH18 5SP
Tel: 01796-481232 Email: r.cam@virgin.net
Clan Donnachaidh (Robertson) Museum
Clan Donnachaidh Centre, Bruar, Pitlochry PH18 5TW
Tel: 01796-483338
Email: clandonnachaidh@compuserve.com
WWW: donkey3@freenetname.co.uk
Clan Menzies Museum
Castle Menzies, Weem, by Aberfeldy, Perthshire, PH15 2JD
Tel: 01887-820982
Dunkeld Cathedral Chapter House Museum
Dunkeld, Perthshire, PH8 0AW Tel: 01350-727601/727249
The Hamilton Toy Collection
111 Main Street, Callander, Perthshire, FK17 8BQ
Tel: 01877-330004
Meigle Museum
Dundee Road, Meigle, Blairgowrie, Perthshire, PH12 8SB
Tel: 01828-640612
Perth Museum & Art Gallery
George Street, Perth, Tayside, PHI 5LB Tel: 01738-632488
Fax: 01738-443505 Email: scpayne@pkc.gov.uk
Regimental Museum and Archives of the Black Watch
Balhousie Castle, Hay Street, Perth, PH1 5HS Tel: 0131-
3108530 Email: bwarchivist@btclick.com
WWW: www.theblackwatch.co.uk
Scottish Horse Regimental Museum
The Cross, Dunkeld, Perthshire, PH8 0AN

Renfrewshire
Mclean Museum & Art Gallery
15 Kelly Street, Greenock, Renfrewshire, PA16 8JX
Tel: 01475-715624
Old Paisley Society
George Place, Paisley PA1 2HZ Tel: 0141-889-1708
Paisley Museum
Paisley Museum and Art Galleries, High Street, Paisley,
Renfrewshire, PA1 2BA Tel: 0141-889-3151
Renfrewshire Council Library & Museum
Central Library & Museum Complex, High Street, Paisley,
Renfrewshire, PA1 2BB Tel: 0141-889-2350
Email: local_studies.library@renfrewshire.gov.uk

Ross-Shire
Dingwall Museum Trust
Town Hall, High Street, Dingwall, Ross-Shire, IV15 9RY
Tel: 01349-865366
The Groam House Museum
High Street, Rosemarkie, Fortrose, Ross-Shire, IV10 8UF
Tel: 01381-620961 Fax: 01381-621730
Highland Museum of Childhood
The Old Station, Strathpeffer, Ross-Shire, IV14 9DH
Tel: 01997-421031 Email: info@hmoc.freeserve.co.uk
WWW: www.hmoc.freeserve.co.uk
Tain & District Museum
Tain Through Time, Tower Street, Tain, Ross-Shire, IV19
1DY Tel: 01862-893054
Email: info@tainmuseum.demon.co.uk
Ullapool Museum & Visitor Centre
7 & 8 West Argyle Street, Ullapool, Ross-Shire, IV26 2TY
Tel: 01854-612987 Email: ulmuseum@wavereider.co.uk

Roxburghshire
Hawick Museum & Scott Gallery
Wilton Lodge Park, Hawick, Roxburghshire, TD9 7JL
Tel: 01450-373457 Fax: 01450-378506
Email: hawickmuseum@hotmail.com
also fionacolton@hotmail.com
Jedburgh Castle Jail Museum
Castlegate, Jedburgh, Roxburghshire, TD8 6BD
Tel: 01835-863254 Fax: 01835-864750
Mary Queen of Scots House and Visitor Centre
Queens Street, Jedburgh, Roxburghshire, TD8 6EN
Tel: 01835-863331 Fax: 01835-863331
Email: hawickmuseum@hotmail.com
also fionacotton@hotmail.com

Scottish Borders
Hawick Museum & Scott Gallery
Wilton Lodge Park, Hawick, Roxburghshire, TD9 7JL
Tel: 01450-373457 Fax: 01450-378506
Email: hawickmuseum@hotmail.com
Mary Queen of Scots House and Visitor Centre
Queens Street, Jedburgh, Roxburghshire, TD8 6EN
Tel: 01835-863331 Fax: 01835-863331
Email: hawickmuseum@hotmail.com

Selkirkshire
Halliwells House Museum
Halliwells Close, Market Place, Selkirk, Selkirkshire, TD7
4BL Tel: 01750-20096 Fax: 01750-23282
Email: museums@scotsborders.gov.uk

Shetland
Fetlar Interpretive Centre
Beach Of Houbie, Fetlar, Shetland, ZE2 9DJ
Tel: 01957-733206 Email: fic@zetnet.co.uk
WWW: www.zetnet.co.uk/sigs/centre
Old Haa Museum
Burravoe Yell, Shetland, Shetland Islands, ZE2 9AY
Tel: 01957-722339
Shetland Museum
Lower Hillhead, Lerwick, Shetland Islands, ZE1 0EL
Tel: 01595-695057 Email: shetland.museum@zetnet.co.uk
WWW: www.shetland-museum.org.uk

Shetland Textile Working Museum The
Weisdale Mill, Weisdale, Shetland, Shetland Islands, ZE2
9LW Tel: 01595-830419
Tangwick HAA Museum
Tangwick, Eshaness, Shetland, ZE2 9RS Tel: 01806-503389
Unst Heritage Centre
Haraldswick, Unst, Shetland, ZE2 9EQ Tel: 01957-711528
Fax: 01957-711387 (Custodian home)

Stirlingshire and Sutherland
Regimental Museum Argyll and Sutherland Highlanders
Stirling Castle, Stirling, Stirlingshire, FK8 1EH Tel: 01786
Stirling
Stirling Smith Art Gallery & Museum
Dumbarton Road, Stirling, FK8 2RQ Tel: 01786 471917
Fax: 01786 449523 Email:
museum@smithartgallery.demon.co.uk
475165 Fax: 01786 446038
Strathnaver Museum
Bettyhill, Sutherland, KW14 7SS Tel: 01641-521418,
Fax: 01641-521315

Wigtownshire
Taylor's Farm Tradition
Barraer, Newton Stewart, Wigtownshire, DG8 6QQ
Tel: 01671-402184 Fax: 01671-404890
Email: j.taylor@bosinternet.com

Northern Ireland
Armagh County Museum
The Mall East, Armagh, County Armagh, BT61 9BE
Tel: (028) 37523070
Ballymoney Museum & Heritage Centre
33 Charlotte Street, Ballymoney, County Antrim, BT53 6AY
Tel: (028) 27662280
Centre for Migration Studies-Ulster American Folk Park
Mellon Road, Castletown, Omagh, County Tyrone, BT78
8QY Tel: 028-8225-6315 Fax: 028-8224-2241
Email: uafp@iol.ie WWW: www.folkpark.com
also www.qub.ac.uk/cms
Down County Museum
The Mall, Downpatrick, County Down, BT30 6AH
Tel: (028) 446615218
Downpatrick Railway Museum
Railway Station, Market St, Downpatrick, County Down,
BT30 6LZ Tel: (028) 446615779
Fermanagh County Museum
Enniskillen Castle Castle Barracks, Enniskillen, County
Fermanagh, BT74 7HL Tel: 028-6632-5000
Fax: 028-6632-7342 Email: castle@fermanagh.gov.uk
Foyle Valley Railway Museum
Foyle Road, Londonderry, County Londonderry, BT48 6SQ
Tel: (028) 712265234
Friends of the Ulster Museum Botanic Gardens
Botanic Gardens, Stranmillas Road, Belfast, County Antrim,
BT9 5AB Tel: (028) 9068-1606
Garvagh Museum
142 Main Street, Garvagh, County Londonderry, BT51 5AE
Tel: 028-295-58216/58188 Fax: 028-295-58993
Email: jclyde@garvaghhigh.garvagh.ni.sch.uk
Northen Ireland Museums Council
66 Donegall Pass, Belfast, County Antrim, BT7 1BU
Tel: (028) 90550215 Fax: (028) 90550216
Email: info@nimc.co.uk WWW: www.nimc.co.uk
Odyssey Science Centre Project Office
Project Office NMGNI, Botanic Gardens, Belfast, County
Antrim, BT9 5AB Tel: (028) 90682100
Roslea Heritage Centre
Church Street, Roslea, Enniskillen, County Fermanagh,
BT74 7DW Tel: (028) 67751750
Route 66
American Car Museum, 94 Dundrum Road, Newcastle,
County Down, BT33 0LN Tel: (028) 43725223
Royal Inniskillin Fusilers Regimental Museum
The Castle, Enniskillen, Co Fermanagh, BT74 7BB
Tel: 028-6632-3142 Fax: (028) 6632-0359

Royal Irish Fusilers Museum
Sovereign's House, Mall East, Armagh, BT61 9DL
Tel: (028) 3752-2911 Fax: (028) 3752-2911
The Royal Irish Regiment Museum
St. Patricks Barracks, Demesne Avenue, Ballymena, County
Antrim, BT43 7BH Tel: (028) 256661355
Royal Ulster Rifles Regimental Museum
5 Waring Street, Belfast, BT1 2EW Tel: (028) 9023-2086
The Somme Heritage Centre
233 Bangor Road, Newtownards, County Down, BT23 7PH
Tel: (028) 91823202 Fax: (028) 91823214
WWW: www.irishsoldier.org
Ulster American Folk Park Project Team Belfast
4 The Mount Albert Bridge Road, Belfast, County Antrim,
BT5 4NA Tel: (028) 9045 2250
Ulster Aviation Society
Langford Lodge Airfield 97, Largy Road, Crumlin, County
Antrim, BT29 4RT Tel: (028) 94454444
Email: ernie@airni.freeserve.co.uk
WWW: www.d-n-a.net/users/dnetrazq/
Ulster Folk & Transport Museum
Cultra, Holywood, Co Down, BT18 0EU
Tel: (028) 90 428428 Fax: (028) 90 428728
The Ulster History Park
Cullion, Lislap, Omagh, County Tyrone, BT79 7SU
Tel: (028) 8164 8188 Fax: (028) 8164 8011
Email: uhp@omagh.gov.uk
WWW: www.omagh.gov.uk/historypark.htm
Ulster Museum
Botanic Gardens, Stranmillis Road, Belfast, BT9 5AB
Tel: (028) 9038 1000 Fax: (028) 9038 3003
Londonderry Harbour Museum
Harbour Square, Londonderry, County Londonderry, BT48
6AF Tel: (028) 713 377331

Ireland
Dublin Civic Museum
58 South William Street, Dublin, 2 Tel: 679-4260
Fax: 677-5954
Irish Jewish Museum
3 - 4 Walworth Road, South Circular Road, Dublin, 8
Tel: 453-1797

Belgium
In Flanders Fields Museum
Lakenhallen, Grote Markt 34, Leper, B-8900
Tel: 00-32-(0)-57-22-85-84 Fax: 00-32-(0)-57-22-85-89
WWW: www.inflandersfields.be

In Praise of Books
Stuart A. Raymond

Where to start? That is the obvious question when we first become interested in family history. Many of us will start with family memories and legends - oral history. Those of us with computers will try the internet. Those anxious to see the original evidence for themselves will head straight for the archives. Those of us who realise how much we do not know about the research process will read a book to find out what we should do, how we should approach the research process, and how we should assess the value of the various bits of evidence that come our way.

Books and other published formats - fiche, CDs, journals - are vital for the genealogist. Other sources of information are useful too, but we do need to understand the relationship between oral history, the internet, archives, and books. In the latter, we will discover how to go about checking the veracity of Great Aunt Minnie's dubious stories, we will find far more information than is ever likely to be available on the internet, we will learn what to expect when we visit the archives, which sources to check, what records are available. Unlike archives, books are not unique; the same titles can be found just as easily in the libraries of Melbourne as they can in London. The overseas researcher who fails to check out the local availability of relevant books before booking his flight to Heathrow is likely to be wasting his money. The computer buff who thinks the Internet has all the information he needs is likely to be missing out on a vast array of potential sources. The researcher in the archives who does not consult books to find out what original source material is available will think he has completed his search when he has barely begun.

It is not too much to say that, for any subject you care to mention, there is a book on it. Millions of books are published every year. The outpourings of the genealogical press alone are staggering. Numerous introductory texts and guides to specific sources are now available, as are a variety of lists of record offices and libraries and calendars of their archival holdings. Publications of sources such as parish registers, inscriptions, wills, estate records, and census returns abound. Family history societies have published thousands of sources on fiche; commercial publishers have re-issued innumerable out of print published registers and trade directories, amongst much else. Libraries and record offices have published many guides to the sources they hold. Innumerable sources have been published by organisations such as the Devon & Cornwall Record Society, the Chetham Society (for Lancashire and Cheshire), and the Harleian Society (heraldic visitations & London parish registers). Specialised societies for publishing parish registers have issued many hundred registers - many of which have since been re-issued on fiche or CD.

We all need to know what publications are available that are likely to be of use to us. There are well over 100,000 publications that are relevant to English genealogical research. That includes over 1,500 CDs, and tens of thousand of fiche, as well as books and journal articles. We also need to know our way around libraries - the public storehouses of the books we need to consult. It is a fact that a high percentage - perhaps 30% - of the questions asked by genealogists on internet newsgroups could easily be answered from books available in good reference libraries throughout the English-speaking world. Such questions rarely betray appreciation of this fact. When we are faced by any genealogical question, it is always sensible to check first to see–

whether there is a book which might contain the answer. In order to do that we need to check relevant bibliographies.

Bibliography is a word which may be unfamiliar to you. Don't be frightened by it! A bibliography is, quite simply, a list of books. Without such lists, you are unlikely to be able to identify all the books which might be of relevance to your research: you cannot afford to ignore them. Some bibliographies are retrospective, that is, they aim to list all the relevant material on the subject covered that has ever been published. Others are current, only listing items which are available for purchase at the time of publication. My county bibliographies are retrospective, and are primarily intended to be used in order to identify material held in libraries; they aim to list everything that has ever been published likely to be of relevance to genealogists searching in the particular county covered. My *British Genealogical Books in Print(F.F.H.S., 1999)*, together - *British Genealogical Microfiche* (F.F.H.S. 1999) and *British Family History on CD* (F.F.H.S., 2001) are current bibliographies, as are Elizabeth Hampson *Current Publications– by Member Societies‘* (10th ed. F.F.H.S., 1999) and John Perkins *Current Publication on - Microfiche from Member Societies‘* (5th ed. F.F.H.S., forthcoming). These are intended to enable - you to identify publications currently available for purchase, and provide details of prices and publishers.

A good genealogical bibliography will reveal the wealth of published materials that are readily available for research. The researcher needs to work through these materials systematically; one-namers in particular would benefit considerably from checking all the publications of sources listed in my county bibliographies - although that is a counsel of perfection, given that most of the many volumes available include over 1,000 citations. It should not, however, take too long to check all the major county-wide printed sources, and publications of vital local sources such as parish registers and monumental inscriptions.

...for any subject you care to mention,there is a book on it...

Once you have identified a book in a bibliography, it should normally be a straight-forward task to locate it in a library. A book is not unique in the way that archives are; at least 500 copies will have been printed, and probably many more. A fair proportion of those copies are likely to have been purchased by libraries throughout the English-speaking world. Many overseas libraries, as well as most English reference libraries, have good collections of English genealogical books. The first edition of my 'English genealogy: a bibliography‘ (now in its 3rd ed. F.F.H.S., 1996) mainly based on books held in the State Library of Victoria, in Melbourne. A number of union lists of books held in various libraries are available, and will help you to locate libraries which hold particular items. Researchers in the United States will find the many hundred volumes of the ‘ National Union Catalog‘ of particular value, listing as it does library locations for millions of books, including most of those identified in my bibliographies. In Australia, the on-line Australian Bibliographic Network performs a similar function, although access to it would normally be through a librarian. Many similar union catalogues are available, and any reference librarian should be able to help you identify which libraries hold particular books. Alternatively, many library catalogues are now available for direct consultation via the internet. If the book you need cannot be found in a

local library, you may be able to ask your librarian to obtain it via the inter-library loan network. This should only be used as a last resort, as there is likely to be substantial cost to the library as well as to you. There are alternative means of acquiring information from books; this is where the internet comes into its own.There are several ways of using the internet to obtain information from books. This is where the Internet comes into its own. Many booksellers, both new and second-hand, now list their stock on the internet and may be able to sell you the book you require. There are also a number of internet sites, where participants offer to check books in their possession for inquirers. Finally, there are hundreds of newsgroups where–genealogists swop information with each other, and it is perfectly possible to ask for checks to be made in particular books that newsgroup members may have in their possession.
Addresses for many genealogical web-sites are listed in my 'Family History on the Web: an internet–directory for

England and Wales'(F.F.H.S., 2001).

The importance of books for genealogical research is often under-rated or ignored by genealogical authors. Too many authors of genealogical textbooks provide insufficient guidance in this area. I have already said it, but it needs to be shouted from the roof-tops: whatever your question, there may well be a book - or perhaps a fiche or CD - which provides the answer. Check it out!

Stuart A Raymond is the author of numerous bibliographies for family historians. He has just published ' Using Libraries: Workshops for Family Historians', which aims to provide basic guidance in the use of libraries and books, and develops the theme of this article. It is available from S.A. & M.J.Raymond, P.O.Box 35, Exeter, EX1 3YZ, price £3.40 (inc p &p). Stuart will also be happy to supply a full listing of his other publications.

Family History Sources in Stirling
Elma Lindsay Local History Officer

Stirling, the Royal Burgh, lies at the geographical and historical heart of Scotland, and is administered by Stirling Council. Two Local Government Reorganisations, in 1975 and again in 1996, have resulted in a give-and-take exchange of communities which may have found themselves variously in Stirlingshire or Perthshire, then Central Region, and now in Stirling District, Falkirk District, or East Dunbartonshire. All this is by way of emphasising that it is important to know the parish where your forebears actually lived so that, if you are coming to this part of Scotland to trace that elusive ancestor, you don't end up at the wrong library in the wrong town.

An article in an earlier edition of 'The Family & Local History Handbook' drew attention to the importance of libraries to the family historian, so where better to start than the Reference Department of Central Library, Corn Exchange Road, Stirling. FK8 2HX (telephone 01786 432106; fax 01786 473094). Central Library is conveniently situated near the town centre, about a ten minute walk from both the bus and the railway stations, and there is metered parking in the surrounding streets. It is a Carnegie building, and in 2002 celebrates the centenary of the laying of the foundation stone. The Reference Library is on the top floor, and unfortunately it is inaccessible to wheelchair users. A new library is at the planning stage, but for the moment those for whom several flights of stairs is a challenge are advised to make their way to Bridge of Allan library. So what genealogical treasures await the intrepid family historian? Those stalwarts of any family history research, the Census returns 1841 – 1891 , are available for the parts of Stirlingshire and Perthshire currently under the aegis of Stirling Council. Parishes now outwith this, but formerly within the County of Stirling, are being added as resources permit. A name index for the 1891 census for Stirlingshire and Perthshire is available on microfiche, and two copies of the Great Britain 1881 Census on CD-Rom are available. The 1851 Census is at present being indexed by Central Scotland Family History Society and published in booklet form, copies of which are purchased for the Reference Library as they become available. There is also a street index for each of the censuses for the parishes of Stirling, St Ninians, and Logie.

Old Parish Registers are available on microfilm for most of the former Stirlingshire parishes and also for parts of Perthshire. For Stirling itself, the earliest record is a baptism of 1585, but researchers should be aware that some of these early records are written in the old Scottish hand and are unintelligible to the average reader. The situation does improve however by the end of the seventeenth century. As elsewhere, births and marriages are indexed , and a local genealogical enthusiast has indexed the deaths from 1819 –1854. The Death and Burial records are particularly rich in Stirling burgh for the Old Town graveyard, as they include details not only of the deceased's name, address , age, date of death, date of burial, and cause of death, but whether or not they merited the church bells being tolled and in which lair of the graveyard they finally were laid to rest.

If finding a particular grave is proving difficult, Mitchell's 'Monumental Inscriptions' may be able to help. The volumes covering East and West Stirlingshire can be consulted in the Reference Library, as well as South Perthshire. A visit to the council Cemeteries Officer might also solve the problem (see section on Cemeteries Department)

The IGI is available on both microfiche and CD-ROM, with printouts available from each. Other material on CD-ROM includes *'Soldiers who died in the Great War'* and *'Soldiers who Died in World War Two'*; *'Retours of Services of Heirs 1544-1699'*; *'Services of Heirs of Scotland 1700-1859'* and

the ever useful *'Index of Occupational Terms'*.

The library holds a range of local newspapers, mostly on microfilm; one, the 'Stirling Journal' which had a lifespan of 150 years, has been indexed in three volumes, each usefully covering a 50 year period. The only surviving newspaper in the burgh, the *'Stirling Observer'* has a 'People' index from 1836 – 1856, under headings such as 'General Reference', and 'Advertisements' in addition to 'Births', 'Marriages' and 'Deaths'. An unlikely section is that on 'Crime', where the names of not only the perpetrator but of the victim may be found. The *'Observer'* is held at the library only from 1970; earlier editions may be consulted at Stirling Council Archives Services. A recent project has seen the indexing of the photographs which appeared in the *'Stirling Observer'* Christmas Annual between 1911 and 1968. Although not yet complete (1911 – 1957) there are currently over 9,000 photographs of named Stirlingshire people which can be produced in minutes, very useful for the family historian.

The library holds a good selection of Street Directories, giving names and addresses of people and businesses from 1869 through to 1932. Although the run is by no means complete, the last years of the nineteenth century are well documented.

Valuation Rolls are available on microfilm, and cover the years 1855 – 1902 for Stirling Burgh. Later years may be seen at the Archives (see section on Stirling Council Archives Services)

The Library has a number of useful maps in various scales, but the largest collection of historical maps is also at the Archives.

A collection of over 400 images of the Stirling Council area has been digitised and these are available for purchase up to size A4. They can be viewed on screen in the Central Reference Library.

Microfilm readers and reader printers are available, but as demand can be very high visitors are strongly advised to book in advance. Photocopying and colour photocopying facilities are also available.

Family History classes are run regularly for the general public, as are training session for new members of staff, including those out in the Community libraries. Although full scale genealogical research is not possible, in-depth searches of material held in Central Reference Library can be carried out. The current charge is £10 per hour, plus photocopying and postage.

Central Library is open 9.30 a.m. – 5.30 p.m. Mondays, Wednesdays , and Fridays; 9.30.a.m. – 7.00p.m. on Tuesdays and Thursdays; 9. 30a.m. – 5.00 p.m. on Saturdays.

The Community Libraries at Bridge of Allan (telephone 01786 833680,) Dunblane (01786 823125), St Ninians (01786 472069), and Drymen (01360 660751) have the IGI on CD-ROM, as well as the 1881 Census. Bridge of Allan also houses material belonging to Central Scotland Family History Society but which the Society generously allows the general public to use. Each of these Community Libraries has good disabled access. Details of their opening can be obtained by telephoning the appropriate library, or by accessing Stirling Council's website (http://web.stirling.gov.uk)

Another very useful source for the family historian is Stirling Council Archives Services. Situated at Unit 6,

Burghmuir Industrial Estate, Stirling FK7 7PY (Telephone 01786 450745; e-mail archive@stirling.gov.uk) the Archives are within easy walking distance of both the railway and bus stations. There is limited disabled access (telephone contact prior to visiting is advised), and nearby parking. Currently, the opening hours are Wednesday to Friday 10.00 – 12.30 and 1.30 – 4. 30. There is no charge for consulting records in the search room, but research on behalf of enquirers is only undertaken by prior agreement and for an agreed fee.

Sources include the records of the Royal Burgh of Stirling, Stirling County Council (including educational records), and the burghs of Callander, Doune and Dunblane. Additionally, there are collections of estate records, maps, church records, burial records (pre-1929), abridgements of sasine, and Calendars of Confirmations and Inventories (1876 - 1936).

Conveniently just across the road from Central Library is Stirling Council Registration Services which hold Birth, Marriage, and Death Registers for the Burgh of Stirling from 1855 onwards. The office is open to the public, but it is preferable to make an appointment before visiting. The hours at present are 9.00-.13.00 and 14.00 – 16.00 Mondays to Thursdays, and 9.00 – 13.00 and 14.00 – 18.00 on Fridays. Personal enquirers are welcome; there is disabled access and nearby metered parking. Current charges are £5 for a particular search (i.e. for a particular name over five years) and for a general search, the fee is £10 for the first hour or part thereof and £5 for a second or subsequent hour or part thereof during the same day. For further information call 01786 432343

A further useful port of call in Stirling is Stirling Council Cemeteries Services, which is housed in the Council Headquarters, New Viewforth, St Ninians Road, Stirling FK8 2HE (Telephone 01786 442559). It is open to the public between 9.00 a.m – 5.00 p.m. Monday to Friday, and it too is within walking distance of the two stations, has parking facilities, and disabled access. There are 56 cemeteries under the care of Cemeteries Services; it holds lair registers and interments registers in general from 1900 onwards which currently staff are in the process of computerising. The department accepts telephone and postal

enquiries, and at present there is no charge for enquiries.

The Smith Art Gallery and Museum
Although staff at the Smith Art Gallery and Museum do not deal with genealogical enquiries, a visit to the Smith is highly recommended for anyone with roots in the area. An independent museum, part-sponsored by Stirling Council, it was funded by a bequest from artist Thomas Stuart Smith and opened its doors in 1874. Two galleries are used for temporary exhibitions, but the main gallery houses 'The Stirling Story', a permanent exhibition which traces the growth and development of Stirling from the Bronze age up to the 1950s. Read all about Dougall Graham, an early war correspondent who followed Charles Edward Stuart's army through the Jacobite uprising of 1745/6 and who produced his eye-witness accounts in a series of chapbooks. Marvel at the world's oldest football, dating from 1540. See the Stirling Jug, one of the oldest measures in Scotland, set up by an Act of Parliament in 1457 which decreed that all the other liquid measures in Scotland were to be calibrated against it. Stirling was given the responsibility of the Jug, because of its pre-eminence as a brewing area. Your maltster forebears were important people. Do you have Bannockburn weavers in your family tree? Admire samples of tartans from the Wilsons' mills of Bannockburn. Although weaving and wearing of tartans by *Highlanders* was banned in an effort to destroy support for the Jacobite cause, *lowland* Bannockburn escaped this edict, and the Wilson family took full advantage of the situation.
Find out about
....Drummond's Tract Enterprise, a local business which began printing religious tracts in 1848 and didn't stop until 1980, having dispatched literally hundreds of millions around the world.
....Howietoun, the world's first commercial fish farm, established in 1873.
...The Homesteads, a social experiment unique in Britain. Wallow in nostalgia with a peek into the window of Mr Hay's music shop

A children's corner provides dressing up, brass rubbing, and quizzes. There is a café, shop, disabled access, a car park, and entry is free. The Smith is open Tuesday – Saturday 10.30 am – 5.00pm, Sunday 2.00pm – 5.00pm.
Check the website at www.smithartgallery.demon.co.uk

2 free issues or a binder when you subscribe to *Local History Magazine*

During 2001 our **News section** covered a wide range of issues from library closures to the possible privatisation of archives, and contained information about local history conferences, day schools, events and hundreds of courses.

'The Rise and Fall of the Turnpike' by the eminent local historian Paul Hindle is just one of **many articles** in recent issues. Other topics have included 'Public Health and Local Pride', 'Homes for Heroes' and a series on enclosure.

News from societies features in every issue. As well as new societies, such as the Milestone Society, we also include progress reports from societies all over the country.

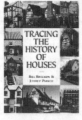

We carry more **book and periodical reviews** than any other magazine. We also sell the best in local history reference books at generous discounts.

In addition to all these features, *Local History Magazine* includes a unique **Noticeboard section** where every subscriber can place **50 words free** in every issue. Subscribers' notices are also included on our website (www.local-history.co.uk) so that your notices can be seen all over the world!

Our normal subscription price is £17.60 per year for six issues, posted direct to your home. Our **introductory offer** means that you can either pay £17.60 and receive 2 free additional issues or pay £32 and receive 12 issues plus a free binder, worth £7.50, which holds 12 copies.

To subscribe, send your cheque for £17.60 or £32, payable to Local History, to: Local History Freepost (NG7 2DS) Nottingham NG7 1BR (no stamp needed).

Offer applies in the UK only. For details of overseas subscription rates, or of how to pay by credit card, e-mail us on editors@local-history.co.uk or telephone us on 0115 9706473.

Libraries

National

Angus Library
Regent's Park College, Pusey Street, Oxford, OX1 2LB
Tel: 01865 288142 Fax: 01865 288121

Birmingham University Information Services - Special Collections
Main Library, University of Birmingham, Edgbaston, Birmingham, B15 2TT Tel: 0121 414 5838 Fax: 0121 471 4691 Email: special-collections@bham.ac.uk
WWW: www.is.bham.ac.uk

Bristol University Library - Special Collections
Tyndall Avenue, Bristol, BS8 1TJ Tel: 0117 928 8014
Fax: 0117 925 5334 Email: library@bris.ac.uk
WWW: www.bris.ac.uk/depts/library

British Genealogical Survey Library
Kingsley Dunham Centre, Keyworth, Nottingham, NG12 5GG Tel: 0115 939 3205 Fax: 0115 936 3200
Email: info@bgs.ac.uk WWW: www.bgs.ac.uk

British Library
British Library Building, 96 Euston Road, London, NW1 2DB Tel: (020) 712-7677 Email: http://www.portico.bl.uk & Reader/admissions@bl.uk

British Library - Early Printed Collections
96 Euston Road, London, NW1 2DB Tel: (020) 7412-7673
Email: rare-books@bl.uk WWW: http://www.bl.uk

Caird Library - National Maritime Museum
Park Row, Greenwich, London, SE10 9NF Tel: (020) 8312 6673 Fax: (020) 8312-6632 Email: ABuchanan@nmm.ac.uk
WWW: http://www.nmm.ac.uk

Cambridge University Library - Department of Manuscripts & University Archives
West Road, Cambridge, CB3 9DR Tel: 01223 333000 ext 33143 (Manuscripts) Tel: 01223 333000 ext 33148 (University Archives) Fax: 01223 333160 Email: mss@ula.cam.ac.uk WWW: www.lib.cam.ac.uk/MSS/

House of Commons Library
House of Commons, 1 Derby Gate, London, SW1A 2DG
Tel: (020) 7219-5545 Fax: (020) 7219-3921

Institute of Heraldic and Genealogical Studies
79 - 82 Northgate, Canterbury, CT1 1BA Fax: 01227-765617 Email: ihgs@ihgs.ac.uk WWW: www.ihgs.ac.uk

Jewish Studies Library
University College, Gower Street, London, WC1E 6BT
Tel: (020) 7387 7050

National Gallery Library and Archive
Trafalgar Square, London, WC2N 5DN Tel: 020 7747 2542
Fax: 020 7753 8179 Email: iad@ng-london.org.uk
WWW: http://www.nationalgallery.org.uk

Nuffield College Library
Oxford, OX1 1NF Tel: 01865 278550 Fax: 01865 278621

Rhodes House Library
Bodleian Library, South Parks Road, Oxford, OX1 3RG
Tel: 01865 270909 Fax: 01865 270912

Robinson Library
University of Newcastle upon Tyne, Newcastle Upon Tyne, NE2 4HQ Tel: 0191 222 7671 Fax: 0191 222 6235
Email: library@ncl.ac.uk
WWW: http://www.ncl.ac.uk/library/

Royal Armouries
H.M Tower Of London, Tower Hill, London, EC3N 4AB
Tel: (020) 7480 6358 ext 30 Fax: (020) 7481 2922
Email: Bridgett.Clifford@armouries.org.uk

Royal Commonwealth Society Library
West Road, Cambridge, CB3 9DR Tel: 01223 33319
 Fax: 01223 333160 Email: tab@ula.cam.ac.uk
WWW: www.lib.cam.ac.uk/MSS/

Society of Antiquaries of London
Burlington House, Piccadilly, London, W1J 0BE Tel: 020 7479 7084
Email: library@sal.org.uk WWW: www.sal.org.uk

Society of Genealogists - Library
14 Charterhouse Buildings, Goswell Road, London, EC1M 7BA Tel: 020-7251-8799 Tel: 020-7250-0291 Fax: 020-7250-1800 library@sog.org.uk - Sales at sales@sog.org.uk
WWW: http://www.sog.org.uk

Sussex University Library
Manuscript Collections, Falmer, Brighton, BN1 9QL Tel: 01273 606755 Fax: 01273 678441

The Kenneth Ritchie Wimbledon Library
The All England Lawn Tennis & Croquet Club, Church Road, Wimbledon, London, SW19 5AE
Tel: (020) 8946 6131 Fax: (020) 8944 6497
WWW: http://www.wimbledon.org Contains the world's finest collection of books and periodicals relating to lawn tennis

Trinity College Library
Cambridge University, Trinity College, Cambridge, CB1 1TQ Tel: 01223 338488 Fax: 01223 338532 Email: trin-lib@lists.cam.ac.uk WWW: http://rabbit.trin.cam.ac.uk

Victoria & Albert Museum - National Art Library
Cromwell Road, South Kensington, London, SW7 2RL Tel: (020) 7938 8315 Fax: (020) 7938 8461

Victoria & Albert Museum Archive of Art and Design
Blythe House, 23 Blythe Road, London, W14 0QF Tel: (020) 7603 1514 Fax: (020) 7602 0980 Email: archive@vam.ac.uk WWW: www.nal.vam.ac.uk

Wellcome Contemporary Medical Archives Centre
183 Euston Road, London, NW1 2BE Tel: (020) 7611 8483 Fax: (020) 7611 8703 Email: library@wellcome.ac.uk
WWW: www.wellcome.ac.uk/library Library catalogue is available through the internet: telnet://wihm.ucl.ac.uk

Wellcome Library for the History of Medicine - Department of Western Manuscripts
183 Euston Road, London, NW1 2BE Tel: (020) 7611-8582 Fax: (020) 7611 8369 Email: library@wellcome.ac.uk
WWW: www.wellcome.ac.uk/library

British Library Newspaper Library
Colindale Avenue, London, NW9 5HE Tel: 020-7412-7353
Fax: 020-7412-7379 Email: newspaper@bl.uk WWW: http://www.bl.uk/collections/newspaper/ The National archive collections of British and Overseas newspapers as well as major collections of popular magazines. Open Mon to Sat 10am to 4.45pm. Readers must be over 18yrs of age and provide proof

British Library of Political and Economic Science
London School of Economics, 10 Portugal Street, London, WC2A 2HD Tel: 020 7955 7223 Fax: 020 7955 7454
Email: info@lse.ac.uk WWW: http://www.lse.ac.uk

British Library Oriental and India Office Collections
96 Euston Road, London, NW1 2DB Tel: (020) 7412-7873
Fax: (020) 7412-7641 Email: oioc-enquiries@bl.uk WWW: http://www.bl.uk/collections/oriental

Caird Library - National Maritime Museum
Park Row, Greenwich, London, SE10 9NF Tel: (020) 8312 6673 Fax: (020) 8312-6632 Email: ABuchanan@nmm.ac.uk
WWW: http://www.nmm.ac.uk

Catholic Central Library
Lancing Street, London, NW1 1ND Tel: (020) 7383-4333
Fax: (020) 7388-6675 Email: librarian@catholic-library.demon.co.uk WWW: www.catholic-library.demon.co.uk

Department of Manuscripts and Special Collections
Hallward Library, Nottingham University , University Park, Nottingham, NG7 2RD Tel: 0115 951 4565 Fax: 0115 951 4558 Email: mss-library@nottingham.ac.uk WWW: www.mss.library.nottingham.ac.uk

Dr Williams's Library
14 Gordon Square, London, WC1H 0AR Tel: (020) 7387-3727
Email: 101340.2541@compuserve.com , The General Registers of Protestant Dissenters (Dr Williams's Library Registers) were surrendered to the Registrar General and are now at The Public Record Office (RG4/4666-4673)

Huguenot Library
University College, Gower Street, London, WC1E 6BT Tel:
(020) 7679 7094 Email: s.massilk@ucl.ac.uk WWW:
http://www.ucl.ac.uk/ucl-info/divisions/library/hugenot.htm
John Rylands University Library
Special Collections Division, 150 Deansgate, Manchester,
M3 3EH Tel: 0161-834-5343 Fax: 0161-834-5343 Email:
spcoll72@fs1.li.man.ac.uk WWW: http://rylibweb.man.ac.uk
Holdings include family muniment collections especially relating to Cheshire
and major Non Conformist Archives Few genealogical records held except for
family muniment collections, especially for Cheshire
Lambeth Palace Library
Lambeth Palace Road, London, SE1 7JU Tel: (020) 7898
1400 WWW: www.lambethpalacelibrary.org
Library of the Religious Society of Friends (Quakers)
Friends House, 173 - 177 Euston Rd, London, NW1 2BJ
Tel: 0207 663 1135 Tel: 0207 663 1001, Email:
library@quaker.org.uk WWW: http://www.quaker.org.uk/library
Limited opening hours. Letter of introduction required. Please send SAE for
details or enclose IRCs
Library of the Royal College of Surgeons of England
35-43 Lincoln's Inn Fields, London, WC2A 3PN Tel: (020)
7869 6520 Fax: (020) 7405 4438 Email: library@rseng.ac.uk
Lifelong Learning Service
Theodore Road, Port Talbot, SA13 1SP Tel: 01639-898581
Fax: 01639-899914 Email: lls@neath-porttalbot.gov.uk
Liverpool University Special Collections & Archives
University of Liverpool Library, PO Box 123, Liverpool,
L69 3DA Tel: 0151-794-2696 Fax: 0151-794-2081 WWW:
http://www.sca.lib.liv.ac.uk/collections/index.html The
University holds the records of a number of charities, especially those which
looked after children or encouraged emigration
Methodist Archives and Research Centre
John Rylands University Library, 150 Deansgate, Manchester,
M3 3EH Tel: 0161 834 5343 Fax: 0161 834 5574
Museum of the Order of St John
St John's Gate, St John's Lane, Clerkenwell, London, EC1M
4DA Tel: (020) 7253-6644 Fax: (020) 7336 0587
WWW: www.sja.org.uk/history
River & Rowing Museum
Rowing & River Museum, Mill Meadows, Henley on
Thames, RG9 1BF Tel: 01491 415625 Fax: 01491 415601
Email: museum@rrm.co.uk WWW: www..rrm.co.uk Thames
linked families especially lock keepers , boat builders
Royal Institute of British Architects' Library
Manuscripts & archives Collection, 66 portland Place,
London, W1N 4AD Tel: 020 7307 3615 Fax: 020 7631 1802
Royal Society of Chemistry Library & Info Centre
Burlington House, Piccadilly, London, W1J 0BA Tel: (020)
7437 8656 Fax: (020) 7287 9798 Email: library@rsc.org
WWW: www.rsc.org
School of Oriental and African Studies library
Thornhaugh Street, Russell Square, London, WC1H 0XG
Tel: 020 7323 6112 Fax: 020 7636 2834 Email:
lib@soas.ac.uk WWW: http://www.soas.ac.uk/library/
South Wales Miners' Library - Swansea
Hendrefoelan House, Gower Road, Swansea, SA2 7NB Tel:
01792-518603 Fax: 01792-518694 Email: miners@swansea.ac.uk
WWW: http://www.swan.ac.uk/lis/swml
The Library & Museum of Freemasonry
Freemasons' Hall, 60 Great Queen Street, London, WC2B
5AZ Tel: (020) 7395 9257
The Science Museum Library
Imperial College Road, South Kensington, London,SW7 5NH
Tel: 020 7938 8234 Tel: 020 7938 8218 Fax: 020 7938 9714
The Women's Library
Old Castle Street, London, E1 7NT Tel: (020) 7320-1189
Fax: (020) 7320-1188 Email: fawcett@lgu.ac.uk
WWW: http://www.lgu.ac.uk./fawcett
Thomas Plume Library
Market Hill, Maldon, CM9 4PZ No facilities for incoming
telephone or fax messages

**Trades Union Congress Library Collections - University
of North London**
236 - 250 Holloway Road, London, N7 6PP Fax: 0171 753 3191
Email: tuclib@unl.ac.uk WWW: http://www.unl.ac.uk/library/tuc
United Reformed Church History Society
Westminster College, Madingley Road, Cambridge, CB3
0AA Tel: 01223-741300 (NOT Wednesdays) Information on
ministers of constituent churches not members
Wellcome Library - History & Understanding of Medicine
183 Euston Road, London, NW1 2BE Tel: (020) 7611-8582 Fax:
(020) 7611 8369 Email: library@wellcome.ac.uk WWW:
www.wellcome.ac.uk/library Library catalogue is available
through the internet: http://library.wellcome.ac.uk

England
Bedfordshire
Bedford Central Library
Harpur Street, Bedford, MK40 1PG Tel: 01234-350931 Fax:
01234-342163 Email: stephensonB@bedfordshire.gov.uk
Local Studies Library
Luton Central Library, St George's Square, Luton, LU1 2NG
Tel: 01582-547420 Tel: 01582-547421 Fax: 01582-547450

Berkshire
Ascot Heath Library
Fernbank Road, North Ascot, SL5 8LA Tel: 01344 884030
Fax: 01344 884030
Binfield Library
Benetfeld Road, Binfield, RG42 4HD Tel: 01344 306663
Fax: 01344 486467
Bracknell Library
(Headquarters), Town Square, Bracknell, RG12 1BH
Tel: 01344 423149 Fax: 01344 411392
Crowthorne Library
Lower Broadmoor Road, Crowthorne, RG45 7LA
Tel: 01344 776431 Fax: 01344 776431
Reading Local Studies Library
3rd Floor, Central Library, Abbey Square, Reading, RG1
3BQ Tel: 0118 901 5965 Fax: 0118 901 5954
Email: info@readinglibraries.org.uk
Reading University Library
University of Reading, Whiteknights PO Box 223, Reading,
RG6 6AE Tel: 0118-931-8776 Fax: 0118-931 6636
WWW: http://www.reading.ac.uk/
Sandhurst Library
The Broadway, Sandhurst, GU47 9BL Tel: 01252 870161
Whitegrove Library
5 County Lane, Warfield, RG42 3JP Tel: 01344 424211

Birkenhead
Wirral Central Library
Borough Road, Birkenhead, CH41 2XB Tel: 0151 652 6106
Tel: 0151 652 6107/8 Fax: 0151 653 7320
Email: birkenhead.library@merseymail.com

Birmingham
**Birmingham Central Library - The Genealogist, Local
Studies & History Service**
Floor 6, Central Library, Chamberlain Square, Birmingham,
B3 3HQ Tel: 0121 303 4549 Fax: 0121 464 0993
Email: local.studies.library@birmingham.gov.uk
WWW: www.birmingham.gov.uk

Bolton
Central Library
Civic Centre, Le Mans Crescent, Bolton, BL1 1SE
Tel: 01204-333185

Bristol
Bristol Central Library
Reference Section, College Green, Bristol, BS1 5TL
Tel: 0117-929-9147 Tel: 0117903 7259 Fax:
Bristol University Library - Special Collections
Tyndall Avenue, Bristol, BS8 1TJ Tel: 0117 928 8014
Email: library@bris.ac.uk WWW: www.bris.ac.uk/depts/library

Buckinghamshire
County Reference Library
Walton Street, Aylesbury, HP20 1UU Tel: 01296-382250
High Wycombe Reference Library
Queen Victoria Road, High Wycombe, HP11 1BD Tel:
01494-510241 Email: hwrlib@hotmail.com
Milton Keynes Reference Library
555 Silbury Boulevard, Milton Keynes, MK9 3HL
Tel: 01908 254160 Fax: 01908 254088

Cambridgeshire
**Cambridge University Library - Department of
Manuscripts & University Archives**
West Road, Cambridge, CB3 9DR Tel: 01223 333000 ext 33143
(Manuscripts) Tel: 01223 333000 ext 33148 (University
Archives) Fax: 01223 333160 Email: mss@ula.cam.ac.uk
WWW: www.lib.cam.ac.uk/MSS/
Homerton College Library
The New Library, Hills Road, Cambridge, CB2 2PH
Norris Library and Museum
The Broadway, St Ives, PE27 5BX Tel: 01480-465101 Fax:
01480 497314 Email: norris.st-ives-tc@co-net.com
The Cambridge Library
Lion Yard, Cambridge, CB2 3QD

Cheshire
Chester Library
Northgate Street, Chester, CH1 2EF Tel: 01244-312935
Crewe Library
Prince Albert Street, Crewe, CW1 2DH Tel: 01270-211123
Fax: 01270-256952 Email: ipcrewe@cheshire.gov.uk
Ellesmere Port Library
Civic Way, Ellesmere Port, South Wirral, L65 0BG Tel:
0151-355-8101 Fax: 0151-355-6849
Halton Lea Library
Halton Lea, Runcorn, WA7 2PF Tel: 01928-715351
Local Heritage Library
Central Library, Wellington Road South, Stockport, SK1
3RS Tel: 0161-474-4530
Email: localherirtage.library@stockport.gov.uk
Macclesfield Library
Jordongate, Macclesfield, SK10 1EE Tel: 01625-422512
Stockport MBC Bibliographical Services Unit
Phoenix House, Bird Hall Lane, Stockport, SK3 0RA
Tameside Local Studies Library
Stalybridge Library, Trinity Street, Stalybridge, SK15 2BN
Tel: 0161-338-2708 Tel: 0161-338-3831 and 0161 303 7937
Fax: 0161-303-8289 Email:
localstudies.library@mail.tameside.gov.uk WWW:
http://www.tameside.gov.uk
Warrington Library & Local Studies Centre
Museum Street, Warrington, WA1 1JB Tel: 01925 442890
Fax: 01925 411395 Email: library@warrington.gov.uk
WWW: www.warrington.gov.uk

Cleveland
Middlesbrough Libraries & Local Studies Centre
Central Library, Victoria Square, Middlesbrough, TS1 2AY
Tel: 01642-263358 Fax: 01642 648077
Stockton Reference Library
Church Road, Stockton on Tees, TS18 1TU Tel: 01642-
393994 Email: reference.library@stockton.bc.gov.uk

Cornwall
**Royal Institution of Cornwall, Courtney Library &
Cornish History Research Centre**
Royal Cornwall Museum, River Street, Truro, TR1 2SJ Tel:
01872 272205 Email: RIC@royal-cornwall-museum.freeserve.co.uk
WWW: www.cornwall-online.co.uk/ric
The Cornwall Centre
Alma Place, Redruth, TR15 2AT Tel: 01209-216760
Email: cornishstudies@library.cornwall.gov.uk
WWW: www.cornwall.gov.uk

County Durham
Centre For Local Studies
The Library, Crown Street, Darlington, DL1 1ND Tel:
01325-349630 Email: crown.street.library@darlington.gov.uk
Durham Arts
Library and Museums Department, County Hall, Durham,
DH1 5TY Tel: 0191-383-3595
Durham City Library
Reference & Local Studies Department, South Street,
Durham, DH1 4QS Tel: 0191-386-4003
Email: durhamcityref.lib@durham.gov.uk
WWW: www.durham.gov.uk
Durham University Library Archives & Special Collections
Palace Green Section, Palace Green, Durham, DH1 3RN
Tel: 0191-374-3032 Email: pg.library@durham.ac.uk

Cumbria
Carlisle Library
11 Globe Lane, Carlisle, CA3 8NX Tel: 01228-607310 Fax:
01228-607333 Email: carlisle.library@cumbriacc.gov.uk
WWW: http://dspace.dial.pipex.com/cumherit/index.htm
Cumbria Record Office and Local Studies Library
Scotch Street, Whitehaven, CA28 7BJ Tel: 01946-
852920Email: whitehaven.record.office@cumbriacc.gov.uk
WWW: , http://www.cumbria.gov.uk/archives
Cumbria Record Office & Local Studies Library
140 Duke St, Barrow in Furness, LA14 1XW Tel: 01229-
894363 Email: barrow.record.office@cumbriacc.gov.uk
WWW: www.cumbria.gov.uk/archives
Kendal Library
Stricklandgate, Kendal, LA9 4PY Tel: 01539-773520Email:
kendal.library@cumbriacc.gov.uk
Penrith Library
St Andrews Churchyard, Penrith, CA11 7YA Tel: 01768-
242100Email: penrith.library@dial.pipexcom
Workington Library
Vulcans Lane, Workington, CA14 2ND Tel: 01900-325170
Email: workington.library@cumbriacc.gov.uk

Derbyshire
Chesterfield Local Studies Department
Chesterfield Library, New Beetwell Street, Chesterfield, S40
1QN Tel: 01246-209292 Fax: 01246-209304
Derby Local Studies Library
25b Irongate, Derby, DE1 3GL Tel: 01332 255393
Family Local Studies Library - Matlock
County Hall, Smedley Street, Matlock, DE4 3AG Tel:
01629-585579 Fax: 01629-585049

Derby City Council
Derby Local Studies Library
25b Irongate, Derby, DE1 3GL Tel: 01332 255393 Fax:
01332 255381

Devon
Devon & Exeter Institution Library
7 The Close, Exeter, EX1 1EZ Tel: 01392-251017Email:
m.midgley@exeter.ac.uk
WWW: http://www.ex.ac.uk/library/devonex.html
Exeter University Library
Stocker Road, Exeter, EX4 4PT Tel: 01392 263870Email:
library@exeter.ac.uk WWW: www.library.exeter.ac.uk

Westcountry Studies Library
Exeter Central Library, Castle Street, Exeter, EX4 3PQ Tel:
01392-384216 Email: dlaw@devon-cc.gov.uk
WWW: http://www.devon-cc.gov.uk/library/locstudy

Dorset
Dorchester Reference Library
Colliton Park, Dorchester, DT1 1XJ Tel: 01305-224448
Dorset County Museum
High West Street, Dorchester, DT1 1XA Tel: 01305 262735
Email: dorsetcountymuseum@dor-mus.demon.co.uk

Poole Central Reference Library
Dolphin Centre, Poole, BH15 1QE Tel: 01202 262424 Fax: 01202 262442 Email: centrallibrary@poole.gov.uk WWW: www.poole.gov.uk The local studies collection was relocated to The Waterfront Museum, Poole Some records moved to Dorset Record Office. Retains only general local history and national family history indexes.

East Sussex
Brighton Local Studies Library
Church Street, Brighton, BN1 1 UD Tel: 01273-296971 Fax: 01273-296962 Email: brightonlibrary@pavilion.co.uk
Hove Reference Library
182 -186 Church Road, Hove, BN3 2EG Tel: 01273-296942

Essex
Central Reference Library - LB of Havering
Reference Library, St Edward's Way, Romford, RM1 3AR Tel: 01708 432393 Email: romfordlib2@rmplc.co.uk
Chelmsford Library
PO Box 882, Market Road, Chelmsford, CM1 1LH Tel: 01245 492758 Email: answers.direct@essexcc.gov.uk WWW: www.essexcc.gov.uk
Colchester Central Library
Trinity Square, Colchester, CO1 1JB Tel: 01206-245917 Email: jane.stanway@essexcc.gov.uk WWW: www.essexcc.gov.uk
LB of Barking & Dagenham Local History Studies
Valence House Museum, Becontree Avenue, Dagenham, RM8 3HT Tel: 020-822-75293 Fax: 020-822-75297 Email: fm019@viscount.org.uk WWW: http://www.bardaglea.org.uk/4-heritage/heritage-menu.html
Heritage service includes a local history museum, and archive section. A list of resources is available upon request. Archives of thethe London Boroughs and Essex Parishes of Barking and Dagenham
LB of Barking & Dagenham Local History Studies
Central Library, Barking, Dagenham, IG11 7NB Tel: (020) 8517-8666 Local History studies from this Library have been centralised at Valence Linbrary, Becontree Avenue, Dagenham, Essex RM8 3HT Tel & (020) 8227 5297 Email:valencelibrary@hotmail.com
Redbridge Library
Central Library, Clements Road, Ilford, IG1 1EA Tel: (020) 8708-2417 Email: Local.Studies@redbridge.gov.uk WWW: www.redbridge.gov.uk
Southend Library
Central Library, Victoria Avenue, Southend on Sea, SS2 6EX Tel: 01702-612621 Email: library@southend.gov.uk WWW: www.southend.gov.uk/libraries/
Thomas Plume Library
Market Hill, Maldon, CM9 4PZ No facilities for incoming telephone or fax messages

Gloucestershire
Cheltenham Local Studies Centre
Cheltenham Library, Clarence Street, Cheltenham, GL50 3JT Tel: 01242-532678 Fax: 01242 532673
Gloucester Library, Arts & Museums
County Library, Quayside, Shire Hall, Gloucester, GL1 1HY Tel: 01452-425037 Email: clams@gloscc.gov.uk WWW: http://www.gloscc.gov.uk
Gloucestershire County Library
Brunswick Road, Gloucester, GL1 1HT Tel: 01452-426979 Email: clams@gloscc.gov.uk WWW: http://www.gloscc.gov.uk
Gloucestershire Family History Society
4 Twyver Close, Upton St Leonards, GL4 8EF Tel: 01452-52344 (RESOURCE CENTRE) Tel: 01452 615143 Fax: 01452 615143 Email: glosearch@hotmail.com WWW: http://www.cix.co.uk/~rd/genuki/gfhs.htm

South Gloucestershire
Thornbury Library
St Mary Street, Thornbury, BS35 2AA Tel: 01454-865655
Yate Library
44 West Walk, Yate, BS37 4AX Tel: 01454-865661

Hammersmith
Hammersmith Central Library
Shepherds Bush Road, London, W6 7AT Tel: 020 8753 3816 Fax: 020 8753 3815 WWW: www.lbhf.gov.uk

Hampshire
Aldershot Library
109 High Street, Aldershot, GU11 1DQ Tel: 01252 322456
Andover Library
Chantry Centre, Andover, SP10 1LT Tel: 01264 352807 Email: , clceand@hants.gov.uk
Basingstoke Library
North Division Headquarters, 19 - 20 Westminster House, Potters Walk, Basingstoke, RG21 7LS Tel: 01256-473901
Eastleigh Library
The Swan Centre, Eastleigh, SO50 5SF Tel: 01703 612513 Email: clweeas@hants.gov.uk
Fareham Library
South Division Headquarters, Osborn Road, Fareham, PO16 7EN Tel: 01329-282715 Email: clsoref@hants.gov.uk
Farnborough Library
Pinehurst, Farnborough, GU14 7JZ Tel: 01252 513838 Email: clnoref@hants.gov.uk WWW: http://www.brit-a-r.demon.co.uk
Fleet Library
236 Fleet Road, Fleet, GU13 8BX Tel: 01252 614213 Email: clnofle@hants.gov.uk
Gosport Library
High Street, Gosport, PO12 1BT Tel: (023) 9252 3431 WWW: clsos@hants.gov.uk
Hampshire County Library
West Division Headquarters, The Old School, Cannon Street, Lymington, SO41 9BR Tel: 01590-675767 Email: clwedhq@hants.gov.uk WWW: http://www.hants.gov.uk
Hampshire Local Studies Library
Winchester library, Jewry Street, Winchester, SO23 8RX Tel: 01962 841408 Email: clceloc@hants.gov.uk WWW: www.hants.gov.uk/library
Lymington Library
Cannon Street, Lymington, SO41 9BR Tel: 01590 673050 Email: clwelym@hants.gov.uk
Portsmouth City Libraries
Central Library, Guildhall Square, Portsmouth, PO1 2DX Tel: (023) 9281 9311 Email: reference.library@portsmouthcc.gov.uk
Royal Marines Museum
Eastney, Southsea, PO4 9PX Tel: (023) 92 819385-Exts-224 Fax: (023) 92 838420 Email: matthewlittle@royalmarinesmuseum.co.uk WWW: www.royalmarinesmuseum.co.uk No charges for research other than material costs. Donations welcome. Visits by appointment Mon to Fri 10am to 4.30pm
Southampton City Libraries - Special Collections
Southampton Reference Library, Civic Centre, Southampton, SO14 7LW Tel: 023 8083 2205 Email: local.studies@southampton.gov.uk WWW: www.southampton.gov.uk Special collections include information on Southampton and Hampshire, genealogy and maritime topics.

Southampton University Library
Highfield, Southampton, SO17 1BJ Tel: 023 8059 3724 Tel: 023 8059 2721 Fax: 023 8059 3007
Waterlooville Library
The Precinct, Waterlooville, PO7 7DT Tel: (023) 9225 4626 Email: clsowvl@hants.gov.uk
Winchester Reference Library
81 North Walls, Winchester, SO23 8BY Tel: 01962-846059 Fax: 01962-856615 Email: clceref@hants.gov.uk

Herefordshire
Bromyard Library
34 Church Street, Bromyard, HR7 4DP Tel: 01885 482657 No Genealogical information held

Colwall Library
Humphrey Walwyn Library, Colwall, Malvern, WR13 6QT
Tel: 01684 540642
Hereford Cathedral Archives & Library
5 College Cloisters, Cathedral Close, Hereford, HR1 2NG
Tel: 01432 374225 Email: library@herefordcathedral.co.uk
Hereford Library
Broad Street, Hereford, HR4 9AU Tel: 01432-272456
Ledbury Library
The Homend, Ledbury, HR8 1BT Tel: 01531 632133
Leominster Library
8 Buttercross, Leominster, HR6 8BN Tel: 01568-612384
Ross Library
Cantilupe Road, Ross on Wye, HR9 7AN
Tel: 01989 567937

Hertfordshire
Hertfordshire Archives and Local Studies
County Hall, Pegs Lane, Hertford, SG13 8EJ Tel: 01438
737333 Email: herts.direct@hertscc.gov.uk WWW:
http://hertsdirect.org/hals Comprised of the former Herts
County Record Office and Herts Local Studies Library
Welwyn Garden City Central Library
Local Studies Section, Campus West, Welwyn Garden City,
AL8 6AJ Tel: 01438 737333 Fax: 01707 897 595

Hull
Brynmor Jones Library - University of Hull
Cottingham Road, Hull, HU6 7RX Tel: 01482 465265
FEmail: archives@acs.hull.ac.uk WWW: www.hull.ac.uk/lib
www.hull.ac.uk/lib/archives
Hull Local Studies Library
Central Library, Albion Street, Kingston upon Hull, HU1
3TF Tel: 01482 210077 Fax: 01482 616827
Email: local.studies@hullcc.gov.uk WWW:
http://www.hullcc.gov.uk/genealogy/

Isle of Wight
Isle of Wight County Library
Lord Louis Library, Orchard Street, Newport, PO30 1LL
Tel: 01983-823800 Email: reflib@llouis.demon.co.uk

Kent
Broadstairs Library
The Broadway, Broadstairs, CT10 2BS Tel: 01843-862994
Canterbury Cathedral Library
The Precincts, Canterbury, CT1 2EH Tel: 01227-865287
Email: catlib@ukc.ac.uk
WWW: www.canterbury-cathedral.org
Canterbury Library & Local Studies Collection
18 High Street, Canterbury, CT1 2JF Tel: 01227-463608
Dartford Central Library - Reference Department
Market Street, Dartford, DA1 1EU Tel: 01322-221133
Dover Library
Maison Dieu House, Biggin Street, Dover, CT16 1DW Tel:
01304-204241
Faversham Library
Newton Road, Faversham, ME13 8DY Tel: 01759-532448 9

Folkestone Library & Local Heritage Studies
2 Grace Hill, Folkestone, CT20 1HD Tel: 01303-256710
Email: janet.adamson@kent.gov.uk
Gillingham Library
High Street, Gillingham, ME7 1BG Tel: 01634-281066
Email: Gillingham.Library@medway.gov.uk
Gravesend Library
Windmill Street, Gravesend, DA12 1BE Tel: 01474-352758
Greenhill Library
Greenhill Road, Herne Bay, CT6 7PN Tel: 01227 374288
Herne Bay Library
124 High Street, Herne Bay, CT6 5JY Tel: 01227-374896

Institute of Heraldic and Genealogical Studies
79 - 82 Northgate, Canterbury, CT1 1BA Fax: 01227-
765617 Email: ihgs@ihgs.ac.uk WWW: www.ihgs.ac.uk

LB of Bromley Local Studies Library
Central Library, High Street, Bromley, BR1 1EX Tel: 020
8460 9955 Email: localstudies.library@bromley.gov.uk

Kent
Margate Library Local History Collection
Cecil Square, Margate, CT9 1RE Tel: 01843-223626
Ramsgate Library and Museum
Guildford Lawn, Ramsgate, CT11 9QY Tel: 01843-593532
Ramsgate Library Local Strudies Collection & Thanet Branch Archives
Ramsgate Library, Guildford Lawn, Ramsgate, CT11 9AY
Tel: 01843-593532 Archives at this library moved to East Kent
Archives CentreEnterprise Zone, Honeywood Road, Whitfield, Dover,
Kent CT16 3EH. A Local Studies Collection remains
Sevenoaks Library
Buckhurst Lane, Sevenoaks, TN13 1LQ Tel: 01732-453118
Sheerness Library
Russell Street, Sheerness, ME12 1PL Tel: 01795-662618
Fax: 01795-583035 WWW: www.kent.gov.uk
Sittingbourne Library
Central Avenue, Sittingbourne, ME10 4AH Tel: 01795-
476545 Fax: 01795-428376 WWW: www.kent.gov.uk
Sturry Library
Chafy Crescent, Sturry, Canterbury, CT2 0BA
Tel: 01227 711479 Fax: 01227 710768
Tunbridge Wells Library
Mount Pleasant, Tunbridge Wells, TN1 1NS
Tel: 01892-522352 Fax: 01892-514657
University of Kent at Canterbury Library
Canterbury, CT2 7NU Tel: 01227 764000
Whitstable Library
31-33 Oxford Street, Whitstable, CT5 1DB
Tel: 01227-273309 Fax: 01227-771812

Lancashire
Barnoldswick Library
Fernlea Avenue, Barnoldswick, BB18 5DW
Tel: 01282-812147 Fax: 01282-850791
Blackburn Central Library
Town Hall Street, Blackburn, BB2 1AG Tel: 01254 587920
Email: reference.library@blackburn.gov.uk
WWW: www.blackburn.gov.uk/library
Bolton Central Library
Civic Centre, Le Mans Crescent, Bolton, BL1 1SE
Tel: 01204-333185
Burnley Central & Local Studies Library
Grimshaw Street, Burnley, BB11 2BD Tel: 01282-437115
Email: burnley.reference@lcl.lancscc.gov.uk
Bury Central Library - References & Info Services
Bury Central Library, Manchester Road, Bury, BL9 0DG
Tel: 0161-253-5871 Email: Bury.lib@bury.gov.uk
WWW: www.bury.gov.uk/culture.htm
Chethams Library
Long Millgate, Manchester, M3 1SB Tel: 0161 834 7961
Fax: 0161 839 5797 Email: chetlib@dial.pipex.com
Colne Library
Market Street, Colne, BB8 0AP Tel: 01282-871155
Heywood Local Studies Library
Heywood Library, Church Street, Heywood, OL10 1LL
Tel: 01706 360947 Fax: 01706 368683
Hyndburn Central Library
St James Street, Accrington, Lancs, BB5 1NQ Tel: 01254-
872385 Email: accrington.localstudies@lcl.lancscc.gov.uk
Lancashire Record Office
Bow Lane, Preston, PR1 2RE Tel: 01772 263039 Fax:
01772 263050 Email: record.office@ed.lancscc.gov.uk
WWW: www.lancashire.gov.uk/education/lifelong/recordindex.shtm
The Lancashire Local Studies Collection is now housed here

Leigh Library
Turnpike Centre, Civic Centre, Leigh, WN7 1EB Tel: 01942-404559 Email: heritage@wiganmbc.gov.uk

Middleton Local Studies Library
Middleton Library, Long Street, Middleton, M24 6DU
Tel: 0161-643-5228 Fax: 0161-654-0745

Oldham Local Studies and Archives
84 Union Street, Oldham, OL1 1DN Tel: 0161-911-4654
Email: archives@oldham.gov.uk & localstudies@oldham.gov.uk
WWW: http://www.oldham.gov.uk/archives
http://www.oldham.gov.uk/local_studies

Prestwich Library
Longfield Centre, Prestwich, M25 1AY Tel: 0161 253 7214
Tel: 0161 253 7218 Email: Prestwich.lib@bury.gov.uk

Radcliffe Library
Stand Lane, Radcliffe, M26 9WR Tel: 0161 253 7160
Fax: 0161 253 7165 Email: Radcliuffe.lib@bury.gov.uk

Ramsbottom Library
Carr Street, Ramsbottom, BL0 9AE Tel: 01706 822484
Fax: 01706 824638 Email: Ramsbottom.lib@bury.gov.uk

Rochdale Local Studies Library
The Esplanade, Rochdale, OL16 4TY Tel: 01706 864915
Temporary address until September 2002: Floor 3
Champness Hall, Drake Street, Rochdale OL16 1PB

Salford Local History Library
Peel Park, Salford, M5 4WU Tel: 0161 736 2649

Salford Museum & Art Gallery
Peel Park, Salford, M5 4WU Tel: 0161 736 2649
Email: info@lifetimes.org.uk WWW: www.lifetimes.org.uk

The Harris Reference Library
Market Square, Preston, PR1 2PP Tel: 01772 404010
Fax: 01772 555527 Email: harris@airtime.co.uk

Working Class Movement Library
Jubilee House, 51 The Crescent, Salford, M5 4WX
Tel: 0161-736-3601 Fax: 0161-737 4115

Lancashire - Wigan
Abram Library
Vicarage Road, Abram, Wigan, WN2 5QX Tel: 1942866350

Ashton Library
Wigan Road, Ashton in Makerfield, Wigan, WN2 9B Tel: 01942 727119

Aspull Library
Oakfield Crescent, Aspull, Wigan, WN2 1XJ Tel: 01942 831303

Atherton Library
York Street, Atherton, Manchester, M46 9JH
Tel: 01942 404817 Tel: 01942 4044816

Beech Hill Library
Buckley Street West, Beech Hill, Wigan, WN6 7PQ

Golbourne Library
Tanners Lane, Golbourne, Warrington, WA3 3AW Tel: 01942 777800

Hindley Library
Market Street, Hindley, Wigan, WN2 3AN Tel: 01942 255287

Ince Library
Smithy Green, Ince, Wigan, WN2 2AT Tel: 01942 255287

Leigh Library
Turnpike Centre, Civic Square, Leigh, WN7 1EB Tel: 01942 404557

Marsh Green Library
Harrow Road, Marsh Green, Wigan Tel: 01942 760041

Orrell Library
Orrell Post, Orrell, Wigan, WN5 8LY Tel: 01942 705060

Shevington Library
Gathurst Lane, Shevington, Wigan, WN6 8HA Tel: 01257 252618

Standish Library
Cross Street, Standish, Wigan, WN6 0HQ Tel: 01257 400496

Tyldesley Library
Stanley Street, Tyldesley, Manchester, M29 8AH Tel: 01942 882504

Wigan Library
College Avenue, Wigan, WN1 1NN Tel: 01942 827619

Wigan M B C - Leisure Services Department
Information Unit, Station Road, Wigan, WN1 1WN

Leicestershire
Hinckley Library Local Studies Collection
Hinckley Library, Lancaster Road, Hinckley, LE10 0AT
Tel: 01455-635106 Fax: 01455-251385

Leicestershire Libraries & Information Service
929 - 931 Loughborough Road, Rothley, LE7 7NH
Tel: 0116-267-8023 Fax: 0116-267-8039

Loughborough Library Local Studies Collection
Granby Street, Loughborough, LE11 3DZ
Tel: 01509-238466 Email: slaterjohn@hotmail.com

Market Harborough Library & Local Studies Collection
Pen Lloyd Library, Adam and Eve Street, Market
Harborough, LE16 7LT Tel: 01858-82127

Melton Mowbray Library
Wilton Road, Melton Mowbray, LE13 0UJ
Tel: 01664 560161WWW: www.leics.gov.uk

Lincolnshire
Boston Library
County Hall, Boston, PE21 6LX Tel: 01205 310010

Gainsborough Library
Cobden Street, Gainsborough, DN21 2NG Tel: 01427 614780

Grantham Library
Issac Newton Centre, Grantham, NG1 9LD Tel: 01476 591411

Lincoln Cathedral Library
Lincoln Cathedral Library, The Cathedral, Lincoln, LN2 1PZ
England Tel: 01522-544544 Fax: 01522-511307

Lincolnshire County Library
Local Studies Section, Lincoln Central Library, Free School
Lane, Lincoln, LN1 1EZ Tel: 01522-510800 Fax: 01522-575011 Email: lincoln.library@lincolnshire.gov.uk
www.lincolnshire.gov.uk/library/services/family.htm

Stamford Library
High Street, Stamford, PE9 2BB Tel: 01780 763442

North East Lincolnshire
Grimsby Central Library Reference Department
Central Library, Town Hall Square, Great Grimsby, DN31
1HG Tel: 01472-323635 Fax: 01472-323634

North Lincolnshire
Scunthorpe Central Library
Carlton Street, Scunthorpe, DN15 6TX Tel: 01724-860161
Email: scunthorpe.ref@central-library.demon.co.uk
WWW: www.nothlincs.gov.uk/library

Liverpool
Liverpool Record Office & Local History Department
Central Library, William Brown Street, Liverpool, L3 8EW
Tel: 0151 233 5817
Email: recoffice.central.library@liverpool.gov.uk
WWW: http://www.liverpool.gov.uk

London
Bishopsgate Institute
Reference Librarian, 230 Bishopsgate, London, EC2M 4QH
Tel: (020) 7247-6198 Fax: (020) 7247-6318

Brent Community History Library & Archive
152 Olive Road, London, NW2 6UY Tel: (020) 8937 3541
Email: archive@brent.gov.uk WWW: www.brent.gov.uk

British Library
British Library Building, 96 Euston Road, London, NW1
2DB Tel: (020) 712-7677 WWW: http://www.portico.bl.uk
Reader/admissions@bl.uk

British Library - Early Printed Collections
96 Euston Road, London, NW1 2DB Tel: (020) 7412-7673
Fax: (020) 7412-7577 Email: rare-books@bl.uk
WWW: http://www.bl.uk

British Library Newspaper Library
Colindale Avenue, London, NW9 5HE Tel: 020-7412-7353
Email: newspaper@bl.uk WWW:
http://www.bl.uk/collections/newspaper/ The National archive
collections of British and Overseas newspapers as well as major
collections of popular magazines. Open Mon to Sat 10am to 4.45pm.

British Library of Political and Economic Science
London School of Economics, 10 Portugal Street, London,
WC2A 2HD Tel: 020 7955 7223 Email: info@lse.ac.uk
WWW: http://www.lse.ac.uk

British Library Oriental and India Office Collections
96 Euston Road, London, NW1 2DB Tel: (020) 7412-7873
Fax: (020) 7412-7641 Email: oioc-enquiries@bl.uk
WWW: http://www.bl.uk/collections/oriental

Caird Library - National Maritime Museum
Park Row, Greenwich, London, SE10 9NF Tel: (020) 8312
6673 Fax: (020) 8312-6632 Email: ABuchanan@nmm.ac.uk
WWW: http://www.nmm.ac.uk

Catholic Central Library
Lancing Street, London, NW1 1ND Tel: (020) 7383-4333
Email: librarian@catholic-library.demon.co.uk
WWW: www.catholic-library.demon.co.uk

Chelsea Public Library
Old Town Hall, King's Road, London, SW3 5EZ Tel: (020)
7352-6056 Tel: (020) 7361-4158 Local Studies Collection on
Royal Borough of Kensington & Chelsea south of Fulham Road

Dr Williams's Library
14 Gordon Square, London, WC1H 0AR Tel: (020) 7387-
3727 Email: 101340.2541@compuserve.com The General
Registers of Protestant Dissenters (Dr Williams's Library Registers) were
surrendered to the Registrar General and are now at The Public Record
Office (RG4/4666-4673)

Ealing Local History Centre
Central Library, 103 Broadway Centre, Ealing, London, W5 5JY
Tel: (020) 8567-3656-ext-37 Email: localhistory@hotmail.com
WWW: www.ealing.gov.uk/libraries Closed Sundays & Mondays

Fawcett Library
London Guildhall University, Old Castle Street, London, E1
7NT Tel: (020) 7320-1189 Email: fawcett@lgu.ac.uk
WWW: http://www.lgu.ac.uk./fawcett

Guildhall Library, Manuscripts Section
Aldermanbury, London, EC2P 2EJ Tel: (020) 7332-1863
Email: manuscripts.guildhall@corpoflondon.gov.uk WWW:
http://ihr.sas.ac.uk/ihr/gh/ Opening hours Mon to Sat 9.30am to
4.45pm (last orders for manuscripts 4.30pm: on Sat no manuscripts
produced bet 12noon and 2pm. Records: City of London parish records,
probate records City Livery

Hammersmith Central Library
Shepherds Bush Road, London, W6 7AT Tel: 020 8753
3816 Fax: 020 8753 3815 WWW: www.lbhf.gov.uk

House of Commons Library
House of Commons, 1 Derby Gate, London, SW1A 2DG
Tel: (020) 7219-5545 Fax: (020) 7219-3921

Huguenot Library
University College, Gower Street, London, WC1E 6BT Tel:
(020) 7679 7094 Email: s.massilk@ucl.ac.uk WWW:
http://www.ucl.ac.uk/ucl-info/divisions/library/hugenot.htm

Imperial College Archives
London University, Room 455 Sherfield Building, Imperial
College, London, SW7 2AZ Tel: 020 7594 8850 Fax: 020
7584 3763 Email: archivist@ic.ac.uk
WWW: http://www.lib.ic.ac.uk

Institute of Commonwealth Studies
28 Russell Square, London, WC1B 5DS Tel: (020) 7862
8844 Fax: (020) 7862 8820 Email: icommlib@sas.ac.uk
WWW: http://sas.ac.uk/commonwealthstudies The Institute of
Commonwealth Studies hosts and leads the CASBAH project which aims
to identify and map research resources for caribbean studies and the
history of Black and Asian people in Britain.

Jewish Museum
The Sternberg Centre for Judaism, 80 East End Road,
Finchley, London, N3 2SY Tel: (020) 8349 1143

Email: jml.finchley@lineone.net
WWW: www.jewmusm.ort.org

Jewish Studies Library
University College, Gower Street, London, WC1E 6BT Tel:
(020) 7387 7050

Lambeth Palace Library
Lambeth Palace Road, London, SE1 7JU Tel: (020) 7898
1400 WWW: www.lambethpalacelibrary.org

Lewisham Local Studies & Archives
Lewisham Library, 199 - 201 Lewisham High Street,
Lewisham, London, SE13 6LG Tel: (020) 8297-0682 Fax:
(020) 8297-1169 Email: local.studies@lewisham.gov.uk
WWW: http://www.lewisham.gov.uk Covering the Parishes of
Lewisham, Lee & St Paul's, Deptford. Appointments advisable.

Library of the Religious Society of Friends (Quakers)
Friends House, 173 - 177 Euston Rd, London, NW1 2BJ
Tel: 0207 663 1135 Email; library@quaker.org.uk
WWW: http://www.quaker.org.uk/library Limited opening
hours. Letter of introduction required. Please send SAE for details or
enclose IRCs

Library of the Royal College of Surgeons of England
35-43 Lincoln's Inn Fields, London, WC2A 3PN Tel: (020)
7869 6520 Email: library@rseng.ac.uk

Linnean Society of London
Burlington House, Piccadilly, London, W1J 0BF Tel: 020
7437 4479 Email: gina@linnean.org WWW: http://www.linnean.org

Local Studies Collection for Chiswick & Brentford
Chiswick Public Library, Dukes Avenue, Chiswick, London,
W4 2AB Tel: (020) 8994-5295 Restricted opening hours for local
history room: please telephone before visiting

LB of Camden Local Studies & Archive Centre
Holborn Library, 32 - 38 Theobalds Road, London, WC1X
8PA Tel: 020 7974 6342 Email: localstudies@camden.gov.uk
WWW: www.camden.gov.uk Closed Wednesday. Open: Mon & Thurs
10 to 7pm; Tues & Fri 10 to 6pm; Sats 10 to 1pm and 2pm to 5pm

LB of Enfield Libraries
Southgate Town Hall, Green Lanes, Palmers Green, London,
N13 4XD Tel: (020) 8379-2724 Fax: (020) 8379 2761

LB of Greenwich Local History Library
Woodlands, 90 Mycenae Road, Blackheath, London, SE3
7SE Tel: (020) 8858 4631 Email: local.history@greenwich.gov.uk
WWW: www.greenwich.gov.uk The library will be moving to a new
Heritage Centre autumn 2002. Please contact the library for more details

LB of Islington Central Reference Library
Central Reference Library, 2 Fieldway Crescent, London,
N5 1PF Tel: (020) 7619-6931 Email:
local.history@islington.gov.uk WWW: http://www.islington.gov.uk
Reorganisation is imminent - planned move to Finsbury Library, 245
St John Street, London EC1V 4NB (020) 7527 6931 (020) 7527
6937 Collection covers the south of the LB of Islington.

LB of Islington Finsbury Library
245 St John Street, London, EC1V 4NB Tel: (020) 7527-
7994 WWW: www.islington.gov.uk/htm

LB of Lambeth Archives Department
Minet Library, 52 Knatchbull Road, Lambeth, London, SE5
9QY Tel: (020) 7926 6076 Email: lambetharchives@lambeth.gov.uk

LB of Newham Archives & Local Studies Library
Stratford Library, 3 The Grove, London, E5 1EL Tel: (020)
8557 8856 Fax: (020) 8503 1525

LB of Wandsworth Local studies
Local Studies ServiceBattersea Library, 265 Lavender Hill,
London, SW11 1JB Tel: (020) 8871 7753 Fax: (020) 7978-
4376 Email: wandsworthmuseum@wandsworth.gov.uk
WWW: www.wandsworth.gov.uk Open Tues & Wed 10am to
88pm, Fri 10am to 5pm, Sat 9am to 1pm - Research service offerred -
£7.00 per half hour (the minimum fee) apointment advised to ensure
archives, hard copy newspapers (if not microfilmed)

London University - Institute of Advanced Studies
Charles Clore House, 17 Russell Square, London,
WC1B 5DR Tel: (020) 7637 1731 Fax: (020) 7637 8224
Email: ials.lib@sas.ac.uk WWW: http://ials.sas.ac.uk

Manuscripts Room
Library Services, University College, Gower Street, London, WC1E 6BT Tel: (020) 7387 7050 Fax: 020 7380 7727 Email: mssrb@ucl.ac.uk WWW: http://www.ucl.ac.uk/library/special-coll/

Museum in Docklands Project Library & Archives
Unit C14, Poplar Business Park, 10 Prestons Road, London, E14 9RL Tel: (020) 7515-1162 Email: docklands@museum-london.org.uk & raspinal@museumoflondon.org.uk

Museum of London Library
150 London Wall, London, EC2Y 5HN Tel: 020 7814 5588 Fax: 020 7600-1058 Email: info@museumoflondon.org.uk WWW: http://museumoflondon.org.uk

Museum of the Order of St John
St John's Gate, St John's Lane, Clerkenwell, London, EC1M 4DA Tel: (020) 7253-6644 WWW: www.sja.org.uk/history

National Gallery Library and Archive
Trafalgar Square, London, WC2N 5DN Tel: 020 7747 2542 Email: iad@ng-london.org.uk WWW: http://www.nationalgallery.org.uk

The Public Library
305 Queens Avenue, London, N6B 3L7 Tel: 519-661-4600

Royal Armouries
H.M Tower Of London, Tower Hill, London, EC3N 4AB Tel: (020) 7480 6358 ext 30 Fax: (020) 7481 2922 Email: Bridgett.Clifford@armouries.org.uk

Royal B of Kensington & Chelsea Libraries & Arts Service
Central Library, Phillimore Walk, Kensington, London, W8 7RX Tel: (020) 7361-3036 Email: information.services@rbkc.gov.uk WWW: www.rbkc.gov.uk

Royal Institute of British Architects' Library
Manuscripts & archives Collection, 66 Portland Place, London, W1N 4AD Tel: 020 7307 3615 Fax: 020 7631 1802

Royal Soc of Chemistry Library & Information Centre
Burlington House, Piccadilly, London, W1J 0BA Tel: (020) 7437 8656 Fax: (020) 7287 9798 Email: library@rsc.org WWW: www.rsc.org

School of Oriental and African Studies library
Thornhaugh Street, Russell Square, London, WC1H 0XG Tel: 020 7323 6112 Fax: 020 7636 2834 Email: lib@soas.ac.uk WWW: http://www.soas.ac.uk/library/

Society of Antiquaries of London
Burlington House, Piccadilly, London, W1J 0BE Tel: 020 7479 7084 6967 Email: library@sal.org.uk WWW: www.sal.org.uk

Society of Genealogists - Library
14 Charterhouse Buildings, Goswell Road, London, EC1M 7BA Tel: 020-7251-8799 Tel: 020-7250-0291 Fax: 020-7250-1800 Email: library@sog.org.uk WWW: http://www.sog.org.uk

Southwark Local Studies Library
211 Borough High Street, Southwark, London, SE1 1JA Tel: 0207-403-3507 Email: local.studies.library@southwark.gov.uk WWW: www.southwark.gov.uk

The Kenneth Ritchie Wimbledon Library
The All England Lawn Tennis & Croquet Club, Church Road, Wimbledon, London, SW19 5AE Tel: (020) 8946 6131 WWW: www.wimbledon.org Contains the world's finest collection of books and periodicals relating to lawn tennis

The Library & Museum of Freemasonry
Freemasons' Hall, 60 Great Queen Street, London, WC2B 5AZ Tel: (020) 7395 9257

The Science Museum Library
Imperial College Road, South Kensington, London, SW7 5NH Tel: 020 7938 8234 Tel: 020 7938 8218 **The Wellcome Trust**
183 Euston Rd, London, NW1 2BE Tel: (020) 7611 8888 Fax: (020) 7611 8545 Email: infoserv@wellcome.ac.uk WWW: www.wellcome.ac.uk

The Women's Library
Old Castle Street, London, E1 7NT Tel: (020) 7320-1189 Fax: (020) 7320-1188 Email: fawcett@lgu.ac.uk WWW: http://www.lgu.ac.uk/fawcett

Tower Hamlets Local History Library & Archives
Bancroft Library, 277 Bancroft Road, London, E1 4DQ Tel: (020) 8980 4366 Ext 129 Fax: (020) 8983-4510

Trades Union Congress Library Collections
236 - 250 Holloway Road, London, N7 6PP Tel: (020) 7753 3191 Email: tuclib@unl.ac.uk WWW: http://www.unl.ac.uk/library/tuc

University of London (Library - Senate House)
Palaeography Room, Senate House, Malet Street, London, WC1E 7HU Tel: (020) 7862 8475 Fax: 020 7862 8480 Email: library@ull.ac.uk WWW: http://www.ull.ac.uk

Victoria & Albert Museum - National Art Library
Cromwell Road, South Kensington, London, SW7 2RL Tel: (020) 7938 8315 Fax: (020) 7938 8461

Victoria & Albert Museum - Archive of Art and Design
Blythe House, 23 Blythe Road, London, W14 0QF Tel: (020) 7603 1514 Fax: (020) 7602 0980 Email: archive@vam.ac.uk WWW: www.nal.vam.ac.uk

Wellcome Library - Contemporary Medical Archives
183 Euston Road, London, NW1 2BE Tel: (020) 7611 8483 Fax: (020) 7611 8703 Email: library@wellcome.ac.uk WWW: www.wellcome.ac.uk/library Library catalogue is available through the internet: telnet://wihm.ucl.ac.uk

Wellcome Library- History & Understanding of Medicine
Wellcome Library for the History of Medicine -
Department of Western Manuscripts
183 Euston Road, London, NW1 2BE Tel: (020) 7611-8582 Fax: (020) 7611 8369 Email: library@wellcome.ac.uk WWW: www.wellcome.ac.uk/library Library catalogue is available through the internet: http://library.wellcome.ac.uk

Westminster Abbey Library & Muniment Room
Westminster Abbey, London, SW1P 3PA Tel: (020) 7222-5152-Ext-4830 Fax: (020) 7226-4827 Email: library@westminster-abbey.org WWW: www.westminster-abbey.org

Westminster University Archives
Information Systems & Library Services, 4-12 Little Titchfield Street, London, W1W 7UW Tel: 020 7911 5000 ext 2524 Fax: 020 7911 5894 Email: archive@westminster.ac.uk WWW: www.wmin.ac.uk The archive is organisationally within the Library but is a separate entity. The University of Westminster Libraries do not have special collections relating to family and local history

Manchester
Chethams Library
Long Millgate, Manchester, M3 1SB Tel: 0161 834 7961 Fax: 0161 839 5797 Email: chetlib@dial.pipex.com

Manchester Archives & Local Studies
Manchester Central Library, St Peter's Square, Manchester, M2 5PD Tel: 0161-234-1979 Fax: 0161-234-1927 Email: lsu@libraries.manchester.gov.uk WWW: http://www..manchester.gov.uk/libraries/index.htm

Methodist Archives and Research Centre
John Rylands University Library, 150 Deansgate, Manchester, M3 3EH Tel: 0161 834 5343

Oldham Local Studies and Archives
84 Union Street, Oldham, OL1 1DN Tel: 0161-911-4654 Email: archives@oldham.gov.uk & localstudies@oldham.gov.uk WWW: http://www.oldham.gov.uk/archives & http://www.oldham.gov.uk/local_studies

Medway
Medway Archives and Local Studies Centre
Civic Centre, Strood, Rochester, ME2 4AU Tel: 01634-332714 Email: archives@medway.gov.uk & local.studies@medway.gov.uk WWW: http://cityark.medway.gov.uk

Merseyside

Crosby Library (South Sefton Local History Unit)
Crosby Road North, Waterloo, Liverpool, L22 0LQ Tel:
0151 257 6401 Email: local-history.south@leisure.sefton.gov.uk The
Local History Units serve Sefton Borough Council area. The South
Sefton Unit covers Bootle, Crosby, Maghull and other communities south
of the River Alt. The North Sefton Unit covers Southport, Formby

Wirral Central Library
Borough Road, Birkenhead, CH41 2XB Tel: 0151 652 6106
Tel: 0151 652 6107/8 Fax: 0151 653 7320
Email: birkenhead.library@merseymail.com

Huyton Central Library
Huyton Library, Civic Way, Huyton, Knowsley, L36 9GD
Tel: 0151-443-3738 Fax: 0151 443 3739
Email: eileen.hume.dlcs@knowsley.gov.uk
WWW: http://www.knowsley.gov.uk/leisure/libraries/huyton/index.html

Southport Library (North Sefton Local History Unit)
Lord Street, Southport, PR8 1DJ Tel: 0151 934 2119 The
Local History Units serve Sefton Borough Council area. The North
Sefton Unit covers Southport, Formby. The South Sefton Unit covers
Bootle, Crosby, Maghull and other communities south of the River Alt

St Helen's Local History & Archives Library
Central Library, Gamble Institute, Victoria Square, St
Helens, WA10 1DY Tel: 01744-456952 Fax: 01744 20836
No research undertaken

Middlesex

LB of Harrow Local History Collection
Civic Centre Library, PO Box 4, Station Road, Harrow, HA1
2UU Tel: 0208 424 1055 Tel: 0208 424 1056 Fax: 0181-
424-1971 Email: civiccentre.library@harrow.gov.uk

Norfolk

Family History Shop & Library
The Family History Shop, 24d Magdalen Street, Norwich,
NR3 1HU Tel: 01603 621152, Fax: Email:
jenlibrary@aol.com WWW: http://www.jenlibrary.u-net.com

Great Yarmouth Central Library
Tolhouse Street, Great Yarmouth, NR30 2SH Tel: 01493-
844551 Tel: 01493-842279 Fax: 01493-857628

Kings Lynn Library
London Road, King's Lynn, PE30 5EZ Tel: 01553-772568
Tel: 01553 761393 Email: kings.lynn.lib@norfolk.gov.uk
WWW: http://www.norfolk.gov.uk/council/departments/lis/nslynn.htm

Norfolk Library & Information Service
Gildengate House, Anglia Square, Norwich, NR3 1AX Tel:
01603-215254 Email: norfolk.studies.lib@norfolk.gov.uk

Thetford Public Library
Raymond Street, Thetford, IP24 2EA Tel: 01842-752048
Fax: 01842-750125 Email: thetford.lib@norfolk.gov.uk
WWW: www.culture.norfolk.gov.uk

Northumberland

Alnwick Library
Green Batt, Alnwick, NE66 1TU Tel: 01665-602689

Berwick upon Tweed Library
Church Street, Berwick upon Tweed, TD15 1EE Tel: 01289-
307320 Fax: 01289-308299

Blyth Library
Bridge Street, Blyth, NE24 2DJ Tel: 01670-361352

Border History Museum and Library
Moothall, Hallgate, Hexham, NE46 3NH Tel: 01434-652349
Fax: 01434-652425 Email: museum@tynedale.gov.uk

Hexham Library
Queens Hall, Beaumont Street, Hexham, NE46 3LS Tel:
01434 652474 Email: cheane@northumberland.gov.uk

Nottinghamshire

Arnold Library
Front Street, Arnold, NG5 7EE Tel: 0115-920-2247

Beeston Library
Foster Avenue, Beeston, NG9 1AE Tel: 0115-925-5168

Eastwood Library
Wellington Place, Eastwood, NG16 3GB Tel: 01773-712209

Mansfield Library
Four Seasons Centre, Westgate, Mansfield, NG18 1NH Tel:
01623-627591 Email: mansfield.library@nottscc.gov.uk

Newark Library
Beaumont Gardens, Newark, NG24 1UW
Tel: 01636-703966 Fax: 01636-610045

Nottingham Central Library : Local Studies Centre
Angel Row, Nottingham, NG1 6HP Tel: 0115 915
2873Email: local-studies.library@nottinghamcity.gov.uk
WWW: www.nottinghamcity.gov.uk/libraries

Retford Library
Denman Library, Churchgate, Retford, DN22 6PE Tel:
01777-708724 Fax: 01777-710020

Southwell Minster Library
Minster Office, Trebeck Hall, Bishop's Drive, Southwell,
NG25 0JP Tel: 01636-812649 Fax: 01636 815904
Email: pat@southwellminster.prestell.co.uk

Sutton in Ashfield Library
Devonshire Mall, Sutton in Ashfield, NG17 1BP
Tel: 01623-556296 Fax: 01623-551962

University of Nottingham
Hallward Library, University Park, Nottingham, NG7 2RD
Tel: 0115-951-4514 Fax: 0115-951-4558
WWW: http://www.nottingham.ac.uk/library/

West Bridgford Library
Bridgford Road, West Bridgford, NG2 6AT
Tel: 0115-981-6506 Fax: 0115-981-3199

Oxfordshire

Abingdon Library
The Charter, Abingdon, OX14 3LY Tel: 01235-520374
Fax: 01235 532643 Email: abingdonlibrary@hotmail.com

Angus Library
Regent's Park College, Pusey Street, Oxford, OX1 2LB
Tel: 01865 288142 Fax: 01865 288121

Banbury library
Marlborough Road, Banbury, OX16 8DF Tel: 01295-262282
Fax: 01295-264331

The Bodelian Library
Broad Street, Oxford, OX1 3BG Tel: 01865 277000
Fax: 01865 277182 WWW: www.bodley.ox.ac.uk

Henley Library
Ravenscroft Road, Henley on Thames, RG9 2DH
Tel: 01491-575278 Fax: 01491-576187

Centre for Oxfordshire Studies
Central Library, Westgate, Oxford, OX1 1DJ
Tel: 01865-815749 Email: cos@oxfordshire.gov.uk
WWW: www.oxfordshire.gov.uk

Middle East Centre
St Anthony's College, Pusey Street, Oxford, OX2 6JF
Tel: 01865 284706 Fax: 01865 311475

Nuffield College Library
Oxford, OX1 1NF Tel: 01865 278550 Fax: 01865 278621

Puysey House Library
Pusey House, 61 St Giles, Oxford, OX1 1LZ Tel: 01865
278415 Fax: 01865 278415

River & Rowing Museum
Rowing & River Museum, Mill Meadows, Henley on
Thames, RG9 1BF Tel: 01491 415625 Fax: 01491 415601
Email: museum@rrm.co.uk WWW: www..rrm.co.uk Thames
linked families especially lock keepers , boat builders

Rhodes House Library
Bodleian Library, South Parks Road, Oxford, OX1 3RG Tel:
01865 270909 Fax: 01865 270912

Wantage Library
Stirlings Road, Wantage, OX12 7BB Tel: 01235 762291

Witney Library
Welch Way, Witney, OX8 7HH Tel: 01993-703659

Peterborough
Peterborough Local Studies Collection
Central Library, Broadway, Peterborough, PE1 1RX Tel:
01733 348343 Email: libraries@peterborough.gov.uk The
telephone number may change in 2002

Shropshire
Wrekin Local Studies Forum
Madeley Library, Russell Square, Telford, TF7 5BB Tel:
01952 586575 Email: wlst@library.madeley.uk WWW:
www.madeley.org.uk

Somerset
Bath Central Library
19 The Podium, Northgate Street, Bath, BA1 5AN
Tel: 01225-428144 Fax: 01225-331839
Bristol University Library - Special Collections
Tyndall Avenue, Bristol, BS8 1TJ Tel: 0117 928 8014
Email: library@bris.ac.uk
WWW: www.bris.ac.uk/depts/library
Bridgewater Library
Binford Place, Bridgewater, TA6 3LF Tel: 01278-450082
Fax: 01278-451027 Email: pcstoyle@somerset.gov.uk
WWW: www.somerset.gov.uk
Frome Library
Justice Lane, Frome, BA11 1BA Tel: 01373-462215
Nailsea Library
Somerset Square, Nailsea, BS19 2EX Tel: 01275-854583
Somerset Studies Library
Paul Street, Taunton, TA1 3XZ Tel: 01823-340300
Weston Library
The Boulevard, Weston Super Mare, BS23 1PL Tel: 01934-
636638 Email: weston.library@n-somerset.gov.uk
Yeovil Library
King George Street, Yeovil, BA20 1PY Tel: 01935-421910
Fax: 01935-431847 Email: ransell@somerset.gov.uk

Staffordshire
Barton Library
Dunstall Road, Barton under Needwood, DE13 8AX
Tel: 01283-713753
Biddulph Library
Tunstall Road, Biddulph, Stoke on Trent, ST8 6HH
Tel: 01782-512103
Brewood Library
Newport Street, Brewood, ST19 9DT Tel: 01902-850087
Burton Library
Burton Library, Riverside, High Street, Burton on Trent,
DE14 1AH Tel: 01283-239556 Fax: 01283-239571
Email: burton.library@staffordshire.gov.uk
Cannock Library
Manor Avenue, Cannock, WS11 1AA Tel: 01543-502019
Email: cannock.library@staffordshire.gov.uk
Cheslyn Hay Library
Cheslyn Hay, Walsall, WS56 7AE Tel: 01922-413956
Codsall Library
Histons Hill, Codsall, WV8 1AA Tel: 01902-842764
Great Wyrley Library
John's Lane, Great Wyrley, Walsall, WS6 6BY
Tel: 01922-414632
Keele University Library
Keele, ST5 5BG Tel: 01782 583237 Fax: 01782 711553
Email: library@keele.ac.uk WWW: www.keele.ac.uk/library
Kinver Library
Vicarage Drive, Kinver, Stourbridge, DY7 6HJ
Tel: 01384-872348
Leek Library
Nicholson Institute, Stockwell Street, Leek, ST13 6DW Tel:
01538-483210 Email: leek.library@staffordshire.gov.uk
Lichfield Library (Local Studies Section)
Lichfield Library, The Friary, Lichfield, WS13 6QG
 Tel: 01543-510720 Fax: 01543-411138

Newcastle Library
Ironmarket, Newcastle under Lyme, ST5 1AT Tel: 01782-
297310 Email: newcastle.library@staffordshire.gov.uk
Penkridge Library
Bellbrock, Penkridge, ST19 9DL Tel: 01785-712916
Perton Library
Severn Drive, Perton, WV6 7QU Tel: 01902-755794 Fax:
01902-756123 Email: perton.library@staffordshire.gov.uk
Rugeley Library
Anson Street, Rugeley, WS16 2BB Tel: 01889-583237
Stoke on Trent City Archives
Hanley Library, Bethesda Street, Hanley, Stoke on Trent,
ST1 3RS Tel: 01782-238420 Fax: 01782-238499
Email: stoke.archives@stoke.gov.uk WWW:
www.staffordshire.gov.uk/archives
Tamworth Library
Corporation Street, Tamworth, B79 7DN Tel: 01827-475645
Email: tamworth.library@staffordshire.gov.uk WWW:
www.staffordshire.gov.uk/locgov/county/cars/tamlib.htm IGI
(Derby, Leics, Notts, Shrops, Staffs, Warks, Worcs). Parish registers for
Tamworth. Census for Tamworth and District, 1841 - 91. Street directories
for Staffs and Warks.
Uttoxeter Library
High Street, Uttoxeter, ST14 7JQ Tel: 01889-256371
William Salt Library
Eastgate Street, Stafford, ST16 2LZ Tel: 01785-278372
Email: william.salt.library@staffordshire.gov.uk
WWW: http://www.staffordshire.gov.uk/archives/salt.htm
Wombourne Library
Windmill Bank, Wombourne, WV5 9JD Tel: 01902-892032

Stockport MBC
Local Heritage Library
Central Library, Wellington Road South, Stockport, SK1
3RS Tel: 0161-474-4530 Fax: 0161-474-7750
Email: localherirtage.library@stockport.gov.uk

Surrey
LB of Merton Local Studies Centre
Merton Civic Centre, London Road, Morden, SM4 5DX Tel:
(020) 8545-3239 Fax: (020) 8545-4037
Email: mertonlibs@compuserve.com
LB of Richmond upon Thames Local Studies Library
Old Town Hall, Whittaker Avenue, Richmond upon Thames,
TW9 1TP Tel: (020) 8332 6820 Fax: (020) 8940 6899
Email: localstudies@richmond.gov.uk WWW:
http://www.richmond.gov.uk Closed Mondays Open Tues 1-5; Wed
1-8pm; Thurs & Fri 10 to 12; Sat 10 to 12 & 1 to 5
Surrey History Service Library
Surrey History Centre, 130 Goldsworth Road, Woking,
GU21 1ND Tel: 01483-594594 Fax: 01483-594595
Email: shs@surreycc.gov.uk WWW: http://.shs.surreycc.gov.uk
Sutton Central Library
St Nicholas Way, Sutton, SM1 1EA Tel: (020) 8770 4745
Email: sutton.information@sutton.gov.uk WWW: www.sutton.gov.uk

Sussex
Sussex University Library
Manuscript Collections, Falmer, Brighton, BN1 9QL
Tel: 01273 606755 Fax: 01273 678441

West Sussex
Worthing Reference Library
Worthing Library, Richmond Road, Worthing, BN11 1HD
Tel: 01903-212060 Fax: 01903-821902
Email: worthinglibrary@hotmail.com Largest library in West
Sussex and specialist centre for family history sources.

Tyne and Wear
City Library & Arts Centre
28 - 30 Fawcett Street, Sunderland, BR1 1RE
Tel: 0191-514235 Fax: 0191-514-8444

Local Studies Centre
Central Library, Northumberland Square, North Shields,
NE3O 1QU Tel: 0191-200-5424 Fax: 0191 200 6118
Email: eric.hollerton@northtyneside.gov.uk
WWW: www.northtyneside.gov.uk/libraries.html

South Tyneside Central Library
Prince Georg Square, South Shields, NE33 2PE Tel: 0191-
427-1818-Ext-7860 Fax: 0191-455-8085
Email: reference.library@s-tyneside-mbc.gov.uk
WWW: www.s-tyneside-mbc.gov.uk

Central Library
Northumberland Square, North Shields, NE3O 1Q
Tel: 0191-200-5424 Fax: 0191-200-611
Email: cen@ntlib.demon.co.uk

Gateshead Central Library & Local Studies Department
Prince Consort Road, Gateshead, NE8 4LN Tel: 0191-477-
3478 Email: a.lang@libarts.gatesheadmbc.gov.uk
WWW: http://ris.niaa.org.ukw & www.gateshead.gov.uk/ls

Newcastle Local Studies Centre
City Library, Princess Square, Newcastle upon Tyne, NE99
1DX Tel: 0191 277 4116 Fax: 0191 277 4118 Email:
local.studies@newcastle.gov.uk WWW: www.newcastle.gov.uk

Robinson Library
University of Newcastle upon Tyne, Newcastle Upon Tyne,
NE2 4HQ Tel: 0191 222 7671 Fax: 0191 222 6235 Email:
library@ncl.ac.uk WWW: http://www.ncl.ac.uk/library/

Warwickshire
Atherstone Library
Long Street, Atherstone, CV9 1AX Tel: 01827 712395
Email: atherstonelibrary@warwickshire.gov.uk

Bedworth Library
18 High Street, Bedworth, Nuneaton, CV12 8NF Tel: 024
7631 2267 Email: bedworthlibrary@warwickshire.gov.uk

Kenilworth Library
Smalley Place, Kenilworth, CV8 1QG Tel: 01926 852595
Email: kenilworthlibrary@warwickshire.gov.uk

Nuneaton Library
Church Street, Nuneaton, CV11 4DR Tel: 024 7638 4027
Email: nuneatonlibrary@warwickshire.gov.uk

Rugby Library
Little ElborowStreet, Rugby, CV21 3BZ Tel: 01788 533250
Email: rugbylibrary@warwickshire.gov.uk

Shakespeare Birthplace Trust - Library
Shakespeare Centre Library, Henley Street, Stratford upon
Avon, CV37 6QW Tel: 01789-204016 Tel: 01789-201813
Fax: 01789-296083 Email: library@shakespeare.org.uk
WWW: http://www.shakespeare.org.uk

Stratford on Avon Library
12 Henley Street, Stratford on Avon, CV37 6PZ Tel: 01789
292209 Email: stratfordlibrary@warwickshire.gov.uk

Sutton Coldfield Library & Local Studies Centre
43 Lower Parade, Sutton Coldfield, B72 1XX Tel: 0121-
354-2274 Tel: 0121 464 0164 Fax: 0121 464 0173
Email: sutton.coldfield.reference.lib@birmingham.gov.uk

University of Warwick Library
Coventry, CV4 7AL Tel: (024) 76524219

**Warwick Library - Warwickshire Local Collection
(County Collection)**
Warwick Library, Barrack Street, Warwick, CV34 4TH
Tel: 01926 412189 Tel: 01926 412488 Fax: 01926 412784
Email: warwicklibrary@warwickshire.gov.uk

Warwickshire County Library
Leamington Library, Royal Pump Rooms, The Parade,
Leamington Spa, CV32 4AA Tel: 01926 74272
Email: leamingtonlibrary@warwickshire.gov.uk

West Midlands
Birmingham University - Special Collections
Main Library, University of Birmingham, Edgbaston,
Birmingham, B15 2TT Tel: 0121 414 5838 Email: special-
collections@bham.ac.uk WWW: www.is.bham.ac.uk

Dudley Archives & Local History Service
Mount Pleasant Street, Coseley, Dudley, WV14 9JR Tel:
01384-812770 Fax: 01384-812770
Email: archives.pls@mbc.dudley.gov.uk
WWW: www.dudley.gov.uk Family History Research

Local Studies Library
Central Library, Smithford Way, Coventry, CV1 1FY Tel:
012476 832336 Fax: 02476 832440
Email: covinfo@discover.co.uk
WWW: www.coventry.gov.uk/accent.htm

Sandwell Community History & Archives Service
Smethwick Library, High Street, Smethwick, B66 1AB
Tel: 0121 558 2561 Fax: 0121 555 6064

Sandwell Community Libraries
Town Hall, High Street, West Bromwich, B70 8DX Tel:
0121-569-4909 Fax: 0121-569-4907
Email: dm025@viscount.org.uk

Solihull Library
Homer Road, Solihull, B91 3RG Tel: 0121-704-6977 The
library is NOT an archive repository, sceondary sources only available for
Solihull MBC area only

Walsall Local History Centre
Essex Street, Walsall, WS2 7AS Tel: 01922-721305Email:
localhistorycentre@walsall.gov.uk WWW:
http://www.walsall.gov.uk/culturalservices/library/welcome.htm

Wolverhampton Archives & Local Studies
42 - 50 Snow Hill, Wolverhampton, WV2 4AG
Tel: 01902 552480 Email: wolverhamptonarchives@dial.pipes.com
WWW: http://www.wolverhampton.gov.uk/archives

West Sussex
Worthing Reference Library
Worthing Library, Richmond Road, Worthing, BN11 1HD
Tel: 01903-212060 Fax: 01903-821902 Email:
worthinglibrary@hotmail.com Largest library in West Sussex and
specialist centre for family history sources.

Wiltshire
Salisbury Reference and Local Studies Library
Market Place, Salisbury, SP1 1BL Tel: 01722 411098
Fax: 01722 413214 WWW: www.wiltshire.gov.uk

Swindon Local Studies Library
Swindon Central Library, Regent Circus, Swindon, SN11QG
Tel: 01793 463240 Email: swindonref@swindon.gov.uk
WWW: http://www.swindon.gov.uk

Wiltshire Archaeological and Natural History Society
Wiltshire Heritage Library, 41 Long Street, Devizes, SN10
1NS Tel: 01380 727369 Email: wanhs@wiltshireheritage.org.uk

Wiltshire Buildings Record Society
Libraries & Heritage, Bythesea Road, Trowbridge, BA14 8BS

Wiltshire Studies Library
Trowbridge Reference Library, Bythesea Road, Trowbridge,
BA14 8BS Tel: 01225-713732 Email:
libraryenquiries@wiltshire.gov.uk WWW: www.wiltshire.gov.uk

Worcestershire
Bewdley Museum Research Library
Load Street, Bewdley, DY12 2AE Tel: 01229-403573

Bromsgrove Library
Stratford Road, Bromsgrove, B60 1AP Tel: 01527-575855

Evesham Library
Oat Street, Evesham, WR11 4PJ Tel: 01386-442291
Email: eveshamlib@worcestershire.gov.uk WWW:
www.worcestershire.gov.uk

Kidderminster Library
Market Street, Kidderminster, DY10 1AD Tel: 01562-
824500Email: kidderminster@worcestershire.gov.uk WWW:
www.worcestershire.gov.uk

Malvern Library
Graham Road, Malvern, WR14 2HU Tel: 01684-561223

Redditch Library
15 Market Place, Redditch, B98 8AR Tel: 01527-63291
Email: redditchlibrary@worcestershire.gov.uk

Worcester Library
Foregate Street, Worcester, WR1 1DT Tel: 01905 765312
Email: worcesterlib@worcestershire.gov.uk WWW:
www.worcestershire.gov.uk/libraries

Yorkshire
York Minster Library
York Minster Library & Archives, Dean's Park, York, YO1
2JQ Tel: 01904-625308 Library Tel: 01904-611118 Archives
Fax: 01904-611119 Email: library@yorkminster.org
archives@yorkminster.org WWW: www.yorkminster.org
Yorkshire Archaeological Society
Claremont, 23 Clarendon Rd, Leeds, LS2 9NZ Tel: 0113-245-
6342 Tel: 0113 245 7910 Fax: 0113-244-1979 Email:
j.heron@sheffield.ac.uk WWW: www.yas.org.uk Opening
Hours: Tues,Wed 2.00 to 8.30pm; Thurs, Fri 10.00 to 5.30; Sat
9.30 to 5.00 Appointment necessary for use of archival material.

Yorkshire Family History - Biographical Database
York Minster Library & Archives, Dean's Park, York, YO1
7JQ Tel: 01904-625308 Library Tel: 01904-611118 Archives
Fax: 01904-611119 Email: library@yorkminster.org
archives@yorkminster.org WWW: www.yorkminster.org

Yorkshire - York
City of York Libraries - Local History & Ref Collection
York Central Library, Library Square, Museum Street, York,
YO1 7DS Tel: 01904-655631 Email:
reference.library@york.gov.uk WWW: http://www.york.gov.uk

Yorkshire - East
Hull Local Studies Library
Central Library, Albion Street, Kingston upon Hull, HU1
3TF Tel: 01482 210077 Fax: 01482 616827
Email: local.studies@hullcc.gov.uk
WWW: http://www.hullcc.gov.uk/genealogy/
Beverley Local Studies Library
Beverley Library, Champney Road, Beverley, HU17 9BG
Tel: 01482-885358 Email: user@bevlib.karoo.co.uk
Bridlington Local Studies Library
Bridlington Library, King Street, Bridlington, YO15 2DF
Tel: 01262-672917 Fax: 01262-670208
East Riding Heritage Library & Museum
Sewerby Hall, Church Lane, Sewerby, Bridlington, YO15
1EA Tel: 01262-677874 Tel: 01262-674265
Email: museum@pop3.poptel.org.uk
WWW: http://www.bridlington.net/sew
Goole Local Studie Library
Goole Library, Carlisle Street, Goole, DN14 5DS Tel:
01405-762187 Email: user@goolelib.karoo.co.uk

North Yorkshire
Catterick Garrison Library
Gough Road, Catterick Garrison, DL9 3EL Tel: 01748
833543 Extensive collection of over 1350 military history books
available for reference or loan. Open Mon 10.am to 12, 1pm to
5.30pm; Wed 10am to 12, 1pm to 5pm; Fri 10am to 12 noon.
Harrogate Reference Library
Victoria Avenue, Harrogate, HG1 1EG Tel: 01423-502744
North Yorkshire County Libraries
21 Grammar School Lane, Northallerton, DL6 1DF
Tel: 01609-776271 Email: elizabeth.melrose@northyorks.gov.uk
WWW: http://www.northyorks.gov.uk
Northallerton Reference Library
1 Thirsk Road, Northallerton, DL6 1PT Tel: 01609-776202
Email: northallerton.libraryhq@northyorks.gov.uk
Pickering Reference Library
The Ropery, Pickering, YO18 8DY Tel: 01751-472185

Scarborough Reference Library
Vernon Road, Scarborough, YO11 2NN Tel: 01723-364285
Email: scarborough.library@northyorks.gov.uk
Selby Reference Library
52 Micklegate, Selby, YO8 4EQ Tel: 01757-702020

Skipton Reference Library
High Street, Skipton, BD23 1JX Tel: 01756-794726
Whitby Library
Windsor Terrace, Whitby, YO21 1ET Tel: 01947-602554

South Yorkshire
Archives & Local Studies
Central Library, Walker Place, Rotherham, S65 1JH
Tel: 01709-823616 Email: archives@rotherham.gov.uk
WWW: www.rotherha.gov.uk/pages/living/learning/islib/callib.htm
Barnsley Archives and Local Studies Department
Central Library, Shambles Street, Barnsley, S70 2JF Tel:
01226-773950 Tel: 01226-773938 Fax: 01226-773955
Email: Archives@Barnsley.govuk
librarian@barnsley.gov.uk
Sheffield Central Library
Surrey Street, Sheffield, S1 1XZ Tel: 0114 273 4711 Fax:
0114 273 5009 Email: sheffield.libraries@dial.pipex.com
Doncaster & District Family History Society Research Centre
For details contact: 'Marton House', 125 The Grove,
Wheatley Hills, Doncaster, DN2 5SN Tel: 01302-367257
Email: tonyjunes@aol.com WWW:
http://www.doncasterfhs.freeserve.co.uk
Doncaster Libraries - Local Studies Section
Central Library, Waterdale, Doncaster, DN1 3JE Tel: 01302-
734307 Fax: 01302 369749 Email:
reference.library@doncaster.gov.uk
Sheffield University Library
Special Collections & Library Archives, Western Bank,
Sheffield, S10 2TN Tel: 0114 222 7230 Fax: 0114 222 7290

West Yorkshire
British Library
Boston Spa, Wetherby, LS23 7BY
The British Library
Boston Spa, Wetherby, LS23 7BQ Tel: 01937-546212
Calderdale Central Library
Northgate House, Northgate, Halifax, HX11 1UN Tel:
1422392631 WWW: www.calderdale.gov.uk
Huddersfield Local History Library
Huddersfield Library & Art Gallery, Princess Alexandra
Walk, Huddersfield, HD1 2SU Tel: 01484-221965
Fax: 01484-221952 Email: ref-library@geo2.poptel.org.uk
WWW: http://www.kirkleesmc.gov.uk
Keighley Reference Library
North Street, Keighley, BD21 3SX Tel: 01535-61821
Email: keighleylibrary@bradford.gov.uk
WWW: www.bradford.gov.uk
Local Studies Library
Leeds Central Library, Calverley Street, Leeds, LS1 3AB
Tel: 0113 247 8290 Email: local.studies@leeds.gov.uk
WWW: www.leeds.gov.uk/library/services/loc_reso.html
Local Studies Reference Library
Central Library, Prince's Way, Bradford, BD1 1NN
Tel: 01274-753661 Fax: 01274-753660
Olicana Historical Society
23 Clifton Road, Ben Rhydding, Ilkley, LS29 8T
Tel: 01943 430798
Pontefract Library & Local Studies Centre
Pontefract library, Shoemarket, Pontefract, WF8 1BD
Tel: 01977-727692
Wakefield Library HQ - Local Studies Department
Balne Lane, Wakefield, WF2 0DQ Tel: 01924-302224 Email:
wakehist@hotmail.com WWW: www.wakefield.gov.uk
Wakefield Metro District Libraries & Info Services
Castleford Library & Local Studies Dept, Carlton Street,
Castleford, WF10 1BB Tel: 01977-722085
Brotherton Library
Department of Special Collections, Leeds University, Leeds,
LS2 9JT Tel: 0113 233 55188
Email: special-collections@library.leeds.ac.uk
WWW: http://leeds.ac.uk/library/spcoll/

Wales

National Library of Wales
Penglais, Aberystwyth, SY23 3BU Tel: 01970-632800
Email: holi@llgc.org.uk WWW: http://www.llgc.org.uk
University of Walwes Swansea library
Library & Information Centre, Singleton Park, Swansea,
SA2 8PP Tel: 01792 295021 Fax: 01792 295851
**South Wales Miners' Library - University of Wales,
Swansea**
Hendrefoelan House, Gower Road, Swansea, SA2 7NB Tel:
01792-518603 Fax: 01792-518694
Email: miners@swansea.ac.uk WWW:
http://www.swan.ac.uk/lis/swml

Blaenau Gwent
Ebbw Vale Library
Ebbw Vale Library, 21 Bethcar Street, Ebbw Vale, NP23
6HH Tel: 01495-303069 Fax: 01495-350547

Caerphilly
Bargoed Library
The Square, Bargoed, CF8 8QQ Tel: 01443-875548 Fax:
01443-836057 Email: 9e465@dial.pipex.com
Caerphilly Library HQ
Unit 7 Woodfieldside Business Park, Penmaen Road,
Pontllanfraith, Blackwood, NP12 2DG Tel: 01495 235584
Fax: 01495 235567 Email: cael.libs@dial.pipex.com

Cardiff
Cardiff Central Library (Local Studies Department)
St Davids Link, Frederick Street, Cardiff, CF1 4DT Tel:
(029) 2038 2116 Email: p.sawyer@cardlib.gov.uk
WWW: www.cardiff.gov.uk

Carmarthenshire
Carmarthen Library
St Peters Street, Carmarthen, SA31 1LN Tel: 01267-224822
Llanelli Public Library
Vaughan Street, Lanelli, SA15 3AS Tel: 01554-773538

Ceredigion
Aberystwyth Reference Library
Corporation Street, Aberystwyth, SY23 2BU Tel: 01970-
617464 Fax: 01970 625059 Email:
llyfrygell.library@ceredigion.gov.uk WWW:
www.ceredigion.gov.uk/libraries
National Library of Wales
Penglais, Aberystwyth, SY23 3BU Tel: 01970-632800
Email: holi@llgc.org.uk WWW: http://www.llgc.org.uk

Flintshire
Flintshire Reference Library Headquarters
County Hall, Mold, CH7 6NW Tel: 01352 704411 Email:
libraries@flintshire.gov.uk WWW: www.flintshire.gov.uk

Glamorgan
Bridgend Library & Information Service
Coed Parc, Park Street, Bridgend, CF31 4BA Tel: 01656-
767451 Fax: 01656-645719 Email: blis@bridgendlib.gov.uk
Dowlais Library
Church Street, Dowlais, Merthyr Tydfil, CF48 3HS Tel:
01985-723051
Merthyr Tydfil Central Library (Local Studies Dept)
Merthyr Library, High Street, Merthyr Tydfil, CF47 8AF
Tel: 01685-723057 Email: library@merthyr.gov.btinternet.com
Neath Central Library (Local Studies Department)
29 Victoria Gardens, Neath, SA11 3BA Tel: 01639-620139
Pontypridd Library
Library Road, Pontypridd, CF37 2DY Tel: 01443-486850
Port Talbot Library
1st Floor Aberafan Shopping Centre, Port Talbot, SA13 1PB
Tel: 01639-763490

Swansea Reference Library
Alexandra Road, Swansea, SA1 5DX Tel: 01792-516753
Email: swanlib@demon.co.uk Extensive holdings of trade
directories, local census returns, newspapers (partially indexed)
University of Wales Swansea library
Library & Information Centre, Singleton Park, Swansea,
SA2 8PP Tel: 01792 295021 Fax: 01792 295851
Treorchy Library
Station Road, Treorchy, CF42 6NN Tel: 01443-773204 Fax:
01443-777407

Gwent
Abertillery Library
Station Hill, Abertillery, NP13 1TE Tel: 01495-212332
Chepstow Library & Information Centre
Manor Way, Chepstow, NP16 5HZ Tel: 01291-635730 Tel:
01291-635731 Email: chepstowlibrary@monmouthshire.gov.uk
WWW: www.monmouthshire.gov.uk/leisure/libraries
Newport Library & Information Service
Newport Central Library, John Frost Square, Newport, NP20
1PA Tel: 01633-211376 Email: reference.library@newport.gov.uk
WWW: http://www.earl.org.uk/partners/newport/index.html The
Local Studies Collection contains information on all aspects of
Monmouthshire and or Gwent. A fee paying postal research service
is available, which uses the library's own resources.
Tredegar Library
The Circle, Tredegar, NP2 3PS Tel: 01495-722687

Gwynedd
Canolfan Llyfrgell Dolgellau Library
FforddBala, Dolgellau, LL40 2YF Tel: 01341-422771
WWW: http://www.gwynedd.gov.uk
Llyfrgell Caernarfon
Lon Pafiliwn, Caernafon, LL55 1AS Tel: 01286-679465
Fax: 01286-671137 Email: library@gwynedd.gov.uk

Merthyr Tydfil
**Merthyr Tydfil Central Library (Local Studies
Department)**
Merthyr Library, High Street, Merthyr Tydfil, CF47 8AF
Tel: 01685-723057 Email: library@merthyr.gov.btinternet.com
Treharris Library
Perrott Street, Treharris, Merthyr Tydfil, CF46 5ET Tel:
01443-410517 Fax: 01443 410517

Monmouthshire
Chepstow Library & Information Centre
Manor Way, Chepstow, NP16 5HZ Tel: 01291-635730 Tel:
01291-635731 Email: chepstowlibrary@monmouthshire.gov.uk
WWW: www.monmouthshire.gov.uk/leisure/libraries

Neath Port Talbot
Lifelong Learning Service
Theodore Road, Port Talbot, SA13 1SP Tel: 01639-898581
Fax: 01639-899914 Email: lls@neath-porttalbot.gov.uk

Pembrokeshire
Pembrokeshire Libraries
The County Library, Dew Street, Haverfordwest, SA61 1SU
Tel: 01437-762070 Email: anita.thomas@pembrokeshire.gov.uk
The Local Studies Library covers peoiple, places and events realting
to The County of Pembrokeshire past and present. The Library also
houses The Francis Green Genealogical Collection

Powys
Brecon Area Library
Ship Street, Brecon, LD3 9AE Tel: 01874-623346 Fax:
01874 622818 Email: breclib@mail.powys.gov.uk
Llandrindod Wells Library
Cefnllys Lane, Llandrindod Wells, LD1 5LD
Tel: 01597-826870 Email: , llandod.library@powys.gov.uk
Newtown Area Library
Park Lane, Newtown, SY16 1EJ Tel: 01686-626934
Fax: 01686 624935 Email: nlibrary@powys.gov.uk

Rhondda Cynon Taff
Aberdare Library
Green Street, Aberdare, CF44 7AG Tel: 01685-885318

Vale of Glamorgan
Barry Library
King Square, Holton Road, Barry, CF63 4RW
Tel: 01446-735722 Fax: 01446 734427

West Glamorgan
West Glamorgan Archive Service - Port Talbot Access Point
Port Talbot Library, Aberafan Centre, Port Talbot, SA13 1PJ
Tel: 01639 763430 WWW: http://www.swansea.gov.uk/archives

Wrexham CBC
Wrexham Library and Arts Centre
Rhosddu Road, Wrexham, LL11 1AU Tel: 01978-292622
Fax: 01978-292611 Email: joy.thomas@wrexham.gov.uk
WWW: www.wrexham.gov.uk

Scotland
St Andrews University Library - Special Collections Department
North Street, St Andrews, KY16 9TR Tel: 01334 462339
Fax: 01334 462282 Email: speccoll@st-and.ac.uk
WWW: http://specialcollections.st-and.ac.uk
Glasgow University Library & Special Collections Dept
Hillhead Street, Glasgow, G12 8QE Tel: 0141 330 6767
Email: library@lib.gla.ac.uk WWW: www.gla.ac.uk/library
Edinburgh University Library, Special Collections Dept
George Square, Edinburgh, EH8 9LJ Tel: 0131 650 3412
Email: special.collections@ed.ac.uk WWW: www.lib.ed.ac.uk
Edinburgh University New College Library
Mound Place, Edinburgh, EH1 2UL Tel: 0131 650 8957
Fax: 0131 650 6579 Email: New.College.Library@ed.ac.uk
WWW: www.lib.ed.ac.uk
Leadhills Miners's Library
Main Street, Leadhills Tel: 01659-74326
National Library of Scotland
George IV Bridge, Edinburgh, EH1 1EW Tel: 0131-226-4531 Email: enquiries@nls.uk WWW: http://www.nls.uk
National Monuments Record of Scotland
Royal Commission on the Ancient & Historical Monuments
of Scotland, John Sinclair House, 16 Bernard terrace,
Edinburgh, EH8 9NX Tel: 0131 662 1456 Fax: 0131 662
1477 or 0131 662 1499 Email: nmrs@rcahms.gov.uk
WWW: www.rcahms.gov.uk Website gives access to the
searchable database of NMRS Records - 'CANMORE'
National Museums of Scotland Library
Royal Museum, Chambers Street, Edinburgh, EH1 1JF Tel:
0131 247 4137 Email: library@nms.ac.uk
WWW: www.nms.ac.uk Holds large collection of family histories
Royal Botanic Garden
The Library, 20a Inverleith Row, Edinburgh, EH3 5LR Tel:
0131 552 7171 Fax: 0131 248 2901
Scottish United Services Museum Library
The Castle, Museum Square, Edinburgh, EH1 1 2NG Tel:
0131-225-7534-Ext-2O4 Fax: 0131-225-3848
Email: library@nms.ac.uk WWW: www.nms.ac.uk
Strathclyde University Archives
McCance Building, 16 Richmond Street, Glasgow, G1 1XQ
Tel: 0141 548 2397 Fax: 0141 552 0775
Scottish Genealogy Society - Library
15 Victoria Terrace, Edinburgh, EH1 2JL Tel: 0131-220 3677
Fax: 0131 220 3677 Email: info@scotsgenealogy.com
WWW: www.scotsgenealogy.com

Aberdeen
Aberdeen Central Library - Reference & Local Studies
Rosemount Viaduct, Aberdeen, AB25 1GW Tel: 01224-652511 Tel: 01224 252512 Fax: 01224 624118 Email:
refloc@arts-rec.aberdeen.net.uk
University of Aberdeen DISS: Heritage Division Special Collections & Archives
Kings College, Aberdeen, AB24 3SW Tel: 01224-272598
Email: speclib@abdn.ac.uk

WWW: http://www.abdn.ac.uk/diss/heritage
Aberdeenshire Library & Information Service
The Meadows Industrial Estate, Meldrum Meg Way,
Oldmeldrum, AB51 0GN Tel: 01651-872707 Tel: 01651-871219/871220Email: ALIS@aberdeenshire.gov.uk
WWW: www.aberdeenshire.gov.uk

Angus
Angus Archives
Montrose Library, 214 High Street, Montrose, DD10 8PH
Tel: 01674-671415 Tel: Fax: 01674-671810 Email:
angus.archives@angus.govuk WWW:
www.angus.gov.uk/history/history.htm Family history
research service. Archive holdings for Angus County,
Arbroath, Brechin, Carnoustie, Forfar, Montrose, Monifieth,
Kittiemuir.

Angus District Montrose Library
214 High Street, Montrose, MO10 8PH Tel: 01674-673256
Tay Valley Family History Society
Family History Research Centre, 179–181 Princes Street,
Dundee, DD4 6DQ Tel: 01382-461845 Fax: 01382 455532
Email: tvfhs@tayvalleyfhs.org.uk
WWW: http://www.tayvalleyfhs.org.uk

Argyll
Argyll & Bute Council Archives
Highland Avenue, Sandbank, Dunoon, PA23 8PB
Tel: 01369-703214
Campbeltown Library and Museum
Hall St, Campbeltown, PA28 6BU Tel: 01586 552366
Argyll & Bute Library Service
Library Headquarters, Highland Avenue, Sandbank, Dunoon,
PA23 8PB Tel: 01369-703214
Email: andyewan@abc-libraries.demon.co.uk

Ayrshire
E Ayrshire Council District History Centre & Museum
Baird Institute, 3 Lugar Street, Cumnock, KA18 1AD
Tel: 01290-421701 Fax: 01290-421701
Email: Baird.institute@east-ayrshire.gov.uk
WWW: www.east-ayrshire.gov.uk
East Ayrshire Libraries
Dick Institute, Elmbank Avenue, Kilmarnock, KA1 3BU Tel:
01563 554310 Tel: 01290 421701 Fax: 01563 554311 Email:
baird.institute@east-ayrshire.gov.uk WWW: www.east-ayrshire.gov.uk
East Ayrshire Libraries - Cumnock
25-27 Ayr Road, Cumnock, KA18 1EB Tel: 01290-422804

North Ayrshire Libraries
Library Headquarters, 39 - 41 Princes Street, Ardrossan,
KA22 8BT Tel: 01294-469137 Fax: 01924-604236
Email: reference@naclibhq.prestel.co.uk
WWW: www.north-ayrshire.gov.uk

South Ayrshire Library
Carnegie Library, 12 Main Street, Ayr, KA8 8ED Tel: 01292-286385 Email: carnegie@south-ayrshire.gov.uk
WWW: www.south-ayrshire.gov.uk

Clackmannanshire
Clackmannanshire Archives
Alloa Library, 26/28 Drysdale Street, Alloa, FK10 1JL Tel:
01259-722262 Email: libraries@clacks.gov.uk
WWW: www.clacksweb,org.uk/dyna/archives
Clackmannanshire Libraries
Alloa Library, 26/28 Drysdale Street, Alloa, FK10 1JL Tel:
01259-722262 Fax: 01259-219469 Email:
clack.lib@mail.easynet.co.uk

Dumfries & Galloway
Ewart Library
Ewart Library, Catherine Street, Dumfries, DG1 1JB Tel:
01387 260285 Tel: 01387-252070 Email: ruth_airley@dumgal.gov.uk
libsxi@dumgal.gov.uk WWW: www.dumgal.gov.uk

Libraries

Dunbartonshire
Dumbarton Public library
Strathleven Place, Dumbarton, G82 1BD Tel: 01389-733273
Fax: 01389-738324 Email: wdlibs@hotmail.com

Dundee
Dundee Central Library
The Wellgate, Dundee, DD1 1DB Tel: 01382-434377 Fax:
01382-434036 Email: local.studies@dundeecity.gov.uk
WWW: http://www.dundeecity.gov.uk/dcchtml/nrd/loc_stud.htm,
Material held mainly Angus and Dundee
Tay Valley Family History Society
Family History Research Centre, 179–181 Princes Street,
Dundee, DD4 6DQ Tel: 01382-461845 Fax: 01382 455532
Email: tvfhs@tayvalleyfhs.org.uk
WWW: http://www.tayvalleyfhs.org.uk

East Ayrshire
Auchinleck Library
Community Centre, Well Road, Auchinleck, KA18 2LA
Tel: 01290 422829
Bellfield Library
79 Whatriggs Road, Kilmarnock, KA1 3RB
Tel: 01563 534266
Bellsbank Library
Primary School, Craiglea Crescent, Bellsbank, KA6 7UA
Tel: 01292 551057
Catrine Library
A M Brown Institute, Catrine, KA5 6RT Tel: 01290 551717
Crosshouse Library
11-13 Gatehead Road, Crosshouse, KA2 0HN
Tel: 01563 573640
Dalmellington Library
Townhead, Dalmellington, KA6 7QZ
Tel: 01292 550159
Dalrymple Library
Barbieston Road, Dalrymple, KA6 6DZ
Darvel Library
Town Hall, West Main Street, Darvel, KA17 0AQ
Tel: 01560 322754
Drongan Library
Mill O'Shield Road, Drongan, KA6 7AY Tel: 01292 591718
Galston Library
Henrietta Street, Galston, KA4 8HQ Tel: 01563 821994
Hurlford Library
Blair Road, Hurlford, KA1 5BN Tel: 01563 539899
Kilmaurs Library
Irvine Road, Kilmaurs, KA3 2RJ
Mauchline Library
2 The Cross, Mauchline Tel: 01290 550824
Muirkirk Library
Burns Avenue, Muirkirk, KA18 3RH Tel: 01290 661505
Netherthird Library
Ryderston Drive, Netherthird, KA18 3AR
Tel: 01290 423806
New Cumnock Library
Community Centre, The Castle, New Cumnock, KA18 4AH
Tel: 01290 338710
Newmilns Library
Craigview Road, Newmilns, KA16 9DQ Tel: 01560 322890
Ochiltree Library
Main Street, Ochiltree, KA18 2PE Tel: 01290 700425
Patna Library
Doonside Avenue, Patna, KA6 7LX Tel: 01292 531538

East Dunbartonshire
**East Dunbartonshire Local Record Offices and
Reference Libraries**
William Patrick Library, 2 West High Street, Kirkintilloch,
G66 1AD Tel: 0141-776-8090 Fax: 0141-776-0408 Email:
libraries@eastdunbarton.gov.uk WWW:
www.eastdunbarton.gov.uk

East Renfrewshire
Giffnock Library
Station Road, Giffnock, Glasgow, G46 6JF Tel: 0141-577-
4976 Email: devinem@eastrenfrewshire.co.uk

Edinburgh
Edinburgh Central Library
Edinburgh Room, George IV Bridge, Edinburgh, EH1 1EG
Tel: 0131-242 8030 Fax: 0131-242 8009 Email:
eclis@edinburgh.gov.uk WWW: www.edinburgh.gov.uk

Falkirk
Falkirk Library
Hope Street, Falkirk, FK1 5AU Tel: 01324 503605 Fax:
01324 503606 Email: falkirk-library@falkirk-
library.demon.co.uk WWW: www.falkirk.gov.uk Holds
Local Studies Collection
Falkirk Museum History Research Centre
Callendar House, Callendar Park, Falkirk, FK1 1YR Tel:
01324 503778 Fax: 01324 503771 Email:
ereid@falkirkmuseums.demon.co.ukcallandarhouse@falkirkmuseums.de
mon.co.uk WWW: www.falkirkmuseums.demon.co.uk Records held:
Local Authority, business, personal and estate records, local
organmisations, trade unions, over 28,000 photographs Falkirk District

Fife
Dunfermline Library - Local History Department
Abbot Street, Dunfermline, KY12 7NL Tel: 01383-312994
Fax: 01383-312608 Email: info@dunfermline.fifelib.net
Fife Council Central Area Libraries
Central Library, War Memorial Grounds, Kirkcaldy, KY1
1YG Tel: 01592-412878 Email: info@kirkcaldy.fifelib.net
St Andrews Library
Church Square, St Andrews, KY16 9NN Tel: 01334-412685
Fax: 01334 413029 Email: info@standres.fiflib.net
St Andrews University Library
North Street, St Andrews, KY16 9TR Tel: 01334-462281
Fax: 01334-462282 WWW: http://www.library.st-and.ac.uk
St Andrews University Library - Special Collections Dept
North Street, St Andrews, KY16 9TR Tel: 01334 462339
Fax: 01334 462282 Email: speccoll@st-and.ac.uk
WWW: http://specialcollections.st-and.ac.uk
Tay Valley Family History Society
Family History Research Centre, 179–181 Princes Street,
Dundee, DD4 6DQ Tel: 01382-461845 Fax: 01382 455532
Email: tvfhs@tayvalleyfhs.org.uk WWW:
http://www.tayvalleyfhs.org.uk

Glasgow
Brookwood Library
166 Drymen Road, Bearsden, Glasgow, G61 3RJ Tel: 0141-
942 6811 Fax: 0141 943 1119
Glasgow City Libraries & Archives
Mitchell Library, North Street, Glasgow, G3 7DN Tel: 0141
287 2937 Fax: 0141 287 2912 Email: history_and_glasgow
@gcl.glasgow.gov.uk WWW:
www.glasgow.gov.uk/html/council/cindex.htm
Glasgow University Library & Special Collections Dept
Hillhead Street, Glasgow, G12 8QE Tel: 0141 330 6767 Fax:
0141 330 3793 Email: library@lib.gla.ac.uk WWW:
www.gla.ac.uk/library
Social Sciences Department - History & Glasgow Room
The Mitchell Library, North Street, Glasgow, G3 7DN Tel:
0141-227-2935 Tel: 0141-227-2937 & 0141-227-2938 Fax:
0141-227-2935 Email: history-and-
glasgow@cls.glasgow.gov.uk WWW: www.libarch.glasgow

Isle of Barra
Castlebay Community Library
Community School, Castlebay, HS95XD Tel: 01871-810471

Isle of Benbecula
Community Library
Sgoil Lionacleit, Liniclate, HS7 5PJ Tel: 01870-602211

Isle of Lewis
Stornoway Library
19 Cromwell Street, Stornoway, HS1 2DA Tel: 01851-703064 Fax: 01851- 708676/708677
Email: stornoway-library1@cne-siar.gov.uk.gov.uk

Kinross-shire
Perth & Kinross Libraries
A K Bell Library, 2 - 8 York Place, Perth, PH2 8EP Tel: 01738-477062 Email: jaduncan@pkc.gov.uk
Tay Valley Family History Society
Family History Research Centre, 179–181 Princes Street, Dundee, DD4 6DQ Tel: 01382-461845 Fax: 01382 455532
Email: tvfhs@tayvalleyfhs.org.uk
WWW: http://www.tayvalleyfhs.org.uk

Lanarkshire
Airdrie Library
Wellwynd, Airdrie, ML6 0AG Tel: 01236-763221
Cumbernauld Central Library
8 Allander Walk, Cumbernauld, G67 1EE Tel: 01236-735964 Fax: 01236-458350 WWW: www.northlan.org.uk

Midlothian
Midlothian Archives and Local Studies Centre
2 Clerk Street, Loanhead, EH20 9DR Tel: 0131 271 3976 Fax: 0131 440 4635 Email: local.studies@midlothian.gov.uk WWW: www.earl.org.uk/partners/midlothian/local.html
Midlothian Libraries Local History Centre
Midlothian Council Libraries Headquarters, 2 Clerk Street, Loanhead, EH20 9DR Tel: 0131-440-2210 Fax: 0131-440-4635 Email: local.studies@midlothian.gov.uk WWW: http://www.earl.org.uk.partners/midlothian/index.html

Morayshire
Forres Library
Forres House, High Street, Forres, IV36 0BJ Tel: 01309-672834 Fax: 01309-675084
Moray Local Heritage Centre
Grant Lodge, Cooper Park, Elgin, IV30 1HS Tel: 01343 562644 Tel: 01343 562645 Fax: 01343-549050 Email: graeme.wilson@techleis.moray.gov.uk WWW: www.morray.org/heritage/roots.html , The Moray District Record Office has now been combined with the Local studies section at Grant Lodge, Cooper Park, Elgin to form the Local Heritage Centre.
Buckie Library
Clunu Place, Buckie, AB56 1HB Tel: 01542-832121 Fax: 01542-835237 Email: buckie.lib@techleis.moray.gov.uk
Keith Library
Union Street, Keith, AB55 5DP Tel: 01542-882223 Fax: 01542-882177 Email: keithlibrary@techleis.moray.gov.uk

North Highland
North Highland Archive
Wick Library, Sinclair Terrace, Wick, KW1 5AB Tel: 01955 606432 Fax: 01955 603000

North Lanarkshire
Kilsyth Library
Burngreen, Kilsyth, G65 0HT Tel: 01236-823147

Motherwell Heritage Centre
High Road, Motherwell, ML1 3HU Tel: 01698-251000 Fax: 01698-253433 Email: heritage@mhc158.freeserve.co.uk
Shotts Library
Benhar Road, Shotts, ML7 5EN Tel: 01501-821556, Fax:

Orkney
Orkney Library
The Orkney Library, Laing Street, Kirkwall, KWI5 1NW Tel: 01856-873166 Email: karen.walker@orkney.gov.uk

Perthshire
Perth & Kinross Libraries
A K Bell Library, 2 - 8 York Place, Perth, PH2 8EP Tel: 01738-477062 Fax: 01738-477010 Email: jaduncan@pkc.gov.uk
Tay Valley Family History Society
Family History Research Centre, 179–181 Princes Street, Dundee, DD4 6DQ Tel: 01382-461845 Fax: 01382 455532
Email: tvfhs@tayvalleyfhs.org.uk
WWW: http://www.tayvalleyfhs.org.uk

Renfrewshire
Renfrewshire Council Library & Museum Services
Central Library & Museum Complex, High Street, Paisley, PA1 2BB Tel: 0141-889-2350 Fax: 0141-887-6468
Email: local_studies.library@renfrewshire.gov.uk

Watt Library
9 Union Street, Greenock, PA16 8JH Tel: 01475-715628

Scottish Borders
Scottish Borders Archive & Local History Centre
Library Headquarters, St Mary's Mill, Selkirk, TD7 5EW Tel: 01750 20842 Tel: 01750 724903 Fax: 01750 22875 Email: archives@scotborders.gov.uk WWW: www.scotborders.gov.uk/libraries

Shetland
Shetland Library
Lower Hillhead, Lerwick, ZE1 0EL Tel: 01595-693868 Fax: 01595-694430 Email: info@shetland-library.gov.uk WWW: www.shetland-library.gov.uk

Stirling
Bridge of Allan Library
Fountain Road, Bridge of Allan, FK9 4AT Tel: 01786 833680 Fax: 01786 833680 Hold the IGI in disc form, the 1881 census on disc and have Internet access, as well as a selection of local history books relevant to their locale. Also holds microfilms of the 1851 census for Stirling
Dunblane Library
High Street, Dunbland, FK15 0ER Tel: 01786 823125 Fax: 01786 823125 Email: dunblanelibrary@stirling.gov.uk
St Ninians Library
Mayfield Centre, St Ninians, FK7 0DB Tel: 01786 472069 Email: , stninlibrary@stirling.gov.uk Hold the IGI in disc form, the 1881 census on disc and have Internet access, as well as a selection of local history books relevant to their locale
Stirling Central Library
Central Library, Corn Exchange Road, Stirling, FK8 2HX Tel: 01786 432106 Fax: 01786 473094 Email: centrallibrary@stirling.gov.uk Hours - Mon, Wed, Fri 9.30-5.30 Tues, Thurs 9.30-7 Sat 9.30-5 Census returns for all Stirling Council area, Old Parish Registers for same, IGI on fiche and disc, 1881 census on disc, local newpapers

Tayside
Dundee University Archives
Tower Building, University of Dundee, Dundee, DD1 4HN Tel: 01382-344095 Email: archives@dundee.ac.uk WWW: http://www.dundee.ac.uk/archives/

West Lothian
West Lothian Council Libraries
Connolly House, Hopefield Road, Blackburn, EH47 7HZ Tel: 01506-776331 Email: localhistory@westlothian.org.uk WWW: http://www.wlonline.org

Northern Ireland
Antrim
North Eastern Library Board & Local Studies
Area Reference Library, Demesne Avenue, Ballymena, BT43 7BG Tel: (028) 25 6641212 Email: yvonne_hirt@hotmail.com WWW: www.neelb.org.uk

Belfast
Belfast Central Library
Irish & Local Studies Dept, Royal Avenue, Belfast, BT1 1EA Tel: (028) 9024 3233 Fax: (028) 9033 2819 Email: info@libraries.belfast-elb.gov.uk
WWW: www.belb.org.uk
Belfast Linen Hall Library
17 Donegall Square North, Belfast, BT1 5GD Tel: (028) 90321707

Co Antrim
Local Studies Service
Area Library HQ, Demesne Avenue, Ballymena, BT43 7BG Tel: (028) 25 664121 Email: yvonne_hirst@hotmail.com WWW: www.neelb.org.uk

Co Fermanagh
Enniskillen Library
Halls Lane, Enniskillen, BT1 3HP Tel: (028) 66322886 Fax: 01365-324685 Email: librarian@eknlib.demon.co.uk

Co Londonderry
Central and Reference Library
35 Foyle Street, Londonderry, BT24 6AL Tel: (028) 71272300 Email: trishaw@online.rednet.co.uk
Irish Room
Coleraine County Hall, Castlerock Road, Ballymena, BT1 3HP Tel: (028) 705 1026 WWW: www.neelb.org.uk

Co Tyrone
Centre for Migration Studies
Ulster American Folk Park, Mellon Road, Castletown, Omagh, BT78 5QY Tel: 028 82 256315 Email: uafp@iol.ie
Omagh Library
1 Spillars Place, Omagh, BT78 1HL Tel: (028) 82244821 Fax: 01662-246772 Email: librarian@omahlib.demon.co.uk

County Down
South Eastern Library Board & Local Studies
Library HQ, Windmill Hill, Ballynahinch, BT24 8DH Tel: (028) 9756 6400 Email: ref@bhinchlibhq.demon.co.uk

Ireland
National Library of Ireland
Kildare Street, Dublin, 2 Tel: 661-8811 Fax: 676-6690 Email: coflaherty@nli.ie
Society of Friends (Quakers) - Historical Library
Swanbrook House, Bloomfield Avenue, Dublin, 4 Tel: (01) 668-7157 Completed computerisation of card index

Co Clare
Clare County Library
The Manse, Harmony Row, Ennis Tel: 065-6821616 Email: clarelib@iol.ie WWW: www.iol.ie/~clarelib

Co Cork
Cork City Library
Grand Parade, Cork Tel: 021-277110 Fax: 021-275684 Email: cork.city.library@indigo.ie
Mallow Heritage Centre
27/28 Bank Place, Mallow Tel: 022-50302

Co Dublin
Dun Laoghaire Library
Lower George's Street, Dun Laoghaire Tel: 2801147 Fax: 2846141 Email: eprout@dlrcoco.ie WWW: www.dlrcoco.ie/library/lhistory.htm

Co Kerry
Kerry County Library Genealogical Centre
Cathedral Walk, Killarney Tel: 353-0-64-359946

Co Kildare
Kildare County Library
Newbridge Tel: 045-431109 Fax: 045-432490
Kildare Hertiage & Genealogy
Kildare County Library, Newbridge Tel: 045 433602 Fax: 045-432490 Email: capinfo@iol.ie WWW: www.kildare.ie

Co Mayo
Central Library
Castlebar Tel: 094-24444 Email: cbarlib@iol.ie

Co Sligo
Sligo County Library
Westward Town Centre, Bridge Street, Sligo Tel: 00-353-71-47190 Fax: 00-353-71-46798 Email: sligolib@iol.ie
Co Tipperary
Tipperary County Libary Local Studies Department
Castle Avenue, Thurles Tel: 0504-21555 Fax: 0504-23442 Email: studies@tipplibs.iol.ie WWW: www.iol.ie/~TIPPLIBS

Co Waterford
Waterford County Library
Central Library, Davitt's Quay, Dungarvan Tel: 058 41231

Co Wexford
Enniscorthy Branch Library
Lymington Road, Enniscorthy Tel: 054-36055
New Ross Branch Library
Barrack Lane, New Ross Tel: 051-21877
Wexford Branch Library
Teach Shionoid, Abbey Street, Wexford Tel: 053-42211 Fax: 053-21097

County Donegal
Donegal Local Studies Centre
Central Library & Arts Centre, Oliver Plunkett Road, Letterkenny Tel: 00353 74 24950 Fax: 00353 74 24950 Email: dgcolib@iol.ie WWW: donegal.ie

County Dublin
Ballyfermot Public Library
Ballyfermot, Dublin, 10

County Limerick
Limerick City Library
The Granary, Michael Street, Limerick Tel: 061-314668 Fax: 061 411506 Email: doyledolores@hotmail.com

Dublin
Dublin Public Libraries
Gilbert Library - Dublin & Irish Collections, 138 -142 Pearse Street, Dublin, 2 Tel: 353-1-677-7662 Fax: 353-1-671-4354 Email: dubcoll@iol.ie WWW: http:/www.iol.ie/ dubcilib/index.html

Australia
ACT
National Library of Australia
Canberra, 2600 Tel: 02 6262 1111
WWW: http://www.nla.gov.au

New South Wales
Mitchell Library
Macquarie Street Sydney, 2000 Tel: 02 9230 1693 Fax: 02 9235 1687 Email: slinfo@slsw.gov.au
State Library of New South Wales
Macquarie Street Sydney, 2000 Tel: 02 9230 1414 Fax: 02 9223 3369 Email: slinfo@slsw.gov.au
Queensland
State Library of Queensland
PO Box 3488, Cnr Peel and Stanley Streets, South Brisbane, Brisbane, 4101 Tel: 07 3840 7775 Fax: 07 3840 7840 Email: genie@slq.qld.gov.au WWW: http://www.slq.qld.gov.au/subgenie/htm

South Australia
South Australia State Library
PO Box 419 Adelaide, 5001 Tel: (08) 8207 7235 Fax: (08) 8207 7247 Email: famhist@slsa.sa.gov.au WWW: http://www.slsa.sa.gov.au/library/collres/famhist/

Victoria
State Library of Victoria
328 Swanston Street Walk Melbourne, 3000 Tel: 03 9669 9080 Email: granth@newvenus.slv.vic.gov.au WWW: http://slv.vic.gov.au/slv/genealogy/index

Western Australia
State Library
Alexander Library, Perth Cultural Centre Perth, 6000 Tel: 09 427 3111 Fax: 09 427 3256

New Zealand
Auckland Research Centre Auckland City Libraries
PO Box 4138, 44 46 Lorne Street Auckland
Tel: 64 9 377 0209 Fax: 64 9 307 7741
Email: heritage@auckland library.govt.nz
National Library of New Zealand
PO Box 1467 Thorndon, Wellington Tel: (0064)4 474 3030 Fax: (0064)4 474 3063
WWW: http://www.natlib.govt.nz
Alexander Turnbull Library
PO Box 12 349 , Wellington, 6038 Tel: 04 474 3050
Fax: 04 474 3063
Canterbury Public Library
PO Box 1466 , Christchurch Tel: 03 379 6914
Fax: 03 365 1751
Dunedin Public Libraries
PO Box 5542, Moray Place Dunedin Tel: 03 474 3651 Fax: 03 474 3660 Email: library@dcc.govt.nz
Fielding Public Library
PO Box 264 , Fielding, 5600 Tel: 06 323 5373
Hamilton Public Library
PO Box 933, Garden Place Hamilton, 2015
Tel: 07 838 6827 Fax: 07 838 6858
Hocken Library
PO Box 56 , Dunedin Tel: 03 479 8873
Fax: 03 479 5078
Porirua Public Library
PO Box 50218 , Porirua, 6215 Tel: 04 237 1541
Fax: 04 237 7320
Takapuna Public Library
Private Bag 93508 , Takapuna, 1309
Tel: 09 486 8466 Fax: 09 486 8519
Wanganui District Library
Private Bag 3005, Alexander Building, Queens Park, Wanganui, 5001 Tel: 06 345 8195 Fax: 06 345 5516 Email: wap@wdl.govt.nz

South Africa
South African Library
PO Box 496 , Cape Town, 8000 Tel: 021 246320
Fax: 021 244848

Canada
Alberta
Calgary Public Library
616 MacLeod Tr SE Calgary, T2G 2M2 Tel: 260 2785
Glenbow Library & Archives
130 9th Avenue SE Calgary, T2G 0P3 Tel: 403 268 4197
Fax: 403 232 6569

British Columbia
British Columbia Archives
865 Yates Street Victoria, V8V 1X4 Tel: 604 387 1952 Fax: 604 387 2072 Email: rfrogner@maynard.bcars.gs.gov.bc.ca

Cloverdale Library
5642   176a Street Surrey, V3S 4G9 Tel: 604 576 1384
Email: GenealogyResearch@city.surrey.bc.ca
WWW: http://www.city.surrey.bc.ca/spl/

New Brunswick
Harriet Irving Library
PO Box 7500 Fredericton, E3B 5H5 Tel: 506 453 4748
Loyalist Collection & Reference Library
PO Box 7500 Fredericton, E3B 5H5 Tel: 506 453 4749

Newfoundland
Newfoundland Provincial Resource Library
Arts and Cultural Centre, Allandale Road St Johns, A1B 3A3
Tel: 709 737 3955 Email: genealog@publib.nf.ca
WWW: http://www.publib.nf.ca

Ontario
National Library
395 Wellington Street Ottawa, K1A 0N4
Tel: 613 995 9481 Fax: 613 943 1112
Email:reference@nlc bnc.ca WWW: http://www.nlc bnc.ca
Toronto Reference Library
789 Yonge Street Toronto, M4W 2G8 Tel: 416 393 7155
James Gibson Reference Library
500 Glenridge Avenue St Catherines, L2S 3A1
Tel: 905 688 5550 Fax: 905 988 5490
Public Library
PO Box 2700, Station LCD 1 Hamilton, L8N 4E4
Tel: 546 3408 Email: speccol@hpl.hamilton.on.ca
Public Library
85 Queen Street North Kitchener, N2H 2H1
Tel: 519 743 0271 Fax: 519 570 1360
Public Library
305 Queens Avenue London, N6B 3L7
Tel: 519 661 4600 Fax: 519 663 5396
Public Library
301 Burnhamthorpe Road West Mississauga, L5B 3Y3 Tel: 905 615 3500 Email: library.info@city.mississauga.on.ca
WWW: http://www.city.mississauga.on.ca/Library
Toronto Public Library
North York (Entral Library) Canadiana Department, 5120 Yonge Street North York, M2N 5N9
Tel: 416 395 5623 WWW: http://www.tpl.tor.on.ca
Public Library
74 Mackenzie Street Sudbury, P3C 4X8
Tel: 01673 1155 Fax: 01673 9603
St Catharines Public Library
54 Church Street St Catharines, L2R 7K2
Tel: 905 688 6103 Fax: 905 688 2811
Email: scpublib@stcatharines.library.on.ca
WWW: http://www.stcatharines.library.on.ca

Quebec
Bibliotheque De Montreal
1210, Rue Sherbrooke East Street , Montreal, H2L 1L9 Tel: 514 872 1616 Fax: 514 872 4654
Email: daniel_olivier@ville.montreal.qc.ca
WWW: http://www.ville.montreal.qc.ca/biblio/pageacc.htm

Saskatchewan
Public Library
PO Box 2311 Regina, S4P 3Z5 Tel: 306 777 6011
Fax: 306 352 5550 Email: kaitken@rpl.sk.ca
Public Library
311   23rd Street East Saskatoon, S7K 0J6 Tel: 306 975 7555
Fax: 306 975 7542

Ancestral Research

National Organisations for Researchers
Association of Genealogists and Researchers in Archives
29 Badgers Close Horsham West Sussex RH12 5RU
Email: agra@agra.org.uk WWW: www.agra.org.uk
See Advert on Page: 18
British Association for Local History
PO Box 1576 Salisbury SP2 8SY Fax: 01722-413242
WWW: www.balh.co.uk See Advert on Page: IFC & 161
Society of Genealogists
14 Charterhouse Buildings Goswell Road London EC1M 7BA
Tel; 020 7253 5235 Email; sales@sog.org.uk Website &
Bookshop; www.sog.org.uk See Advert on Page: 203 & 415

Comprehensive Research and all Counties
Achievements (Est 1961)
Centre for Heraldic & Genealogical Research & Artwork 79
- 82 Northgate Canterbury Kent CT1 1BA Fax: 01227
765617 Email: achievements@achievements.co.uk WWW:
www.achievements.co.uk See Advert on Page: 53
Back to Roots Family History Service
16 Arrowsmith Drive Stonehouse Gloucestershire GL10
2QR Email: mike@backtoroots.co.uk WWW:
http://www.backtoroots.co.uk See Advert on Page: 416 &
IBC
Len Barnett Research
22 Park Avenue South Hornsey London N8 8LT
Email: lenny@barnettresearch.freeserve.co.uk WWW:
www.barnettresearch.freeserve.co.uk See Advert on Page: 75
Colin Dale Researches (GSD)
1 Furham Field Pinner Middlesex HA5 4DX See Advert
on Page: 99
Geoff Nicholson BSc
57 Manor Park Concord Washington Tyne and Wear
NE37 2BU Email: geoff@genic.demon.co.uk WWW:
http://www.genic.demon.co.uk/index.html See Advert on
Page: 15
Kinship Genealogical Research
23 Friar Road Brighton East Sussex BN1 6NG Email:
kinship2@hotmail.com See Advert on Page: 30
Link Investigations
296 High Street Dorking Surrey RH4 1PN Fax: 01306-
888077 Email: info@linkinvestigations.co.uk WWW:
http://www.linkinvestigations.co.uk
See Advert on Page: 17
Sydney G Smith
59 Friar Road Orpington Kent BR5 2BW
Email: ss.famhist@virgin.net See Advert on Page: 81
Tim Hughes & Associates - Historical Research
PO Box 401
Twickenham TW1 4FE Fax: (020) 8395 6281 Email:
mail@timhughes.com WWW: www.timhughes.com See
Advert on Page: 200
David L Williams
7 Buckbury Heights Newport Isle of Wight PO30 2LX
Email: david@genpix.fsnet.co.uk
See Advert on Page: 112
www.bigfamily.co.uk
The Gatehouse Fen Road Milton Cambridgeshire CB4
6AF Fax: 01223 864767 Email: mark@bigfamily.co.uk
WWW: www.bigfamily.co.uk See Advert on Page: 105
Worthington Clark PTY Ltd
PO Box 161 Lane Cove New South Wales 1595 Australia
Fax: +(612)-9428-4242 Email:
jworth@worthclark.bu.aust.com See Advert on Page: 21
UK Searches
14 Merchant Street Bognor Regis West Sussex PO21 1QH
Fax: 01243 841418 Email: hac@abel.co.uk WWW:
www.uksearches.com See Advert on Page: 157

England

Bedfordshire
Victor Longhorn
53 Theydon Avenue Woburn Sands Milton Keynes MK17
8PN Email: victor.longhorn@btinternet.com See Advert on
Page: 99
Mrs Carolynn Boucher
1 Ivinghoe Close Chiltern Park St Albans Hertfordshire
AL4 9JR Email: carolynn.boucher@tesco.net
See Advert on Page: 12
Timothy P Saxon, BA, AGRA
229 New Bedford Road Luton Bedfordshire LU3 1LN
Fax: 01582 727790
Email: timothy@saxonlu31ln.freeserve.co.uk
See Advert on Page: 85

Berkshire
M & P Barnes 138 Ermin Street Stratton St Margaret
Swindon Wiltshire SN3 4NQ See Advert on Page: 180

Birmingham
**Birmingham & Midland Society for Genealogy and
Heraldry**
2 Castle Croft Oldbury West Midlands B68 9BQ Email:
birmingham@terrymorter.fsnet.co.uk WWW:
www.bmsgh.org See Advert on Page: 245

Bristol
Robert J Haines, BSc. (Hons)
25 Lynch Road Berkeley Gloucestershire GL13 9TA
See Advert on Page: 99

Buckinghamshire
Mrs Carolynn Boucher
1 Ivinghoe Close Chiltern Park St Albans Hertfordshire
AL4 9JR Email: carolynn.boucher@tesco.net See Advert on
Page: 12
Victor Longhorn
53 Theydon Avenue Woburn Sands Milton Keynes MK17
8PN Email: victor.longhorn@btinternet.com
See Advert on Page: 99
Timothy P Saxon, BA, AGRA
229 New Bedford Road Luton Bedfordshire LU3 1LN
Fax: 01582 727790
Email: timothy@saxonlu31ln.freeserve.co.uk See Advert on
Page: 85
Kathleen Wilshaw, BA
The Shieling Duns Tew Oxfordshire OX25 6JS
Email: kathywilshaw@hotmail.com
 See Advert on Page: 112

Cheshire
Chris E Makepeace Local History Consultancy
5 Hilton Road Disley Cheshire SK12 2JU Fax: 01663
764910 Email: chris.makepeace@talk21.com
See Advert on Page: 44

Cumbria
Sydney G Smith
59 Friar Road Orpington Kent BR5 2BW
Email: ss.famhist@virgin.net See Advert on Page: 81

Dorset
M & P Barnes
138 Ermin Street Stratton St Margaret Swindon Wiltshire
SN3 4NQ See Advert on Page: 180

Durham
Neil W Richardson 12 Banbury Way South Beach Estate
Blyth Northumberland NE24 3TY Email:
k.richardson@ukonline.co.uk WWW:
http://www.ukonline.co.uk/northumweb/index.htm See
Advert on Page: 110

County Durham(East)
County Durham Expert &Seaham Super Index
53 Longlands Court Westbourne Grove London W11 2QF
Email: Kch66@dial.pipex.com
WWW: http://dspace.dial.pipex.com/town/street/Kch66
See Advert on Page: 12

Gloucestershire
Robert J Haines, BSc. (Hons)
25 Lynch Road Berkeley Gloucestershire GL13 9TA
Email: See Advert on Page: 99
Herefordshire Family History Research
"Rosenallis" 17 Whitefriars Road Hereford Herefordshire
HR2 7XE Email: eleanor.harris@which.net WWW:
www.herefordshireresearch.co.uk See Advert on Page: 85

Hampshire
M & P Barnes
138 Ermin Street Stratton St Margaret Swindon Wiltshire
SN3 4NQ Email: See Advert on Page: 180
Ancestral Research by Paul Lister
4 Sergison Road Haywards Heath West Sussex RH16 1HS
Email: piggleston@aol.com WWW:
http://members.aol.com/piggleston/ancestralresearch/index/h
tml See Advert on Page: 94

Herefordshire
Herefordshire Family History Research
"Rosenallis" 17 Whitefriars Road Hereford Herefordshire
HR2 7XE Email: eleanor.harris@which.net WWW:
www.herefordshireresearch.co.uk See Advert on Page: 85

Hertfordshire
Victor Longhorn
53 Theydon Avenue Woburn Sands Milton Keynes MK17
8PN Email: victor.longhorn@btinternet.com See Advert on
Page: 99
Timothy P Saxon, BA, AGRA
229 New Bedford Road Luton Bedfordshire LU3 1LN
Fax: 01582 727790
Email: timothy@saxonlu31ln.freeserve.co.uk
See Advert on Page: 85
Mrs Carolynn Boucher
1 Ivinghoe Close Chiltern Park St Albans Hertfordshire
AL4 9JR Email: carolynn.boucher@tesco.net
See Advert on Page: 12
Kent
Brickwall Research
41 Reachfields Hythe Kent CT21 6L
Email: jennifer.killick@virgin.net
WWW: www.brickwallresearch.co.uk
See Advert on Page: 99
Kent County Archives Service
Sessions House County Hall Maidstone Kent ME141XQ
Fax: 01622 694379 Email: archives@kent.gov.uk
WWW: www.kent.gov.uk/e&l/artslib/ARCHIVES/archiveshome.htm
See Advert on Page: 326
Ancestral Research by Paul Lister
4 Sergison Road Haywards Heath West Sussex RH16 1HS
Email: piggleston@aol.com
WWW: http://members.aol.com/piggleston/ancestralresearch/index/html
See Advert on Page: 94
Kin in Kent
Boundary House Stodmarsh Road Canterbury Kent CT3
4AH Fax: 01227 455267 Email: Kentkin@lineone.net See
Advert on Page: 199

Lancashire
Jane Hamby
22 St Michaels Road Preston Lancashire PR1 6LY See
Advert on Page: 10
Chris E Makepeace Local History Consultancy
5 Hilton Road Disley Cheshire SK12 2JU Fax: 01663
764910 Email: chris.makepeace@talk21.com
See Advert on Page: 44
Sydney G Smith
59 Friar Road Orpington Kent BR5 2BW
Email: ss.famhist@virgin.net See Advert on Page: 81

Leicestershire
Record Office for Leicestershire, Leicester & Rutland
Long Street Wigston Magna Leicestershire LE18 2AH
Fax: 0116-257-1120 Email: recordoffice@leics.gov.uk See
Advert on Page: 300

London
Victor Longhorn
53 Theydon Avenue Woburn Sands Milton Keynes MK17
8PN Email: victor.longhorn@btinternet.com See Advert on
Page: 99
Ancestral Research by Paul Lister
4 Sergison Road Haywards Heath West Sussex RH16 1HS
Email: piggleston@aol.com
WWW: http://members.aol.com/piggleston/ancestralresearch/index/html
See Advert on Page: 94
Timothy P Saxon, BA, AGRA
229 New Bedford Road Luton Bedfordshire LU3 1LN
Fax: 01582 727790
Email: timothy@saxonlu31ln.freeserve.co.uk
See Advert on Page: 85
Sydney G Smith
59 Friar Road Orpington Kent BR5 2BW Email:
ss.famhist@virgin.net See Advert on Page: 81
Seaham Super Index
53 Longlands Court Westbourne Grove London W11 2QF
Email: Kch66@dial.pipex.com
WWW: http://dspace.dial.pipex.com/town/street/Kch66/
See Advert on Page: 12
Rosie Taylor BA
103 Pemberton Road London N4 1AY Email:
rosietay@supanet.com See Advert on Page: 112

Manchester
Chris E Makepeace Local History Consultancy
5 Hilton Road Disley Cheshire SK12 2JU Fax: 01663
764910 Email: chris.makepeace@talk21.com See Advert on
Page: 44

Northamptonshire
Sue Comont Research Services
26 St Margaret's Avenue Rushden Northamptonshire
NN10 9YH Email: sue.comont@hotmail.com See Advert
on Page: 39

Northumberland
Neil W Richardson
12 Banbury Way South Beach Estate Blyth
Northumberland NE24 3TY Email:
k.richardson@ukonline.co.uk WWW:
http://www.ukonline.co.uk/northumweb/index.htm See
Advert on Page: 110

Nottinghamshire
David Hallam
62 Chetwynd Road Toton Nottinghamshire NG9 6FT See
Advert on Page: 110

Oxfordshire
M & P Barnes
138 Ermin Street Stratton St Margaret Swindon Wiltshire
SN3 4NQ See Advert on Page: 180
Kathleen Wilshaw, BA
The Shieling Duns Tew Oxfordshire OX25 6JS Email:
kathywilshaw@hotmail.com See Advert on Page: 112

Rutland
Record Office for Leicestershire, Leicester &Rutland
Long Street Wigston Magna Leicestershire LE18 2AH
Fax: 0116-257-1120 Email: recordoffice@leics.gov.uk See
Advert on Page: 300

Shropshire
Mrs Sue Cleaves, BSc, ALA.
3 Gilbert Close Newport Shropshire TF10 7UU Fax:
01952 812060 Email: suecleaves@care4free.net See Advert
on Page: 30

Staffordshire
Birmingham & Midland Society for Genealogy and Heraldry
2 Castle Croft Oldbury West Midlands B68 9BQ Email: birmingham@terrymorter.fsnet.co.uk WWW: www.bmsgh.org See Advert on Page: 245
Mrs Sue Cleaves, BSc, ALA.
3 Gilbert Close Newport Shropshire TF10 7UU Fax: 01952 812060 Email: suecleaves@care4free.net See Advert on Page: 30

Surrey
Ancestral Research by Paul Lister
4 Sergison Road Haywards Heath West Sussex RH16 1HS Email: piggleston@aol.com WWW: http://members.aol.com/piggleston/ancestralresearch/index/html See Advert on Page: 94

Sussex
Ancestral Research by Paul Lister
4 Sergison Road Haywards Heath West Sussex RH16 1HS Email: piggleston@aol.com
WWW: http://members.aol.com/piggleston/ancestralresearch/index/html
See Advert on Page: 94

Warwickshire
Birmingham & Midland Society for Genealogy and Heraldry
2 Castle Croft Oldbury West Midlands B68 9BQ Email: birmingham@terrymorter.fsnet.co.uk WWW: www.bmsgh.org See Advert on Page: 245
Kathleen Wilshaw, BA
The Shieling Duns Tew Oxfordshire OX25 6JS Email: kathywilshaw@hotmail.com See Advert on Page:112

Westmorland
Sydney G Smith
59 Friar Road Orpington Kent BR5 2BW Email: ss.famhist@virgin.net See Advert on Page: 81

West Sussex
West Sussex Record Office
County Hall
Chichester West Sussex PO19 1RN Fax: 01243-533959
Email: records.office@westsussex.gov.uk
WWW: www.westsussex.gov.uk/cs/ro/rohome.htm
See Advert on Page: 326

Wiltshire
M & P Barnes
138 Ermin Street Stratton St Margaret Swindon Wiltshire SN3 4NQ See Advert on Page: 180
Worcestershire
Birmingham & Midland Society for Genealogy and Heraldry
2 Castle Croft Oldbury West Midlands B68 9BQ Email: birmingham@terrymorter.fsnet.co.uk
WWW: www.bmsgh.org See Advert on Page: 245
Herefordshire Family History Research
"Rosenallis" 17 Whitefriars Road Hereford HR2 7XE
Email: eleanor.harris@which.net
WWW: www.herefordshireresearch.co.uk
See Advert on Page: 85

Yorkshire - North
yorkshireancestors.com
Studley House Farm 67 Main Street Ebberston Scarborough North Yorkshire YO13 9NR Fax: 01723 859285 Email: brenda@yorkshireancestors.com WWW: http://www.yorkshireancestors.com See Advert on Page: 201

Yorkshire
Derwent Communications
Riversdale House 7 Church Street Bubwith East Riding of Yorkshire YO8 6LW Fax: 01757 288313 Email: rogerwitt@derwentpr.co.uk See Advert on Page: 21
Hull Central Library Family and Local History Club
Central Library Albion Street Kingston upon Hull HU1 3TF Fax: 01482 616827 Email: gareth2ukorigins.co.uk WWW: http://www.hullcc.gov.uk/genealogy See Advert on

Page: 12
M R Pickard
76 Conference Road Armley Leeds West Yorkshire LS12 3DX Tel: 07887 563657 Fax: 0113 263 6198 See Advert on Page: 21
www.yorksgenresearch.com
36 Kirkwood Way Cookridge Leeds West Yorkshire LS16 7EX Email: CBuck785@aol.com WWW: http://members.aol.com/cbuck785/postcardindex.htm See Advert on Page: 17
Yorkshire
Yorkshire Family History - Biographical Database
York Minster Library & Archives Dean's Park York Yorkshire YO1 7JQ Tel: 01904-611118 Archives Fax: 01904-611119 Email: library@yorkminster.org archives@yorkminster.org WWW: www.yorkminster.org See Advert on Page: 292

Wales
Association of Genealogists & Researchers in Archives
29 Badgers Close Horsham West Sussex RH12 5RU Email: agra@agra.org.uk WWW: www.agra.org.uk See Advert on Page: 18
CARW
4 Rhodfa Anwyl Rhuddlan Denbighshire LL18 2SQ Email: DThomas715@aol.com See Advert on Page: 128
Welsh Genealogy Holidays
Snowdonia Holidays Limited Plas Blaenddol Llan Ffestiniog Gwynedd LL41 4PH Fax: 01766 762796 Email: welshroots@snowdonia-holidays.co.uk WWW: www.welshroots.com See Advert on Page: 131

Scotland
John Adams Genealogical Research
8 North Gardner Street Partickhill Glasgow G11 5BT Tel: 0141 334 1021 Email: jadams@primex.co.uk See Advert on Page: 135
CO LEIS THU? Research Centre
Seallam! Visitor Centre Northton (Taobh Tuath) Isle of Harris HS3 3JA Tel: 01859 520488 (Home) Fax: 01859 520258 Email: lawsonbill@cs.com WWW: www.seallam.com See Advert on Page: 135
First Scottish Searching Services Limited
Bonnington Bond Anderson Place Edinburgh EH6 5NP Fax: 0131-554-6006 Email: fss@btinternet.com See Advert on Page: 135
Leslie Hodgson
5 St Stephen Place Edinburgh EH3 5AJ Scotland Tel: 0131 225 2723 See Advert on Page: 136
Scots Ancestry Research Society
8 York Road Edinburgh EH5 3EH Fax: 0131 5522028 Email: scotsanc@aol.com
WWW: http://www.royalmile.com/scotsancestry
See Advert on Page: 135
Scottish Family History Research Service
Flat B The Lodge 2 East Road North Berwick EH39 4HN Fax: 01620 894672 Email: wbigwood@compuserve.com See Advert on Page: 142
Scottish Roots
16 Forth Street Edinburgh EH1 3LH Fax: 0131-550-3701 Email: stuart@scottish.roots.co.uk WWW: http://www.scottish-roots.co.uk See Advert on Page: 135

Northern Ireland
Banbridge Genealogy Services
Gateway Tourist Information Centre 200 Newry Road Banbridge County Down BT32 3NB Northern Ireland Fax: 028 4062 3114 Email: banbridge@nitic.net See Advert on Page: 156
Historical Research Associates
Glen Cottage Glenmachan Road Belfast BT4 2NP Northern Ireland Tel: (028) 9368502 See Advert on Page: 148
Ulster Historical Foundation
Balmoral Buildings 12 College Square East Belfast BT1 6DD Northern Ireland Fax: 028 9023 9885 Email: enquiry@uhf.org.uk & andrew@uhf.org.uk WWW:

http://www.uhf.org.uk
www.ancestryireland.com See Advert on Page: 150

Ireland
Eneclann - Irish Research
Unit 1 Trinity College Enterprise Centre Pearse Street
Dublin 2 Ireland Fax: +353 1 671 0281 Email:
genealogy@eneclann.ie WWW: www.eneclann.ie See Advert
on Page: 150
Historical Research Associates
Glen Cottage Glenmachan Road Belfast BT4 2NP
Northern Ireland Tel: (028) 9368502 See Advert on Page:
148
Mary P. McConnon M.A. - MC Research Service
Seabank Castlebellingham Dundalk County Louth Ireland
Fax: +353-42-9372046 Email: mcres@iol.ie WWW:
www.mc-research.com See Advert on Page: 154
Angela Murphy LRPS
4 Nutley Park Donnybrook Dublin 4 Ireland Email:
angelamurphy@oceanfree.net See Advert on Page: 149
Ulster Historical Foundation
Balmoral Buildings 12 College Square East Belfast BT1
6DD Northern Ireland Fax: 028 9023 9885 Email:
enquiry@uhf.org.uk & andrew@uhf.org.uk WWW:
http://www.uhf.org.uk www.ancestryireland.com See Advert
on Page: 150

Australia
Genealogical Society of Victoria
Ancestor House 179 Queen Street Melbourne 3000
Victoria Australia Fax: +61-03-9670-449
 Email: gsv@gsv.org.au WWW: www.gsv.org.a
 See Advert on Page: 258
Worthington Clark PTY Ltd
PO Box 161 Lane Cove New South Wales 1595 Australia
Fax: +(612)-9428-4242 Email:
jworth@worthclark.bu.aust.com See Advert on Page: 21

New Zealand
Worthington Clark PTY Ltd
PO Box 161 Lane Cove New South Wales 1595 Australia
Fax: +(612)-9428-4242 Email:
jworth@worthclark.bu.aust.com See Advert on Page: 21

Local History Research

England
Cheshire, Lancashire & Manchester
Chris E Makepeace Local History Consultancy
5 Hilton Road Disley Cheshire SK12 2JU Fax: 01663
764910 Email: chris.makepeace@talk21.com See Advert on
Page: 44

Scotland
Rosemary Philip
15 Beresford Gardens Edinburgh EH5 3ER Scotland
Email: rsmry@philip63.freeserve.co.uk See Advert on Page:
135

Specialist Subjects

Clothing
Identify Your Ancestors Through Their Clothing
100 Chester Terrace Brighton East Sussex BN1 6GD
Email: Jayneshrimpton@photographdating.freeserve.co.uk
WWW: www.photographdating.freeserve.co.uk See Advert
on Page: 10

Criminal & Convicts
**Black Sheep Research (Machine Breakers, Rioters &
Protesters)**
4 Quills Letchworth Garden City Hertfordshire SG6 2RJ
Email: J_M_Chambers@compuserve.com See Advert on
Page: 21

Durham Coalfield
Seaham Super Index
53 Longlands Court Westbourne Grove London W11 2QF
Email: Kch66@dial.pipex.com WWW:
http://dspace.dial.pipex.com/town/street/Kch66/ See Advert
on Page: 12

Emigration & Immmigration
Hull Central Library Family and Local History Club
Central Library Albion Street Kingston upon Hull HU1
3TF Fax: 01482 616827 Email: gareth2ukorigins.co.uk
WWW: http://www.hullcc.gov.uk/genealogy See Advert on
Page: 12

Fine Art Picture Research
Timothy P Saxon, BA, AGRA
229 New Bedford Road Luton Bedfordshire LU3 1LN
Fax: 01582 727790 Email:
timothy@saxonlu31ln.freeserve.co.uk
See Advert on Page: 85

Machine Breakers & Rioters
**Black Sheep Research (Machine Breakers, Rioters &
Protesters)**
4 Quills Letchworth Garden City Hertfordshire SG6 2RJ
Email: J_M_Chambers@compuserve.com See Advert on
Page: 21

Maritime
Len Barnett Research
22 Park Avenue South Hornsey London N8 8LT Email:
lenny@barnettresearch.freeserve.com.uk
WWW: www.barnettresearch.freeserve.co.uk
See Advert on Page: 75
National Maritime Museum
Romney Road Greenwich London London SE10 9NF
Fax: (020) 8312-6632 Email: WWW:
http://www.nmm.ac.uk See Advert on Page: 39
David L Williams
7 Buckbury Heights Newport Isle of Wight PO30 2LX
Email: david@genpix.fsnet.co.uk See Advert on Page: 112

Mariners / Seamen
Len Barnett Research
22 Park Avenue South Hornsey London N8 8LT Email:
lenny@barnettresearch.freeserve.com.uk WWW:
www.barnettresearch.freeserve.co.uk See Advert on Page: 75
CARW 4 Rhodfa Anwyl Rhuddlan Denbighshire LL18
2SQ Wales Email: DThomas715@aol.com
See Advert on Page: 128

Military
**David J Barnes (Military & Aviation Research 1914 -
1919)**
148 Parkinson Street Burnley Lancashire BB11 3LL See
Advert on Page: 241
Bartletts Battlefield Tours
Broomhill Edlington Horncastle Lincolnshire LN9 5RJ
Fax: 01507-523130 Email: info@battlefields.co.uk WWW:
www.battlefields.co.uk See Advert on Page: 242
Border Regiment & Kings Own Royal Border Regiment Museum
Queen Mary's Tower The Castle Carlisle Cumbria CA3
8UR Fax: 01228-521275 Email:
rhq@kingsownborder.demon.co.uk See Advert on Page: 242
Cross & Cockade International
The First World War Aviation Historical Society
5 Cave Drive Downend Bristol BS16 2TL WWW:
www.crossandcockade.com See Advert on Page: 240
Holts Tours Ltd Battlefields and History
Golden Key Building 15 Market Street Sandwick Kent
CT13 9DA Tel: 01932 242011 (Home) Fax: 01304 614930
Email: info@holts.co.uk WWW:
http://www.battletours.co.uk See Advert on Page: 243
Lest We Forget
30 Coniston Road Coulsdon Surrey CR5 3BS Email:
drkevin@blueyonder.co.uk See Advert on Page: 230
National Maritime Museum
Romney Road Greenwich London London SE10 9NF
Fax: (020) 8312-6632 WWW: http://www.nmm.ac.uk See

Advert on Page: 39

Murder Files
Murder Files
81 Churchfields Drive Bovey Tracy Devon TQ13 9QU
Fax: 01626-835797 Email: enquiry@murderfiles.com
WWW: www.murderfiles.com See Advert on Page: 24

Napoleonic Wars
1st or Grenadier Foot Guards & Other Regiments
39 Chatterton Letchworth Garden City Hertfordshire SG6
2JY Email:
http://members.aol.com/bjcham2809/homepage.html See
Advert on Page: 241

Newspaper Library
Colin Dale Researches (GSD)
1 Furham Field Pinner Middlesex HA5 4DX
 See Advert on Page: 99

Railway Employees
CARW
4 Rhodfa Anwyl Rhuddlan Denbighshire LL18 2SQ
Wales Email: DThomas715@aol.com See Advert on Page:
128

Records of the Tower
Records of the Tower
PO Box 2884 Westbury BA13 3WE
Email: tcr@records-of-the-tower.co.uk
WWW: www.records-of-the-tower.co.uk See Advert on
Page: 61

Support Services

Accommodation
Ashley Hotel
15 - 17 Norfolk Square Hyde Park London W2 1RU Fax:
(020) 7723 0173 Email: ashhot@btinternet.com WWW:
www.ashleyhotels.com See Advert on Page: 75
yorkshireancestors.com
Studley House Farm 67 Main Street Ebberston
Scarborough North Yorkshire YO13 9NR Fax: 01723
859285 Email: brenda@yorkshireancestors.com WWW:
http://www.yorkshireancestors.com See Advert on Page: 201
www.hotelstruro.com
Marcorrie Hotel : Brookdale Hotel 20 Falmouth Road :
Tregolls Road Truro Cornwall TR1 2HX : TR1 1JZ Tel:
01872 273513 Brookdale Hotel Fax: 01872-241666 and
01872 272400 Email: marcorrie@aol.com
brookdale@hotelstruro.com WWW: www.hotelstruro.com
See Advert on Page: 202
Welsh Genealogy Holidays
Snowdonia Holidays Limited Plas Blaenddol Llan
Ffestiniog Gwynedd LL41 4PH Wales Fax: 01766 762796
Email: welshroots@snowdonia-holidays.co.uk WWW:
www.welshroots.com See Advert on Page: 131

Armorial & Heraldry
Achievements (Est 1961)
Centre for Heraldic & Genealogical Research and Artwork
79 - 82 Northgate Canterbury Kent CT1 1BA Fax: 01227
765617 Email: achievements@achievements.co.uk WWW:
www.achievements.co.uk See Advert on Page: 53
Marie Lynskey
109 Nutcroft Grove Fetcham Surrey KT22 9LD Fax:
01372-372334 Email: ml@clara.net WWW:
http://www.ml.clara.net See Advert on Page: 39
The Name Shop
20 Barnes Wallis Drive Leegomery Telford Shropshire
TF1 4XT Fax: 01952 410689 Email:
gary.huston@cableinet.co.uk WWW: http://www.family-
name.co.uk/history See Advert on Page: 125

Battlefield Tours
Bartletts Battlefield Tours
Broomhill Edlington Horncastle Lincolnshire LN9 5RJ
Fax: 01507-523130 Email: info@battlefields.co.uk WWW:

www.battlefields.co.uk See Advert on Page: 242
Holts Tours Ltd Battlefields and History
Golden Key Building 15 Market Street Sandwich Kent
CT13 9DA Tel: 01932 242011 (Home) Fax: 01304 614930
Email: info@holts.co.uk WWW:
http://www.battletours.co.uk See Advert on Page: 243

Book Sales & Supply
Aberdeen & N E Scotland Family History Society
164 King Street Aberdeen AB24 5BD Scotland Fax:
01224-639096 Email: enquiries@anefhs.org.uk WWW:
http://www.anesfhs.org.uk See Advert on Page: 253
ABM Publishing Ltd
61 Great Whyte Ramsey Huntington Cambridgeshire
PE26 1HJ Fax: 01487-711361 Email: family-tree-
magazine@mcmail.com WWW: www.family-tree-
magazine.co.uk See Advert on Page: 65 & 89
Back to Roots Family History Service
16 Arrowsmith Drive Stonehouse Gloucestershire GL10
2QR Email: mike@backtoroots.co.uk WWW:
http://www.backtoroots.co.uk See Advert on Page:416 &
IBC
M & P Barnes
138 Ermin Street Stratton St Margaret Swindon Wiltshire
SN3 4NQ See Advert on Page: 180
British Association for Local History
PO Box 1576 Salisbury SP2 8SY Fax: 01722-413242
Email: WWW: www.balh.co.uk See Advert on Page: IFC &
161
Federation of Family History Societies Publications Ltd
Units 15 & 16 Chesham Industrial Estate Oram Street Bury
Lancashire BL9 6EN Fax: 0161 797 3846
Email: sales@ffhs.org.uk
WWW: www.familyhistorybooks.co.uk
See Advert on Page: 159
GENfair
9 Fairstone Hill Oadby Leicestershire LE2 5RL Email:
info@genfair.com
WWW: www.genfair.comSee Advert on Page: 18
Genealogical Society of Victoria
Ancestor House 179 Queen Street Melbourne 3000
Victoria Australia Fax: +61-03-9670-4490
Email: gsv@gsv.org.au WWW: www.gsv.org.au
See Advert on Page: 258
Gould Books
PO Box 126 Gumeracha South Australia 5233 Australia
Tel: +61 8 8389 1611 Fax: 08 8389 1599 Email:
gould@adelaide.on..net WWW: http://www.gould.com.au
See Advert on Page: 139
Interlink Bookshop & Genealogical Services - Interlink
Bookshop 1505 Fell Street Victoria British Columbia
V8N 4G2 Canada Fax: 250-595-2495
Email: ibgs@interlinkbookshop.com
WWW: http://www.InterlinkBookshop.com
See Advert on Page: 53
Institute of Heraldic and Genealogical Studies
79 - 82 Northgate Canterbury Kent CT1 1BA Fax: 01227-
765617 Email: ihgs@ihgs.ac.uk WWW: www.ihgs.ac.uk See
Advert on Page: 13
Chris E Makepeace Local History Consultancy
5 Hilton Road Disley Cheshire SK12 2JU Fax: 01663
764910 Email: chris.makepeace@talk21.com
See Advert on Page: 44
National Maritime Museum
Romney Road Greenwich London London SE10 9NF
Fax: (020) 8312-6632 Email: WWW:
http://www.nmm.ac.uk See Advert on Page: 39
Public Record Office Book Shop
Ruskin Avenue Kew Richmond Surrey TW9 4DU Fax:
(020) 8392 5266 Email: bookshop@pro.gov.uk WWW:
http://www.pro.gov.uk/ See Advert on Page: 59
S.A. & M.J. Raymond
PO Box 35 Exeter Devon EX1 3YZ
Email: stuart@samjraymond.softnet.co.uk
WWW: www.soft.net.uk/samjraymond/igb.htm See Advert
on Page: 289, 373 & 375

Sessions of York
Ebor Press Division Huntington Road York YO3 9HS Fax:
01904-637068 Email: ebor.info@sessionsof york.co.uk
WWW: www.sessionsofyork.co.uk
See Advert on Page: 94

Society of Genealogists Enterprises Ltd 14 Charterhouse
Buildings Goswell Road London EC1M 7BA Tel; 020
7253 5235 Email; sales@sog.org.uk Website & Bookshop;
www.sog.org.uk
See Advert on Page: 203 & 415

S & N Genealogy Supplies
Greenacres Salisbury Road Chilmark Salisbury Wiltshire
SP3 5AH Fax: 01722 716160 Email:
100064.737@compuserve.com WWW:
http://www.genealogy.demon.co.uk See Advert on Page: 4

Stepping Stones
PO Box 295 York YO31 1YS Email:
jud@mjudson.freeserve.co.uk422351 WWW:
http://www.stepping-stones.co.uk See Advert on Page: 56

Sutton Publishing
Phoenix Mill Thrupp Stroud Gloucestershire GL5 2BU
Fax: 01453 731117 Email: sales@sutton-publishing.co.uk
See Advert on Page: 160

Computing
Back to Roots Family History Service
16 Arrowsmith Drive Stonehouse Gloucestershire GL10
2QR Email: mike@backtoroots.co.uk
WWW: http://www.backtoroots.co.uk See Advert on Page:
416 & IBC

GENfair
9 Fairstone Hill Oadby Leicestershire LE2 5R
 Email: info@genfair.com WWW: www.genfair.com See
Advert on Page: 18

Gensearch
7 Victoria Place Lymington Hampshire SO41 3TD Email:
john@gensearch.co.uk
WWW: www.gensearch.co.uk See Advert on Page: 85

Gould Books
PO Box 126 Gumeracha South Australia 5233 Australia
Tel: +61 8 8389 1611 Fax: 08 8389 1599 Email:
gould@adelaide.on..net
WWW: http://www.gould.com.au See Advert on Page: 139

Custodian - P A & S Smith
PO Box 180 2 Church Cottages Bishopstone Hereford
HR4 7YP Tel: 07801 503144 Email: PandSSmith@aol.com
WWW: www.custodian2.co.uk See Advert on Page: 24

Stepping Stones
PO Box 295 York YO31 1YS
Email: jud@mjudson.freeserve.co.uk422351
WWW: http://www.stepping-stones.co.uk
See Advert on Page: 56

S & N Genealogy Supplies
Greenacres Salisbury Road Chilmark Salisbury Wiltshire
SP3 5AH Fax: 01722 716160 Email:
100064.737@compuserve.com WWW:
http://www.genealogy.demon.co.uk See Advert on Page: 4

Generations Family Tree
Sierra Home ' Generations' 2 Beacontree Plaza Gillette
Way Reading Berkshire RG2 0BS
Email: info@vvp-interactive.co.uk
WWW: www.sierra-online.co.uk See Advert on Page: 102

yorkshireancestors.com
Studley House Farm 67 Main Street Ebberston
Scarborough North Yorkshire YO13 9NR Fax: 01723
859285 Email: brenda@yorkshireancestors.com WWW:
http://www.yorkshireancestors.com See Advert on Page: 201

Date by Clothing Service
Identify Your Ancestors Through Their Clothing
100 Chester Terrace Brighton East Sussex BN1 6GD
Email: Jayneshrimpton@photographdating.freeserve.co.uk
WWW: www.photographdating.freeserve.co.uk See Advert
on Page: 10

Education & Courses
Institute of Heraldic and Genealogical Studies
79 - 82 Northgate Canterbury Kent CT1 1BA Fax: 01227-
765617 Email: ihgs@ihgs.ac.uk WWW: www.ihgs.ac.uk See
Advert on Page: 13

Scottish Family History Research Service
Flat B The Lodge 2 East Road North Berwick EH39 4HN
Scotland Fax: 01620 894672 Email:
wbigwood@compuserve.com See Advert on Page: 142

Family History Fairs
Yorkshire Coast Family History Fair
90 Prospect Road Scarborough North Yorkshire YO12 7JY
Email: greenfairs@scarborough-1.fsnet.co.uk See Advert on
Page: 412

Family History Fairs
5 Cottesmore Hanworth Bracknall Berkshire RG12 7YL
Email: Fhfairs@aol.com WWW:
www.3w.co.uk/familyhistoryfairs See Advert on Page: 408

Keighley & District Family History Society
2 The Hallows Shann Park Keighley West Yorkshire
BD20 6HY See Advert on Page: 248

Northern Family History Fairs
206 Moseley Wood Gardens Leeds West Yorkshire LS16
7JE Email: stanley@nfhistoryfairs.co.uk WWW:
nfhistoryfairs.co.uk See Advert on Page: 408

North West Group of FHS Family History Fairs
North West Group of Family History Societies 4 Lawrence
Avenue Simonstone Burnley Lancashire BB12 7HX
Email: ed@gull66.freeserve.co.uk
See Advert on Page: 411

West Yorkshire Archive Service
Registry of Deeds Newstead Road Wakefield West
Yorkshire WF1 2DE Fax: 01924-305983
Email: hq@wyashq.demon.co.uk WWW:
http://www.archives.wyjs.org.uk See Advert on Page: 409

Yorkshire Family History Fair
1 Oxgang Close Redcar Cleveland TS10 4ND Fax: 01642-
486615 See Advert on Page: 410

House Histories
Achievements (Est 1961)
Centre for Heraldic & Genealogical Research and Artwork
79 - 82 Northgate Canterbury Kent CT1 1BA Fax: 01227
765617 Email: achievements@achievements.co.uk WWW:
www.achievements.co.uk See Advert on Page: 53

Derwent Communications
Riversdale House 7 Church Street Bubwith East Riding of
Yorkshire YO8 6LW Fax: 01757 288313 Email:
rogerwitt@derwentpr.co.uk See Advert on Page: 21

Insurance
British Association for Local History
PO Box 1576 Salisbury SP2 8SY Fax: 01722-413242
Email: WWW: www.balh.co.uk See Advert on Page: IFC &
161

Location Photography
Angela Murphy LRPS 4 Nutley Park Donnybrook
Dublin 4 Ireland Email: angelamurphy@oceanfree.net See
Advert on Page: 149

Magazines & Periodicals
**ABM Publishing Ltd - Family Tree Magazine &
Practical Family History**
61 Great Whyte Ramsey Huntington Cambridgeshire
PE26 1HJ Fax: 01487-71136
 Email: family-tree-magazine@mcmail.com
WWW: www.family-tree-magazine.co.uk
See Advert on Page: 65 & 89

Diamond Publishing Group - Family History Monthly
45 St Mary's Road Ealing London W5 5RQ
See Advert on Page: 31

Irish Roots
Belgrave Publications Belgrave Avenue Cork Co Cork
Ireland Fax: 021 4500067 Email: irish@iol.ie
WWW: http://www.iol.ie/~irishrts See Advert on Page: 150

Ancestors Magazine
Public Record Office Ruskin Avenue Kew Richmond
Surrey TW9 4DU Fax: (020) 8392 5266
Email: bookshop@pro.gov.uk
WWW: http://www.pro.gov.uk/ See Advert on Page: 59
Family Chronicle Magazine
PO Box 1111, Niagara Falls NY 14092-1111 USA WWW:
http://www.familychronicle.com See Advert on Page: 49
Local History Press Limited
3 Devonshire Promenade Lenton Nottingham
Nottinghamshire NG7 2DS Fax: 0115 970 5237 Email:
editors@local-history.co.uk WWW: http://www.local-
history.co.uk See Advert on Page: 376
Old Yorkshire Magazine
111 Wrenbeck Drive Otley West Yorkshire LS21 2BP Fax:
01943 464702 Email: brian@oldyorkshire.co.uk WWW:
www.oldyorkshire.co.uk See Advert on Page: 336

Military Uniform Identification
David J Barnes (Military & Aviation Research 1914 - 1919)
148 Parkinson Street Burnley Lancashire BB11 3LL
 See Advert on Page: 241

Postcards
Old Picture Postcards
9 St Swithins Walk Holgate York YO26 4UG Email:
postcardsuk@yahoo.co.uk See Advert on Page: 290
Picture Past
47 Manor House Park Codsall Staffordshire WV8 1ES
 See Advert on Page: 322
Postcard Index
36 Kirkwood Way Cookridge Leeds West Yorkshire LS16
7EX Email: CBuck785@aol.com WWW:
http://members.aol.com/cbuck785/postcardindex.htm See
Advert on Page: 373

Published Material
**Black Sheep Research (Machine Breakers, Rioters &
Protesters)**
4 Quills Letchworth Garden City Hertfordshire SG6 2RJ
Email: J_M_Chambers@compuserve.com See Advert on
Page: 21
Cottage Books
The Cottage Gelsmoor Coleorton Leicester Leicestershire
LE67 8HR See Advert on Page: 172
Eneclann - Irish Research
Unit 1 Trinity College Enterprise Centre Pearse Street
Dublin 2 Ireland Fax: +353 1 671 0281 Email:
genealogy@eneclann.ie WWW: www.eneclann.ie See
Advert on Page: 150
Federation of Family History Societies Publications Ltd
Units 15 & 16 Chesham Industrial Estate Oram Street Bury
Lancashire BL9 6EN Fax: 0161 797 3846 Email:
sales@ffhs.org.uk WWW: www.familyhistorybooks.co.uk
See Advert on Page: 159
Gensearch
7 Victoria Place Lymington Hampshire SO41 3TD Email:
john@gensearch.co.uk WWW: www.gensearch.co.uk See
Advert on Page: 85
Local History Press Limited
3 Devonshire Promenade Lenton Nottingham
Nottinghamshire NG7 2DS Fax: 0115 970 5237 Email:
editors@local-history.co.uk WWW: http://www.local-
history.co.uk See Advert on Page: 376
Chris E Makepeace Local History Consultancy
5 Hilton Road Disley Cheshire SK12 2JU Fax: 01663
764910 Email: chris.makepeace@talk21.com See Advert
on Page: 44
Mapped Out
Applecross Cicelyford Trellech Monmouthshire NP25
4PT Wales Tel: 01600 860521 Fax: 01600 860521 Email:
sales@allmappedout.com WWW: www.allmappedout.com
See Advert on Page: 175
MM Publications
The White Cottage The Street Lidgate Near Newmarket
Suffolk CB8 9PP Fax: 01638 500777 Email:
michael@mmpublications.softnet.co.uk

WWW: www.mmpublications.co.uk See Advert on Page:375
Murder Files
81 Churchfields Drive Bovey Tracy Devon TQ13 9QU
Fax: 01626-835797 Email: enquiry@murderfiles.com
WWW: www.murderfiles.com See Advert on Page: 24
Northern Writers Advisory Services
77 Marford Crescent Sale Cheshire M33 4DN Email:
grovesjill@aol.com See Advert on Page: 184
Postcard Index
36 Kirkwood Way Cookridge Leeds West Yorkshire LS16
7EX Email: CBuck785@aol.com WWW:
http://members.aol.com/cbuck785/postcardindex.htm See
Advert on Page: 373
S.A. & M.J. Raymond
PO Box 35 Exeter Devon EX1 3YZ
Email: stuart@samjraymond.softnet.co.uk
WWW: www.soft.net.uk/samjraymond/igb.htm See Advert
on Page: 289
Sessions of York
Ebor Press Division Huntington Road York YO3 9HS Fax:
01904-637068 Email: ebor.info@sessionsof york.co.uk
WWW: www.sessionsofyork.co.uk
See Advert on Page: 94
Stepping Stones
PO Box 295 York YO31 1YS
Email: jud@mjudson.freeserve.co.uk422351
WWW: http://www.stepping-stones.co.uk
See Advert on Page: 56
yorkshireancestors.com
Studley House Farm 67 Main Street Ebberston
Scarborough North Yorkshire YO13 9NR Fax: 01723
859285 Email: brenda@yorkshireancestors.com WWW:
http://www.yorkshireancestors.com See Advert on Page: 201
Wiltshire Index Service
11 Ardmore Close Tuffley Gloucester Gloucestershire
GL4 0BJ WWW wiltshireancestors.co.uk See Advert on
Page: 44

Microfiche & Microfilm
Marathon Microfilming Ltd
27-29 St Mary's Place Southampton SO14 3HY Fax: 023
80 230452
Email: sales@marathon-microfilm-cdrom.co.uk
WWW: www.marathon-microfilm-cdrom.co.uk
See Advert on Page: 42
Mercury Visuals
426 Flixton Road Flixton Manchester M41 6QT
mercvis@lineone.net See Advert on Page: 199
Microfilm Shop
Hammond Close Nuneaton Warwickshire CV11 6RY Fax:
024-7638-2319 Email: sales@microfilm.com WWW:
http://www.microfilm.com See Advert on Page: 64
M W Microfilm Supplies
18 Watling Place Houghton Regis Dunstable Bedfordshire
LU5 5DP Fax: 01582 867045 Email: margaret@mw-
microfilm.co.uk WWW: www.mw-microfilm.co.uk See
Advert on Page: 24

Presentation Services
Allen & Todd
9-11 Square Street Ramsbottom Bury Lancashire BL0
9BE Fax: 01706 827988 See Advert on Page: 180
APC Clothing
Unit 6A Guardian Park Station Road Industrial Estate
Tadcaster North Yorkshire LS24 9SG Fax: 01937 832649
Email: sales@apc-clothing.co.uk See Advert on Page: 409
Marie Lynskey
109 Nutcroft Grove Fetcham Surrey KT22 9LD Fax:
01372-372334 Email: ml@clara.net WWW:
http://www.ml.clara.net See Advert on Page: 39
The Name Shop
20 Barnes Wallis Drive Leegomery Telford Shropshire
TF1 4XT Fax: 01952 410689 Email:
gary.huston@cableinet.co.uk WWW: http://www.family-
name.co.uk/history See Advert on Page: 125
CW & S Parkinson
16 Foxhills Close Ashurst Southampton Hampshire SO40

7ER Email: cws@sirdar.demon.co.uk WWW:
http://www.sirdar.demon.co.uk/cws/ See Advert on Page: 199
Secol Limited Howlett Way Thetford Norfolk IP24 1HZ
See Advert on Page: 81

Plans & Maps
Gould Books
PO Box 126 Gumeracha South Australia 5233 Australia
Tel: +61 8 8389 1611 Fax: 08 8389 1599 Email:
gould@adelaide.on..net WWW: http://www.gould.com.au
See Advert on Page: 139
Chris E Makepeace Local History Consultancy
5 Hilton Road Disley Cheshire SK12 2JU Fax: 01663
764910 Email: chris.makepeace@talk21.com See Advert on
Page: 44
Mapped Out
Applecross Cicelyford Trellech Monmouthshire NP25
4PT Wales Tel: 01600 860521 Fax: 01600 860521 Email:
sales@allmappedout.com WWW: www.allmappedout.com
See Advert on Page: 175

Printing Services
AWP
718 Ripponden Road Oldham Lancashire OL4 2LP
WWW: www.awpdigital.co.uk See Advert on Page: 413
Parchment Oxford Limited
Printworks Crescent Road Cowley Oxford Oxfordshire
OX4 2PB Fax: 01865 747551 Email: parch2000@cs.com
WWW: www.PrintUK.com See Advert on Page: 68

Private Investigations
Link Investigations
296 High Street Dorking Surrey RH4 1PN Fax: 01306-
888077 Email: info@linkinvestigations.co.uk WWW:
http://www.linkinvestigations.co.uk See Advert on Page: 17

Promotional Clothing & Corporate Wear
APC Clothing
Unit 6A Guardian Park Station Road Industrial Estate
Tadcaster North Yorkshire LS24 9SG Fax: 01937 832649
Email: sales@apc-clothing.co.uk See Advert on Page: 409

Publications

England

Federation of Family History Societies
PO Box 2425 Coventry CV5 6YX Fax: 01564 703100
Email: admin@ffhs.org.uk See Advert on Page: 6
Birmingham
**Birmingham & Midland Society for Genealogy and
Heraldry**
2 Castle Croft Oldbury West Midlands B68 9BQ
birmingham@terrymorter.fsnet.co.uk WWW:
www.bmsgh.org See Advert on Page: 245

Cheshire
North Cheshire Family History Society
2 Denham Drive Bramhall Stockport Cheshire SK7 2AT
Email: roger@demercado.demon.co.uk
WWW:
http://www.genuki.org.uk/big/eng/CHS/NorthChesFHS See
Advert on Page: 251
Northern Writers Advisory Services
77 Marford Crescent Sale Cheshire M33 4DN
grovesjill@aol.com See Advert on Page: 184

Cleveland
Cleveland Family History Society
1 Oxgang Close Redcar Cleveland TS10 4ND Fax: 01642
486615 See Advert on Page: 248

Cornwall
Cornwall Family History Society
5 Victoria Square Truro Cornwall TR1 2RS Email:
secretary@cornwallfhs.com WWW:
http://www.cornwallfhs.com See Advert on Page: 251

Cumbria, Cumberland
Cumbria Family History Society
"Ulpha" 32 Granada Road Denton Manchester M34 2LJ
WWW:
http://www.genuki/big/eng/CUL/cumbFHS/membership.html
See Advert on Page: 252

Derbyshire
Derbyshire Family History Society
Bridge Chapel House St Mary's Bridge Sowter Road
Derby Derbyshire DE1 3AT WWW: www.dfhs.org.uk See
Advert on Page: 245

Dorset
Somerset & Dorset Family History Society
PO Box 4052 Sherborne Dorset DH9 6YL Fax: 01935
389611 Email: society@sdfhs.org WWW: www.sdfhs.org
See Advert on Page: 250

Durham
Cleveland Family History Society
1 Oxgang Close Redcar Cleveland TS10 4ND Fax: 01642
486615 See Advert on Page: 248

Essex
Essex Society for Family History
Research Centre, Essex Record Office Wharf Road
Chelmsford Essex CM2 6YT Email: secretary@esfh.org.uk
WWW: www.esfh.org.uk See Advert on Page: 409

Herefordshire
Herefordshire Family History Society
6 Birch Meadow Gosmore Road Clehonger Hereford
Herefordshire HR2 9RH Email: prosser_brian@hotmail.com
WWW: www.roortsweb.com~ukhfhs See Advert on Page:
252

Lancashire
Manchester and Lancashire Family History Society
Clayton House 59 Piccadilly Manchester M1 2AQ Fax:
0161-237-3512 Email: office@mlfhs.demon.co.uk WWW:
www.mlfhs.demon.co.uk See Advert on Page: 252
Lancashire - North
Cumbria Family History Society
"Ulpha" 32 Granada Road Denton Manchester M34 2LJ
WWW:
http://www.genuki/big/eng/CUL/cumbFHS/membership.html
See Advert on Page: 252

Manchester
Manchester and Lancashire Family History Society
Clayton House 59 Piccadilly Manchester M1 2AQ Fax:
0161-237-3512 Email: office@mlfhs.demon.co.uk WWW:
www.mlfhs.demon.co.uk See Advert on Page: 252

Somerset
Somerset & Dorset Family History Society
PO Box 4052Sherborne Dorset DH9 6YL Fax: 01935
389611 Email: society@sdfhs.org WWW: www.sdfhs.org
See Advert on Page: 250

Staffordshire
**Birmingham & Midland Society for Genealogy and
Heraldry**
2 Castle Croft Oldbury West Midlands B68 9BQ Email:
birmingham@terrymorter.fsnet.co.uk WWW:
www.bmsgh.org See Advert on Page: 245

Warwickshire
**Birmingham & Midland Society for Genealogy and
Heraldry**
2 Castle Croft Oldbury West Midlands B68 9BQ Email:
birmingham@terrymorter.fsnet.co.uk WWW:
www.bmsgh.org See Advert on Page: 245

Westmorland
Cumbria Family History Society
"Ulpha" 32 Granada Road Denton Manchester M34 2LJ
WWW:
http://www.genuki/big/eng/CUL/cumbFHS/membership.html
See Advert on Page: 252

Worcestershire
Birmingham & Midland Society for Genealogy and Heraldry
2 Castle Croft Oldbury West Midlands B68 9BQ Email: birmingham@terrymorter.fsnet.co.uk WWW: www.bmsgh.org See Advert on Page: 245

Yorkshire - North
Cleveland Family History Society
1 Oxgang Close Redcar Cleveland TS10 4ND Fax: 01642 486615 See Advert on Page: 248

Yorkshire - South
Doncaster & District Family History Society
'Marton House' 125 The Grove Wheatley Hills Doncaster South Yorkshire DN2 5SN Email: tonyjunes@aol.com WWW: http://www.doncasterfhs.freeserve.co.uk See Advert on Page: 254

Sheffield & District Family History Society
10 Hallam Grange Road Sheffield South Yorkshire S10 4BJ Email: secretary@sheffieldfhs.org.uk WWW: www.sheffieldfhs.org.uk See Advert on Page: 248

Yorkshire - West
Huddersfield & District Family History Society
292 Thornhills Lane Clifton Brighouse West Yorkshire HD6 4JQ WWW: http://www.hdfhs.or.uk See Advert on Page: 253

Keighley & District Family History Society
2 The Hallows Shann Park Keighley West Yorkshire BD20 6HY See Advert on Page: 248

Pontefract & District Family History Society
Mrs B Graham, 10 Saddlers ~Grove, Badsworth, Pontefract WF9 1PE See Advert on Page: 274

Wakefield & District Family History Society
11 Waterton Close Walton Wakefield West Yorkshire WF2 6TT Tel: 01924 250882 (Membership Secretary) Email: ronaldpullan@hotmail.com WWW: http://homepage.virgin.net/wakefield.fhs See Advert on Page: 250

Yorkshire - York
City of York & District Family History Society
4 Orchard Close Dringhouses York Yorkshire YO24 2NX WWW: www.yorkfamilyhistory.org.uk See Advert on Page: 246

Wales
Federation of Family History Societies
PO Box 2425 Coventry CV5 6YX Tel: 024 7667 7798 (Not for Publication) Fax: 01564 703100 Email: admin@ffhs.org.uk See Advert on Page: 6

Brecknockshire
Powys Family History Society
Oaker's Lodge The Vineyards Winforton Herefordshire HR3 6EA Fax: 01544 327103
Email: 114251,2276@compuserve.com
WWW: http://ourworld.compuserve.com/homepages/michaelmacsorley/powys1.htm
and also via Genuki See Advert on Page: 251

Carmarthenshire
Dyfed Family History Society
38 Brynmelyn Avenue Llanelli Carmarthenshire SA15 3RT Email: johnhtjames@lineone.net
WWW: http://www.westwales.co.uk/dfhs/dfhs.htm
See Advert on Page: 256

Ceredigion
Dyfed Family History Society
38 Brynmelyn Avenue Llanelli Carmarthenshire SA15 3RT Email: johnhtjames@lineone.net WWW: http://www.westwales.co.uk/dfhs/dfhs.htm See Advert on Page: 256

Clwyd
Clwyd Family History Society
The Laurels Dolydd Road Cefn Mawr Wrexham LL14 3NH WWW: www.clwydfhs.org.uk
See Advert on Page: 255

Denbighshire
Clwyd Family History Society
The Laurels Dolydd Road Cefn Mawr Wrexham LL14 3NH WWW: www.clwydfhs.org.uk See Advert on Page: 255

Dyfed
Dyfed Family History Society
38 Brynmelyn Avenue Llanelli Carmarthenshire SA15 3RT Email: johnhtjames@lineone.net WWW: http://www.westwales.co.uk/dfhs/dfhs.htm See Advert on Page: 256

Flintshire
Clwyd Family History Society
The Laurels Dolydd Road Cefn Mawr Wrexham LL14 3NH WWW: www.clwydfhs.org.uk See Advert on Page: 255

Montgomeryshire
Powys Family History Society
Oaker's Lodge The Vineyards Winforton Herefordshire HR3 6EA Fax: 01544 327103 Email: 114251,2276@compuserve.com WWW: http://ourworld.compuserve.com/homepages/michaelmacsorley/powys1.htm and also via Genuki See Advert on Page: 251

Pembrokeshire
Dyfed Family History Society
38 Brynmelyn Avenue Llanelli Carmarthenshire SA15 3RT Email: johnhtjames@lineone.net WWW: http://www.westwales.co.uk/dfhs/dfhs.htm See Advert on Page: 256

Powys
Powys Family History Society
Oaker's Lodge The Vineyards Winforton Herefordshire HR3 6EA Fax: 01544 327103 Email: 114251,2276@compuserve.com WWW: http://ourworld.compuserve.com/homepages/michaelmacsorley/powys1.htm and also via Genuki See Advert on Page: 251

Radnorshire
Powys Family History Society
Oaker's Lodge The Vineyards Winforton Herefordshire HR3 6EA Fax: 01544 327103 Email: 114251,2276@compuserve.com WWW: http://ourworld.compuserve.com/homepages/michaelmacsorley/powys1.htm and also via Genuki See Advert on Page: 251

Northern Ireland
Ulster Historical Foundation
Balmoral Buildings 12 College Square East Belfast BT1 6DD Northern Ireland Fax: 028 9023 9885 Email: enquiry@uhf.org.uk
andrew@uhf.org.uk WWW: http://www.uhf.org.uk www.ancestryireland.com See Advert on Page: 150

Scotland
Aberdeen
Aberdeen & North East Scotland Family History Society
164 King Street Aberdeen AB24 5BD Scotland Fax: 01224-639096 Email: enquiries@anefhs.org.uk WWW: http://www.anesfhs.org.uk See Advert on Page: 253

Argyll, Ayrshire, Bute, Dunbartonshire, Glasgow, Lanarkshire, Renfrewshire, Stirlingshire, North West Scotland
Glasgow & West of Scotland Family History Society
Unit 5 22 Mansfield Street Partick Glasgow G11 5QP Fax: 0141-339-8303 WWW: http://www.gwsfhs.org.uk See Advert on Page: 253

CO LEIS THU? Research Centre
Seallam Visitor Centre Northton (Taobh Tuath) Isle of Harris HS3 3JA Tel: 01859 520488 (Home) Fax: 01859 520258 Email: lawsonbill@cs.com WWW: www.seallam.com See Advert on Page: 135

Scottish Genealogy Society
15 Victoria Terrace Edinburgh EH1 2JL Scotland Tel: 0131 220 3677 Fax: 0131 220 3677 Email: scotgensoc@sol.co.uk WWW: www.scotsgenealogy.com See Advert on Page: 257

Australia
Genealogical Society of Victoria
Ancestor House 179 Queen Street Melbourne 3000 Victoria Australia Fax: +61-03-9670-4490 Email: gsv@gsv.org.au WWW: www.gsv.org.au See Advert on Page: 258

South Africa
The South African War 1899 - 1902
14a Pembroke Crescent Glendowie Auckland 1005 New Zealand Email: smgray@ihug.co.nz See Advert on Page: 223

Photographic & Reproductive
M & P Barnes
138 Ermin Street Stratton St Margaret Swindon Wiltshire SN3 4NQ See Advert on Page: 180
Creative Digital Imaging
3 Post Office Row Legbourne Louth Lincolnshire LN11 8LL Tel: 01507-600059 Email: cdilouth@cs.com WWW: http://ourworld.cs.com/cdilouth/ See Advert on Page: 15
Angela Murphy LRPS
4 Nutley Park Donnybrook Dublin 4 Ireland Email: angelamurphy@oceanfree.net See Advert on Page: 149
Zebrafoto
55 Walsingham Road Woodthorpe Norringham Nottinghamshire NG5 4NQ Email: ian@zebrafoto.co.uk WWW: www.zebrafoto.co.uk See Advert on Page: 64

Publishers
GR Specialist Information Services
33 Nursery Road Nether Poppleton York YO26 6NN Email: publishers@genealogical.co.uk WWW: www.genealogical.co.uk See Advert on Page: 413 & 415

Specialist Indexes
Seaham Super Index
53 Longlands Court Westbourne Grove London W11 2QF Email: Kch66@dial.pipex.com WWW: http://dspace.dial.pipex.com/town/street/Kch66/ See Advert on Page: 12
Wiltshire Index Service
11 Ardmore Close Tuffley Gloucester Gloucestershire GL4 0BJ WWW:www.wiltshireancestors.com See Advert on Page: 44

Stationery & Storage
Back to Roots Family History Service
16 Arrowsmith Drive Stonehouse Gloucestershire GL10 2QR Email: mike@backtoroots.co.uk WWW: http://www.backtoroots.co.uk See Advert on Page: 416 & IBC
CW & S Parkinson
16 Foxhills Close Ashurst Southampton Hampshire SO40 7ER Email: cws@sirdar.demon.co.uk WWW: http://www.sirdar.demon.co.uk/cws/ See Advert on Page: 199
Secol Limited
Howlett Way Thetford Norfolk IP24 1HZ See Advert on Page: 81

Record Offices and Archives
Probate Service
Probate Sub Registry Duncombe Place York YO1 7EA See Advert on Page: 302
Public Record Office
Public Record Office Ruskin Avenue Kew Richmond Surrey TW9 4DU WWW: http://www.pro.gov.uk/ See Advert on Page: 59

England
Barnet
Hertfordshire Archives and Local Studies
County Hall Pegs Lane Hertford Hertfordshire SG13 8EJ Fax: 01923 471333 Email: herts.direct@hertscc.gov.uk WWW: http://hertsdirect.org/hals See Advert on Page: 301

Cumbria
Border Regiment & Kings Own Royal Border Regiment Museum
Queen Mary's Tower The Castle Carlisle Cumbria CA3 8UR Fax: 01228-521275 Email: rhq@kingsownborder.demon.co.uk See Advert on Page: 242

Hertfordshire
Hertfordshire Archives and Local Studies
County Hall Pegs Lane Hertford Hertfordshire SG13 8EJ Fax: 01923 471333 Email: herts.direct@hertscc.gov.uk WWW: http://hertsdirect.org/hals See Advert on Page: 301

Hull
Hull Central Library Family and Local History Club
Central Library Albion Street Kingston upon Hull HU1 3TF Fax: 01482 616827 Email: gareth2ukorigins.co.uk WWW: http://www.hullcc.gov.uk/genealogy See Advert on Page: 12

Kent
Kent County Archives
Sessions House County Hall Maidstone Kent ME141XQ Fax: 01622 694379 Email: archives@kent.gov.uk WWW: www.kent.gov.uk/e&l/artslib/ARCHIVES/archiveshome.htm See Advert on Page: 326

Lancashire
Lancashire Record Office
Bow Lane Preston Lancashire PR1 2RE Fax: 01772 263050 Email: record.office@ed.lancscc.gov.uk WWW: www.lancashire.gov.uk/education/lifelong/recordindex.shtm See Advert on Page: 328

Leicester, Leicestershire & Rutland
Record Office for Leicestershire, Leicester and Rutland
Long Street Wigston Magna Leicestershire LE18 2AH Fax: 0116-257-1120 Email: recordoffice@leics.gov.uk See Advert on Page: 300

London
London Metropolitan Archives
40 Northampton Road London EC1R 0HB Tel: Mini com 020 7278 8703 Fax: 020 7833 9136 Email: ask.lma@ms.corpoflondon.gov.uk WWW: www.cityoflondon.gov.uk See Advert on Page: 296

National Maritime Museum
Romney Road Greenwich London London SE10 9NF Fax: (020) 8312-6632 Email: WWW: http://www.nmm.ac.uk See Advert on Page: 39

Public Record Office
Public Record Office Ruskin Avenue Kew Richmond Surrey TW9 4DU Fax: (020) 8392 5266 Email: bookshop@pro.gov.uk WWW: http://www.pro.gov.uk/ See Advert on Page: 59

Middlesex
Hertfordshire Archives and Local Studies
County Hall Pegs Lane Hertford Hertfordshire SG13 8EJ Fax: 01923 471333 Email: herts.direct@hertscc.gov.uk WWW: http://hertsdirect.org/hals See Advert on Page: 301

Suffolk
Suffolk Record Office Lowestoft Branch
Central Library Clapham Road Lowestoft Suffolk NR32 1DR Fax: 01502-405350 Email: lowestoft.ro@libher.suffolkcc.gov.uk. WWW: www.suffolkcc.gov.uk/sro/ See Advert on Page: 405
Suffolk Record Office - Bury St Edmunds Branch
77 Raingate Street Bury St Edmunds Suffolk IP33 2AR Fax: 01284-352315 Email: bury.ro@libher.suffolkcc.gov.uk WWW: http://www.suffolkcc.gov.uk/sro/ See Advert on Page: 405

Suffolk Record Office Ipswich Branch
Gatacre Road Ipswich Suffolk IP1 2LQ Fax: 01473-584533
Email: ipswich.ro@libher.suffolkcc.gov.uk WWW:
www.suffolkcc.gov.uk/sro/ See Advert on Page: 405

West Sussex
West Sussex Record Office
County Hall Chichester West Sussex PO19 1RN Fax: 01243-533959 Email: records.office@westsussex.gov.uk WWW:
www.westsussex.gov.uk/cs/ro/rohome.htm See Advert on
Page: 326

Yorkshire - East Yorkshire
Hull Central Library Family and Local History Club
Central Library Albion Street Kingston upon Hull HU1 3TF
Fax: 01482 616827 Email: gareth2ukorigins.co.uk WWW:
http://www.hullcc.gov.uk/genealogy See Advert on Page: 12

Yorkshire - West
West Yorkshire Archive Service
Registry of Deeds Newstead Road Wakefield West
Yorkshire WF1 2DE Fax: 01924-305983 Email:
hq@wyashq.demon.co.uk WWW:
http://www.archives.wyjs.org.uk See Advert on Page: 409

Wales
National Library of Wales
Penglais Aberystwyth Ceredigion SY23 3BU Wales Tel:
01970 632902 Marketing Fax: 01970-615709 Email:
holi@llgc.org.uk WWW: http://www.llgc.org.uk See Advert
on Page: 128

Scotland
General Register Office for Scotland
New Register House Edinburgh EH1 3YT Scotland Tel:
Certificate Order 0131 314 4411 Fax: 0131-314-4400 Email:
records@gro-scotland.gov.uk
WWW: http://www.gro-scotland.gov.uk
Pay per view search site: http://www.origins.net
See Advert on Page: 136

During the recent epidemic of smallpox the Admiralty lent the Metropolitan Asylums Board one of the few old wooden vessels which are still extant—the *Atlas* a 100-gun line-of-battle ship of some 5000 tons. At the outset the vessel was intended to be moored off Greenhithe, but was ultimately, however, transferred to Greenwich. The labour of clearing the vessel of her fighting gear, &c., was considerable, but in a very short space of time she was fitted with all the requisites of an hospital. Three wards were erected between decks, the lowest, or orlop deck, having been made available by cutting thirty-four new ports through the sides of the vessel, and a deckhouse was erected for the accommodation of doubtful cases, as

𝓣owing the 𝓢mallpox 𝓗ospital 𝓢hip
The Graphic November 11, 1882

well as a set of six small isolated wards and a laundry.

The vessel was originally intended to receive 300 patients, but this r number was subsequently restricted to 180, viz., 70 on the main deck, 60 on the lower, and 50 on the orlop decks. While the vessel e was off Greenwich 1,105 patients were treated, of whom 120 died— a percentage of 10.8 per cent and a rate of mortality which compares favourably with the results shown by shore hospitals.

Our engraving represents her being towed from her moorings before Greenwich Hospital, where, like the old *Dreadnought,* she has for some time been a picturesque element in the river view, to her original berth off Greenhithe. Her removal, which will certainly leave a blank in the Lower Thames was due, it is said, to the remonstrances of the good people of Greenwich, who objected to a floating hospital ship for so eminently infectious a disease being moored in such close proximity to their town, and whose representatives prevailed upon the powers that be to waive their opposition to the original mooring berth at Greenhithe.

This position is decidedly more suitable, having a fair expanse of water, and being surrounded by open country. Patients will be far better treated there than on a mud bank, which was the resting-place at Greenwich.

The Church of Jesus Christ of Latter Day Saints and Genealogical Resources

The International Genealogical Index (IGI)

Arising from its religious beliefs The Church of Jesus Christ of Latter Day Saints has produced the marvellous International Genealogical Index (known as the I.G.I.). The Index is unique source of information on family histories gathered world-wide. For many researchers it is the first location they check for leads in their quest for information on ancestors being as it is an index to millions of records of births, deaths and marriages recorded in church records in many countries from medieval times prior to civil registration.

Currently the I.G.I. is available on microfiche and CD-ROM viewable at the Family History Centres of the Church (UK Centres listed later in the GSD) and also at many public locations such as libraries, record centres, etc. It is also available on-line on the internet via Church

Stationery and Recording Aids

The Church also produces a very useful range of forms for recording family history details which may be purchased by non-Church members at very reasonable

charges from the Family History Centres usually located at the local Church premises referred to above.

Support for computer storage of information

The Church also caters for those who use computers as tools in their family history researches in producing the very fine 'Personal Ancestral File' (PAF) computer program for organising and managing genealogical information plus supplementary programs which enhance the basic program. Copies of the PAF program can obtained via the Web Site: www.lds.org and the other items are obtainable from the Distribution Centres now detailed:

Church of Jesus Christ of Latter Day Saints - North America Distribution Centre
1999 West 1700 South, Salt Lake City, Utah, 84104, United States of America
Church of Jesus Christ of Latter Day Saints - UK Distribution Centre
399 Garretts Green Lane, Birmingham, West Midlands, B33 0HU Tel: 0870-010-2051

Family History Centres ~ The Church of Jesus Christ of The Latter Day Saints

England

Bedfordshire
St Albans Family History Centre London Road/Cutenhoe Road, Luton LU1 3NQ Tel: 01582-482234

Berkshire
Reading Family History Centre 280 The Meadway, Tilehurst, Reading RG3 4PF Tel: 0118-941 0211

Bristol
Family History Centre 721 Wells Road, Whitchurch, Bristol, BS14 9HU Tel: 01275-838326

Cambridgeshire
Cambridgeshire Family History Centre 670 Cherry Hinton Road, Cambridge CB1 4DR Tel: 01223-247010,
Peterborough Family History Centre
Cottesmore Close off Atherstone Av, Netherton Estate, Peterborough, PE3 9TP Tel: 01733-263374

Cheshire
Chester Family History Centre
Clifton Drive, Blacon, Chester CH1 5LT Tel: 01244-390796

Cleveland
Billingham Family History Centre
The Linkway, Billingham TS23 3HG Tel: 01642-563162

Cornwall
Helston Family History Centre
Clodgey Lane, Helston Tel: 01326-564503

Cumbria
Carlisle Family History Centre
Langrigg Road, Morton Park, Carlisle CA2 5HT Tel: 01228-26767

Devon
Exeter Family History Centre
Wonford Road, Exeter Tel: 01392-250723
Plymouth Family History Centre
Mannamead Road, Plymouth PL3 5QJ Tel: 01752-668666

Dorset
Poole Family History Centre
8 Mount Road, Parkstone, Poole BH14 0QW Tel: 01202-730646

East Sussex
Crawley Family History Centre
Old Horsham Road, Crawley RH11 8PD Tel: 01293-516151

East Yorkshire
Hull Family History Centre 725 Holderness Road, Kingston upon Hull HU4 7RT Tel: 01482-701439

Essex
Romford Family History Centre
64 Butts Green Road, Hornshurch RM11 2JJ Tel: 01708-620727

Gloucestershire
Cheltenham Family History Centre Thirlestaine Road, Cheltenham GL53 7AS Tel: 01242-523433
Forest of Dean Family History Centre
Wynol's Hill, Queensway, Coleford, Tel: 01594-542480

Greater Manchester
Manchester Family History Centre
Altrincham Road, Wythenshawe Road, Manchester, M22 4BJ Tel: 0161-902-9279

Hampshire
Portsmouth Family History Centre
82 Kingston Crescent, Portsmouth PO2 8AQ Tel: (023) 92696243

Isle of Wight
Newport Family History Centre Chestnut Close, Shide Road, Newport PO30 1YE Tel: 01983-529643

Kent
Maidstone Family History Centre
76b London Road, Maidstone ME16 0DR Tel: 01622-757811

Lancashire
Ashton Family History Centre
Patterdale Road, Ashton-under-Lyne OL7 Tel: 0161-330-1270
Blackpool Family History Centre
Warren Drive, Cleveleys, Blackpool, FY5 3TG Tel: 01253-858218
Chorley Family History Centre
Preston Temple, Chorley, PR6 7EQ Tel: 01257-226147
Lancaster Family History Centre
Ovangle Road, Lancaster, LA1 5HZ Tel: 01254-33571
Rawtenstall Family History Centre
Haslingden Road, Rawtenstall, Rossendale, BB4 6PU Tel: 01706-213460

Leicestershire
Leicestershire Family History Centre
Wakerley Road, Leicester LE5 4WD Tel: 0116-233-5544

Lincolnshire
Lincoln Family History Centre
Skellingthorpe Road, Lincoln LN6 0PB Tel: 01522-680117
Email: dann.family@diamond.co.uk

London
Hyde Park Family History Centre
64 - 68 Exhibition Road, South Kensington, London, SW7 2PA Tel: (020) 789-8561

Wandsworth Family History Centre
149 Nightingale Lane, Balham, London, SW12 Tel: (020) 8673-6741

Merseyside
Liverpool Family History Centre
4 Mill Bank, Liverpool L13 0BW Tel: 0151-228-0433

Middlesex
Staines Family History Centre
41 Kingston Road, Staines TW14 0ND Tel: 01784-462627

Norfolk
Kings Lynn Family History Centre
Reffley Lane, Kings Lynn PE30 3EQ Tel: 01553-67000
Norwich Family History Centre
19 Greenways, Eaton, Norwich NR4 6PA Tel: 01603-452440

North East Lincolnshire
Grimsby Family History Centre
Linwood Avenue (NO LETTER BOX), Scartho, Grimsby DN33 2NL Tel: 01472-828876

North Yorkshire
Scarborough Family History Centre
Stepney Drive/Whitby Road, Scarborough

Northamptonshire
Northampton Family History Centre
137 Harlestone Road, Duston, Northampton NN5 6AA
Tel: 01604-587630

Nottinghamshire
Mansfield Family History Centre
Southridge Drive, Mansfield NG18 4RJ Tel: 01623-26729,
Nottingham Family History Centre
Hempshill Lane, Bulwell, Nottingham, NG6 8PA Tel: 0115-927-4194

Shropshire
Telford Family History Centre 72 Glebe Street, Wellington

Somerset
Yate Family History Centre
Wellington Road, Yate BS37 5UY Tel: 01454-323004
Yeovil Family History Centre
Forest Hill, Yeovil, BA20 2PH Tel: 01935-26817

South Yorkshire
Sheffield Family History Centre
Wheel Lane, Grenoside, Sheffield S30 3RL Tel: 0114-245-3124

Staffordshire
Lichfield Family History Centre
Purcell Avenue, Lichfield WS14 9XA Tel: 01543-414843,
Newcastle under Lyme Family History Centre
PO Box 457, Newcastle under Lyme, ST5 0TD Tel: 01782-620653

Suffolk
Ipswich Family History Centre
42 Sidegate Lane West, Ipswich IP4 3DB Tel: 01473-723182
Lowestoft Family History Centre
165 Yarmouth Road, Lowestoft, Tel: 01502-573851

Tyne and Wear
Sunderland Family History Centre
Linden Road off Queen Alexandra Road, Sunderland SR2 9BT
Tel: 0191-528-5787

West Midlands
Coventry Family History Centre
Riverside Close,Whitley, Coventry Tel: (024) 76301420
Harborne Family History Centre
38 Lordswood Road, Harborne, Birmingham, B17 9QS
Tel: 0121-427-9291,
Sutton Coldfield Family History Centre
185 Penns Lane, Sutton Coldfield, Birmingham, B76 1JU
Tel: 0121-386-1690,
Wednesfield Family History Centre
Linthouse Lane, Wednesfield, Wolverhampton, Tel: 01902-724097

West Sussex
Worthing Family History Centre
Goring Street, Worthing,West Sussex, BN12 5AR

West Yorkshire
Huddersfield Family History Centre
12 Halifax Road, Birchencliffe, Huddersfield HD3 3BS
Tel: 01484-454573

Leeds Family History Centre
Vesper Road, Leeds, LS5 3QT Tel: 0113-258-5297

Worcestershire
Redditch Family History Centre 321 Evesham Road, Crabbs Cross, Redditch B97 5JA Tel: 01527-550657

York
Family History Centre
West Bank, Acomb, York, Tel: 01904-785128

Wales
Denbighshire
Rhyl Family History Centre
Rhuddlan Road, Rhyl, Denbighshire
Glamorgan
Merthyr Tydfil Family History Centre
Swansea Road, Merthyr Tydfil CF 48 1NR Tel: 01685-722455
Swansea Family History Centre
Cockett Road, Swansea, SA2 0FH Tel: 01792-419520
South Glamorgan
Cardiff Family History Centre
Heol y Deri, Rhiwbina, Cardiff CF4 6UH Tel: (029) 20620205

Scotland
Edinburgh Family History Centre
30a Colinton Road, Edinburgh, EH4 3SN Tel: 0130-337-3049,
Glasgow Family History Centre
35 Julian Avenue, Glasgow, G12 0RB Tel: 0141-357-1024
Ayrshire
Kilmarnock Family History Centre
Wahtriggs Road, Kilmarnock KA1 3QY Tel: 01563-26560
Dumfrieshire
Dumfries Family History Centre
36 Edinburgh Road, Albanybank, Dumfries DG1 1JQ Tel: 01387-254865
Fife
Kirkcaldy Family History Centre
Winifred Crescent, Forth Park, Kirkcaldy KY2 5SX Tel: 01592-640041
Grampian
Aberdeen Family History Centre
North Anderson Dr, Aberdeen AB2 6DD Tel: 01224-692206
Highlands
Inverness Family History Centre
13 Ness Walk, Inverness IV3 5SQ Tel: 01463-231220
Johnstone
Paisley Family History Centre
Campbell street, Paisley PA5 8LD Tel: 01505-20886
Shetland
Lerwick Family History Centre
Baila Croft, Lerwick, Shetland, ZE1 0EY Tel: 01595-695732 Tel: 01950-431469
Tayside
Dundee Family History Centre
22 - 26 Bingham Terrace, DundeeDD4 7HH Tel: 01382-451247

Isle of Man
Douglas Family History Centre
Woodbourne Road, Douglas IM2 3AP Tel: 01624-675834

Channel Islands
Jersey
St Helier Family History Centre La Rue de la Vallee, St Mary, Jersey, JE3 3DL Tel: 01534-82171

Northern Ireland
Belfast Family History Centre
401 Holywood Road, Belfast, BT4 2GU Tel: (028) 90768250,
Londonderry Family History Centre
Racecourse Road, Belmont Estate, Londonderry, Tel: Sun-only-(028) 71350179

Republic of Ireland
Co Dublin
Dublin Family History Centre The Willows, Finglas, Dublin, Co Dublin, 11 Tel: ++-353-4625609

West Yorkshire Archive Service

The Archives for Bradford, Calderdale (Halifax), Kirklees (Huddersfield, Leeds & Wakefield:

Tel: Bradford 01274 731931
         Calderdale 01422 392636
         Kirklees 01484 221 966
         Leeds 0113 214 5814
         Wakefield 01924 305980
         Yorkshire Archaeological
         Society 0113 245 6362

Website: http://www.archives.wyjs.org.uk

For details of
The Local & Family History Day 2002
(Autumn)

contact by email:
gparker@wyjs.org.uk

Your first date for 2003?

The
ESSEX SOCIETY FOR FAMILY HISTORY
in association with the
Federation
invite you to register your possible interest in a major conference..

A
little of what you fancy ...
to be held at the University in
Colchester during the weekend of
Friday 29th - Sunday 31st August **2003**
A Victorian research theme with a background of Music Hall and Gilbert and Sullivan's works.
For details and brochuure
e-mail
<heather@feather1.demon.co.uk>
or telephone 01702 522992

GARMENTS PRINTED & EMBROIDERED

APC CLOTHING

bags
T-shirts
caps
sweatshirts

for all your club and corporate clothing
printed and embroidered with your design

*Contact Nick Hall for further details
and a full colour brochure*

APC Clothing Ltd
**Unit 6a Guardian Park
Station Road Industrial Estate
Tadcaster North Yorkshire LS24 9SG**

*Tel: 01937 833449 Fax: 01937 832649
e-mail: sales@apc-clothing.co.uk*

**Privileged to supply
The Public Record Office and
The Genealogical Services Directory
amongst many others**

---

www.genealogical.co.uk
If you have missed the deadline for Advertising in this Edition
it is never *too* early to reserve your place in the *next* Edition !

Until that time
why not
take some space in the
WebServices® Section
at
www.genealogical.co.uk

YORKSHIRE
FAMILY HISTORY FAIR
KNAVESMIRE EXHIBITION CENTRE
YORK RACECOURSE

SATURDAY 29TH JUNE 2002
10.00.a.m. to 4.30.p.m.

Many Stalls including:
Society of Genealogists, Federation Publications
The Family & Local History Handbook
(The Genealogical Services Directory)
Family Tree Magazine, Local Archives,
Family History Societies from all over Great Britain
Maps, Postcards, Printouts,
New & Second-hand Microfiche Readers
Genealogy Computer Programs
Advice Table

FREE CAR PARKING
ADMISSION £2.50

Further Details from:
Mr A Sampson
1 Oxgang Close, Redcar TS10 4ND
Tel: 01642 486615

NOTE FOR YOUR DIARY:

YEAR 2003 - YORKSHIRE FAMILY HISTORY FAIR
SATURDAY 28TH JUNE 2003
YEAR 2004 - YORKSHIRE FAMILY HISTORY FAIR
SATURDAY 26TH JUNE 2004
YEAR 2005 - YORKSHIRE FAMILY HISTORY FAIR
SATURDAY 25TH JUNE 2005
YEAR 2006 - YORKSHIRE FAMILY HISTORY FAIR
SATURDAY 24TH JUNE 2006

About the Editor

Robert Blatchford LL.B (Hons)
has been involved in genealogy for several
years. He is a member of Cleveland,City of
York & District, Devon, Dyfed, East
Yorkshire, Glamorgan and Gwent Family
History Societies and Poppleton History
Society. A former Chairman of The City of
York & District Family History Society and
former Vice Chairman of the North East
Group of Family History Societies. He has
undertaken research in the United Kingdom &
Australia.

NorthWest Group of Family History Societies

Family History Fair
held every
Autumn
in the North West of England
For Details of the biggest and best
Family History Fair in the North West
contact:
Mr E W Gullick
4 Lawrence Avenue, Simonstone, Burnley
Lancashire BB12 7HX
(Please enclose a Stamped addressed envelope)

**Lectures
Throughout
The Day**

Exhibitors:
Family History Societies, Local History Societies
Local studies libraries, Record offices
Booksellers, Computers, Recording Aids, Fiches
Readers
and

**Car Park
Refreshments**

The Family & Local History Handbook
published by The Genealogical Services Directory

Greenfairs PROMOTIONS

THE YORKSHIRE COAST FAMILY HISTORY FAIR
2002
28th September 10am to 5pm

SPA GRAND HALL
SCARBOROUGH

Admission £2 accompanied children free

Telephone: 01723 363665
email: greenfairs@btinternet.com

In association with Back to Roots.co.uk Ltd

Published by
The Genealogical Services Directory
(a trading name of GR Specialist Information Services)
33 Nursery Road, Nether Poppleton YORK, YO26 6NN England

E Mail: publishers@genealogical.co.uk
WWW: http://www.genealogical.co.uk

The Genealogical Services Directory
First Edition Published 1997
Second Edition Published January 1998 (Revised & Reprinted April 1998)
Third Edition Published January 1999
Fourth Edition Published January 2000
© Robert Blatchford and Geoffrey Heslop

Family & Local History Handbook
5th Edition Published January 2001   ISBN 0 9530297 4 3

6th Edition Published February 2002 ISBN 0 9530297 5 1
© 2002 Robert Blatchford

ISSN 1368-9150   **ISBN 0 9530297 5 1**

Printed by
AWP
9 Advance Workshops, Wild Street, Dukinfield SK16 4DL   Tel: 07041 428220

Disclaimer

The Editor and Publishers of The Family & Local History Handbook make every effort to verify all information published. Nearly every organisation in this handbook has been contacted and asked to confirm that our information is correct. We provided reply paid envelopes and are grateful to those organisations who took the time to reply. We must express our disappointment that there were some organisations who did not reply. We cannot accept responsibilty for any errors or omissions or for any losses that may arise.

Advertisers are expected to provide a high standard of service to our readers. If there is a failure to provide such a service the Editor and Publishers reserve the right to refuse to accept advertising in future editions.

The Editor and Publishers cannot be held responsible for the errors, omissions or non performance by advertisers. Where an advertiser's performance falls below an acceptable level readers are asked to notify The Genealogical Services Directory in writing.

The views and opinions expressed in each of the articles are those of the author and do not necessarily reflect the opinions of the Editor.

Email and Internet or Web Addresses

Email and Web addresses shown in this book have been notified to us by the Organisation or advertiser. Unlike a normal postal address these addresses are subject to frequent change especially since the introduction of Free Internet Service Providers (e.g. Freeserve).

In the case of businesses Email forwarding and Website transfer are usually provided by links to the original address. This does not always happen and the only solution is to use the various search engines available on the internet.

Many of the Browsers and Search engines will accept an address beginning with either http:// or www

Index to Advertisers

BACK TO ROOTS (UK) LTD

Computer Programs, Data CD's and Disks, Books and Acid Free Items

Family Tree Maker V9 (1 CD) (p&p 75p)	£29.95
Family Tree Maker Upgrade V9 (p&p75p)	£19.95
Generations Grande Suite V8(p&p £3.50)	£46.00
Generations Starter Kit V8 (p&p £3.50)	£27.00
Generations Deluxe V4 CD Set (p&p £2)	£ 9.95
Ultimate Family Tree Basic (p&p 75p)	£10.00
LDS Companion (p&p 75p)	£16.50
Genmap (p&p 75p)	£24.95

**p & p - discs 50p each - 1 CD 75p, 2 CDs £1,
3 CDs £1.25 - 5 CDs or more FREE**

Muster Rolls 1781-82 (disc) £3.99 each	
- covering every county in England and Wales	
Dambusters (CD)	£5.99
Royal Naval Marriages (disc)	£4.50
Criminal Registers 1805-1816 (disc)	£5.99
each covering every county in England &	
Monmouthshire	
Criminal Registers 1805-1816 (CD)	£14.50
each - covering every county in England	
Criminal Registers 1817-1828 (disc)	£5.99
each - for Cornwall, Dorset, Bedfordshire, Devon,	
Bristol, Leicester	
Criminal Registers 1829-1840 (disc)	£5.99
each - for Cornwall, Dorset	
Criminal Registers 1817-1828	
(CD) - Devon & Cornwall	£14.50
Military Courts (CD)	£7.99
Death Sentences (CD)	£9.99
Serious Crimes (CD)	£9.99
Transportations (CD)	£9.99
1851 Census for Gloucestershire, Bristol &	
Somerset (CD)	£18.00

Directories on CD:

Birmingham Private Residents Dir 1777 Street &	
Trade Dir 1896	£11.99
Bristol Slater's Trade Dir 1852-3	£11.99
Bristol & Suburban District Street Dir 1896	
	£11.99
Cambridgeshire Trade Dir 1830	£11.99
Cambridgeshire Trade Dir 1833	£11.99
Cambridgeshire Post Office Dir 1883	£11.99
Cheshire Pigot's Trade Dir 1828-29	£11.99
Cornwall Kelly's Dir 1919	£11.99
Cumberland Pigot's Trade Dir 1834	£11.99
Derbyshire Pigot's Trade Dir 1842	£11.99
Devonshire Pigot's Trade Dir 1830	£11.99
Durham & surrounding villages Trade Dir 1834	£11.99
Essex Pigot's Trade Dir 1832-33	£11.99
Essex Trade Dir 1828-29	£11.99
Gloucestershire Trade & Court Dir 1894	£11.99

Gloucestershire Post Office Dir 1894	£11.99
Gloucester City & District Street Dir 1920	£11.99
Hampshire Pigot's Trade Dir 1830	£11.99
Hertfordshire Trade Dir 1828-29	£11.99
Huddersfield Street Dir 1937	£11.99
Hull & surr. villages Kelly's Dir 1897	£11.99
Hull Street Dir 1892	£11.99
Hull Trade Dir 1892	£11.99
Hull Alphabetical Dir 1892	£11.99
Huntingdonshire PO & Trade Dir 1877	£11.99
Kent Trade Dir 1832-34	£11.99
Kent Trade Dir 1828-29	£11.99
Lancashire Slater's Trade Dir 1848	£11.99
Leeds Street Dir 1853	£11.99
Leeds Street Dir 1907	£11.99
Leeds Alphabetical Named List of Private	
Residents Part 1 A-J; Part 2 K-Z £11.99 each	
Leeds & Bradford City Centre Street & Trade Dir	
1822	£11.99
Leicestershire Trade Dir 1828	£11.99
Lincolnshire Post Office Dir 1876	£11.99
Liverpool Slater's Trade Dir 1848	£11.99
London Street Dir 1865 - (A-K)	£11.99
London Street Dir 1865 - (L-Z)	£11.99
London Trade Dir 1865 (A-L)	£11.99
London Trade Dir 1865 (L-Z)	£11.99
London 1828	£11.99
Manchester & Salford Slater's 1848	£11.99
Manchester & Salford PO & Trade 1824-25	£11.99
Manchester & Salford Alphabetical & Addresses	
Dir 1824-25	£11.99
Middlesborough City Centre 1897	£11.99
Middlesex Trade Dir 1828-29	£11.99
Middlesex Trade Dir 1839	£11.99
Newcastle First Trade Dir 1778	£11.99
Norfolk Trade Dir 1830	£11.99
Norfolk Post Office Dir 1888	£11.99
Norfolk Trade Dir 1888	£11.99

We carry many more directories on CD's and also a great number of data disks, too many to list here. We also carry large stocks of acid free products such as certificate and photo binders, polypockets, acid free pens and glue.

Back to Roots also has a very large range of books and research recording aids. Please send for a comprehensive brochure or alternatively check our web page which is regularly updated.

**16 Arrowsmith Drive,
Stonehouse, Glos. GL10 2QR
Freephone 0800 2985894
E-mail: mike@backtoroots.co.uk
Web page: www.backtoroots.co.uk**

We reserve the right to
change prices
without notice.